Microsoft® Word Version 2002

INSIDE OUT

The CD that helps you put your software to work!

Dig in—for the work-ready tools and resources that help you go way beyond just using Word. You'll conquer it! Just like the Inside Out book, we've designed your Inside Out CD to be both comprehensive and supremely easy to use. All the tools, utilities, and add-ins have been tested against final Word Version 2002 code—not beta. The sample chapters from other Inside Out books help take your Microsoft Office XP learning experience even deeper. You get essential links to online software updates, product support, and more—direct from the Microsoft Office team. And with the CD's intuitive HTML interface, you'll always know exactly where you are and what else you can do!

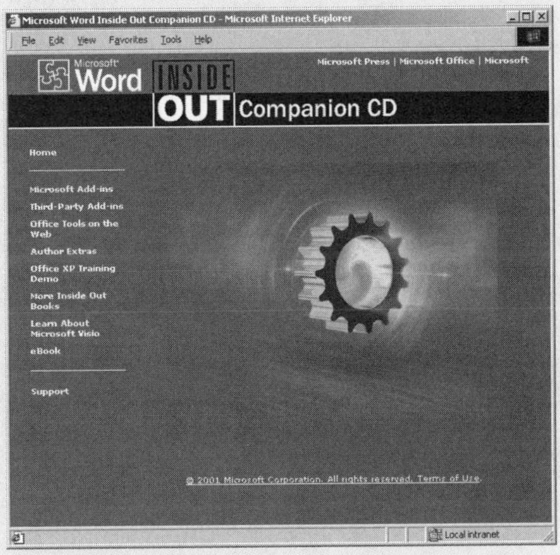

Your Inside Out CD features:

- **Microsoft and Third-Party Add-Ins**—dozens of must-have tools, utilities, demos, and trial software
- **Office Tools on the Web**—complete descriptions and links to official Microsoft Office resources on line
- **More Inside Out Books**—sample chapters from other Inside O
- **Complete Microsoft Press® eBook**—the entire Microsoft W book in easy-search electronic format
- **Step by Step Interactive Tutorials**—trial version of official training for Office XP

Want to learn more? Read on for full details, including System Requirements (last page of this section).

Microsoft
Word
Version 2002
INSIDE
OUT

Microsoft Add-Ins

Get Microsoft add-ins and tools for Word Version 2002—straight from the source.

Includes:

- **Microsoft Word Templates**—jump-start your own projects with these timesaving templates
- **Microsoft Office Visual Keyboard**—type in multiple languages on the same computer by using an on-screen keyboard for other languages
- **Microsoft Outlook® Mobile Manager**—install this cutting-edge add-in on your desktop PC and receive e-mail, calendar, and reminders on a whole range of mobile devices—so you get the information you need no matter where you go!
- **Microsoft Office Internet Free/Busy Service Wizard**—publish the blocks of time when you are free and busy to a shared Internet location, so people who don't normally have access to your Microsoft Outlook Calendar can check your schedule over the Web

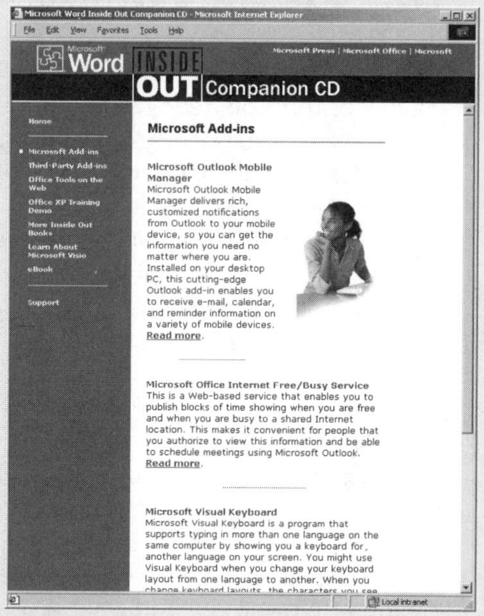

- **Microsoft Visio® Auto-Demos**—use these customizable auto-demos to see how to put Visio diagramming software to work on your next project
- **Step by Step Interactive Tutorials**—try official Microsoft interactive training for Office XP, and teach yourself common tasks and key features and functions

Microsoft Word Version 2002 INSIDE OUT

Third-Party Utilities, Demos, and Trials

All the third-party add-ins on this CD have been tested for use with Word Version 2002. Find all the details you need about each tool—including a full description, application size, system requirements, and installation instructions.

Includes:

- **HiSoftware's JITI Builder™ Office**—expand the Microsoft Office document property management tools and make your documents easier to find, explore, manage, and archive
- **Nereosoft's ProWrite™**—use existing information from the contact manager to create new e-mail and letter merges, faxes, memos, labels, and envelopes in a flash
- **J&R Software's Seal-It!™**—help ensure the security of your Word documents by digitally signing them using your unique voice imprint together with an RSA-generated public key signature algorithm
- **ConvertAll's ConvertAll**—convert money and units of measurement effortlessly in Word and Excel—everything from $ to €, km to miles, and lbs to kilos!
- **Avery Dennison's Avery Wizard™**—design and print professional-looking labels, dividers, cards, and more without ever leaving Word
- **AnvilLogic's AcroWizard™**—collect acronyms and their definitions from your docs, build a list, and update a database of acronyms for reuse
- **Seaview Software's Mark-A-Text™**—quickly find, mark, index, and extract specific text from contracts and other documents
- **Systemik Solutions' PerformX™ Designer and Author**—design, author, and publish documentation based on templates you create using the PerformX Designer Wizard
- **HiSoftware's metaPackager™**—encapsulate your files in *pure* XML so they're easy to index and manage

Microsoft Word Version 2002 INSIDE OUT

Office Tools on the Web

Here you'll find ready links to the most helpful and informative online resources for Office XP, direct from Microsoft. Find out exactly how each site can help you get your work done—then click and go!

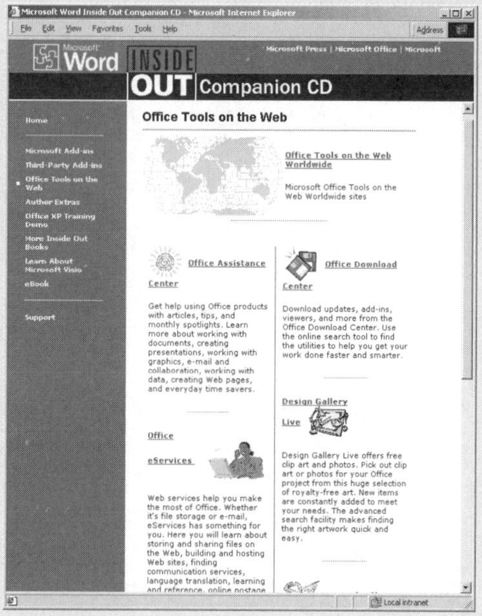

Office Assistance Center

Get help using Office products with articles, tips, and monthly spotlights. Learn more about working with documents, data, and graphics; using e-mail and collaboration features; creating presentations and Web pages; and using everyday time-savers.

Office eServices

Use these Web services to get the most from Office. Learn how to store and share files on the Web; build and host Web sites; find communication services, language translation, learning and reference, and online postage resources; tune up your computer; and much more!

Office Product Updates

Obtain recommended and critical updates to enhance your Office XP experience.

Office Download Center

Download updates, add-ins, viewers, and more from the Office Download Center. Use the online search tool to find the utilities to help you work faster and smarter.

Design Gallery Live

Pick out clip art or photos for your Office project from this huge royalty-free selection. New items are constantly added to meet your needs. The advanced search facility makes finding the right artwork quick and easy.

Microsoft Office Template Gallery

Instead of starting from scratch, download a template from the Template Gallery. From calendars to business cards, marketing material, and legal documents, Template Gallery offers hundreds of professionally authored and formatted documents for Microsoft Office.

Office Tools on the Web (continued)

Online Troubleshooters

Microsoft has developed Office XP online troubleshooters to help you solve problems on the fly. Access them using the links on the CD and get the diagnostic and problem-solving information you need.

More Inside Out Books

The INSIDE OUT series from Microsoft Press delivers comprehensive reference on the Office XP suite of applications. On this CD, you'll find sample chapters from the companion titles listed below, along with details about the entire line of books:

- Microsoft FrontPage® Version 2002 Inside Out
- Microsoft Office XP Inside Out
- Microsoft Outlook Version 2002 Inside Out
- Microsoft Excel Version 2002 Inside Out
- Microsoft Visio® Version 2002 Inside Out

Microsoft Word Version 2002 INSIDE OUT

Complete Microsoft Press eBook

You get the entire MICROSOFT WORD VERSION 2002 INSIDE OUT book on CD—along with sample chapters from other INSIDE OUT books—as searchable electronic books. These Microsoft Press eBooks install quickly and easily on your computer (see System Requirements for details) and enable rapid full-text search.

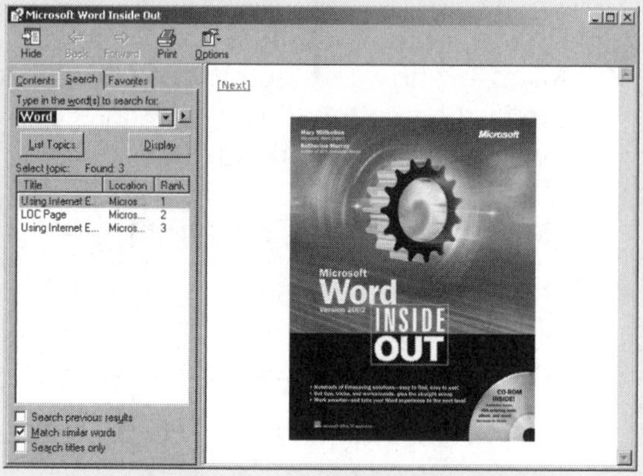

Features:

- Super-fast HTML full-text search
- Full-size graphics and screen shots
- Copy, paste, and *print* functions
- Bookmarking capabilities
- A saved history of every file viewed during a session

CD Minimum System Requirements

- Microsoft Windows® 95 or higher operating system (including Windows 98, Windows Millennium Edition, Windows NT® 4.0 with Service Pack 3, Windows 2000, or Windows XP)
- 266-MHz or higher Pentium-compatible CPU
- 64 megabytes (MB) RAM
- 8X CD-ROM drive or faster
- 46 MB of free hard disk space (to install the eBook and interactive tutorials)
- 800 x 600 with high color (16-bit) display settings
- Microsoft Windows-compatible sound card and speakers
- Microsoft Internet Explorer 4.01 or higher
- Microsoft Mouse or compatible pointing device

NOTE

System Requirements may be higher for the add-ins available on the CD. Individual add-in system requirements are specified on the CD. An Internet connection is necessary to access the hyperlinks in the Office Tools on the Web section. Connect time charges may apply.

Mary Millhollon
Microsoft Word Expert
Katherine Murray
Author of 40+ computer books

Microsoft

Microsoft Word Version 2002 INSIDE OUT

- Hundreds of timesaving solutions—easy to find, easy to use!
- Get tips, tricks, and workarounds, plus the straight scoop
- Work smarter—and take your Word experience to the next level

PUBLISHED BY
Microsoft Press
A Division of Microsoft Corporation
One Microsoft Way
Redmond, Washington 98052-6399

Library of Congress Cataloging-in-Publication Data
Millhollon, Mary.
Microsoft Word Version 2002 Inside Out / Mary Millhollon, Katherine Murray.
p. cm.
Includes index.
ISBN 0-7356-1278-1
1. Microsoft Word. 2. Word processing. I. Murray, Katherine, 1961- II. Title.

Z52.5.M52 M56 2001
652.5'5369--dc21 2001030871

Printed and bound in the United States of America.

1 2 3 4 5 6 7 8 9 QWT 6 5 4 3 2 1

Distributed in Canada by Penguin Books Canada Limited.

A CIP catalogue record for this book is available from the British Library.

Microsoft Press books are available through booksellers and distributors worldwide. For further information about international editions, contact your local Microsoft Corporation office or contact Microsoft Press International directly at fax (425) 936-7329. Visit our Web site at mspress.microsoft.com. Send comments to *mspinput@microsoft.com.*

Acquisitions Editor: Kong Cheung
Series Editor: Sandra Haynes
Project Editor: Kristen Weatherby

Body Part No. X08-06072

"By a single thought that comes into the mind,
In one moment a hundred worlds are overturned."

—Rumi

Contents At A Glance

Table of Contents

Chapter 10
Using Styles to Increase Your Formatting Power 227

Chapter 11
Outlining Documents for Clarity and Structure 251

Chapter 16
Enlivening Documents with Drawings and AutoShapes 381

Chapter 23
Using Word's Desktop Publishing Features 549

Chapter 24
Drawing Attention to Your Document with Borders and Shading 575

Part 7
Taking Advantage of Web and Networking Features 659

Chapter 29
Keeping an Eye on Word's Online Features 661

Chapter 30
Collaborating On Line with E-Mail, NetMeeting, Discussions, and Faxes 671

Chapter 39
Putting Speech and Handwriting Recognition Features to Work 927

Chapter 40
Creating and Working with VBA Macros 959

Acknowledgments

First and foremost, our thanks goes out to Claudette Moore and Debbie McKenna at the Moore Literary Agency, and Kong Cheung, the acquisitions editor at Microsoft Press, for making this book possible in the first place. In addition, we sincerely appreciate the work and almost superhuman effort exerted by the entire group of people who had a hand in seeing this book to fruition. In particular, we thank Kristen Weatherby, project editor at Microsoft Press, for her persistent and personable shepherding; Steve Sagman for his ever-watchful eye as the project coordinator; Gail Taylor and Jennifer Harris for their conscientious and professional editing; Jack Beaudry, for his terrific work and helpful suggestions as he tech-edited his way through this entire book; Sharon Bell, the principal compositor, for the great-looking, easy-to-read pages; and Tom Speeches, the principal proofreader. Furthermore, we thank Al Gordon, an expert in on-line speech and handwriting technologies, for sharing his knowledge in Chapter 39, "Putting Speech and Handwriting Recognition Features to Work." And, we thank Archie Millhollon, a networking and hardware guru (and the originator of Frankenstein computers), for sharing his expertise in Appendix D, "Quick Guide to Peer-to-Peer Networks," that readers will certainly find useful.

Writing computer books is often an isolating process that matches up three odd companions: a person, a computer, and a program. But in writing this book with my co-author Mary Millhollon, I was blessed to be a part of a team, to give and receive support, trading both technical information and stories about our sons (which turned out to be really important stress-reducers when the deadlines loomed large!). Thanks, Mary, for your partnership and your friendship. I also found the Microsoft Press team to be among the most responsive and supportive publishing groups I've ever worked with. I especially enjoyed working with Kristen Weatherby, Steve Sagman, and Gail Taylor, who made this extremely challenging project not only possible, but pleasurable. I hope we all get the opportunity to work together again sometime.

Last but not least, (now it's Mary's turn) I'm extremely grateful for having the opportunity to collaborate with Kathy Murray; her unique blend of intelligence, wit, and insight is truly phenomenal. After typing at least a dozen sentiments here and deleting all of them because they sounded a tad too smarmy, I think simplicity says it best—Thanks Kathy! I'm also grateful to the Microsoft Press team—especially Kristen, Steve, Jennifer, and Jack—whose professionalism and responsiveness helped to make this project a success. Also, thanks to friends and family for tolerating my invisibility while I wrote my share of this book. Most notably, thanks to Jeff Castrina for providing constant inspiration; Julie Pickering, because, in a perfect world, everyone would have a sister like her just to keep life interesting; and Jason Millhollon, who periodically knocked on my door to make sure I was getting those chapters wrapped up (now, let's catch a movie!). Finally, as always, my heartfelt thanks goes to Cale and the two boys who spontaneously bring sunshine and color (and lizards and worms) into my life on a daily basis, Robert and Matthew.

We'd Like to Hear from You!

Our goal at Microsoft Press is to create books that help you find the information you need to get the most out of your software.

The INSIDE OUT series was created with you in mind. As part of an effort to ensure that we're creating the best, most useful books we can, we talked to our customers and asked them to tell us what they need from a Microsoft Press series. Help us continue to help you. Let us know what you like about this book and what we can do to make it better. When you write, please include the title and author of this book in your e-mail, as well as your name and contact information. We look forward to hearing from you.

How to Reach Us

E-mail: nsideout@microsoft.com
Mail: Inside Out Series Editor
Microsoft Press
One Microsoft Way
Redmond, WA 98052

Note: Unfortunately, we can't provide support for any software problems you might experience. Please go to http://support.microsoft.com *for help with any software issues.*

Conventions and Features Used in This Book

This book uses special text and design conventions to make it easier for you to find the information you need.

Text Conventions

Convention	Meaning
Abbreviated menu commands	For your convenience, this book uses abbreviated menu commands. For example, "Choose Tools, Track Changes, Highlight Changes" means that you should click the Tools menu, point to Track Changes, and select the Highlight Changes command.
Boldface type	**Boldface** type is used to indicate text that you enter or type.
Initial Capital Letters	The first letters of the names of menus, dialog boxes, dialog box elements, and commands are capitalized. Example: the Save As dialog box.
Italicized type	*Italicized* type is used to indicate new terms.
Plus sign (+) in text	Keyboard shortcuts are indicated by a plus sign (+) separating two key names. For example, Ctrl+Alt+Delete means that you press the Ctrl, Alt, and Delete keys at the same time.

Design Conventions

newfeature!

This text identifies a new or significantly updated feature in this version of the software.

InsideOut

These are the book's signature tips. In these tips, you'll get the straight scoop on what's going on with the software—inside information on why a feature works the way it does. You'll also find handy workarounds to different software problems.

tip Tips provide helpful hints, timesaving tricks, or alternative procedures related to the task being discussed.

Troubleshooting

Look for these sidebars to find solutions to common problems you might encounter. Troubleshooting sidebars appear next to related information in the chapters. You can also use the Troubleshooting Topics index at the back of the book to look up problems by topic.

Cross-references point you to other locations in the book that offer additional information on the topic being discussed.

on the CD This icon indicates sample files or text found on the companion CD.

caution Cautions identify potential problems that you should look out for when you're completing a task or problems that you must address before you can complete a task.

note Notes offer additional information related to the task being discussed.

Sidebar

The sidebars sprinkled throughout these chapters provide ancillary information on the topic being discussed. Go to sidebars to learn more about the technology or a feature.

Part 1

Introducing Word 2002—Fast and Functional

Chapter 1

Gearing Up with Word 2002

Welcome to Word 2002—the fast-moving, streamlined, full-featured new edition of one of the world's most popular word processing programs. Are you looking for a way to create professional documents faster and better than ever? Word can help you with that. Would your life be easier if you had a program capable of a powerful but easy-to-use mail merge? Word's Mail Merge is now better than ever. Do you want a program that will help you leverage the data you create in other applications, enabling you to create something once and use it many times?

Word is the word processing program in the Microsoft Office suite, but it's much more than a simple word processor. Word can be an e-mail editor, Web page generator, long-document manager, newsletter publisher, and more. Word literally puts a world of possibilities at your fingertips and gives you the tools you need to package your information for print or Web use.

Finding Out What's New

If you've been using Word for a while, you've probably gone through a number of program revisions and upgrades. Each new version brings a new face, a fix of buggy-but-functional features, and some cool new capabilities that are worth learning to use.

And this version of Word has a number of new and interesting features. Some of the features—such as the task pane, smart tag improvements, and the new and improved Clipboard—make using Word easier, faster, and more intuitive. Others are exciting new additions, like speech and handwriting technologies and the powerful new organization chart generator and diagramming feature. Still other changes make your use of Word safer, reducing the frustration and potential damage done by untimely computer crashes.

Checking Out the New, Streamlined Look

What you'll notice first is that Word 2002 has a new look—sleek and streamlined. Designed to give you maximum room on-screen in which to work, the new interface includes several features that help you create faster, cleaner documents:

- **Make your choices faster, thanks to improved graphical menus.** The menus now include a gray sidebar that houses the tool icons to the left of the commands, enabling you to see at a glance how the text options and the icons relate. (See Figure 1-1.) No more hunting for the tool you need or waiting for ScreenTips to appear—just open the menu and choose the item you want quickly.

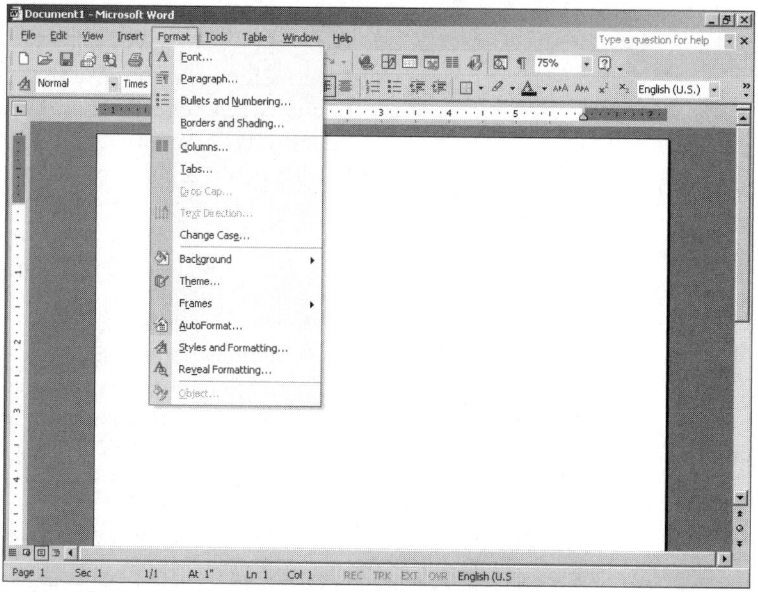

Figure 1-1. Tool icons appear to the left of commands in a new gray sidebar, helping you see at a glance which tool you need.

- **Choose new input methods using the Language bar.** The Language bar appears in the upper right corner of the screen and gives you choices for text input. (See Figure 1-2.) You can choose to dictate using the Microphone or write additional notes or drawings by hand and add them to your document easily.

Figure 1-2. The Language bar makes your choices for text input available at the click of a button. You can choose to give Word voice commands, handwrite notes, change your options, or make corrections using the Language bar.

InsideOut

This is one of those quirky Word issues—on some systems, the Language bar appears by default; on others, it doesn't. If your Language bar doesn't appear automatically, look for the small EN symbol in the lower right area of your screen, beside the system clock in your taskbar. Double-click the symbol to display the Language bar.

For more information on how to set up and use Word 2002's new speech and handwriting recognition features, see Chapter 2, "Creating Documents from Start to Finish."

- **Find what you need easily with the task pane.** The task pane is an effective, out-of-the-way, multi-purpose panel that automatically opens when you choose certain commands. The pane displays items you might need to access quickly—like new document choices, styles, templates, document options, Clipboard contents, formatting selections, search tools, and Document Recovery choices. (See Figure 1-3.)

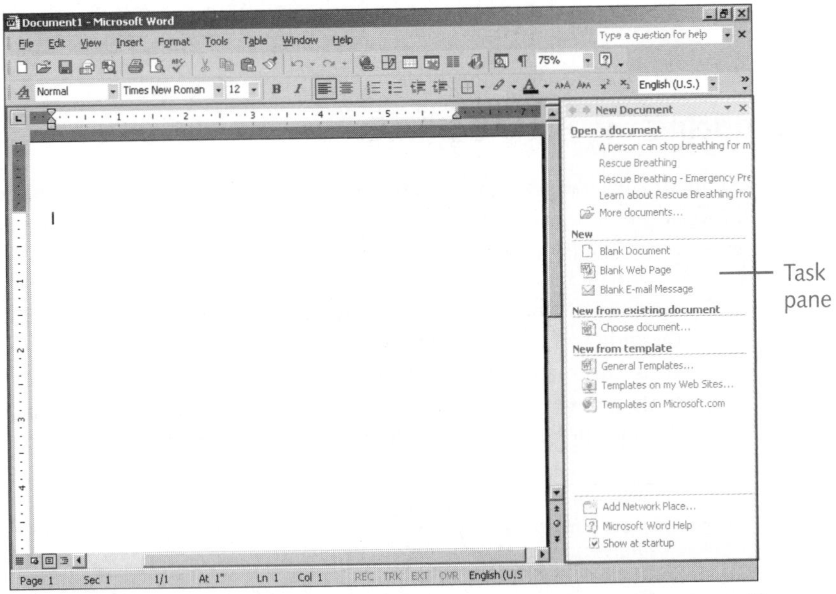

Figure 1-3. The task pane brings choices to you by providing options, files, styles, and other selections in a side panel along the right side of the work area. Other features in Word—including Clipboard, Mail Merge, and Document Recovery—also use the task pane, keeping the look and feel consistent.

- **Get focused help, faster, with the Ask A Question box.** The Ask A Question box gives you quick, question-style help anytime you need it. Instead of waiting for the Office Assistant to do its animated bit, you can simply click in the Ask A Question box, type your puzzlement, and press Enter. The answer appears in the task Pane, positioned to the right of your work space.

- **Get quick info from smart tags.** Smart tags are contextual prompts that help you work flexibly and fast. When you position the pointer over a tag in a document, a prompt allows you to retrieve or add data from Microsoft Outlook, check your schedule, set meetings, and display and access address, phone, and e-mail information.
- **See what you're pasting from the new, improved Clipboard.** Now the Clipboard shows you up to 24 items stored there—including thumbnails of text or pictures. This enables you to see what's actually on the Clipboard so that you can figure out at a glance which item you want to paste. The Clipboard appears in the task pane, along the right side of the work area.

For more information on working with the new and improved Clipboard, see Chapter 2, "Creating Documents from Start to Finish."

- **Find, store, and organize clips more easily in the Media Gallery.** The Microsoft Media Gallery has been revamped to carry the familiar look and feel of Microsoft Windows Explorer. Now you can select the categories and folders by clicking your choice in the left panel and make your choice in the right. There is also expanded support for clips of all types on line.

Introducing the Big Additions

Many of the changes in Word 2002 have more to do with *enhancement* than innovation—but these three new features give you additional choices for the way you enter your data (be it words or pictures):

- **Speak your piece.** Now you aren't limited to the keyboard or scanner as the only means of getting your text into Word. You can use Word 2002's voice command and dictation features to open and close menus, choose tools, and enter information. The Speech Training Wizard walks you through the feature setup the first time you use it.

For more information about using Word's voice command and dictation features and handwriting recognition, see Chapter 2, "Creating Documents from Start to Finish," and Chapter 38, "Customizing Word and Maximizing Accessibility."

- **Add handwritten notes to your documents.** Now you can add your customized signature to documents, add handwritten notes, circle key points, and more, using Word 2002's handwriting feature.
- **Create organization charts and diagrams in your document.** You can create organization charts and five different types of conceptual diagrams without leaving your document. The new Diagram button on the Drawing toolbar gives you quick access to the feature and makes it easy for you to add to, edit, and wrap text around the charts and diagrams you create.

- **Add drawings more easily with the drawing canvas.** Now you can add drawings without interrupting your editing process. When you choose Insert, Picture and click New Drawing, an easy-to-use drawing canvas is presented so that you can create custom drawings without leaving Word. (See Figure 1-4.)

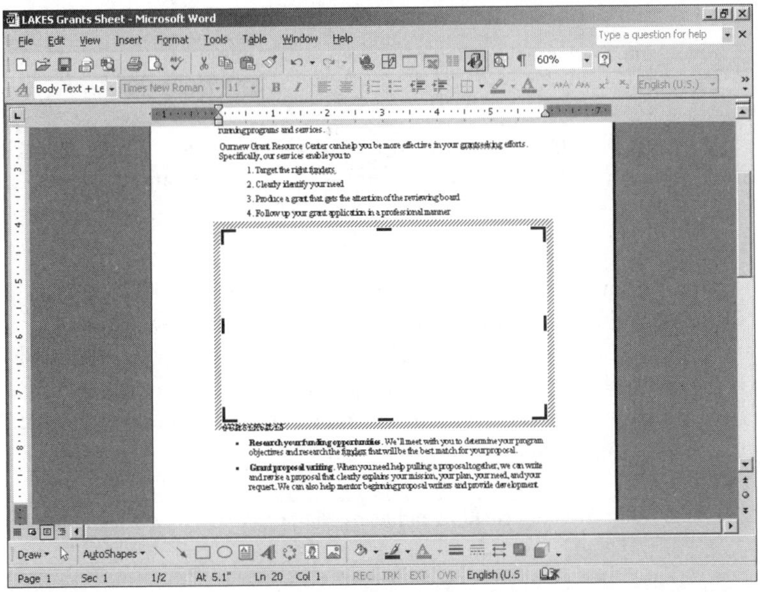

Figure 1-4. The drawing canvas opens up a drawing space right in your current document—which means you don't have to leave what you're doing in order to create an illustration to accompany your words.

For more about using the drawing canvas, see Chapter 16, "Enlivening Documents with Drawings and AutoShapes."

Collaborative Document Enhancements

Today's fast-paced business environment demands the efficient and effective use of the talents of many people. Collaboration is big. And a number of improved Word features help you make cooperative document creating and editing easier than ever.

- **Faster access for multiuser documents.** You no longer have to wait for a file to be unlocked before working on a collaborative document. The new multi-user document support in Word 2002 makes copies of the file being accessed and then merges the different changes after the fact. This reduces your wait time and takes care of the necessary coordination behind the scenes.

- **Compare and combine documents more easily.** If you often compare and merge changes in team documents, you'll find it easier to review comments and coordinate changes. Now Compare And Merge Documents is a single command available in the Tools menu, and the Merge action gives you the means to control the way in which you merge documents.

For more information on working with compare and merge features, see Chapter 30, "Collaborating On Line with E-Mail, NetMeeting, Discussions, and Faxes."

- **View document changes more clearly.** Now you can turn tracking on and off with the selection of a single command, and control of tracking—viewing, adding, accepting, and rejecting changes—is easier from the revised Reviewing toolbar.
- **Guarantee the authenticity of your documents with a digital signature.** With the increased need for ensuring reliability and authenticity in an often virtual workplace, Word 2002 includes the ability to add digital signatures to documents. You secure the signature for your document or macro project through an Internet certification authority or your system administrator or IT professional.

For more information on creating and using digital signatures, see Chapter 34, "Addressing Security Issues."

- **Better support for ODMA.** If you rely on the Open Document Management API (ODMA) to make data generation and reuse seamless for others in your department or company, you'll like having ODMA support available when you're using mail merge and comparing and merging documents. You can also work with ODMA when you insert field data, add files or pictures, and use the Save As command.

Formatting Enhancements

High on the list of "top ten headaches" experienced by Microsoft Word users are the hassles that formatting often brings. And while Word 2002 won't wave all your woes away, the program does make some gains in making formatting generally easier to use, relaxing the strict use of styles, making table generation easier, and streamlining some of the more cumbersome formatting features in Word 2000.

- **Apply and clear formats—simple and fast.** One of our favorite changes in the formatting realm is the easy application of formats—no styles required. Styles are great when you're creating a format you'll use over and over throughout a document, a project, or a company. But new features in Word let you apply a simple format you want to use more than once *without* having to go through the sometimes confusing process of creating a style. You can apply the format with a clean point-and-click. Another addition, the Clear Formatting command, enables you to remove formatting and hyperlinks and return selected text to the Normal style.

- **Select multiple blocks of text anywhere in your document.** The previous incarnation of Word forced you to select text in a continuous block—but this is no longer true. If you want to pick and choose words, paragraphs, or sections, you can simply press Ctrl while selecting multiple blocks.

> newfeature!
> **tip** **Find and highlight the text you want—fast**
>
> Another small change that makes life easier is the ability to find and highlight text blocks using an option in the Find And Replace dialog box. You no longer need to page through your documents or find occurrences one by one—now you can do a search and automatically select the text you want to work with.

- **Control your bullets and numbered lists.** The benefit of having list formatting brings with it the pitfalls of styles that behave the way they want to. In earlier versions of Word, it was hard to predict when and how list formats would change if you did anything at all unpredictable. With Word 2002, you can easily drag list items, renumber and reorder lists, and create custom list styles without that element of surprise. And for those occasional stubborn list formats that might occur, a smart tag appears, giving you the ability to turn the format off if desired.
- **Enter and organize table data more easily.** Now you can easily copy table data from one table to another by dragging the selected information and you can apply the new custom table styles in the process. The table sort feature has also been improved, giving you more control over the way you organize your information.
- **Get clear about footnotes.** Word 2002 makes adding footnotes and endnotes easier by combining all related options on a single page in the Footnote And Endnote dialog box.
- **See the formatting applied to your document.** Now you have the option of using the Reveal Formatting command (in the Format menu) to display in the task pane the variety of formats applied to the text at the insertion point. (See Figure 1-5, on the next page.)

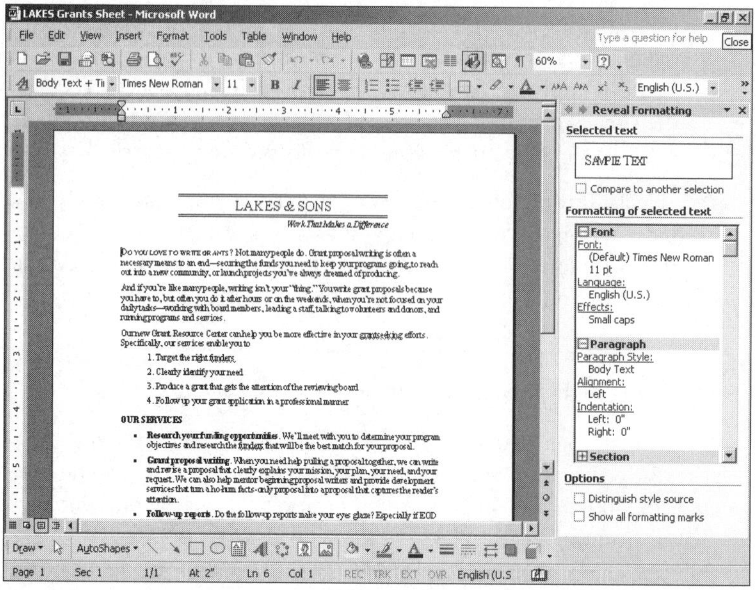

Figure 1-5. Now you can reveal the formatting codes in your document as you work, which enables you to spot inconsistencies and weed them out.

Editing Enhancements

A few editing changes in Word 2002 improve and extend the reach of existing features. Nothing earthshaking here, but the small improvements make some of the routine Word tasks easier to manage.

- **Find And Replace** dialog box now enables you to locate and highlight words, phrases, paragraphs, or entire sections of text.
- **Custom dictionaries** are modifiable and easier to create and select.
- **AutoCorrect** now provides information about how to insert the suggested word and automatically corrects misspellings caused by common typographical errors
- **Word Count** now displays a running total while you work on your document. Additionally, you control whether footnotes and endnotes are included as part of the total count. (See Figure 1-6.)

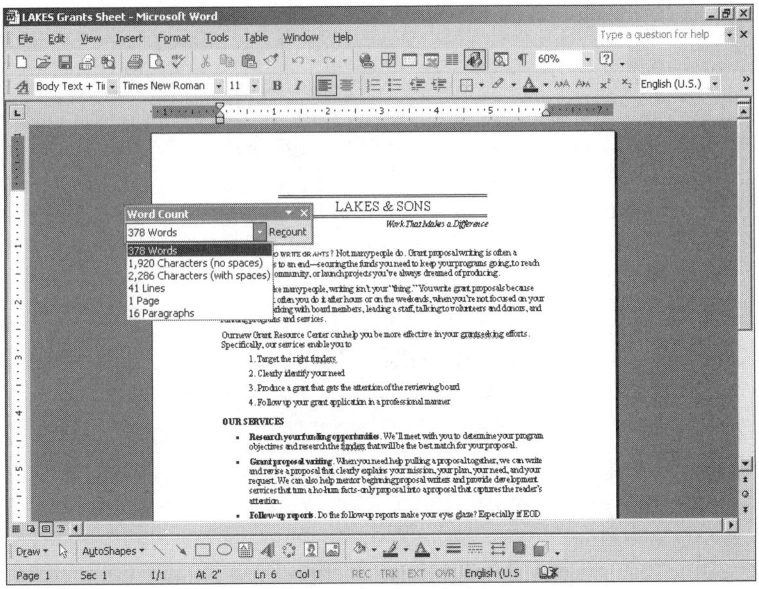

Figure 1-6. No more pointing and clicking to find a word count—now you can display a running total on the Word Count toolbar as you work.

Mail Merge Revamped

If you're tired of piecing together Word's mail merge process, you'll like the restructuring of mail merge in Word 2002. Now you have the option of working with the Mail Merge Wizard, which leads you through creating letters, e-mail messages, envelopes, labels, and directories. The wizard appears as a series of steps in the task pane, so it works alongside your document, prompting you to select your data file, edit your list, and make your selections as needed.

The addition of a Mail Merge toolbar makes your self-directed work easier, enabling you to control the mail merge process as you see fit. Create the data document, insert fields, search and sort records, and merge to another document, printer, e-mail, or fax.

For more about using mail merge effectively, see Chapter 35, "Performing Mail Merges."

Printing Changes

New printing features extend Word's capabilities by enabling you to zoom the print display when printing in landscape mode. You also have the option of printing folios, pamphlets, and booklets and controlling duplex printing by selecting Options in the Print dialog box.

Web Improvements

In addition to making Word easier for collaborative document creation—which could take place on an intranet or the Internet—a number of Web enhancements improve and extend Word's Web page development capabilities.

- **Easy-to-use picture bullets.** Now you can use pictures as you would any other bullet on a Word Web page. You can choose the pictures you want and apply them to various outline levels.

- **Better control of cascading style sheets.** If you work with HTML, you know how important cascading style sheets (CSS) are to the Web documents you create. Word 2002 gives you additional control over style sheets by enabling you to select the ones you want and prioritize them for your pages.

- **Word 2002 as the default e-mail editor.** By default, Word 2002 is selected as the Office default e-mail editor. (See Figure 1-7). This is a good idea for several reasons: It gives you the additional text-editing and formatting features Word offers. It also adds an Introduction field, which gives you a way of writing an introduction to your message (similar to a comment you might add on a fax cover sheet).

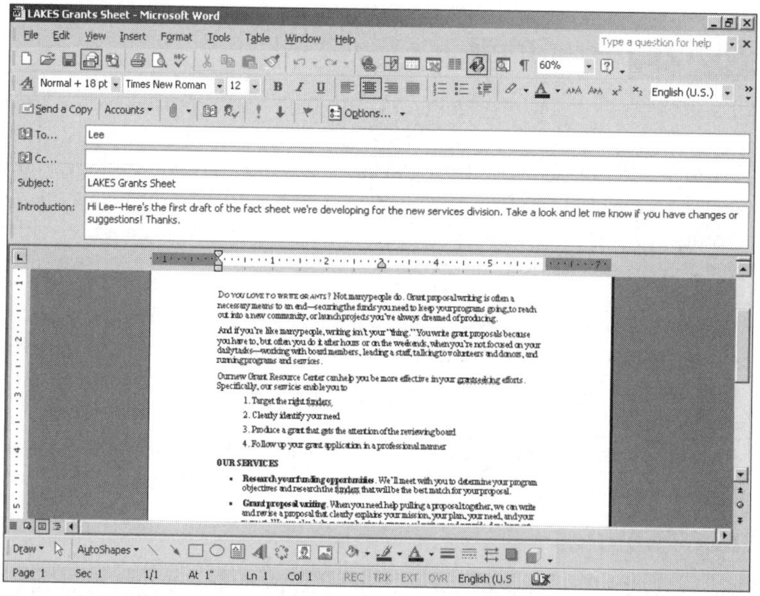

Figure 1-7. Using Word as your default e-mail editor enables you to control the document format and text styles.

For more about using Word to create Web pages, see Chapter 31, "Creating Professional Web Sites."

Crash Protection

When Word quits—unexpectedly—can you be sure you've saved your important document and taken all the precautions you can take to protect your data? Word 2002 helps you do that. With a number of new crash protection features, Word will step in to lessen the chances of data loss and recover your open files. The crash protection features included in Word 2002 are as follows:

- **Save On Crash.** Word automatically lists in the Document Recovery task pane the files that were active at the time of the crash and prompts you to save them.
- **Open And Repair.** If a bad crash results in a corrupted file, Word gives you the means to open and repair the damaged file. (See Figure 1-8.)

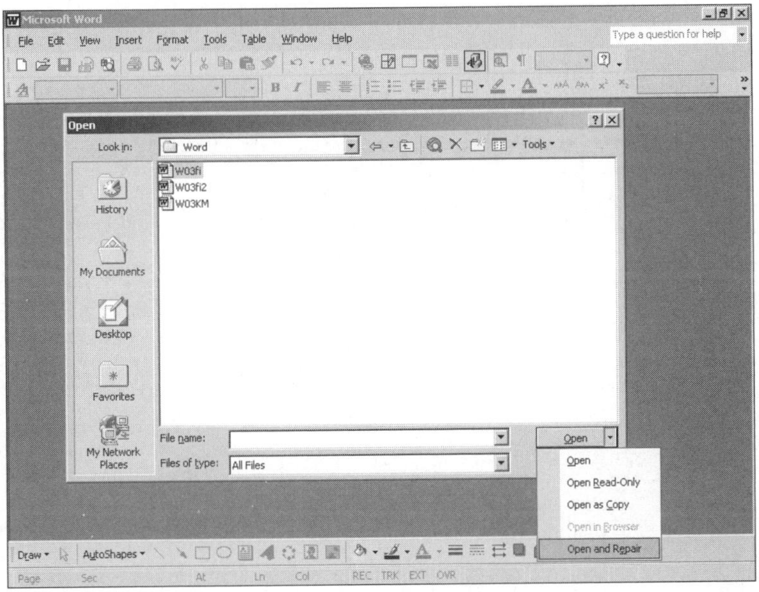

Figure 1-8. In the event that a crash causes a file corruption, you have a way to attempt recovery of the file with the Open And Repair command in the Open dialog box.

- **Reporting Crashes.** If you have an Internet connection when the crash occurs, an message box asks whether you'd like to report the problem to Microsoft. If you click Yes, a problem report is created and sent in electronically.

note When Word runs into problems and crash recovery kicks in (don't worry—your system will crash sooner or later and you'll get to see this feature!), the program gives you the option of sending a crash report to Microsoft for analysis. Do you wonder what they'll do with your report? The technical team at Microsoft reviews the report, categorizes it, and tries to find a resolution, which might involve a program update, a knowledge base article, or a code fix.

Investigating Word's Interface Tools

Start Word by clicking Start, Programs, Microsoft Word. The Word document window opens and a new blank document is displayed. Figure 1-9 shows the Word 2002 interface and the various screen elements and tools you'll use as you create and work with documents.

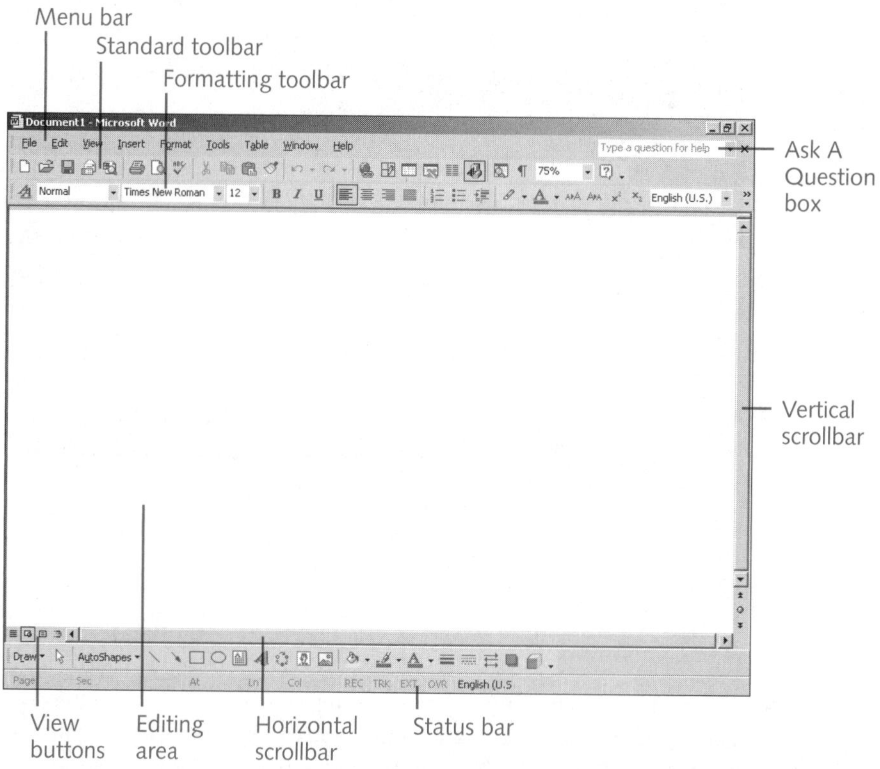

Figure 1-9. The interface changes in Word 2002 give you a flatter, more open document surface. The tools you need are within easy reach and positioned around the periphery of the work area.

If you need help installing Word, see Appendix A, "Installing or Upgrading Word."

Working with Menus

You have several different ways to work with Word. From personalized menu selections to shortcut menus to customizable toolbars, you have a range of flexible options for the way you make your selections. What's more, Word attempts to learn the way you work, personalizing your menus and toolbars with the items you use most often and leaving off other items until you select them.

Personalized Menus

With an intentional focus on keeping the screen uncluttered, the personalized menus in Word allow you to use the menu's "short form," unless you need a command that doesn't appear initially on the shortened menu. When you first open a menu, Word displays a shortened list of the most commonly used commands in that menu. An Expand button at the bottom of the menu enables you to display the remaining commands if necessary. (See Figure 1-10.)

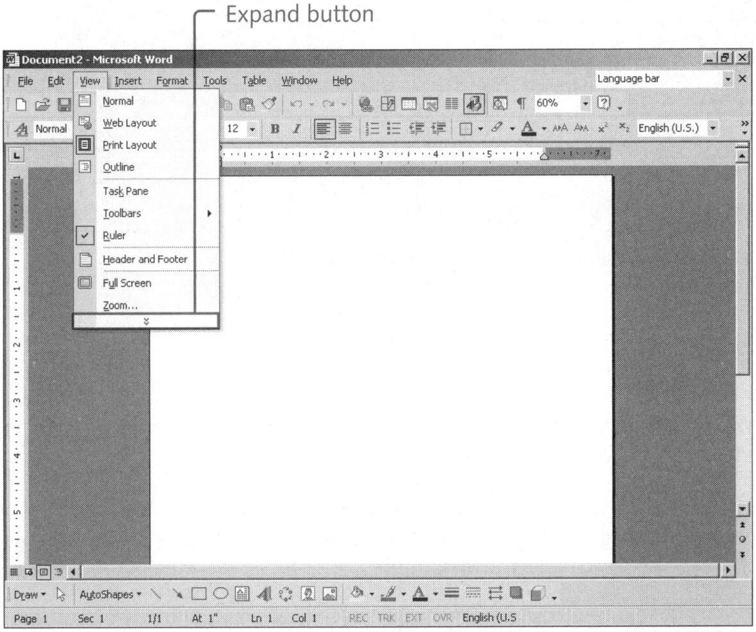

Figure 1-10. A personalized menu appears first in a short form; when you click the Expand button and select a command, it's added to the menu automatically.

Shortcut Menus

Another type of menu that helps streamline your use of Word is the shortcut menu. You display shortcut menus by right-clicking the mouse button in the editing window. The content of the menu varies, depending on what you're doing and what you clicked. For example, if you're editing a paragraph and you right-click, the menu shown in Figure 1-11 might appear.

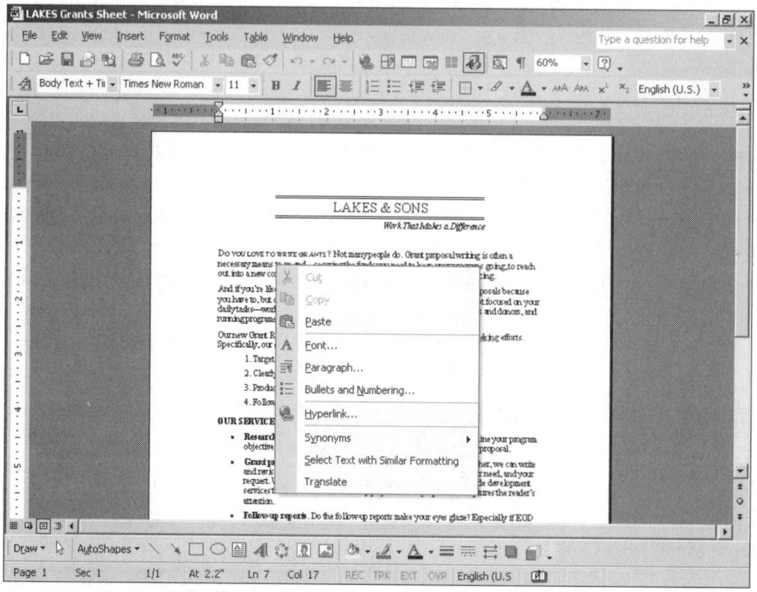

Figure 1-11. The shortcut menu displays commands that are related to the task you're carrying out and the type of data with which you're working.

By contrast, if you're adding a graphical object and right-click the object, the shortcut menu in Figure 1-12 appears.

tip **Don't like using the horizontal scrollbar?**

You can wrap the text in your document to contain it within the window—then you won't need to use the horizontal scrollbar at all. Choose Tools, Options and click the View tab. On the View tab of the Options dialog box , select the Wrap To Window check box and click OK.

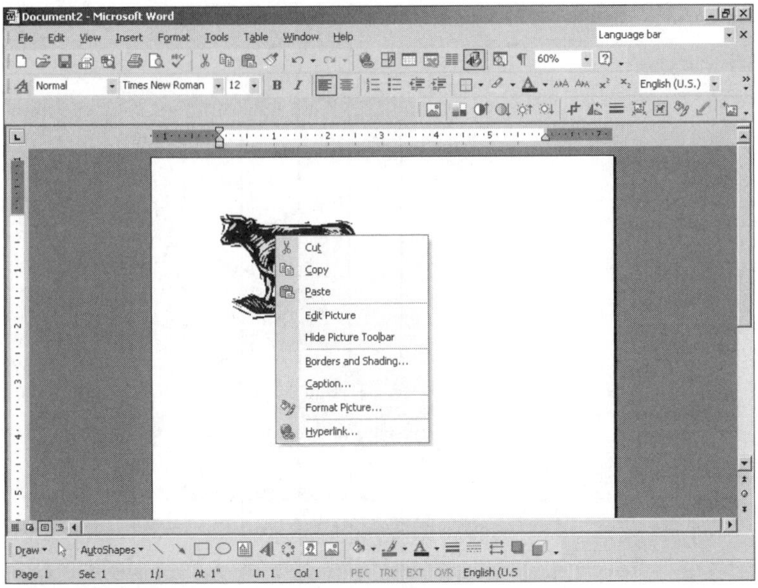

Figure 1-12. The shortcut menu for a graphical object shows a different collection of commands.

Putting Scrollbars to Work

Scrollbars have been around for a long time—they are a staple in Windows applications. Word scrollbars give you a quick method for moving through the document. Simply drag the scroll box down the vertical scrollbar or to the right on the horizontal scrollbar to move through your document. A ScreenTip appears to show you the heading nearest to the scroll box position as you move the box on the scrollbar.

Using the Document Browser

Another way to move quickly through your document involves using the document browser. The browser is an effective little tool that enables you to move through your document in a variety of ways. For example, you might browse by graphics, by headings, by section, or by page. To use the document browser, follow these steps:

1. Click the Select Browse Object button. The Select Browse Object menu appears. (See Figure 1-13, on the next page.)

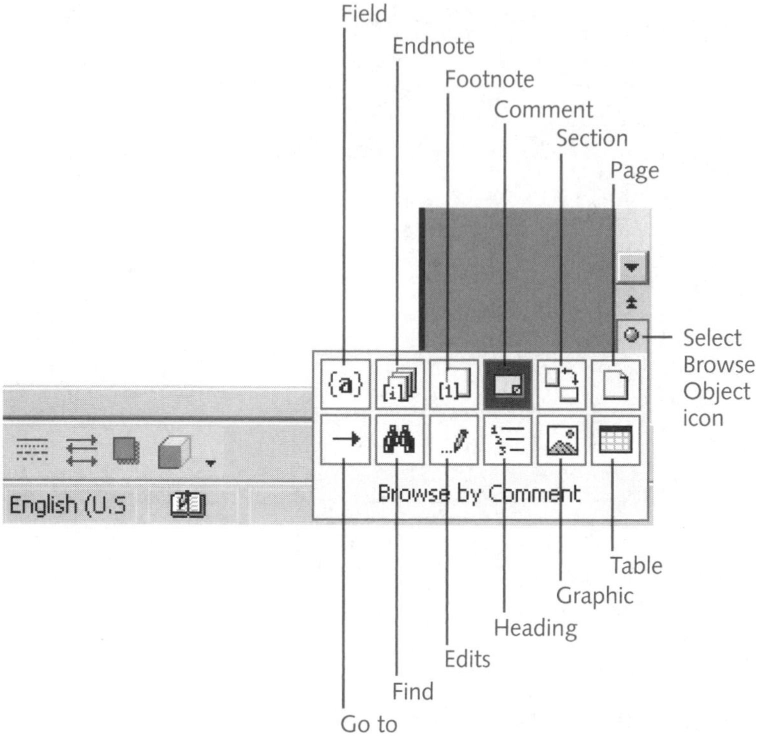

Figure 1-13. The Select Browse Object menu gives you a range of elements to select as your stopping points.

2. Click your choice on the Select Browse Object menu. Word moves the insertion point to the next occurrence of the item you selected.
3. To continue browsing forward in the document, click the double down arrows below the Select Browse Object icon.
4. To browse backward, click the double up arrows above the Select Browse Object icon.

> **tip** **Identify elements in the document browser**
>
> If you forget which element you've selected in the Select Browse Object menu, position the mouse pointer over the navigation arrows. If you've selected Browse By Comment, for example, Next Comment appears when you position the pointer over the double down arrows.

Using Keyboard Shortcuts

If you're a consistent—if not fast—typist, you might be most comfortable moving through your document and making command selections by using the keyboard. Word includes a library of keyboard shortcuts you can use to get your work done quickly.

Displaying Key Functions

Not sure what your function keys do? You can have Word display a toolbar of functions if you choose. Choose Tools, Customize and click the Toolbars tab. Locate the Function Key Display check box in the list and select it. The Function Key toolbar then appears at the bottom of the screen. (See Figure 1-14.)

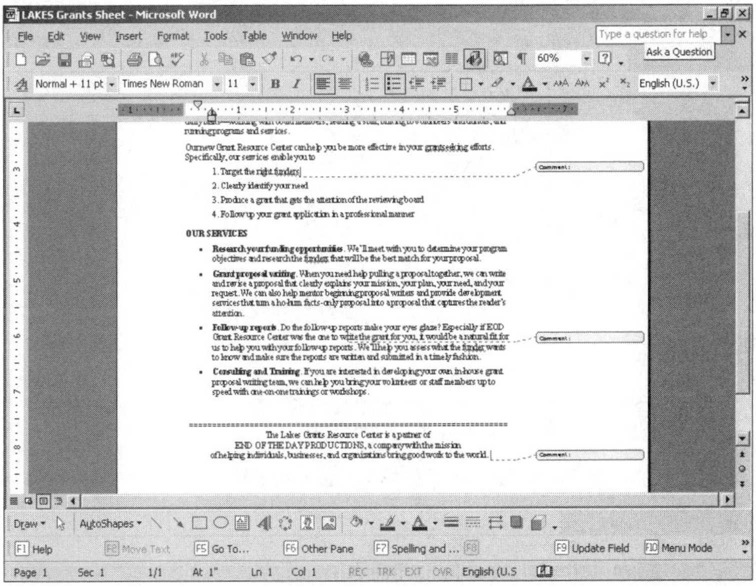

Figure 1-14. If you don't mind giving up the screen real estate, you can display the function key listing at the bottom of the work area.

Additionally, you can make many of the most common menu selections by using keyboard shortcuts, as shown in Table 1-1, on the next page.

Table 1-1. Bypassing Menu Selections Using Keyboard Shortcuts

Button	Menu and Command Selection	Shortcut
	File, New	Ctrl+N
	File, Open	Ctrl+O
	File, Save	Ctrl+S
	File, Print	Ctrl+P
	Edit, Undo	Ctrl+Z
	Edit, Redo	Ctrl+Y
	Edit, Cut	Ctrl+X
	Edit, Copy	Ctrl+C
	Edit, Paste	Ctrl+V
N/A	Edit, Select All	Ctrl+A
	Edit, Find	Ctrl+F
N/A	Edit, Replace	Ctrl+H
N/A	Edit, Go To	Ctrl+G
	Insert, Hyperlink	Ctrl+K
	Tools, Spelling And Grammar	F7
N/A	Tools, Language, Thesaurus	Shift+F7
	Tools, Track Changes	Ctrl+Shift+E
	Tools, Macro, Macros	Alt+F8
N/A	Tools, Macro, Visual Basic Editor	Alt+F11
N/A	Tools, Macro, Microsoft Script Editor	Alt+Shift+F11
	Help, Microsoft Word Help	F1
	Help, What's This?	Shift+F1

Viewing Documents in Various Lights

Word provides many different ways for you to see what you're doing—from outline form to full screen display to something in between, you determine what you want on-screen as you go about your work.

Document Views

Print Layout is one of the first views you'll see when you begin using Word. This view shows you the way your document will look when printed. As you work in this view, you'll see all elements—text formats, graphics, rules, borders and shading—that you add to the page.

The different views in Word each give you a different perspective of the developing document. Table 1-2 lists the various views and gives suggestions for their use.

Table 1-2. Comparing Word Views

View	Description	Use	Access
Normal	Displays single page with simple text the formatting. No drawings, comments, or columns.	For entering text quickly and doing simple text editing	Choose View, Normal or click the Normal View button to the left of the horizontal scrollbar.
Web Layout	Displays the page width and text position and format as the document would appear on the Web. Inserted drawings, graphics, and columns will appear.	For testing a page you're creating for the Web	Choose View, Web Layout or click the Web Layout View button.
Print Layout	Displays the document as it will appear in print, with text formatting, graphics, headers and footers, columns, and all special elements.	For proofing the design, layout, and treatment of text and graphics before you print	Choose View, Print Layout or click the Print Layout View button.
Outline	Displays the headings and subheads in your document, providing the organizational structure.	For structuring the content of your document or organizing sections	Choose View, Outline or click the Outline View button.
Document Map	Displays the document in two different frames. On the left, the headings of the document enable you to navigate through the text on the right.	For moving through the document quickly, checking headings and corresponding sections	Choose View, Document Map or click the Document Map button on the Standard toolbar.

(continued)

Table 1-2. *(continued)*

View	Description	Use	Access
Full Screen	Displays the editing window of your document in full-screen view, without rulers, toolbars, or the menu bar.	For viewing the maximum work-space available on-screen.	Choose View, Full Screen; to return to the Preview view, click Close Full Screen on the Full Screen toolbar.

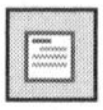
Normal

Displaying Your Document in Normal View Normal view is touted as the fastest and easiest view for entering and editing text quickly. If you need to just "get text in there," without seeing special layouts like columns and additional elements like headers and footers, Normal view enables you to work with text efficiently and get the task done. In Normal view, you *won't* see these elements:

- Multiple columns
- Drawings
- Headers and footers
- Footnotes and endnotes

Additionally, the page and section breaks in Normal view are shown as dotted lines and it's a bit more difficult to get a feel for how the text will actually look on the printed page. To know how the text will look in relation to the page, switch to Print Layout view.

Web Layout

Working in Web Layout View The Web Layout view shows the document the way it will appear in a Web browser—as one long page with no page breaks. Here the text will wrap to a wider margin and you'll see how your headings, formatting, background color, and graphics will look. Working in this view is helpful when you're creating a Web page in Word and also when you're creating a printed publication that you want to be able to port easily to a Web page.

Print Layout

Showing Print Layout View Print Layout view is the most complete view of the lot. With this view, you'll see the document as it will appear in print, with graphics, special formats, page breaks, and additional elements like headers, footers, endnotes, and more. Your special formats, like multiple columns, will appear.

Outline

Working with Outline View The Outline view enables you to see the organizational structure of your document. And not only can you *view* the levels, but you can also reorganize the outline, change heading subordination, and add and delete sections from within Outline view. Figure 1-15 shows a document displayed in Outline view. The outline has been collapsed to the first two organizational levels.

For more information on working with documents in Outline view, see Chapter 11, "Outlining Documents for Clarity and Structure."

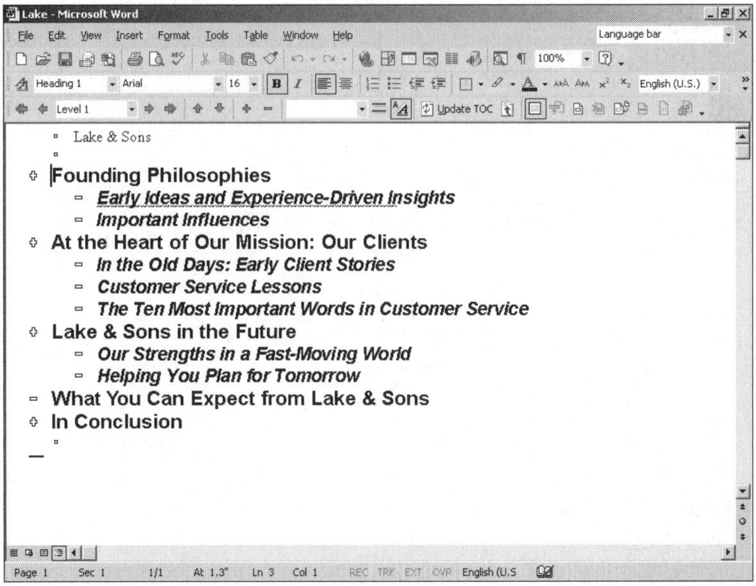

Figure 1-15. Outline view gives you the means to check the structure of your document and reorder sections as needed.

Document Map

Displaying the Document Map Word's Document Map enables you to see both the structure of your document and the content at the same time. Display it by choosing View, Document Map or by clicking the Document Map button on the Standard toolbar. Although the left panel doesn't show the actual outline *per se*, it does give you the means to navigate through your document by clicking the headings on the left to scroll the document to the desired section. (See Figure 1-16, on the next page.)

InsideOut

The Document Map might decide not to leave when you're finished with it. If the Document Map stays on when you switch to a different view, click the Document Map button once more.

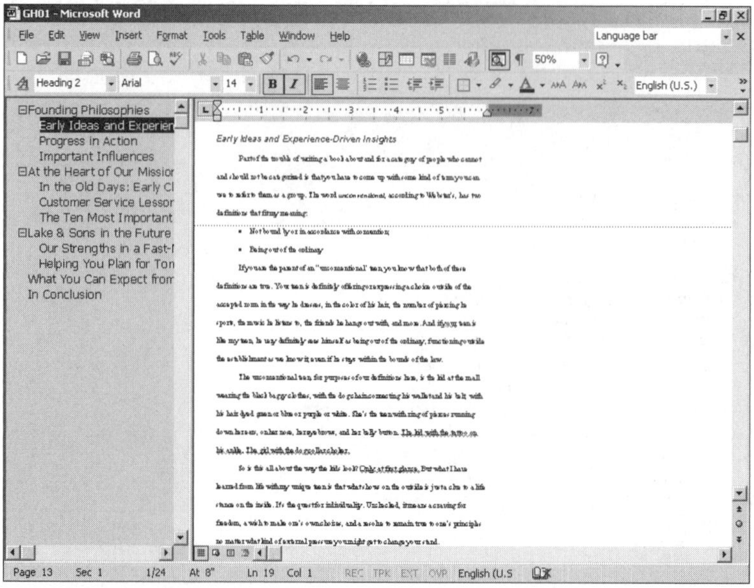

Figure 1-16. The Document Map gives you the means to see both the structure and the content at the same time.

Working in Full Screen View Full Screen view isn't exactly considered a document view, but it does change the way in which you see and work with your document. Full Screen view gets rid of everything except the text and a small toolbar, giving you the means to write and edit flat out without menus, the Task Pane, or—heaven forbid—the Office Assistant interrupting you. (See Figure 1-17.) To select Full Screen view, choose View, Full Screen. When you're ready to return to your previous view mode, click Close Full Screen.

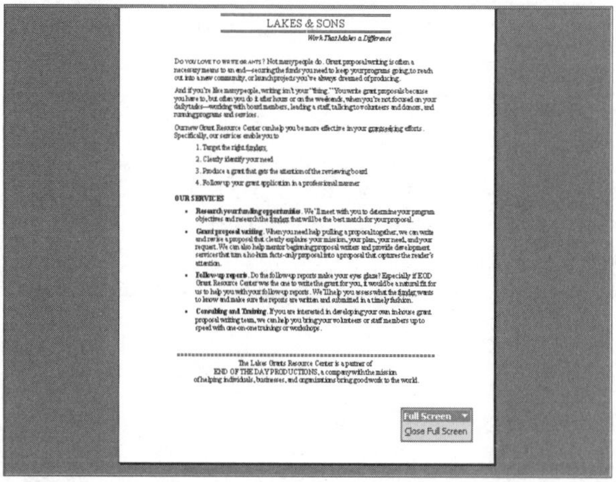

Figure 1-17. Full Screen gives you the maximum amount of room on-screen for text entry and editing.

Other Ways to Control and Customize Your View

There are other ways you can change the view of your document while you're working. You might want to change the display percentages using Zoom, split the display, or customize the View options used for document defaults.

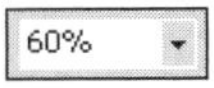

Zooming In on Your Document The Zoom control enables you to "get closer" or "move away from" the page while you work. The percentage you set controls the size of the document display. (See Figure 1-18.) A percentage of 100 displays the document at actual size. Percentages of less than 100 make the document display smaller. Percentages greater than 100 enlarge the text and graphics, enabling you to work "up close" for special spacing tasks, line drawing, or positioning techniques.

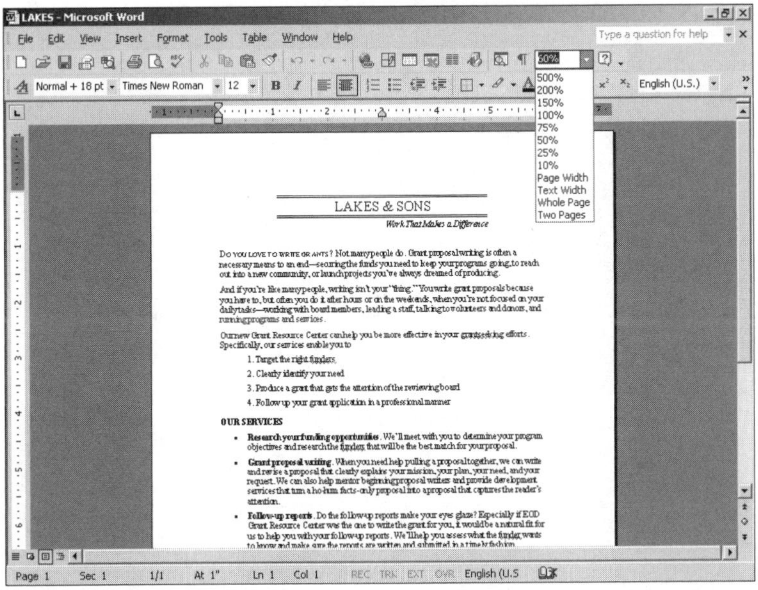

Figure 1-18. Click the Zoom down arrow to display the list of choices. Click your choice to make the change.

tip **Choose Page Width or Text Width with Zoom**

The Zoom list box offers Page Width, which enables you to choose a size that matches the width of the page; Text Width, which shows the display at the width of the text; and Whole Page and Two Pages, which reduce the display to fit one or two pages in the display area, respectively.

Earlier in this chapter, you learned about the new Reveal Formatting command, which displays in the task pane the various formats you've applied to your current document. For more about working with Reveal Formatting, see Chapter 5, "Adding Panache with Text Formatting and Special Characters."

Displaying Two Areas Simultaneously The work you do in some documents might require that you split the screen so that you can see two sections of a document at the same time. Perhaps you refer in an early part of your document to a section covered later and you want to make sure you've described the section accurately. You can have Word split the screen, as shown in Figure 1-19, into two sections that you can navigate independently by following these steps:

1. Position the pointer on the split box at the top of the vertical scroll bar. The pointer changes to a double-headed arrow.
2. Drag the box down to reveal the upper pane of the split window. When the pane is the size you want, release the mouse button.

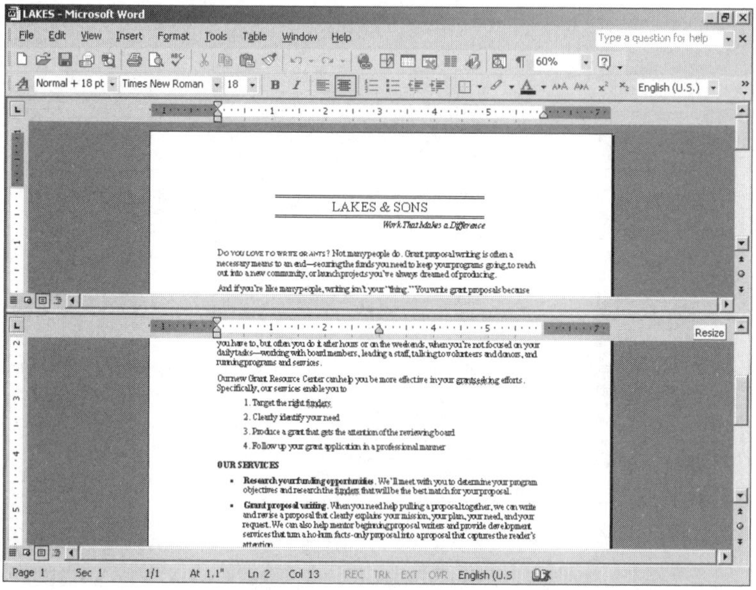

Figure 1-19. Clicking the split box and dragging it down opens a second document display window at the mouse pointer position. You can then scroll through the document as needed to locate the text you need.

> **tip** **Perform multi functions in multi windows**
>
> You can perform other functions in the split document window, as well: You can search, format, scroll, zoom in and out, and edit text as you would in a singular window.

Customizing View Options You can make some major choices about the way your Word screen appears by changing the view options. Choose Tools, Options and click the View tab. (See Figure 1-20.) You'll find a number of options related to different aspects of the document display.

- **Show** section options control whether additional elements appear in the Word window.
- **Formatting Marks** section options determine whether the formatting characters like tabs, characters, hidden text, and paragraph marks are displayed.
- **Print And Web Layout Options** control whether drawings, anchors, text boundaries, white space, and vertical rules are displayed.
- **Outline And Normal Options** allow you to choose whether text wraps to the window, whether a draft font is used, and if a style area is specified, the width of the area assigned to the style column.

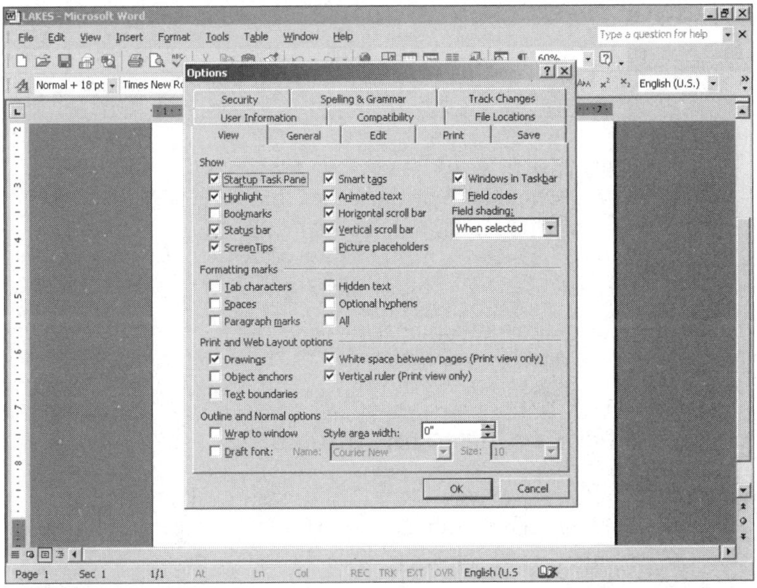

Figure 1-20. Setting View options enables you to control the elements that are displayed on the screen by default.

Creating Convenient Toolbar Displays

For several versions now, Word has given us customizable toolbars. The graphical nature of Word makes it easier to point and click than to open menus and search for commands. In Word 2002, the menus and the toolbars meet in a happy middle ground. Now the menus have the tools embedded in them, reinforcing what to look for when you don't feel like opening menus to find the same command.

To display a toolbar, simply choose View, Toolbars and select the toolbar you want to display. To remove a toolbar, just repeat the action, selecting to hide.

Know Your Staples: the Standard and Formatting Toolbars

The two toolbars most often used, and the ones that are displayed by default, are the Standard toolbar and the Formatting toolbar. The Standard toolbar includes the tools you'll use to manage files, create and edit documents, and add special but common elements to your document, such as tables, graphics, or charts. (See Figure 1-21.)

Figure 1-21. Tools on the Standard toolbar take care of file management, document creation, and editing tasks.

> **note** The order and selection of the tools shown on your Standard and Formatting toolbars might differ slightly from those shown here. As you work with Word, the program adds any previously undisplayed tools you select to the displayed toolbar, where they'll be within easy reach.

The Formatting toolbar includes the tools you'll use to control the font, size, style, alignment, format, and color of text. (See Figure 1-22.) Also on the Formatting toolbar are tools for controlling indents and alignment.

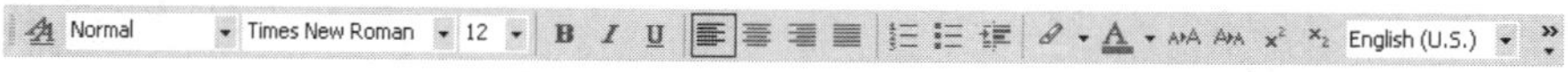

Figure 1-22. Formatting tools enable you to change the look, alignment, and color of text.

newfeature!

Introducing the New or Improved Toolbars

In addition to the better menu look, Word has added new toolbars, improved others, and subtracted one: The Clipboard toolbar is now displayed in a task pane all on its own. New or improved toolbars include the following:

- **Mail Merge**, now selectable from the View menu, offers tools for creating new documents, opening a data file, working with fields, searching and sorting data, and merging to printer, fax, e-mail, or other documents (see Figure 1-23).

  Figure 1-23. The Mail Merge toolbar lets you create your own mail merge operation without relying on the wizard.

- **Outlining**, now also available from the View menu, gives you the means to promote or demote headings or sections, choose outline levels, update the table of contents, and move to the table of contents. (See Figure 1-24.)

Figure 1-24. The Outline toolbar gives you a way to change heading and text levels and prepare and work with a table of contents.

note The Outline toolbar that appears as a selectable toolbar and the tool set that appears in Outline view are slightly different. The toolbar in Outline view is more complete and offers you the choice of working with master and subdocuments as well.

- **Word Count** is a simple little toolbar that gives you a running count of the words in your document. (See Figure 1-25.)

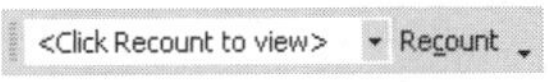

Figure 1-25. Small and simple, the Word Count toolbar keeps track of the number of words in your document.

Relocating Toolbars

If you like to work with a number of toolbars but don't want your document overloaded at the top of the window, you can move toolbars to any of the four edges of the screen. Additionally, you can create a *floating toolbar* by dragging the toolbar out into the work area.

To move a toolbar, follow these steps:

1. Display the toolbar you want to use.
2. Position the mouse pointer on the move handle at the far left edge of the toolbar. The pointer changes to a four-pronged arrow.
3. Drag the toolbar to the new location.

Toolbars are "sticky," which means you can drag them to one of the borders of the work area and they will suddenly adhere to the edge of the screen. For example, the Formatting toolbar shown in Figure 1-26, on the next page, is positioned along the left edge of the work area.

Quickly Adding and Removing Buttons

As we mentioned earlier in this chapter, Word attempts to learn the way you use the program by adding the tools you select to the toolbars as you go along. This enables the menus to stay relatively light until you select the tools you need to add. But there's another way to add tools to the toolbars—you can click the Toolbar Options button (located at the far right end of each toolbar) and point to Add Or Remove Buttons.

When the tools are displayed, click the one you want to add to select it. Alternatively, to remove a tool, click the tool and click to remove the check mark. The tool will be removed from the current display.

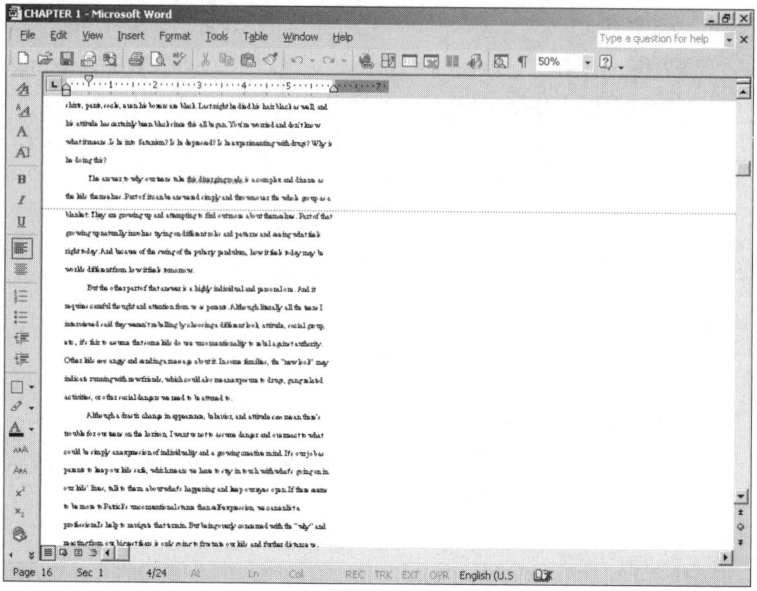

Figure 1-26. You can move toolbars to other positions on-screen simply by dragging them to the new location. If you want to create a floating toolbar, simply leave the toolbar in the document work area.

To find out how to create your own custom toolbars, see Chapter 38, "Customizing Word and Maximizing Accessibility."

Interpreting Status Bar Data

The status bar, located along the bottom edge of the Word window, helps you keep your bearings as you're working on a document. The information in the status bar tells you important information about where you are in the document, which features are currently enabled, and what mode you're using.

The left side of the status bar shows your location in the document. The page and section numbers, as well as the current and total page count and line number and column location, all indicate the insertion point in the current document. On the right side of the status bar, you see information about active modes and features.

Listed below are the four modes that can appear in the status bar:

- REC is highlighted when you are recording a macro.
- TRK is highlighted when Tracking Changes is enabled.
- EXT is highlighted when selected text is extended.
- OVR indicates that Overtype mode (as opposed to Insert mode) is in effect.

Chapter 2

Creating Documents from Start to Finish

If you've been using Microsoft Word through its last few versions, you might have noticed that Word has been steadily growing beyond a basic word processing tool. If you haven't been using Word lately, you might have heard through the grapevine (and be pleasantly surprised to find) that Word has evolved into a word processing application that can also be used to create e-mail messages, conduct mail merges, perform desktop publishing tasks, create Web pages, and on and on. All these features add value to Word's complete package, but the root of Word's power remains in its fundamental capability—*document creation*.

Fortunately, Word's functionality has expanded without diminishing its word processing features. In fact, in Word 2002 you'll find word processing features are abundant and more powerful than ever. You'll be pleased to see that you can find many standard word processing features and tools available in predictable and comfortable places. For example, the Exit command is still located at the bottom of the Find menu; the Minimize, Restore, and Close buttons are still in the window's upper-right corner; and you can still press Ctrl+S to save your current document. In addition, Word 2002 provides a number of new tools and innovative twists on familiar features that extend Word's capabilities and ease of use. Because document creation is Word's primary functionality, this chapter is dedicated to the process—from start to finish—of creating documents. Along the way, you'll learn about Word's new and revised tools, features, and procedures. Whether you're a new user or an old hand, this chapter will help you master Word's document creation tasks.

Getting Started with Blank Documents

Frequently, the first task in Word is opening a blank document. This procedure sounds pretty straightforward, but just to warm you up a little, let's look at the various ways you can go about creating a blank document. First you must open Word. The simplest, most direct method is to:

- Click Start, point to Programs, and click Microsoft Word 2002.

By default, a blank document opens whenever you start Word by clicking the Word application icon.

To create a new blank document from within Word, you can use any of Word's traditional methods, including the following:

New Blank Document

- Click the New Blank Document button on the Standard toolbar.
- Press Ctrl+N.

You can also create documents using Word's New Document task pane. To open the task pane, choose File, New. To create a blank document, click the Blank Document link. The New Document task pane also enables you to quickly perform a variety of other tasks, including opening existing documents, accessing templates, and more.

newfeature!

Working with the New Document Task Pane

When you open Word 2002, the New Document task pane appears docked along the right side of the window by default, as shown in Figure 2-1.

The New Document task pane provides the following features:

- **Open A Document** provides links to recently opened documents as well as a More Documents link that you can click to access the Open dialog box. The Open dialog box is discussed in more detail in the section "Retrieving Documents" on page 63.
- **New** provides links to create a new blank document, a blank Web (.htm) page, or an e-mail message. To create a blank document, a Web page, or an e-mail message, simply click the desired link in the task pane.
- **New From Existing Document** provides a Choose Document that you can click to open the New From Existing Document dialog box, which looks similar to the Open dialog box. When you create a new document from an existing document, it may seem as if you're working on an existing document, but the new document actually contains only a copy of the existing

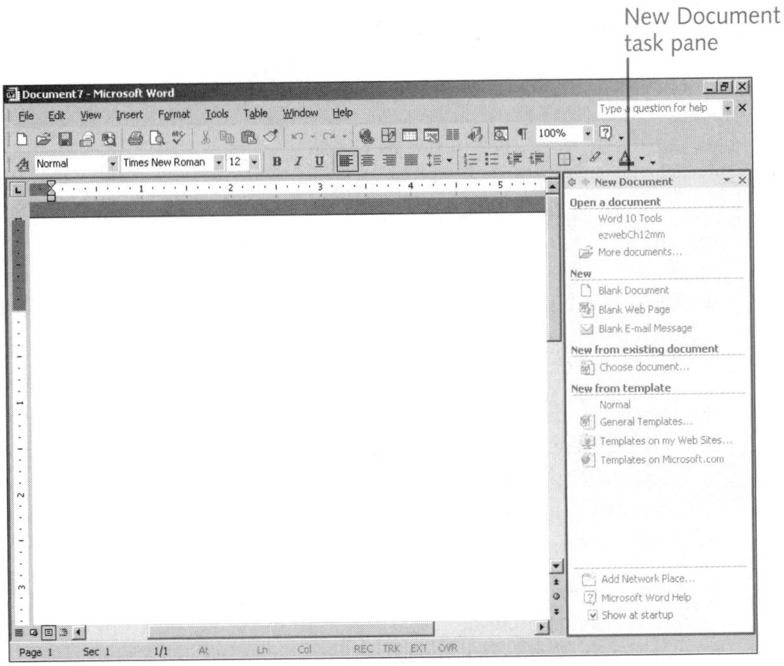

Figure 2-1. The New Document task pane provides a variety of methods you can use to create and access files.

file's contents. When you save the new document, Word will automatically display the Save As dialog box so that you can save the file as a new file instead of replacing the existing document.

- **New From Template** enables you to create new documents based on existing templates. By default, recently used templates are listed in this section along with links to Word's general templates, any templates you've stored on your Web site (if you have a Web site), and Microsoft's online templates.

For more information about templates, see Chapter 22, "Formatting Documents Using Templates, Wizards, and Add-Ins."

- **Task Pane Options** enables you to quickly add a Network Place to your system, access Word Help topics, and specify whether the task pane should be displayed each time you start Word.

For more information about Word's Help features, see Chapter 3, "Getting the Most from Help."

Displaying and Hiding the Task Pane

As mentioned, the task pane appears by default when you open Word. You can move the task pane, close the task pane at any time to maximize your work area, reopen the task pane when you want to use its options, and configure the task pane to not be displayed automatically when you start Word. If you view other contents in the task pane, you can easily redisplay the New Document options with a click of your mouse. The techniques for achieving these effects are described here:

- **Move the task pane.** To move the task pane from its docked position, drag the task pane's title bar. To redock the task pane, drag the task pane's title bar to the pane's original right-aligned position.
- **Toggle the display of the task pane.** To toggle the task pane's display, choose View, Task Pane, or choose View, Toolbars, and then select Task Pane. After the task pane has been displayed at least once during the current session, you can right-click any open toolbar and select the Task Pane command.
- **Close the task pane manually.** Similar to floating (or undocked) toolbars, the task pane includes a Close button in the upper-right corner of its title bar that you can click to close the task pane at any time.
- **Redisplay the New Document options.** You can specify which task pane options will be displayed by clicking the down arrow on the task pane's title bar, as shown in Figure 2-2. To display the New Document options in the task pane, choose the New From Existing Document option on the task pane's drop-down menu.

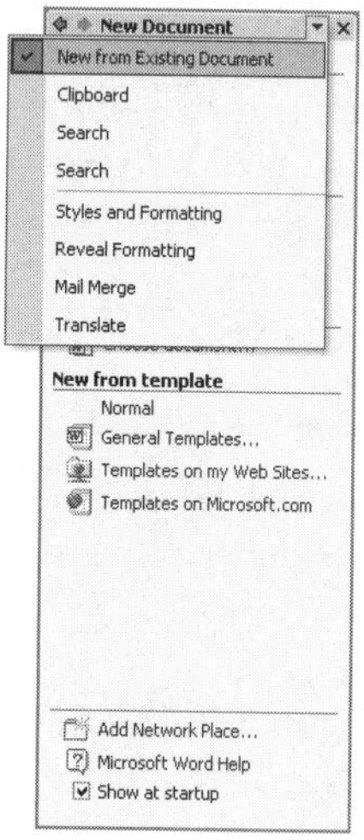

Figure 2-2. The task pane offers a variety of views.

Chapter 2

- **Control whether the task pane is displayed automatically at startup.** The lower section of the task pane includes a Show At Startup option. You can clear this check box if you do not want the task pane to be displayed by default when Word opens. You can also access this option by choosing Tools, Options and then clicking the View tab. The Startup task pane check box appears in the Show section on the View tab. Select the check box if you want the task pane to be displayed at startup, or clear the check box if you don't want the task pane to appear when you start Word.

InsideOut

Be aware that if you configure the task pane to not be displayed when Word starts, you won't be able to right-click a toolbar to select the Task Pane command at first. Instead, you will have to choose View, Task Pane. After you display the task pane during your current session, you'll be able to right-click any toolbar and choose the Task Pane command to toggle the task pane's display.

Configuring the Task Pane's List of Recently Opened Documents

In addition to hiding and displaying the task pane, you can customize the New Document task pane somewhat by specifying how many recently opened documents will be listed under the Open A Document heading. To configure this setting, choose Tools, Options, click the General tab, and type a number from 0 through 9 in the Recently Used File List box to display up to nine recently used documents in your task pane.

InsideOut

You might think that clearing your document history from the Windows Start menu (by clicking Start, Settings, Taskbar & Start Menu, clicking the Advanced tab, and then clicking Clear) would automatically clear the Open A Document list in the task pane—but it doesn't. To clear the task pane's document history list, you must choose Tools, Options, click the General tab, and then clear the Recently Used File List check box or type **0** in the Recently Used File List box.

Implementing Templates and Wizards

You can also create new documents based on *templates*. Templates are predesigned documents that contain formatting and, in many cases, generic text. They are used as a foundation for creating new documents based on predetermined settings. For example, to create a basic left-aligned Web page, you could use the Left-Aligned Column template, as shown in Figure 2-3. (The Left-Aligned Column template is a Word template that you can access on the Web Pages tab in the Templates dialog box.)

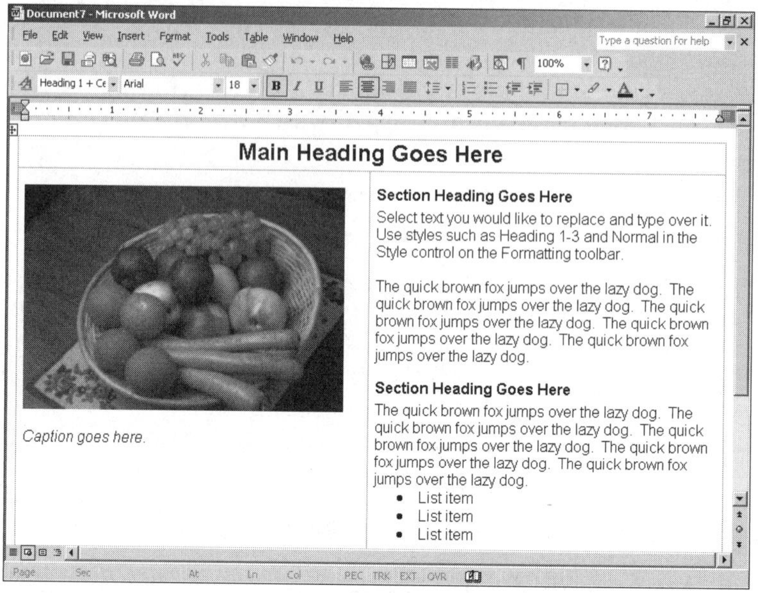

Figure 2-3. Templates can contain standard text elements and font styles as well as provide placeholder text and graphics—as seen here in the Left-Aligned Column Web page template.

By default, templates carry the .dot extension and blank Word documents are based on the standard Normal.dot template. The Normal template contains default styles but no generic text. You can access other general templates provided with Word by selecting the New From Template links in the task pane. The New From Template links include the following:

- **List of Recently Used Templates.** The task pane automatically displays links to recently used templates. This feature can dramatically speed the process of applying a template to multiple documents because you won't need to continually open the Templates dialog box to apply a previously accessed template.
- **General Templates.** When you click the General Templates link, the Templates dialog box opens, as shown in Figure 2-4. The Templates dialog box contains templates and wizards that can assist you in creating basic documents organized by category: General (Blank Document, Web Page, and E-Mail Message), Legal Pleadings, Letters & Faxes, Mail Merge, Memos, Other Documents (including résumé templates), Publications, Reports, and Web Pages.

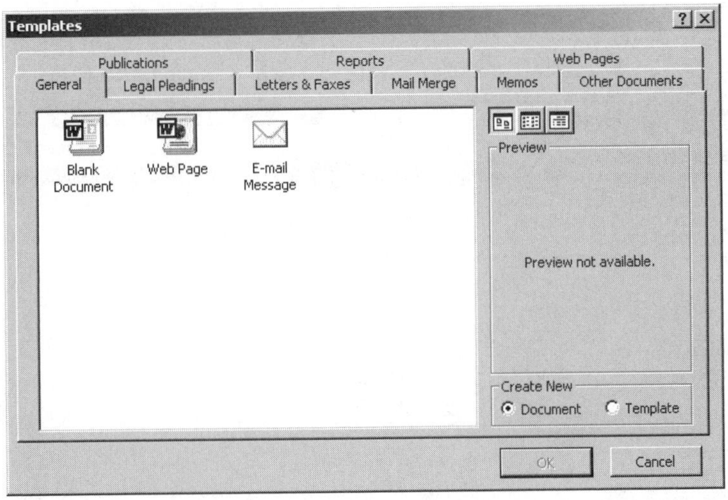

Figure 2-4. The Templates dialog box enables you to quickly access standard templates installed with Word.

- **Templates On My Web Sites.** If you (or an associate) have set up a Web site on a network or the Internet and stored templates on the site, you can click the Templates On My Web Sites link to access the templates on the site.

tip **Store templates on line**

Occasionally, you might want to store templates on line. If you don't have a Web site, you can work around this limitation without spending a dime by using MSN's free online file storage space (referred to as *File Cabinets*) at *communities.msn.com*. You can use the free space to store templates (and other files), thereby making the files easily accessible on the Internet. You can also configure the Templates On My Web Sites link in the New Documents task pane to include a shortcut to your File Cabinet's contents. For more information about storing templates on a Web site and using MSN File Cabinets, see Chapter 32, "Sharing Information on Networks."

- **Templates On Microsoft.com.** Clicking this link opens the Microsoft Office Template Gallery Web page in your Web browser, as shown in Figure 2-5, on the next page. The Template Gallery provides a selection of templates ranging from staffing and management documents to stationery.

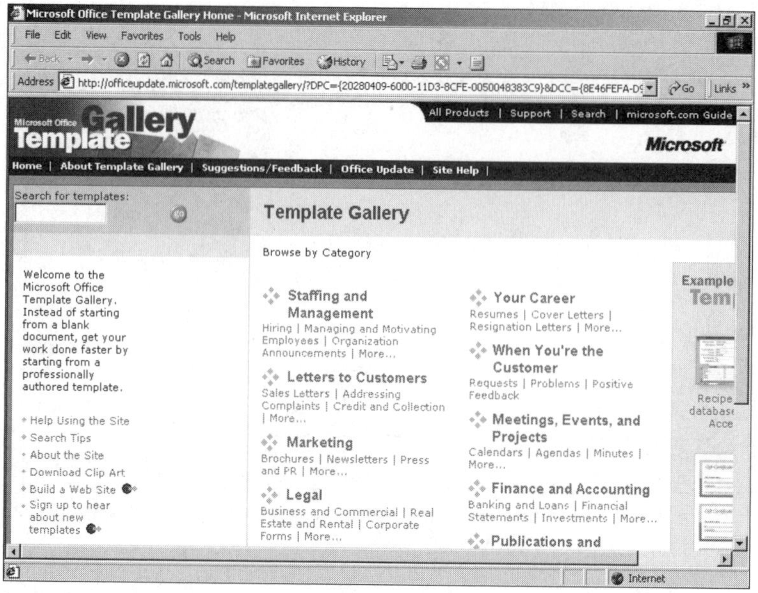

Figure 2-5. The Microsoft Office Template Gallery provides free templates, arranged by category, that you can open in Word and modify to suit your purposes.

> **tip** **Add a custom template to the list of recently used templates**
>
> Templates downloaded from the Microsoft Office Template Gallery are not displayed in the New From Template recently used templates list in the task pane. If you want to add a custom template to the task pane (whether you create the template or download it from the Template Gallery), you can do so fairly easily.
>
> To include a custom template in the New From Template recently used templates list, create a custom template (or copy an existing custom template), and save it in ...\Application Data\Microsoft\Templates. (You might have to display hidden folders to see the Application Data folder.) Then, when you are working in Word, click General Templates in the task pane and select your custom template, which should appear on the General tab in the Templates dialog box. A link to the template will be added to the New From Template recently used templates list in the task pane.

Mastering Document Content Fundamentals

After you open a new document—whether it's blank or based on an existing document or template—the next order of business is to insert information into the document and format it. Granted, that's a fairly obvious observation, but it's well worth discussing. Working with document information is what this book's all about, so just to be sure we cover all our bases, we'll address content fundamentals here. First we'll look at inputting information, and then we'll look at ways to navigate through documents and perform standard editing tasks. These topics might sound basic, but you should be able to pick up a few pointers here and there throughout the upcoming sections. If nothing else, scan the tables included on the next few pages to learn a new trick or two to help streamline your working style.

Inputting Information

You have a few options when it comes to inserting information into Word 2002 documents:

- **Click in the document and begin typing in the editing window.** Typed text appears to the left of the insertion point. You can reposition the insertion point by clicking elsewhere within the editing window.

> **tip** **Change from Insert Mode to Overtype Mode**
>
> By default, new text you type in the middle of a line will be inserted between existing text. To change from Insert mode to Overtype mode, you can choose Tools, Options and then clear the Overtype Mode check box on the Edit tab. For quicker results, double-click OVR on the status bar or press Insert to toggle between Insert and Overtype modes.

- **Copy and paste information.** Using the Office Clipboard (as described in the section "Using the Office Clipboard," on page 50,and in Chapter 6, "Putting Text Tools to Work"), you can easily copy information from within the current document, from other Word documents, and from other applications, including online information displayed within your browser, data from other Office applications, and information from almost any other application that allows you to copy selected data. After you copy existing data, you can paste the information directly into Word documents.
- **Insert the contents of another Word document or text file.** You can insert the contents of another document within the current document without copying and pasting by choosing Insert, File, navigating to the file that contains the information you want to insert into the current document, and then double-clicking the document. The document's contents are inserted into the currently displayed document (and the existing document remains unchanged).

newfeature!

- **Use the new Speech Recognition features.** You can speak your piece by configuring and working with the new Speech Recognition features. Using speech recognition, you can dictate content and use voice commands by talking into a high-quality headset.

newfeature!

- **Handwrite content using the mouse or a stylus.** Word can recognize handwritten marks you make with your mouse or a *stylus*, which is a pencil-like tool used on an electronic writing or drawing pad. When you use the Handwriting Recognition feature, you can retain your written marks or you can configure Word to interpret your handwriting and display the information as typed text.

For more information about Speech and Handwriting Recognition features, see Chapter 39, "Putting Speech and Handwriting Recognition Features to Work."

Moving Within Documents Using Keyboard Shortcuts and Function Keys

After you enter information in documents, you'll frequently need to move around within your documents so that you can add, edit, and format your documents' contents. As you most likely know, you can move around within a document using the scroll bars located along the right and bottom edges of the editing window, and you can reposition the insertion point by clicking anywhere within your document. By learning a few keyboard shortcuts, you can speed up your text navigation tasks considerably. Table 2-1 lists common keyboard shortcuts that you might find handy as you work your way through Word documents.

tip **Use Shift to select text**

By pressing Shift in combination with a keyboard shortcut, you can generally select all the text from the insertion point's current location to the location to which the shortcut takes you. For example, if you press End, the insertion point moves to the end of the line, but if you press Shift+End, you'll select all the text from the insertion point to the end of the line.

In addition to the common keyboard shortcuts listed in Table 2-1, you can take advantage of the function keys to perform a variety of other tasks. An easy way to view the commands associated with function keys is to display the Function Key Display toolbar on your desktop. To do so, choose Tools, Customize, select Function Key Display on the Toolbars tab, and then click Close.

Table 2-1. **Keyboard Shortcuts for Navigating Within Documents**

Keyboard shortcut	Action
Alt+F1 (or F11)	Moves to the next field
Alt+F4	Quits Word
Alt+F7	Moves to the next misspelled word if the Check Spelling As You Type feature is turned on (the default)
Alt+Page Down	Moves to the bottom of the current column
Alt+Page Up	Moves to the top of the current column
Arrow keys	Move the insertion point left, right, up, or down
Ctrl+Alt+Home	Opens the Select Browse Object menu
Ctrl+Alt+Page Down	Moves the insertion point to the bottom of the window
Ctrl+Alt+Page Up	Moves the cursor to the top of the window
Ctrl+Alt+Y (or Shift+F4)	Finds the next instance of a search term
Ctrl+Alt+Z (or Shift+F5)	Moves to the previous insertion point location
Ctrl+Down Arrow	Moves to the next paragraph
Ctrl+End	Moves to the end of the document
Ctrl+F	Displays the Find tab in the Find And Replace dialog box
Ctrl+F6	Displays the next window
Ctrl+G (or F5)	Displays the Go To tab in the Find And Replace dialog box
Ctrl+Home	Moves to the beginning of the document
Ctrl+Left Arrow	Moves one word to the left
Ctrl+O (or Ctrl+Alt+F2)	Displays the Open dialog box
Ctrl+Page Down	Moves to the top of the next page
Ctrl+Page Up	Moves to the top of the preceding page
Ctrl+Right Arrow	Moves one word to the right
Ctrl+S (or Alt+Shift+F2)	Saves the current document
Ctrl+Shift+F6	Displays the previous window
Ctrl+Up Arrow	Moves to the previous arrow location

(continued)

Table 2-1. *(continued)*

Keyboard shortcut	Action
End	Moves to the end of the current line
Esc	Closes an open menu
F6	Moves to the next pane or frame
Home	Moves to the beginning of the current line
PageDown	Displays the next screen
PageUp	Displays the previous screen
Shift+F6	Moves to the previous pane or frame
Shift+Tab	Moves to the previous cell in a table
Tab	Moves to the next cell in a table

By default, the Function Key Display toolbar shows the basic function key commands. You can press Shift, Ctrl, Alt, or any combination of those three buttons to display other available commands on the Function Key Display toolbar. To help illustrate this little toolbar trick, Figure 2-6 shows the Function Key Display toolbar in normal, Shift, Ctrl, and Alt mode. Table 2-2 lists a few common navigation-related function key commands.

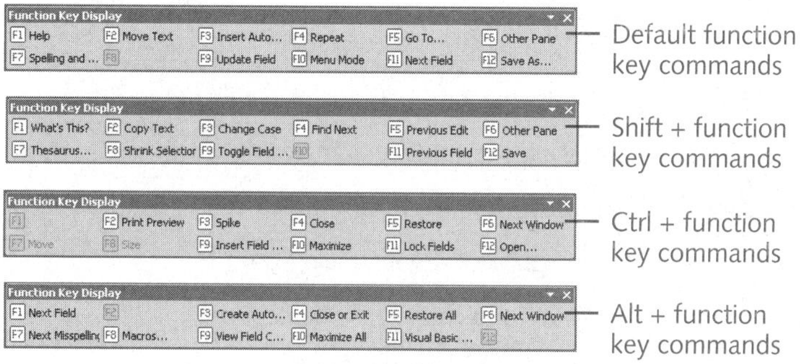

Figure 2-6. The Function Key Display toolbar adjusts to show various options when you press Shift, Ctrl, and Alt alone or in any combination.

> **note** You can also browse through documents using the Go To tab in the Find And Replace dialog box. To access the Go To tab, press F5, press Ctrl+G, or choose Edit, Go To. For more information about using the Find And Replace dialog box, see Chapter 12, "Honing Document Navigation Skills."

Table 2-2. **Function Keys for Navigating Within Documents**

Command	Action
Alt+F1 (or Alt+F11)	Moves to the next field
Alt+F4	Quits Word
Alt+F7	Moves to the next misspelled word
Alt+Shift+F2 (or Ctrl+S)	Saves the current document
Ctrl+Alt+F2 (or Ctrl+O)	Displays the Open dialog box
Ctrl+F6	Displays the next window
Ctrl+Shift+F6	Displays the previous window
F5 (or Ctrl+G)	Displays the Go To tab in the Find And Replace dialog box
F6	Moves to the next pane or frame
Shift+F4 (or Ctrl+Alt+Y)	Finds the next instance of a search term
Shift+F5 (or Ctrl+Alt+Z)	Moves to previous insertion point location (even if the insertion point was in a different Word document)
Shift+F6	Moves to the previous pane or frame

Performing Basic Editing Tasks

As you know, merely entering information into a Word document doesn't usually create a finished product. Instead, your documents are the result of entering information, and editing and formatting the entered text. Now that we've covered entering text and navigating within documents, it's time to work with text by performing basic editing tasks. This section provides information about selecting, copying, cutting, and pasting text; using the Clipboard; and undoing, redoing, and repeating changes—in other words, some of the common tasks you'll perform every time you work on a document in Word.

For more information about formatting text, see Chapter 5, "Adding Panache with Text Formatting and Special Characters."

Using the Browse Object Feature

Another way to browse through documents is to use the Select Browse Object menu and its associated buttons. You can find the three browse buttons—Previous, Select Browse Object, and Next—in the lower-right corner of the editing window, as shown here:

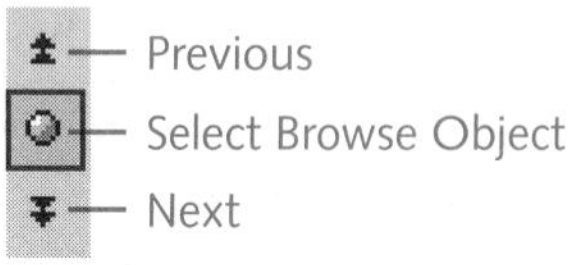

To use the Browse Object feature, follow these steps:

1. Open the Select Browse Object menu by pressing Ctrl+Alt+Home or by clicking the Select Browse Object button on the vertical scroll bar.
2. Select the type of document element you want to browse for (such as browsing from heading to heading).
3. Click the Previous and Next buttons to navigate from one browse object to the next.

The Select Browse Object menu, shown below, displays the types of objects you can use to browse through a document. Table 2-3 describes the available options.

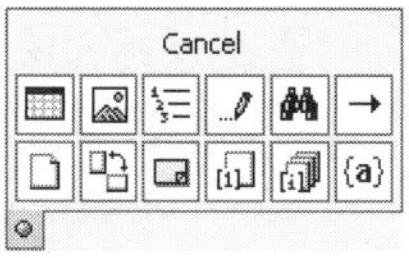

Table 2-3. Select Browse Object Menu Options

Button	Description
	Browses by moving from table to table
	Browses by moving from graphic to graphic
	Browses by moving from heading to heading
	Browses by moving from edit to edit (if the Track Changes feature has been used)
	Browses by using the Find tab in the Find And Replace dialog box
	Browses by using the Go To tab in the Find And Replace dialog box

(continued)

Using the Browse Object Feature *(continued)*

Table 2-3. *(continued)*

Button	Description
	Browses by moving from page to page
	Browses by moving from section to section
	Browses by moving from comment to comment
	Browses by moving from footnote to footnote
	Browses by moving from endnote to endnote
{a}	Browses by moving from field to field

Selecting Text

Generally speaking, you can streamline many editing tasks by first selecting the text you want to edit. In fact, you can speed up most text modification tasks by mastering precise selection techniques. You can select text in a variety of ways. Usually (and not too surprisingly), you will select text using the mouse or keyboard commands. (You can also select text that contains similar formatting by using the Styles And Formatting task pane, but because that topic is slightly more advanced and is related to creating and using styles, that technique is addressed in Chapter 10, "Using Styles to Increase Your Formatting Power.") Regardless of how you select text, you can deselect it by clicking any area outside of the selected text.

note You can access text selection options by choosing Tools, Options, and then clicking the Edit tab in the dialog box. On the Edit tab, you can specify whether to automatically select paragraph marks when you select paragraphs (the Use Smart Paragraph Selection check box) and whether to automatically select entire words when you're selecting text (the When Selecting, Automatically Select Entire Word check box). Both text selection settings are activated by default.

Selecting information using the mouse Selecting information using the mouse is the most common way to select text and other elements (such as graphics, tables, and so forth) in Word documents. To select information using the mouse, you can use any of the options described in Table 2-4.

Table 2-4. Methods of Selecting Text Using the Mouse

Selection	Method
Contiguous text or elements	Position the insertion point at the beginning of the text to be selected, click and drag to select the desired text, and then release the mouse button.
Word or single element	Double-click the word or element.
Paragraph	Triple-click within the paragraph, or double-click in the left margin next to the paragraph.
Entire line	Click in the left margin.
Multiple lines	Click and drag in the left margin.
newfeature! Multiple noncontiguous instances of text or elements	Select the first item (as described above), press Ctrl, and then select additional text or elements elsewhere within your document.
Entire section	Display your document in Outline view, and double-click a heading.
Large block of text	Click at the start of the selection, scroll to the end of the selection, and then hold down Shift as you click.
Blocks of text using Extend mode	Click at the beginning of the text you want to select, double-click EXT on the status bar, and then click at the end of the text you want to select. To deactivate Extend mode, press Esc or double-click EXT again so that it appears dimmed on the status bar.
Vertical block of text	Press Alt, and then drag over the text.
Entire document	Triple-click in the left margin or press Ctrl+A.

note In Word 2002, you can select noncontiguous blocks of text as well as contiguous blocks of text. When you want to select large areas of contiguous text, consider using Extend mode, which enables you to select contiguous blocks of text without holding down the mouse button.

newfeature!

tip **Select all instances of an element**

You can select all instances of a word, a symbol, or a phrase. To do so, select the Find tab in the Find And Replace text box (press Ctrl+F), type the text you want to select in the Find What box, select the Highlight All Items Found In check box, select Main Document in the drop-down list if necessary, and click the Find All button.

Chapter 10, "Using Styles to Increase Your Formatting Power," discusses how to select text based on formatting attributes.

Selecting text using keyboard commands As most people's Word proficiency increases, so does their desire to take advantage of Word's numerous keyboard commands. Keyboard commands increase productivity by limiting how frequently you move your hand away from your keyboard to your mouse and back again. For the most part, selecting text using keyboard commands requires you to press Shift along with the keyboard combination that moves the insertion point in the direction of the text you want to select. If you know the keyboard combinations used to move the insertion point (shown in Table 2-1), you can generally select text by using the same keyboard combination while holding down Shift. For example, Ctrl+Right Arrow moves the insertion point to the next word, and Shift+Ctrl+Right Arrow selects the text from the insertion point to the beginning of the next word. Table 2-5 identifies the text selection keyboard commands that might be most useful for you.

tip Remember to combine cursor movement keyboard commands with text-selection commands to keep selection practices precise (for example, press Home to move to the beginning of a line before you select the line; see Tables 2-1 and 2-2).

tip To select multiple noncontiguous areas, make your first selection, hold down Ctrl, and then select other items.

Table 2-5. Keyboard Commands for Selecting Text

Keyboard Command	Selection
Ctrl+A	Entire document.
Ctrl+Alt+Shift+Page Down	To the end of the current window
Ctrl+Shift+Down Arrow	To the end of the current paragraph
Ctrl+Shift+End	To the end of the current document
Ctrl+Shift+F8 + arrow keys or mouse	Vertical or horizontal blocks of text beginning at the insertion point (Press Esc to cancel the selection mode.)
Ctrl+Shift+Home	To the beginning of the current document
Ctrl+Shift+Left Arrow	To the beginning of a word (To select preceding words, press Left Arrow repeatedly as you hold down Ctrl+Shift.)
Ctrl+Shift+Right Arrow	To the end of a word (To select subsequent words, press Right Arrow repeatedly as you hold down Ctrl+Shift.)

(continued)

Table 2-5. *(continued)*

Keyboard Command	Selection
Ctrl+Shift+Up Arrow	To the beginning of the current paragraph
Esc (or double-click EXT on the status bar)	To turn off Extend mode
F8	To turn Extend mode on and increase the size of a selection. (Press F8 twice to select a word, three times to select a sentence, and so forth.)
F8+F8	Current word
F8+F8+F8	Current sentence
F8+arrow key	To a specific location in a document. (Press Esc to cancel selection mode.)
F8+Left Arrow or Right Arrow	To select the nearest character
Shift+Down Arrow (or Shift+Up Arrow)	Entire line, beginning at the insertion point
Shift+Down Arrow+ Down Arrow	Current line and following lines, beginning at the insertion point (To select multiple lines, press Down Arrow repeatedly as you hold down Shift.)
Shift+End	To the end of the current line
Shift+F8	To reduce the size of a selection
Shift+Home	To the beginning of the current line
Shift+Left Arrow	One character to the left
Shift+Page Down	One screen down
Shift+Page Up	One screen up
Shift+Right Arrow	One character to the right
Shift+Up Arrow+Up Arrow	Current line and preceding lines, beginning at the insertion point (To select multiple lines, press Up Arrow repeatedly as you hold down Shift.)

tip **Use F8 to select text**

You can use the F8 key to progressively select the current word, sentence, paragraph, and so forth. For example, to select the current word, press F8 twice. To select the current sentence, press F8 three times. To select the current paragraph, press F8 four times.

Copying, Cutting, and Pasting

Copying, cutting, and pasting are probably among the top word processing features responsible for saving countless trees. Thousands of sheets of paper have been conserved as people copy, cut, and paste text instantaneously instead of painstakingly retyping documents on fresh paper each time a sentence or paragraph needs to be moved or revised. Using Word, you can easily copy, cut, and paste selected text without retyping or wasting a single sheet of paper.

Word provides a number of ways to go about your copying, cutting, and pasting business, as shown in Table 2-6. To use the Copy and Cut features, select the text you want to manipulate and then choose one of the listed commands. To paste information, position the insertion point where you want to insert the information, and then choose one of the Paste commands. Alternatively, you can right-click selected text and choose Cut, Copy, or Paste from the shortcut menu.

Table 2-6. Copy, Cut, and Paste Features

Action	Menu Command	Keyboard Shortcut	Toolbar Button
Copy	Edit, Copy	Ctrl+C	
Cut	Edit, Cut	Ctrl+X	
Paste	Edit, Paste	Ctrl+V	

tip You can configure your Insert key to serve as a Paste key. To do so, click Tools, Options, Edit tab, and then select the Use The INS Key For Paste check box.

You can also reposition text by using Word's drag-and-drop feature, which essentially enables you to use the mouse to cut and paste text without using the Cut and Paste commands.

newfeature!

In Word 2002, when you paste an item, Word displays the Paste Options smart tag, as shown in Figure 2-7, on the next page. This smart tag provides paste-specific formatting options. To apply any of the options, position the mouse pointer over the Paste Options smart tag to open the drop-down menu, and then choose a command. To ignore a smart tag after pasting, simply continue to work within your document—the smart tag will quietly disappear until the next time you paste an object.

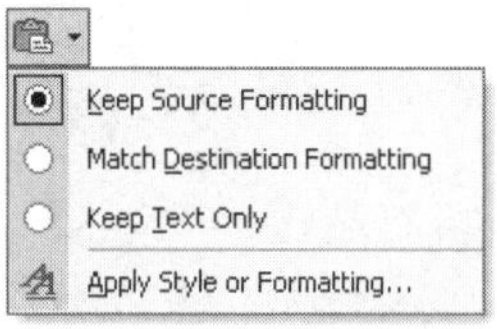

Figure 2-7. By default, the Paste Options smart tag appears whenever you paste an element into your Word document.

Using the Office Clipboard

You can copy, cut, and paste within the same document, between multiple documents, and even between different applications, thanks to the Office Clipboard. The Office Clipboard has been upgraded in Word 2002—it now allows you to store up to 24 items, including text and graphics, which means you can copy or cut 24 elements from various applications without losing data in the digital abyss. (Of course, as soon as you copy item 25, the first item you copied to your Clipboard is removed.) In addition, the newly revised Clipboard provides a much easier means of seeing which Clipboard item contains the information you want to access. As shown in Figure 2-8, the Clipboard contents are displayed in the task pane. In this example, five items are stored on the Clipboard (notice the *5 of 24* in the task pane's title bar), including a Microsoft Excel spreadsheet, a Jasc Paint Shop Pro image, some text copied from Word documents, and a clip art image. Each Clipboard item's parent application is identified by an accompanying icon.

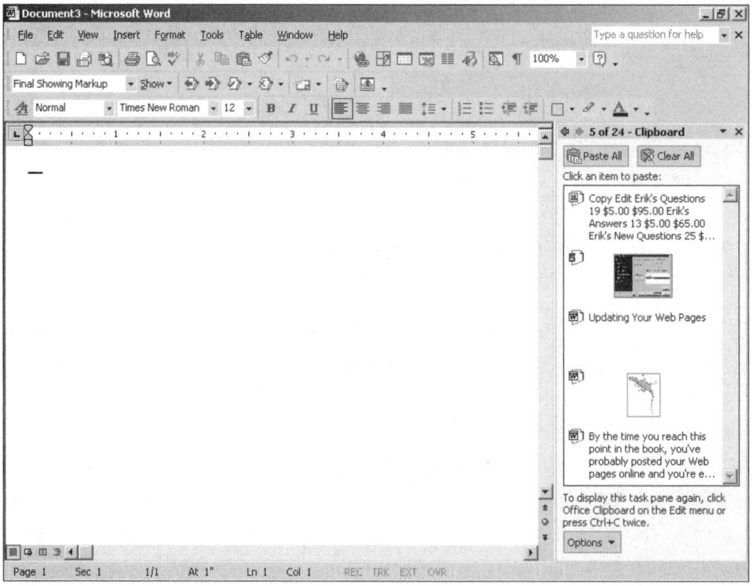

Figure 2-8. The Clipboard now holds up to 24 items and displays some of the copied and cut items' contents to help you more easily identify the item you want to paste into a document.

Opening the Clipboard To open the Clipboard manually, choose Edit, Office Clipboard, or select Clipboard in the task pane's drop-down menu. Otherwise, the Clipboard opens automatically when you perform any of the following actions:

- Copy or cut two items consecutively in the same program.
- Copy and paste an item and then copy another item in the same program.
- Copy one item twice either by double-clicking the Copy button on the Standard toolbar or by pressing Ctrl+C twice. (You can hold down the Ctrl key while you press the C key twice.)

You can also open the Clipboard using the Clipboard icon, shown in Figure 2-9, which appears on the taskbar by default whenever the Clipboard is displayed in any Office program. You double-click the icon to open the Clipboard in the current window. For example, if the Clipboard is open in Word, you can open Excel and then double-click the Clipboard icon on the taskbar to open the Clipboard in Excel.

Figure 2-9. Whenever the Clipboard is open in an Office application, the Clipboard icon appears in the status area of the Windows taskbar.

> **tip** To opt out of displaying the Office Clipboard icon on the taskbar, click the Options button in the Clipboard task pane, and clear the Show Office Clipboard Icon On Taskbar check box.

Pasting Clipboard information After information is stored on the Clipboard, you can paste the information into a document by positioning the insertion point where you want to insert the information, displaying the Clipboard, and then clicking the item you want to paste. If you want to paste everything stored on the Clipboard into your document, click the Paste All button in the task pane.

Deleting Clipboard information To delete items from the Clipboard, you can either click the down arrow that appears when you position your mouse pointer over the Clipboard item or right-click an item to open the drop-down menu, as shown in Figure 2-10, on the next page, and then choose Delete. If you want to clear the entire Clipboard, click the Clear All button in the task pane.

Figure 2-10. You can delete Clipboard items one at a time, or you can clear the entire Clipboard by clicking the Clear All button.

The Office Clipboard and the System Clipboard

You might be wondering how the Office Clipboard relates to the system Clipboard. Here's a quick rundown of how the two Clipboards interrelate:

- The last item you copy to the Office Clipboard is stored on the system Clipboard.
- Clearing the Office Clipboard also clears the system Clipboard.
- When you click the Paste toolbar button, choose Edit, Paste, or click Ctrl+V to paste information, you paste the contents of the system Clipboard (which by default is the last item you added to the Office Clipboard).

For more information about the ins and outs of the Clipboard feature, see Chapter 6, "Putting Text Tools to Work."

Undoing, Redoing, and Repeating

Fortunately, changes you make to documents are not immediately set in stone. You have ample opportunity to change your mind when it comes to editing text—not only can you undo edits you've recently made but you can also redo undone edits and even repeat an action if you need to. Most likely, you'll use the Undo command more frequently than the Redo and Repeat commands, so let's look at that feature first.

Using the Undo feature The Undo feature enables you to undo one or many changes to a document made during the current session. In fact, the Undo feature can store over 100 actions, so you have plenty of time during the current session to discard your edits. Keep in mind that some actions are too large to store, such as reformatting large tables. When Word encounters a change that the Undo command can't handle, you'll receive a warning message indicating that you won't be able to undo a particular action. In addition to not being able to undo the current action, you'll also lose the ability to undo prior actions. If you're sure that's OK, you simply proceed, and Word will begin a new Undo list.

InsideOut

If you receive a message that you won't be able to undo a current action and you're a little leery about moving ahead without the Undo safety net, you can take precautionary action. One easy approach is to simply perform the "risky" action last so that you won't lose your current Undo list until you're sure you'll no longer need it. Another workaround is to copy the element you want to perform the action on, paste the information into a blank document, perform the desired action on the copied version of your information, and then copy and paste the modified information into the original document. Using this method, you can ensure that if the action doesn't go as planned, your original document remains intact.

To Undo an action or numerous actions, use any of the following procedures:

- Choose Edit, Undo to undo the last action.
- On the Standard toolbar, click the Undo button to undo the last change (or click it multiple times to undo a series of changes).
- On the Standard toolbar, click the Undo down arrow and click the action you want to undo. (If you don't see the action you're looking for, scroll through the list.) When you undo an action on the drop-down list, you also undo all the actions that appear above it in the list.
- Press Ctrl+Z to undo the last action.
- Press Alt+Backspace to undo the last action.

Using the Redo feature As soon as you undo an action, you automatically activate the Redo command. The main role of the Redo command is to enable you to redo an undone action before you make any further changes. If you want to redo an undone action, use any of the following techniques:

- Choose Edit, Redo immediately after you've undone an action (before you've made any other changes).
- On the Standard toolbar, click the Redo button to redo the last undone change (or click it multiple times to undo a series of changes).

- On the Standard toolbar, click the Redo down arrow, and click the action you want to redo. (If you don't see the action you're looking for, scroll through the list.) When you redo an action on the drop-down list, you also redo all the actions that appear above it in the list.
- Press Ctrl+Y to redo the last undone change.
- Press Alt+Shift+Backspace to redo the last undone change.
- Press F4 to redo the last undone change.
- Press Alt+Enter to redo the last undone change.

caution If you type or perform any other action after you undo a change, you lose the ability to redo the undone action.

Using the Repeat feature The Repeat command is related to the Undo and Redo commands. When the Redo feature isn't activated (Redo is activated only after you undo an edit), the Edit menu displays a Repeat command. The Repeat feature is fairly self-explanatory—choosing this command repeats the last action you performed. For example, if you typed your name in a form, you could use the Repeat command to insert your name elsewhere on the form. To do so, simply click to reposition the insertion point, and then choose the Repeat command. To execute the Repeat command after you have added content to your document, you can perform any of the following actions:

- Choose Edit, Repeat. (If you clicked the Undo command immediately before opening the Edit menu, the Redo command is displayed in place of the Repeat command.)
- Press Ctrl+Y.
- Press F4.
- Press Alt+Enter.

The Repeat command comes in handy when you use it as a cut-and-paste shortcut.

Positioning Content Effectively

Whenever you create documents (reports, brochures Web pages, and so forth)—regardless of their purpose—you'll need to position (and reposition) text, graphics, and other elements within the documents. You can easily align and move contents within a Word document by using the Formatting toolbar buttons and the Click And Type and drag-and-drop features.

For a full discussion on aligning information in Word documents, see Chapter 7, "Aligning Information and Styling Paragraphs."

Aligning Text Using the Toolbar

Word offers four quick-and-dirty paragraph and element alignment options:

- **Left** aligns text and other elements (such as graphics, tables, and so on) along the left margin, leaving a ragged right edge. Left alignment is the default setting in most versions of Word.
- **Center** aligns the midpoint of the selected element with the centerpoint between the page's margins.
- **Right** aligns text and other elements along the document's right margin, leaving the left margin ragged.
- **Justified** creates straight (or flush) left and right edges by adding white space between text to force the text to align with the left and right margins.

To apply an alignment setting, click anywhere within the paragraph or element you want to align, highlight the text or element you want to align, or select multiple elements within the document and then use one of the command options shown in Table 2-7.

Table 2-7. Text Alignment Options

Setting	Toolbar Button	Keyboard Shortcut
Left		Ctrl+L
Center		Ctrl+E
Right		Ctrl+R
Justified		Ctrl+J

tip **Activate the automatic hyphenation feature**

To steer clear of having too much white space inserted within justified text, you might want to activate the automatic hyphenation feature. To do so, choose Tools, Language, and then choose Hyphenation to open the Hyphenation dialog box. Select the Automatically Hyphenate Document check box, and then click OK. To learn more about character spacing issues, see Chapter 5, "Adding Panache with Text Formatting and Special Characters," and to learn more about hyphenation, see Chapter 7, "Aligning Information and Styling Paragraphs."

Using the Click And Type Feature

The Click And Type feature, which was introduced in Word 2000, is still available in Word 2002. This feature enables you to click anywhere on a page to position the insertion point and add text, graphics, tables, or other items in a blank area of a document. Before Click And Type came along, you had to insert carriage returns, tabs, and spaces before you could properly position your insertion point away from existing page elements.

By default, the Click And Type feature is enabled in Word 2002. You can verify whether the feature is currently activated by choosing Tools, Options, Edit tab, and making sure that the Enable Click And Type check box is selected.

To use Click And Type, you must be working in Print Layout or Web Layout view (choose View, Print Layout, or View, Web Layout). From Layout view, double-click on the page to position the insertion point (Watch the insertion point, it'll indicate the default alignment of the text you enter.)

Keep in mind that you can't use the Click And Type feature to position text in the following situations:

- With multiple columns.
- With bulleted and numbered lists.
- With floating objects. (You can't position text next to them.)
- To the left or right of pictures that have top and bottom text wrapping.
- To the left or right of indents.
- While recording macros.

Using the Drag-and-Drop Feature

The drag-and-drop feature is a favorite with most people because it seems to come naturally. It reflects how we arrange our lives—we pick up items and put them down elsewhere, without issuing a complex series of cut and paste commands.

To use the drag-and-drop feature, select the text (or other element, such as a graphic or table) that you want to move, click and hold down the mouse button within the selected area, and then drag the selected element to another area within your document or in another document. When you release the mouse button, the element will be repositioned in your document and the Paste Options smart tag will be displayed (because when you use the drag-and-drop feature, you are essentially cutting and pasting). If you right-click when you perform this action, a shortcut menu opens when you release the mouse button, which provides Move Here, Copy Here, Link Here, and Cancel commands.

Saving Documents

Whenever you create and edit documents, you need to save your work—an obvious statement, but one well worth emphasizing. You should save your work as frequently as possible, not just when you're closing a document. In this section, we'll take a quick look at techniques you can use when saving documents to help make saving as seamless as possible.

Saving Changes in Existing Documents

Saving your document in the same location with the same name is easy. Simply follow any of these procedures:

- Choose File, Save.
- Click the Save button on the Standard toolbar.
- Press Ctrl+S.
- Press Shift+F12.
- Press Alt+Shift+F2.

tip **Save, save, save**

Take advantage of the simplicity of the save procedure. Whenever you're about to take a break, press Ctrl+S as you start to roll your chair away from your desk. When your phone rings, click the Save button as you reach for the receiver. Saving your work periodically helps you avoid major data-loss headaches when you least expect them (because, as everyone knows, system crashes or disasters usually strike at the most inopportune times).

Saving Files Using the Save As Dialog Box

The Save As dialog box appears every time you save a new document or opt to save an existing document as a new file or in a new location by choosing File, Save As (or by pressing F12). Figure 2-11, on the next page, shows the latest incarnation of the Save As dialog box in Word 2002, which looks very similar to the Save As dialog box in Word 2000.

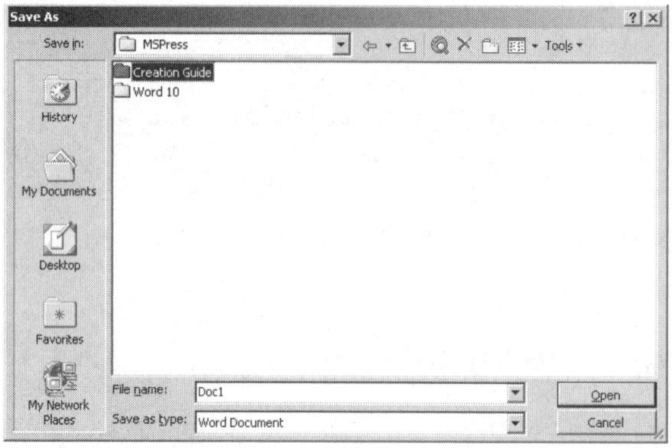

Figure 2-11. The Save As dialog box provides all the options you need to specify how and where to save new and existing documents.

To save a new document using the Save As dialog box or to save an existing document with new parameters (including a new location, a new file type, or a new file name), follow these steps:

1. Choose File, Save As, or press F12. (Or, if you're saving a newly created document for the first time, click the Save button on the Standard toolbar.)
2. Navigate to the folder in which you want to save the current document, type a file name in the File Name box, and select the file type in the Save As Type list. Most of the time, you'll probably use the Word Document file type (which is displayed by default and saves documents with the .doc extension). You can, however, save Word documents using a variety of file types, which can come in especially handy if you're saving a file for someone who is using an application other than Word. (Table 2-8, in the following section, lists the file formats available in the Save As dialog box.)
3. Click Save.

note Keep in mind that the Save feature replaces an existing file with an updated version of the file and the Save As feature creates a new file. When you use the Save As feature while working on an existing file, you create a new version of the file, and the original copy of the file remains intact in its original location.

Reviewing Available File Formats in the Save As Dialog Box

The file format types available in the Save As dialog box's Save As Type list are described in Table 2-8.

Table 2-8. **File Formats Available in the Save As Type List**

Format type	Description
Word Document	Saves the file as a Word 2002 document.
Web Page	Saves the file as a Web page with full Word editing capabilities.
newfeature! Web Archive	Saves all the elements of a Web site, including text and graphics, as a single file.
Document Template	Saves the file as a template that you can use to build similar documents.
Rich Text Format	Saves the file using a standard text format that's widely recognized among word processing applications and used to exchange word processing information.
Plain Text	Eliminates all formatting; converts lines, section breaks, and page breaks to paragraph marks; and uses the ANSI character set. A useful option for cross-platform availability when formatting isn't a major consideration.
newfeature! Web Page, Filtered	Saves a document as a Web page without including extraneous HTML source code that enables many Word editing features. Using this option creates smaller HTML files than saving with the Web Page option.
MS-DOS Text	Emulates formatting somewhat by using additional spaces to indicate indents, tabs, tables, and other formatting and uses the MS-DOS extended ASCII character set. This option is useful when you're saving documents that will be accessed in non-Windows applications.
Text With Layout	Similar to the MS-DOS Text With Layout format except that Text With Layout doesn't support the extended ASCII character set.
Word 2.x For Windows	Saves the file in the Word 2.x for Windows format.
Word 4.0 For Macintosh	Saves the file in the Word 4 for Macintosh format.
Word 5.0 For Macintosh	Saves the file in the Word 5 for Macintosh format.
Word 5.1 For Macintosh	Saves the file in the Word 5.1 for Macintosh format.
Word 6.0/95	Saves the file so that both Windows and Macintosh systems can open the file using Word 6, and enables Word 95 users to open the file if they're working on Windows 95, Windows 98, and Windows NT systems.

(continued)

Table 2-8. *(continued)*

Format type	Description
Word 97-2000 & 6.0/95 - RTF	Saves the file in Rich Text Format, which can be recognizedby Word 6, Word 95, Word 97, and Word 2000.
WordPerfect 5.0	Saves the file in WordPerfect 5 format.
WordPerfect 5.0 Secondary File	Creates a WordPerfect 5 secondary file.
WordPerfect 5.1 For DOS	Saves the file in WordPerfect 5 for MS-DOS format.
WordPerfect 5.1 Or 5.2 Secondary File	Creates a WordPerfect 5.1 or 5.2 secondary file.
WordPerfect 5.x for Windows	Saves the file in a WordPerfect 5.x for Windows format.
Works 2000	Saves the file in MS Works 2000 format.
Works 4.0 For Windows	Saves the file in MS Works 4 for Windows format.

note You might have to install a filter from your Office CD-ROM or a network drive (if you installed Office from a network) before you can save and open files using some of the formats shown in Table 2-8.

Obtaining Additional File Format Converters

At some point, you might find yourself facing the task of converting a document for which Word has not supplied a converter and no converter for the file type is available on the Office CD-ROM. When this situation arises, you'll have to install another converter. In some cases, you can easily obtain a converter from the Microsoft Office Web site or in the Microsoft Office Resource Kit. If you have an Internet connection, you can access the Microsoft Office Web site by choosing Help, Office On The Web. If the Web site or the Office Resource Kit don't provide what you're looking for, your next step should be to dig up a third-party solution. One well-known, third-party, file-conversion solution is Dataviz's Conversions Plus software. In addition, you can search shareware sites (such as *www.tucows.com*) for file conversion programs.

Specifying a Default Save Format

The default setting when you save Word documents is to save the documents using the Word Document (*.doc) format. You have the opportunity to save files as other file types when you save a file using the Save As dialog box (to do so, select another file type in the Save As Type drop-down list.) If you frequently save your documents in a format other than the default .doc format, you can change the default setting to another file format by configuring the Save tab in the Options dialog box. When you change the default file format setting, all documents will be saved with the specified format unless otherwise configured during the save process. To change the default file format setting, follow these steps:

1. Choose Tools, Options, and select the Save tab, as shown in Figure 2-12.

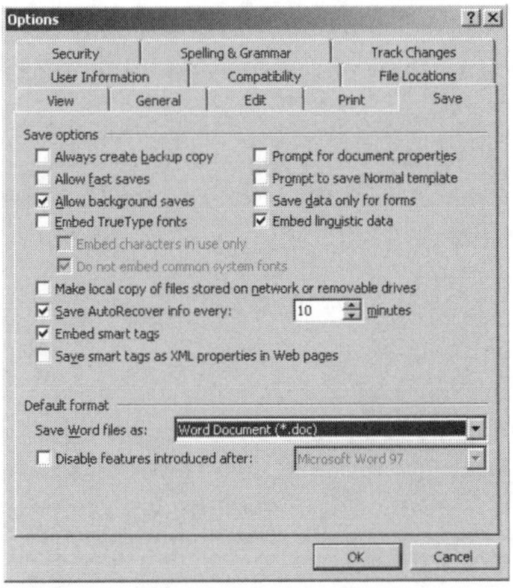

Figure 2-12. The Save tab enables you to configure default Save settings.

2. In the Default Format section, select a new default format setting in the Save Word Files As list, and click OK.

> **tip** At times, you'll want to create a folder to contain a newly created file. You can easily create a new folder during the save procedure by clicking the Create New Folder button on the Save As dialog box's toolbar.

Saving a File as a Web Page

As Word continues to evolve, creating and saving documents as Web pages in Word is becoming increasingly feasible for Web page developers. In short, you can save any document in Word as a Web page by using the Save As Type drop-down list in the Save As dialog box. In Word 2002, three Web-related file types are available in the Save As Type list:

- Web Page
- Web Page, Filtered
- Web Archive

When you're creating Web pages in Word, you'll probably want to begin by saving the document in the Web Page file type format. This format creates an HTML document and enables you to continue using all the Word editing features while you work. Later, when you're ready to upload your Web page to a network or the Internet, you might want to then save the document using the Web Page, Filtered option to streamline your document's HTML code and create a smaller HTML file than is created by the Web Page option. (The Web Page, Filtered option removes some of the HTML source code that's inserted into Word-generated Web pages for the sole purpose of providing Word editing capabilities.) Finally, when you're ready to archive a Web site or you want to send an entire Web site as a single file to someone, you'd probably use the Web Archive file type, which saves all the elements of your Web site—graphics and text—as a single .mhtml file.

For more information about creating Web pages in Word, see Chapter 31, "Creating Professional Web Sites."

Saving a File on a Network

Saving a file in a network location is similar to saving a file in a folder on your local computer. The main difference is that you navigate to a network location instead of to a local folder within the Save As dialog box. Word 2002 makes saving a file in a network location even easier by providing the My Network Places button on the Places bar. (The Places bar is discussed in the section "Taking a Closer Look at the Places Bar," on page 64.) Figure 2-13 shows the My Network Places button selected in the Save As dialog box.

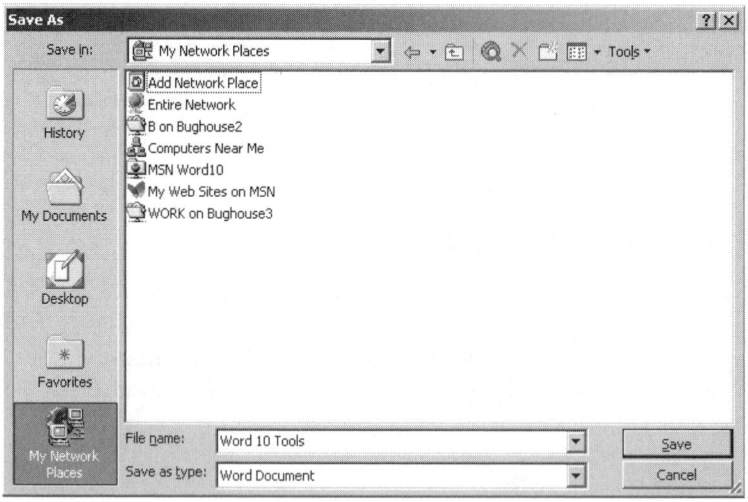

Figure 2-13. The My Network Places button simplifies the process of navigating to networked locations.

Creating Automatic Backups

By default, Word's AutoSave feature stores unsaved changes to a file at specified intervals. For added assurance, you can configure Word to create a backup file every time you save a file. To set this option, choose Tools, Options, Save tab, and select the Always Create Backup Copy check box. When this feature is activated, you'll notice that your folders contain two versions of each document you've saved: one file displays the standard file name, and the other file is named "Backup of *file name*.wbk." To open a backup file, simply double-click the file in the same manner you double-click other files to open them.

note You can't use the fast save feature and the automatic backup feature at the same time. The automatic backup feature creates a backup file each time you save your document. When the Allow Fast Saves check box is selected on the Save tab in the Options dialog box, Word saves only the changes you make to a document (instead of saving the entire document). When the list of changes grows fairly large, Word performs a normal save and integrates all the changes. By default, neither the fast save nor the automatic backup feature is activated.

Retrieving Documents

The poet William Wordsworth once claimed that he wrote his best works in a single sitting. But most of us living people don't work that way—instead, we return to documents time and again for one reason or another. Therefore, Word provides a few techniques you can use to retrieve existing documents. This section lays out the various document retrieval options—you can sift through and determine which method best suits your working style.

Displaying Existing Documents

As with other files in Windows, you can retrieve documents in a variety of ways using the Windows interface. For example, you can choose the Documents option on the Start menu, open My Computer, navigate to a document within your browser, and so forth. In Word, the best sources for retrieving Word documents are the Open dialog box and the New Document task pane.

Surveying the Updated Open Dialog Box

The Open dialog box, shown in Figure 2-14, on the next page, is your key to finding and retrieving Word documents. (Notice that the Open dialog box provides features similar to the options in the Save As dialog box, shown in Figure 2-11.)

To display the Open dialog box, perform any of the following actions within Word:

- Choose File, Open.
- Click the Open button in the Standard toolbar.
- Click the Documents link in the New Document task pane.
- Press Ctrl+O.
- Press Ctrl+F12.
- Press Ctrl+Alt+F2.

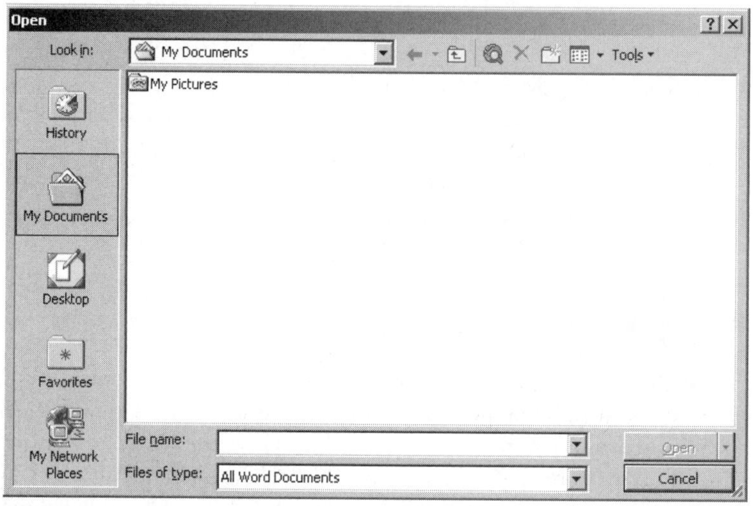

Figure 2-14. The Open dialog box serves as a gateway to existing files on your system, your network, and the Internet.

Taking a closer look at the Places bar The Places bar enables you to move quickly around your system and network as you retrieve documents. The default Places bar buttons are described in Table 2-9.

To learn how to customize the Places bar, see Chapter 38, "Customizing Word and Maximizing Accessibility."

Selecting views in the Open dialog boxes As with most Windows applications, you can specify how you'd like to display the documents and folders listed in the Open dialog box. To do so, you click the down arrow on the Views toolbar button and select a view from the list. You can display files and folders in the Open and Save As dialog boxes using the following views:

- Large Icons
- Small Icons

Table 2-9. Default Places Bar Buttons

Button	Name	Function
	History	Displays Windows shortcuts to every file you've opened, listed in date and time order, starting with the most recently used document. If you've worked on a document a number of times, clicking the shortcut in the History folder takes you to the most recent version.
	My Documents	Opens the default document folder named My Documents.
	Desktop	Displays the contents of your desktop. You should probably avoid saving Word documents to your desktop so that you don't clutter up your desktop (especially if you've turned on the Automatic Backups feature, because you'll have twice as many files fighting for space on your desktop).
	Favorites	Displays the files you've added to your Favorites folder because you think you'll access them frequently. This folder might seem familiar because it's the same Favorites folder used in Internet Explorer and Windows Explorer.
	My Network Places	Displays your network locations (shown in Figure 2-13).

- List
- Details
- Properties
- Preview
- Thumbnails
- WebView

In addition, you can arrange the sort order of documents and folders by clicking the column heading buttons, such as Name, Size, Type, and Modified.

Perfecting the Art of Opening Existing Documents

After you become familiar with the ins and outs of the Open dialog box, opening documents is fairly straightforward. The basic premise behind opening files using the Open dialog box is to select a file name and click the Open button or simply double-click a file name.

Troubleshooting

I Don't See the File I'm Looking for in the Open Dialog Box

At times, you might run into a bit of trouble finding a document, and you won't see the file you're looking for in the Open dialog box. If you don't see your file, first verify that you're looking in the proper location, especially if you're working on a network. (Checking your location is the word processing equivalent of checking to see whether your TV is plugged in.) If you're on the right track, select All Files in the Files Of Type list to ensure that the file you're looking for isn't being filtered out of the displayed file names. If you really get stuck, try searching for the file using the Basic Search or Advanced Search task panes, as described in Chapter 12, "Honing Document Navigation Skills."

tip To open multiple files from within the Open dialog box, select files while pressing Ctrl, and then click the Open button.

As you might have noticed, the Open button in the Open dialog box sports a drop-down menu that provides a few extra commands, as shown in Figure 2-15. This menu enables you to open a file as read-only, open a copy of a file, open a file in a browser (if the document's an HTML file), or open and repair a faulty file.

tip Remember, when you open a read-only file, you must use the Save As feature to save any changes you make to the document (in which case, you create a new document based on the read-only document without affecting the original file).

To bypass the Open dialog box altogether when opening documents, you can use one of these methods:

- Double-click a Word document's icon in a folder.
- Drag a Word document's icon from its folder into the Word application.
- Click a document link listed under the Open A Document heading in the New Document task pane.

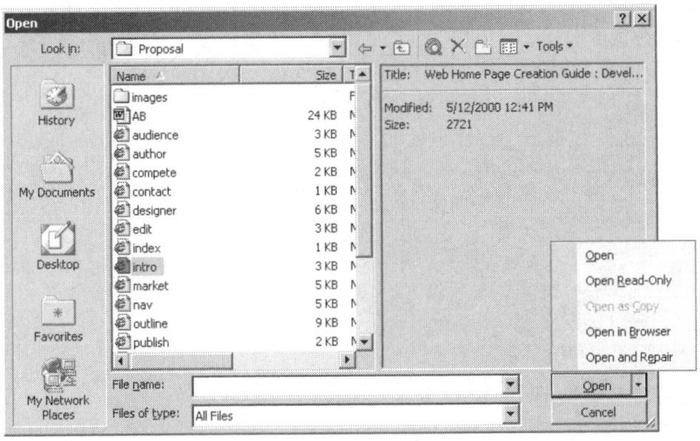

Figure 2-15. The Open button drop-down menu provides options that let you control how you open a document.

note Take special note of the Open And Repair command. You can use Open And Repair to attempt to open a file that's been damaged or corrupted.

newfeature!

Searching for Files

Search

Finding files isn't much of an issue when you know where you stored the file or the name of a specific file. But in some cases, you might have to search for a file stored on your local computer or network. Word provides two new search utilities—Basic Search and Advanced Search—which are displayed in the task pane and enable you to conduct fairly specific and wide-reaching search operations. You can display the Basic Search task pane by choosing File, Search or by clicking the Search button on the Standard toolbar. To switch to the Advanced Search task pane, click the Advanced Search link in the Basic Search task pane. Figure 2-16, on the next page, shows the Basic Search and Advanced Search task panes. To learn how to use the Word Search features, see Chapter 12, "Honing Document Navigation Skills."

Working with Multiple Files

Working with multiple files open is a common situation for many Word users. For example, if you're writing a chapter for a book, you might need to open the chapter document, a style sheet, a template, a test document, the book's outline, and a notes file. Fortunately, Word simplifies the process of working with multiple files in a few ways—most of which you're probably familiar with if you've been using Microsoft Office applications recently. The main issues you face when working with multiple documents are switching among open files and closing and saving all documents when you're ready to pack it up.

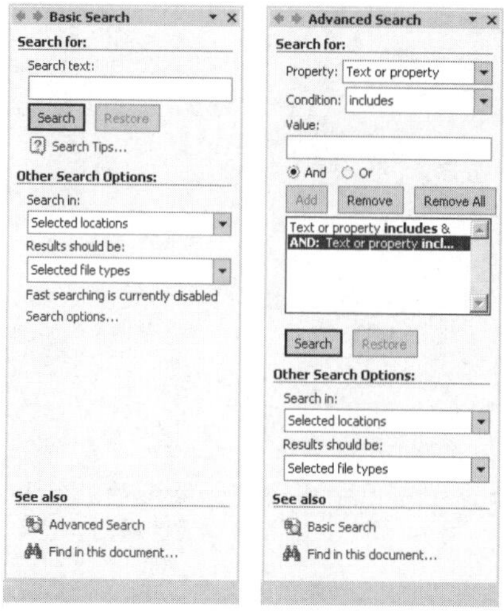

Figure 2-16. You can conduct basic and advanced searches within the new task pane.

Switching Among Open Files

Many Word users were disappointed to find that Word 2000 created a Windows taskbar icon for every opened Word document. For people who opened numerous Word documents during a session, the new setup up forced ridiculously small icons across the width of the taskbar. Therefore, many users might be glad to find that Word 2002 offers a choice in this matter. (Of course, by now, you might be accustomed to accessing files from amidst the multiple icons in the taskbar.) You can configure Word 2002 to display an icon for each opened Word document or to show a single taskbar icon that indicates the currently displayed Word document. (This window organization, which displays multiple document windows all within the same application, is called multiple-document interface [MDI] behavior in Word 97.) To access the taskbar setting, choose Tools, Options, View tab, and select or clear the Windows In Taskbar check box. When the Windows In Taskbar check box is selected, you'll see a taskbar icon for each opened document; when the check box is cleared, only one taskbar icon will represent the Word application. By default, the Windows In Taskbar check box is selected, which reflects the Word 2000 way of managing taskbar icons.

The taskbar also comes into play when you want to control the display of all windows. By right-clicking a blank area of the Windows taskbar, you can arrange your open windows in cascading or tiled pattern. Similarly, you can use Arrange All on the Window menu in Word to access and control how Word files are displayed.

Last but not least, you can navigate among open files using the old standby Alt+Tab technique, if you're not in MDI mode. As an experienced user, you've probably used Alt+Tab to select a document's icon to bring the selected document to the foreground. (If you haven't used this technique, you can quickly review how the feature works by opening a few applications and documents and then pressing Alt+Tab.)

Saving All Open Documents Simultaneously

When you want to shut down in a hurry but you have multiple documents open, you can save all open documents at the same time. To do so, press Shift and then choose File, Save All. Word saves all the open documents and templates at the same time. If you have open documents that have never been saved, the Save As dialog box appears so that you can name any newly created files.

tip You can close all documents without saving them by pressing Shift and choosing File, Close All.

Taking Advantage of AutoRecovery and Background Saves

As all computer users intuitively know, there's always a risk of losing data when you least expect it. To help reduce the risk of inadvertently losing data, Word is installed with the AutoRecovery and background saves features activated. These two features work together to help save your information without interrupting your workflow too much. These features can be summarized as follows:

- **AutoRecovery** automatically stores information about an active document that might be useful if your system crashes or if there's a power failure. By default, Word gathers AutoRecovery information every 10 minutes.
- **Background Saves** enables you to continue working in Word while you save a document. A pulsing disk icon appears on the status bar when a background save is taking place.

To verify that your system has these two features activated, choose Tools, Options, Save tab, and make sure that the Save AutoRecovery Info Every and Allow Background Saves check boxes are selected.

Keep in mind that the AutoRecovery feature isn't a replacement for saving your file. Instead, it's a tool Word can use when it attempts to recover a file after a system crash. You need to continue to save your documents regularly. If your system seems a bit shaky, you can also configure AutoRecovery to gather information more frequently by clicking the Save tab in the Options dialog box and changing the interval time in the Save AutoRecover Information Every box.

note By default, AutoRecovery files are stored in ...Application Data\Microsoft\Word. You can change the default location using the File Locations tab in the Options dialog box. (See Chapter 38, "Customizing Word and Maximizing Accessibility" for instructions about changing default file locations.)

newfeature!

If you experience a system crash while working in Word, Word displays a Document Recovery task pane after you restart your system and reopen Word, as shown in Figure 2-17.

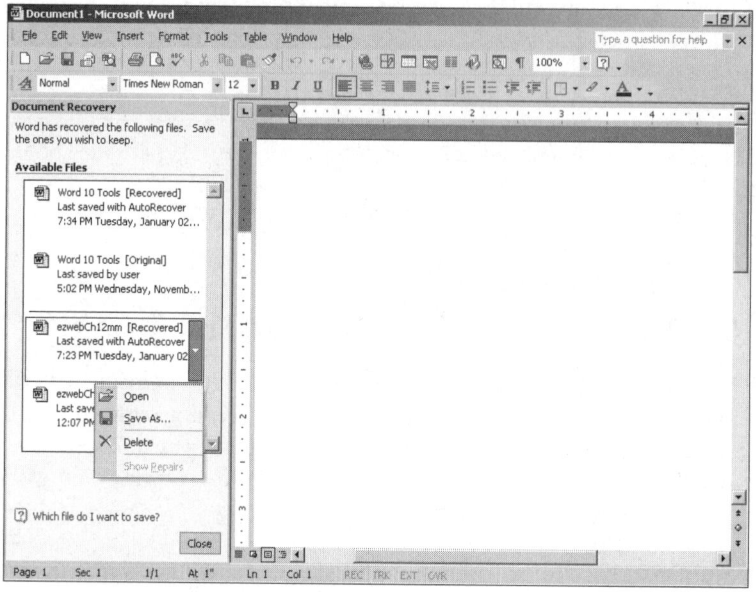

Figure 2-17. The Document Recovery task pane enables you to control how Word manages recovered files after a system crash.

You can select which files you want to recover from among the available recovered versions of documents within the Document Recovery task pane. The documents are referred to as recovery files, and they carry the .asd extension. To open a recovered document, double-click the entry in the task pane or choose Open on the item's drop-down menu. In addition, you can save or delete a recovered file or view repairs made to a recovered file by clicking the item's down arrow and selecting the desired command.

> **tip** **Recover the Most Recent Versions of Files**
>
> Frequently, you'll see a few versions of the same file listed in the Document Recovery task pane's Available Files list. When this occurs, keep in mind that a recovered file with *"[Recovered]"* in its title is usually in better shape than a file with *"[Original]"* in its title. Be sure to check the Last Saved time listed with each recovered document to verify that you're recovering the most recent version.

After you've made your recovery decisions, click the Close button in the lower-right corner of the Document Recovery task pane to close the pane. If you have not taken specified recovery action (such as deleting, saving, or opening and closing without saving) for each file in the Document Recovery task pane, a message box will appear asking whether you want to view the recovered files later or remove the files because you've saved the file you need. Select the action you want Word to take, and then click OK to complete the recovery process.

caution When you close a recovery file without saving it, the recovery file is deleted—you can't recover a deleted recovery file.

Troubleshooting

Recovery Files Aren't Displayed in Word After a Crash

In some instances, your recovery files might not appear when you reopen Word. Don't worry (yet)—all is not lost at this point. You can try to locate and open a recovery file manually when necessary. To do so, follow these steps:

1. Click the Open button on the Standard toolbar, and navigate to Windows\Application Data\Microsoft\Word or Windows\Profiles*username*\Application Data\Microsoft\Word.
2. In the Files Of Type box, select All Files. You'll be looking for .asd files, but Word doesn't include a drop-down list item for that file type. (If you want to get really fancy, you can simply search for recovered files using the parameter *AutoRecovery*.** in the Windows Search Results dialog box. To open the Windows Search Results dialog box, choose Start, Search, For Files Or Folders.)
3. Find the recovery file named "AutoRecovery save of *file name*.asd", and then open the document.
4. Click Save on the Standard toolbar, type or select the file name of the existing document, and then choose Yes when you're asked whether you want to replace the existing file.

Chapter 3

Getting the Most from Help

Word 2002 includes a multifaceted help system that enables you to find the answers to your questions—in the form you want them. You can rely on an interactive feature called the Office Assistant to lead you through processes, offer suggestions when you appear to get stuck, and prompt you to add common signatures and salutations as you type.

Some experienced users find the Office Assistant a bit annoying, because at first it pops up unexpectedly and takes some time and focus away from what might be a fast-paced production. Although the Assistant lives on in Word 2002, the control is in your court: Not only can you hide the Assistant, but you can also remove it if that's your preference. Beyond the Assistant-level help, Word 2002 adds two solid help features that will enable you to work better and more safely with your documents. The first new feature we cover in this chapter is the Ask A Question box, which appears in the upper right corner of your Word work space. The second is a new crash recovery feature that enables you to recover from those badly timed lockups.

Finding Answers Quickly

If you're an experienced user of Word, the features you need help with are often those you seldom use. You might need to remember how to add a symbol to a footer or how to insert a field code on a merge document you're preparing. Word includes several features that will help you find the help you need quickly.

newfeature!

Using the Ask A Question Box

Word 2002 adds a new help feature in the right side of the menu bar that enables you to ask an English-style question or enter a word or phrase and get help on the topic you entered. This feature is called the Ask A Question box, for obvious reasons. (See Figure 3-1.)

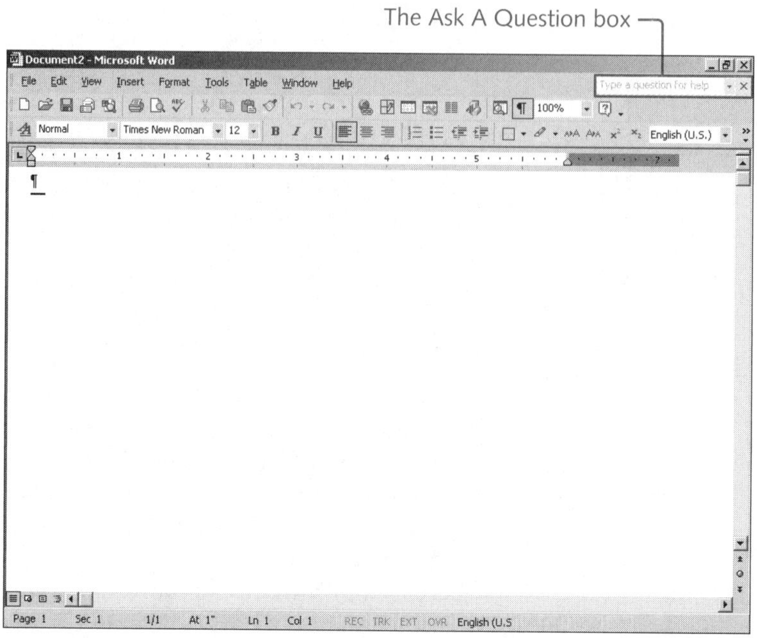

Figure 3-1. Use the Ask A Question box to ask a question or enter a phrase related to a specific topic you want to find out about.

After you type your question or phrase and press Enter, a list of specific Help topics appears. You can then click on the Help topic that will tell you more about your selected subject or click See More to display additional related Help topics.

After you click a Help topic, the full Help entry is displayed in the Microsoft Word Help window, located to the right of the document work area.

Suppose that you look up help on how to add a field code and then get busy doing something else for a while. You don't have to re-enter your search phrase and navigate to the help you seek; you can simply recall your help question by clicking the Ask A Question box's down arrow and selecting the help you want to review. However, the Ask A Question box is cleared each time you exit Word.

Using What's This?

What's This?

You'll find the What's This? option in the Word Help menu, which is no big surprise if you've used previous versions of Word. What's This? can help you get quick help about commands, features, and dialog box elements, and it can also provide helpful information about the formatting of selected items in your document.

Using What's This? to Describe Screen Elements and Commands

To use What's This?, choose Help, What's This? and then simply position the pointer on the item for which you want help and click. A Help window appears with the descriptor you need. (See Figure 3-2.)

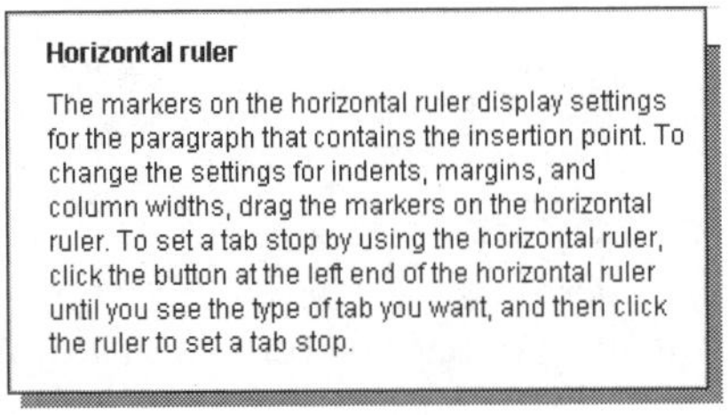

Horizontal ruler
The markers on the horizontal ruler display settings for the paragraph that contains the insertion point. To change the settings for indents, margins, and column widths, drag the markers on the horizontal ruler. To set a tab stop by using the horizontal ruler, click the button at the left end of the horizontal ruler until you see the type of tab you want, and then click the ruler to set a tab stop.

Figure 3-2. To discover the function of screen elements, commands, and dialog box options, use the What's This? command.

newfeature!

Using What's This? to Reveal Formatting

In the previous version of Word, What's This? was also used to display the formatting of selected text. In Word 2002, What's This? displays even more formatting information in the task pane, as Figure 3-3, on the next page, shows. To display the formatting information for selected text, choose Help, What's This? and click the text with the format you want to view. The information is shown in the task pane and is linked so that you can move directly to the appropriate formatting dialog boxes to modify or set options as needed.

For more information on working with Reveal Formatting and using the task pane to choose and modify formatting choices, see Chapter 7, "Aligning Information and Styling Paragraphs," and Chapter 10, "Using Styles to Increase Your Formatting Power."

Using What's This? in Dialog Boxes

The What's This? button can also be found in many of the dialog boxes you'll be using in Word. The What's This? button actually resembles the Help button (it looks like a question mark) and it's placed to the left of the dialog box Close button. To find out more about a feature or command, click the What's This? button and then click the item you want to know more about. If help is available, a ScreenTip appears, giving you additional information about the choice. To close the ScreenTip, simply click anywhere in the dialog box outside the tip.

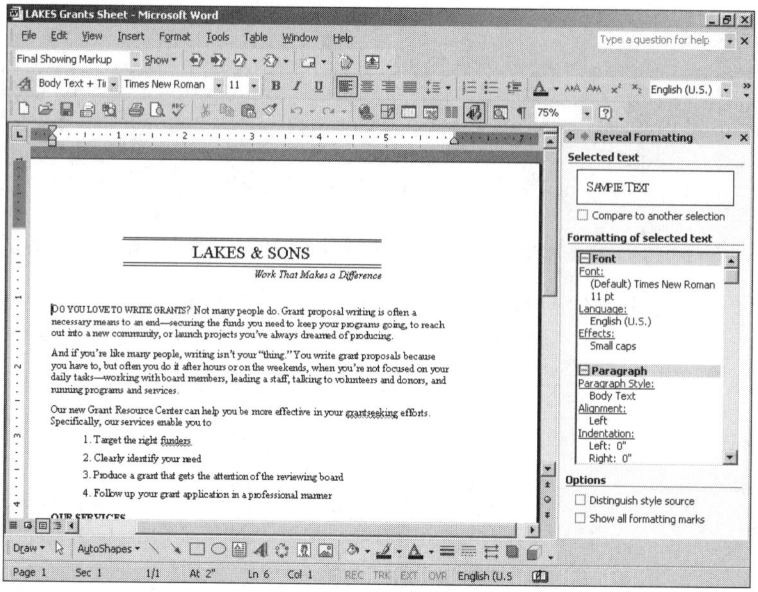

Figure 3-3. When used to check the formatting of selected text, What's This? displays a range of formatting information in the task pane.

Training Your Office Assistant

Few people are lukewarm about the Office Assistant. They either really appreciate the help, waiting there patiently to suggest next steps, or they resent the interruptions and the time spent navigating to the answers they need. Whichever description fits you best, you can customize the way you work with the Office Assistant to get just the type (and amount) of help you want to receive.

Getting Help from the Assistant

The Assistant pops up whenever it observes you working with a common process or seeming to labor over a particular task. You can display the Assistant in a number of ways:

- Choose Help, Microsoft Word Help.
- Choose Help, Show Office Assistant (this option is available only if the Assistant is not currently enabled).
- Press F1.
- Click the Microsoft Word Help button on the Standard toolbar.

The Assistant appears, asking you what you'd like help with. Type your question, and click Search.

In other cases, the Assistant will appear with a balloon, asking you to explain what you want to know. You can simply type your question or phrase (the more complete the better the result) and click Search. After selecting a Help topic, the Assistant then displays the help in the task pane. (See Figure 3-4.)

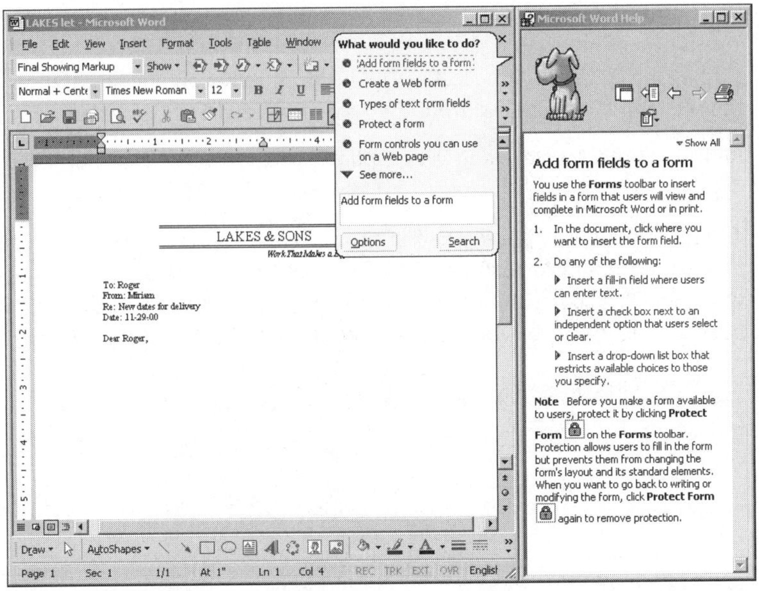

Figure 3-4. After you select the help you want, the Assistant displays the specific information in the task pane.

For more information on navigating through help in the task pane, see "Working with Microsoft Word Help," later in this chapter.

Hiding Your Assistant

When you first install and begin working with Word, the Assistant greets you. By default, your companion is Clippit, the personable paper clip. He watches over what you do and makes suggestions when you take on some of the tasks he's programmed to help with.

If you want to hide the Assistant while you work (which is a temporary fix—we'll tell you how to disable the fellow later in this section), simply right-click the Assistant and choose Hide from the shortcut menu that appears.

tip **Ask the right question the right way**

The Office Assistant is programmed to understand questions asked in general English, but you can save a few clicks by following a simple rule: Use an entire phrase or sentence as opposed to a single word. For example, entering the phrase *Create a Web page* will get you much more targeted help than entering the single word, *Web*.

Changing Assistant Behavior

Working with the Assistant isn't an all-or-nothing proposition. You can make a number of changes to the Assistant to control and customize the way it helps. You can choose a different assistant entirely, limit the way it behaves, or disable it entirely. Here's how to customize the Assistant:

1. Display the Assistant, if necessary. If you need to review the steps, refer to the section, "Getting Help from the Assistant," earlier in this chapter.
2. Right-click the Assistant and click Options. The Office Assistant dialog box appears.
3. The set of options in the top half of the dialog box on the Options tab concern the use of the Office Assistant. (See Figure 3-5.) To further limit when and where the Office Assistant pops up to help you, clear some of these check boxes. Table 3-1 gives you an overview of the Office Assistant options.

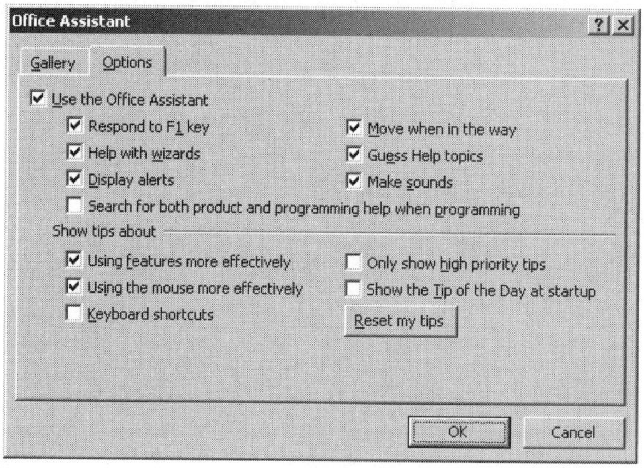

Figure 3-5. Change or limit the actions of the Office Assistant by clearing check boxes on the Options tab of the Office Assistant dialog box.

Table 3-1. Office Assistant Options

Assistant Option	Description
Respond To F1 Key	Displays context-sensitive help when you press F1
Help With Wizards	Displays the Office Assistant automatically when you elect to work with a wizard
Display Alerts	Uses the Assistant to display Word alerts; clearing this check box displays the alert in a traditional message box

(continued)

Table 3-1. *(continued)*

Assistant Option	Description
Search For Both Product And Programming Help When Programming	Disabled by default; this option provides both programming and regular help when you're working in programming areas
Move When In The Way	Moves the Office Assistant to a new location if it interferes with your work
Guess Help Topics	Enables the Assistant to make "best guesses" about Help topics it's unsure of
Make Sounds	Adds audio output to the actions of the Assistant motions

Displaying Tips

One feature the Assistant offers is the ability to display tips that can make working with Word easier. Word includes a library of tips that the program cycles through, one at a time. To turn on the tips, right-click the Office Assistant, choose Options, and on the Options tab select the check boxes for the tips settings you want.

If you have Tip of the Day turned on, when you launch Word for the first time each day, a tip appears in the startup dialog box. Additionally, if you've turned on the tip feature and the Office Assistant is displayed as you work, a light bulb will appear above the Assistant's head when there's a tip to be shared. (See Figure 3-6.)

Figure 3-6. If you elect to get additional tips about ways to be most effective with Word, a light bulb above the Assistant's head alerts you to a tip.

If you hide the Assistant but leave the tips selected, a light bulb icon appears beside the Help button in the Standard toolbar when there's a tip Word thinks you might want to read.

Selecting a Different Assistant

One of the ways you can control the Office Assistant is to choose a different one. Word 2002 comes with eight different personalities you can try, each with a different movement, sound, and style (see Table 3-2, on the next page). To change Assistants, follow these steps:

1 Display the Assistant, if necessary. Turn to the section, "Getting Help from the Office Assistant," for more information.

2. Right-click the Office Assistant.
3. Click Choose Assistant.
4. When the Office Assistant dialog box appears, on the Gallery tab, browse through the Assistants by clicking Next.
5. To make your choice, click OK.

tip You can also get other Office Assistants on line by choosing Help, Office On The Web.

Table 3-2. Assistant Choices

Assistant	Name	Comments
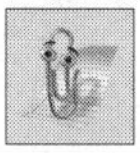	Clippit	The personable wire paper clip—the default Assistant
	The Dot	A little bouncing dot that changes into various shapes as you work
	F1	A robot character with a metallic sound that's sure to wake the cat
	Office Logo	The Office logo highlights and plays a chime sound when activated
	Merlin	An automated wizard that speaks, twirls, and appears and disappears
	Mother Nature	An earth logo that also changes to a flower or volcano and sounds a harmonic chime.
	Links	A cat with a loud purr (this will *really* wake the cat up!)
	Rocky	The cartoon dog that was the default Office Assistant in previous versions

note If you haven't installed any additional Office Assistant yet, Word will prompt you to insert your Office CD.

Getting Rid of Your Assistant

If you want to turn off the Office Assistant until further notice, clear the Use The Office Assistant check box in the Options tab of the Office Assistant dialog box. The Assistant will disappear until you invoke him choosing Help, Show The Office Assistant.

tip **Get help with programming**

While you're programming with Word, you can get high-level help. Right-click the Office Assistant, and click Options. To make the programming help available, select the Search For Both Product And Programming Help When Programming check box. Then, when you're programming, both regular help and more specialized programming help will be available to you.

Working with Microsoft Word Help

Although the Ask A Question box and the Office Assistant are the two most obvious help sources, you have a number of other options available to you. The older-style Contents and Index options are ready for your use, and the Answer Wizard enables you to move directly to the help you seek.

Displaying Help

To display Help in a separate window, first disable the Office Assistant as described in the preceding section and then choose Help, Microsoft Word Help. The help information is displayed in the Microsoft Word Help window, to the right of the work area (see Figure 3-7).

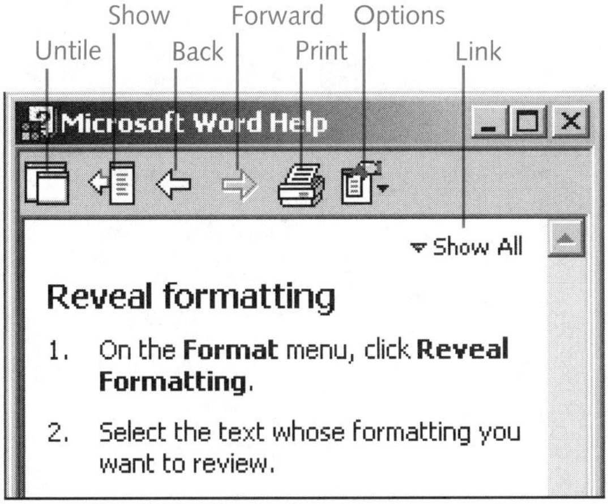

Figure 3-7. The Microsoft Word Help window provides a number of different controls that enable you to choose your help and customize the view.

To select a help topic, click the link, and the help for that item will be displayed. To return to the previous help screen, click Back.

InsideOut

It might seem like the Office Assistant is everywhere. If you have the Office Assistant enabled and you choose Microsoft Word Help or press F1, the Assistant will appear instead of the Microsoft Word Help window. If you want to display the task pane without the intervention of the Assistant, turn the Assistant off in the Office Assistant dialog box before you begin.

Controlling Help Displays

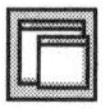
Untile

The Help options give you several choices about the way in which you view help. The default display, in the Task Pane, tiles the help windows so you see only one portion at a time. Click Untile if you want to position the window on top of your document (as opposed to changing the width of the document so both the document and the Task Pane are displayed in the screen area).

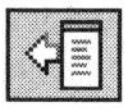
Show

Click the Show button to display the complete Help window. The left panel of the Help window will appear. This panel includes the Contents, Answer Wizard, and Index tabs. (See Figure 3-8.)

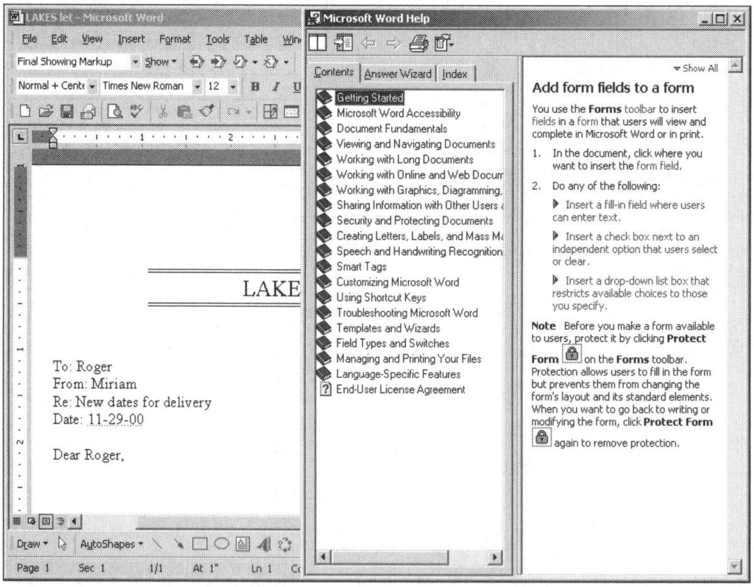

Figure 3-8. Click Show to extend the display of the Help window; here you can work with the Content, Answer Wizard, and Index tabs.

Using the Answer Wizard

The Answer Wizard is similar to the Office Assistant in that you can receive answers to English-style questions. Unlike the animated presence of the Assistant, however, the Answer Wizard simply leads you through various help categories until you get to the topic you want.

The Answer Wizard is open when you extend the Help window. Type your phrase or question and click Search; a list of topics is displayed in the list area. (see Figure 3-9.) Click the help item you want to see and the right panel displays that help.

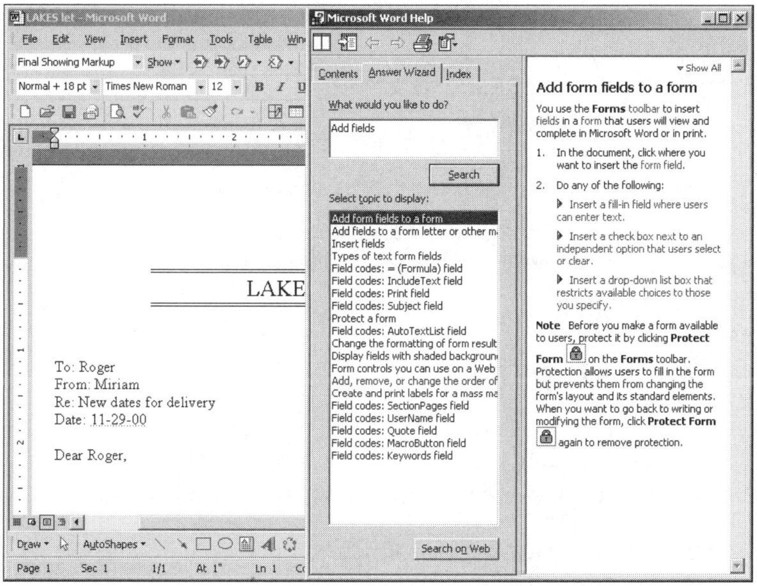

Figure 3-9. The Answer Wizard tab gives you a quick way to display the help you seek.

Using the Help Contents to Get Help

If you've used Word for a while, you're probably used to the Help Contents list—those task-focused Help screens that give you in-depth information on key Word features. To use the Help Contents, click the tab and double-click the topic you want to investigate. A list of subtopics appears. Click the topic you want to find out more about, and the more specific level of help, with additional links for more information, appears in the right panel of the Task Pane. (See Figure 3-10, on the next page.) Using Contents is helpful when you want to get general information about a certain feature in Word, and also when you want to find out about specific tasks. For example, you can begin in Contents with a general introduction to "Working with long documents" and continue choosing subtopics until you find the specific information on "Inserting headers and footers."

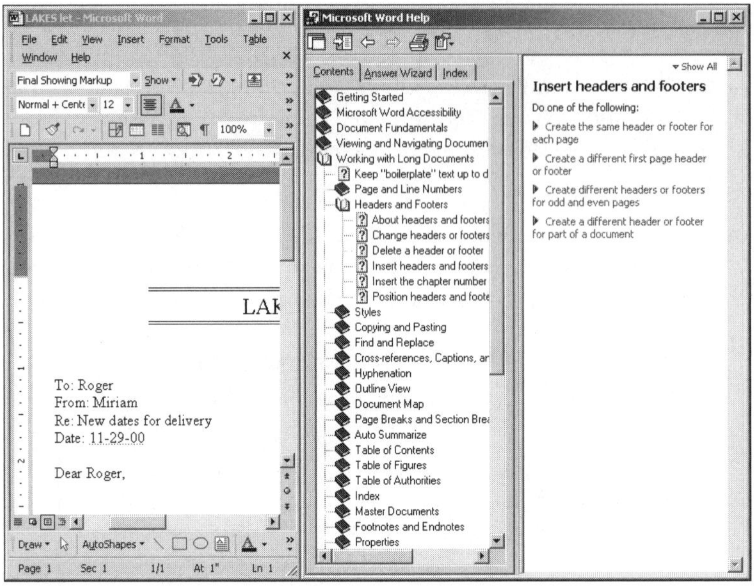

Figure 3-10. The Contents gives you both conceptual and practical help about common Word tasks.

Working with the Help Index

Finally, the Index tab offers another text-based help resource. The Index allows you to search for specific help topics when you might not be quite sure about the task or the topic terminology that you need. To use the Index, follow these steps:

1. Display the Microsoft Word Help window.
2. Click Show to extend the Help window, and click the Index tab.
3. Type the word or phrase you're looking for, and click Search. A list of topics with the word or words you entered is displayed in the Choose A Topic list.
4. Click the topic you want to view. The help you want appears in the right panel of the Help window.
5. Click the right arrows or highlighted text in the right pane to display specific procedures for the task you've identified. (See Figure 3-11.)

> **tip** **Print the help you want**
>
> If you need to print a copy of help information, click the Print button. The Print dialog box appears so that you can enter your options and click Print. Remember to display help at the level you want before printing.

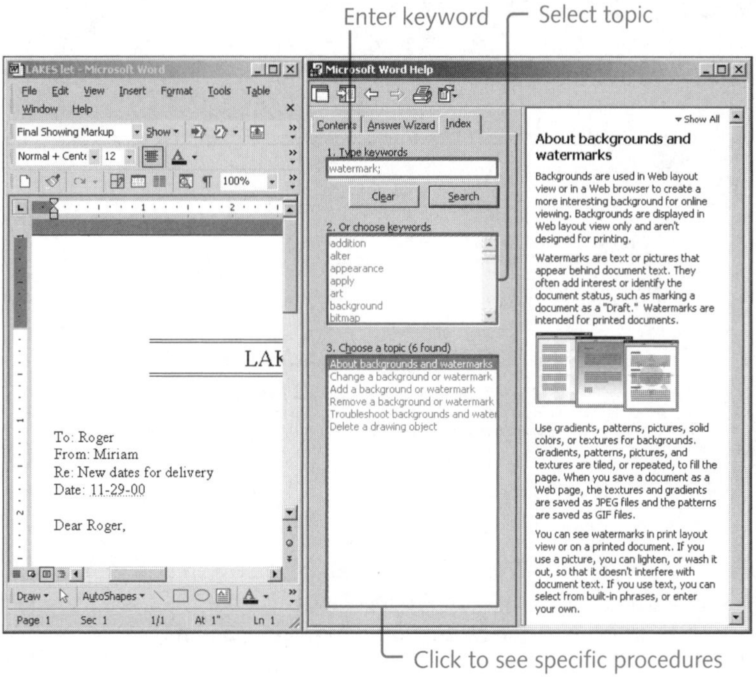

Figure 3-11. Use the Index to search for help on a specific keyword; then choose the topic you want to display help information.

InsideOut

One annoying aspect to the Index is the limitation you have in typing any keyword you want. Instead, Word limits you to typing only keywords that it recognizes. Your only workaround here is to enter a keyword and then navigate through the topics to the one you want to see.

Getting Help with Office on the Web

Microsoft hosts a wealth of technical support information online; the most obvious way to access it is to choose Help, Office On The Web. Selecting this command takes you to the Microsoft Office Product Updates page (see Figure 3-12, on the next page), where you can scout Microsoft services, download templates and updates, chat with others about your Word headaches, and learn ways to optimize your Office use.

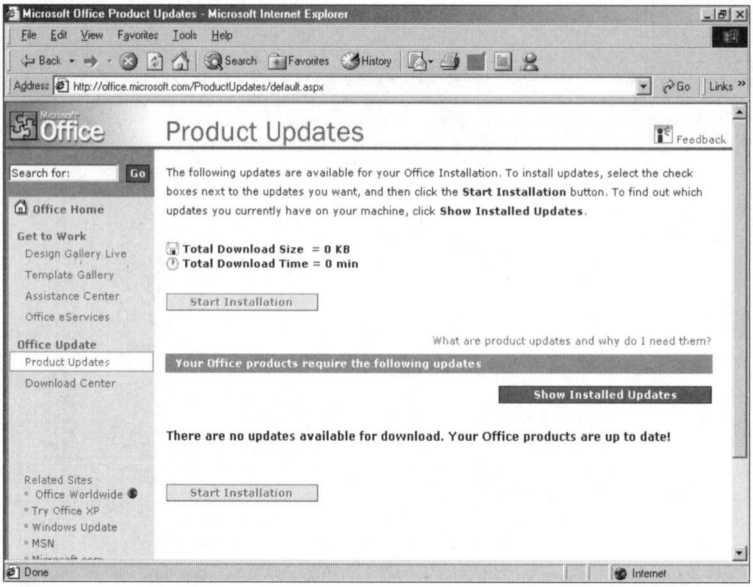

Figure 3-12. The Microsoft Office Product Updates page gives you a number of links for updates, downloads, technical support information, and more.

Using Microsoft's Knowledge Base

The Microsoft Knowledge Base is a huge compilation of articles on line, written to provide technical support information and provide users with a resource for sleuthing out their own technical problems. (See Figure 3-13.) To access the Knowledge Base, follow these steps:

1. Connect to the Internet and launch your Web browser.
2. Go to *www.microsoft.com* (you can also choose Help, Office On The Web).
3. Position the pointer over the Support tab in the upper right corner of the screen. (If you've accessed the Knowledge Base from within Word, you will need to click this tab.) When the Support menu appears, click Knowledge Base.
4. On the Knowledge Base Search page, choose the product you want help with (conceivably, Word 2002), choose the way in which you want to search, and type your question. Finally, click Go. After a few seconds, the results are shown in a Search Results screen. The titles of the articles are linked so that by clicking the one you want, you can move to it directly.

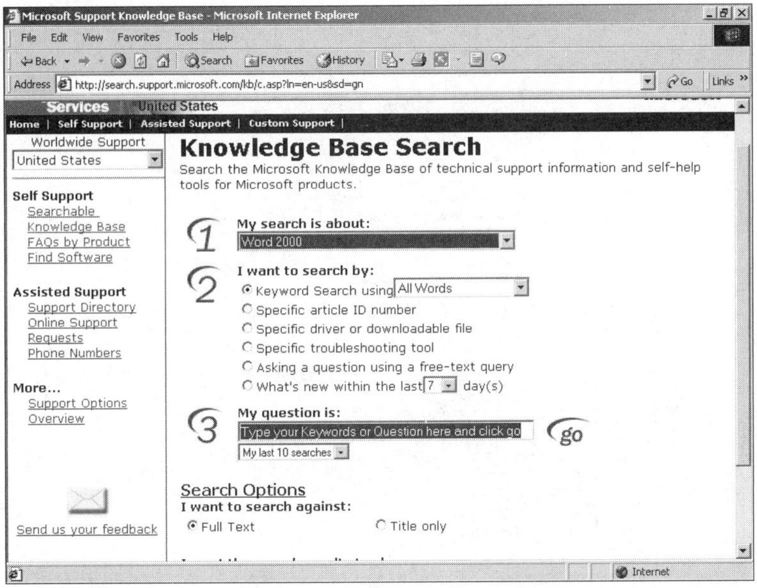

Figure 3-13. The Knowledge Base is a kind of tech support encyclopedia on line.

Researching FAQs

The Knowledge Base is considered part of Microsoft's "self support" system; another self-support help option is available in the Word-specific FAQs available on line. FAQs are frequently asked questions about a particular product, operating system, or feature. FAQs are valuable resources in that they compile user-submitted questions and problems and list resolutions offered by tech support in the past. To find FAQs to help with your use of Word (or other Office products), search the Support site for Word at *www.microsoft.com.*

Getting Newsgroup-Style Support

Yet another way to get help and trade tips and tricks with other Word users is available in the Office and Word newsgroups sponsored by Microsoft. You can use your newsreader (available in both Microsoft Outlook and Microsoft Outlook Express) to access list servers that distribute mail discussing topics such as Word issues. Some newsgroups are hosted by Microsoft IT, so you can get real help in a newsgroup if you're willing to participate (and filter out the spam that might come flying your way). Figure 3-14, on the next page, shows a screen with one of the Microsoft-supported newsgroups.

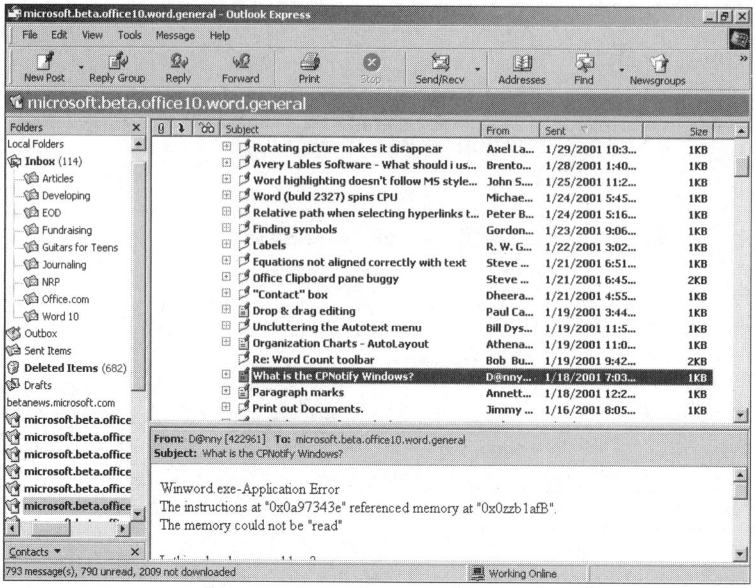

Figure 3-14. Newsgroups can give you the means to ask your questions directly and benefit from the shared knowledge of other users.

Getting Help for System Recovery

System crashes happen—and they are often hard to recover from. The phrase "save early and often," is a common reminder to help us prepare against the moment when we *finally* get the document entered the way we want it and the system goes down, zapping our files and costing us valuable time. Word 2002 attempts to make crashing less traumatic for users with a few crash recovery features—some visible, some transparent.

Using Application Recovery

Word, Microsoft PowerPoint, Microsoft Excel, and Outlook all have available a feature that interrupts a crashing system to allow open files to be saved. You can use Application Recovery to regain control of your system by following these steps:

1. Click Start and point to Programs, Microsoft Office Tools, and click Microsoft Office Application Recovery.
2. The Application Recovery window appears, as shown in Figure 3-15. In the figure, you can see that both Word and Outlook are active.
3. To try to stabilize the affected application, click the application name and click Recover Application; if that doesn't work, close the application by clicking End Application.

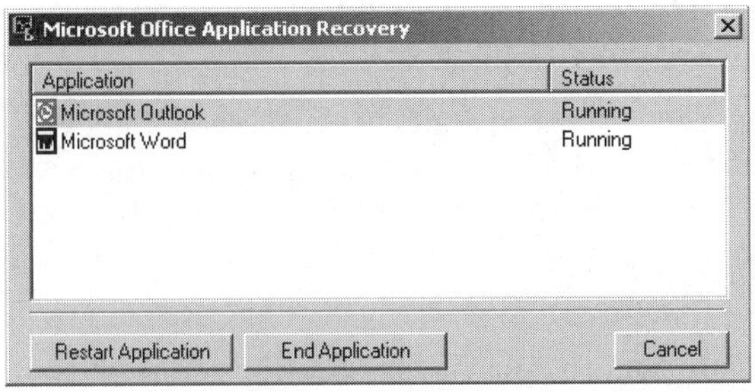

Figure 3-15. The Microsoft Office Application Recovery utility enables you to recover a failing application or exit a program that's locking up.

> **note** If your system is too far gone to interrupt with Application Recovery, try using the Task Manager. In Microsoft Windows 2000, press Ctrl+Alt+Delete, and when the Windows Security dialog box appears, click Task Manager. You can then click the application that is having trouble and click either Switch To, to try to get some response from it, or End Task, to exit the application. If you're using another version of Windows, you can press Ctrl+Alt+Delete and click End Task.

Crash Reporting

When your Word application is heading for a crash, you'll notice a few telltale signs. Processing will slow down considerably; the screen update will piece onto the screen. Then a dialog box appears, apologizing for the error (not a bad public relations move) and giving you the option of having Word recover your work and restart Word.

You are also given the option of sending an Error Report to Microsoft so that your crash will be logged and, conceivably, someone in technical support can begin working on the problem. (See Figure 3-16.)

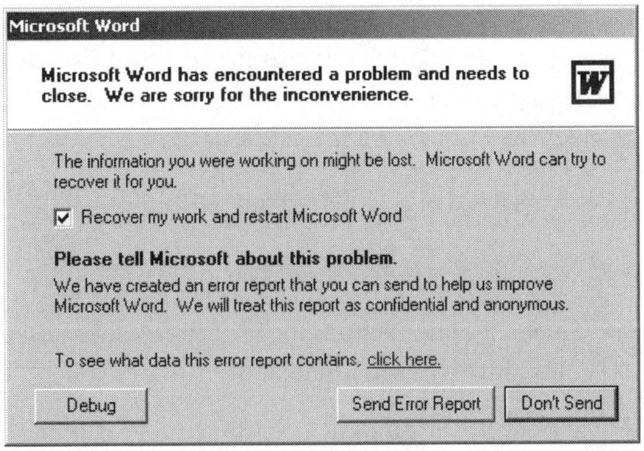

Figure 3-16. When a crash occurs, a Microsoft Word dialog box appears, asking whether you'd like to send an error report to Microsoft for evaluation. If you currently have an active Internet connection, click Send Error Report.

tip **Click don't send to finish without reporting**

If the crash dialog box appears and your Internet connection is not active, you can attempt to establish the connection before continuing. If your system is failing, however, you might need to click Don't Send to finish the process. No report is sent, and Word displays a message telling you it is recovering your documents; then the program restarts.

Click Send Error Report. An Error Reporting dialog box appears, showing that the report is being transmitted over a secure connection. When the report transmission is complete, click the Close button and Word will restart and display your recovered files.

What's in an Error Report?

The information sent to Microsoft when your system fails includes the context of the error (what you were trying to do when it occurred), which operating system you're using, the technical specifications of your system, your registration ID, and the IP address of your system. No personal information or data is sent. Links in the crash report dialog box can take you to Microsoft's error reporting and data sharing policies on the Web.

newfeature!

Recovering Documents

One of the most visible crash recovery features—and one that you'll meet as soon as you experience a crash while using Word 2002—is the new Document Recovery task pane, which displays the files that were saved when the crash occurred. (See Figure 3-17.) Word then gives you the option of saving the file that was open during the crash.

Setting AutoRecover Intervals

One of the features of that "save-early-and-often" mindset is the AutoRecover feature. You can have Word automatically save your open files at regular intervals—and you can determine how long or short you want those intervals to be.

To check and change the AutoRecover settings, follow these steps:

1. Choose Tools, Options to open the Options dialog box.
2. Click the Save tab. In the Save Options section, locate the Save AutoRecover Info Every check box and make sure that it is selected.
3. The default value for AutoRecover is 10 minutes. To shorten that period of time, click the down arrow in the box. (See Figure 3-18.)

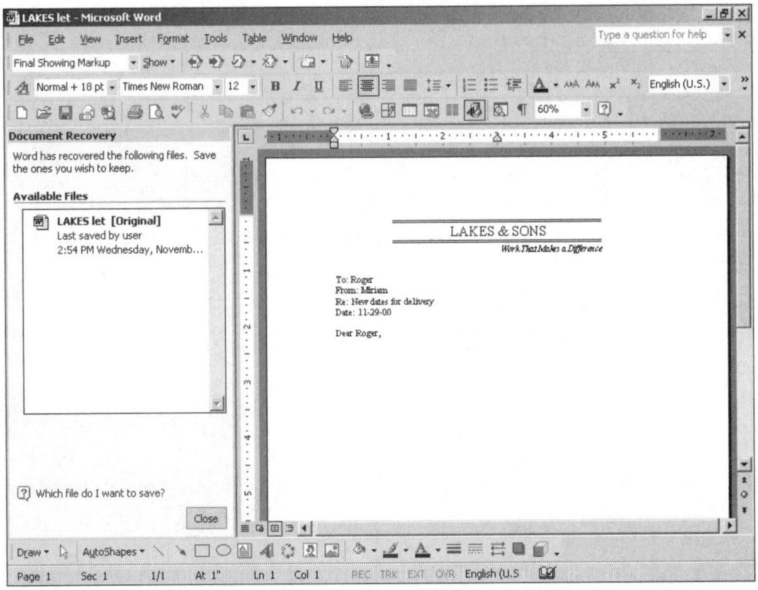

Figure 3-17. Document Recovery displays the file that was open when the crash occurred so that you can save it normally before proceeding with your work.

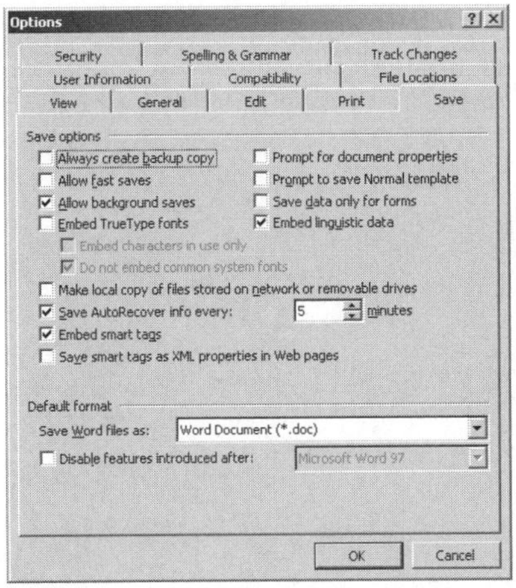

Figure 3-18. Change the length of time between AutoRecover saves by adjusting the value in the Save AutoRecover Info Every box.

> **tip** **Save your recovered file**
>
> Don't rely only on AutoRecover for saving your files, however. And when your Document Recovery task pane displays the available recovered files, you must go ahead and save the file (saving it under its original name is OK) in order to preserve your most recent changes.

Chapter 3

tip **When you can't find a recovered file**

Where's the recovery file? Depending on how hard your computer is working, it can take several minutes to create the recovery file in AutoRecover. If the computer locks up before the file is finished, your changes will be lost.

Files saved by AutoRecover are given the file extension .asd temporarily, until you save the file. If you can't find a recovered file you need, search your hard disk for *.asd files.

Chapter 4

Printing with Precision

The phenomenal surge of personal computing in the 1980s and 1990s introduced the concept of a "paperless" society, but the world has yet to realize that ideal (as plenty of buried desks and bulging file cabinets can attest). For the most part, people continue to rely fairly heavily on printed matter. And chances are, when you work in Microsoft Word, you'll probably need to print information frequently. In most cases, printing a document requires you simply to click the Print button on the Standard toolbar—not a complex task. But as a more experienced Word user, you might want a higher level of control over your print jobs–especially if you want to do more than simply print single copies of entire documents. For example, you might want to print selected sections of a document, print more than one copy of a document, print multiple document pages per printed page, or print a summary of the formatting styles used in a document. Fortunately, you can achieve additional printing control by using the printing options included in Word—and that's what this chapter's all about.

Previewing Before Printing

Even before you familiarize yourself with the nuances of printing, you should make a habit of using the Print Preview feature. Like a painter stepping back from her canvas, Print Preview enables you to take a big-picture look at a page or series of pages before you commit the information to hard copy. In Print Preview mode, you can examine entire pages at once, checking for obvious page setup errors and oddities and even applying minor fixes to correct some of the errors you discover. For example, using Print Preview, you can quickly see when an image box overlays text (or vice versa), a single line runs onto the next page, or indented text is out of whack.

Getting Comfortable in Print Preview Mode

Print Preview gives you a chance to view your document from a variety of perspectives before you print. By default, Print Preview shows the current page when you activate the feature. To activate Print Preview mode, open your document in Word, and then use one of the following techniques:

- Choose File, Print Preview.
- Click the Print Preview button on the Standard toolbar.
- Press Ctrl+Alt+I.

Print Preview

Figure 4-1 shows a document in Print Preview mode. The Print Preview toolbar buttons are described in Table 4-1.

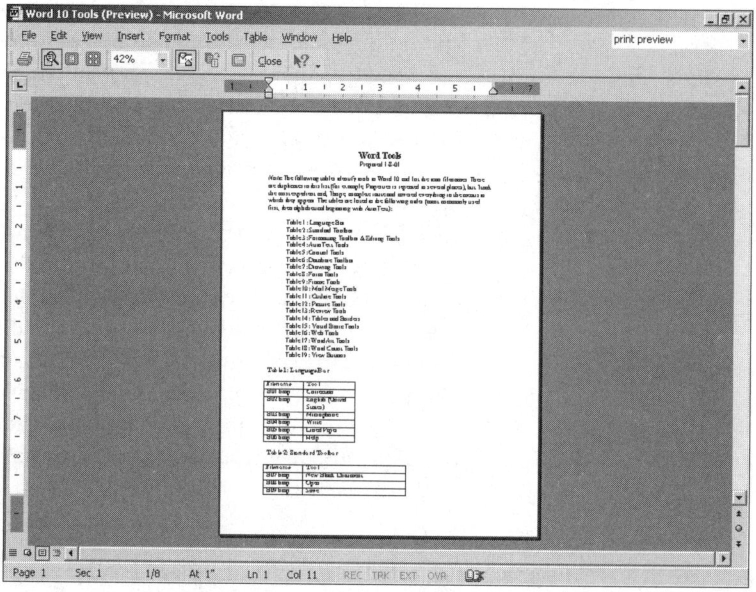

Figure 4-1. Previewing documents can help you troubleshoot page layout issues before you print.

To exit Print Preview mode, you can use one of the following methods:

- Choose View, Normal.
- Press Esc.
- Click Close on the Print Preview toolbar.
- Click a view button (located to the left of the horizontal scroll bar).

When you exit Print Preview, Word returns the insertion point to the location it was at before you selected Print Preview.

Table 4-1. Print Preview Toolbar Buttons

Name	Button	Description
Print		Prints a single copy of the previewed document without opening the Print dialog box
Magnifier		Enlarges and reduces the view, as well as enables you to edit content
One Page		Displays a single page in Print Preview
Multiple Pages		Enables you to arrange and display one or more pages at one time
Zoom drop-down list	50%	Enables you to enlarge or reduce the current view
Ruler		Toggles rulers on and off. Rulers enable you to modify margins and indents and set tabs from within Print Preview mode.
Shrink To Fit		Avoids the problem of a small amount of text spilling onto an extra page by reducing the number of pages in the current document by one
Full Screen		Maximizes the viewing area by hiding standard Word window components, such as the title bar, menu bar, status bar, and scroll bars
Close Full Screen	Close	Exits Print Preview mode and returns to the same page and view displayed before Print Preview was activated
What's This?		Activates the Context Sensitive Help feature

Controlling How Print Preview Displays Documents

In Print Preview mode, you can examine your document by zooming in to see details. You can also maximize your viewing area by shifting to Full Screen mode, pull back to display the flow of content on multiple pages, or select a specific page to focus on. Let's look at each viewing option:

- **Zooming in on information.** You can increase the size of your document by using the Magnifier button (which displays the document at actual size) or by indicating a size in the Zoom box (either by selecting a size in the Zoom drop-down list or by typing a percentage value). To zoom in on a selected area, click the Magnifier button, and then click the area of

Differentiating Between Print Layout View and Print Preview

Keep in mind that *Print Layout view* and *Print Preview* are two different views. (Print Layout view and Print Preview are discussed in detail in the section "Viewing Documents in Various Lights," on page 20.) To summarize:

- Print Layout View displays your document as it will print within the standard Word interface. Print Layout view enables you to work with standard Word editing controls while viewing how page elements will print. To switch to Print Layout view, choose View, Print Layout.
- Print Preview displays your document in a custom interface containing the Print Preview toolbar. In Print Preview mode, you can view multiple pages at one time as well as make editing and formatting changes before you print.

In general, Print Layout View should be used as a working environment, and Print Preview mode should be used to verify your document's layout when you're almost ready to print and to make minor fixes.

the document that you want to see more closely. You can use the Zoom box to further modify your view, if necessary. To revert your document to its original size, make sure that the Magnifier button is selected (it remains selected until you click another toolbar button), and then click the document. In other words, you click once to enlarge your view to 100 percent, and click a second time to reduce the view. As you'll see in the next section, you can also use the Magnifier button to activate Print Preview mode's editing options.

- **Working in Full Screen mode.** To maximize your screen's viewable area, click the Full Screen button. Figure 4-2 shows a document in Full Screen mode. Notice that all standard window elements are hidden except the Print Preview toolbar and a small floating toolbar containing the Close Full Screen button. To display menu options in Full Screen mode, position the mouse pointer at the top of the window. To revert to standard Print Preview mode, click the Close Full Screen button on the Full Screen toolbar, click the Full Screen button, or press Esc.

- **Displaying multiple pages.** One of the greatest benefits of Print Preview is the ability to view multiple pages at once. This feature enables you to see how your document will flow from page to page before you create a hard copy. You can view up to 24 pages (3 rows by 8 columns). To show multiple

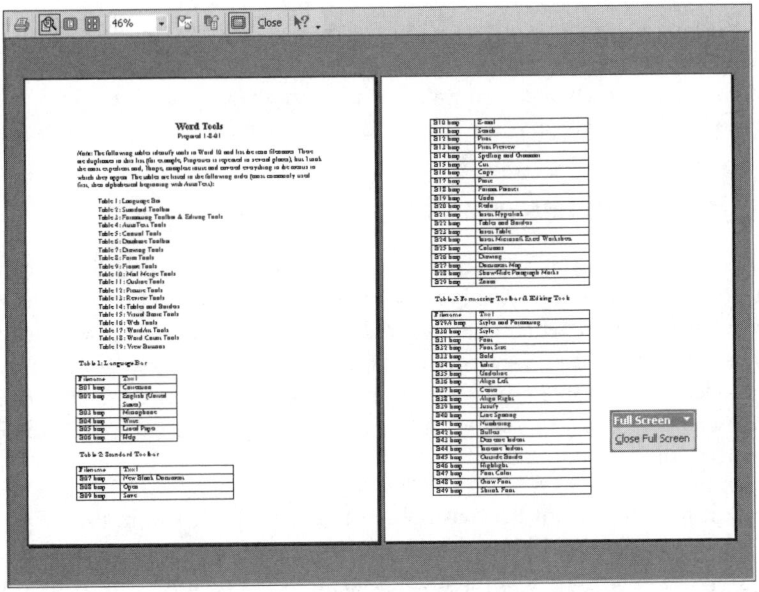

Figure 4-2. Full Screen mode maximizes your Print Preview viewing area.

pages, click the Multiple Pages button, and drag to select the number of rows and columns you want to display. Figure 4-3 shows two rows and four columns of pages in the Print Preview window.

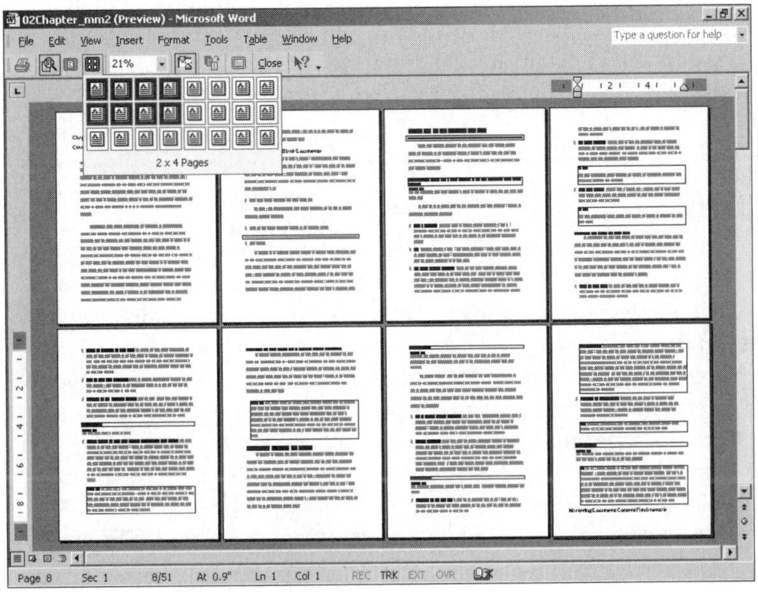

Figure 4-3. Using the Multiple Pages feature, you can display up to 24 thumbnail-sized pages at a time.

- **Viewing a selected page.** Obviously, you can click the One Page button on the Print Preview toolbar to display a single page. Nicely enough, you can also select which page you want to view if multiple pages are displayed. To do so, click the page you want to view, and then click the One Page button.

Editing in Print Preview Mode

As you zoom in, out, and around in Print Preview, you'll occasionally see details you want to adjust. If you exit Print Preview mode to fix the problems, you'll be returned to your original location, which means you'll have to search all over again for the areas you identified in Print Preview mode. Fortunately, you don't have to leave Print Preview mode to make some minor editing adjustments. If you need to edit some text, tighten up a document, or adjust content alignment, you can do so in Print Preview mode using the techniques described here:

- **Editing text in Print Preview mode.** You can modify text in Print Preview mode by deleting, adding, cutting, copying, pasting, moving, and formatting text and other document components—in much the same way you edit documents in other views. To activate text editing mode in Print Preview mode, click the Magnifier button, which changes the insertion point to a magnifying glass. To edit at actual size (100 percent), position the magnifying glass on the page in the area you want to edit, click to zoom in to 100 percent, and then click the Magnifier button again to change the magnifying glass to an insertion point. Keep in mind that you don't have to edit in 100 percent view; you can edit in any view size. At 100 percent, you can edit text in detail; at smaller sizes with multiple pages displayed, you can easily drag elements from page to page.

InsideOut

When you exit Print Preview, your insertion point returns to the location it was at before you selected Print Preview. In some instances, you might prefer to go directly to the page you were viewing in Print Preview mode. Unfortunately, Word doesn't provide an option to display the current page in Print Preview mode in other views—you're forced to return from whence you came. The quickest workaround to this little impediment is to take note of the relevant page number while you're in Print Preview mode (click the page, and check out the page number on the status bar), close Print Preview, and then use Go To (press Ctrl+G or open the Select Browse Object menu) to move to the desired page.

- **Condensing text to shorten a document by one page.** You can use the Shrink To Fit feature to tighten up a document that's just a tad too long. To do so, click the Shrink To Fit button on the Print Preview toolbar. Be forewarned that you might not like the changes Word implements (fonts can be reduced up to four point sizes). In some cases, Word will simply give up and present a message box stating that it was unable to shrink the document by one page.

caution If you want to print but not store the Shrink To Fit results, click the Shrink To Fit button to shrink your document, click Print on the Print Preview toolbar, and then undo the Shrink To Fit action before you save the document. (See the InsideOut box below for information about undoing actions in Print Preview mode.) Once you save the document, you can't undo the Shrink To Fit changes.

InsideOut

Notice that the Print Preview toolbar doesn't contain an Undo button. Luckily, this doesn't mean that you can't undo changes in Print Preview mode. To undo changes, choose Edit, Undo, or press Ctrl+Z. If you find that you need to undo changes in Print Preview mode on a regular basis, display the Formatting toolbar (choose View, Toolbars, Formatting) in Print Preview mode, or customize the Print Preview toolbar by adding the Undo button, as described in Chapter 38, "Customizing Word and Maximizing Accessibility."

- **Adjusting margins, indents, and tabs.** You can click the Rulers button on the Print Preview toolbar to toggle rulers on and off in Print Preview mode. When the rulers are displayed, you can drag the margin, indent, and tab icons to adjust margins, indents, and tabs. If you're displaying multiple pages, the rulers move to the top and left of the page that's currently selected. In Figure 4-3, the rulers correspond to page 8, the last page in the second row.

For more information about using rulers to adjust margins, indents, and tabs, see Chapter 7, "Aligning Information and Styling Paragraphs."

> **tip** **Access Page Setup options quickly**
>
> When rulers are showing, you can quickly open the Page Setup dialog box, which enables you to reset a document's margins, page orientation, and other page setup options. To open the Page Setup dialog box, double-click anywhere within the ruler areas except the white portion of the top ruler. If you click the white area of the top ruler, you might end up setting unwanted tabs.

Printing Quickly and Efficiently

After you've approved your document's appearance using Print Preview mode, you're ready to print. By far the easiest and most common printing task is printing an entire document. You've probably done this a million times, but to make sure we don't overlook any obvious procedures, here's a quick rundown of the ways you can print a single copy of the current document:

- Choose File, Print, and then click OK.
- Click Print on the Standard toolbar.
- Press Ctrl+P or Ctrl+Shift+F12, and then click OK.

Print

You can also print a Word document without opening it by right-clicking the file's icon and choosing Print on the shortcut menu. To print multiple documents stored in the same folder at one time, follow these steps:

1. Choose File, Open.
2. In the Open dialog box, open the folder that contains the documents you want to print, and then select the documents.
3. In the Open dialog box, click the Tools down arrow, and then choose Print on the drop-down menu.

> **note** To print from Word, you must have a printer and printer driver installed. If you're in charge of configuring your own printer, remember to check your printer manufacturer's Web page for any updated drivers that you should download if you run into any Word 2002 compatibility issues.

> For more information about printing envelopes and labels, see Chapter 38, "Performing Mail Merges."

Canceling a Print Job

Sometimes, you might decide at the last moment that you want to cancel a print job. How you cancel a print job varies, depending on whether background printing is turned on. By default, background printing is activated, which means that you can continue working while you print a document. To change this setting, choose Tools, Options, select the Print tab, and clear the Background Printing check box. To halt printing from within Word while your computer is sending a document to the printer, follow one of these two procedures:

- If background printing is disabled, click Cancel or press Esc.
- If background printing is enabled, double-click the animated printer icon on the status bar while the document is being sent to the printer. If you're printing a short document, the animated printer icon might not be visible long enough for you to cancel the printing task.

Managing Print Jobs Using the Print Queue Window

You can also manage your print jobs within the print queue window after they have been sent to the printer. To open the print queue window, double-click the Printer icon on the Windows taskbar after you've sent a document to the printer. You can perform the following key tasks from the print queue window:

- **Delete a single print job.** Select the print job you want to cancel, and choose Document, Cancel Printing to remove it from the print queue.
- **Reprioritize print jobs** Drag print icons up or down within the print queue list to change the order in which documents are printed.
- **Cancel all print jobs** Choose Printer, Purge Print Documents to delete all documents from the print queue.

Controlling Print Jobs

As an experienced user, you probably need to perform print tasks that are more complex than merely printing single copies of entire documents. Thus, instead of clicking the Print button on the Standard toolbar, you'll probably benefit more by pressing Ctrl+P or choosing File, Print so that you can take advantage of the options available in the Print dialog box, shown in Figure 4-4, on the next page. In this section, you'll learn how to customize and control many of these printing settings. Notice too that the Print dialog box includes a Properties button in the Printer section. The Properties button enables you to access some of the same settings you can access by choosing Start, Settings, Printers in Windows.

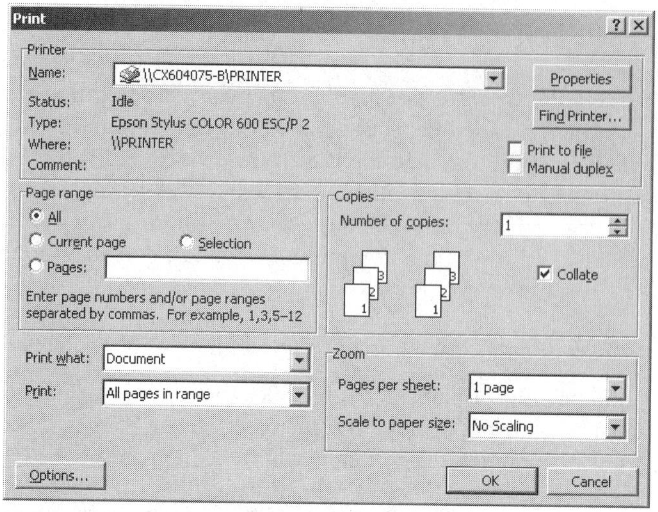

Figure 4-4. The Print dialog box provides many of the options that you can use to control your print jobs.

Printing More Than One Copy of a Single Document

To print multiple copies of a document, open the Print dialog box, and type a value in the Number Of Copies box or click the up and down arrows. By default, Word collates multiple copies of a print job. (Notice that the Collate check box is selected in the Copies section in the Print dialog box.) When collating is enabled, Word sends one copy of your print job to the printer, waits a moment, then sends the next copy to the printer, and so on. The result is that the entire selection or document is printed, and then the next copy is printed, and so forth. In the long run, this method is probably easier for an end user, but it takes longer to process and can cause bottlenecks in a print queue if the document contains numerous large graphics or extensive formatting. If you prefer, you can clear the Collate check box. Word will then send to the printer all copies of the first page, all copies of the second page, and so forth, leaving you to collate the copies manually. On some laser printers, printing without collating might speed the process and avoid bottlenecks in the print queue because the printer won't have to reprocess information for each copy of a page.

Printing Ranges

In many cases, you'll want to print a selection of pages instead of an entire document. For example, you might want to select and print a few paragraphs of text instead of an entire Web page, or you might want to print two or three noncontiguous sections within a long report, or you might want to print the cover letter attached to your updated résumé. To print specific pages and sections within a document, use the following options in the Page Range section of the Print dialog box:

- **All** prints the entire document; the default selection. To print an entire document, open the Print dialog box, and click OK.
- **Current Page** prints the page in which your insertion point is currently located. To use this option, click on the page you want to print, open the Print dialog box, click Current Page, and click OK.
- **Selection** prints selected text. To use this option, select the text you want to print, open the Print dialog box, click Selection, and click OK.

To review text selection methods, see Chapter 2, "Creating Documents from Start to Finish."

- **Pages** prints only the pages, page ranges, and sections you specify. You can use commas and hyphens along with the letters *s* (for *section*) and *p* (for *page*) to delimit which pages, sections, and page ranges you want to print. For example, enter **1-5,9,15-18** to print pages 1 through 5, page 9, and pages 15 through 18; enter **s2,s4** to print sections 2 and 4; and enter **p3s4-p6s5** to print from page 3, section 4, to page 6, section 5.

For more information about defining and using sections, see Chapter 9, "Formatting Columns and Sections for Advanced Text Control."

Printing Odd and Even Pages to Simulate Duplex Printing

If you want to print using both sides of paper but you don't have a *duplex printer* (a printer that can automatically print on both sides of paper), you can use the Odd Pages and Even Pages print options in Word to work around the limitation. To accomplish this, you can print all the odd pages first, turn the printed pages over, reinsert the paper into your printer's paper tray, and then print the even pages. You'll probably have to experiment with your printer tray a little to ensure that you insert the paper properly. (Usually, the odd pages would go in face down and forward.) Bear in mind that printing in this manner too frequently can cause printers to jam over time due to ink buildup from inked pages passing through your printer. If you do a lot of two-sided printing, you should probably invest in a printer that is designed to handle it.

To configure a print job to print only odd or even pages, open the Print dialog box and select either Odd Pages or Even Pages in the Print drop-down list. By default, the All Pages In Range option is selected.

You can use the Odd Pages and Even Pages options in combination with specified page ranges. For example, you can print only the odd pages included in the range from page 110 through page 213 by specifying **110-213** in the Pages box and selecting Odd Pages in the Print drop-down list.

Printing Document Elements

As you know, documents consist of much more than just the content that appears on a page. Documents can include property settings, editing marks, comments, keyboard shortcut assignments, formatting styles, and so forth. In some cases, you might want to print a document's informational elements instead of the actual document. The Print dialog box enables you to easily print some common document elements by selecting them in the Print What drop-down list. Using this technique, you can print the following elements:

- **Document** prints the entire document; the default setting.
- **Document Properties** prints basic information about a file, such as the file name, author, creation date, last saved date, number of words, and so forth. This information is similar to the information stored in the file's Properties dialog box. You can view a file's properties without printing the information by opening a document and choosing File, Properties.

newfeature!

- **Document Showing Markup** prints the document and all the tracked changes made in the text. In addition, each comment inserted in the document is printed in the corresponding page's margin in a box called a *bubble box*, with dashed lines indicating the insertion point of each comment. You can see how a marked-up document will be printed by previewing the document in Print Preview mode, as shown in Figure 4-5.

For information about using markup features, see Chapter 33, "Revising Documents Using Markup Tools."

newfeature!

- **List Of Markup** prints each tracked change made in a document on a separate line below a color-coded heading. The color-coding is based on who made each change, and each heading's text indicates page number, action (deleted, inserted, or comment), name of the user who made the change, and the date and time of the modification. This printout provides a very detailed list of changes. If the document contains more than a few changes or comments, this print job could take a few minutes to queue and even longer to print. Keep in mind that this option can create fairly large print files, so use this option sparingly and with discretion.

tip **Print additional document information**

You can print other document components in addition to those in the Print What drop-down list. For example, to print hidden text and field codes, display them in your document before you print (as described in the section "Setting Print Options," later in this chapter); to print an outline of your document, display the document in Outline view before you print; and to print a Web page's HTML source code, choose View, HTML Source before printing.

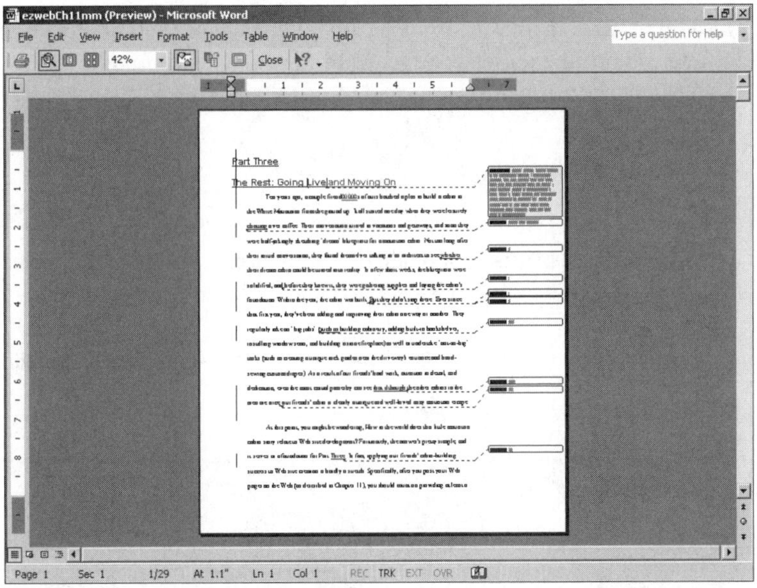

Figure 4-5. A document printed with markup shows all tracked changes and comments along with the document's contents, similar to how a marked-up document appears in Print Preview mode.

- **Styles** creates an alphabetic list of styles used in the current document. Each list entry includes the style's parameters, in reveal formatting style. For example, an excerpt from a Styles printout might look like this:

> **Bull List**
>
> Normal + Indent: Left: 0", Hanging: 0.25", Line spacing: 1.5 lines, Space Before: 3 pt, After: 6 pt, Tabs: 0.5", Left, Bulleted
>
> **Caption**
>
> Style for Next Paragraph: Normal
>
> Normal + Font: Italic, Indent: First line: 0", Line spacing: 1.5 lines, Space Before: 0 pt, After: 6pt
>
> **Comment Reference**
>
> Default Paragraph Font + Font: 8pt

For more information about creating and using styles, see Chapter 10, "Using Styles to Increase Your Formatting Power."

- **AutoText Entries** prints a complete, alphabetic list of the AutoText entries associated with the template attached to the current document. By default, the Normal.dot template is attached to documents if no other template has been specified.

For more information about AutoText, see Chapter 6, "Putting Text Tools to Work."

- **Key Assignments** prints an alphabetic list of custom shortcut keys created for standard Word commands or macros.

For more information about working with macros, see Chapter 44, "Creating, Running, and Editing VBA Macros."

Troubleshooting

Printing a Markup List for a Page Range Doesn't Work

Unfortunately, you can't print a markup list for a range of pages—you have to print either a complete list of all the changes made to an entire document or none at all. Luckily, if you're feeling flexible, you can work around this limitation. The easiest way is to forget about the list and instead print a range of pages using the Document Showing Markup option. You'll be able to see the tracked changes and comments in this view—it just won't be printed in list format (and in many cases, the changes make more sense when you see them in a document instead of listed one after another). Of course, in some instances, you might really need to print a list of markups for a range of pages. Don't worry—there's still hope. One way you can accomplish this is to follow these easy steps:

1. Make sure the marked-up document is open in Word with the changes showing.
2. Select the range you want to use to generate a markup list, and copy it to the Clipboard (by clicking the Copy button on the Standard toolbar).
3. Click the New Blank Document button.
4. Paste the copied selection into the new blank document.
5. Open the Print dialog box (by pressing Ctrl+P or choosing File, Print), select List Of Markup in the Print What drop-down list, and click OK.
6. After the list is printed, close the new blank document without saving it.

Printing Draft Copies

In some instances, you might want to quickly print a document's text without "extras" like formatting and graphics. In these cases, you can print a draft copy, if your printer supports this option. You can activate the draft printing feature using one of these techniques:

- Choose Tools, Options, Print tab, and select the Draft Output check box.
- Open the Print dialog box, click the Options button, select the Draft Output check box, and click OK.

When you print a document using Draft mode, your printed document will contain minimal formatting and no graphics.

Printing Several Pages per Sheet

Beginning in Word 2000, you can print more than one document page on a single sheet of paper. This feature helps you to better see a document's layout and can be used to present information in a visually concise manner. You'll find that printing several pages per sheet is similar to previewing multiple pages in Print Preview mode. (The difference is that the printed pages generally provide a clearer view of the pages' contents.) When you print multiple pages on a single sheet of paper, Word shrinks the pages to the appropriate size for printing purposes. To set up this arrangement, follow these steps:

1. Choose File, Print.
2. In the Zoom section of the Print dialog box, select the number of pages per page you want to print in the Pages Per Sheet drop-down list.

note The Pages Per Sheet feature comes with a few limitations. First, you must use the values in the Pages Per Sheet drop-down list to specify the number of pages to be printed—you can't type in a value. In addition, the feature is available only when the Document or Document Showing Markup option is selected in the Print What drop-down list.

Scaling Printed Documents

Just as you can reduce and enlarge copies when you use a photocopy machine, you can reduce and enlarge your print output in Word by using the Scale To Paper Size feature. Scaling documents can come in handy when you are printing on nonstandard paper sizes or when you want to shrink your output slightly to ensure that information isn't cut off by margin settings.

The key to scaling documents is to use the Scale To Paper Size drop-down list, which is located in the Zoom section in the Print dialog box. The Scale To Paper Size drop-down list includes a variety of sizing options, including Letter, Legal, A4, various envelope sizes, and so forth. To view the list of options, click the Scale To Paper Size down arrow. By default, the No Scaling option is selected.

note Scaling a document in the Print dialog box scales your document for the current printing session only; it doesn't resize or alter the document's contents, unlike the Shrink To Fit feature in Print Preview mode (which modifies the formatting in your document).

Creating a Print File

At times, you might want to create a print file instead of sending your document to your local printer. Usually, print files are created when a file needs to be printed on another (generally higher-quality) printer. For example, if you create a document in your home office, you might want to create a print file so that you can print the document on your company's high-quality color printer. Or perhaps you have developed a magazine or newsletter on your computer at work, but you want to submit a print file to a print shop so that they can create the final version.

Essentially, when you create a print file, you save your document in a format that another printer can recognize. When you print to a file, Word preserves the document's layout information, such as font spacing, line breaks, and page breaks.

To create a print file, follow these steps:

1. Determine which printer (for example, a PostScript printer) will be used, and install a printer driver for that printer, if necessary. (Ask your print shop for a copy of the appropriate printer driver if you need one, or download it from the Web.)
2. Open the Print dialog box (by choosing File, Print, or pressing Ctrl+P).
3. In the Name drop-down list, select the printer that will ultimately print the file.
4. Select the Print To File check box, and click OK to open the Print To File dialog box, which looks similar to the Save As dialog box.
5. Navigate to the location in which you want to save the print file, type a name for the print file in the File Name box, and then click OK. The file is saved with a .prn extension.

Setting Print Options

In addition to the options available in the Print dialog box, Word offers a number of other printing options. You can find these options on the Print tab in the Options dialog box (which is opened by choosing Tools, Options), shown in Figure 4-6. You can access the same options by clicking the Options button in the Print dialog box. Table 4-2, on the next page, summarizes the options available in the Printing Options section of the Print tab.

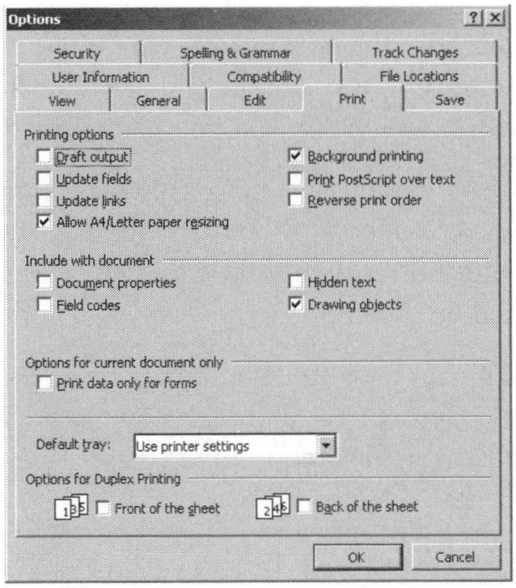

Figure 4-6. You can configure a number of Print options in addition to the print controls available in the Print dialog box.

In addition to the options listed in Table 4-2 on the next page, the Print tab offers options that enable you to perform the following tasks:

- Print various document elements in addition to your print tasks, such as printing a summary of the document properties, field codes (instead of field contents), hidden text (as discussed in Chapter 5, "Adding Panache with Text Formatting and Special Characters"), and drawing objects (as discussed in Chapter 16, "Enlivening Documents with Drawings and AutoShapes").
- Print only the data inserted into a form. This option works for the current document only, which means you can't set this option to be a global default.
- Specify a default paper source.
- Configure duplex printing options for printers that can print on both sides of a sheet of paper.

Table 4-2. Printing Options

Option	Description
Draft Output	Prints a document without formatting and graphics (as described in the section "Printing Draft Copies," on page 107).
Update Fields	Updates fields before printing. For example, when this option is selected, date and time fields will be updated when you print.
Update Links	Updates links to other documents before printing. For example, if a linked document has changed, the linked content will be updated before printing.
Allow A4/Letter Paper Resizing	Enables automatic switching between standard 8 ½-by-11 paper and the narrower, slightly longer A4 paper size used in most countries. This option is selected by default.
Background Printing	Enables you to continue working while print tasks are being processed (although you might notice a slight slowing in response times as you work). This option is enabled by default.
Print PostScript Over Text	Prints PostScript code (such as watermarks or overprinted text) inserted in a Word for Macintosh document above text, not beneath it.
Reverse Print Order	Prints a document in reverse order, beginning with the document's last page.

For more information about selecting paper sources, see Chapter 21, "Mastering Page Setup and Pagination."

Troubleshooting

A Printing Error Message Appears After I Send a Document to Be Printed

First and foremost, if your printer generally works without a hitch but it's not responding at the moment, check your hardware. Perform the following simple (yet important and sometimes overlooked) checks:

- Make sure that the toner or ink cartridge isn't empty.
- Verify that the paper tray contains paper.
- Clear any paper jams, and reset the printer if necessary.
- Check that the printer connections (wires, plugs, and contacts) are secure and firmly in place.
- Make sure that the online light is lit, if the printer is an older model.
- Verify that you can manually print a test page. (Refer to your printer's manual for instructions on manually printing a test page.)

If all the hardware components seem to be in working order, your next step is to look at the software side of the problem. The main software-related tasks you might have to perform if Word can't find a printer when you send your document to be printed are listed here:

- **Installing or reinstalling a default printer driver.** You might have to install printer drivers from the printer's installation CD-ROM or Windows CD-ROM, or download a driver from the printer manufacturer's Web site.
- **Fixing a damaged Windows registry entry.** You can try to fix a damaged Windows registry entry for your default printer by setting another printer as the default printer and then resetting your original printer as the default to overwrite the damaged Windows entry.
- **Correcting a device conflict on the printer port.** If you can't print on your local printer, you might have a printer port conflict. To correct this conflict, try using the Windows Device Manager to remove and reinstall the printer port.

For detailed instructions regarding these procedures, visit the Microsoft Knowledge Base on line, at *support.microsoft.com*.

Part 2

Manipulating Text with Authority

Chapter 5

Adding Panache with Text Formatting and Special Characters

The next order of business after you create and save a document is usually to enhance your text by applying text formatting attributes and adding any necessary symbols or special characters. As an experienced user, you probably perform some of these formatting tasks while you enter text, and you're likely familiar with at least a few text formatting techniques. However, Word provides numerous approaches to applying formatting such as text fonts, sizes, attributes, and more. In this chapter, we'll look at the various text formatting options (including inserting symbols, special characters, and basic date and time elements). With any luck, you'll discover a new technique or two or three along the way. More advanced formatting techniques, such as formatting paragraphs, are discussed in Chapter 7, "Aligning Information and Styling Paragraphs."

Formatting Text Efficiently

As with most Word tasks, you can format text using menu options, keyboard shortcuts, or toolbar buttons. In addition, you can set formatting options before you enter text, or you can apply formatting to existing text. One of the most common methods of formatting text is by using the buttons readily available on the Formatting toolbar, shown in Figure 5-1, on the next page.

Figure 5-1. The Formatting toolbar is displayed by default; it provides quick access to the most frequently used formatting commands.

tip **Add and remove toolbar buttons**

You can easily add buttons to and remove buttons from the Formatting toolbar by clicking the down arrow at the right end of the Formatting toolbar, pointing to Add Or Remove Buttons, selecting Formatting, and then selecting the buttons you want to show or hide. The following Formatting toolbar buttons can be added: Grow Font, Shrink Font, Superscript, Subscript, and Language.

For more information about customizing toolbars, see Chapter 38, "Customizing Word and Maximizing Accessibility."

Using the Formatting toolbar is often the quickest way to get formatting results, but once you memorize the key combinations, keyboard shortcuts also enable you to format text quickly and efficiently. And although choosing menu options to format text is generally the slowest method, menus can provide more control and flexibility when you are formatting text as well as allow you to apply multiple formatting settings at one time.

Regardless of whether you use toolbar buttons, keyboard shortcuts, or menu options, the procedure is basically the same: you select the text you want to format (or position the insertion point where you want formatting to begin when you start typing) and then click the appropriate toolbar button, press the keyboard shortcut, or choose a menu option. In this section, you'll learn how to manipulate text using all three techniques.

note Most toolbar buttons and keyboard shortcuts are *toggle commands,* which means that you perform the same action both to apply and to remove a formatting attribute. For example, selecting unformatted text and pressing Ctrl+B (or clicking the Bold button on the Formatting toolbar) applies boldface formatting to the selected text, and then pressing Ctrl+B (or clicking Bold) again removes the boldface formatting from the selected text.

Specifying Fonts and Sizes

As you know, the world of documents embraces numerous fonts. Thus, it should come as no surprise that Word can handle thousands of Windows-compatible fonts, including Adobe PostScript fonts (if the Adobe Type Manager is installed) and TrueType fonts. The quickest way to specify a font is to select the text you want to format and then select a font in the Font drop-down list located on the Formatting toolbar, as shown in Figure 5-2. The Font drop-down list contains all the currently available fonts.

note The default fonts installed with Microsoft Office are all TrueType fonts. With TrueType fonts, the text displayed on your screen is the same as the text in your printed document.

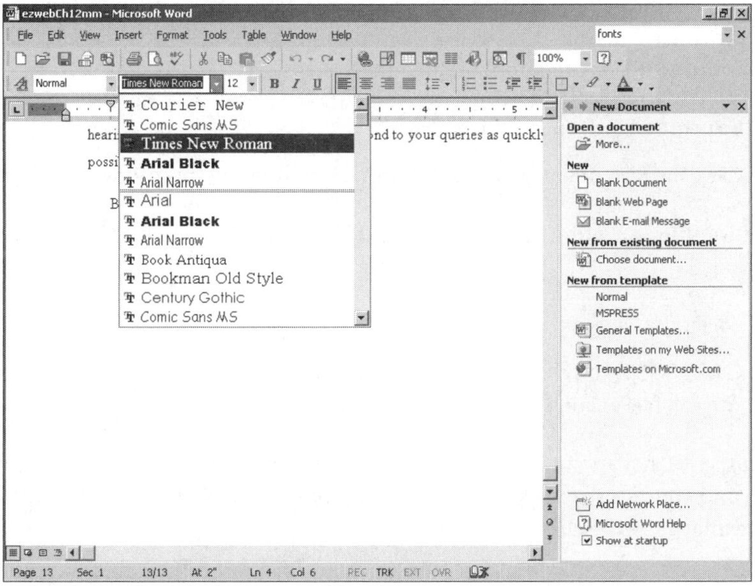

Figure 5-2. By default, the Font drop-down list displays font names in their respective fonts.

You can specify whether the font names in the Font drop-down list are displayed in their respective fonts or in plain text. To configure this setting, follow these steps:

1. Choose Tools, Customize, and then click the Options tab in the Customize dialog box.
2. Select or clear the List Font Names In Their Font check box.

Serif vs. Sans Serif Fonts

All fonts can be classified as *serif* or *sans serif*. You can easily differentiate between the two font types. Serif fonts add "hooks" to their letters, similar to the font used in the following paragraph's text. Examples of serif fonts are Times and Times New Roman. In contrast, sans serif fonts have plain-edged letters, like the font used to create the headings throughout this book. Examples of sans serif fonts are Arial and Helvetica. Using sans serif fonts for headings and serif fonts for body text is common practice in the print community because most readers find it easiest to read.

After you select a font for your text, you'll most likely want to specify a size. The quickest way to size text is by using the Size drop-down list, located to the right of the Font drop-down list on the Formatting toolbar (see Figure 5-1). As you probably know, font sizes are measured in points, and 72 points equals an inch. By default, the Size drop-down list provides a variety of common point sizes. To apply a font size using the Size drop-down list, you simply follow these steps:

1. Select the text you want to resize.
2. Click the Size down arrow, and select a size from the drop-down list.

If you want to use a font size not listed in the Size drop-down list, you need to do the following:

1. Select the text you want to resize.
2. Click the Size box to select the currently displayed font size (or press Ctrl+Shift+P), and then enter a new value.

You can enter half-point sizes in the Size box using decimal notation (for example, 10.5), and you can specify sizes as tiny as 1 point and as large as 1,638 points (which is approximately two feet high).

tip When you type large numbers in the Size box, don't include a comma separator—it'll only confuse Word and slow you down.

As a Word veteran, you won't be surprised to hear that you can also resize text using keyboard shortcuts. Table 5-1 lists the keyboard shortcuts you can use to change the font size.

Applying Multiple Font Attributes at One Time

Formatting toolbar buttons and keyboard shortcuts are great for simple formatting needs. But in other instances, you might want to take advantage of a not-so-readily accessible formatting effect (such as Emboss or Superscript) or apply a number of

Table 5-1. Keyboard Shortcuts for Sizing Text

Keyboard Shortcut	Sizing Effect
Ctrl+Shift+P, and then enter a font size or press the Up and Down Arrow keys to choose a font size from the Size drop-down list	Changes font size to a specified size
Ctrl+]	Enlarges font by 1 point
Ctrl+[	Reduces font by 1 point
Ctrl+Shift+>	Increases font to the next larger size in the Size drop-down list
Ctrl+Shift+<	Decreases font to the next smaller size in the Size drop-down list

formatting attributes at one time. In those cases, a better approach would be to use the Font dialog box, shown in Figure 5-3. To format text using the Font dialog box, follow these steps:

1. Select the text you want to format, click within the word you want to format, or position the insertion point where you want formatting to start when you begin typing.
2. Choose Format, Font (or right-click the text and choose Font on the shortcut menu).

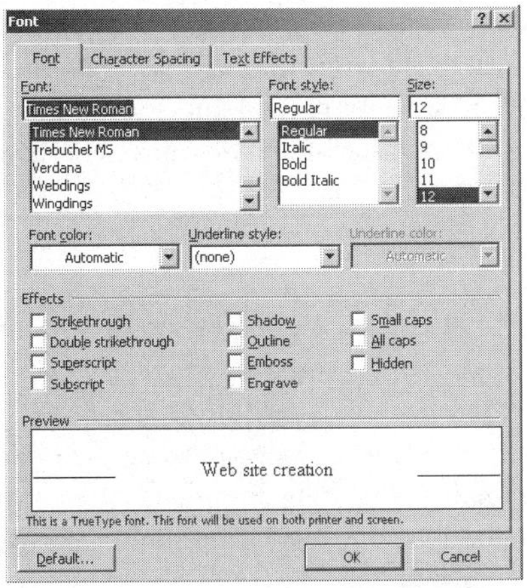

Figure 5-3. The Font dialog box enables you to select additional formatting effects as well as format multiple font attributes at one time, including font, size, color, and effects.

Chapter 5

In the Font dialog box, you can specify the font name, font style (including italic, bold, and bold italic), size, underline style, effects, and more. The Font dialog box also contains a preview window, so you can see how your font selections will appear in your document.

Applying Bold, Italic, and Underline Attributes

In addition to selecting fonts and resizing text, you can apply formatting attributes. The Formatting toolbar includes buttons for the three most commonly used formatting attributes—Bold, Italic, and Underline. To apply boldface, italic, and underlining to your text, simply click the appropriate toolbar button or press the keyboard shortcut, as listed in Table 5-2.

Table 5-2. Toolbar Buttons and Keyboard Shortcuts for Applying Boldface, Italic, and Underlining

Format	Toolbar Button	Keyboard Shortcut
Bold	B	Ctrl+B
Italic	I	Ctrl+I
Underline	U	Ctrl+U
Underline Words Only	None	Ctrl+Shift+W
Double Underline	None	Ctrl+Shift+D

The Underline button and keyboard shortcuts allow you to quickly apply standard underlining, but you can access a greater variety of underline styles using the Font dialog box. To choose an underline style in the Font dialog box, click the Underline Style down arrow in the Font dialog box (see Figure 5-3) and select an underline style from the list. Figure 5-4 shows some of the Underline Style options in action.

tip **Remove or change a custom underline**

To quickly remove a custom underline or to change the underline to a standard underline, select the underlined text (or click within the word you want to remove the underline from), and press Ctrl+U or click the Underline button on the Formatting toolbar once to remove the custom underline and twice to remove the underline altogether. The first time you execute the Underline toggle command, the custom line changes to a standard (straight-line) underline, and the second time you execute the command, the standard underline is removed.

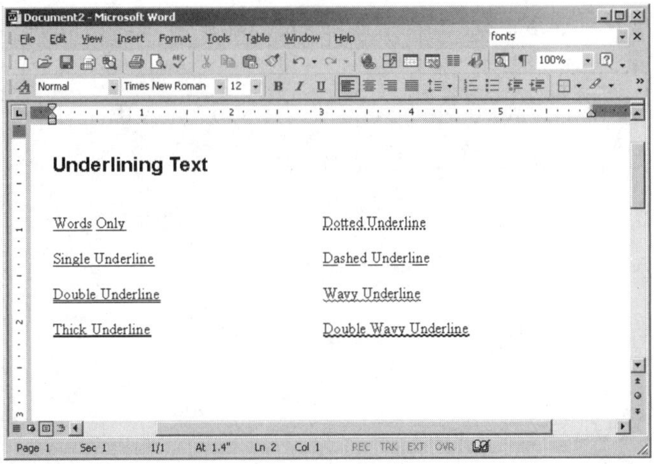

Figure 5-4. Word provides a variety of underline styles, including the styles shown here, which you can apply to text by using the Font dialog box.

Troubleshooting

Word Won't Let Me Underline a Blank Line

In Word, you can't underline a blank line. Instead, you must create the appearance of an underline by using any of the following procedures:

- Use the Border feature to add a border to the bottom of the line (by clicking the Border down arrow on the Formatting toolbar and choosing Bottom Border on the drop-down menu). (See Chapter 7, "Aligning Information and Styling Paragraphs," for more information about adding borders.)
- Press Shift+hyphen (creates an underscore; usually located to the right of the 9 key) repeatedly.
- Create nonbreaking spaces by pressing Ctrl+Shift+Spacebar (you can hold down the keys to quickly create a series of nonbreaking spaces), select the nonbreaking spaces, and then apply underlining using the technique described above.

Changing Text Color

Applying color to text and underlining provides another avenue by which you can customize text attributes. By default, Word displays and prints black text on a white background. (You can configure your view in Word to display white text on a blue background by choosing Tools, Options, clicking the General tab, and selecting the Blue Background, White Text check box, but keep in mind that this setting changes your *view*, not the printed text color.) In many cases, you might want to color your text to add pizzazz to your documents. For example, you might color text when you're creating a brochure, a Web page, an e-mail message, or any other document in which the text will be displayed on a colored background.

The most straightforward way to apply color to text is to follow these steps:

1. Select the text you want to color.
2. Click the Font Color down arrow on the Formatting toolbar.
3. Select a color from the color palette, shown in Figure 5-5.

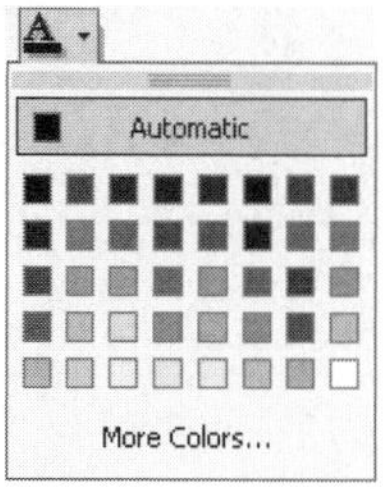

Figure 5-5. You use the color palette to specify the color you want to apply to selected text.

After you've colored some text, the Font Color button retains that color setting throughout your current session (or until you select another color in the color palette). The underline below the *A* on the Font Color button reflects the most recently selected color. You can select other text and simply click the Font Color button to color the text using the same color (instead of having to repeatedly select the same color in the color palette each time you want to apply the color). By default, the Font Color button is set to Automatic (which generally equates to black).

If you're going to be coloring text frequently within a document, you can drag the top bar of the color palette to display it as a floating toolbar that remains available as you work, as shown in Figure 5-6. To close the Font Color toolbar after you've detached it from the Formatting toolbar, simply click the Close button—the color palette will be available to you again via the Font Color down arrow on the Formatting toolbar whenever you need it.

In addition to these methods of changing font color, you can also color text using the Font dialog box, shown in Figure 5-3. Notice that you can specify a font color as well as an underline color. Clicking either color down arrow in the Font dialog box opens the color palette, which you can use to apply an appropriate color to your text.

For more information about creating custom colors, see Chapter 16, "Enlivening Documents with Drawings and AutoShapes."

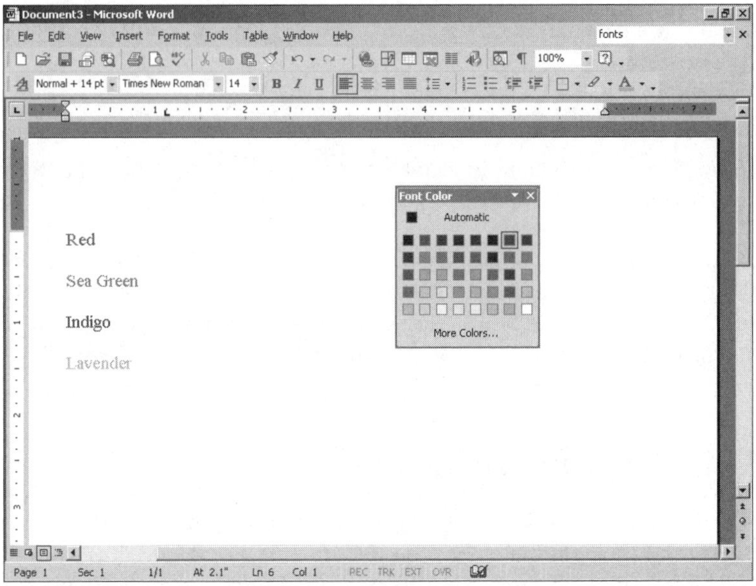

Figure 5-6. You can drag the color palette by its top bar to display it as a floating toolbar.

Copying Styles Using the Format Painter

After you've formatted your text, you might want to apply similar attributes to other text. For example, suppose you've used the following settings to style a book title that's embedded in body text: bold, italic, 12 points, Arial, red. When you type the next book title in your document, you could either manually apply all the formatting settings or use the Format Painter tool to copy and paste the settings from the last book title to the current book title. Usually, the quick-and-convenient route of copying formatting specifications will be preferable to manually reapplying attributes.

Using the Format Painter tool is a breeze. By default, the Format Painter tool is available on the Standard toolbar. To use the Format Painter, follow these steps:

Format Painter

1. Select the text containing the formatting you want to apply to other text.
2. Click the Format Painter button.
3. Select the text you want to format.

To format multiple instances of text using the Format Painter, select the text you want to emulate and double-click the Format Painter, which keeps the Format Painter turned on until you turn it off. All text you select while the Format Painter is activated will be reformatted. To turn off the Format Painter, click the Format Painter button on the Standard toolbar.

You can also use keyboard commands to access the Format Painter tool. To do so, follow these steps:

1. Select the formatted text you want to emulate, and press Ctrl+Shift+C.
2. Select the text you want to format, and press Ctrl+Shift+V to apply the formatting attributes.

The advantage of using keyboard shortcuts in this case is that you can repeat the Ctrl+Shift+V command as many times as necessary on various instances of selected text—the formatting settings are retained during the current session until you execute another Ctrl+Shift+C command. Sometimes, having a group of formatting commands available with a single keyboard shortcut can prove to be a real time-saver.

Adding Text Effects and Animation

In addition to basic formatting, Word provides a number of other text effects that you can access from the Font dialog box (see Figure 5-3). Figure 5-7 illustrates these text effects. The following options are available in the Effects section of the Font tab:

- Strikethrough
- Double Strikethrough
- Superscript (Ctrl+Shift+=)
- Subscript (Ctrl+=)
- Shadow
- Outline
- Emboss
- Engrave
- Small Caps (Ctrl+Shift+K)
- All Caps (Ctrl+Shift+A)
- Hidden (Ctrl+Shift+H)

Adding an effect to text using the Font dialog box is accomplished in a predictable manner:

1. Click within a word, select the text you want to format, or position the insertion point where you want an effect to begin when you start typing.
2. Choose Format, Font.
3. Select the appropriate check box on the Font tab, and click OK.

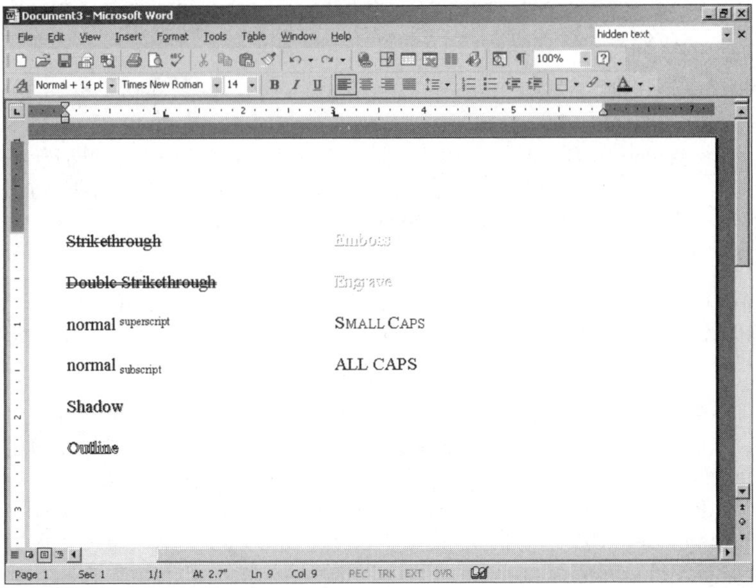

Figure 5-7. Word offers a number of font effects that you can apply to existing text.

You can also add animation effects by clicking the Text Effects tab in the Font dialog box. The animations available in Word are shown here:

- **(None)** applies no animation effects (the default selection).
- **Blinking Background** creates a blinking effect by alternating reverse text within a black rectangle with regular text.
- **Las Vegas Lights** surrounds selected text with a looping series of blinking colored shapes.
- **Marching Black Ants** borders selected text with a black dashed line that moves clockwise.
- **Marching Red Ants** borders selected text with a red dashed line that moves clockwise.
- **Shimmer** repeatedly blurs and unblurs selected text.
- **Sparkle Text** displays moving colored "sparkles" on top of the selected text.

Working with Hidden Text

You can't see it in Figure 5-7, but the word *Hidden* is inserted below *ALL CAPS* and formatted using the Hidden text effect. You can create hidden text by selecting text and then selecting the Hidden check box on the Font tab in the Font dialog box or by pressing Ctrl+Shift+H. Hidden text is useful for making notes to yourself. Word uses hidden text for certain components, including index fields, bookmarks, and table of contents fields.

Show/Hide

To display hidden text on screen, click the Show/Hide button on the Standard toolbar or press Ctrl+Shift+8 to toggle your display. Hidden text is identified with a dotted underline.

Keep in mind that if you print your document while hidden text is displayed on your screen, the text will be printed by default. Likewise, if you click the Show/Hide button to hide all hidden text, the hidden text will not be printed when you print your document by default. But if you desire, you can print hidden text that's in a document even if the hidden text isn't displayed on screen. To do so, verify that the hidden text is not displayed on screen, choose Tools, Options, click the Print tab, select the Hidden Text check box on the Print tab, click OK, and then print the document.

The Text Effects tab in the Font dialog box is shown in Figure 5-8. To see each effect in action, press Ctrl+D to open the Font dialog box, click the Text Effects tab, and then click each option in the Animations list. The Preview section at the bottom of the Text Effects tab shows a small animated display as you select each option.

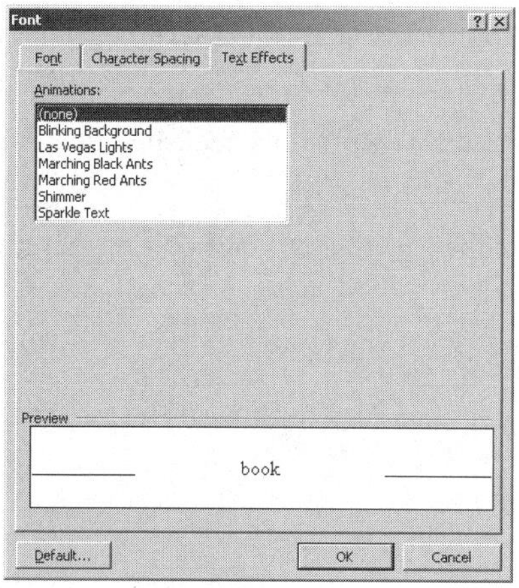

Figure 5-8. Word provides a number of animated text effects that you can use within your documents.

tip **Animate with care**

Animated text should be used sparingly. Animation can serve a purpose in a few select cases, but the effects are frequently distracting and can be downright annoying when overused. In addition, you need to consider software limitations when you use animated text. For example, earlier versions of Word such as Word 95 and Word 6, don't recognize animations, and of course animated text can't be printed (which could be a concern).

InsideOut

Although using the text animation feature seems like a natural fit for creating Web pages, the feature doesn't work in Word documents saved as Web pages. When you save a document containing animated text, Word displays a message box stating that the animated text will be displayed as italicized text. If you truly need to show animated text in a document on line, the only workaround at this time is to create a link on your Web page that points to the Word document containing the animation.

Changing Case

Occasionally, you might want to change lowercase text to all caps, all caps to lowercase, or mixed-cased text to all caps or all lowercase. Fortunately, you can perform these potentially tedious maneuvers without opening the Font dialog box or retyping text. In fact, all you need to do is to select the text you want to change and press Ctrl+Shift+A to alternate between all lowercase and all uppercase or press Shift+F3 to cycle through all lowercase, initial capped, and all uppercase.

In addition, Word offers more advanced capitalization schemes in the Change Case dialog box. To open the Change Case dialog box, shown in Figure 5-9, choose Format, Change Case. Notice that you can format selected text using the following options: Sentence Case, Lowercase, Uppercase, Title Case, or Toggle Case.

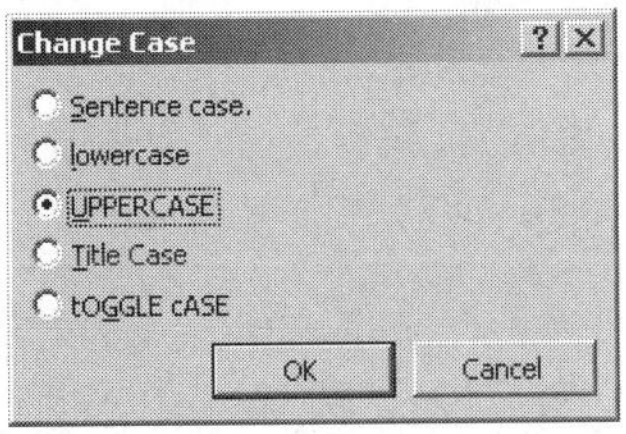

Figure 5-9. The Change Case dialog box enables you to quickly revise uppercase and lowercase letters.

Controlling Character Spacing

Another key font formatting issue is character spacing. Word provides space-tweaking features that were once available only to professional typesetters. You can (and should) use character spacing features to improve the look and readability of your documents. To view the primary character spacing options, choose Format, Font, and click the Character Spacing tab, as shown in Figure 5-10.

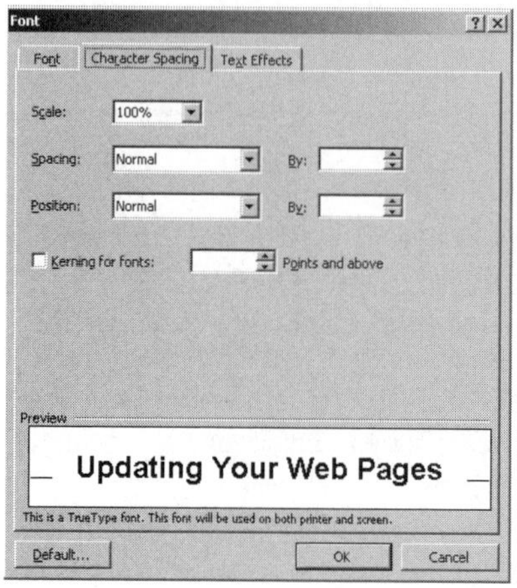

Figure 5-10. The Character Spacing tab in the Font dialog box enables you to rescale selected text, adjust spacing between characters, and reposition text.

You can control the following spacing parameters:

- **Scale** lets you stretch or compress selected text characters horizontally as a percentage of the text's current size for design purposes. You can choose a scaling option from the drop-down list, or you can manually enter a scaling value from 1% to 600%. The Scale option is set to 100% for normal text.
- **Spacing** enables you to expand or condense the spacing between text characters by the amount you enter in the By box. If you decide you don't like the expanded or condensed spacing settings, you can choose Normal in the Spacing drop-down list to revert to standard letter spacing.

note To reiterate, the Scale option narrows and widens the actual text characters, whereas the Spacing option adjusts the space between letters.

- **Position** allows you to raise or lower selected text relative to the text's baseline by the amount you enter in the By box. To reset the text on the baseline, choose Normal in the drop-down list.

- **Kerning For Fonts** enables Word to automatically adjust the amount of space between specific character combinations so that words and letters look evenly spaced. You can specify the minimum font size that should be automatically kerned in the Points And Above box. Generally, kerning is used for headings and larger fonts sizes (12 to 14 points and larger). In Word, kerning works only with TrueType or Adobe Type Manager fonts. Be aware that turning on the Kerning For Fonts feature can slow processing. If you want to manually kern characters, select the characters and use the Spacing option to tighten or loosen the characters' positions.

The Character Spacing tab also includes a Default button. This Default button enables you to store all the current settings for the Font, Character Spacing, and Text Effects tabs in the Font dialog box as the default settings for the active document as well as for all new documents based on the current template. If your current document uses the Normal template, clicking the Default button will change the defaults for all new blank documents you create, so be careful.

Clearing Formatting Attributes

Up to now, we've been looking at how to add font formatting attributes, but at times, you might want to remove all formatting attributes from within a paragraph. Word provides a quick way to clear all formatting attributes from text at one time. To clear all formatting from a single word or selected text, follow these steps:

1. Select the word or text you want to convert to plain text.
2. Press Ctrl+Spacebar.

> **Tip** You can remove formatting from an entire document by pressing Ctrl+A to select the entire document and then pressing Ctrl+Spacebar.

newfeature!

Similarly, you can remove formatting by using the new Styles And Formatting task pane. To do so, follow these steps:

1. Select the word or text you want to clear.

Styles and Formatting

2. Click the Styles And Formatting button on the Formatting toolbar (or select Styles And Formatting in the Task Pane drop-down list if the task pane is already open).
3. In the Pick Formatting To Apply section, choose Clear Formatting in the list.

Troubleshooting

I Want to Remove a Single Character Formatting Attribute (Such as Boldfacing) That's Scattered Throughout a Paragraph

Word offers a couple of handy ways to clear all formatting from selected text, but you're still left to your own devices if you want to clear multiple instances of a single formatting attribute from text. Fortunately, there's an easy workaround. To quickly remove all instances of a single formatting attribute from an entire paragraph (or other selected text), follow these steps:

1. Select the paragraph (triple-click within the paragraph) from which you want to clear a formatting attribute.
2. Execute the formatting attribute's command as follows:
   - Choose the command once if the attribute is applied to the first letter in the paragraph. (Word toggles a format property based on the formatting of the first letter in the selected text.)
   - Choose the command twice if the text at the beginning of the paragraph doesn't contain the formatting attribute you are removing.

For example, let's say you want to remove all the boldface formatting within a paragraph that begins with a non-boldface word but contains a few words formatted as boldface scattered throughout the remainder of the paragraph. To remove the boldfacing, you'd select the paragraph and press Ctrl+B, Ctrl+B. The first Ctrl+B would apply boldfacing to the entire paragraph, and the second Ctrl+B would remove the boldfacing throughout. Similarly, if you want to remove all the boldface formatting from a paragraph that begins with a boldface word, you press Ctrl+B only once.

Inserting Symbols and Special Characters

Sometimes, your text will require symbols and special characters that aren't readily available on your keyboard. For example, you might want to show a copyright symbol, insert foreign-language words containing accent marks, include small "dingbat" graphics, insert a nonbreaking space, and so forth. Quite a few symbols and special characters are available in Word if you know where to look. Nicely enough, when you find what you're looking for, Word makes it easy to insert and reuse symbols and special characters in the future.

Adding Symbols

Word provides the Symbol dialog box to take care of your symbol and special character needs. (To access the Symbol dialog box, choose Insert, Symbol.) Figure 5-11 shows the new and improved Symbols tab in the Symbol dialog box. In earlier versions of Word, the Symbols tab showed miniature versions of symbols; you had to click each symbol to obtain a larger view. The process was fairly tedious when you were selecting among similar symbols. In Word 2002, the Symbol dialog box has been updated, most notably in the following ways:

- The symbols are displayed at a larger size, which makes them much easier to identify.

newfeature!

- A collection of recently used symbols is gathered in a separate, easy-to-access section below the symbol table.

newfeature!

- The Symbol dialog box can be resized by dragging the lower right corner.

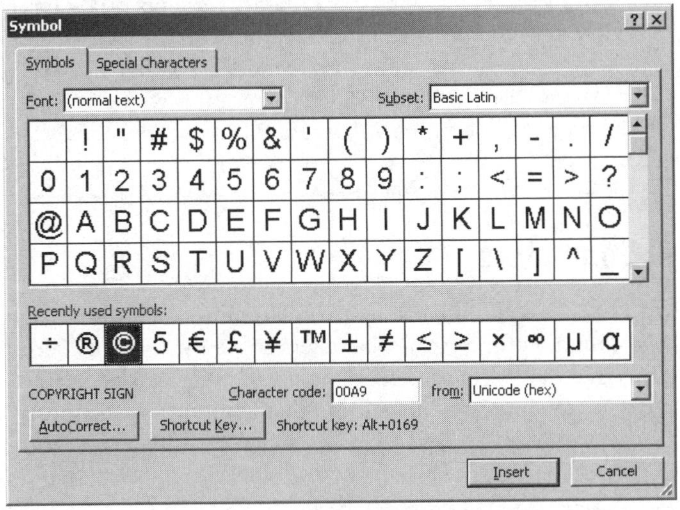

Figure 5-11. The Symbols tab in the Symbol dialog box has been revamped to make symbol selection easier.

You can insert symbols in three main ways:

- Click a symbol in the symbol table, and then click the Insert button.
- Double-click a symbol in the symbol table.
- Press the symbol's shortcut key. (This method inserts a symbol without opening the Symbol dialog box.)

When you're inserting symbols from within the Symbol dialog box, keep in mind that you can insert multiple symbols during a single visit. In fact, inserting all the symbols you'll need for a while can prove to be fairly efficient. (After all, cutting and pasting inserted symbols is quicker and easier than repeatedly accessing the Symbol dialog box.) When you've inserted the symbols you need, click Close to close the Symbol dialog box.

Troubleshooting

I Want to Insert Symbols Without Repeatedly Reopening the Symbol Dialog Box

In some instances, you can reopen the Symbol dialog box quickly by double-clicking a symbol that's been inserted into your document. Unfortunately, you can't always count on this being the case. For example, you can double-click smiley faces and arrows to open the Symbol dialog box, but you can't open the Symbol dialog box by double-clicking copyright and registered trademark symbols.

If you're going to need more than a few symbols, you can either paste in a number of symbols you think you'll need or leave the Symbol dialog box open while you work. Fortunately, you can enter text in your document while the Symbol dialog box is open. The main annoyance with this approach is that the Symbol dialog box stays on top, so you'll probably have to drag the dialog box out of your way a few times as you work. And although you can resize the new Symbol dialog box by making it larger, you can't make it smaller. The capability to reduce the Symbol dialog box can't be too far off in the future, however, now that resizable dialog boxes are starting to work their way into Word.

Adding Special Characters

Inserting special characters is similar to inserting symbols. Logically enough, special characters can be found on the Special Characters tab in the Symbol dialog box, as shown in Figure 5-12. Most of the special characters are typesetting characters that you use when refining document text. You will find that a number of the special characters can also be inserted from the Symbols tab or by using the AutoCorrect feature.

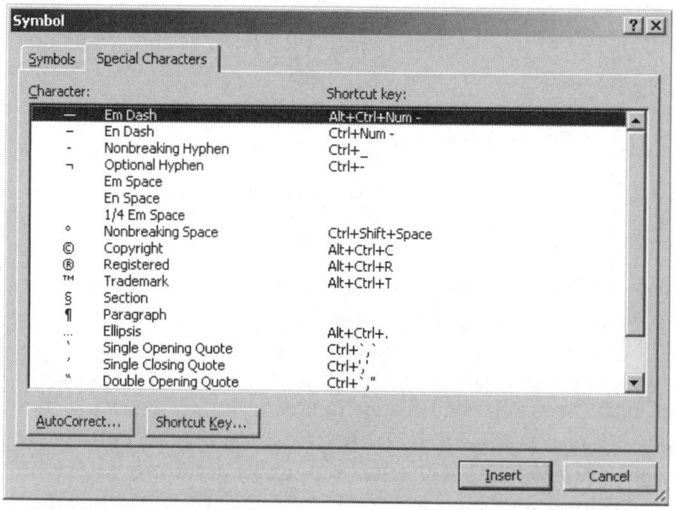

Figure 5-12. The Special Characters tab in the Symbol dialog box provides quick access to special characters.

You can insert special characters using any of these techniques:

- Double-click an entry on the Special Characters tab.
- Select an entry on the Special Characters tab, and click Insert.
- Press an assigned keyboard shortcut.

Using Keyboard Shortcuts to Insert Symbols and Special Characters

You can simplify your life if you regularly need to insert a symbol or special character that requires you to access the Symbol dialog box by memorizing preassigned keyboard shortcuts or by creating custom keyboard shortcuts. In Figures 5-11 and 5-12, you can see that both tabs in the Symbol dialog box contain a Shortcut Key button. In addition, both tabs display currently assigned keyboard shortcuts for quick reference. On the Symbols tab, available keyboard shortcuts are displayed next to the Shortcut Key button when a symbol is selected; on the Special Characters tab, keyboard shortcuts are listed in the Shortcut Key column.

If you find that you use a symbol or special character that isn't already assigned a keyboard shortcut (or if you want to associate your own command with a symbol or special character even though it already has a shortcut), you can create a custom shortcut for future use. To do so, follow these steps (from either the Symbols or the Special Characters tab):

1. Select a symbol or special character.
2. Click the Shortcut Key button. The Customize Keyboard dialog box opens.
3. Click the Press New Shortcut Key box, and then type the keyboard shortcut you'd like to assign to the symbol. If the combination is already in use by another operation, the dialog box indicates which operation uses the keyboard shortcut. If the keyboard shortcut is not already associated with another operation, the dialog box indicates that the combination is currently unassigned, as shown in Figure 5-13, on the next page.
4. Click Assign, and then click Close twice to close the remaining open dialog boxes.
5. Test your newly created keyboard shortcut within your document to verify that it is working properly.

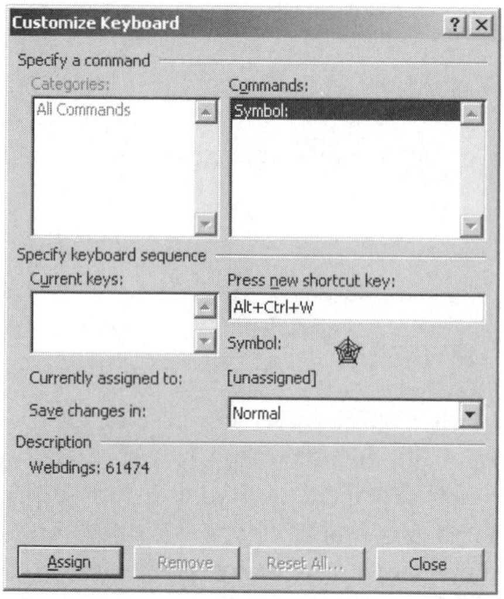

Figure 5-13. The Customize Keyboard dialog box enables you to assign a custom keyboard shortcut to a symbol or special character.

Inserting Symbols Automatically

In addition to manually inserting symbols and using keyboard shortcuts, Word enables you to automatically create symbols as you're typing, without opening the Symbol dialog box. The magic behind this trick is the AutoCorrect feature. When the AutoCorrect feature is turned on, you can automatically insert symbols that are included in the built-in list of AutoCorrect entries. Table 5-3 lists the symbols you can create using the AutoCorrect feature.

When symbols are inserted automatically, Word 2002 accompanies the symbol with a smart tag. (If the smart tag isn't displayed immediately, hover the mouse pointer over the symbol until it appears.) Figure 5-14 shows the AutoCorrect smart tag associated with the automatically generated right arrow symbol.

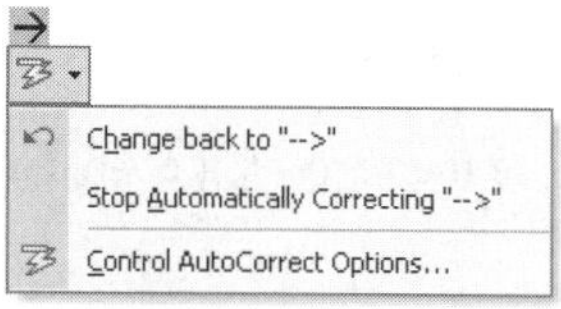

Figure 5-14. The AutoCorrect smart tag enables you to control whether automatically generated symbols should replace typed text.

Table 5-3. Symbols That Can Be Inserted Using AutoCorrect

Symbol	Keyboard Shortcut
©	(c)
®	(r)
™	(tm)
…	...
☺	:) or :-)
😐	:| or :-|
☹	:(or :-(
→	-->
←	<--
➔	==>
🡸	<==
⇔	<=>

If an AutoCorrect symbol is inserted but you would prefer to display the typed text, simply press the Backspace key once after you type the text. For example, if you want to display (c) instead of ©, type an opening parenthesis, **c**, and then a closing parenthesis (at which point, the text changes to the copyright symbol automatically), and then press the Backspace key (which removes the copyright symbol and redisplays the (c) text).

In some cases, you might find yourself removing a symbol repeatedly. Instead of driving yourself crazy, hold the mouse pointer over the symbol's smart tag before you remove it, click the down arrow, and then choose the Stop Automatically Correcting command on the smart tag's drop-down menu. This action forces Word to stop converting the typed combination to a symbol throughout the remainder of the document.

tip **Eliminate an automated replacement action**

If you want to permanently eliminate a particular automated replacement action, you can control the AutoCorrect feature's settings by configuring the AutoCorrect tab in the AutoCorrect dialog box (choose Tools, AutoCorrect Options, AutoCorrect tab). For more information about AutoCorrect and smart tags, see Chapter 6, "Putting Text Tools to Work."

Inserting Date and Time Elements—The Quick Way

You might also want to insert date and time elements into your documents. Basically, date and time elements are fields (which are discussed in greater depth in Chapter 36, "Working with Field Codes and Custom Forms"), but Word provides a quick-and-easy method of inserting date and time components without your having to delve into the nitty-gritty of fields. If you want to simply enter the current date and time without manually configuring fields, you can do so as follows:

1. Choose Insert, Date And Time. The Date And Time dialog box opens, as shown in Figure 5-15.

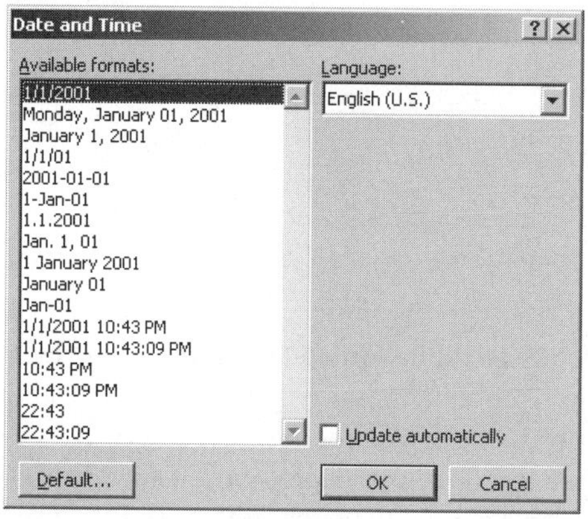

Figure 5-15. The Date And Time dialog box enables you to insert date and time elements that will show the original date and time (when the element was inserted) or update automatically each time the document is opened or printed.

2. Select a date and time format in the Available Formats list, and choose a language in the Language drop-down list.
3. If you'd like the date and time to be updated automatically, select the Update Automatically check box; if you prefer to keep the date and time unchanged, leave the check box cleared.
4. Click OK. The date and time information is inserted into your document and is accompanied by a smart tag (which enables you to schedule a meeting or display your calendar). You can format the date and time elements just as you format other text within your document.

You can also insert a current time that is updated when you update the document's fields by pressing Alt+Shift+T. (By default, fields are updated each time you open a Word document, as specified on the General tab in the Options dialog box. In addition, you can choose to update fields when you print by selecting the Update Fields check box on the Print tab in the Options dialog box.)

Chapter 6

Putting Text Tools to Work

Part of the challenge of working with a word processing program that's as full-featured and powerful as Word is getting to the tools you need quickly. Some tasks are very simple—entering text, running the spelling checker, printing a quick page. Others are more complicated and require an investment of time and effort. Applying a format to a heading, for example, requires you to think about the overall design of your document (or the standards for publication in your department) and to choose the text font, size, style, and spacing settings you want in order to create just the right effect. But to cut down on the time you spend making those choices, Word includes an automated tool called AutoFormat that enables you to quickly apply and change formats in your documents. And if you want to reuse formats from other documents or sections of your work, you can use another feature—Reveal Formatting—to view the formats applied to selected text sections.

You also spend time going back and netting out the bugs that sneak into your documents. Word includes tools to help you cut down on error-correction time. AutoText is a feature that inserts words or phrases you use often in your work (you can train AutoText to use terms native to your business or industry). AutoCorrect also corrects typos as you go, giving you a cleaner document right from the start. This explores all of these tools as well as the new, improved Word 2002 Office Clipboard, which now holds up to 24 different items and offers a "smart" paste feature that helps you easily repeat routine tasks.

Applying Quick Format Changes

Word 2002 includes a number of automatic features that help you control the formatting in your document. AutoFormatting, which enables you to add predesigned formats to paragraphs, headings, and tables, is covered in detail in the next section. Here we'll take a look at the Format Painter, which gives you the means to copy formats from place to place, and a new offering that enables you to copy formats without creating new styles to do it.

Automatic? Your Call

If you granted three wishes to experienced Word users, at the top of the list would be improved control over automatic features. Until you understand what's going on behind the scenes with the various tools—including spelling, font choice, leading, and more—you don't often know where to go when Word begins indenting lists you don't want indented, adding numbers you don't want added, or swapping words against your will. Such is the downside of automated functionality.

But the good news is that with Word 2002, you have increased control over auto features. You can turn each of the automatic features on and off and control the items you want Word to change on the fly. This chapter looks at each of these features individually and shows you how you can set them up to work most efficiently for you.

newfeature!

Copying Formats Without Styles

In Chapter 1, you learned about the new task pane, which appears along the right side of your work area, offering options and choices that apply to the procedure you're performing. Now, in Word 2002, you can use the task pane to select and apply formats you've used in other parts of your document (or in other documents). To use the task pane to copy formats, follow these steps:

1. Start by opening the document you want to work with.
2. Create (or select) the text with the format you want to copy.
3. Choose Format, Styles And Formatting. The Styles And Formatting task pane appears, as Figure 6-1 shows.
4. Select the text to which you want to apply the format.
5. Click the format you want to use in the Styles And Formatting task pane. The format is then applied to the selected text.

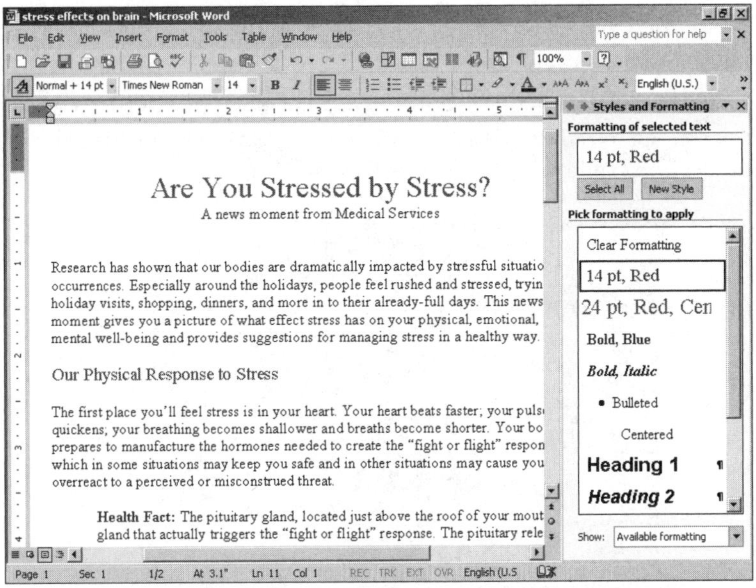

Figure 6-1. The Styles And Formatting task pane lists all the formats used in the current document, whether they've been saved as styles or not.

note Styles sometimes get a bad rap for being difficult to create and use. But styles can save you valuable time and effort, especially when you have specific formats and text treatments you use often. An individual style can include your choices for the font, size, color, style, spacing, and alignment of text. If you need to use a consistent standard for headings, body text, captions, or list items in your document, styles can save you time in applying the same format throughout your work.

Choosing Formats to View

You can change the formats that are available in the Styles And Formatting task pane by clicking the Show down arrow in the Styles And Formatting task pane and choosing one of the following options:

- **Available Formatting** displays all the formats that are currently available to the open document.
- **Formatting In Use** shows only the styles that are currently being used in the open document.
- **Available Styles** shows only the created and named styles available to the open document. This option does not display the unnamed styles you might have added to the entered text.

- **All Styles** displays all styles available in the style sheets available to Word and the open document.
- **Custom** opens a dialog box that enables you to choose the elements used to gather styles displayed in the Styles And Formatting task pane. (See Figure 6-2.)

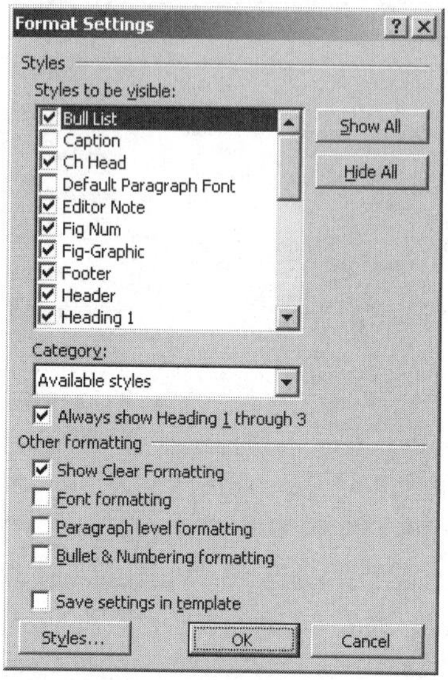

Figure 6-2. You can control where Word looks for styles by changing the selection in the Category drop-down list.

For more information about creating, applying, and organizing styles, see Chapter 10, "Using Styles to Increase Your Formatting Power."

Employing the Format Painter

The Format Painter is a quick-use tool that enables you to copy and apply a format you've used by clicking a simple toolbar button. The button is found in the center of the Standard toolbar.

To use the Format Painter, follow these steps:

1. Select the text with the format you want to use.
2. Click the Format Painter button.
3. Click in the text or phrase to which you want to apply the format. The format is automatically applied.

Format Painter

Format Painter Tricks

- If you want to apply the format multiple times in your document, double-click the Format Painter to activate it, apply the format as needed, and then click Format Painter again or press Esc to deactivate it.
- If you want to apply the format to a single word, click once anywhere in the word to be formatted.
- To apply the format to an entire paragraph, click to the left of the paragraph.
- To apply the format to a phrase, select the entire phrase you want to be affected by the format.
- To cancel a Format Painter operation, press Esc.
- To copy and paste the format quickly, use Ctrl+Shift+C to copy and Ctrl+Shift+V to paste.

Painless AutoFormatting

A good format is worth its weight in gold. A format that is inviting, professional, and easy to read can make the difference between your document's getting a second look or a toss in the trash. Because of a clean format, your grant proposal might get closer scrutiny; your book might catch an editor's attention; and your report could get passed up the line of command to the CEO's desk.

Word makes formatting easier by anticipating what you need and automating format changes with AutoFormat. You have the option of working with AutoFormat as you type or applying AutoFormat to an existing document. By default, AutoFormat is activated, so as soon as you begin using Word 2002, AutoFormat will kick in and help you.

What Can You Do with AutoFormat?

AutoFormat can jump in and quickly format items you use often in your documents. You might use AutoFormat to do the following:

- Format numbered lists in the way you want them.
- Assign a particular bullet style to a bulleted list.
- Take care of typographical issues, such as inserting open and close quotation marks.
- Format fractions and font style changes as needed.

Applying AutoFormatting

When you open an existing document in Word, you have the option of applying AutoFormat to go through and correct any inconsistencies or errors in the format. You can choose both the form of the document you want Word to check (select from General Document, Letter, or Email styles) and the way in which Word alerts you about the changes that need to be made.

Start the process by choosing Format, AutoFormat. The AutoFormat dialog box is displayed. (See Figure 6-3..

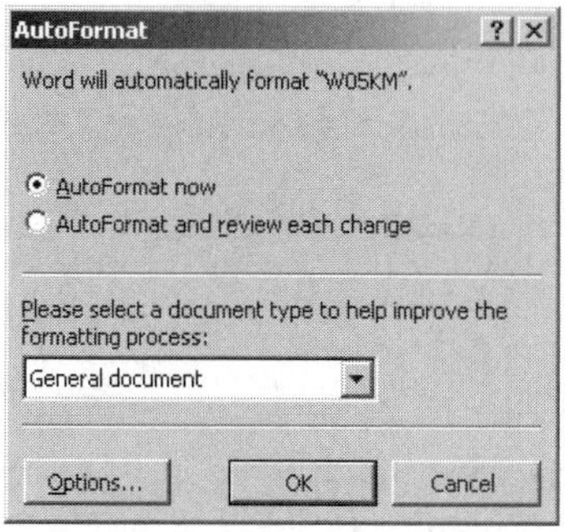

Figure 6-3. You can choose the document type and set AutoFormat options in the AutoFormat dialog box.

Your first major decision here is whether you want to review each AutoFormat suggestion as it arises or give AutoFormat carte blanche to make changes. If you want to apply AutoFormat now to the entire document, click AutoFormat Now. Word goes through the document and makes changes according to the AutoFormat options selected by default.

If you want to see the changes AutoFormat wants to make before they're made, click the AutoFormat And Review Each Change option. After you click OK, Word begins to AutoFormat the document and displays the AutoFormat dialog box so that you can accept or reject the changes it proposes. (See Figure 6-4.)

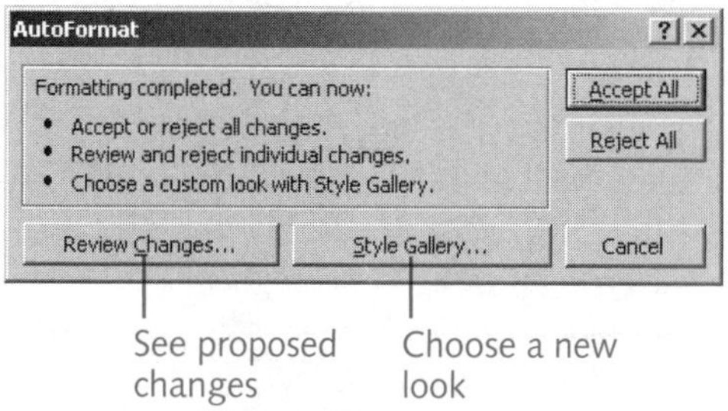

Figure 6-4. When you elect to have accept-and-reject privileges with AutoFormat, you're asked to make decisions about each change as it's proposed.

tip **Select what you want to AutoFormat**

If you want to apply AutoFormat to a selected portion of your document, select it before you display the AutoFormat dialog box.

Setting AutoFormat Options

You control the types of items you want AutoFormat to format for you. Display the choices by clicking the Options button in the AutoFormat dialog box. The AutoFormat tab is displayed, and you can review all the AutoFormat options set by default for your document. (See Figure 6-5.) Table 6-1, on the next page, provides a quick description of the various AutoFormat options and gives an example of when they might affect your work.

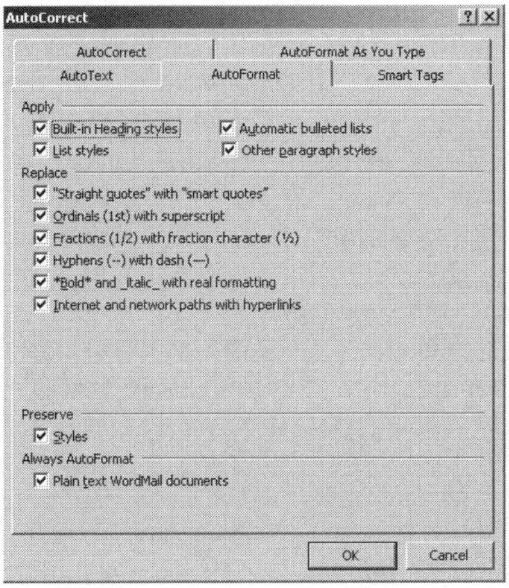

Figure 6-5. The check boxes on the AutoFormat tab control the various items Word looks for when it AutoFormats your document.

note If you try to use dashes in your current document and AutoFormat doesn't automatically change them for you, make sure you don't include spaces before and after the hyphens. Word will AutoFormat the hyphens as dashes, but only when you type the hyphens between two text characters.

Table 6-1. AutoFormat Options Selected by Default

AutoFormat Check Box	Description	Use
Built-in Heading Styles	Formats the headings in your document	You have a particular style sheet you want to apply to a long document.
List Styles	Uses the default list style to automatically	You have a multistep process indent and number your lists. that you want to format in a consistent way.
Automatic Bulleted Lists	Takes its cue from the first bullet you enter and formats subsequent quent lines accordingly	You want to use standardized bulleted lists throughout your document.
Other Paragraph Styles	Anticipates the styles of your paragraphs, adding spacing and indent levels according to paragraph styles in your document, letter, or e-mail message	You want to use spacing consistent with that already used in your document and existing styles.
"Straight Quotes" With "Smart Quotes"	Replaces straight quotation marks with open and close quotation marks	You want to create a document that is typographically accurate with correct punctuation.
Ordinals (1st) With Superscript	Inserts ordinals (such as 1st, 2nd, 3rd) when you type full-character sized ordinals	You want to increase the professional look of your document and make ordinals easier to read.
Fractions (1/2) With Fraction Character (½)	Replaces full-character sized fractions (1/2) with reduced fraction (½)	Again, you want to increase the professional look of your publication and make the fraction easier to read.
Hyphens (--) With Dash (—)	Replaces two hyphens (--) with a dash character (—)	You want to add to the professional look of your document.
Bold And _Italic_ With Real Formatting	Applies text styles Bold and Italic to words as you type	You want to type quickly without interrupting your process to choose bold and italic styles.

(continued)

Table 6-1. *(continued)*

AutoFormat Check Box	Description	Use
Internet And Network Paths With Hyperlinks	Adds hyperlinks automatically to text strings Word recognizes as URLs and network paths.	You want to create hyperlinks to other documents on line.
Preserve Styles	Keeps any styles you create in the existing document and does not replace them with named styles.	You want to keep custom styles in the current document and don't want other formatting applied automatically.
Always AutoFormat Plain Text WordMail Documents	Enables you to use automatic formatting in e-mail messages.	You want to include formatting in your e-mail messages and you've selected Word as your e-mail editor.

Disabling AutoFormat Features You Don't Use

No big surprise here—if you want to disable AutoFormat features, clear the check box to the right of the option you want to leave out. Which options might you want to disable in AutoFormat?

- **List Styles.** If you have customized lists or need to enter project-specific codes as you type, clear the List Styles check box so Word doesn't apply its own format.
- **Automatic Bulleted Lists.** If you have a specific style you want to apply to your document, or you want to use the dashes or asterisks commonly used to denote bullets, clear the Automatic Bulleted Lists check box.
- **Preserve Styles.** If you want Word to automatically update styles in a document to fit the styles in the applied style sheet, clear the Styles check box. Word will then automatically format modified paragraphs to fit accepted styles.

AutoFormatting As You Type

Word also gives you the option of automatically formatting your text as you type, allowing you to enhance the consistency of your document as you create it. Because AutoFormat is enabled by default, the feature will already be turned on as you begin to type. If you want to change the formatting options, however, you can change the settings on the AutoFormat As You Type tab of the AutoFormat dialog box. To set AutoFormat As You Type options, choose Format, AutoFormat. Click the Options button in the AutoCorrect dialog box and then click the AutoFormat As You Type tab. The options are similar to the options you've just set on the AutoFormat tab, but there are a few differences, as you can see in Figure 6-6.

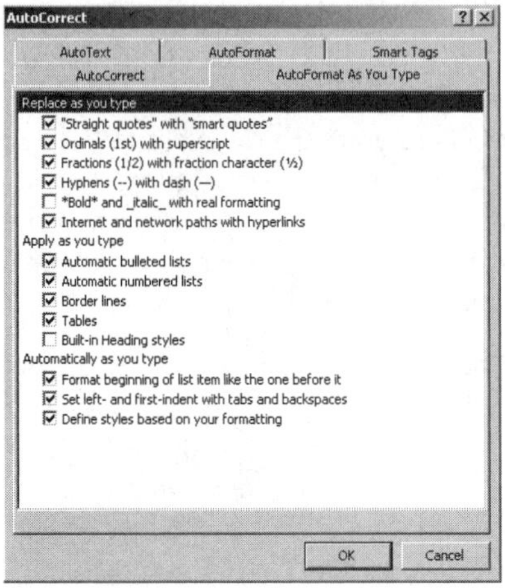

Figure 6-6. Catching formatting problems while you type is the function of the AutoFormat As You Type options.

newfeature!

The only options that are not enabled by default are the ones that replace words enclosed in asterisks and underscores with bold and italic, respectively, and the Built-in Heading Styles option. One option that is new to Word 2002 is the Set Left- And First-Indent With Tabs And Backspaces item, available in the Automatically As You Type section. This feature "picks up" the indents you set as you type, replicating them in subsequent similar paragraphs.

After you've finished setting the options for AutoFormat As You Type, click OK to close the AutoCorrect dialog box.

newfeature!

Seeing What's Going On with Reveal Formatting

In previous versions of Word, you could use the What's This? command in the Help menu to display formatting information about text at the insertion point. Word 2002 gives you the means not only to display but also to change formatting information with a few simple clicks.

To display the Reveal Formatting task pane, follow these steps:

1. Select the text you want to work with.
2. Choose Format, Reveal Formatting. The Reveal Formatting task pane appears along the right side of the screen. (See Figure 6-7.)

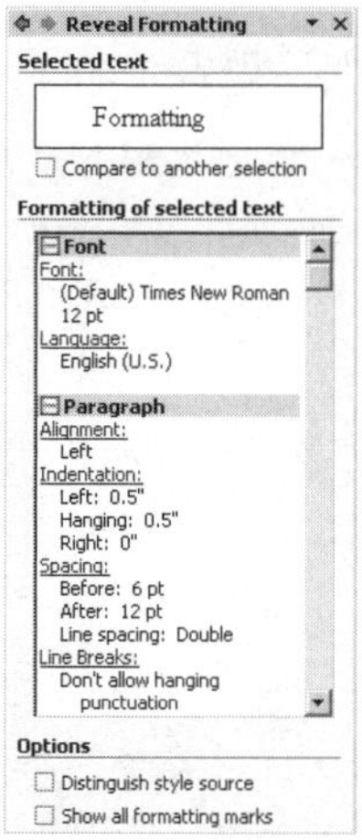

Figure 6-7. The Reveal Formatting task pane lists the various format settings for the text at the insertion point.

The Reveal Formatting task pane lists all the different format specifications for the selected text. The format items are divided into three groups:

- **Font.** This section includes format items that have to do with the characters used in the document, including the font type and size in use, as well as the language selected for the document.
- **Paragraph.** This section contains format items that control the paragraph choices for the selected text. These items list the selected paragraph style, the text alignment, indentation settings, and paragraph spacing (before and after spacing, as well as line spacing settings).
- **Section.** This section includes the format settings you use to control larger portions of the document, including overall margin settings, page layout choices, and paper selections.

Making Changes from Reveal Formatting

You can make formatting changes to the text at the insertion point right from the Reveal Formatting task pane. By simply clicking the formatting item you want to change (the links are shown in blue, underlined text), you can move directly to that dialog box. To make formatting changes directly from the task pane, follow these steps:

1. Select the text for which you want to change the format.
2. Choose Format, Reveal Formatting. The Reveal Formatting task pane appears.
3. Click the formatting item you want to change. For example, click the Spacing link in the task pane. The Paragraph dialog box appears with the Indents And Spacing tab displayed, as shown in Figure 6-8.
4. Make your changes as needed and close the dialog box. You are returned to your displayed document.

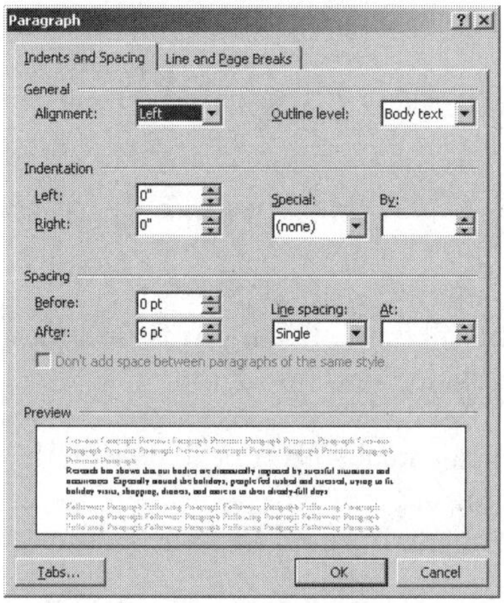

Figure 6-8. You can save time and effort by moving directly to the changes you want to make from the Reveal Formatting task pane.

Displaying Formatting Marks from Reveal Formatting

Do you work with formatting marks showing in your documents? For those times when you need to grab the last paragraph mark, move blocks of text from one section to another, or make sure you have only one space between words, you can display and work with paragraph marks in your document.

You can display formatting marks easily from the Reveal Formatting task pane by selecting the Show All Formatting Marks check box at the bottom of the task pane. The marks are then displayed in your document, as Figure 6-9 shows.

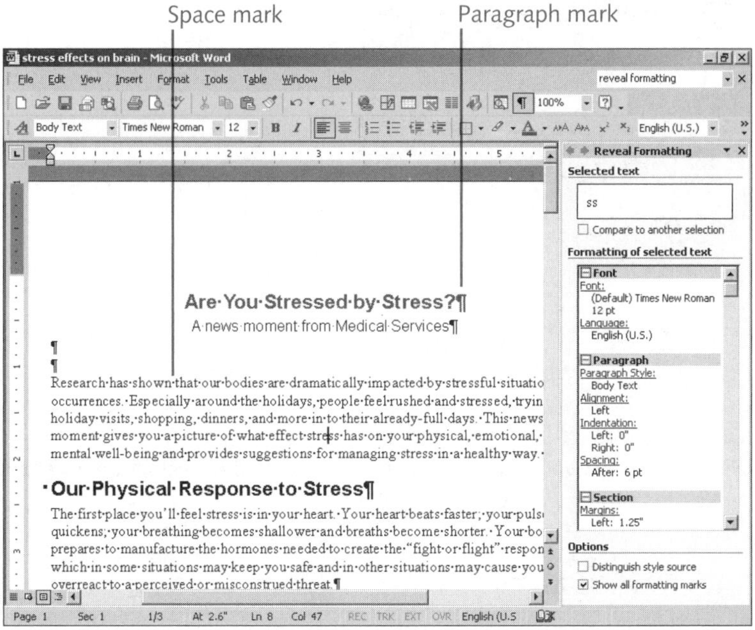

Figure 6-9. Display formatting marks by selecting the check box at the bottom of the Reveal Formatting task pane.

Changing the Displayed Formatting Marks

By default, all available formatting marks—tabs, spaces, paragraph marks, hidden text, and hyphens—are shown when you select Show All Formatting Marks in the Reveal Formatting task pane. You can change the marks that are displayed by following these steps:

1. Choose Tools, Options. The Options dialog box is displayed. (See Figure 6-10, on the next page.)
2. Click the View tab, if necessary. In the Formatting Marks section, select the check boxes you want to include.

tip **Avoid screen clutter**

Some people are able to work with formatting marks on and barely notice them; others are distracted by the dots and symbols stuffed between words and paragraphs in their text. You can hide formatting marks quickly by clicking the Show/Hide button on the Standard toolbar.

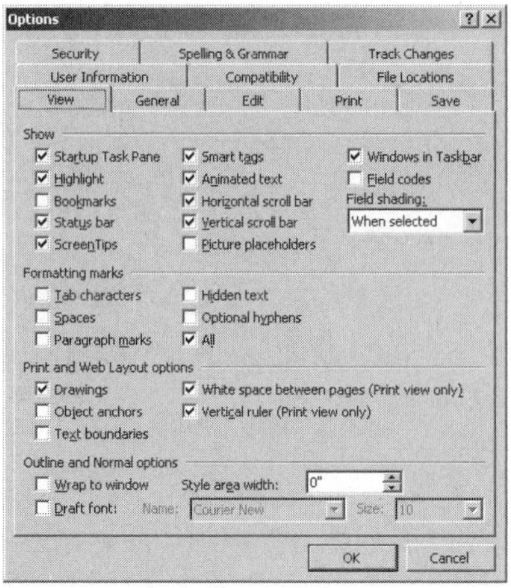

Figure 6-10. Switch to the View tab in the Options dialog box to change which formatting marks are displayed.

Comparing Other Text Formats

Another option available to you in the Reveal Formatting task pane is the ability to compare and contrast similar-but-different text styles. Have you ever spent time studying a heading, wondering why it doesn't look quite right when compared to another heading in your document? Now Reveal Formatting enables you to click on one text item and then compare it to another, showing the differences in font styles and sizes, spacing, and so forth.

To compare two text segments in your document, follow these steps:

1. Select the text you want to start with. You can either select a block of text or simply click the mouse pointer in the text you want to use.
2. Display the Reveal Formatting task pane, if needed, by choosing Format, Reveal Formatting.
3. Select the Compare To Another Selection check box, just beneath the Selected Text box in the Reveal Formatting task pane. Another text selection box opens in the task pane, showing a duplicate of the text you selected.
4. Now select the text to which you want to compare the original text. The task pane shows the formatting differences between the two selections, as Figure 6-11 shows.

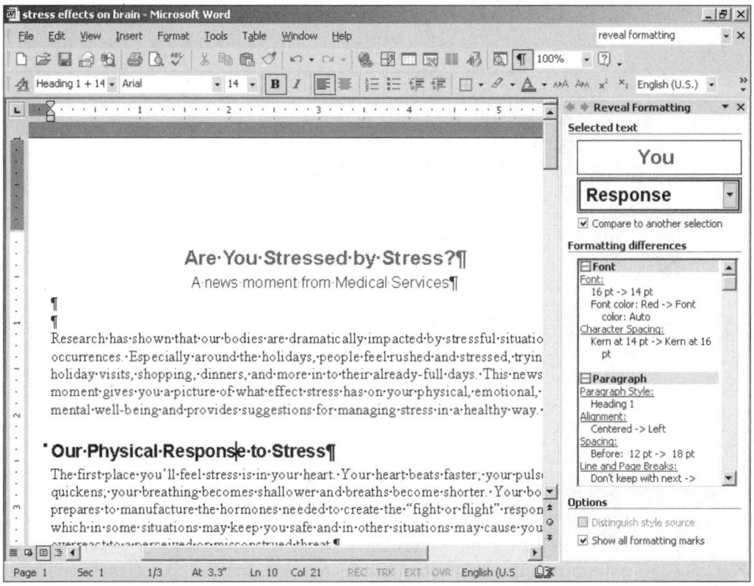

Figure 6-11. The Reveal Formatting task pane displays the formatting differences between the two text selections.

Making Changes in Compared Text

Suppose that comparing two different types of heading reveals the need to reformat one type of heading throughout your entire document. Word gives you the means to do this easily. Right there in the Reveal Formatting task pane, you can choose the option that will modify every heading formatted with those particular settings throughout the rest of your document. To make this kind of change, follow these steps:

1. Click the down arrow to the right of the compared text. A drop-down menu appears (see Figure 6-12, on the next page).

   You can choose Select All Text With Similar Formatting, which highlights all text in the document with the same specifications; Apply Formatting Of Original Selection, which applies the format of the first item to the second item; or Clear Formatting, which clears the formatting of the second item.

> **tip** **Find similar formats**
>
> When the Reveal Formatting task pane is not displayed, you can easily find and highlight all text with the same format as the text at the insertion point. Just right-click the text and choose Select Text With Similar Formatting from the shortcut menu. All similar text items throughout your document will be selected, and you can make your changes as needed.

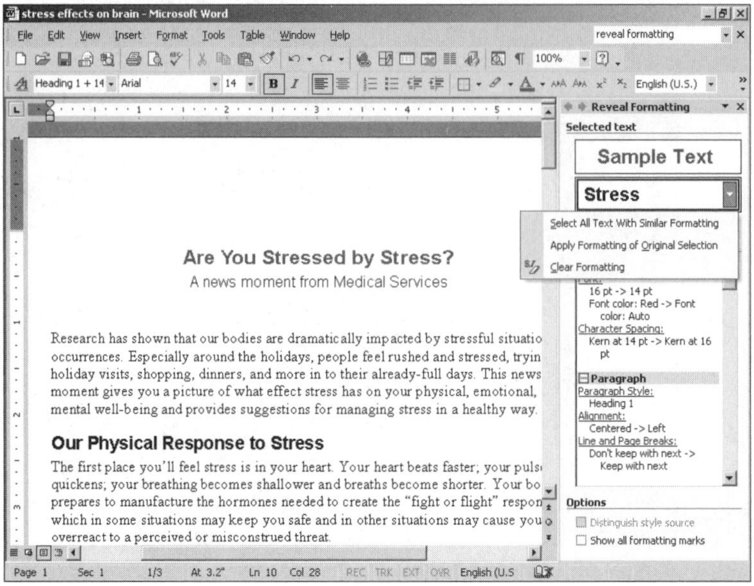

Figure 6-12. Select the action to take in the Reveal Formatting task pane.

2 Choose the option you want and Word reformats the text accordingly. If you don't like the change, choose Edit, Undo to reverse your changes.

Where Did That Style Come From?

One final offering in the Reveal Formatting task pane that's worth a mention: You can find out what the source of a particular style is by selecting the Distinguish Style Source check box at the bottom of the Reveal Formatting task pane.

Selecting this check box causes Word to display the style from which the new style was created; for example, if a Note style applied to a segment of text in your document was created based on your Body Text style, the task pane will show you that information. That's helpful to know if you're planning to change the Body Text style at some point—you'll be able to see at a glance which other items in your document will be affected by the change.

AutoCorrecting Your Typos Away

AutoCorrect is a terrific Word feature that anticipates your possible errors and corrects them—almost before you know you made them. AutoCorrect comes with a library of more than a thousand different items, and it learns from you as you go along. Are you forever typing **yuor** when you mean to type **your**? AutoCorrect will automatically reverse the characters in words it recognizes without any further action from you.

AutoCorrect locates a number of different types of problems in your document. You can relax and let the thoughts flow, knowing that Word will catch and correct the following types of situations:

- **Problems with capitalization.** If you accidentally type too many capital letters in a row, forget to capitalize the beginning of a sentence or a table heading, or enter the name of a day of the week in lowercase (tuesday), Word will fix it for you.

> **newfeature!**
> **note** The AutoCorrect feature that looks for and capitalizes words in table cells is new with Word 2002.

- **Problems with garbled typing.** If your fingers get tied up in a knot when you try to type the word **can** and type **acn** instead, Word will untangle the characters for you.
- **Problems with spacing.** If your words run together, as in **nextime** instead of **next time**, Word will add the missing letter and character space.
- **Inserting special symbols.** Instead of going through the menu selections needed to insert a special symbol like a Wingding, you can rely on AutoCorrect to substitute the symbol for the text you type (replacing (r) with ®).

> **tip** **Check existing text**
>
> Although AutoCorrect doesn't go through and check words in an existing document against the items in the AutoCorrect list, you can download a macro from the Microsoft Knowledge Base that will take care of this for you. Go to *www.microsoft.com* and choose Support; then search for Knowledge Base Article number Q210869. This is a macro written for Word 2000, but it works in Word 2002 as well.

Controlling AutoCorrect

AutoCorrect is one of those great features that can cut down on the time and effort you spend ensuring the accuracy and professionalism of your documents. It can also get in your way at times, when you *mean* to enter a word in all caps, or you want to spell something incorrectly, or you purposefully lowercase the labels in a table. You have the option of changing AutoCorrect options one at a time, while you're working in your document, and all at once, by changing the selections in the AutoCorrect dialog box.

Working with AutoCorrect in Your Document

The first time you notice AutoCorrect might be when it has just changed something you've typed. Suppose, for example, that you began typing a sentence and neglected the first capital letter. AutoCorrect makes the change. You then have the option of continuing on and accepting the change or stopping and undoing it (assuming, of course, you *meant* to leave the character lowercase). To see your AutoCorrect choices after a change is made, follow these steps:

1. Position the pointer over the word that was changed. A blue underline appears at the beginning of the word.

AutoCorrect Options

2. Hover the mouse pointer over the line for a second, and the line changes to the AutoCorrect Options button. To the right of the button is a down arrow.
3. Click the down arrow to see a menu of choices. These choices reflect the type of change that's been made and give you the option of undoing the change or changing other AutoCorrect options. (See Figure 6-13.)
4. Click the command you want in the drop-down menu and Word makes the change. You can then continue with your text entry and editing.

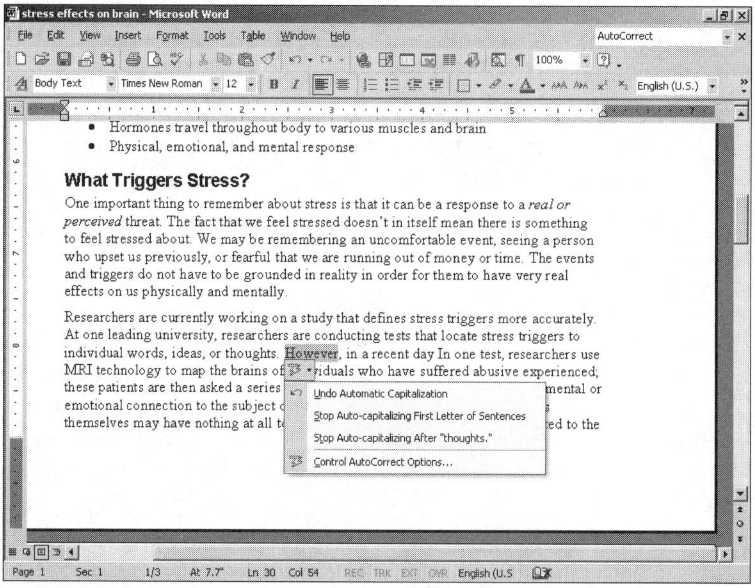

Figure 6-13. You can make changes to the way AutoCorrect does things while continuing to work in your document.

Setting AutoCorrect Options

It's good to know how to set the AutoCorrect options just the way you want them. You can control the items that AutoCorrect fixes; you can also create your own words and phrases AutoCorrect inserts (you can even add images in place of text, if you choose). You can have AutoCorrect pull correct spellings from the spelling checker as you type.

To open the AutoCorrect dialog box shown in Figure 6-14, choose Tools, AutoCorrect Options. The AutoCorrect dialog box allows you to control the various changes Auto-Correct makes for you. Table 6-2 describes your choices in the AutoCorrect dialog box.

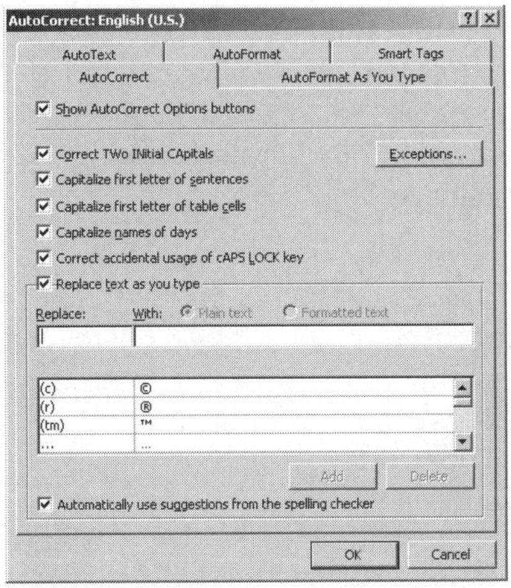

Figure 6-14. You can make changes to the way AutoCorrect does things while continuing to work in your document.

Table 6-2. Setting AutoCorrect Options

AutoCorrect Option	Description	Use
Show AutoCorrect Options Buttons	Displays the AutoCorrect Options button when a change is automatically made in your document	You want to be able to go back and undo AutoCorrect changes.
Correct TWo INitial CApitals	Finds and changes any capitalization inconsistencies such as two capital letters in the middle of a word	You are not entering data with acronyms or unusual capitalization.
Capitalize First Letter Of Sentences	Capitalizes the first word in a new sentence	You are typing sentences.

(continued)

Table 6-2. *(continued)*

AutoCorrect Option	Description	Use
Capitalize First Letter Of Table Cells	Capitalizes the data entered in the cells of a table	You want to capitalize table data.
Capitalize Names Of Days	Capitalizes any full names of days of the week in your document	You want the days of the week to be shown traditionally; if you want days to occur lowercase as part of a design element, clear this check box.
Correct Accidental Usage Of Caps Lock Key	Catches the accidental pressing of the Caps Lock key, releases it, and changes the erroneous capitalization of characters	You want AutoCorrect to watch for and catch unusual capitalization.
Replace Text As You Type	Enables AutoCorrect to make changes as you type. If you disable this option, AutoCorrect will not make changes on the fly	You want AutoCorrect to make changes as you work.
Replace: With:	Enables you to add your own AutoCorrect entries to the AutoCorrect library	You have words, phrases, text blocks, or graphics that you want to insert automatically in your document.
Automatically Use Suggestions From The Spelling Checker	Looks for suggestions for misspelled words by consulting the spelling checker's dictionary	You want to include words and phrases the spelling checker recognizes as part of the AutoCorrect library.
Exceptions	Enables you to "teach" AutoCorrect which items *not* to correct automatically	You have particular words, phrases, acronyms, or items that you don't want AutoCorrect to change.

Adding AutoCorrect Entries

One of the great things about AutoCorrect, besides the fact that it catches your errors and makes you look good, is that you can cut down on data entry time by having Word automatically insert words, phrases, or even logos or graphics when it finds an AutoCorrect item you've entered.

For example, suppose that it's part of your company's policy to use the real company logo whenever the name of the company is shown in text. You can create an AutoCorrect entry that does that for you, automatically. Here's how:

1. Start by creating the item you want to place in the document, complete with the formatting, coloring, and spacing you want.
2. Select the item.
3. Choose Tools, AutoCorrect Options. The AutoCorrect dialog box appears.
4. Click Formatted Text in the Replace Text As You Type section if you've added formatting features to the word or phrase.
5. Type the characters you want to use to trigger the replacement in the Replace box (see Figure 6-15).
6. Click Add. Word then adds the new AutoCorrect entry to the list.
7. Test it. Click in your document and type the characters you entered in the Replace box. AutoCorrect will place the new addition at the insertion point.

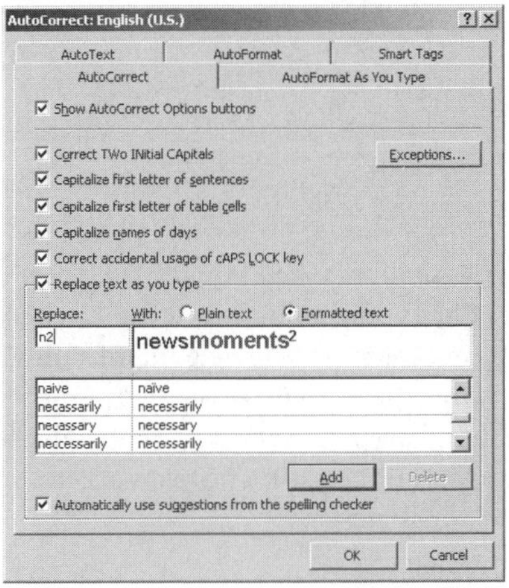

Figure 6-15. You can create AutoCorrect entries that replace the text you type with words, phrases, logos, graphics, and even blocks of text you enter.

tip **Save keystrokes**

You can use AutoCorrect to enter blocks of text you type often, saving you the trouble of retyping text over and over again. For example, if you include your organization's mission statement on everything you print, you can create an AutoCorrect entry that inserts the entire mission statement when you type the letters **ms**.

Replacing and Deleting AutoCorrect Entries

You can edit the AutoCorrect entries you create by simply recreating and then replacing them. For example, if you want to modify the logo you entered as an AutoCorrect item, you can simply make the change, select the item, and then enter the same trigger word in the Replace box on the AutoCorrect tab of the AutoCorrect dialog box. The button beneath the list changes from Add to Replace. Click Replace to add the new AutoCorrect entry in place of the original. Word will display a message box asking you to confirm the action. Click Yes, and the AutoCorrect entry is replaced.

You can delete entries in a similar way. Display the AutoCorrect dialog box and type the characters for the trigger item in the Replace box on the AutoCorrect tab. When AutoCorrect displays the item you want to delete, click it to select it; then click Delete.

tip **Catch accidental deletions**

A warning about deleting AutoCorrect entries, however: Word doesn't prompt you to confirm that you do, in fact, mean to delete the item. It's simply removed from the list. If you clicked Delete accidentally and want to save the AutoCorrect entry you've just deleted, you have one last chance—until you click OK or select another entry, AutoCorrect displays the item just deleted in the Replace and With boxes. You can click Add to add the item back to the list, if you catch the error in time.

Entering Exceptions

As great as AutoCorrect is, there will be times when you don't want it interfering with what you're trying to do. You might be typing a document full of chemical compounds, for example, or creating a list of access codes for the new mainframe. You don't want AutoCorrect to get in there and change the capitalization and perhaps your character order while you type. In this case, you have two options: You can disable AutoCorrect while you're working on this document, or you can create an exception to teach AutoCorrect what you don't want it to change.

tip **Add exceptions automatically**

If you've selected Automatically Add Words to List in the AutoCorrect Exceptions dialog box, Word automatically updates your list of selections if you press Backspace after Word AutoCorrects a word and then type the word as you want it to appear. If you use Undo, Word will not update your list with your change.

To enter AutoCorrect exceptions, you click the Exceptions button on the AutoCorrect tab in the AutoCorrect dialog box. The AutoCorrect Exceptions dialog box shown in Figure 6-16 appears.

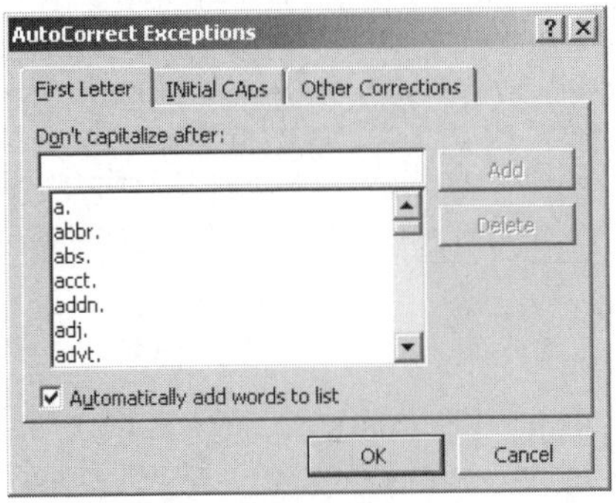

Figure 6-16. You can teach AutoCorrect not to correct certain items that are unique to the documents you create.

AutoCorrect lets you create three different kinds of exceptions:

- **First Letter** capitalization controls abbreviations and the words immediately following them (For example, you might have a phrase such as "after the merging of Lake Ltd. and Smith Co.," in which the word "and" should not be capitalized.)
- **INitial CAps** allows you to enter words and phrases with unusual capitalization that you don't want changed. This might include company names or abbreviations or terms unique to your business or industry.
- **Other Corrections** enables you to add additional items you don't want AutoCorrect to change. This might include names, locations, unique spellings, and phrases that reflect terminology particular to your work.

To add an exception to one of the Exception lists, follow these steps:

1. Display the AutoCorrect Exceptions dialog box, if necessary, by clicking the Exceptions button in the AutoCorrect dialog box.
2. Click the tab for the exception type you want to enter.
3. Click in the text box and type the item you want to add.
4. Click Add to add the exception to the AutoCorrect Exceptions list.
5. Click OK to close the dialog box and return to your document.

Making AutoText Work for You

Although AutoCorrect and AutoText can be used in similar ways—cutting down on the time and effort you spend entering text—AutoText really has a different function. Instead of catching errors in spelling, capitalization, and spacing, the focus of AutoText is simply to help you enter text as quickly as possible. AutoText works with the AutoComplete feature to anticipate the words you are preparing to enter and to insert them for you. By spending the time to educate Word about the terms, phrases, and descriptions often used in your documents, you can both save text entry time and reduce your margin for error.

newfeature!

Inserting AutoText Entries

AutoText includes a long list of entries, from the attention line to mailing instructions, to company name, to salutations. Word 2002 expands the list with the timely addition of E-mail options (which includes a full listing of the e-mail addresses Word recognizes from your Outlook Address Book) and the addition of a Person selection, which lists the individuals in your Address Book by name.

You begin the process of using AutoText by choosing Insert, AutoText. A menu of AutoText choices appears, and you can point to the selection you want to display specific AutoText choices. (See Figure 6-17.)

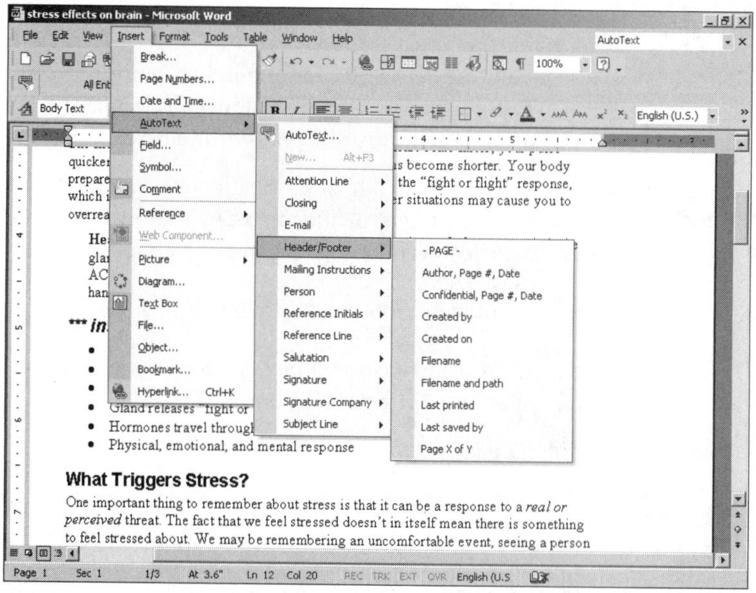

Figure 6-17. AutoText leverages the text you often add and the text you've already entered to create the fastest means of text entry for your documents.

Chapter 6

AutoText in Headers and Footers

When you want to add AutoText to a header or footer in your document, start by displaying the Header And Footer toolbar by choosing View, Header And Footer. Then click in the header (or footer) and follow these steps:

1. Choose Insert, AutoText. A list of Header and Footer AutoText items appears.
2. Choose the item you want to add as AutoText. The text is added at the insertion point.

You'll notice that although the AutoText submenu item is Author, Page #, Date, for example, once it's placed in the document, it displays the actual data—your name, the current page number, and today's date. This happens because the Header and Footer AutoText entries are actually field codes, meaning they are replaced with data when used in the document. Each time you open a document, these fields will be updated as needed.

Inserting AutoText in Your Document

AutoText is another one of those options that is enabled by default. When you begin typing a word or phrase AutoText recognizes, it displays the rest of the phrase in a ScreenTip above the word you are typing, with the instruction "press ENTER to Insert," as Figure 6-18 shows.

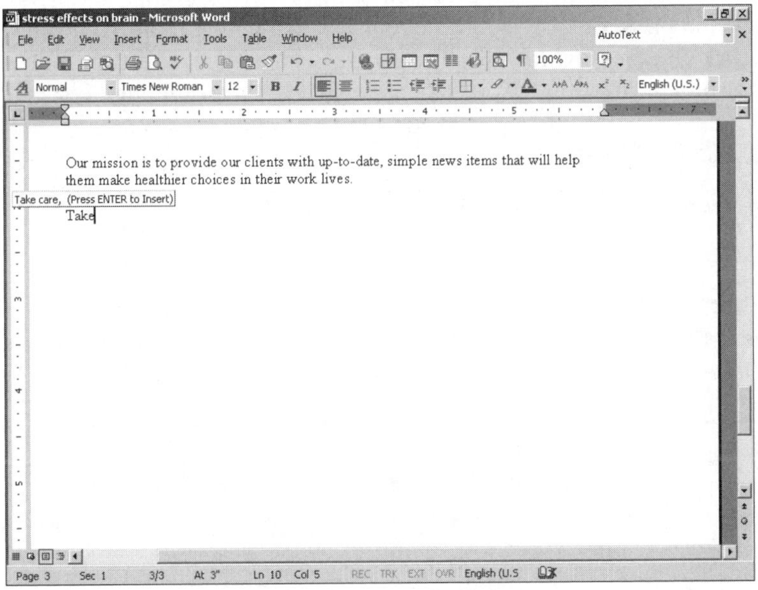

Figure 6-18. AutoComplete jumps in and offers to complete a word or phrase for you. Press Enter to add the text as prompted.

Although entering AutoText on the fly, as you're prompted, offers the fastest way of inserting the AutoText entries, you can add entries from the AutoText tab of the AutoCorrect dialog box if you choose. Simply scroll through the AutoText entry list until you find the item you want; click it and then click Insert. Word adds the text you selected at the insertion point in your document.

InsideOut

Confused about the difference between AutoComplete and AutoText? The two terms are actually two parts of the same process. AutoText entries are those words and phrases you enter by choosing the AutoText selection from the Insert menu. AutoComplete is the process of finishing a half-typed word or phrase for you. But when you want to enter new phrases for AutoComplete, where do you go? The AutoText tab of the AutoCorrect dialog box.

Adding Your Own AutoText Entries

What other entries will AutoText insert for you? Months, days of the week, and names it recognizes. The best way to get the full effect of AutoText, however, is to teach it to enter the words and phrases you use most often. This is really a simple thing to do.

The quickest way to add AutoText entries is just to proceed typing happily along in your document. When you get to a word or phrase that you'd like to enter as an AutoText entry, select it and press Alt+F3. The Create AutoText dialog box appears, and all you need to do is click OK. (See Figure 6-19.) The phrase is added to your list and will be suggested for insertion the next time Word recognizes that you're beginning to type the phrase.

Figure 6-19. Fast and simple—add an AutoText entry by selecting the phrase and pressing Alt+F3.

note You can also add AutoText entries on the AutoText tab of the AutoCorrect dialog box. Simply type the entry in the Enter AutoText Entries Here box, and click Add. Using this method is best when you have a number of entries to create at once. When you're finished adding entries, click OK to return to your document.

Managing AutoText Entries

You've already spent some time in the AutoCorrect dialog box, which includes a tab for AutoText. Here you have another option for the way you add your own AutoText entries. You can also manage the entries you've got by inserting and deleting them. Figure 6-20 shows the AutoText tab in the AutoCorrect dialog box.

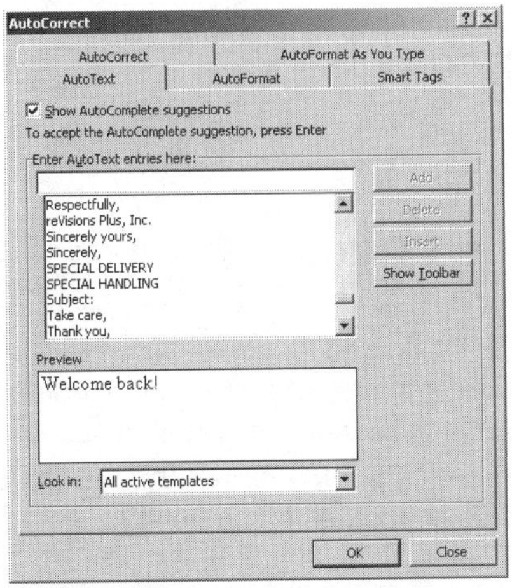

Figure 6-20. You can manage the AutoText entries you add and insert on the AutoText tab of the AutoCorrect dialog box.

Disabling AutoText

If AutoText just gets under your skin and you want to disable the feature (but *why?*), you can do so easily by displaying the AutoCorrect dialog box (choose Tools, AutoCorrect Options), clicking the AutoText tab, and clearing the Show AutoComplete Suggestions check box. That suppresses the display of the ScreenTips that come to your rescue as you type. When and if you want to use AutoText once again, simply repeat the steps and select Show AutoComplete Suggestions check box.

> **tip** **Improve speed by disabling AutoText**
>
> Some users feel that, especially in large documents and documents that are heavily loaded with graphics, the ScreenTips slow Word down. If you find this to be true on your system, try disabling AutoText to see whether the change makes a difference in performance.

Choosing Templates for AutoText

By default, AutoText looks in all active templates to gather the AutoCorrect entries used in your document. The items you add are saved in Normal.dot, the global template on which Word traditionally bases newly created files (unless you specify otherwise). To choose a different template, click the Look In down arrow on the AutoText tab of the AutoCorrect dialog box, and click the template you want to use.

Saving AutoText Entries to Other Templates

If you've added other templates to Word, you can save AutoText entries to them by following these steps:

1. Choose Tools, Templates And Add-Ins to display the Templates And Add-ins dialog box.
2. Click the Organizer button and click the AutoText tab. The listing on the left shows the AutoText entries in Normal.dot, the global template. The listing on the right shows the AutoText entries in the current document. If you want to change the template from which you are copying the AutoText entries, click the Close File button on the left to close the selected file and then click Open File and choose the file you want to use.
3. Select the AutoText entries in the left listing that you want to copy to the file in the right side of the Organizer dialog box. (See Figure 6-21.) Click Copy. The AutoText entries are added to the template on the right.
4. Click Close to exit the Organizer dialog box and return to your document.

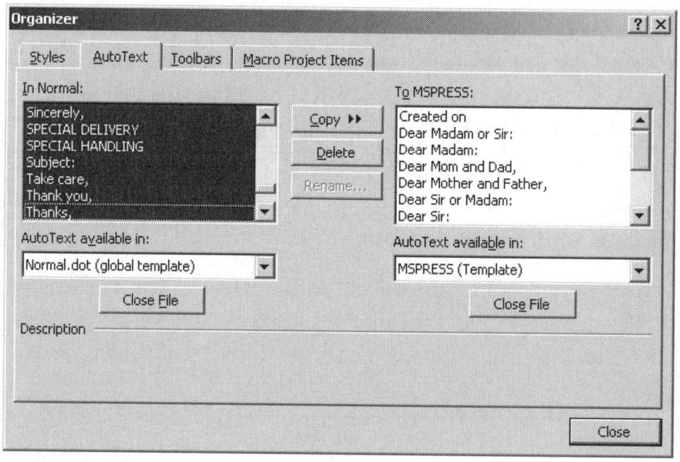

Figure 6-21. Copying AutoText entries to another document template is a simple matter when you use the Organizer available through Tools, Templates And Add-ins.

> **tip** **Why copy AutoText entries?**
>
> If AutoText is capable of looking in all available templates for possible entries, why is it necessary to copy entries from one template to another? If you're creating a standard template for your department or group, or you simply want a backup copy for yourself, having all the same AutoText entries saved in the template you use helps ensure consistency in the documents you create. It also can save your coworkers some time, depending on how complete your AutoText entries are.

Using the AutoText Toolbar

Word includes an AutoText toolbar you can use to insert entries, add new words and phrases, and display the AutoText options. You can display the toolbar in one of two ways:

- Choose View, Toolbars and click AutoText.
- Click the Show Toolbar button on the AutoText tab of the AutoCorrect dialog box.

The AutoText toolbar is shown in Figure 6-22. You can use this toolbar to insert, create, and manage your AutoText entries.

Figure 6-22. The AutoText toolbar gives you tools for displaying the dialog box, inserting, and adding entries.

> **tip** **List AutoText entries**
>
> Want to see a full listing of all your AutoText entries? You can print a list from the Print dialog box. Press Ctrl+P to display the Print dialog box, choose your printing options, and in the Print What drop-down list, select AutoText Entries; then click OK. A full listing of your AutoText entries will be printed.

newfeature!

Getting the Scoop on Smart Tags

One of the exciting new features Word 2002 offers is smart tags. Smart tags actually deliver something very similar to what their name suggests—they provide links to additional information that give you more data on a recognized item, person, place, or thing. They make you "smarter" by giving you wider access to the data in your applications.

Smart tag functionality is included with both Word and Excel, with support for their display in Microsoft Internet Explorer. A smart tag is meant to be an intuitive link, an easy connection made for the user to get to more information about the tagged item.

For example, suppose that you're writing a report that summarizes new research your department has recently completed. When you enter the list of contributing writers, you see the name of a person you recognize, but you can't recall her department. In theory, if the information about the employee has been entered, you should be able to position the pointer over the employee's name and see a ScreenTip of information about her, complete with her name, e-mail address, and other contact information. The fact that this data is retained in Excel and potentially in Web documents makes this transfer of data smarter and more consistent.

> **note** In earlier version of Word, this kind of "smart" technology helped users locate URLs and e-mail addresses. Now this functionality, officially named "smart tags," has been expanded to offer more meaningful information, including full contact information and customized data.

Following a Smart Tag

A smart tag in your document appears like a ScreenTip in other uses. The first item you see is a small circular tag and a purple dotted underline. When you click the circular tag, a menu appears, as Figure 6-23 shows. Table 6-3 describes the different functions of the smart tag choices.

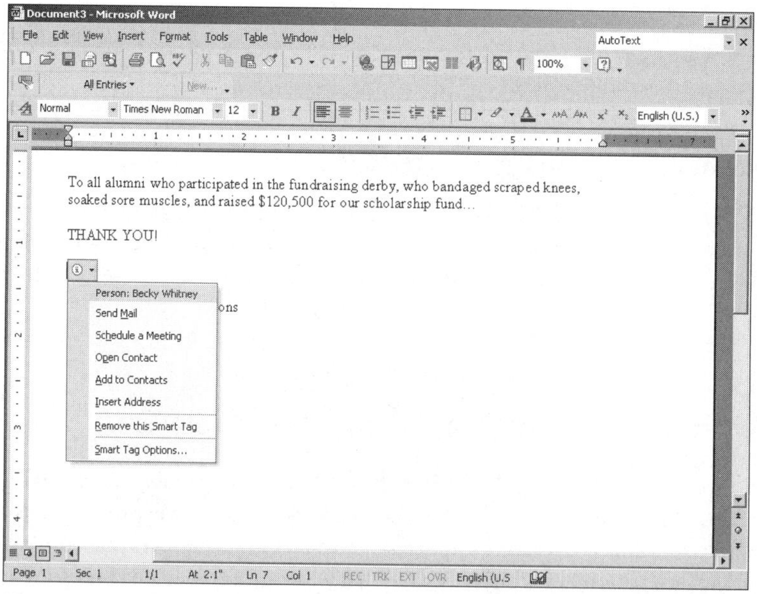

Figure 6-23. Smart tags broaden your use of data among applications, enabling you to create mail, schedule meetings, add contacts, and insert addresses as you work.

Table 6-3. Smart Tag Choices

Smart Tag Option	Description
Send Mail	Opens an e-mail message with Word as the editor
Schedule A Meeting	Opens Outlook so that you can schedule a meeting and invite the selected person
Open Contact	Displays the Outlook Contact List so that you can look up, add to, or edit the person's information
Add To Contacts	Adds the selected person to Outlook's Contact List
Insert Address	Inserts the address of the person at the current insertion point
Remove This Smart Tag	Deletes the smart tag at this occurrence in the document
Smart Tag Options	Displays the Smart Tags tab, enabling you to choose additional options

Turning Off Smart Tags

If you decide that you don't want to use smart tags in your document, simply display the Smart Tags tab of the AutoCorrect dialog box (see Figure 6-24) and clear the Label Text With Smart Tags check box; then click OK. Smart tags will be disabled for your current document.

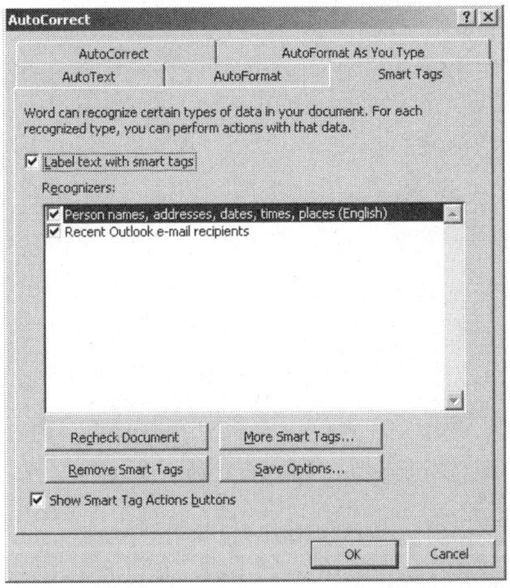

Figure 6-24. You turn smart tags on and off and select the options you want on the Smart Tags tab of the AutoCorrect dialog box.

Understanding Recognizers

A *Recognizer* is an item that the smart tag recognizes; a person, place, date, time, or thing that has been added to your application data. By default, both types of Recognizers are selected. To disable either Recognizer type, simply clear the check box to the left of the item. Word will then use only the selected item to display information in smart tag form in the document.

Rechecking Your Document

After you make a change to smart tags, you might want to recheck your document by clicking the Recheck Document button on the Smart Tags tab of the AutoCorrect dialog box. Word warns you that changes made by the grammar checker might be reversed as you go through the process of rechecking smart tags. If you want to continue, click Yes; otherwise, click No.

Getting Additional Smart Tags

You can get additional smart tags from the Microsoft Web site. Start by establishing your Internet connection and then display the Smart Tags tab of the AutoCorrect dialog box. Click More Smart Tags, and Word will launch Internet Explorer and display the Office Update Worldwide page. Follow the prompts on-screen to navigate to and download the smart tags you'll use to extend Word 2002's functionality.

Removing Smart Tags

You might want to remove selected smart tags in your document, depending on how many you have and how often you need them. Word gives you the option of removing selected tags or getting rid of them all at once.

Removing an Individual Smart Tag

To remove a specific smart tag, follow these steps:

1. In your document, click the smart tag to display the menu for the tag you want to remove.
2. Choose Remove This Smart Tag from the menu. The underline and the identifier are removed for that particular smart tag.

> **note** If you've cleared the Label Text With Smart Tags check box and then copied text into your document that has a smart tag attached, the smart tag will appear even though you've turned smart tags off.

Removing All Smart Tags

If you want to do something really drastic and get rid of all the smart tags in your document, display the Smart Tags tab in the AutoCorrect dialog box and click Remove Smart Tags. Word will display a warning that the action will remove all smart tags permanently—both in the existing document and in any copies of this document that eventually wind up on someone else's computer. If you want to remove the smart tags, click Yes; otherwise, preserve them by clicking No.

Exploring the New and Improved Clipboard

Using the Clipboard isn't rocket science—we've all been working with the Windows Clipboard since the earliest incarnations of Word. The Office Clipboard in Word 2002, however, is truly a "new and improved" Clipboard, with broader paste capabilities and a task pane you can display while you work.

What's more, you can display the Office Clipboard by choosing Edit, Office Clipboard. The Clipboard opens in a task pane along the right side of your work area. (See Figure 6-25, on the next page.)

note The new and improved Clipboard can store up to 24 items. In addition to the old standby keystrokes—Ctrl+C to copy and Ctrl+V to paste—you can opt to paste all Clipboard items at once by clicking a single button in the Clipboard task pane.

Pasting from the Office Clipboard

When you've saved an item to the Clipboard, you can paste it in several different ways:

- You can press Ctrl+V.
- You can choose Edit, Paste.
- You can position the pointer over the item in the Clipboard task pane. A down arrow appears. Click the arrow to display a short menu, offering you the Paste and Delete commands. This is a handy feature when you want to remove items from the Clipboard in order to free up the memory used.

Setting Clipboard Options

The Office Clipboard includes a number of options you can control from the Clipboard task pane. When you click the Options button in the lower left corner of the task pane, you're given four different commands in the drop-down menu. Table 6-4, on the next page, gives you an overview of each.

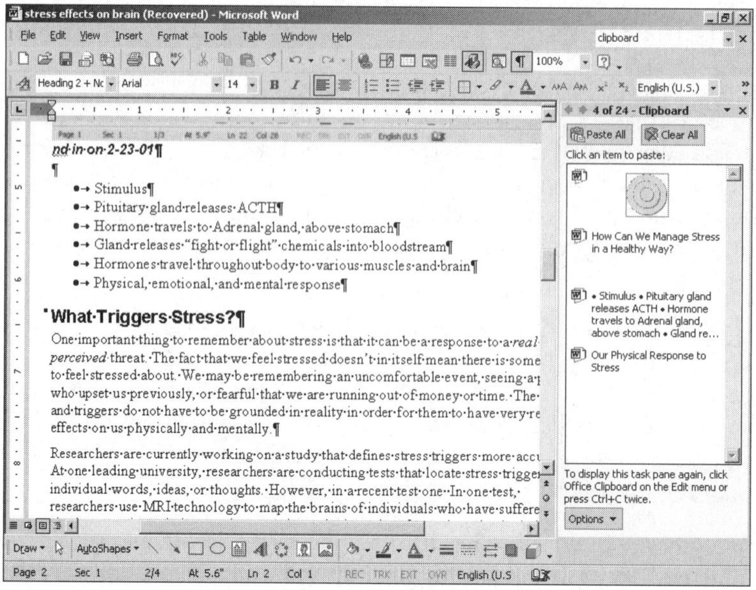

Figure 6-25. Now the Clipboard is available in a task pane so that you can easily see and manipulate the images and text stored there.

Table 6-4. Office Clipboard Options

Office Clipboard Option	Description	Use
Built-in Heading Styles	Formats the headings in your document	You have a particular style sheet you want to apply to a long document.
Show Office Clipboard Automatically	Automatically displays the Clipboard task pane whenever the Clipboard is used	You want to see what is stored on the Clipboard.
Collect Without Showing Office Clipboard	Hides the display of the Clipboard but collects up to 24 items	You want maximum available space on-screen.
Show Office Clipboard Icon On Taskbar	Displays a small Clipboard icon in the lower right corner of the Windows taskbar	You want to be reminded when something is stored on the Clipboard without having an application maximized.
Show Status Near Taskbar When Copying	Displays a ScreenTip showing how many items of 24 are currently stored on the Clipboard	You want to keep an eye on the resources you're using for the Clipboard, particularly if you're switching among Office applications.

Chapter 7

Aligning Information and Styling Paragraphs

Professional-looking documents rely on accurate content alignment and styling—no matter how avant-garde a document's layout happens to be. Typesetters and layout artists have long recognized that effectively aligning page elements plays a large role in increasing a document's readability and "keeping the reader's eye on the page." Even people untrained in design can quickly see that "something's wrong" when they view a page that's been slapped together without regard to formatting and alignment. Therefore, when you work in Word, you should give serious thought to formatting and aligning your document's elements. If you learn to use Word formatting and alignment tools effectively—maybe even automatically—you'll be able to seamlessly integrate design tasks throughout the document creation process.

In this chapter, we'll look at formatting and alignment commands associated with a single type of element: *paragraphs*. Paragraph formatting and alignment isn't as narrow a topic as it might sound at first. As a Word veteran, you probably know (or can intuit) that Word addresses document formatting and layout issues on three levels: character, paragraph, and section (or page). Character formatting issues include applying font styles and attributes (as discussed in Chapter 2, "Creating Documents from Start to Finish"). At the other end of the formatting spectrum, section formatting options control margins, headers, footers, gutters, and other page setup configurations (as covered in Chapter 21, "Mastering Page Setup and Pagination"). Paragraph formatting represents the middle ground of document formatting and alignment. Clearly, paragraph issues aren't as narrowly focused as character formatting tasks, and they aren't as encompassing as section setup commands. But don't let paragraph formatting's midlevel classification fool you—working with paragraphs is one of the most fundamental and essential skills you need to master to effectively use Word.

Understanding the Significance of Paragraphs in Word Documents

¶ Show/Hide

Surprisingly, even experienced Word users aren't fully aware of how extensively Word formatting relies on paragraphs. Part of this emphasis on paragraphs stems from the fact that, in Word, the term *paragraph* refers to far more than a group of sentences related to a theme. Instead, a paragraph in Word includes a paragraph mark (¶) along with all content preceding the paragraph mark, up to (but not including) the preceding paragraph mark. Each time you press Enter after a letter, heading, graphic, table, chart, or any other element, you insert a paragraph mark and create what Word considers a paragraph. Figure 7-1 illustrates the concept of various paragraph elements in Word; notice the paragraph marks after each bulleted list item, each paragraph of text, each heading, and the graphic. You can display paragraph marks (along with other hidden text) in your documents by clicking the Show/Hide button on the Standard toolbar or by selecting Show All Formatting Marks in the Reveal Formatting task pane.

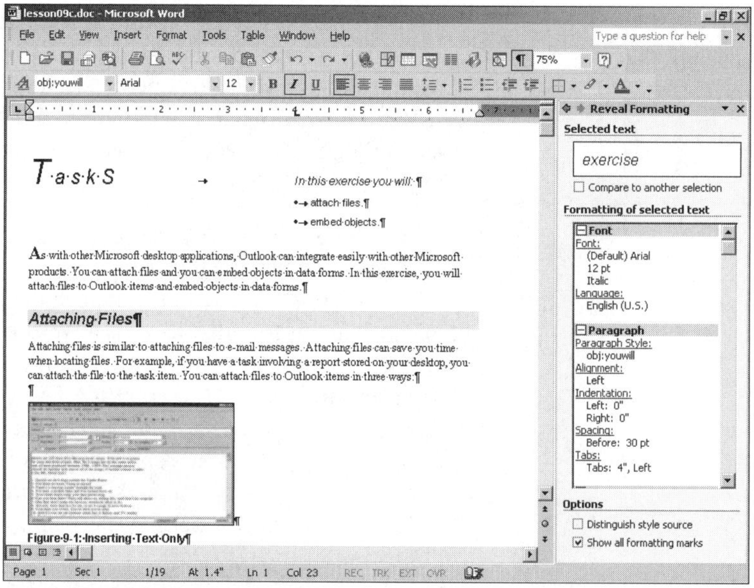

Figure 7-1. In Word, any content followed by a paragraph mark is considered a paragraph.

InsideOut

The Show/Hide button on the Standard toolbar provides a quick way to display paragraph marks along with other typically hidden characters (like spaces and tab marks). In some cases, you might find that having hidden characters displayed all over your document is a bit distracting. Fortunately, showing hidden characters isn't an all-or-nothing proposition. You can easily circumvent the Show/Hide button and configure your view to show selected hidden characters as follows:

1. Choose Tools, Options, View tab.
2. In the Formatting Marks section on the View tab, clear the All check box (if it's selected), and select the hidden characters you want to display. For example, select only the Paragraphs check box to show only paragraph marks.

After you specify which formatting marks you want to display, those marks will appear in your document, regardless of whether you click the Show/Hide button. (Note that the Show/Hide button continues to show all hidden characters when you toggle the button on, regardless of your View tab settings.) To hide formatting marks activated using the View tab, you'll need to revisit the View tab to reconfigure the formatting marks settings.

In addition to imposing a broader definition of paragraphs, Word enables you to associate specific formatting information with your paragraphs. When you format a paragraph, the formatting information is stored in that paragraph's paragraph mark. Word can then use the information stored in paragraph marks to apply paragraph properties to text inserted within a formatted paragraph. This setup also enables Word to apply a current paragraph's formatting to subsequent paragraphs when you press Enter at the end of the paragraph. This process is fairly logical. When you click at the end of a paragraph, the insertion point is positioned before the existing paragraph mark by default. (You can easily demonstrate this behavior by displaying paragraph marks and then clicking at the end of any paragraph—you'll be able to click to the left but not to the right of a paragraph mark.) Pressing Enter at the end of a paragraph essentially simulates the act of inserting information anywhere else within the existing paragraph, so the paragraph formatting is retained.

In Word, you can format paragraphs by setting the following paragraph formatting parameters:

- Paragraph alignment
- Indentation
- Spacing between lines
- Spacing before and after paragraphs
- Tabs

- Line and page breaks
- Hyphenation

In the following sections, you'll learn how to manage these paragraph features. The final section of this chapter describes how to create drop caps, because drop caps are most commonly used when formatting paragraphs.

Technically speaking, some tasks performed while you are in Outline view relate to paragraph formatting, but those topics aren't addressed in this chapter. Word offers a comprehensive collection of outlining tools and features; for a more in-depth look at outlining, see Chapter 11, "Outlining Documents for Clarity and Structure."

Avoiding Mixed Formatting in Merged Paragraphs

In some instances, you might be tempted to delete paragraph marks to merge paragraphs. This method works nicely if the paragraphs contain identical paragraph formatting information. But be aware that if you're merging paragraphs with dissimilar paragraph formatting settings, you'll most likely be left staring at a newly created paragraph that contains a patchwork of formatting.

Mismatched formatting occurs because when you merge two paragraphs by deleting a paragraph mark, neither paragraph takes on the other paragraph's formatting (which means that both blocks of text retain their original formatting settings). If the paragraph formatting for both is the same, no harm, no foul. But if the paragraph formatting varies, you'll end up with a formatting hodgepodge. To avoid formatting confusion, cut and paste information without the paragraph mark (or drag the text) from one paragraph into another, instead of deleting paragraph marks.

You can specify how to format the pasted text using the new Paste smart tag. In Word 2002, after you paste information, Word automatically displays a Paste smart tag, which provides the following formatting options:

- **Keep Source Formatting** retains the pasted information's original formatting.
- **Match Destination Formatting** changes the pasted text's formatting to match the formatting of the destination location.
- **Keep Text Only** retains only the text portion of the pasted information and removes all graphics and document formatting, such as shaded backgrounds and borders.
- **Apply Styles Or Formatting** opens the Styles And Formatting task pane, which you can use to apply a style to the pasted text.

Formatting Paragraphs by Aligning and Indenting Text

One of the most common paragraph formatting tasks is aligning paragraphs within a document. As you know, you can set margins to specify overall page and document alignment. But alignment matters don't stop there. You can also control alignment at the paragraph level by specifying text alignment and indentation. You can configure paragraph alignment settings using these familiar methods:

- Click buttons on the Formatting toolbar or press keyboard shortcuts to quickly format paragraphs.
- Use the horizontal ruler to align paragraphs visually.
- Configure settings in the Paragraph dialog box.

In this section, we'll examine the intricacies of each of these techniques.

For more information about setting margins and configuring overall page setup parameters, see Chapter 21, "Mastering Page Setup and Pagination."

Aligning Paragraphs Using Toolbar Buttons and Keyboard Shortcuts

The quickest way to apply paragraph formatting is to click within a paragraph or select a few paragraphs and then click a button on the Formatting toolbar or press a keyboard shortcut. Of course, these processes are limited by their default settings, but in many cases, the easiest route proves to be the best when it comes to paragraph formatting. To review which Formatting buttons and keyboard shortcuts can assist you in formatting paragraphs, see Table 7-1, on the next page.

Numbered and bulleted lists also use paragraph formatting settings. For more information about lists, see Chapter 8, "Enumerating with Lists, Lists, and More Lists."

Aligning Paragraphs Using the Ruler

Formatting toolbar buttons and keyboard shortcuts supply quick access to paragraph formatting options, but the Word ruler offers visually oriented people an intuitive and more precise method for controlling paragraph alignment. The trick to effectively using the ruler is to become comfortable with the ruler's markers. To get up to speed, have a look at Figure 7-2, which shows the latest incarnation of the Word ruler (which looks extremely similar to the ruler used in earlier versions of Word). The next few sections describe how to use the ruler markers to format paragraphs.

Table 7-1. Formatting Toolbar Buttons and Keyboard Shortcuts for Aligning and Formatting Paragraphs

Format	Toolbar button	Keyboard shortcut	Description
Align Left		Ctrl+L	Aligns information along the left margin of the page or specified area, with a jagged right edge.
Align Center		Ctrl+E	Aligns the midpoint of each line with the horizontal center of the page or area.
Align Right		Ctrl+R	Aligns information along the right margin of the page or specified area, with a jagged left edge.
Justify	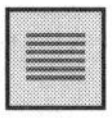	Ctrl+J	Aligns text flush with both the left and right margins of the page or specified area.
Line Spacing	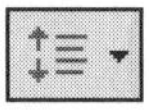	Ctrl+1 (single space), Ctrl+2 (double-space), or Ctrl+5 (1.5 space)	Controls the vertical spacing between lines of text. The Line Spacing tab includes a drop-down list of line spacing options.
Decrease Indent	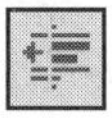	Ctrl+Shift+M	Decreases a paragraph's indent by one tab stop. By default, tab stops are set every 0.5 inch.
Increase Indent	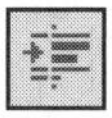	Ctrl+M	Increases a paragraph's indent by one tab stop. By default, tab stops are set every 0.5 inch.
Border	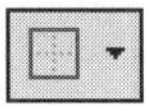	None	Applies a border to specified text. Clicking the Borders down arrow opens a drop-down menu of common border options.

Displaying and Configuring the Ruler

By default, Word displays the ruler in all views except Outline view. If you don't see the ruler, you can display it by choosing View, Ruler.

As you can see in Figure 7-2, the *0* spot on the ruler corresponds to the left margin setting. By default, the left and right margins are set to 1.25 inches on 8.5–by-11-inch paper. Thus, the default setup provides 6 inches between the margins for content (see Figure 7-1).

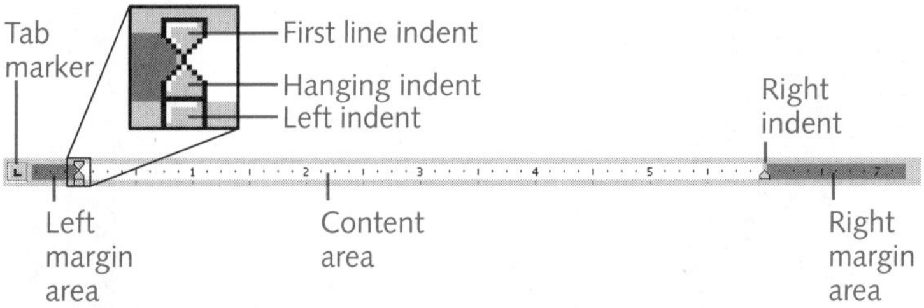

Figure 7-2. You can use the Word ruler to quickly and accurately align document information.

You've probably noticed that the ruler measurements are displayed in inches. If you prefer to use other units of measurement, you can change the default measurement unit setting as follows:

1. Choose Tools, Options, and click the General tab.
2. On the General tab, click the Measurement Units down arrow, select a measurement unit from the drop-down list, and click OK. Available options are Inches, Centimeters, Millimeters, Points, and Picas.

Adjusting Left and Right Indents

To adjust left and right indents using the ruler, click within the paragraph or select the paragraphs you want to adjust, or select the entire document (press Ctrl+A). Then click and drag the Left Indent or Right Indent marker on the ruler.

tip To move the First Line Indent marker along with the Hanging Indent marker, drag the small rectangle below the Hanging Indent marker on the ruler. Dragging the Left Indent rectangle retains the relative settings of the first line and left margin.

When you're working with tables, the ruler offers additional alignment markers, as shown in Figure 7-3. Namely, you can drag column markers to alter margin widths and row height markers to adjust row height; the margin markers move to correspond to the currently selected row and column. You can also indent table cell contents or entire columns.

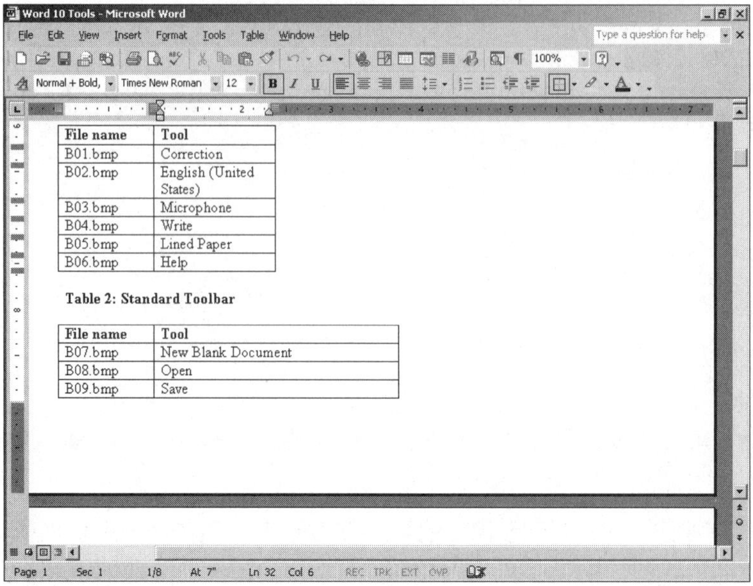

Figure 7-3. When you're working with tables in Print Layout view, you can use the vertical and horizontal rulers to adjust row heights and column widths.

For more information about resizing and aligning tables and table contents, see Chapter 18, "Organizing Concepts in Tables."

Creating First-Line and Hanging Indents

You can use the ruler to create a hanging indent or a first-line indent, as illustrated in Figure 7-4. To do so, click in the paragraph you want to format or select multiple paragraphs, and then drag the First Line Indent marker left or right to the desired location.

tip You can press Ctrl+T to create a hanging indent that aligns body text with the first tab marker. (By default, tabs are set every 0.5 inch.) You can press Ctrl+Shift+T to "unhang" an indent, regardless of how the hanging indent was created.

Aligning Paragraphs Using the Paragraph Dialog Box

Using toolbar buttons, keyboard shortcuts, and ruler markers to align paragraphs can be quick, but aligning paragraphs by using the Paragraph dialog box offers its own advantages. By configuring settings in the Paragraph dialog box, you can align paragraphs precisely as well as apply a number of paragraph formatting settings at one time.

To open the Paragraph dialog box, shown in Figure 7-5, choose Format, Paragraph, or right-click a paragraph (or selected paragraphs) and choose Paragraph on the shortcut menu.

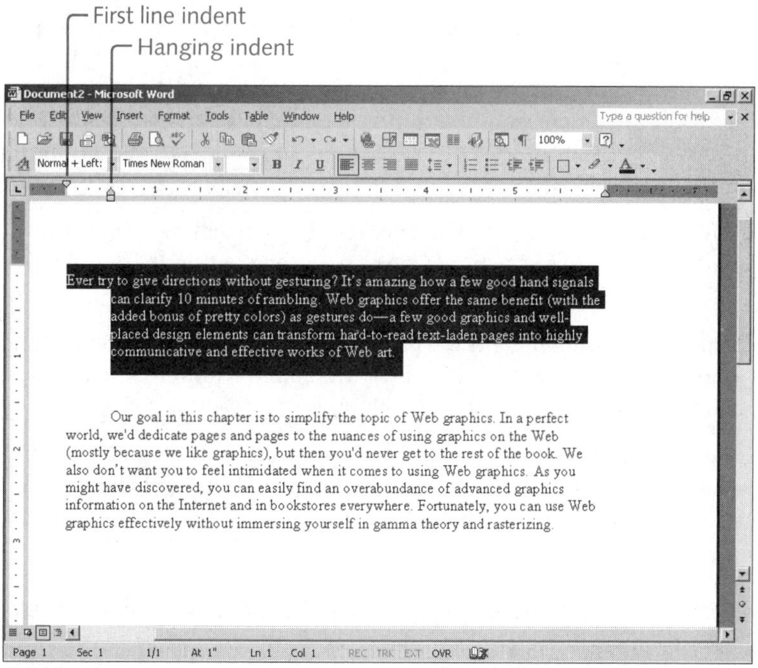

Figure 7-4. You can drag the First Line Indent marker to create a hanging indent or a first-line indent.

tip You can also access the Paragraph dialog box by clicking the Alignment or Indentation link in the Reveal Formatting task pane, as described in the section "Modifying Paragraph Attributes Using Reveal Formatting," on page 188.

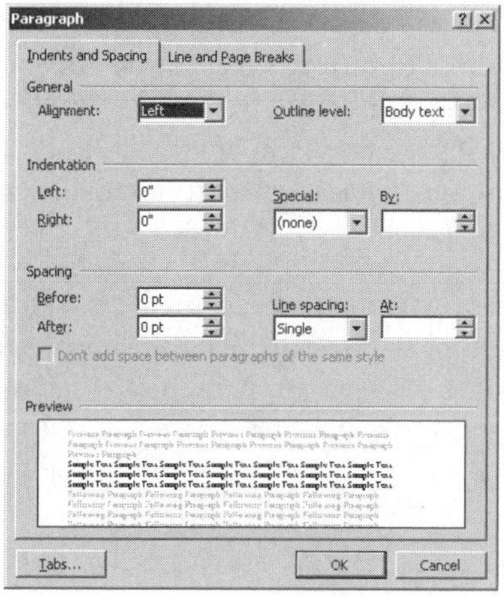

Figure 7-5. The Paragraph dialog box provides precise and complete control of paragraph formatting.

The Indents And Spacing tab offers the following paragraph alignment options:

- **Alignment** sets the position of paragraph contents, relative to the margins. Available alignment options are Left, Centered, Right, and Justified. The options in this drop-down list correspond to the alignment buttons on the Formatting toolbar.
- **Left Indentation** indents the paragraph from the left margin by the amount you specify. To display text or graphics within the left margin, enter a negative number in the Left box.
- **Right Indentation** indents the paragraph from the right margin by the amount you specify. To display text or graphics within the right margin, enter a negative number in the Right box.
- **Special and By** control the paragraph's first-line indentation. The Special drop-down list has three options: (None), First Line, and Hanging. The (None) option is selected by default. To specify the first-line indent, enter a value in the By box.

You can configure other paragraph settings in the Paragraph dialog box, including paragraph spacing parameters, as you'll see next.

Addressing Spacing Issues

You can adjust line spacing in your documents to help create a stylistic impression or improve readability. In particular, you can control line spacing within paragraphs as well as specify the amount of space above and below paragraphs.

Specifying Line Spacing

Long gone are the days when you had to press Return twice at the end of each line of text to double-space your paragraphs. Now creating line spacing is a simple matter of configuring paragraph settings before, during, or after you enter text. In Word, you can adjust line spacing in several ways, including using the Formatting toolbar, keyboard shortcuts, and the Paragraph dialog box.

newfeature!

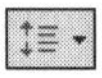

Line spacing

One fast way to configure a paragraph's line spacing is to click in the paragraph you want to configure or select multiple paragraphs and then click the Line Spacing button on the Formatting toolbar. The Line Spacing drop-down menu offers the following options: 1.0, 1.5, 2.0, 2.5, 3.0, or More. Selecting a number option instantly adjusts the selected paragraphs' line spacing. If you select More, the Paragraph dialog box opens.

tip **Apply line spacing to subsequent paragraphs**

After you select a line spacing option on the Line Spacing drop-down menu, you can click the Line Spacing button to apply the specified line spacing to subsequently selected paragraphs. To view the current line spacing setting, simply hover the mouse pointer over the Line Spacing button. The ToolTip will display the current setting in parenthesis–for example, *Line Spacing (3)*.

Using the Paragraph dialog box, you can adjust paragraph line spacing to a precise 1/10 of a point by using the Line Spacing option in conjunction with the At box on the Indents And Spacing tab (see Figure 7-5). By default, Word formats paragraphs using single-line spacing that is adjusted automatically based on the paragraph font's size. The Line Spacing drop-down list provides the following options:

- **Single** accommodates the largest font per line plus a small amount of extra space to create the appearance of a single-spaced paragraph. This is the default setting.
- **1.5 Lines** inserts one-and-one-half times the space allotted for a single line space to selected paragraph(s).
- **Double** inserts twice the space allotted for a single line space to the selected paragraph(s).
- **At Least** sets a minimum space for each line as specified in the At box. When Word encounters a larger font size or a graphic that won't fit in the minimum space, Word increases that line's spacing to accommodate the text or graphic.
- **Exactly** forces Word to apply an exact line spacing, as specified in the At box, regardless of what size text or graphics Word encounters. (By default, Word automatically accommodates the largest text or graphic in a line.)
- **Multiple** allows you to use the At box to specify a line spacing setting from 0.06 through 132 lines, in increments of 1/100 of a line. This option provides extra-fine control over line spacing.

To apply a line spacing setting using the Paragraph dialog box, click in the paragraph you want to format or select multiple paragraphs, and then choose Format, Paragraph, and click the Indents And Spacing tab, or right-click, choose Paragraph on the shortcut menu, and click the Indents And Spacing tab. Specify your line spacing settings, and click OK.

Last but not least, you can quickly adjust a paragraph's line spacing by clicking in a paragraph or selecting multiple paragraphs and pressing any of the following keyboard shortcuts:

- Ctrl+1 applies single-line spacing to selected paragraphs.
- Ctrl+2 applies double-line spacing to selected paragraphs.
- Ctrl+5 applies 1.5-line spacing to selected paragraphs.

Adjusting Spacing Above and Below Paragraphs

In addition to adding spacing between lines within your paragraphs, you can configure the space displayed above and below paragraphs. Adding space around paragraphs is an old typesetters' trick used to create a particular look-and-feel for a document and to improve readability. In Word, adding space above and below paragraphs produces the desired typesetting results and provides added control during document adjustments tasks. For example, you're not limited to separating paragraphs by one or two lines—you can separate paragraphs by 0.5 inch, 3.2 inches, and so forth. In addition, if you use spacing consistently within your document and you find that your document (or a section within your document) runs a little long or comes up a tad short, you can select the entire document, a section, or a few paragraphs and adjust the paragraph spacing options using the Paragraph dialog box to tighten up or lengthen your document.

To add spacing above and below selected paragraphs, follow these steps:

1. Click in the paragraph you want to configure, or select multiple paragraphs.
2. Choose Format, Paragraph, and click the Indents And Spacing tab.
3. Enter values in the Before and After boxes in the Spacing section, and click OK. The Before and After spacing options require you to specify in points how much space to insert before and after paragraphs. Keep in mind that 72 points equals approximately 1 inch.

If you create styles for your documents, you'll want to consider configuring the Before and After settings when you create paragraph styles. Adding before and after spacing to paragraph styles helps to ensure that spacing will be applied consistently and automatically throughout your document.

For more information about creating styles, see Chapter 10, "Using Styles to Increase Your Formatting Power."

tip **Add line spaces before paragraphs**

You can instantly add a full line space before a paragraph by selecting the paragraph(s) you want to format and pressing Ctrl+0 (zero). If you select multiple paragraphs, pressing Ctrl+0 adds a blank line space before each paragraph included in the selection.

Controlling Alignment Using Tabs

Back in the typewriter's heyday, tab stops were the end-all when it came to formatting tables, charts, and columns. Now Word offers a variety of text alignment tools, including specific features you can use to create columns, tables, and charts. But even with the advanced Word formatting features, tab stops continue to play a key role in aligning text and performing other tab-related activities. For example, tabs frequently come into play when you want to create simple lists, tables of contents (including dotted leader lines between titles and page numbers), center-aligned or decimal-aligned text, and so forth. Figure 7-6 shows a variety of tab styles in action.

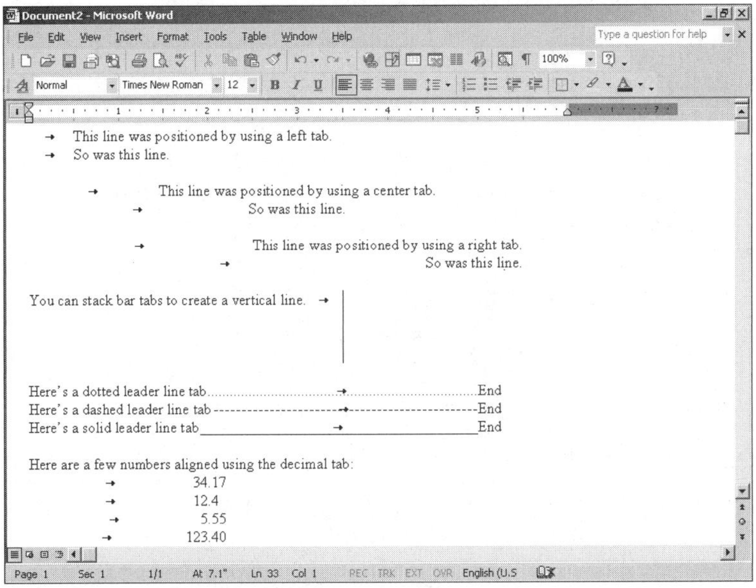

Figure 7-6. Word enables you to select from a variety of tab styles when you're adding tab stops.

New documents based on the default Normal.dot template include left-aligned tab stops every 0.5 inch, without displaying the tab settings in the ruler. You can adjust the default tab stop setting, add custom tabs, clear all tabs, and create tabs with leader lines. To adjust tabs, use the ruler or Tabs dialog box, as discussed in the following sections.

> **tip** **Display hidden characters**
>
> You can see where tabs are inserted in your document by displaying characters that are typically hidden. To do so, click the Show/Hide button on the Standard toolbar, or choose Tools, Options, click the View tab, select Tab Characters, and then click OK. Tabs appear as arrows, as shown in Figure 7-6.

Putting the Ruler to Work to Set Tabs

You can set tabs using the horizontal ruler in Word. Using the ruler has several advantages: you get visual feedback as soon as you set the tabs, and you can drag the ruler tabs to the left or right until you're satisfied with their positions. (You can even drag tabs off the ruler to delete them.) As soon as you set a tab on the ruler, your selected text moves to reflect the setting. To set tabs using the ruler, you need to complete the following three steps:

1. Click in a paragraph or select multiple paragraphs in which you want to set tabs, or position the insertion point at the location where you want to create a new paragraph containing the tab settings.
2. Set the desired tab style by clicking the button at the left end of the horizontal ruler. To cycle through the available tab styles, click the button repeatedly. Table 7-2 lists the available tab styles.
3. After you select a tab style, click the ruler to insert a tab. If you misposition a tab, you can drag it off the ruler to delete it or drag it left or right to reposition it.

Table 7-2. Ruler Markers

Button	Name	Description
	Left Tab	Text begins at the tab stop and continues right. This is the most commonly used tab style.
	Center Tab	Text is centered on the tab stop as you type.
	Right Tab	Text begins at the tab stop and moves left as new text is typed.
	Decimal Tab	Rows of numbers are aligned on the decimal point, regardless of the number of decimal places in each number.
	Bar Tab	Creates a vertical line. This setting enables you to draw vertical lines that span any number of horizontal lines of text.

(continued)

Table 7-2. *(continued)*

Button	Name	Description
	First Line Indent	Activates the First Line Indent feature. Click the ruler to set a first-line indent. (Using this method, you can create a first-line indent with a single click instead of dragging the ruler marker.)
	Hanging Indent	Activates the Hanging Indent feature. Click the ruler to position a hanging indent.

Carrying Tabs from One Paragraph to the Next

If you set tabs in a paragraph, the tab settings will automatically be included in the next paragraph if you press Enter at the end of the paragraph and continue typing to create a new paragraph. On the other hand, if you format tabs in a paragraph that's already embedded among other paragraphs, the tab settings will not automatically extend to subsequent paragraphs.

If you want to extend tab formatting to existing paragraphs, you need to select all the paragraphs you want to format before you set the tabs, or you can format a single paragraph and then use the Format Painter to copy the paragraph attributes to other paragraphs. Be sure to use the Format Painter option cautiously—Format Painter copies all paragraph formatting attributes, not just the tab settings. (For more information about the Format Painter, see Chapter 5, "Adding Panache with Text Formatting and Special Characters.")

Finally, if you want to set tabs throughout an entire document, press Ctrl+A to select the document, and then set your tabs on the ruler. Be aware that setting tabs for an entire document might affect existing tabs, so be sure to review your document after you make wide-ranging changes. Also, you might want to clear any existing tabs before inserting your new "global" tags. The process of deleting tabs is described in the section "Clearing Custom Tabs," on page 187.

Creating Tabs Using the Tabs Dialog Box

In addition to clicking the ruler to create tabs, you can add tabs using the Tabs dialog box. When you use the Tabs dialog box, you can set tabs using precise measurements. You can also create tabs that use leader lines. (*Leaders* insert formatting, such as dots or dashes, in the space leading up to the tab stop.) Neither of these tasks can be accomplished using the ruler. The main drawback of creating tabs using the Tabs dialog box is that you won't be able to see how your tabs affect your text until after you close the dialog box and view your document. To access the Tabs dialog box, perform any of the following actions:

- Choose Format, Tabs.
- Click the Tabs button in the Paragraph dialog box.
- Double-click an existing tab on the horizontal ruler.

Figure 7-7 shows the Tabs dialog box. If the currently selected paragraph contains any tabs when you open the Tabs dialog box, the tab positions will be listed in the Tab Stop Position list. Notice that the Default Tab Stops option is set to *0.5* by default.

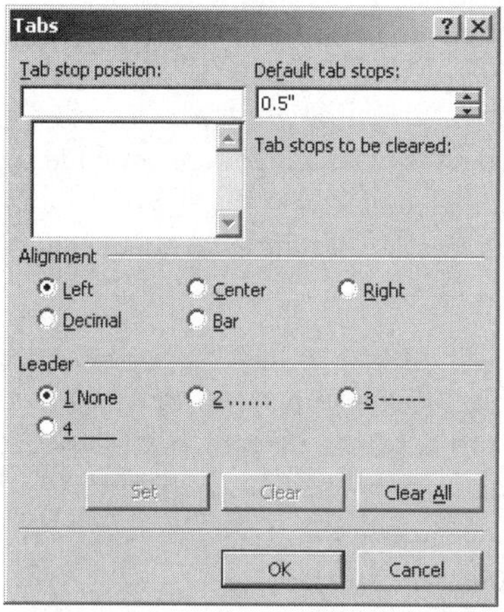

Figure 7-7. The Tabs dialog box enables you to modify the default tab stop settings, insert tabs at precise positions, create leader lines, and clear existing tabs.

To set tabs using the Tabs dialog box, follow these steps:

1. Click in the paragraph or select multiple paragraphs in which you want to set tabs, or position your insertion point at the location where you want to create a new paragraph containing the tab settings.
2. Open the Tabs dialog box (by choosing Format, Tabs or double-clicking an existing tab).
3. Type a tab location, such as **1.75**, in the Tab Stop Position box.
4. In the Alignment section, specify whether you want a left, center, right, decimal, or bar tab.
5. Select a leader line style, if desired, and then click Set. The tab will be listed in the Tab Stop Position list.
6. Add more tabs, if necessary, by repeating steps 3 and 4, and then click OK to close the Tabs dialog box when you've finished setting tabs.

tip **Adjust the default tab and indent setting**

To change the default tab and indent setting, you can type a new setting in the Default Tab Stops box in the Tabs dialog box. For example, you could change the default 0.5-inch setting to 0.75 inch. The default setting is used if custom tabs aren't set when you press Tab or click the Increase Indent and Decrease Indent buttons on the Formatting toolbar.

Clearing Custom Tabs

Just as you can add custom tabs using the horizontal ruler and the Tabs dialog box, you can also clear tabs using these same tools. You can even clear all tabs at one time if you're really in "spring cleaning" mode. To remove tabs, select the paragraph(s) you want to modify, and then perform one of the following procedures:

- Drag the tab markers off the ruler. (Simply click a tab marker and drag it down into the document area.)
- Open the Tabs dialog box (by choosing Format, Tabs or double-clicking an existing tab), select the tab you want to delete, and click Clear.
- Open the Tabs dialog box, and click Clear All.
- Click the Tabs link in the Reveal Formatting task pane (as described in the following section).

Troubleshooting

Ruler Options Are Unavailable When Multiple Paragraphs Are Selected

In some instances, you might want to modify paragraphs that have different tab settings so that they have consistent tab settings. You can do so using both the horizontal ruler and the Tab dialog box. The easiest way to accomplish this task is shown here:

1. Select the paragraph(s) you want to format. If the tab markers on the horizontal ruler appear grayed, the tab settings aren't currently applied to the entire selection. (You probably already know this, so the grayed tab markers shouldn't phase you.)
2. Double-click a grayed tab marker (or choose Format, Tabs) to open the Tabs dialog box.
3. Click the Clear All button, click OK, and then click the horizontal ruler to define tab settings that will apply to the entire selection.

newfeature!

Modifying Paragraph Attributes Using Reveal Formatting

After you apply paragraph alignment settings (as well as font and section formatting settings), you can view your settings in the Reveal Formatting task pane. To open the Reveal Formatting task pane, choose Format, Reveal Formatting, or select Reveal Formatting on the task pane's drop-down menu. Figure 7-8 shows the Reveal Formatting task pane in action.

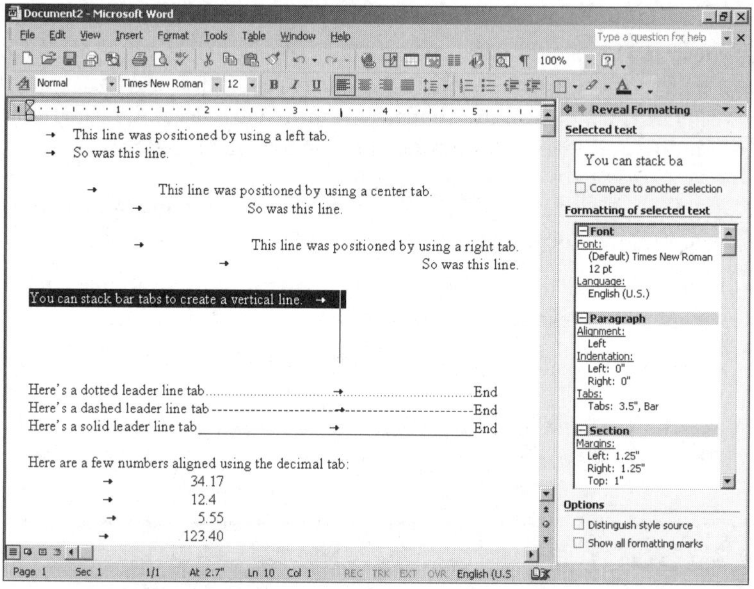

Figure 7-8. The Reveal Formatting task pane provides quick access to font, paragraph, and section formatting settings. Click a link to open the appropriate formatting dialog box.

As you can see, the Reveal Formatting task pane is a wellspring of formatting information, but its usefulness doesn't stop there. The Reveal Formatting task pane also provides links to the appropriate dialog boxes if you need to modify any format settings. Notice that the task pane is divided into Font, Paragraph, and Section sections (representing the three levels of formatting used in Word documents). Within each section, you can see links to formatting attributes set within the current selection. You can click any link to open the dialog box associated with the selected settings. For example, if you click the Tabs link, the Tabs dialog box opens so that you can easily configure tab settings for the current paragraph. Table 7-3 lists more examples of which dialog box opens when you click a formatting link.

Table 7-3. **Reveal Formatting Links and Dialog Box Associations**

Link	Associated Dialog Box and Tab
Font	Font dialog box, Font tab
Language	Language dialog box
Alignment	Paragraph dialog box, Indents And Spacing tab
Indentation	Paragraph dialog box, Indents And Spacing tab
Tabs	Tabs dialog box
Margins	Page Setup dialog box, Margins tab
Layout	Page Setup dialog box, Layout tab
Paper	Page Setup dialog box, Paper tab

After you click a link in the task pane and modify settings in a particular dialog box, click OK to returned to the task pane and document window. You'll be able to see your new format settings implemented in the document.

Controlling Line and Page Breaks

In addition to aligning paragraphs, adjusting line spacing, and setting tabs, you can fine-tune the flow of your paragraphs by controlling line and page breaks. The main area to turn to when you want to control line and page breaks is the Line And Page Breaks tab in the Paragraph dialog box, shown in Figure 7-9.

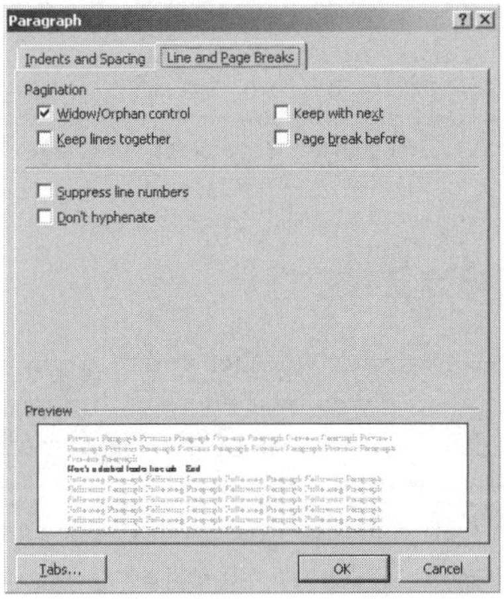

Figure 7-9. You can control line and page breaks to some extent in Word by selecting check boxes on the Line And Page Breaks tab.

To apply the line and page break settings, select the text you want to format, display the Line And Page Breaks tab, and select the appropriate check boxes. The following line and page break options are available:

- **Widow/Orphan Control** ensures that the last line of a paragraph doesn't appear by itself at the top of a new page (a widow) or that the first line of a paragraph isn't displayed by itself at the bottom of a page (an orphan). Typesetters have been struggling to avoid widows and orphans for centuries. The Widow/Orphan Control check box is selected by default.
- **Keep Lines Together** prevents page breaks from occurring within selected paragraphs. When a page break is needed, Word moves the entire paragraph to the next page.
- **Keep With Next** prevents a page break from occurring between the selected paragraph and the following paragraph. This feature can come in handy when you're using paragraphs that work together to create a single element, such as a table and a table caption.
- **Page Break Before** inserts a manual page break before the selected paragraph. You might want to configure this option if you think the selection might cause pagination problems or if you want to ensure that content, such as a section title, appears at the top of a new page.

tip To apply the pagination controls found on the Line And Page Breaks tab in the Paragraph dialog box to an entire document, press Ctrl+A to select the entire document before configuring the pagination check boxes.

The Line And Page Breaks tab also contains a Suppress Line Numbers check box, which prevents line numbers from appearing if you're using the line numbering feature. For more information about line numbering, see Chapter 21, "Mastering Page Setup and Pagination."

Taking Charge of Hyphenation

When you work with paragraphs, you need to decide whether you're going to hyphenate words at the ends of lines to create more evenly aligned edges within paragraphs. By default, hyphenation is turned off in Word. This means that if a word is too long to fit on a line, the entire word is moved to the beginning of the next line. If you prefer, you can activate Word's built-in Hyphenation feature to eliminate white space and gaps along the edges of your text. When you use the Hyphenation feature, you can opt to apply hyphenation manually or automatically, as follows:

- **Automatic Hyphenation.** Word automatically hyphenates an entire document. If you later change the document's contents, Word re-hyphenates the document as needed, while you work.

- **Manual Hyphenation.** Word searches for instances in which hyphenation is needed, and then you manually confirm whether to add a hyphen at each proposal. If you later modify the document, Word displays and prints only the hyphens that fall at the ends of lines. To re-hyphenate the document, you would have to repeat the manual hyphenation process.

Either way, the process of adding hyphenation begins in the Hyphenation dialog box, shown in Figure 7-10. To access the Hyphenation dialog box, choose Tools, Language, Hyphenation. The followings sections briefly describe how to control hyphenation.

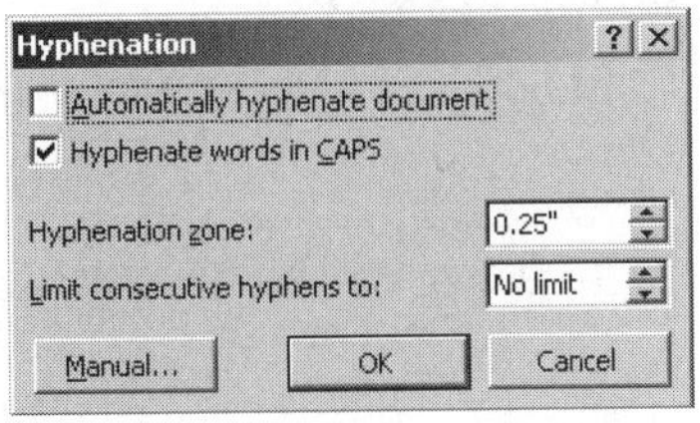

Figure 7-10. The Hyphenation dialog box enables you to automatically or manually hyphenate your documents.

> **tip** **Insert nonbreaking hyphens**
>
> You can format nonbreaking hyphens to prevent a hyphenated word, number, or phrase from breaking if it falls at the end of a line. For example, you might not want to break a phone number at the end of the line. To insert a nonbreaking hyphen, press Ctrl+Shift+hyphen.

Hyphenating an Entire Document Automatically

To hyphenate an entire document automatically, follow these steps:

1. Choose Tools, Language, Hyphenation to open the Hyphenation dialog box.
2. Select the Automatically Hyphenate Document check box.
3. In the Hyphenation Zone box, enter the amount of acceptable white space to leave between the end of the last word in a line and the right margin. If you want fewer hyphens, make the Hyphenation Zone value larger; if you want to reduce jagged edges, make the Hyphenation Zone value smaller.
4. In the Limit Consecutive Hyphens To box, type the maximum number of consecutive lines that can end with a hyphen.

> **tip** If you want to turn off the Automatic Hyphenation feature as well as remove automatically inserted hyphens, simply open the Hyphenation dialog box, clear the Automatically Hyphenate Document check box, and click OK.

Hyphenating Part of a Document Automatically

To hyphenate part of a document automatically, follow these steps:

1. Select the text you don't want to hyphenate.
2. Choose Format, Paragraph, Line And Page Breaks tab. Select the Don't Hyphenate check box, and click OK.
3. Choose Tools, Language, Hyphenation to open the Hyphenation dialog box.
4. Select the Automatically Hyphenate Document check box.
5. Configure the Hyphenation Zone and Limit Consecutive Hyphens To settings as described above, and then click OK.

This procedure will hyphenate your document in all areas except the section you've excluded.

Hyphenating All or Part of a Document Manually

When you hyphenate a document manually, you can hyphenate the entire document or you can select part of the document before you open the Hyphenation dialog box. To hyphenate text manually, either select the text you want to hyphenate or make sure that no text is selected if you want to hyphenate the entire document, and then follow these steps:

1. Choose Tools, Language, Hyphenation to open the Hyphenation dialog box.
2. Click Manual to have Word scan the document. When Word identifies a word or phrase that should be hyphenated, the Manual Hyphenation dialog box opens, as shown in Figure 7-11. You can click Yes to insert the specified hyphen; use the arrow keys to reposition the hyphen location and then click Yes; click No to ignore the suggestion and move to the next word; or click Cancel to end the hyphenating process.

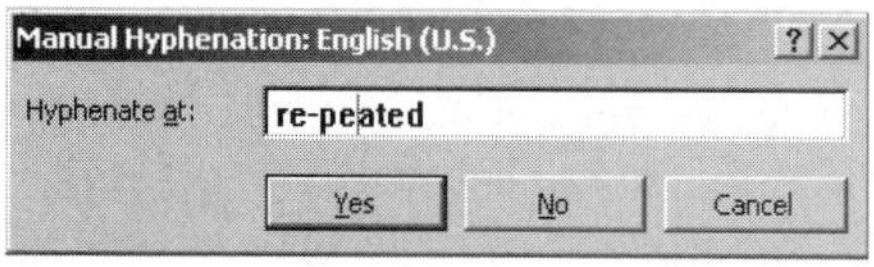

Figure 7-11. When you manually hyphenate a document, the Manual Hyphenation dialog box is displayed each time a word needs to be hyphenated. You then specify how to handle the hyphenation for that instance.

Creating Drop Caps in Existing Paragraphs

A popular formatting task frequently associated with paragraphs is the creation of drop caps. *Drop caps* refer to the large letters that appear at the very beginning of chapters or sections, as shown in Figure 7-12.

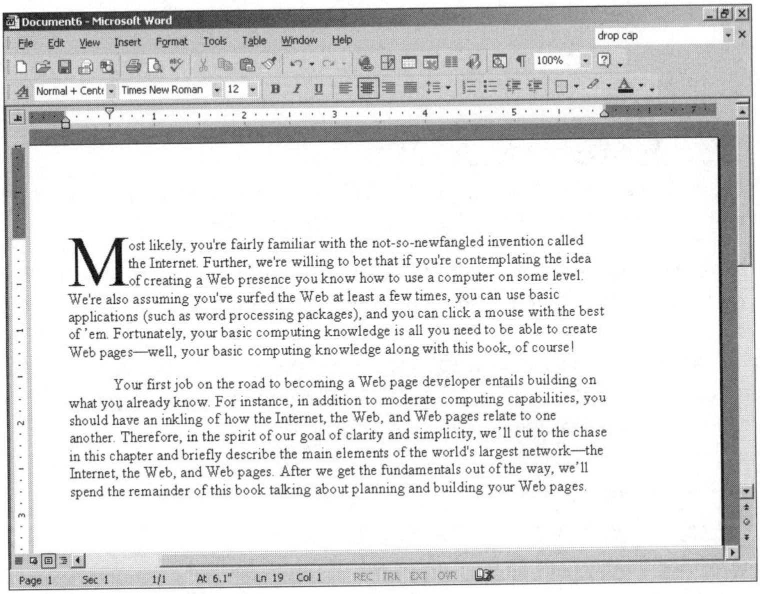

Figure 7-12. Drop caps are large, stylized letters that are frequently used to identify the beginning of a prominent section in a document, such as a chapter.

Word provides an easy way for you to add drop caps to paragraphs. When you use the Drop Cap feature, Word basically converts the first letter of a paragraph to a graphic. After the graphic is automatically created and situated, you can further modify the drop cap just as you modify any graphic element. To create a drop cap, follow these steps:

1. Click in the paragraph that you want to customize with a drop cap.
2. Choose Format, Drop Cap. The Drop Cap dialog box opens, as shown in Figure 7-13.

For more information about working with graphics, see Part III "Adding Value with Graphics and Objects."

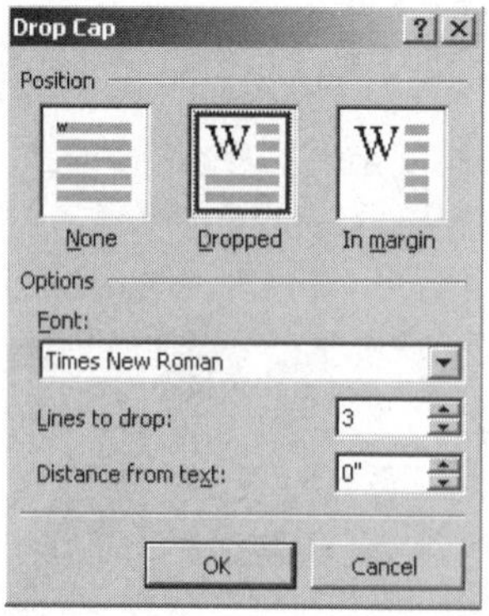

Figure 7-13. The Drop Cap dialog box enables you to set parameters before the first-letter graphic is created and inserted in your document.

3. Click the Dropped option, configure any formatting parameters you want to customize Font, Lines To Drop, and Distance From Text), and then click OK.

If you decide you prefer not to display a drop cap in your paragraph, you can easily remove the formatting. To do so, click in the paragraph containing the drop cap, open the Drop Cap dialog box, click None, and click OK.

Perking Up Paragraphs with Borders and Shading

Another common method of customizing paragraphs is to add borders around and add shading behind selected paragraphs. To accomplish this simple feat, follow these steps:

1. Select the paragraph you want to format.
2. Choose Format, Borders And Shading.
3. Select the border or shading options you want to apply to the selected paragraph, and then click OK.

For more information about the ins and outs of creating borders and shading, see Chapter 24, "Drawing Attention to Your Document with Borders and Shading."

Chapter 8

Enumerating with Lists, Lists, and More Lists

Are you a list maker? Do you organize your shopping trips by lists, your to-do tasks by lists, and your team members by lists? And do you often find yourself turning chaos into process by using lists? "No, Jason—put your homework in your folder, *then* in your book bag, and *then* by the front door!"

Our lives are filled with items, people, places, and things that need to be ordered into some kind of system that works. Our documents are no different. They need organization and clarity. And they need a format that works. Lists help us create that format.

Adding bulleted and numbered lists to your document can go a long way toward making your document more readable, which is an achievement your readers will be grateful for. Lists can also help you make your point clearly and succinctly, enabling the ideas to stand out instead of being lost inside a larger paragraph. This chapter shows you how to create lists—both bulleted and numbered—in your Microsoft Word documents. You'll learn the ins and outs of list-making and discover how lists can make your work easier and more effective, whether you create short articles, long dissertations, or something in between.

List-Making the Effective Way

Like its predecessors, Word 2002 includes automated features that make creating lists a fairly simple process. Within that process, however, you have a number of choices to make—and some quirks to navigate around.

Throughout this chapter, both bulleted and numbered lists are referred to simply as lists, because they behave the same way. When you choose a bullet, of course, you're using a special symbol, character, or graphic to start the text line. When you use a number, you're selecting the font, size, and color of the numeral you want to use. In addition, you can use roman numerals, letters, and other line identifiers in numbered lists (a technique covered later in this chapter in the section "Improving Numbered Lists").

When Bullets Work

Word gives you the capacity to create bulleted lists with a number of different looks. You can change the character that leads off the item; you can change color; you can change indents. You can place bulleted lists side by side in a multi-column format, if you choose. Here are some guidelines to remember when you create bulleted lists:

- **Be concise.** Fewer words make a bigger impact. Unless you *must* include paragraphs of text for each bullet item, pare your prose down to fewer than three sentences if you can.
- **Stick to the point.** A general rule is "one point, one bullet." Don't try to cram more than one idea into each bullet item.
- **Be clear.** Flowery language isn't necessary—clear and simple is best.
- **Don't overdo it.** Bullets can be so much fun (and easier than big blocks of text) that you might be tempted to use them liberally throughout your document. Resist the temptation to over-bulletize your work and use them only when they bring clarity to your content.
- **Choose a bullet that makes sense.** If your report is about a new model of fishing boat your company is manufacturing, would baby-bottle bullet characters really make sense? Probably not. Be sure to fit the bullet characters you choose with the style and expectation of your audience.
- **Don't use too many at once.** Research shows that the average Web page visitor moves on after seven seconds, and logic says that the average reader tunes out after too many steps or bullets. Don't make your lists burdensome for your readers. Say what you need to say in five to seven bullet points and move back to paragraph style.

> **tip** **Bullet them in any order**
>
> Bullets are ideal for those times when you want to convey short, to-the-point pieces of information. The fact that you use bullets instead of numbers implies to your reader that the points can be read and applied in any order; there's no necessary sequence in a bulleted list.

When Numbers Matter

Whether you need numbered lists in your documents will be determined by the type of work you create. If you're writing a how-to manual on fly-fishing, you might have quite a few numbered steps, explaining important steps like preparing equipment, finding the right spot, and setting up for your first cast. If you're creating a marketing plan with a timeline and an action sequence, your steps will define a process that builds a bigger promotions system. Whatever the purpose of your numbered list, you can make sure it's most effective in these ways:

- **Remember the white space.** Whether you're working with bulleted or numbered lists, the white space in your document is as important as the text on the page—it might be a humbling statement, but it's true. White space gives your readers' eyes a rest, so don't crowd your list items together too closely.
- **Use numbers that fit your style.** In an upbeat publication, you might want to use specialty numbers or a casual font with oversized numbers. In a more serious piece, you'll want the numbers you select to carry a more professional tone.
- **Alignment matters.** Similar to the spacing issues for bulleted and numbered lists, the alignment of your list matters. Make sure the indents on the second line of the list item align with the first character of text.

tip **Number list items when order matters**

The items in a numbered list actually communicate a sequence: First we have the team meeting; then we do the plan; then we write the report and present it. These items, in a list, would be numbered because they show a process. Numbered lists are used to explain processes or to show the pieces of a whole (such as, "Four key ideas contribute to this finding").

Preparing to Create Lists

You need to make sure that you have AutoFormat configured for lists and bullets if you want to create bulleted and numbered lists automatically as you type. Begin by following these steps:

1. Choose Tools, AutoCorrect Options. The AutoCorrect dialog box appears.
2. Click the AutoFormat As You Type tab and make sure the Format Beginning Of List Item Like The One Before It check box is selected in the Automatically As You Type section.
3. Next, click the AutoFormat tab and make sure that List Styles and Automatic Bulleted Lists are both selected in the Apply section at the top of the tab.

4 Click OK to return to your document.

For more about working with automatic text tools like AutoFormat, AutoCorrect, and AutoText, see Chapter 6, "Putting Text Tools to Work."

Creating a Quick List

Word enables you to create both lists on the fly and lists from text you've already entered. To create a quick list while you type, follow these steps:

1. Place the insertion point where you want to add the list.

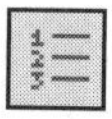

Numbering

2. Click the Numbering button on the Formatting toolbar if you want to create a numbered list.
   OR

   Click the Bullets button on the Formatting toolbar if you want to create a bulleted list.

Bullets

3. Type your first item and press Enter. The list item is added and the next bullet or number is added. (See Figure 8-1.)
4. Continue entering your list as needed.

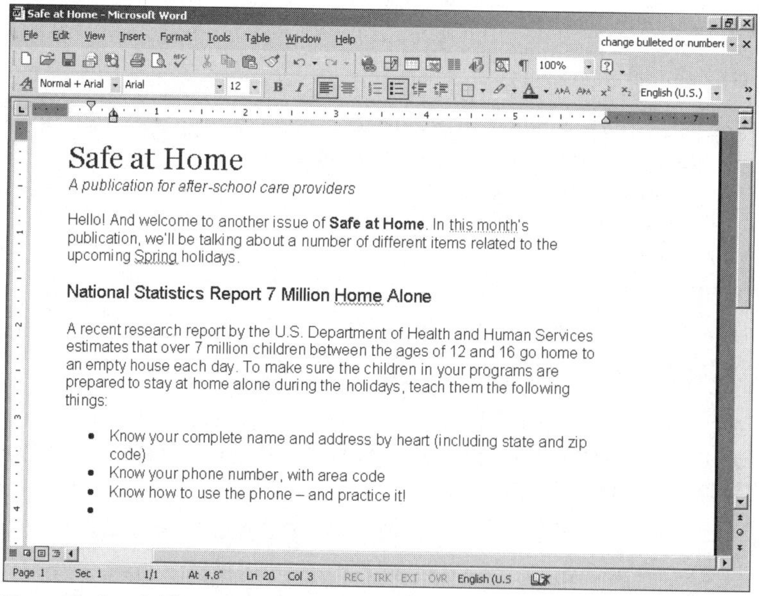

Figure 8-1. Adding a quick list uses Word's default bullet style.

This simple list uses only the Word default bullet or number style—you didn't have any say in the font, color, design, or spacing of the list. But those items are all easily changed and controlled, which you'll discover as you read through the rest of this chapter.

> newfeature!
> **tip** **Copy a format in the Styles And Formatting task pane**
>
> You can easily copy a format you've created in Word 2002, and you don't need to create a style to do it. Just display the Styles And Formatting task pane by choosing Format, Styles And Formatting. Click the new text to which you want to apply the format you've just created. Then, in the Pick Formatting To Apply section in the task pane, scroll to the format you want to apply. Word applies the format as selected.

Ending a List—the Way You Want

One of the challenges users often face with bulleted and numbered lists is that the lists seem to want to continue on forever. After you press Enter on your last list entry, yet another bullet (or number) shows up. Get rid of the extra bullet or number by doing one of three things:

- Click the Bullets or Numbering toolbar button to turn off the feature.
- Press Backspace to delete the item.
- Press Enter twice after the last item instead of once.

> **caution** If spacing is important in your document, avoid the last option because it adds an unnecessary line space in your document.

Customizing Lists

The default Word settings for bulleted and numbered lists are fine when you're creating a quick, simple document that will be passed around the office and eventually end up in the dumpster. But what about those special reports you create or the procedure manuals that others rely on? Those need to have a more professional look and feel, and the treatment of the lists in your document suddenly become more important.

Enhancing Bulleted Lists

You can improve a basic bulleted list in several different ways. You might want to customize your list by choosing your bullet style from the bullet library, selecting a picture bullet, creating your own bullets, or changing indents and spacing for your bullet items.

Choosing a New Bullet from the Palette

Word 2002 gives you a palette of seven preset bullet styles to choose from and a virtually unlimited supply of bullet options you can pull from symbol typefaces, graphical libraries, and more. To choose a new bullet character for your list, follow these steps:

1. Select the list items with the bullets you want to change.
2. Choose Format, Bullets And Numbering. The Bullets And Numbering dialog box appears. (See Figure 8-2.)
3. Select the new bullet you want to use by clicking the preview box of your choice.
4. Click OK to return to your document. The bullet character is added and your list is updated with the new style.

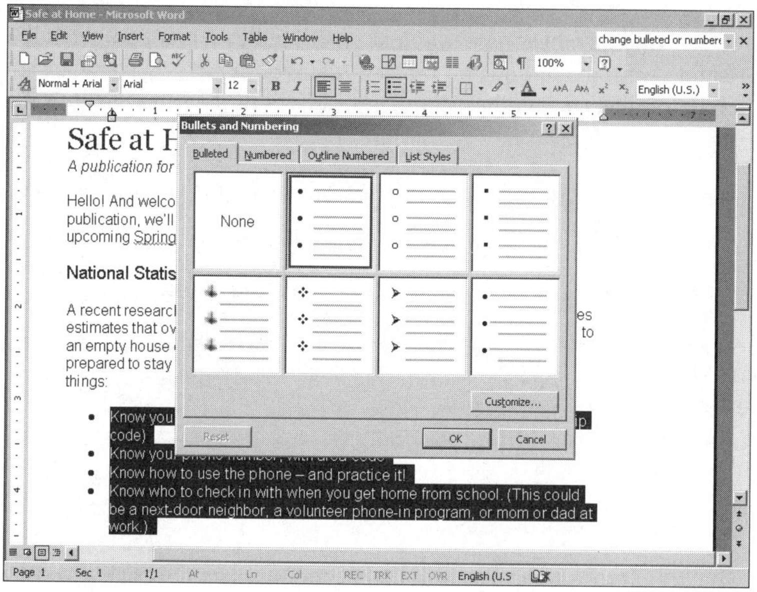

Figure 8-2. Changing the default bullet to another Word bullet style is a simple matter of point-and-click.

tip **Right-click to add bullets or numbering**

A quick way into the Bullets And Numbering dialog box is to select your list and then right-click. Choose Bullets And Numbering from the shortcut menu, and the dialog box appears.

Selecting a Different Bullet Character

If one of the preset palette offerings doesn't work for you, you can click the Customize button in the Bullets And Numbering dialog box to start the process of changing your bullet character choices. In the Customize Bulleted List dialog box, you see the bullet character choices across the top of the dialog box. Beneath the current bullet selections are buttons that allow you to choose three very different types of bullet modifications: Font, Character, and Picture. (See Figure 8-3.)

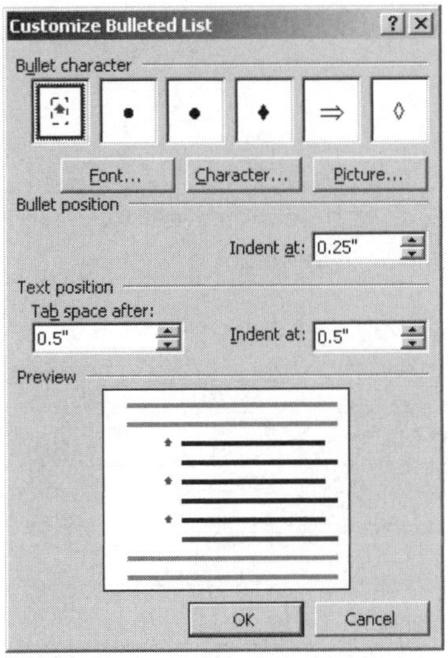

Figure 8-3. The Customize Bulleted List dialog box gives you the means to change the font and character you use for bullets. You can also change bullet spacing and text position here.

Changing the Bullet Font

When you click the Font button in the Customize Bulleted List dialog box, the Font dialog box is displayed. (See Figure 8-4, on the next page.) Here you can select a different typeface and change font settings for the bullet character you choose.

There are a number of different typefaces in Word that include symbols that can be used as bullet characters, as Table 8-1, on the next page, shows. (Actually, you can use *any* character, alphabetic or otherwise, as a bullet character. But unless you're creating an outline, letters as bullets can be less clear for readers than graphical symbols.)

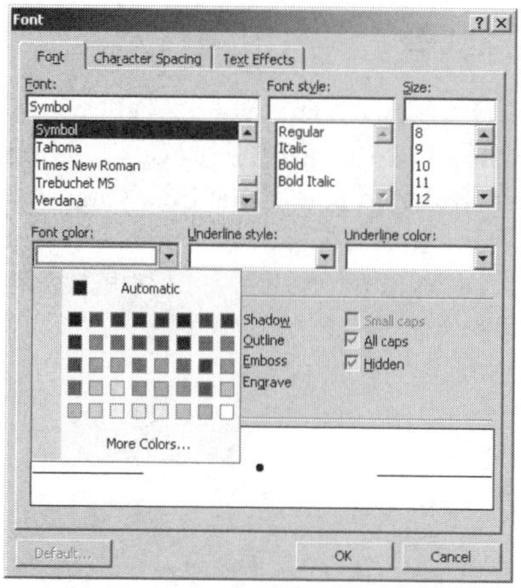

Figure 8-4. The Font dialog box enables you to choose a different typeface and change style, color, and text effects for the bullet character you use.

Table 8-1. Fonts Used for Bullets in Word 2002

Typeface	Sample
MS Outlook	
MT Extra	∩ □ … ⋯ ⋮ ⋰ ⋱
Symbol	∞ *f* ♣ ♦ ♥ ♠ ↔ ← ↑ → ↓
Webdings	
Wingdings	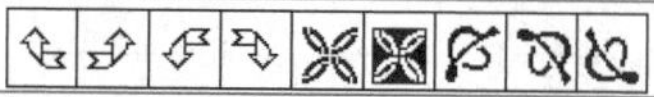
Wingdings2	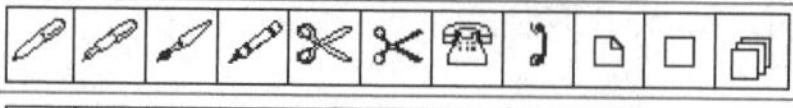
Wingdings3	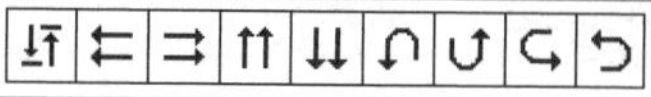

Changing the Character

When you click the Character button in the Customized Bulleted List dialog box, the display of characters for the selected font appears. (See Figure 8-5.) You also have the option of choosing a different font from this dialog box if you choose, by clicking the Font down arrow and choosing the typeface you want from the list; otherwise, you can click the character you want and click OK.

newfeature!

One new addition in Word 2002: Now you can see the numeric character code for the character you select. This enables you to be sure you've used the same bullet throughout your document and in other documents you produce that need a consistent style.

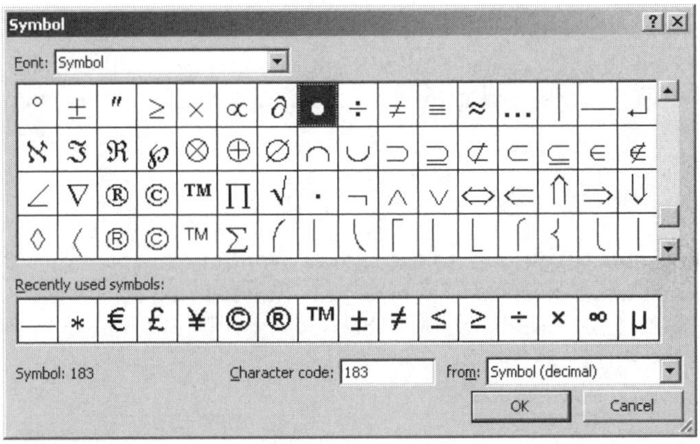

Figure 8-5. Click the symbol you want to select a new bullet character. Make note of the character code of the item you select if you need to be consistent with lists in other documents.

Using a Picture Bullet

We live in an age of graphical everything—the Web has raised the bar on what we expect in terms of aesthetic design of our information. No longer will boring round and black bullets hold readers' interest for long—now you can use picture bullets in your documents to add spots of color and interest to your traditional text.

What is a picture bullet? Simply a graphic image that's small enough to use as a bullet character. Word offers a range of bullet styles and shapes. To display the Picture Bullet dialog box and see what the offerings are, click Picture in the Customize Bulleted List dialog box. A range of picture bullets is displayed, as Figure 8-6 shows.

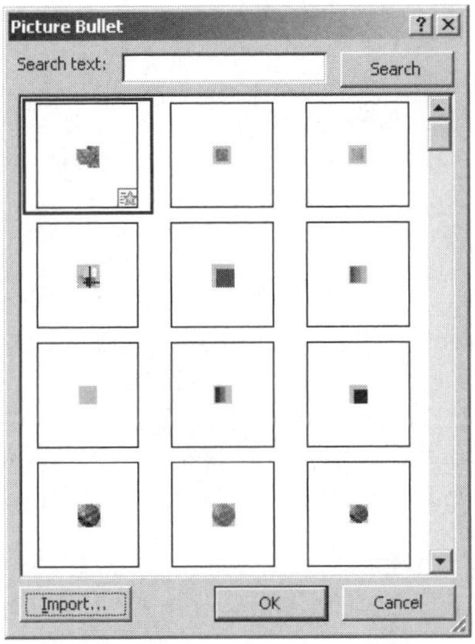

Figure 8-6. Picture bullets are displayed in a dialog box offering search capabilities.

To select a picture bullet, simply click the one you want, and Word adds it to the bullet character choices in the Customize Bulleted List dialog box. You'll then be able to select it as the bullet of choice in the Bullets And Numbering dialog box (which is where we started).

Creating Your Own Bullets

If you create other bullets you want to use in your Word documents, you can add them in the Picture Bullet dialog box. Display the Picture Bullet dialog box by clicking Picture in the Customize Bulleted List dialog box; then click the Import button in the bottom left corner of the dialog box.

tip To use your images as Word picture bullets, save the files in GIF, BMP, or JPEG format.

The Add Clips To Gallery dialog box appears, as shown in Figure 8-7. Navigate to the folder containing the file you want to add; click it and click Add. Word adds the bullet to the Picture Bullet dialog box and you can select it as you would any of the predesigned bullets displayed.

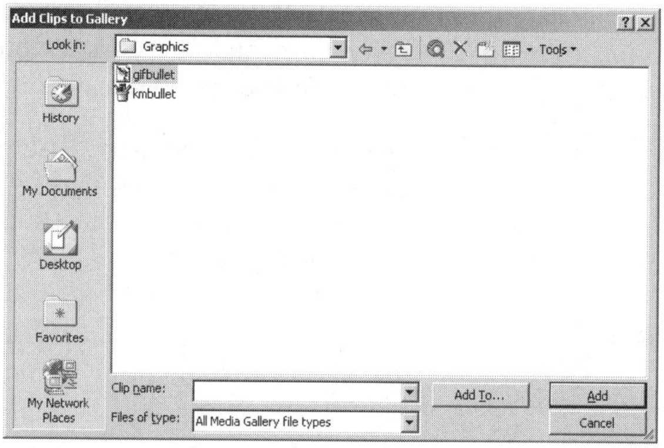

Figure 8-7. Add your own picture bullets by clicking the Import button in the Picture Bullet dialog box, selecting the file you want, and clicking Add.

Changing the Bullet Indent

When you first create a bullet the Word-default way, the program indents the bullet by ¼ of an inch, or .25 on your ruler. Text begins at the .5 marker. Although this is the default setting, you might want to change the indent level to either move the bullet farther out toward the text margin, or inward, to put more space between the edge of the page and the bullet character and text. Make your changes in one of two ways:

- **Increase indent.** To increase the space between the left edge of the page and the bullet character, click the Indent At up arrow in the Bullet Position section of the Customize Bulleted List dialog box. You can also click in the box and type the value you want.

- **Decrease indent.** To decrease the indent, click the down arrow or click in the Indent At box and type the value you want.

tip To display the ruler quickly in your Word work space, choose View, Ruler.

Modifying Text Position

Depending on the bullet character you choose, you might want to add more space between the character and the beginning of the text. By default, Word separates the bullet and the text beginning by ¼ of an inch, or .25 on your ruler. The text itself begins at the .5 marker.

You can change both these settings by changing the Text Position settings. Here's how:

1. Make sure the bullet items are selected in your document.
2. Choose Format, Bullets And Numbering.
3. In the Bullets And Numbering dialog box, click Customize. The Customize Bulleted List dialog box appears.
4. In the Text Position section of the dialog box, click the up or down arrow in the Tab Space After box, to change the setting as needed. This setting controls the amount of space between the bullet character and the beginning of the text.
5. In the Indent At box, click the up or down arrow to increase or decrease the position at which you want the text to begin. In both this and the previous step, you can click in the text box and type the value if you prefer.
6. Click OK to accept the new bullet settings and return to your document.

note As always, if you don't like the changes, you can press Ctrl+Z to undo your last operation.

Improving Numbered Lists

Similar to bulleted lists, numbered lists allow you to make your own choices about the look and format of the numerals used. Specifically, you can make modifications by choosing a different font, selecting the number style you want, and choosing the number and text position of your list text.

note Because the process of changing the font, number position, and text position in the Customize Numbered List dialog box is the same as for changing the bullet and text font and position (covered earlier in this chapter in the sections, "Changing the Bullet Indent" and "Modifying Text Position"), those steps are not repeated here for numbered lists. See also "Changing the Bullet Font" on page 201 to learn how to change the font for the numbers you use.

Choosing a Numbering Scheme

Numbers provide a lot of character for the numbered lists they lead. You might use simple traditional characters or larger, colorful characters, depending on the nature of your publication. Begin by selecting the numbered list you want to change. Then follow these steps:

1. Choose Format, Bullets And Numbering. The Bullets And Numbering dialog box is displayed with the Numbered tab selected. (See Figure 8-8.)
2. Click one of the numbering styles shown in the dialog box, if you see one to your liking.
3. Click OK; Word updates the numbering style in your list to match your selection.

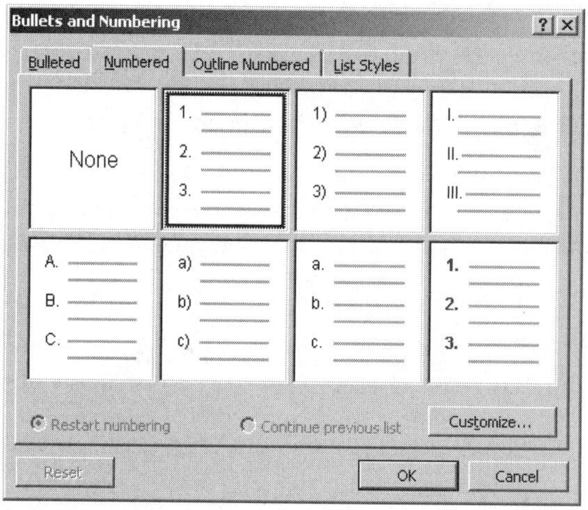

Figure 8-8. The Bullets And Numbering dialog box automatically displays the numbering styles available so that you can make your selection.

Modifying the Numbering Style

If you aren't particularly happy with the numbering styles available in the default palette, you can customize the numbering style you use. Display the Numbered tab of the Bullets And Numbering dialog box and click the Customize button. The Customize

Numbered List dialog box appears, giving you a number of choices for the way you want your numbers to look. (See Figure 8-9.)

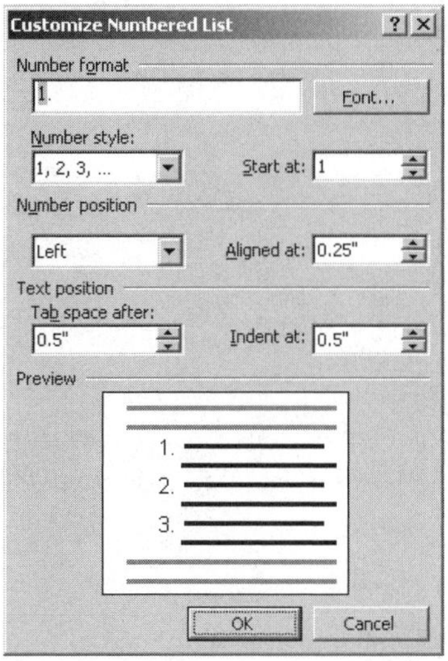

Figure 8-9. The Customize Numbered List dialog box gives you the means to change the number style you use in your list. You can also change number spacing and text position here.

Choose the Font you want to use by clicking the Font button and using the Font dialog box, and then click the Number style down arrow to see the style choices available to you. You can determine what you want the starting number to be by clicking in the Start At box and typing the number for the start point. If you prefer, you can use the up and down arrows to increase or decrease the number by one.

Continuing Numbering

Some of your numbered list items might be separated by things like charts or sidebars. But instead of starting over again with number 1, as Word will do by default, you want to pick back up with the next step in your process. You can have Word do this for you by making a choice in the Bullets And Numbering dialog box. Here's how:

1. Begin by selecting the second of the numbered lists—the one in which you want to continue the numbering.
2. Choose Format, Bullets And Numbering.
3. Click the Continue Previous List option in the lower portion of the Bullets And Numbering dialog box. The numbering scheme you've selected changes to show the additional numbers. (See Figure 8-10, on the next page.)
4. Click OK to return to the document. The numbers will continue in sequence from the previous list, as you selected.

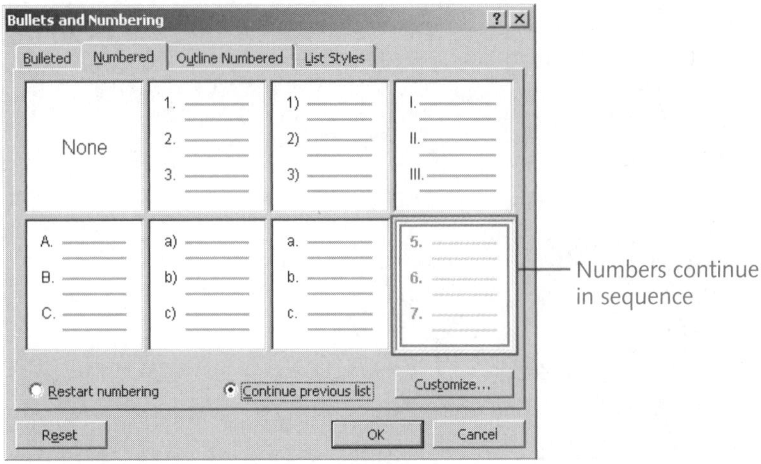

Figure 8-10. When you click Continue Previous List, the styles update to show the extended numbering sequence.

Resolving List Challenges

Word's bulleted and numbered list feature is basically simple to use, but a few headaches occur now and then. Here are a few workarounds for list challenges.

Turning Off AutoFormat Features

Sometimes the automatic features can conflict with your desire to format things yourself. If you want to make your own changes to Word's bullet and numbering schemes, disable AutoFormat before you begin list making. To do that, follow these steps:

1. Choose Tools, AutoCorrect Options and the AutoFormat tab.
2. Clear the List Styles and Automatic Bulleted Lists check boxes on the AutoFormat tab.
3. On the AutoFormat As You Type tab, clear the Automatic Bulleted Lists and Automatic Numbered Lists check boxes.

Dropped Formatting

Having a feature that enables you to easily create consistent bulleted and numbered lists is a great thing—especially when it works. But sometimes Word doesn't duplicate the correct format in the second line of a list item that has more than one formatting change. For example, suppose that in a bulleted list, you begin with the first word bold and the rest of the item in regular style. When you create the second bullet item, Word doesn't apply the bold style. For example,

1. **Bold item.** Regular item.
2. Bold item. Regular item.

You can fix this by clicking at the end of the first bullet item and pressing Enter. This re-applies the format to the second list item, making it appear as follows:

2. **Bold item.** Regular item.

Go Custom, Not Default

When you create a new style to handle commonly used formats for your bulleted and numbered lists, don't base the new style of any of Word's list styles. Instead, choose to create a custom style. When you use the default list styles, Word returns to its default settings at shutdown, which means that when you open your document the next time, your changes will be gone.

Styles of Your Own

Here's one way to ensure that you've got all the bullet and numbering styles you want saved the way you want them: you can create your own template of new styles. For more information on creating styles, see Chapter 10, "Using Styles to Increase Your Formatting Power."

Chapter 9

Formatting Columns and Sections for Advanced Text Control

Depending on the types of documents you create, in all probability you rely heavily on Word's ability to create columns and sections. When you combine these two elements, you can control how the text flows in various parts of the same document. You can create single or multiple columns, even or uneven columns, columns with line dividers or with blank spaces, or gutters, in between. Using columns enables you to change the format of a single-column document, creating newspaper-style documents and pages with interesting new looks. Word also enables you to create sections in your document, which give you additional control over the way the text flows in your publication. In addition, by creating sections in your document, you can control changes in format—you can use a single column in the first section, multiple columns in the second, and go back to a single-column finish at the end. This chapter explores both columns and sections in Word and helps you create interesting formats for your newsletters, reports, and more.

Planning Your Document

If the design of your document is up to you, it's a good idea to start out not at the computer keyboard but at the drawing board, literally sketching out how you want your pages to look. Will you use two columns or three? Do you want them to have equal widths or will one be narrow and the other two wide? Thinking carefully about your document's final appearance will go a long way toward helping you create it that way.

Word gives you the capability of creating up to 12 columns, but in all but the most rare of circumstances (such as a simple word or number list) you won't use 12 columns—the width of each column is a scant 0.5 inch! Most traditional documents use one, two, or three columns. In some instances, you might use four, but even those columns provide little room for more than a few small words on a line.

As you prepare your document plan, consider these questions:

- How many columns do you want? Table 9-1 lists the column widths Word uses by default for the first six multi-column choices of an 8.5-by-11-inch portrait page.
- Will you include graphics around which your columns need to flow?
- How much space do you want to leave between columns?
- Do you want your columns to be of equal width or varied?
- Will you include a table of contents column that might require more space than a traditional text column?
- Do you want the column settings to extend the full length of the page, or do you want to include a section at the top of the page that is only a single column?

Table 9-1. Word's Default Column Widths

Number of Columns	Width of Each Column
1	6.0 inches
2	2.75 inches with 0.5 spacing
3	1.78 inches with 0.33 spacing
4	1.32 inches with 0.24 spacing
5	1.05 inches with 0.19 spacing
6	0.87 inches with 0.16 spacing

Choosing Predesigned Columns

Word includes a number of professionally designed templates that help you get a jump start on using columns in your documents. The Brochure and the Directory templates are two of these. You can get a closer look at the templates by following these steps:

1. Choose File, New. The New Document task pane appears in the right side of your work area.
2. Click General Templates. The Templates dialog box appears. Click the Publications tab. (See Figure 9-1.)

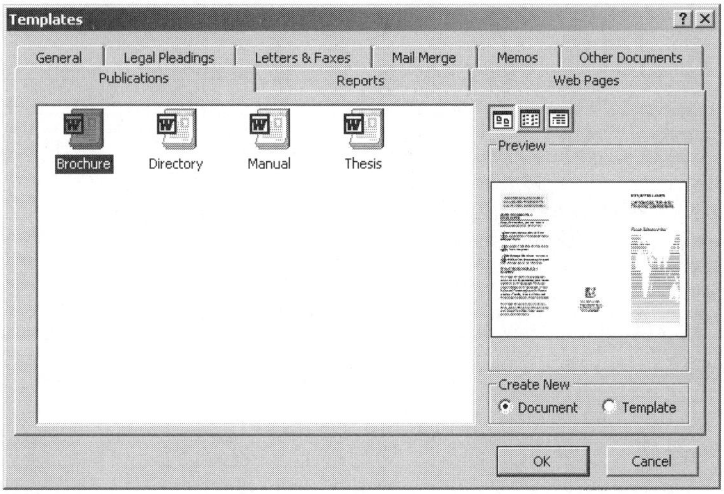

Figure 9-1. You can begin working with columns by using Word's predesigned templates.

3. To see a preview of the different document templates, click the one you want to see. The Brochure and Directory types both include the use of columns.

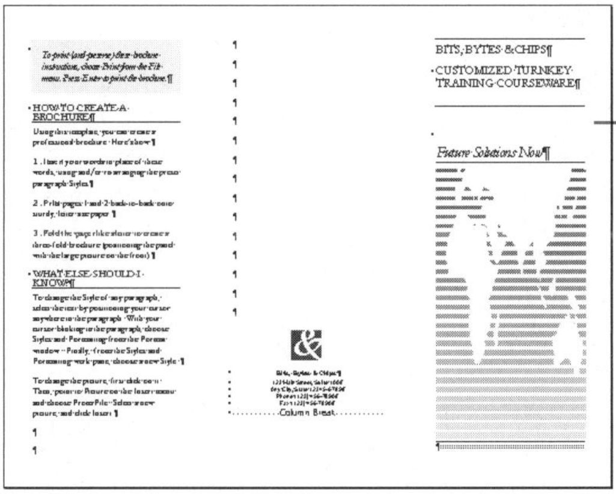

Brochure uses a three-column layout in landscape mode to create a tri-fold brochure.

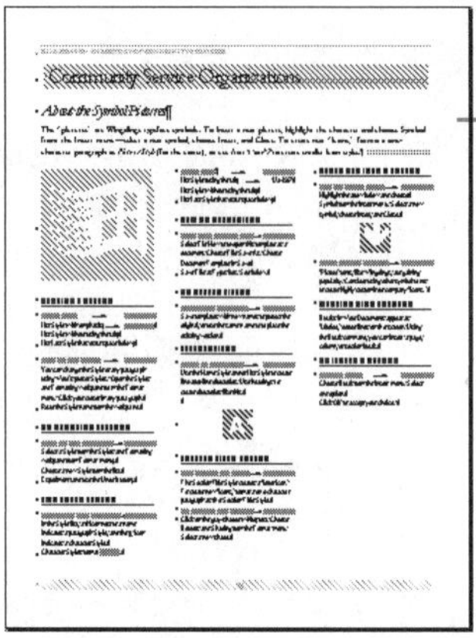

Directory uses a three-column layout in portrait mode to provide the template for a directory-type document.

4 To open one of the templates, simply click your choice and click Open.

note The terms *landscape* and *portrait* are layout terms used to describe the way in which a page is positioned for printing. In landscape mode, the document is printed so that the long edge of the paper is the top of the document, in 11-by-8.5-inch layout. In portrait mode, the document is printed in the traditional 8.5-by-11-inch layout.

For more about working with Word's templates, see "Implementing Templates and Wizards" on page 35.

Creating a Multi-Column Document

There are several ways to format your document in multiple columns. If you want to create columns on the fly, use the Columns button. If you have certain specifications—for example, exact column measurements, a spacing requirement of a certain size, or more than four columns—use the Columns dialog box to choose those settings.

tip **Switch to Print Layout view**

Be sure to display your document in Print Layout view before you begin working with columns. Normal view, Web Layout view, and Outline view won't enable you to see columns as they will appear in print. To display Print Layout view, Choose View, Print Layout or click the Print Layout View button to the left of the horizontal scroll bar.

Using the Columns Button

Columns

The easiest way to create a multi-column document is to use the Columns button on the Standard toolbar. When you click the button, a drop-down menu presents the choice of between one and four columns. (See Figure 9-2.) Click the column setting you want, and Word automatically updates the layout in your document.

tip **Define columns the quick way**

If you want to create columns for only a portion of the document, select the area to which you want to apply the column format before you click the Columns button.

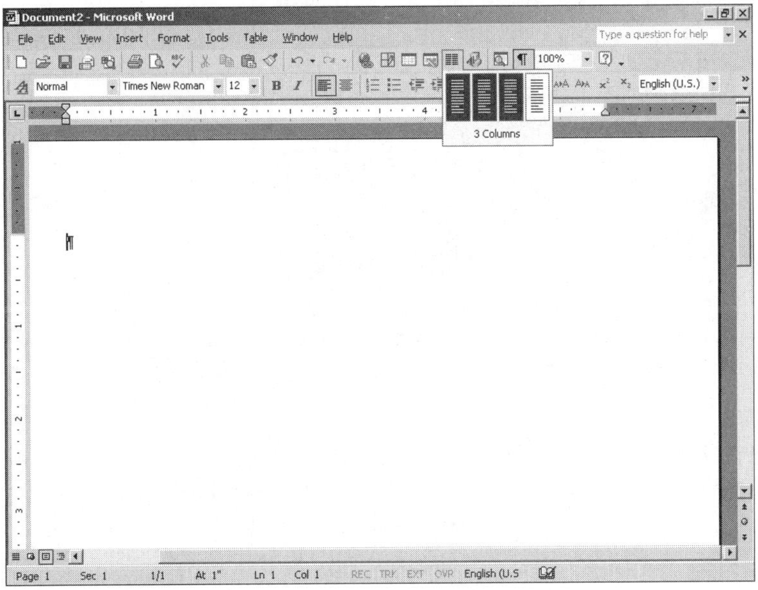

Figure 9-2. The Columns button allows you to select up to four columns from the Standard toolbar.

note The only way you can see that Word has, in fact, created columns in your document is that the margins on the ruler will show the new boundaries. If the ruler isn't currently displayed in your document, choose View, Ruler to display it.

Choosing Column Specs in the Columns Dialog Box

If you have certain column specifications that you need to enter—for example, you're creating a follow-up report based on a format your department has adopted as its report format of choice—you can create and work with columns by using the Columns dialog box. Here are the steps:

1. Choose Format, Columns. The Columns dialog box is displayed.
2. Click the preset column format you want, if you see one that meets your needs. The Preview section shows you the format you've selected. (See Figure 9-3.)

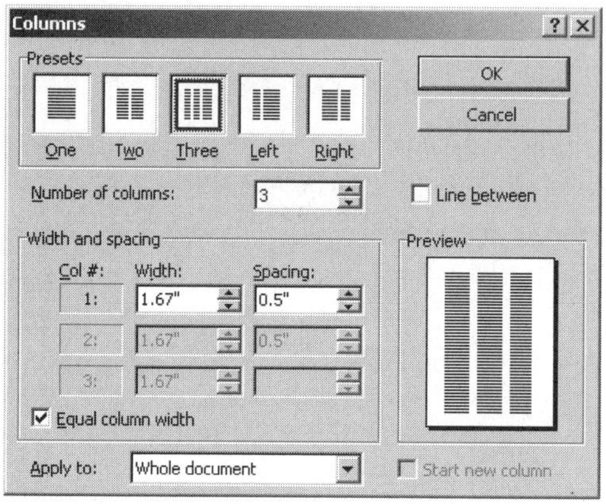

Figure 9-3. You can enter more specific column settings in the Columns dialog box.

By default, Word assumes that you want your columns to be created equally (unless you choose either the Left or Right preset selection) and that you don't want a line to be placed between the columns you create. If you want to add a line between columns, select the Line Between check box, and Word will add the necessary rule.

Creating Columns for Part of a Document

Another assumption Word makes is that you want to apply the column format to the entire document. If you want to apply the format only from this point forward, click the down arrow in the Apply To box and select This Point Forward. You might want, for example, to open your document with a paragraph or two in single-column format and then break the rest of the document up into three columns. (See Figure 9-4.)

note Once you add section breaks to your document, you'll discover that This Section becomes one of your choices in the Apply To box.

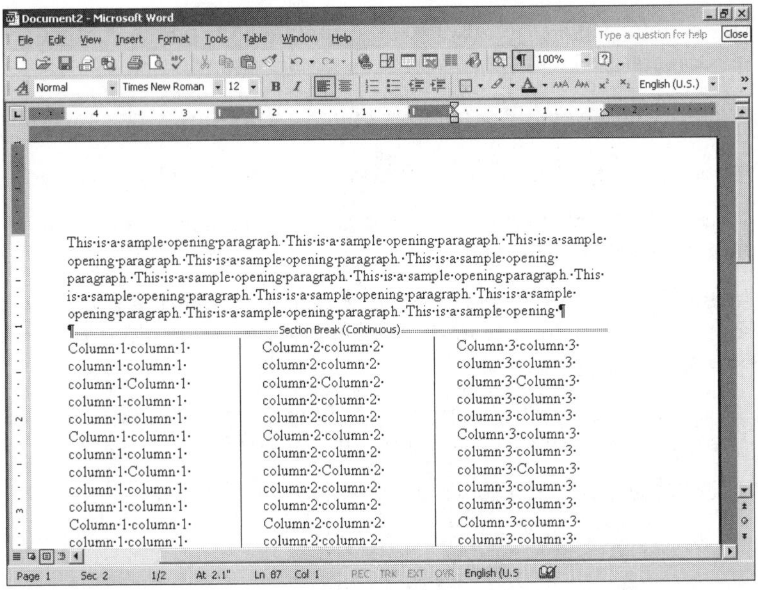

Figure 9-4. You can mix single-column and multi-column formats in the same document.

To create a mixed format, follow these steps:

1. Type the opening paragraph, leaving the document set to single-column format.
2. At the point where you want to create columns, Choose Format, Columns. The Columns dialog box is displayed.
3. Choose the number of columns you want; enter any spacing specifications as needed.
4. Select the Line Between check box if you want a line to be displayed between columns.
5. Click the Apply To down arrow and choose This Point Forward. Click OK.

   The Columns dialog box closes and you're returned to the document. Notice that, at the point where the format is changed from a single column to multiple columns, Word adds a Section Break marker.

Creating Unequal Column Widths

Although Word sets a number of options for you in the Columns dialog box, you can change those options to create columns that suit your document specifications. By choosing the Left or Right preset format, you can tell Word to create unequal formats, meaning the columns are not of equal width. When you choose the Left preset format, the column to the left is proportionately smaller than the one to the right. When you choose the Right preset, the right column is the smaller one.

To customize column widths using the Columns dialog box, follow these steps:

1. Choose Format, Columns to display the Columns dialog box.
2. Click in the Number Of Columns box and type the number of columns you want to create.
3. Clear the check box to the left of Equal Column Width. The Width settings become available for columns 1 through 3 so that you can customize the settings. (See Figure 9-5.)
4. Modify the Width and Spacing settings for your columns to get the effect you want. The Preview section shows the result of your choices.
5. Click OK to save your choices and return to the document.

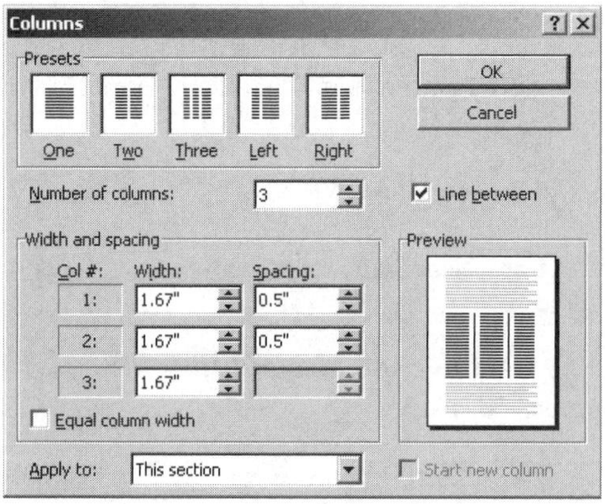

Figure 9-5. Use the Columns dialog box to specify the width and spacing for unequal columns.

Changing Column Width on the Ruler

You can also change the width of columns by dragging the column margins in the ruler at the top of your work area. If you want to keep the spacing the same between columns, position the pointer on the center of the spacing bar. When the pointer changes to a double-headed arrow, move the spacing bar in the direction you want to change the column. For example, to make the left column narrower, drag the spacing bar to the left. To make the left column wider, drag the spacing bar to the right. (See Figure 9-6.)

You can also increase or decrease the amount of spacing between columns by dragging the edge of the spacing bar to the right or left. For example, to expand the spacing into the right column, drag the right edge of the spacing bar to the right. The size of the right column is reduced by the same amount of space you added to the spacing bar.

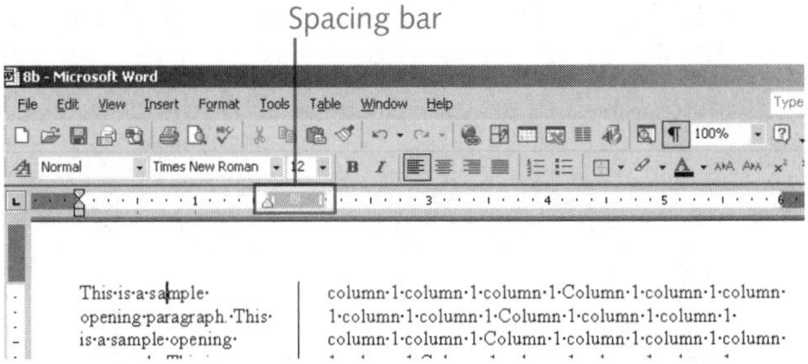

Figure 9-6. You can easily change the width of a column by dragging the spacing bar in the ruler.

Getting Text into a Column Layout

Everything in Word should be this simple. When you're turning a single-column document into a multiple-column document, Word does all the work for you. You simply display the Columns dialog box, choose the number of columns you want, specify any width and spacing settings, choose whether you want a line divider, and click OK. Word then puts the text in the format you selected, whether you already have a document full of text or an empty page.

> **tip** **Create columns before or after: which is easier?**
>
> This is a matter of personal preference, but most people seem to prefer to do the writing, editing, and reworking in single-column format and then put the prepared document into columns as a last step. From that point on, it's just a matter of tweaking spaces, line breaks, and word wrap to get the document to its finished stage.

If you're entering text in columns as you go, no text will appear in the second column until the previous column has been filled; that is, if you intend to have only headings in the left column and flow your text into the right column of a two-column format, you'll need to fill the column with line spaces between headings until you get to the end of the column and Word wraps back up to the top of column 2. For example, in the two-column report in Figure 9-7, on the next page, you can see the paragraph marks showing the line spacing inserted to cause the text to wrap to the next column.

> **note** There *is* a quicker way to do this, if your left column is going to be blank except for perhaps a heading at the top. When you know you've entered all you want in a column, you can add a column break. You'll learn how later in this chapter in the section "Inserting Column Breaks," on page 222.

Chapter 9

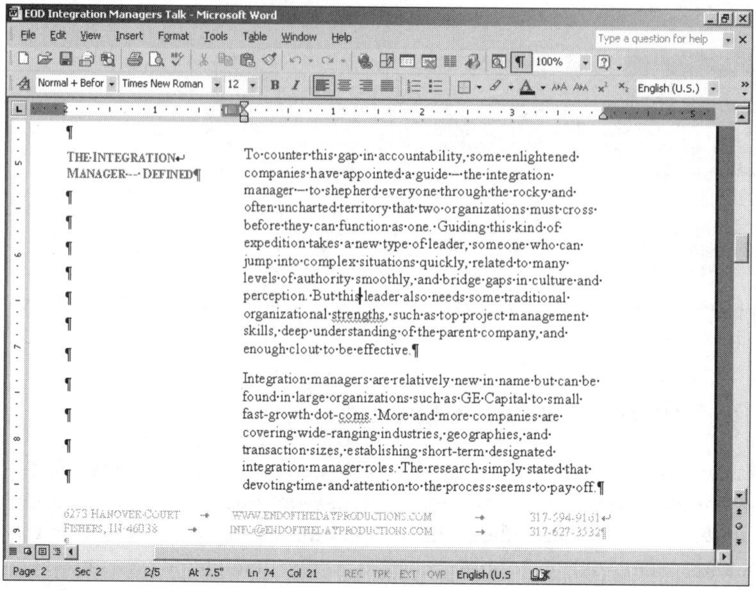

Figure 9-7. Before text will wrap to the second column, the first column must be filled.

Choosing Text Alignment

The way your text looks—and how readable your readers think it is—has a lot to do with the alignment you choose for the text. Traditional document alignment is often left-justified, in which the text is aligned along the left margin of the page only. Other alignments include centered, which is often used for headings, and right-justified, which aligns text along the right margin and is used rarely for traditional documents. Another alignment, full-justified text, aligns text along both the left and right margins, adding spaces in between words to spread out the text enough to make the both-edge alignment possible. Table 9-2 gives you a look at alignment differences.

Table 9-2. Text Alignment Differences

Example	Alignment Type	Use
This·is·a·sample·opening·paragraph.·This·is·a·sample·opening·paragraph.·This·is·a·	column·1·column·1·column·1·column·1·Column·1· (×4)	Left	For traditional body text, headlines, captions, and more
This·is·a·sample·opening·paragraph.·This·is·a·sample·opening·paragraph.·This·is·a·	column·1·column·1·column·1·column·1·Column·1· (×4)	Centered	For headlines, special text effects, captions or callouts
This·is·a·sample·opening·paragraph.·This·is·a·sample·opening·paragraph.·This·is·a·	column·1·column·1·column·1·column·1·Column·1· (×4)	Right	For specialty text designs, table text, captions
This·is·a·sample·opening·paragraph.·This· is· a· sample· opening· paragraph.· This· is· a·	column·1·column·1·column·1·column·1·Column·1· (×4)	Full	For text in columns, some special text elements, quotes

Users often prefer left-justified text for just about everything; but some people like using full-justified text for documents with multiple columns. In some cases, formats work well with the left column right-justified, lining up along the leftmost edge of the right column, which is full-justified. (See Figure 9-8.)

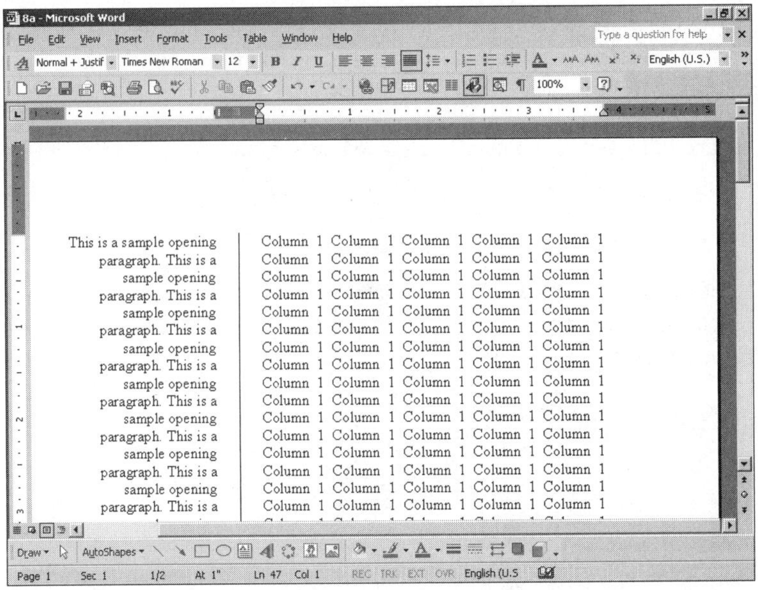

Figure 9-8. Mix and match alignment to see what looks best in your particular publication.

Beginning a New Column Layout

Longer documents often require a number of different general layouts—the introduction and summary of your report might read, story-like, in a single-column format. When you begin to talk about the specification of your new product line, however, you might go to a multi-column format that presents information in the clearest way possible. You might also want to incorporate graphs and tables in the body of those columns.

How can you easily switch between column layouts without messing up the way text flows in your document? The easiest way to change to a multi-column format is to place the insertion point where you want to start the new column layout and then follow these steps:

1. Choose Format, Columns. Select the number of columns you want to include in the Columns dialog box; add width and spacing settings, if necessary.
2. Select the Line Between check box if you want a line separating the columns.
3. In the Apply To box, click the down arrow and choose This Point Forward.
4. Select the Start New Column check box.

5 Click OK to return to the document. Word moves to the top of the next column, and your column settings are in effect.

Inserting Column Breaks

When you've entered everything you want in a specific column and you're ready to wrap text to the next column, you can add a column break to force the wrap. To add a column break, follow these steps:

1. Place the insertion point where you want to insert the column break.
2. Choose Insert, Break. The Break dialog box appears, as shown in Figure 9-9.
3. In the Break Types section, click Column Break.
4. Click OK. You're returned to the document, and Word adds a Column Break at the insertion point. The text in the column past that point is wrapped to the top of the next column.

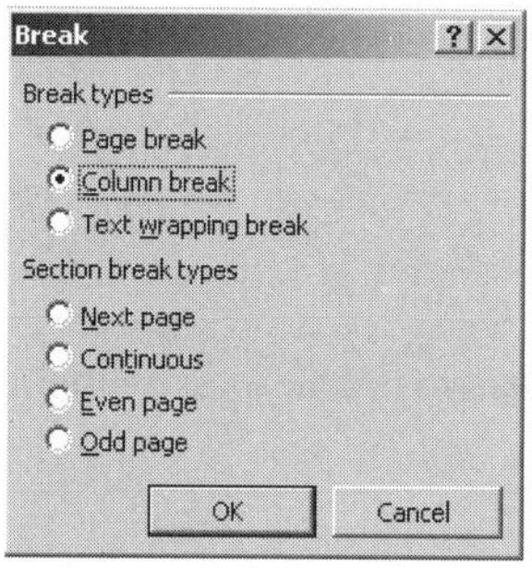

Figure 9-9. You can force a column break to cause text remaining in that column to wrap to the top of the next column.

Removing Column Breaks

In Word, you can delete columns as easily as you add them. They can be removed as easily as removing a simple character—just position the insertion point immediately following a break and press Backspace (or select the break itself and press Delete). The column break is removed and the text is flowed back into the column.

Balancing Your Columns

Lining text up isn't always easy, and Word includes a feature that can help you automatically balance the text in your columns. When you create a column break, as described in the preceding section, you can have Word create a continuous break, which ensures that the columns will balance out. The "continuous" part of the break gives Word permission to end the column wherever necessary to even out the text placement.

To create a continuous break, follow these steps:

1. Place the insertion point where you want the break to be added.
2. Display the Break dialog box by choosing the Insert, Break.
3. Select Column Break as usual and, in the Section Break Types section, click Continuous. Word then adds the continuous break, which will break the text at the appropriate point to balance the text columns most effectively.

Working in Sections

Because Word includes features that stretch to give you a variety of formats and controls for long documents, you need a way to limit the changes to make to individual portions of your document. That's what sections are all about. By using sections, you can control a change from a single-column format to multiple columns and back again. You can create layouts that look different on odd and even pages. You can modify the margins of a section and then revert to the regular document formatting when the section is completed.

Creating a Section

Starting a section is almost as easy as starting a column. You can begin a new section anywhere—in the middle of a page or at the beginning of a new one. To start a new section, follow these steps:

1. Place the insertion point where you want to start the new section.
2. Choose Insert, Break. The Break dialog box appears (refer to Figure 9-9, on previous page).
3. Click one of the section break types (further described in Table 9-3, on the next page) and click OK. The section is created, and the text is flowed accordingly.

> **tip** **Create sections in Page Setup**
>
> If you have a larger vision of your document when you first use Page Setup, you can elect to create sections there as well. Choose File, Page Setup to display the Page Setup dialog box, and then click the Layout tab. The first group of settings on the Layout tab in the Page Setup dialog box deals with sections. You can choose Continuous, New Column, New Page, Even Page, and Odd Page in the Section Start drop-down list, just as you can in the Break dialog box. As always, you can change any of your selections at any time, and making changes in the Break dialog box later will carry through to the settings you entered in the Page Setup dialog box.

Table 9-3. A Quick Look at Section Types

Section Type	Description	Use
Next Page	Creates a new section at the top of the next page	You want to start a new section with different formatting specifications at the next page in the document.
Continuous	Creates a new section beginning at the document insertion point	You want to begin a new section in the middle of the current page.
Even Page	Creates a new section beginning on an even page. If the current page is an even page, an odd page is inserted and left blank	You want to create a new section with a format used uniquely for even pages.
Odd Page	Creates a new section beginning on an odd page. If the current page is an odd page, an even page is inserted and left blank	You want to create a section for odd pages only.

newfeature!

Selecting Multiple Sections

Now Word gives you the means of selecting different portions of your document at the same time. Whether you want to copy large and nonsequential sections, run the spelling checker on selected text, or reformat or delete selected blocks, you can use the new multiple-select feature in Word 2002 to select noncontiguous blocks and sections. To select multiple sections, follow these steps:

1. Select the first section you want to work with.
2. Press and hold the Ctrl key, and scroll to the next section and select it.
3. Continue adding sections as necessary and then perform the operation you have in mind. No longer is Word limited to an all-or-nothing selection method, which means you can work with just the text you want, when and how you want it.

Removing Section Breaks

You can remove the section breaks in your Word document in the same way you delete column breaks—simply select them and press Delete. Once you delete a section break, the document settings that were in effect before the break are applied to that section.

A Plug for Your Own Templates

Once again, a reminder: Any time you go to any significant trouble to create your own formats, especially if there's a chance you'll use the formats again, consider saving the format you've created as a template you can use again as the basis for other documents.

To create a template from a document you've made, follow these steps:

1. Choose File, Save As. The Save As dialog box appears.
2. Type a name for the template in the File Name box.
3. Click the Save As Type down arrow and choose Document Template.
4. Click Save to save the template file.

Chapter 10

Using Styles to Increase Your Formatting Power

Formatting takes on new meaning when you create complex or long documents that contain recurring elements, such as headings, formatted paragraphs, figure captions, table headings, and so forth. Spending time formatting components one by one in a document that contains a variety of elements can easily lead to hours of tedium and increased chances of formatting errors. Conveniently, you can eliminate repetitive formatting tasks in Word by using *styles*.

A style is a named set of formatting characteristics that you can apply to text, tables, and lists. When you use styles, you can quickly apply multiple formatting commands to specified text. In addition, styles enable you to easily modify the look of a document by changing a style (or styles) instead of manually reformatting components throughout your document. Styles also enable you to take advantage of the following powerful automation and organization features available in Word:

- **AutoFormat** (See Chapter 6, "Putting Text Tools to Work.")
- **AutoSummarize** (See Chapter 13, "Maximizing Electronic Reference Tools.")
- **Master Documents** (See Chapter 25, "Creating and Controlling Master Documents.")
- **Outlining** (See Chapter 11, "Outlining Documents for Clarity and Structure.")
- **Tables of contents, tables of figures, and similar elements** (See Chapter 26, "Generating First-Class Tables of Contents and Related Elements.")

- **Themes, templates, and add-ins** (See Chapter 22, "Formatting Documents Using Templates, Wizards, and Add-Ins.")
- **Web page wizards and templates** (See Chapter 31, "Creating Professional Web Sites."

The bottom line is that instead of formatting each paragraph in a document separately by using toolbar buttons, keyboard shortcuts, menu commands, and dialog box options, you can make better use of your time and resources by creating and using styles.

Unfortunately, the concept of styles tends to make most Word users feel a bit uncomfortable, and even some experienced Word users rarely bother with styles (or they use styles sporadically). Fortunately, if you're comfortable using Word but are new to styles, you needn't worry—creating, using, and modifying styles are skills that are well within your grasp. Most cases of the style heebie-jeebies are quickly eliminated with a little information and some hands-on experience. If you take a little time to understand and experiment with the concepts presented in this chapter, you'll be able to easily use styles whenever you need them during document creation and modification. More importantly, you'll discover that using styles can dramatically improve productivity.

Understanding Styles

In Word, the term *style* refers to a collection of formatting commands that are grouped together and given a name. To apply a style, you simply select the text you want to format (or position the insertion point in a new paragraph where you want the formatting to begin when you enter text) and then select a style from the Style drop-down list on the Formatting toolbar—all with a single click instead of many. When you apply a style, all the formatting settings contained in the style are applied at once. In Word 2002, styles come in four types:

- **Paragraph** affects all the properties associated with a paragraph's appearance, such as text alignment, tab stops, line spacing, borders, and shading. Paragraph styles can include character formatting.
- **Character** formats selected text within a paragraph, including properties such as font, size, boldface, italic, and underlining.

newfeature!

- **Table** gives a uniform appearance to table borders, colors, shading, alignment, and fonts.

newfeature!

- **List** affects alignment, numbering or bullet components, and fonts used within lists.

> **note** Prior to Word 2002, you could create and use only two types of styles: paragraph and character. The table and list styles are new additions to the style scene.

You create, use, and modify the four types of styles in the same basic manner, and you can access all style types in the Styles And Formatting task pane, the Style drop-down list on the Formatting toolbar, and the Style dialog box. But before you start customizing your documents using homegrown styles, you should take a look at the sizable collection of built-in styles provided with Word, described next.

Working with Word's Default Styles

As you probably know, Word uses the Normal.dot template to create new documents, and you use the Normal default style when you start entering text in a new, blank document. (By default, the Normal style settings are Times New Roman, 12 point, left aligned, single spaced.) The Normal.dot template includes over 110 built-in styles, including paragraph, character, list, and table styles. Five of the most widely used built-in styles also have keyboard shortcuts. Two additional keyboard shortcuts let you promote and demote headings by one level. Table 10-1 summarizes these built-in style-related keyboard shortcuts.

> **note** Remember, a *template*, such as Normal.dot, is a document that contains the formatting settings and other layout components used within a document, including styles, standard (or *boilerplate*) text, graphics, page components, and so forth. For more information about templates, see Chapter 22, "Formatting Documents Using Templates, Wizards, and Add-Ins."

Table 10-1. Built-In Style-Related Keyboard Shortcuts

Style	Keyboard shortcut
Normal	Ctrl+Shift+N
List Bullet	Ctrl+Shift+L
Heading 1	Ctrl+Alt+1
Heading 2	Ctrl+Altl+2
Heading 3	Ctrl+Alt+3
Demotes Heading Level	Alt+Shift+Right Arrow
Promotes Heading Level	Alt+Shift+Left Arrow

For more information about creating a keyboard shortcut for any style, see "Assigning Keyboard Shortcuts to Styles," on page 245.

When you work in a Word document, the default styles are available for you to use and customize. You can opt to use only the default styles (which are effective, albeit a bit conservative), customize existing styles on a document-by-document basis, create custom styles from scratch and save them in the document or in a custom template, or customize the Normal.dot template if you want the changes to appear in all new documents. We'll look at each of these alternatives in the following sections.

Getting to Know the New Styles And Formatting Task Pane

In this version of Word, you can view available styles in three places: the Style drop-down list on the Formatting toolbar, the Style dialog box (accessed by double-clicking a style name in the Style Area or by clicking Styles in the Format Settings dialog box), and the new Style And Formatting task pane. The Style drop-down list and the Style dialog box are familiar tools that have been around for a few versions of Word. Their functionality remains fairly consistent with earlier versions of Word, although the Style dialog box has had a minor face-lift to make working with the options easier, as shown in Figure 10-1.

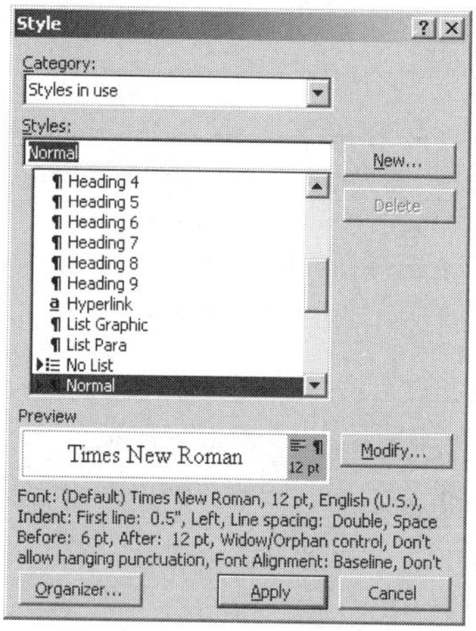

Figure 10-1. The Style dialog box has been slightly revamped to more clearly show sample text style, eliminating the Paragraph Preview section used in Word 2000.

On the other hand, the Styles And Formatting task pane, shown in Figure 10-2, is a completely new feature in Word 2002, and it's designed to make using, creating, and modifying styles easier and more intuitive than ever. In fact, the Styles And Formatting task pane makes working with styles so convenient that it might significantly weaken the barriers many users have erected concerning styles.

Styles And Formatting

To open the Styles And Formatting task pane, click the Styles And Formatting button on the Formatting toolbar (to the left of the Style drop-down list), or if your task pane is open, click the task pane's drop-down arrow and choose Styles And Formatting. The Styles And Formatting task pane contains the following elements:

- **Formatting Of Selected Text drop-down list** displays the style of the current paragraph or selected text.

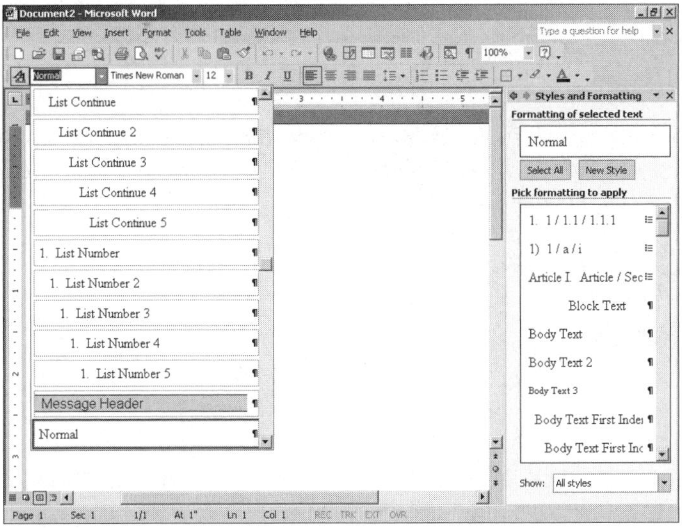

Figure 10-2. The Style drop-down list provides quick access to available styles, and the Styles And Formatting task pane displays style names with their associated formatting.

- **Select All button** selects all instances of the current style, as indicated in the Formatting Of Selected Text drop-down list as well as in the Style drop-down list on the Formatting toolbar.
- **New Style button** opens the New Style dialog box, where you can create and modify styles and templates. (The New Style dialog box is discussed in detail in the section "Creating New Styles," on page 237.)
- **Pick Formatting To Apply list** displays a list of styles, as specified in the Show drop-down list. Most styles are accompanied by a symbol to the right of the style name. The symbols identify the style type—character, paragraph, list, or table. If no symbol appears next to a list item, the item represents a formatting combination, used within the document, that hasn't been named and saved as a style.
- **Show drop-down list** enables you to specify which styles are displayed in the Pick Formatting To Apply list and in the Style drop-down list on the Formatting toolbar. You can choose Available Formatting, Formatting In Use, Available Styles, All Styles, or Custom.

tip **Display all built-in Word styles**

When you first open a blank document in Word 2002, the Styles And Formatting task pane and Style drop-down list show only four built-in styles: Heading 1, Heading 2, Heading 3, and Normal. To show all the built-in Word styles in the Styles And Formatting task pane and in the Styles drop-down list, select All Styles in the Show drop-down list in the Styles And Formatting task pane.

Customizing the Style List in the Styles And Formatting Task Pane

You can temporarily customize the Styles And Formatting task pane by selecting Custom in the Show drop-down list. When you select Custom, the Format Settings dialog box opens, as shown in Figure 10-3.

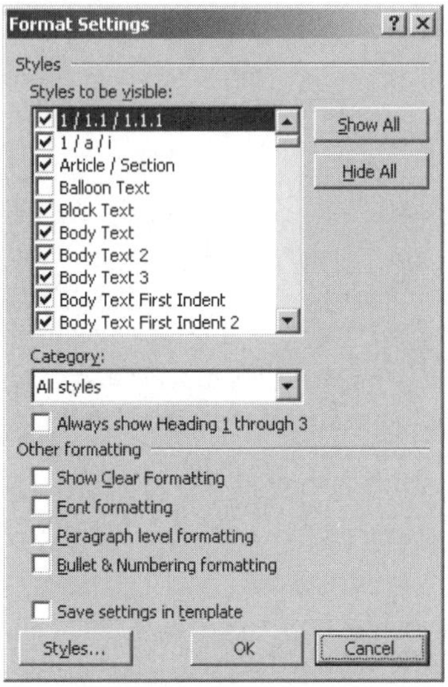

Figure 10-3. The Format Settings dialog box enables you to control which styles display in the Styles And Formatting task pane.

In the Format Settings dialog box, you can specify which styles will be displayed by selecting a style category and then selecting check boxes in the Styles To Be Visible list. You can configure additional settings in the Other Formatting section, including the Show Clear Formatting option, which adds the Clear Formatting option to the Style list. The Clear Formatting option is discussed in the section "Clearing Formatting in Selected Text," on page 236.

Finally, you can customize the Style And Formatting task pane view for all documents that use the template that's attached to the current document. To do so, select the styles you want to make visible, choose the Save Settings In Template check box, and click OK. Word will automatically display the selected styles in the Style And Formatting task pane for the current document as well as future documents created using the same template. Nicely enough, you can change which styles display at any time by revisiting the Format Settings dialog box.

Configuring the Width of the Style Area

Often you'll find it convenient to view applied styles while you work. For example, you might want to verify that you're properly applying a defined set of styles, or you might need to differentiate between styles with similar appearances. When you view styles as you work, you can easily distinguish which styles are applied to which paragraphs because Word displays each paragraph's style name in the Style Area.

To display styles while you work, first make sure that you're in Normal or Outline view, and then configure the Style Area Width display setting. By default, Style Area Width is set to 0 inches, so it is hidden from view. To increase the width of the Style Area, follow these steps:

1. Choose Tools, Options, and click the View tab.
2. In the Styles Area Width box near the bottom of the View tab, type an appropriate value. Figure 10-4 shows the result of specifying a Style Area Width of 1 inch.

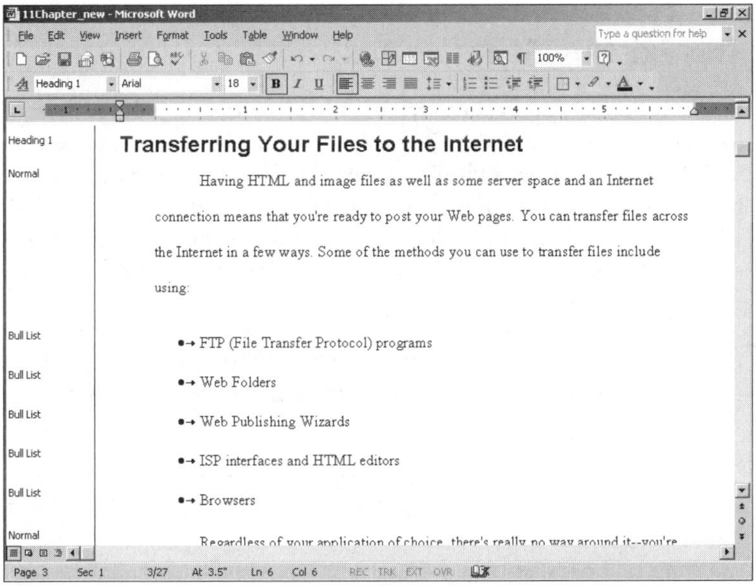

Figure 10-4. The Style Area identifies each paragraph's style in an adjustable-width column located to the left of a document's content.

After you display the Style Area, you can change its width by dragging the border left or right. You can select a paragraph (or paragraphs) in your document by clicking the paragraph's style name in the Style Area, and you can access the Style dialog box by double-clicking a style name. To hide the Style Area, either drag the border all the way to the left or change the Style Width Area setting on the View tab to **0**.

Making Styles Work for You

Before you begin creating and customizing styles to suit your purposes, you should be comfortable using and applying existing styles. Word provides plenty of styles that you can use to format your documents while you hone your style skills. Incidentally, the quickest way to apply styles to documents is to use the styles that already exist. Don't be intimidated when it comes to using styles. In Word 2002, you can easily change all occurrences of a style. In fact, after you've applied styles, you'll be able to select and modify all instances of a style as well as clear formatting if you determine you'd rather not use a specified style. The next few sections look at how to apply, select, change, and clear existing styles.

Applying Existing Styles to Text

Logically enough, applying a style entails first specifying the element you want to format. You can specify text to be styled by clicking within a paragraph, selecting text within a paragraph or multiple paragraphs, or positioning the insertion point at the beginning of an empty paragraph in which you want the selected style to be applied when you type. After you've specified what you want formatted, you can perform any of the following procedures to apply an existing style to the text:

- Choose a style in the Style drop-down list on the Formatting toolbar. You can click the Style down arrow or press Ctrl+Shift+S to display the drop-down list and then use the Up Arrow and Down Arrow keys to navigate through the style options.

tip To avoid scrolling through the Style drop-down list, click the Style down arrow, and then type the first letter of the style name. Styles are listed alphabetically, so the list will jump to the style names starting with the typed letter.

- Select a style in the Pick Formatting To Apply list in the Styles And Formatting task pane.
- Double-click the paragraph's existing style name in the Style Area, and choose a style in the Style dialog box.
- Press a preassigned keyboard shortcut (see Table 10-1) or a custom keyboard shortcut.

When you apply a style, the selected text is immediately reformatted in that style. If you find that the newly applied style isn't what you were looking for, you can replace it by applying another style or undo the formatting by clicking Undo on the Standard toolbar, pressing Ctrl+Z, or choosing Edit, Undo.

Troubleshooting

Character Formatting Disappears When I Apply a Style

When you apply a style, you might notice that manual formatting such as boldface, italics, and underlining disappears. For instance, if you apply the built-in Heading 1 style to underlined text, the text will be formatted as Heading 1 (Arial, 18 point), and the underline will be removed. To work around this default action, you can add boldface, italics, and underlining after you apply a style to selected text so that the manual formatting commands won't be lost.

newfeature

Selecting and Changing All Instances of a Style

After you apply styles to your text, you can easily select all instances of a style whenever the need arises. In earlier versions of Word, you had to use the Find And Replace dialog box to find instances of a formatting style, and you were limited to finding instances one at a time—in other words, you couldn't select all instances of similarly styled text at once. In Word 2002, you can use the Style And Formatting task pane to quickly select all instances of a specified style. This new capability can considerably speed up a number of global style-related tasks. For example, you might want to select all instances of styled text because you want to replace one style with another style, or you might want to delete all text that appears in a particular style, or you might want to copy all similarly styled elements to a new document. Regardless of your reasons, you can select all instances of a style by following these steps:

1. Click a paragraph that uses the style you want to select. (You can display the Style Area to simplify the process of selecting a paragraph that has been formatted with the sought-after style.)
2. Click the Styles And Formatting button on the Formatting toolbar to open the Styles And Formatting task pane if it isn't already displayed.
3. Click Select All, or hover the mouse pointer over the text in the Formatting Of Selected Text section, click the drop-down arrow, and choose Select All *x* Instance(s), as shown in Figure 10-5, on the next page.

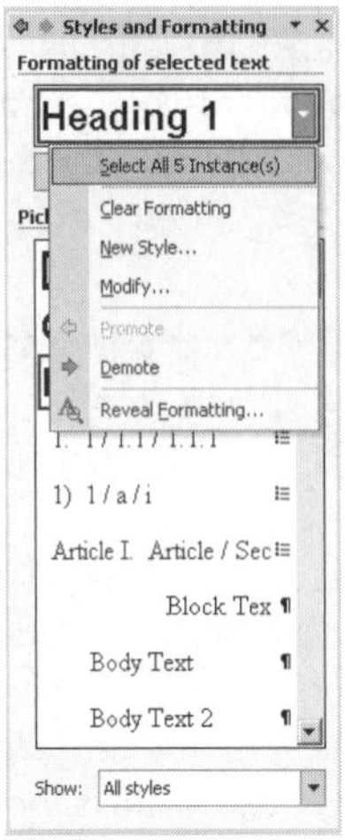

Figure 10-5. Using the Formatting Of Selected Text drop-down list, you can see exactly how many times a style is applied in the current document.

After you select all instances of text with a particular style, you can reformat the selected text by selecting another style in the Style drop-down list on the Formatting toolbar or by selecting a style in the Pick Formatting To Apply list in the Styles And Formatting task pane. You can delete all selected text with the specified style by pressing Backspace or Delete.

For information about modifying a style's settings, see the section "Modifying Existing Styles," on page 245.

newfeature!

Clearing Formatting in Selected Text

In addition to simplifying the process of selecting all instances of styled text, the Styles And Formatting task pane enables you to quickly clear formatting commands. In this version of Word, both the Pick Formatting To Apply list in the Styles And Formatting task pane and the Style drop-down list on the Formatting toolbar include a Clear Formatting option. You can use this option to remove all formatting settings in selected text, paragraphs, or entire documents. To do so, follow these steps:

1. Select the text or click within the paragraph you want to clear.
2. Display the Styles And Formatting task pane (by choosing Format, Styles And Formatting).
3. Perform any of the following actions:
   - Choose Edit, Clear, Formats.
   - In the Pick Formatting To Apply list in the Styles And Formatting task pane, select the Clear Formatting option.

- Select Clear Formatting in the Style drop-down list on the Formatting toolbar.
- Hover the mouse pointer over the text in the Formatting Of Selected Text drop-down list, click the down arrow, and select Clear Formatting.

After you clear the formatting, the text reverts to Normal style (Times New Roman, 12 point, left aligned, single spaced). If you realize immediately that you don't want to clear the formatting, click Undo on the Standard toolbar, press Ctrl+Z, or choose Edit, Undo.

tip **Clear formatting**

To clear all text formatted with a particular style, select all instances of the style (as described in the section "Selecting and Changing All Instances of a Style," on page 235), and then select Clear Formatting in the Formatting Of Selected Text drop-down list in the Styles And Formatting task pane.

Troubleshooting

The Clear Formatting Option Isn't Shown in the Pick Formatting To Apply List

If you select text and then find that the Clear Formatting option isn't listed in the Styles And Formatting task pane, it might be because the All Styles option is selected in the Show drop-down list. By default, the All Styles view doesn't include the Clear Formatting option. To eliminate this little annoyance, click the Show down arrow, and choose Available Formatting, Formatting In Use, or Available Styles, all of which are configured to show the Clear Formatting option by default. The Clear Formatting option will be displayed near the top of the list after you change the Show setting.

Creating New Styles

Up to now, we've been looking at existing styles. Most likely, you could create the majority of your documents using the built-in styles found in the Normal.dot template. Doing so would ensure that your documents look consistent, your formatting time is reduced, and your documents are able to interact with the Word tools that rely on styles. But keep in mind that millions of other people use Word as well, and your documents might look rather familiar (and possibly mundane) to them (and to you). And even though Word includes more than 110 styles in the Normal.dot template, you might find that you need a style that's not provided, such as a boxed tip element or a shaded sidebar. When you want to add some formatting spice or find you need an additional style, you can create your own styles, as described in this section.

Your primary tool when you create new styles is the New Style dialog box. The New Style dialog box offers options specific to the type of style you're creating (paragraph, character, table, or list), as shown in Figure 10-6. To access the New Style dialog box, click the New Style button in the Styles And Formatting task pane.

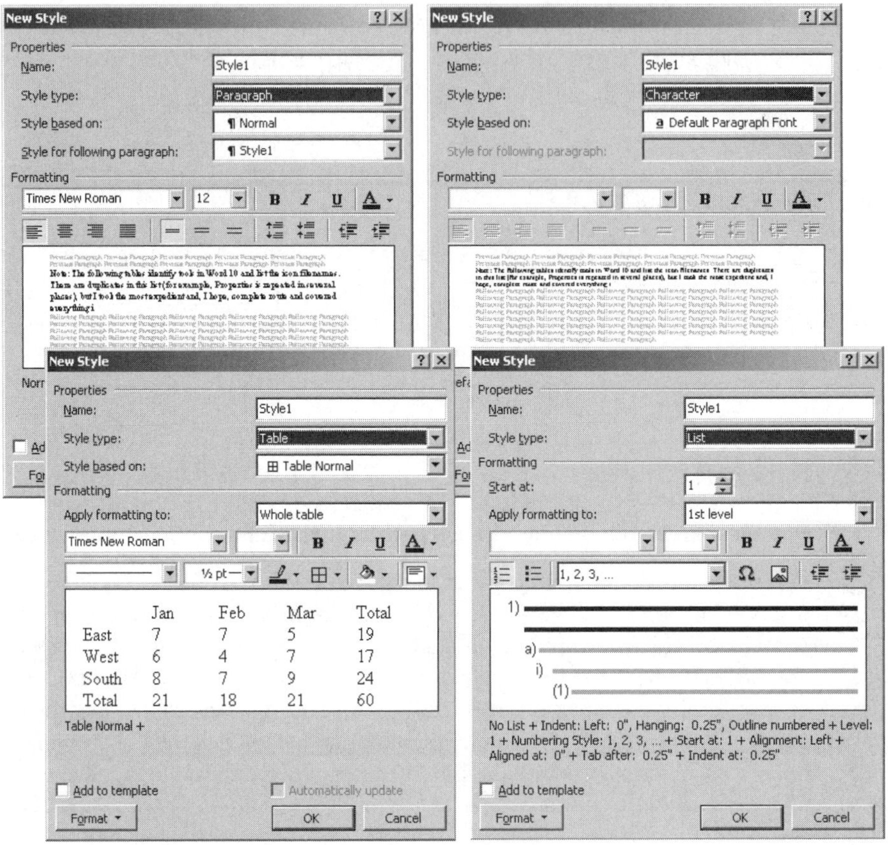

Figure 10-6. The New Style dialog box enables you to configure numerous properties when you create a new style; its options change slightly based on whether you're creating a paragraph, character, table, or list style.

> **tip** **Find more information about formatting**
>
> Formatting paragraphs, characters, lists, and tables from within the New Style dialog box is similar to formatting the same elements from within the main Word window. If you're unsure of a formatting feature in the New Style dialog box that's not addressed in this chapter, check the table of contents for a related chapter that clarifies a formatting feature's effect. For example, table formatting options are discussed in Chapter 18, "Organizing Concepts in Tables."

Creating New Styles Based on Preformatted Text

One of the easiest ways to create a style is to format existing text and then define a style based on the formatted text. To successfully create a style using this technique, select and format text within your document (remember to consider font characteristics as well as paragraph settings), and then perform any of the following actions:

- Click the Style box on the Formatting toolbar or press Ctrl+Shift+S, and type a name for the new style. You can create only paragraph styles using this method.
- Display the Styles And Formatting task pane, and click New Style. In the New Style dialog box, type a style name in the Name box, configure any other settings, and click OK. Notice the Style Type drop-down list, where you can specify whether you want to create a paragraph, character, table, or list style, as described in the section "Creating New Styles," on page 237.
- Double-click a style name in the Style Area to open the Style dialog box, and click New to open the New Style dialog box. In the New Style dialog box, type a style name in the Name box, specify the style type, select any other formatting options, and click OK.

When you create a new style using the New Style dialog box, you can define the style for the current document only (which is the default action), or you can apply the style to the current template. To add a style to the current template (which is Normal.dot by default, if no other template has been attached to the document), select the Add To Template check box. This option saves the style information as part of the current template and makes the style available to other documents using the same template.

For a more in-depth discussion of the New Style dialog box, see the section "Creating New Styles using the New Style Dialog Box," on page 240, and for more information about the Add To Template option, see the section "Adding a Style to a Document or Template," on page 244.

Using the AutoFormat Feature to Create Styles as You Type

In Word, you can also create styles automatically while you work. By using the AutoFormat feature, you can configure Word to automatically create styles for the current document based on your formatting commands. After you turn on the AutoFormat feature, you'll notice that the formatting and styles you use are automatically added to the Styles And Formatting task pane. To best see the feature in action while you work, open the Styles And Formatting task pane and select Formatting In Use in the Show drop-down list. To automatically create styles while you format text, follow these steps:

1. Choose Tools, AutoCorrect Options to open the AutoCorrect dialog box.
2. Click the AutoFormat As You Type tab.

3. In the Apply As You Type section, select the Built-In Heading Styles check box. (The other check boxes should already be selected by default).
4. In the Automatically As You Type section, select the Define Styles Based On Your Formatting check box.
5. Click OK to close the AutoCorrect dialog box.

After you activate the AutoFormat As You Type feature, Word will automatically apply heading and text styles (such as Heading 1, Body Text, List, and so forth) to text as you type. If you don't agree with the AutoFormat feature's treatment, you can apply a different style to a text component. If AutoFormat seems to regularly misinterpret your formatting needs, you might consider turning the feature off. To do so, you simply undo the settings you used to turn the feature on, as follows:

1. Choose Tools, AutoCorrect Options, and click the AutoFormat As You Type tab.
2. Clear the Built-In Heading Styles check box, and clear the Define Styles Based On Your Formatting check box.

For more information about using the AutoFormat feature, see Chapter 6 "Putting Text Tools to Work."

Creating New Styles Using the New Style Dialog Box

As you've seen, you can create styles by formatting text and basing a style on the text. But if you want a somewhat higher degree of control over your style creation endeavors, you should consider creating styles using the New Style dialog box (shown in Figure 10-6). When you use the New Style dialog box, you can easily incorporate alignment, line spacing, indents, paragraph spacing, font colors, and more into your style. To create a new style using the New Style dialog box, follow these steps:

1. Click the Styles And Formatting button on the Formatting toolbar to display the Styles And Formatting task pane, and then click the New Style button. The New Style dialog box opens.
2. In the New Style dialog box, type a name for your new style in the Name box. Be thoughtful when you consider names to associate with styles—the more descriptive your style names are, the easier it will be for you (and others) to identify each style's purpose and apply the proper style within documents.
3. In the Style Type drop-down list, specify whether your style will be a paragraph, character, table, or list style. The majority of styles in the list are paragraph styles.

4 In the Formatting section, configure your style's properties using the Font and Size lists as well as the formatting, color selection, alignment, line spacing, above and below spacing, and indent buttons.

5 If necessary, click the Format button to access additional formatting options, as shown in Figure 10-7.

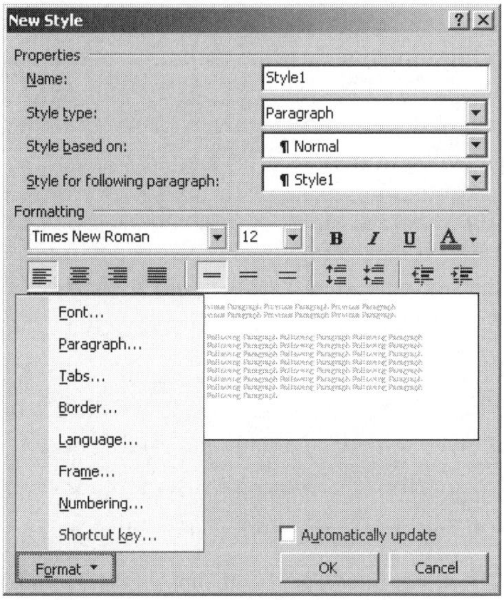

Figure 10-7. The Format button enables you to access dialog boxes that provide more detailed formatting options.

6 When you've finished configuring formatting options, click OK.

The newly created style will appear in the Styles And Formatting task pane as well as in the Style drop-down list. You can use, modify, and delete your new styles just as if they were built-in styles. The next few sections address some of the additional configuration options found on the New Style dialog box.

Basing New Styles on Existing Styles

By default, the styles you create in the New Style dialog box (or by typing a name in the Style box on the Formatting toolbar, for that matter) are based on the Normal style. This means that your styles contain all the settings for the Normal style plus whatever modifications you make to the style.

Word makes it easy for you to create a new style based on an existing style of your choice. When you base a new style on an existing style, some of the new style's properties are already configured, which can simplify the style creation process. In addition, whenever you alter a base style, all styles created using the base style are automatically altered as well—this provides an added level of consistency. (But it can also create a mess if you're not careful.)

To illustrate the trickle-down theory of base styles, let's look at an example. Suppose you want to create a style named Heading 1 Centered that's based on the existing Heading 1 style. By default, the Heading 1 style is Arial, 18 point, left aligned. You can create Heading 1 Centered by basing the new style on the existing Heading 1 style and changing the Alignment setting to Centered. Now let's say that a few days down the road, you learn that the headings in your document should be formatted using the Verdana font, not Arial. You can alter the Heading 1 style to use Verdana, and because you based the Heading 1 Centered style on the Heading 1 style, the text formatted with the Heading 1 Centered style will automatically be reformatted to use Verdana as well.

By default, many built-in Word styles are based on the Normal style. The styles you create will also be based on the Normal style unless you specify otherwise. To review, the Normal style includes the settings listed in Table 10-2 by default.

Table 10-2. Default Normal Style Settings

Font type	Settings
Font	Times New Roman, 12 point, and English (U.S.)
Paragraph	Left aligned, 0" left indentation, 0" right indentation, single spaced, and 0" spacing above and below paragraphs
Section	1.25" left margin, 1.25" right margin, 1" top margin, 1" bottom margin, section starts new page, and 8.5" x 11" paper

tip **View a style's formatting in the Reveal Formatting task pane**

You can view a style's formatting settings by clicking a paragraph that's formatted with the style you want to investigate and then displaying the Reveal Formatting task pane. The Reveal Formatting task pane shows all the details about the style's font, paragraph, and section properties.

To indicate that you want to base a style on an existing style other than Normal or to specify that you don't want to base your style on any existing style, you can use the Style Based On drop-down list in the New Style dialog box, shown in Figure 10-8. This list contains a (No Style) option that enables you to avoid basing your new style on any existing style.

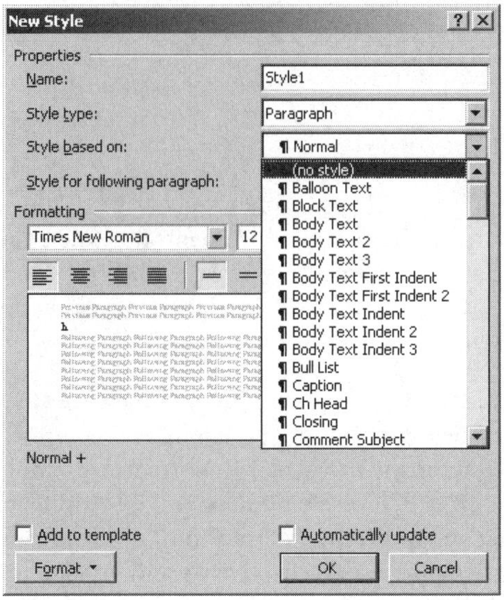

Figure 10-8. You can select any existing style to serve as a base style when you're creating new styles.

Specifying Styles for Following Paragraphs

Some styles are fairly predictable—you can predict which style elements are likely to precede or follow them 99 percent of the time. For example, most of the headings in your documents are probably followed by Normal text, or maybe your documents use a figure number element that's almost always followed by a figure caption. You can take advantage of style predictability and save yourself from having to perform unnecessary formatting steps by configuring settings for the following paragraph.

When you specify a following paragraph style, you essentially tell Word that you want to apply a particular style after you press Enter at the end of the current style. You can easily instruct Word regarding the nuances of a following paragraph while you're creating a new style. To do so, choose a style in the Style For Following Paragraph drop-down list in the New Style dialog box.

note If you don't specify a following paragraph style, Word continues to use the current style for following paragraphs until you choose another style.

After you configure the Style For Following Paragraph option and click OK, Word takes care of the rest. The next time you press Enter after the configured style, the style for the following paragraph will automatically come into play. If you display your Style Area while you work, you can easily verify that you've configured your following paragraph styles correctly.

You can modify the following paragraph setting for existing styles as well, as described in the section "Adjusting Style Properties," on page 247.

Adding a Style to a Document or Template

By default, Word adds a new style to the active document only. If you change a built-in style, that change too applies only to the existing document. But when you create a style, Word gives you the opportunity to add a style to the template attached to the active document. You can easily add a new style to a template by selecting the Add To Template check box in the New Style dialog box before you click OK.

Keep in mind that when you add a style to a template, you add the style to the template that's attached to the current document. As you might imagine, because the Normal.dot template is the default template in Word, the Normal.dot template is associated with a great number of documents. Therefore, when you add a style to a template, there's a high likelihood that you're adding the style to the Normal.dot template. When you modify the Normal.dot template, you effectively modify the template associated with all those other documents. Adding a style to a template grants users access to the style in the list of available styles in all documents that are based on the same template. Even so, you don't want to change an existing style that might negatively affect another document's appearance. Instead, consider creating a custom template, as described in Chapter 22, "Formatting Documents Using Templates, Wizards, and Add-Ins."

tip **Identify the attached template**

To identify the active document's attached template, choose Tools, Templates And Add-Ins. In the Templates And Add-Ins dialog box, the name of the currently attached template is displayed in the Document Template box. In many instances, you'll see that the Normal template serves as the active document's attached template.

For more information about the interrelationship of templates and styles, see Chapter 22, "Formatting Documents Using Templates, Wizards, and Add-Ins."

Controlling Automatic Style Updates

When you create a paragraph style, you can configure Word to update the style whenever you apply manual formatting to text formatted in the selected style. To illustrate, let's say a style automatically applies boldface formatting to text. While working in a document, you decide that you don't want the paragraph style to include boldface text, so you select a paragraph that uses the style you want to adjust (including the paragraph mark) and then press Ctrl+B to turn off the Bold attribute. When you alter text that's configured with an automatically updating style, you adjust all text that's formatted with the same style. In addition, the style definition is adjusted to match your manual change.

To activate automatic updating, select the Automatically Update check box in the New Style dialog box. Keep in mind that an automatic update made to a style is reflected only in the active document, even if the style is saved in the attached template.

> **note** When a paragraph style is configured to update automatically, you can still perform character formatting tasks within the paragraph without affecting the style or other paragraphs formatted with the style. Automatic updates come into play only when you select the entire paragraph (paragraph mark and all) and apply a formatting change.

Modifying Existing Styles

After you learn how to create styles, modifying existing styles is a snap. The main difference between creating and modifying styles is that you use the Modify Style dialog box instead of the New Style dialog box. To access the Modify Style dialog box, perform any of the following actions:

- In the Style Area, double-click the style name you want to modify to open the Style dialog box, and then click the Modify button.
- In the Styles And Formatting task pane, hover the mouse pointer over a style in the Formatting Of Selected Text drop-down list or Pick Formatting To Apply list, click the down arrow, and choose Modify.
- In the Styles And Formatting task pane, right-click a style in the Formatting Of Selected Text box or Pick Formatting To Apply list, and choose Modify.

The Modify Style dialog boxes for paragraph, character, table, and list styles look very similar to their counterpart New Style dialog boxes. These dialog boxes allow you to configure most of the same settings that are available when you create a new style.

Assigning Keyboard Shortcuts to Styles

One style modification trick that will come in handy when you're working with styles is assigning keyboard shortcuts to commonly used styles. If you use the same few styles as you work your way through a document, you might find it tiresome to repeatedly click a style in the Styles And Formatting task pane or select a style in the Style list. In those cases, it's quicker to create a keyboard shortcut that you can press whenever you need a particular style. Creating a shortcut is quick and easy. To do so, follow these steps:

1. In the Styles And Formatting task pane, right-click the style you want to associate with a keyboard shortcut, and choose Modify. The Modify Style dialog box opens.

2 In the Modify Style dialog box, click the Format button, and then click the Shortcut Key menu option. The Customize Keyboard dialog box opens, as shown in Figure 10-9.

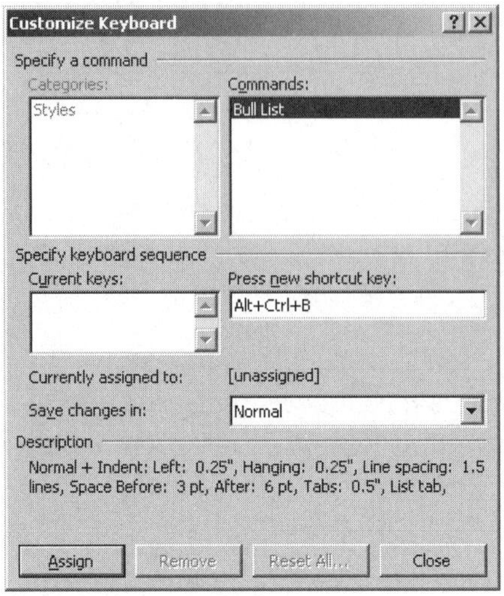

Figure 10-9. You can use the Customize Keyboard dialog box to create keyboard shortcuts for styles.

3 Press the keyboard shortcut you want to use. If the combination is already in use, the dialog box will indicate which feature uses the keyboard shortcut; if the combination is available, the Currently Assigned To label will indicate that the keyboard command is unassigned.

4 In the Save Changes In drop-down list, specify whether you want to save the keyboard shortcut in the global Normal template, in another template, or in the active document.

5 Click Assign.

After you create a keyboard shortcut, you can type text, click within the paragraph or select the text you want to format, and then press the keyboard shortcut.

Renaming a Style

Sometimes you might want to rename a style—maybe the style's purpose has changed since the style was created, or maybe you want to make the style's name more descriptive. Regardless of your reasons, you can change a style name easily by following these steps:

1 Right-click a style name in the Styles And Formatting task pane, and choose Modify.

2 In the Modify Styles dialog box, click in the Name box, edit the style's name, and click OK.

Keep in mind that the name change is effective only in the active document. If you want to apply the name change globally, you need to save the style in the active template by selecting the Add To Template check box before you click OK.

You can also rename styles stored in documents and templates using the Organizer, as discussed in the section "Copying Styles from One Document to Another," on page 249.

Adjusting Style Properties

As we've seen, you can select all instances of a given style of text and then apply formatting. But an easier and more efficient method (especially if the document is still in the creation stage) is to modify the style's properties. When you modify an existing style's properties, all text currently formatted with that style is updated to match the new settings. This reaction to modifications enables you to change the look of your document rapidly and efficiently, without having to revisit every instance of a style and manually applying formatting changes. This benefit can potentially help you avoid making hundreds of changes by hand.

To modify a style's properties, open the Modify Style dialog box, and remove and apply the appropriate formatting settings. You can use the controls in the Formatting section as well as the Format button's drop-down menu. After you've made your changes, click OK. Your document will be reformatted with the modified style settings.

tip **Modify the default style settings**

Because many styles are based on the Normal style, you can easily change the entire look of your document by modifying the Normal style's default font—for example, you might want to use Bookman Old Style in place of Times New Roman to create a more "open" look. (The Bookman Old Style font is wider than Times New Roman, which is considered fairly narrow.) The modifications you make to a style will apply only to the active document if the Add To Template check box is cleared when you implement style modifications.

caution Changing a built-in style and saving it in a template—especially the Normal template—can wreak havoc on documents that are based on the template.

Updating an Existing Style to Match Selected Text

In addition to modifying style properties and using the Automatically Update feature, Word 2002 provides another shortcut to reformatting styles used in an active document. Namely, you can change an existing style by instructing Word to modify the style to conform to selected text. To take advantage of this backdoor approach to formatting, follow these steps:

1. In your Word document, format and select the text you want to use to modify a style.
2. In the Styles And Formatting task pane, right-click the style you want to change, and choose Update To Match Selection.

After you choose the Update To Match Selection option, the style is modified to match the selected text's formatting, and all text formatted with the style takes on the new formatting settings. The changes you make using this option apply to the active document only.

Deleting Styles

Naturally, when you create and modify styles, you'll probably want to delete a few as well. You can delete styles from the active document's task pane or completely obliterate a style from a template. This section describes how to delete styles from the active document.

To learn more about editing templates (including deleting styles from templates), see Chapter 22 "Formatting Documents Using Templates, Wizards, and Add-Ins."

When you delete a style from an active document, you are essentially either deleting a custom style you created for the active document or instructing Word to not use a particular style found in the document's template. If you delete a paragraph style, Word applies the Normal style to all text that was formatted with the deleted style and removes the style definition from the task pane. You can delete styles in two main ways:

- Right-click a style in the Styles And Formatting task pane, and choose Delete.
- Double-click a style name in the Style Area, select the style (if necessary) in the Style dialog box, and click Delete.

note You can't delete the built-in Word styles from the All Styles view in the Styles And Formatting task pane. You can delete built-in styles from other views in the Show drop-down list in the Styles And Formatting task pane, because in those cases you're merely configuring the active document's task pane view, not modifying the template.

Copying Styles from One Document to Another

After you've created a document using just the right styles, you might want to share those styles with another document. You can easily copy styles from one document to another, without having to create or modify templates. In a nutshell, the procedure entails opening the Organizer window (by choosing Tools, Templates And Add-ins, Organizer), displaying the style lists on the Styles tab for the two documents involved in the copying endeavor, and copying styles from one document to another. Here's the procedure:

1. Choose Tools, Templates And Add-ins, and then click the Organizer button. The Organizer opens, as shown in Figure 10-10.

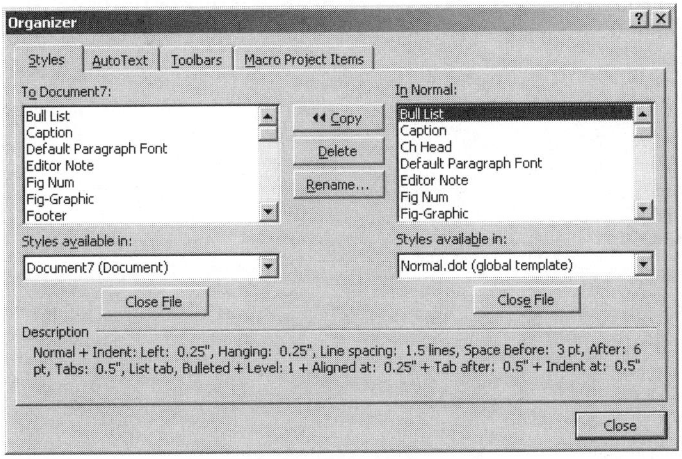

Figure 10-10. The Organizer assists you when you want to copy styles, templates, and other features from one document to another. You can also delete and rename styles within the Organizer if desired.

2. At this point, on the Styles tab, you want to navigate to the two documents you want to work with. Therefore, if necessary, click the Close File button below the left style list. The style list is cleared, and the button changes to an Open File button.
3. Click the Open File button. The Open dialog box appears.
4. In the Open dialog box, click the Files Of Type down arrow, choose All Files, and then double-click the name of the file you want to copy styles to.
5. Now you need to display the document styles you want to copy into a document. To do so, click the Close File button below the right style list. The style list is cleared, and the button changes to an Open File button.

6. Click the Open File button. The Open dialog box appears.
7. In the Open dialog box, double-click the name of the file that contains the styles you want to copy.
8. To select all the styles in the right style list, you can click the first style, press and hold Shift, and then click the last style. Or, if you prefer, you can pick and choose which styles you want to copy by clicking one style and then pressing Ctrl and clicking additional styles.
9. After you select the styles you want to copy, click Copy, and then click Yes To All (or click Yes each time Word asks whether you want to overwrite an existing style with the same name).
10. Click Close, and click Yes to save the modified document.

In addition to copying styles from one document to anther in the Organizer, you can also delete and rename styles as well as copy, delete, and rename AutoText entries, custom toolbars, and macros. These topics are covered in chapters devoted to each subject.

Chapter 11

Outlining Documents for Clarity and Structure

With all the "wizard" technology around, wouldn't you think somebody would come up with a wizard that can write your document for you? Word 2002 doesn't go quite that far, but by using the outlining capabilities of the program, you can make planning, structuring, drafting, and reorganizing your document a clean and simple process. Many professional writers (present company included) use outlining to provide a kind of "road map" for the documents they'll eventually create. Outlines enable you to think first about the logical foundation of your document so that when it's time to write, you can let your creative energies flow from your fingertips.

In this chapter, you'll learn all about the outlining capabilities of Word. Whether you love outlining and want to make the best use of all available tools or you're only creating the blasted thing because your supervisor asked for it, you'll find the tools easy to understand and use. And with practice and a few tips and techniques, you might find yourself actually enjoying it.

10 Reasons to Outline Your Next Long Document

Remember those awful research paper projects you had to do in junior high school, the ones where you had to turn in first your outline, then your note cards, then your draft, and then your final? Composing in Word isn't like that, thank goodness. Once you create an outline in Word, you've got something to start with. Not something you'll type once and then type again later—something you can use to build your document, edit it, and organize (or reorganize) it. And with that outline you create, you can even move seamlessly to and from a table of contents, linked accurately to the work in progress.

So if you have a resistance to outlining (and you're not alone), consider these reasons for outlining long documents in Word:

1. **You're more likely to meet your goals.** If your job involves writing grant proposals, producing product evaluations, writing annual reports, or composing print publications, you know that your document must reach a particular goal. You need to know where you're going, why you're going there, and who you're trying to take along with you. When you first type the document headings in Word, you're defining the steps that will take you to the goal of your publication. Your headings reflect the major categories of information your audience will want to know. As you create the outline, you can make sure you're completely covering all the topics that you need to reach your end result.

2. **You can create an organized, thoughtful document.** Your outline will list not only the large-ticket categories but also smaller subtopics within each category. The multi-level capabilities Word outlines offer (up to nine levels) enable you to organize your thoughts down to the smallest detail.

3. **The headings remind you where you're going.** Once you have an outline that you're happy with, you're free to write the document as the muse strikes. If you're a stream-of-consciousness writer, you can simply go with the flow and let the words fly—in the appropriate sections, of course. (Actually, you can always move them later if you choose.) If you're more of a left-brained, analytical writer, you can craft your sentences within the structured topics, making sure you've got the requisite topic sentence, supporting sentences, and closing or transition sentence.

4. **You can easily reorganize your document later.** Because Word offers you the means of moving parts of your document easily, even after your long document is filled with text, you can collapse topics to their headings and move them around as you like. And of course, Undo always reverses your action if you decide it was a bad move afterward.

5. **You can expand and collapse topics.** The expand and collapse features of Word's outline enable you to change what you're viewing in the document. A fully expanded outline will show everything entered thus far—so all the text you've written, subheadings you've added, and notes you've inserted will be visible in a fully expanded outline view. If you want to limit the display to only headings and subheadings, you can collapse the outline to show only those items. This enables you to check to make sure that your organization is logical, that you've covered everything you want to cover, and that you've got your topics in the right order.

6. **You can divide up long documents and make assignments to get documents done faster.** Word's Master Document feature enables you to break long documents up into smaller chunks that you can then assign to other writers. When you pull the document back together, all the pieces can be merged into one coherent whole. Using the outlining feature enables you to see at a glance where the most logical places for divisions would be.

For more about creating and working with Master Documents, see Chapter 25, "Creating and Controlling Master Documents."

7. **You can see what doesn't fit.** Outlining also gives you the means to see what *doesn't* work in your document. If there's a topic that really needs to be a separate document, or a heading that is begging for a rewrite, it will stick out like a sore thumb. Of course, you can edit, move, and enter text in Outline view, so making those changes is a simple matter.

8. **You can easily change heading levels.** Word's outlining feature comes with its own toolbar, giving you the means to promote or demote headings and text. If you want to change a level 1 heading to a level 2 heading, for example, you can do that with a click of a button. This also works for text you want to raise to a heading or headings you want to drop to body text level.

9. **You can work seamlessly with the TOC.** If you've created a table of contents for your document, you can update the TOC on the fly and move directly to the TOC to make changes, if needed. This saves you the hassle—and potential error—of creating a separate document with a TOC that might not get updated when the document does.

10. **You can print your outline for handouts, reviews, or talking points.** Word gives you the option of printing only the outline for your publication, which is a nice feature when you want to show others key points in a document or presentation but don't want them reading along word for word. Whether you do this in outline review stage, as part of a collaborative effort, or you condense your finished document down to a printable outline, you can display and print only the headings you want your readers to see.

Using the Document Map vs. the Outline

Document Map

You might have already discovered a Word feature that gives you a quick-look outline in a side panel along the left edge of your work area. Word's Document Map creates a listing of headings in your document that are linked so that you can move easily from one part to another. (See Figure 11-1.) To display the Document Map, click the Document Map button on the Standard toolbar or choose View, Document Map.

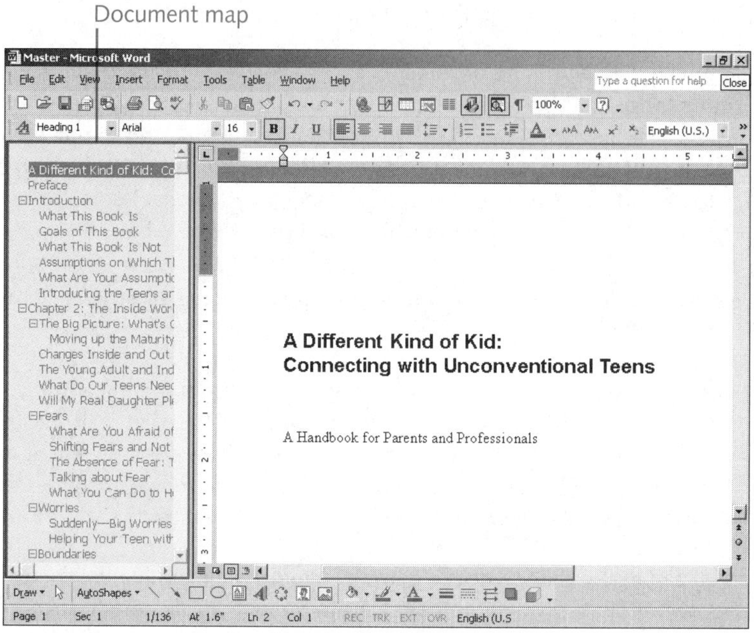

Figure 11-1. Document Map view gives you a quick look at the way your natural outline occurs. The headings listed are those to which you've applied heading styles.

> **tip** **Think Document Map perks**
>
> Two great things about the Document Map: You can view your document two ways at once—in outline form and in print layout (or Web) form—and you can easily move to the topic you want to see by clicking the heading in the left panel of the work area.

Why have a Document Map *and* an outlining feature? First, the Document Map is a handy tool when you want to do things like check the wording of a topic, make sure the text you've added fits the heading, and see at a glance that you've covered all the topics you intended to cover.

What you *can't* do in Document Map view is what makes Word's outline capabilities necessary: You can't change the heading levels of text, reorganize parts, or affect the table of contents in any way. For major structuring changes, text reorganizations, heading modifications, and more, you'll want to work in Outline view. For simple, lay-of-the-land operations, the Document Map will give you a clear picture of your document in a way that you can access and navigate quickly.

note Does it seem as if the Document Map appears in some views but not in others? This is a purposeful thing—the Document Map will not appear (even if you select it) when you choose Outline view. In fact, if you already have the Document Map open and choose Outline view, the Document Map will go away. No worries, though—you don't need two outlines showing at once.

Viewing a Document in Outline View

Whether you're just starting a document from scratch or you're working with an existing one, with text and headings already entered and formatted, you can use outlines to your benefit. To display Outline view, click the Outline View button to the left of the horizontal scroll bar.

tip You can also change to Outline view by pressing Ctrl+Alt+O or by choosing View, Outline.

If you've entered headings in your document and formatted them with one of Word's heading styles (Heading 1, Heading 2, and Heading 3), they'll appear as headings in Outline view. (See Figure 11-2, on the next page.) The basic text styles applied to your document will be reflected in the outline, but all paragraph formatting (indents, before and after spacing, and line spacing) is suppressed. When you return to Print Layout or Web Page Layout view, the paragraph formatting will be intact.

Troubleshooting

Headings Don't Show Up in Outline View

When you switch to Outline view, why don't any of your headings appear as you expected? If you didn't use the built-in heading styles Word offers—Heading 1, Heading 2, or Heading 3—Word won't automatically recognize the headings as outline levels you want to use. To correct the problem, click the headings one by one, click the Outline Level down arrow on the Outlining toolbar, and choose the heading level you want from the list. If you want to do it all at once, select all your headings, choose Outline Level 1, and then use Demote as needed to reduce headings to Level 2 and Level 3.

Several different types of symbols appear in Outline view, as shown in Table 11-1, on the next page. They provide clues as to what action to take while working in an outline.

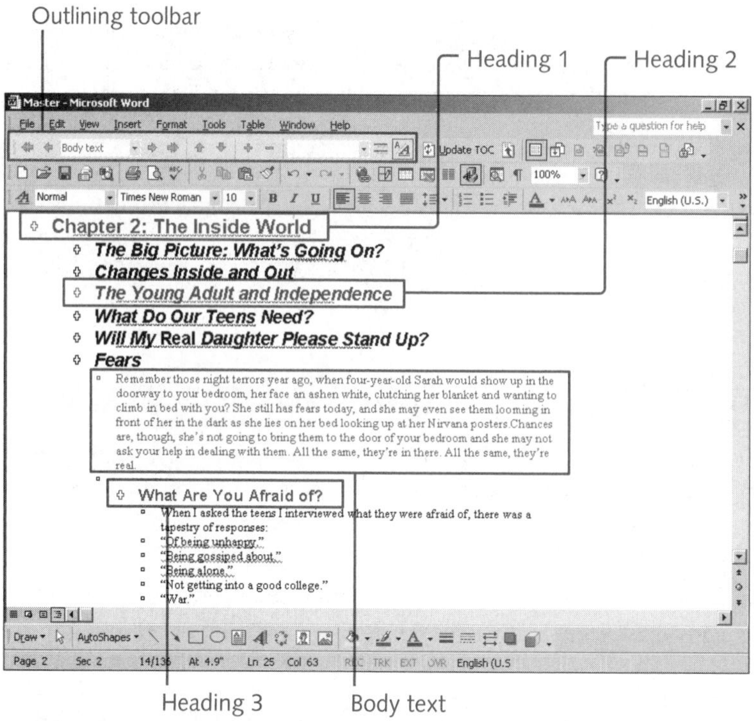

Figure 11-2. Outline view makes use of the headings you've formatted in your document. Paragraph text also appears by default when you first display the outline.

Table 11-1. Outline Symbols

Symbol	Name	Description
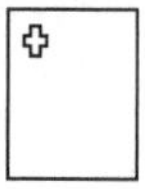	Expand button	If double-clicked, alternately displays and hides subordinate headings and text paragraphs
	Collapse button	Indicates that there are no subordinate headings or text paragraphs
Testing	Underlined heading	Shows that the topic includes body text
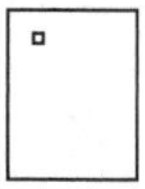	Topic marker	Symbol applied to lowest-level outline entry, formatted as body text

Exploring the Outlining Toolbar

When you display your document in Outline view, the Outlining toolbar appears automatically. Like other Word toolbars, the Outlining toolbar is dockable, which means you can move it to any place on screen you think is convenient. Figure 11-3 shows the work space with the Outlining toolbar in the document area as a floating toolbar. Table 11-2, on the next page, lists and describes the various tools on the Outlining toolbar.

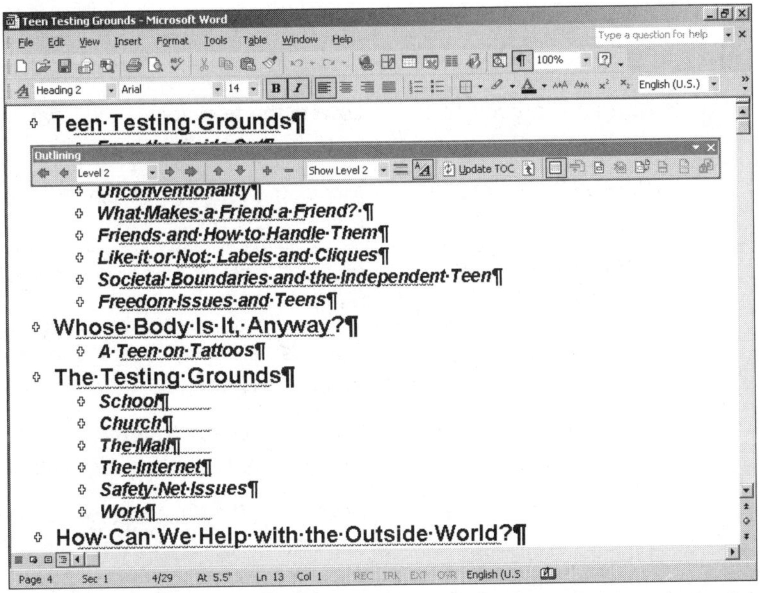

Figure 11-3. The Outlining toolbar can be docked along the edges of your document window or pulled anywhere on the screen as a floating toolbar.

> **note** When you display the Outlining toolbar by choosing View, Toolbars and selecting Outlining, only the tools shown in Table 11-2 are displayed. When you change to Outline view, the Outlining toolbar and the Master Document tools appear in the same button row.

> **newfeature!**
> **tip** **Explore new tools on the Outlining toolbar**
>
> In Word 2002, you can choose the outline level right from the Outlining toolbar by clicking the Outline Level down arrow and choosing the level you want from the displayed list. You can also update the table of contents (TOC) from Outline view and go directly to the TOC while you work.

Chapter 11

Table 11-2. Outlining Tools

Tool	Name	Description
	Promote To Heading 1	Raises the outline level of the selection to the highest outline level, Heading 1
	Promote	Raises the outline level of the selection by one level
Outline Level	Outline Level	Enables you to view and change the outline level of the selection
	Demote	Lowers the selection by one outline level
	Demote To Body Text	Lowers the selection to the lowest outline level, body text
	Move Up	Moves the selection up one level in the outline
	Move Down	Moves the selection down one level in the outline
	Expand	Expands the outline heading to show subheadings and text
	Collapse	Reduces selection to top-level headings, hiding subordinate headings and text
Show Level 3	Show Level	Displays a list of heading levels; select the level to which you want the outline displayed
	Show First Line Only	Reduces text entries to show a single line; good for reviewing paragraph topics
	Show Formatting	Alternately hides and displays the character formatting shown in Outline view
	Update TOC	Automatically updates a table of contents you've generated for the current document
	Go To TOC	Moves the display to the table of contents (usually positioned at the end of the document)

Creating a New Outline

Creating a new outline in Word is a simple matter. If you're just starting a document, simply click the Outline View button to the left of the horizontal scroll bar. Follow these steps to start the new outline:

1. Type the text for your heading. The heading is automatically formatted in the Heading 1 style.

2. Press Enter. The insertion point moves to the next line in the outline.

Demote

3. To create a sublevel, click Demote on the Outlining toolbar. Word indents the insertion point and changes the first outline symbol (-) to a plus (+) symbol, indicating that the heading level now has a subordinate entry. Type the text for that entry.

4. Press Enter to move to the next line in your outline. By default, Word creates the same level heading as the heading you last entered. If you want to create another sublevel, click Demote.

Promote

5. To raise an entry one heading level, click the Promote button. If you want to move all the way out to the left margin and create a Heading 1 outline level, click the Promote To Heading 1 button.

6. Continue typing entries until your outline is completed. Figure 11-4 shows a sample outline with multiple outline levels.

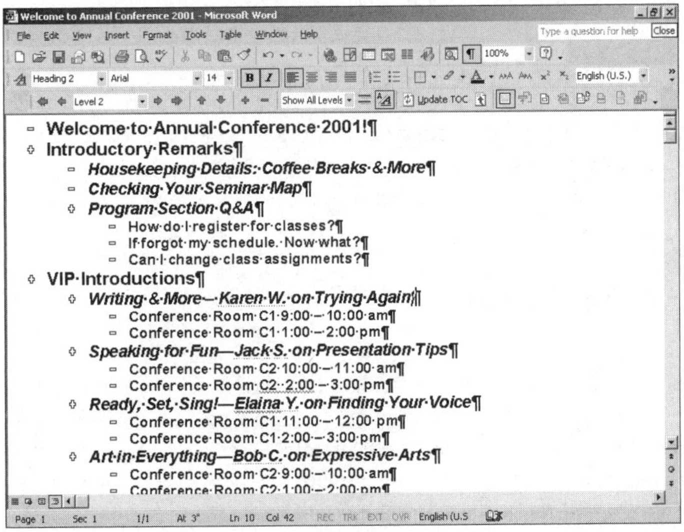

Figure 11-4. Outlining is a simple matter of identifying key topics in your document, naming them, and ordering them the way you want them.

tip **Change the look of Heading 1**

It's true that you must have your headings formatted in the styles Word will recognize—Heading 1, Heading 2, or Heading 3—in order for them to act and display properly in the Outline window, but you do have the choice of creating the styles you like for those headings. You can use the Reveal Formatting task pane to change the formatting choices for those styles and save the changes in the current document. You can also have Word automatically make the changes to all similar heading styles in your document. For more information on using the Reveal Formatting task pane to format headings easily, see Chapter 6, "Putting Text Tools to Work."

caution In some instances, you might want to use the Tab key not to indent a heading level in your outline but to actually insert a Tab character between words. When you want to insert a tab as a tab in your outline, press Ctrl+Tab instead.

Choosing the Way You Want Your Outline Displayed

Working in Word's Outline view enables you to customize the display so you see only the heading levels you want to work with. For example, you might want to see only the first-level heads in your outline so that you can check to make sure all your most important topics are covered. Or perhaps you want to see every level, to check the completeness of the subtopics. You can easily move back and forth between various outline displays by using the buttons on the Outlining toolbar.

Displaying Different Levels of Text

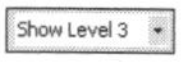

Show Level

You can easily control how much of the outline you want to see. If you want to limit the display of your outline to only Heading 2 levels, for example, you click the Show Level down arrow to display the list of levels. Click Show Level 2 to display every level down to and including level 2. (See Figure 11-5, on page 262.)

InsideOut

Being able to collapse the outline display to headings only gives you a quick look at the overall organization of your document. If only you could copy and paste only the headings of your outline as well. Unfortunately, when you highlight the entire outline, copy it, and paste it into another document, the whole thing—headings and subordinate text—goes along for the ride. The workaround is to create a table of contents (Chapter 26 tells you how) and then convert the TOC to regular text by pressing Ctrl+Shift+F9. Then you can copy the headings and paste them into a document.

Dictating Your Outline

Now, with Word 2002, you can "speak" your outline into being. If you've enabled the Speech Recognition feature, created a profile, and taught Word how to recognize your speech patterns by using the Speech Recognition Training Wizard, you can dictate your outline as you would any other document. To dictate your outline, follow these steps:

1. Open a new document and click Outline view or choose View, Outline.
2. Place the insertion point where you want to begin.
3. Display the Language bar, if necessary (double-click the EN symbol to the left of the clock on the Windows taskbar).
4. Make sure your microphone is connected and turned on and click Microphone on the Language bar.
5. Click Dictation. Word begins "listening" to your speech.
6. Slowly and clearly speak your first heading. After a brief delay, Word enters the words at the insertion point.

The first few times you use Word 2002's new Dictation feature, don't expect miracles. It's a long process of training the program to learn to recognize your words, the way you say them. Using the training wizard and creating your own profile help, but it's a continual process. It's fun, and hopefully worth the effort, but a process nonetheless.

One word of caution, however: If you forget to turn your microphone off and you mutter to yourself as you work, you can have odd words appear in your paragraphs. A laugh apparently sounds like "Lincoln" to Word, and the phrase "You talkin' to me?" was interpreted as "Utah in the." So be forewarned: remember to turn your microphone off when you're no longer using dictation. Somebody's listening to every word you say.

For more about setting up and learning to use Word 2002's speech features, see Chapter 39, "Putting Speech and Handwriting Recognition Features to Work."

note You have other methods of changing displayed heading levels: You can click the Expand or Collapse button on the Outlining toolbar, or you can double-click the Expand button to the right of a heading to display subordinate items.

Showing the First Line of Text

When you get the to the point in your outline work where you're ready to take a look at the paragraph text you've entered, you can have Word display only the first line of text so that you can see what the content of the paragraph is without displaying the entire paragraph. Why might you want to display only the first line of text?

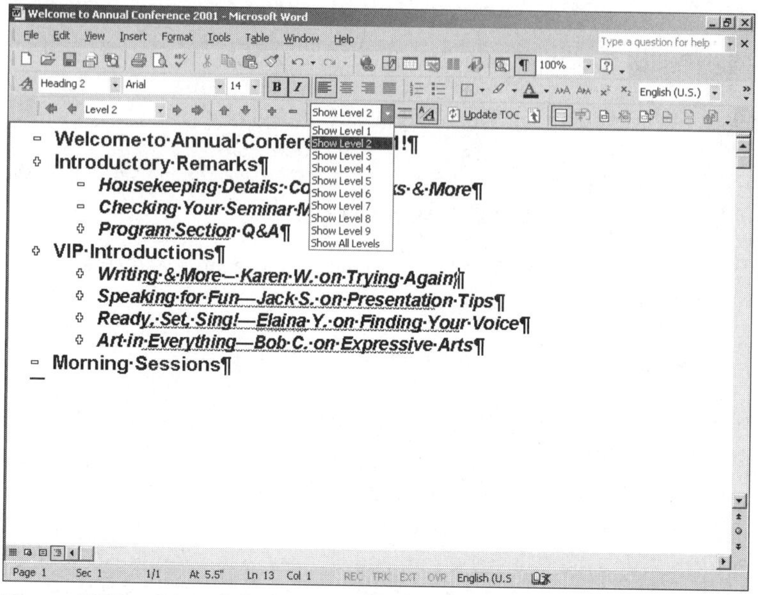

Figure 11-5. Control the levels displayed in Outline view by choosing what you want to see in the Show Level drop-down list.

Show First Line Only

- You might want to check the order in which you discuss topics.
- You're considering whether to move text to a different part of the document.
- You're reviewing the primary points you've covered under subheadings.

To display only the first line of text for the paragraphs in your document, click the Show First Line Only button on the Outlining toolbar. The display changes to show the first text lines, as Figure 11-6 shows. To redisplay full paragraphs, click the button a second time.

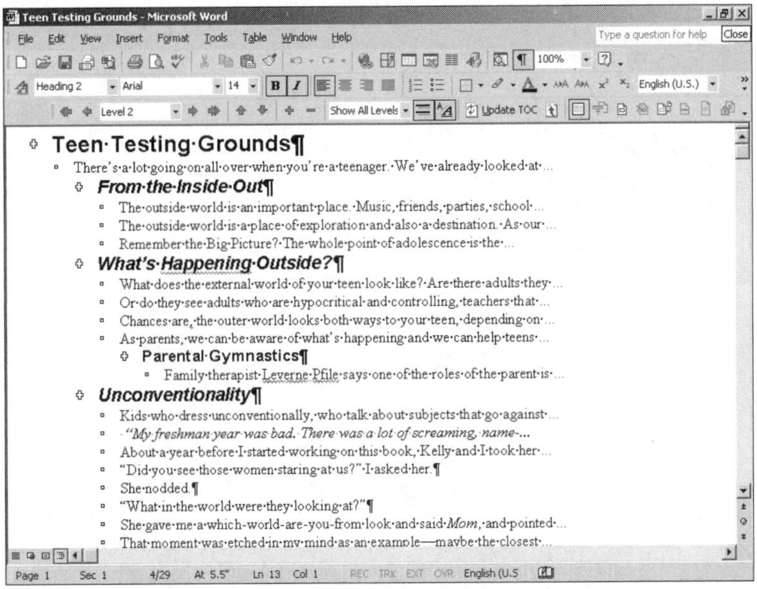

Figure 11-6. Displaying only the first line of text allows you to see the general subject of your text so that you can make informed choices about reordering topics.

Removing and Redisplaying Formatting

Another quick display change you might want to try: suppressing the display of formatting in your outline. As you know, when you change to Outline view, the headings are shown with whatever character formatting they're assigned in the other Word views. Heading 1, by default, shows Arial 18 Point type, for example. When you're working in the outline, however, you might find the formatting differences distracting while you consider the content and organization of your topics.

Show Formatting

To hide the formatting assigned to heading levels in your outline, click the Show Formatting button on the Outlining toolbar. This button actually functions as a toggle, meaning that the first click hides the formatting and the second redisplays it. Figure 11-7, on the next page, shows you what a simple outline looks like when all formatting has been suppressed.

Working with Headings in Outline View

Whether you create an outline from scratch or use the outline created as part of your existing document, you'll invariably want to change some headings around and insert and delete others. Headings are easy to work with in Outline view—with a simple click of a tool, you can change heading levels, move headings in the outline, and even demote the heading to body text, if you like.

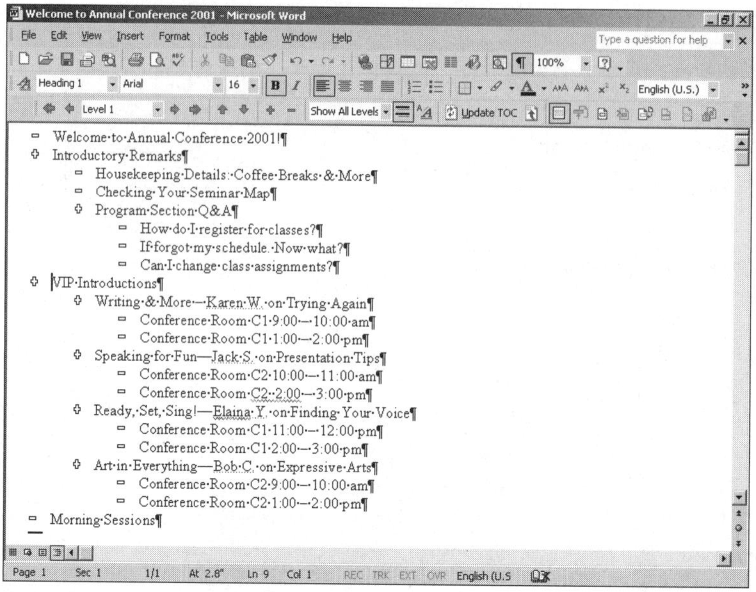

Figure 11-7. When you want to focus only on the thoughts in your outline, you might want to hide the formatting applied to heading levels.

Adding a Heading

When you want to insert a heading in an existing outline, in Outline view, simply place the insertion point following the heading where you want to insert the new heading and press Enter. If you want the heading to be at the same level as the level preceding it, simply type your new heading. If you want to promote or demote the heading level, click the appropriate button before typing your text.

Applying Outline Levels

Outline Level

You can choose the outline level for your heading by using the Outline Level drop-down list on the Outlining toolbar. Simply click in the heading to which you want to apply the outline level; then click the Outline Level down arrow to display the list, as Figure 11-8 shows. Click your choice, and the format is applied to the heading.

> **tip** **Get different document perspectives**
>
> You can easily view your document in both Outline view and Print Layout view at the same time. Just drag the screen divider (located at the top of the vertical scroll bar) down the scroll bar; another pane opens above the current one. To change that area to another view, click in it to make it active and select the view you want. You can then see how your document looks while you're working in Outline view.

Chapter 11

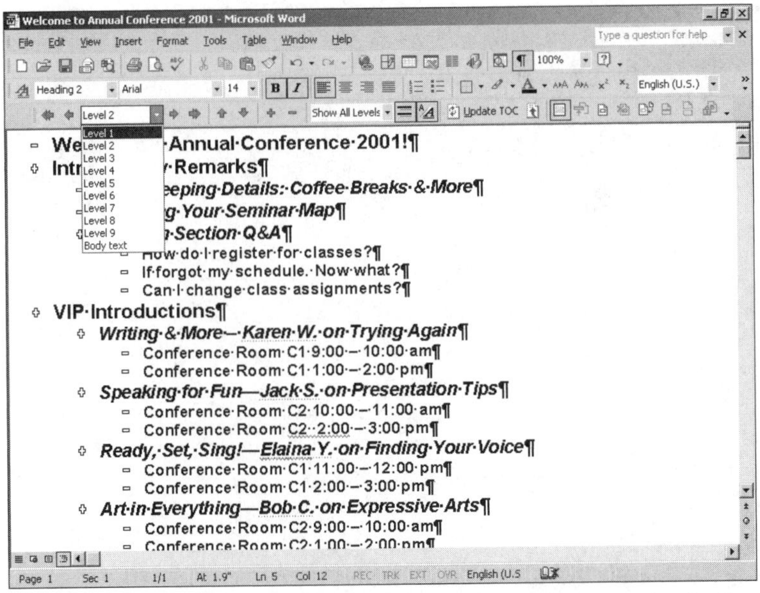

Figure 11-8. If you know which outline level you want to assign to the new heading, choose it directly from the Outline Level drop-down list.

Promoting and Demoting Headings

Promote

Demote

Demote To Body Text

Promote To Heading 1

Once you have text in your outline, you can easily change outline levels, moving a heading from level 1 to level 2, for example, or from body text up to level 3. Put simply, promoting a heading takes it one level higher in the outline, and demoting a heading moves it one level down in the outline. Figure 11-9, on the next page, shows the various levels available as you promote and demote headings.

Each time you click Demote, Word moves the heading one level down the Outline Level scheme. Outline view shows the change by indenting the heading another 0.5 inch and changing the displayed formatting. Conversely, Promote raises the heading level of the selected text until you reach Heading 1, which is the highest outline level available.

When you want to demote and promote in larger increments, moving a heading all the way to the topmost level, for example, or changing a heading to body text, use the Promote To Heading 1 or Demote To Body Text button.

When might you want to promote or demote text? You could be working on a report, for example, and realize that a topic you've placed at a Heading 2 level really belongs as part of another topic. You can first change the heading levels to reflect the levels they need to be so that they'll fit in the outline where you need them to go; then you can move the selection to that point.

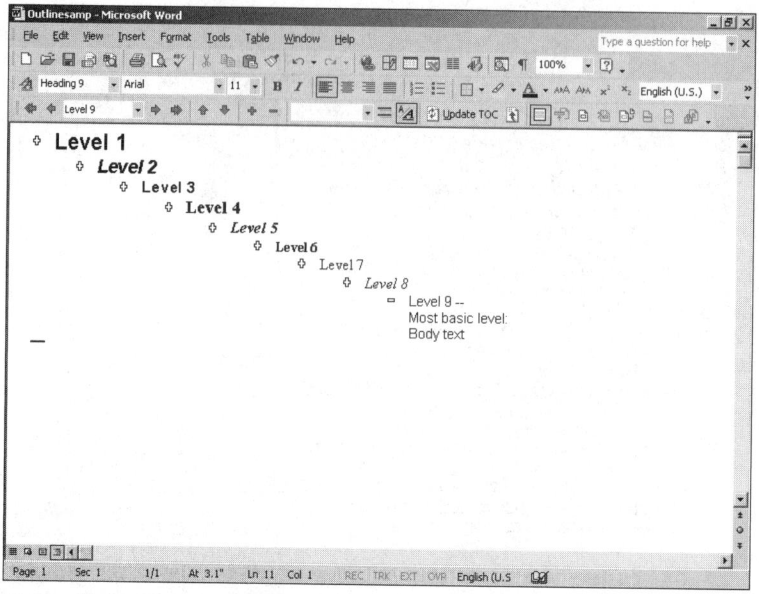

Figure 11-9 Promote and Demote give you a simple way to change the outline level of selected headings.

Changing Your Outline

Once you have all the heading levels set the way you want them, you might decide that you want to move some of your outline topics around. That's one of the biggest benefits of using Outline view—you can see easily which topics fit and which don't, or which topics would work better somewhere else.

Expanding and Collapsing the Outline

As you learned earlier in this chapter, items in the Outline window give you clues about what, if anything, is subordinate to the level displayed in the outline. The visual clues are as follows:

- A minus sign means a heading has no subordinate headings or text.
- A plus sign means subheadings appear beneath the heading level.
- An underlined heading indicates body text is present.
- A small square shows you that the item is body text, the lowest outline item available.

Expand

You'll find two easy methods for expanding and collapsing the topics in your outline: You can double-click the plus sign to the left of the heading you want to expand. Or, if you prefer, you can simply make sure the heading is selected and then click Expand. Figure 11-10 shows the expanded outline.

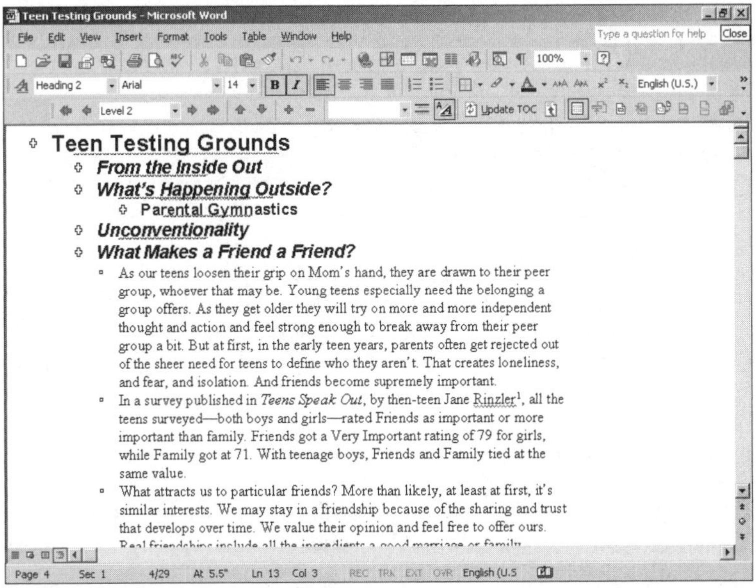

Figure 11-10. When you click Expand, Word expands the selection to the level previously displayed. If you've selected Show First Lines Only, Word will stop at first-line display.

Collapse

Collapse works the same way; simply click in the heading of the topic you want to hide; then double-click the plus sign or click Collapse on the Outlining toolbar.

Moving Outline Topics

Another benefit to Outline view is that you can easily move entire topics in your document. Whether you choose to use Word's Outlining tools, cut and paste text using the Office Clipboard, or drag what you've selected from place to place, you can easily move portions of your document as needed.

Moving Topics Up and Down

Move Up

When you want to move part of an outline to an earlier point in your document or closer to the end, you can use two of Word's Outlining tools—Move Up and Move Down—to do the trick. Start by selecting the entire part you want to move; then click Move Up to move the selection up one heading. If you want to move it more than one level up, click Move Up as many times as needed to position the selection in the right place.

Move Down

You use Move Down the same way: Select the part of your outline and click Move Down on the Outlining toolbar. If you want to move the selection more than one heading farther down, keep clicking Move Down. When you get it to where it will remain, remember to press Ctrl+S to save the file.

> **tip** **Move only a heading**
>
> If you want to move only a heading—not an entire topic—simply click in the heading before choosing Move Up or Move Down. Word moves only the selected heading and leaves any subordinate headings and text in place.

Cutting and Pasting Parts of the Outline

You can also cut and paste parts of your documents in Outline view. This is helpful for those times when you know you want to move a topic, but you're not exactly sure where you want to put it. You can cut and paste part of an outline by following these steps:

1. Select the entire portion you want to move.

Cut

2. Click Cut on the Standard toolbar. The selected portion is removed from the outline and stored on the Office Clipboard.
3. Scroll through the outline until you find the place where you'd like to paste it and click to place the insertion point there.

Paste

4. Click Paste on the Standard toolbar. The portion is pasted at the new location.

> newfeature!
>
> **tip** **Forget what's on the clipboard?**
>
> Word 2002 enables you to take a look at what you've placed on the Office Clipboard. Choose Edit, Office Clipboard to view the Clipboard task pane along the right side of your document window.

Dragging to a New Location

If the part of your outline you want to move is within dragging distance of the new location, you can simply highlight it and drag it to the new position. As you drag, the pointer changes, showing a small box beneath the arrow. A text insertion bar moves from line to line, tracking the point at which the selection will be inserted when you release the mouse button.

tip **Keep it at a high level**

For best results, show only high-level headings before you move part of your outline. This enables you to display more of your outline on the screen and you'll have to drag what you're moving a shorter distance. Even if text is not displayed, subordinate headings and text will be moved with the heading.

newfeature!

Updating Your Table of Contents

One of the new features in Word 2002 is the ability to update a table of contents easily. With the click of a button right on the Outlining toolbar, you can update a table of contents you've already generated. This allows you to record any changes you've made while outlining, whether you've moved headings around, changed word choice, or deleted headings altogether.

tip **Create your TOC**

You must have created a table of contents previously before you attempt using the Update TOC button or Word will display a message that there's no TOC to update. You create a table of contents by placing the insertion point where you want to add it and then choosing Insert, Reference, Index And Tables. When the Index And Tables dialog box appears, click the Table Of Contents tab. Make any necessary changes and click OK to generate the TOC.

Update TOC

To update your table of contents from Outline view, simply click Update TOC. Word goes through your document, checking the headings as they now stand, and modifying the TOC in your document.

To find out more about creating a table of contents for your documents, see Chapter 26, "Generating First-Class Tables of Contents and Related Elements."

Go to TOC

If you want to move to the TOC to take a look for yourself, simply click Go To TOC on the Outlining toolbar. Word moves to the place in your document you've placed the table of contents. (See Figure 11-11, on the next page.)

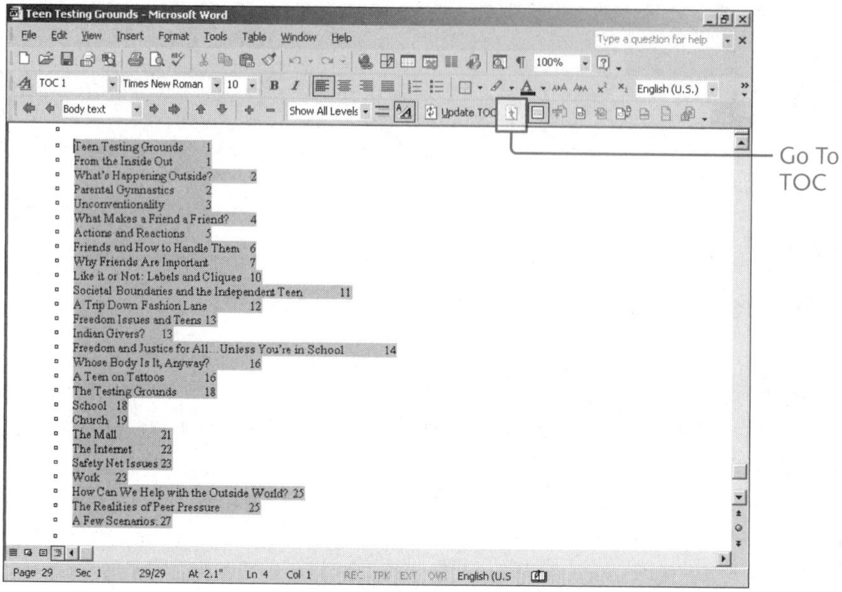

Figure 11-11. You can move directly to the table of contents in your document by clicking Go To TOC.

Numbering Your Outline

For some of your documents, you might need to use Word's Outline Numbering feature. This enables you to choose one of Word's preset numbering schemes (seven are displayed by default) or create one of your own. When might you need to use outline numbering?

- You're creating a long paper that will be reviewed by other people. (Having the numbers is helpful for those times when Arnie in sales says, "Hey, I'm not sure I get what you're saying in paragraph 34.")
- You're drawing up a contract for a new associate to sign.
- You're drafting an outline for a book and want the chapters to be numbered automatically.
- You've finally decided to go back to finishing that dissertation.

Adding a Numbering Scheme

You can add numbers to an existing outline or you can create a numbered outline as you go. To add numbers to an outline you've already created, follow these steps:

1. Display the outline to which you want to add numbers.

2 Choose Format, Bullets And Numbering. The Bullets And Numbering dialog box appears.

3 Click the Outline Numbered tab, as shown in Figure 11-12.

4 Review the preset selections; click your choice, and click OK. The style you selected is applied to your outline.

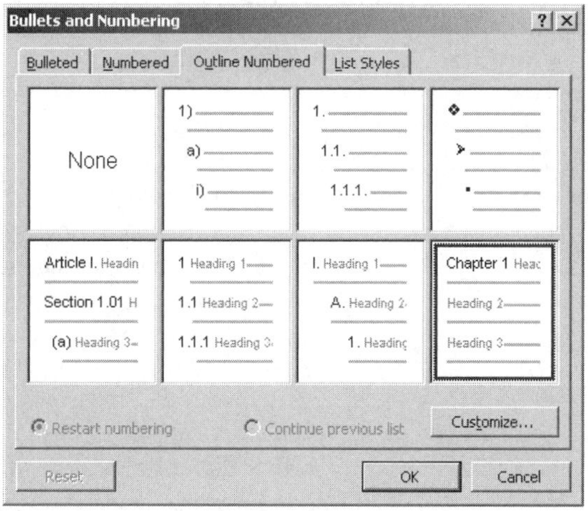

Figure 11-12. Word offers a number of preset outline numbering styles you can use as they are or customize to meet your needs.

You'll notice that the preset numbering schemes each include different character styles (some use numbers; some use symbols; some use a mix of numbers and letters, etc.). The preset numbering schemes act differently depending on which elements in your outline you want to number, as well. Table 11-3, on the next page, gives you a quick look at the different preset numbering schemes in Word's outline numbering feature.

tip **Display and hide outline numbers**

You might want to use numbering in your outline only while the document is in its draft stages. While you're working on it and others are reviewing it, you might find it helpful to have numbers in the outline so that others can make references to sections without a lot of searching. When you're finished with the document and you're ready to finalize it, you can simply remove the numbering by selecting the entire document, right-clicking, and choosing Bullets And Numbering from the shortcut menu. On the Outline Numbered tab, select None and click OK.

Table 11-3. Preset Outline Numbering Schemes

Scheme	Characters Used	Use
1)——— a)——— i)———	Numbers, letters, and Roman numerals	You're following a traditional outlining format.
1.——— 1.1.——— 1.1.1.———	Numbers	You have a multi-level document with multiple subtopics.
◆——— ➢———— ■———	Symbol characters	You want to call attention to the major points in your document and don't need a more traditional numbering sequence.
Article I. Headin Section 1.01 H (a) Heading 3–	Article and Section numbering plus letters	You're creating a paper that is a compilation of multi-level documents or a reference work of several fully developed pieces.
1 Heading 1——— 1.1 Heading 2— 1.1.1 Heading 3	Numbers	You want to number main points and provide a numeric reference among subpoints.
I. Heading 1—— A. Heading 2 1. Heading	Roman numerals, letters, and numbers	You want to use a traditional literary outline style.
Chapter 1 Head Heading 2——— Heading 3———	Chapter numbering plus numbers	You're creating an outline for a book project and want only major headings labeled in the outline.

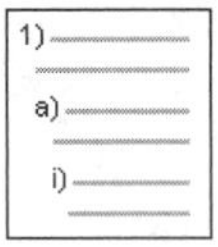

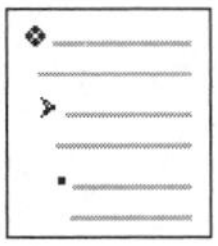

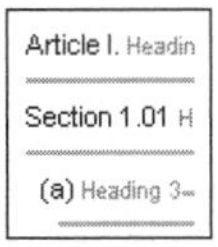

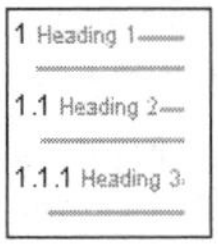

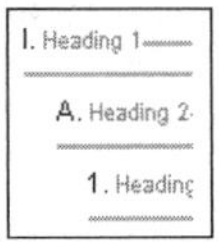

Customizing the Numbering Scheme

If you're working on a unique project and you want to create your own numbering scheme, you can customize one of the outline numbering sequences to get what you want. To start the customizing process, follow these steps:

1. Display the outline you want to number.
2. Right-click in the work area. The shortcut menu appears.
3. Click Bullets And Numbering. The dialog box opens.
4. Click the Outline Numbered tab.
5. Select the numbering scheme that's closest to the one you want and then click Customize. The Customize Outline Numbered List dialog box is displayed. (See Figure 11-13.)

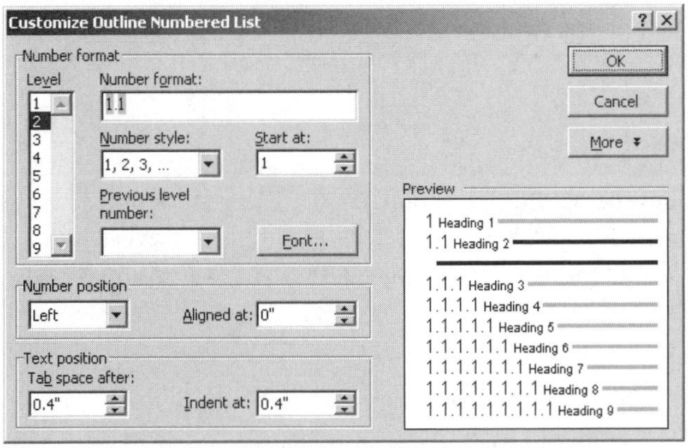

Figure 11-13. You can create your own outline numbering scheme based on one of Word's preset styles.

tip **Renumber safely**

If you try one outline numbering sequence and then want to change to another, first remove the previous outline numbering sequence by displaying the Bullets And Numbering dialog box, clicking the Outline Numbered tab, clicking None, and clicking OK. That removes the numbering scheme from your outline. Now go back and repeat the steps to choose the numbering scheme you want. If you go directly from one numbering style to another, you might get unexpected results; occasionally Word changes outline levels and could introduce errors into your document.

Troubleshooting

The Numbers in the Numbered Outline Disappear

You're creating a numbered outline and you selected the style you want in the Outline Numbered tab of the Bullets And Numbering dialog box. But when you return to the outline, not all the headings are numbered as you selected. What's going on?

Word only "sees" and formats headings that are assigned to the built-in heading styles. If only a portion of your headings are formatted with the built-in styles, Word numbers only those headings. If you've created custom styles for your outline, you can still use those styles (and number them the way you want). In order to do this, you need to create a link that ties the custom style to one of Word's outline levels. Take care of creating this link by right-clicking in the work area and choosing Bullets And Numbering. Click the Outline Numbered tab and click Customize. In the Customize Outline Numbered List dialog box, select the outline level you want, click More (if necessary), and click the Link Level To Style down arrow. Choose the name of the style you used for the heading and click OK. Word links the style you selected to the outline level in the numbering scheme.

Selecting the Level

Word provides the option of customizing the different outline levels separately. Click the level you want to work with by selecting it in the Level list, on the left side of the Customize Outline Numbered List dialog box. In the Preview section, you see the outline level you've selected.

tip **Change a portion of your outline**

By default, Word applies to the entire document the changes you make in the Customize Outline Numbered List dialog box. If you want to apply a change only to a portion of your outline, however, you can display the dialog box, click More (if necessary) to display the advanced options, and click the Apply Changes To down arrow. Choose Current Paragraph to apply the changes to the paragraph at the insertion point, This Point Forward to apply the changes throughout the remainder of the document, or Selected Text to apply the changes only to the text that's selected.

Choosing Your Style

The number style you select determines whether the numbering scheme uses numbers, letters, words, or characters. You can choose from 16 different styles, which include several bullet styles and a picture bullet style. To choose the number style you want to use for your customized outline, click the Number Style down arrow in the Customize Outline Numbered List dialog box and click your choice.

> **tip** **Create legal briefs**
>
> If your work involves preparing legal briefs on a regular basis, you'll be pleased to know that there's a single option that can do the legal style numbering for you. Right-click in the Outline window and choose Bullets And Numbering from the shortcut menu. Click the Outline Numbered tab and click Customize. Click the More button in the Customize Outline Numbered List dialog box. Select the Legal Style Numbering check box. Finally, click OK, and Word renumbers your outline.

Controlling the Format of Outline Numbers

All the selections you make in the Customize Outline Numbered List dialog box, with the exception of the indent for a particular item, are shown in the Number Format box at the top of the dialog box. The number format controls the way your numbering scheme is displayed. If you want to use additional characters or words in your numbering scheme, enter them here. For example, you might want to use some of the following: (1) 1: 1 –New Item! ** 1 ** <1> ~ 1 ~.

As you make each change, the Preview window shows you how your new outline format will look. You can continue revising the format as many times as you want; Word doesn't record the change until you click OK.

Customizing Your Start Point

You also have the option of starting the numbering of your outline with a number other than 1. To choose a new number, click the Start At up and down arrows or click in the text box and type the number you want to use.

> **tip** **Link outline levels to styles**
>
> Don't want all these changes to go to waste? You can link the changes you make in your outline levels to corresponding styles in the style sheet of the current document. To do so, display the Customize Outline Numbered List dialog box, choose the Level style you want to use, and click the More button. Click the Link Level To Style down arrow and choose the style to which you want to link the outline level; then click OK.

Customizing the Font Selection

You aren't stuck with the fonts Word assigns by default—or even the fonts you've already used in your document heading styles—when it comes to customizing your outline. To select a different font, click the Font button in the Customize Outline Numbered List dialog box. When the Font dialog box appears, make your choices and click OK. The Number Format box and the Preview section in the Customize Outline Numbered List dialog box will reflect the changes you made.

Fonts for Outlines

Which fonts work best for intricate outlining? By default, Word uses Arial 18 for Heading 1, Arial 14 Bold Italic for Heading 2, and Arial 14 Regular for Heading 3. Pretty unexciting stuff. The point, however, when you're in Outline view, is to create something that's easy to read. Arial, while it's not going to make anybody's pulse race, is a straightforward, readable font.

The most readable fonts for text, according to typographically savvy designers, are serif fonts like Times Roman, New Century Schoolbook, and Garamond. The most interesting fonts for headings are often those that give a contrast to the rest of your document—so if you have page upon page of Times New Roman text, looking at an Arial heading isn't such a bad idea. Funny fonts that have personality, like Comic Sans, are great for an occasional attention getter but won't go far toward readability in an outline.

The best advice for choosing fonts for your particular outline is to try a few in your document to see which font best complements the text.

Changing Number and Text Position

If you're creating a custom outline and want to change the alignment and spacing of the numbers in your outlining scheme, you can make those changes in the Number Position section of the Customize Outline Numbered List dialog box. To change alignment, click the alignment down arrow in the Number Position section and make your choice. You can select Left, Centered, or Right.

To indent the text so that it's aligned where you want it, click the up or down arrow in the Aligned At box. You might want to increase the alignment value, for example, if you want the outline to be indented within another section of text or printed within a customized layout scheme.

newfeature!

A new choice in Word 2002 enables you to control where you set a tab for text following an outline number. Now you can enter the spacing for the tab, which helps you with text alignment throughout the list series of your outline. The default setting is 0.4 inch; to increase the setting, in the Text Position section, click the Tab Space After up arrow or type the new value. To decrease the amount of space, click the down arrow or enter the setting you want.

Finally, you can change the amount of space by which you indent the text following the number or letter in your numbering scheme. If you're placing a phrase instead of a single character, you might want to increase the indent to give readers more white space as they read. Changing the text position simply requires entering another value in the Indent At box in the Text Position section. Again, the Preview section shows the change.

Printing Your Outline

At various stages throughout the process of viewing, editing, arranging, reorganizing, and formatting the headings in your outline, you might want to print a copy to see how things are shaping up. Printing is the same basic process, whether you're printing a long document or a simple outline. Here are the steps:

1. Switch to Outline view and display your outline.
2. Display only those headings you want to print by using Collapse and Expand and selecting the outline levels you want to see.
3. Click the Print button on the Standard toolbar. The outline will be printed as displayed on the screen.

Print

Troubleshooting

Too Many Page Breaks in Printed Outlines

You've finished working on the outline for the new product report, and the development team is waiting to see what you've come up with. You've gone back over it several times to make sure you've got all the sections organized properly and the outline levels set correctly. Everything looks good.

But when you print the outline, there are big blank spots in the center of the pages. In the file, the text looks fine—what's the problem? Chances are the blank spots are due to Word's treatment of manual page breaks. If you've inserted manual page breaks in your document, you'll need to remove them before printing the outline; otherwise, the blank spots will prevail.

To remove the manual page breaks, click Show All to display all the formatting marks in your outline; then move to the page break symbols and press Delete to delete them. Save your document and print again. The unwanted breaks should be gone.

Chapter 12

Honing Document Navigation Skills

As an experienced Microsoft Word user, you've undoubtedly grown accustomed to using a few standard techniques for finding files and winding your way through documents. For instance, most people locate and open documents using common navigation tools such as Windows Explorer and the Open dialog box. They can then navigate seamlessly through open Word documents using scroll bars, keyboard keys (such as Page Up and Page Down), and keyboard shortcuts. In addition to these standard means of document navigation, you can use several other Word tools to find and navigate through documents—most notably, the Document Map, Find, Replace, Go To, and Search features.

This version of Word retains the Document Map, Find, Replace, and Go To features from earlier versions of Word. In addition, Word 2002 provides expanded searching capabilities. The key document searching utilities are the new Search task pane and the Search dialog box (which is a modified version of the Find dialog box found in Word 2000, by choosing File, Open, Tools, Find). This chapter takes a look at Word's document navigation tools—the ones that go above and beyond basic document navigation.

The Many Faces of Document Navigation

Word provides numerous document navigation tools, some of which don't even seem like document navigation tools on the surface. This chapter presents the main navigation tools beyond basic browsing, but other means of moving through documents are discussed elsewhere in this book. For example, you can move through documents using the following techniques:

- Jump to marked locations within your document by using bookmarks. (Bookmarks are introduced in the section "Jumping to Document Areas Using the Go To and Select Browse Object Options," on page 300, and are described in more detail in Chapter 28, "Configuring Footnotes, Endnotes, and Cross-References.")
- Browse from component to component using the Select Browse Object options. (Browsing is introduced in Chapter 2, "Creating Documents from Start to Finish," and is discussed further in the section "Jumping to Document Areas Using the Go To and Select Browse Object Options," on page 300.)
- Move from section to section quickly using outline levels. (See Chapter 11, "Outlining Documents for Clarity and Structure.")
- Work with multiple-file documents using Master Documents. (See Chapter 25, "Creating and Controlling Master Documents.")

Keep in mind that the ultimate goal is to become comfortable with the various document navigation tools so that you can access the information you need efficiently and almost automatically.

Conducting Basic and Advanced Searches

Before you learn how to search within documents, you should take a look at how to search among documents. As mentioned, in this version of Word, you can find documents using the Search task pane and the Search dialog box. Using these tools, you can conduct basic and advanced searches. You use the Basic Search view of the Search task pane when you want to find files, Microsoft Outlook items, or Web pages containing various forms of text, and you use the Advanced Search view of the Search task pane when you want to find files based on file properties, such as author name, file name, date last modified, and so forth.

newfeature!

To access the Search task pane, use any of the following methods:

- Choose File, Search.
- Click the Search button on the Standard toolbar.

Search

- If the task pane is open, click the down arrow on the task pane's title bar and choose Search on the drop-down menu.

By default, the Search task pane opens in the last search view you used to conduct a search. If the Advanced Search view is displayed, you can access the Basic Search options by clicking the Basic Search link in the Search Also section of the task pane. Likewise, if the Basic Search view is displayed, you can access the Advanced Search view by clicking the Advanced Search link in the See Also section of the task pane. Figures 12-1 and 12-2 show the Basic Search and Advanced Search task pane views.

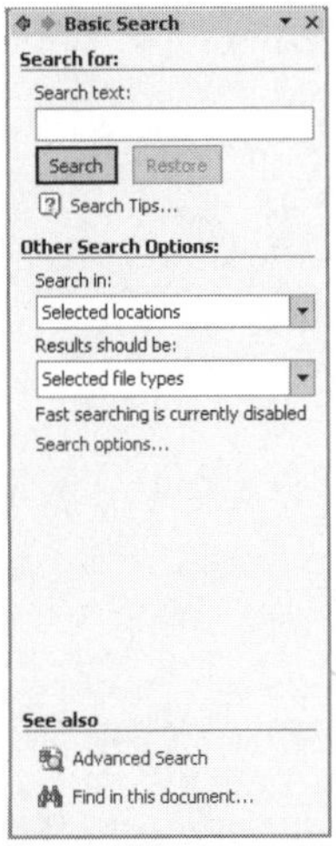

Figure 12-1. The Basic Search task pane view enables you to search documents using text strings.

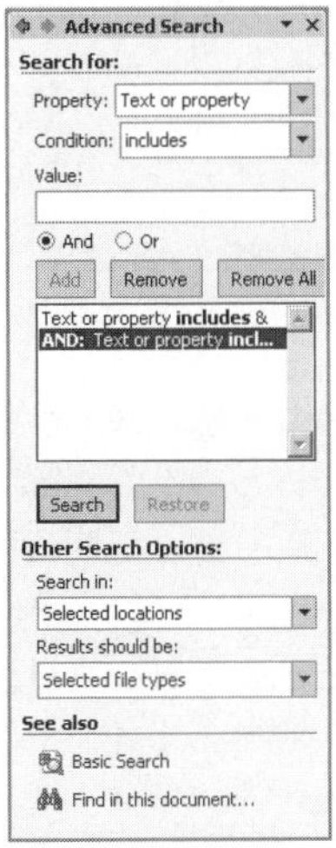

Figure 12-2. The Advanced Search task pane view enables you to search for documents based on properties and conditions.

The Search dialog box offers search capabilities similar to those of the Search task pane. You open the Search dialog box from within the Open dialog box. This approach to searching for documents is handy if you're already in the Open dialog box and you're not sure where a particular document is stored. To view the Search dialog box, perform the following steps:

1. Choose File, Open, or click the Open button on the Standard toolbar to display the Open dialog box.
2. In the Open dialog box, choose Tools, Search.

The Search dialog box contains Basic and Advanced tabs, shown in Figures 12-3 and 12-4, on the next page, which provide options similar to those available in the Search task pane's Basic Search and Advanced Search views (compare Figures 12-1 and 12-2).

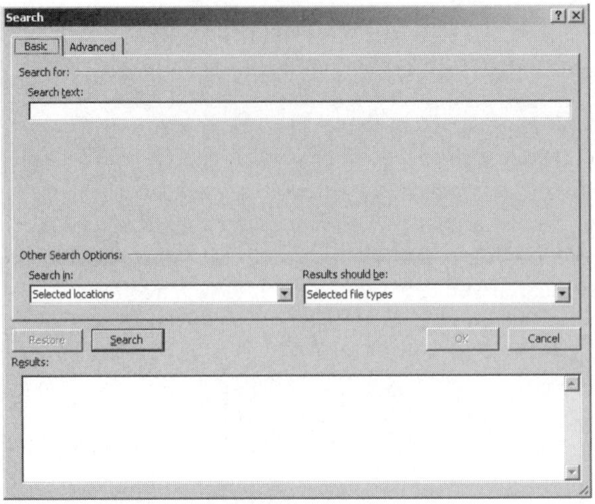

Figure 12-3. The Basic Search options in the Search dialog box.

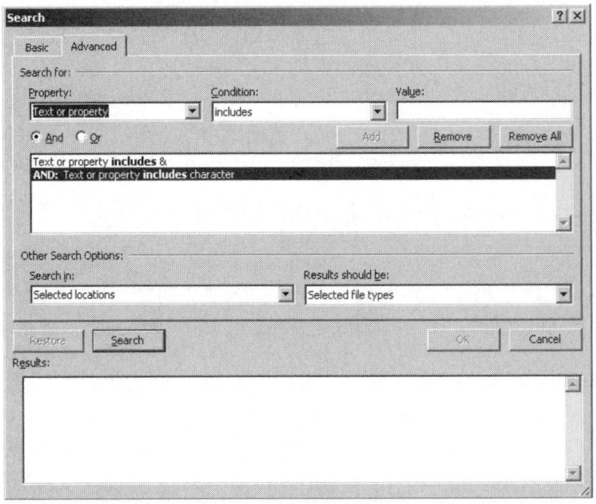

Figure 12-4. The Advanced Search options in the Search dialog box.

To use the Search dialog box and the Search task pane options, you perform similar procedures. In this chapter, we'll look primarily at how to use the Search task pane options, but you can use the same techniques in the Search dialog box.

newfeature!

Using Basic Search to Find Documents

One of the most common ways to search for documents is to look for a particular character, word, or phrase within your documents' file names and contents. In Word 2002, you can search among documents located on your computer and in your Network Places by entering text strings in the Basic Search task pane view.

Using Basic Search is similar to using online search engines such as Alta Vista or Lycos. Word (and other Microsoft Office applications, for that matter) lets you base your search on one or more words. Entering more than one word in the Search Text box makes your search more specific and generally reduces the number of documents returned. In addition, keep in mind the following search tips:

- By default, a basic search finds files containing various forms of a word. For example, searching for **run** would find any document containing the words *run*, *running*, or *ran*.
- You can use the asterisk (*) wildcard to represent any group of letters. For example, entering **l*st** would return any documents containing *last*, *least*, *lowest*, and so forth.
- You can use the question mark (?) wildcard to represent any single character. For example, entering **l?st** would return any documents containing *last*, *lest*, *list*, *lost*, or *lust*.
- If you're searching among Outlook items only (including e-mail messages, calendar items, contacts, tasks, journal entries, and notes) and you're using an English-language version of Word 2002, you can use *natural language searching*. With natural language searching, you can enter word phrases, such as **Find all tasks completed yesterday**, to find information. (Note that natural language searches have some limitations—for example, you can't use a natural language search to look through Outlook public folders.)

tip For additional search tips, click the Search Tips link in the Basic Search task pane view.

After you define your search text, you can choose to search any of the following document storage areas, found in the Search In drop-down list:

- **Everywhere** searches all folders and embedded folders included in My Computer, My Network Places, and Outlook.
- **My Computer** includes all the drives and folders on your computer. You can select My Computer to search through everything on your computer, or you can pick and choose which folders and files you want to include in your search.
- **My Network Places** includes all folders stored on network file servers, Web servers, or Microsoft Exchange servers that are configured as Network Places. Keep in mind that some networked locations don't support searching.
- **Outlook** searches all the messages, appointments, contacts, tasks, and other information stored in your Outlook folders.

> **tip** If you know exactly where the folder you want to search is located, you can type the folder's path directly in the Search In box.

The steps for conducting a basic search are as follows:

1. Click the Search button on the Standard toolbar to open the Search task pane, and click Basic Search in the See Also section, if necessary.
2. In the Search For section of the Basic Search task pane view, type your search text in the Search Text box.
3. In the Other Search Options section, click the Search In down arrow. Select check boxes for the drives, folders, files, or whatever you want to search for in the intended document, as shown in Figure 12-5, and then click outside the drop-down list to close it. If you select folder check boxes other than Everywhere, My Computer, My Network Places, or Outlook, you can use multiple clicks to achieve the following results:
   - One click selects the folder.
   - Two clicks selects the folder and folders within it.
   - Three clicks selects only the folders within the top-level folder.
   - Four clicks deselects all folders within the folder.

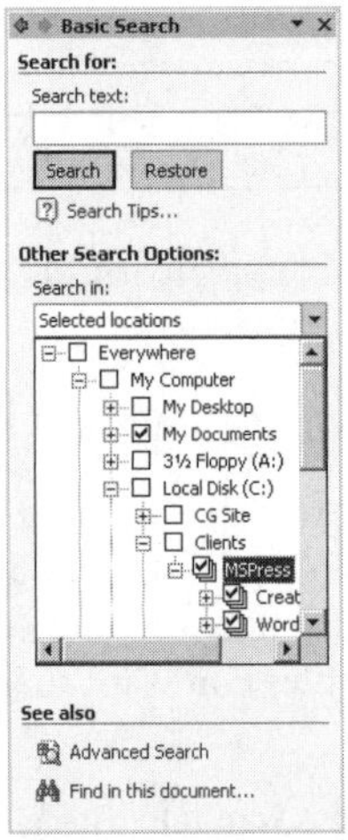

Figure 12-5. Click plus sign icons to expand your view, and select check boxes to indicate that you want Word to search within a selected drive, folder, or file. Notice the "stacked" check boxes, which indicate that subfolders will be included in the current search.

4 Click the Results Should Be down arrow, select which types of files you want to include in your search, and click outside the drop-down list to close it. For example, if you want to search only Word files, make sure that only the Word check box is selected under Office Files, as shown in Figure 12-6.

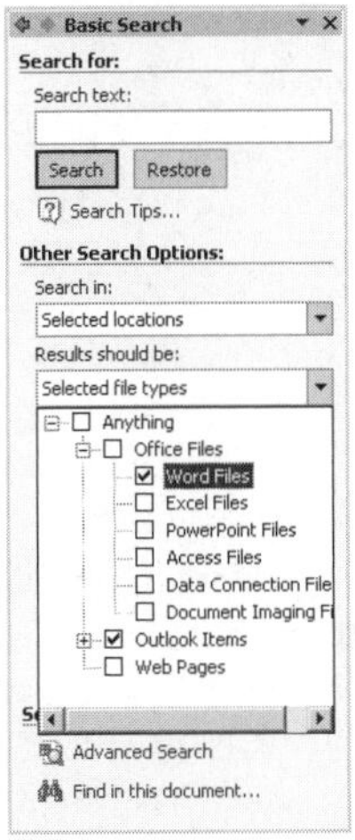

Figure 12-6. You can pick and choose which types of files you want to include in your document search.

The Results Should Be options include the following:

- **Anything** specifies the broadest set of file types, including file types not typically associated with Microsoft Office.
- **Office Files** specifies Microsoft Office documents. You can limit which Office documents to search among by selecting the check boxes next to specific Office applications.
- **Outlook Items** specifies e-mail messages, calendar items, contacts, tasks, notes, and journal entries.
- **Web Pages** specifies Web pages (.htm or .html), Web archives (.mht or.mhtml), and other Web-related formats (such as .asp).

5 After you've configured your basic search parameters, click Search.

When you click Search, the Basic Search task pane view changes to the Search Results task pane view. The search results are divided into My Computer, My Network Places, and Outlook categories. While the search is being processed, you'll see *(Searching)* next to category headings. If no results are found in a particular category, you'll see *(No Results Found)* next to the category heading. If the search seems to be taking too long, you can click the Stop button to end the procedure. (After the search is completed, the Stop button changes to the Modify button.) Figure 12-7, on the next page, shows the results of a completed search.

Figure 12-7. You can perform a variety of actions on your search results using the drop-down menu commands associated with each item.

After the search is completed, you can perform any of the following actions on the returned items in the Search Results task pane view:

- **View document properties.** Hover the mouse pointer over an item in the search results list, or hover over the item and then click the item's down arrow and choose Properties on the drop-down menu to view a more comprehensive summary of the document's properties.
- **Open an item in its default application.** Click a search result item.
- **Edit an item using an Office application.** Click the item's down arrow (as shown in Figure 12-7), and choose to edit the document.
- **Open an item in a browser.** Click the item's down arrow, and choose Open In Browser.
- **Create a new document based on the existing document.** Click the item's down arrow, and choose New From This File.
- **Store a hyperlink to an item on the Office Clipboard.** Click the item's down arrow, and choose Copy Link To Clipboard.
- **View additional search result items.** Click the Next *x* Results link at the bottom of the list of search results.
- **Conduct a new search or modify the search text.** Click the Modify button, and change your search parameters.

InsideOut

Unfortunately, when you open a document from the search results list, the search term isn't selected within the document. To further compound the problem, you can't reliably use the Find utility (as described in the section "Finding Text and Elements Within the Current Document," on page 292) to highlight your search term(s) within documents because all forms of the search term are included in the results (such as *eat*, *eating*, and *ate* for the search term *eat*). To help eliminate extraneous documents in your search results list, consider using at least two-word target phrases when searching and enclose exact phrases in quotations marks whenever possible. By enclosing multiple words or phrases in quotation marks, you indicate that the search terms should be combined to make a single search string.

Conducting Advanced Searches Based on Document Properties

As mentioned, in addition to searching for text strings in documents, you can conduct advanced searches based on document properties. Advanced searches enable you to enter more detailed search criteria by specifying document properties, conditions, and values. To conduct an advanced search, follow these steps:

1. Click the Search button on the Standard toolbar, and if necessary, click the Advanced Search link in the See Also section of the Search task pane to display the Advanced Search task pane view.
2. In the Advanced Search task pane view, click the Property down arrow, and select the document property you want to use to conduct your search.
3. Click the Condition down arrow, and select a condition. Only certain conditions are available for each property.
4. In the Value box, type a value associated with the specified property and condition.
5. Click Add. The search parameter (consisting of the property, condition, and value you specified) will appear in the list, which is located below the Add button.

note If you type a value that's invalid for a property or condition, the Add button will remain unavailable.

6 You can narrow your search by adding more search parameters if desired. To do so, select another property and condition, type a value, and then click And or Or. If you click And, the documents must match both search parameters before they can be included in your search results. If you click Or, any document containing either search parameter is included in your search result.

7 Click Add.

> **tip** If you add a search parameter to an advanced search that you later decide you don't want to include, select the search parameter, and click Remove. Or if you want to clear your search parameters entirely, click Remove All.

8 After you've specified your search parameters, select an item in the Search In and Results Should Be drop-down lists. (The settings in these lists are described in the section "Using Basic Search to Find Documents," on page 282.) Then click Search.

Figure 12-8 shows an example of an advanced search, with two search parameters set and a third search parameter about to be added to the list.

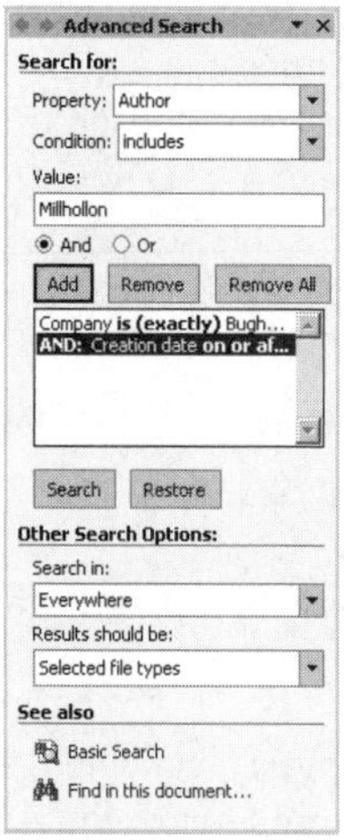

Figure 12-8. Using the And option narrows an advanced search, whereas using the Or option expands your search.

You can perform the same actions on advanced search results as on basic search results, as described in the preceding section. For example, you can hover the mouse pointer over a search result item to view document properties, or you can click a search result item to open the item in its default application.

Speeding Search Tasks Using the Indexing Service

You can speed up your searches by enabling Fast Searching and keeping your index up to date. Fast Searching speeds up your searches by taking advantage of the Indexing Service. The Indexing Service extracts information from a set of documents and organizes the information in a way that makes searching quick and easy. This information includes text (content) as well as characteristics (properties) of documents.

Fast Searching is enabled by default in Microsoft Windows 98, Windows Me, and Windows NT 4 systems. To enable Fast Searching in Windows 2000 or to verify your Fast Searching status if you're using another version of Windows, perform these steps:

1. Click the Search button on the Standard toolbar to display the Basic Search task pane view, and then click the Search Options link. If Fast Searching isn't enabled, you'll see the Indexing Service Settings dialog box.

2. In the Indexing Service Settings dialog box, choose Yes, Enable Indexing Service, as shown in Figure 12-9, and then click OK. The Indexing Service will begin to scan documents to create your search index.

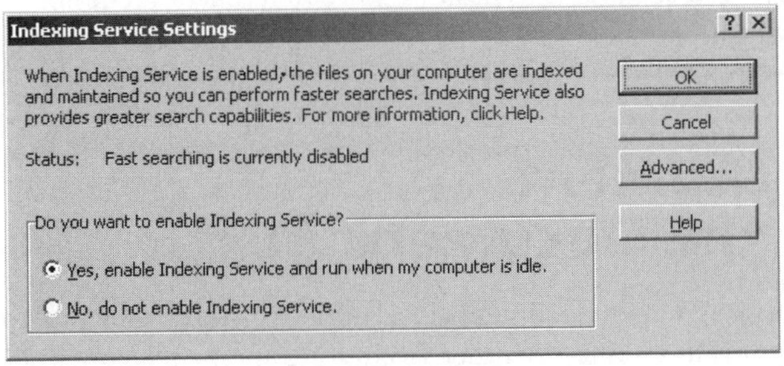

Figure 12-9. You can enable the Indexing Service from within Word.

Troubleshooting

No Search Results Appear for a Search Term After the Indexing Service Is Enabled

When the Indexing Service indexes documents, it ignores the words, letters, and numbers found in the Noise-Word List. If you try to search for a term that appears on the Noise-Word List, you won't get any search results.

Noise-Word List files are named Noise.*xxx*, where the three-letter extension indicates the language of the list. For example, Noise.enu refers to an English Noise-Word List. You can view the words your index's disregards by choosing Start, Search, For Files Or Folders and searching for a file named Noise.*. You can edit the Noise.* document in any text editing program (such as WordPad). If you see a word on the list that you want indexed, simply delete the word from the Noise-Word List and save the file.

Adhering to Search Query Rules After the Indexing Service Is Enabled

After you start the Indexing Service, keep the following search query rules in mind when you search for documents:

- Queries are not case-sensitive.
- You can't search for words appearing in the Noise-Word List.
- If you use a special character in your query (such as &, |, ^, #, @, or $), you must enclose the query in quotation marks to identify the enclosed information as a single search string unit.
- Date and times values should be in the form *yyyy/mm/dd hh:mm:ss* or *yyyy-mm-dd hh:mm:ss*. The first two characters of the year and the entire time can be omitted.
- Numeric values can be decimal or hexadecimal. Hexadecimal values should be preceded by *0x*.
- You can use the following Boolean operators or symbols: AND (&), OR (|), and NOT (&!). You can also use NEAR (~) in content queries (but not in property queries).

Accessing Document Areas Using the Document Map

You can navigate through open documents in a number of ways. One way to navigate through a document is to use the Document Map feature. The Document Map is displayed as a separate pane along the left side of your window and contains a list of the headings in the document. The Document Map enables you to quickly jump to specific sections in your document; it also serves as a quick reminder of your current location within the open document. Figure 12-10 shows a document with the Document Map opened.

To use the Document Map effectively, your document must be formatted with built-in heading styles or outline-level paragraph formats. If your document doesn't use either of these built-in formatting settings, Word attempts to identify paragraphs that seem to be headings and displays them in the Document Map, but this approach is only nominally effective. To navigate through a document using the Document Map, follow these steps:

1. Click the Document Map button on the Standard toolbar, or choose View, Document Map. By default, all levels of headings are displayed. To change the default setting, right-click the Document Map, and choose a heading level. You can also click the plus and minus signs next to headings that have subheadings to expand and collapse sections.

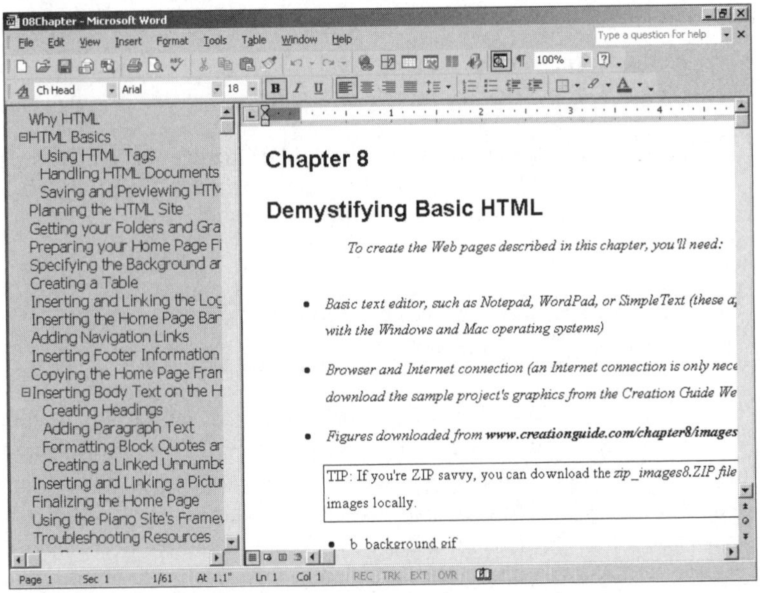

Figure 12-10. Click a section heading to display the section.

Troubleshooting

The Text in the Document Map Is Too Large

You can format the text in the Document Map to make working with it easier. For example, changing the font and font size can make the Document Map text easier to read and headings easier to find. (When you reformat the Document Map text, you do not alter the actual heading styles in the document.) To modify the Document Map text, follow these steps:

1. Click the Document Map button on the Standard toolbar, or choose View, Document Map.
2. Click the Styles And Formatting button on the Formatting toolbar, or choose Format, Styles And Formatting.
3. In the Styles And Formatting task pane, click the Show down arrow, and select Custom.
4. In the Format Settings dialog box, select the Document Map check box in the Style To Be Visible list, and then click OK to return to the Styles And Formatting task pane.
5. Right-click Document Map, choose Modify, configure the font style and size, and then click OK.

2 Click a heading to jump to the corresponding section in the document window. The current section's heading is highlighted, so you can quickly see the current position of the insertion point within the document.

3 Close the Document Map by clicking the Document Map button, double-clicking the Document Map's resize bar (the bar adjacent to the vertical scroll bar), or choosing View, Document Map.

Finding Text and Elements Within the Current Document

In addition to searching for documents and navigating through documents using the Document Map, you can search for text, graphics, and other document elements within the current document by using the Find, Replace, and Go To features. Find, Replace, and Go To are extremely popular tools among seasoned Word users because they are quick, accurate, and easy to use. And as an added bonus, Word 2002 tosses in a couple new twists to these tried-and-true favorites without eliminating any existing functionality. In this section, we'll take a closer look at the Find feature; we'll look at Replace and Go To in the two sections that follow.

To access the Find tab in the Find And Replace dialog box, shown in Figure 12-11, choose Edit, Find, or press Ctrl+F. Alternatively, you can click the Find button on the Select Browse Object menu. (To display the Select Browse Object menu, click the Select Browse Object button located near the bottom of the vertical scroll bar, or press Ctrl+Alt+Home.)

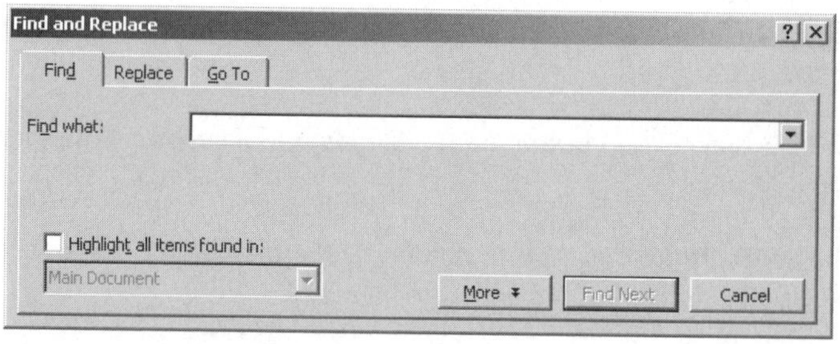

Figure 12-11. You can use the Find tab to locate instances of words, phrases, special characters, styles, and more.

In this section, you'll learn how to use the Find tab's various options; many of these options also appear on the Replace tab.

> **tip** **Add the Find Button to the Standard Toolbar**
>
> To add the Find button to the Standard toolbar, click the down arrow on the right end of the Standard toolbar, choose Add Or Remove Buttons, point to Standard, and then click the Find option.

newfeature!

Finding and Selecting Items

As an experienced Word user, you know that you can find characters, words, phrases, and text elements by typing a search string in the Find dialog box and then clicking Find Next to move from one instance of the search string to the next. In addition to the standard instance-by-instance Find capabilities, this version of Word lets you select every instance of a character, word, phrase, or text element at one time with a single click. To select every instance of a search text string, follow these basic steps:

1. On the Find tab in the Find And Replace dialog box, type your search text in the Find What box.
2. Select the Highlight All Items Found In check box, ensure that Main Document is selected in the drop-down list, and then click Find All. (The Find Next button changes to the Find All button after you select the Highlight All Items Found In check box.)
3. Click Close to close the dialog box.

When all instances of a search string are selected, you can globally format the selected text by clicking toolbar buttons or applying Format menu options. You can also delete all the selected text by pressing Delete or Backspace. To deselect the selected text, simply click an unhighlighted area within your document.

Configuring Options on the Find Tab

In many cases, conducting a simple text search using the Find tab adequately serves your needs. But you'll also encounter situations when you want to further refine your search parameters. To define more specific searches or to search for document elements, you'll need to use the Find And Replace dialog box's additional options. To view the additional options on the Find tab, click the More button. The fully expanded Find tab is shown in Figure 12-12, on the next page.

The Find options in Word 2002 are fundamentally the same as the Find options in Word 2000, so taking advantage of the advanced Find capabilities in this version of Word will be very familiar to Word 2000 users. But let's take a moment to review the expanded Find tab's options. (Keep in mind that most of these options are also available on the Replace tab.)

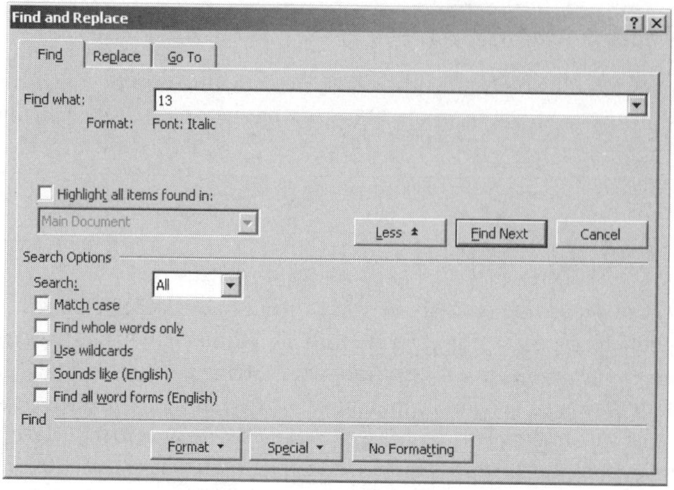

Figure 12-12. The expanded version of the Find dialog box provides access to search options as well as the Format, Special, and No Formatting buttons. Notice that the More button has changed to a Less button; you can click the Less button to shrink the dialog box to its original view.

The following Search options are available on the expanded Find tab:

- The **Search** box enables you to specify whether to search Down, Up, or All. When you choose All, Word searches the entire document by starting at the insertion point, searching to the end of the document, moving to the beginning of the document, and then searching until reaching the insertion point again. When you choose Down or Up, Word starts from the insertion point and searches only in the specified direction; with the Up and Down options, Word does not search headers, footers, footnotes, or comments.
- **Match Case** specifies a search that distinguishes between uppercase and lowercase letters based on the text entered in the Find What box.
- **Find Whole Words Only** searches only for whole words, not parts of longer words. For example, if you type **the** in the Find What text box and select Find Whole Word Only, Word will ignore words that contain *the*, such as *them, there, other,* and so forth.
- **Use Wildcards** enables you to use wildcard characters in place of text to expand and refine your searches. If you enter wildcard characters in the Find What box without selecting the Use Wildcards option, Word will treat the wildcards as plain text. Table 12-1 lists the wildcards you can use in the Find And Replace dialog box. When the Use Wildcard check box is selected and you want to search for a character that is also a wildcard, precede the character with a backslash (\). For example, to search for an asterisk, you must enter *.

- **Sounds Like** searches for terms that sound like the word or words entered in the Find What box. For example, if you enter **eight** in the Find What box and then select the Sounds Like check box, Word will find all instances of *eight* as well as *ate*. This feature works only with legitimate words—entering the number **8** and selecting the Sounds Like check box won't return *eight*, *ate*, or *8*, and entering **u r** won't return *you are*.
- **Find All Word Forms** searches for all forms of the word entered in the Find What box. For example, if you enter **speak** in the Find What box, Word will find *speak*, *speaking*, *spoke*, *spoken*, *speaks*, and so forth. This option is unavailable when you select the Use Wildcards or Sounds Like check box.

Table 12-1. Using Wildcards in the Find And Replace Dialog Box

Wildcard	Specifies	Example
?	Any single character	**p?t** finds *pet*, *pat*, *pit*, and so forth.
*	Any string of characters	**p*t** finds *pest*, *parrot*, *pit*, and so forth.
<	Finds the text at the beginning of a word	**<(mark)** finds *market* but not *demark*.
>	Finds the text at the end of a word	**(ter)>** finds *winter* but not *terrain*.
[ ]	Finds one of the enclosed characters	**t[oa]n** finds *ton* and *tan*.
[-]	Finds any character within the specified range	**[r-t]ight** finds *right*, *sight*, and *tight*.
[!x-z]	Finds any single character except characters in the range inside the brackets	**cl[!a-m]ck** finds *clock* and the *cluck* but not *clack* or *click*.
{*n*}	Finds exactly *n* occurrences of the preceding character or expression	**ble{2}d** finds *bleed* but not *bled*.
{*n*,}	Finds at least *n* occurrences of the preceding character or expression	**fe{1,}d** finds *fed* and *feed*.
{*n*,*m*}	Finds from *n* to *m* occurrences of the preceding character or expression	**10{1,3}** finds *10*, *100*, and *1000*.
@	Finds one or more occurrences of the preceding character or expression	**mo@d** finds *mod* and *mood*.

Finding Instances of Formatting

In addition to finding text strings, you can find (and replace) various formatting settings. To view the available formatting parameters on the expanded Find tab, click the Format button, as shown in Figure 12-13.

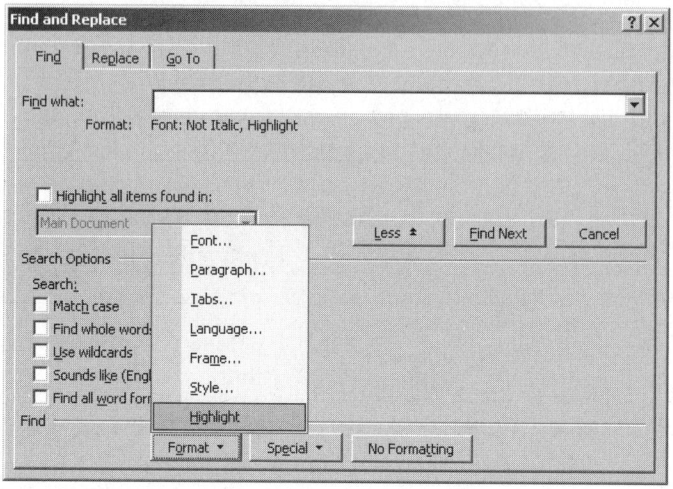

Figure 12-13. You can find instances of formatting by choosing options available on the Format drop-down menu.

Choosing Font, Paragraph, Tabs, Language, Frame, or Style on the Format drop-down menu opens the corresponding formatting dialog box. For example, choosing Font opens a dialog box named Find Font, which looks very similar to the Font dialog box. Choosing the Highlight option lets you specify highlighted or unhighlighted text in the Find What box. For example, choose Highlight once to find highlighted text, choose Highlight again to indicate that you want to find text that is not highlighted, and choose Highlight a third time to find all instances of the search text regardless of highlighting. When formatting is applied to text in the Find What box, the formatting information appears below the Find What box, as you can see in Figure 12-13.

tip **Control Formatting Using Keyboard Shortcuts**

You can control basic character formatting by using keyboard shortcuts. To do so, click in the Find What box and press keyboard shortcuts such as Ctrl+B (bold), Ctrl+I (italic), and Ctrl+U (underline) to toggle among applied, not applied, and neither (which equates to no formatting) settings.

You can find instances of formatting without entering text in the Find What box. For example, the configuration shown in Figure 12-13 will find only instances of highlighted text that isn't italic in the current document. You can, of course, specify text in combination with formatting settings if that's what you need to find.

To clear all formatting commands in the Find What box, click the No Formatting button. You'll want to clear formatting when you complete one Find operation and are ready to conduct another.

Finding Special Characters Using Codes

Word further expands your search capabilities by providing special codes you can use to find document elements, such as paragraph marks, tab characters, endnote marks, and so forth. To view the available special characters, click the Special button in the Find And Replace dialog box, as shown in Figure 12-14.

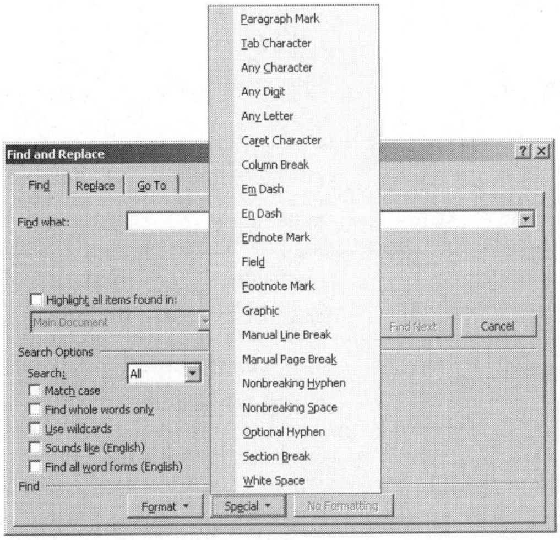

Figure 12-14. You can search for special character and document elements by choosing options on the Special drop-down menu or by inserting character codes directly in the Find What box (or the Replace With box on the Replace tab).

When you choose an option on the Special drop-down menu, a code is inserted in the Find What box. If you'd prefer, you can enter a code directly in the Find What box. Table 12-2 lists some commonly used special character codes. (Notice that some codes can be used only in the Find What or in the Replace With box, and that the Use Wildcards option must be turned on or off in certain instances.)

Table 12-2. Using Special Character Codes in the Find And Replace Dialog Box

Special character	Code	Find And Replace box
ANSI or ASCII characters	^0*nnn* (where *nnn* is the character code)	Find What; Replace With
Any character	^?	Find What (with the Use Wildcards check box cleared)
Any digit	^#	Find What (with the Use Wildcards check box cleared)
Any letter	^$	Find What (with the Use Wildcards check box cleared)
Caret	^^	Find What; Replace With
Column break	^n	Find What; Replace With
Contents of the Find What box	^&	Replace With
Em dash	^+	Find What; Replace With
En dash	^=	Find What; Replace With
Endnote	^e	Find What (with the Use Wildcards check box cleared)
Field	^d	Find What (with the Use Wildcards check box cleared)
Footnote	^f	Find What (with the Use Wildcards check box cleared)
Graphic	^g	Find What (with the Use Wildcards check box selected)
Manual line break	^l	Find What; Replace With
Nonbreaking hyphen	^~	Find What; Replace With
Nonbreaking space	^s	Find What; Replace With
Optional hyphen	^-	Find What; Replace With
Paragraph mark	^p	Find What (with the Use Wildcards check box cleared); Replace With
Section break	^b	Find What (with the Use Wildcards check box cleared)
Tab	^t	Find What; Replace With

(continued)

Table 12-2. *(continued)*

Special character	Code	Find And Replace box
White space	^w	Find What (with the Use Wildcards check box cleared)
Windows Clipboard contents	^c	Replace With

Replacing Text

Often, you'll want to find text to replace it with something else. In Word, you use the Replace tab in the Find And Replace dialog box. The Replace tab contains the options available on the Find tab, but it also includes a Replace With box, as shown in Figure 12-15. You can enter text, wildcards, formatting, and special characters codes in the Replace With box in the same way you enter information in the Find What box.

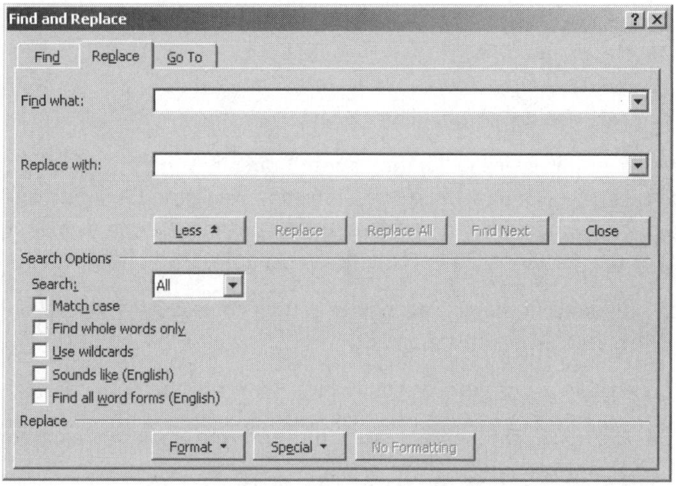

Figure 12-15. The expanded view of the Replace tab offers the same options found on the expanded Find tab in the Find And Replace dialog box.

To access the Replace tab in the Find And Replace dialog box, choose Edit, Replace, or press Ctrl+H. Type the text you want to find in the Find What box, and type the replacement information in the Replace With text box. Then click one of the following buttons:

- **Replace** replaces the currently selected instance of the Find What information with the Replace With information and selects the next instance.
- **Replace All** replaces all instances of the Find What information with the Replace With information. (Be careful when using Replace All—unless you

have a very specific search element, it's usually safer to replace text and components on a case-by-case basis.)

- **Find Next** skips the currently selected instance of the Find What information without replacing it and selects the next instance.

tip **Transpose Words Using the Replace Feature**

Just as you did on the Find tab, you can use wildcards on the Replace tab. Here's a wildcard trick that uses parentheses and backslash wildcards to transpose words. It's especially useful when you'd like to switch a name from last name first to first name first. For example, type (Dunn), (Matthew) in the Find What box and type \2 \1 in the Replace With box. Select the Use Wildcards check box, and click Replace. Word finds *Dunn, Matthew* and replaces it with *Matthew Dunn*. olacing the comma outside the parentheses ensures that it's eliminated when the replacement text is inserted.

Troubleshooting

I Can't Replace Text with a Graphic or an Object

Although the Find And Replace dialog box doesn't directly support replacing text with graphics or objects, you can easily perform this action using the Clipboard and the ^c wildcard. You might want to use this feature to insert elements such as margin icons or recurring field combinations. To execute this procedure, follow these steps:

1. If not already present, enter placeholder text (such as **@@@**) where you want to insert the graphic or other element.
2. Copy the graphic or component you want to insert to the Clipboard.
3. Press Ctrl+H to open the Replace tab in the Find And Replace dialog box.
4. In the Find What box, type the placeholder text.
5. In the Replace With text box, enter **^c;** to indicate the last item copied to the Clipboard.
6. Click Replace or Replace All.

Jumping to Document Areas Using the Go To and Select Browse Object Options

The third tab in the Find And Replace dialog box is the Go To tab, shown in Figure 12-16, which enables you to move quickly through a document, and go just about anywhere you'd like. For example, you can go directly to a page, section, line, bookmark, comment, footnote, endnote, field, table, graphic, equation, object, or heading.

To access the Go To tab in the Find And Replace dialog box, perform any of the following actions:

- Choose Edit, Go To.
- Press F5 or Ctrl+G.
- Click the Go To button in the Select Browse Object menu. (To open the Select Browse Object menu, click the Select Browse Object button toward the bottom of the vertical scroll bar.)

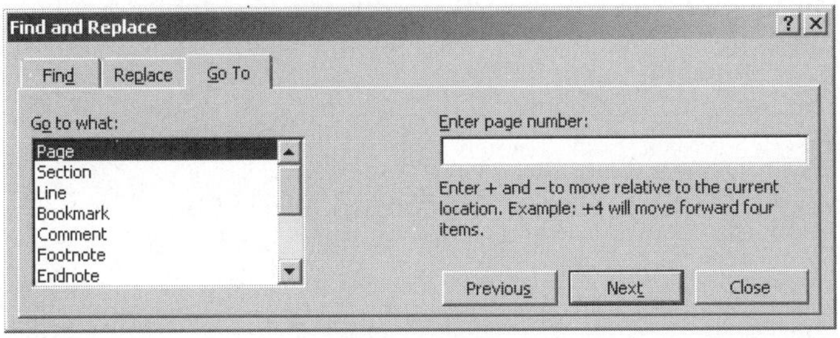

Figure 12-16. You can literally jump from area to area within a document using the Go To feature.

To use the Go To tab, select a component in the Go To What list, enter the appropriate value or parameter in the box to the right if necessary, and then click Go To (or click Previous or Next if no value or parameter is specified). Here are two possible uses for the Go To feature:

- To display a particular page in the document, select Page in the Go To What list, type the page number in the Enter Page Number box, and click Go To.
- To display the next heading in the document, select Heading in the Go To What list, and then click Next (without entering text in text box).

You can also use the Select Browse Object menu to move from document element to document element. To open the Select Browse Object menu, click the Select Browse Object button on the vertical scroll bar. The Select Browse Object menu, shown in Figure 12-17, on the next page, contains buttons that enable you to perform the following tasks:

- Browse by table (see Chapter 18, "Organizing Concepts in Tables")
- Browse by graphic
- Browse by heading
- Browse by edits (see Chapter 33, "Revising Documents Using Markup Tools")

- Display the Find tab in the Find And Replace dialog box
- Display the Go To tab in the Find And Replace dialog box
- Browse by page
- Browse by section (see Chapter 9, "Formatting Columns and Sections for Advanced Text Control")
- Browse by comment (see Chapter 33, "Revising Documents Using Markup Tools")
- Browse by footnote (see Chapter 28, "Configuring Footnotes, Endnotes, and Cross-References")
- Browse by endnote (see Chapter 28, "Configuring Footnotes, Endnotes, and Cross-References")
- Browse by field (see Chapter 36, "Working with Field Codes")

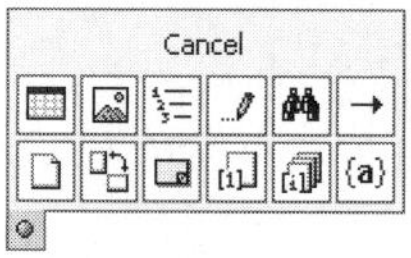

Figure 12-17. The Select Browse Object menu enables you to jump from component to component within a document.

After you choose an option on the Select Browse Object menu, you can click the Previous and Next arrow buttons (located above and below the Select Browse Object button on the vertical scroll bar) to move to the next and previous instances of the selected object.

Creating Bookmarks for Document Navigation

In addition to using the Go To tab in the Find And Replace dialog box and the Select Browse Object menu, you can navigate documents by creating bookmarks. If you frequently need to access a particular area within a document, you can insert a bookmark to make returning to the area a snap. To insert and name a bookmark, follow these steps:

1. Position the insertion point where you want to insert a bookmark, and choose Insert, Bookmark.
2. In the Bookmark dialog box, type a name for the bookmark, click Add, and click OK.

After you insert a bookmark, you can use the Go To tab to find the bookmarked area, or you can choose Insert, Bookmark to open the Bookmark dialog box, select the bookmark's name, and click Go To.

Chapter 13

Maximizing Electronic Reference Tools

Microsoft Word adds resources to your reference library without taking up an inch of shelf space. By default, when you install Word, you also install several standard reference tools such as a dictionary, a grammar guide, a thesaurus, a translation tool, and a document statistics tool.

The greatest advantage reference tools in Word have over traditional reference books is that you can access and customize the Word tools while you work—without stopping midsentence, digging out your trusty dictionary or grammar guide, flipping through pages, and then modifying your text after you find the answer to your spelling or grammar question. Furthermore, Word reference tools enable you to apply spelling and grammatical changes automatically, thereby speeding your word processing tasks even more. Once you learn how to use Word reference tools properly, you'll find that they can be extremely handy. In this chapter, we'll focus on getting the most out of the electronic reference tools that are readily available every time you work in Word.

Building a Document's Credibility Using Spelling and Grammar Tools

The two most frequently used reference tools in Word are the spelling and grammar tools. The popularity of these tools is understandable—most people know that nothing detracts from a document's credibility more than spelling and grammatical errors. To help you avoid the pitfalls of these types of errors, let's look at the ins and outs of the spelling and grammar tools in Word.

> **caution** Using the spelling and grammar tools to check your documents shouldn't replace proofreading. These features are helpful, but they can't definitively correct your text in all instances. Instead of thinking of the spelling and grammar checking tools as a teacher correcting your work, visualize an assistant who taps you on the shoulder whenever your text seems to go astray and then offers advice on how to fix the problem. Ultimately, you'll need to carefully read through your document to ensure its accuracy.

Benefiting from Automated Spelling and Grammar Checking

By default, Word checks spelling and grammar whenever you open a document or type information in a document. With automatic spelling and grammar checking, Word flags potential spelling errors with a wavy red underline and potential grammatical errors with a wavy green underline, as shown in Figure 13-1 (although you won't be able to differentiate between green and red here).

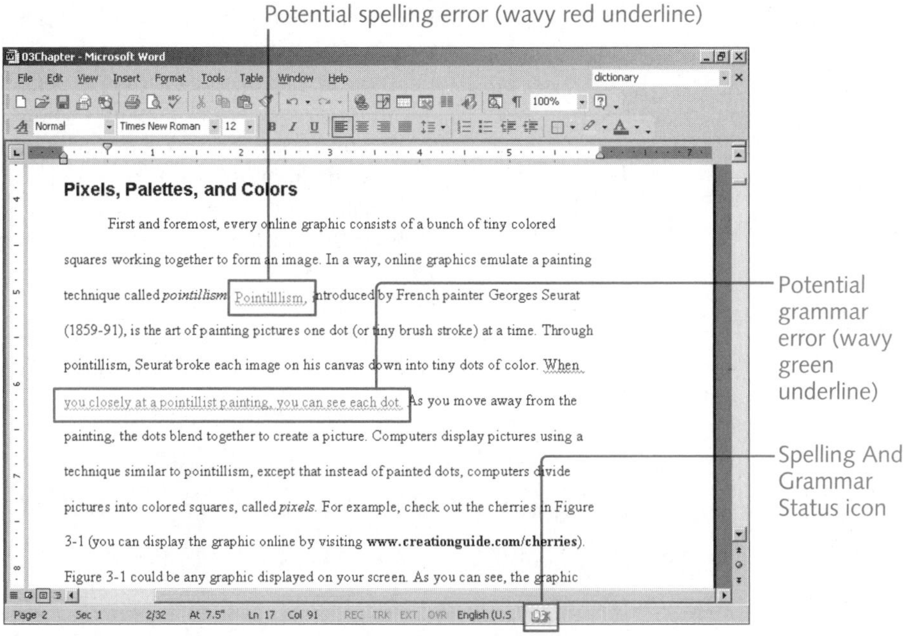

Figure 13-1. By default, Word automatically checks your document for spelling and grammar errors and flags the errors with wavy underlines.

note The red and green wavy underlines used to flag spelling and grammar errors are not printed when you print your document—they appear only on screen.

Word also displays the Spelling And Grammar Status icon on the status bar. This icon indicates whether your document contains any potential errors. If errors are detected, the icon contains an X mark; if no errors are found, the icon contains a check mark. (In the example document in Figure 13-1, the Spelling And Grammar Status icon contains an X, indicating that the document contains potential spelling or grammar errors.)

tip **Flag formatting inconsistencies**

In addition to displaying red and green wavy underlines to denote spelling and grammatical issues, you can configure Word to flag formatting inconsistencies with a blue wavy underline. Word marks text when it appears similar but not exactly the same as other formatting in your document. For example, Word can recognize when a list is formatted slightly differently than other lists in your document or when normal text appears in boldface in paragraph text. To use the formatting checker, choose Tools, Options, click the Edit tab, and then select the Mark Formatting Inconsistencies check box. In addition, the Keep Track Of Formatting check box must be selected on the Edit tab (the default setting).

Fixing Marked Text Quickly

After Word marks potential spelling and grammar errors, you can resolve each issue on a case-by-case basis. To access options for fixing potential errors, you can right-click text that has a wavy underline or double-click the Spelling And Grammar Status icon to select the next instance of a potential error. Both techniques open a shortcut menu containing error fixing options. The available options vary depending on whether the potential error is a spelling issue or a grammar issue.

The shortcut menu for a spelling issue is shown in Figure 13-2, on the next page.

The possible remedies are as follows:

- **List of possible replacement words** provides one or more words that might represent the correctly spelled version of the incorrectly spelled word in your text. To replace a misspelled word with a correctly spelled word, simply click the word on the shortcut menu.
- **Ignore All** instructs Word to ignore all instances of the flagged spelling within the current document. When you ignore all instances of a particular flagged word, the red wavy underline is removed from the specified text throughout the document.

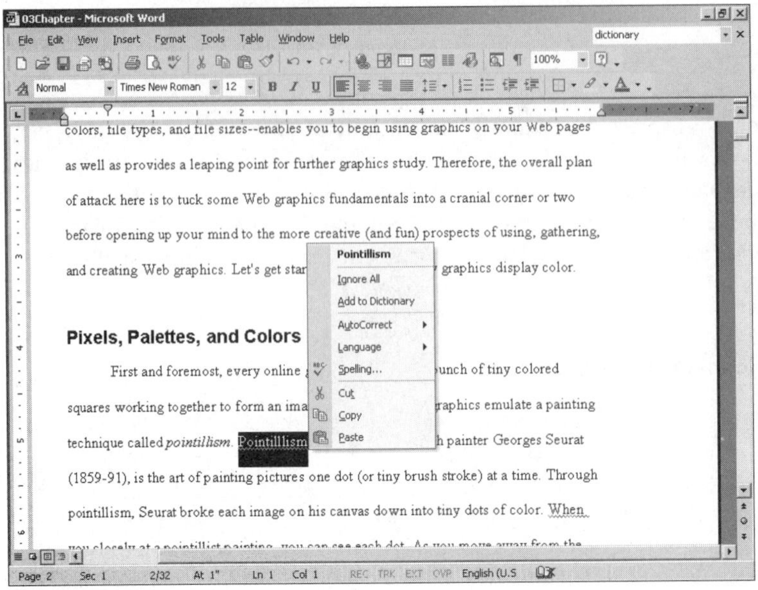

Figure 13-2. Word provides a selection of relevant error correction options when you right-click text flagged as a potential error.

- **Add To Dictionary** adds the word (as it's spelled in your document) to your custom dictionary, which ensures that the term won't be flagged as a potential error in future instances. (Custom dictionaries are discussed in detail in the section "Managing Custom Dictionaries," on page 314.)
- **AutoCorrect** enables you to configure an AutoCorrect setting for the misspelled word. You can automatically replace the misspelled word with the correctly spelled word in the future by clicking the correctly spelled word on the AutoCorrect submenu, as shown in Figure 13-3. Alternatively, you can manually configure an AutoCorrect entry in the AutoCorrect dialog box by clicking AutoCorrect Options on the AutoCorrect submenu.
- **Language** enables you to specify that a particular word or phrase is written in another language. If proofreading tools are installed for that language, Word uses the appropriate language dictionary to check the text. If you don't have a corresponding language dictionary installed, Word will skip the specified words without marking them as potential errors.
- **Spelling** opens the Spelling dialog box, which provides additional spelling checking options. The Spelling dialog box is similar to the Spelling And Grammar dialog box, which you can access by choosing Tools, Spelling And Grammar or by pressing F7.
- **Cut** deletes the selected text and puts it on the Clipboard.

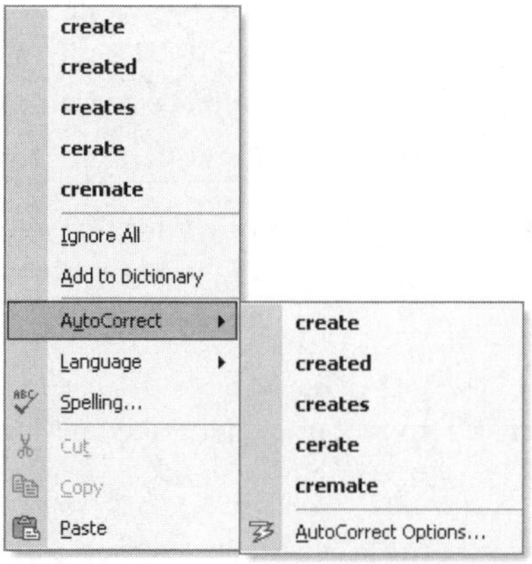

Figure 13-3. You can select a correctly spelled word on the AutoCorrect submenu so that future instances of the selected mistyped text are replaced with the correctly spelled word automatically.

- **Copy** copies the selected text to the Clipboard.
- **Paste** pastes the last item copied to the Clipboard. To replace a misspelled word using Paste, be sure that the entire misspelled word is selected.

Grammar correction options are accessed in much the same way as spelling correction options. In this case, you right-click text flagged with a green wavy underline or double-click the Spelling And Grammar Status icon. Both techniques display a shortcut menu containing the following options:

- **Short error explanation or replacement text** provides a brief description of the problem or possible replacement text. For example, the error explanation might state *Fragment (Consider Revising)*, or it might show the flagged phrase followed by the plural form of the verb instead of the singular form.
- **Ignore Once** disregards the current instance of the grammatical error but doesn't disregard other text that breaks the same grammar rule. You might want to ignore an error once if a particular construct is acceptable in a specific area of your document but you don't want to ignore the construct in other areas. For example, you might want to allow a sentence fragment in a figure caption but still want Word to continue to scan for sentence fragments within the rest of your document.
- **Grammar** opens the Grammar dialog box, which provides additional grammar checking options. The Grammar dialog box is similar to the Spelling And Grammar dialog box; you can access it by choosing Tools, Spelling And Grammar or by pressing F7.
- **About This Sentence** provides additional information about the potential error flagged by Word.
- **Cut** deletes the selected text and puts it on the Clipboard.

- **Copy** copies the selected text to the Clipboard.
- **Paste** pastes the last item copied to the Clipboard. To replace a word using Paste, be sure that the entire word is selected.

You can also resolve spelling and grammar issues by correcting your text without accessing the shortcut menus. When you correct a misspelling or a grammatical error, Word removes the wavy underline.

tip To jump to the next spelling or grammatical error without opening the Spelling And Grammar dialog box, double-click the Spelling And Grammar Status icon or press Alt+F7.

Disabling Automatic Spelling and Grammar Checking

Word automatically checks for spelling and grammar errors by default, but you can turn off one or both of these features at any time. For instance, many users appreciate the spelling checker but find that the grammar checker doesn't serve their needs particularly well. To control automatic spelling and grammar checking, perform one of the following actions:

- Right-click the Spelling And Grammar Status icon, and choose Hide Spelling Errors or Hide Grammatical Errors on the shortcut menu.
- Choose Tools, Options, and click the Spelling & Grammar tab (or right-click the Spelling And Grammar Status icon, and choose Options). On the Spelling & Grammar tab, shown in Figure 13-4, clear the Check Spelling As You Type check box to turn off the spelling checker, or clear the Check Grammar As You Type check box to turn off the grammar checker.

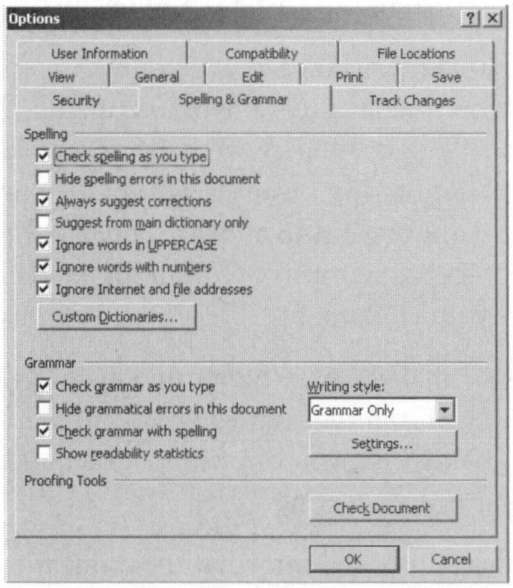

Figure 13-4. The Spelling & Grammar tab enables you to customize how Word performs spelling and grammar checking tasks.

tip **Turn off the wavy lines**

If you want to use the Spelling Checking and Grammar Checking features but you don't want to see red and green wavy underlines throughout your document, you can turn off the underlines. To do so, choose Tools, Options, click the Spelling & Grammar tab, and then select the Hide Spelling Errors In This Document check box to hide red (spelling) underlines and select the Hide Grammatical Errors In This Document check box to hide green (grammar) wavy underlines. Or you can right-click the Spelling And Grammar Status icon and choose Hide Spelling Errors or Hide Grammatical Errors on the shortcut menu.

Scrutinizing Your Spelling

At times, you might prefer to check your spelling and grammar in one fell swoop instead of right-clicking every instance of a potential error. In those cases, your best bet is to work through your document using the Spelling And Grammar dialog box. To access the Spelling And Grammar dialog box, perform any of the following actions:

- Choose Tools, Spelling And Grammar.
- Click the Spelling And Grammar button on the Standard toolbar.
- Press F7.

Spelling And Grammar

When the Spelling And Grammar dialog box opens, it displays the first potential error it encounters after the insertion point in the current document. For each potential problem, the word or phrase in question is displayed in color: red for a spelling issue, and green for a grammar issue. Figure 13-5, on the next page, shows the Spelling And Grammar dialog box when a potential spelling error is being addressed, and Figure 13-6, also on the next page, shows the Spelling And Grammar dialog box when a potential grammar error is being reviewed. Take a moment to compare the options in the two versions of the dialog box—you'll notice many similarities and a few differences. In this section, you'll learn how to handle potential spelling errors. The grammar options are discussed in the section "Brushing Up Your Grammar," on page 320.

InsideOut

You can control whether the grammar checker is activated by selecting or clearing the Check Grammar check box in the Spelling And Grammar dialog box, but you can access this option only when you choose Tools, Spelling And Grammar or press F7. If you open the Spelling dialog box or the Grammar dialog box by right-clicking an underlined potential error, this check box will not be available.

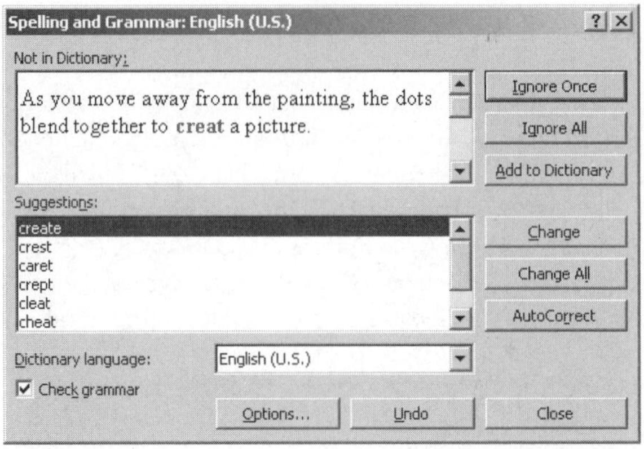

Figure 13-5. When you use the Spelling And Grammar dialog box to correct errors, you have a greater selection of suggestions and options to pick from than when you right-click potential errors. This version of the dialog box shows the options available for a potentially misspelled word.

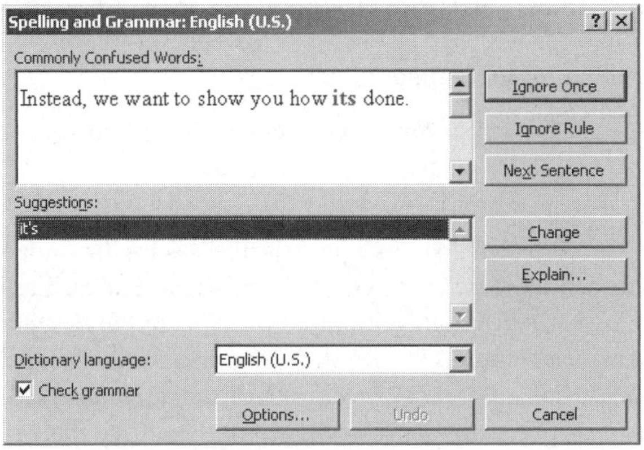

Figure 13-6. The grammar checker provides error checking options similar to the options available in the spelling checker.

Specifying How to Handle Spelling Errors

When a potential spelling problem is displayed in the Spelling And Grammar dialog box, you can modify the highlighted text by typing in the top text box, or you can handle the flagged text using one of the following techniques:

- **Ignore the current instance.** You can disregard the current instance of a particularly spelled word by clicking Ignore Once. If the ignored misspelling occurs elsewhere in your document, the spelling checker will continue to flag subsequent instances.

- **Ignore all instances.** You can disregard all instances of a particularly spelled word throughout the current document by clicking Ignore All. After you click Ignore All, Word won't flag or query you about any other instances of the misspelled word.
- **Add a word to the dictionary.** You can add the current instance of a particularly spelled word to your dictionary by clicking Add To Dictionary. The word will be added to your custom dictionary without further configuration on your part. For more information about controlling your custom dictionary, see the section "Managing Custom Dictionaries," on page 314.
- **Change the current instance.** You can replace the selected text with a suggested word by double-clicking the correct word in the Suggestions list or by selecting a word in the Suggestions list and then clicking Change.
- **Change all instances.** You can replace the selected text and all other instances of the same text with a particular word by selecting a word in the Suggestions list and then clicking Change All.
- **Add terms to the AutoCorrect list.** You can add a correction to the AutoCorrect list by selecting a word in the Suggestions list and then clicking AutoCorrect. The misspelled and correctly spelled words are automatically added to your AutoCorrect list without further configuration on your part.

For more information about the AutoCorrect list, see Chapter 6, "Putting Text Tools to Work."

After you resolve the current spelling issue, Word automatically jumps to the next potential spelling error. If you change your mind about a spelling modification, you can undo the last spelling change by clicking Undo in the Spelling And Grammar dialog box or by clicking the Undo button on the Standard toolbar (after you close the dialog box or click in the document).

tip **Edit text while checking spelling and grammar**

You can click in your document and make changes directly to your text while the Spelling And Grammar dialog box is open. After you finish making changes to your document, you can continue your spelling check by clicking the Resume button in the Spelling And Grammar dialog box.

When every spelling issue has been addressed, Word displays a message box informing you that the spelling check is complete. If you want to stop the spelling checker before you've checked the entire document, simply click Close in the Spelling And Grammar dialog box.

Selecting the Text You Want to Check

By default, when you use the Spelling And Grammar dialog box, you check the entire document, starting at the current location of the insertion point. But if you prefer, you can check only selected text. To check only selected text, select the text, and then click the Spelling And Grammar button on the Standard toolbar. (Of course, if you select a single word, you can right-click to access the word replacement options on the shortcut menu.) The spelling checker works through the selected text. When the end of the selected text is reached, Word displays a dialog box stating that Word has finished checking the selected text and asking whether you'd like to continue checking the remainder of the document.

tip **Omit selected text from spelling and grammar checking**

In addition to selecting specific text you want to check, you can also indicate that portions of text should never be checked for spelling or grammar errors. (When you use this feature, you have to eliminate both spelling and grammar checking—you can't turn off only one feature for selected text.) To turn off spelling and grammar checking procedures for specific text, select the text you want to omit, choose Tools, Language, Set Language, and then select the Do Not Check Spelling Or Grammar check box and click OK.

Configuring Spelling Options

As mentioned, you can control a few spelling checker options by configuring settings on the Spelling & Grammar tab in the Options dialog box (accessed by choosing Tools, Options, and clicking the Spelling & Grammar tab; see Figure 13-4). The first two options in the Spelling section of the Spelling & Grammar tab—Check Spelling As You Type and Hide Spelling Errors In this Document—are discussed in the section "Disabling Automatic Spelling and Grammar Checking" on page 308. The other options you can configure are described here:

- **Always Suggest Corrections.** By default, Word provides a list of suggested corrections for each misspelled word. If you find that Word doesn't provide the correct spelling in the majority of instances (for example, you might be working on a document that contains highly specific jargon, such as a medical document), you can clear this check box to save time.
- **Suggest From Main Dictionary Only.** Word checks all open dictionaries during spelling checks, including the main dictionary and your custom dictionaries. If you prefer to use only the main dictionary, select the Suggest From Main Dictionary Only check box.
- **Ignore Words In UPPERCASE.** This check box excludes words in all uppercase from spelling checks. The spelling checker would be hard pressed to understand all acronyms, so this check box is selected by default.

If you use a number of acronyms and you'd like to check them, you can add the acronyms to your custom dictionary and clear the Ignore Words In UPPERCASE check box.

- **Ignore Words With Numbers.** By default, any words that contain numbers are ignored by the spelling checker. You'll especially appreciate this option if you're proofreading documents such as catalog or price lists in which product codes are combinations of numbers and letters.
- **Ignore Internet And File Addresses.** By default, the spelling checker ignores Internet addresses, file path names, and e-mail addresses. For example, text such as *C:\clients\microsoft* and *www.microsoft.com* is automatically ignored by the spelling checker. If you prefer to check these types of elements, clear the Ignore Internet And File Addresses check box.

By configuring these spelling checker options, you can customize spelling tasks to be as streamlined as possible for particular document types.

Rechecking Your Document

Once you've checked a document using the appropriate spelling checker options, Word doesn't recheck any of the spelling or grammar issues that you've addressed or dismissed. If you want to recheck your document a second (or third) time, you'll have to tell Word to recatch previously caught spelling and grammar issues. To do so, follow these simple steps:

1. Click the Options button in the Spelling And Grammar dialog box, or choose Tools, Options, and click the Grammar & Spelling tab in the Options dialog box.
2. Click the Recheck Document button. A message box appears, stating that the operation will reset the spelling and grammar checkers so that Word can recheck your document for potential errors, even if you've previously dismissed the error marks.
3. Click Yes to close the message box, and then click OK to close the Options dialog box.
4. After Word has finished rechecking your document, press F7 to open the Spelling And Grammar dialog box, and then check your document.

You can recheck a document as many times as necessary. This feature is especially handy if you've ignored particular corrections and later want to change the ignored text.

Managing Custom Dictionaries

When you install Word, you also install a main dictionary. The spelling checker uses the main dictionary whenever it checks your document for spelling errors. You can also add words to your custom dictionary or add existing dictionaries to the list of dictionaries Word uses to check documents.

When you click Add To Dictionary in the Spelling And Grammar dialog box, Word adds the selected term to your custom dictionary. After you add terms to your custom dictionary, Word checks both the main dictionary and your custom dictionary (named CUSTOM.DIC by default) whenever you run the spelling checker. You can also edit and delete terms in your custom dictionary, as well as create additional custom dictionaries that you can use whenever necessary.

Modifying Custom Dictionaries

As mentioned, you can add terms to your default custom dictionary by clicking Add To Dictionary in the Spelling And Grammar dialog box. You can also add terms to your custom dictionary by right-clicking words that are flagged by a red wavy underline and choosing Add To Dictionary on the shortcut menu. Because adding terms to the custom dictionary is so easy, many users mistakenly add words that shouldn't be included, such as words or abbreviations that should be ignored in one document but might be incorrect in other documents. For example, you might want to allow the word *lite* in a marketing piece but have Word catch the misspelling in other documents. If you regularly add terms to your custom dictionary or if you suspect that you've added incorrect terms, you should review and manually correct your dictionary to ensure accuracy.

To access and modify your custom dictionary, follow these steps:

1. Display the Spelling & Grammar tab (by choosing Tools, Options and clicking the Spelling & Grammar tab; by pressing F7 and clicking Options; or by right-clicking the Spelling And Grammar Status icon and choosing Options).
2. On the Spelling & Grammar tab, click Custom Dictionaries. The Custom Dictionaries dialog box opens, as shown in Figure 13-7. Notice that the CUSTOM.DIC dictionary is selected by default.
3. Select a dictionary in the Dictionary List, and then click Modify to open a dictionary editing dialog box, as shown in Figure 13-8.

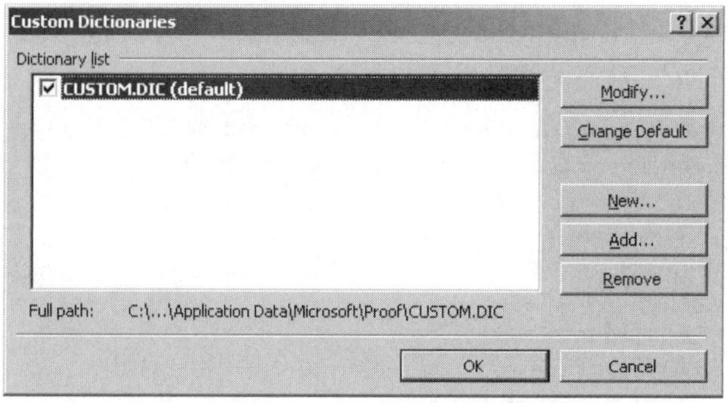

Figure 13-7. The Custom Dictionaries dialog box provides options for creating and modifying custom dictionaries used by Word in conjunction with the main dictionary.

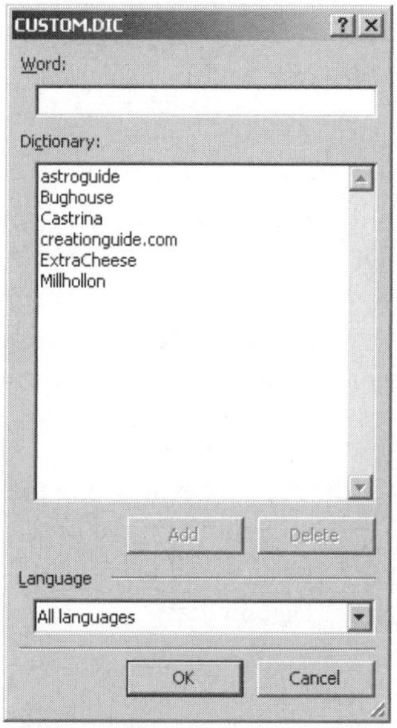

Figure 13-8. The dictionary editing dialog box provides an easy way to create and modify custom dictionaries. In earlier versions of Word, editing dictionaries entailed modifying a plain text file.

Within this dialog box, you can perform the following actions:

- **Manually add a term to a custom dictionary.** Enter a term in the Word box, and click Add. The dictionary arranges terms alphabetically.

- **Delete a term included in a custom dictionary.** Choose a word in the Dictionary list, and click Delete.
- **Specify a language for a custom dictionary.** Click the Language down arrow and choose a language in the drop-down list. By default, the CUSTOM.DIC dictionary is set to All Languages.

4 Click OK when you have finished modifying your custom dictionary.

> **tip** When you add terms to a custom dictionary, be sure that the words are 64 characters or fewer and do not contain spaces.

With careful maintenance of your custom dictionary, including adding frequently used terms, you can keep your spelling checker working in peak condition. By properly managing your custom dictionary, you automatically increase your efficiency because you'll avoid having to continually dismiss terms that appear regularly in your documents but aren't included in the main dictionary.

Creating New Custom Dictionaries

At times, you might work on jargon-laden documents that use very specific terminology or example, if you occasionally work on medical documents that contain terms such as *brachytherapy, echography,* and *osteotomy,* you could create a custom dictionary named Medical that you could activate whenever you're using medical terminology. To create a custom dictionary that you can use in addition to CUSTOM.DIC, follow these steps:

1 Display the Spelling & Grammar tab in the Options dialog box (by choosing Tools, Options and clicking the Spelling & Grammar tab; by pressing F7 and clicking Options; or by right-clicking the Spelling And Grammar Status icon and choosing Options), and click Custom Dictionaries.

2 In the Custom Dictionaries dialog box, click New. The Create Custom Dictionary dialog box opens. This dialog box displays a list of the custom dictionaries currently available to Word in the Proof folder. Figure 13-9 shows the Create Custom Dictionary dialog box, which contains the CUSTOM.DIC file and two additional custom dictionaries.

3 Type a name for the new custom dictionary in the File Name box, and click Save. When you create a custom dictionary, the file is saved with the .dic extension in the Proof folder, along with the Custom.dic file and any other custom dictionaries you've created.

After you create a new dictionary, it is added to the Dictionary List in the Custom Dictionaries dialog box and its check box is selected. When the spelling checker runs, it refers to the main dictionary and all custom dictionaries that are selected in the Dictionary List.

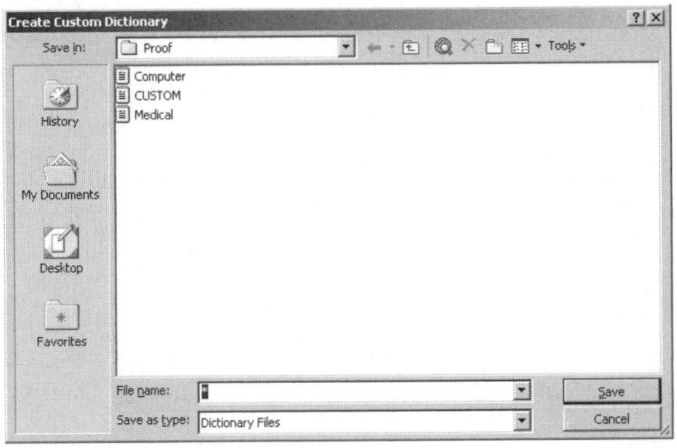

Figure 13-9. The Create Custom Dictionary dialog box enables you to create new dictionaries that you can use on an "as-needed basis" whenever you check documents.

> **tip** **Avoid suggestions from the main dictionary only**
>
> When you use custom dictionaries, make sure that the Suggest From Main Dictionary Only check box is cleared (the default setting) on the Spelling & Grammar tab in the Options dialog box. If this check box is selected, Word won't refer to your custom dictionaries when the spelling checker is started.

To add terms to a new custom dictionary, you can click Modify in the Custom Dictionaries dialog box and then manually enter terms. You can also add terms to the dictionary as you work, as described in the section "Choosing a Default Dictionary," on page 318.

> **tip** **Create a Names dictionary**
>
> You might want to create a Names dictionary that contains the names of people you interact with on a regular basis. Not only will this streamline your spelling checker processes by not repeatedly flagging correctly spelled names, but you'll also avoid misspelling people's names in your documents because your custom dictionary will be keeping an eye on your spelling.

Adding Custom Dictionaries

Most of the time, you'll either use the CUSTOM.DIC dictionary or create a new custom dictionary. But you can also add existing dictionaries to the Dictionary List in the Custom Dictionaries dialog box. Adding an existing dictionary is similar to creating a new custom dictionary. To do so, follow these steps:

1. On the Spelling & Grammar tab in the Options dialog box, click Custom Dictionaries.

2. In the Custom Dictionaries dialog box, click Add to open the Add Custom Dictionary dialog box, which looks almost identical to the Create Custom Dictionaries dialog box.

3. Navigate to the desired dictionary file, and double-click the dictionary's file name. The dictionary will be displayed in the Dictionary List and its check box will be selected.

By default, custom dictionaries are stored in the ...\Application Data\Microsoft\Proof folder. If you have a custom dictionary file (with a .dic extension), you can store the file in the Proof folder; it will then be easily accessible from the Custom Dictionaries dialog box.

Converting an Existing List of Terms to a Custom Dictionary

If you have an existing list of terms or a style sheet containing terms you frequently use, you can create a custom dictionary without having to retype or copy all the terms in the dictionary editing dialog box. To convert a list to a custom dictionary, follow these steps:

1. Verify that each term is displayed on a separate line with no blank lines inserted between terms. Then save your document as a plain text (.txt) file, and close the file.

2. Right-click the file name in Windows Explorer, and rename the file using the .dic extension. (You might have to clear the Hide File Extensions For Known File Types check box on the View tab in the Folder Options dialog box in Windows Explorer in order to view file name extensions.)

3. After you rename the file, store it in ...\Application Data\Microsoft\Proof.

The next time you open the Add Custom Dictionary dialog box, you'll see your newly created dictionary listed among the available custom dictionaries. Double-click the newly added dictionary to add it to the Dictionary List in the Custom Dictionaries dialog box.

Choosing a Default Dictionary

By default, all terms you add to a dictionary while running a spelling check are added to the CUSTOM.DIC dictionary. You can change the custom dictionary in which added words are stored by changing the default custom dictionary. By reconfiguring your default dictionary, you can quickly build very specific custom dictionaries without having to manually enter terms. Let's return to the Medical dictionary example. While you're working on a medical document, you could specify the Medical dictionary as your default custom dictionary. Then whenever you click Add To Dictionary, the specified term would be added to the Medical dictionary instead of CUSTOM.DIC. Configuring Word in this way would serve two purposes: it would avoid adding unnecessary terms to the CUSTOM.DIC dictionary, and it would save you from manually typing terms into the Medical dictionary.

To specify which custom dictionary serves as the default file, perform the following simple actions:

1. Choose Tools, Options, click the Spelling & Grammar tab, and then click the Custom Dictionaries button to open the Custom Dictionaries dialog box.
2. Select the custom dictionary you want to be the default in the Dictionary List.
3. Click Change Default.

The default custom dictionary will appear at the top of the list with *(default)* after its name, as shown in Figure 13-10. Now when you click Add To Dictionary in the Spelling And Grammar dialog box or right-click a word with a red wavy underline and click Add To Dictionary on the shortcut menu, the term will be added to the new default custom dictionary.

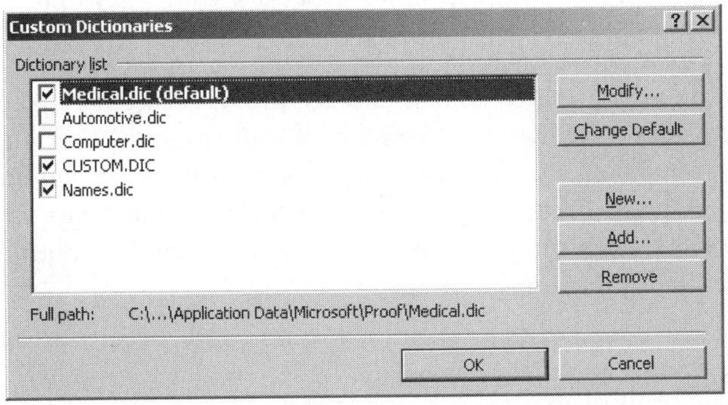

Figure 13-10. The default custom dictionary appears at the top of the Dictionary List, above the alphabetic list of custom dictionaries.

Disabling, Removing, and Deleting Dictionaries

Most of the time, you won't need to have Word check all your custom dictionaries every time you're working on a document. Therefore, you might want to disable some custom dictionaries until you need them. Other times, you might want to remove a custom dictionary from your Dictionary List altogether. Word allows you to do this without deleting the dictionary file. Or you might want to completely delete a dictionary file because you no longer use it. You can perform all these tasks easily, from within the Custom Dictionaries dialog box, as follows:

- **Disable a dictionary.** Clear the dictionary's check box in the Dictionary List. When a dictionary's check box is cleared, Word doesn't reference the dictionary during spelling checking operations.
- **Remove a dictionary.** Select the dictionary name you want to remove in the Dictionary List, and click Remove. This action does not delete the file; it simply removes it from the Dictionary List.
- **Delete a dictionary.** Click New or Add, select the dictionary file name in the Create Custom Dictionary or Add Custom Dictionary dialog box, and press Delete (or right-click the dictionary file name, and choose Delete on the shortcut menu). Click Yes in the Confirm File Delete message box, and then click Cancel to close the dialog box. This operation sends the dictionary file to your Recycle Bin.

Brushing Up Your Grammar

As we've seen, in addition to checking spelling, Word can check documents for grammatical accuracy. In a nutshell, Word's grammar checker works by reviewing standard grammar-related issues in your documents and flagging any potential errors with a wavy green underline. By design, the grammar checker focuses only on the most typical and frequent types of grammar problems, meaning that most but not every grammar issue will be flagged by the grammar checker.

As you become familiar with the grammar checker and its capabilities, you'll find that its usefulness fluctuates quite markedly from one document to the next. In some documents, the grammar checker will catch all sorts of useful errors, but in other documents, the grammar checker might flag numerous potential errors that are in fact grammatically correct. Therefore, you'll probably want to turn the Grammar Checking feature on and off depending on the current document.

tip **Control the grammar checker**

You can turn the grammar checker on and off by selecting or clearing the Check Grammar check box in the Spelling And Grammar dialog box. Similarly, you can hide the green wavy underlines without disabling grammar checking by right-clicking the Spelling And Grammar Status icon and choosing Hide Grammatical Errors on the shortcut menu.

Using the grammar checker in Word is similar to using the spelling checker. But the grammar checker has a few grammar-specific features of its own, which we'll look at now.

Checking Your Grammar

To run the grammar checker, right-click a potential grammar error and choose Grammar from the shortcut menu, or choose Tools, Spelling And Grammar, as described in the section "Benefiting from Automated Spelling and Grammar Checking," on page 304. To resolve a grammar issue in the Spelling And Grammar dialog box (or in the Grammar dialog box), you can modify the highlighted text by typing in the top text box, or you can choose from among the following options:

- **Ignore Once** leaves the selected text as it is, without making any changes. Word removes the green wavy underline and displays the next grammar issue. If you click in the body of your document while the dialog box is open, the Ignore Once button changes to Resume, which you can click to continue the grammar checking process whenever you're ready to move on.
- **Ignore Rule** ignores the highlighted text and all other grammar issues that are classified as the same type of error. Word removes the green wavy underline from all instances and displays the next grammar issue.
- **Next Sentence** retains the currently selected text without making changes and jumps to the next grammatical error.
- **Change** replaces existing text with the text selected in the Suggestions list.
- **Explain** opens the Office Assistant, which briefly describes the currently selected grammatical error.

In addition to these options, you can also choose a dictionary language (by selecting a language in the Dictionary Language drop-down list), undo the last implemented correction (by clicking Undo), or display the grammar options (by clicking Options), as described next.

Configuring Grammar Options

Like the spelling checker, the grammar checker has options that you can configure on the Spelling & Grammar tab in the Options dialog box. As we've seen, the first two check boxes in the Grammar section—Check Grammar As You Type and Hide Grammatical Errors In This Document—control whether the grammar checker is turned on or off and whether green wavy underlines are displayed in the document.

The third option—the Check Grammar With Spelling check box—performs essentially the same function as the Check Grammar check box in the Spelling And Grammar dialog box: it enables you to turn off the grammar checker while you're using the spelling checker. When you clear this check box, you can check spelling without addressing grammar issues. (The green wavy underlines used to flag potential grammar problems will continue to be displayed in your document if the Check Grammar As You Type check box is selected.) Selecting this option usually speeds up document checking because Word skips the grammar issues and presents only the potential spelling errors.

The remaining options on the Spelling & Grammar tab, the Writing Style and Settings options, enable you to define grammar rules that Word should follow, as discussed in the next section.

For more information about the Show Readability Statistics check box in the Grammar section on the Spelling & Grammar tab, see the section "Judging a Document's Readability Level," on page 330.

Specifying Grammar Rules

The grammar checker in Word can check up to 32 types of fundamental grammar rules, ranging from finding double negatives and clichés to identifying incorrect verb tenses and passive sentence structures. To specify grammar rule settings, follow these steps:

1. Choose Tools, Options, click the Spelling & Grammar tab, and then specify whether you want the grammar checker to check grammar only or grammar and style (by selecting the appropriate option in the Writing Style drop-down list).

2. Click Settings. The Grammar Settings dialog box opens, as shown in Figure 13-11.

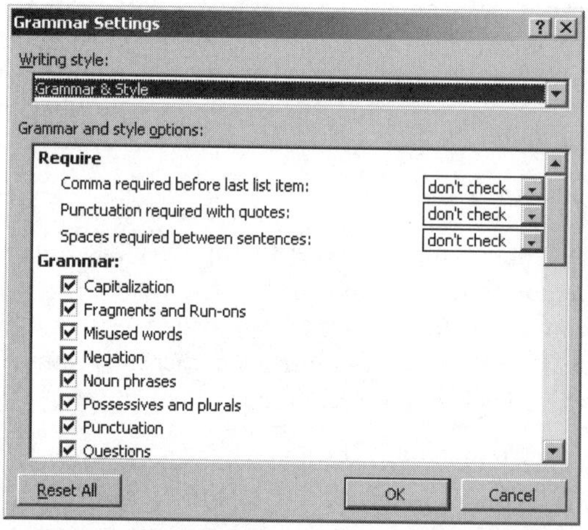

Figure 13-11. You can pick and choose which grammar rules you want Word to use when it searches for potential grammatical errors.

3. Select and clear the check boxes to configure which grammar rules you want Word to use when it searches for potential grammatical problems.

tip **View details of grammar and style options**

To view brief descriptions of the grammar and writing style settings you can configure in the Grammar Settings dialog box, type grammar options in the Ask A Question search box on the menu bar, and press Enter. Then click the Grammar And Writing Style Options entry in the Results list. To view details about each option, click the Show All link in the Microsoft Word Help window. The Help window presents a brief summary of each grammar rule.

Enlivening Your Vocabulary Using the Thesaurus

As you write, you might encounter instances when you just can't think of the right word or you find yourself using the same word repeatedly. At those times, you should consider turning to a thesaurus. Now, instead of lugging out a heavy book every time you want to find a synonym, you have a much lighter resource on hand—the Word thesaurus. Just as the Word spelling and grammar checkers suggest replacement text for potential spelling and grammar errors, Word provides a thesaurus that lists alternative terms you can use in your document.

Replacing Existing Text with a Synonym or an Antonym

You can use the Word thesaurus to look up synonyms and antonyms for selected words. To use the thesaurus, right-click the word you want to replace and then choose Synonyms on the shortcut menu to display a list of potential synonyms and antonyms, as shown in Figure 13-12, on the next page.

InsideOut

You can't right-click to open the thesaurus for a word that's flagged as a potential spelling or grammar error (a word marked with a red or green wavy underline). When you want to replace a flagged word with a synonym, you need to right-click and address the spelling or grammar error first. Then you can right-click the word again to access the thesaurus.

To replace existing text with a suggested term, click the appropriate suggestion; the original text is automatically replaced with the alternative.

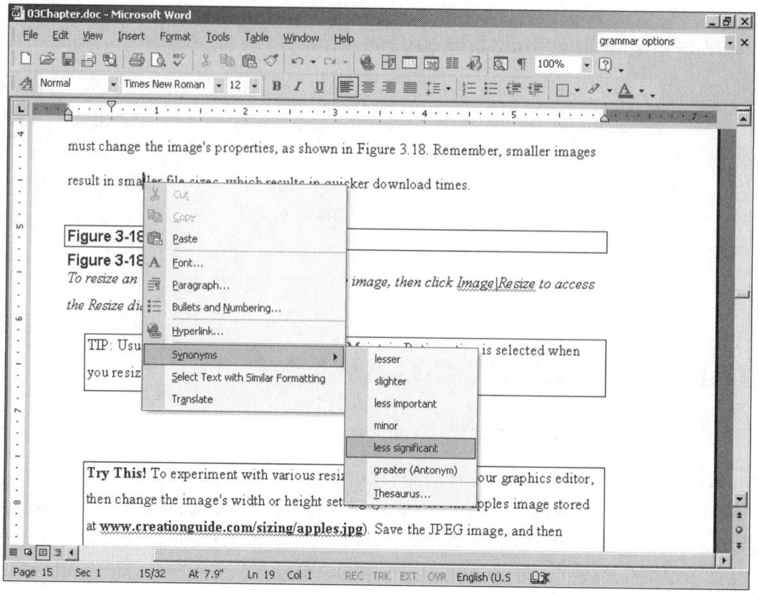

Figure 13-12. Notice that this synonym list for the word "smaller" includes an antonym, which is identified by the word *(Antonym)* after the suggested term.

Thumbing Through the Virtual Pages of the Online Thesaurus

If you right-click a word to access a list of synonyms (or antonyms) and none of the alternatives suit your purposes, you can click Thesaurus to open the Thesaurus dialog box, as shown in Figure 13-13. You can use the Thesaurus dialog box to search for additional terms.

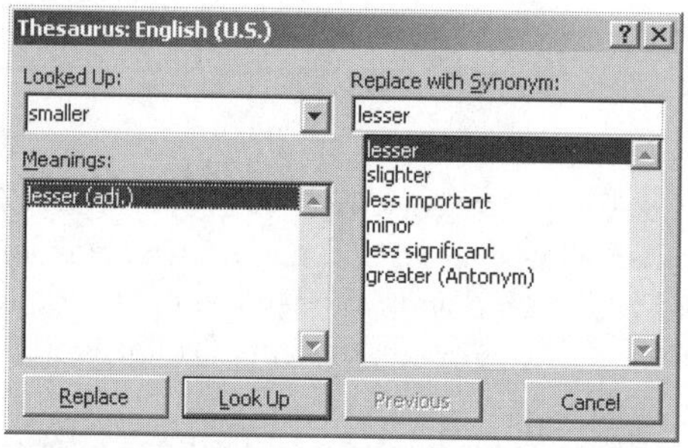

Figure 13-13. The Thesaurus dialog box enables you to jump from term to term in the same fashion you might flip through a hard-copy thesaurus.

The Thesaurus dialog box enables you to look for synonyms and antonyms that you can use to replace existing text by searching through a wider scope of suggestions than the terms available using the right-click method. To open the Thesaurus dialog box, position the insertion point in or near the word you want to look up, and then use one of the following procedures:

- Choose Tools, Language, Thesaurus.
- Press Shift+F7.
- Right-click the word you want to replace, and choose Thesaurus from the shortcut menu.

The word you looked up appears in the Looked Up list box in the Thesaurus dialog box. (See Figure 13-13.) (You can look up a different word by typing the word in the Insert box and pressing Enter.) You can then select the preferred meaning of the word you want to look up in the Meanings list and click Look Up to find additional suggestions. If you find a word that suits your needs in the Replace With Synonym list, select it, and click Replace to insert the selected word in place of the original word.

tip If you don't find an acceptable replacement word in the Replace With Synonym list after clicking Look Up, you can click Previous to return to the previous selected meaning and associated synonyms.

newfeature!

Translating Text into Other Languages

Using Word 2002, you can perform basic translation tasks, such as translating words or phrases and inserting translated text into your documents. The main interface you use when using the new Word Translate feature is the Translate task pane, which is shown in Figure 13-14.

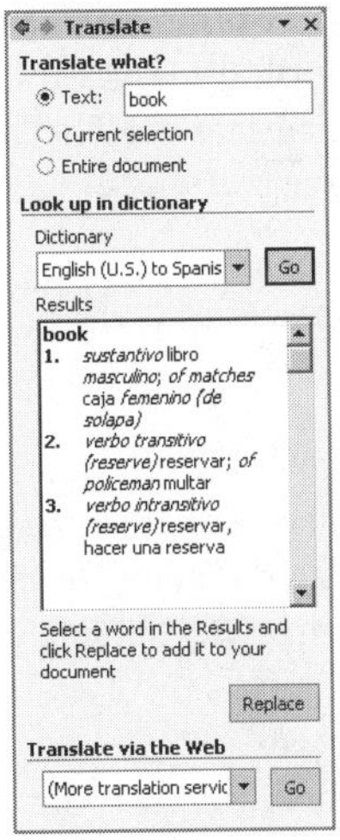

Figure 13-14. The Translate task pane helps you translate words and phrases.

To open the Translate task pane, use one of the following methods:

- Choose Tools, Language, Translate.
- Click Translate on the drop-down menu in the Translate task pane.
- Right-click a word in your document that you want to translate, and choose Translate on the shortcut menu.

> **note** You might be asked to install the Word translation components from the setup CD or the network setup location (if you installed Word from a network location) the first time you use the Translate feature and subsequently when you first select a translation dictionary in the Dictionary drop-down list in the Translate task pane. If you don't see the translation dictionary you want in the Dictionary drop-down list, you might have to install the dictionary from your Office setup disks.

To use the Translate task pane, follow these steps:

1. Specify the text you want to translate by choosing one of the following options:
   - **Text.** Choose Text, and type the word or phrase you want to translate in the Text box.
   - **Current Selection.** Select a word or phrase in your document that you want to translate, and choose the Current Selection option, or right-click a word in your document, and choose Translate on the shortcut menu (to open the Translate task pane and automatically choose the Current Selection option).
   - **Entire Document.** Choose the Entire Document option to translate the entire current document. Choosing this option dims all other options in the Translate task pane except the Translate Via The Web drop-down list. When you want to translate large sections of text, Word defers to Web translation services.

> **tip** **Translate documents using online translation services**
>
> When you select a translation service in the Translate Via The Web drop-down list and then click Go, you're most likely accessing services that use computers to translate your text automatically. These services can help you determine the main ideas in documents, but they shouldn't be used for important or sensitive documents because computers cannot preserve your text's full meaning, detail, or tone. To translate critical documents, you should hire a professional (human) translator.

2 Select a translation dictionary in the Dictionary drop-down list. For example, you can select English (U.S.) to French (France), English (U.S.) to Spanish (Spain-Modern Sort), French (France) to English (U.S.), Spanish (Spain-Modern Sort) to English (U.S.), and so forth.

3 Click Go in the Look Up In Dictionary section. Your translation results are displayed in the Results list. You can select a word in the Results list and click the Replace button to insert the translated text into your document.

If you are having trouble finding appropriate translations, try looking up the singular form of nouns (for example, *child* instead of *children*) and search using the infinitive form of verbs (for example, *swim* instead of *swam*). Searching for root words generally results in greater success during translation. Also keep in mind that the Word translation tool serves approximately the same function as a language dictionary—it's not a full-service translation utility, but it's a nice way to interpret a few words or phrases.

Scrutinizing Document Statistics

In addition to the standard reference book features included in Word, you have several other electronic reference tools that you can use to analyze your documents. Namely, you can instruct Word to quickly summarize the content in a document by using the AutoSummarize feature, you can analyze a document's readability level using Flesch Reading Ease and Flesch-Kincaid Grade Level scores, and you can display word count statistics to track the length of your text while you work.

Getting to the Point with AutoSummarize

Word can automatically summarize key points in your documents, enabling you to create a brief version of documents that can be quickly scanned. You'll find that AutoSummarize works best on structured documents such as reports, white papers, technical documents, articles, and so forth. AutoSummarize doesn't work especially well for fiction, correspondence, and other more loosely structured documents.

The AutoSummarize feature determines key points in your document by analyzing and scoring sentences. Sentences are given higher scores if they contain words that are frequently used in the document.

You can choose one of the following four options for displaying the summary information:

- **Highlight Key Points** summarizes the current document by highlighting summary information (in yellow, by default). The remainder of the document text appears in gray. The AutoSummarize toolbar is displayed by default; it includes a Highlight/Show Only Summary button, a Percent Of Original slider that enables you to adjust the percentage of the document included in the summary, and a Close button that returns you to your original document. Figure 13-15 shows a sample document with key points highlighted; notice the AutoSummarize toolbar in the upper right corner.

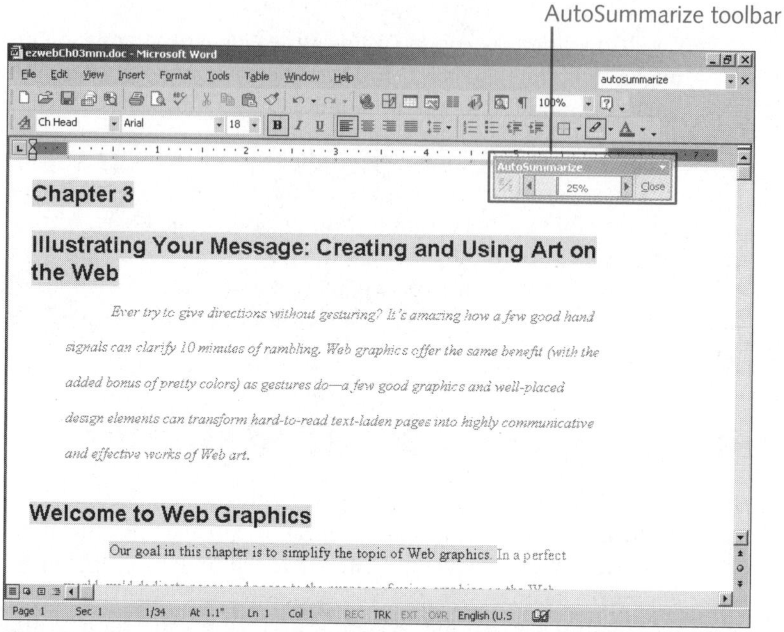

Figure 13-15. You can temporarily highlight a document's key points using the AutoSummarize feature. The AutoSummarize toolbar is displayed.

- **Create A New Document And Put The Summary There** displays the summarized information in a new document. This option creates a separate document with no link to the original text. The only way you can adjust the percentage of information in this type of summary is to re-create the summary. This type of summary is helpful if you want to create an abstract or executive summary of a document.
- **Insert An Executive Summary Or Abstract At The Top Of The Document** inserts the summary at the beginning of the document under the heading *Summary*. Using this option, the summary becomes part of your document.
- **Hide Everything But The Summary Without Leaving The Original Document** hides all document text except the text included in the summary. This option doesn't change your text; it merely hides the text not included in the summary temporarily. If you print your document, only the summary will be printed. To return to your document's complete display, click Close on the AutoSummarize toolbar.

Chapter 13

AutoSummarize can't summarize text in textboxes, frames, or tables. For more information about text boxes and frames, see Chapter 23, "Styling Document Layouts Using Text Boxes, Frames, Backgrounds, and Themes," and for more information about tables, see Chapter 18, "Organizing Concepts in Tables."

To summarize a document using the AutoSummarize tool, follow these steps:

1 Choose Tools, AutoSummarize to open the AutoSummarize dialog box, shown Figure 13-16.

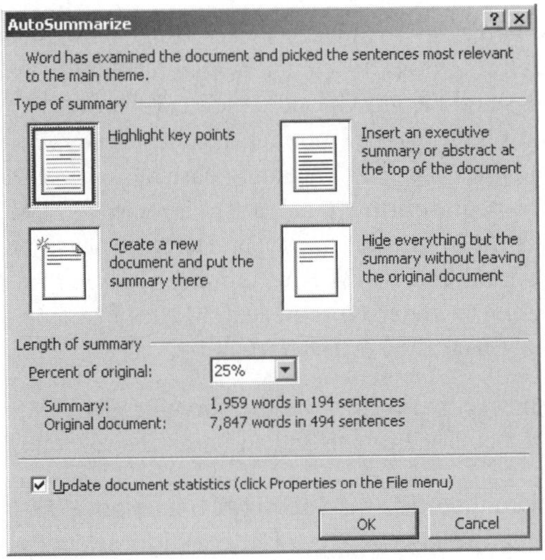

Figure 13-16. AutoSummarize provides various options for displaying a summary of the current document.

tip The AutoSummarize processing can take a few moments to complete. If you find the processing is taking too long, you can stop it by pressing Esc.

2 In the AutoSummarize dialog box, choose the type of summary you want to create.

3 In the Percent Of Original box, specify the level of detail that you want to include in your summary. You can choose anywhere from 10 sentences to 75 percent of your document. (A higher percentage includes more details in your summary, whereas a lower percentage includes less detail.)

4 Specify whether you want AutoSummarize to replace existing keywords and comments on the document's Summary tab in the document's Properties dialog box (by choosing File, Properties, and clicking the Statistics tab). If you don't want AutoSummarize to replace this information, clear the Update Document Statistics check box.

5 Click OK to create the summary.

After you create a summary using the AutoSummarize feature, you should proofread and edit the summary to smooth any rough edges, especially if you chose to create a new document or inserted the summary at the beginning of your document. Sometimes, you might find that it's better to include more in your summary at first and then pare down the information as needed—generally, it's easier to cut text than to put text back in.

Judging a Document's Readability Level

You can configure Word to display a readability level for a document after you finish spelling and grammar checking tasks. Word determines readability levels by assigning Flesch Reading Ease scores and Flesch-Kincaid Grade Level scores to documents. These scores are obtained by rating the average number of syllables per word and average number of words per sentence. The Flesch Reading Ease score is based on a 100-point scale, in which a higher score means that a document is easier to read. You should aim for scores ranging from 60 to 70 in most cases. The Flesch-Kincaid Grade Level score rates text based on U.S. school grade level. For example, a score of 8.0 means that an eighth grader should be able to understand the text. Most documents intended for the general public should score near the 7.0 or 8.0 level.

To display reading statistics, you must turn on the Show Readability Statistics option and completely check your documents spelling and grammar as follows:

1. Choose Tools, Options, and click the Spelling & Grammar tab. Select the Check Grammar With Spelling check box (if necessary), select the Show Readability Statistics check box, and click OK.

2. Run a complete spelling and grammar check by choosing Tools, Spelling And Grammar. When the check is complete, Word automatically displays information about the reading level of the document, as shown in Figure 13-17.

Displaying Word Count Statistics

At times, you might want to show word count statistics without obtaining readability information. For example, you might have been given a limit on how many words a document can be for a particular assignment—magazines commonly set this type of limitation. You can easily count the words in your document in Word. To do so, choose Tools, Word Count. The Word Count dialog box opens, displaying word count information, as shown in Figure 13-18.

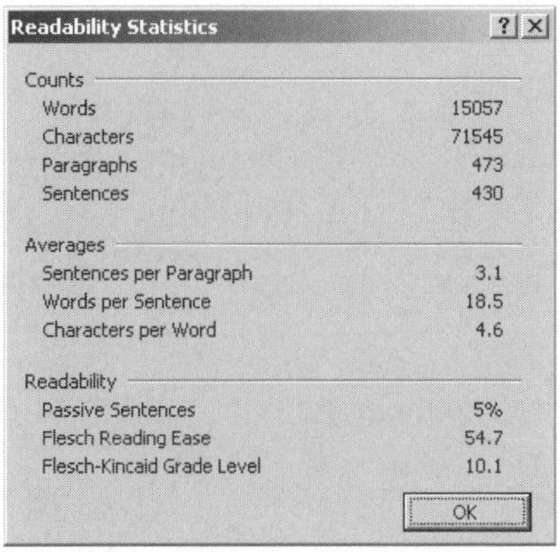

Figure 13-17. The Readability Statistics dialog box shows readability levels in addition to other details, such as word count, average words per sentence, and so forth.

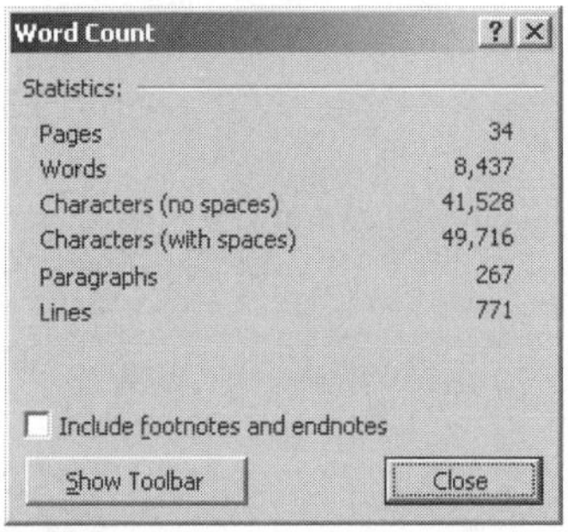

Figure 13-18. The Word Count dialog box gives you a quick summary of your document's statistics.

newfeature!

The Word Count dialog box contains a Show Toolbar button. Click this button to display the Word Count toolbar, shown in Figure 13-19, and then close the Word Count dialog box. The Word Count toolbar is a new toolbar that remains on your desktop while you work; you can click Recount at any time to quickly check your word count statistics.

Figure 13-19. You can display various word count statistics on the Word Count toolbar by selecting the type of statistic from the drop-down list.

In addition to displaying the number of words in your document, the Word Count toolbar can be configured to display the number of characters (counting or not counting spaces), lines, pages, or paragraphs in your document. Click the down arrow and select the count you want to display from the drop-down list.

Part 3

Adding Value with Graphics and Objects

Chapter 14

Adding Visual Impact with Pictures

You've probably heard that "a picture is worth a thousand words," and that's not just rhetoric. Think about what we see around us on the Web, in our mailboxes, in the newspaper, on TV—words alone don't cut it. We want color; we want pictures; we want style. All by themselves, words don't capture our attention or ignite our imaginations. Even this book, although it's communicating information you want and need, wouldn't be as effective without the careful design of the pages (making it easier for you to read) and the pictures of screens, captured to show you what to look for as you try the procedures for yourself.

A picture can show at a glance what it takes words time to create. In a report, you'll need an entire paragraph (or a page!) to explain how a new product goes through a development cycle, but showing a photo of the process —or better yet, a diagram—will let your readers know instantly what the whole process looks like. This chapter explores ways you can use Word to bring images into your documents that add spark, interest, and more effective communication elements to the work you create.

What a Difference an Image Makes!

Need reasons to put images in your documents? There are many different reasons to use clip art, pictures, photos, drawings, and special graphic designs in the publications you produce. The goals of your publication will determine whether artwork would enhance the document. Here are a few ways in which images help you reach your audience in an effective way:

- **Capture—and hold—the reader's interest.** In this time of colorful, slick marketing pieces and MTV-style Web pages, we need something that will make us take notice. A well-planned picture, whether it's a photo, a logo, or a drawing, can catch the reader's eye and get your document a closer look.
- **Give the reader's eyes a break.** It's a well-established fact that readers won't struggle through page after page of single-spaced text. They want healthy margins on the page, and they want both visual interest and rest—something images on your page can give them. A well-placed image in a brochure can help lead the reader's eye from place to place. A diagram in a long report can provide a much-needed reading break.
- **Support an idea in your story or report.** An image in your document or on your Web page can help reinforce the theme or concept of your writing. If you're the publications director for a women's health center, for example, and you're creating your organization's annual report, photos of healthy, happy women help to communicate your message and your mission. Likewise, in other documents, photos of products help build brand identity in your readers' minds, and organizational charts help befuddled staff understand who they report to in the aftermath of a corporate merger.

Finding Art You Can Use

What kind of art do you want to use? The kind you can import into Word—drawing, paintings, images you create in high-end graphics programs, and art you download off the Web. There's room for everything, and unless you've got an art file created in an ancient (or virtually unheard-of) format, you'll be able to get a filter that enables Word to import it.

Paint and Draw Distinctions

When you work with graphics, you create one of two types of images: bitmapped and vector graphics. You might see bitmapped graphics referred to as paint graphics or raster images. These types of images are created based on a pattern of pixels (or a map of bits). When you enlarge bitmapped graphics, the dots are stretched, resulting in a loss of clarity because the larger the dots, the greater the space between the dots.

This chapter deals specifically with placing, importing, and working with images, both clip art and drawn images. For more about using Word's drawing tools to create images within your documents, see Chapter 16, "Enlivening Documents with Drawings and AutoShapes."

Vector images (also called draw graphics and object-oriented graphics) are drawings made of shapes, lines, and curves. Because these items are based on mathematical calculations, the images can be grouped into a single object and later divided again into individual objects. They also can be resized and enlarged with no loss of quality. Table 14-1 lists some popular images you'll use, identifies their type, lists the common file formats, and suggests possible sources or programs.

Table 14-1. Paint and Draw File Types

Item	Image type	File formats	Source
Clip art	Depends on the image—bitmapped or vector graphics	.bmp, .dib, .gif, .jpg, .pcx, .png, .tif, .wmf	Microsoft Clip Organizer, purchased clip art collections, Web clip art sources
AutoShapes	Vector graphics	.wmf	Windows programs
Scanned images	Bitmapped graphics	.bmp, .gif, .png, .jpg	Windows Paint Adobe Photoshop Paint Shop Pro
Web graphics	Usually bitmapped graphics	.gif, .png	Available on line and in some Web generation programs
Page backgrounds	Bitmapped graphics	.bmp, .dib, .gif, .pcx, .png, .jpg, .tif, .htm	Paint images HTML files
Picture bullets	Bitmapped graphics	.gif	Images created in paint programs such as Windows Paint

newfeature!

Enhancing Your Documents with Clip Art

Word includes a gallery of clip art you can use in your own documents. Both bitmapped and vector images are included in the collection—and you'll find all sorts of different topics represented, from animals to transportation to people and holidays.

And if you're used to the Clip Gallery in Word 2000, be forewarned: The Clip Organizer is a major overhaul of this former feature and it doesn't behave the same way. Whereas the Clip Gallery was a fully functional utility—meaning that you selected, organized, and inserted art from the Clip Gallery, now Word 2002 separates the "insert clip art" and "organize clip art" tasks. When you want to insert clip art, you'll use the Insert Clip Art task pane to do so. It's an easy and intuitive process. In this respect, it's a great improvement over the Clip Gallery, which could be cumbersome and, at times, buggy.

The Clip Organizer is a full-fledged art collection utility, tracking not only images but sounds and motion files as well. You'll use the Clip Organizer to organize, add, review, and sometimes delete media clips of all types. You'll also use the Clip Organizer to access additional clips and services on the Web, a feature that's built right into the Clip Organizer interface.

Inserting Art from the Task Pane

Word 2002 speeds up the process of placing clip art by using the task pane. With just a few simple commands, you can display the pane and search for the clips you want to insert quickly in your documents. Here's the process for adding images quickly to your document:

1. Place the insertion point where you want to add clip art.
2. Choose Insert, Picture, Clip Art. The Insert Clip Art task pane appears, as Figure 14-1 shows.

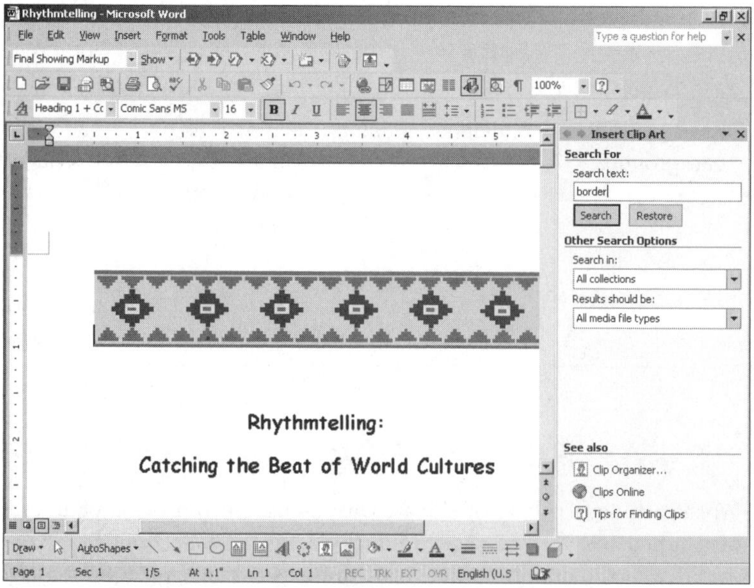

Figure 14-1. The Insert Clip Art task pane gives you a fast and easy method of placing images in your document.

note If this is the first time you've use Clip Art, the Add Clips To Gallery dialog box appears so that you can add your own clip art to the Clip Organizer. To have Word automatically scan your hard disk for media clips, which can include video segments, sound, or pictures, click OK. Otherwise, click Cancel.

1. Enter a word or phrase in the Search Text box that describes the type of art you're looking for. You don't need to know the name of a specific category—simply enter a word that describes the topic you want, such as "border."

2. Click Search. A list of clips that meet your criteria is displayed in the task pane. (See Figure 14-2.)

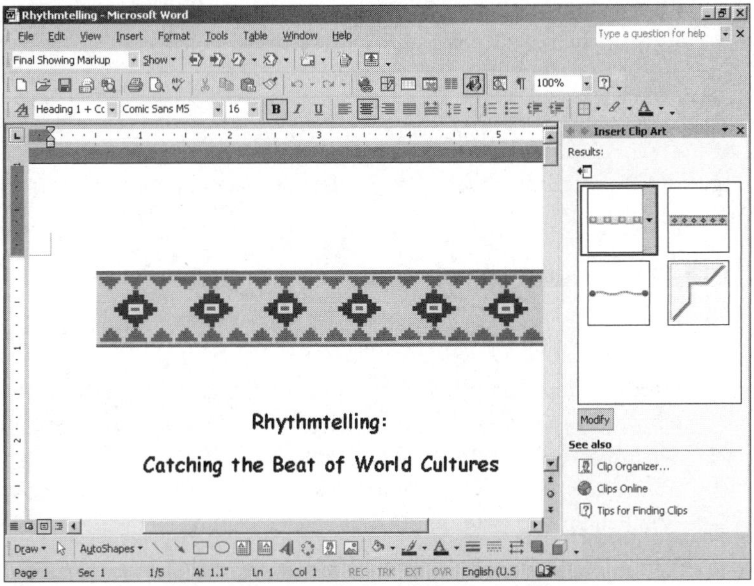

Figure 14-2. Choose from the list of clips that meet your criteria.

3. Click the clip art you want to insert. Word adds the image at the insertion point.

Searching for Art in the Task Pane

When you search for a specific piece of clip art, Word searches by default all available categories: My Collections, Office Collections, and Web Collections. View the available collections by clicking the Search In down arrow in the Other Search Options section of the task pane. (See Figure 14-3, on the next page.)

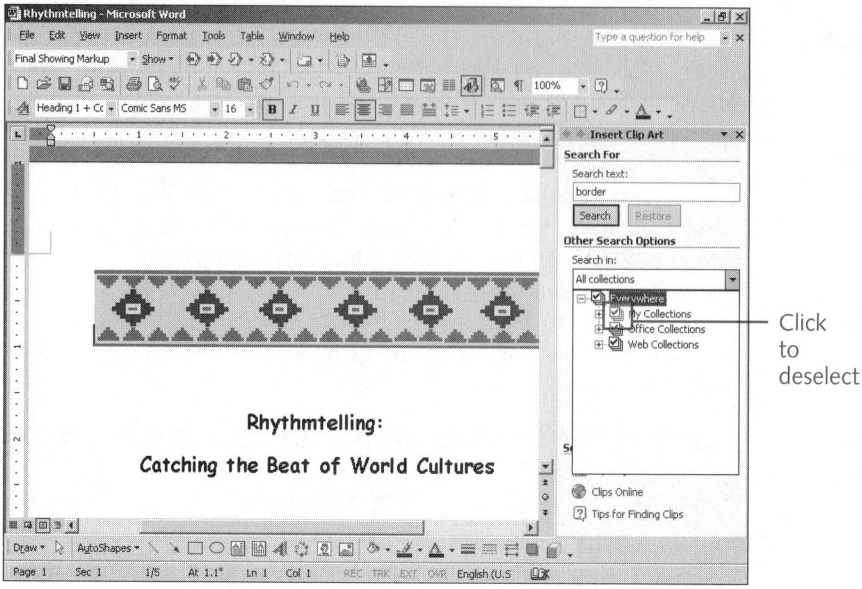

Figure 14-3. You can change Word's default search options by selecting only the collections you want.

You'll find three different collections:

- **My Collections** includes the art you bring into the Clip Organizer.
- **Office Collections** includes the following 43 different major categories, where you're sure to find something that fits your topic (there are also subcategories in some groups):

Academic	Communications	Maps	Sites
Agriculture	Concepts	Nature	Sports
Animals	Decorative Elements	Occupations	Symbols
Arts	Emotions	People	Tools
Astrology	Fantasy	Personal appearance	Technology
AutoShapes	Flags	Plants	Transportation
Banners	Food	Religion	Travel
Backgrounds	Government	Sciences	Weather
Buildings	Healthcare	Seasons	Web Elements
Business	Household	Signs	
Character	Industry	Special Occasions	
Collections	Leisure		

- **Web Collections** includes all the Web-friendly graphics included in the Clip Organizer. When you click Clips Online for the first time, the Gallery creates a folder for storing clips downloaded from the Web.

At the bottom of the Insert Clip Art task pane, you see further choices that take you to the Microsoft Clip Organizer, onto the Web for more clip gathering, and to tips that can help you locate the right art for your documents.

newfeature!

Using the Clip Organizer

The Microsoft Clip Organizer is a clip-organizing tool that helps you keep all your image, sound, and motion files in one place, arranged according to topic. To launch the Microsoft Clip Organizer, click the Clip Organizer link at the bottom of the Insert Clip Art task pane. Figure 14-4 shows the Microsoft Clip Organizer as it first appears.

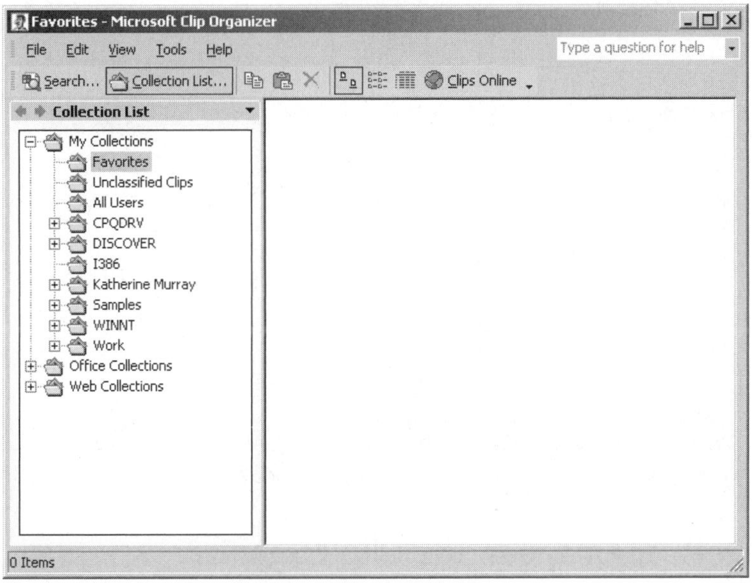

Figure 14-4. Click the folder of the collection you want to view.

The layout of the Microsoft Clip Organizer resembles that of the Windows Explorer; you can easily see the number of collections available for your selection. You'll use the following items to help you locate and work with the clips you need:

- **Menu bar** contains the commands you need to create new categories, organize your clips, copy and paste clips between collections, view individual images, search for more help on the Web, and get help with using the Clip Organizer.
- **Toolbar** provides tools for searching, choosing collections, copying, pasting, and deleting images, controlling the display in the Microsoft Clip Organizer window, and accessing the Web to search for more clips.

- **Collection List** panel shows all available folders in which you can search for images.
- **Display window** shows selected clips. By positioning the pointer on a specific clip, you can display information about the file. In Figure 14-5, the file description shows the name of the file, the width and height in pixels, the file size, and the file format.

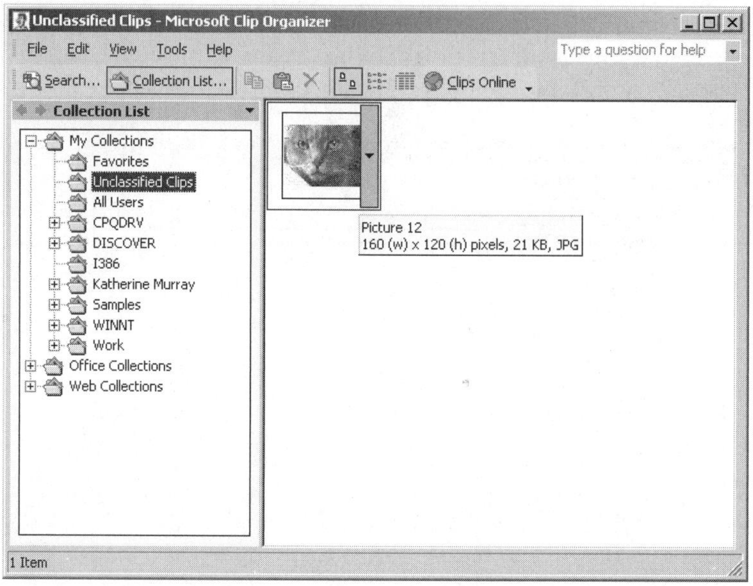

Figure 14-5. The Clip Organizer has a new look and feel in Word 2002.

Working with an Image in the Clip Organizer

To choose a clip from the Microsoft Clip Organizer, simply navigate to the clip you want and select it in the view window. The image is selected and a down arrow appears along the right edge of the image. Click the down arrow to display the drop-down menu; a range of choices appears, as Figure 14-6 shows.

How will you use the Clip Organizer to work with your images? Most of the things you'll do in the Clip Organizer have to do with organizing and accessing your images. For example, you can use the Clip Organizer to do the following:

- Scan your hard drive for clip art images to add to the Gallery.
- Copy and paste images into other folders, files, and applications.
- Reorganize art collections.

- Locate images with a similar style.
- Add and edit keywords that describe individual images.
- Access Web tools for working with Clip Organizer images.
- Display the properties of an individual image.

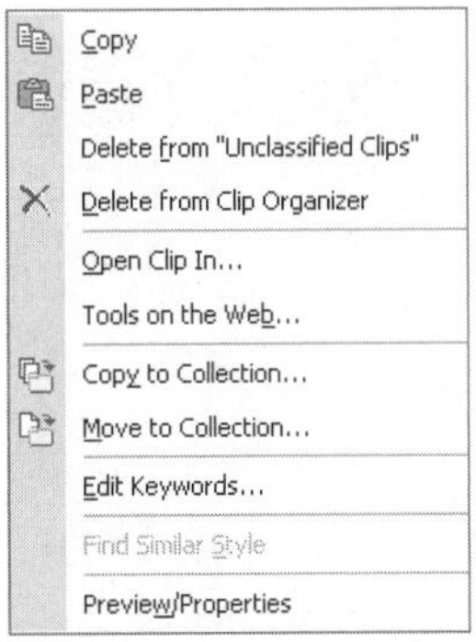

Figure 14-6. Right-click an image and choose an option to work with your Gallery images.

Accessing Microsoft Clip Organizer eServices Online

To access Web tools for working with Clip Organizer images, select the clip art image in the view window, click the down arrow, and choose Tools On The Web from the drop-down menu. The Microsoft Clip Organizer eServices window appears, and you can explore the various offerings on the site.

Saving Favorite Clips

Over time, you might find that you have a group of images that qualify as "favorites." You can save those clips to your Favorites collection so that you can access them easily. Here's how:

1. Display the Microsoft Clip Organizer by choosing Insert, Picture, Clip Art; then click Clip Organizer in the See Also section of the task pane.
2. Expand your My Collections section so that the Favorites folder is visible.
3. Navigate to the collection and folder storing the clip art you want to copy.
4. Drag the clip art image from the view window to the Favorites folder. (See Figure 14-7, on the next page.) The Clip Organizer makes a copy of the file and leaves the original in the Collection folder.

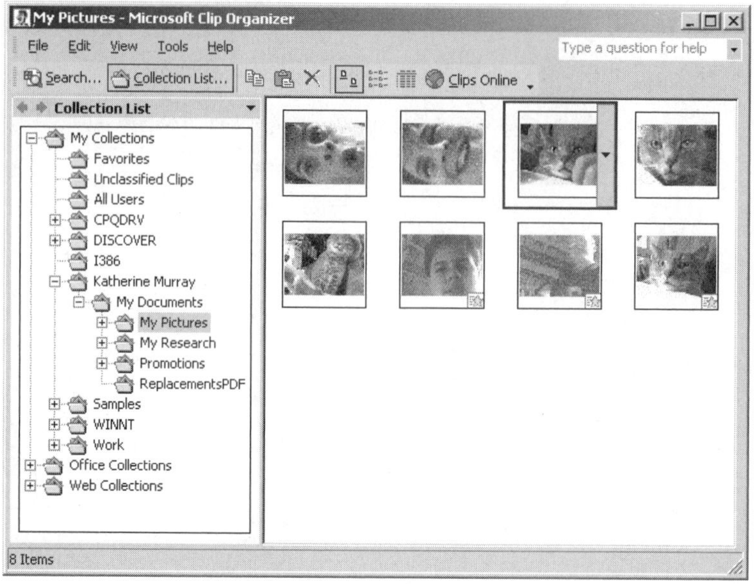

Figure 14-7. You can drag a copy of an image to your Favorites folder to keep a collection of files you use often.

> **tip** **Copy images from the Task Pane**
>
> You can copy an image from the Insert Clip Art task pane to your Favorites folder in the Clip Organizer by clicking the image down arrow and choosing Copy To Collection. When the Copy To Collection dialog box appears, you can choose your Favorites collection (or another collection as applicable) and click OK. The image is then copied to the specified collection.

Adding Your Own Images—Automatically

If you're using your own clip art collections or you want to use clip art from a previous Office version, you can have the Clip Organizer search and add clips automatically. To add the clips to the Clip Organizer, follow these steps:

1. Display the Microsoft Clip Organizer by choosing Insert, Picture, Clip Art; then click Clip Organizer in the See Also section of the task pane.

2. In the Microsoft Clip Organizer window, choose File, Add Clips To Gallery Automatically to have Word search and add the clips it finds without any intervention from you. The Add Clips To Gallery dialog box appears, alerting you that Word will catalog all media files (including picture, sound, and motion files) if you were to click OK.

3. Click Options in the Add Clips To Gallery dialog box t to specify which folders the Clip Organizer will search for the files you want to add. The Auto Import Settings dialog box appears, listing all found folders on your system. (See Figure 14-8.) If you want the Clip Organizer to skip any of the selected folders, simply clear the folder check boxes.

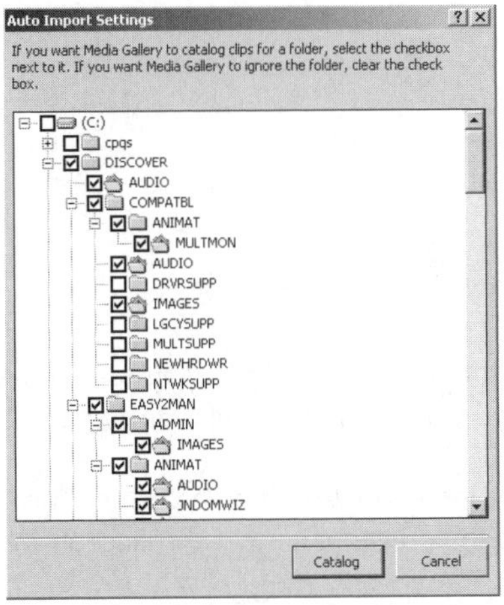

Figure 14-8. The Clip Organizer will search all available folders on your computer unless you specify otherwise.

4. Click Catalog in the Auto Import Settings dialog box to begin the process. The Clip Organizer displays a status dialog box showing you the progress of searching for clips and adding keywords to link the clips to the gallery. You can click Stop at any time you want to cancel the process.

Adding Images On Your Own

The Clip Organizer also gives you the option of adding images manually, that is, by selecting the ones you want to add and specifying where they go. You can also add keywords that you'll use to refer to the images later. To add images on your own, follow these steps:

1. Display the Microsoft Clip Organizer.

2. Choose File, Add Clips To Gallery and select On My Own. The Add Clips To Gallery dialog box appears, as Figure 14-9 displays, on the next page.

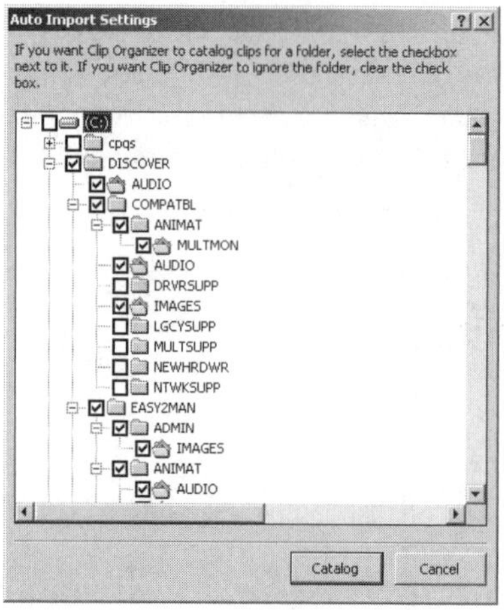

Figure 14-9. You can add your clips to the Clip Organizer manually by navigating to the folder you want and choosing a destination collection.

3. Click the file you want to add; then click the Add To button. The Import To Collection dialog box appears so you can choose the collection folder for the clip you are importing.

4. Click the folder, click OK, and then click Add. You're returned to the Clip Organizer and the clip is added to your collection as specified.

Creating a New Collection

You can create a new collection in two ways: by clicking New in the Import To Collection dialog box or by choosing File, New Collection in the Clip Organizer. The New Collection dialog box appears, where you can choose a parent folder, if necessary, and enter a name for the collection. (See Figure 14-10.)

Figure 14-10. You can create new collections in the Clip Organizer to store clips specific to your interests or industry.

tip **Review clip properties**

For some of your documents, you'll need to look carefully for just the right images to fit the design and layout of your project. In these cases, you might want to see the file type, the size, the orientation, and any keywords associated with the image. To view the properties of an image, select the image and choose Preview/Properties from the drop-down menu. The Preview Properties dialog box displays file specifications and lists the full path to the file, along with any caption and keywords entered.

Adding and Editing Keywords

Keywords are important in helping you find the images you want. Each of the files in the Clip Organizer is assigned a certain number of keywords—these words help characterize the image so that the Clip Organizer knows what to display when you enter a certain word in the Search box. Keywords are what make it possible for you to enter *cat* in either the Microsoft Clip Organizer or the Insert Clip Art task pane and display the images of cats included in the collections.

To display the keywords for a specific image, follow these steps:

1. Select your image in either the Microsoft Clip Organizer or the Insert Clip Art task pane, and click its down arrow.
2. Choose Edit Keywords. The Keywords dialog box appears, as Figure 14-11 shows.

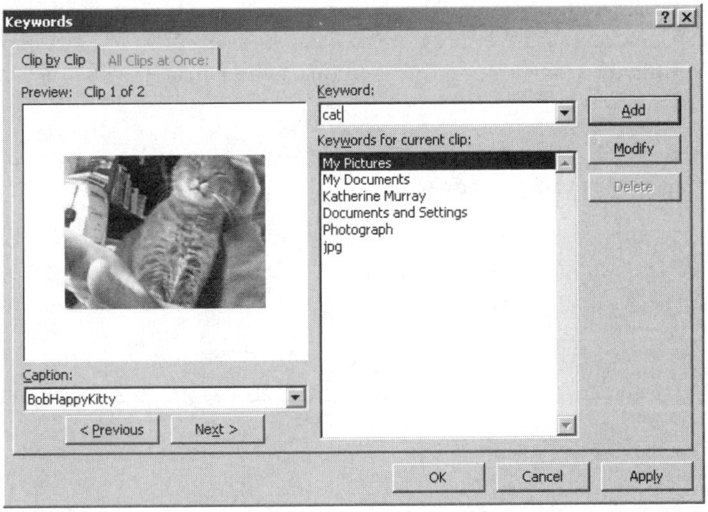

Figure 14-11. You can review, add, edit, or delete keywords in the Keywords dialog box.

3 By default, the name of the image is displayed in the Caption drop-down list. You can click in the edit portion of the list and enter the caption (or name) you want to appear.

4 Click in the Keyword drop-down list and choose a word from the list or type a word you want to use to refer to the image. Click Add to add the keyword.

tip If you want to delete any of the keywords currently in the list for the selected clip, simply select it and click Delete.

Deleting Unwanted Images

If the Clip Organizer acquires files you don't want included, you can select and delete them using the image drop-down menu. Click the file you want to delete, and you'll see two delete options on the drop-down menu: You can delete the clip from the selected folder, or you can delete the file from the Clip Organizer completely. If you choose the first option, the image is deleted without any further action from you. If you choose the second option, the Clip Organizer alerts you that the action will cause the image to be deleted from all collections on your system. Click OK to proceed, or press Esc to cancel.

Inserting Pictures

Although letting the Clip Organizer scan your computer and add files for you is a nice, timesaving feature, there will be those times when you want specifically to import files you've created in another program or brought in on disk. You can import images from other programs, and you can bring in images you created with your scanner or digital camera.

tip **Use pictures as backgrounds**

You can turn a picture you like into a background for your Word document. Choose Format, Background; click Fill Effects and click the Picture tab. Click the Select Picture button to display the Select Picture dialog box in which you can choose the picture for your background. Click the image and click Insert. The image is copied, tile-fashion, the width and length of your document.

Importing Images into Word

The process of importing an image simply involves choosing Insert, Picture, From File. Word automatically goes to your My Pictures folder and displays all importable files. (See Figure 14-12.) Click the file you want and click Insert; Word adds the file to the document at the insertion point.

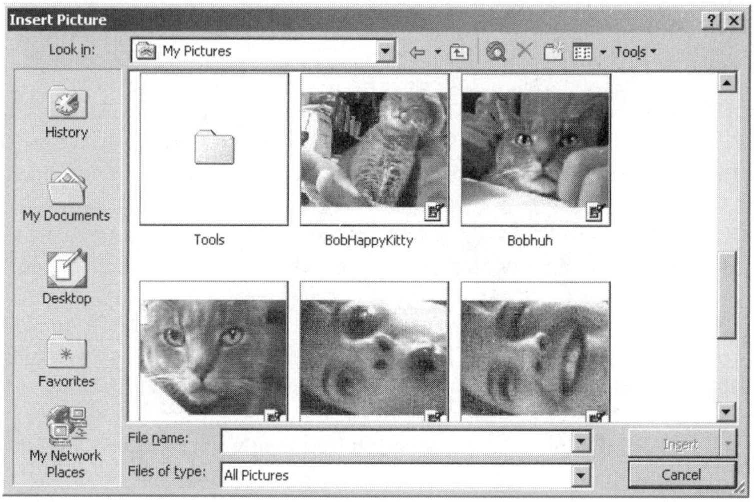

Figure 14-12. Word displays all file types it recognizes.

tip **Limit file display**

If you want to see only files of a certain type, click the Files Of Type down arrow and choose the file format you want to see from the displayed list. Only those files with the extension you selected will appear in the Insert Picture window.

Using Scanned and Digital Images in Word

Many of the best images you use in your documents might be real, live photos of real, live people. Your annual report could show the smiling faces of real people helped by your organization; your business plan could include scanned images of the site where your new building will be erected; your classroom project could include the 22 smiling faces of the students who helped prepare it.

To scan an image or use a digital photograph in Word, follow these steps:

1. Open the document to which you want to add the image.

2 Choose Insert, Picture, From Scanner Or Camera. The Insert Picture From Scanner Or Camera dialog box appears. (See Figure 14-13.)

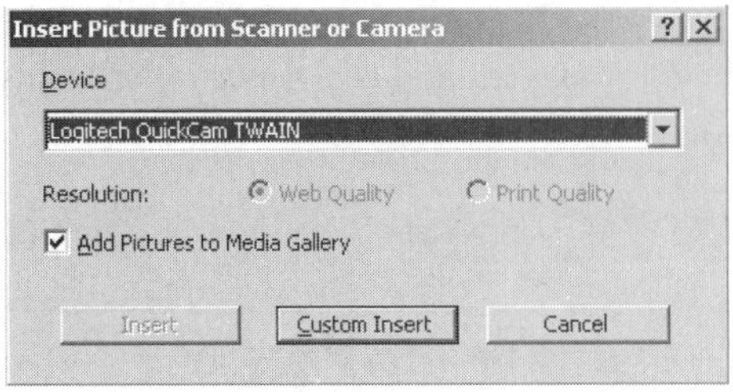

Figure 14-13. The Insert Picture From Scanner Or Camera dialog box gives you the means to scan your photos or pictures directly into your Word document.

3 If you have more than one scanner or camera installed on your system, click the Device down arrow and choose the one you want to use.

4 Choose the resolution you want to use. Web Quality is of lower quality (fewer pixels and colors are used to create the image) than Print Quality, but the files are smaller and they're fine for screen display.

5 If you want the image to be added to the Clip Organizer by default, leave the Add Pictures To Clip Organizer check box selected.

6 Finally, if you want to add a picture from your scanner, click Insert; if you want to add a picture from a digital camera, click Custom Insert.

> **tip** **Find lost images**
>
> If you elected to have the scanned image or captured photo saved to the Clip Organizer, look for it in your Unclassified Clips collection. You can then drag it to your Favorites folder or another collection of your choosing.

Working with Pictures

The pictures we've been talking about thus far in this chapter have been pictures you choose from the Insert Clip Art task pane, pictures you import from another program, or images you scan or capture with a digital camera. These different ways of bringing images into Word produce different types of files:

- Clip art can be either bitmapped or vector images.
- Imported files can also be either bitmapped or vector images.
- Scanned images and captured photos are always bitmapped images.

Although bitmapped images and vector images each require some different techniques in editing, you'll use basically the same procedures with them in Word. The primary difference between the two types of image files is what happens to them when you resize them. A bitmapped image will become stretched and blurrier as the graphic is enlarged; a vector image can be resized with no loss of quality or clarity.

Graphics File Type is Unlisted

Word comes equipped with a number of graphics filters that enable the program to convert files from other programs easily. But if you don't see the file type you need listed in the Files Of Type box (in the Insert Picture dialog box), you can still use the picture. Open the file in Windows Paint or another graphics program; copy the image, and then switch to Word and paste the picture into your document.

Checking Out the Picture Toolbar

When you click one of the images you've added to your document, the Picture toolbar appears by default. This toolbar includes all the items you need to make simple changes to the images you bring into Word. Table 14-2, on the next page, takes a look at each of the Picture toolbar buttons and gives you an idea of when you will use each one.

From Color to Black & White and Back

The first button on the Picture Toolbar to the right of the Insert Picture button offers you the choice of turning your color photograph or picture into a grayscale or black and white image. By default, the image is assigned Automatic coloring. If you're preparing a document that will be printed in black and white only, you can change the image to grayscale (which transforms all the coloring differences into shades of gray) or to black and white, which does away with subtleties and gives you a sharply defined black and white image. Figure 14-14 shows the results when a color photo is first changed to Grayscale and then to Black & White.

Figure 14-14. Grayscale and Black & White give you two dramatic ways to modify photos and pictures.

Table 14-2. Picture Tools for Editing Images

Button	Name	Description	Use
	Insert Picture	Displays the Insert Picture dialog box so you can import a new file	You want to add another picture as you work in your document.
	Color	Gives you a set of four options that range from full color to black and white	You want to use a special treatment on an image—removing color, turning it to black and white.
	More Contrast	Makes the darks darker and the lights lighter	You want to make an image appear more abstract, less blended.
	Less Contrast	Lessens the division between dark and light, blurring the image	You want to create a subtle effect with no sharp contrasts.
	More Brightness	Increases the lightness of the overall image	You want to lighten a too-dark photo or captured image.
	Less Brightness	Tones down the brightness, taking the edge off light colors and reflections	You want to darken a too-light photo or image.
	Crop	Appears to "cut" the edges of an image (in reality preserves the entire image)	You want to select a portion of a photo or image to be used in a document.
	Rotate Left	Rotates image to the left 90 degrees each time you click on its side	You want to turn the image, angle text, or skew a line or border.
	Line Style	Sets the width of the line style used to border the image	You want to create a boundary or frame for the image.

(continued)

Table 14-2. *(continued)*

Button	Name	Description	Use
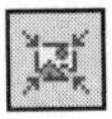	Compress Pictures	Reduces the space required to save picture files (Web or Print resolution)	You're concerned about file size and want to optimize your document for the Web.
	Text Wrapping	Controls the way text wraps around the selected object	You're creating a document that incorporates text and images together in a continuing layout.
	Format Picture	Displays the Format Picture dialog box so that you can make choices in one place about cropping, brightness, compression, and more	You want to choose a number of settings for your picture at once.
	Set Transparent Color	Creates a "see through" effect in an image when you click the areas you want changed	You're creating an image with a special effect—for example, a stylized photo or drawing.
	Reset Picture	Returns the picture to its size, shape, and brightness and contrast levels before you made any changes to it	You've modified an image and want to discard the changes you've made.

Changing Picture Contrast and Brightness

Contrast and Brightness are two of those controls that have been around for a long, long time. Remember the brightness button on the old color television? The knob you always turned by accident when you meant to twist the vertical hold? In Word, the contrast and brightness controls for your images influence the overall effect of the image in a significant way.

The Contrast setting controls the amount of differentiation between light and dark. When you increase the contrast by clicking More Contrast, the darks get darker and the lights get lighter. When you decrease the contrast by clicking Less Contrast, the darks lighten and the lights darken.

The brightness of your image controls the light-to-dark ratio your graphic displays. Click More Brightness to increase the brightness, and the entire image lightens. When you click Less Brightness, the entire image darkens. The buttons are incremental, meaning that each time you click them, Word changes the amount of brightness just a bit.

tip **Test brightness and contrast levels**

There's no hard and fast rule for brightness and contrast settings for your images. Test out different settings and see what looks best. If you're creating a print document, remember to print a copy as a test, because what you see on the screen won't exactly match the quality of what you see in print.

Cropping Pictures

Cropping images is a pretty simple process. With the image displayed on your screen, click the Crop button on the Picture toolbar. The pointer changes to a cropping tool. You can then place the tool on the edge or corner of the image where you want to begin cropping and drag the side or corner of the image inward until the amount you want to remove has been cropped out.

tip **Spare the crop and spoil the picture**

If you decide after you've cropped an image that you liked it better the way it was before you changed it, you can undo the operation by clicking Undo on the Standard toolbar. If you want to reverse not only the cropping but other changes as well, you can return the picture to its original state by clicking Restore Picture on the Picture toolbar.

Resizing Pictures

Another operation that goes hand in hand with cropping is resizing the images you import. This is one technique you'll be using all the time—pictures rarely come into your documents at just the right size.

To resize a picture in word, click the image. Handles appear around the edge of the object. If you want to enlarge the image, click in one corner of the picture and drag the handle outward. A dotted outline follows the pointer, showing the new size of the image. (See Figure 14-15.) When the image is the size you want it, release the mouse button.

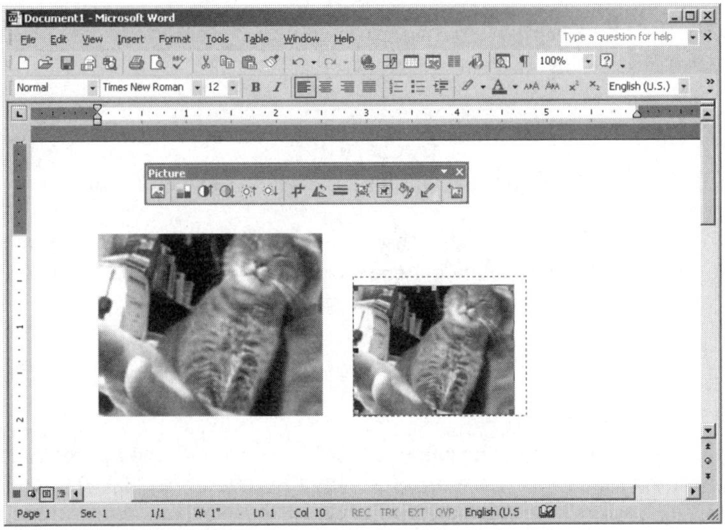

Figure 14-15. Resizing follows the same rule of thumb in Word as it does in other applications—click and drag to resize quickly.

> **tip** **Resize accurately**
>
> If you need to resize your picture to fit a precise specification, click the Format Picture button on the Picture Toolbar to display the Format Picture dialog box; then select the Size tab and enter the exact measurements for your picture.

If you're working with bitmapped graphics, like the one shown in Figure 14-15, you'll notice a loss of clarity when you enlarge the image. To maintain the best clarity possible for scanned and digitized images, keep their sizes as small as your design allows. Several small focused images are better than one large fuzzy one.

> **One of the headaches with image size and placement is how well—or how poorly—the text wraps (or doesn't wrap) around the picture. For more about text wrap, see "Controlling Text Wrap" on page 358 later in this chapter.**

newfeature!

Rotating Pictures

Rotating is fun. If you're creating a special border effect, a text-and-graphics look in which your logo pitches sideways, a rolling star, or some other creative addition to your documents, the Rotate tool will come in handy.

Although rotating in general isn't new to Word, what's new is its inclusion on the Picture toolbar. And now, instead of having to select a series of different commands to do block rotates and free rotation, you can do it all in one smooth sequence. To rotate an image in Word, follow these steps:

1. Display your document in Print Layout view.
2. Select the image you want to rotate. The Picture Toolbar appears.
3. Click Rotate Left. Word rotates an image to the left 90 degrees each time you click. A small green handle appears at the top edge of the rotated image; this is the handle that enables you to freely rotate the image.
4. Position the pointer over the handle. The pointer changes shape to a curved arrow.
5. Drag the handle in the direction you want to free rotate the image. You can control the rotation in either direction, right or left, and modify the rotation as many times as you like. (See Figure 14-16.)

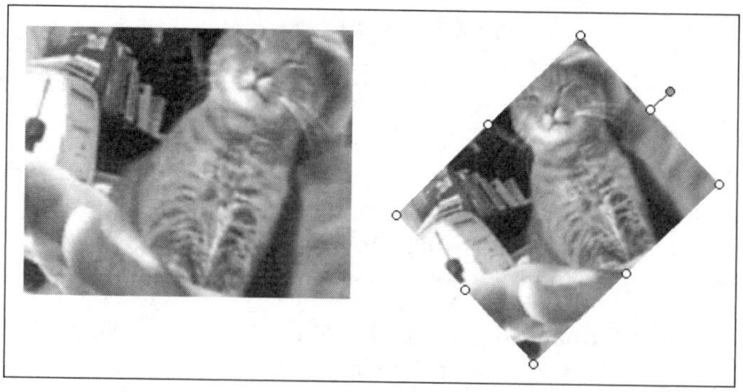

Figure 14-16. You can use both block rotate and free rotate functions right from the Picture Toolbar in Word 2002.

note A block rotate is the process of turning the picture by a certain number of degrees, in this case, 90 degrees. A free rotate is the process of grabbing an image by a handle and moving it to the desired rotation position.

Controlling Line Style

Not all images need a frame—you'll discover how best you want to use the line style control settings on a case-by-case basis. With the Line Style options you can select a variety of line styles and widths, and you can further control them in the Format Picture dialog box, which appears when you choose More Lines at the bottom of the Line Style drop-down menu. (See Figure 14-17.) To choose the line style you want, simply click the picture, click Line Style, and make your choice.

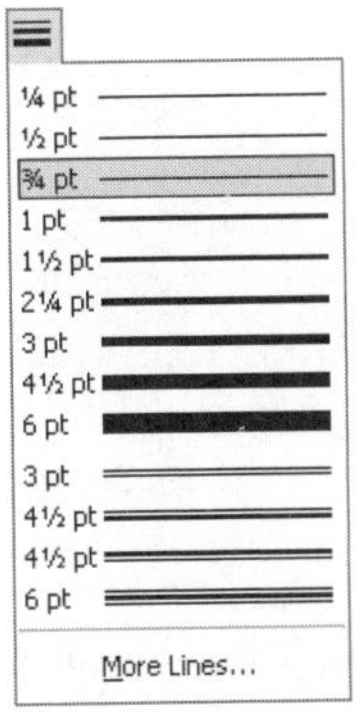

Figure 14-17. Word offers a number of different line styles to border your image.

Compressing Pictures

newfeature!

Pictures can take up a hefty amount of disk space as well as use your computer resources in printing. Because of the amount of data stored in an image—especially a color image—the files tend to be huge. Word offers the Compress Pictures tool as an option for reducing the amount of space taken up by your picture files. To compress the pictures in the current document, follow these steps:

1. Select one of the pictures in the document. The Picture Toolbar appears.
2. Click the Compress Pictures button. The Compress Pictures dialog box appears, as Figure 14-18 shows.

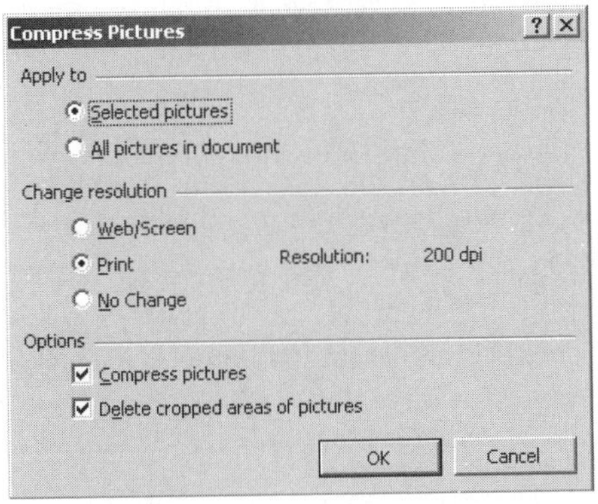

Figure 14-18. You can reduce the amount of space a graphics-heavy file requires by compressing images.

3. If you want only the selected picture compressed, leave the default setting on Selected Pictures. If you want to compress all pictures in the document, click the All Pictures In Document option.

In choosing resolution, you can tell Word to lower the resolution for the screen (which also affects Web viewing) or for printouts only.

note If you elect to have Word change the resolution to Web/Screen, the image will be displayed at 96 dots per inch (dpi) on your monitor. If you choose Print, Word reduces resolution to 200 dpi. For best results, test both resolution changes and see whether either works for you. If not, choose No Change and Word will compress the file as much as possible without affecting the display or print resolution.

4. For optimum compression, leave the last two check boxes, Compress Pictures and Delete Cropped Areas Of Pictures, selected. They ensure that the pictures are compressed as fully as possible.

5. Click OK to compress the images. Word displays a warning that compression might reduce the quality of the picture and asks you whether you want to apply picture optimization. If you want Word to step in and attempt to optimize your picture in light of the lost resolution, click Apply. If you click Cancel, the compression process is stopped.

Cut Your Files Down to Size

If you're working on high-quality documents and file size is a concern but not a priority, you might want to think of ways to creatively reduce the size of your file without resorting to compression features. In our experience, compressing images can cause a dramatic loss of quality, and if your objective in using pictures is to make your documents look their best, including a fuzzy or ill-defined image might not be quite good enough.

There are ways, however, that you can control file size as you work:

- **Limit your use of photos.** Because of the information stored in a digitized image file, it can be very large. Consider how many photos you want to use in your document and use them effectively.
- **Watch your file types.** Some files are larger than others. A small JPG or GIF file takes up less space than the average BMP or TIF file.

Controlling Text Wrap

The whole point to adding pictures is to illustrate your text, right? So you need a way to help your text and graphics flow together naturally. You coordinate this text-and-art relationship by using the Text Wrap tool, which is available on the Picture Toolbar.

> **tip** **Make a Text Wrap toolbar**
>
> You can grab the top of the Text Wrap list and drag it off in a toolbar by itself. This is convenient if you're working repeatedly with text wrap considerations and want to save yourself a few toolbar clicks.

To set up text wrap in your document, follow these steps:

1. Select the picture you want to wrap text around. The Picture Toolbar appears.
2. Click the Text Wrapping button. A list of Text Wrap choices appears, as Figure 14-19 shows.

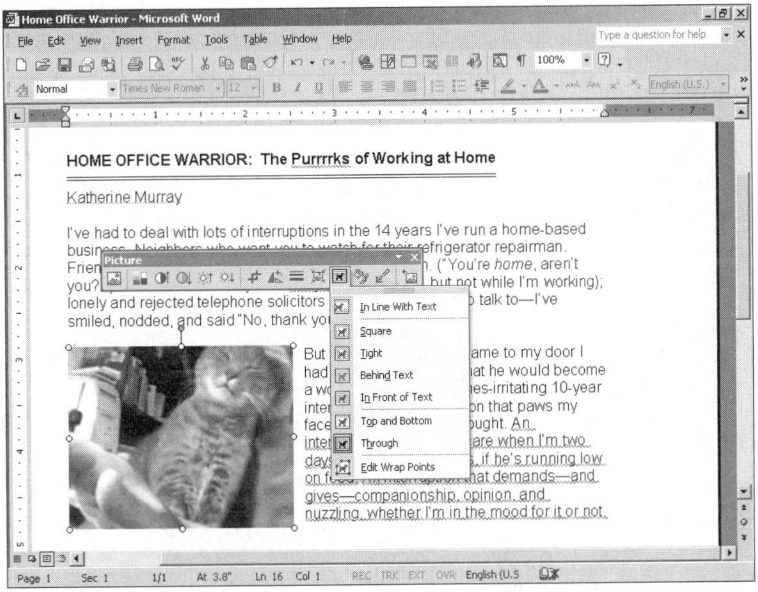

Figure 14-19. Choose from a list of Text Wrap styles to position your picture and text together the way you want them.

3. Select the Text Wrap style you want to apply to your picture. Experiment if you like; you can always Undo your choice if you don't like the effect. The Text Wrap options are these:
   - **In Line with Text** is selected by default; positions the picture in line with text as it appears at the current position.
   - **Square** causes the text to wrap left and right of the bounding box enclosing the picture.

- **Tight** secures the text to the picture itself, not the bounding box (which might appear to be the same border, depending on the picture you are working with).
- **Behind Text** causes the text to flow over the top of the picture.
- **In Front Of Text** flows the text behind the picture.
- **Top And Bottom** wraps the text above and below the image in the document, if there's room. White space is left bordering the picture on the sides.
- **Through** wraps text up against the border of your picture, which is a nice effect if you have an uneven boundary that text could fill.
- **Edit Wrap Points** enables fine-tuning of the way the text wraps around the picture. By controlling individual points, you can set a boundary for the text that follows the line of the picture.

Adding and Editing Wrap Points

Word gives you the means to create your own kind of text wrap by creating boundaries for text to flow along. You do this using the Edit Wrap Points button on the Picture toolbar. For example, consider the example shown in Figure 14-20. In this example, the bottom edge of the wrap area was extended to make room for some graphic "paw prints" around the base of the photo.

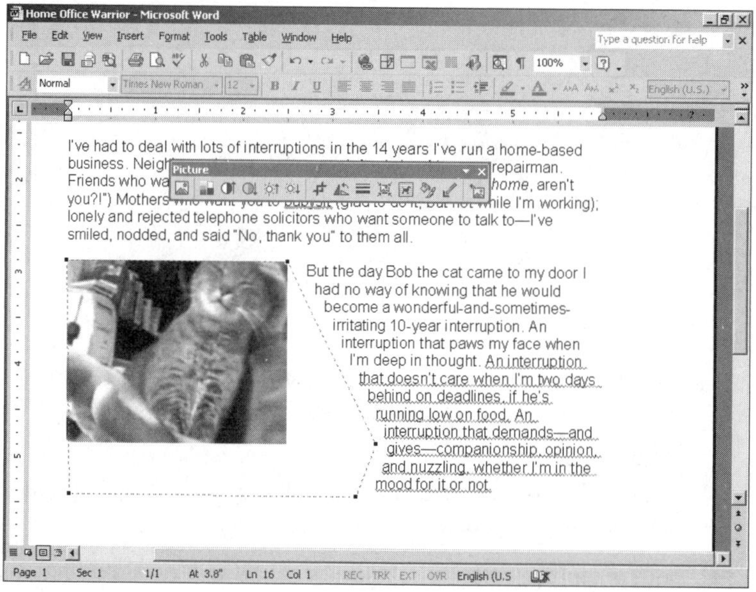

Figure 14-20. You can create your own text wrap boundaries with Edit Wrap Points.

Here's the process for creating and working with edit wrap points for your picture and text wrap boundaries:

1. Select the picture you want to work with. The Picture Toolbar appears.
2. Click the Text Wrapping button and choose Edit Wrap Points from the drop-down menu. A red dashed boundary with several black handles appears around your picture.
3. Grab one of the handles with the mouse pointer and drag it outward, to the edge of the boundary you want to create. The line stays where you put it.
4. To create another handle (you aren't limited to following the shape of the image—you can stretch and add edit points any place you choose), simply click in the boundary line and drag it out to the point at which you want it. This creates another handle at that point and establishes the boundary where you put it.
5. After you finish creating your text boundary, click the Text Wrapping button again and click Through. The text wraps up to, but not into, the new text boundary you created.

Troubleshooting

Only Part of My Image Is Displayed

If only part of your picture displays properly, make sure that the spacing isn't the problem. Select the picture and choose Format, Paragraph. Click the Indents And Spacing tab and, if you want the picture to display in line with the selected text, click the Line Spacing down arrow and choose Single.

Formatting Pictures

When you're comfortable working with pictures, making your choices, and fitting your color, shading, brightness, and text wrap choices to a norm, you might want to handle all these different choices in one place rather than selecting them individually. That's what the Format Picture dialog box is for. Also available from the Picture Toolbar, the Format Picture dialog box enables you to make choices for colors and lines, picture size, text wrap, alignment, brightness and contrast, cropping settings, and Web text settings. (See Figure 14-21, on the next page.)

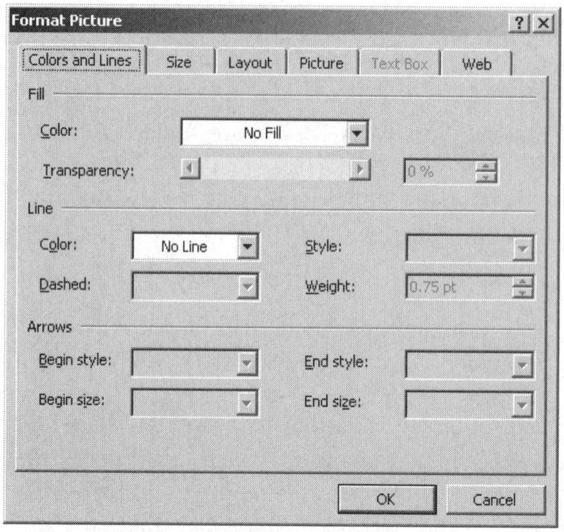

Figure 14-21. The Format Picture dialog box combines many of the options you've worked with individually in using the Picture toolbar.

Because we've covered most of this elsewhere in this chapter, and because finding your way around a dialog box is no doubt a technique you mastered long ago, it's only necessary to describe one item in the Format Picture dialog box: setting alternative text for Web display.

Creating Web Alternative Text

If you're using Word to create a Web page, when you position graphics on a page, it's possible that the visitors to your site won't ever view them. That's not because of bandwidth issues; that's because some users prefer to browse with their graphics capabilities disabled. It enables them to move more quickly through Web pages and get on with the business of surfing. But if your visitors don't have their graphics enabled and you've got all these great pictures on your site, what are they going to see?

That's where alternative text comes in. You can add a text message that explains what the image *would* look like if the user chose to view it. Also, alternative text can provide a message while a large file loads or alert a user if a file is missing.

To add alternative text to your document, follow these steps:

1. Click the picture to which you want to add alternative text; make sure the Picture Toolbar appears. (If it doesn't appear automatically, right-click the image and choose Show Picture Toolbar from the menu.)

2. Click the Format Picture button. The Format Picture dialog box appears.

3 Click the Web tab. This tab gives you a large open space where you can type the message you want to appear in place of the picture. (See Figure 14-22.)

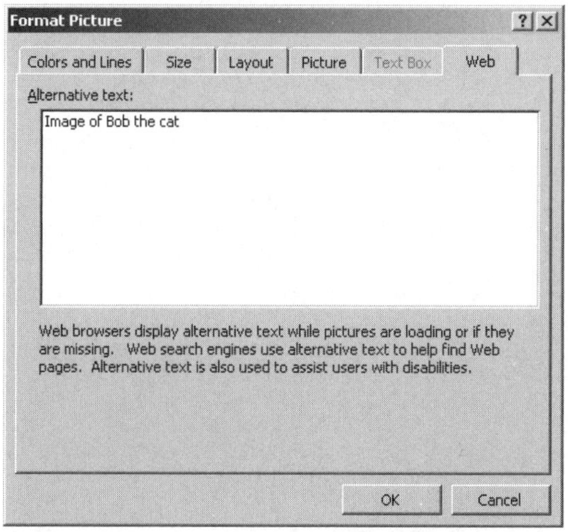

Figure 14-22. Alternative text gives Web visitors something to view if they don't have graphics enabled in their browsers.

Troubleshooting

Graphics Are Missing from My Document

If you don't see graphics in your document, make sure that you haven't enabled the Picture Placeholders option in the Options dialog box. This feature helps speed up screen display by showing only the outline of graphics. Choose Tools, Options and click the View tab. Make sure the Picture Placeholders check box is not selected.

Chapter 15

Inserting Objects for Multimedia and More

Text is text is text, but Microsoft Word offers much more than simple text management and enhancement techniques. Your Word documents can literally sing, if you choose to add audio clips or voice-overs. They can tell a story, if you choose to add a video segment. Your Web pages can teach, if you want to add a Microsoft PowerPoint presentation to the page you create in Word.

Word makes it easy to both link and embed files (which are called *objects* for this operation). That means you can work with files you create in other programs, whether they're Microsoft Office applications or not. This chapter gets you up to speed on incorporating objects in your documents, whether you want to add multimedia effects or something more sedate, like a Microsoft Excel spreadsheet or a bit of Microsoft Access data.

What kinds of things might you want to link? You've got all sorts of choices: a sound file, a table, a video clip, an equation, data tables, images, a presentation file, or another Word document.

Create It Once, Use It Again

One of the great things about using a multi-application suite like Office is the way you can reuse what you create. You can open your Excel spreadsheet in your sales report. You can attach an organization chart to the announcement of the new spring promotions. You can add a voice-over segment to a section of a speech you're testing out with your coworkers. You can use these different items in your Word document by importing them as objects.

Although you can copy and paste these items into a document, keeping the data current can be a problem if your information changes often. If you paste a segment of your Excel worksheet in your document, and then the original worksheet changes, your document will be out of date. To resolve this so that you can create these multidimensional documents and still keep your documents current, you can link the objects to their original files using object linking and embedding (OLE) and Dynamic Data Exchange (DDE).

note You can import objects from programs outside the Office applications. As long as the program supports OLE and DDE, you can link and edit that program's objects.

Linking vs. Embedding: A Comparison

Linking and *embedding* a file might seem like the same process at first. In fact, they are two very different processes, each providing a different function:

- **Linking** a file establishes a link between the original (source) file and the file to which you copied the data (destination). Whenever you change the information in the source file, the destination file is updated.
- **Embedding** a file places an intact copy of the source in the destination file. Although changing the source doesn't affect the destination file, you can *edit* the object in the destination file by double-clicking it. You can then edit the object without quitting Word.

tip **Cut to the Chase**

The biggest difference between linking and embedding is the file in which the data is stored (source or destination) and how it's updated (at the source, or originating program, or in the destination document).

Good Candidates for Linking and Embedding

Linking an object is a good choice when you need to keep data in your documents up to date. Here are a few examples:

- You're creating a draft of a report that includes slides from a PowerPoint presentation that's not yet finished. If the document is linked to the presentation file, when you finish the presentation, the document will reflect the changes.

- You have a new logo design for your business, and you're trying it out on letterhead. If you maintain the link to the draw file in which the logo is stored, when you change the logo, the letterhead will reflect the changes.
- You have a sales report due this afternoon, but not all the numbers are in from your regional sales staff. If you import the part of the Excel spreadsheet that's ready and establish a link when you update the information later, the file will reflect the changes.

Embedding objects is a good idea when you don't need to maintain a link but want to edit the object in your document. Here are some examples of embedding:

- You want to send a snapshot of current Excel data to a coworker, but the information is likely to change.
- You want to add a finished spreadsheet object. You don't need to maintain the link, but you might want to change the format or values later.
- You've added an organization chart, but when you send the document to different audiences, you need to change the roles that are displayed.

note Linking an object to a file establishes a one-way link to the source document. When you change the information in the source—for example, when you change the name of a product in the PowerPoint presentation you've imported—the same change is reflected in the document to which you've linked the information.

tip **Link for Small File Size**

When you want to keep your files small, linking is your best bet. Because linked files store only a pointer to the source file, the destination file size increases only a little. Although these types of links introduce other potential problems (such as broken links to deleted or moved source files), they give you the flexibility you might need when size is a consideration.

Linking Objects

Word provides two different ways for you to bring linked objects into your documents. You can use the Insert Object dialog box to place an existing object in your document, and you can use the Paste Special command to use the basic copy-and-paste procedure to establish and maintain a link with the source file.

Inserting a Linked Object

Suppose you have a great new banner ad design that you want to incorporate in the document you're preparing for a client. Although the banner ad isn't quite finished, you want to show the client how the ideas are developing in the presentation. You decide to add the entire presentation to your document as a link in the report.

To insert the object and create a link to the source file, follow these steps:

1. Place the insertion point where you want to include the object.
2. Choose Insert, Object. The Object dialog box appears.
3. Click the Create From File tab. (See Figure 15-1.) Here you can enter the name for the file you want to insert and choose whether to link or embed the file.

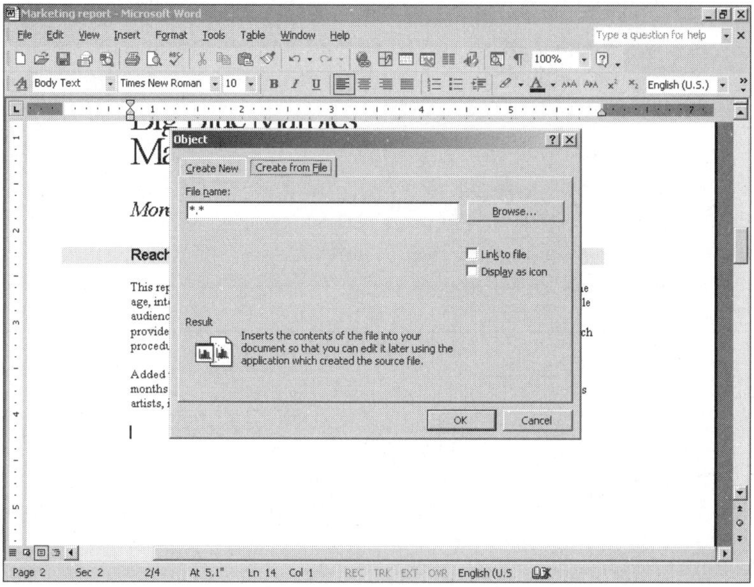

Figure 15-1. The Object dialog box gives you the means to link or embed objects.

4. Click Browse. The Browse dialog box is displayed. Navigate to the folder in which the file you want to link is stored, select the file, and click Insert. You are returned to the Object dialog box.
5. Select the Link To File check box. This tells Word to establish the link to the source.

6 Click OK. The object is inserted, as Figure 15-2 shows.

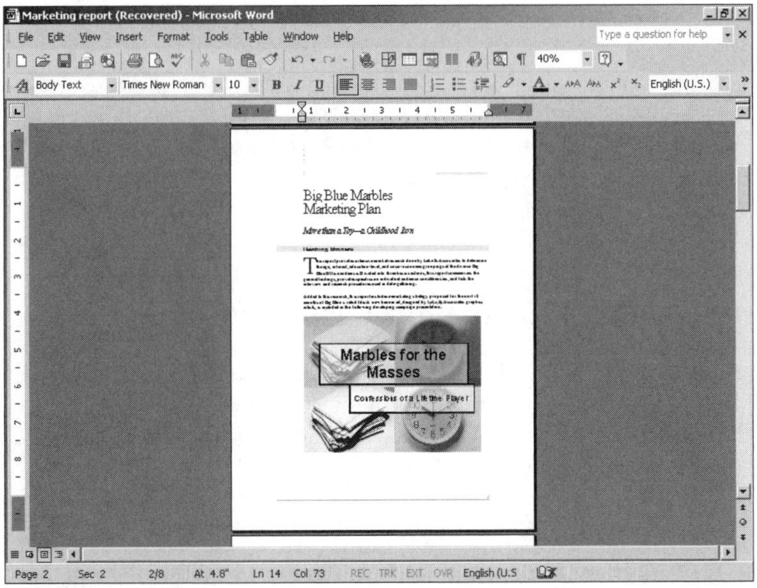

Figure 15-2. The object is placed at the insertion point.

> **tip** **Run a Presentation**
>
> If your linked object is a PowerPoint presentation, run the presentation by double-clicking it. You won't be able to edit the presentation, however, without opening the source file.

Troubleshooting

The Linked Object Is Missing

So after you go through the steps to insert a linked object, it starts to appear in your file and then—nothing. Just an outline, no object. What's going on?

If you have enabled Picture Placeholders in the Options dialog box, Word is saving memory and screen update time by showing only the outline of the object. You can fix this by choosing Tools, Options and clearing the Picture Placeholders check box on the View tab.

tip **Create Objects with Create New**

The process of embedding uses the Create New tab in the Object dialog box. Embedding an object enables you to include in your document objects you have created in other programs, and it also lets you actually create the objects from scratch while you are working with Word. When you use the items in the Create New tab to create an embedded object, Word launches the program you used to create the object; and then after you save and close the other program, you are returned to Word, and the object is embedded in your current document.

Adding Linked Objects with Paste Special

Another way to add a linked object in your document is to use Paste Special. This command (available from the Edit menu) copies and pastes not only the data but also a link to the source file. Start in the Word document to which you want to add the linked object, and then follow these steps:

1. Position the insertion point where you want to add the object.
2. Launch the program in which you have created the object to be linked. Select the section or object, and copy the item to the Clipboard.
3. Return to Word, and choose Edit, Paste Special. The Paste Special dialog box appears. (For an example of the Paste Special dialog box, see Figure 15-5, on page 226.)
4. Click the Paste Link option, select the object type in the As list box, and click OK. Word adds the data and the link to your document. Note: The Paste Link option is available only for objects you've created in programs that support linking.

tip When you want to review the links in your current document, choose Edit, Links to display the Links dialog box.

Changing Linked Objects

Any editing you do on a linked object actually takes place in the source file. You can edit a linked object in several different ways:

- You can double-click the object to launch the source program.
- You can click the object, choose Edit, Linked Object, and click Edit Link.

- You can right-click the object to display the shortcut menu. You can then click Linked Object and select Edit Link. (See Figure 15-3.) This takes you to the source file so that you can make changes as needed.

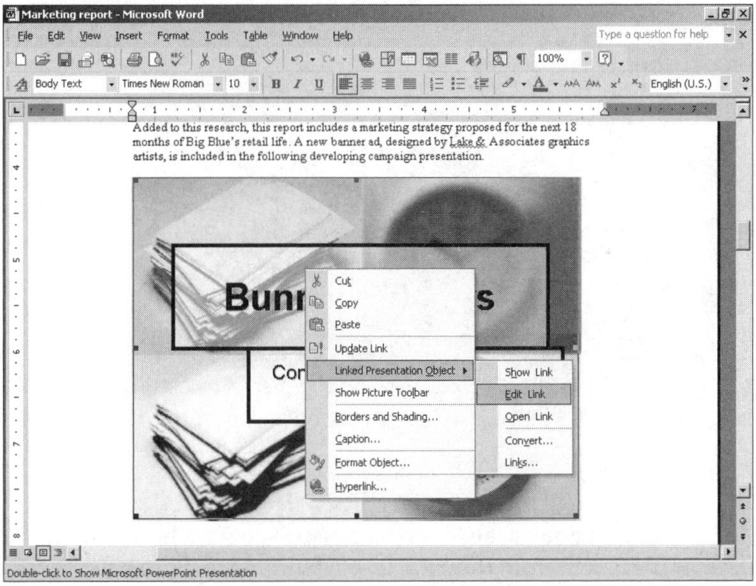

Figure 15-3. You can modify a linked object and update the changes.

To modify the source object directly, make your changes in the originating program. Save and close the object as you would normally.

When you return to the linked document, select the linked object and choose Edit, Update Link (or press F9). Depending on how you've set up your options for updates, the destination file might be updated as soon as you return to it or it might be delayed until you manually choose an update.

For more information on controlling the update of linked objects, see the section "Updating Links" on page 222.

Working with Links

The only tricky part to working with linked objects in your documents is that managing a variety of links can be confusing and a drain on your system's resources. For this reason, Word pulls link management together in one place—the Links dialog box. To display this box, choose Edit, Links. (See Figure 15-4, on the next page.)

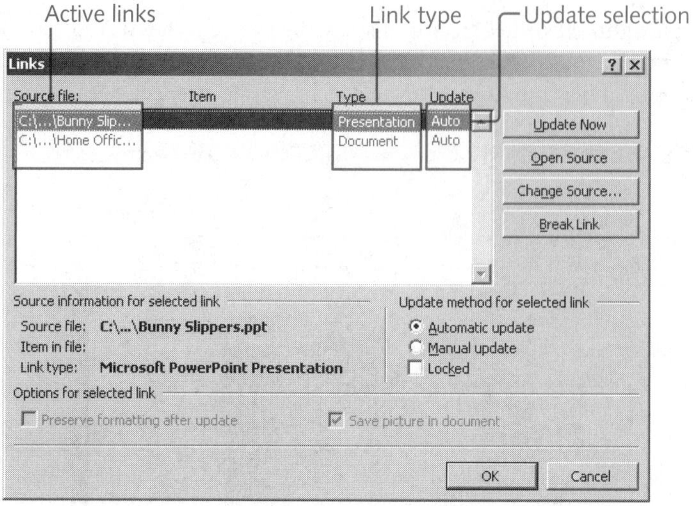

Figure 15-4. The Links dialog box gives you the means to review, change, update, and remove links to objects you've inserted in your document.

Reviewing Links

In the Source File section of the Links dialog box, you see a list of the currently active links in your document. You can scroll through the list to determine the following:

- The source file for the object
- The type of object that's linked
- The type of update assigned to the object

Using the various options in the Links dialog box, you can change the update method of the link, check the source file, modify the location of the source file, and review information about the link. You can also lock the link or break it to protect the destination document from any further changes.

> **tip** **Update Now**
>
> It's possible for you to have some links in the Source File list in the Links dialog box that show Auto updates and others that show Manual updates. You can force the update of a Manual link by selecting it in the Source File list and clicking Update Now.

Updating Links

By default, Word updates any links in your document. Each time you open the file, Word checks whether any links have changed—a process that can take a few minutes if you've added many links to your current document. Similarly, when you make a change to the source file and the destination file happens to be open, Word updates the destination file if you've got the updating options set to update automatically.

Manually Updating Links

Word gives you the option of updating links automatically or manually. Automatic is nice—you don't have to worry about it—unless sharing files is an issue and you want to limit others' ability to change or modify the linked document by editing the source. When you want to set a link in your document to be manually updated, follow these steps:

1. Choose Edit, Links. The Links dialog box appears.
2. Select the linked object in the Source File list.
3. In the Update Method For Selected Link section, click the Manual Update option.
4. Click OK. The object will be updated only when you choose Update Link from the Edit menu or press F9.

Locking a Link

When you get an object just the way you want it—your PowerPoint presentation is finished, for example, or that logo has finally been approved—you can protect the destination from further changes by locking the link. When you lock a link, it will no longer be updated, even if the source file is modified.

To lock a link, display the Links dialog box, select the linked object in the Source File list, and select the Locked check box in the Update Method For Selected Link section. You can unlock a link later if you choose by repeating the first two steps and clearing the Locked check box.

Troubleshooting

My Changes Are Lost

If Word crashes and then AutoRecover restores your document, you might find that your linked object has lost its most recent changes and is appearing as an outline instead of a fully displayed object. To fix these problems, save the document, click the object, and choose Tools, Options. Clear the Picture Placeholders check box on the View tab, and click OK to close the dialog box. Then, with the object still selected, press F9 to force a manual update. Word compares the object against the source file and updates any missing changes.

Going to the Source

When you want to look at the source file for your document, you can use the Open Source button in the Links dialog box to get to it. Simply select the link in the Source File list and click Open Source. The source program is opened and the file is displayed.

tip **Edit Your Slide Show**

If your source's native application is PowerPoint, Open Source will run a slide show rather than displaying editing mode for the presentation. To launch PowerPoint so that you can make changes in the file, right-click the object in your Word document and choose either Edit Link or Open Link. The PowerPoint work area will be displayed with the first slide shown in Slide view.

Changing the Source

When you want to move a source file, the linked document needs to know a move has taken place. To tell Word the source has moved, choose Edit, Links and, with the link selected, click Change Source in the Links dialog box. The Change Source dialog box appears. Navigate to the folder where the source file is now located, click the file, and click Open. Click OK to close the Links dialog box.

Breaking Links

After you have a file in its finished state, you might want to break a link to keep the object from future modifications. To break the link of a selected object, follow these steps:

1. Display the Links dialog box by choosing Edit, Links.
2. In the Source File list, select the link you want to break.
3. Click Break Link. Word displays a message box asking you to confirm that you want to proceed with the operation.
4. Click Yes to break the link. The link is removed from the list, although the object remains in your document. Any further changes to the source file will not affect your document.
5. Click Close to close the Links dialog box.

note If you want to reestablish the link you just broke, you can press Ctrl+Z or select Undo to reestablish the link.

Linking Considerations for Shared Files

As you can see, managing the links for your documents could be a fairly complicated process, especially if you create a number of links to each document and choose to have some updated automatically and others updated manually. Reviewing your links regularly, as well as keeping a list of active links for current files, is a way to ensure that an important source file doesn't disappear 15 minutes before a major meeting.

If your document is linked to a source file on a network server, you run the risk that the document might be changed, moved, or deleted by another user. Although Word looks for the missing file, there's no guarantee it will find it. Make sure that you keep active backups of important files and that you review your links often.

Another network consideration: If your source file is stored in a shared directory, it's possible that another user can access your file and make a change without your knowledge. This is fine if the change makes things better, but what if the change introduces an error you miss? To control the access to the file, you can choose to manually update the link when you add the linked object.

Troubleshooting

The Source File Has Moved

If you get an error when you try to edit a linked or embedded object, check to see whether the source file has been moved. To do this, click the linked object, choose Edit, Links. Use the Change Source button in the Links dialog box to reconnect the links.

Embedding Objects

Embedding objects, by contrast to linking objects, is a pretty straightforward process. There are no links to worry about or maintain. You simply place an object in the document and there it stays. Pretty clean and simple.

The downside of embedded objects is the size of the file they create. When you add a PowerPoint presentation to your destination document, for example, your Word file takes on the weight of the additional file. With a linked file, only the link to the source file is actually stored in the document.

You also have an additional choice with embedded objects that you didn't have with linked objects: You can create a new embedded object on the fly. That is, you can create a new object while you're working in your Word document. This section explores ways to embed data sections, create new embedded objects, edit your objects, and convert them to other file formats.

Pasting Data as an Embedded Object

When you want to embed a portion of a file, you can use Paste Special to import the information, keeping the formatting intact. Here are the steps for embedding a section of data:

1. In the source program, open the data file from which you want to copy data.
2. Select the data, and copy it to the Clipboard.
3. Open your destination document, and place the insertion point where you want to add the data.
4. Choose Edit, Paste Special. The Paste Special dialog box appears, as Figure 15-5 shows.

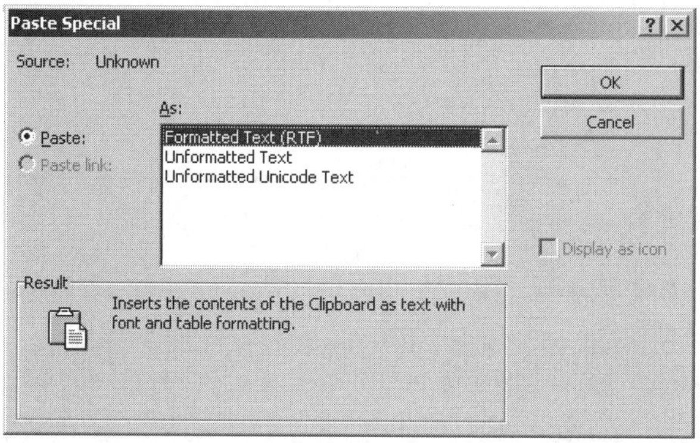

Figure 15-5. The Paste Special dialog box enables you to both link and embed data.

Creating an Embedded Object

What kind of object would you like to add as you're working on your Word document? Word enables you to create embedded objects as you work in Word, using programs such as Microsoft Equation 3.0, PowerPoint, Paintbrush, and RealNetworks' RealPlayer. You also can add data from Excel, a slide from PowerPoint, a wave (sound) file from Microsoft Sound Recorder, a video segment from Media Clip, or any number of other programs you might have installed on your system.

To create an embedded object in Word, follow these steps:

1. Start in the document to which you want to add the embedded object.
2. Place the insertion point where you want to add the object.
3. Choose Insert, Object. The Insert Object dialog box appears, with the Create New tab selected, as Figure 15-6 shows.

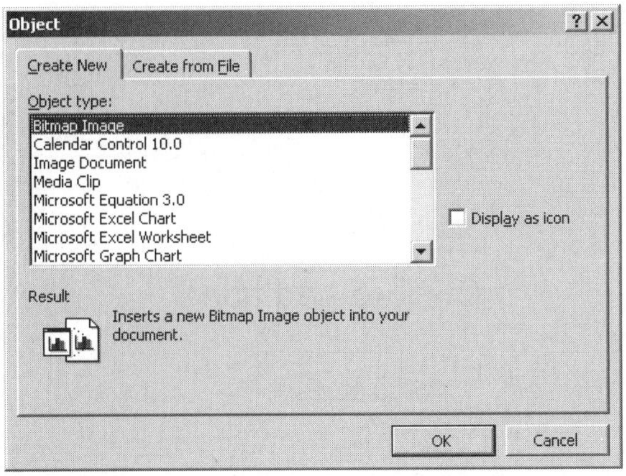

Figure 15-6. You can create an embedded object from within your Word document.

4 Scroll through the Object Type list, and select the one you want.

5 If you want to have the embedded object displayed as an icon instead of a file, select the Display As Icon check box.

6 Click OK to close the dialog box and launch the program. Figure 15-7, on the next page, shows the screen that appears when Microsoft PowerPoint Slide is selected.

note Depending on the program you're using to create the embedded object, the menus you see might differ from those you see here. Different programs offer different levels of support for object linking and embedding. If you need help with the program you're using to create the embedded object, consult that program's help system or your program documentation.

7 In the source program, choose File and select the command that enables you to close the program and return to Word. The program is closed, and you are returned to the destination document. If you chose to display the object as an icon, the icon is displayed at the insertion point. If you chose to clear the Display As Icon check box, the file is displayed in full.

tip **Change the Icon**

If you elect to display the embedded object as an icon, a Change Icon button appears in the Insert Object dialog box that changes the icon used in your document. To see the list of displayed icons, click the Change Icon button, and scroll through the list to see the available icons. Click Browse if necessary, and select the file you want. Click in the Caption box, add a caption and click OK to accept the change.

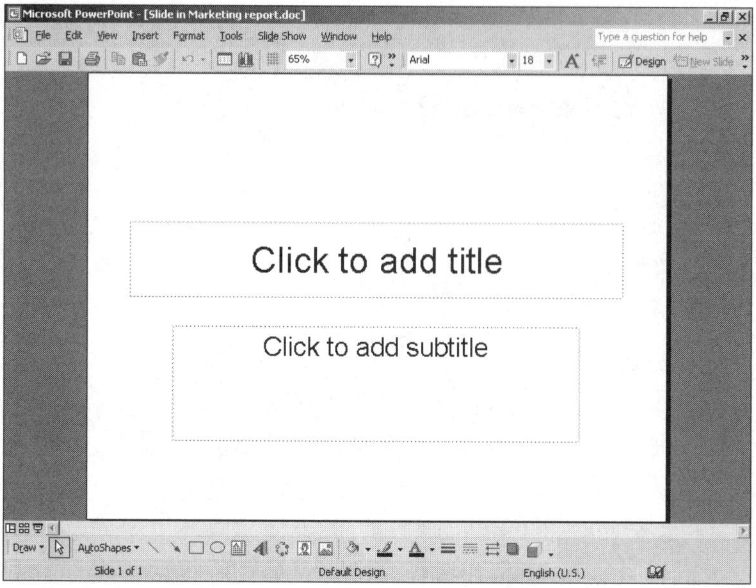

Figure 15-7. Creating an embedded object in Word involves working in the source program.

Adding an Existing Object

Adding a file or data section to your document as an embedded object allows you to keep all the data in one place, which makes your file portable. The benefit of embedding a file as opposed to copying it in your document is that you can edit an embedded object—in its originating program—from within your Word document.

To add an existing object to your Word document, follow these steps:

1. Place the insertion point where you want to add the embedded object.
2. Choose Insert, Object.
3. Click the Create From File tab. (See Figure 15-8.) Click Browse, select the file you want to embed, and click Insert.
4. If you want the embedded object to appear as an icon, select the Display As Icon check box.
5. Click OK to add the object.

note The process for embedding an object is only one step removed from adding a linked object: In the Create From file tab, you *don't* select the Link To File check box. By leaving this check box unselected, you tell Word that the file is to be incorporated as an embedded object in the current document.

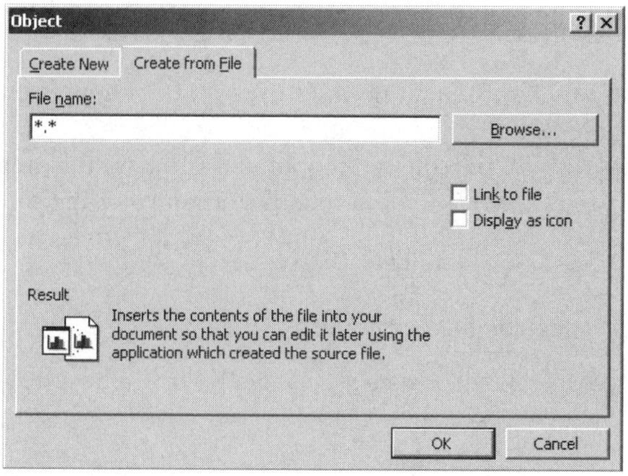

Figure 15-8. Use the Create From File tab in the Insert Object dialog box to embed an existing file.

Editing an Embedded Object

You edit an embedded object by double-clicking it—whether the object is a section of a file or an entire embedded file. Double-clicking opens the program in which the file was created. You can make your changes as needed and choose File, Close And Return To Microsoft Word to accept the changes in your document.

Troubleshooting

I Can't Edit an Embedded Object

You double-click an object to edit it, and nothing happens. What's going on? These are the possibilities:

- Make sure the source program is still installed. If it's not, install it or convert the embedded object to a file format you can use.
- Make sure that you're not running low on system memory. If that appears to be the problem, close all other programs to free up space.
- If you're working with a linked object on a network, make sure that no one else has the source file open at the same time.
- Make sure that the source file hasn't been moved or renamed. Check this by clicking the object and choosing Edit, Links.

Converting Embedded Objects to Other Formats

Your embedded file has all the data it needs in order to be complete. But what happens when you copy the file to a disk and take it to another computer that doesn't have the source file? You could install the source program—if you have it handy. If not, another option is to convert the embedded object to a file format you can use.

To convert an embedded object, follow these steps:

1. Right-click the embedded object.
2. On the shortcut menu, choose Object, Convert. The Convert dialog box appears, as Figure 15-9 shows.

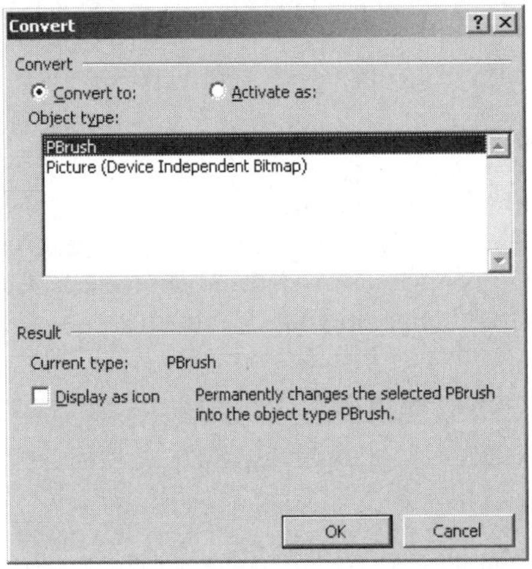

Figure 15-9. Converting an embedded object enables you to save it in another file format.

3. Choose the file format to which you want to convert the embedded file, and click OK. The file is converted as you selected.

> **note** Use Activate As if you want to open an object as the type you select in the Object dialog box and then allow it to return to its natural object type when you close it.

Chapter 16

Enlivening Documents with Drawings and AutoShapes

You can liven up your Word documents with two types of graphics—pictures and drawing objects. A *picture* in Word is a graphic created from another file, such as a bitmap, a scanned image, a photograph, or most types of clip art. *Drawn graphics* (also called *vector drawings*) are created from lines, curves, rectangles, and other objects that can be changed, formatted, moved, and enhanced. In Word, you can create drawings by combining objects such as AutoShapes, freeform shapes, diagrams, curves, lines, arrows, WordArt, and similar constructs. In this chapter, we'll focus on creating and inserting drawing objects in Word.

For more information about working with pictures in Word, including clip art, see Chapter 14, "Adding Visual Impact with Pictures," and for more information about WordArt, see Chapter 17, "Customizing Documents with WordArt."

Getting Acquainted with Drawing Features in Word

Semantically, it might sound a little odd that you can *draw* in *Word*, but drawing capabilities have been steadily evolving in Word throughout the last few versions. As an experienced Word user, you're probably familiar with the basic drawing tasks you can perform in Word, such as creating lines and inserting shapes. In Word 2002, the drawing capabilities continue to grow with the addition of an optional drawing canvas, which can help you to further control how drawings are displayed in your documents. (The drawing canvas is discussed in more detail in the section "Understanding the Role of the Drawing Canvas," on page 384.) As you know, Word is a document creation program, not a painting program, so you should expect some drawing limitations in Word, and you should count on creating detailed graphics in a true painting program. On the other hand, the Word drawing tools are advanced enough to be extremely handy when you want to create particular types of drawings, including the following:

- Arrows or connection lines
- Simple iconlike illustrations
- Bare-bones office or room layout illustrations
- Diagrams, flowcharts, and organizational charts (See Chapter 20, "Diagramming Projects, Process, and Relationships.")
- Images created by combining regular shapes, such as squares, ovals, and lines
- Splash starbursts and shapes containing text blocks
- Stylized WordArt text (See Chapter 17, "Customizing Documents with WordArt.")

You can access the tools required to create drawing objects by using the Drawing toolbar and the AutoShapes drop-down menu (which is on the Drawing toolbar). In addition, you can effectively control your drawings by mastering the relationship between drawing objects and the drawing canvas.

Familiarizing Yourself with the Drawing Toolbar and the AutoShapes Drop-Down Menu

When you create drawings in Word, you must work with the Drawing toolbar, which provides a central location for drawing tools. To display the Drawing toolbar, click the Drawing button on the Standard toolbar, or choose View, Toolbars, Drawing. Table 16-1 describes the buttons available on the Drawing toolbar.

Table 16-1. Drawing Toolbar Buttons

Button	Name	Function
	Draw	Provides a drop-down menu with drawing and editing commands, such as Order, Group, and Text Wrapping
	Select Objects	Enables you to select one or more drawing objects
	AutoShapes	Provides ready-made shapes, including lines, basic shapes, arrows, stars, banners, callouts, and others

(continued)

Table 16-1. *(continued)*

Button	Name	Function
	Line	Enables you to click and drag to draw a line
	Arrow	Enables you to click and drag to draw an arrow
	Rectangle	Enables you to click and drag to create a square or a rectangle
	Oval	Enables you to click and drag to draw a circle or an oval
	Text Box	Enables you to create a text box so that you can add text to drawing objects
	WordArt	Opens the WordArt Gallery
newfeature!	Diagram	Opens the Diagram Gallery
	Clip Art	Opens the Insert Clip Art task pane in the current view
	Picture	Opens the Insert Picture dialog box
	Fill Color	Enables you to control the color, texture, pattern, or picture used to fill drawing objects
	Line Color	Enables you to control the color, texture, pattern, and effect of line objects
	Font Color	Enables you to color text
	Line Style	Provides a variety of line styles and settings you can apply to lines and borders
	Dash Style	Provides a variety of dashed line styles and settings you can apply to lines and borders
	Arrow Style	Provides a variety of arrow styles and settings you can apply to lines
	Shadow Style	Enables you to add and control shadow effects for drawing objects
	3-D Style	Enables you to add and control 3-D settings for drawing objects
	Select Multiple Objects	Opens the Select Multiple Objects dialog box; not shown by default

In addition to using Drawing toolbar buttons to draw shapes, you can insert standard shapes into your documents by using the AutoShapes drop-down menu, which is accessed by clicking AutoShapes on the Drawing toolbar, as shown in Figure 16-1. The AutoShapes drop-down menu provides a library of shapes that you can use to create custom drawings. After you insert an AutoShape, you can color, resize, reshape, and otherwise customize the object, as you'll see throughout this chapter. You can also combine AutoShapes and other drawing components to create more complex graphics.

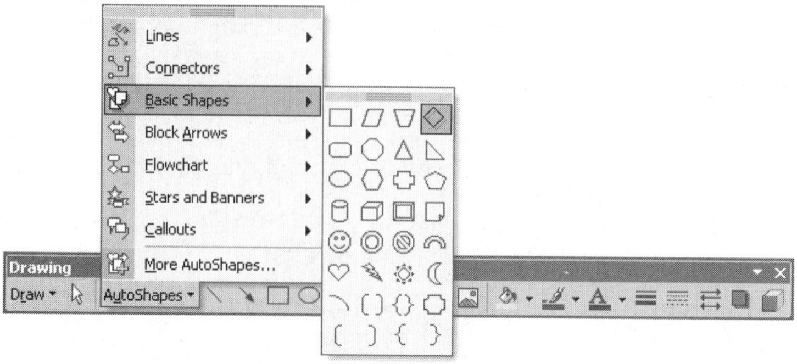

Figure 16-1. The AutoShapes drop-down menu provides a collection of shapes you can insert and combine to create custom graphics.

newfeature!

Understanding the Role of the Drawing Canvas

Before you create a drawing using the Word drawing tools, you should understand how drawings work in Word 2002. By default, when you create a drawing in Word, the drawing is placed on a drawing canvas. You don't have to use the drawing canvas when you create drawings, but you will probably find it useful. After all, the drawing canvas is designed to help you control drawing objects combined to create a single drawing as well as control how completed drawings are displayed within your document.

To display a new drawing canvas, perform one of the following actions:

- Choose Insert, Picture, New Drawing.
- On the Drawing toolbar, choose an AutoShape on the AutoShapes drop-down menu.
- On the Drawing toolbar, click the Line, Arrow, Rectangle, Oval, or Text Box button.

Figure 16-2 shows a couple of objects placed on an active drawing canvas.

Notice that the drawing canvas displays a framelike boundary while you work. The frame outlines the drawing canvas's current working area, and it includes solid black lines and corners that you can drag to resize the canvas. By default, the drawing canvas doesn't have borders or background formatting, but you can customize the drawing canvas just as you can customize any other drawing object. For example, you can add

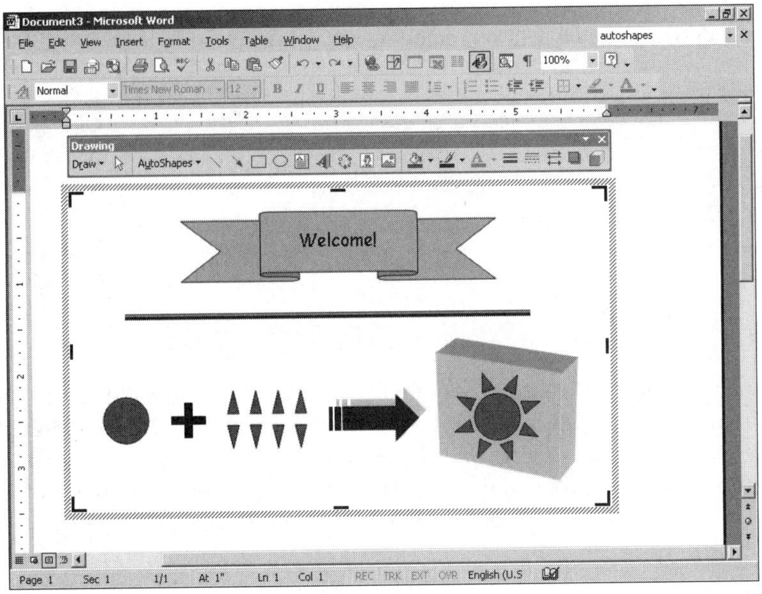

Figure 16-2. The drawing canvas helps you control drawing objects relative to other drawing objects in a drawing and control the overall relationship between the complete drawing and the document's contents.

color, apply shading, resize the frame, add 3-D effects, and so forth. To access formatting options for the drawing canvas, you can right-click the drawing canvas and choose Format Drawing Canvas on the shortcut menu, double-click a blank area of the drawing canvas, or click in the drawing canvas and choose Format, Drawing Canvas. Each of these techniques opens the Format Drawing Canvas dialog box, which is discussed in more detail in the section, "Integrating the Drawing Canvas with Document Text" on page 418.

If you prefer that the drawing canvas not appear by default each time you insert a drawing object, you can change this setting. To do so, follow these steps:

1. Choose Tools, Options, and click the General tab.
2. Clear the Automatically Create Drawing Canvas When Inserting AutoShapes check box, and click OK.

Keep in mind that the drawing canvas is highly customizable and helps you to easily move combined drawing objects as a unit. For the most part, you'll probably want to use the drawing canvas when you create drawings unless you're inserting a single object, such as a line or an arrow.

tip **Delete a drawing canvas without deleting a drawing**

If you create a drawing on a drawing canvas and later decide that you don't want to use the drawing canvas, you can drag your drawing off the drawing canvas, select the drawing canvas, and then press Delete (or right-click the drawing canvas and choose Cut on the shortcut menu). This action enables you to retain your drawing while deleting the drawing canvas.

Drawing Basic Lines and Shapes

Although drawing capabilities continue to expand in Word, the old standby tools remain intact and readily available. As with earlier versions of Word, Word 2002 enables you to draw basic lines and shapes in your documents by clicking Drawing toolbar buttons. Basic lines and shapes frequently serve as the foundation for more complex drawings that you create by combining and formatting objects.

note When you draw in Word, you must work in Print Layout or Web Layout view. If you're in any other view when you click a line or shape button on the Drawing toolbar, Word automatically changes your view to Print Layout.

Working with Straight Lines and Arrows

In Word, you can use the Drawing toolbar to create straight lines and arrows. To do so, follow these steps:

1. Click the Line or Arrow button on the Drawing toolbar. The mouse pointer changes to a crosshair pointer whenever a drawing tool is selected.
2. Click in the drawing canvas where you want to start the line or arrow.
3. Drag to draw the line or arrow.

After you draw a line or an arrow, you can manipulate and control it in the following ways:

- **Change the appearance of a line or an arrow.** Click the line or arrow to select it; click the Line Style, Dash Style, or Arrow Style button on the Drawing toolbar; and choose a new style for the line or arrow on the drop-down menu. You can apply multiple settings to a single object. For example, you can apply a dash style and an arrow style to the same object. Figure 16-3 shows the Arrow Style drop-down menu.

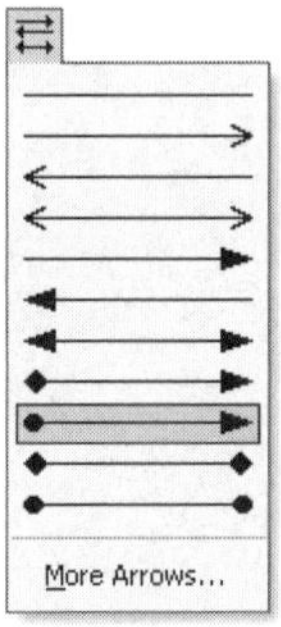

Figure 16-3. You can change the appearance of arrows and lines by choosing options on the Line Style, Dashed Style, and Arrow Style drop-down menus.

- **Constrain a line or an arrow to 15-degree-angle increments from the starting point.** Press Shift as you draw the line or arrow. As you move the mouse pointer, the angle of the object will change in 15-degree increments.
- **Lengthen a line or an arrow in opposite directions.** Press Ctrl as you draw the line or arrow.
- **Reposition a line or an arrow.** Click the line or arrow to select it, click the selected object (but do not click a selection handle), and then drag the object to a new location.
- **Resize a line or an arrow.** Select the line or arrow, and drag a selection handle to lengthen, shorten, or change the angle of the object.

You can also double-click an existing line or arrow to open the Format AutoShape dialog box, shown in Figure 16-4, on the next page. The Format AutoShape dialog box enables you to configure a number of shape formatting settings. The techniques for formatting objects are discussed throughout this chapter.

tip **Add a vertical line between columns**

When you want to add a line between columns, you can do so without creating a drawing canvas or using Drawing toolbar buttons. To add a vertical line between columns, click in a column, and then choose Format, Columns. In the Columns dialog box, select the Line Between check box. For more information about working with columns, see Chapter 9, "Formatting Columns and Sections for Advanced Text Control."

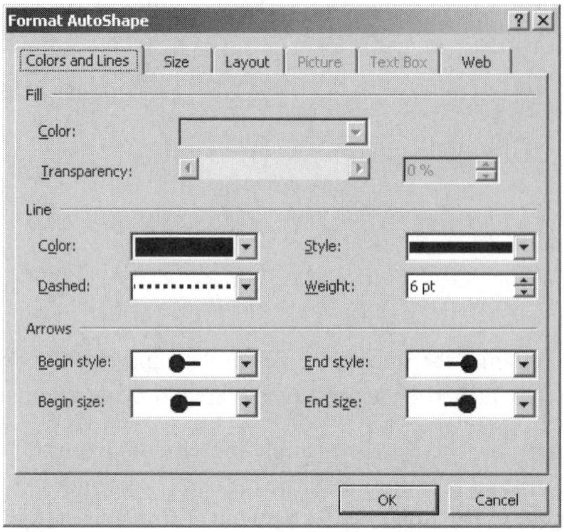

Figure 16-4. You can double-click an object on the drawing canvas to access the object's formatting dialog box.

Creating Ovals and Rectangles

Creating ovals, circles, rectangles, and squares is similar to creating lines and arrows. To create an oval or a rectangle, click the Oval or Rectangle button on the Drawing toolbar, click in the drawing canvas, and then drag to create the object. To create an exact circle or square, click the Oval or Rectangle button, and press Shift as you drag to create your shape. You can move and resize an oval or a rectangle by selecting and dragging the object to move it or by dragging the object's selection handles to resize it.

tip **Create a box around paragraph text**

If you want to draw a box around text, use the Borders drop-down menu on the Formatting toolbar. For more information about adding borders, see Chapter 24, "Drawing Attention to Your Document with Borders and Shading."

Working with AutoShapes

As mentioned, AutoShapes are ready-made shapes that you insert into your documents by choosing a shape on the AutoShapes drop-down menu. AutoShapes come in a variety of forms, including basic shapes, lines, connectors, flowchart symbols, stars, banners, callouts, and other common shapes. (See Figure 16-1.) After you insert an AutoShape, you can format, move, resize, and otherwise manipulate the shape in the same way you manipulate other drawing objects, as described in the section "Customizing Lines and Shapes," on page 397, and the section "Controlling Objects in Drawings," on page 411.

tip **Display a menu as a floating toolbar**

If you find that you use a particular AutoShape submenu repeatedly, you can drag the menu by its top bar to create a floating toolbar. When you've finished with the floating toolbar, simply close it; you'll be able to access the submenu in its regular position on the AutoShapes drop-down menu.

Automatically Format a Series of Objects

At times, you might want to create a series of AutoShapes that use the same formatting. For example, maybe you're creating coupons and you want to draw four rectangles with two 1/4-inch-thick dashed lines. Instead of formatting each rectangle separately, you can format the first rectangle and then copy the settings before you create the next three rectangles.

You can easily create a default drawing style that will be implemented automatically when you create new shapes. To do this, right-click the AutoShape that contains the formatting you want to use to create new objects, and then choose Set AutoShape Defaults on the shortcut menu. The next objects you draw (regardless of their shapes) will automatically be formatted with the settings you applied to the object you used to set the defaults.

Drawing Nonstandard Lines and Freeform Shapes

The first submenu on the AutoShapes drop-down menu is Lines. The Lines submenu enables you to draw lines that are more complex than the straight lines and arrows you can create using the Line and Arrow buttons on the Drawing toolbar. To use one of these more complex lines, choose an AutoShape on the Lines submenu, and then click and drag on the drawing canvas to create your line, shape, or arrow. The Lines submenu provides the following tools:

- **Line** draws a straight line, similar to using the Line button on the Drawing toolbar.
- **Arrow** draws a standard arrow, similar to using the Arrow button on the Drawing toolbar.
- **Double Arrow** draws an arrow with arrowheads on both ends of the line.
- **Curve** draws a smooth-turning line or shape that curves at each point you click in the drawing canvas. To turn off the Curve tool, double-click or press Esc.
- **Freeform** draws objects by using straight lines and hand-drawn lines. To create straight lines, click two points; to create curvy lines, hold down the

mouse button as you draw. To delete your most recent freeform action while you're creating your object, press Delete, and to turn off the Freeform tool, double-click or press Esc. To change the shape of a freeform object, click Draw on the Drawing toolbar and choose Edit Points, and then drag the edit handles to modify the object.

- **Scribble** draws a line wherever you click and drag. To turn off the Scribble tool, release the mouse button. The Scribble tool draws a single line and is then automatically deactivated.

> **tip** Freeform drawings, curved lines, and scribble lines can be formatted with fill effects, color, and line style options in the same manner other drawing objects are formatted, as described throughout this chapter.

Adding Basic Shapes and Block Arrows

As mentioned, the AutoShapes drop-down menu provides a number of basic shapes and arrows that you can insert into your document. Figure 16-5 shows the Block Arrows and Basic Shapes submenus as floating toolbars. After you insert a shape or an

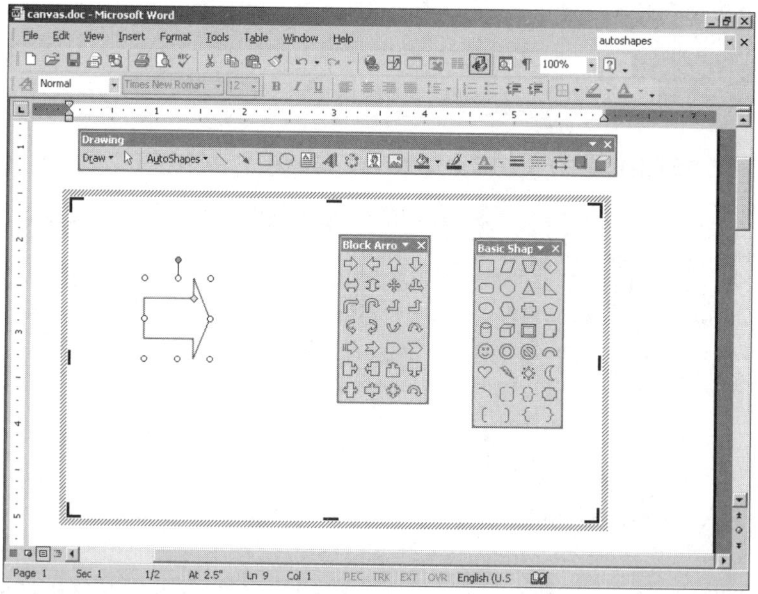

Figure 16-5. The Block Arrows and Basic Shapes submenus—shown here as floating toolbars—provide a variety of shapes that you can insert into your documents and customize to your needs.

arrow, you can drag the object to reposition it, drag selection handles to resize or reshape it, and format the object's line and fill settings, as described in the section

"Customizing Lines and Shapes," on page 397, and the section "Controlling Objects in Drawings," on page 411.

Changing a Shape Without Losing Formatting

You can always replace an existing AutoShape or standard shape (such as a rectangle or an oval) with a different shape without losing your format settings. To do so, follow these steps:

1. Select the AutoShape, click Draw on the Drawing toolbar, and choose Change AutoShape. The Change AutoShape submenu opens, which includes submenus for Basic Shapes, Block Arrows, Flowchart, Stars And Banners, and Callouts.
2. Choose a shape on any of the Change AutoShape submenus to replace the existing shape.

Keep in mind that you can replace only standard shapes. For example, you can replace a rectangle or an AutoShape with another AutoShape, but you can't replace a line or a freeform shape with an AutoShape.

newfeature!

Using Connectors

Connectors are a new drawing feature in Word 2002. If you want to use a line or an arrow to connect shapes and keep them connected, you might want to draw a connector instead of a standard line or arrow. A connector joins two shapes at specified points (called *connection sites*) on the shapes. If you move or resize shapes joined by a connector, the connector adjusts and continues to connect the two objects at the connection sites using the predetermined line shape. Connectors can be lines or arrows, as shown in Figure 16-6.

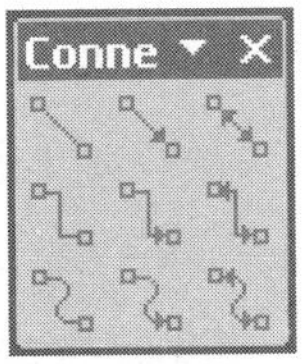

Figure 16-6. A connector creates a line or an arrow between shapes and remains connected even when the shapes are moved, reshaped, or resized.

To join objects using a connector, follow these steps:

1. On the Drawing toolbar, click AutoShapes, choose Connectors on the drop-down menu, and then click the type of connector you want to create.

2. Hover the mouse pointer over the first shape you want to attach to the connector. When you choose a connector and position the mouse pointer over a shape, connection sites are displayed as blue circles on the shape.
3. Click a blue connection site on the first object, and hover the mouse pointer over the object you want to connect to. (Blue connection sites will appear on the second shape when you position the mouse pointer over the shape.) Then click a connection site on the second object.

Figure 16-7 illustrates the process of creating a connector and shows how the objects remain connected even after they have been moved and resized.

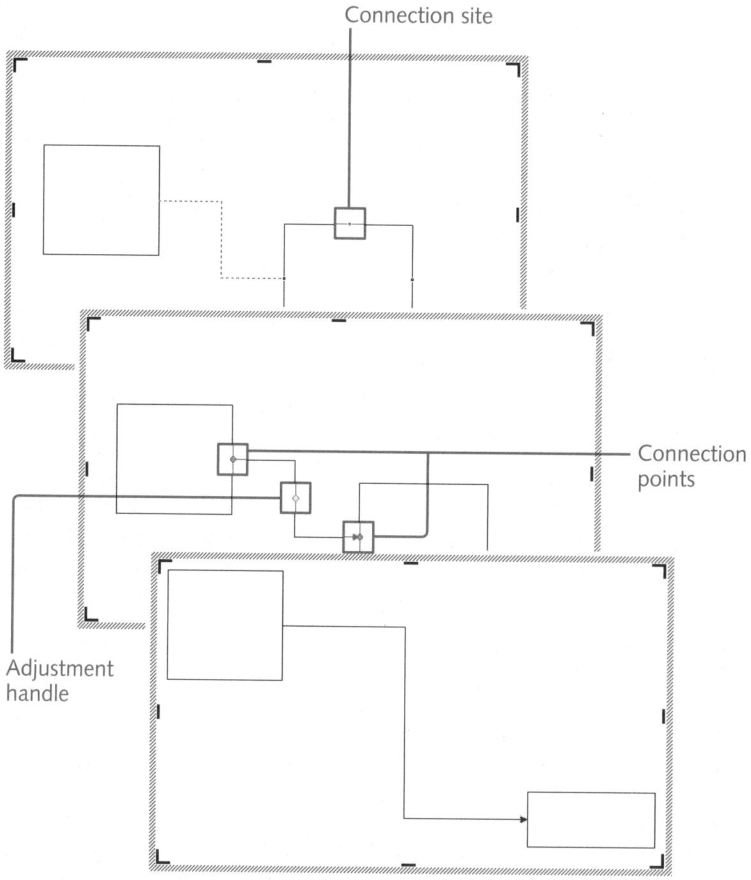

Figure 16-7. A connector is a line between objects that remains connected even if the connected objects are moved or resized.

After you connect two objects, you can move, reshape, and resize the objects without losing the connection. To modify a connector, you can drag the end points (indicated by red circles) to a new connection site, or you can right-click the connector to access shortcut menu commands. The shortcut menu enables you to sever the connection (by choosing Cut), change the connector's style (by choosing the straight, elbow, or curved options), or reroute the connector (by choosing Reroute Connectors). You can also automatically reroute connectors by clicking Draw on the Drawing toolbar and choosing Reroute Connectors.

tip Some connectors have a yellow diamond-shaped adjustment handle. You can drag the handle to change the shape of the connector line without detaching the line from the connection sites on the connected objects.

Creating Flowcharts

Another group of AutoShapes available in Word are flowchart shapes. You can draw a flowchart fairly easily in Word by using the flowchart AutoShapes and connector lines. To access the flowchart objects, click AutoShapes on the Drawing toolbar, and choose Flowchart to open the Flowchart submenu and view the flowchart AutoShapes. The Flowchart floating toolbar, shown in Figure 16-8, contains 28 flowchart AutoShapes that you can use to create standard flowcharts.

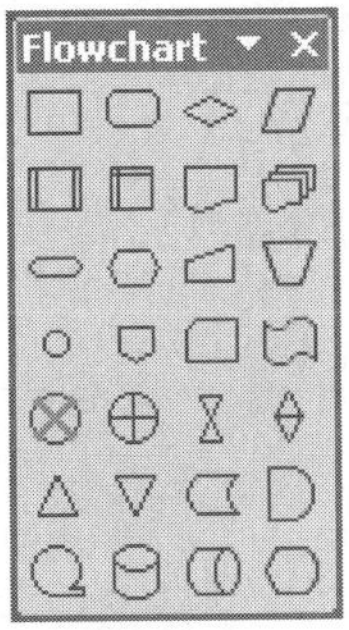

Figure 16-8. Word includes flowchart AutoShapes that you can combine with connectors to create flowcharts.

Flowcharts are frequently used to illustrate processes and relationships in an abbreviated form. For example, you might use a flowchart to illustrate a decision-making process (for instance, if you choose Yes, you follow one path, and if you choose No, you follow another), or you might use a flowchart to illustrate relationships among pages in a small Web site. To create a flowchart, you combine a number of drawing tasks, as summarized here:

1 Draw the shapes you need for your flowchart using the flowchart AutoShapes.

2 Arrange the shapes by dragging them on the drawing canvas, and then connect the shapes using connectors. Connectors work better than standard

lines and arrows when you're creating flowcharts because you might have to move or resize the flowchart shapes.

3 Right-click each flowchart shape, choose Add Text on the shortcut menu, and type the appropriate text.

After you create a flowchart, you can color and format lines and shapes in the flowchart, as described in the section "Customizing Lines and Shapes," on page 397.

Creating and Customizing Stars and Banners

When you want to create a visual splash on a flyer, an advertisement, a newsletter, or another eye-catching publication, you can use objects from the Stars And Banners AutoShapes submenu. Inserting a star or banner is similar to inserting other AutoShapes, as shown here:

1 Click AutoShapes on the Drawing toolbar, and choose Stars And Banners on the drop-down menu.

2 Choose a star or banner, and then click and drag in the drawing canvas to create the object.

An example of an inserted star and banner is shown in Figure 16-9.

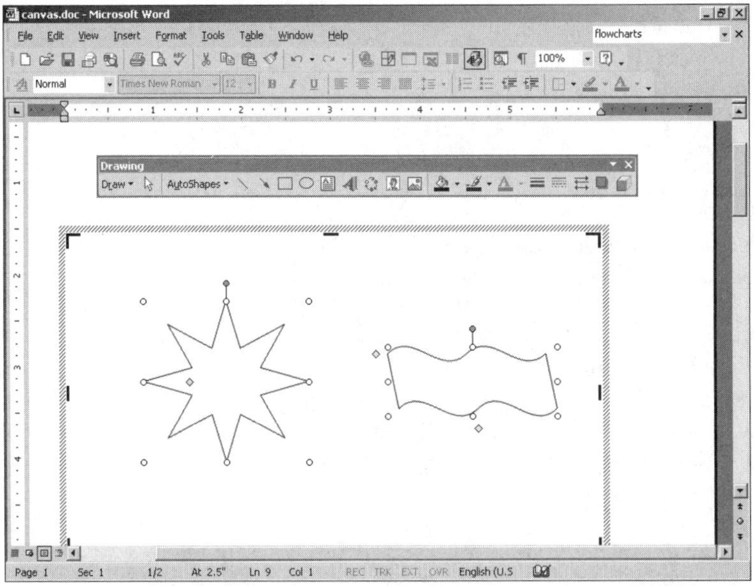

Figure 16-9. You can modify how stars and banners are displayed by using the rotation, adjustment, and sizing handles. See "Controlling Objects in Drawings," on page 411.

As with most AutoShapes, stars and banners are customizable, as described in the section "Customizing Lines and Shapes" on page 397. For example, you can customize stars and banners in the following ways:

- By adding text
- By applying color or a fill effect
- By modifying the outline style
- By rotating the object
- By adjusting the shape of the star or banner
- By resizing the star or banner

Keep in mind that the purpose of using star and banner objects in documents is to draw attention to particular bits of information or sections of your documents. If you overuse these types of objects, you'll tend to drive readers away instead of attract them.

Drawing Callouts

Sometimes, you might want to associate bits of information with a particular spot on a graphic, or you might want to annotate areas of a document. You can easily do so by using *callouts*. A callout object combines a text box with an arrow, a line, or a pointer. Word provides 20 types of callout AutoShapes, which can be accessed from the Callouts floating toolbar, shown in Figure 16-10.

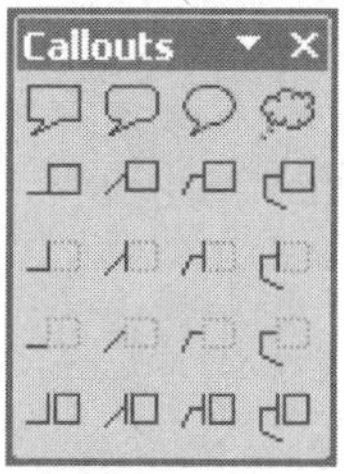

Figure 16-10. Word provides a variety of callout objects that you can use to annotate documents, identify areas in graphics, or present other types of information.

To use a callout, follow these steps:

1. Click AutoShapes, choose Callouts, and then choose a callout style on the Callouts submenu.
2. Click the location on the drawing canvas where you want to insert the callout, and drag to create the object.
3. After you insert a callout, you can drag the yellow diamond-shaped adjustment handle to reposition the callout's leader line, and drag selection handles to resize the callout.

4 Click in the callout's text area, and type the relevant information.

As with other AutoShapes, you can format callouts using standard formatting techniques, such as applying colors, adding fill effects, resizing, and moving.

Accessing More AutoShapes in the Clip Art Task Pane

If you find that you need an object not available on the seven AutoShapes submenus, you can access additional shapes by choosing More AutoShapes, located at the bottom of the AutoShapes drop-down menu. When you click this option, Word opens the Insert Clip Art task pane, shown in Figure 16-11.

Figure 16-11. When you choose the More AutoShapes option, you gain quick access to additional drawing objects that are easily customizable.

The additional AutoShapes include the following:

- Room layout objects, such as outlines of desks, chairs, wastebaskets, and door swing marks
- Computers and computer-related objects, such as mainframes, modems, firewalls, and folders
- Commonly used objects, such as musical notes, light bulbs, and padlocks
- Web site–related objects, such as objects that represent a home page, a film clip, a feedback form, and an e-mail icon

You insert items associated with the More AutoShapes category in the same way you insert other clip art items—simply by clicking the object you want to insert. The main difference between the More AutoShapes objects and standard clip art is that you can more easily format the AutoShapes as drawing objects than you can most clip art.

tip **Integrate clip art into drawings**

In addition to the clip art items associated with the More AutoShapes option, you can add any other clip art item to a drawing. You can also right-click a clip art item and choose Edit Picture on the shortcut menu to customize the clip art as a drawing object. If you've inserted a clip art item that's a picture and not a drawing object, Word displays a message box when you click Edit Picture that asks whether you want to convert the picture to a drawing object. Click Yes to make the conversion.

If you convert a complex picture to a drawing object, consider grouping the drawing's components after Word converts the picture. (Converted pictures tend to have numerous components, as you'll see by the constellation of selection handles that appear after you convert a picture to a drawing object.) Grouping objects is described in more detail in the section "Grouping and Ungrouping Objects," on page 416.

Customizing Lines and Shapes

Most likely, you'll want your drawings to be displayed in color rather than in black, white, and shades of gray. In Word, you can colorize your lines and fill objects using standard and custom colors, including a full range of gray shades. You can also customize your shapes by using fill effects to insert multicolor gradient blends, textures, and pictures.

note When you use colors, keep in mind how your document will be displayed and printed. If your document will always be viewed as an electronic document or printed on high-quality paper with four colors, you won't have to worry too much about color reproduction. On the other hand, if your document will be printed on a black-and-white printer (even if it's also viewed on line) or on colored paper, you'll want to make sure that the colors you use in your drawings create adequate contrast; otherwise, your drawings might be printed as indiscernible blobs.

Specifying Line and Fill Colors

As a rule, drawing objects created in Word have two main areas that can contain color: borders (called *lines*) and interior spaces (called *fills*). The easiest way to color lines and fills is to use the Drawing toolbar, as follows:

- **Color a line.** Select an object, click the Line Color down arrow on the Drawing toolbar, and choose a color in the color palette, shown in Figure 16-12, on the next page.
- **Color a fill.** Select an object, click the Fill Color down arrow, and choose a color in the color palette. The Fill Color drop-down menu is similar to the Line Color drop-down menu.

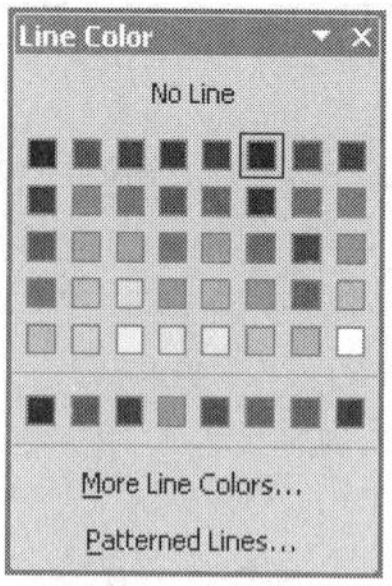

Figure 16-12. To color a line or fill, simply click a color on the Line Color or Fill Color drop-down menu or floating toolbar. The row of colors below the default color palette contains the last eight custom colors you've used for either lines or fills.

The Line Color and Fill Color drop-down menus also contain No Line or No Fill options. You can use these options to display an object without any lines (not even black) or with no fill color (which means that the background color will show through the object's outlined form).

Using Custom Colors and Transparent Colors

You can apply custom colors and transparent colors to objects by choosing the More Fill Colors command on the Fill Color drop-down menu or the More Line Colors command on the Line Color drop-down menu. Either option displays the Colors dialog box, shown in Figure 16-13.

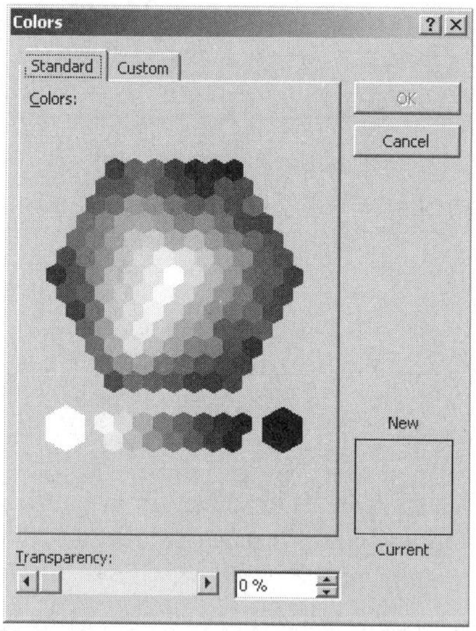

Figure 16-13. Choose more colors in the Colors dialog box.

Using Custom Colors and Transparent Colors *(continued)* Click a color on the Standard tab to use it and add the color to your custom color area in the color palette. If you want to choose from 16 million predefined colors, click the Custom tab, shown in Figure 16-14.

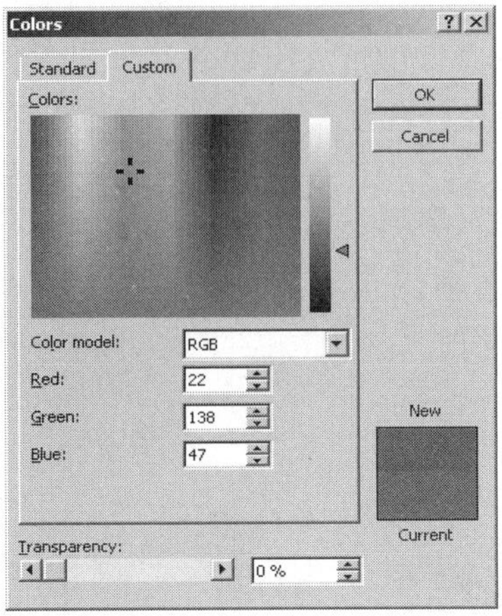

Figure 16-14. You can choose from 16 million predefined colors on the Custom tab.

Choose a color using the crosshair and slider bar. The Custom tab also includes Red, Green, and Blue value boxes that reflect the color values indicated by the crosshair and slider bar. The Red, Green, and Blue value boxes specify exact RGB color values for graphics. If you know a color's RGB values, you can enter them in the appropriate boxes, or you can click the up and down arrows to scroll through values. In addition to using the RGB Color Model option, you can click the down arrow to access HSL (hue, saturation, luminance), CMYK (cyan, magenta, yellow, black), and PANTONE color models. HSL is generally used to control colors for devices that transmit light, such as video monitors, and CMYK and PANTONE are color models used for printed publications.

Both the Standard and Custom tabs include a Transparency option. This option helps you to assign a particular color to serve as a transparent or semitransparent color. In a nutshell, a transparent color lets a page's background color or texture show through. When you make a color transparent or semitransparent and you place your picture on a page that has a background color or texture, the background color or texture shows through the picture wherever the transparent color is applied. For example, let's say you have a drawing of a mouse and you want to show the mouse on your Web page without the rectangular picture background. You could color all areas in the mouse picture—except the mouse—pink. Then you could choose pink on the Standard or Custom tab and set the Transparency option to 100%. After you specify that pink is transparent, all pink areas within your picture will allow the page's background

(continued)

Using Custom Colors and Transparent Colors *(continued)* color or texture to show through in certain applications (such as Web browsers and HTML editors).

Transparency is frequently used in Web graphics to create images that seem to be cut out (instead of rectangular). For example, in the Web page graphic shown in Figure 16-15, the picture of the cherries on the left doesn't use transparency, whereas the picture on the right has White set to 100% transparency. (Notice that the colored background shows through in the image on the right but that the background is solid white in the image on the left.)

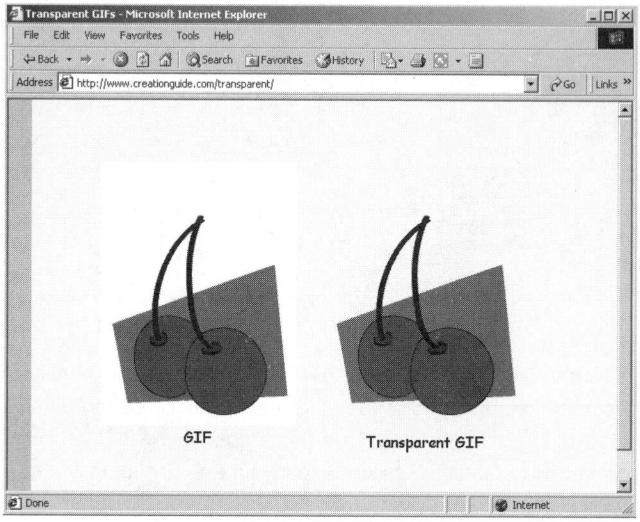

Figure 16-15. The picture on the left does not use transparency.

Adding Fill Effects and Patterns

In addition to coloring lines and fills, you can apply fill effects and patterns to further customize drawing objects. To add a fill effect to an object, select the object, click the Fill Color down arrow on the Drawing toolbar, and then choose the Fill Effects command on the Fill Color drop-down menu to open the Fill Effects dialog box. To add a pattern to a line, select the line, click the Line Color down arrow on the Drawing toolbar, and then choose Patterned Lines on the Line Color drop-down menu to open the Patterned Lines dialog box. The available effects are discussed in this section.

tip **Copy an object's formatting**

After you format an object—including adding color and fill effects—you can copy the object's formatting to other objects. To do so, select the formatted object, click Format Painter on the Standard toolbar, and then click the object you want to contain the same formatting.

If you want to apply the formatting to multiple objects, select the formatted object, double-click the Format Painter button on the Standard toolbar, and click the objects you want to format. You then press Esc or click the Format Painter button to turn off the feature.

Adding Color Gradients to Shapes

The Gradient tab in the Fill Effects dialog box is shown in Figure 16-16. This tab enables you to custom blend color gradients for selected objects. You can create a gradient from one or two colors, or you can choose from among a number of preset gradients, such as Daybreak, Horizon, and Chrome. In addition, you can specify the direction of your gradient in the Shading Styles section of the Gradient tab.

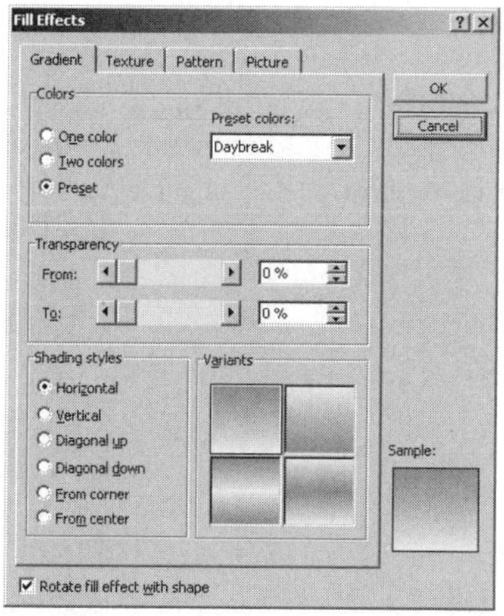

Figure 16-16. The Gradient tab enables you to blend colors to create shading effects in to your objects.

To create a gradient, follow these steps:

1. Double-click the object you want to format with a color gradient. The Formatting dialog box opens.
2. Click the Colors And Lines tab, and in the Fill section, click the Color down arrow, and choose Fill Effects. The Fill Effects dialog box opens.

3. In the Colors section on the Gradient tab, click the Two Colors option and choose colors in the Color 1 and Color 2 drop-down lists to create a custom gradient, or click Preset to select from a group of built-in gradient schemes in the Preset Colors drop-down list.
4. Choose a Shading Styles option, and click a Variants option. Notice that the Sample window displays a preview of your gradient options; you can experiment with a few shading styles and variants until you find the effect you're after.
5. When you're satisfied with your color gradient settings, click OK to close the Fill Effects dialog box, and then click OK to apply the gradient to the selected object.

note The Fill Effects dialog box contains two options that appear on each of the tabs in the Fill Effects dialog box: the Sample window, which lets you preview each fill effect as you select or create it, and the Rotate Fill Effect With Shape check box, which enables you to control whether the fill effect should be repositioned whenever you rotate or flip an object. (This option is unavailable when you're working with the Patterns tab.)

Applying Textures to Shapes

The Texture tab in the Fill Effects dialog box, shown in Figure 16-17, lets you add textures to drawing objects. By default, Word includes 24 textures that you can use to customize objects. You can import your own textures, if you have any.

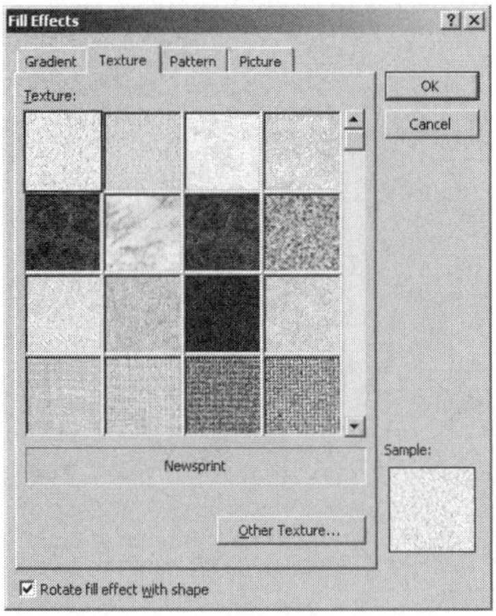

Figure 16-17. The Texture tab provides textures that you can apply to selected objects.

To apply a texture to a shape, follow these simple steps:

1. Select the drawing object you want to fill with a texture.
2. Click the Fill Color down arrow on the Drawing toolbar, choose Fill Effects on the drop-down menu, and click the Texture tab in the Fill Effects dialog box.
3. On the Texture tab, click the texture you want to use, or click the Other Texture button to open the Select Texture dialog box, navigate to and select your custom texture file, and click Insert.
4. Click OK in the Fill Effects dialog box to complete the procedure.

If you find that you don't like a texture's appearance, simply click Undo on the Formatting toolbar (or press Ctrl+Z), or apply a new texture to the object using the same procedure.

InsideOut

Because textures are images that you insert into an object's background, you can't apply a color and a texture to an object at the same time. If you apply a texture to an object that contains a color fill, the texture replaces the color. Likewise, if you apply color to an object that contains a texture, the color replaces the texture. A workaround might be to colorize a texture image in a painting program or to use a pattern, as described in the next section.

Creating Patterns for Shapes and Lines

Patterns can be used to create fill and line effects that are not as complex as textures and yet not as flat as solid color fills. Word offers 48 patterns that you can apply to objects and lines. In addition to adding a pattern to an object, you can also specify foreground and background colors to be used by the pattern. The processes of adding patterns to fills and lines are similar, as you can see here:

- **Add a pattern to a fill.** Select an object, click the Fill Color down arrow on the Drawing toolbar, choose Fill Effects on the drop-down menu, click the Pattern tab, select a pattern, specify foreground and background colors, and click OK.
- **Add a pattern to a line.** Select an object, click the Line Color down arrow, choose Patterned Lines on the drop-down menu, select a pattern, specify foreground and background colors, and click OK.

Figure 16-18, on the next page, shows the Pattern tab, which is available for both lines and fills.

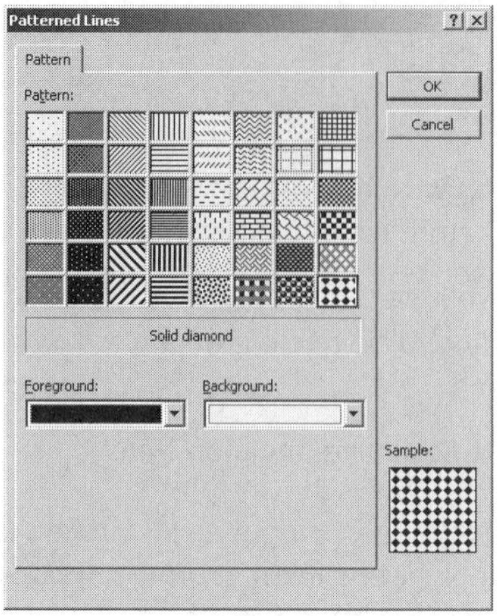

Figure 16-18. The Pattern tab enables you to apply patterns with custom colors to selected objects.

You can use custom colors to create patterns, and you can preview your patterns in the Sample window before you apply the patterns to your objects.

Inserting Pictures into Shapes

Similar to adding a background graphic to your objects, you can insert a picture to serve as a fill effect. To use a picture as a fill, follow these steps:

1. Select the object, click the Fill Color down arrow on the Drawing toolbar, and choose Fill Effects on the drop-down menu.
2. In the Fill Effects dialog box, click the Picture tab, shown in Figure 16-19, and then click the Select Picture button to display the Select Picture dialog box.

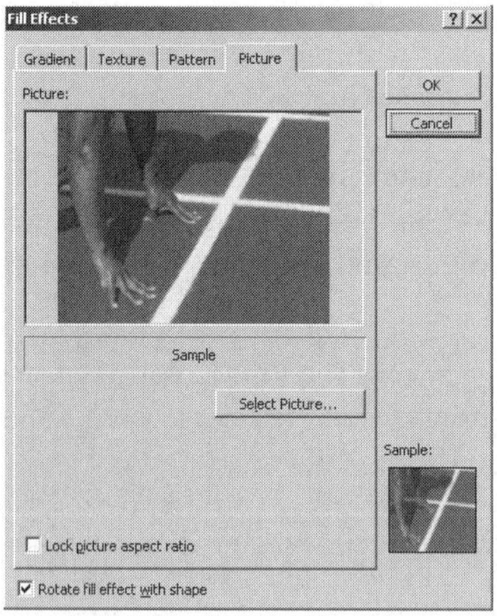

Figure 16-19. The Picture tab enables you to fill objects with picture backgrounds.

3 In the Select Picture dialog box, navigate to the location of your picture, and then double-click the picture. The picture is displayed in the Picture tab and in the Sample area.

4 Click OK to display the picture as the selected object's fill.

Figure 16-20 shows an object formatted with a picture fill.

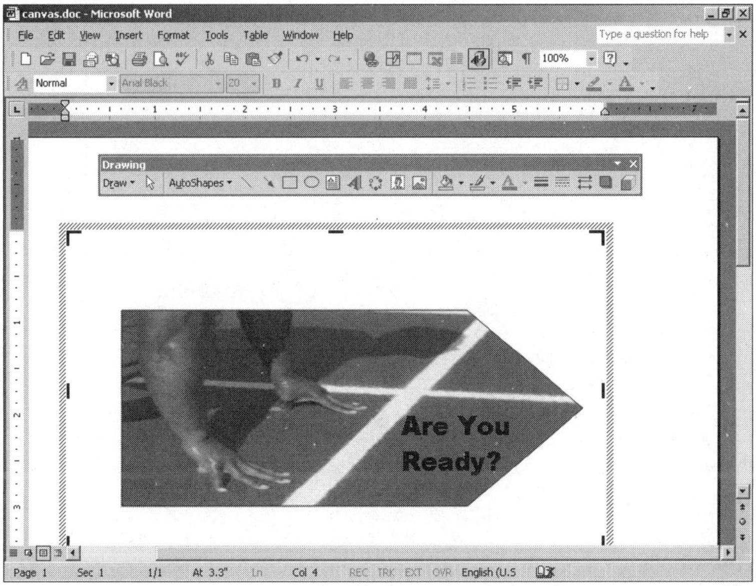

Figure 16-20. You can use graphics images to create a custom fill.

Formatting Shadows and 3-D Effects

In addition to adding textures and colors, you can apply 3-D and shadow effects to lines, arrows, shapes, AutoShapes, backgrounds, and freeform shapes. Generally, you'll want to use 3-D and shadow effects when you want to create a sense of depth in your drawing. Both the shadow and the 3-D effects are accessible from the Drawing toolbar.

note You can apply either a shadow or a 3-D effect to an object—but you can't apply both. This means that if you apply a 3-D effect to a drawing object that has a shadow, the shadow will disappear. Likewise, if you add a shadow effect to a 3-D object, the 3-D formatting will be removed.

Adding and Controlling Shadows

You can instantly add depth to drawing objects in Word by adding a shadow to the edge of an object. The Shadow Style effects in Word enable you to add various shadow styles to objects, adjust shadow position, and change shadow color. Figure 16-21 shows a few flowchart objects formatted using the Shadow Style effects.

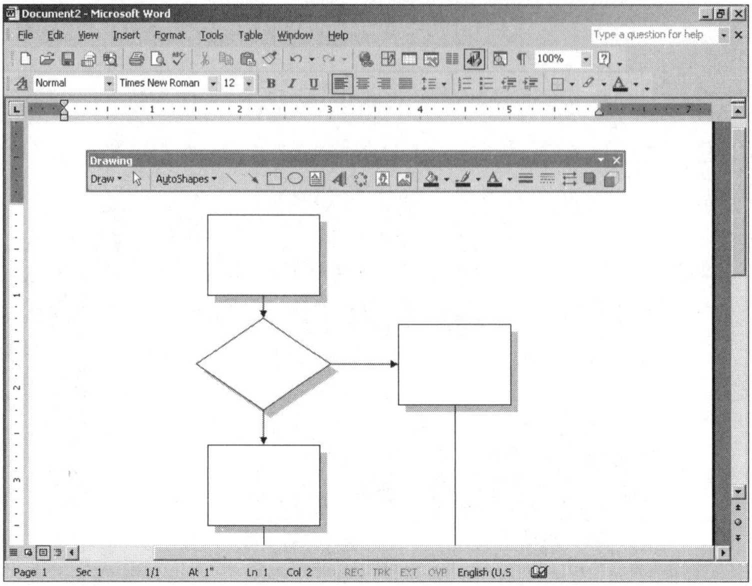

Figure 16-21. You can add shadows to basic objects, as shown in this flowchart structure.

Creating Shadows

You can add a 50-percent gray shadow to any selected object by using a preset shadow style in Word. To do so, you use the Shadow Style drop-down menu on the Drawing toolbar, shown in Figure 16-22.

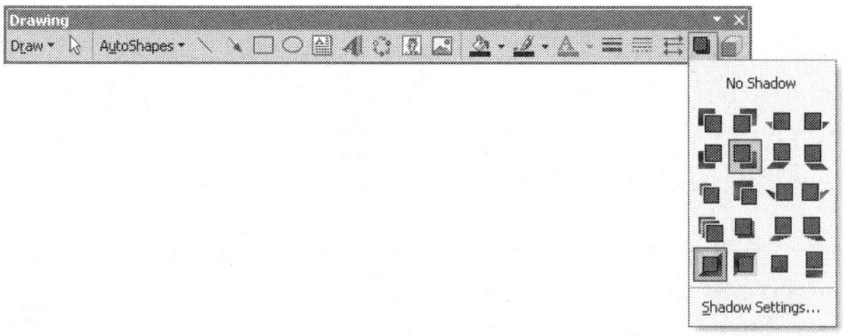

Figure 16-22. Word provides 20 preset styles on the Shadow Style drop-down menu.

To add a preset shadow style to an object, select the object you want to add a shadow to, click the Shadow Style button on the Drawing toolbar, and choose a shadow style on the Shadow Style drop-down menu. To remove a shadow, select the object, and click No Shadow on the Shadow Style drop-down menu.

Changing the Position of Shadows

After you apply a shadow, you can manually adjust the shadow's position relative to the object. To do so, follow these steps:

1. Select the object whose shadow you want to adjust.
2. Click the Shadow Style button on the Drawing toolbar, and choose Shadow Settings on the drop-down menu. The Shadow Settings toolbar opens.

   The buttons on the Shadow Settings toolbar are described in Table 16-2.
3. Click the appropriate buttons to reposition the shadow. Each time you click a nudge button, the shadow moves 1 point in the specified direction.

Table 16-2. Shadow Settings Toolbar Buttons

Button	Name	Description
	Shadow On/Off	Adds or removes an object's shadow
	Nudge Shadow Up	Moves an object's shadow up by 1 point
	Nudge Shadow Down	Moves an object's shadow down by 1 point
	Nudge Shadow Left	Moves an object's shadow left by 1 point
	Nudge Shadow Right	Moves an object's shadow right by 1 point
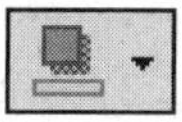	Shadow Color	Opens a color palette that you can use to color a shadow

tip To nudge a shadow 6 points instead of 1 point, press Shift while you click the appropriate nudge button on the Shadow Settings toolbar.

Coloring Shadows

In addition to adjusting a shadow's position, you can also color a shadow. To do so, follow these steps:

1. Select the drawing object that contains the shadow you want to change.
2. Click the Shadow button on the Drawing toolbar, and choose Shadow Settings from the drop-down menu. The Shadow Settings toolbar opens.

Chapter 16

3 On the Shadow Settings toolbar, click the Shadow Color down arrow, and choose the color you want to apply to the shadow from the drop-down menu.

If you don't see the color you want on the Shadow Color drop-down menu, click More Shadow Colors to access the Standard and Custom tabs in the Colors dialog box (as discussed in the section "Specifying Line and Fill Colors," on page 397). The Shadow Color drop-down menu also includes a Semitransparent option. This option is selected by default; it creates a lighter shadow that you can see text through. Clear the Semitransparent selection if you want to make your shadow darker and make sure that text is not visible through the shadow.

InsideOut

If you apply an embossed or engraved shadow to an object (Shadow Style 17 or Shadow Style 18 on the Shadow Style drop-down menu), Word hides the object's borders by default. If you later apply a different shadow effect to the object, you might have to redraw the object's borders (especially if the object is the same color as the background). To do so, select the object, and choose a line color on the Line Color drop-down menu on the Drawing toolbar.

Applying and Customizing 3-D Effects

By using 3-D effects, you can format and customize simple 3-D objects. To add a 3-D effect to an object, Word adjusts the two-dimensional object by expanding (or extruding) the object's edges and rotating the object to an angle. In Word, you can control the depth of a 3-D object's extrusion as well as the object's angle. In addition, you can specify how light and shadow reflect off the shape, and you can specify how the object's surface should be formatted by choosing the Wire Frame, Matte, Plastic, or Metal option.

Adding 3-D Effects

To create a 3-D effect, you use the 3-D Style drop-down menu, shown in Figure 16-23.

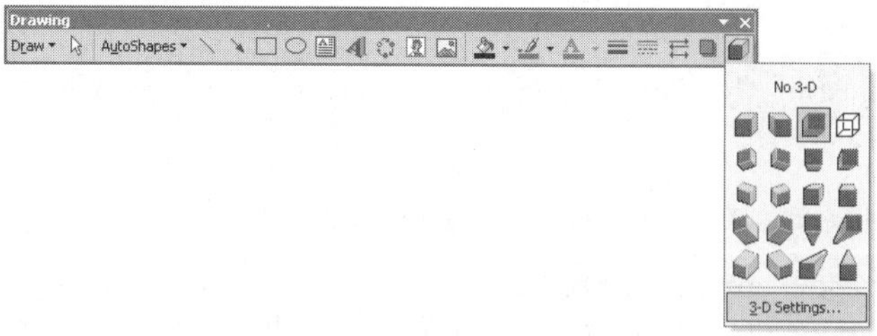

Figure 16-23. Word provides 20 preset styles on the 3-D Style menu.

To format a 3-D object, follow these steps:

1. Select the object you want to modify.
2. On the Drawing toolbar, click the 3-D Style button, and then click a 3-D setting on the 3-D Style drop-down menu.

After you create a 3-D object, you can remove a 3-D effect by choosing No 3-D on the 3-D Style drop-down menu. You can also change which 3-D setting is applied by selecting the 3-D object and choosing a different setting on the 3-D Style drop-down menu.

tip To add the same 3-D effect to several objects at one time (including applying the same lighting effects and other settings), select or group the objects before you apply the 3-D settings.

Controlling Light, Color, Angle, and Other Settings

After you apply a 3-D style to an object, you can change the 3-D style's appearance, including its color, rotation, depth, lighting, and surface texture. To modify an object's 3-D effects, you select the object, click the 3-D button on the Drawing toolbar, and then click 3-D Settings on the 3-D Style drop-down menu to open the 3-D Settings toolbar. Table 16-3 describes the buttons available on the 3-D Settings toolbar.

To use any of the 3-D Settings toolbar buttons, select the 3-D object and then click the appropriate toolbar button. Similar to the color settings available for other objects, the 3-D Color drop-down menu enables you to create custom colors for a 3-D object's extrusion by choosing the More 3-D Colors option to display the Colors dialog box. (The Colors dialog box is shown in Figures 16-13 and 16-14.)

Table 16-3. 3-D Settings Toolbar Buttons

Button	Name	Description
	3-D On/Off	Adds or removes a 3-D effect.
	Tilt Down	Tilts the object down by 5 degrees. Press Shift while clicking to move the object in 45-degree increments. Press Ctrl while clicking to move the object in 1-degree increments.
	Tilt Up	Tilts the object down by 5 degrees. Press Shift while clicking to move the object in 45-degree increments. Press Ctrl while clicking to move the object in 1-degree increments.

(continued)

Table 16-3. *(continued)*

Button	Name	Description
	Tilt Left	Tilts the object 5 degrees to the left. Press Shift while clicking to move the object in 45-degree increments. Press Ctrl while clicking to move the object in 1-degree increments.
	Tilt Right	Tilts the object 5 degrees to the right. Press Shift while clicking to move the object in 45-degree increments. Press Ctrl while clicking to move the object in 1-degree increments.
	Depth	Opens a drop-down menu that enables you to change the size of the object's extrusion.
	Direction	Opens a drop-down menu that enables you to control the direction of the object's extrusion. You can choose from nine preset values as well as specify a diminishing perspective (Perspective) or a flat-plane perspective (Parallel).
	Lighting	Opens a drop-down menu that enables you to choose a light direction. You can choose from nine preset values as well as Bright, Normal, or Dim.
	Surface	Opens a drop-down menu containing four surface options you can assign to the selected object: Wire Frame, Matte, Plastic, and Metal.
	3-D Color	Opens a color palette that you can use to control the color of the 3-D object's extrusion.

Adding Text to Drawings

A picture may be worth a thousand words, but you'll often find that you want to add text to your drawings. You can add text as a separate element by drawing a text box, or you can enter text directly into an existing object. For example, you might want to insert text into a star shape or a banner. To add text to drawings, use one of the following methods:

- **Add text box properties to an existing shape.** To enter text directly into an object, right-click the object, and choose Add Text on the shortcut menu. The shape will become a text box, with an insertion point inside. You simply type and format the text you want to appear in the shape.

- **Create a text box.** To create a freestanding text box, click the Text Box button on the Drawing toolbar, and draw a text box on the drawing canvas. After you draw a text box, you simply type text into the box. Text boxes can be treated as shapes, which means that they can be resized and formatted in many of the same ways shapes are formatted, including modifying fills, borders, shadow, and 3-D effects.

In addition to entering text in text boxes and objects, you can add WordArt to your drawings. To add a WordArt object, click the Word Art button on the Drawing toolbar, which opens the WordArt Gallery. WordArt enables you to add highly stylized text to your drawings so that you can create custom text art, such as title bars, logos, and buttons.

For more information about working with text boxes, see Chapter 23, "Using Word's Desktop Publishing Features," and for more information about WordArt, see Chapter 17, "Customizing Documents with WordArt."

InsideOut

As mentioned, when you create a freehand drawing, you can't right-click the drawing and choose Add Text. To work around this limitation, you can click the Text Box button on the Drawing toolbar and draw a text box on top of your freehand drawing. Then type and format text in the text box. If you want to ensure that the text and drawing aren't separated or layered incorrectly in the future, choose the shape and the text box (by pressing Shift as you click the objects), and then click the Draw button on the Drawing toolbar and choose Group on the drop-down menu to group the two objects together.

tip **Create Web page buttons**

By combining basic objects and text boxes, you can create custom buttons for Web pages. To make these custom buttons active hyperlinks, you simply add hyperlink properties to your drawing objects, as described in Chapter 31, "Creating Professional Web Sites."

Controlling Objects in Drawings

When you create a drawing using objects, you'll find that you frequently need to adjust existing objects in a number of ways. Because drawn pictures are made of lines and shapes, you can reshape, group and ungroup, reorder, and change the color of one or all parts of a picture. This section describes the numerous ways you can work with existing objects when you create drawings in Word.

Modifying Objects

Rarely will you create a shape in the exact position and size required by your drawing. Thus, you need to become proficient at resizing, reshaping, rotating, and flipping objects before you can successfully create drawings in Word.

Resizing Objects

To resize an object, select the object and then drag the object's selection handles. You can resize a single shape, a group of selected shapes, or the entire drawing canvas. When you resize drawing objects, Word redraws the lines and shapes to meet the newly designated dimensions.

Reshaping Objects

Many AutoShapes display a yellow diamond-shaped adjustment handle when you select them. This adjustment handle enables you to change the most prominent feature of a shape. For example, you can change the length and width of a star's points by dragging the star's adjustment handle. Figure 16-24 shows a star shape that has been modified using this technique.

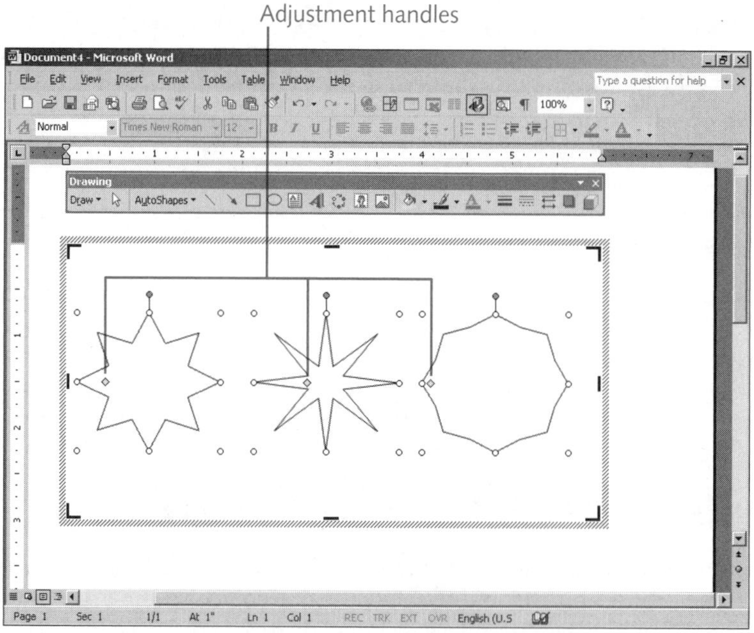

Figure 16-24. These stars were created from the same AutoShape; each has been modified by dragging its yellow diamond-shaped adjustment handle.

Rotating Objects

In addition to resizing and reshaping objects, you can rotate them. To do so, use either of the following methods:

- Drag the green round rotation handle located near the top of the object, and then click outside the object to set the rotation position.
- On the Drawing toolbar, click Draw, choose Rotate Or Flip on the drop-down menu, and then choose Free Rotate, Rotate Left, or Rotate Right. When you choose Rotate Left or Rotate Right, you rotate the object by 90 degrees. When you choose Free Rotate, you can rotate the object to any angle by using the provided rotation handles.

Remember, if your object contains a fill effect, you must make sure that the Rotate Fill Effect With Shape check box is selected in the Fill Effects dialog box if you want the fill to rotate with the object.

tip To restrict the rotation of objects to 15-degree angles, press Shift while you drag the rotation handle.

Flipping Objects

Flipping an object literally means to flip an object over. (It might help to visualize flipping pancakes when using this feature.) You can flip an object horizontally or vertically. To flip an object, select the object, click Draw on the Drawing toolbar, choose Rotate Or Flip on the drop-down menu, and choose Flip Horizontal or Flip Vertical. Figure 16-25, on the next page, shows the results of flipping an object horizontally and vertically.

note You can flip AutoShapes, pictures, clip art, and WordArt objects.

Selecting Multiple Drawing Elements at One Time

At times, you might want to select multiple objects at one time because you want to perform one of the following tasks:

- Apply formatting to all selected objects.
- Move all the selected objects without losing the spacing between the objects.
- Delete all the selected objects.
- Prepare to group the objects (as described in the next section).

To select multiple objects, press Shift and click each object you want to include, or click the Select Objects button on the Drawing toolbar and drag to encompass the objects you want to select in the selection rectangle. You can tell which objects have been selected because they are displayed with selection handles. After a group of objects is selected, you can right-click to apply shortcut menu options, click Drawing toolbar buttons to apply formatting, or drag the selected items to move them as a group.

Repositioning Drawing Objects with Precision

As an experienced Word user, you know that you can reposition drawing objects by clicking and dragging them. Moving objects this way to create drawings is especially effective now that Word includes the drawing canvas. At times, however, you might want to position objects with more precision. You can control how objects are positioned by using a drawing grid, nudging objects into place, and using the aligning and distributing options provided on the Drawing toolbar, as described here:

- **Using the drawing grid.** You can use the drawing grid inside the drawing canvas to help you position graphics within your drawing. To turn on the drawing grid, click in the drawing canvas, click Draw on the Drawing toolbar, and choose Grid on the drop-down menu. In the Drawing Grid dialog box, select the Display Gridlines On Screen check box, as shown in Figure 16-26, and then click OK. The drawing grid appears. To turn off the grid, clear the Display Gridlines On Screen check box in the Drawing Grid dialog box.

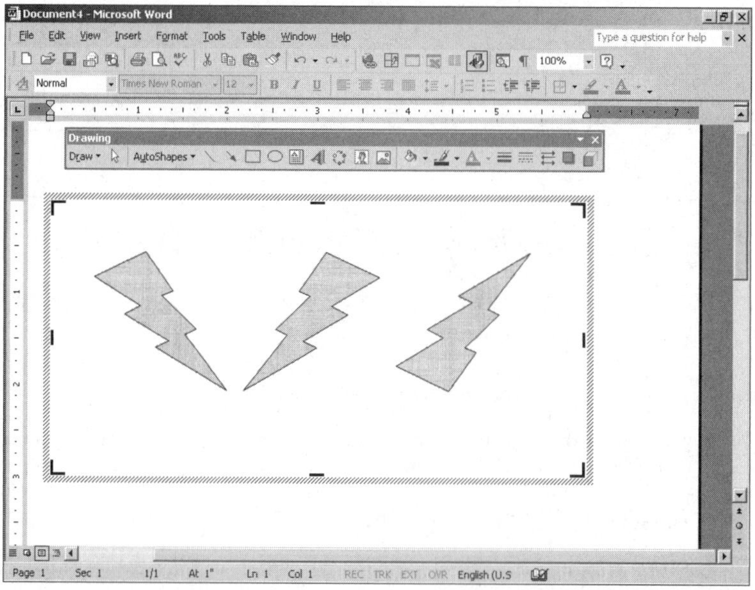

Figure 16-25. The lightning bolt in the center has been flipped horizontally, and the lightning bolt on the right has been flipped vertically.

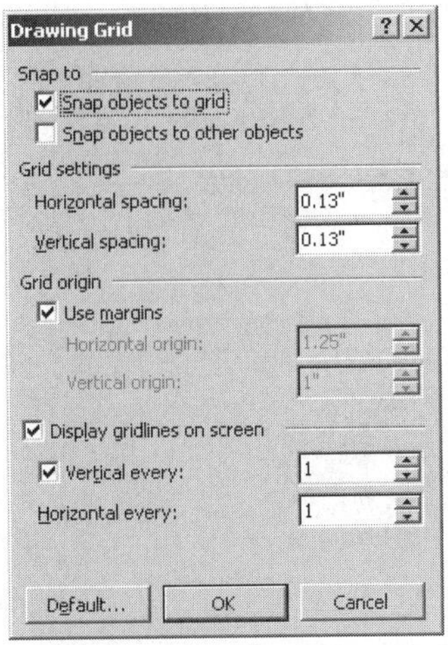

Figure 16-26. The Drawing Grid dialog box provides options you can use to control how the drawing grid looks and behaves.

- **Nudging objects into place.** You can move (nudge) an object up, down, left, or right by 1 pixel by selecting the object and then pressing the arrow keys or by selecting the object and then clicking Draw on the Drawing toolbar, choosing Nudge on the drop-down menu, and choosing Up, Down, Left, or Right. If you have the Snap Objects To Grid option turned on while you are using the drawing grid, as shown in Figure 16-27, on the next page, choosing the Nudge option moves your object one grid measurement. You can also nudge objects in smaller increments while using the grid by pressing Ctrl while you press the arrow keys.

note If you have the Snap Objects To Grid feature turned on while you work on the drawing grid, you can override the feature by pressing Alt while you drag an object.

- **Aligning and distributing objects.** To help you align and arrange objects evenly relative to each other, you can use the alignment and distribution options on the Draw drop-down menu. To do so, select the objects you want to position, click Draw on the Drawing toolbar, and choose Align Or Distribute on the drop-down menu. As shown in Figure 16-28, on the next page, you can align objects vertically (Left, Center, or Right), horizontally (Top, Middle, or Bottom), and distribute selected objects evenly horizontally or vertically. By default, objects are distributed relative to the drawing canvas.

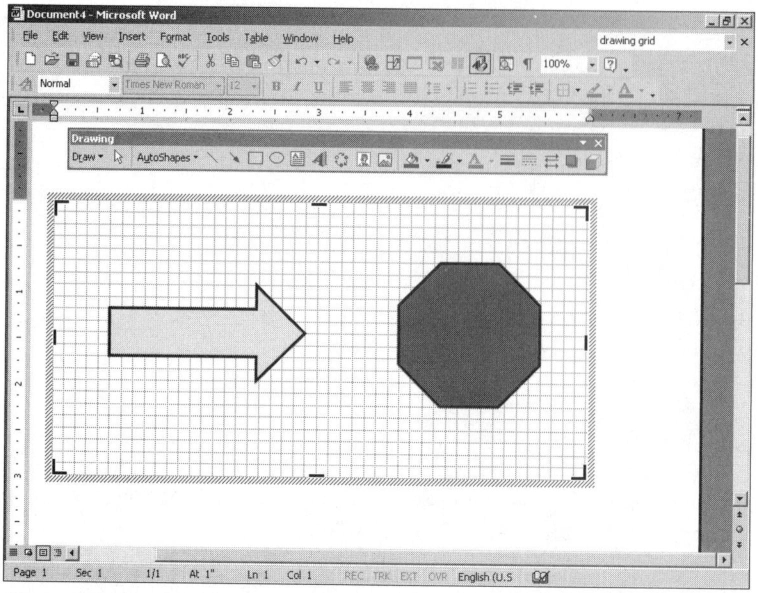

Figure 16-27. You can use the drawing grid to help size and align objects accurately.

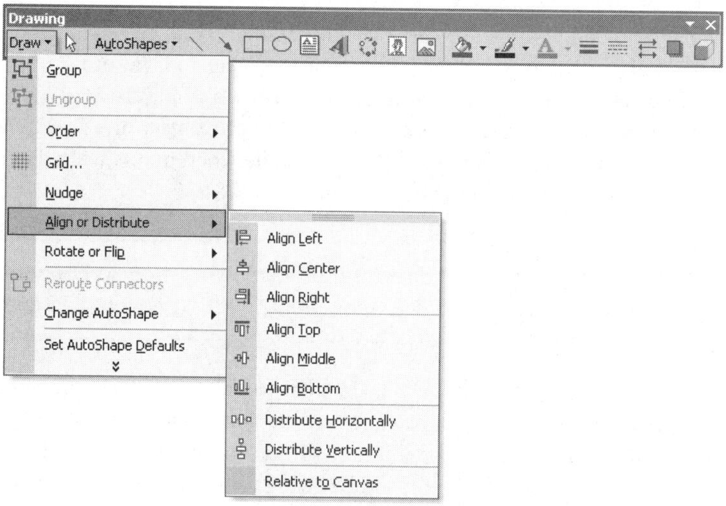

Figure 16-28. After you learn how to align and distribute objects, you'll find that you use these alignment options frequently to create professional-looking drawings.

Grouping and Ungrouping Objects

You can group objects to ensure that certain objects stay together no matter what. For example, if you've overlaid a text box on an AutoShape, you might want to group the two objects so that you won't have to reposition the text box within the shape every time you move the shape. (In addition, you won't have to worry about the text box being accidentally layered beneath the object, which would hide the text.) You can ungroup grouped items at any time, which enables you to edit any part of a grouped object whenever necessary.

To group objects, select the objects you want to group (by pressing Shift and clicking each object you want to include), click Draw on the Drawing toolbar, and choose Group from the drop-down menu. Or select the objects you want to group, right-click, choose Grouping on the shortcut menu, and then choose Group.

To ungroup objects, click the group to select it, click Draw on the Drawing toolbar, and choose Ungroup. Or right-click the group, and choose Grouping on the shortcut menu, and then choose Ungroup.

tip **Regroup your objects**

If you ungroup a group to make a minor change—maybe you want to resize an object in the group, for example—you can easily regroup the objects after you make your changes. To do so, select any object that was part of the group, click Draw on the Drawing toolbar, and choose Regroup on the drop-down menu. Or right-click the object, choose Grouping on the shortcut menu, and then choose Regroup.

Controlling Object Layering

When you create a drawing that contains many objects, you'll need to control which objects are layered above and below other objects. Paying attention to how objects are layered can save you from inadvertently obscuring parts of your drawings that should be displayed. The order in which objects are stacked is sometimes referred to as the *z-order,* based on standard coordinate references, in which *x* refers to horizontal positioning, *y* refers to vertical positioning, and *z* refers to depth positioning. To control the z-order of objects in your drawing, select an object, click Draw on the Drawing toolbar, and choose Order on the drop-down menu (or right-click an object and choose Order on the shortcut menu) to access the layering options, as shown in Figure 16-29, on the next page. You can position an object in front of all layers, in back of all layers, in front of the next layer, or in back of the next lower layer. In addition, you can specify drawing canvases to be placed in front of or behind text.

tip If you're having trouble selecting an object (maybe it's almost completely buried under other objects), you can press Tab repeatedly to move your selection focus from one object to the next.

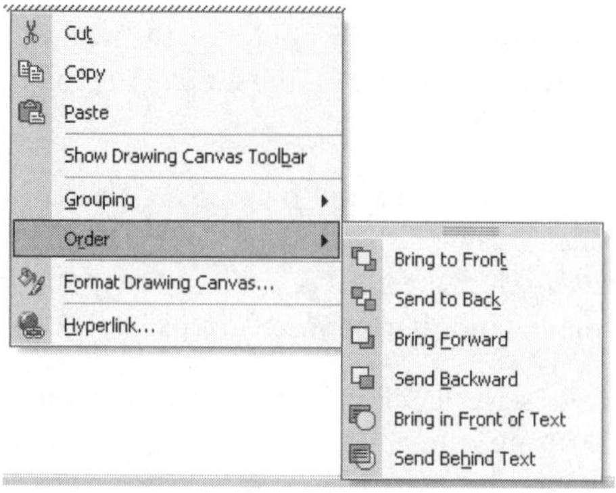

Figure 16-29. Layering objects helps you to control which objects should be displayed in the foreground of your drawing and which should appear in the background.

newfeature!

Integrating the Drawing Canvas with Document Text

Most of this chapter describes how to work with drawing objects, both inside and outside the drawing canvas. If you create a drawing within the drawing canvas, you can control how the drawing canvas wraps around the drawing as well as how the drawing canvas is positioned relative to a document's text. To configure the drawing canvas settings, you use the Drawing Canvas toolbar, shown in Figure 16-30.

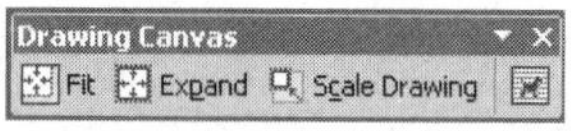

Figure 16-30. You can resize the drawing canvas as well as specify how text should wrap around the canvas by using the Drawing Canvas toolbar buttons.

To display the Drawing Canvas toolbar, right-click a blank area in the drawing canvas and choose Show Drawing Canvas Toolbar on the shortcut menu. The Drawing Canvas toolbar buttons are described in Table 16-4.

You can also access drawing canvas options by opening the Format Drawing Canvas dialog box using one of the following methods:

- Click a blank area in the drawing canvas, and choose Format, Drawing Canvas.
- Double-click a blank area of the drawing canvas or the drawing canvas frame.
- Right-click a blank area in the drawing canvas frame, and choose Format Drawing Canvas on the shortcut menu.

The Format Drawing Canvas dialog box is shown in Figure 16-31. This dialog box is similar to the formatting dialog box that appears when you double-click drawing objects.

Table 16-4. **Drawing Canvas Toolbar Buttons**

Button	Name	Description
Fit	Fit	Reduces the drawing canvas frame to the size of the drawing.
Expand	Expand	Expands the drawing canvas. You can click this button multiple times to expand the canvas incrementally.
Scale Drawing	Scale Drawing	Displays selection handles on the drawing canvas that enable you to resize the drawing canvas and the drawing at the same time.
	Text Wrapping	Opens the Text Wrapping drop-down menu, which enables you to specify how text should wrap around the drawing canvas. The text wrapping options are the same options you use when formatting pictures. (See Chapter 14, "Adding Visual Impact with Pictures," for more information about text wrapping options.)

Using the Format Drawing Canvas dialog box, you can customize the color, line, size, and layout options. You can also enter alternative text (called ALT text) if you'll be using the drawing on a Web page. ALT text is displayed in Web pages in place of graphics when graphics are turned off in a browser or a user is using a text-only browser. (See Chapter 31, "Creating Professional Web Sites," for more information about ALT text.)

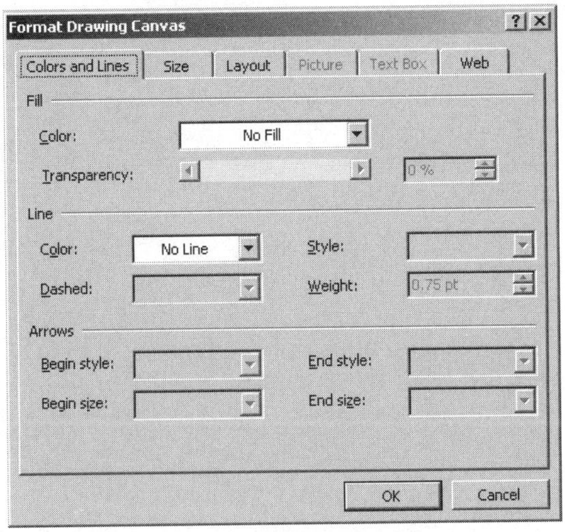

Figure 16-31. The Format Drawing Canvas dialog box enables you to precisely control your drawing canvas settings.

Chapter 16

You can also control the drawing canvas directly in a few ways. For example, you can reposition a drawing canvas in a document by dragging the drawing canvas frame. In addition, you can drag drawings off the drawing canvas and then delete the drawing canvas, if desired, by right-clicking it and choosing Cut on the shortcut menu. Last, you can delete an entire drawing—canvas and all—by right-clicking the drawing canvas and choosing Cut on the shortcut menu or pressing Delete.

Chapter 17

Customizing Documents with WordArt

As word-processing software capabilities expand, so do the opportunities to liven up documents. At one time, most people were satisfied with creating neat-looking documents by typing pages of information. Nowadays, many users find themselves creating complex page layouts and more graphics intensive pieces. A popular method of adding a bit of pizzazz to a document is to include graphical text, such as title bars, banners, Web page buttons, logos, and so forth. To help users bridge the gap from plain yet functional to visually provocative yet informative, Word provides a handy graphical text feature called WordArt.

Introducing WordArt

If your Word documents leave you with that nagging "it's just missing something" feeling, you might want to add some graphical text. Graphical text works especially well in intentionally eye-catching types of documents, such as brochures, flyers, newsletters, Web pages, and advertisements. If after considering the purpose of your document you determine that adding graphical text seems like a viable option, you're in luck—the WordArt feature helps you create and customize graphical text quickly and easily.

Used creatively (and sparingly), WordArt can add a splash of color, a bit of dimension, a touch of originality, and a professional polish to your documents. The example document in Figure 17-1, on the next page, illustrates how a couple of default WordArt styles can be combined to create a Web page logo. These default WordArt styles and colors are certainly adequate, but if creating a unique look is a concern, you should seriously consider customizing WordArt objects whenever you use them—otherwise, people might recognize that you're using a standard WordArt style. If you master the WordArt features described in this chapter, you'll be able to create highly customized graphical text for your documents.

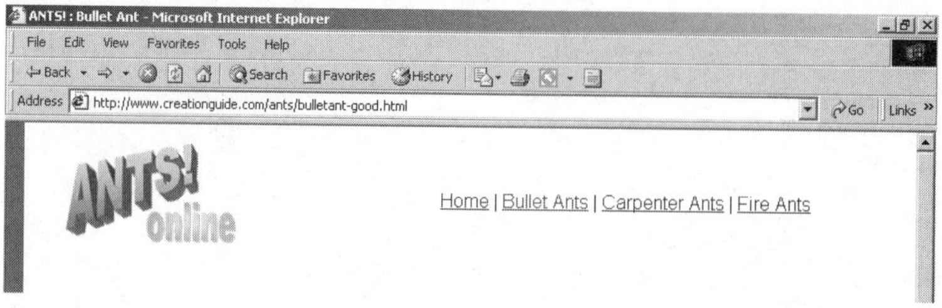

Figure 17-1. Two WordArt styles combined to create a simple fictitious Web page logo.

> After you create WordArt objects, you can manipulate them much like other drawing objects in Word. For more information about drawing objects, see Chapter 16, "Enlivening Documents with Drawings and AutoShapes."

Inserting WordArt Using the WordArt Gallery

At the most basic level, including a WordArt object in your document entails selecting a WordArt style and entering the WordArt object's display text. To accomplish these two tasks, you'll use the WordArt Gallery, shown in Figure 17-2, and the Edit WordArt Text dialog box, shown in Figure 17-3.

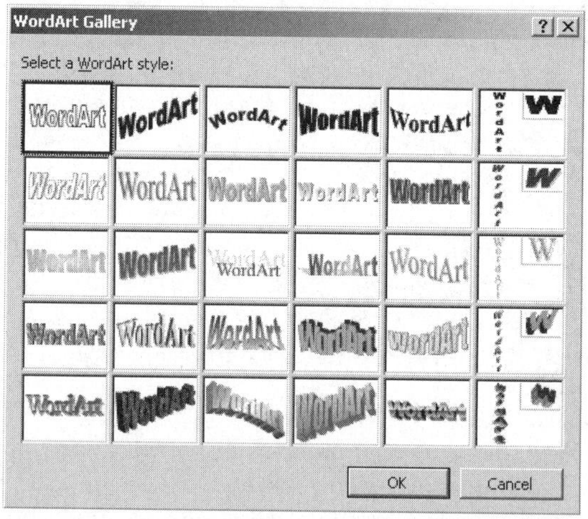

Figure 17-2. The WordArt Gallery offers 30 base styles that you can use as a foundation when you create a WordArt object.

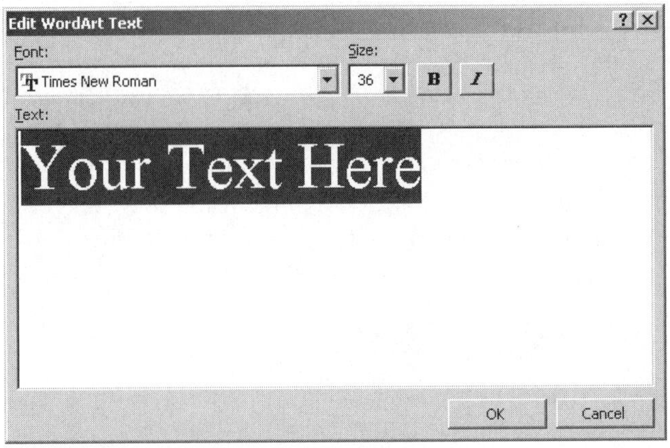

Figure 17-3. You can enter custom text for a WordArt object in the Edit WordArt Text dialog box, as well as configure font, size, boldface, and italic formatting settings.

To create a WordArt object, follow these steps:

1. In your document, position the insertion point where you want to insert the WordArt object.
2. Verify that you're working in either Print Layout view or Web Layout view, and then choose Insert, Picture, WordArt, or display the Drawing toolbar (by clicking the Drawing button on the Standard toolbar) and click the WordArt button.
3. In the WordArt Gallery, select a WordArt style, and click OK (or simply double-click the WordArt style of your choice). The Edit WordArt Text dialog box appears.
4. Type the WordArt object's display text in the Text box, and configure the Font, Size, Bold, and Italic text attributes. (You can easily reconfigure these settings later, so don't be overly worried about getting them right the first time.)
5. After you configure the WordArt object's text, click OK. The WordArt object appears in your document.

tip If you want to convert existing text to a WordArt object, select the text before you choose Insert, Picture, WordArt. The selected text will be displayed automatically in the Text box in the Edit WordArt Text dialog box.

Customizing WordArt Objects

After you insert a WordArt object, you'll most likely want to customize the object to suit your purposes. You can customize WordArt objects in a number of ways. For example, you can adjust a WordArt object's content and style, change the object's shape, combine WordArt objects, control text alignment, and so forth. To assist you in making changes to your WordArt objects, Word provides the WordArt toolbar, shown in Figure 17-4.

Figure 17-4. The WordArt toolbar contains most of the tools you need to fully customize WordArt objects.

The next few sections describe the various ways you can alter WordArt characteristics to morph standard WordArt objects into custom graphical text elements. As you'll discover, customizing WordArt is a breeze.

Adjusting WordArt Style and Text

After you create a standard WordArt object, you might decide that you want to change your basic font selection, apply a different WordArt base style, or edit the text. To do this, you'll have to return to the WordArt Gallery or the Edit WordArt Text dialog box. Backtracking is easy:

WordArt Gallery

- **To apply a different WordArt base style to an existing WordArt object,** click the WordArt object you want to modify, click the WordArt Gallery button on the WordArt toolbar, and double-click a style in the WordArt Gallery.

Edit Text

- **To edit text in an existing WordArt object,** double-click the WordArt object, or click the WordArt object (which selects the WordArt object and opens the WordArt toolbar by default) and click the Edit Text button on the WordArt toolbar. In the Edit WordArt Text dialog box, make any desired changes, including adjusting text and formatting, and click OK.

When you apply a different style using the WordArt Gallery or edit WordArt text in the Edit WordArt Text dialog box and click OK, the changes are instantly reflected in your WordArt object.

Positioning WordArt Objects in Documents

After you create a WordArt object, you'll probably want to specify how and where the object will be displayed in your document. By default, a WordArt object is inserted as an *inline object*. This means that the object is inserted at the insertion point and embedded within a regular line of text, as shown in Figure 17-5. You can drag inline WordArt objects from line to line and from paragraph to paragraph. You can also resize inline WordArt objects just as you resize other objects (by dragging the object's sizing handles or configuring the object's Size properties, as described in the section "Changing the Shape of WordArt," on page 427). But if you want to wrap text around a WordArt object, rotate the object, angle the object's text, position the object behind or in front of document text, or drag the object around a page that doesn't contain text, you'll need to change the WordArt object's text wrapping setting.

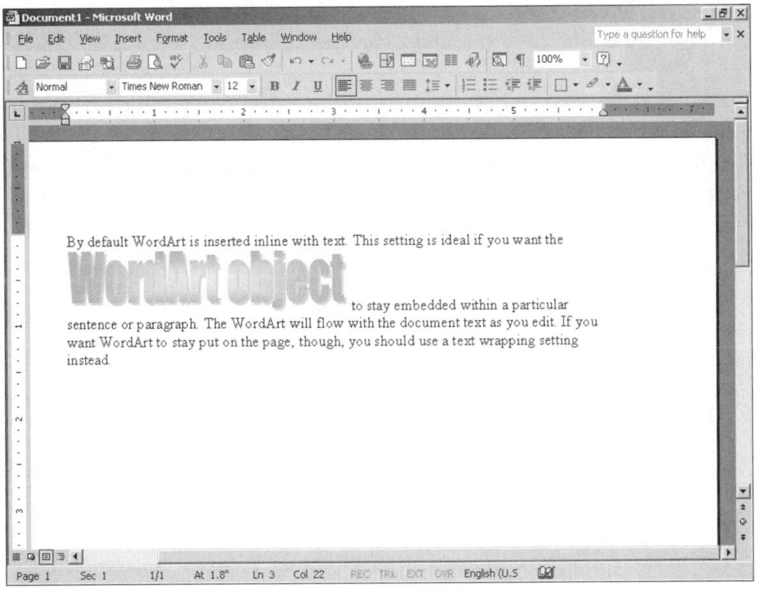

Figure 17-5. By default, WordArt objects are formatted as inline objects.

To change a WordArt object's text wrapping setting, follow these steps:

Text Wrapping

1. Click the WordArt object, and click the Text Wrapping button on the WordArt toolbar.
2. On the Text Wrapping drop-down menu, choose a text wrapping setting.

The Text Wrapping drop-down menu, shown in Figure 17-6, provides the following standard text wrapping styles: In Line With Text (the default setting), Square, Tight, Behind Text, In Front Of Text, Top And Bottom, Through, and Edit Wrap Points.

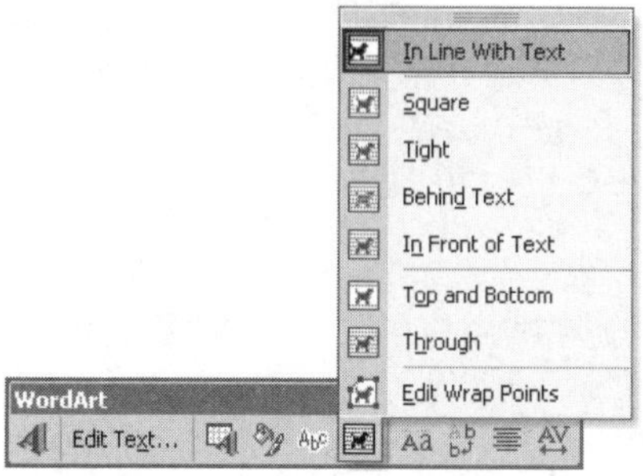

Figure 17-6. You can control how WordArt is displayed relative to document text by configuring the text wrapping setting.

After you specify how you'd like a WordArt object to be positioned within text, you can move the object by dragging it around your page in Web Layout or Print Layout view. In addition, you can specify exact object placement settings by configuring the Layout tab in the Format WordArt dialog box.

> **tip** **Move WordArt Objects Incrementally**
>
> You can move WordArt objects in small increments using the arrow keys. To nudge a WordArt object, click the object to select it, and then press the Up Arrow, Down Arrow, Left Arrow, and Right Arrow keys to move it in the desired direction.

To access advanced layout properties for a selected WordArt object, you need to display the Advanced Layout dialog box. To do so, follow these steps:

Format WordArt

1. Click the WordArt object, and click the Format WordArt button on the WordArt toolbar (or right-click the WordArt object, and choose Format WordArt on the shortcut menu) to open the Format WordArt dialog box.
2. In the Format WordArt dialog box, click the Layout tab. The Layout tab provides basic text wrapping and text alignment settings.
3. On the Layout tab, click the Advanced button. The Advanced Layout dialog box opens, as shown in Figure 17-7. Notice that the Advanced Layout dialog box contains two tabs: Picture Position and Text Wrapping.

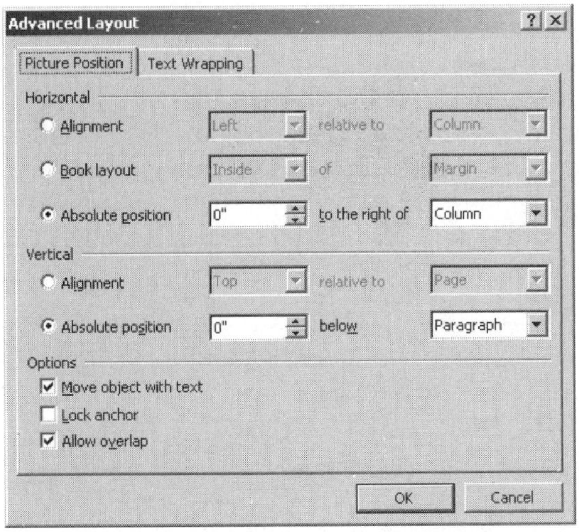

Figure 17-7. The Advanced Layout dialog box enables you to precisely configure a WordArt object's position, alignment, and text wrapping settings.

4. Configure your settings on both tabs, click OK to close the Advanced Layout dialog box, and then click OK in the Format WordArt dialog box to apply the settings.

> **For more information about setting Advanced Layout options, see Chapter 14, "Adding Visual Impact with Pictures."**

If you're attempting to apply advanced layout settings to a WordArt object but find that the Picture Position options are unavailable, change the Wrapping Style setting on the Text Wrapping tab to something other than In Line With Text. The Picture Position tab also contains a Move Object With Text check box. If you want to position a WordArt object on a particular page regardless of text flow, be sure to clear this check box.

Changing the Shape of WordArt

After you insert and position a WordArt object, you'll probably want to resize and reshape the object to suit your purposes. You can resize and reshape WordArt using three key tools: handles, WordArt shapes, and the Format WordArt dialog box.

Putting Handles to Work

As with other objects and graphics, you can display handles on WordArt objects and use these handles to modify the size and appearance of the objects. Both inline and floating WordArt objects provide sizing handles, which you can drag to resize the object.

To display a WordArt object's handles, simply click the object. Inline WordArt objects display standard black square sizing handles that you can drag to resize the object horizontally, vertically, and diagonally (which resizes the height and width proportionally). WordArt objects that aren't formatted as inline objects display a more colorful set of handles. Namely, a non-inline object provides clear circle handles for resizing, a green circle handle for rotating, and a yellow diamond handle for angling text. Figure 17-8 shows a WordArt object and its handles. To use any handle, simply drag the handle to the desired position.

note Remember, when you are working with an inline WordArt object, you can only drag the sizing handles to resize the WordArt object—you can't rotate or angle the text.

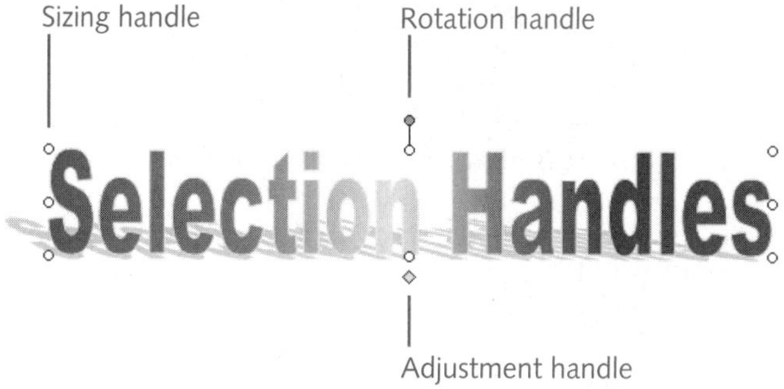

Figure 17-8. Handles enable you to resize, rotate, and angle WordArt text.

tip Keep an eye on the dashed lines when you rotate, angle, and resize WordArt text. Dashed lines are displayed as you drag handles so that you can get an idea of how you are reshaping a WordArt object.

Applying WordArt Shapes

In addition to resizing, rotating, and angling WordArt text, you can distort a WordArt object's shape. To do so, select the WordArt object, click the WordArt Shape button on the WordArt toolbar, and choose one of the 40 shapes available on the WordArt Shape menu, shown in Figure 17-9.

Figure 17-9. To get a feel for WordArt shapes, experiment with the WordArt Shape menu by applying various shapes to selected WordArt objects.

Sizing, Rotating, and Scaling WordArt with Precision

As you've seen, you can use handles to resize, rotate, and adjust WordArt objects until they look just right, but you can also perform these actions by specifying precise measurements. Using precise measurements to define your WordArt objects is an effective method when you want to create a uniform appearance among documents or among similar components within the same document. To precisely control WordArt size and rotation settings, you configure the settings on the Size tab in the Format WordArt dialog box, shown in Figure 17-10. To access the Size tab, right-click a WordArt object, choose Format WordArt on the shortcut menu, and click the Size tab. You can set sizing options for WordArt objects just as you set sizing options for other graphics or objects. After you configure Size And Rotate and Scale options, click OK to apply the settings.

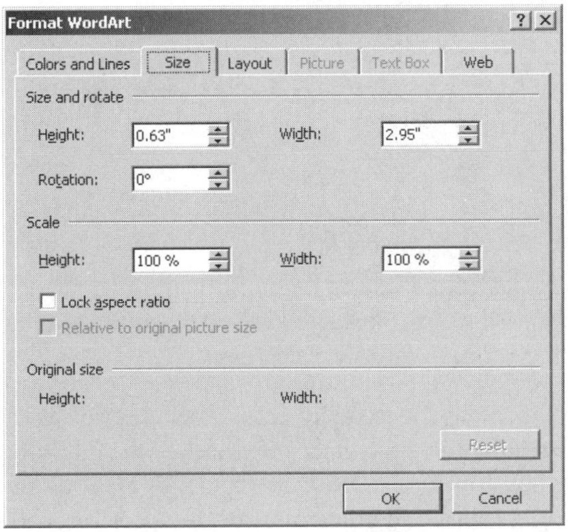

Figure 17-10. The Size tab enables you to precisely configure the size, rotation, and scale settings for your WordArt objects. Notice that the Size tab includes a Lock Aspect Ratio check box, which allows you to proportionally resize the height and width of a WordArt object based on a percentage of its current size.

Modifying WordArt Colors and Line Properties

Whenever you use WordArt, you should modify the default style so that you can present custom graphical text. Because so many people use Word, applying a default WordArt style without adding your own flair can result in others recognizing your use of WordArt. This recognition isn't necessarily a negative factor, but you'd probably prefer people to admire your graphical text, read the content, and move on, without pondering the sources of your design. Originality has its benefits. One of the most notable ways in which you can customize a WordArt object is to change the object's colors, texture, and line properties.

Changing a WordArt object's color scheme is as simple as selecting the WordArt object, clicking the Format WordArt button on the WordArt toolbar, and configuring the Colors And Lines tab in the Format WordArt dialog box. Figure 17-11 shows the Colors And Lines tab with the Color drop-down menu open. The Color setting in the Line section comes into play when you use a WordArt style that incorporates an outline around the graphical text.

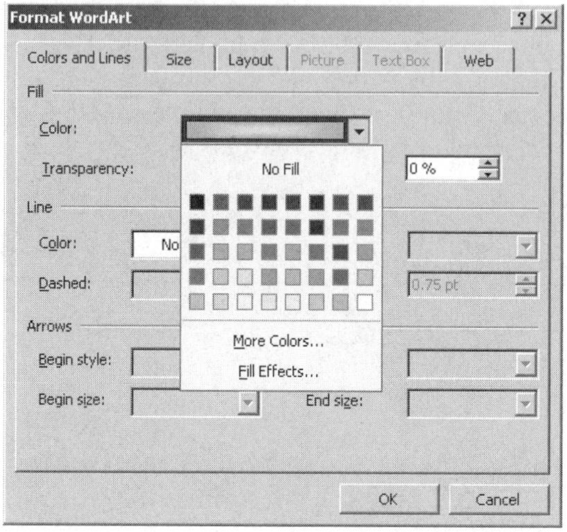

Figure 17-11. You can modify WordArt colors and line settings by configuring the Colors And Lines tab in the Format WordArt dialog box.

The Color drop-down menu includes the standard color palette as well as options that allow you to access additional colors and fill effects. If you click the Fill Effects command, the Fill Effects dialog box appears, as shown in Figure 17-12. You can use this dialog box to configure shading colors and gradients, textures, patterns, and pictures used to fill the WordArt object.

Changing the Shading or Texture of a WordArt Object

Some WordArt objects use a two-color (or more) gradient and shading scheme. If you apply a single color to those types of WordArt objects, the objects will look a bit flat due to the one-dimensional coloring scheme. If you want to change the color of a two-tone WordArt object, you have to modify the object's colors on the Gradient tab in the Fill Effects dialog box. You can also select a preset gradient color scheme by choosing the Preset option on the Gradient tab.

If you want to change the texture used in a default WordArt style, click the Texture tab in the Fill Effects dialog box. You can choose from a number of additional textures as well as navigate to any textures or graphics stored on your system.

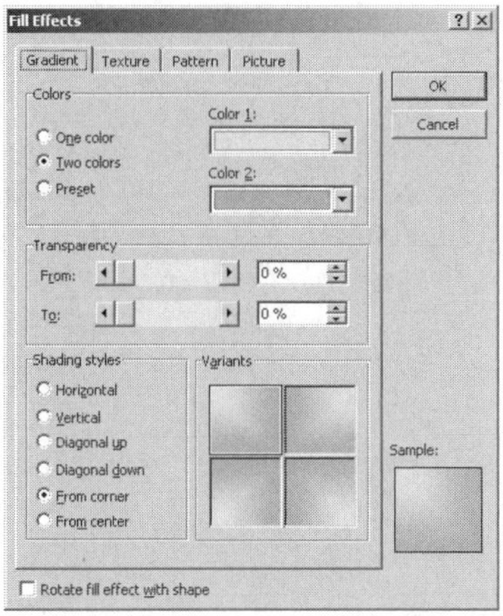

Figure 17-12. If a default WordArt style uses gradients, multiple colors, textures, or patterns, you can change the default configurations using the Fill Effects dialog box.

Formatting WordArt as Vertical Text

WordArt Vertical Text

At times, you might want to display WordArt vertically instead of horizontally. You can create a vertical WordArt object by choosing one of the five vertical WordArt styles in the WordArt Gallery, or you can select an existing WordArt object and click the WordArt Vertical Text button on the WordArt toolbar.

You can also create columns of WordArt text by pressing Enter after each word you type in the Edit WordArt Text dialog box. Then, after the WordArt is displayed in your document, click the WordArt Vertical Text button. You WordArt text will look something like the example in Figure 17-13, on the next page.

Aligning and Justifying WordArt Text

WordArt Alignment

If your WordArt object includes multiple words on more than one line, you can control how the WordArt text is aligned. Aligning WordArt text is similar to aligning standard paragraph text. To view the available WordArt alignment options, select the WordArt object, and click the WordArt Alignment button on the WordArt toolbar, as shown in Figure 17-14, on the next page.

The WordArt Alignment drop-down menu provides the following commands:

- **Left Align** aligns the text along the left edge of the WordArt frame.
- **Center** centers the text within the frame.
- **Right Align** aligns the text along the right edge of the frame.
- **Word Justify** justifies the text within the frame by adding space between words.

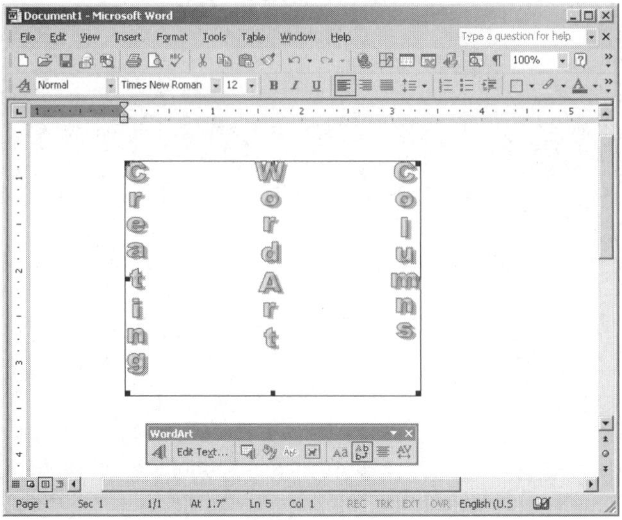

Figure 17-13. You can convert horizontal WordArt to vertical text by using the WordArt Vertical Text button on the WordArt toolbar.

Figure 17-14. You can align WordArt text within the object's frame by choosing alignment options on the WordArt Alignment drop-down menu.

- **Letter Justify** justifies the text within the frame by adding space between letters and increasing existing spaces between words. Single-word lines are treated the same as they would be using the Word Justify option.
- **Stretch Justify** justifies the text within the frame by stretching the letters and the spaces between words.

> **tip** **Align Vertical Columns**
>
> You can use the alignment options to align vertical columns of WordArt text as well. To top-align vertical columns of text, choose the Left Align option on the WordArt Alignment drop-down menu; to bottom-align vertical columns of text, choose the Right-Align option.

Using the WordArt Same Letter Heights Option

WordArt Same Letter Heights

Another effect you can apply to WordArt is to display lowercase letters the same height as uppercase letters. You might want to use this option to create a somewhat avant-garde artistic effect in a flyer or newsletter. To apply this formatting option, select the WordArt object, and click the WordArt Same Letter Heights button on the WordArt toolbar. Like other WordArt formatting options, you can't selectively apply this format setting within a WordArt object—it's an all-or-nothing proposition unless you use a workaround, as described in the following sidebar.

Adjusting WordArt Character Spacing and Kerning

Before word processing applications came along, most people left concepts like *character spacing* and *kerning* to professional typesetters. But now everyone who uses a word processing application is a bit of a typesetter. Thus, character spacing and kerning issues have made it to the fringe of mainstream document creation. If you've been ignoring character spacing and kerning options lately, here are a couple quick definitions to get you going:

- **Character spacing** refers to the space between characters. You can expand or condense space evenly between all WordArt characters.
- **Kerning** refers to adjusting spacing between pairs of characters to create the appearance of even spacing. For example, you might want to tighten the space between letter pairs such as *YO* and *WA*.

To adjust character spacing and kerning in WordArt objects, you can click the WordArt Character Spacing button on the WordArt toolbar, as shown in Figure 17-15. The WordArt Character Spacing drop-down menu lets you specify whether you want to set character spacing as Very Tight, Tight, Normal, Loose, Very Loose, or Custom. In addition, you can turn on or off the Kerning Character Pairs option to suit your preferences.

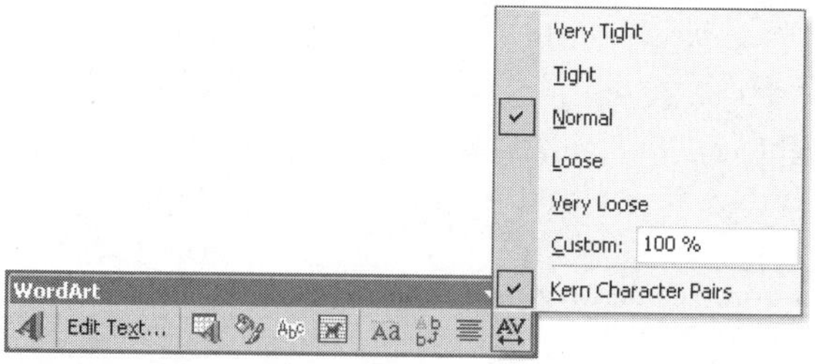

Figure 17-15. The WordArt Character Spacing drop-down menu provides options for expanding or condensing WordArt text.

Troubleshooting

Formatting Applies to the Entire WordArt Object, but I Want to Format Only Part of the Object

Nicely enough, Word provides numerous formatting options when it comes to customizing WordArt objects, but one drawback sticks out like a sore thumb—WordArt formatting options almost always apply to the entire WordArt object. If you want to format various parts of a WordArt object differently, you have to get a little creative. Specifically, you have to create separate pieces of WordArt, format the pieces as individual objects, and then group the objects together. You can accomplish this in two ways: by using the Grouping option, or by using the drawing canvas.

To use the Grouping option, create two or more WordArt objects, apply custom settings, and then group the WordArt objects as follows:

1. Verify that the objects aren't configured as inline objects. (To do so, click the Text wrapping button on the WordArt toolbar, and confirm that an option other than In Line With Text is selected.)
2. Drag the objects to where you want them to appear relative to each other.
3. Select all the objects (by pressing Ctrl and clicking each object).
4. Right-click the selected objects, and choose Grouping, Group on the shortcut menu.

When you choose the Group command, the WordArt objects are stored as a group. If you need to modify any portion of the WordArt grouping, right-click the grouped object, and choose Grouping, Ungroup on the shortcut menu.

To use the drawing canvas to combine custom WordArt objects, follow these steps:

1. Position the insertion point where you want to create the object, and then choose Insert, Picture, New Drawing to insert a drawing canvas.
2. Create and configure as many WordArt objects as necessary in the drawing canvas area. (Notice that the Drawing toolbar includes a WordArt button.)
3. Position your WordArt objects where you want them to appear relative to each other.

As an added bonus, when you use the drawing canvas to combine WordArt objects, you can include any other drawing elements in your graphic as well.

For more information about using the drawing canvas, see Chapter 16, "Enlivening Documents with Drawings and AutoShapes."

Formatting WordArt for Web Pages

Web page creation has introduced an entire new genre of word processing, and Word offers a number of Web-friendly features. Among the plethora of Word features, WordArt seems to be a natural fit for creating Web page components. In fact, WordArt can be customized using a couple of Web-specific options. In particular, you can add *alternative text* (usually referred to as *ALT text* by Web designers) to WordArt, and you can format WordArt objects as hyperlinks. The next two sections describe these two basic Web formatting options.

For more information about creating Web pages in Word, see Chapter 31, "Creating Professional Web Sites."

Adding ALT Text to WordArt for Web Page Use

ALT text is text that is displayed on Web pages in place of graphics if a user has graphics capabilities turned off or if the user is using a text-only browser. ALT text is also displayed while graphics are loading (to give users a hint about the graphic before it loads) and when users hover the mouse pointer over a graphic. Basically, ALT text helps users identify the purpose of a Web page graphic. To add ALT text to a WordArt object, follow these steps:

1. Select the WordArt object, and click the Format WordArt button on the WordArt toolbar, or right-click the WordArt object, and choose Format WordArt on the shortcut menu.

2. In the Format WordArt dialog box, click the Web tab. By default, the WordArt text is displayed as the ALT text, as shown in Figure 17-16.

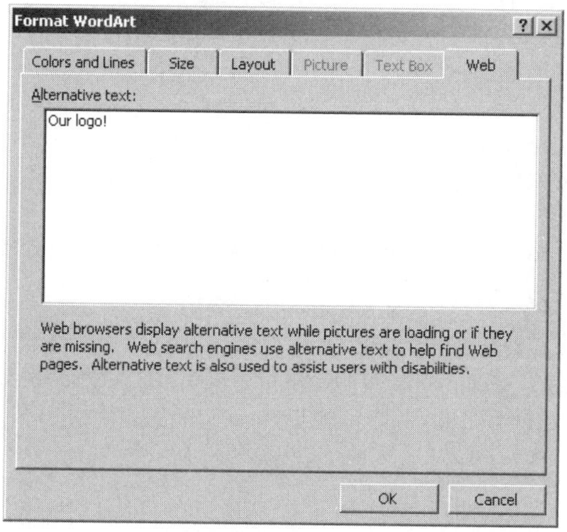

Figure 17-16. The Web tab in the Format WordArt dialog box is used to set the ALT text displayed for a WordArt object.

3 To change the ALT text (by default, the ALT text is the same as the WordArt text), select the existing ALT text, type the text you want to associate with your WordArt object, and then click OK.

When your WordArt is displayed as part of a Web page, the ALT text will be displayed in place of your graphic as the graphic downloads and whenever users opt to hide graphics or use a text-only browser.

Formatting WordArt as a Hyperlink

Another Web-related way in which you can configure a WordArt object is to format the object as a hyperlink. Often, graphics (and remember, graphical text is fundamentally the same as a graphic) also serve as Web page hyperlinks. When you use WordArt on a Web page, you're basically inserting a graphic in your page. You might want to convert your WordArt object to a hyperlink for a number of reasons. For example, you might want to use a WordArt object as a button that links to a subpage, or you might want to use WordArt to create a linked logo image that users can click to return to your home page.

Configuring WordArt as a hyperlink is done using the same procedure as adding a hyperlink to other graphics or objects. To link a WordArt object, follow these steps:

1 Select the WordArt object, and click the Hyperlink button on the Standard toolbar, or right-click a WordArt object, and choose Hyperlink on the shortcut menu. The Insert Hyperlink dialog box opens, as shown in Figure 17-17.

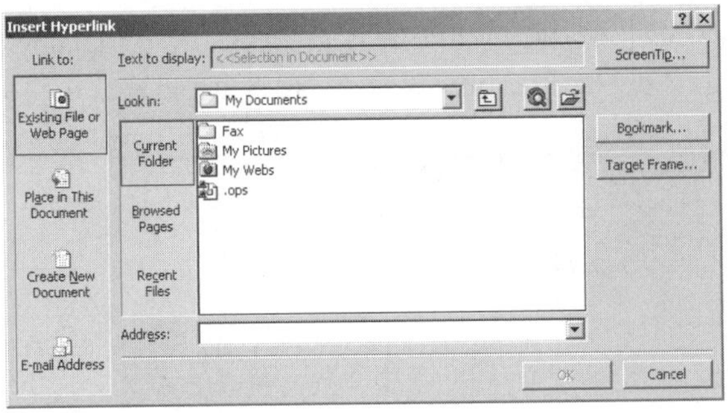

Figure 17-17. The Insert Hyperlink dialog box enables you to format a WordArt object as a hyperlink.

2 In the Insert Hyperlink dialog box, specify the type of link you want to create in the Link To list. You can link to an existing file, another place in the current document, a new file, or an e-mail address. Then insert the link's address by navigating to a file or typing the address in the box.

Using linked WordArt, you can easily add clickable banners, logos, buttons, and icons to your online documents.

Part 4

Clarifying Concepts with Tables, Charts, and Diagrams

Chapter 18

Organizing Concepts in Tables

Not everybody has an organized mind. Just look around your office—how many people do you know who have "a place for everything, and everything in its place"? For those times when words need to be organized into columns and rows, when concepts can be made clearer with comparison and contrast, Word's powerful table features really come in handy.

Word might surprise you with the flexibility it offers when it comes to creating tables. You can use the left-brained approach—planning your table, choosing the right number of columns and rows, and designing it to an exact specification—or you can use the right-brained approach—just click the Draw Table button on the Tables And Borders toolbar and draw what you want on the page.

Whichever table generation method suits your style best, Word complements the table-creating basics with a wealth of special table features. You'll be able to apply styles to give your tables a professional look; search for and sort table information according to your specifications; easily add, delete, and reorder rows and columns; drag table data; create your own custom styles; and much more. This chapter sprints you through the basics and spends some time on features you can use to really make your Word documents stand out.

Creating Effective Tables

Half the battle in creating a logical, usable table is in the planning. What do you want to show in table form? What will your readers be looking for, and how can you best organize that data to help them find what they need? Here are some additional questions to ask as you're thinking out the table you're going to create:

- Do you need to create the table in a limited space in your document?
- How many rows and columns will you need?
- Will the table content include text, numbers, or both?
- Will you use functions for totaling and averaging columns?
- Will you have similar tables in your document?
- Will you use a predesigned table style or create your own?

Knowing ahead of time what you want to create helps you get a "big picture" of the resulting table. Throughout this chapter, you'll find the necessary procedures for creating tables with each of these characteristics.

Creating a Simple Table

Word gives you several different ways to create a table, and a full set of tools to use after the creation is done. Table 18-1 describes the various options for table creation. The easiest way to create a simple table is to use the Insert Table button on the Standard toolbar. Here are the steps:

1. Place the insertion point where you want to create the table in your document.
2. Click the Insert Table button on the Standard toolbar. A drop-down menu displays a grid of rows and columns.
3. Drag the mouse pointer down and to the right until you've highlighted the number of rows and columns you want to create. (See Figure 18-1.)

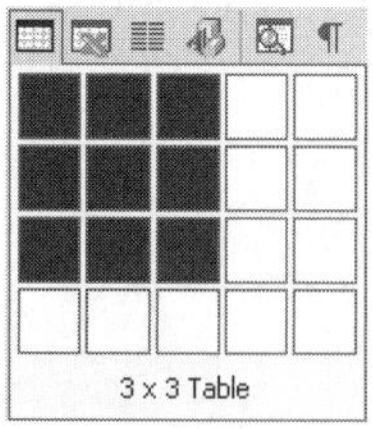

Figure 18-1. Select the number of rows and columns by highlighting them in the Insert Table drop-down menu.

4 When you have highlighted the number of cells you want to create, release the mouse button. The resulting table is placed at the insertion point. (See Figure 18-2.)

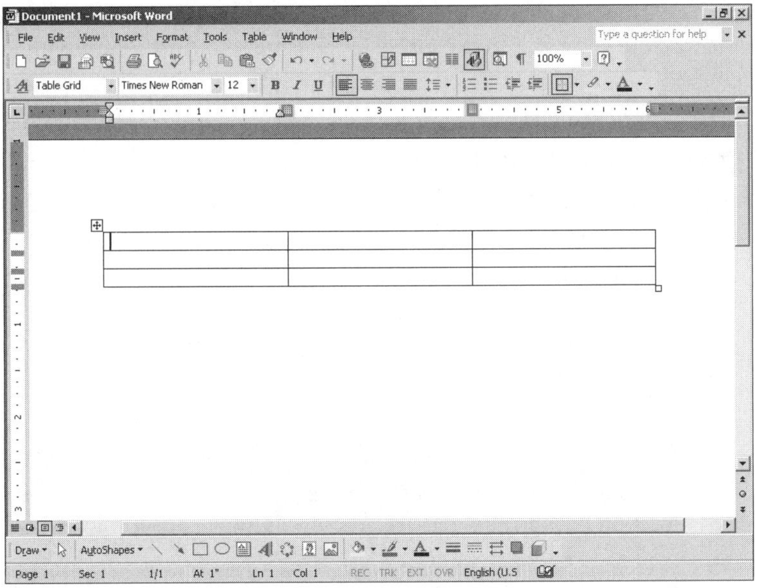

Figure 18-2. The table created with the Insert Table button on the Standard toolbar is uniform in size and shape.

Table 18-1. Comparing Table Creation Approaches

Method	Description	Use
 Insert Table	Displays a drop-down menu so that you can choose the number or rows and columns	You want to enter a simple table that spans the width of the current column.
Choose Table, Draw Table or click the Tables And Borders Toolbar button on the Standard toolbar	Gives you a drawing tool with which you can draw the table, including rows and columns, on the page	You want to draw a table "freehand" and create a table of a table of a particular size, customizing row and column widths and heights.
Choose Table, Insert, Table	Displays the Insert Table dialog box so that you can enter specific table values	You want to create a table to a particular specification, including the number of rows and columns and the fit of table entries.

Chapter 18

Drawing a Table Freehand

If you prefer to draw tables as you go rather than relying on menus and tools, you can choose Table, Draw Table or click the Table And Borders button on the Standard toolbar. This tool enables you to take an electronic pencil of sorts and draw the table the way you want it. You can also add lines for rows and columns and make editing changes while you work.

> **tip** **Create special table effects easily**
>
> Using Word's Draw Table feature, you can create uneven rows and columns, remove line segments in areas of your table you want to open up, and control borders and shading, all with the click of the mouse.

To draw a table in your Word document, follow these steps:

1. Place the insertion point where you want to create the table.

Tables And Borders

2. Click the Tables And Borders button. The pointer changes to a pencil tool and the Tables And Borders toolbar appears. Table 18-2 describes the various tools on this toolbar.
3. Drag the pointer down and to the right to draw the table. You can create the table to the exact size and specification you want, using the horizontal and vertical rulers as a guide, or you can later resize the table by dragging a corner. Release the mouse button when you're finished.

> **tip** **Wrap text automatically**
>
> If you want to create a table in the middle of a text section and have the text automatically wrap around it, press Ctrl while you draw the table.

4. Use the mouse pointer to draw rows and columns. Word adds the straight line as you draw. Figure 18-3, on page 444, shows a table created with the Draw Table tool. Both rows and columns have been added.

> **tip** **Use the eraser**
>
> 
>
> Eraser
>
> If you don't want a segment of a line to extend all the way across the table (you might want to underline only the totals columns in a table, for example), you can erase the pieces of the line you don't want. Simply click the Eraser button and click the line segment you want to erase.

Table 18-2. Buttons on the Tables And Borders Toolbar

Button	Name	Description
	Draw Table	Enables you to draw a table freehand
	Eraser	Erases line segments you don't want
Border Style	Line Style	Displays choices for the style of the table border line
Border Width	Line Weight	Sets the width of the border line
	Border Color	Displays choices for the color of the border line
	Outside Border	Enables you to choose whether (and how) you want to border the table
	Shading Color	Displays shade color choices for selected cells
	Insert Table	Displays the Insert Table dialog box
	Merge Cells	Merges cells together in a specified segment
	Split Cells	Splits selected cell into individual cells
	Cell Alignment	Lets you choose the alignment for data in cell entries
	Distribute Rows Evenly	Arranges data evenly within a row
	Distribute Columns Evenly	Arranges data evenly within a column
	Table AutoFormat	Displays the Table AutoFormat dialog box so that you can choose a predesigned table format or create your own
	Change Text Direction	Rotates text in the selected cell
	Sort Ascending	Sorts selected cells in ascending (A to Z) order
	Sort Descending	Sorts selected cells in descending (Z to A) order
	AutoSum	Totals the values in the cells in the corresponding row or column and places the result in the current cell

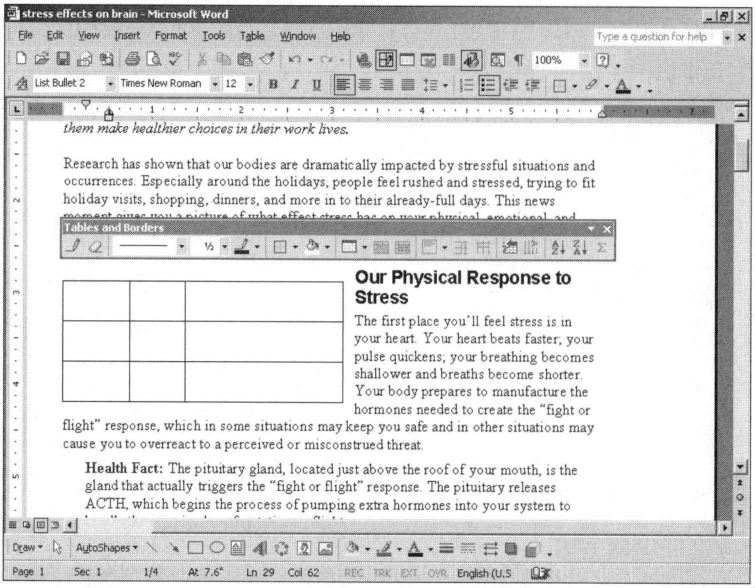

Figure 18-3. You can draw a table at any point in your document using the Draw Table tool.

> **tip** **Move or delete a line**
>
> If you don't like where you just drew a line in your table, you have one of two options: You can press Ctrl+Z to delete the line, or you can close the Tables And Borders toolbar and position the text cursor over the line. The pointer changes to a double-headed arrow. You can now click the line and drag it to where you wanted it in the first place.

Setting Rows and Columns

If drawing a table freehand is too free-wheeling an approach for you, you can use the Insert Table dialog box to set up the table the way you want it. Use this method when you want to create a table to precise dimensions, with a set number of rows and columns. Follow these steps:

1. Place the insertion point where you want to begin the table.
2. Choose Table, Insert, Table. The Insert Table dialog box appears, as Figure 18-4 shows.
3. Enter the number of columns and rows you want to create in the table.
4. Choose the AutoFit Behavior option that best suits your needs.

You can apply a predesigned style to your table by using Table AutoFormat. For more information see "Producing a Finished Table with AutoFormat," on page 455.

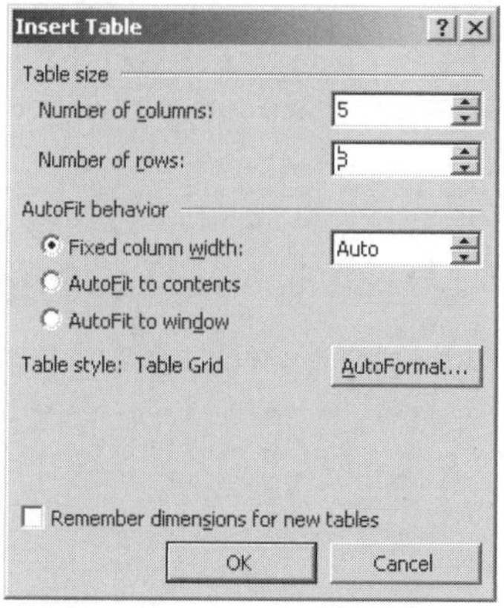

Figure 18-4. The Insert Table dialog box enables you to plan the table first by choosing the number of columns and rows, the fit behavior, and the predesigned format used, if any.

tip **Apply table dimensions across the board**

If you want Word to apply the table selections you make in the Insert Table dialog box to other new tables you create in the current document, select the Remember Dimensions For New Tables check box.

Entering Table Data

Getting the data into the table is the easy part. You might enter data by hand, copy it from a Microsoft Excel spreadsheet, drag it from another table, or import it from a text-delimited file. To add data by hand, simply click in the cell in which you want to add data and type. Move to the next cell by pressing the Right Arrow key, if there's no data in the cell, or by pressing Tab. To move back to a previous cell, press the Left Arrow key or Shift+Tab.

newfeature!

Now in Word 2002, you can copy tables and table data by using the drag-and-drop technique. If you want to copy an entire table, simply click the table move handle in the upper left corner of the selected table, press Ctrl, and drag to the new location. (If you don't press Ctrl while you drag, the entire table will be moved, not copied.)

Troubleshooting

Drag-and-Drop Technique Doesn't Work

If you've been trying to drag-and-drop text from one place to another in your document and find that it doesn't work, check to make sure you've got the feature enabled. To find out, follow these steps:

1. Choose Tools, Options.
2. Click the Edit tab, and select the Drag-And-Drop Text Editing check box.

This activates the feature, and you should be able to drag-and-drop items as needed.

Editing Tables

Getting the data into table form is only half the battle. Once you get your data entered, you'll no doubt want to reorganize, edit, add to, and delete some of it. That means adding rows and columns, perhaps moving the rows you've already got, and deleting others. You might decide to rearrange the order of columns, which means moving data from one side of the table to the other. That's where Word's formatting features come in.

Displaying Table Formatting Marks

One of the secrets in moving and editing table data successfully lies in seeing the unseen. Each table cell, row, and column is given a marker that delineates the end of the items in the table format. When you move, copy, or paste information, those unseen markers might go along, giving you unexpected results at best, or overwriting your existing data at worst. To display the hidden marks in your current Word table, select it by clicking the table move handle and then click Show/Hide on the Standard toolbar. The various table formatting marks appear, as shown in Figure 18-5.

Selecting Table Cells

To move and copy rows, columns, and cells, you start simply by selecting them to let Word know which data you want to work with. As you get comfortable working with tables, you'll discover the tricks to selecting just the data you want for various operations. Table 18-3 lists selection methods you'll use in working with tables.

newfeature!

tip **Use multiple table selections**

In Word 2002, you can select noncontiguous sections of a table by pressing and holding Ctrl while you click additional selections. In a product listing, for example, this capability enables you to choose only the products that will be included in the 2002 catalog and copy them to a new table, leaving all the 2001 offerings behind.

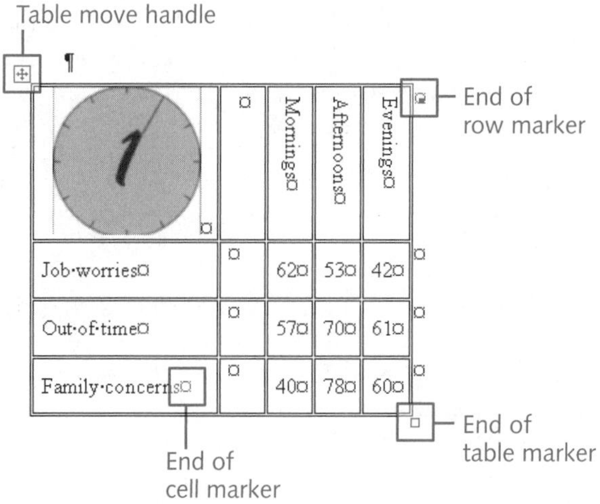

Figure 18-5. Table Formatting Marks identify the end of individual cells, rows, columns, and the table itself.

Table 18-3. Selecting Table Segments

Selection	Method	Use
Entire table	Click the table, and click the table move handle that appears in the upper left corner of the table.	You want to move, copy, format, or delete an entire table.
Single row	Click outside the table to the left of the row.	You want to reorder, format, copy, move, insert, or delete a row.
Single column	Click outside the table just above the column.	You want to move, format, copy, insert, or delete a column.
Single cell	Click to the left of any data entered in the cell.	You want to move, copy, delete, or clear that cell.
Multiple cells, rows, or columns	Drag across the elements you want to select.	You want to move, format, copy, or delete sections of a table.

Copying Table Data

Although copying is basically a simple operation, copying table data can be a pain. The data can sometimes go where you don't expect it; for example, if you want to copy all the information into one cell in the new table, the data might instead be spread over the entire row, replacing existing data. If you want to copy multiple cells to multiple cells in the new table, the incoming cells might all be lumped into the cell at the insertion point. How do you avoid these kinds of copy surprises?

First, know what you're copying. The trick is to select cell data if you want to copy cell data; to select cells themselves (or rows, or columns) if that's what you want to copy. By capturing the table formatting marks when you highlight the section you want to copy, you can be sure you get the results you expect.

Next, know where you're copying to. If you are copying a row or a column, make sure you've allowed enough room for the incoming data so important entries won't be overwritten and lost.

newfeature!

Once you've selected what you want to copy and you've planned the copy destination, press Ctrl+C to copy and Ctrl+V to paste, as usual. You can also use the new, improved Clipboard by choosing Edit, Office Clipboard. You can select the copied items in the Clipboard task pane and paste as needed.

Inserting Columns

You can expand and add to your table easily. One way to do this is by adding new columns. You have two different ways to add columns to the right or left of an existing column. One method causes Word to reconfigure the width of the existing columns, so the width of the overall table is no wider than it was before you inserted a column. The other method keeps the widths of existing columns and widens the table by the width of the new column.

To add a new column in your table, select the column beside which you want to create the new column. To select the entire column, click on the top border of the column. When the column is selected, the Insert Table button on the Standard toolbar changes to the Insert Column button. Click the button to add the new column. If your table is already the width of the text column, the column is added without the table widening. If your table is narrower than the text margins allow, the column is inserted and the columns to the right of the column move to make room.

tip **Choose right or left, above or below**

The buttons on the Standard toolbar don't give you quite the flexibility that menu commands do. Here's an example: By default, Word inserts columns to the left of the selected column and rows above the selected row. If you use the Insert Column button to add a column to your table, you must accept this default. However, if you choose Table, Insert and then select Columns To The Right or Rows Below, you can tell Word exactly where to insert a column or row.

Inserting Rows

Insert Rows Above

Insert Rows Below

Inserting rows is similar to inserting columns. Begin by selecting the row below which you want to insert a new row. Select the entire row by clicking to the left of the first cell of the row. The entire row is highlighted.

Click the Insert Rows button on the Standard toolbar (this button replaces the Insert Table button when a row is selected). Word inserts the new row just above the currently selected row.

tip **Insert multiple rows and columns**

If you want to insert more than one row or column, select the number of rows or columns you want to add. For example, if you want to insert three rows, select three rows in the current table before choosing the commands necessary to add the rows.

Inserting Cells

Insert Cells

In some circumstances, you might want to insert cells in a table without adding an entire row or column. You might do this, for example, when you overlooked a product name and number in your listing and need to add it without changing the entire table. To insert cells in a table, follow these steps:

1. Select the cell (or cells) below which you want to insert new cells.
2. Choose Table, Insert, Cells. The Insert Cells dialog box appears, as shown in Figure 18-6.
3. Click Shift Cells Down to place the new cells above the selected cells. Click Shift Cells Right if you want to move the existing cells to the right to make room for the new cells.
4. Click OK to insert the cells. The cells are added and the existing cells are moved as specified.

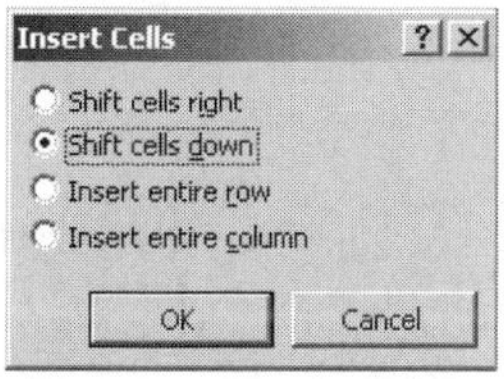

Figure 18-6. You can insert individual cells or groups of cells without moving an entire row or column.

Deleting Columns and Rows

Delete Cells

If you decide that you don't need certain rows or columns after all, or you have empty rows you didn't use, you can easily delete them. Simply highlight the rows or columns, choose Table, Delete, and choose what you want to delete from the Delete submenu.

When you choose to delete cells in a table, Word displays the Delete Cells dialog box (similar to the Insert Cells dialog box shown in Figure 18-6) so that you can identify where you want remaining cells to be shifted. Click your selection, and click OK to return to the document.

Moving Rows and Columns

In some instances, you might want to select parts of your table and move them to other parts of your document, perhaps creating a new table, moving rows to another position in the table, or turning the table information into text. When you want to move rows or columns, simply select the rows or columns you want to move and drag the selected block to the new location. The table rows (or columns) are moved as you selected.

Merging Cells

Sometimes tables seem to grow out of proportion. If this has happened to your table and you're looking for a way to consolidate data, you can use Word's Merge Cells command to take data from separate cells and combine it in one cell. To merge cells in your table, select the rows or columns you want to merge and choose Table, Merge Cells. The data is combined. Figure 18-7 shows an example of a table in which the first two columns, Item Number and Title, have been combined in a single cell in a single column.

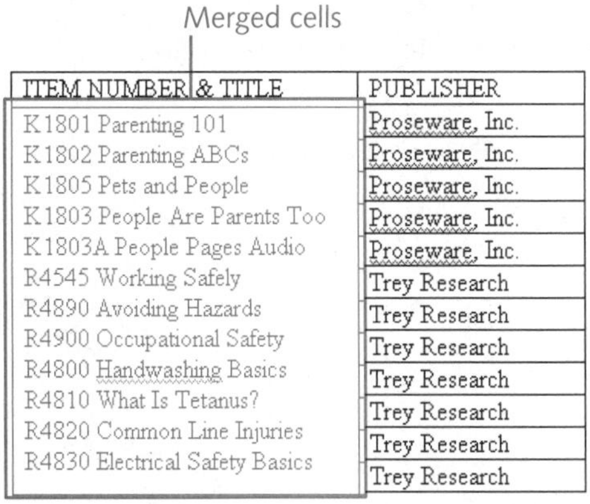

ITEM NUMBER & TITLE	PUBLISHER
K1801 Parenting 101 K1802 Parenting ABCs K1805 Pets and People K1803 People Are Parents Too K1803A People Pages Audio R4545 Working Safely R4890 Avoiding Hazards R4900 Occupational Safety R4800 Handwashing Basics R4810 What Is Tetanus? R4820 Common Line Injuries R4830 Electrical Safety Basics	Proseware, Inc. Proseware, Inc. Proseware, Inc. Proseware, Inc. Proseware, Inc. Trey Research Trey Research Trey Research Trey Research Trey Research Trey Research Trey Research

Figure 18-7. Merging cells puts separate cells together in a single cell, row, or column.

note You'll probably need to do some editing to get your data looking the way you want after a merge. Data takes on the format of the receiving cell, and you might wind up with extra lines and odd capitalization as a result.

Splitting Cells

As you might imagine, splitting cells is the opposite of merging them. When you've got a collection of data that you want to divide into separate cells, rows, or columns, you can use the Split Cells button on the Tables And Borders toolbar (or the Split Cells command on the Table menu). To split cells, follow these steps:

1. Select the cells, row, or column you want to split.
2. Click the Split Cells button on the Tables And Borders toolbar. The Split Cells dialog box appears, as Figure 18-8 shows.

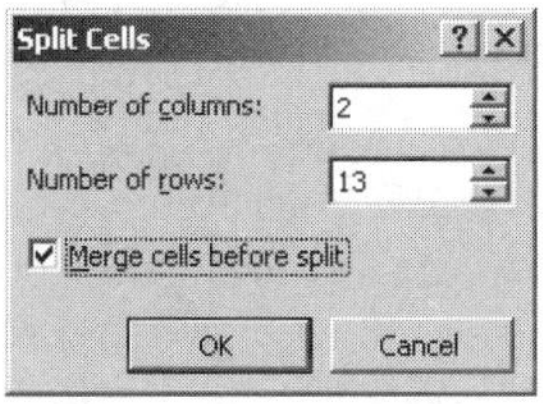

Figure 18-8. Splitting cells divides data into separate cells, rows, or columns.

3. Enter the number of columns and rows over which you want to divide the data.

   If you have previously merged the data you are now splitting, Word "remembers" the number of columns and rows and suggests those values for the division.

4. To retain the basic format and apply existing row and column formatting to the new columns and rows, leave the Merge Cells Before Split check box selected.
5. Click OK to split the cells.

tip **Adjust column sizes**

After you split cells in your table, you'll probably need to redistribute the space in the columns. To resize a column quickly, point to the column border in the top row of the column you want to change. When the pointer changes to a double-headed arrow, drag the column border in the direction you want to resize the column. When the column is the size you want it, release the mouse button.

Resizing Tables

You won't always know how large a table is going to be when you first begin creating it. Word provides options for helping you control the size of your table and offers flexibility for resizing your table exactly the way you want. This section explains how you can work with Word to best handle table-sizing issues.

Understanding AutoFit

When you first create a table using the Insert Table dialog box, you're given the option of choosing AutoFit for your table. AutoFit enables you to automatically resize your window as needed, and it is already working, by default, to create fixed column widths in your table. AutoFit offers three options:

- **Fixed Column Width** enables you to choose a specific width for the columns you create.
- **AutoFit To Contents** adjusts the width of columns to accommodate the data you enter.
- **AutoFit To Window** sizes a table so that it fits within a Web browser window. This size changes depending on the size of the window, which means that the table will be automatically redrawn many times as the user resizes his or her browser window.

tip **Test AutoFit To Window**

If you want to see how resizing your table will affect the rest of the text displayed in your document, you can easily test AutoFit To Window by creating your table, choosing AutoFit To Window (you can do this before you create the table or after the fact), and then displaying the table in Web Layout view. When the table is displayed, resize your document window. The table is automatically reformatted so that it always fits within the borders of the window.

Resizing an Entire Table

Although AutoFit does a fine job of keeping on top of the way your table needs to grow (or shrink), there will be times when you want to make those changes yourself. Resizing a table is a simple matter of click-and-drag editing. Start by selecting the table (click the table move handle). Then follow these steps:

1. Scroll to the end of the table. In the lower right corner, you see a table resize handle.

2. Position the pointer over the table resize handle. The pointer changes to a double-headed arrow.
3. Drag the corner of the table in the direction you want the table to be resized. The cells of the table are redrawn to reflect the new size.

note You can resize tables only in Print Layout and Web Layout views. Although you can see a table in Normal view, the table resize handle is not available.

Setting Preset and Percent Table Sizes

The Table Properties dialog box gives you two very different sizing options. To open this dialog box, click in the table and choose Table, Table Properties. To create a table based on a fixed measurement, click the Table tab, and in the Size section, select the Preferred Width check box and enter the width for the table you're going to create. Click the Measured In down arrow and select Inches; then click OK.

The best use of this feature, however, is in creating a table that reformats automatically based on the size of the browser window. This means if you're viewing your table in a Web page, and you reduce the size of your browser window, the table will reformat so that it will stay visible, even in the smaller window. This is a great feature if you're often switching back and forth between applications and want to keep your information open on the screen. To create a changing Web table that's based on a percentage of screen display, click the Measure In down arrow, select Percent, and then click OK. The table will be reformatted as needed to stay within the size of the Web browser window.

Changing Column Width

The fastest way to change the width of a column is also the easiest. You simply position the pointer over the dividing line of the column you want to change and, when the pointer changes to a double-headed arrow, drag the border in the direction you want. Be sure that you've grabbed the border for the entire column, however; it's possible to move the border for a single cell, which won't help if you want to make an entire column wider or narrower. (You'll be able to tell that you've "grabbed" the entire column when you see the dotted column guide along the length of the table.)

Changing Row Height

Changing row height is similar to changing column width. Position the pointer on the row border you want to change. When the pointer changes to a double-headed arrow, drag the border in the direction you want to change the height.

> **tip** **Add space to table rows**
>
> We don't need statistics to tell us that nobody wants to read a cramped table. You can help the readers of your document get your point more easily by providing enough space in your table rows. By default, Word is a bit skimpy on row height (less than a quarter of an inch); you might want to increase your rows to at least 0.25 if the space in your document allows.

Distributing Data Evenly in Rows and Columns

Distributing your data refers to the process of spacing and aligning data within cells. By default, when you create a basic table and enter text, the text aligns along the left border of the cell, placed in the first line of the cell. To distribute your data evenly in the row (which spaces it evenly between the top and bottom margins of the row), click the Distribute Rows Evenly button on the Tables And Borders toolbar.

To distribute the data evenly among the columns in your table, click Distribute Columns Evenly. See Figure 18-9 for an example.

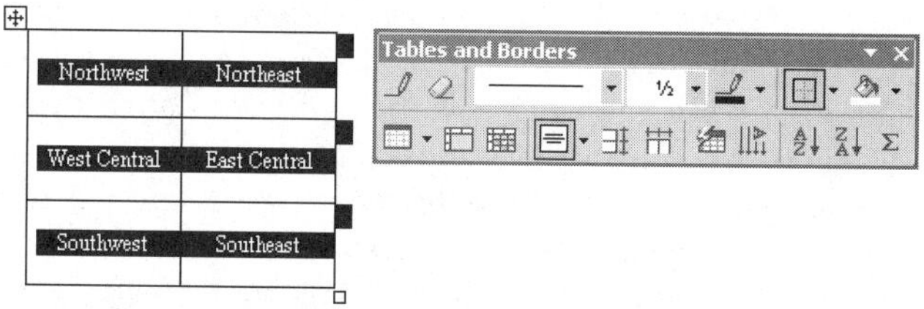

Figure 18-9. Data is distributed evenly among columns and rows in the selected table.

Changing Text Direction

While we're talking about distributing data, how about rotating the text in your table cells? Word provides a capability that enables you to turn your horizontal text to the vertical, which gives you the means to create interesting column headings for your tables.

You can change the direction of your text whether you've already entered table cell data or you're just beginning to add data to your table. If you're changing the direction of existing text, select the text, and then click the Change Text Direction button on the Tables And Borders toolbar. Clicking this button rotates the text 90 degrees to the left. The vertical column headings in the table in Figure 18-10 were created using this button.

If you want to change the direction yet again, click Change Text Direction a second time. Now the text rotates a further 180 degrees, so that it faces the other edge of the table. Click the button again, and the text returns to normal. If you're setting the direction for the text you are about to enter, simply click the button and then type your text.

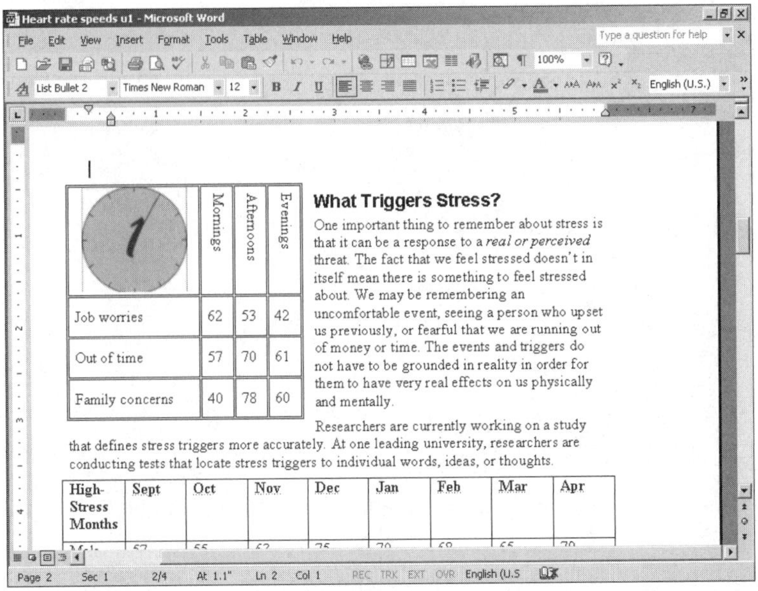

Figure 18-10. The column headings in this table have been rotated 90 degrees.

newfeature!

Enhancing Your Tables with Formatting

Tables come in all shapes and sizes—from simple to sophisticated. Word includes a number of formatting features you can apply to your tables to give them just the look you want. Word now supports custom table styles, which means you can create your own Table AutoFormats from scratch or modify existing formats to meet your needs. In this section, you'll also find out about creating borders, adding shading, and using table colors.

Producing a Finished Table with AutoFormat

Word's Table AutoFormat feature gives you a library of different formats you can apply to your tables. When you want to create a table in a hurry, you can rely on Word's Table AutoFormat to give you the look you want—you can then just plug in the data. Or, if you've already created a basic table, as discussed in the first half of this chapter, you can apply an AutoFormat to the table you've already begun. To apply an AutoFormat to a table you've created, follow these steps:

1. Click in the table you want to AutoFormat.
2. Choose Table, Table AutoFormat. The Table AutoFormat dialog box appears, as Figure 18-11, on the next page, shows.

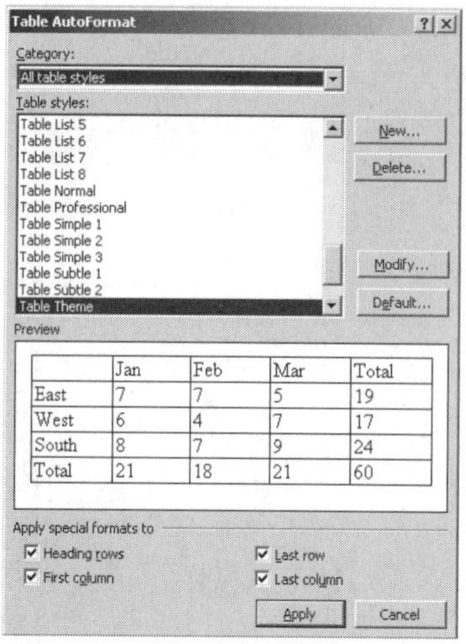

Figure 18-11. Table AutoFormat enables you to apply predesigned table styles to your tables.

3. Scroll through the formats in the Table Styles list to find the one you want. Notice that some formats lend themselves more to the display of numeric data than to straight text. You can modify any of the settings used in a Table AutoFormat style.
4. Click OK to close the Table AutoFormat dialog box and apply the selected style.

In the Table AutoFormat dialog box, you have the option of disabling any of the special features Table AutoFormat applies that you *don't* want to use. You can select the Heading Rows, First Column, Last Row, and Last Column check boxes if you want the entire table to be formatted in a uniform fashion.

tip **Select a default table style**

If you want to choose a particular Table AutoFormat as the default table style for your document, click it in the Table Styles list and click Default. Word displays the Default Table Style dialog box, asking whether you want to make this style the default style for this document only or for all documents based on the Normal template. Click your choice, and click OK.

AutoFormatting a New Table

If you want to start right off the bat using AutoFormat to set up a new table, you can do so by clicking Insert Table on the Tables And Borders toolbar. The Insert Table dialog box appears. Enter the number of columns and rows you want to create; then click the AutoFormat button. This action takes you to the Table AutoFormat dialog box, where you can choose the style you like.

Modifying an Existing Table AutoFormat

Once you get used to working with Table AutoFormats, you might discover that you like some styles more than others. Perhaps you like light shading behind columns but find it distracting in heading rows. You might prefer one color to another, or perhaps a certain font really goes with the standard design of your business documents.

You can modify an existing AutoFormat to create a new style that accommodates the settings you like best. Here are the steps:

1. Click in the table that's been formatted with the Table AutoFormat style you want to enhance.
2. Choose Table, Table AutoFormat. The Table AutoFormat dialog box appears. The current AutoFormat style is selected in the Table Styles list.
3. Click Modify. The Modify Style dialog box appears. (See Figure 18-12.)

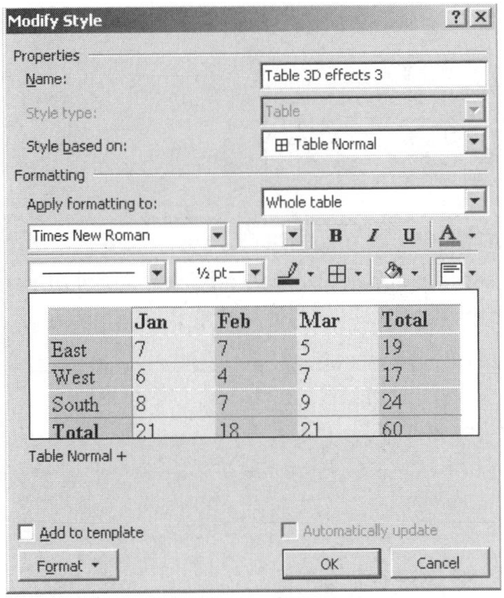

Figure 18-12. You can modify an existing Table AutoFormat style to create a unique table style.

4. Enter a name for the new table style.

> **tip** Name any new styles you create in such a way that you'll be able to identify the style later. For example, you might name a new shaded table BlueShade1 if that will help you remember what's unique about that style.

5 By default, the table style already applied to the table (if applicable) is shown in the Style Based On drop-down list. Click the down arrow and choose a different style if you want to change the format the new style is based on.

6 In the Formatting section, choose the item you want to modify.

tip For those times when you want to modify only a single element of the table format (for example, removing the bold from the last row in the table), choose just the item you want to change, select the new format settings, and click OK.

7 Make your formatting changes in the Modify Style dialog box. (See Figure 18-13.) When you're finished, click OK to return to the Table Auto-Format dialog box and then click Close to return to the document. Your changes will be reflected in the table.

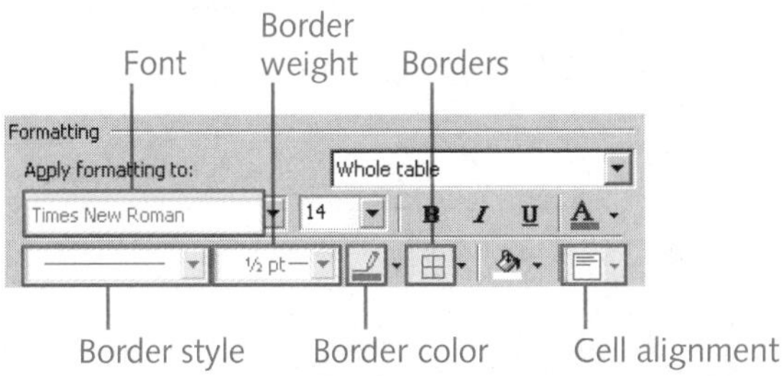

Figure 18-13. Enter settings for your modified Table AutoFormat style in the Formatting section of the Modify Style dialog box.

tip If you want to add the new Table AutoFormat style you create to the template for this document, select the Add To Template check box.

Creating Your Own Table Style

The process of modifying an existing Table AutoFormat isn't too different from creating your own from scratch. To create your own AutoFormat table style, click the Table AutoFormat button on the Tables And Borders toolbar to display the dialog box; then click the New button. The New Style dialog box appears, and it contains all the same choices you worked with in the Modify Style dialog box (refer to Figure 18-12).

Adding Borders and Shading

Borders and shading are two of those fun Word features in which the caveat "a little goes a long way" is particularly meaningful. Think carefully about how and why you'll use borders, shading, and colors, and then create the table effect to match your thoughtful vision.

Using Borders: Do's and Don'ts

Applying borders to your documents isn't rocket science, of course. But by following these simple guides, you can make sure your use of borders is a help to your readers rather than a hindrance:

Do

- Use a border to set a table off from surrounding text.
- Create a type of border that allows the reader's eye a rest.
- Use gridlines when your table includes columns of numbers.

Don't

- Create a heavy, overwhelming border that crowds the text.
- Mix heavy line weights, dark colors, and multi-line styles for traditional documents.
- Use designer lines as a grid in the center of your table.

Choosing Borders

Word provides a number of border styles for your table. When you want to add a border to your table, follow these steps:

1. Click in the table (anywhere in the table will do).
2. Click the Border Color button on the Tables And Borders toolbar. The Borders And Shading dialog box appears, as Figure 18-14, on the next page, shows.
3. Select the Setting type you want to use. Word offers five different choices:
   - **None** doesn't apply a border to the table.
   - **Box** draws a boundary around the table.
   - **All** includes an outer border and an internal grid between table cells and applies a shadow format and current style and width settings to the table.

- **Grid** creates a three-dimensional effect with an internal grid.
- **Custom** enables you to create a custom border, using the settings you select in the Preview section. You might, for example, elect to have only top and bottom borders for your table and forgo any side boundaries or gridlines.

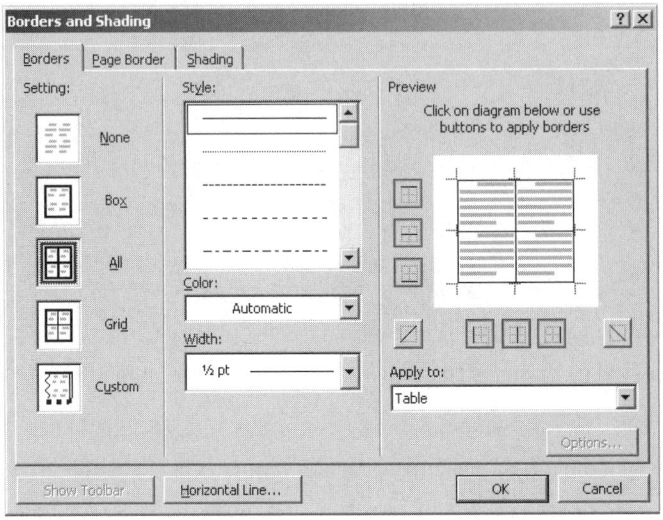

Figure 18-14. Choose from a number of preset border styles in the Borders And Shading dialog box.

4 Choose the style for the line used in the border. You can scroll through the Style list to find and select the line style you want.

5 Click the Color down arrow to locate and select the color you want to use for the border.

6 Click the Width down arrow, and select your choice of width.

7 If you want to customize the display of the selected border by adding or removing border edges, click your selections in the Preview section.

> **tip** If you want to apply a border to a single cell, display the Borders And Shading dialog box and make your selections. Then click the Apply To down arrow, and select Cell.

Selecting Shading

Right behind the Borders and Page Borders tabs in the Borders And Shading dialog box, you'll find the Shading tab. Shading is often used effectively in tables to perform different functions. For example, shading can be used for these purposes:

- Help the reader see a distinction between data types (for example, the column showing last year's revenue might be light gray, while this year's is white).
- Call attention to important data items.
- Enhance design. Table headings and column labels are often placed in shaded bars.

When you want to add shading to your table, you can use either the Borders And Shading dialog box or the Shading Color button on the Tables And Borders toolbar. Here are the steps for using the toolbar:

1. Click in the table you want to shade.

> **note** If you want to apply shading to a selected portion of a table, select those cells (or rows or columns) before opening the Borders And Shading dialog box.

2. Click Tables And Borders on the Standard toolbar to display the Tables And Borders toolbar.
3. Click the Border Color button on the Tables And Borders toolbar.
4. In the Fill section on the Shading tab, click the Fill color you want to apply to the table. The Preview section shows your change.
5. Click the Style down arrow and select a list of percentage shades. These settings control the density (darkness) of the color you chose in step 4.
6. Click OK to return to the table. Your choices are reflected in the updated table.

> **note** If you want to see additional color choices, or enter your own custom color (with RGB percentages), click the More Colors button. This option comes in handy when you need to match a specific hue for professional documents.

You can later change the table color quickly by clicking the Shading Color button on the Tables And Borders toolbar. This displays the Borders And Shading dialog box, and you can make your changes as needed.

Working with Table Properties

Now that you've been through many of these table features on your own—from creating tables to editing, resizing, and formatting them—you can work on some of the finer points of table management. The Table Properties dialog box enables you to make choices about how you want your table to behave—with text in a document and in a browser window on the Web. To display the Table Properties dialog box, click in the table and then choose Table, Table Properties. (See Figure 18-15.)

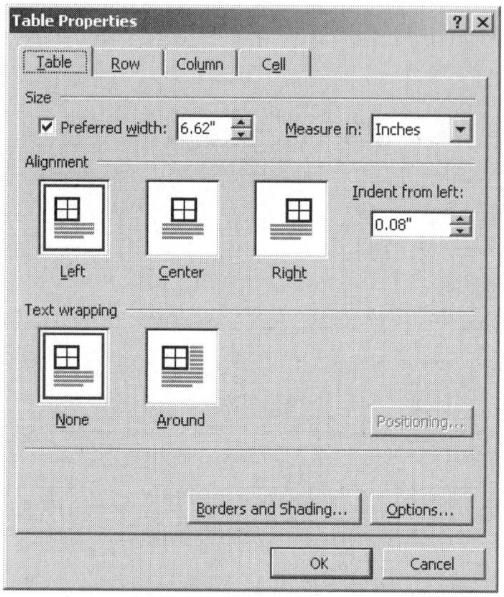

Figure 18-15. The Table Properties dialog box enables you to make sizing and behavior choices for your tables.

Controlling Table Size

In the Table Properties dialog box, the Size options in each of the tabs—Table, Row, Column, and Cell—include the choices you need to set the preferred width or height measurements for each item.

- **Preferred Width** refers to the size at which the item is displayed by default, if space allows.
- **Measure In** determines whether the size is kept to a precise measurement or is figured as a percentage of available display space.

note The Percent option in the Measure In box enables you to create a table that's reformatted to fit the Web page each time a user resizes his or her browser window. Having this kind of flexibility makes your tables that much more effective. Table, Column, and Cell tabs all have the capacity to accept a Percent setting. The Row tab doesn't need the Percent option because that's controlled by the Column settings for the table.

Aligning Tables with Text

The way in which your text aligns with the table you create is controlled on the Table tab in the Table Properties dialog box. You can choose Left, Center, and Right alignment, which act as follows:

- **Left** positions the table along the left text margin.
- **Center** places the table centered between the left and right text margins.
- **Right** aligns the table along the right text margin.

Another option in the Alignment section of the Table tab in the Table Properties dialog box enables you to indent the table from the left margin by a specific increment. The default is set to 0 inch, and you can increase that setting as needed.

Aligning Cells

The Cell tab in the Table Properties dialog box also includes an alignment setting that controls the vertical alignment of data in table cells. This setting enables you to choose the alignment of text within the cell, and it's related to the choices you can make on the Tables And Borders toolbar when you select the Align button.

Controlling Text Wrap

Text wrap becomes a very important consideration when you're working with multiple tables in a long document. On the Table tab in the Table Properties dialog box, you have the option of choosing None, which means text doesn't wrap around text at all but appears above and below it, or Around, which flows text up to and around the table.

When you click Around, the Positioning button becomes available. Click Positioning to make choices that control where the table is positioned in your document by default. (See Figure 18-16, on the next page.)

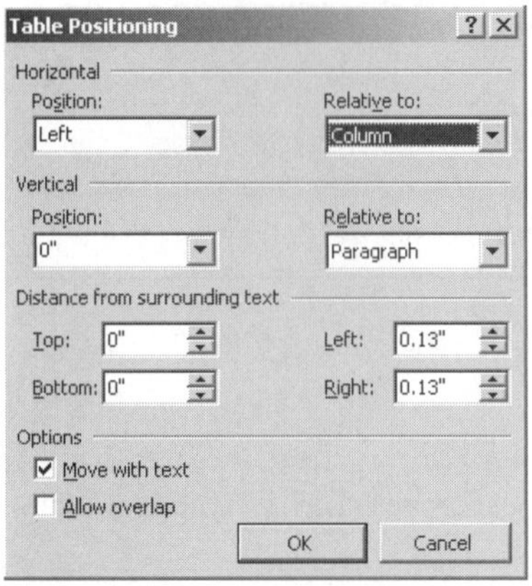

Figure 18-16. The Table Positioning dialog box enables you to control the default table position for your document.

These choices include the following:

- The horizontal and vertical positioning of the table (choose Left, Right, Center, Inside, or Outside)
- The element to which the table position is relative (choose Margin, Page, Column for the horizontal position and Margin, Page, Paragraph for the vertical position)
- The space you want to leave between the table and surrounding text
- Whether you want to allow the text to overlap the table boundary and whether you want the table to stay fixed in place or move with text if it is reformatted

tip Different tables require different settings. Take the time to experiment with the best effects for your particular table.

Controlling Table Breaks

Two options on the Row tab of the Table Properties dialog box control the way in which the table is divided in the event of a section or page break. If you want to allow Word to break the table at a specified point in the table, click the Next Row or Previous Row button to select the row after which you would allow a break. Then select the Allow Row To Break Across Pages check box. (See Figure 18-17.)

If you want to repeat the column headings in the second section of the divided table, select the Repeat As Header Row At The Top Of Each Page check box. This will cause your table heads to be replicated at the beginning of the next table segment.

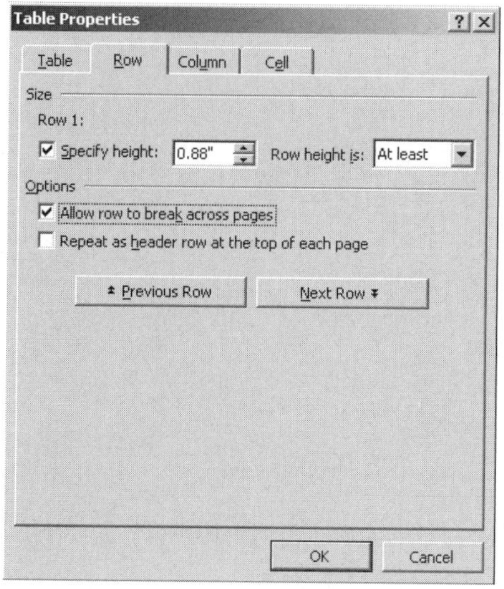

Figure 18-17. Choose whether you want to allow a table to be divided by a page or section break on the Row tab in the Table Properties dialog box.

Sorting Your Table Data

One of the great things about Word tables is that they provide more than a clear way of organizing data—they also give you a means of *reorganizing* data. Because Word includes a Sort function, you can easily reorder the information in your table by searching and sorting on certain key words or phrases.

> newfeature!
> **tip** **Try the beefed-up sort capabilities**
>
> Sort capabilities have been improved in Word 2002. Now you can do a multilevel sort in a single column. For example, you can sort first by last name and then by first name in a single column of data.

The easiest way to sort data in a Word table is to simply click in the table and click Sort Ascending or Sort Descending on the Tables And Borders toolbar. Figure 18-18, on the next page, shows two tables with the same data. The table on the left is sorted in ascending order, and the table on the right is in descending order.

If you want to use Word to do a more specialized sort, you can display the Sort dialog box by clicking in the table and then choosing Table, Sort. The Sort dialog box provides you with the means to sort by three different fields, data types, and document elements. (See Figure 18-19, on the next page.)

Product	Type	Shelf
11100	Book	B
12400	Book	B
12944	Video	C
13100	Book	A
13200	Book	A
13411	Video	C
13500	Book	B
13500	Book	A
13999	Video	D
14999	Video	D
15211	Video	C

Product	Type	Shelf
15211	Video	C
14999	Video	D
13999	Video	D
13500	Book	B
13500	Book	A
13411	Video	C
13200	Book	A
13100	Book	A
12944	Video	C
12400	Book	B
11100	Book	B

Figure 18-18. Word sorts data in ascending or descending order based on the data in column 1.

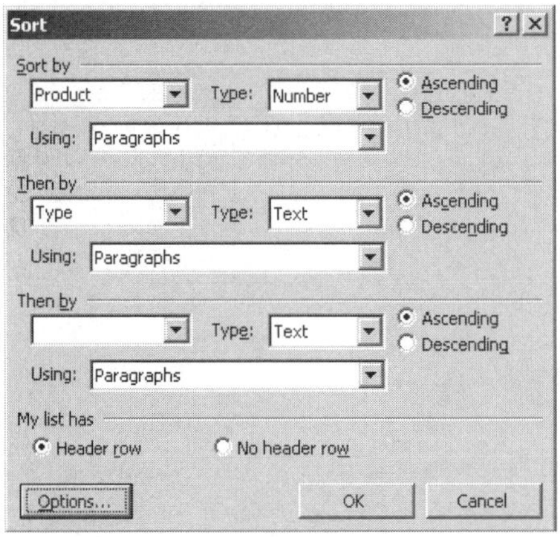

Figure 18-19. The Sort dialog box gives you the means to search on three fields.

To enter sort specifications in the Sort dialog box, follow these steps:

1. In the Sort By section, click the down arrow of the first item and choose the name of the column by which you want to sort.
2. Click the Type down arrow and select the data type (Number, Text, or Date).
3. Leave Ascending selected if that's the sort order you choose; otherwise, click Descending.
4. If you have a secondary sort, select that column in the Then By section. (For example, you might want to arrange the products first by Type, then by Shelf, and finally by Product number).
5. Select the data type for the secondary sort and select the sort order.
6. Define a third sort in the second Then By section if needed.
7. If you want Word to leave the header row out of the sort, click the Header Row option.
8. Click OK to perform the sort.

note Word includes options that enable you to search information that isn't in table form. To sort non-tabular data, highlight it and choose Table, Sort. Click the Options button in the Sort dialog box to open the Sort Options dialog box and specify the character you've used to separate data entries. If you want Word to distinguish between uppercase and lowercase letters (which it ignores by default), select the Case Sensitive check box. Click OK to return to the Sort dialog box.

Troubleshooting

Two-Name Search Produces Unexpected Results

If your two-name search doesn't give you the results you expect, make sure that you've used the right character to separate the words. If you're searching for <FirstName> <LastName>, you need to insert a space to separate the words. If you're searching <LastName>, <FirstName>, you need to include a comma and space between the words. To enter the separator character, choose Table, Sort and click Options. Select the separator you want in the Separate Fields At section.

Working with Functions in Tables

Although Word is happy to leave the truly complicated calculations to its suite-sister, Excel, the program includes support for working with a number of functions in your tables. Some of the Word tables you create will no doubt include numbers—and some of those columns will require totals, averages, and more.

Adding with AutoSum

The function you'll use most often will probably be AutoSum, included as a button on the Tables And Borders toolbar. AutoSum will total the cell values in contiguous cells in a column or row. To use AutoSum, follow these steps:

1. Click in the cell at the end of a column of numbers (or the right end of a row).
2. Click the AutoSum button on the Tables And Borders toolbar. Word automatically totals the column or row of numbers and inserts the total at the insertion point.

note Whenever you change a value in the column used to create the AutoSum total, the change will be reflected in the sum. To force an update of calculations in your table, press F9.

Using Other Functions

AutoSum isn't the only function you can include in your Word tables. You can create a number of calculations, depending on what you want the data in your tables to do. You can create your own formulas and work with other Word functions by using the Formula dialog box shown in Figure 18-20.

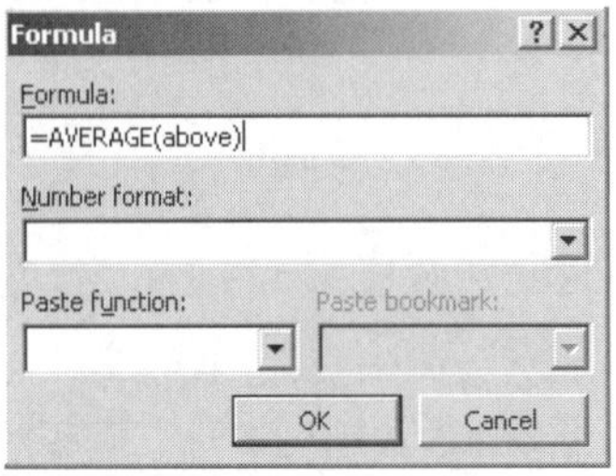

Figure 18-20. You can create your own formulas in the Formula dialog box.

You can display the different functions Word allows by clicking the Paste Function down arrow. These functions are available for your selection:

ABS	IF	OR
AND	INT	PRODUCT
AVERAGE	MAX	ROUND
COUNT	MIN	SIGN
DEFINED	MOD	SUM
FALSE	NOT	TRUE

To insert your own formula in a table, follow these steps:

1. Click in a cell at the end of a column of numbers where you want to add the formula.
2. Choose Table, Formula. The Formula dialog box is displayed.
3. Type = in the Formula box to tell Word you're entering a formula.
4. Click the Paste function down arrow and choose the function you want from the displayed list. (For this example, AVERAGE was selected.) The function is added to the Formula box, and parentheses are supplied.
5. Type **ABOVE** within the Parenthesis as shown in Figure 18-20. This tells Word to gather the average value of all items listed in the column above the current cell.
6. Click OK to close the Formula dialog box. Word calculates the answer and displays it in the table cell.

tip **Choose a number format**

You can have Word display a numeric result in the format you want. Simply click the Number Format down arrow and choose from the displayed options.

Converting Tables to Text

What happens when you don't want a table to be a table anymore? Suppose that you've created a great table for the annual report, but now someone in marketing wants it in text form—no tables allowed. How do you preserve the data and lose the grid? Follow these steps to convert a table to text:

1. Click in the table.
2. Choose Table, Convert, Table To Text. The Convert Table To Text dialog box is displayed.
3. In the Separate Text With section, select the character you want Word to use to delineate individual text entries. You might have Word separate your table entries by inserting commas, paragraph marks, or another character between them.
4. Click OK to convert the table.

Changing Text to a Table

The process for changing from text to table is equally simple. When you select text in Word to be formatted as a table and you choose Table, Convert, Text To Table, the Convert Text To Table dialog box asks for input similar to what you entered in the Insert Table dialog box. The program will want to know how many columns and rows you want to use, how you want to use AutoFit, which Table AutoFormat you want to use, if any, and finally, which characters have been used to delineate the individual text entries. Click your choices and click OK, and Word converts the text to a new table.

Chapter 19

Showcasing Data with Charts and Graphs

A chart can give you an image and an understanding of your data in a way that words alone can't. With a single picture, you can show how sales in all four regions compare—you know at a glance who comes out the winner. You can capture and portray important buying trends among your customers; you can give upper management a picture of staff productivity; you can give an instant picture of the healthy progress your business is making in new venues.

note What's the difference between a chart and a graph? Nothing, really. The terms are used interchangeably to describe the graphical depiction of data—early on, the term *charting* referred to a type of mapmaking. *Graphing*, on the other hand, involved plotting data points and discerning trends and relationships. Today, the terms mean essentially the same thing; for example, you use Microsoft *Graph* to create *charts* in your Word documents.

The Smart Use of Charts and Graphs

Charts are used to illustrate relationships—how one item relates to another, how an item this year relates to the same item last year. There are several different types of charts available to you as you create your Word documents. Some of the most commonly used charts include the following:

- **Column charts.** A column chart is used to show data comparisons. You might show, for example, how two data series "stack up" against each other for the first quarter.
- **Bar charts.** Word 2002 shows a bar chart as horizontal bars, graphing data items over time (or other categories). You might use a bar chart to compare the stages of different products in a production cycle.
- **Line charts.** A line chart plots data points over time or by category. You might use a line chart to show a trend in product returns over a six-month period.
- **Pie charts.** A pie chart shows the relationship of different data items to the whole. Each pie comprises 100 percent of the series being graphed, and each slice is shown as a percentage of the pie. You might use a pie chart to show the relative size of individual departments in the northeastern sales division of your company.
- **XY (Scatter) charts.** An XY chart enables you to plot pairs of data points over time. You might use an XY chart to contrast the test scores of a battery of exams given at two different universities.
- **Area charts.** An area chart gives you the means to compare data two different ways: You can show the accumulated result of the data items, and you can show how the data (and their relationship to one another) change over time. For example, you might use an area chart to show how many students took each module of the exam at two different universities.
- **Doughnut charts.** A doughnut chart is similar to a pie chart in that it shows the relationship between data items. Doughnut charts enable you to compare two sets of data and the way in which they relate to the whole and to each other. You might use a doughnut chart to portray two different sales campaigns. The sections of the doughnut could represent the different sales channels, and you could compare and contrast the different effects of each channel.
- **Radar charts.** A radar chart plots multiple data points and shows their relation to a center point. You might use a radar chart to show how each regional sales division fared in the recent sales competition.
- **Bubble charts.** A bubble chart enables you to plot three different data series. Each item is plotted at a particular point in time and shows, as a bubble, the data value. This would enable you to see, for example, which accounts had the highest charges during the second quarter.

Introducing Microsoft Graph

Word 2002 relies on Microsoft Graph to help you create the charts you want in your documents. Microsoft Graph is a full-featured graphing utility that enables you to use any of the 14 different standard charts or the 20 built-in custom charts. You can also create your own custom chart types for those times when you need to show unique data relationships for your particular documents. Table 19-1 lists the various chart types you can create in Microsoft Graph.

Table 19-1. Microsoft Graph Chart Types

Standard	Custom
Column	Area Blocks
Bar	B&W Area
Line	B&W Column
Pie	B&W Line – Timescale
XY (Scatter)	B&W Pie
Area	Blue Pie
Doughnut	Colored Lines
Radar	Column – Area
Surface	Columns with Depth
Bubble	Cones
Stock	Floating Bars
Cylinder	Line-Column
Cone	Line-Column on 2 Axes
Pyramid	Lines on 2 Axes
	Logarithmic
	Outdoor Bars
	Pie Explosion
	Smooth Lines
	Stack of Colors
	Tubes

note Microsoft Graph is built into Word, and all other Office applications as well. You begin a chart by choosing Insert, Picture, Chart. When you want to edit a chart, simply double-click the chart and Microsoft Graph launches.

Creating a Basic Chart

When you're ready to create a simple chart with Microsoft Graph, start by selecting the data you want to use. You can do this by entering the data in the datasheet Graph gives you, by copying the data from another program, or by selecting data you have in your current Word document.

Starting with Word and Selecting Chart Data

The easiest way to create a chart is to begin with a table of data you've created in your Word document. Create your information as you want it, and then follow these steps to use it to create a chart:

1. Click in the table and then choose Table, Select, Table (or click the table move handle to select the entire table).
2. Choose Insert, Picture, Chart. Microsoft Graph launches and creates a chart based on the information in the table you selected. (See Figure 19-1.)

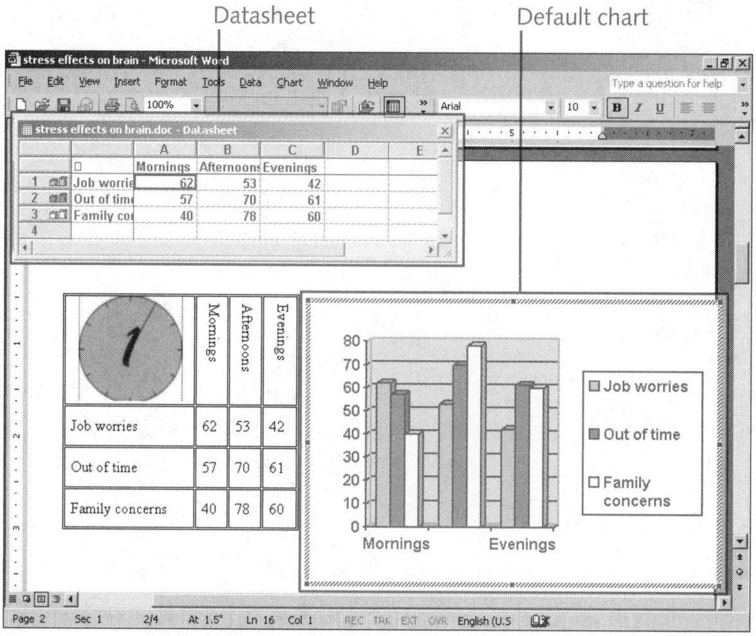

Figure 19-1. You can easily create a chart based on data you've already entered in your Word document.

> **tip** **Select table sections only**
>
> If you want only a portion of the table to be used for your chart, select only the segment you want to use; then choose Insert, Picture, Chart.

Checking Out the Microsoft Graph Window

When Microsoft Graph launches in Word, it brings along with it several key components. Graph inserts additional menus in the Word menu bar and adds graph-related buttons in the Standard toolbar. The default chart Microsoft Graph draws based on the data you selected is a column chart.

- **Default chart.** Microsoft Graph chooses a column chart as the default chart type for the data you select. You can easily change the chart type to better represent the data you're working with.
- **Datasheet.** The information you selected in your Word document is shown in the datasheet. Here you can modify information as needed to customize the values and labels shown in the chart.
- **Additional menus.** Microsoft Graph brings two additional menus—Data and Chart—that enable you to work with the data and charts you create. The commands in the other menus are also changed to reflect chart-related commands.

> **tip** **Get Graph help**
>
> Microsoft Graph comes with a fully developed Help system of its own, which means that you can get help on any chart operations you're attempting. Simply press F1 to launch the Help utility.

Importing Data from Other Programs

Although you're creating a chart for use in your Word document, you might want to use data from other programs to create the chart. Because Microsoft Office is built on the "create it once, use it many times" idea, you can import data from Microsoft Excel, as well as other popular programs. You can import data in the following formats:

- Microsoft Excel
- Text files
- SYLK files
- Lotus 1-2-3

When you're ready to import a data file to use as the basis for your Microsoft Graph chart, follow these steps:

View Datasheet

Import File

1. Double-click the chart with the datasheet you want to modify.
2. Make sure the datasheet is displayed. If it isn't in view, click the View Datasheet button on the Standard toolbar.
3. Choose Edit, Import File or click the Import File button on the Standard toolbar. The Import File dialog box appears.
4. Click the down arrow in the Files Of Type box and select the format of the file you're importing.

5 Navigate to the folder you want, select the file, and click Open. The Import Data Options dialog box appears, as Figure 19-2 shows.

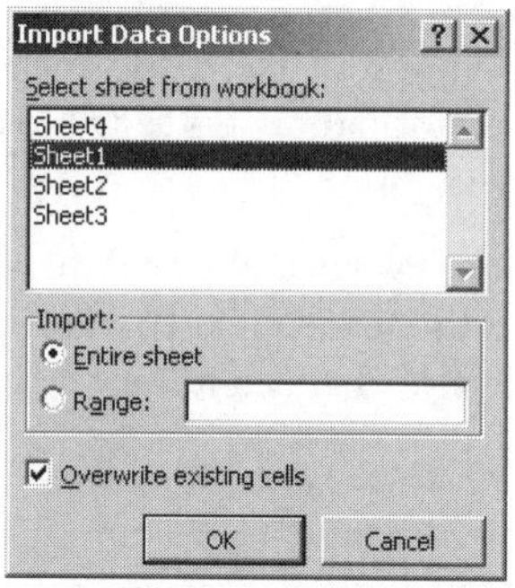

Figure 19-2. You can use data from other programs in the charts you create in Microsoft Graph.

6 Choose the worksheet from which you want to import the chart data.

7 Enter the data range of cells you want to import if you're importing only selected data; otherwise, leave the Entire Sheet option selected.

8 If you want to be prompted before Microsoft Graph overwrites the existing data in your datasheet, clear the Overwrite Existing Cells check box. (By default, Microsoft Graph selects this check box, which causes your data to be overwritten without any action by you.)

9 Click OK. The data is brought into the datasheet and the chart is changed accordingly.

tip **Link or embed**

You can choose to link or embed chart data in a Word document. If you link a chart, the chart in your Word document will be updated whenever the source document changes. If you embed a chart in your document, you'll be able to edit the chart as you would normally, by double-clicking it in the hosting document.

Creating the Right Chart for the Job

Making sure you've got the right chart for the data you're displaying is key to communicating your point most effectively. Some charts, such as the bar and column charts, are best for comparing data items—for example, tracking the sales of apples compared to oranges. Other charts are better for showing the relation of individual items to a whole—such as the sales of apples and oranges as they compare to total produce sold in May 2001.

> **tip** **Create your own custom chart types**
>
> You can also create your own custom chart types with Microsoft Graph. When there's a specific type of chart you want, or a mix of chart types, you can create your own specifications and save them with the current document. To find out more about creating a custom chart type, see "Creating Your Own Chart Types," on page 479 later in this chapter.

Checking Out the Chart Types

Chart Type

Microsoft Graph makes it simple for you to select and change chart types. Start by creating a new chart or by displaying the chart you've already created. Double-click the chart, if necessary, so that the Microsoft Graph additions to the Standard toolbar are displayed. Then choose Chart, Chart Type. The Chart Type dialog box appears and contains all the different charts—both Standard and Custom—that are available to you. (See Figure 19-3.)

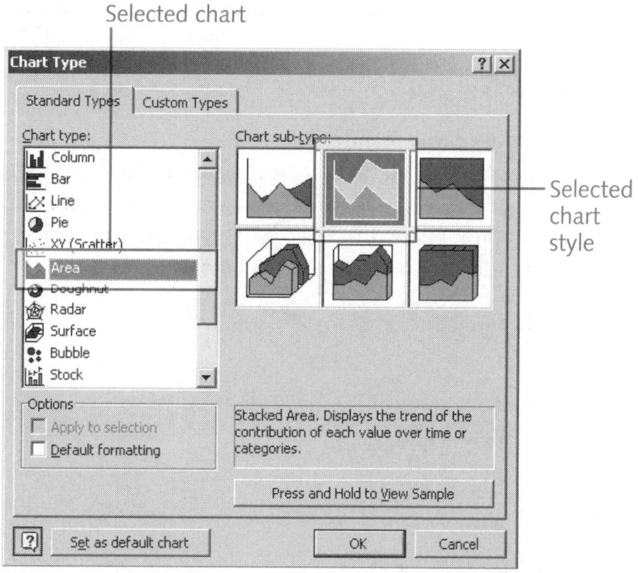

Figure 19-3. The Chart Type dialog box includes over 30 different chart types you can use to illustrate your data.

> **tip** **Change chart types—the fast way**
>
> If you've used the Chart Type dialog box before, Microsoft Graph will have placed its button on the Standard toolbar. To change a chart type quickly, simply click the Chart Type button's down arrow and select the chart you want from the drop-down menu. The selected chart is automatically replaced with the new chart type you select.

Selecting a Standard Chart Type

The Standard Types tab in the Chart Type dialog box is the first to be displayed. The type of chart selected in the Chart Type list (and in the Chart Sub-Type section) depends on the type of chart selected in your document.

To choose another chart type, simply scroll through the Chart Type list and select the one you want. The examples in the Chart Sub-Type section change to reflect your new choice. Select the sub-type you want by clicking it as well. When you click OK, you are returned to Microsoft Graph, and your chart is updated to show the new chart type.

tip **Test your choice**

If you're not sure how your choice will look and want to test it out before you make the change, select the type and the sub-type and then click the Press And Hold To View Sample button On the Standard Types tab in the Chart Type dialog box. Microsoft Graph gives you a preview of your chart, redrawn in the new type. If you like what you see, click OK, and the chart is replaced in your document.

Choosing a Custom Chart Type

If you don't see what you want on the Standard Types tab of the Chart Type dialog box, you can try the Custom Types tab. Click that tab and scroll through the list of Custom Chart Types. You'll see many different styles of all kinds and colors. (See Figure 19-4.) When you find the one you want, select it in the Chart Type list and click OK. You are returned to your document and the chart change is made.

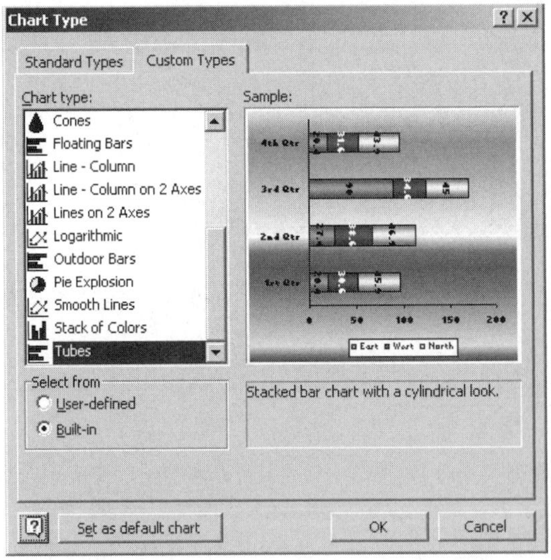

Figure 19-4. The Chart Type Custom Types tab gives you additional choices for more specialized graphs.

Setting a New Default Chart Type

If you really like the chart type you've selected, you can make it the default chart Microsoft Graph automatically uses when you create a new chart. Double-click the chart in your document and choose Chart, Chart Type. Click the Set As Default Chart button to store this chart type as the type Microsoft Graph uses when you create a new chart.

Creating Your Own Chart Types

If you just can't find the exact chart you want, or if your data needs are specialized for a particular document type, you can create a custom chart type to handle your unique situation. Similar to the way in which you create styles, you base the creation of a custom chart style on an existing style. You can tailor the existing style by changing colors, bar type, 3-D or 2-D effects, background, titles and labels, and more.

To create your own custom chart type, follow these steps:

1. Place the insertion point where you want to create the chart.
2. Choose Insert, Picture, Chart. The default chart and datasheet are displayed.
3. Change the data as needed and close the datasheet; and select other chart options such as chart type, color, and style in the way you want them to appear.
4. Click Chart, Chart Type. The Chart Type dialog box appears.
5. Click the Custom Types tab.
6. In the Select From section, click the User-defined option. The Custom Types tab changes to show the default chart type. An Add button appears so that you can add the new chart type to the Chart Type list.
7. Click Add. The Add Custom Chart Type dialog box appears. (See Figure 19-5.)

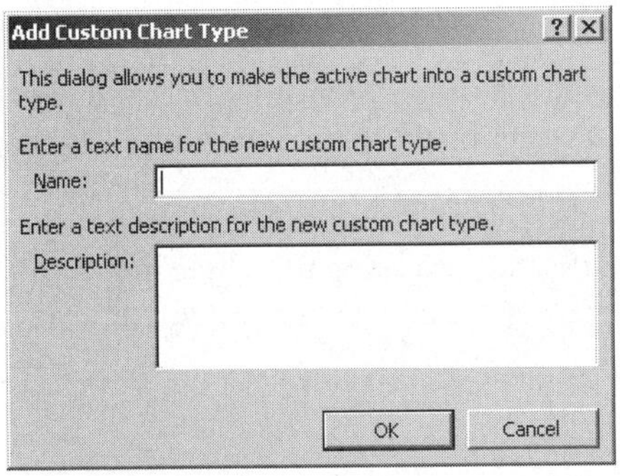

Figure 19-5. When you create a custom chart type, you name the type and add a description in the Add Custom Chart Type dialog box.

8. In the Name box, type a name for the chart type.

9. If you want to add a description of the chart or the way in which it is to be used, click in the Description box and type the chart type's explanation.
10. Click OK to add the custom chart type; then click OK in the Chart Type dialog box to finish creating the custom chart type.

> **tip** **Use your own chart types**
>
> When you want to use one of your own custom-designed chart types in a document, choose Insert, Picture, Chart, click the Custom Types tab in the Chart Type dialog box, and click the User-Defined option. Select the chart you want to use from the Chart Types list, and click OK. Microsoft Graph inserts the custom chart in your document.

Working with the Datasheet

When you first create a chart, whether you're basing the information on data in your current Word document or entering it as you go, Microsoft Graph displays a datasheet along with the newly created chart. The datasheet shows you the data, including categories, data series, and values, that's used to make your chart. (See Figure 19-6.)

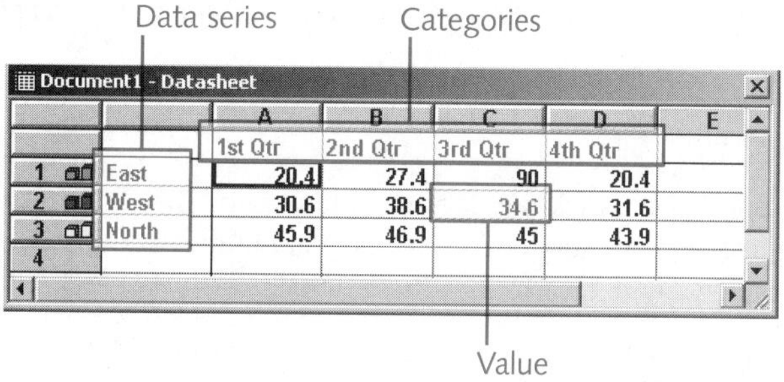

Figure 19-6. The datasheet displays the data values and labels used to create your chart.

You can easily modify this data and change the way the chart is drawn by editing the values on the datasheet. The datasheet includes the following elements:

- **Categories.** The items in the columns are the categories placed along the horizontal axis of the chart. Categories might include months, quarters, stages of a project, or some other unit by which value can be measured.
- **Data Series.** The data series show the items that are being graphed, according to the categories selected.
- **Values.** The data entered in the cells of the datasheet is compared against the value axis, which is the vertical axis in the created chart.

Datasheet Tips

Here are some quick tips for working with your chart's datasheet:

- To select everything in the datasheet quickly, click the Select All button (the gray rectangle in the top left corner of the datasheet).
- To hide a data series, double-click the row label of the series you want to hide.
- To add a data series, simply click in the next available row, type a label, and enter your data.
- To control the way the datasheet treats empty cells, choose Tools, Options and click the Chart tab in the Graph Options dialog box. Click the desired empty cell option, and click OK.
- To copy datasheet values for use in a Word table, select the information you want and press Ctrl+C. This places a copy on the Clipboard, and you can paste the data as needed by pressing Ctrl+V.

tip If you close the datasheet, you can redisplay it while editing the chart by clicking the View Datasheet button on the Standard toolbar.

Changing the Data Arrangement

By default, Microsoft Graph displays the categories along the horizontal axis and the values along the vertical axis, but if you choose, you can flip that arrangement to display your data differently. Consider, for example, the chart shown in Figure 19-7, on the next page. Although the default configuration for the chart compares the quarterly sales results of each region, the flipped version compares the regions with each other, spotlighting how well each did during the different quarters of the year.

You can change the data arrangement of your chart in two different ways:

By Column

By Row

- Choose Data, Series In Columns or Series In Rows (the default).
- Click the By Column or the By Row button on the Standard toolbar while editing the chart to change the data arrangement. By Row is the default setting.

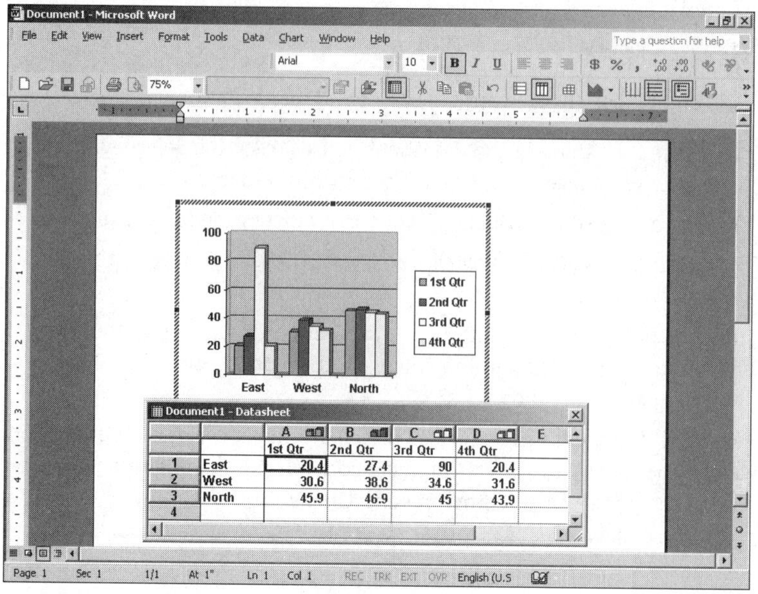

Figure 19-7. Flipping the data arrangement in your chart enables you to see in a new way the data you've used to build your chart.

Editing and Adding to Chart Information

Creating your chart is only half the fun. Once you decide on the basic style you want, you can add to, edit, and enhance your chart by using chart options to add titles and labels, and you can make other modifications as well. You use the Chart Options dialog box to add titles, axes controls, gridlines, legends, labels, and more. To display the Chart Options dialog box, double-click the chart in your document; then choose Chart, Chart Options. (See Figure 19-8.)

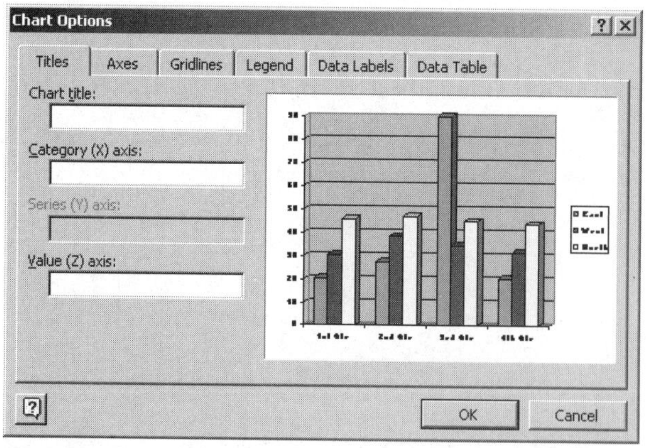

Figure 19-8. You add titles, labels, and other chart elements in the Chart Options dialog box.

Although most of the elements you'll find in the Chart Options dialog box apply to all the different chart types, some controls are disabled for certain charts. For example, the Series (Y) Axis box is disabled in a default column chart, shown in Figure 19-8. And the only tabs available in the Chart Options dialog box for a pie chart are Titles, Legend, and Data Labels.

Titling the Chart and Axes

When you first display the Chart Options dialog box, the Titles tab is selected by default. In this tab, you'll add an overall title for your chart and specify titles for each axis, as desired. Click in the Chart Title box and type your title. The preview window is automatically updated to reflect your change.

tip **Choose chart titles that work**

Chances are that you won't have a lot of room in your document for lengthy chart titles. Try to choose a title that pulls out key words reflecting what the chart's portraying. If you're comparing product sales, "Product Sales Comparison" works. If you're comparing your private school's test results with the local public school system, "Test Score Comparison" would be accurate. Not exciting, but accurate. If you can think of something exciting too, all the better.

The process of naming the axes is similar to naming the chart; simply click in the appropriate box and type your title. The Category (X) Axis is the horizontal axis; the Value (Z) Axis is the vertical axis. Remember that each title you enter takes up space around your chart and you run the risk of giving the readers too much to read—so make sure your axes titles, if you choose to use them, truly add to the information you're trying to convey.

After you name the chart and the axes, click OK to return to the document in Microsoft Graph. You can now edit and format the chart title as you would any other text; you can change the font, style, color, and size.

Controlling the Axes

You can further customize the way information is displayed in your chart by changing what's shown along the chart axes. When you first create a chart, Microsoft Graph notches off the axes by adding tick marks, small marks that indicate increments, or categories by which your data is measured.

If you want to suppress the display of the tick marks used along the axes, choose Chart, Chart Options to display the Chart Options dialog box and click the Axes tab. (See Figure 19-9, on the next page.) The Axes tab gives you the choice to display or hide the marks and labels along the Category (X) axis and the Value (Z) axis. (If your chart has a Series (Y) axis, like the one in Figure 19-9, this option will be enabled as well.) By default, all labels and marks are displayed. To suppress the display, clear the check box beside the axis items you want to hide.

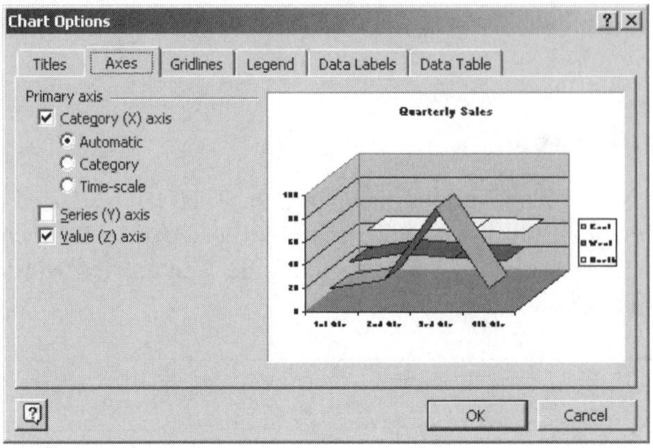

Figure 19-9. If you're pressed for space in your document, you can suppress the display of axis labels and tick marks.

> ## Troubleshooting
>
> **I Can't See Axis Titles in My Chart**
>
> If you're having trouble seeing the axis titles along the Category and Values axes on your chart, the chart area might be too small to display all the chart information successfully. Try resizing the chart by clicking it and dragging one of the resize handles outward, enlarging the chart. If that doesn't do the trick, click the axis title while editing the chart and choose a smaller Font Size in the Formatting toolbar.

To Gridline or Not to Gridline

For complicated charts with multiple data series especially, gridlines can help clarify the comparisons and conclusions you want readers to draw from your chart. Gridlines are easy to both add and remove, so there's no reason not to experiment with them to see whether they suit your needs for your current chart type.

Category Axis Gridlines

To add gridlines to your chart, select the chart in Microsoft Graph and click one of the following buttons on the Standard toolbar:

Value Axis Gridlines

- **Category Axis Gridlines** adds vertical gridlines that correspond to the categories of your data.
- **Value Axis Gridlines** adds horizontal gridlines that correspond to the value data segments along the Value axis.

By default, Microsoft Graph adds gridlines at each major category or value mark in your chart. But you can add additional gridlines in smaller increments, if you find that your data needs warrant it. With the chart selected, choose Chart, Chart Options to display the Chart Options dialog box and click the Gridlines tab. You'll find a series of options that enable you to select both Major and Minor gridlines for your chart.

Be forewarned, however: With gridlines, a little goes a long way. Be sure to add only what your reader needs in order to understand your data—too many lines will clutter up your chart and make it more difficult for readers to decipher.

> **tip** **Get the particulars right**
>
> If you want more control over where gridlines are placed and how tick marks appear, select the axis you want to change and then right-click and choose the Format Axis command on the shortcut menu. In the Format Axis dialog box, click the Scale tab and enter the settings you want for the display and number of tick marks used.

Working with a Legend

Legend

Microsoft Graph assumes that you want a legend for your chart when you first create it. If this is a mistaken assumption, you can have Graph remove the legend by clicking the Legend button on the Standard toolbar. This hides the legend and causes your chart to be enlarged to fill the space the legend previously occupied.

You can control where in the chart the legend is placed by selecting the chart in Microsoft Graph and choosing Chart, Chart Options to display the Chart Options dialog box. Click the Legend tab, and you'll see a number of options that enable you to hide the legend (simply clear the Show Legend check box) or, in the Placement section, place it by clicking Bottom, Corner, Top, Right, or Left. Microsoft Graph repositions or hides the legend after you click OK.

Entering Data Labels

Data labels are helpful in those instances when you need to give the reader further clues about which data items go with which series or category. Microsoft Graph gives you the ability to add several different kinds of data labels to your charts. You might want to add percentages to pie slices, for example, or category labels to stacked bars.

To add data labels, choose Chart, Chart Options to display the Chart Options dialog box and click the Data Labels tab. (See Figure 19-10, on the next page.) The options you see will depend on the type of chart you're working with, but you'll see at least the Series Name and Category Name labels if you're working with a chart that has horizontal and vertical axes. Choose the labels you want to display by selecting the check box to the left of the label type:

- **Series Name** adds the name of the data series (in the example, East, West, and North).
- **Category Name** displays the name of the category, which in this example is already listed along the Category (X) axis.
- **Value** displays the actual numeric value of the data plotted at each category.
- **Percentage** (available for pie and doughnut charts) displays the percentage of the whole each data item represents.
- **Bubble Size** (available for bubble charts) lists the size of each bubble, which is tied to the value.

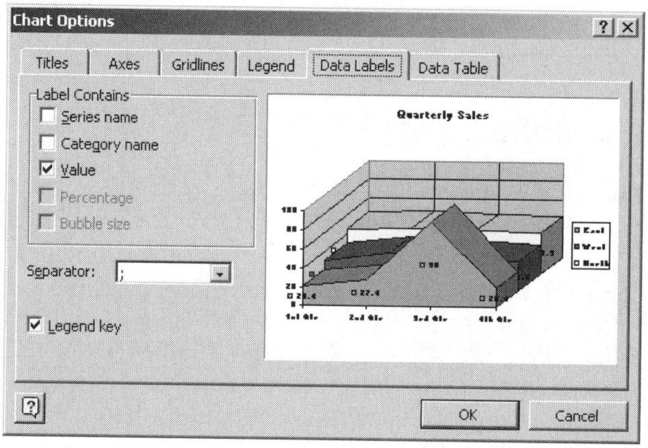

Figure 19-10. Data labels can add a bit of extra description to the data series in your chart.

> **tip** **Choose multiple labels**
>
> You can choose to display more than one type of label if you choose. For example, you might want to display both percentages and category names on a pie chart. If you select more than one label type, use a separator to separate the labels. Click the Separator down arrow to display a list of choices and click the separator you want to use.

One more way you can make sure readers get the connection between your data trends and the categories being plotted: You can use the Legend Key feature to add small legend tags to the left of each data label. Readers will be able to see at a glance which items relate to the categories displayed in your chart legend.

> **tip** **Change labels in the datasheet**
>
> The data labels Microsoft Graph uses are taken right from your datasheet. If you want to change a data label on the chart, it's best to go back to the datasheet and make the change. Otherwise, the label change might not "stick" and you might see the same old label displayed the next time you display your chart.

Creating a Data Table from Chart Options

Data Table

There's yet another way to make sure your readers understand how the data in your chart directly relates to the values they've seen in your document. You can create a data table in Microsoft Graph to show the numeric data beneath the actual chart. This gives readers different ways to understand the data being graphed.

To create a data table for your chart, click the Data Table button on the Standard toolbar. A data table is added, as Figure 19-11 shows.

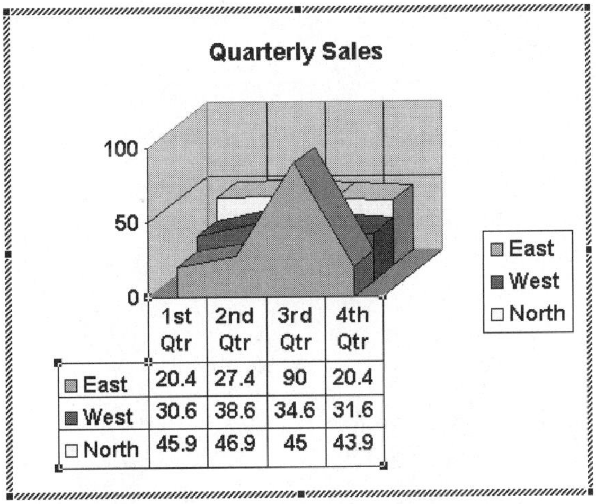

	1st Qtr	2nd Qtr	3rd Qtr	4th Qtr
East	20.4	27.4	90	20.4
West	30.6	38.6	34.6	31.6
North	45.9	46.9	45	43.9

Figure 19-11. Data tables display the actual data used to create your chart in table format beneath the chart area.

> **tip** **Add a data table within a chart**
>
> You can also add a data table from within the Chart Options dialog box. Simply click the Data Table tab and select the Show Data Table check box. Click OK to return to your chart and the data table will be added.

Formatting Charts

Microsoft Graph gives you the ability to format all the different elements your chart includes. You might want to change the font of a title, resize the labels, change the background color, change the line thickness, apply a pattern, or do any number of other things.

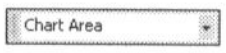

Chart Objects

To choose the chart object you want to work with, double-click the chart and click the Chart Objects down arrow on the Standard toolbar. A list of possible objects appears. (See Figure 19-12.) Click your choice, and Microsoft Graph selects that item in the chart. You can then right-click the item to display a format choice—for example, right-clicking a legend displays a shortcut menu with the Format Legend command. When you select that command, a formatting dialog box appears in which you can select the Patterns, Font, and Placement for the legend.

note The formatting commands available—and the tabs in the different Formatting dialog boxes—vary widely depending on the type of chart you're creating and the chart element you've selected. Right-clicking a chart axis, for example, displays a very different set of choices than right-clicking the legend does.

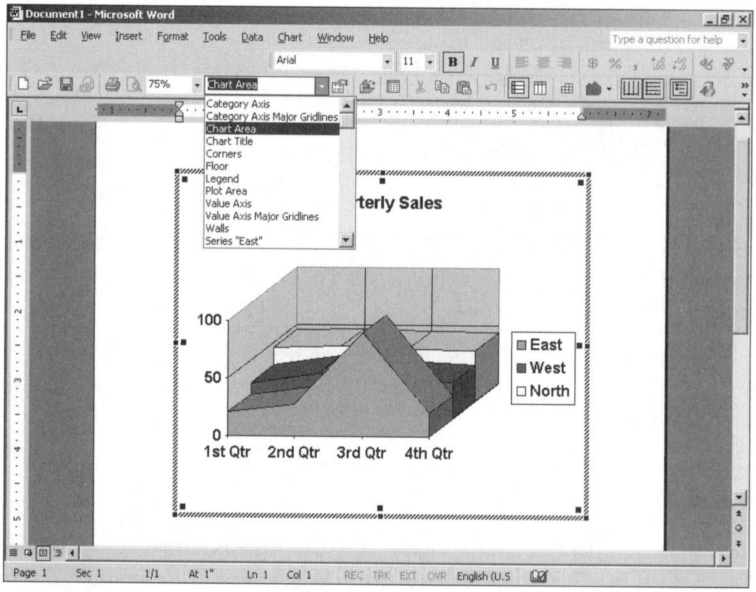

Figure 19-12. Use the Chart Objects list to select the chart element you want to work with.

Working with Patterns

You work with patterns in Microsoft Graph to tell the program how you want to format a number of different items:

- Do you want a border around your chart? If so, what kind? You make those choices on the Patterns tab of the Format dialog box.
- Do you want to choose a different color for the lines in your chart?
- Would you like to add a drop shadow to the chart?
- Do you plan to recolor any or all of the data series lines or bars in your chart?

You can change each of these items by displaying the Format dialog box and clicking the Patterns tab. (See Figure 19-13.) By default, Microsoft Graph includes a single-line border, but you can customize and modify the lines used to enclose your chart. Additionally, you can experiment with fill colors for the chart area. The Sample preview box in the lower left corner shows you the effect of your changes.

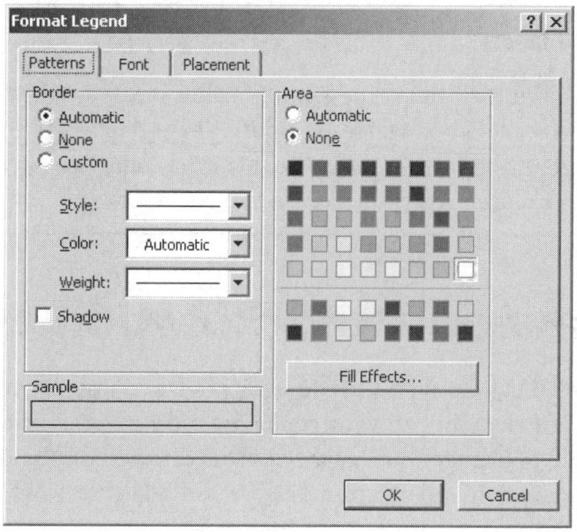

Figure 19-13. You can modify settings on the Patterns tab of the Format Legend dialog box to change the chart's border and color scheme.

Changing Fonts

There's no big secret about changing fonts in a chart—simply select the text you want to change and change it as you would choose text in your document. You can use the buttons on the Formatting toolbar (which is available even when Microsoft Graph is active), or you can choose Format, Font. The Format dialog box appears with the Font tab selected, as Figure 19-14, on the next page, shows, and you can modify the font, style, size, underline, color, background, and effects.

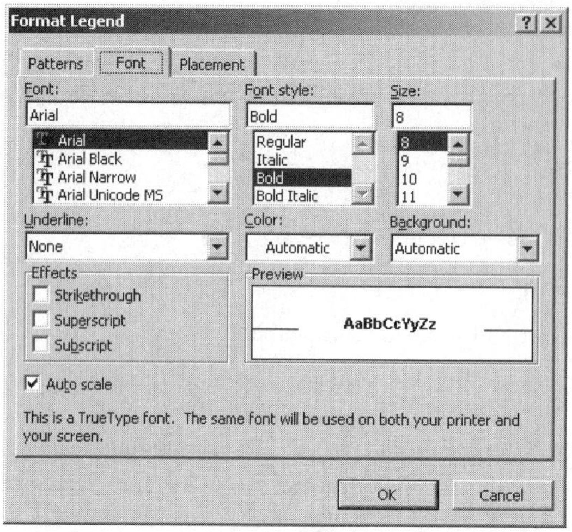

Figure 19-14. You can easily change the fonts used for titles and labels in your chart by using the Font tab in the Format Legend dialog box.

tip **Control the size of titles and labels**

The Auto Scale check box on the Font tab in the Format dialog box is selected by default—this means that Microsoft Graph will resize your titles and labels to fit the chart if you resize it. If you want the titles and labels to stay the same size no matter how the chart is increased or reduced, clear the Auto Scale check box.

Changing the Elevation and Rotation

You might notice that your 3-D chart angles to the left by default. You might find, however, that the other design elements on your page have a different orientation. In this case, you need to be able to change the way the chart is directed on the page. Microsoft Graph provides elevation and rotation options for 3-D charts, which enable you to do just that:

- **Elevation** is the vertical distance from which the reader's perspective of the chart is measured. For example, with an elevation of 30, the elevation is twice as "high" as the same chart viewed with an elevation of 15.
- **Rotation** is the degree to which the chart is rotated away from the straight-on view. Raising Microsoft's default value of 20 to 40 turns the chart further to the left.
- **Perspective** is another option that's available for some charts. This option enables you to change the depth of the chart by increasing or decreasing the value.

To change the elevation, rotation, and perspective for your 3-D chart, follow these steps:

1. Double-click the 3-D style chart to select it and display the Microsoft Graph additions to the menus and Standard toolbar.
2. Choose Chart, 3-D View. The 3-D View dialog box appears, as Figure 19-15 shows.
3. Experiment with Elevation options by clicking the up and down arrows until you get the effect you want.
4. Click the Rotation buttons to turn the chart right and left as needed.
5. Click the up and down arrows above the Perspective box to modify the depth of the 3-D chart.
6. Click Apply to apply the new settings to the selected chart.
7. Click OK to close the dialog box and return to Microsoft Graph.

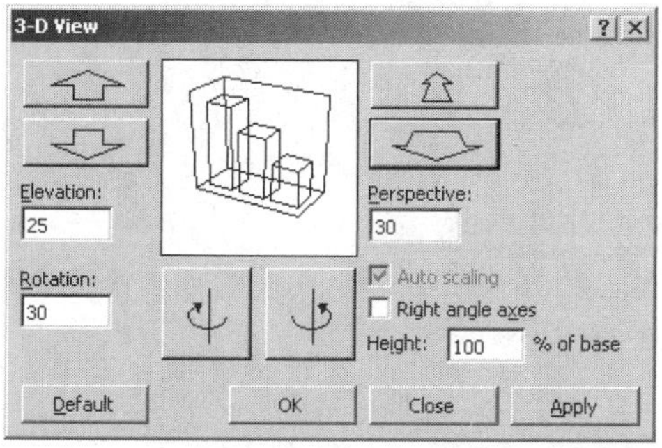

Figure 19-15. Use Elevation, Rotation, and Perspective settings to change the way a 3-D chart is displayed in your document.

Adding Error Bars and Trendlines

Two additional visual cues, error bars and trendlines, can help your readers understand your data more quickly. Error bars show the error margin built into each data marker, and trendlines use an analysis of existing data to predict future behavior.

Inserting Error Bars

You can create error bars for the data series in your 2-D area, bar, column, and line charts, as well as bubble and xy (scatter) charts. To add error bars to your chart, follow these steps:

1. Double-click your chart to select it.
2. Use the Chart Objects list to select the data series to which you want to add error bars.

3. Right-click the selected series and choose Format Data Series on the shortcut menu.
4. Click the Y Error Bars tab and select the Display option you want. You can choose one of the following, as Figure 19-16 shows:
   - **Both** displays an error amount above and below the displayed value
   - **Plus** displays an error amount above the displayed value.
   - **Minus** shows an error amount below the displayed value.
5. In the Error Amount section, choose the amount of the difference between actual and plus or minus you want to show.
6. Click OK to add the error bars and return to the chart.

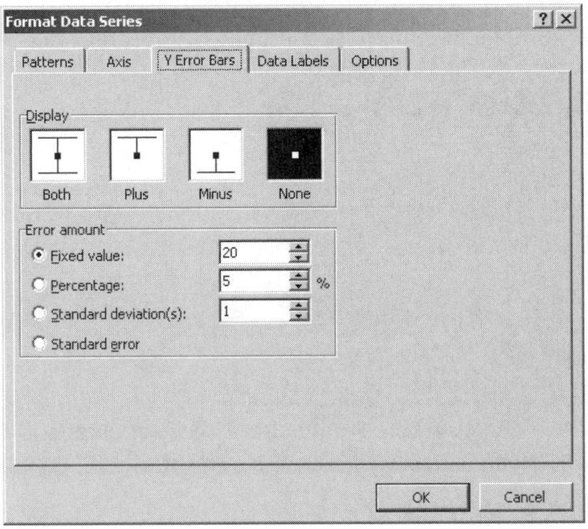

Figure 19-16. Use the Format Data Series dialog box to add error bars that show a margin for error in which the result could be a bit higher or lower than what's shown in your chart.

Plotting Trendlines

Trendlines are helpful when you want to use your chart as a basis for either looking ahead to future possibilities or seeing trends in the past. You can add trendlines to area, bar, bubble, column, line, stock, and xy (scatter) charts. When you've created one of these chart types, adding a trendline is simple. Here are the steps:

1. Double-click the chart to select it.

2 Choose Chart, Add Trendlines. The Add Trendline dialog box appears (see Figure 19-17).

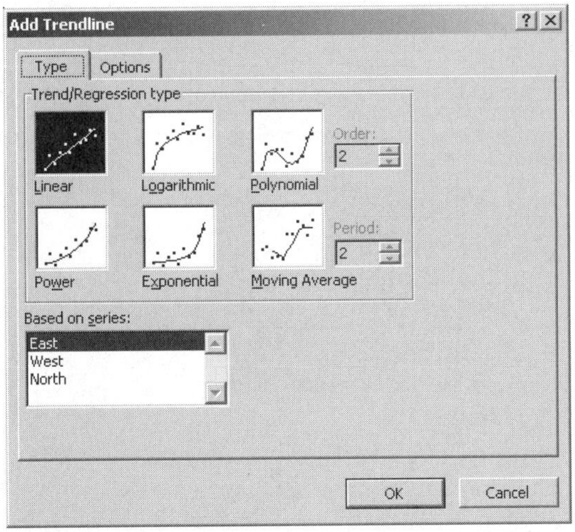

Figure 19-17. In the Add Trendline dialog box, select the formula you want Microsoft Graph to use to plot your projections.

3 In the Trend/Regression Type section, choose the type of trendline you want to create. Each of these types is based on a formula that calculates and projects data patterns based on the information in your datasheet.

4 In the Based On Series section, select the data series you want to use to create the trendline.

5 Click the Options tab. Here you'll enter a name for the trendline (if necessary), choose the length of the periods forward and backward you want to project, and choose whether you display equations or values on the chart. Make your choices, and click OK. You're returned to Microsoft Graph, and the trendline has been added. (See Figure 19-18, on the next page.)

tip **Find out more about trendlines**

If you want to understand more about the equations the trend types use to calculate trends in your data, click the What's This? button in the Add Trendline dialog box and click the trend type you want to see. A ScreenTip gives you more information about the trend type you've selected.

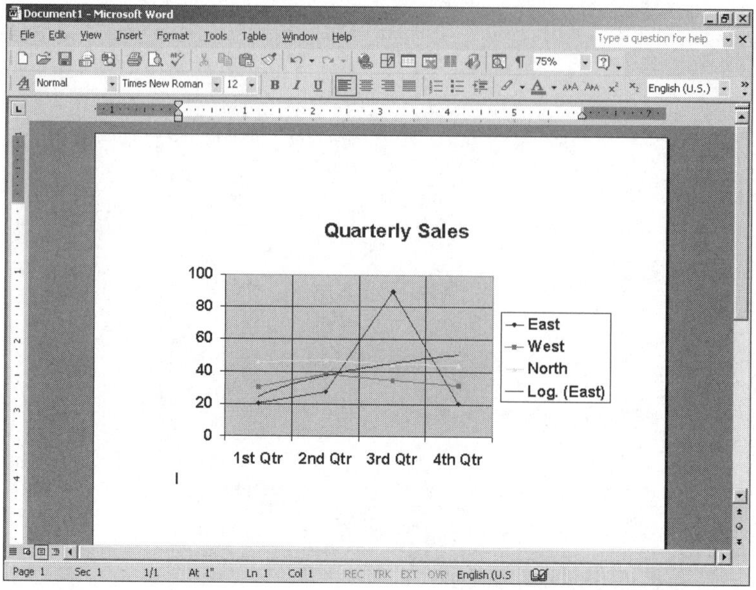

Figure 19-18. A trendline in your chart can show a general direction for your data and helps readers understand at a glance what the significant changes in your data might be.

Chapter 20

Diagramming Projects, Process, and Relationships

If you've been relying on third-party programs to create organization charts and diagrams, you'll like the new built-in diagramming tools of Word 2002. Now you can add an organization chart as easily as a piece of clip art, and a diagram with two clicks of a mouse button. This chapter shows you how you can add and work with organization charts and diagrams in your Word documents.

Charting and Diagramming for Clarity

Organization charts and diagrams can add clarity to documents in which you need to show relationships—whether those relationships are between the workers in a company or the stages of a project. You might use organization charts to

- Show all employees and their reports in a specific department
- Illustrate the role each person plays in a particular project

Diagrams are helpful in illustrating not people relationships as much as relationships between parts of a project, steps toward a goal, or the process of building toward a desired end. For example, you might use diagrams to

- Show how the responsibilities of departments overlap

- Identify the steps needed to resolve the current inventory problem
- Show all the reasons to produce a new product
- Illustrate the foundation of a new business and the incremental steps involved in bringing ideas to market

You use two different procedures to add organization charts and diagrams. The next section shows you how to insert, edit, and enhance organization charts.

Adding Organization Charts

When you create an organization chart in Word, you can create a new chart on the fly and enter text as you go, or you can use existing text in Word, Microsoft PowerPoint, or Microsoft Excel and build your chart from that. Either way, creating the organization chart is a simple process that gives you the flexibility you need to fit the chart in your document and format it the way you want.

Creating an Organization Chart

When you're ready to create an organization chart from scratch, follow these steps:

1. Place the insertion point where you want to create the chart.
2. Choose Insert, Picture, Organization Chart. Word creates your basic chart—now you can enter text and add shapes as needed. (See Figure 20-1.)

Organization Chart Elements

There aren't a lot of parts to deal with in an organization chart. You'll use basic shapes to create relationships—subordinates, peers, and assistants—and you'll design, move, and change branches that show the relationships among people or processes. Here are the items you'll be working with in your organization charts:

- **Shapes** are the boxes used to name a person, identify a role, or describe a step or department.
- **Connector lines** are the lines that connect each of the shapes in your chart.
- **Chart frame** is the border surrounding the organization chart. This is a nonprinting border, although you can add a border to the chart if you choose.
- **Organization Chart toolbar** provides the menus and tools you need to add, move, and wrap text around the chart in your document. Table 20-1 introduces the tools and gives examples of when each could be used.

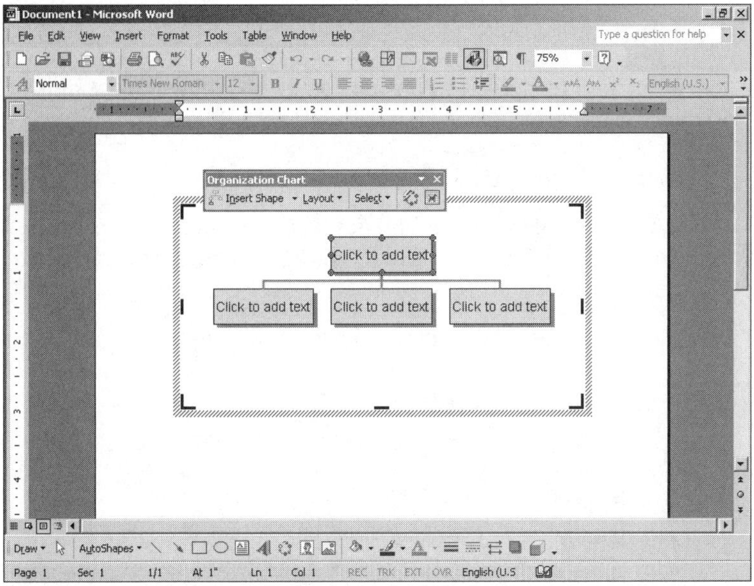

Figure 20-1. Word draws a simple organization chart and gives you the tools to add shapes as needed.

Table 20-1. Organization Chart Tools

Button	Name	Description	Use
	Insert Shape	Adds subordinate, coworker, or assistant shapes	You want to add a new position, person, or project to your chart.
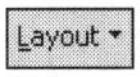	Layout	Changes the layout of the organization chart	You want to display the chart information in a different form.
	Select	Displays choices for selecting chart elements	You want to select a particular level, type of shape, or branch.
	AutoFormat	Provides a gallery from which you can choose predesigned chart styles	You want a professional look with coordinated colors and lines.
	Text Wrapping	Displays text wrap options for the placement of text around the chart	You want to arrange text around, up against, or even through your chart.

Entering Text

Once you create the basic chart, you're ready to add text in the individual shapes. Here are the steps:

1. Click in the shape at the top of the chart.
2. Type the name of the person, position, or process. The text appears as you type, left-aligned in the shape. Figure 20-2 shows names entered in each of the four shapes.
3. Click in another box; continue adding text as needed.

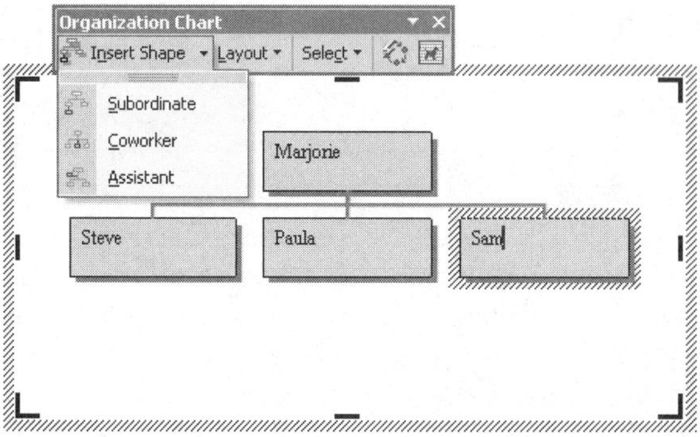

Figure 20-2. Word adds text in the default font for the current template; you can change the font, style, color, and alignment as needed.

note Your typical text navigation keys—Enter, Tab, and the arrow keys—don't work in the organization chart. Just move the mouse pointer and click to move from shape to shape.

Inserting Shapes

When you first create an organization chart, Word gives you one superior (lead) shape and three subordinates. For most charts, you'll want to add and reorder shapes as you continue to build your chart.

To insert shapes in your organization chart, follow these steps:

1. Click the shape to which you want to add a relationship. The frame for the shape changes, showing that it's selected.

2 Click the Insert Shape down arrow on the Organization Chart toolbar or simply click Insert Shape to add a subordinate. If you displayed the shortcut menu, choose the relationship you want to add from the drop-down menu:

- **Subordinate** adds a shape beneath the selected shape.
- **Coworker** adds a shape on the same level.
- **Assistant** adds a shape below and to one side, off the main branch. (See Figure 20-3.)

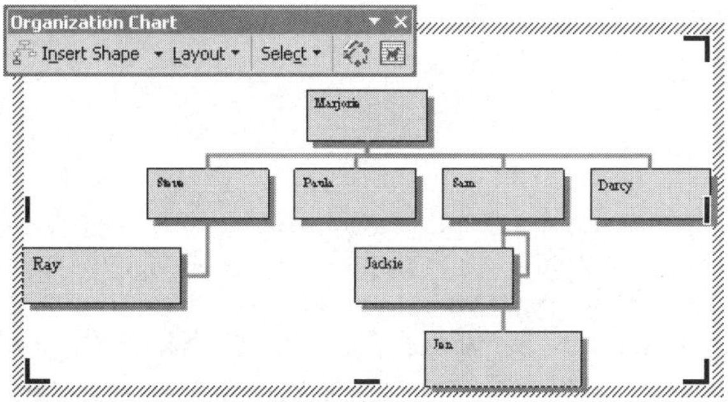

Figure 20-3. Add new shapes and relationships to expand the organization chart.

Changing the Layout

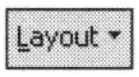

Layout

The basic tree structure is the default arrangement for new organization charts, but you have other layouts to choose from. To see the different layouts, click the Layout button on the Organization Chart toolbar. (See Figure 20-4.)

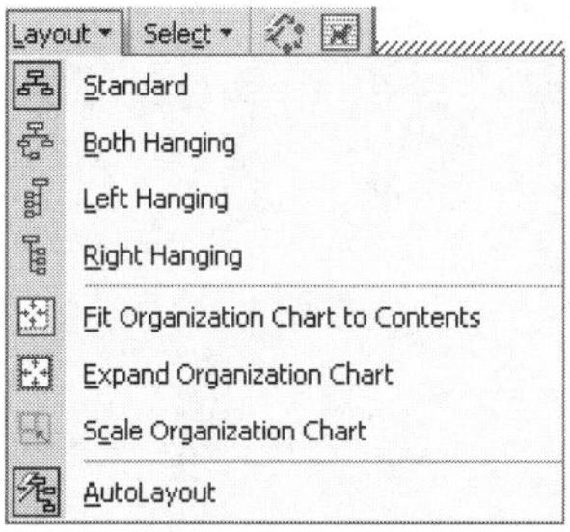

Figure 20-4. You can select a different layout for the organization chart.

Different types of organizations will lend themselves to different chart layouts, so try experimenting with the different choices to see what works best for your data. Also consider where the chart appears on the page, how it fits with your overall design, and which alignment might help lead the reader's eyes in the most effective way. Figure 20-5, on the next page, shows an organization chart displayed in the Right Hanging layout.

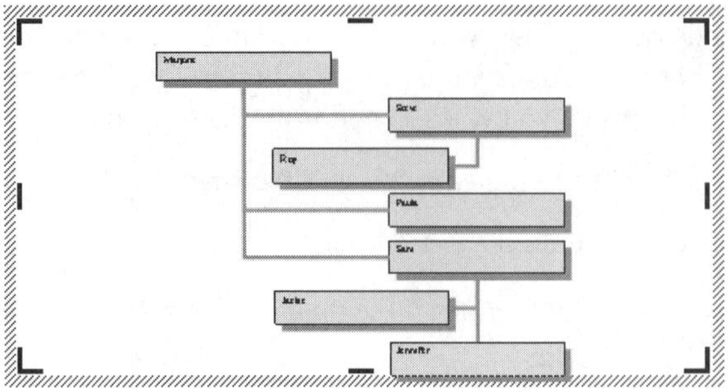

Figure 20-5. Experimenting with the layout styles gives you a sense of what works best in your document.

Selecting Branches

As you work with your organization chart, you might find that you want to work with several items at once. You might, for example, want to change the line color for all connector lines to blue. Or you might want to add a drop-shadow to all management level shapes. Or you might want to change the fill color of individual shapes. Whatever change you want to make, you need to select the shapes before you can modify them.

You tell Word which items you want to select by using the Select drop-down menu. (See Figure 20-6.) Then make your selection from the following choices:

- **Level** selects all shapes on the current level.
- **Branch** selects all shapes in the current branch.
- **All Assistants** selects all assistant shapes in the chart.
- **All Connecting Lines** selects all lines in the chart so that you can change color, thickness, etc.

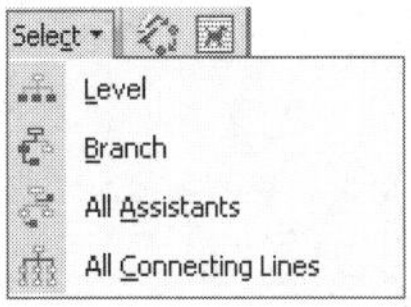

Figure 20-6. Choose chart elements from the Select drop-down menu.

> **note** Can you raise a shape from one level to another? No—but you can simply delete the existing shape and create a new one, showing the correct relationship.

Moving Shapes and Sections

Once you select the shape or branch you want to work with, you can reorder the selections the way you want. To move a shape in an organization chart, follow these steps:

1. Click the shape you want to move. If the frame appears around the shape, click the item again to display the shape handles.
2. Position the pointer over one of the handles. The pointer changes to a four-sided arrow.
3. Drag the shape to the new location in an equal position in the chart. (The shape will not move if you try to move it to a superior position.) An outline moves with the shape, and when you release the mouse button, the shape is moved to the new location.

To move a branch, follow these steps:

1. Click the shape at the top level of the branch you want to move so the handles appear.
2. Click Select on the Organization Chart toolbar, and choose Branch from the drop-down menu. All shapes in that branch are selected.
3. Position the pointer over one of the shapes. When the pointer changes to a four-sided arrow, drag the branch to the new location. A dotted outline follows the movement of the mouse pointer.
4. Release the mouse button, and the branch is moved to the new place in the organization chart.

Using AutoFormat to Modify the Look

You can apply predesigned formatting to your organization chart, using AutoFormat. Click in the chart and then click the AutoFormat button on the Organization Chart toolbar, and the Organization Chart Style Gallery dialog box appears. (See Figure 20-7, on the next page.) Click through the various Gallery styles to find the one you want. When you find a style that fits your document, click Apply.

Resizing an Organizational Chart

Word creates an organization chart at a standard size, one that uses most of your page width. If you want to reduce the size of the chart, perhaps so that you can include text in a column to one side, you can resize the chart. You can resize an organization chart in three different ways:

- Click the resize handle at any of the four corners and drag to resize the chart in the direction you want. The diagram and text are resized accordingly.

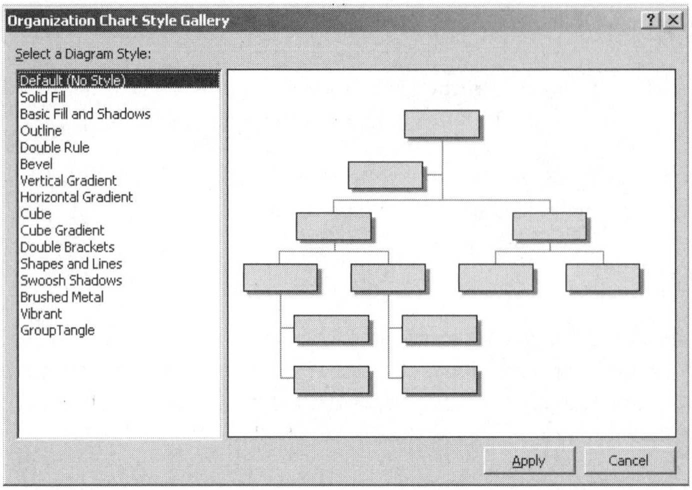

Figure 20-7. Select a style from the Organization Chart Style Gallery dialog box.

- Click the Layout button on the Organization Chart toolbar and choose Fit Organization Chart To Contents to reduce the white space around the chart.
- Click the Layout button on the Organization Chart toolbar and choose Expand Organization Chart to increase the white space around the chart and expand the overall area.

Controlling Text Wrap Around Charts and Diagrams

Chances are, you'll have more than a single organization chart in your document—you'll need to combine text and charts together in a layout that works for your readers. Start by clicking the Text Wrapping button on the Organization Chart toolbar. Then choose the option that fits for you:

- **In Line With Text** places the chart on the same line as the current text.
- **Square** runs text up to the edge of a squared area around the chart.
- **Tight** wraps the text tightly against the outline of the organization chart.
- **Behind Text** runs text over the top of the chart.
- **In Front Of Text** places text behind the chart.
- **Top And Bottom** wraps text above and below the chart.
- **Through** runs text through the white space in the organization chart.
- **Edit Wrap Points** allows you to add custom points so that you can create your own text wrap boundary around the chart. (See Figure 20-8.)

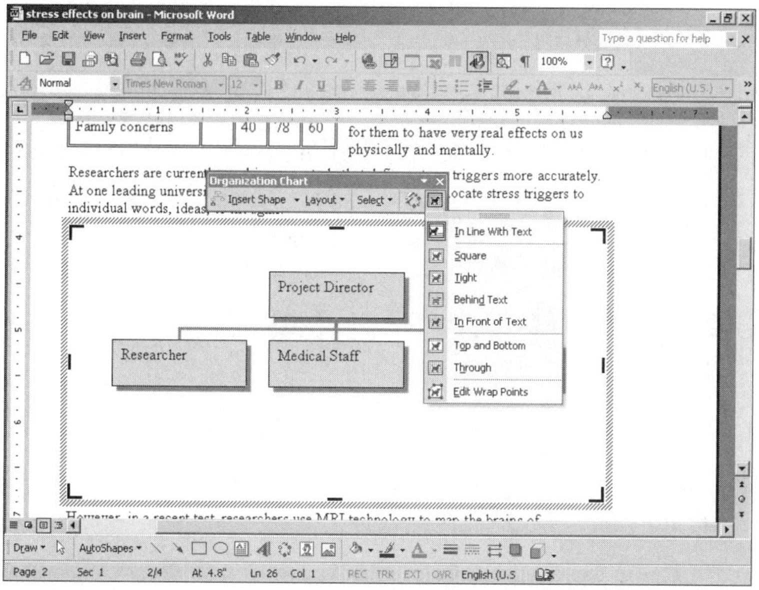

Figure 20-8. You can control the text wrap around an organization chart.

newfeature!

Designing Conceptual Diagrams

Another new feature in Word 2002 is the built-in ability to create diagrams. Beyond an organization chart, a diagram enables you to show more complicated relationships, dependencies, processes, and more. Word gives you five different diagram types to choose from—a full complement of tools for illustrating data concepts.

Selecting the Right Diagram for the Job

In addition to the Organization Chart type, Word includes these diagram types that you can use and customize for your documents:

- **Cycle** shows a cyclical process.
- **Radial** shows how different elements relate to a core element.
- **Pyramid** shows how various elements build on a foundation.
- **Venn** shows how elements overlap with other elements.
- **Target** shows individual relationships to a core element or goal.

Creating the Diagram

Adding a diagram is a simple two-click process. Here are the steps:

1. Click at the point in the document where you want to add the diagram.
2. Choose Insert, Diagram or click the Diagram button on the Drawing toolbar. The Diagram Gallery dialog box appears, displaying the different diagram types. (See Figure 20-9.)

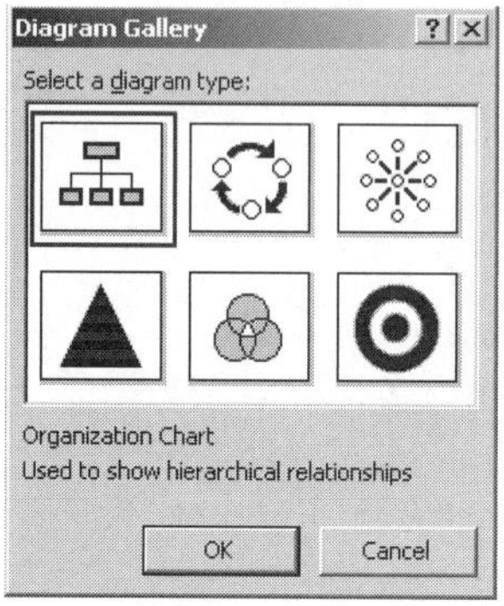

Figure 20-9. Choose the diagram type you want to create in the Diagram Gallery dialog box.

3. Click the diagram you want to create, and click OK. The diagram is added to your document, and the Diagram toolbar is displayed. Table 20-2 describes each of the buttons you'll find on the Diagram toolbar.

Adding to the Diagram

The default diagram appears with several preset shapes—but you'll want to add more on your own. Simply select the shape beside or above which you want to add a shape. Click the Insert Shape button on the Diagram toolbar. A new shape is added to the diagram. The type of shape depends on which diagram you're creating:

- A stripe for a Pyramid
- An overlapping circle for a Venn chart
- A circle and connector line for a Radial chart
- A segment for a Cycle chart
- A ring for a Target diagram

tip Adding text is as simple as clicking and typing. If you want to edit text in your diagram, click the item you want to change and type the desired text.

Table 20-2. Diagram Tools

Button	Name	Description	Use
Insert Shape	Insert Shape (Note: This tool changes based on the type of diagram you select.)	Enables you to add a shape in the form fitting to the diagram type	You want to add another element in your diagram.
	Move Shape Backward	Moves the currently selected shape one item down or back	You want to change the order of the elements in your diagram.
	Move Shape Forward	Moves the currently selected shape one item forward or up	You're reordering diagram elements.
	Reverse Diagram	Switches the order of the selected diagram element	You want to move the top element to the bottom of the diagram.
Layout ▾	Layout	Provides options for resizing the diagram	You're reducing the size of the chart to make room for text wrap.
	AutoFormat	Displays a Gallery of preset diagram formats	You want to create a professional-looking diagram.
Change to ▾	Change To	Displays options for other diagrams	You want to change your current diagram into another diagram type.
	Text Wrapping	Shows the options for wrapping text around diagrams	You want to flow text around the select diagram.

Moving Diagram Elements

Moving shapes in a diagram is a slightly different process than moving shapes in an organization chart. Instead of selecting and moving an entire branch, you work with single elements. Here are the steps:

1. Select the shape you want to move.

2 Use one of the following tools to accomplish what you want to do:

- **Move Shape Backward** moves the shape down.
- **Move Shape Forward** moves the shape up.
- **Reverse Diagram** moves the shape to the opposite side (or end) of the diagram.

Changing the Diagram Layout

Resizing your diagram involves the use of the Layout button on the Diagram toolbar. When you click the Layout button, you're given three different choices in addition to the AutoLayout option:

- **Fit Diagram To Contents** tightens up the white space surrounding the diagram.
- **Expand Diagram** widens the diagram box.
- **Scale Diagram** resizes the actual diagram. Resize handles appear at the outer edges of the diagram box. Click a handle and drag the diagram box inward or outward. (See Figure 20-10.)

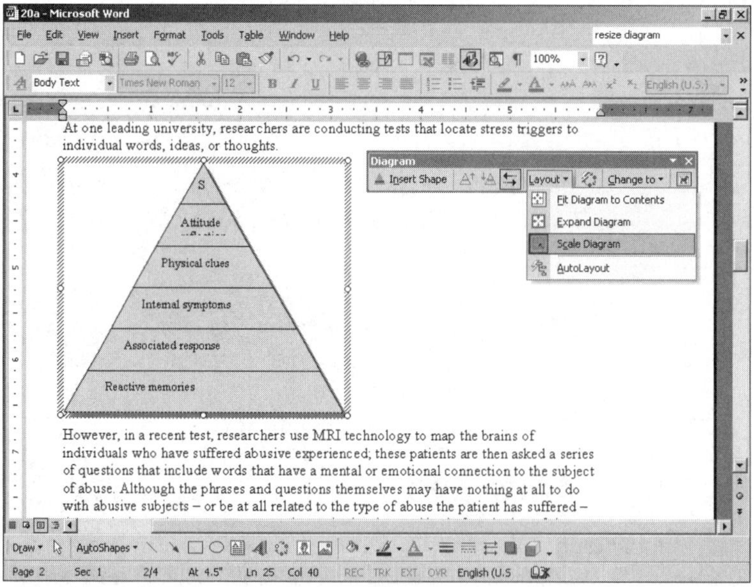

Figure 20-10. Resize the diagram by selecting Scale Diagram and dragging a handle.

Using AutoFormat for Diagrams

The AutoFormat button displays the Diagram Style Gallery dialog box. (See Figure 20-11.) Similar to the Organization Chart Style Gallery dialog box, this AutoFormat collection displays different styles you can apply to your diagram. You'll find different color schemes and shapes for each of the different diagram types. Experiment with the different formats until you find a style that suits your document. Click Apply to apply the style to your diagram.

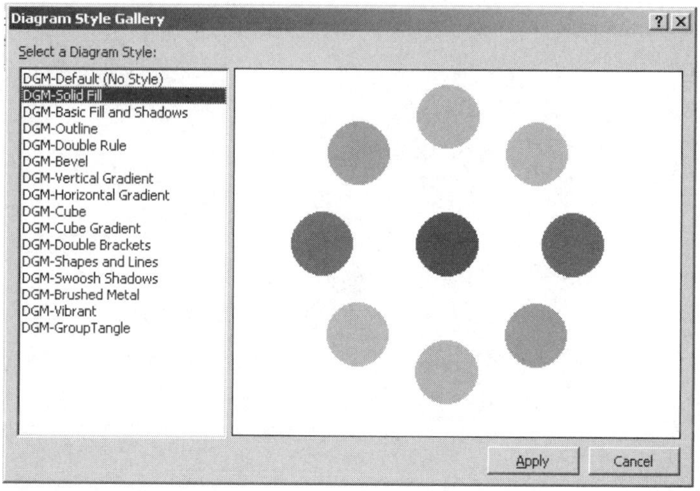

Figure 20-11. Choose a style from the Diagram Style Gallery dialog box.

Changing to Another Diagram Type

One great feature about the new diagramming capability is the ease with which you can change from type to type. For example, if you use a cycle diagram to show the process of bringing a new product to market and it just doesn't seem quite right, you can switch the diagram—with data intact—to a radial diagram type. To change to another diagram type, click in the diagram and then click the Change To button on the Diagram toolbar and click the type of diagram you want. The diagram is redrawn in the type of diagram you selected.

note For specifics about using the Text Wrapping tool to control the way text flows around your diagram, see the section, "Controlling Text Wrap Around Charts and Diagrams," on page 502 earlier in this chapter.

Part 5

Designing Pages for Maximum Visual Impact

Chapter 21

Mastering Page Setup and Pagination

Have you ever started creating a document with one goal in mind and then seen it change (sometimes against your will) into something entirely different? A single-column publication suddenly becomes a multiple-column document. A piece that wasn't supposed to be a booklet now is. Everything changes—margins, orientation, column specifications, and headers and footers. These aren't the kind of changes you want to be making when you have a 2:00 P.M. deadline to meet.

Whether you plan your publication in advance or change strategies mid stream, Microsoft Word's page setup features control the page basics. Specifically, when you plan your pages, you'll be making choices about the following things:

- The size of top, bottom, left, and right margins
- The space between columns
- Whether you want to print one or two pages per sheet
- The size of paper you plan to use
- The orientation of your document
- The tray or cartridge from which the paper will be fed
- Layout considerations for sections, headers, and footers

Planning Page Setup

Although you can select your page settings at any point during the creation or editing of your document, taking time up front to think about and plan basic document settings can save you time, trouble, and corrections later. Additionally, if you're creating a standard document for others in your department to use, getting the basics set early can ensure that you don't have to go into multiple documents to readjust margin settings, page size, and more.

When you make drastic changes in your document setup—such as changing the page from portrait to landscape orientation—the content of your page will be dramatically affected. If you switch orientation after you've entered text and graphics, set headers and footers, and created section divisions, you'll have lots of changing to do.

Preparing Your Document

You'll use the Page Setup dialog box to enter the page settings. To display the dialog box, choose File, Page Setup. The Page Setup dialog box appears, as Figure 21-1 shows.

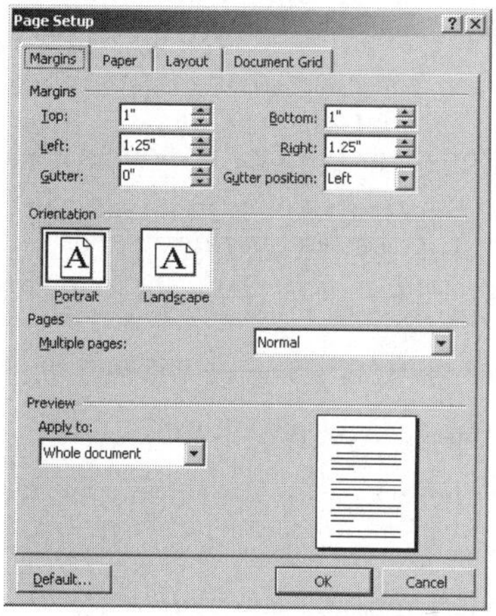

Figure 21-1. The Page Setup dialog box enables you to choose the settings that affect the margins, paper type, layout, and spacing of your document.

newfeature!

The Page Setup dialog box has a new look in Word 2002—in addition to the reordering of options on the individual tabs, a new tab called Document Grid has been added. Use the following tabs to enter the page basic settings:

- **Margins.** The Margins tab allows you to enter the top, bottom, left, right, and gutter margins; choose the page orientation; and select the format for multiple pages.

- **Paper.** The Paper tab includes all the choices you need to choosing the paper size and source for the paper and envelopes on which you'll print your information.
- **Layout.** The Layout tab enables you to make choices about sections, headers and footers, and the alignment of text.
- **Document Grid.** The Document Grid tab enables you to control the horizontal and vertical spacing of characters in your document. From within this tab, you can also specify drawing grid settings, which give you spacing control over document drawings.

Setting Up the Document as a Whole

One of the first choices you'll make controls how far-reaching you want the page setup settings to be. You can choose to apply the page settings to the entire document or apply the settings from the cursor position forward. To make your choice, choose File, Page Setup to display the Page Setup dialog box and, on the Margins tab, click the Apply To down arrow. To have Word apply the settings to the entire document, select Whole Document. Any other changes you make in the Page Setup dialog box will be applied to your document as you selected.

tip **Choose both document and section settings**

You can mix and match choices you make for the entire document and for selected sections. For example, you can set a specific left margin for the entire document and add line numbers only for a section. Be sure to make your selection in the Apply To list before you enter the page setting you want.

Working in Sections

If you want to enter page setup settings for a selected section only, start by placing the insertion point where you want to make the change. Then choose File, Page Setup to display the Page Setup dialog box, and click the Apply To down arrow. Select the option From This Point Forward, and then make your page setup changes. The settings you enter are applied throughout the rest of the document, and Word inserts a Section Break marker at the insertion point.

If you want to end the page setup settings at a certain point (for example, perhaps you increased the right indent for a particular section but want to return to the normal margin after that section), start by placing the insertion point where you want to make the change. Then choose File, Page Setup to display the Page Setup dialog box a second time, click the Apply To down arrow, choose From This Point Forward, and return the settings to normal. Finally, click OK to return to your document.

Setting Page Setup Defaults

Once you get the page settings set up the way you want them, you can save the specifications as your page setup defaults. To do this, follow these steps:

1. Place the insertion point where you want new page settings to take effect.
2. Choose File, Page Setup to display the Page Setup dialog box.
3. Click the Apply To down arrow, and choose whether you want the changes applied to the entire document or from the insertion point forward.
4. Enter the other page setup choices you want reflected in the document.
5. Click the Default button in the lower left corner of the Page Setup dialog box. A message box appears (see Figure 21-2), asking whether you'd like to change the default settings in the current template. To do so, click Yes; otherwise, click No.

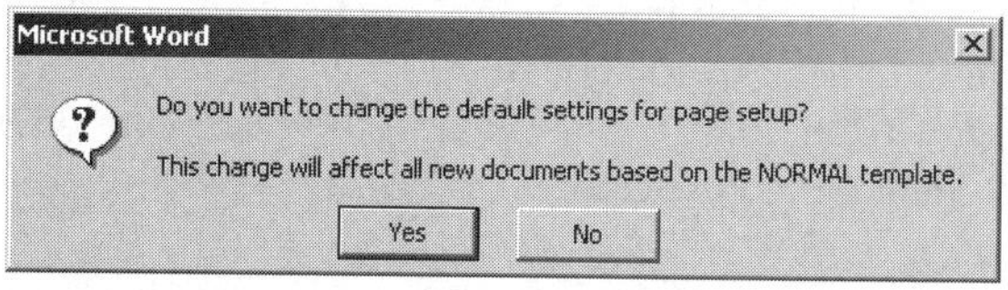

Figure 21-2. Making the current page setup settings the new default changes the existing template.

> **tip** **Make a backup copy**
>
> For best results, always keep a clean backup copy of your standard template in another directory on your hard disk or server. That way, if you need to return to earlier default specifications, you can do so without having to re-enter the original Word settings.

newfeature!

Changing Margins and Orientation

The page setup items you'll change most often are likely to be the margins and orientation settings. The margins of your document control the amount of white space at the top, bottom, right, and left edges of the document. You can also control the amount of space used for the gutter, which is the space reserved for binding. Now, in Word 2002, you can customize the gutter setting along the left or top margins of the page.

tip **Plan your margins for double-sided printing**

If you'll be binding the document you create, be sure to specify a gutter margin large enough to accommodate the binding. If your document is printed single-sided, every gutter margin will show the spacing you enter along the left margin. If your document is to be printed double-sided, click the Multiple Pages down arrow and choose Mirror Margins to make sure the margin settings are applied to the left and right internal margins.

Entering Margin Settings

When you first begin working with a new Word document, the left and right margins are set to 1.25 inches. You can change margin settings in Word in two different ways:

- Drag the Left Indent and Right Indent markers on the horizontal ruler to the setting you want.
- Change the margins in the Page Setup dialog box by clicking in the appropriate box and typing the value.

note When you select a value in the Gutter Position drop-down list, Word adds the gutter setting to the left margin (or alternating right and left, if you've selected Mirror Margins in the Multiple Pages drop-down list).

Choosing Orientation

The orientation of your document affects the way in which the text is printed on the page. Portrait orientation prints documents in traditional, 8.5-by-11-inch format; landscape orientation prints documents in a horizontal, 11-by-8.5-inch format. When should you use which orientation? Here are a few ideas:

- **Portrait orientation** might be used for traditional documents, letters, reports, newsletters, and invoices.
- **Landscape orientation** might be used for slides, signs, title pages, charts, and tables.

To change the orientation of your document, choose File, Page Setup to display the Page Setup dialog box and click the Margins tab. Click Landscape to change the orientation so that the document is printed with the long edge of the paper serving as the top of the page.

note You can change the orientation from landscape to portrait and back again in a single document, if you choose. Simply place the insertion point where you want to change the orientation, display the Page Setup dialog box, click the Margins tab, and choose the appropriate setting in the Apply To drop-down list. Now click the orientation you want. After you click OK, Word begins a new page and shows the change in the page orientation as you specified.

Working with Multiple Pages

When you're working with more complex documents, you'll want to vary the margins depending on the type of document you're creating. A standard report might have equal margins on the right and left, but a document you want to bind, or a publication that's designed so that the left and right pages complement each other, requires a little flexibility in the page settings.

When you want to set up multiple pages so they have different page settings, follow these steps:

1. Choose File, Page Setup to display the Page Setup dialog box.
2. Enter the Margin, Paper, and Layout settings on their respective tabs.
3. In the Pages section on the Margin tab, click the Multiple Pages down arrow. Table 21-1 shows the different effects of the Multiple Pages choices.
4. Click your choice; then click OK. Word applies the changes to the existing document.

Table 21-1. Choosing Page Settings for Multiple Pages

Setting	Preview	Description
Normal		Creates single pages, with the same margin and header and footer selections for every page.
Mirror Margins		Creates a document in which the margins on the left and right pages to mirror each other.
Two Pages Per Sheet		Divides the current page into two pages.
Book Fold	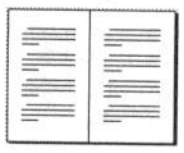	Treats each left and right page as a spread, using a gutter and mirroring margins as applicable.

Selecting Paper Size and Source

The next step involves preparing your document for the eventuality of final printing. What size paper or envelope will you use, and what is the paper source? Word 2002 now offers a huge range of paper sizes. The standard basics are there—from letter (traditional 8.5-by-11-inch) to legal (8.5-by-14-inch) to traditional business envelopes. But in addition to the usual paper sizes, Word supports Statement, Executive, Folio, Quarto, and Note sizes. You'll also find German and Japanese paper size choices, as well as many other envelope options.

Choosing a Paper Size

To choose a paper size, begin by choosing File, Page Setup to display the Page Setup dialog box; then click the Paper tab. The options displayed all have to do with the paper size and source you'll use. (See Figure 21-3.) Click the Paper Size down arrow, and choose the size you want from the displayed list.

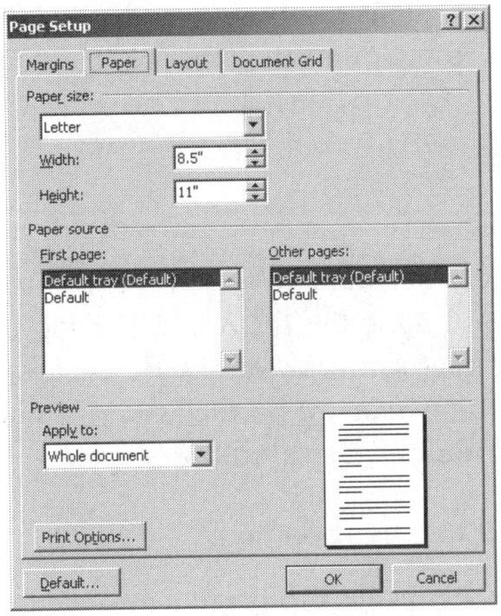

Figure 21-3. Choose the size and source for paper on the Paper tab of the Page Setup dialog box.

Selecting the Paper Source

The paper source is where you send Word to get the paper you'll use in printing your documents. If you're working with a printer that has several trays, you can customize the documents you print, for example, printing one page on letterhead in one tray and printing subsequent pages on blank stock.

To choose a new paper source, click the Paper tab of the Page Setup dialog box and simply click the tray you want to use as the source. When you click OK, Word saves your setting and prints your document accordingly.

tip **Choose print options from the Paper tab**

It seems like an obvious place to stop and check that all your print options are in working order. Because so many of the choices overlap in Print and Page Setup settings, take a moment to check your print options by clicking the Print Options button in the bottom left corner of the Paper tab in the Page Setup dialog box. If you want to use A4 or legal paper sizes, or you plan to use duplex printing, you can select those settings here.

For more information on printing in Word 2002, see Chapter 4, "Printing with Precision."

Making Layout Choices

Depending on the specific characteristics of the document you create, you might need to make layout choices that affect the number of columns you use, the settings you choose for headers and footers, text alignment, line numbering, and more. The Layout tab of the Page Setup dialog box brings all those options together so that you can make your choices in one place.

Section Selection

Word gives you the option of choosing where you want your new sections to begin. Whenever you choose the This Point Forward option in the Apply To drop-down list, Word begins a new section and applies the page settings you've selected. Display your section choices by clicking the Section Start down arrow on the Layout tab of the Page Setup dialog box. Then select your choice from the displayed list:

- **Continuous** begins the new section at the insertion point.
- **New column** starts a new column when you elect to begin a new section.
- **New page** jumps to a new page to begin a new section.
- **Even page** moves to the next even page to begin a new section.
- **Odd page** moves to the next odd page to begin a new section.

For more information on working with sections, see Chapter 9, "Formatting Columns and Sections for Advanced Text Control."

Controlling Header and Footer Placement

Headers and footers are an important part of longer documents. You'll use headers and footers to provide readers with important information about the publication, which could include the title, the author, the page number, and other data items. When you want to create headers and footers that are different for odd and even pages, you enter that setting in the Page Setup dialog box. Here are the steps:

1. Choose File, Page Setup to display the Page Setup dialog box.
2. Click the Layout tab. Make your selections in the Headers And Footers section. You have three options:
   - **Different Odd And Even** enables you to create headers and footers that are different for right and left pages. This would allow you, for example, to place the page numbers in the outside bottom corner of every page, whether you're printing an odd or even page.
   - **Different First Page** enables you to disable the display of headers or footers on the first page. Or, if you prefer, you can enter header or footer information that prints on only that page.
   - **From Edge** controls the amount of spacing between the edge of the page and the headers and footers. To enter this setting, type in the value box or use the up and down arrow buttons to adjust the measurement.

Aligning Sections Vertically

Word also gives you the option of indicating how you want the text between the top and bottom margins of your page to be aligned. On the Layout tab of the Page Setup dialog box, click the Vertical Alignment down arrow to see a list of your choices. You can choose Top, Center, Justified, or Bottom. If you click Center, for example, Word will center the document between top and bottom margins. If you choose Bottom, Word aligns text with the bottom margin.

Adding Line Numbers

If you're working on a document that requires line numbering, you can use Page Setup settings to add the numbers automatically. As with the other settings, you can choose whether you want to number the entire document or a selected section. To turn on line numbering, follow these steps:

1. Choose File, Page Setup. The Page Setup dialog box is displayed.
2. Enter Margins, Paper, and Layout settings as needed.

3 On the Layout tab, click the Line Numbers button. The Line Numbers dialog box appears, as Figure 21-4 shows.

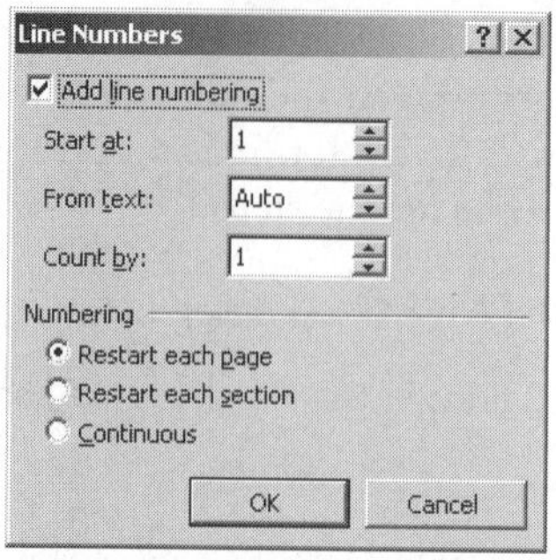

Figure 21-4. In the Line Numbers dialog box, you can elect to add line numbering for a section or for the entire document.

4 Select the Add Line Numbering check box. In the Start At box, type the number with which you want numbering to begin.

5 In the Numbering section, click Restart Each Page if you want each page to be individually numbered, Restart Each Section if you want the numbering to begin again with each subsequent section, or Continuous if you want numbers to increase throughout the document.

6 Click OK to close the Line Numbers dialog box and return to the Page Setup dialog box. Click OK to close the Page Setup dialog box.

InsideOut

If you've created heading styles that extend all the way to the left margin of your page, you might find them truncated when you add line numbering. You can fix this by displaying the Line Numbers dialog box and changing the From Text setting. By default, From Text is set to Auto, but by increasing the amount of space between numbering and text, you can make room for both line numbering and headings.

Creating a Page or Section Border

If you want to set up the page and section borders for your document while you're taking care of the rest of your page settings, you can do so in the Page Setup dialog box. Click the Layout tab, and click the Borders button. The Borders And Shading dialog box appears; here you can make the selections you want for the border.

For full coverage about this process, see Chapter 24, "Drawing Attention to your Document with Borders and Shading."

Controlling Page Breaks

As you know if you've created documents of any length, Word automatically adds page breaks at the appropriate points to indicate page divisions and show you how printed pages will look. An automatic page break looks truly like a break between pages—you can see where one page ends and another begins. There will be other instances in which you want to add breaks, however. You might want to add your own manual breaks, section breaks, and column breaks.

Adding Manual Page Breaks

In some cases, you might want to enter your own page break to control where data before of after the break is positioned on the page. You might want to insert a manual page break in the following instances:

- To prevent a paragraph from being divided across two pages
- To begin a new section with a heading at the top of a page
- To end a section when you don't want anything else printed on the current page

To enter a manual page break, place the insertion point where you want to make the break and press Ctrl+Enter. Or, if you prefer, you can choose Insert, Break. The Break dialog box appears, as Figure 21-5 shows.

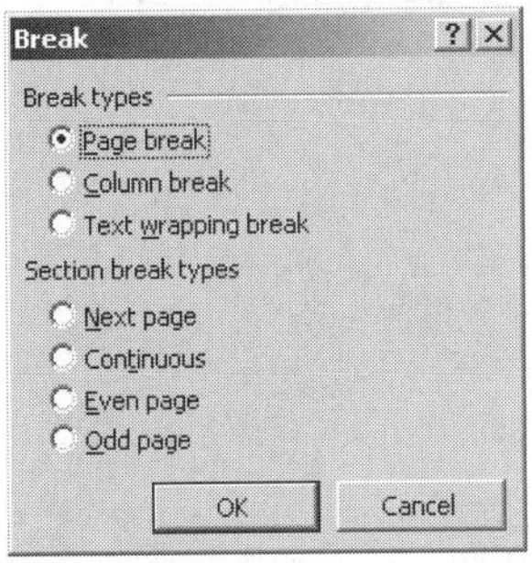

Figure 21-5. You can choose to insert a page, column, or text wrapping break using the Break dialog box.

Inserting Column and Text Breaks

Other breaks you can add include column breaks and text wrapping breaks. When you add a column break by choosing the Insert, Break and selecting Column Break in the dialog box, Word inserts a column break at the insertion point and wraps any remaining text to the next available column.

You'll use the Text Wrapping Break option when you need to force a text break because of an inline graphic, chart, or other element around which you need to wrap text. Instead of leaving a portion of a line or a stray line above an image, for example, you can insert a text wrapping break so the text begins immediately following the graphic.

Troubleshooting

My Printed Document Includes Unwanted Breaks

You finish your document and print a draft. What's this? The document is breaking at odd places…you seem to have mysterious phantom page breaks somewhere in your document. To resolve this problem, click the Show All button on the Standard toolbar. This displays all formatting characters, and you'll be able to look for and delete the unwanted page break character before you print.

For more information on working with sections, see Chapter 9, "Formatting Columns and Sections for Advanced Text Control."

newfeature!

Working with the Document Grid

For those times when text flow, precise character placement, and spacing control are important, you can turn on Word's Document Grid feature to align and space the characters in your document. You choose grid settings on the Document Grid tab of the Page Setup dialog box. (See Figure 21-6.)

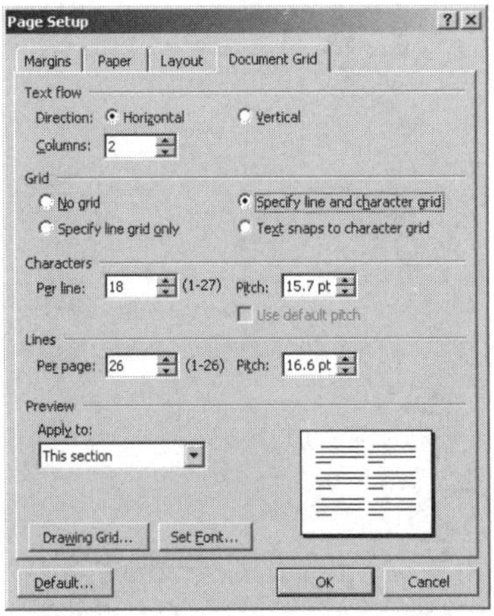

Figure 21-6. The Document Grid enables you to control precisely the line and character spacing in your document.

To use the Document Grid features, follow these steps:

1. Choose File, Page Setup. The Page Setup dialog box appears.
2. Click the Document Grid tab.
3. If you want to text to be displayed vertically, appearing top to bottom as you type, click Vertical in the Text Flow section. Otherwise, for traditional right-to-left text display, leave Horizontal selected.
4. To turn on the grid feature, select one of the following:
   - **Specify Line Grid Only** enables only the settings in the Lines section, so that you can choose the amount of space between lines (by selecting the number of lines you want to appear on the page) and the pitch, or spacing between lines.
   - **Specify Line And Character Grid** makes all settings in both Character and Lines sections available. This setting enables you to choose both the number of characters per line and the number of lines per page. You can also choose the pitch of both characters and lines.
   - **Text Snaps To Character Grid** disables the Pitch settings and gives you the means to choose number of Characters Per Line and Lines Per Page.
5. Click the Apply To down arrow, and choose the option reflecting the portion of the document to which you want to apply the grid. You can choose This Section, This Point Forward, or Whole Document.
6. Click OK to apply the grid settings and close the dialog box.

If you changed the text direction from horizontal to vertical, Word starts a new page and the grid choices are in effect. If you left the text direction as it was, Word applies the grid effects as soon as you begin typing. As you type, you'll be able to see the effects of the new spacing selections you've chosen.

Displaying the Document Grid

If you want to see the grid while you work, choose File, Page Setup to display the Page Setup dialog box; then click the Document Grid tab. In the lower left portion of the dialog box, click the Drawing Grid button. In the Drawing Grid dialog box, select the Display Gridlines On Screen check box. (See Figure 21-7, on the next page.) Click OK twice to return to the document. The gridlines are displayed throughout the entire document.

note If you want to see the document grid while you work, be sure to display your document in Print Layout view by choosing View, Print Layout. The document grid does not appear in Normal, Web Layout, or Outline view.

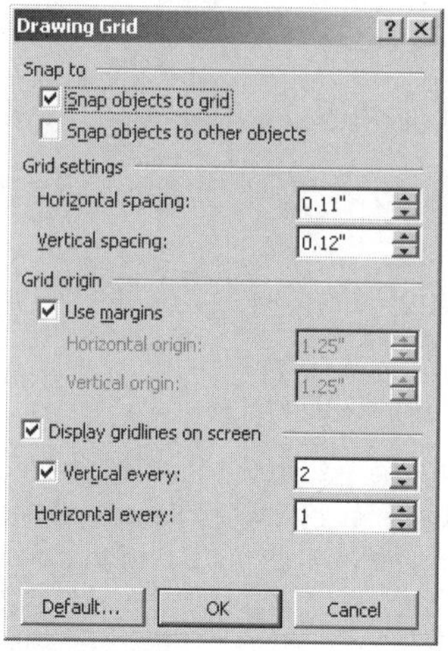

Figure 21-7. Customize the grid display by using the Document Grid settings.

Inserting Page Numbers

One of the first things you'll want to do with a multi-page document is add page numbers to the pages. Word gives you the option of controlling the placement, alignment and format of the page numbers you add. To add page numbers, choose Insert, Page Numbers. The Page Numbers dialog box appears. Here you make the following choices:

1. Click the Position down-arrow, and choose the place on the page where you want the page number to appear. The Top Of Page choice inserts the page number in the header; the Bottom Of Page choice adds the page number to the footer. Other choices include Vertically Center Of Page, Vertically Outside, and Vertically Inside. As you choose each type, Word shows the effect of your selection in the Preview window.
2. Click the Alignment down-arrow, and choose the way in which you want the page number to be aligned. Choices include Left, Center, Right, Inside, and Outside.
3. Click Show Page Number On First Page if you want the page number to appear on your title page.
4. Click Format to display the Page Number Format dialog box so that you can choose the type, style, and numbering sequence for your page numbers.
5. Click OK twice to close the dialog boxes and add the page numbers to your document.

Chapter 22

Formatting Documents Using Templates, Wizards, and Add-Ins

Computers are powerful, but they still need to be told what to do at times—no matter how "automated" a task might seem. It should come as no surprise, therefore, that whenever you create a new document in Word, your document is based on a *template* that provides default document creation settings. Templates serve as patterns for documents; they define styles, AutoText entries, toolbars, standard (or *boilerplate*) text, placeholder text, and so forth. You can control how documents and templates interact in a number of ways. For example, you can base documents on existing templates, create custom templates for new and existing documents, attach templates to documents, load global templates, and edit templates.

In addition to controlling documents using templates, you can use interactive *wizards* to create particularly styled documents. Word provides a set of wizards, and each wizard presents a series of dialog boxes that walks you through the construction of a particular type of document. For instance, you can use wizards to create memos, Web pages, résumés, letters, and other common documents.

You can also control your Word environment by adding custom commands and features with *add-ins*. Add-ins are supplemental programs that add specific capabilities to Word. For example, some add-ins install Microsoft Office updates, proofreading tools, troubleshooter tools, sound files, graphic filters, and additional templates and wizards. In this chapter, you'll learn how to use and control templates, wizards, and add-ins to enhance and automate document creation, editing, and formatting.

Understanding How Templates Work

As mentioned, every Word document is based on a template. A template is a .dot file (or group of related files) that contains the structure and tools for shaping the style and page layout of finished files. Templates can contain settings for fonts, styles, page layout parameters, toolbars, macros, AutoText entries, key assignments, menus, and special formatting. By default, Word bases new blank documents on the Normal template (discussed in more detail in the section, "Getting the Scoop on Word's Normal Template," on page 527).

The main purpose of templates is to make formatting and inserting information into documents as efficient and automatic as possible. The fewer formatting and typing tasks you have to perform, the better. In addition to speeding document creation, templates enable you to provide custom editing environments for particular projects and clients because templates can include interface tools (such as toolbars, macros, and menus) as well as formatting and layout settings. To clarify, templates can assist in document creation tasks in the following ways:

- **Provide all relevant styles for a particular document.** As described in Chapter 10, "Using Styles to Increase Your Formatting Power," you can create and use a series of styles to generate a particular look for a document. By creating a template that contains a set of styles, you can easily access and consistently apply the styles throughout similar and related documents.
- **Include boilerplate text, AutoText entries, and placeholder text.** Templates can save you from repeatedly typing information that recurs in related documents by enabling you to create new documents that automatically contain default text, include relevant custom AutoText entries (such as company names and contract text), and display placeholder text. For more information about AutoText entries, see Chapter 6, "Putting Text Tools to Work."
- **Display necessary and customized toolbars and menus.** If a particular type of document always uses specific Word tools, you can create a template that displays a Word interface that caters to the tasks associated with the document type. To learn about customizing toolbars and menus, see Chapter 38, "Customizing Word and Maximizing Accessibility."

- **Include specialized macros for a particular document type.** To help streamline tasks in certain types of documents, you can include macros in a template. Macros are routines that are created to perform a task or set of tasks, and are assigned to a toolbar button or keyboard shortcut. For more information about macros, see Chapter 40, "Creating and Working with VBA Macros."

Regardless of the information included in templates, you can use two main types of templates as you work in Word: *global templates* and *document templates.* Global templates (most notably the Normal template) contain settings that are available to all documents. In contrast, document templates, such as memo and Web page templates, contain settings that are available only to documents based on that template. When a document is based on a template, the template is attached to the document. (For more information about attaching templates, see the section "Attaching Templates to Documents," on page 538.) If this difference between global and document templates seems a little cloudy at the moment, don't despair. Once you review the information in this chapter and experiment with templates for a while, you'll quickly see the value of knowing how to use and customize global and document templates as you work.

Getting the Scoop on Word's Normal Template

No matter what template you use to format a specific document, the Normal global template is always open. Normal.dot is stored in the ...\Application Data\Microsoft\Templates folder by default. Whenever you start Word, it automatically looks for the Normal template in the location specified on the File Locations tab in the Options dialog box. (You access this dialog box by choosing Tools, Options.)

For more information about changing the default location of template files, see Chapter 38, "Customizing Word and Maximizing Accessibility."

The Normal template contains default styles and built-in AutoText entries (but no boilerplate text) that are automatically available whenever you create new, blank documents. As you work in a document, any styles, AutoText entries, macros, or other customizations you save are stored in the Normal template unless you specify otherwise. In addition, you can modify the Normal template to change the default document formatting in Word. As you can imagine, the longer you work with Word, the more customized your Normal.dot file becomes.

If the Normal template is damaged, moved, missing, or renamed, Word creates a new Normal template the next time you start Word, which is based on the default settings. This automatically generated Normal template won't include any customizations you've made to a previously existing version of Normal.dot. Of course, if you've intentionally renamed your Normal template to force Word to create a new Normal template, you can copy components from the renamed template into the newly generated Normal template by using the Organizer, as described in the section "Renaming, Deleting, and Copying Styles Using the Organizer," on page 543.

Troubleshooting

Word Crashes During Startup

If Word crashes during startup, you can quickly determine whether the problem is due to a damaged registry entry or a corrupt Normal.dot file. To get to the root of the problem, try starting Word while bypassing these two items, as follows:

1. Click Start, and choose Run.
2. In the Run dialog box, type **"c:\program files\microsoft office\office10\winword.exe" /a** (or replace the text in quotation marks with a different path if you installed Word elsewhere) in the Open box, and click OK.

If Word opens properly using this method, you can deduce that you have a damaged registry or a corrupt Normal.dot file. To test whether the Normal.dot file is the culprit in your startup woes, use Windows Explorer to find and rename the Normal.dot file, and then attempt to start Word normally. If Word starts, a new Normal.dot file will be created, and you can use the Organizer to copy any components you need from the renamed file into the newly created Normal.dot file.

If Word still doesn't start properly after you rename your existing Normal.dot file, you probably have a damaged registry. You can try to correct this problem by opening Word using the Run dialog box (as described above) and choosing Help, Detect And Repair. Alternatively, you can run the Windows Installer. To do so, choose Start, Settings, Control Panel. In Control Panel, double-click Add/Remove Programs, select Microsoft Office or Microsoft Word on the Install/Uninstall tab of the Add/Remove Programs Properties dialog box, and click Add/Remove. In the setup dialog box, choose the repair option to restore your original Word files and registry settings.

caution Because the Normal template is so necessary and so widely used, it's often the first target of macro virus authors. Therefore, if you work with a highly customized Normal template, you might want to back up your system's Normal.dot file every few weeks. If you don't need to change your Normal.dot file on a regular basis, you can provided added security by making the Normal template read-only. Making your Normal template read-only protects it from virus attacks that attempt to overwrite or add information to Normal.dot files.

Creating New Documents Based on Existing Templates

When you install Word, the setup program provides numerous wizards and templates. You can find additional wizards and templates on the Web, most notably by accessing the Microsoft Office Template Gallery (at *officeupdate.microsoft.com/templategallery*). With all these prebuilt templates at your disposal, you can easily create new documents based on templates without having to create a custom template. In this section, you'll learn how to create new documents based on templates that you have on hand or can access easily.

Troubleshooting

Some Built-In Word Templates Aren't Available

When Word is installed as part of a typical Office installation, some built-in wizards and templates are installed directly onto your computer, but other wizards and templates are loaded by the Windows Installer the first time you try to access them. If you click Customize instead of Install Now when you first run the setup program, you can choose to install additional templates and wizards at that time.

To make additional built-in templates available after Word is installed, follow these steps:

1. Run the setup program, choose the Add Or Remove Features option, and click Next.
2. In the Features To Install list, expand the Word section, and then expand Wizards And Templates to view the list of built-in wizards and templates.
3. Click the Wizards And Templates down arrow, and choose Run All From My Computer on the drop-down menu. To install only a few additional templates and wizards, click the icon next to each wizard or template you want to add, and choose Run From My Computer.
4. Click Update to install the wizards and templates.

By indicating that you want templates and wizards to run on your computer, you'll be able to access the templates and wizards easily, without having to run the Windows Installer program.

Using the Templates Dialog Box to Create New Documents

As mentioned, Word provides a number of built-in templates that you can use to create new documents. For easy access, Word displays links to templates in the New Document task pane. To access the Word templates, choose File, New to display the

New Document task pane, and then click the General Templates link. The Templates dialog box will appear, as shown in Figure 22-1.

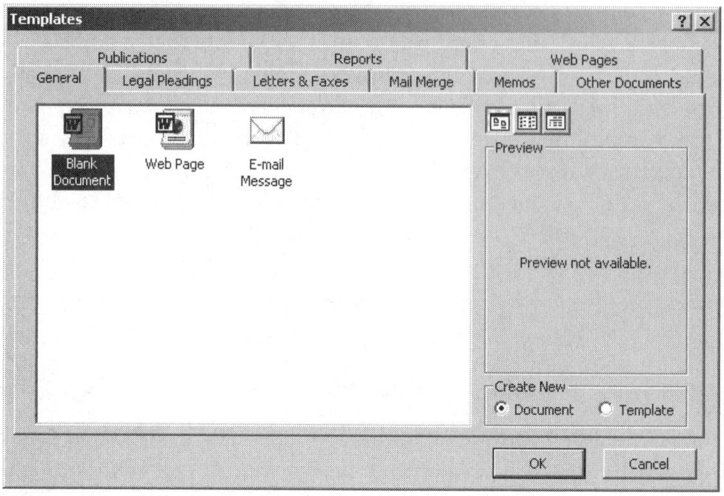

Figure 22-1. The Templates dialog box provides easy access to built-in Word templates as well as custom templates.

The Templates dialog box lets you access all default Word templates (which are stored in the location shown for the Workgroup Templates File Types entry when you choose Tools, Options and click the File Locations tab) as well as any templates you create and save in the ...Application Data\Microsoft\Templates folder. Each tab in the Templates dialog box indicates a subfolder. When you create or copy custom templates (as described in the section "Creating Custom Templates" on page 534), you can include your custom templates in the Templates dialog box by storing the files in the Templates folder.

To create a new document using a template stored in the Templates dialog box, follow these steps:

1. Choose File, New to open the New Document task pane, and then click General Templates in the New From Template section.
2. In the Templates dialog box, click the tab for the subfolder that contains the template you want to use for the new document.
3. In the Create New section, make sure that Document is selected, and then double-click the template (or select the template, and click OK).

If you're opening a template or wizard that's located on your computer, Word immediately creates a new document. If the template isn't on your computer, Windows Installer loads it and then Word creates the document.

> **tip** **Access Word templates from the Start Menu**
>
> If you have Microsoft Office installed, you can open Word and a new document based on a template simultaneously. To do so, click Start, choose New Office Document, and then double-click any Word template displayed in the New Office Document dialog box.

newfeature!

Obtaining Templates from Microsoft.com

If you find that the Templates dialog box doesn't contain the template you need, you might want to download additional templates from the Microsoft Office Template Gallery Web site. Figure 22-2 shows some of the template categories available on the Office Template Gallery Web site.

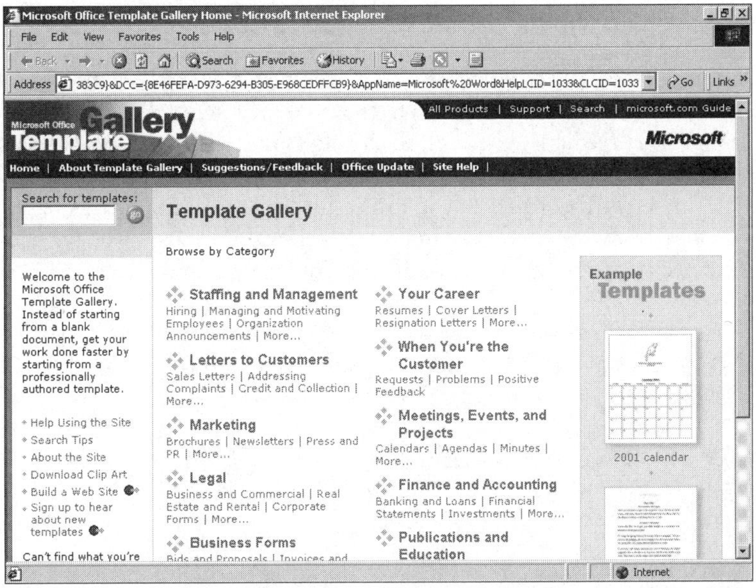

Figure 22-2. In addition to clicking category headings to find templates, you can type a search string in the Office Template Gallery's Search For Templates box.

To use the Office Template Gallery, verify that you're connected to the Internet, and then follow these basic steps:

1. Choose File, New, and then click the Templates On Microsoft.com link in the New Document task pane.

2 On the Office Template Gallery Web page, click a main category or a subcategory listing, and then scan the available templates. To preview a template, click the Go To Preview hyperlink associated with the template. You might be asked to accept a template agreement; if so, click Accept to continue.

3 When you find a template that suits your needs, click the Edit In Microsoft Word hyperlink.

The template will be downloaded to your system and displayed in Word. At that point, you can edit the template and save it as a local document or template. You should spend some time checking out the templates on the Office Template Gallery Web site—the selection is fairly extensive, ranging from marketing and business forms to stationery and résumés.

newfeature!

Using Templates Stored on Your Web Sites

In addition to retrieving templates from the Templates dialog box and the Office Template Gallery, you can access templates stored on a network or Web site. Frequently, workgroups need to share templates, so storing templates on line provides an ideal way to share templates and ensure that the most up-to-date templates are readily available to team members. In Word 2002, you can easily create new documents based on templates that are stored on Web sites and in networked locations. To do so, make sure you're connected to the Internet, and then follow these steps:

1 Choose File, New, and then click the Templates On My Web Sites link in the New Document task pane. The New From Templates On My Web Sites dialog box opens, as shown in Figure 22-3.

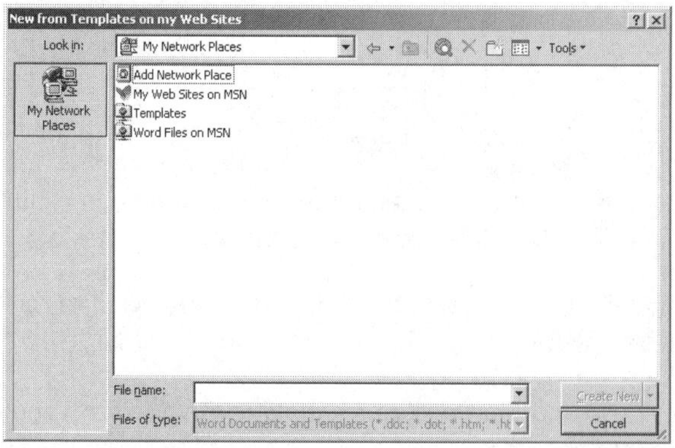

Figure 22-3. The New From Templates On My Web Sites dialog box serves as a gateway to templates stored on your network or Web sites.

2 Double-click the shortcut to the folder on the Web server that contains the template you want to use.

3. If necessary, double-click the folder that contains the template you want to use, and then double-click the template file.

After you open an online template file, a new document is created on your desktop that's based on the template settings. You can then type the contents of the new file and save the document locally or store it on the server, just as you can any other document.

Troubleshooting

Links to Templates Are Not Displayed When I Click the Templates On My Web Sites Link

Before you can create a new document based on a template that's stored on line, the template must be stored in an online folder, and you need to create a shortcut to the network or Web server that contains the template you want to use. If these conditions aren't met, you won't have any Web site shortcuts in the New From Templates On My Web Sites dialog box.

If you don't have a Web site or network server space, you can obtain file storage space on line in a number of ways. Here are a couple of techniques for accessing free Internet space that you can use to store files:

- You can create a File Cabinet on the MSN Communities Web site, at *communities.msn.com*.
- You can access recommended entities providing free server space by visiting the Microsoft Office Update page (*officeupdate.microsoft.com*). On the Microsoft Office Update page, click the eServices hyperlink, and then click the Store Files On The Web hyperlink (which appears below the My Data On The Web hyperlink).

After you have created an online folder in which you can store files and templates, the next order of business is to create a shortcut to the online folder. To do so in Windows 2000, follow these steps:

1. Click Add Network Place in the New Document task pane.
2. In the Add Network Place Wizard, click Create A Shortcut To An Existing Network Place, and click Next.
3. Type the URL of the Web server, type a name for the shortcut to the Web server, and then click Finish.

After you create shortcuts to Web site locations, you can click the links to the sites in the New From Templates On My Web Sites dialog box to access the online folder and any files or templates stored within the folder.

Creating Custom Templates

Once you're familiar with how templates work and how to use existing templates, you're ready to start creating your own templates. In Word, you can create templates in three ways. You can base a template on an existing document, base a new template on an existing template, or create a template from scratch. The method you use should depend on the resources you have on hand, as follows:

- **Create a template based on a document** when you have a document that contains most or all of the settings you want to use in your template.
- **Create a template based on an existing template** when you have a template that contains many of the settings you want to use in your new template but you want to add or change a few settings without affecting the existing template.
- **Create a template from scratch** when you have no usable model to use as a starting point for your template.

When you create custom templates, you should save your templates in the ...\Application Data\Microsoft\Templates folder so that they'll be easily accessible in the Templates dialog box. Templates you save in the Templates folder appear on the General tab in the Templates dialog box (which means, logically enough, that templates stored elsewhere won't appear in the Templates dialog box). If you want to store your templates on a custom tab in the Templates dialog box, create a new subfolder (or a few subfolders, if necessary) in the Templates folder, and save your templates in that subfolder. The custom tab labels are the same as the subfolders' names, so name your subfolders carefully. Keep in mind that you must save at least one template in each subfolder; otherwise, the subfolder won't appear as a tab in the Templates dialog box.

Now that we have a few details out of the way, let's look more closely at the three ways you can create templates.

note You should save your template with the .dot extension, but any document file that you save in the Templates folder will also act as a template by default.

Document templates can be stored on your hard disk, included in a document library, or used as a workgroup template. For more information about document libraries and workgroup templates, see Chapter 32, "Sharing Information on Networks."

Basing a Template on an Existing Document

When you base a template on an existing document, you create a template that contains all the styles, macros, toolbars, menus, layout, and other settings contained in the document. Most likely, you'll want to modify the document's settings slightly to fine-tune your template. You can do so, but be careful. You don't want to modify the document—you want to modify the template. So create your template first, close the existing document (if necessary), and then make all your modifications within the template document at that point, as follows:

1. Choose File, Open.
2. In the Open dialog box, open the document that contains the formatting and/or text you want to include in your template.
3. Choose File, Save As.
4. In the Save As dialog box, select Document Template in the Save As Type drop-down list, as shown in Figure 22-4.

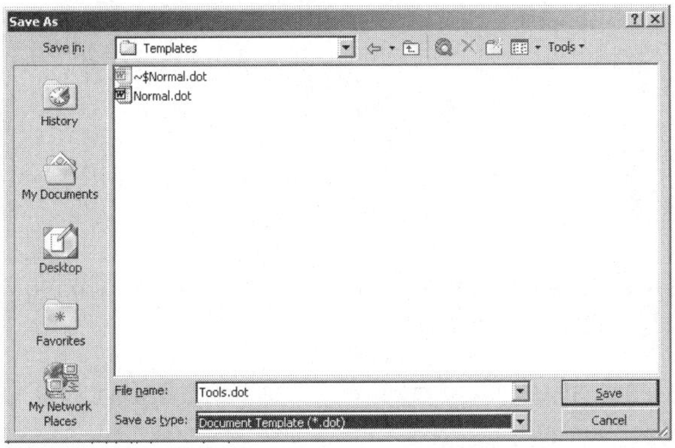

Figure 22-4. When you select Document Template in the Save As Type drop-down list, Word displays the Templates folder by default.

5. By default, the document will be saved in the Templates folder, and the template will appear on the General tab in the Templates dialog box. To display the template on a custom tab, create a new subfolder. The subfolder's name will also appear as the name of the tab.
6. In the File Name box, type a name for the new template, and click Save.
7. In the new template, add any text or graphics you want to appear in new documents that you base on the template, and delete any information you don't want to appear in documents using the template.
8. Make setup changes in the new template, if desired. For example, you can change the margin settings, page size and orientation, styles, paragraph formatting, header or footer information, and so forth.
9. Save and close the new template.

After you create a new template, you should test the template to verify that it works as intended by creating a document using the template. To do so, click the General Templates link in the New Document task pane, click the tab on which the template is located (if necessary), make sure that the Document option is selected in the Create New section in the Templates dialog box, and then double-click the new template.

Creating a New Template Based on an Existing Template

If you have a template that you want to use as a starting point for a new template, you can do so in much the same way you create a template based on an existing document. The main procedural difference is that you open a template (.dot) file instead of a document (.doc) file.

To create a template based on an existing template, follow these steps:

1. Choose File, New.
2. In the New Document task pane, click the General Templates link in the New From Template section. The Templates dialog box opens.
3. Click a template similar to the one you want to create, click the Template option in the Create New section, and then click OK.
4. After the template opens, choose File, Save As, and save the template as a new template with a new name.
5. In the new template, add and modify settings as necessary, and then save the template.

Customizing existing templates comes in especially handy when you download templates using the Templates On Microsoft.com link in the New Document task pane. The Web site provides a wide variety of generic templates; you can customize the generic templates by modifying them to suit your specific needs and then save the modified templates as your own.

For more information about the Office Template Gallery, see the section "Obtaining Templates from Microsoft.com" on page 531.

Building a Template from Scratch

In addition to basing templates on existing documents and templates, you can build templates from scratch. Building a template from scratch is similar to creating a document from scratch. To create a new, blank template, follow these steps:

1. Choose File, New, and then click General Templates in the New Document task pane.

2 In the Templates dialog box, choose Template in the Create New section, and then double-click Blank Document on the General tab.

tip Another way to create a blank template is to open a new, blank document, open the Save As dialog box, and then save the document as a template.

After you create a blank template file, you can add styles, boilerplate text, custom toolbars, macros, and any other elements you want to include in your template.

tip **Use themes to create template settings**

When you create templates, you might want to incorporate built-in *themes* to streamline the template creation process. A theme is a set of colors, fonts, and graphics elements (such as ruled lines and bullets) that work together to provide a unified look for you document. Even if you don't see a built-in theme that exactly meets your needs, you can use a theme as a starting point to help identify some of the elements you might want to include in your template. After you apply a theme to your template, you can reformat the theme components to suit your style. For more information about themes, see Chapter 23, "Using Word's Desktop Publishing Features."

Previewing Templates Using the Style Gallery

One of the nicer aspects of using templates is that you aren't forever committed to using a particular template's styles. You can change a document's styles at any time. If you're considering changing a document's styles, you should visit Word's Style Gallery. The Style Gallery enables you to preview how an entire document will look if styles are applied from another template. If you like what you see, you can copy the styles from within the Style Gallery directly into your document.

To preview a document with other template styles and to apply new styles to the document, follow these steps:

1 Choose Format, Theme.

2 In the Theme dialog box, click Style Gallery. The Style Gallery opens, as shown in Figure 22-5, on the next page.

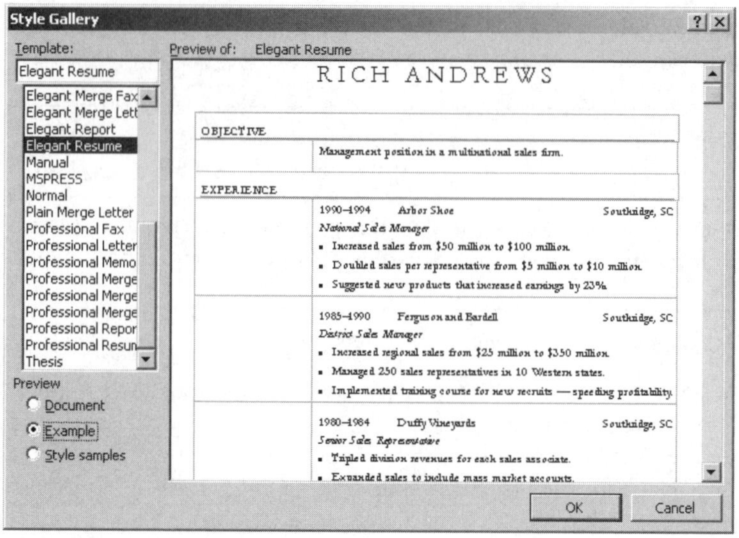

Figure 22-5. The Style Gallery enables you to preview and apply styles from other templates to the current document.

3. Select a template in the Template list, and choose an option in the Preview section, as follows:

   - **Document** displays how your document will appear if it's formatted with the selected template.
   - **Example** displays an example of another file formatted with the template.
   - **Style Samples** displays the format for each style included in the template in list format.

4. To apply the selected template to the current document, click OK.

Keep in mind that when you apply styles using the Style Gallery, you aren't changing the template that's attached to the current document. Instead, the Style Gallery lets you view and apply styles from other templates. To attach a different template to a document, follow the instructions in the next section.

Attaching Templates to Documents

Every document has a template associated with, or "attached" to, it that controls the basic layout and settings used in the document by default. If you create a new, blank document, the Normal template is attached to the document. When you create a document from an existing template, that template is automatically attached to the document. You can specify which template you want to attach to a document, regardless of which template is currently attached. And when you replace the existing document template with a new one, you can specify to automatically update the document's text with the new styles.

To attach a new template to a document and update the document's styles, follow these steps:

1. Choose Tools, Templates And Add-Ins. The Templates And Add-Ins dialog box opens, as shown in Figure 22-6.

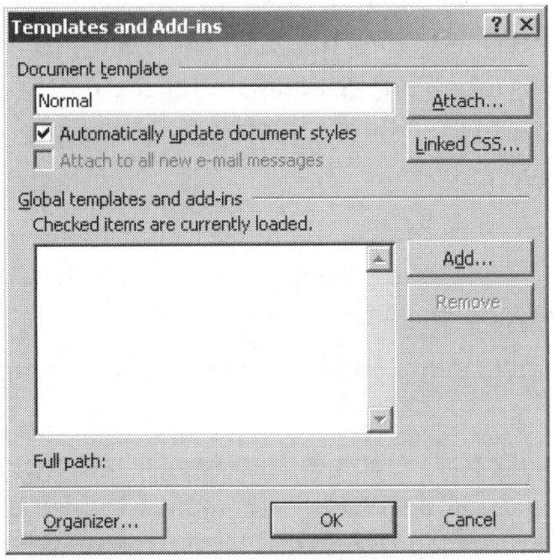

Figure 22-6. The Templates And Add-Ins dialog box helps you attach a different template to a document, automatically update styles, and control global templates and add-ins.

2. Click Attach to open the Attach Template dialog box, which looks very similar to the Open dialog box. The contents of the Templates folder are displayed by default.

3. Select the template you want to attach to the current document, and then click Open (or simply double-click the desired template).

4. To automatically apply the newly attached template's styles to the current document, select the Automatically Update Document Styles check box in the Templates And Add-Ins dialog box.

5. Click OK to attach the selected template to the current document.

If you direct Word to automatically update styles, keep in mind that the document text must be formatted with styles that have the same names as the styles in the newly attached template. If the style names are the same, Word will update the text formatting to match the new template's style formats. If the document's style names are different from the new template's style names, you'll have to select and replace instances of each style. If you find that you're faced with changing styles manually, consider using the new Select All feature to choose all instances of an "old" style, and then click the new style name in the Styles And Formatting task pane to replace the styles.

For more information about changing all instances of a style, see Chapter 10, "Using Styles to Increase Your Formatting Power."

Modifying Attached Templates

Instead of replacing an attached template with a different template, you might occasionally want to modify an attached template. You might want to modify a template when you're satisfied with the current template for the most part but you want to do some minor tweaking or add a new component. Modifying an attached template has the following effects:

- Macros, AutoText entries, custom toolbars, and custom command settings in the modified template are available for use in any document based on the template, including existing documents.
- Modified styles are not immediately updated in existing files to match the template's new styles.
- Added or modified boilerplate text, graphics, and format settings (such as page margins, column settings, and so forth) are applied to new documents subsequently based on the modified template. Existing documents aren't affected.

If you want to update an existing file that was created using a template before it was modified, open the document, display the Templates And Add-Ins dialog box (by choosing Tools, Templates And Add-Ins), and select the Automatically Update Document Styles check box. After you click OK, the document will be reformatted using the template's new settings.

For more information about how to modify existing templates, see the section "Modifying Existing Templates," on page 543.

Working with Global Templates

As mentioned, Word uses two types of templates: global and document. All documents have access to the Normal global template, and many documents have document templates attached that provide formatting instructions. In addition, you can load other templates as needed to serve as global templates. Keeping all these template possibilities in mind, you can see that the styles available in a current document are based on the following templates:

- The Normal template, which is a global template
- The document template attached to the document, which is the template you based the document on if you based it on a template other than Normal
- Any currently loaded global templates

If several templates are open that define the same style name, the attached document template's settings override all global template settings. The reason document templates take precedence when it comes to styles is because the purpose of global templates is to store macros, AutoText entries, and custom toolbar, menu, and keyboard shortcut settings that you can use while you work with any document, not just documents based on a particular document template. By design, templates should be used as global templates when they contain features that are beneficial to any open document.

Typically, when you work on a document, you use only the settings stored in the attached document template or in the Normal template. But when you need to use any items that are stored in another template, you can load the other template as a global template. This enables you to use the template's features without having to modify the Normal.dot file or replace the attached document template. After you load a global template, items stored in the template are available to any document during the remainder of the Word session.

Loading Global Templates

When you load global templates, you can specify whether they are to be available for the current session only or available whenever you start Microsoft Word. To load a global template for the current session, follow these steps:

1. Choose Tools, Templates And Add-Ins to open the Templates And Add-Ins dialog box.
2. In the Global Templates And Add-Ins section, click Add to open the Add Template dialog box, and then double-click the name of a template that you want to include in the global template list.
3. Select the check boxes next to any templates you want to load during the current session, as shown in Figure 22-7, on the next page.
4. Click OK to complete the setup.

If you often load the same global template, you can configure Word to load the global template automatically whenever you start Word. The easiest way to accomplish this is to copy the template into the Word Startup folder, which is located at ...Application Data\Microsoft\Word\Startup by default.

caution Be careful when choosing to load global templates automatically. Configuring your system to load global templates each time Word starts uses up system memory and slows the Word startup process.

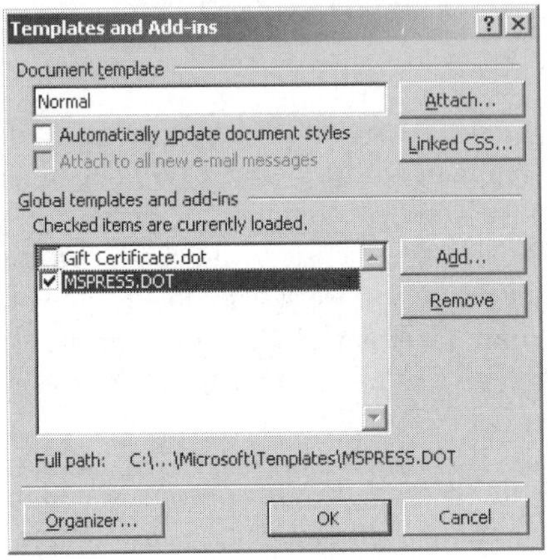

Figure 22-7. You can pick and choose which templates you want to load as global templates during the current session.

Unloading Global Templates

By default, global templates are unloaded when you exit Word, unless you've placed the global template in your Word Startup folder. But if you prefer, you can unload global templates before then. When you've finished with a global template, you can unload it or remove it from the global template list. Note that neither action deletes the template file; you'll merely stop the template from serving as a global template. To unload a global template, perform either of the following actions:

- Open the Templates And Add-Ins dialog box, and clear the check box next to the template's name in the global templates list to stop using the global template.
- Select the global template in the global templates list, and then click Remove to stop using the global template and to remove the template from the global templates list.

InsideOut

The Remove button in the Templates And Add-Ins dialog box is unavailable when the global template you select to remove is stored in your Startup folder. To work around this, cut and paste the template in the Startup folder to a new location, or if you have another copy of the template, simply delete the template in the Startup folder.

Modifying Existing Templates

You can modify existing templates by opening and manually changing the template file, or you can copy, delete, and rename template components using the Organizer. Either way, when you modify a template, the modifications affect new documents that you create based on the template, but the content of existing documents is not affected by template modifications unless you specifically instruct Word (by configuring options in the Templates And Add-Ins dialog box) to apply the new template settings to the document.

Modifying an Existing Document Template

To modify an existing document by working directly in the template, you must first open the file as a template from the Open dialog box, as follows:

1. Choose File, Open, select Document Templates in the Files Of Type drop-down list, and then locate and open the template you want to modify. By default, templates are stored in the ...\Application Data\Microsoft\Templates folder.

2. Change any of the template's text and graphics, styles, formatting, macros, AutoText entries, toolbars, menu settings, and keyboard shortcuts, and then click Save on the Standard toolbar.

Remember, whenever you make changes to a document template, you should take the time to test the changes by creating a sample new document based on the template.

Renaming, Deleting, and Copying Styles Using the Organizer

In addition to working directly in a template file, you can use the Organizer to manage template components. The Organizer dialog box contains tabs for Styles, AutoText, Toolbars, and Macro Project Items, as shown in Figure 22-8, on the next page.

To use the Organizer to copy and manage any of these types of elements in documents and templates, follow these steps:

1. Choose Tools, Templates And Add-Ins, and then click the Organizer button.

2. In the Organizer dialog box, click the tab for the items you want to copy, delete, or rename.

3. To copy items to or from templates or files, click Close File to close the active document and its attached template or to close the Normal template. Then click Open File, and select the template or file you want to open by double-clicking it in the Open dialog box. Select the items you want to copy, delete, or rename, and then click the Copy, Delete, or Rename button as appropriate.

4 Click Close when you've finished with the Organizer.

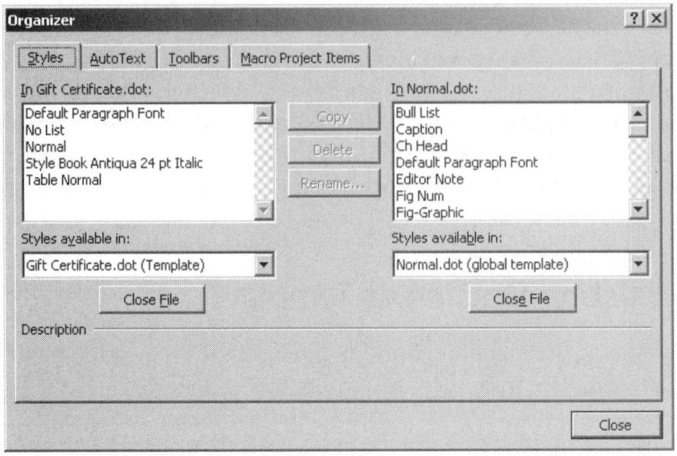

Figure 22-8. You can copy, delete, and rename styles, AutoText, toolbars, and macros stored in specific documents and templates by using the Organizer.

Troubleshooting

I Can't Copy Items to a Particular Template

If you try to copy styles, macros, toolbars, or other items to a template that's protected in some way, you might not be able to open the template, accept or reject tracked changes in the template, or save changes to the template. This problem might be due to any of the following reasons:

- The template is protected for tracked changes, comments, or forms.
- The template is encrypted and requires you to enter a password.
- You must enter a file sharing password to modify a document. If you don't know the password, you can open the template only as a read-only file.
- You don't have access to the server on which the template is stored.
- The template might be open on another computer on your network.

To save changes to a template, the protection settings must be removed from the template, you must gain the proper access permissions, or you must wait until the template is no longer open on another networked computer.

In some instances, you might want to protect templates. To learn more about protecting documents, see the next section, "Protecting Templates."

Protecting Templates

Protecting your templates can help ensure that templates remain intact, without unintentional alterations. You can protect templates in the same manner you protect documents. In particular, you can protect your templates in the following ways:

- **Suggest that they be opened as read-only.** Choose Tools, Options, click the Security tab, select the Read-Only Recommended check box, and then click OK.
- **Protect tracked changes, comments, or forms.** Choose Tools, Protect Document, enter a password, click OK, re-enter your password, and then click OK again.

For more information about tracking changes and adding comments see Chapter 33, "Revising Documents Using Markup Tools," and for more information about creating and protecting forms, see Chapter 36, "Working with Field Codes and Custom Forms."

- **Encrypt the template.** Choose Tools, Options, click the Security tab, enter a password in the Password To Open box, click OK, re-enter your password, and then click OK again.
- **Create a file sharing password.** Choose Tools, Options, click the Security tab, enter a password in the Password To Modify box, click OK, re-enter your password, and then click OK again.

Protecting your templates can be especially important if you're sharing them with other people.

For more information about security in Word, see Chapter 34, "Addressing Security Issues."

Constructing Documents Using Word's Wizards

By now, most experienced Word users are familiar with Word's wizards. These wizards provide a set of interactive dialog boxes that walk you through the document construction process. In other words, the wizard asks questions, you provide responses, and then an item is created, such as a form or a Web page, in accordance with your answers. The aim of a wizard is to create a foundation for a document. After the document is created, you fill in the gaps with more detailed and refined information.

By default, wizards are stored in the Templates dialog box, alongside document templates. You can easily identify wizards in the Templates dialog box because wizard icons include a magic wand. To open a wizard, you simply double-click the wizard of your choice. To work through a wizard, you simply follow the on-screen instructions.

For example, the Web Page Wizard welcome screen is shown in Figure 22-9. As you can see, the wizard steps are listed on the left side of the screen; the current step is shown in green. By referring to this area while you work, you can see where you are in the construction process at any time.

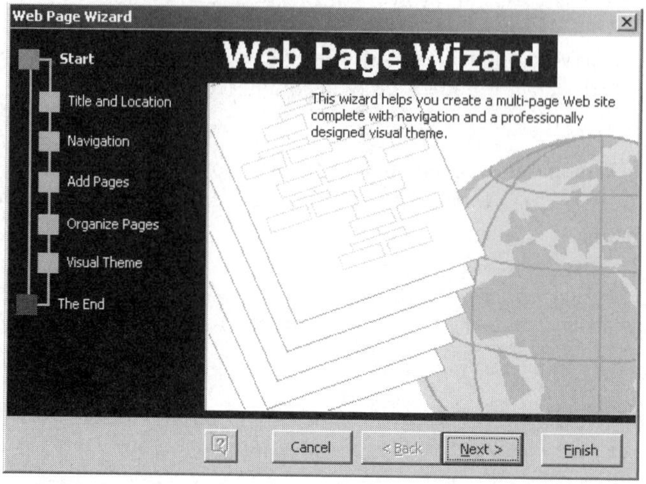

Figure 22-9. Wizards apply information you supply to create a document or set of documents.

Customizing Word with Add-Ins

The final way in which you can modify your Word environment is to use add-ins. An add-in is a supplemental program that adds custom commands or custom features to Word. Like global templates, some add-ins can be loaded for the current session only or whenever you start Word. (For loading instructions, see the section "Loading Global Templates," on page 541.) Other types of add-ins (such as Office updates) run automatically after you install them when you start Word.

Examples of typical add-ins offered by Microsoft and other third-party vendors include the following:

- **Stamps.com** enables you to print your own postage.
- **Supplement Templates And Wizards** provides additional wizards for home and work use.
- **Office Troubleshooters** includes troubleshooting tools that can help you diagnose and correct common Office problems.

- **Microsoft Office XP Proofing Tools** contains proofreading tools that Microsoft makes for over 30 languages, including fonts, spelling and grammar checkers, AutoCorrect lists, AutoSummarize rules, translation dictionaries, and for Asian languages, Input Method Editors (IMEs).

To find add-ins on the Microsoft Office Update site, follow these steps:

1. In Word, choose Help, Office On The Web. The Word page should be displayed by default.
2. Click the Downloads hyperlink.
3. On the Downloads For Word page, select the Add-Ins And Assistants check box, clear the other check boxes, and then click Search Now.

To find Microsoft-approved add-ins provided by third parties, click the Word Downloads From Third Parties hyperlink on the Microsoft Office Update Web site's Downloads For Word page (*officeupdate.microsoft.com/downloadCatalog/Word_thirdpartydl.htm*).

Keep in mind that when you download an add-in, you might have to follow specific installation procedures to ensure that the add-in runs properly. Generally, the download site provides the information you need for correct installation. Before you download an add-in, you should print the installation instructions so that you'll have them on hand for easy reference.

> **tip** You can remove most add-ins by using the Windows Add/Remove Programs dialog box. To access this dialog box, choose Start, Settings, Control Panel, and then in Control Panel, double-click Add/Remove Programs.

Chapter 23

Using Word's Desktop Publishing Features

When you work in Microsoft Word, you probably take for granted how Word seamlessly flows text from margin to margin and page to page. On occasion, however, you might want to venture beyond basic word processing and into the realm of desktop publishing. For example, instead of filling up a page with text, you might want to precisely position and format blocks of text in your document, or you might want to customize the overall "look" of your document by applying a uniform color scheme. Although Word doesn't offer all the bells and whistles incorporated in high-end desktop publishing applications, it does include a nice collection of desktop publishing tools that can serve the majority of your workaday desktop publishing needs.

Specifically, the desktop publishing capabilities in Word let you control text layout by using text boxes, AutoShapes formatted to serve as text containers, and frames. And you can add pizzazz to your page layouts by including backgrounds and themes in on-screen documents and watermarks in printed documents. In this chapter, you'll learn how to use these common desktop publishing tools to create professional and imaginative document layouts.

Controlling Text Placement and Formatting with Text Boxes

When you use Word, you might occasionally find that you need control over your text layout beyond setting margins, formatting paragraphs, and creating columns. At those times, you might benefit from entering your information into shapes that can contain text, such as AutoShapes that can serve as *text containers* or *text boxes*. Text boxes are free-floating objects, independent of your regular document, that you can use to enclose information. You can then format these objects in the same ways you format drawings (by using the Drawing toolbar).

For more information about working with AutoShapes and the Drawing toolbar, see Chapter 16, "Enlivening Documents with Drawings and AutoShapes."

In Word, you can use two main types of text boxes: standard text boxes and AutoShapes formatted to serve as text containers. Generally, you'll want to use text boxes and AutoShapes when you want to position several blocks of text on a page or flow a continuing story from one area in your document to another. For example, you might be creating a newsletter in which a story starts on the cover page but concludes on another page, later in the newsletter.

note In Word, text and graphics contained within a single text box or a chain of linked text boxes is referred to as a *story*.

In addition to creating interesting page layouts and continuing a story from one text block to another, you might also want to use text boxes to accomplish the following tasks:

- Format text blocks using Drawing toolbar buttons
- Rotate or flip text
- Change text orientation
- Group text blocks and change the alignment or distribution of them as a group

This section describes how you can manipulate and control text using text boxes—both standard rectangular text boxes and AutoShapes formatted as text containers. Keep in mind that when you're working with text boxes and AutoShapes, you must work in Print Layout view. In Print Layout view, the text boxes and AutoShapes are displayed on screen as you work. Figure 23-1 shows a Print Layout view of a text box and an AutoShape formatted to contain text.

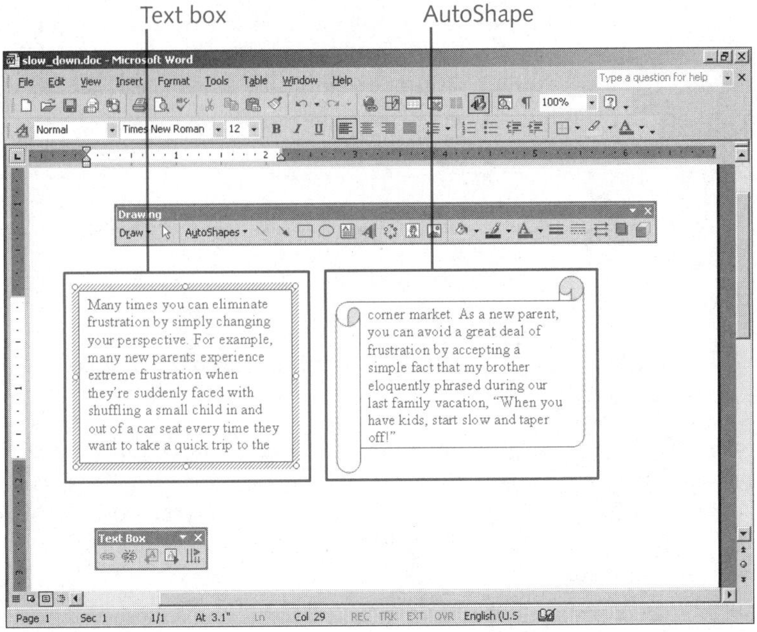

Figure 23-1. You can control text placement and generate unique page designs using text boxes and AutoShapes.

As you can see, the active text box is displayed surrounded by a frame-like border. This border appears whenever you click a text box, and it serves a number of purposes, including enabling you to move and resize the text box as well as access text box properties.

Creating Text Boxes

Creating a text box is as easy as drawing a box or shape on the drawing canvas. You can create a text box by performing any of the following actions:

Text Box

- Choose Insert, Text Box, and then drag the mouse pointer in your document to draw a text box.
- Click the Text Box button on the Drawing toolbar, and then drag the mouse pointer in your document to draw a text box.
- Create an AutoShape, right-click the AutoShape, and choose Add Text on the shortcut menu.

For more information about creating AutoShapes, see Chapter 16, "Enlivening Documents with Drawings and AutoShapes."

By default, when you draw a text box or an AutoShape, a drawing canvas appears. You can work with a text box on the drawing canvas, or you can drag the text box off the drawing canvas and then delete the canvas. (To delete the drawing canvas, select it, and press Delete.) If you prefer to avoid placing text boxes and AutoShapes on the drawing canvas in the first place, you can turn off the drawing canvas's default action by configuring the Options dialog box, as follows:

1. Choose Tools, Options, and click the General tab.
2. Clear the Automatically Create Drawing Canvas When Inserting AutoShapes check box.
3. Click OK.

After you close the Options dialog box, the drawing canvas will not appear when you create text boxes and drawings.

Regardless of whether you work on or off the drawing canvas, you'll notice that the Text Box toolbar opens automatically after you create a text box. (See Figure 23-1.) This toolbar is displayed whenever a text box is selected. When no text boxes are selected, the Text Box toolbar is hidden. To redisplay the toolbar, simply click a text box in your document.

tip **Redisplay the Text Box toolbar**

By default, the Text Box toolbar appears when you select a text box and disappears when the text box is no longer selected. If you manually close the Text Box toolbar while you're working by clicking its Close button, the toolbar won't appear automatically when you click text boxes. To redisplay the Text Box toolbar after you close it, you need to click a text box and then choose View, Toolbars, Text Box. The Text Box option appears on the Toolbars menu only when you've selected a text box within your document.

As you create text boxes in your document, you can move and resize the text boxes in the same manner you move and resize drawing objects—by dragging them by their borders. To move a text box, click anywhere on its border other than a sizing handle, and then drag the text box. To resize a text box, you can drag the sizing handles (which appear as circles in text box frames) to change the text box's width and height. (Figure 23-1 shows a selected text box along with its border and sizing handles.)

Inserting Text into Text Containers

After you create text boxes, you are ready to add text and formatting. You can insert text into text boxes in a few predictable ways, including the following:

- Type text directly into the text box.
- Paste copied information into the text box.

- Drag information into the text box.
- Click a text box, and choose Insert, File to insert a file's contents into the text box.

If you're planning to insert a longer story into a text box, you should consider typing and editing the story in a plain Word document before importing the information into a text box. That way, you can conduct most of your editing, formatting, and fine-tuning tasks in a standard document, which generally provides a larger viewing area.

tip **Format text in text boxes**

You can format text in text boxes in the same manner you format document text. First click in the text box, and then format the text using keyboard shortcuts, Formatting toolbar buttons, Font and Paragraph dialog boxes, and the Styles And Formatting task pane.

In addition to inserting text, you can insert graphics, tables, and some fields into text boxes. Among the items that you can't include in text boxes are the following:

- Columns
- Comments
- Drop caps
- Endnotes
- Footnotes
- Indexes
- Page and column breaks
- Tables of contents

To be able to include these elements in a text container, you'll have to convert your text box to a floating frame, as described in the next section, or you'll need to use a framed document, as discussed in the section "Adding Frames When Designing Online Documents," on page 560.

note A nice feature of text containers is that when you run the spelling checker and grammar checker, Word also checks the information in text containers.

Using Comments, Footnotes, Tables, and Fields in Floating Frames

Generally, your best bet when it comes to placing text in text containers is to use text boxes and AutoShapes, because they are highly customizable. But if you need to insert text that contains comments, footnotes, endnotes, tables, or certain fields (such as table of contents and index fields) in a text container, you'll have to use a *floating frame* instead of a text box, because text boxes can't properly support these types of elements. A floating frame looks like a text box, but you can't format it as extensively as a text box and it supports Word fields.

You can easily convert an existing text box to a floating frame whenever necessary by following these steps:

1. If the text box you want to convert is on the drawing canvas, drag the text box off the canvas.
2. Click the text box you want to convert, and then right-click the text box's frame.
3. Choose Format Text Box on the shortcut menu, and then click the Text Box tab in the Format Text Box dialog box.
4. Click the Convert To Frame button. A message box appears, warning you that you are about to change the text box to a frame and that some drawing formatting might be lost. Click OK.

After you convert a text box to a frame, the Text Box toolbar and some Drawing toolbar buttons, such as the Fill Color and Line Color buttons, will be unavailable.

Formatting Text Boxes and AutoShapes

By default, when you create a text box, it appears as a white (not transparent) box surrounded by thin (0.75 point) black lines. Fortunately, text boxes don't have to be limited to plain white rectangles strategically placed around your document. You can format text boxes and AutoShape text containers in the same manner you format other drawing objects. For example, you can apply fill and line colors by using the Fill Color and Line Color buttons on the Drawing toolbar, or you can add a shadow to a text box by using the Shadow Style button. To format text boxes and AutoShapes using the Drawing toolbar, select the text box or AutoShape, and then click the appropriate Drawing toolbar button.

In addition to the standard formatting buttons available on the Drawing toolbar, you can format text boxes using the Format Text Box dialog box. Namely, you can control the position of text within text boxes and AutoShapes, you can change a text box's shape, and you can instruct Word to automatically resize a text box or an AutoShape to accommodate a story's complete text. For more information about using the Drawing toolbar buttons to format drawing objects, see Chapter 16, "Enlivening Documents with Drawings and AutoShapes."

Controlling Text in Text Boxes and AutoShapes

You can control how close or far away text is placed relative to a text box or an AutoShape's edges. You do this by changing the text box's internal margin settings, as described here:

1. Click a text box or an AutoShape, and then double-click the container's frame (or right-click the frame, and choose Format Text Box or Format AutoShape on the shortcut menu; or click a text container, and then choose Format AutoShape or Format Text Box). The Format Text Box or Format AutoShape dialog box opens, depending on the type of text container you're formatting.
2. Click the Text Box tab, shown in Figure 23-2. The Text Box tab appears the same in both the Format Text Box and Format AutoShape dialog boxes.

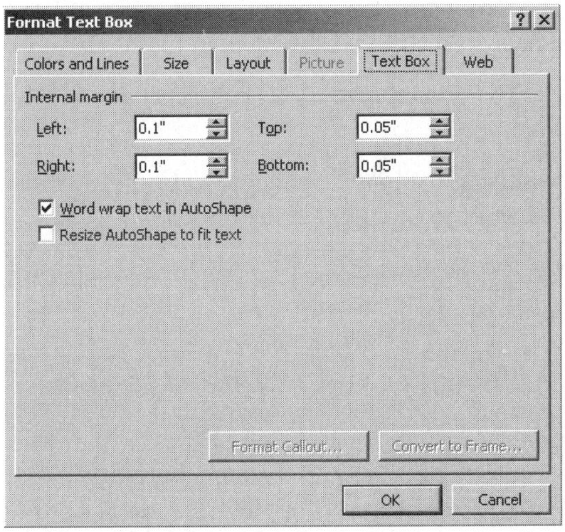

Figure 23-2. You can control the spacing around text placed in text boxes and AutoShapes by configuring the internal margin settings on the Text Box tab.

3. In the Internal Margin section, increase or decrease the left, right, top, and bottom margin measurements to control the distance between the text and the selected object's edges. Click OK to apply the settings.

Change Text Direction

In addition to controlling internal margins, you can change the direction of text within text boxes. To do so, click in a text box, and click the Change Text Direction button on the Text Box toolbar. You can continue to click the button to cycle through the available text direction options: down, up, and standard.

caution When you change the text direction in a linked text box, you change the text direction in all linked text boxes included in the story. In other words, you can't change the text direction in a single text box if it's part of a linked series of text boxes. For more information about linked text boxes, see the section "Linking Text Boxes to Flow Text from One Text Box to Another," below.

Changing Text Box Shapes

The beauty of using AutoShapes is that you can change your mind regarding which AutoShape you want to use at any time, even if the AutoShape is formatted as a text box. Changing the shape of a text box or an AutoShape is similar to changing shapes that don't contain text. To do so, ensure that you're working in Print Layout view, and then follow these basic steps:

1. Click the text box whose shape you want to modify. To select multiple text boxes, press and hold Shift while clicking each of the text boxes.
2. On the Drawing toolbar, click Draw, and choose Change AutoShape on the drop-down menu.
3. On the Change AutoShape submenu, choose a category, and then click the shape you want to apply to the selected text boxes.

All selected shapes take on the new shape but retain all other format settings, such as color, internal margins, and so forth.

Resizing Text Boxes or AutoShapes Automatically to Show All Text

You can automatically resize a text box or an AutoShape that contains text so that it is as long or as short as necessary to display all the text inserted in it. You can use this option only with nonlinked (stand-alone) text boxes because linked text boxes are designed to flow text to the next linked text box if text is longer than the current text box's boundaries. To automatically size a nonlinked text container to accommodate inserted text, follow these steps:

1. Double-click a text container's frame, and then click the Text Box tab in the Format Text Box or Format AutoShape dialog box.
2. Select the Resize AutoShape To Fit Text check box, and click OK.

The text container will automatically stretch or shrink to accommodate the text.

Linking Text Boxes to Flow Text from One Text Box to Another

If you've ever created a newsletter or a brochure, you know how tricky it can be to properly fill text areas and manage jumps from one page to another. In Word, you can simplify these types of tasks by linking text boxes. When you link text boxes, you indicate that any text you insert into one text box will automatically flow into the next text box when the first text box cannot fit all of the inserted text. After you insert text into linked text boxes, you can edit the text to make your story longer or shorter, and Word will automatically reflow the text throughout the series of linked text boxes.

> **note** The maximum number of links you can have in one document is 31, which means that you can have up to 32 linked text containers in one document.

When you want to link text boxes or AutoShapes, you need to keep the following limitations in mind:

- Linked text boxes and AutoShapes must be contained in a single document.
- Each text box or AutoShape must be empty.
- Each text box or AutoShape must not already be linked to another series or story.

Before you flow text into a series of linked text boxes, you should be sure that you've made most of your changes to your text. Then draw the text boxes you want to link and import your story into. When your text is ready and your text boxes are drawn, follow these steps to link the text boxes and insert the text:

Create Text Box Link

1. In Print Layout view, click the first text box you want to insert text into, and then click the Create Text Box Link on the Text Box toolbar. The mouse pointer changes to an upright pitcher.

2. Move the mouse pointer to the text box you want link to the first text box. When you move the upright pitcher pointer over a text box that can receive the link, the pitcher tilts and turns into a pouring pitcher. Click the second text box to link it to the first text box.

3. To link a third text box, click the text box you just linked to the first text box, click the Create Text Box Link button, and then click the third text box. You can create a chain of linked text boxes using this method.

> **tip** If you click the Create Text Box Link button and then decide that you don't want to link to another box, press Esc to cancel the linking process.

4 After you link your text boxes, click in the first text box, and insert text by typing, pasting, or choosing Insert, File. The latter approach is recommended because it enables you to insert prepared and edited text into your linked text boxes.

InsideOut

Word excludes all text in text boxes from both the word and line count statistics when you use the Word Count command on the Tools menu to perform counts on your entire document. If you need to obtain word count statistics for text in text boxes, you can work around this limitation with a little effort. Basically, you can count the text in each text box and then add the numbers together to get a total count for the story. To do this, click a text box, press Ctrl+A to select all the text in the text box, and then choose Tools, Word Count. You'll need to repeat the process in each text box, even if the text boxes are linked, and then add the numbers to produce a grand total.

Moving Among Linked Text Boxes

Next Text Box

Previous Text Box

After you link text boxes, you can easily jump from one text box to another by using the Text Box toolbar. To do so, select a text box that's part of a linked series of text boxes. Then, on the Text Box toolbar, click the Next Text Box button to move to the next linked text box, or click the Previous Text Box button to jump to the previous text box. You can also move to the next text box by positioning your insertion point at the end of text in a text box and pressing the Right Arrow key, or you can jump to the preceding text box by positioning your insertion point at the beginning of the text in a text box and pressing the Left Arrow key.

Copying or Moving Linked Text Boxes

You can copy or move a story (including text boxes and their contents) to another document or location in the same document. To accomplish this, you must select all the linked text boxes in a story if the story consists of multiple linked text boxes. If you copy just some of the text boxes in a story, you'll copy the text boxes but not the text inside the text boxes. If your story is contained in a single text box, Word automatically includes the content when you copy the text box.

To copy or move an entire story that's contained in a single text box or a series of linked text boxes, follow these steps:

1 In Print Layout view, select the first text box in the story by clicking the text box's frame.

2 Press Shift and select all other text boxes you want to copy or move, and then click the Copy or Cut button on the Standard toolbar (or press Ctrl+C or Ctrl+X).

3 Click where you want to reposition the text boxes, and click Paste on the Standard toolbar (or press Ctrl+V).

To copy or move text that appears within a text box without copying or moving the text box, select just the text, and then copy or move it in the same manner you normally copy or move text in Word documents. Unfortunately, you can't select and copy all the text in a linked story at once—instead, you have to select and copy the text in each text box one at a time.

InsideOut

If you want to copy all the text in a story that appears in a series of linked text boxes, you might be able to avoid copying the story piece by piece if your story isn't too long. One way to streamline the copying of a story that's spread across a series of linked text boxes is to resize the first text box so that it's large enough to contain the entire story. The story will automatically reflow into the first text box, which will make it easy for you to select and copy the text as a whole. After you copy the text, click Undo on the Standard toolbar (or press Ctrl+Z) to restore the text box to its previous size and automatically reflow the story.

Breaking Text Box Links

You can break links between text boxes just as easily as you create them. When you break a link, you remove only the link between the selected text box and the text box that follows it in the series—you don't remove all the links throughout a linked series. Essentially, when you break a link, you divide a story into two series of linked text boxes. By default, the first series of linked text boxes contains the story, and the second series of linked text boxes are emptied.

To break a link between text boxes, follow these steps:

1 In Print Layout view, click the border of the text box where you want the text to stop flowing from. The selected text box will become the last text box in the first linked series of text boxes.

2 On the Text Box toolbar, click the Break Forward Link button.

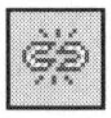

Break Forward Link

At this point, text will stop flowing in the last text box before the broken link, and the second series of linked text boxes will be empty. If the text doesn't fit in the first series of linked text boxes after you break a link, you can create and link additional text boxes or enlarge existing text boxes to provide enough room to display the text.

tip **Eliminate a text box in the middle of a story**

You can cut a text box in the middle of a linked series of text boxes without deleting any parts of your story. To do so, simply right-click a text box's border, and choose Cut on the shortcut menu. When you cut a linked text box, the story readjusts and flows the text into the next text box.

Deleting Linked Text Boxes Without Losing Text

To delete a text box, you simply select a text box and press Delete. Performing this action on a nonlinked text box deletes both the text box and its contents. In contrast, when you delete a text box that's part of a linked series of text boxes, the text from the deleted text box automatically flows into the remaining linked text boxes. If the remaining text boxes aren't large enough to properly display the story in its entirety, you'll have to resize the remaining text boxes, create additional text boxes, or edit your story to fit in the existing text boxes. Keep in mind that Word doesn't notify you when text overflows the final text box's boundaries, so you should always be extra diligent about checking the flow of stories and making sure that no text is hidden.

tip To avoid deleting an entire story when you delete a stand-alone, nonlinked text box, click in the text box, press Ctrl+A to select the story, and then either drag or copy the selected story into your document before you delete the text box.

Adding Frames When Designing Online Documents

If you're creating documents that will be viewed on line, you can take advantage of *frames* to organize your documents. Frames enable you to create areas for text on screen that allow you to divide a window into multiple areas so that you can show several documents at one time. Frames are most frequently used in Web page design. In fact, you've probably used frames while surfing the Web.

Web designers commonly use frames to create a number of window regions that show specific types of information. For example, frames are sometimes used to create a menu bar that contains links to main pages in a Web site. Users click links on the menu bar in one frame to display selected information in another "target" frame that serves as the main content area. Figure 23-3 shows a Web page that uses three frames—one title area frame, a navigation bar frame, and a body frame.

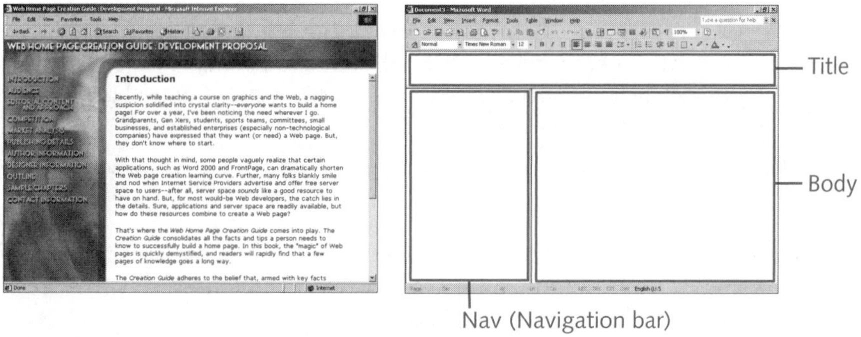

Figure 23-3. The Web page design on the left is based on a framework of three frame areas, as shown on the right.

The basic philosophy behind a *frames page* is that you create a page that defines how the window will be divided and then you specify the documents that should be displayed in each frame. When you upload a page that uses frames to a server, you must copy the frames page as well as the files that contain the frames' content to your server. When you save a document that uses frames in Word—whether you save the document as a Word document or a Web page—Word creates a separate file for the content in each area as well as a frames page that defines the view. Thus, the Web page shown in Figure 23-3 would consist of four files at a minimum—the title bar file, the navigation bar file, the main body text file, and the frames page file (which defines how the content files are displayed in the window). To reopen a document that uses frames in Word, you simply open the frames page document.

> **note** Using frames to create Web pages can take some finagling. If you're new to frames and you're creating a Web page, you should do some research about frames on line or consult some of the many Web page design books.

Adding Frames to Documents

You can add frames to a document using any of the following techniques:

- Choose Format, Frames, New Frames Page to open a new document and display the Frames toolbar, which you can use to add frames to the new document.
- Choose View, Toolbars, Frames to open the Frames toolbar, which you can use to create frames in the current document.
- Choose Format, Frames, Table Of Contents In Frame to create a left-side frame that contains links to the headings in the current document. (The document must be formatted with built-in Word headings for this option to work properly.)

- Choose File, New to open the New Document task pane. Click the General Templates link, click the Web Pages tab in the Templates dialog box, and then double-click the Web Page Wizard icon to create a frames-based Web site.

For more information about creating Web pages, see Chapter 31, "Creating Professional Web Sites."

The tools you need to create and manage frames can be found on the Frames toolbar, shown in Figure 23-4. (You can also access frames options when you're working in a frames page by choosing Format, Frames.)

Figure 23-4. You can click buttons on the Frames toolbar to add and delete frames in a frames page.

Using the Frames toolbar, you can add a frame to the current document by clicking one of the position buttons: New Frame Left, New Frame Right, New Frame Above, or New Frame Below. After you add a frame, you can resize it by dragging the frame's border.

Table Of Contents In Frame

In addition to creating standard frames, you can have Word automatically generate a frame that contains links to the headings in your document. If your document uses built-in Word heading styles, you can click the Table Of Contents In Frame button (or choose Format, Frames, Table Of Contents In Frame) to create a linked table of contents in a left frame, as shown in Figure 23-5. You can format an automatically generated table of contents frame in the same manner you format other frames and documents.

tip To use the links in a table of contents frame in Word, press Ctrl as you click the link. If you want to be able to click links normally, choose Tools, Options, click the Edit tab, and then clear the Use Ctrl+Click To Follow Hyperlink check box.

tip If you're going to include top or bottom frames in your document along with a left or right frame, you should create the top or bottom frames first. That way, the top or bottom frame will span the entire width of the page.

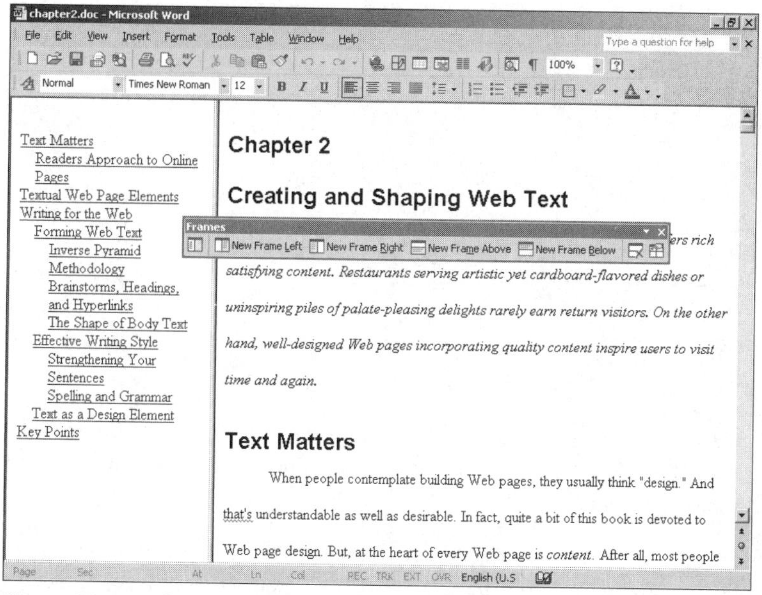

Figure 23-5. The Tables Of Contents In Frame option enables you to quickly create a left frame that contains links to each heading in your document.

Controlling Frame Properties

Frame Properties

As with most constructs created in Word, you can control a frame's properties by configuring settings in a Properties dialog box. The two main areas of concern when you're working with frames are the content and the appearance of the frame itself. You can access content and appearance settings for frames by opening the Frame Properties dialog box. To do so, click the frame you want to format, and then click the Frame Properties button on the Frames toolbar or choose Format, Frames, Frame Properties. The Frame Properties dialog box is described in more detail in the following sections.

Assigning Documents and Names to Frames

When you create a frames page, Word displays a different document in each frame. You might have to tell Word which document to display in which frame. (If you create a frames page from scratch, Word will automatically generate file names and documents for you.) You can specify documents to associate with a frame by configuring settings on the Frame tab in the Frame Properties dialog box, shown in Figure 23-6, on the next page.

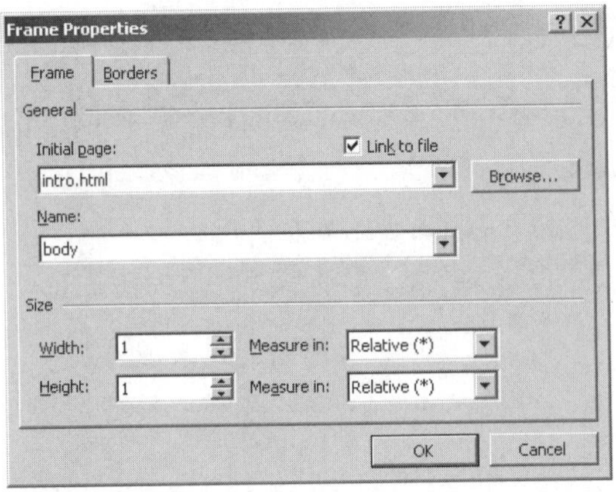

Figure 23-6. Using the Frame tab, you can perform a number of frame configuration tasks, including naming a frame and assigning a document to display in the frame when the frames page opens.

On the Frame tab, you can indicate which page to display in a frame by inserting the file's path and name in the Initial Page box. The file specified in the Initial Page box is the file that is displayed each time the frames page is opened. You can also select the Link To File check box to ensure that the document used in your frames page is updated each time the Initial Page file is changed.

In addition to specifying which file is initially displayed in a frame, you can assign a name to each frame. When you use frames, the frames must be named so that you can refer to specific frames when you create hyperlinks. For example, the Frame tab shown in Figure 23-6 specifies that the intro.html file is displayed in a frame named *body*. The Introduction hyperlink in the navigation frame in Figure 23-3 is configured to open the intro.html file in the frame named *body* when the hyperlink is clicked. The frames page shown in Figure 23-3 contains frames named *title*, *body*, and *nav* (short for navigation bar).

To learn more about creating hyperlinks and specifying frame targets, see Chapter 31, "Creating Professional Web Sites."

note Frame names are case-sensitive and can include numbers and letters. Also, because each frame must have a name, Word automatically provides default frame names for frames that aren't named manually.

The remaining frame parameters you can configure on the Frame tab are the frame's height and width. You can assign height and width measurements in the Height and

Troubleshooting

Some of My Frame Pages Are Missing

If you find that a frame doesn't display an initial page when you open your frames page, you need to check the Initial Page setting in the frame's Frame Properties dialog box.

To display the Frame Properties dialog box, choose Format, Frames, Frame Properties and click the Frame tab. After you display the Frames tab, ensure that the path and file name in the Initial Page box is accurate and points to a valid file. Keep in mind that whenever you rename a file that's referred to in a frames page, you must modify the frames page's Frame Properties settings as well.

Width boxes and use the Measure In drop-down lists to specify whether the measurements are a percentage of the screen size, a fixed size in inches, or relative to the other frames, as follows:

- **Percent** specifies that a frame's height or width should be sized as a percentage of the window. For example, if a frame's width is set to 50 percent, the frame will consume half the width of a user's window, regardless of the window size.
- **Inches** specifies a fixed width or height in inches. The frame will always be displayed at the specified height, regardless of the window size.
- **Relative** (*) indicates that the frame's height or width should fill the remaining area of the window after the other frame settings are applied. For example, if a top frame is set to 1 inch and a bottom frame is set to 1 inch, the body frame could be set to Relative so that the frame fills the area between the top and bottom frames, regardless of the window size.

Frequently, you'll find that your document uses a combination of Percent, Inches, and Relative settings. Fortunately, if you arrange your document by dragging frame borders, Word will automatically configure your frame size settings for you.

Controlling Frame Borders, Resizing Capabilities, and Scroll Bars

In addition to controlling which documents are displayed in frames and assigning sizes and names to frames, you can control frame borders. To access frame border properties, follow these steps:

1. Click the frame you want to format.
2. Click the Frame Properties button on the Frames toolbar, or choose Format, Frames, Frame Properties.

3 Click the Borders tab, shown in Figure 23-7.

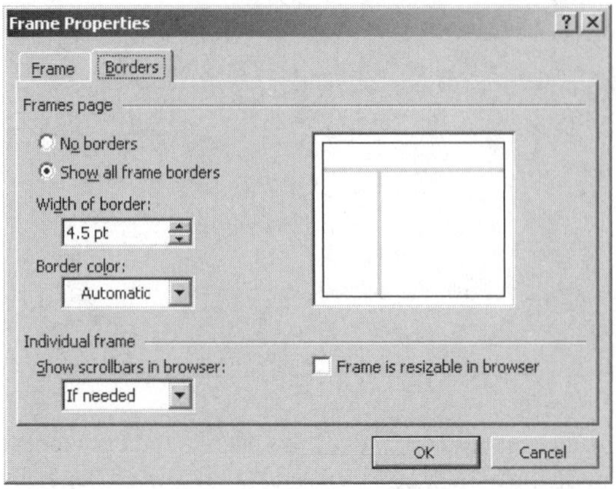

Figure 23-7. The Borders tab in the Frame Properties dialog box provides settings you can use to specify how frame borders appear in the current document.

The settings available on the Borders tab are listed here:

- **No Borders.** Choose this option if you want your frames to be displayed seamlessly, without borders.
- **Show All Frame Borders.** Choose this option if you want borders to be displayed.
- **Width Of Border.** If you choose to show frame borders, you can type a value in this box or click the up or down arrow to specify the size of the border that is displayed between frames.
- **Border Color.** Click the Border Color down arrow to access the standard color palette, which enables you to specify the color of frame borders displayed in your document.
- **Show Scrollbars In Browser.** Click the down arrow and choose an option on the drop-down menu to specify whether you want scroll bars to be displayed for the selected frame always, never, or only when needed.
- **Frame Is Resizable In Browser.** Select this check box if you want users to be able to resize the selected frame. If you want the frame to always appear according to your frame size settings, clear the check box. Keep in mind that if you want the current frame to be resizable, adjacent frames must also be formatted as resizable.

As you configure border settings, notice that the preview box shows how your borders will appear. When you finish configuring border settings, click OK to apply the settings to the current document.

Chapter 23

Deleting Frames

If you decide to modify a frames page, you can easily delete a frame. Remember, when you delete a frame, you delete only the frame in the frames page—you don't delete the file that contains the content that is displayed in the frame. To delete a frame, click the frame, and then click the Delete Frame button on the Frames toolbar or choose Format, Frames, Delete Frame.

caution When you delete a frame, you can't click Undo to revert to the previous frame setup. If you want to restore a deleted frame, you'll have to re-create the frame by using the Frames toolbar. Then you'll need to configure the frame's Initial Page setting so that the frame can display the document that was displayed in the frame before you deleted it.

Using Backgrounds and Watermarks

To add information or visual interest to your documents, you can add *backgrounds* to online documents and *watermarks* to printed documents. Backgrounds are visible in Web Layout view or in a Web browser, and they are generally used to create interesting backdrops for online documents. Backgrounds are displayed in Web Layout view only and aren't designed for printing. If you want to create a printable background, you need to create a watermark. A watermark is faded text or a pale picture that appears behind document text. Watermarks are often used to add visual appeal to a document or to identify a document's status, such as marking the document as a "Draft" or "Confidential." You can see watermarks in Print Layout view or in a printed document. In this section, you'll learn how to create, control, and delete backgrounds and watermarks in your Web pages and printed documents.

Creating Backgrounds and Watermarks

You can create custom backgrounds for online pages and custom watermarks for printed documents. When you create a background for an online document, you can use color gradients, patterns, pictures, solid colors, or textures that repeat, or "tile," to fill the page. When you create a watermark for a printed document, you can use a light-colored picture (usually gray) or light-colored text to appear behind your document's contents. If you use text, you can choose from built-in phrases or enter your own.

Adding Backgrounds to Online Pages

To add a background to an online page (such as a Web page, an online document, or an e-mail message), choose Format, Background, and then perform any of the following actions:

- Click a color on the color palette to add a background color.

- Choose More Colors to access additional colors that you can apply to your background.
- Choose Fill Effects to access the Gradient, Texture, Pattern, and Picture tabs in the Fill Effects dialog box, which enable you to create custom backgrounds.

For more information about using fill effects, see Chapter 16, "Enlivening Documents with Drawings and AutoShapes."

After you choose a color or create a fill effect, Word automatically applies the background to the current document. You can see the background only in Web Layout view (by choosing View, Web Layout); if you display the page in any other view, you won't see the background, and if you print the document, the background won't be printed.

note When you save a Web page with a background, Word saves background textures and gradients as JPEG files and patterns as GIF files.

newfeature!

Adding Watermarks to Printed Documents

To add a watermark to a printed document, display your document in Print Layout or Normal view, and then choose Format, Background, Printed Watermark. The Printed Watermark dialog box opens, as shown in Figure 23-8.

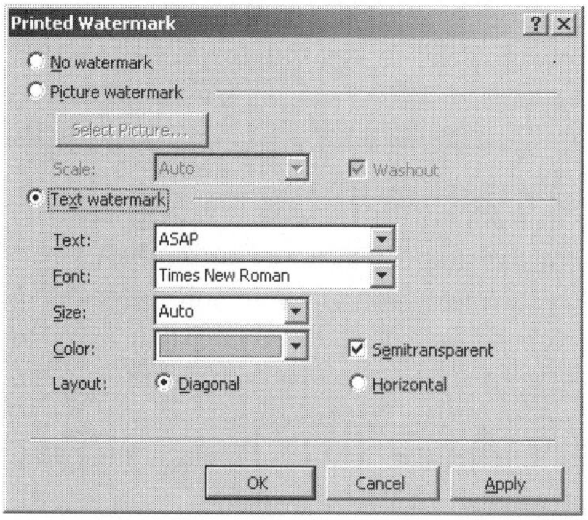

Figure 23-8. In Word 2002, you can use the Printed Watermark dialog box to add picture and text watermarks to your documents.

You can insert a picture or text watermark by configuring the settings in the Printed Watermark dialog box, as described here:

- **Picture watermark.** If you want to insert a picture watermark, click the Picture Watermark option, and then click the Select Picture button to choose a picture for the watermark. You can use color or grayscale pictures for watermarks. The Scale option lets you specify a size for the watermark picture. In most cases, you should select the Washout check box so that the watermark doesn't interfere with your document's readability.

- **Text watermark.** To insert a text watermark, click the Text Watermark option, and type custom text in the Text box or choose from text in the Text drop-down list. Then configure the Text, Font, Size, Color, and Layout settings. You can display the watermark text diagonally or horizontally. In most cases, you should select the Semitransparent check box so that the watermark doesn't interfere with your document's readability.

After you configure your picture or text watermark settings, click OK to apply the watermark to the current document. Figure 23-9 shows a document in Print Preview mode that has a *Confidential* watermark.

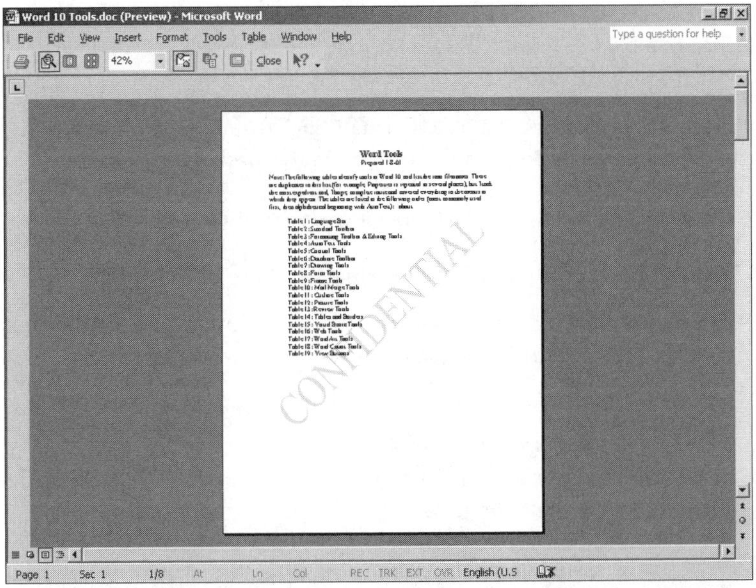

Figure 23-9. You can easily add watermarks to documents in Word 2002.

Including Watermarks in Document Headers

Before Word 2002, many people created watermarks by adding objects (such as AutoShapes) and images to document headers. You can continue to create watermarks in this manner. To do so, you manually paste or insert the watermark object or image into the document header. If you create watermarks this way, you can't use the Printed Watermark dialog box to configure the watermark's settings. For simplicity's sake, you should use the Printed Watermark dialog box to create watermarks whenever possible.

Changing and Removing Backgrounds and Watermarks

After you add backgrounds to online pages and watermarks to printed documents, you're free to change your mind at any time. You can easily change or remove backgrounds and watermarks that have been added to documents. To change backgrounds or watermarks, use one of the following methods:

- **Change a background.** Choose Format, Background, and choose new background settings.
- **Change a watermark.** Choose Format, Background, Printed Watermark, and specify new settings in the Printed Watermark dialog box.

To remove backgrounds and watermarks, use one of these methods:

- **Remove a background.** Choose Format, Background, No Fill.
- **Remove a watermark.** Choose Format, Background, Printed Watermark. In the Printed Watermark dialog box, click the No Watermark option, and then click OK.

When you remove a background from a Web page, the page will be displayed using the default background colors specified by the user's Web browser. Generally, default background colors are white or gray.

note If you created a watermark by inserting a watermark in a document's header, you must open the header and manually delete or change the watermark. You can't use the Printed Watermark dialog box to modify and remove watermarks inserted into headers.

Styling Documents with Themes

If you want to go one step beyond adding backgrounds when you format online documents, you can apply *themes* to Web page documents, e-mail messages, and documents that you know will be viewed in Word only. A theme is a set of unified design elements and color schemes. When you apply a theme to an online document, an e-mail message, or a Web page, Word customizes the background colors, bullets, heading styles, body text, lists, horizontal lines, hyperlinks, colors, tables, and so forth. For information about adding a theme to e-mail messages, see Chapter 30, "Collaborating On Line with E-Mail, NetMeeting, Discussions, and Faxes."

You can also use themes when you create a Web site using the Web Page Wizard and when you create custom templates. For more information about using the Web Page Wizard, see Chapter 31, "Creating Professional Web Sites," and for more information about creating custom templates, see Chapter 22, "Formatting Documents Using Templates, Wizards, and Add-Ins."

Previewing and Implementing Themes

Your gateway to using themes is the Theme dialog box. You can use the Theme dialog box to preview and apply themes. In addition, you can use the Theme dialog box to configure the following settings for a selected theme:

- **Vivid Colors** changes the colors used for styles and table borders to brighter settings. You can instantly see the difference the Vivid Colors setting makes to a selected theme by keeping an eye on the preview box as you select and clear the Vivid Colors check box.
- **Active Graphics** includes animated graphics, such as spinning bullets, when the page is displayed in a Web browser. For the most part, you'll probably want to avoid active graphics because they generally require users' browsers to perform extra processing for little visual gain.
- **Background Image** applies the background image shown in the preview box to the current document. If you prefer to use a solid color background, clear the Background Image check box.
- **Set Default** sets the selected theme as the default theme. When you click this button, the theme will be applied automatically whenever you create a new, blank document or a new, blank Web page (depending on the type of document that's currently opened when you click the Set Default button).
- **Style Gallery** displays the Style Gallery dialog box, which enables you to access a variety of templates.

To apply a theme to a document, follow these steps:

1. Open a document that you want to format, or open a blank document or blank Web page.
2. Choose Format, Theme.
3. In the Theme dialog box, click theme names in the Choose A Theme list to preview available themes. (If a theme isn't installed on your system, Word provides an Install button, which enables you to install the theme from the installation CD, as described in the next section, "Installing Additional Themes.") Figure 23-10 shows the Theme dialog box, with the Nature theme selected.

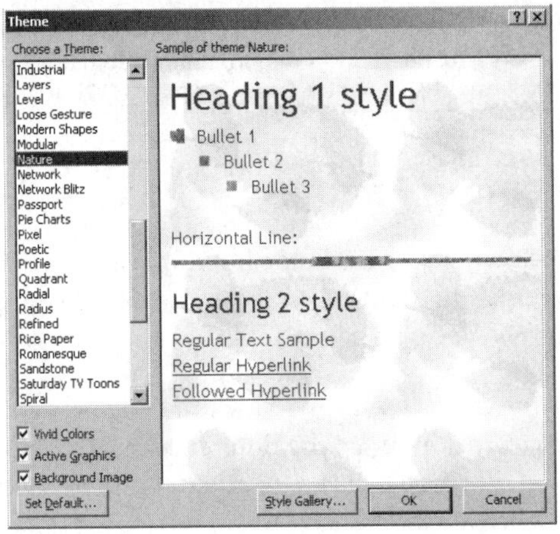

Figure 23-10. Word provides a selection of themes that you can use to format Web pages and online documents.

4. Select a theme, and then select the Vivid Colors, Active Graphics, or Background Image check boxes, if desired.
5. Click OK to apply the theme to the current document.

For more information about the Style Gallery, see Chapter 22, "Formatting Documents Using Templates, Wizards, and Add-Ins."

After you select a theme and configure its settings, click OK to apply the theme to the current document. If you clicked the Set Default button in the Theme dialog box, you can create new documents based on the theme by choosing File, New to open the New Document task pane and then clicking Blank Web Page or Blank Document.

Installing Additional Themes

If you select a theme in the Theme dialog box that isn't installed on your system, the Theme dialog box presents an Install button in place of the preview box. To install the additional themes, insert the installation CD, and then click Install. You'll see a progress dialog box as the theme is installed onto your system, as shown in Figure 23-11. When the installation is complete, the theme will be displayed in the preview box in the Theme dialog box.

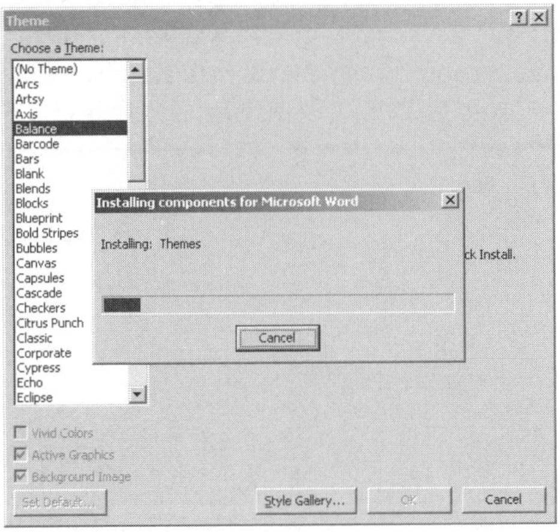

Figure 23-11. By default, Word doesn't install all themes when you perform a typical installation; in some cases, you might need to install additional themes from the installation CD.

> **tip** You can download additional themes from the Microsoft Office Update site. To access the site, make sure you're connected to the Internet, and then choose Help, Office On The Web.

Changing and Removing Themes

You can easily change or remove the currently displayed document's theme or the default theme at any time. To change and remove themes, perform any of the following procedures:

- **Change the current document theme.** Choose Format, Theme to open the Theme dialog box, select a new theme, and then click OK.
- **Change the default theme.** Display a document or Web page to specify the type of default page you want to format, and then choose Format, Theme. In the Theme dialog box, select a new theme, click Set Default, and click Close.

- **Remove a theme from the current document.** Choose Format, Theme to open the Theme dialog box, select (No Theme) in the Choose A Theme list, and then click OK.
- **Reset the default to create new Web pages or blank documents without a theme.** Choose Format, Theme to open the Theme dialog box, select (No Theme) in the Choose A Theme list, click the Set Default button, and then click Close.

tip As mentioned, you can also use themes to format e-mail messages. For more information about using Word to create and format e-mail messages, see Chapter 30, "Collaborating On Line with E-Mail, NetMeeting, Discussions, and Faxes."

Chapter 24

Drawing Attention to Your Document with Borders and Shading

Sometimes producing a simple document on a clean white page is the best approach for communicating your message as clearly as possible. But there are those times when you want to wow your audience, when you're looking for ways to enhance the look, spark up the design, and show your readers you really know what you're doing. When you're looking for more than a simple text-on-paper appeal, you can use borders and shading to create effective, eye-catching document designs.

How will you use borders in your publication? Here are a few ideas, but you'll no doubt have many more of your own:

- Create a border around a table that's placed in text.
- Set your headline as white text in a dark blue box.
- Showcase a special section of text that goes along with a primary article.
- Set off your table of contents so that readers can see it easily.

> **tip** **Make custom border choices**
>
> The borders you create don't have to go all the way around an item. You can use rules to border only the top or bottom, or sides, of an object. For more information on using rules to enhance an object, see the section, "Inserting a Horizontal Line," on page 589 later in this chapter.

Adding a Simple Border

Tables and Borders

The easiest way to add a nothing-fancy border to an item in your document is to select it and then click the Tables And Borders button on the Standard toolbar. This displays the Tables And Borders toolbar, as Figure 24-1 shows.

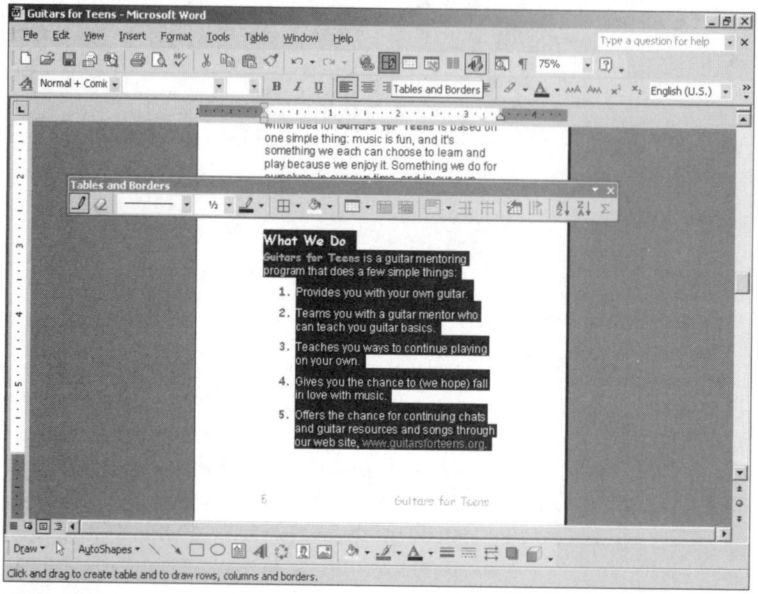

Figure 24-1. You can use the Tables And Borders toolbar to draw tables and add borders of various weights and colors.

> **note** If you've previously used the Table And Borders toolbar, it will appear in the place you left it, with the tool you last used displayed. For example, if your last use involved the Outside Border button, that button will be displayed as the representative border style selected.

To add a quick border, click the Borders down arrow. A list of border choices appears. Table 24-1 describes the different choices available to you. To create a simple border that outlines your selection, click Outside Border.

The various buttons on the Tables And Borders toolbar are described in Table 18-2 on page 443.

Table 24-1. Border Choices

Button	Name	Description
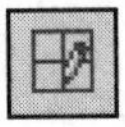	All Borders	Encloses the item with a border (if text, horizontal and vertical lines are added between each item)
	No Border	No borders are shown
	Outside Border	Encloses only the outline of the table, text item, or image
	Inside Border	Places a border between rows and columns but excludes the outside border
	Top Border	Applies a border only to the top of the selected text or graphic
	Bottom Border	Applies a border only to the bottom edge of selected text or graphic
	Left Border	Applies a border only to the left edge of the text or graphic
	Right Border	Applies a border only to the right edge of the selected text or graphic
	Inside Horizontal Border	Inserts a horizontal line through the center of the selected text
	Horizontal Line	Adds a horizontal line through the cell at the cursor position
	Inside Vertical Border	Adds a vertical line through the center of the selected text
	Descending Diagonal Border	Draws a diagonal border down through the created table or text area
	Ascending Diagonal Border	Draws a diagonal line up through the selected table or text area

Creating Enhanced Borders

When you want to create a border that has a more dramatic look than a simple line, you can take matters into your own hands using the Borders And Shading dialog box. By setting the options in this dialog box, you can choose a different look for your border (including 3-D and shadow effects) and change the style, color, and width of the line you use. You can also create partial borders by selecting only the line segments you want to appear.

To create a customized border, begin by placing the insertion point where you want the border to begin or by selecting the data around which you want to create the border. Then choose Format, Borders And Shading. The Borders And Shading dialog box appears, as Figure 24-2 shows.

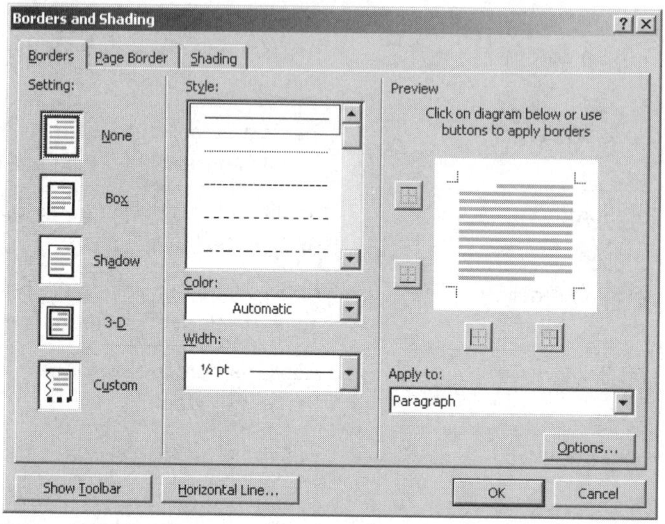

Figure 24-2. Use the options in the Borders And Shading dialog box to select the border type and line style, color, and width you want.

Word 2002 offers five different selections for the borders you create, although you have an almost unlimited number of combinations you can create, using the different styles, colors, widths, and line selections. The border type is the first major choice you'll make. It controls the overall look and feel of the border itself. You can choose from the following options:

- **None** is the default, of course, showing no border around selected text and objects.
- **Box** encloses the selection in a simple line box.
- **Shadow** outlines the selection with a box and adds a drop shadow below and to the right of the selection.
- **3-D** creates a three-dimensional effect for the selected border, making it appear to "stand out" from the page.
- **Custom** enables you to create the look you want yourself by choosing only the line segments you want to display.

tip **Mix and match borders**

You can mix and match different border types to get the effect you want. For example, you might start with a 3-D border type and click Shadow to add a shadow behind it. You can further combine border options such as color and line width to make the border unique.

On the Borders tab of the Borders And Shading dialog box, click the border type you want to apply. If you don't want to make any additional changes, you can simply click OK to return to your document. The border will be added to the text or object you selected. If you didn't select anything before choosing Format, Borders And Shading, the border simply appears around the line at the insertion point; the border will expand as you type.

tip **Undo or change a border**

If you add a border and decide you really don't like it, you can do away with it altogether by pressing Ctrl+Z. Or, if you prefer, you can choose Format, Borders And Shading and select a different border type.

Selecting a Style

Word 2002 gives you 25 different line styles you can use to create the border effects you want. From simple, straight lines to dotted, double, and triple lines, you can create a variety of looks by changing the line style. Figure 24-3, on the next page, shows a few examples of borders with different line styles.

To choose a different line style, open the Borders And Shading dialog box and select a line style in the Style list on the Borders tab. The Preview section shows the effect of your choices. Set any other border choices you want and click OK. The document is updated with your changes.

Troubleshooting

There's Not Enough Contrast in My Double Line

If you create a double line and can't see enough contrast between lines of different weights, you can play around with the line widths you've selected to get a better contrast. Start by selecting the area with the border and choosing Format, Borders And Shading to display the Borders And Shading dialog box. In the Preview section in the dialog box, click the line you want to modify. Then try selecting a heavier line width by clicking the Width down arrow and choosing a thicker line. This action magnifies the effect of the lines and, in a multi-line style with different weights, it increases the contrast.

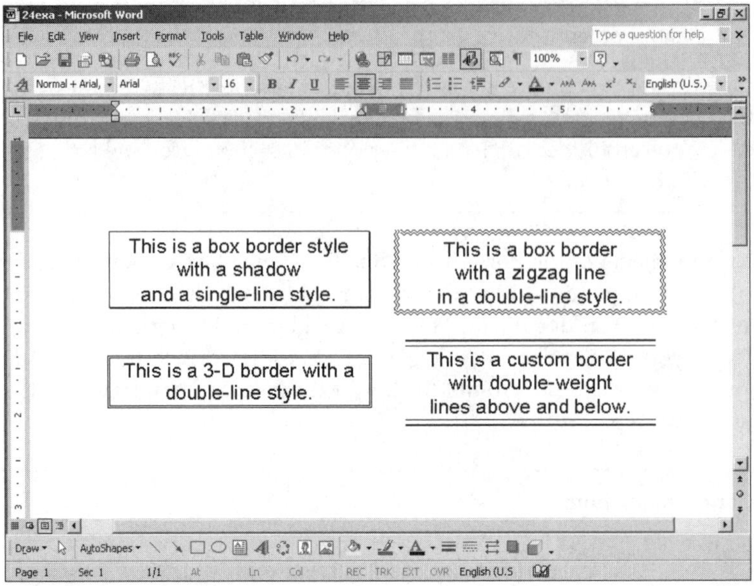

Figure 24-3. The line style you choose has a dramatic effect on the overall look of the border.

Choosing Color

When you first start adding lines and borders to your publication, Word selects black by default. But you have all the colors of Word at your disposal, so you can get as colorful as your needs allow. To choose a color for your border, follow these steps:

1. Select the border you want to change or place the insertion point where you want to add the border.
2. Choose Format, Borders And Shading. The Borders And Shading dialog box appears.
3. Select the border type and line style you want.
4. Click the Color down arrow. The color palette appears, as shown in Figure 24-4.
5. Click the color you want to use from the color palette, or, if you don't see the color you were hoping for, click More Line Colors. The Colors dialog box appears so that you can find the color you're looking for. Click the color you want, and then click OK. The change you selected is displayed in the Preview section.
6. When you're happy with the selection, click OK.

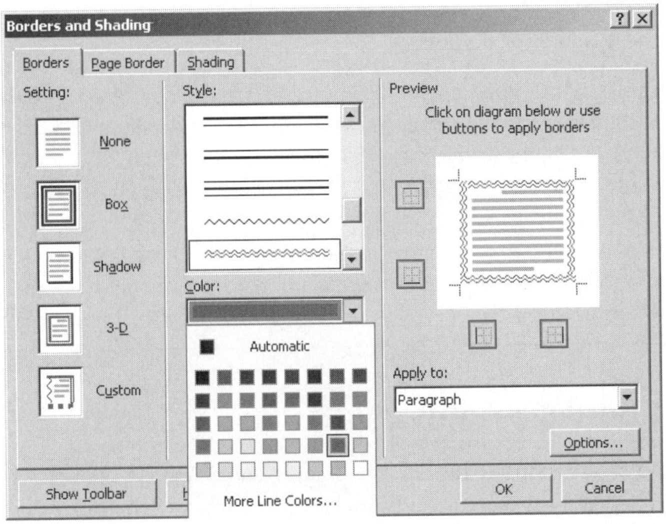

Figure 24-4. Use the color palette to select the color for lines and shading.

When You Need to Match Colors Exactly

Suppose that you're using Word to create a Web page that has the look and feel of your department's annual report, which was published on line last year. When you've been asked to match color schemes, choosing the right color for your borders can become an important issue. For these times, you can use the Custom tab in the Colors dialog box to find and then enter the exact Red, Green, and Blue percentages of the custom color you seek.

To determine the custom color of an item (such as the color you need to replicate from last year's annual report), right-click the item, choose Font on the shortcut menu, and in the Font dialog box, click the Font Color down arrow. The color palette appears. Choose More Colors, and click the Custom tab. At the bottom of the Custom tab, you see three percentages—Red, Green, and Blue if you've selected RGB as your color model, and Hue, Sat, and Lum if you've selected HSL. The numbers shown in the text boxes indicate the percentages of those colors used to create your custom color. Write the numbers down so that you'll have them when you return to the Borders And Shading dialog box to replicate the color. Close the Colors and Font dialog boxes.

tip **Pick the best colors for borders**

The trick to selecting good colors for your text, image, and table borders is to select a color that complements the rest of your design. If you've used a dark blue for headings, for example, you might want to use the same blue for borders and lines. Or if you have a variety of colors in your publication—some used for text, and others used for icons and other types of graphics—be consistent with the colors already used for similar design elements. What you *don't* want to do is create an effect that's interruptive or distracting—the point is to help readers find and understand your information more easily, not to leave them wondering about why you chose that loud color for your border.

Controlling Border Width

When you create a simple border, the default line width is ½ point, which is a simple, thin line. If you want to create a more dramatic effect—whether you leave the line black or add color—you can change the width of the line. To change the line width, display the Borders And Shading dialog box and click the Width down arrow. Then click the width you want, in increments, up to 6 points.

tip **Add special effect separator lines**

You can use line widths to create a special effect for partial borders. Select the area you want to enclose in a border, choose Format, Borders And Shading, and click the Custom border type. Select the line style and click the Width down arrow and choose 3 point. In the Preview section, click the top horizontal border. The line changes to show the 3 point thickness. Next, click the bottom horizontal border; then click OK. Word adds the thick line border above and below the selected area.

Creating Partial Borders

Not every paragraph, table, or object you enclose in a border will need four lines all the way around. You might want to add two lines, along the top and right side of a paragraph, for example, to help set it apart from an article that's displayed beside it. You might use only a top and bottom rule to contain your table of contents. Or you might use a single line to split a quotation off from the main text in your report.

Creating a partial border is a simple matter. You use the Custom border type to do it, and then simply click the sides you want to add. Here are the steps:

1. Select the information around which you want to create the border.
2. Choose Format, Borders And Shading. The Borders And Shading dialog box appears.

3 Click the Custom border type. Select the line style, color, and width settings you want to apply.

4 In the Preview section, click the button that corresponds to the side you want to add. Table 24-2 describes the different choices available in the Preview section.

Table 24-2. Border Button Choices

Button	Description
	Adds a line at the top
	Adds a line at the bottom
	Adds a line at the left
	Adds a line at the right

Applying a Page Border

The techniques you've learned for adding a border to a section or object in your document can be used to add a border to the entire page, as well. Start the process, as usual, by choosing Format, Borders And Shading. When the Borders And Shading dialog box appears, click the Page Border tab.

The only visual difference is the addition of the Art drop-down list (covered in the next section), but you can make all your border choices, and the border will be applied to the entire page. Here's the process:

1 Choose Format, Borders And Shading to display the Borders And Shading dialog box.

2 On the Page Border tab, click the border type you want (Box, Shadow, 3-D, or Custom).

3 Select a line style you want in the Style list.

4 Select a color, if applicable.

5 Click the Width down arrow and choose the line width you want. Each of these settings is reflected in the Preview section.

6 Click OK to close the dialog box. By default, the border is added to all the pages in the current document. (See Figure 24-5, on the next page.) If you want to apply the border to a specific section, you can click the Apply To down arrow and make that selection.

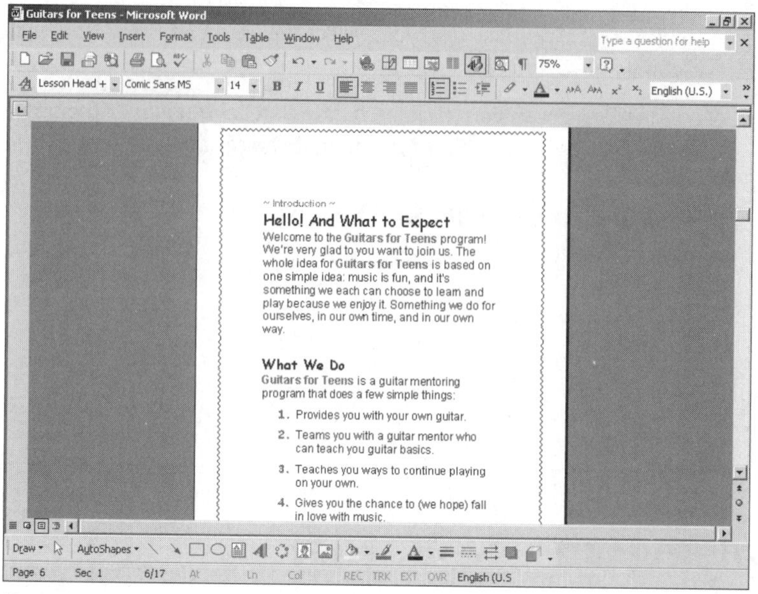

Figure 24-5. The page border settings you select are applied to all pages in your document.

> **tip** **Skip the first page border**
>
> When you add a page border, Word applies the border to all the pages in your document. What if you want to skip the border on one page? To suppress the display of the border for first pages, choose Format, Borders And Shading, click the Page Border tab, click the Apply To down arrow, and select This Section – All Except First Page.

Art Border, Anyone?

Another feature, known in earlier versions of Office as BorderArt, enables you to add an artistic touch to entire pages in your document. Special graphics are placed in patterns—both black and white and color—and used to border the page. To apply an art page border, follow these steps:

1. Start anywhere in the document to which you want to add the border.
2. Choose Format, Borders And Shading. The Borders And Shading dialog box appears.
3. Click the Page Border tab. Most of the options remain the same, but now the Art drop-down list is available.
4. Click the Art down arrow and scroll through the art borders. Select the one you want. The Preview section shows your change. (See Figure 24-6.)

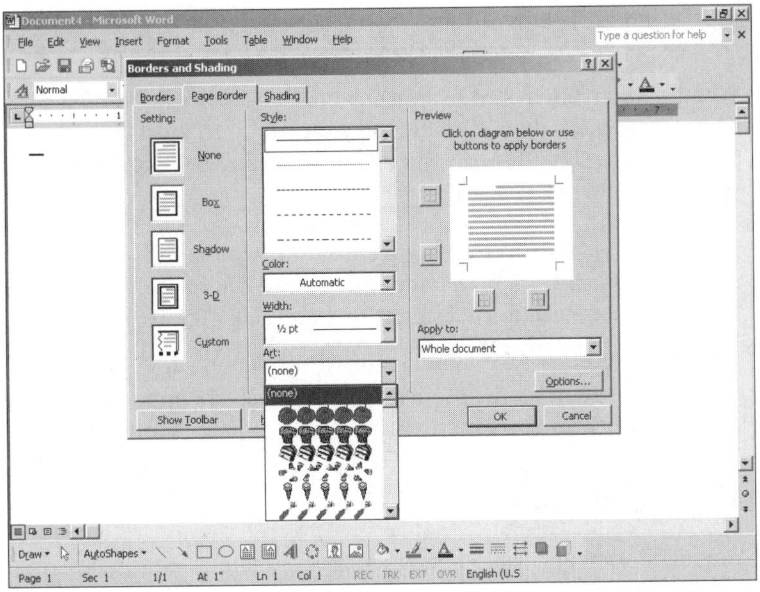

Figure 24-6. The page border settings you select are applied to all pages in your document.

5 When you've selected the art border you want, click OK. The border is added to all pages.

note As you can see, art borders are colorful and vibrant—and they can also be a bit much for some professional documents. For that reason, use art borders sparingly.

Troubleshooting

I Accidentally Created Separate Tables

You've selected the text you want to surround with a border, but when you create the border, Word divides the selection and draws one border around the heading and another around the text. How do you combine both borders into one rectangular border? There are two workarounds for this problem: First, try selecting a larger section that extends at least one line both before and after the item you want to border. Then select the border as you would normally. If the border's still breaking the text into two separate boxes, copy the information in the second box, place the insertion point following the line of text where the break occurs, and press Shift+Enter to add a "soft" line break, and press Ctrl+V to paste. You might have to do a little reformatting to get your information to look right, but this should resolve the border break problem.

Adding Borders to Sections and Paragraphs

Whether you're interested in applying borders to a single word, a paragraph, a section, or a page, you can do it easily by using the Apply To drop-down list in the Borders And Shading dialog box. The tab you choose—Borders or Page Border—depends on the element you want to enclose in a border:

- If you want to create a border around a section in your document, click the Page Border tab. In the Apply To drop-down list on that tab, you'll find what you need to choose section bordering options.
- If you want to add a border around a paragraph, text, or selected cells in your document, click the Borders tab. The Apply To options in that tab will give you the item-specific choices you need to apply borders to portions of text.

Bordering Sections

You might want to create a border around a section when you have specific information you want to highlight or when you want to set a section apart from the regular flow of the text. To create a section border, start by placing the insertion point in the section you want to border. Choose Format, Borders And Shading to display the dialog box, and click the Page Border tab. Next, simply choose all the border effects you want—the border type and line style, color, and width—and then click the Apply To down arrow and select your choice. Depending on the border you're creating (these options are not available for every type of border), you might see the following options:

- **Whole document** adds a border to every page in your document.
- **This Section** adds a border only to the pages between the previous section break and the next section break.
- **This Section—First Page Only** finds the first page after the previous section break and adds a border only to that page.
- **This Section—All Except First Page** adds a border to all pages in the current section except the first page after the preceding section break.

Simply click the selection you want, and click OK to close the dialog box. The border is added to the section as you selected. If you want to see how the border looks for the entire section, choose File, Print Preview, and click the Multiple Pages button on the Print Preview toolbar and select the number of pages to display. The document appears in multi-page format so that you can see the effect of your border selection. Click Close on the Print Preview toolbar to return to the document window.

tip **Add write-in spaces with a border**

Here's a great way to add horizontal lines for write-in spaces in your documents. Press Enter to insert a number of blank lines in your document. Then highlight the area to which you want to add horizontal lines and click the Tables And Borders button. Click the Borders down arrow on the Tables And Borders toolbar, and select Inside Horizontal Border from the menu. The lines are added automatically, extending from the left to the right margin, and they're spaced evenly.

Bordering Paragraphs

If you want to create a border around a smaller portion of text, such as a paragraph, selected text, or the cells in a table, you use a different set of choices. Start by selecting the text item you want to create the border around; then choose Format, Borders And Shading. When the dialog box appears, leave the Borders tab selected, make your border choices as usual, and click the Apply To down arrow. Depending on the text you've selected, you might see the following choices:

- **Paragraph** creates a border around the currently selected paragraph.
- **Text** adds a border to the highlighted text.
- **Cell** draws a border around the cells you've selected in the document.
- **Table** borders the entire table at the insertion point.

Click your selection, and then click OK to close the Borders And Shading dialog box. The border is added to the selection as you specified.

Choosing Border Options

Word makes a few assumptions about the way you want to display the borders in your documents. By default, Word applies a small margin to borders you apply to a paragraph and a larger margin to borders for sections and pages. When you add a border to a paragraph, Word adds a 1-point margin to the top and bottom and a 4-point margin along the left and right edges of the border. When you add a page or section border, Word adds a 24-point margin all the way around.

Display the Border options by choosing Format, Borders And Shading. Leave the Borders tab selected if you're changing the options for a paragraph border; if you're working with a document or section border, click the Page Border tab. Then click the Options button in the lower right corner of the dialog box. The Border And Shading Options dialog box appears, as Figure 24-7, on the next page, shows.

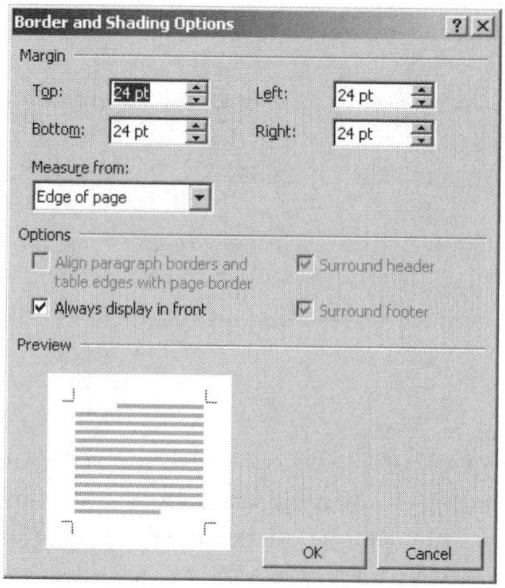

Figure 24-7. You control border margins and make choices about border alignment in the Border And Shading Options dialog box.

To make changes to the border margins, click in the box you want to change and type the new value, or use the arrows to increase or decrease the value shown.

Word automatically measures the margin beginning at the edge of the page, but you can change that setting so that the measurement reflects spacing between surrounding text and the selected border. To make this change, click the Measure From down arrow and choose Text.

The other options in the Border And Shading Options dialog box are available only if you're working with a page or section border. By default, Word includes any headers and footers inside the bordered area and, also by default, enables the Always Display In Front check box, which causes the border to be displayed in front of any text or graphic objects that might overlap it. If you have other borders or tables within the bordered section, the Align Paragraph Borders And Table Edges With Page Borders check box will also be available to you. If you want Word to align all these borders evenly, select this check box.

After you've finished choosing border options, click OK to close the dialog box; then click OK a second time to return to your document.

> **note** If you select a table before you display the Borders And Shading dialog box, your options in the Apply To list will show Paragraph, Table, and Cell.

Inserting a Horizontal Line

In some situations, you'll want only a divider line, not a complete border, to set off sections or special elements in your document. For example, if you're creating a Web page, you might want to add a line to mark the end of one section and the beginning of the next. Word provides a feature that gives you a library of graphical lines—special design effects you can place in your document as needed.

Adding a Line

To add a horizontal line to your document, follow these steps:

1. Place the insertion point where you want to add the line.
2. Choose Format, Borders And Shading. The Borders And Shading dialog box appears.
3. Click the Horizontal Line button. This action displays the Horizontal Line dialog box, as Figure 24-8 shows.
4. Scroll through the selections until you find the one you want. Click your choice, and click OK to add the line.

Figure 24-8. The Horizontal Line dialog box displays the predesigned graphical lines you can insert in your document.

> **tip** Once you place a horizontal line in your document, you can select, copy and paste, and move it as you would any graphical item.

Importing a Custom Line

If you create your own graphical lines in another program (which could be Windows Paint, Microsoft PowerPoint, or even Word), you can add those files to your Horizontal Line gallery. Word can import files in the following formats:

- BMP, RLE, DIB (Microsoft Windows Bitmap)
- EMF (Enhanced Metafile)
- EPS (Encapsulated Postscript)
- GIF (Graphics Interchange Format)
- JPG (Joint Photographic Experts Group)
- PNG (Portable Network Graphics)
- TIFF (Tagged Image File Format)
- WMF (Windows Metafile)

For more information on importing objects and files into your Word documents, see Chapter 15, "Inserting Objects for Multimedia and More."

To add a custom line to your Horizontal Line gallery so that it's available in the Horizontal Line dialog box, follow these steps:

1. In the graphics program you're using, save the file in one of the supported file formats.
2. In Word, choose Format, Borders And Shading to display the Borders And Shading dialog box.
3. Click the Horizontal Line button. The Horizontal Line dialog box appears.
4. Click the Import button. The Add Clips To Organizer dialog box is displayed.
5. Navigate to the file you want to use; click it and click Add. The line is added to the gallery and remains selected.
6. Add the clip to your document by clicking OK. The Horizontal Line dialog box closes and the line is placed at the insertion point in your document.

Troubleshooting

My Border Isn't Printing Correctly

If your page border doesn't print along one edge of the page or is positioned too close to one edge or another, check the margin options you've set for the border. To do this, choose Format, Borders And Shading, click the Page Border tab, and click Options. In the Margin section, increase the margin values to make sure the border is not placed in your printer's nonprinting range.

If you've set up your border to be measured from Text, the space between the text and the border might be pushing the border into the nonprintable range. (Most printers will not print in the 0.5-inch area around the perimeter of the page.)

Shading Sections

Sometimes you need more than a border—you need something to help the text, headline, or image really stand out as different from the rest of the publication. For those times, you might want to consider adding a shade to provide color, contrast, or interest to your document.

Applying Shades to Tables and Paragraphs

Word includes a number of predesigned table formats that include many different shading possibilities. You can use one of the preset shades by selecting the table and choosing Table, Table AutoFormat. You can then click each of the format choices to see the shading that's been used in the AutoFormats.

When you want to apply your own shade to a paragraph, table, or headline, follow these steps:

1. Select the item to which you want to add a shade.
2. Choose Format, Borders And Shading. The Borders And Shading dialog box appears.
3. Click the Shading tab. You see the various options you'll use for adding and modifying shades. (See Figure 24-9, on the next page.)

note The borders and shading features of Word work independently, which means that if you add shading without adding a border, the item will appear with only the shade behind it—no outer border will be added automatically. To add a border to the shade, select it and choose Format, Borders And Shading; then choose your border choices on the Borders tab, and click OK.

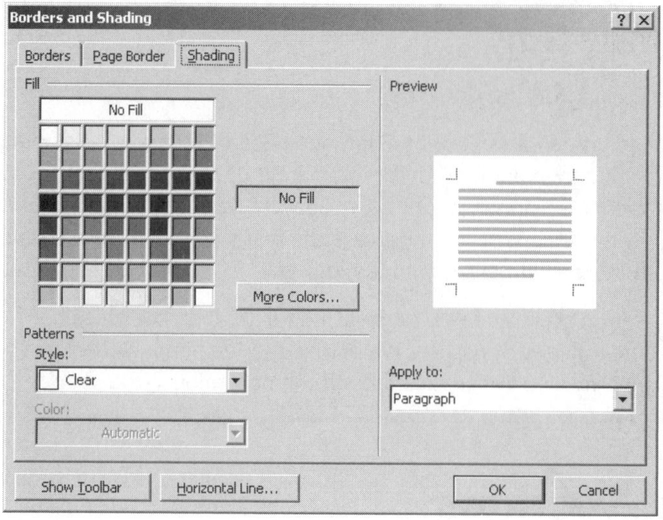

Figure 24-9. Adding shading can be as simple as choosing the color you want.

In the Fill section, click the color you want to apply. If you don't see the color you want, you can click More Colors to open the Colors dialog box and choose from another selection. Alternatively, you can click the Custom tab in the Colors dialog box to enter the values for your own custom color.

In the Patterns section, click the Style down arrow to display your choices for the density of the color you select. Choose a lower percentage for a lighter shade. The Preview section shows the effect of your choices. Click OK to make your changes. The shade is added to the selected item in your document.

Shading Considerations

Similar to the caveat given earlier about art borders, remember that a little shading goes a long way. Done thoughtfully and with the reader in mind, shades can be very effective in calling attention to certain elements and helping special design objects to stand out on the page. But overusing shading or using the wrong mix of colors and patterns can make your document or Web page harder for people to read, which means they'll turn the page or click through your site—and you'll lose your audience.

To use shading effectively, stay close to these guidelines:

- **Use shades on a need-to-use basis.** Don't sprinkle shades all the way through your document at random. Give a shade a reason, such as, "Every time we mention a new board member we'll provide a brief biography in a shaded sidebar."

- **Choose intensities carefully.** A shade that looks light on-screen might show up to be much darker in print.
- **Test your contrasts.** When you add a colored shade behind text, be sure to increase the contrast between the color of the shade and the color of text. If you choose a dark blue background, black text won't show up clearly. If you choose a dark background, select a light-colored (white or yellow) text.
- **Do test prints on a printer of comparable output.** If you're printing colored shades, be sure to print a test page on a color printer.
- **If you're creating a Web page, use Web-safe colors for your shades.** Most Web browsers today can support the standard colors used in the Windows palette. If you choose customized colors, however, other browsers might not display the color accurately. Test the display of the page with different browsers to check the colors you've selected.

Troubleshooting

The Border Changes I Made in My Table Disappeared

If you change the border or shading of a table and find out, when you close the Borders And Shading dialog box, that the changes you selected weren't made, try this fix: Click the Show All button on the Standard toolbar to display all the formatting characters in your document. Now reselect the table, making sure to include the end-of-cell marks at the ends of rows. Next, choose Format, Border And Shading to display the Borders And Shading dialog box, and re-enter your changes. Because the table formatting marks were included, the changes should stick this time.

Part 6

Publishing Long Documents

Chapter 25

Creating and Controlling Master Documents

When you begin to work on longer documents, consistency and continuity become important. You need to make sure that all the various parts of your document use the same styles, treat tables and figures the same way, and have consistent headers and footers. You need to be able to check the overall organization of your document, making sure that the topics flow logically and that you've arranged them in the best possible order.

This is easy to do when you're working with 10, 20, or even 30 pages. But what about those book-length projects for which various team members are taking a chapter or two, somebody else is plugging in the charts, and yet another person is checking the citations and references? It's in this type of situation that Word's master and subdocument features really shine. By using those features, you can divide a large document up into pieces—for example, giving a chapter to each team member—and then integrate them back into one piece; you can have both the benefit of working with a team to get a major project done and the insurance that the consistency and continuity of your document are intact.

Using Master Documents

At its most basic level, a master document holds together a number of separate files. You might create a master document to handle the following projects:

- A book-length manuscript in which each team member writes and edits one chapter.

- A grant proposal in which different committee members are responsible for different pieces (for example, your executive director writing the Executive Summary, your financial officer providing the budget, and your development committee chairperson writing the objective and evaluation sections).
- An annual report that's a compilation of a number of different sections, including the introduction, the program descriptions, the donor thank-you section, and letters from clients served. Each person on your publications team could research and write a different piece of the report.
- A technical manual that's a collaborative effort between your IT department and a technical illustrator. After each chapter is written, you can send it as a subdocument to the illustrator, who can create and place the illustrations and then return the subdocument to be integrated into the master.

> **note** Master and subdocuments create a great opportunity for you to use Word's team review and collaboration features. For more about tracking, comparing, and integrating changes in a collaborative document, see Chapter 30, "Collaborating On Line with E-Mail, NetMeeting, Discussions, and Faxes."

No matter what type of project you're working on—whether you're working with a team or doing it all yourself—you can use master documents to do the following things:

- Keep track of disparate sections and open and print them all rather than working with individual files
- Display and collapse subdocuments to switch between views easily
- Coordinate pieces of a project that are distributed to other team members
- Review and easily reorganize a long document
- Control styles, margins, and other formats throughout a long document
- Work with a long document as a whole for operations such as printing, checking spelling, and Find and Replace

What's in a Master Document?

In Chapter 11, "Outlining Documents for Clarity and Structure," you worked in Outline view to create, check, and change the basic organization of your document. The idea behind master documents builds on this basic philosophy and takes it to a higher level. By working with the "big picture" of your document, you can easily see how your sections or chapters compare, what needs to be moved, and which pieces you want to assign to other team members. The best place for this big picture approach is Outline view. That's where you'll do all your work with master and subdocuments.

When you first change to Outline view, either by choosing View, Outline or by clicking the Outline View button to the left of the horizontal scroll bar, the Outlining toolbar appears. On the toolbar, you'll see the master document buttons. Table 25-1 introduces you to these different tools.

note For a review of the other buttons on the Outlining toolbar, see Chapter 11, "Outlining Documents for Clarity and Structure."

Table 25-1. Master Document Buttons

Button	Button Name	Description
	Master Document View	Switches the display to master document view so that you can see subdocument icons
	Collapse Subdocuments	Hides the display of subdocument sections to their heading levels
	Create Subdocument	Creates a subdocument of the current selection
	Delete Subdocument	Removes the subdocument designation and returns the selection to a normal part of the master document
	Import Subdocument	Inserts an existing document as a subdocument
	Merge Subdocument	Puts two or more selected subdocuments together
	Split Subdocument	Divides a subdocument into two subdocuments
	Protect Subdocument	Secures the subdocument so that no further changes can be made

Master documents can include text, graphics, charts—anything you put in your documents. One of the best things about working with master and subdocuments is the ability it gives you to build documents from segments and vice versa. Once you set up your master document to include subdocuments, you'll see a number of items in Outline view, as Figure 25-1, on the next page, shows.

- **Subdocument icons.** Once you create a subdocument from a selection in a document, Word displays the subdocument with an icon, in outline form.
- **Document text.** When the master document is fully expanded, you can see everything in your document, all the way to document text level.
- **Subordinate headings.** The subdocument headings enable you to see at a glance how your document is organized. You can also determine easily how to assign the various portions for other team members.
- **Master and subdocument buttons on the Outlining toolbar.** Any time you work in Outline view, the master and subdocument buttons are available at the right end of the Outlining toolbar.

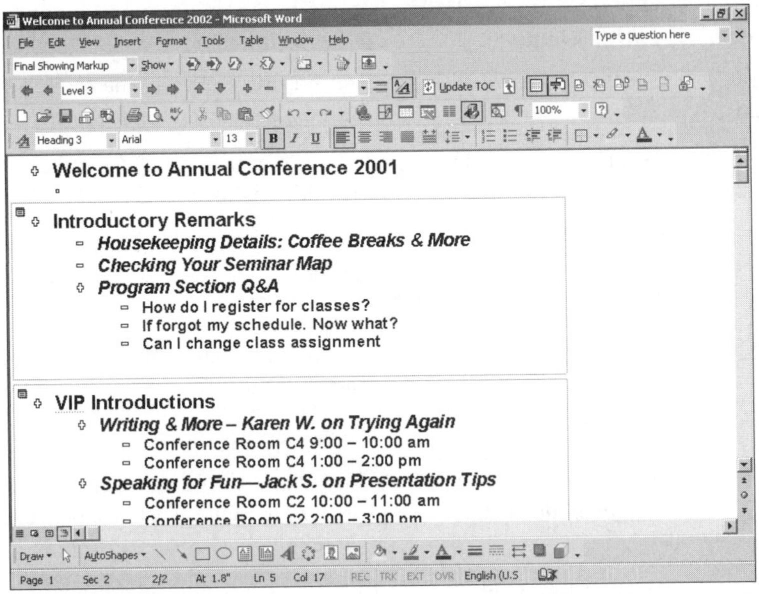

Figure 25-1. Working with master documents in Outline view, you can easily see and work with the subdocuments you create.

Preparing Master Documents and Subdocuments

You can see the benefits of working with master and subdocuments—especially if you're managing a large project. Like anything else that requires the cooperation of a number of people, it's best to start with a plan. Take some time to consider all the different aspects of your document and plan the types of assignments you want to make before you get started. Be sure to create a table or listing of various part assignments that will enable you to track the different parts of your document.

tip **Create an assignment list**

You might want to use Word's Table of Contents (TOC) feature to automatically generate a table of contents that you can use as an assignment list. If you have a large project with many different pieces (and as many team members), you'll need to track the list so you know who has which piece. For more about using Word's TOC feature, see Chapter 26, "Generating First-Class Tables of Contents and Related Elements."

File Organization for Master and Subdocuments

In addition to the organization of the various pieces and people, you'll need to think about a physical location for the files as they come and go. All files for master and subdocuments must be stored in the same folder—otherwise, Word won't know where to look to integrate the various pieces.

Choose a folder in which you'll store both the master and subdocument files. If you're working on a network system, make sure this is a place created on a shared drive to which all team members have access. If you'll be using existing documents to build the master document, be sure to move those documents to the newly created directory before you begin the process of creating the master document.

Creating a Master Document

You have two different options for creating a master document—and both procedures are simple ones:

- You can start with an existing document and turn it into a master document by creating subdocuments within it.
- You can create a master document from scratch, creating the outline headings and subdocuments as you go along.

Starting with an Existing Document

If you have a document you want to use as a master document, start by opening the file you want to use by choosing File, Open, navigating to and selecting the file you want, and clicking Open. Change to Outline view by choosing View, Outline. The document appears in Outline view, with the heading styles you've selected. (See Figure 25-2, on the next page.)

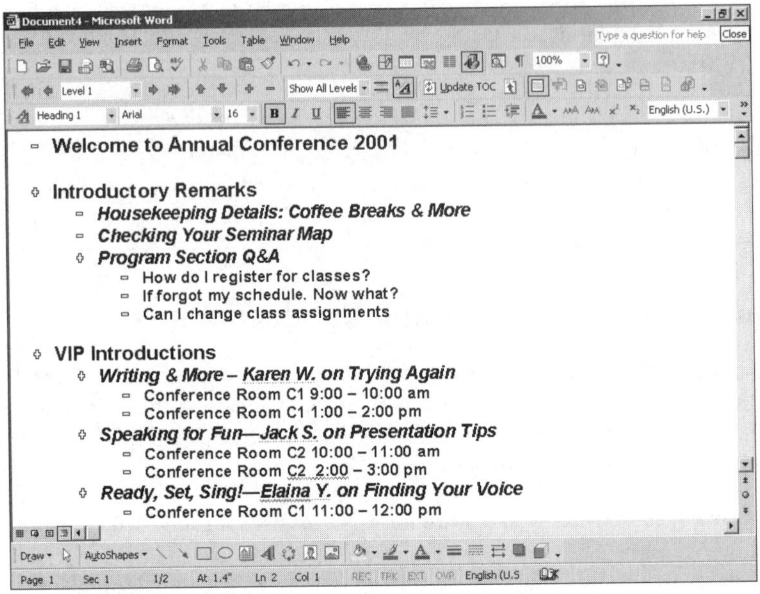

Figure 25-2. When you start with an existing document for your master, Word displays the existing heading levels in Outline view.

The heading styles you've assigned to the text in your document tell Word which headings to use for the master document outline. You divide the master by selecting the portion you want to mark as a subdocument; then Word inserts a link in place of the actual text in the master and saves the text as a subdocument. In the section "Creating Subdocuments" on the next page, you'll learn how to select sections and create the subdocuments you need.

Troubleshooting

Document Headings Don't Appear as Headings in Outline View

When you change to Outline view, you might find that Word doesn't show your headings as the headings you thought they were. If you created your own styles and didn't base them on Word's Heading 1 or Heading 2 styles, or you simply entered the headings using the Normal style, Word won't recognize your headings.

Promote

To fix this easily, click the Promote button to raise the text to Level 1, which also assigns the Heading 1 style. You can easily modify your custom styles and base them on the Heading 1 style so that you can get the look you want and still be able to work with the Outline view and Master Documents. For more on setting up and working with styles, see Chapter 10, "Using Styles to Increase Your Formatting Power."

Starting from Scratch

You can create a master document right from the beginning of your project. Once you've got a concept and thoughts for a beginning outline, you can create the outline in Outline view and then make the assignments for your subdocuments as needed. Here are the steps for starting a new master document from scratch:

1. Start a new document and change to Outline view by choosing View, Outline.
2. Enter the headings for the document title and subdocument titles. Word automatically creates the headings with the default style Heading 1. Make sure each heading you intend to turn into a subdocument is assigned the Heading 1 style. This is the style Word will use in dividing into subdocuments.

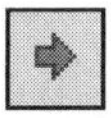
Demote

3. Create subheadings (sections within the subdocument) by clicking Demote to assign Heading 2 to subhead text.

Save

4. When you've got your outline the way you want it, save the file by clicking the Save button on the Standard toolbar, typing a name for the file, and clicking Save.

> **tip** **Create a backup copy**
>
> If you think you might like to keep a copy of your outline before it's been divided into subdocuments, use Save As to save a backup copy of the outline file. Although you can easily remove subdocument divisions and integrate subdocuments into the master at a later time, that's a lot of hassle if you simply want an original version of the outline to play around with.

Creating Subdocuments

Once you've got the basic outline in place, you can determine how you want to divide up the master document. Create a subdocument by following these steps:

1. Make sure that all headings and subheadings you want to include in the subdocument are displayed by clicking the Show Level down arrow on the Outlining toolbar and selecting Show All Levels.
2. Click the symbol to the left of the heading of the portion you want to use for the subdocument. For example, if you want to create a subdocument of the "Introductory Remarks" in Figure 25-3, on the next page, click the plus symbol, and the entire topic is selected.

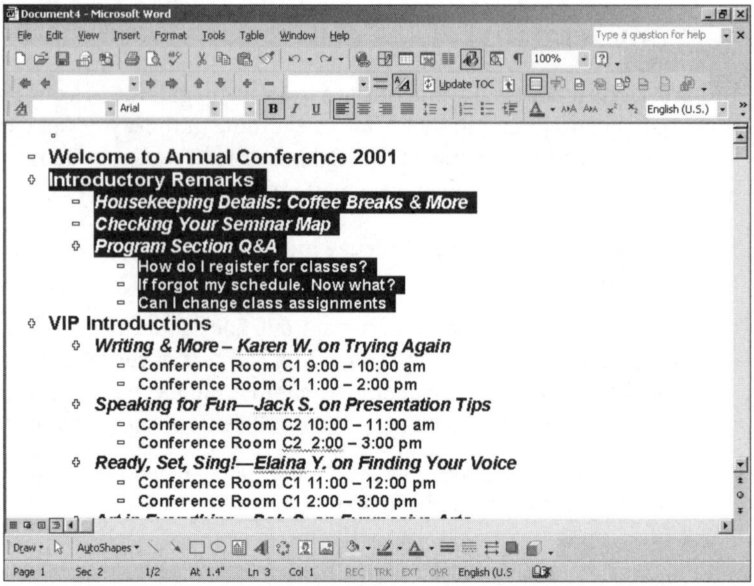

Figure 25-3. Be sure to display and select all text you want to include in your subdocument before clicking the Create Subdocument button.

Create Subdocument

3 Click the Create Subdocument button on the Outlining toolbar. The topic is marked as a subdocument, as Figure 25-4 shows.

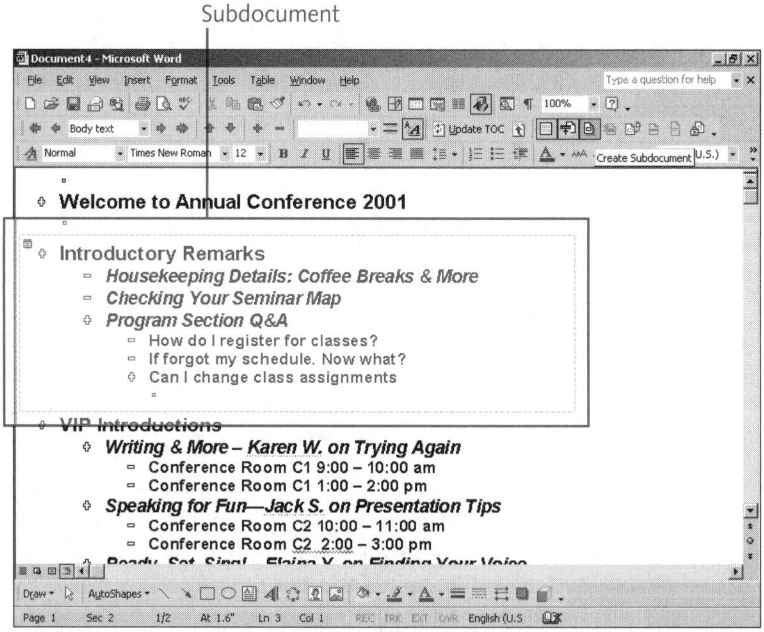

Figure 25-4. Word creates the subdocument and names it according to the text in the first line of the selection.

4 Save the document. Word saves the subdocument as a separate file in the same folder. The Heading 1 text at the beginning of the file is used as the file name.

> **caution** This is one of those reasons to create a different folder for each master document you work with—if there's any chance you'll have subdocuments with the same name in two different master documents, one subdocument might overwrite the other if you have too many files together. Better to be safe than sorry—create a new folder for each master document project.

Importing Data for Subdocuments

You can also create subdocuments by importing other files into your master document. In this case, you might have a partial outline you're working with, or you might start a new file for your master and then open existing files into it. However you choose to get the document pieces together, here are the steps for turning them into subdocuments:

1 Start with the master document open on the screen.

2 Place the insertion point where you want to add the subdocument.

Import Subdocument

3 Click Import Subdocument on the Outlining toolbar. This opens the Insert Subdocument dialog box. (See Figure 25-5.)

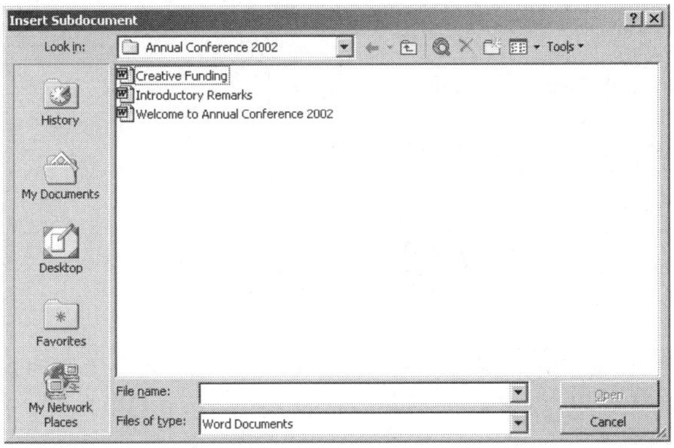

Figure 25-5. Importing an existing file into a master to be used as a subdocument saves you data entry and organizing time.

4 Navigate to the file you want to import, select it, and click Open. The subdocument is added to the master document at the insertion point.

5 Add or create other subdocuments as needed. When you're finished creating subdocuments, save the file. Word saves the master and the subdocuments in the folder you specify.

Navigating to and from the Master Document

So the basic idea behind master documents is that you can have one large file in which all pieces are represented, but for convenience and expediency's sake, you can have each of these different pieces in different places, theoretically being worked on by different people. As you begin to work with and edit the text of your long document, you'll need to know how to navigate among the files in order to make the changes you want to make.

Working with the Master Document

After you create a master document and create subdocuments within it, Word changes the way it saves the file information. No longer is everything stored within the single document. Now the master document contains links to the subdocuments, and when you expand and work with the subdocuments within the master, you are really, through links, working in the individual subdocument files themselves.

After you save and close your master document, reopen it and notice the change. As Figure 25-6 shows, the master document for the Annual Conference publication now stores links to the subdocuments.

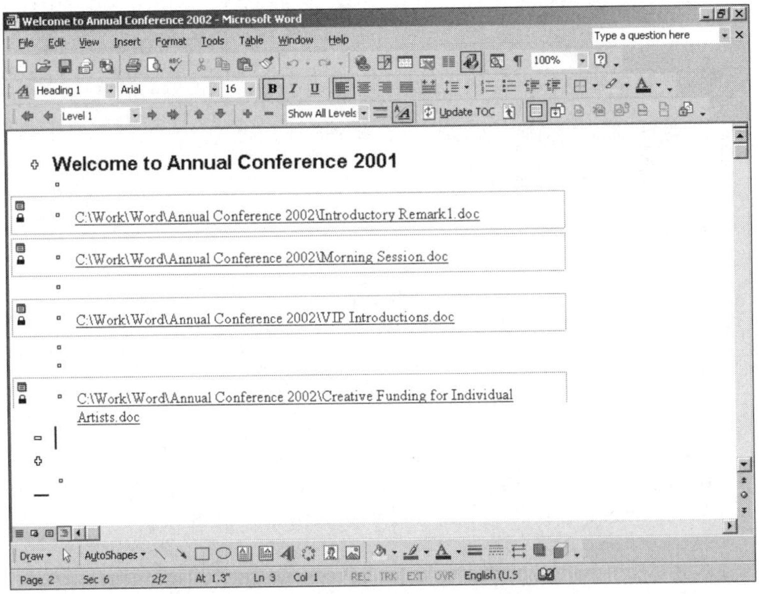

Figure 25-6. After you save, close, and reopen the master document, Word shows the links to the subdocuments in place of the text.

> **tip** **See the path**
>
> To review the path to the folder in which the subdocument is stored, position the mouse pointer over the subdocument link. A ScreenTip shows the link and tells you to press and hold Ctrl while clicking the link to move to the subdocument.

Following Links to Subdocuments

To move to the subdocument by using the link, press and hold Ctrl while clicking on the link. The subdocument file opens in a new Word window on your screen. (See Figure 25-7.) You can now expand and edit the file as needed.

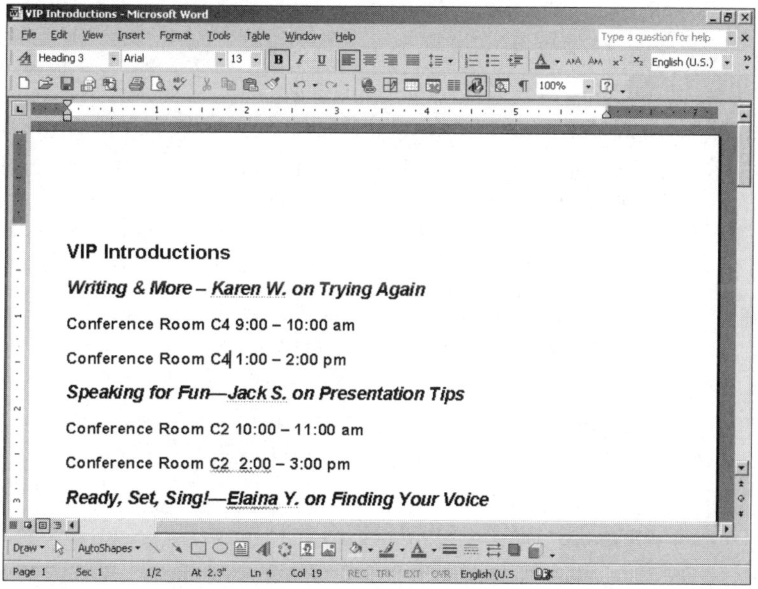

Figure 25-7. When you want to add to or edit a subdocument, follow the link to the document and make the changes you want.

> **caution** If you later reorganize your files and move subdocuments from one place to another—even if you are moving them within the same directory to new subfolders, Word will display the message "Error! Hyperlink reference not valid." To re-establish links between your master and subdocuments, delete the broken subdocument link and use the Import Subdocument button on the Outlining toolbar to relink the document.

Controlling Subdocument Display

As you begin to work with the master and subdocuments you create, you might want to change the level to which text, headings, and graphics are displayed. You can suppress the display of text and graphics, for example, when you're thinking about reorganizing the document and want only to see first and second-level headings.

Similarly, you'll want to be able to view the contents of the master document when you want to do global searches, work with formats and styles, check spelling, and print the publication. This will require that you expand the subdocuments to show the complete contents of the master. To change the display of subdocuments in this way, you'll use the master and subdocument buttons at the right end of the Outlining toolbar. Table 25-2 introduces the buttons you'll use to control the display of subdocuments.

Table 25-2. Outlining Toolbar Buttons for Hiding and Displaying Subdocuments

Button	Button Name	Description	Use
	Expand Subdocuments	Replaces the links in the master document with the text displayed from the subdocument	You want to see all headings, graphics, and text in your master document.
	Collapse Subdocuments	Shows in the master document only the links to the subdocuments	You want to view only the structure and links of the overall document.
	Collapse	Collapses all text except headings	You want to view only the headings in your subdocument.
	Expand	Expands a document that has previously been collapsed	You want to see all text in the subdocument.
	First Line Only View	Displays only the first line of text in individual paragraphs	You want to reorganize paragraphs in a section or document.
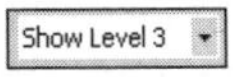	Show Level	Shows text below the level selected	You want to see text in sections below a specific level.

Expanding and Collapsing Subdocuments

You can collapse an outline to move and reorganize the document easily. As you learned when working in Outline view, however, you can collapse and expand only text that's been formatted with Word's built-in heading styles or preset outline levels.

Displaying Subdocuments

To display the subdocuments in the master, you need to expand the display. Follow these steps:

1. Open your master document.
2. Place the insertion point at the beginning of the document.
3. Change to Outline view by choosing View, Outline, if necessary.
4. Click the Expand Subdocuments button on the Outlining toolbar.
   All subdocuments in your master are displayed, as Figure 25-8 shows.
   The subdocument icon and any subordinate text and graphics also appear.

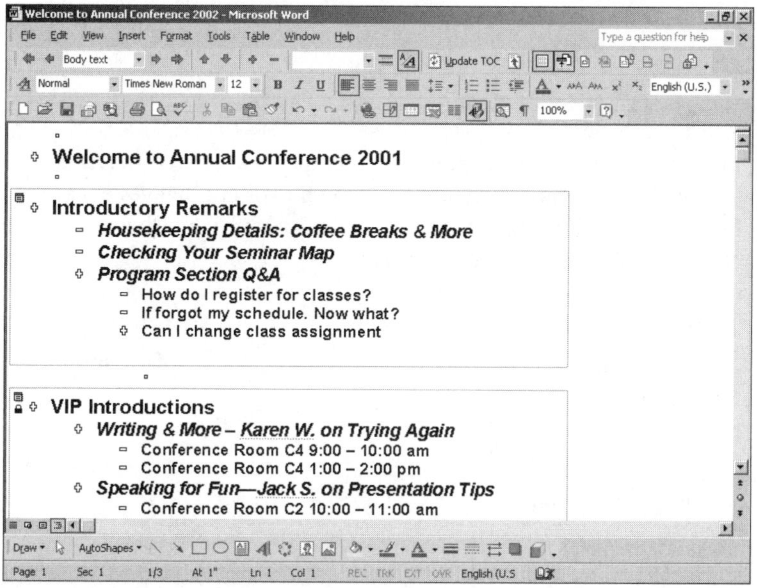

Figure 25-8. Expanding subdocuments shows all text in the master, keeping the subdocument breaks and icons intact.

> **tip** **Check things out in Print Layout view**
>
> When you expand subdocuments in the master document, you can change to Print Layout view to see how the sections will look in print form. You can make formatting changes, check spelling, and use Find and Replace to your heart's content while you're in Print Layout view. Then return to Outline view to finish working with the master document and move sections, if needed.

Hiding Subdocuments

Once you've expanded the subdocuments in the master, the button changes to Collapse Subdocuments so that you can again suppress the display of the subdocuments. You'll want to do this before you reorder subdocuments in your master document. To collapse the master display, click anywhere in the document and select Collapse Subdocuments. The master goes back to its links-only display.

> **tip** If you want to collapse only the heading levels within a subdocument, use the traditional Collapse button on the Outlining toolbar to control that display.

Editing Master and Subdocuments

Because master documents and subdocuments are two different kinds of files, each storing different things, you'll make different editing changes in each of them. Table 25-3 lists the various editing tasks you'll want to perform and shows where you'll make those changes in master and subdocuments.

Table 25-3. Editing Master and Subdocuments

Editing Task	Master Document	Subdocument
Text editing and correction		✔
Applying heading levels	✔	
Changing topic order	✔	
Checking spelling	✔	
Global formatting	✔	
Local formatting of individual elements	✔	✔
Changing margins and page setup	✔	
Adding headers and footers	✔	
Adding borders and shading to specific objects		✔

Making Master Changes

The types of changes you'll make to your master document include those that will affect the entire publication. For example, you'll add styles to a template in the master document so that all the styles can be consistent among the various pieces of the publication. You'll also change margins, specify column settings, and do things like run the spelling checker and print while you have everything together in your master document.

You'll also add headers and footers to your master document so that you can ensure consistent treatment throughout all your subdocuments.

Entering Subdocument Changes

Especially if you are assigning subdocuments to different team members to write, edit, proofread, and ultimately return to the master, the most basic changes will have to happen in the subdocuments. The line-by-line editing, word choice, and object work (such as the addition of tables, graphics, and text boxes) all need to happen in the subdocument file.

Each person working on a subdocument can make changes as needed and then save the file in the designated folder. When the master document is opened and the document is expanded, all changes made in the various subdocuments will be reflected in the master. The person working with the master can then change global formatting options, check spelling, add headers and footers, and print the document as needed.

Troubleshooting

Different Styles Appear in Master Document and Subdocuments

If you notice that the headings in your master document and subdocuments look different, check the template you've applied by choosing Tools, Templates And Add-Ins. In the Document Template section, check each file to make sure that both the master and the subdocument have the same template selected and that the Automatically Update Document Styles check box is selected. If necessary, attach a different template by clicking the Attach button and, in the Attach Template dialog box, navigating to the template file you want. Make your selection and click Open; click OK to close the Template And Add-Ins dialog box and return to the document.

Locking Subdocuments

Word provides a subdocument locking feature that enables you to protect documents so that no further changes can be made to them. This is particularly helpful if you're working as part of a team and want to make sure another team member doesn't modify a file after it's been finalized.

Protect Document

To lock a subdocument, simply click the subdocument icon and click the Protect Document button on the Outlining toolbar. A small lock symbol appears beneath the subdocument icon to the left of the subdocument text. (See Figure 25-9.)

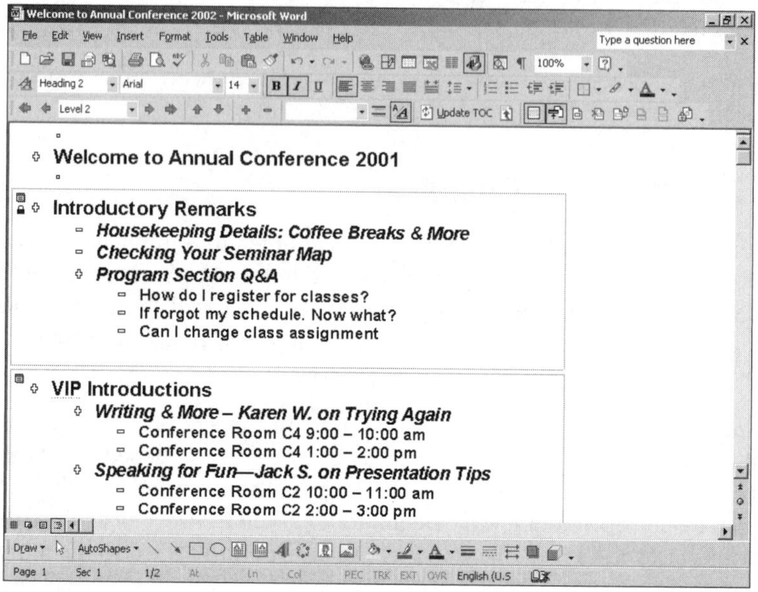

Figure 25-9. Once you finish editing a subdocument, you can lock it against further changes by clicking Protect Document on the Outlining toolbar.

Rearranging a Master Document

One of the greatest perks of working in a master document is the ease with which you can rearrange subdocuments. Start by opening your master document and reviewing the order of the subdocuments you've got listed. Here are the steps:

Open the master document.

1. Choose View, Outline (or click the Outline View button to the left of the horizontal scroll bar). The master document appears in Outline view.
2. Click Expand Subdocuments on the Outlining toolbar. The master document expands to show headings and text of the subdocuments.
3. Drag the subdocument icon of the item you want to move to the new location. A heavy indicator line moves with the pointer, showing you the placement of the subdocument. (See Figure 25-10.)

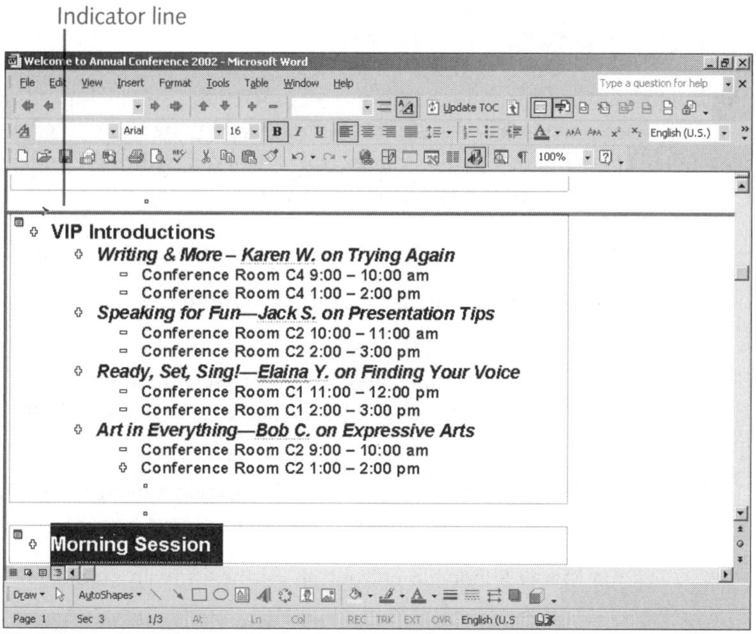

Figure 25-10. When you rearrange subdocuments, the indicator line shows you where the subdocument will be placed when you release the mouse button.

4 When the indicator line is positioned where you want to insert the subdocument, release the mouse button. The subdocument is then moved to that position.

tip **Don't accidentally bury your subdocument**

Be sure to place the indicator line outside another subdocument boundary before you release the mouse button. Otherwise, Word will create a "nested" subdocument, placing the subdocument you just moved inside another subdocument. If this was not your intention, drag the subdocument icon to a new location outside an existing subdocument area.

tip **Work with multiple subdocuments**

You can select multiple subdocuments by pressing and holding Shift while clicking the subdocument icons. If you want to select noncontiguous subdocuments, press and hold Ctrl while selecting the subdocuments you want to move.

Merging Subdocuments

Although splitting documents into subdocuments for organizing, editing, and enhancement purposes is a useful function, there will be times when you want to combine subdocuments together after you've worked with them independently. To merge two subdocuments, follow these steps:

1. Open the master document with links to the subdocument files.
2. Click Expand Subdocuments to display the contents of the subdocument files.
3. Make sure that the subdocuments you want to combine are next to one another. For more on moving subdocuments, see "Rearranging a Master Document," on page 612.
4. Select both subdocuments by clicking their subdocument icons. (Press and hold Shift while you select the second subdocument.)
5. Click the Merge Subdocument button on the Outlining toolbar. The second subdocument is combined with the first.

note When Word combines subdocuments, the first file "takes on" the addition of the new data and everything is saved into that file.

Separating Subdocuments

If you create a new topic or want to divide a subdocument into two, simply create a new heading at the point where you want to make the break (or raise an existing heading to a Heading 1 level); then click Split Subdocument on the Outlining toolbar. The subdocument is divided at the insertion point. (See Figure 25-11.)

Converting Subdocuments

Depending on the nature of the document you're creating, you might at some point want to convert all the subdocuments back to a single document. This is an easy process: Start with the master document open on your screen and display the document in Outline view. Select the first subdocument you want to convert; press and hold Shift while clicking subsequent subdocuments.

Remove Subdocument

When you've selected all the subdocuments you want to convert, click the Remove Subdocument button on the Outlining toolbar. The subdocument icons and boundaries are removed and the subdocuments become part of the master document—once again you have a whole document. Save your file by pressing choosing File, Save, or press Ctrl+S.

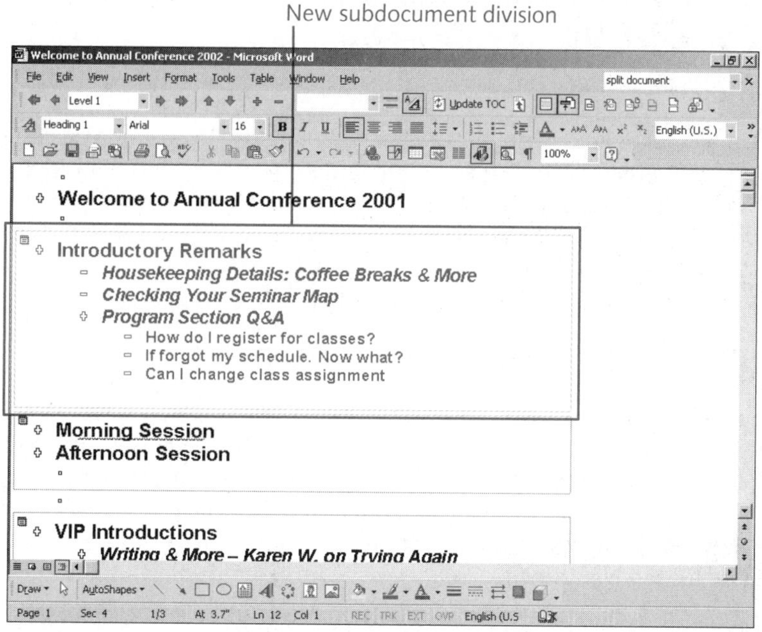

Figure 25-11. You can create a new subdocument by splitting a portion off from an existing subdocument.

Printing a Master Document

When you're ready to print your master document, begin by opening the master document and expanding the document display to the level you want to print. First click Expand Subdocuments on the Outlining toolbar to show the headings of all subdocuments; then use the Expand buttons to expand the text level as desired. Finally, change to Print Layout view by choosing View, Print Layout, or clicking the Print Layout View button to the left of the horizontal scroll bar.

Choose File, Print, select any necessary print options, and click Print. The entire master document, including the subdocument text, is printed.

tip **Get a bird's eye view**

Take a look at the document as it will appear in print by choosing File, Print Preview. You can select a multi-page view to see the overall look applied to the combined subdocuments in the master document. Click Close to return to the Print Layout view and make any necessary changes before printing.

Troubleshooting

Master Document Is Incomplete When Printed

If, when you print your master document, you find that there are some sections missing, return to Outline view and scroll through the document to make sure all sections have been expanded. Anything left collapsed will not be printed, so make sure that you expand the entire document, if that's your intention, before selecting Print.

Managing Master Documents

As you can see, working with master and subdocuments is a great way to manage and manipulate large files. The only downside to Master Documents is the sometimes complicated task of keeping your files straight. Some procedures you take for granted with ordinary files—such as saving, opening, renaming, and moving—take a little more thought when it comes to working with master documents. Here are some reminders for those times when you need to manage your master document files.

Saving Subdocument Files

Word saves the master document and all subdocuments when you choose File, Save or press Ctrl+S. The master document is saved under the name you entered the first time you saved the file, and Word names all the subdocuments automatically, using the first words of the heading as the file name. If you have several headings with the same title, Word adds numbers to the file names, such as "Lesson Plan1," "Lesson Plan2," and so on.

If you want to save a master document to a new location, choose File, Save As. Remember to create a new folder for the new master document and files. Then you'll need to select each individual subdocument and use Save As to save it to the new folder. Otherwise, the next time you open your master document, you'll see an error message telling you that the subdocument link is missing. Click Close to save the file and return to the document.

Renaming Subdocuments

If you want to rename a subdocument, start in the master document and select the subdocument you want to rename. Then choose File, Save As. When the Save As dialog box appears, enter the new name for the file and click Save. Because you renamed the file from within the master document, the link will be updated and preserved within the master information.

Selecting Subdocuments

One of the tricks to dividing a document into subdocuments accurately is in displaying and selecting the text you want to include. Make sure that you expand the selection fully before clicking Create Subdocument; otherwise, Word might not include all the text you want in the new subdocument.

tip If you don't get the whole subdocument the first time, click Remove Subdocument to merge the text back in with the master document; then select all the text for the subdocument again and click Create Subdocument.

Chapter 26

Generating First-Class Tables of Contents and Related Elements

Each of us needs a good road map once in a while. Even if you're the type of person who refuses to stop for directions, having a good table of contents (TOC) handy when you need to find something quickly in a long document can be a lifesaver. It's three minutes until the board meeting and you can't remember the name for the new program you're championing (oops). Where's that section on fall programs? If only you'd added that TOC....

A TOC lists the important headings in your document, providing you a quick glance at the topics, along with page numbers, so that you can easily move to the parts of the document you want. Whether you're creating a print document or a Web page, you can generate the tables you need for reference using Word's TOC feature.

This chapter introduces you not only to the TOC feature in Microsoft Word, but also to other quick-look reference tables, including the table of authorities and the table of figures. You'll learn to create, edit, customize, and update your table of contents and add entries for special reference tables, which make it easy to locate figures, citations, and more in your long documents.

Tips for Creating an Effective TOC

Headings are the real secret in creating a helpful table of contents. If you've written clear, understandable headings, your readers will know where to turn for the information they want. The next consideration is the way in which you format those headings—if you don't use styles Word recognizes, the program won't collect the headings the way you want it to. To create the TOC you want, keep these guidelines in mind:

- **Use Word's built-in heading styles—or create your custom styles based on them.** When you're working in Outline view or working with master documents, it's important that you use Word's built-in headings styles—Heading 1, Heading 2, or Heading 3. Additionally, you can use the various outline levels—1 through 9—but any other style won't be included in the table of contents Word generates for you.
- **Make your headings clear and concise.** The best headings are short—between 4 and 10 words—and communicate the subject clearly. The headings for your document will vary, of course, depending on content, but if your objective is to help readers find what they want quickly, you'll be closer to meeting your goal if you keep your headings short, sweet, and smart.
- **Avoid confusing headings.** If the tone of your document is conversationally hip, you might be tempted to throw in little humorous sayings or quips as headings throughout your text. As a wise editor once asked, "Would readers understand what this heading means if they opened the book at this page?" If helping readers is your main goal, avoid phrases that might confuse them.

note You can literally include any text in your document as part of the TOC by selecting the entries manually. For more information on manual table of contents entries, see "Adding TOC Entries Manually," on page 622.

Creating a Table of Contents

Once you've checked your headings to make sure they're clear and concise and that you've assigned a heading style Word will recognize, you can generate the table of contents. Here are the steps:

1. Place the insertion point where you want to add the table of contents.
2. Choose Insert, Reference, Index And Tables. The Index And Tables dialog box appears.

3 Click the Table Of Contents tab. Here you choose options for the table of contents you generate. (See Figure 26-1.)

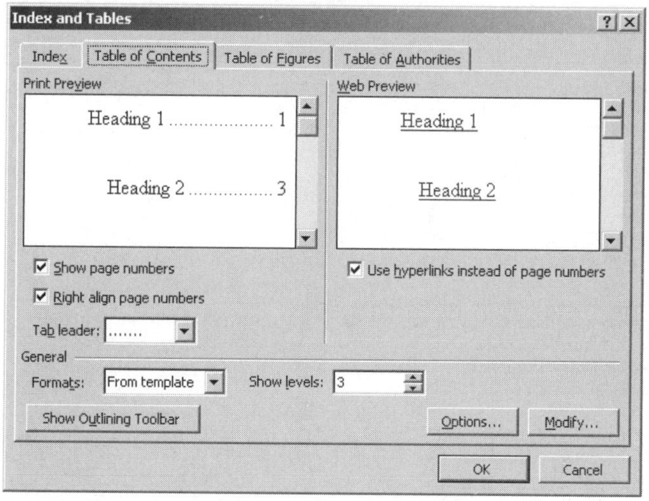

Figure 26-1. You generate a table of contents in the Index And Tables dialog box.

4 By default, Word right-aligns the page numbers in your table of contents. If you want no page number displayed, clear the Show Page Numbers check box; if you want to left-align the page numbers, clear the Right Align Page Numbers check box.

5 Click the Tab Leader down arrow. Click the leader character you want to use, if any. You can choose from None, periods, en dashes (–), or em dashes (—).

6 Click OK to generate the TOC. Word places the table at the insertion point. (See Figure 26-2, on the next page.)

tip **Take a look at your TOC**

You can view the table of contents you create in two different ways: When you change to Print Layout view, you see the TOC complete with page numbers and leaders. If you display the TOC in Web Layout view, you'll see hyperlinks in the document.

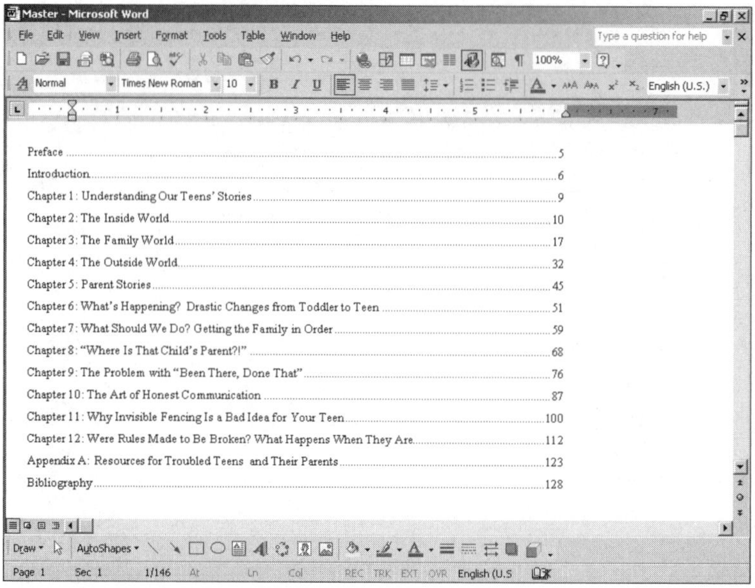

Figure 26-2. The table of contents Word generates by default right-aligns page numbers and includes dot leaders.

Adding TOC Entries Manually

You aren't limited to using headings alone in your table of contents. You can select any word or phrase in your document for inclusion in the TOC by following these steps:

1. Select the text you want to use in the TOC.
2. Press Alt+Shift+O. The Mark Table Of Contents Entry dialog box appears, as Figure 26-3 shows. The entry you selected appears in the Entry box.

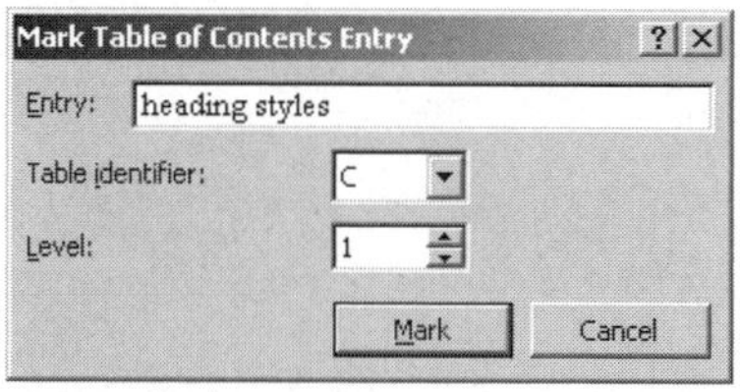

Figure 26-3. Enter TOC entries manually in the Mark Table Of Contents Entry dialog box.

3. If you use more than one TOC listing in a document, click the Table Identifier down arrow to assign this entry to a TOC. (This step is unnecessary if you're creating only one TOC.)
4. Enter the level at which you want the entry to be listed in the Level box. The first-level entry is the default.

5. Click Mark to add the entry. Word adds the table of contents field code to the entry.
6. For subsequent entries, select the text you want to use in your document, click in the Entry box (which causes the word to be added to the box), and click Mark.
7. When you're finished adding entries, click Close.

Next, to generate the table of contents to include the manual TOC entries, follow these steps:

1. Place the insertion point where you want to insert the TOC.
2. Choose Insert, Reference, Index And Tables.
3. Click the Options button on the Table Of Contents tab.
4. In the Table Of Contents Options dialog box, select the Table Entry Fields check box. This adds the TOC entries to the table of contents. (To find out more about the Table Of Contents Options dialog box, see "Customizing a Table of Contents" on page 626.)
5. Click OK twice to close the dialog boxes; click OK once more if you are replacing an existing TOC to confirm the operation. Word adds the new TOC at the cursor position.

tip **Display the entries you want**

If you want your table of contents to include only the entries you've added manually, clear the Styles and Outline Levels check boxes. If you want all the elements included, leave those items selected and select the Table Entry Fields check box as well.

Choosing a Format

The simple table of contents format gives you a standard TOC with right-aligned page numbers, dot leaders, and left-aligned headings. You can choose from a number of specially designed TOC formats so that your table of contents fits the style of your publication.

You can choose a format for your table of contents when you first generate it. When you choose Insert, Reference, Index And Tables and the Index And Table dialog box appears, click the Formats down arrow on the Table Of Contents tab. The formats shown there—From Template, Classic, Distinctive, Fancy, Modern, Formal, and Simple—offer different combinations of text styles used for your TOC. Click the one you want; the style is shown in the Print Preview window. When you find the one you want, click OK. The table of contents is created and formats are assigned as you selected.

tip **Update the TOC format after the fact**

If you want to change the format for a table of contents you've already created, select the table, and then choose Insert, Reference, Index And Tables. Click the Table Of Contents tab, select the Formats down arrow, and choose the style you want. Finally, click OK. Word displays a message box asking whether you want to replace the selected TOC. Click OK to replace the selected TOC, and Word updates the TOC with the new format.

Troubleshooting

Headings Are Missing in My TOC

After you generate a table of contents for your Word document, review the document and check your headings carefully. If any headings are missing in the TOC, determine whether you've added text boxes or callouts in the drawing layer.

Word creates your table of contents by gathering all the headings and table of contents entry fields; if you've added text to the drawing layer, the entries won't be found automatically. To add these items to the TOC, just select the items, copy them, and paste them on the text layer. Finally, press F9 to update the TOC.

Editing and Updating a TOC

As you continue to work with your document, you might move sections around and add and edit headings and text. That means as soon as you make a heading change, your TOC is out of date because it won't reflect your most recent changes. You can update the table of contents in two different ways:

Update TOC

- Press F9 to update the table of contents.
- Click Update TOC on the Outlining toolbar to update the TOC.

Word searches the document and updates the TOC to reflect any changes you've made to headings.

Go To TOC

You can also move to the table of contents in case you want to do additional formatting or editing there. Just click the Go To TOC button on the Outlining toolbar. The display moves to the TOC so that you can make your changes.

Preparing a TOC for the Web

When you generate a table of contents for your document, a preview for the TOC in the Web page is displayed beside the TOC print preview on the Table Of Contents tab of the Index And Tables dialog box. Try out a Web TOC in your document by first placing the insertion point where you want to add the TOC and then clicking Insert, Reference, Index And Tables, and clicking the Table Of Contents tab. Make sure the Use Hyperlinks Instead Of Page Numbers check box is selected; then click OK. The TOC is added at the insertion point. To see the TOC in Web format, choose View, Web Layout. The TOC is shown as a table of active hyperlinks, each of which takes you to the corresponding document section. (See Figure 26-4.)

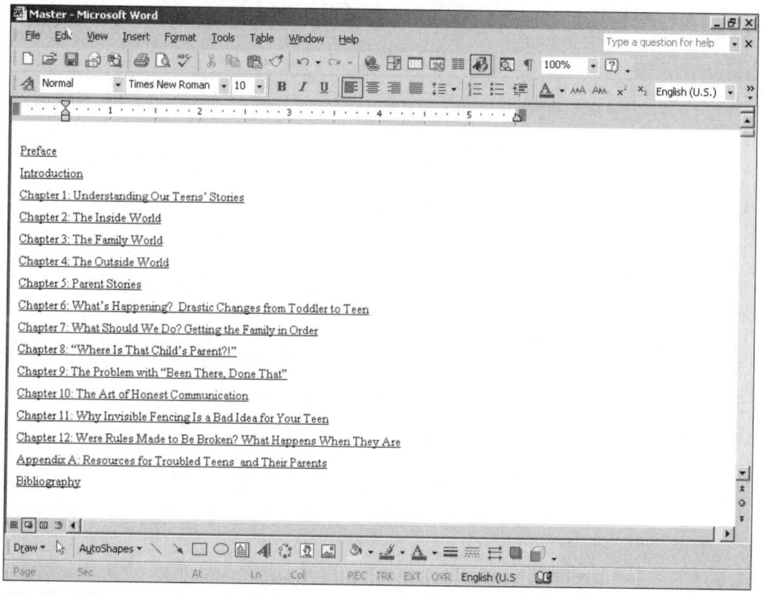

Figure 26-4. When you display Web Layout view, you'll see hyperlinks in your Web TOC.

Creating a Web TOC in a Frame

If you use frames in your Web page, you have the ability to show more than one item, file, or image on the screen at any one time. Using a TOC frame in your document allows your users to access the various sections of a document easily. By simply clicking a topic heading in the TOC frame, users can display in another frame the content of a topic.

Just as with traditional TOCs for your document, you must use Word's built-in heading styles in order for Word to recognize the headings for the table of contents. If the headings are based on the built-in styles, you can automatically create a TOC that appears in the left frame of a framed Web page. You can click the link in the left frame, and the frame on the right shows the page you've selected.

1. To create the table of contents in your Web page, follow these steps:
2. Select Format, Frames, Table Of Contents In Frame. If prompted, click Yes and save the document. Word displays the Web page, with the new TOC in the left frame, as shown in Figure 26-5.

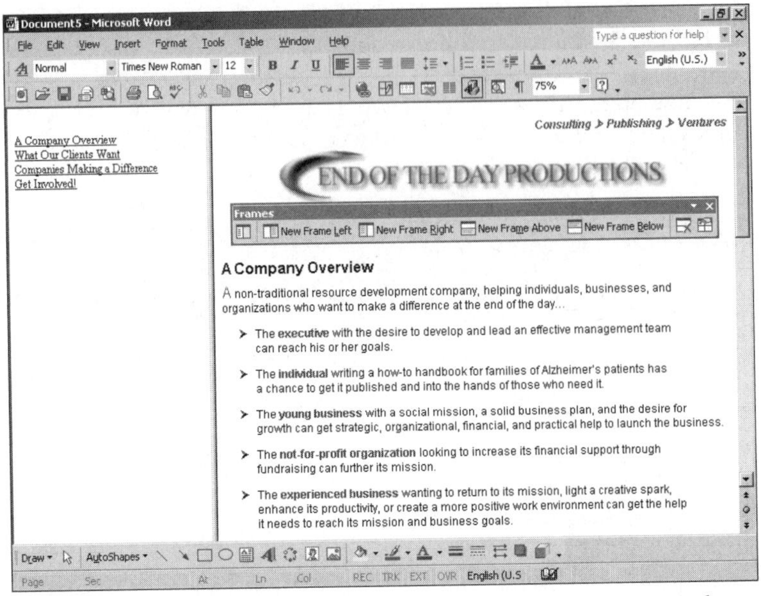

Figure 26-5. You can create a table of contents in the left frame of your Web page.

For more about working with frames in your Web pages, see Chapter 29, "Keeping an Eye on Word's Online Features."

note If you've created a table of contents for your Web page and the TOC appears in a Web frame, click inside the TOC frame before you press F9 to update; otherwise, the table will not be updated correctly.

Customizing a Table of Contents

You can make additional changes to your table of contents by customizing both the elements you include in the TOC and the styles you use to include them. Figure 26-6 shows the Table Of Contents Options dialog box and the features available to you. To display these options, choose Insert, Reference, Index And Tables, and select the Table Of Contents tab. Finally, click Options.

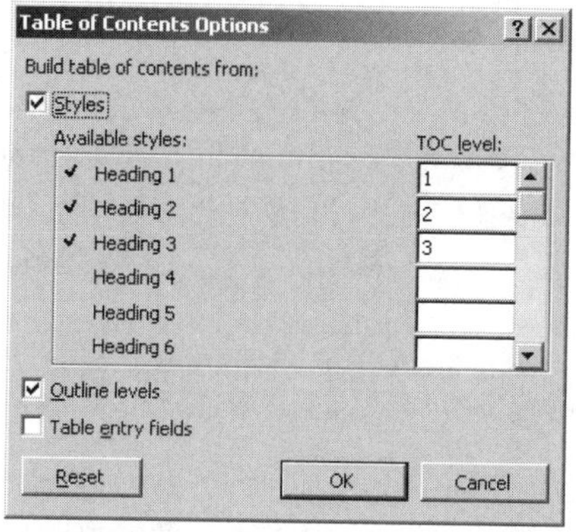

Figure 26-6. You can choose the elements you want to use in the Table Of Contents Options dialog box.

In the Table Of Contents Options dialog box, you can also select the styles you apply to the different elements in your table of contents. For example, in Figure 26-6, Headings 1, 2, and 3 are assigned to TOC levels 1, 2, and 3. If you choose, however, you can scroll down through the list to find other styles in your document—either styles you've created or existing styles—and enter a TOC level in the text boxes on the right. They'll be included in the TOC when it's generated. Click OK to update the table of contents.

tip If you want to undo your changes and reset the options to their default settings, click Reset in the Table Of Contents Options dialog box.

tip **Modify styles in your document template**

If you've selected From Template in the Formats drop-down list on the Table Of Contents tab, the Modify button is available. When you click Modify, the Style dialog box appears, and you're given the choice of adding, deleting, or changing the styles used in the table of contents. When you click the Modify button in the Style dialog box, the Modify Style dialog box appears, so that you can make font and formatting changes to the selected style.

Incorporating Other Reference Tables

TOCs aren't the only reference tables you'll use as you work with long documents. If you use illustrations, tables, diagrams, or equations, you'll like having the choice of numbering and labeling those elements automatically. If you work with legal briefings and citations, the ability to create a table of authorities will save you considerable time and trouble.

Building a Table of Figures

When you have Word generate a table of figures to use as a reference tool in your document, Word searches for and collects the figure captions in your document. This means that you need to set up your captions before you generate the table.

Adding Captions

First things first. Start by adding labels to the items you want to include in your table of figures. You can add captions while you work by using Word's AutoCaption feature. Here are the steps:

1. Choose Insert, Reference, Caption. The Caption dialog box appears.
2. Click the AutoCaption button. The AutoCaption dialog box, shown in Figure 26-7, appears.

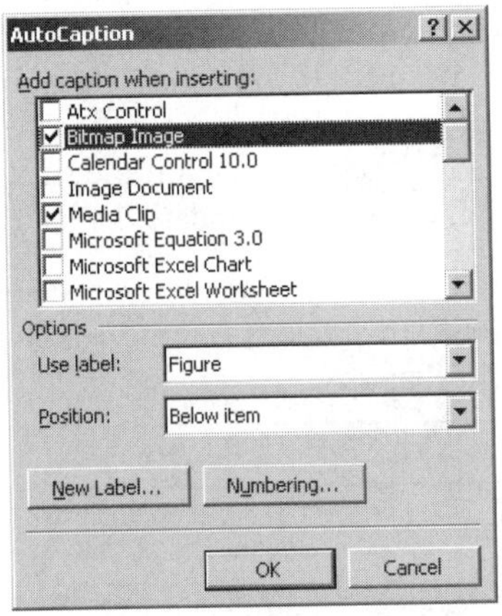

Figure 26-7. AutoCaption enables you to add labels and numbers to your figures automatically.

3. In the Add Caption When Inserting list, select the check boxes next to the elements for which you want to add captions.
4. In the Options section, choose the label you want to use, click the Position down arrow, and select Above Item or Below Item.
5. Click OK to have Word search for and update the elements in your document.

> **note** To view and work with the various options available for your table of figures, choose Insert, Reference, Index And Tables, and then click the Table Of Figures tab.

Controlling Figure Numbering

If you want to add figure numbering to your captions, choose Insert, Reference, Captions to display the Captions dialog box. Select the element to which you want to add the numbering (or update your other caption choices), and then click the Numbering button. The Caption Numbering dialog box appears, as Figure 26-8 shows.

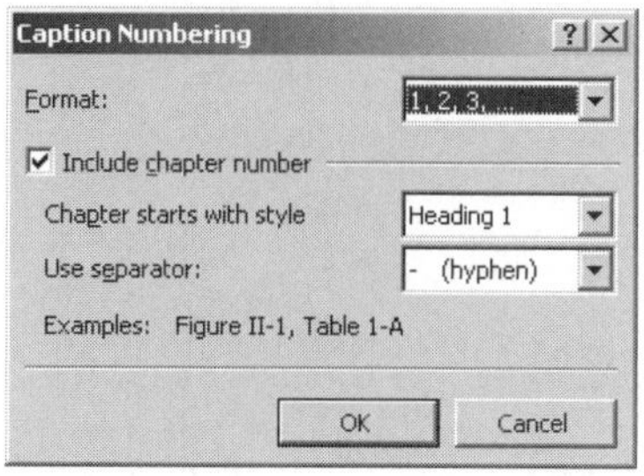

Figure 26-8. The Caption Numbering dialog box enables you to choose the format and style of the numbering sequence.

Begin by choosing the format you want to use for the numbering sequence. You can choose the traditional 1, 2, 3 or A, B, C, or you can choose roman numerals for figure numbering in the Format drop-down list. If you want to include chapter numbers (which Word picks up from the text), select the Include Chapter Number check box; then specify the heading style the chapter starts with (this shows Word where to begin looking), and select a separator character from the Use Separator drop-down list (Word will place this between the chapter number and the figure number in the caption). Click OK to save the settings. When you add your next figure, the caption will be applied automatically.

Generating a Table of Figures

After you've added captions to your illustrations by choosing Insert, Reference, Captions, you can use those captions to create a table of the figures in your document. Follow these steps to generate a table of figures:

1. Place the insertion point where you want to create the table of figures.
2. Click Insert, Reference, Index And Tables. The Index And Tables dialog box appears.
3. Click the Table Of Figures tab. The default selections for the table are displayed in the preview boxes. (See Figure 26-9, on the next page.)
4. Change the settings as needed, and click OK to create the table. The table of figures is placed in the document at the insertion point.

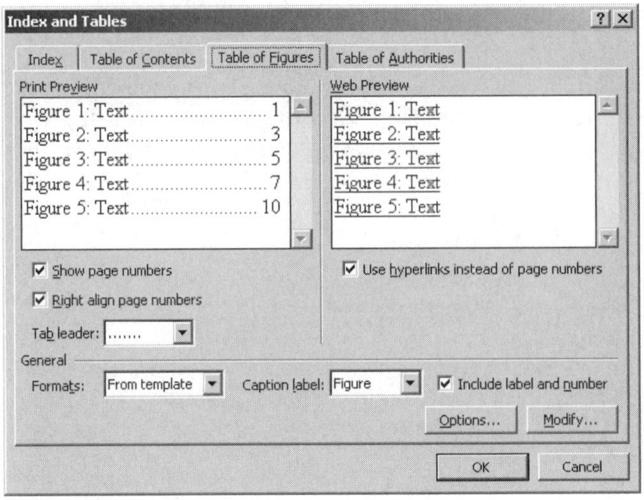

Figure 26-9. The preview boxes in the Index and Tables dialog box show the default selections.

Building a Table of Authorities

A table of authorities is a more specialized table reference that helps you track, compile, and display citations included in your document. You'll use this feature most often for legal documents that reference cases, rules, treaties, and other documents. Before you can create a table of citations, obviously, you need to have placed those citations within the body of the document.

Adding Citations Manually

You can easily track citations for inclusion in the table of authorities as you work in your document. To begin the process of adding a citation, follow these steps:

1. Select the citation in the document.
2. Press Alt+Shift+I. The Mark Citation dialog box appears with the selected citation displayed in the Selected Text box, as Figure 26-10 shows.
3. Click the Category down arrow and choose the type of citation you're creating.
4. Edit the citation, if needed, in the Short Citation box.
5. Click Mark. Word adds the necessary codes in your document to identify the citation for inclusion in the table of authorities.

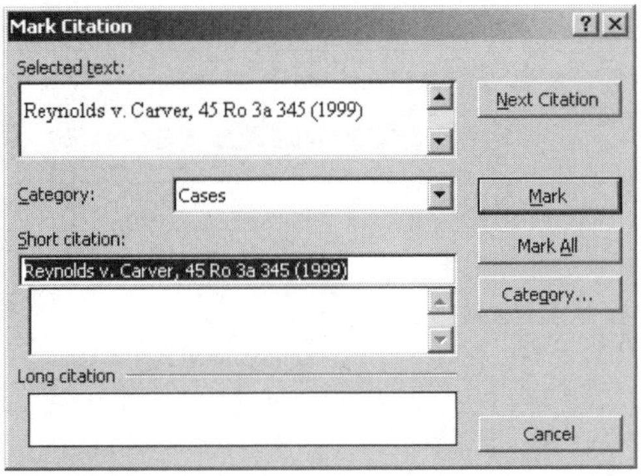

Figure 26-10. Use the Mark Citation dialog box to include citations in your table of authorities.

6. In your document, select another citation, and then click in the Selected Text box. This adds the citation to the box. Again, click Mark to add the citation.
7. Click Close to close the dialog box when you're finished adding citations.

> **tip** **Add citations directly**
>
> You can also add citations from the Table Of Authorities tab in the Index And Tables dialog box. To display the tab, choose Insert, Reference, Index And Tables, and then click the Table Of Authorities tab. Click Mark Citation to display the Mark Citation dialog box. Enter your citation as needed and click Mark to complete the entry.

Generating the Table of Authorities

After you've entered the citations you want to reference, you can start the process of creating a table of authorities by following these steps:

1. Click Insert, References, Index And Tables.
2. Click the Table Of Authorities tab, and enter your choices for the table of authorities you create. (See Figure 26-11, on the next page.)
3. Choose your category from the list on the right.
4. Choose the formatting and styles you want, and then click OK to create the table of authorities.

> **tip** If you've created multiple tables in your document, be sure to update each table independently. To update, click in the table and press F9.

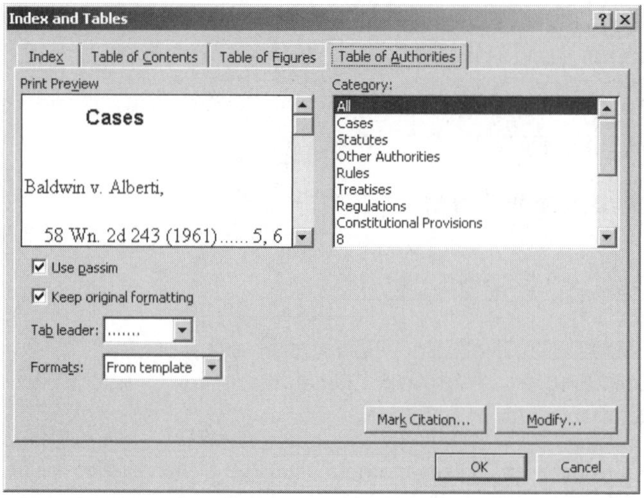

Figure 26-11. The Table Of Authorities tab includes everything you need for entering and formatting the table.

Chapter 27

Creating Effective Indexes

If you're creating a long document that covers a lot of ground—a textbook on the principles of modern economics, a procedural manual for a new computer program, or a parts catalog for an auto supply store—it's important for readers to find the subjects they're looking for. Creating a good index is part of making your document accessible for readers, by providing a listing of topics and subtopics and the pages on which they can be found. It's been said that your table of contents might be what helps readers decide whether to read your document in the first place, but the index determines whether or not they'll come back to it. If your index helps readers find what they're looking for quickly, they'll turn to it again and again.

In this chapter, you'll learn how to create indexes for your Microsoft Word documents. Whether you create entries one by one or use a table to automate index entries, you'll find the process fairly intuitive and fast.

Constructing a Good Index

There are a number of things you can do to ensure that the index you create is one that readers will use. Think of the various indexes you've used in the past—no doubt some were better than others. Some seemed to lack all the main topics you were looking for, or they seemed disorganized. Here are some characteristics you should be sure to include in the indexes you create:

- **Usability.** An index is first and foremost a reader service. Make sure that you've included all major topics, and that you've thought through the alternate ways readers might be looking for those topics. Include topics, subtopics, and references to other topics for related information (for example, "*See* Parenting teens").
- **Readability.** Using terms your readers will recognize—whether or not they're familiar with the content of your document—is important. If you're unsure about the various ways a reader might reference a certain topic, ask around. Talk to others on your team or in your department to make sure you've used words and phrases that will be easily understood.

> **tip** **Ask for feedback on your topic list**
>
> After you identify key words and phrases for your index, create a list and send it to others in your department, asking for input, additions, and suggestions. Testing the topics in your index before you create it can save you editing time later.

- **Cross-references.** Cross-references in an index refer readers to other topics where they'll find more information. For example, a listing with a subentry that sends others to the section on *Needs assessment* might look like this:

```
Feasibility studies, 3-10
  Creating audience surveys, 3-4. See Needs assessment
  Hosting focus groups, 4-6
  Tabulating results, 6-8
```

- **Logical structure.** One mistake new indexers often make is to include every important-sounding word—plus the kitchen sink. You'll help your readers find what they are looking for if you think carefully through your index. Which topics are most important? How many different ways might a reader refer to them? What are the words that will be searched out most often?

> **tip** **Find the index topics you need**
>
> One place you can get clues for important index terms is your table of contents. Which words and phrases are used in your headings? Definitely include those topics in your index, and look for plenty of opportunities to create subentries from the topics within those sections.

Indexing with Word

Creating indexes in Word is an interactive process that is part hands-on and part automatic. You create a Word index in three basic stages:

1. Mark index entries in your document (or create a concordance file, which allows you to automatically mark index entries).

> **tip** **Use a concordance file to add entries automatically**
>
> If you have a number of terms you're sure to include in your index, you can create them in a concordance file. Word will use the file to quickly mark the index entries you want. For more about creating a concordance file, see "AutoMarking Entries with a Concordance File," on page 644.

2. Choose Insert, Reference, Index And Tables, and click the Index tab to set indexing options, which control the way the index is placed and formatted in your document.
3. Create the index by choosing Insert, Reference, Index And Tables.

Word then sorts all the index entries in alphabetical order, adds the page numbers, and deletes any repeated entries. Figure 27-1, on the next page, shows an example of a completed index.

¶ Show/Hide

When Word compiles your index, the program inserts codes that mark the beginning and end of a topic and lists the page numbers on which the topics appear. Word marks each entry with the code XE, but the codes are hidden. You can display the hidden codes by clicking the Show/Hide button on the Standard toolbar.

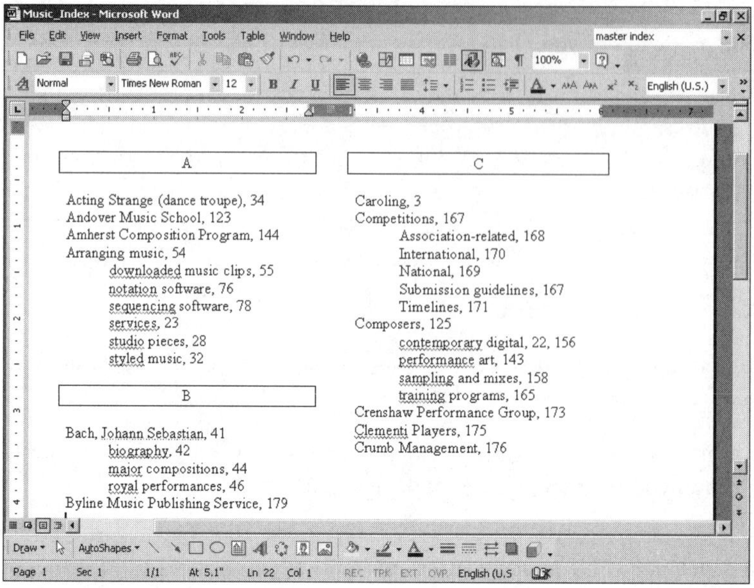

Figure 27-1. Word alphabetizes your entries, subordinates subentries, and adds alphabetic headings.

Creating Index Entries

Word makes it easy for you to enter index entries as you go along—and once you display the Mark Index Entries dialog box, you can mark additional entries, add subentries, and add cross-references and page ranges.

Marking Index Entries

You can create an index entry in two different ways:

- If you want to begin with text that is already in the document, select and use existing text.
- If you want to add an entry that does not key off an existing word or phrase in your document, click to place the insertion point in the paragraph where you want to add the index entry.

To add index entries, follow these steps:

1. Select the text or place the insertion point, and then press Alt+Shift+X. The Mark Index Entry dialog box appears, as Figure 27-2 shows.

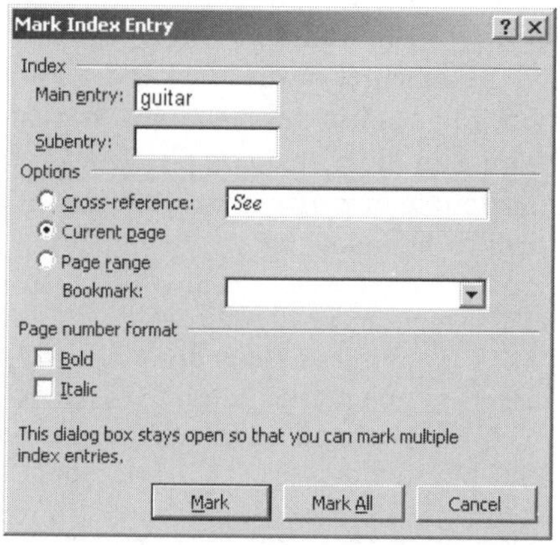

Figure 27-2. You use the Mark Index Entry dialog box to enter index entries and subentries.

2. If you selected text before opening the Mark Index Entry dialog box, the text appears in the Main Entry box. If necessary, edit the text that appears. If you placed the insertion point rather than selecting text, type the entry you want in the Main Entry box.
3. Click Mark to mark the entry and close the dialog box.

> **tip** **Create clear index entries**
>
> Edit the entry in the Mark Index Entry dialog box to make it as clear as possible. For example, instead of a phrase that appears in your document, such as "served in the state legislature," you might enter the phrase "legislature," or "government service."

Creating Subentries

A subentry is a secondary topic you use to narrow the search on a specific topic. For example, if your report is about a new HR training program your company offers, one main index entry and the related subentries might look like this:

```
Life Essentials / Work Skills program, 5
  Overview, 6
  Program timeline, 7
  Reporting procedures, 7
  Retreat sessions, 8
  Training opportunities, 8
```

A subentry provides readers with additional references they can look up. It also adds depth and functionality to your index as a whole, and it makes reading the index easier on the eye.

Here's a quick way to enter subentries if you want to avoid repeat clicks in the dialog box: Just type the main entry and the subentry in the Mark Index Entries dialog box, separating the entries with a colon. You can use this technique to create up to seven levels of subentries, although creating an index that complex would no doubt baffle your readers! For best results, stick to one or perhaps two subentry levels. Examples of subentries entered in this way include the following:

```
Life Essentials / Work Skills program: Overview
  Life Essentials / Work Skills program: Program timeline
  Life Essentials / Work Skills program: Reporting procedures
  Life Essentials / Work Skills program: Retreat sessions
  Life Essentials / Work Skills program: Training opportunities
```

tip **Divide long subentry lists**

If you find yourself entering too many subentries for a particular topic, you might want to think of a way to create another main entry to divide up the list. If your index lists a whole column of subentries, your readers might get lost in the list and not remember the main entry heading above.

Selecting Repeated Entries

When you're putting together a quick index and want to reference all occurrences of a particular word or phrase, you can do that easily using the Mark Index Entry dialog box. Start by selecting the text you want to index, and then pressing Alt+Shift+X to display the Mark Index Entry dialog box. Change the Main Entry text to show the entry you want, and then enter a subentry, if you want to include one. Finally, click Mark All. Word searches for the word or phrase and applies an index entry to every occurrence.

note One of the limitations of Mark All is that the program marks every occurrence as it appears. This means that not only will you have the same index entry for each item (which doesn't give you the flexibility of creating multiple references to the same topic), but Word will find only the words or phrases that match exactly the text you've entered. Words like *composers* will be found, but not *composing* or *composition*.

Formatting Entries

As you add index entries, you can specify formatting for the characters and page numbers, thus cutting down on the editing and formatting time you'll spend after you create the index. Here are the steps to apply formatting to your index entries:

1. Select the text for the index entry.
2. Press Alt+Shift+X to display the Mark Index Entry dialog box.

3. Edit the text in the Main Entry box as needed.
4. Select the text in the Main Entry box you want to format.
5. Press Ctrl+B to apply bold, Ctrl+I for italic, or Ctrl+U for underline styles.
6. Complete the entry as desired, and click Mark to create the entry.

> **note** Word won't allow you to add any specialized formatting to entries at this stage. If you add color, change the font, or make any other changes beyond a change to bold, italic or underline style, the change will be applied to the selected text in the document and not to the index entry.

You can also control the format of the page numbers Word adds to the index by selecting or clearing the check boxes in the Page Number Format section. You might want to use bold or italic to highlight certain entries. For example,

- A bold page number might indicate the most in-depth coverage of an item.
- An italic page number might include biographical information or reference another work.

Adding Cross-References

Not all your entries will provide page number references for your readers. Some might point them instead to other topics in your index. A cross-reference gives readers a pointer to an entry (or group of entries) for related information. To create a cross-reference in your index, follow these steps:

1. Select the text for the index entry, or position the insertion point in the document.
2. Press Alt+Shift+X to display the Mark Index Entry dialog box.
3. Enter the Main Entry text, if needed.
4. Click the Cross-Reference option.
5. After the word *See*, type the index entry you want to refer readers to. For example, you might create cross-references that look like this:

   `Training sessions. `*`See`*` Retreat sessions.`

Specifying Page Ranges

By default, Word assigns the index entry the number of the current page. If you select and create an entry on page 3, for example, Word shows that page number along with the index entry. If you want to indicate a span of pages so that you can provide for your readers the full range of pages on which a specific topic is covered, you can do so by using bookmarks you've already created.

If you haven't created bookmarks to mark places in your document and want to find out how, see Chapter 12, "Honing Document Navigation Skills."

To use a bookmark to indicate a page range in your index, follow these steps:

1. Press Alt+Shift+X to display the Mark Index Entry dialog box.
2. Enter the text you want in the Main Entry and Subentry boxes, if needed.
3. Click the Page Range option.
4. Click the Bookmark down arrow to display the list of bookmarks in the current document; click the bookmark you want to use.
5. Click Mark to add the entry.

When you create the index later, Word will insert an en dash (a long dash) between the page numbers in the range. A page range entry looks like this:

```
Physical response to stress, 1-2
```

Generating the Index

Once you've marked all the entries you want to include in your index, you're ready for Word to compile the document and place it in your document. When Word compiles the index, it gathers all the entries you've marked, assigns page numbers as you've specified, and alphabetizes the entries. Finally, after you click OK, Word places the index at the insertion point.

tip **Review your document**

Although you can update an index easily by pressing F9 (which means you can go back and edit your index entries if you choose), you'll lose any additional formatting choices you make after the index is compiled. So it's worth your time, *before* Word compiles the index, to go back through the document and review your index entries to make sure you haven't missed anything important. To display the index entry codes, click the Show All button on the Standard toolbar. Then page through the document to review important headings, sections, and captions for inclusion in your index.

Start the process of creating the index by placing the insertion point where you want to create the index and clicking Insert, Reference, Index And Tables. The Index And Tables dialog box appears, with the Index tab selected. In this dialog box you'll choose the format for both the text entries and page numbers. (See Figure 27-3.)

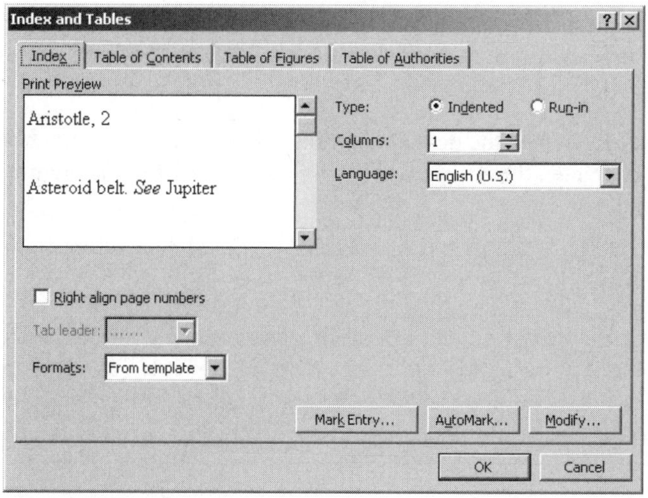

Figure 27-3. The Index tab includes the options and commands you need to create the index.

note Notice the Mark Entry button on the Index tab in the Index And Tables dialog box. If you begin making your formatting choices for the index and suddenly remember a topic you want to include in the index, you can click Mark Entry to open the Mark Index Entry dialog box.

Choosing the Index Format

One of the most important choices you'll make on the Index tab in the Index And Tables dialog box involves the format you select for the compiled index. How do you want the index to look? When you click the Formats down arrow, Word gives you the following choices:

- **From Template**, which is selected by default, leaves out headings.
- **Classic** centers the alphabetic headings over the index column.
- **Fancy** encloses the heading in a shadowed box.
- **Modern** italicizes the heading and places a rule above it.
- **Bulleted** formats the heading as a block letter and centers it over the index column.
- **Formal** right-aligns page numbers, adds dot leaders, italicizes the heading, and indents the heading from the left margin.
- **Simple** removes all alphabetic headings and special formats.

Choosing each of these different options produces a different index format, which is displayed in the preview window. To make your choice, click the Formats down arrow and click the selection you want.

If you later decide to change the default alignment of the numbering or choose a different leader character, those changes will override the settings belonging to the different formats.

> **tip** **Choose your format**
>
> Experiment with the different formats before selecting the one you want by clicking your different choices in the Formats drop-down list on the Index tab in the Index And Tables dialog box. When you choose a format style, the Print Preview box shows your selection so you can see the formatting effect of each style.

Choosing Alignment

After you create your index, you might want to make changes to the alignment and leaders the format applied. You can change these settings so that page numbers are aligned along the right edge of the index column, and dot leaders are added to help lead the reader to the related page number. To change the alignment of page numbers in your index, follow these steps:

1. Display the Index And Tables dialog box by choosing Insert, References, Index And Tables.
2. On the Index tab, click the Indented option if necessary and then select the Right Align Page Numbers check box.
3. Click the Tab Leader down arrow, and select the type of leader you want.
4. Click OK to create the index, and the page numbers are formatted as you selected.

Changing the Way Entries Are Displayed

Another choice in the Index And Tables dialog box allows you to choose whether you want index subentries to be run in with the index main entries or indented below them. Simply click your choice and Word will format the index accordingly.

When you choose Indented, your index subentries are indented beneath the main entries, like this:

```
Stress,
  controlling, 3
  managing, 5
  reducing, 7
```

When you choose Run-In, the subentries are placed on the same line with the main entries, such as

```
Stress: controlling, 3; managing, 5; reducing, 7
```

tip **Save space in cramped documents**

If you're getting to the end of your document and you're running out of space, you can use the Run-In setting to pick up extra space your index might otherwise use. To do this, choose Insert, Reference, Index And Tables, click Run-In, and then click OK.

Troubleshooting

Error Messages Appear in My Index

You've gone through the process of marking your index entries and created the index by choosing Insert, Reference, Index And Tables. But after Word places the index in your document, you notice that error messages appear instead of the page numbers. The most likely cause of this is that you created the index in a subdocument rather than in the master document of your publication.

To resolve the problem, close the current document by choosing File, Close, and open the master document. (For more information on working with master documents, see Chapter 25, "Creating and Controlling Master Documents.") Expand all subdocuments by clicking the Expand Subdocuments button in the Master Document tools on the Outlining toolbar; then press F9 to update your index. The page numbers should be displayed correctly.

Changing Index Columns

Depending on the length of your document and the index you're creating, you might want to format your index in multiple columns. By default, Word compiles your index in two columns, but you might want to change this setting if you have a short outline that will occupy only a partial column, or you want to run text in the column beside the index you create.

You can create up to four columns for the index. To make a change, display the Index And Tables dialog box and on the Index tab, click the Columns up or down arrow to increase or decrease the number of columns you want.

Troubleshooting

My Index Columns Don't Line Up

You've finally finished marking all the entries in your long document. You choose Insert, Reference, Index And Tables, click the Index tab, and select the format you want. You elect to create an indented index that's displayed in three columns. With a second look over your choices, you click OK to have Word compile the index. But when you see the index on the screen, you notice that the middle column seems out of alignment with the other two. What's going on?

Although Word automatically creates a section break both before and after your index, it's possible that an extra line space is preceding the first line in the second column. Click the Show All button on the Standard toolbar to display hidden paragraph marks in your document and review the top and bottom entries in each column. If you see an unwanted paragraph mark, select it and press Delete to remove it. Then press F9 to have Word update your index and balance the columns.

Updating an Index

You can update an index at any time by pressing F9. This means that after you have a chance to look at the compiled index, you can go back into the document and add entries you missed.

When you're ready to update the index, simply click it to select it and press F9. The index is updated, and the choices you made in the Index And Tables dialog box are preserved.

note If you've made any formatting changes, such as selecting a different format style or changing from Indented to Run-in style, Word asks you whether you want to replace the existing index with the new one. If you haven't made any editing changes in the current index—or you're willing to re-enter the changes you've made—select Yes. Word replaces the existing index with the new, updated one, and you'll need to re-enter those edits. If you select Cancel, the operation is canceled and your changes are not made.

AutoMarking Entries with a Concordance File

A concordance file is really a simple table you create to track and enter index entries easily. The table you create is a two-column table in which you enter the text you want

Word to mark as the entry in the first column and the index entry you want to use in the second column. Here are the steps:

Insert Table

1. Create a table in a new document by clicking the Insert Table button on the Standard toolbar and creating a two-column table.
2. In the first column, enter the words or phrases you want Word to mark for the entry.
3. In the second column, type the index entry for the text in the first column. Be sure to type each entry in a separate cell.
4. Save and close the concordance file.
5. Choose File, Open, select the name of the file you want to index in the Open dialog box, and then click Open.
6. Choose Index, Reference, Index And Tables. In the Index And Tables dialog box, click the Index tab.
7. Click the AutoMark button to open the Open Index AutoMark File dialog box.
8. Navigate to and select the concordance file, and click Open. Word automatically searches your document and locates each entry with the words you specified in the concordance file. (Word marks only the first occurrence of an entry in any one paragraph.)

InsideOut

You think you're saving lots of time and trouble by creating a concordance file that lists topics you want to be sure to include in your index. After you finish creating and saving the list, you create the index, but you wind up with all kinds of unnecessary entries. For example, in your publication on contemporary music, you wanted to index references to *jazz*, but found instead that the word *jazz* was included in many different places and contexts. As a result, there are many more references than you need.

A workaround for compiling huge indexes full of unnecessary AutoMarked entries is to create the majority of the index entries manually, using the Mark Index Entry dialog box (which you display by pressing Alt+Shift+X). Then use the concordance file, and the AutoMark button on the Index tab in the Index And Tables dialog box, to add to your basic index entries, including in a limited fashion only those key words or phrases that are used in the sections to which you want to refer your readers.

Chapter 28

Configuring Footnotes, Endnotes, and Cross-References

Most of us dread the kind of documents that demand the careful and painstaking attention that footnotes, endnotes, and cross-references require. Who has time to do all that notating?

Luckily, Microsoft Word makes it easy to insert, edit, and work with footnotes, endnotes, and cross-references in your documents. You make a few choices and enter your text, and Word takes care of the numbering, even if you move the notes from one place to another in your document. This chapter shows you how to quickly add and work with these kinds of notes—so they give you the added accuracy you need without the extra hassle.

Adding Footnotes and Endnotes

If you're working on a document that's based on research, that points to other documents, or that references a URL, you can easily add the source information at either the bottom of the page or at the end of the document.

Footnotes appear in an area at the bottom of your page, with a separator line and a note reference mark to identify the note. (See Figure 28-1, on the next page.) A matching note reference mark appears in the text at the place you create the footnote.

Endnotes look similar to footnotes, except that they're placed at the end of a document. Only one separator line separates the text and the endnotes, and the note reference marks are placed to the left of the noted items.

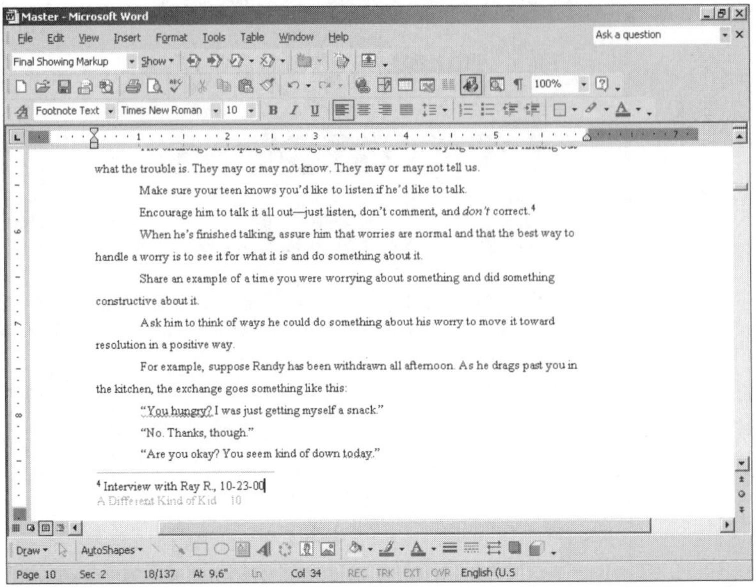

Figure 28-1. Footnotes appear at the bottom of the page and include a separator line and a note reference mark.

You can enter footnotes and endnotes of any length, but because the notes are placed in a typeface that's smaller than regular text and because they take up room in your document otherwise reserved for text, your reader will be happier if you keep your footnotes and endnotes as short as possible.

Inserting Footnotes and Endnotes

When you're ready to insert a footnote or endnote in your document, follow these steps:

1. Place the insertion point where you want to add the footnote or endnote.
2. Choose Insert, Reference, Footnote. The Footnote And Endnote dialog box appears, as Figure 28-2 shows.
3. In the Location section of the Footnote And Endnote dialog box, click either the Footnotes or Endnotes option.
4. In the Format section, click the Number Format down arrow and choose the numbering scheme you want to use for the note reference marks that identify your footnotes and endnotes. You'll find all the traditional choices—numeric, alphabetic, and roman numerals—plus something different: a collection of special symbols.
5. If you want to start the footnote or endnote with a number other than 1, click in the Start At box and type the number you want.

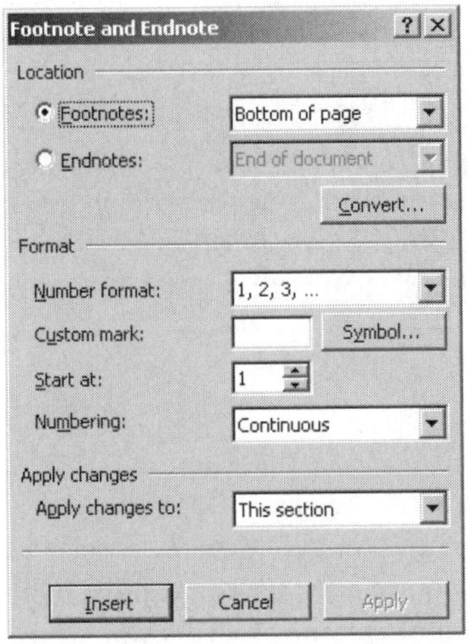

Figure 28-2. Enter footnote and endnote format choices in the Footnote And Endnote dialog box.

6 Click Insert to add the note. Word adds the note reference mark and, if you're viewing the document in Normal view, opens either the Footnotes pane (shown in Figure 28-3) or the Endnotes pane at the bottom of the Word window so that you can enter and later edit the note. If you're working in Print Layout view, Word places the insertion point following the footnote or endnote identifier at the bottom or end of the document.

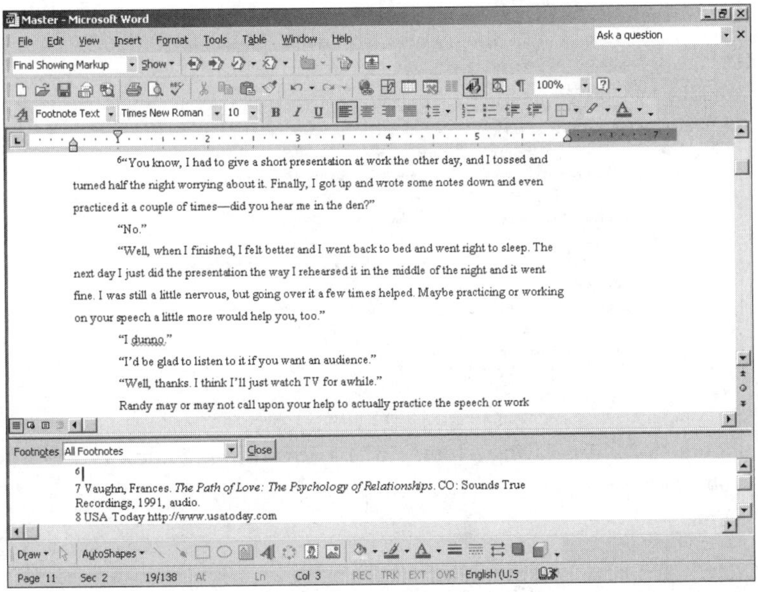

Figure 28-3. Word opens the Footnotes pane so that you can enter footnotes.

Chapter 28

tip **Add notes in sections**

If you want to apply the changes you make in the Footnote And Endnote dialog box to only a section in your document, begin by clicking in the section and displaying the dialog box by choosing Insert, Reference, Footnote. Make your changes in the dialog box, and then click the Apply Changes To down arrow. Choose This Section to apply the changes only to the current section, and then click Apply.

Viewing Footnotes

As you work with the text in your document, the only clue you'll get about the placement of your footnotes and endnotes are the note reference marks inserted in the text. If you want to view the footnotes or endnotes you've entered, you can do so by displaying them as ScreenTips, by double-clicking the note reference mark, or by opening the Footnotes or Endnotes pane.

To display a footnote as a ScreenTip, position the pointer over the note reference mark in the document. The footnote appears as a tip above the pointer. (See Figure 28-4.)

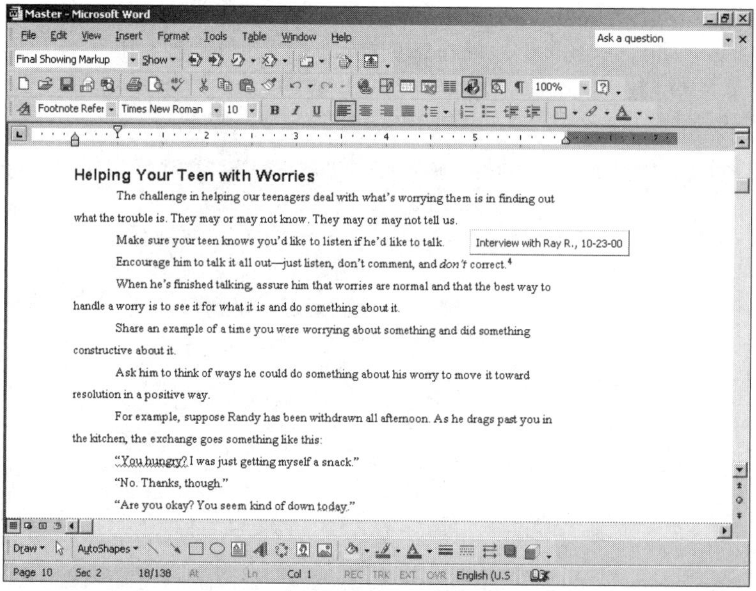

Figure 28-4. Displaying a footnote as a ScreenTip is a quick way to review a footnote you've entered.

tip You can display a footnote or endnote in the Footnotes or Endnotes pane quickly by double-clicking the note reference mark.

To have Word display your footnotes in the Footnotes pane at the bottom of your screen, follow these steps:

1. Choose View, Normal or click the Normal View button to the left of the horizontal scroll bar.
2. Choose View, Footnotes. If you have both footnotes and endnotes, the View Footnotes dialog box appears. Click either View Footnote Area or View Endnote Area, and click OK.

note The Footnotes option on the View menu is available only after you've chosen Insert, Reference, Footnote to add a footnote to your document.[1]

Editing Footnotes and Endnotes

When you want to edit a footnote or endnote, you need to display the Footnotes or Endnotes pane for the item you want to edit. You can then edit and enhance the text as needed. Here are the steps:

1. Double-click the note reference mark of the footnote or endnote you want to edit. The Footnotes or Endnotes pane appears at the bottom of the Word window.
2. Edit the note as needed.
3. Click Close to close the pane.

Moving Footnotes and Endnotes

If you want to move a footnote or endnote from one position to another, select and drag the mark to the new location. If you want to move the mark to a location that's too far away to drag, you can cut and paste the mark by using Ctrl+X to cut and Ctrl+V to paste.

note If the position to which you move the footnote precedes another footnote, Word changes the numbering automatically.

Copying Footnotes and Endnotes

If you have a footnote or endnote you plan to use more than once in your document, you can copy a note reference mark instead of typing a duplicate entry. Simply select the note reference mark, and press and hold Ctrl while dragging the mark to the new place in the document.

---

[1] a sample

Deleting Footnotes and Endnotes

When you want to remove a footnote or endnote from your document, go to the place in the document where the note reference mark appears and delete it. Simply removing the text in the Footnotes or Endnotes pane doesn't remove the note itself—Word will still keep the note reference mark in place and reserve the space at the bottom or end of your document for the note.

Troubleshooting

Deleted Footnotes Won't Go Away

If you've deleted a footnote or endnote that keeps reappearing, chances are that a portion of the note has been left behind. To find the culprit character, click the Show All button on the Standard toolbar. All the paragraph marks will appear, and you can move to the footnote area and delete the stray paragraph mark. The reference in the text will then be deleted.

Adding Symbols to Footnotes

If you want to use a symbol instead of a numeric or alphabetic character as the identifier in your note reference marks, display the Footnote And Endnote dialog box by choosing Insert, Reference, Footnote. Then click the Symbol button. The Symbol dialog box appears, as shown in Figure 28-5. Choose the font and character you want to use, and then click OK. Word adds the symbol to the Custom Mark box in the Footnote And Endnote dialog box and, when you click Insert, the symbol is added as the note reference character in the text and in the Footnotes or Endnotes pane.

Troubleshooting

My Footnotes Disappeared on My Web Page

If you created a document, complete with footnotes and endnotes, and then saved it as a Web page, your footnotes haven't disappeared completely; they've simply been moved to the end of the Web document. The footnotes are turned into hyperlinks, so you can access them easily from within the page.

Click the note reference mark to activate the link; the footnote is then displayed in your browser. To return to the Web page, click your browser's Back button to return to the previous page.

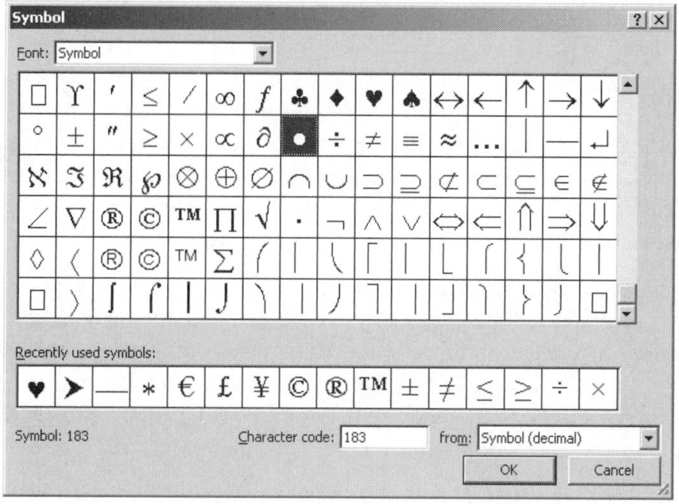

Figure 28-5. You can use symbols as note reference marks instead of numbers.

Creating a New Separator Line

The separator line Word uses to show where the document text ends and the footnote text begins is a pretty nondescript line that extends a short distance across the page. If you want to change the separator line—perhaps to add color or choose a different line style or thickness—use the Borders And Shading dialog box to make the change. Here are the steps:

1. In Normal view, choose View, Footnotes to open the Footnotes pane.
2. Click the Footnotes down arrow, and select Footnotes Separator from the Footnotes drop-down list.
3. Delete the existing separator line by clicking it and pressing Delete.
4. Choose Format, Borders And Shading. The Borders And Shading dialog box appears.
5. Click the Borders tab.
6. In the Style list, select the border style you want.
7. Click the bottom and side segments in the Preview section to remove them, leaving only the top line.
8. Click OK to add the new separator line to the document.

Troubleshooting

My Footnote Is Split Across Two Pages

Sometimes getting footnotes to print just where you'd intended can be a bit tricky. You might wind up with too many additional blank lines on the page after the footnote, or you could find that your footnote has been divided, with one line appearing on the first page and a second line printing on the next page.

If you find that part of your footnote is moved to the next page, take a look at the margin settings you have for the page. The text on the page, the margins, and the footnote length all play a part in the amount of space reserved for your footnote area. Click File, Page Setup to display the Page Setup dialog box, and note the space you have entered for the margins. Try reducing the Bottom Margin setting to allow more room for the footnote; click OK to return to the document.

For best results, try to keep your footnotes short—to one or two lines if possible. If you need to insert a long footnote, consider converting it to an endnote so that it can be placed at the end of the document.

Using Cross-References

When you're working on a long document in which you want to refer to other portions, you can use cross-references to help readers find the information they seek. Word lets you refer to a number of different elements in your document—including captions, headings, footnotes and endnotes, and bookmarks you've created.

tip **Expand subdocuments before referencing**

You can create cross-references only within the current document. You might create a reference in the beginning of a long report, for example, that points readers to a table in a later section that lists statistics related to a new study you're releasing. You can't create a cross-reference to refer to a table in another document, however.

If you're working with master and subdocuments, be sure to expand the master by clicking the Expand Subdocuments button on the Outlining toolbar. This makes all text accessible before you enter cross-references.

Creating a Cross-Reference

When you're ready to create a cross-reference, start by placing the insertion point where you want the cross-reference in your document. Then follow these steps:

1. Add the text that refers to the cross-reference (for example, you might use a phrase such as "To review the results of our survey, see").
2. Choose Insert, Reference, Cross-Reference. The Cross-Reference dialog box appears, as shown in Figure 28-6.

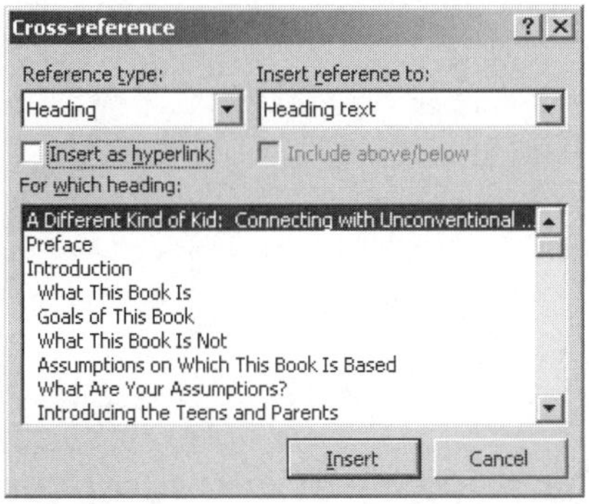

Figure 28-6. Cross-references enable you to point readers to different elements in your document.

3. Click the Reference Type down arrow and make your selection. You can choose from the following document elements:
   - **Numbered Item** lists all the text entries beginning with a number throughout the document.
   - **Heading** shows all headings based on Word's Heading 1, 2, 3 styles or outline levels.
   - **Bookmark** displays all the bookmarks currently listed in the document.
   - **Footnote** shows all footnotes inserted in the document.
   - **Endnote** lists the endnotes you have created.
   - **Equation** shows any equations you've inserted in the document.
   - **Figure** lists all figure references.
   - **Table** shows all available tables in the document.

Chapter 28

4. Click the Insert Reference To down arrow and choose what you want Word to insert in the document. This item will be inserted at the insertion point.
5. Select the item to which you want to refer by clicking it in the For Which list.
6. Click Insert, and Word adds the cross-reference to your document as you selected.
7. Click Close to return to your document.

tip **Create links for a Web page**

If you plan to save your document as a Web page or make it available as an electronic file, you can have Word turn your cross-references into hyperlinks, so that visitors to your site can move from one page to another easily. To create links for cross-references, select the cross-reference you've created and display the Cross-Reference dialog box by choosing Insert, Reference, Cross-Reference. Select the Insert As Hyperlink check box, and click Insert. The inserted cross-reference is created as a link to the other location in the document.

Modifying, Moving, and Updating Cross-References

You can edit and delete the text that introduces a cross-reference the same way you would modify any other text in your document. If you want to modify the item to which a reference refers, you need to make a different kind of change. Here are the steps:

1. Select the item inserted as the cross-reference (for example, you might select *Table 1-1*).
2. Display the Cross-Reference dialog box by choosing Insert, Reference, Cross-Reference.
3. In the For Which list in the Cross-Reference dialog box, click the new item to which you want the cross-reference to refer.
4. Click Insert and then Close to close the Cross-Reference dialog box.

tip **Make a reference relative**

You can have Word create a relative reference to a cross-reference you enter by selecting the Include Above/Below check box in the Cross-Reference dialog box. Create your cross-reference as usual, and then after selecting the item you want inserted in the Insert Reference To drop-down list, select the Include Above/Below check box. If the insertion point is on the same page as the section or item referenced, Word will insert "above" or "below," based on the position of the reference.

If you want to move a cross-reference, simply select the reference in your document and cut and paste it as you would normally. Once you have the reference in the location you want, press F9. Word updates the reference and makes the connection to the new location. If you want to update all references in a document, select the entire document before pressing F9.

note When you want to delete a cross-reference in your document, simply select the reference and delete it as you would any other text.

Troubleshooting

Cross-Referencing in My Document Produces an Error Message

If you go through the steps to create a cross-reference and instead of the reference you expect, you get an error message saying, "Error! Reference source not found," check to make sure that the information you're referring to hasn't been removed from your document. If the item is still in your document but the reference still displays an error message, try fixing the problem by selecting the cross-reference and pressing F9 to update the reference. If the problem is caused by a broken link or a moved reference, the item should now be displayed properly.

Part 7

Taking Advantage of Web and Networking Features

Chapter 29

Keeping an Eye on Word's Online Features

Now that the Internet has emerged from its infancy, businesses and individuals are continually finding innovative ways to take advantage of the Internet's rapidly improving features and capabilities. As you know, the Internet—which was once limited to serving as a collection of text files, File Transfer Protocol (FTP) file repositories, bulletin boards, and newsgroups—now offers full-service online businesses, streaming video, real-time data, software updates, support services, interactive forms, and much more. Not surprisingly, Microsoft has had its eye on seamlessly integrating desktop applications and the Internet for years. (In fact, Microsoft clearly stated its vision in the early 1990s.) As you'll see in this chapter, Microsoft continues its trend toward incorporating Internet capabilities into Microsoft Word.

Accessing the Web Using the Web Toolbar

One of the most obvious means by which Word integrates with the Web is the Web toolbar, shown in Figure 29-1. As an experienced Word user, you're probably familiar with the Web toolbar. It has been around since Microsoft Word 97, and its appearance and functionality haven't changed since its introduction. Primarily, this toolbar is provided as a convenience so that you can access Web pages and browse hyperlinks included in documents displayed in Word.

Figure 29-1. The Web toolbar enables you to access Web pages from within Word.

To open the Web toolbar, choose View, Toolbars, Web. The Web toolbar provides buttons that are frequently found in Web browsers, as follows:

- **Back** takes you to the previously displayed document. You can display Word documents or Web pages using the Back button.
- **Forward** takes you to the next document if you've clicked the Back button.

tip You can use keyboard shortcuts to move back and forward between pages while surfing the Internet. To move back, press Alt+Left Arrow, and to move forward, press Alt+Right Arrow.

- **Stop** stops the current page loading process.
- **Refresh** reloads the currently displayed page in Word.
- **Start Page** opens your browser and displays the first page that appears when you open your default Web browser. A start page can be a Web site or a local file on your hard disk or network.
- **Search The Web** opens your browser and loads the default search page.
- **Favorites** opens your Favorites list, which can contain local files and folders as well as locations on networks and the Internet. This list is the same Favorites list available to you from within Internet Explorer.
- **Go** provides a drop-down menu with options that enable you to open a hyperlink, move back or forward, display the start or search page, and set the default start or search page to the currently displayed page.
- **Show Only Web Toolbar** maximizes your viewing area by hiding all toolbars except the Web toolbar and the menu bar. When you'd like to redisplay the hidden toolbars, click the Show Only Web Toolbar button again.
- **Address** lets you enter a local or an online path name to access information. You can click the Address down arrow to display the same history list links that are available from the Internet Explorer Address box.

tip **Specify a Start Page**

You can control which Web page opens when you click the Start Page button by configuring your browser's start page settings. For example, in Internet Explorer, you control your start page by choosing Tools, Internet Options and then configuring the Home Page section on the General tab in the Internet Options dialog box.

newfeature!

Using the Task Pane to Initiate Online-Related Tasks

As you know by now, one of the principal innovations in Word 2002 is the task pane, which is designed to provide a standard area for commands, files, and functionality. Among its many features, you'll find a number of Web-related options that enable you to use the task pane to integrate Web capabilities as you work. In particular, you can open the task pane by choosing File, New and then use the task pane to perform the following Internet-related tasks:

- **Create a new, blank Web page or e-mail message.** In the New Document task pane, click the Blank Web Page or Blank E-mail Message link.
- **Access templates stored on your Web sites and in the online Microsoft Office Template Gallery.** In the New Document task pane, click the Templates On My Web Site or Templates On Microsoft.com link.
- **Add a Network Place so that you can access online sites from within Word.** In the New Document task pane, click the Add Network Place link.
- **Obtain online help.** In the New Document task pane, click the Microsoft Word Help link.
- **Search for additional clip art items on line.** In the Insert Clip Art task pane, click the Clips Online link.
- **Translate documents via the Web.** In the Translate task pane, click Go in the Translate Via The Web section.

For more information about downloading clip art from the Web, see Chapter 14, "Adding Visual Impact with Pictures." For more information about using templates and wizards from the Microsoft Office Template Gallery, see Chapter 22, "Formatting Documents Using Templates, Wizards, and Add-Ins." For more information about obtaining online technical assistance from Microsoft (including information about Office On The Web features), see Chapter 3, "Getting the Most From Help."

Looking at Your Documents from the Web's Perspective

As you might know, the latest features in Word make the application a viable interface for creating and editing Web pages. Many Web page developers found the Web page capabilities in Word 2000 intriguing but not particularly practical, because Word automatically generated HTML source code that was bloated with lots of extra Word-specific commands. Now, in Word 2002, developers can easily strip out the extra code before sending their pages on line. This makes Word much more appealing as a Web page development tool.

For more information about creating Web pages in Word, see Chapter 31, "Creating Professional Web Sites."

When you create and edit Web pages in Word, you can use the following Web-specific views:

- **Web Page Preview** displays the current document in your Web browser so that you can see how it will look as a Web page. To preview a document as a Web page, choose File, Web Page Preview. If your Web browser is not running when you choose Web Page Preview, Word starts it automatically. You can return to your document in Word at any time.
- **Web Layout view** enables you to work on a document while displaying it in Word in a manner that simulates how the document will appear in a Web browser. For example, in Web Layout view, your documents appear as one long page (without page breaks), text and tables wrap to fit the window, and backgrounds are displayed. You should work in Web Layout view when you are creating Web pages or documents that will be viewed on screen. To change to Web Layout view, choose View, Web Layout.

When you're working in Web Layout view, keep in mind that Word offers a few additional configurable options for this view. Namely, you can control whether *object anchors* and *text boundaries* are displayed while you work. Object anchors indicate where objects are attached to paragraphs or positioned within tables, and text boundaries are dotted lines that show spacing and cell padding settings within page margins, columns, tables, and objects. To access the Object Anchors and Text Boundaries options, choose Tools, Options and click the View tab; the options are included in the Print And Web Layout Options section. Figure 29-2 shows a sample Web page with the Text Boundaries check box selected. (Notice that the page's graphics links are broken so that you can see the margin and spacing lines more clearly.)

Working with My Network Places

In the true spirit of Web and desktop integration, you can use Word to create, copy, save, and manage folders and files that reside on a network, the Web, or FTP servers. After you create shortcuts to online folders (and if you have the proper permissions), you can work with online files and folders as though they were on your local computer. Of course, taking advantage of working with networks and the Web implies that you are connected to a network or have a connection to the Internet.

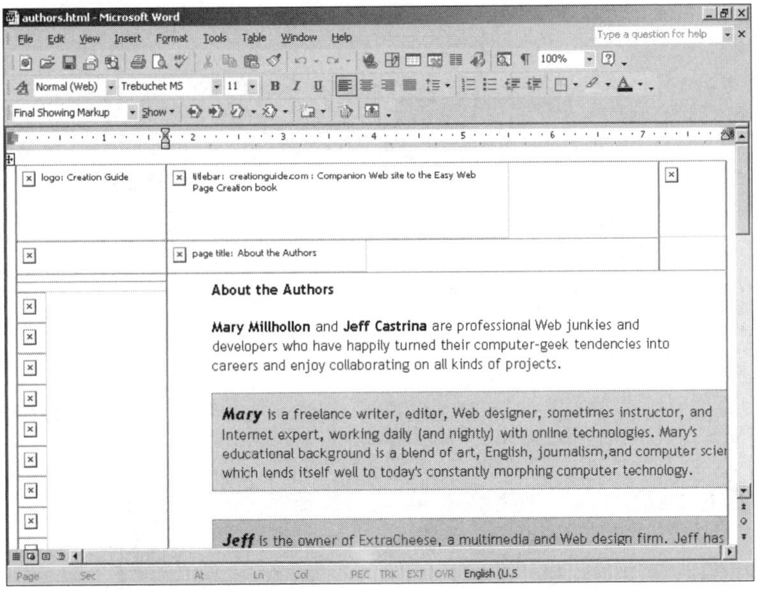

Figure 29-2. When you configure the Web Layout view to show margin spacing, Word uses dotted lines to indicate margin and spacing settings within pages, tables, and columns.

Troubleshooting

Word Doesn't Allow Me to Create a Network Place

Although you can create shortcuts and folders in existing Network Places from within Word (by clicking the Add Network Place link in the New Document task pane), you need to set up links to new Network Places initially by using the Add Network Place Wizard in Microsoft Windows.

To create a Network Place in Windows 2000, follow these steps:

1. Double-click My Computer on the desktop.
2. Click the My Network Places link, and double-click the Add Network Place icon.
3. Work through the Add Network Place Wizard's pages to create a link to the Network Place.

After you add a Network Place, you can create shortcuts to the Network Place or new folders in the Network Place from within Word.

Creating a New Folder and Setting Up a Shortcut at the Same Time

Although it's not readily apparent, you can create a new folder within an existing network location while creating a shortcut. To do so, follow these steps:

1. Choose File, New to open the New Document task pane, and then click Add Network Place.
2. Click Create A New Network Place, and then click Next.

   If necessary, double-click the link to the Network Place you want to use to store the new folder.
3. Right-click in the folder area in the Add Network Place Wizard, and choose New, Folder on the shortcut menu, as shown here:

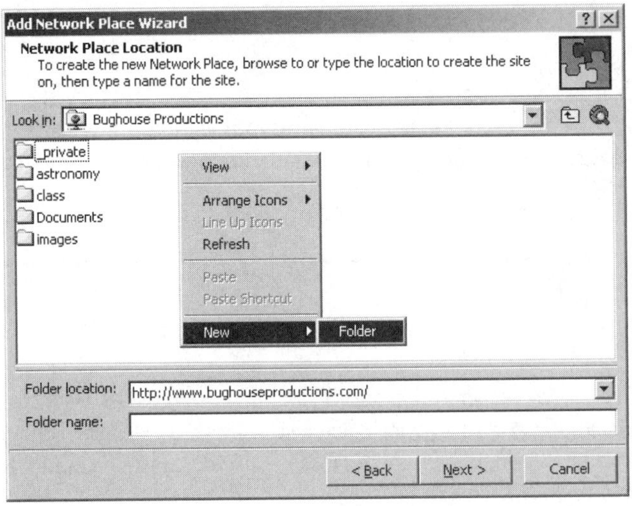

4. Type a name for the new folder, press Enter, verify that the new folder is selected, enter a shortcut name in the Folder Name box, and then click Finish.

   A shortcut to the newly created folder will be added to the My Network Places list.

Adding a Shortcut to a Network Place

After you've established Network Places, you can access them from within Word as well as save files and folders to the online locations. To create shortcuts to Network Places from within Word, follow these steps:

1. Click File, New to open the New Document task pane.
2. In the New Document task pane, click the Add Network Place link to open the Add Network Place Wizard.
3. Click Create A Shortcut To An Existing Network Place, and then click Next.

> **tip** To add a folder to a network location without creating a shortcut, choose Create A New Network Place instead of Create A Shortcut To An Existing Network Place.

4. Enter the URL of the Web site, or double-click the network location and its subfolders to select a particular location.
5. Type a name in the Shortcut Name box, and then click Finish.

After you create a shortcut, the shortcut will appear as a top-level link whenever you access the My Network Places area. Having a top-level link simplifies working with files stored in the network location, as described in the next section.

Linking to FTP Sites

In the same way you access other Network Places, you can add FTP sites to your list of Internet sites if you have access to a network or the Internet. To create shortcuts to FTP sites, follow these steps:

1. Click Open on the Standard toolbar to open the Open dialog box.
2. Click the Look In down arrow, and choose Add/Modify FTP Locations. The Add/Modify FTP Locations dialog box opens.
3. In the Name Of FTP Site box, enter the address of the FTP site (for example, **ftp.microsoft.com**).
4. Specify whether you need to log on anonymously or by providing a user name by clicking either Anonymous or User. If you must supply a user name, type the user name in the User box, and type a password (if necessary) in the Password box. A sample completed Add/Modify FTP Locations dialog box is shown in Figure 29-3, on the next page.
5. When you finish configuring the Add/Modify FTP Locations dialog box, click Add to add the new FTP location, and click OK to close the dialog box.

After you create an FTP link, you can double-click the link in the Open dialog box to access the contents of the FTP site. To modify or delete the link to an FTP site, right-click the link, and choose Remove or Modify on the shortcut menu.

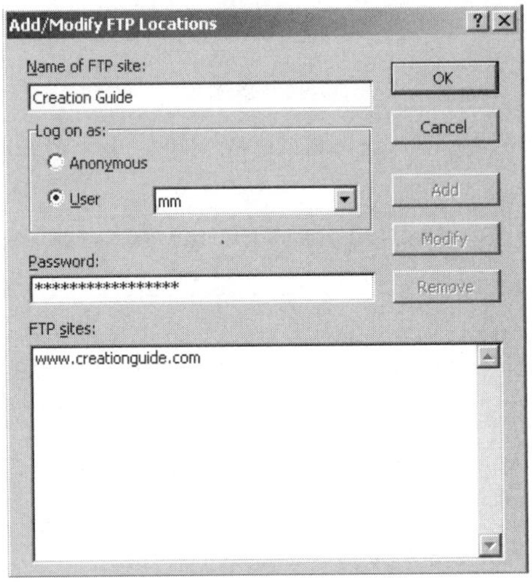

Figure 29-3. Adding FTP locations to your list of available network locations can streamline FTP procedures such as transferring large files and uploading Web pages to servers.

Accessing Resources Stored in Network Locations

You access network locations in the same way you access local files and folders—you simply navigate to the online file and folder locations within the Open dialog box and then create a local shortcut to the document, if desired. To open an online folder or file using the Open dialog box, follow these steps:

1. Choose File, New to open the New Document task pane, and then click More Documents in the Open A Document section (or click the Open button on the Standard toolbar).
2. Click the Look In down arrow, choose My Network Places or FTP Locations, and then double-click the location you want to access.

When you access network locations, Word identifies the types of network connections with icons. Table 29-1 summarizes the common icons you'll see associated with network locations.

Table 29-1. Network Location Icons

Icon	Description
	FTP server.
	Web site hosted by MSN. (Other hosting companies might provide their own icons.)
	Shared folder on a network.
	Folder on a Web site.

Saving Documents to a Network Location

In addition to opening files from network locations, you'll most likely want to save files to online locations. After you create shortcuts to network locations, the process of saving files to online locations is similar to saving files locally. To save a file to an online location, follow these steps:

1. Choose File, Save As.
2. In the Save As dialog box, click My Network Places.
3. Double-click the shortcut to the network location where you want to save the document, and double-click any subfolders you want to access as well.
4. In the File Name box, type a name for the file (or retain the current name), and then click Save.

Whenever you work with online files, you need to consider how other people will be (or are) interacting with files. For example, if you're updating Web pages, make sure no other people are working on the pages when you replace existing files. Otherwise, you might overwrite each other's changes, which can be an extremely annoying experience. For more information about sharing files and folders on networks, see Chapter 32, "Sharing Information on Networks."

Chapter 30

Collaborating On Line with E-Mail, NetMeeting, Discussions, and Faxes

In this era of telecommuting, long-distance associations, and on-the-move lifestyles, online communication plays a much larger role in collaboration than it has in the past. Online communication gives people a convenient way to work together by sharing documents and ideas in near real time across networks, regardless of where participants are located. To help make online communication possible, Microsoft Office XP offers a number of online collaboration features.

The online collaboration features found in Microsoft Word work in conjunction with other Office applications to expand the Internet and network options available to you from within Word. For example, Word works with Microsoft Outlook to enable you to create and send e-mail messages using the Word window, and Word works in conjunction with Microsoft Internet Explorer to provide Microsoft NetMeeting conferencing capabilities. In this chapter, you'll learn about a few of the most common online collaboration tools accessible from within Word. In particular, you'll learn how to use Word to send e-mail messages, conduct online conferences and meetings, participate in Web discussions, and send faxes. Let's start by looking at the most common online communication activity—sending e-mail messages.

Using Word as an E-Mail Editor

Almost everyone has had at least a brush with e-mail in one form or another. As an experienced Word user, you've probably sent more e-mail messages than you care to count. What you need to know about sending e-mail messages in Word is rooted in the Word-specific "how-tos." In this section, you'll see how you can get the most out of the e-mail features in Word.

As you might imagine, you can use Word to send messages formatted as plain text, rich text, or HTML. Most new and updated versions of e-mail applications (including Outlook 2002) offer a choice of plain text or HTML; earlier or scaled-down versions of e-mail applications generally support plain-text messages only. When you use Word, you can use any of the three listed formats. The following pros and cons should help you decide which format best suits your needs:

- **Plain-text e-mail messages.** By far, the most common e-mail message format is plain text. Plain-text e-mail messages are small, which makes sending and receiving messages quick. In addition, plain-text e-mail messages are easily interpreted by all e-mail applications. The main drawback of plain-text e-mail messages is that they are just that—plain text. You can't specify fonts, create layouts, include color, or apply any other text or document formatting; you can send only a typed message (with an occasional emoticon to spice up your note). To work around this limitation, most people send a plain-text e-mail message and attach document files that contain desired formatting. For more information about attaching files to e-mail messages, see the section "Sending an Attachment," on page 680.
- **HTML e-mail messages.** HTML messages represent the newer wave of e-mail messaging. Using HTML messages, you can send highly formatted messages that incorporate font formatting, color, backgrounds, themes, and so forth. You can also use existing documents as e-mail messages without losing the document formatting. The drawbacks of HTML e-mail messages are somewhat significant. First, not all e-mail applications support HTML messages. When an HTML message is sent to a person who's using a text-only e-mail application, the recipient might have to wade through some HTML code gobbledygook before getting to the body of your message. A second drawback of HTML messages is that they are larger, which means that the messages can take longer to send and receive if they contain a lot

of formatting and graphics. (This might be a particular concern if you know the recipient will be using a dial-up connection to receive your message.) Before you send HTML messages, make sure that the recipient can view HTML messages and has a relatively speedy Internet or network connection.

- **Rich-text e-mail messages.** You can also format e-mail messages in Word as rich text, which sends a plain-text e-mail message along with a .dat file (usually named Winmail.dat) containing information about message formatting as well as other data, such as voting button information. If recipients are using Outlook or the Exchange Client, a rich-text message will appear fully formatted. If recipients aren't using Outlook or the Exchange Client, they will receive a plain-text message with the Winmail.dat file attached (and the file's contents will seem meaningless). Unless you're working on an intranet and you need to use some of Outlook's special features, you'll usually want to format your e-mail messages using either the Plain Text or HTML setting.

By default, Word formats new, blank e-mail messages using the HTML format. You can change this setting by configuring the Mail Format tab in the Options dialog box in Outlook. To access this setting, follow these steps:

1. In Outlook, choose Tools, Options, and click the Mail Format tab in the Options dialog box.
2. Click the Compose In This Message Format down arrow, and choose HTML, Rich Text, or Plain Text in the drop-down list. (HTML is selected by default.)
3. Click OK.

Keep in mind that if you format a document before you convert the document to an e-mail message, Word will automatically retain your formatting and send the message as an HTML e-mail message—even if you've specified plain text as your default e-mail message format. The default setting comes into play only when you create new, blank e-mail messages, as described in the section "Sending a Document, E-Mail Style," on page 674.

> Many e-mail options provided by Word are available only if you're using Outlook in conjunction with Word. For more information about using Outlook, see *Microsoft Outlook Version 2002 Inside Out*, also from Microsoft Press.

Turning Word On or Off as Your E-Mail Editor or Viewer

By default, Outlook is configured to use Word as your e-mail editor. This means that when you click the New Mail Message button on the Standard toolbar in Outlook, a blank e-mail document opens in a Word window. To verify this setting, open a new e-mail message in Outlook (by choosing File, New, Mail Message or pressing Ctrl+Shift+M), and look at the message's title bar. The title bar displays *Untitled Message – Microsoft Word*, and the window contains the standard Word features (including toolbars, view buttons, Browse By buttons, and so forth).

Although Word offers numerous formatting advantages over the standard Outlook message window, you can specify to not use Word as your e-mail editor if you prefer to use a scaled-down version of the Outlook message window. To control this setting, follow these steps:

1. In Outlook, choose Tools, Options, and click the Mail Format tab in the Options dialog box.
2. Select or clear the Use Microsoft Word To Edit E-Mail Messages check box, and then click OK.

You can change this setting at any time if you find you prefer one message window over the other.

Sending a Document, E-Mail Style

If you want to use Word to send an e-mail message, you can open an e-mail pane, which appears across the top of your Word window. This e-mail pane contains a number of buttons and text boxes that you can use to format and send your e-mail messages.

You can create new, blank e-mail messages in Word or you can create e-mail messages from existing Word documents, as follows:

E-mail

- **To create a new, blank e-mail message**, choose File, New to open the New Document task pane, and click the Blank E-Mail Message link. The e-mail pane opens above a new, blank document, as shown in Figure 30-1.
- **To create an e-mail message from an existing document**, open an existing document or enter information in a new, blank document, and then click the E-Mail button on the Standard toolbar. The e-mail pane opens above the document's contents, as shown in Figure 30-2. Notice that the Subject box contains the document's file name. (If the document has been saved, the file name is displayed in the Subject box automatically.)

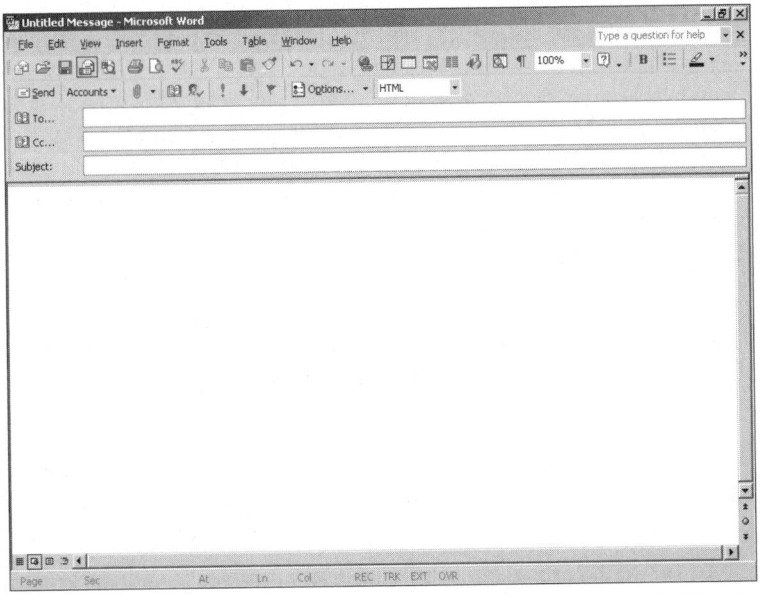

Figure 30-1. You can create a new, blank e-mail message by clicking the Blank E-Mail Message link in the New Document task pane.

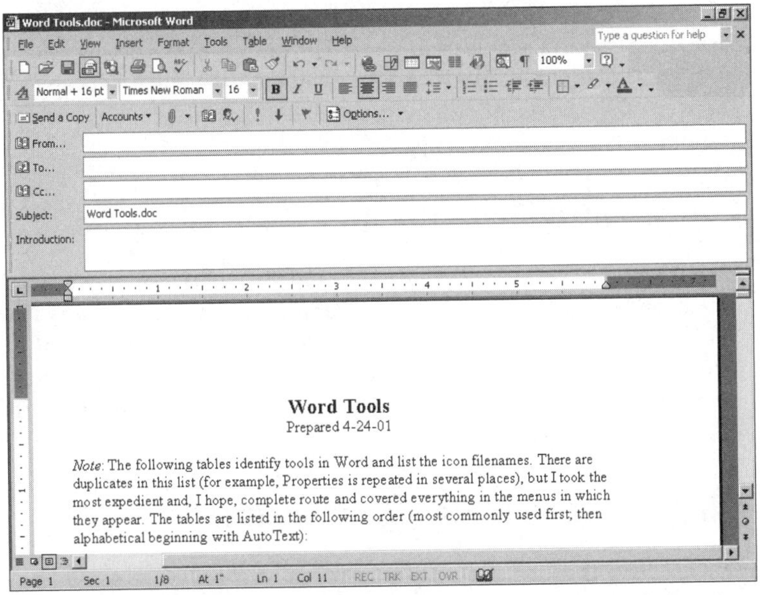

Figure 30-2. You can display the e-mail pane in an existing document, which enables you to send the entire document in an e-mail message.

As you can see in Figures 30-1 and 30-2, the e-mail pane varies slightly depending on how you create your e-mail message. When you click the E-Mail button on the Standard toolbar to add the e-mail pane to an existing document, the e-mail pane includes an Introduction box (discussed in more detail in the section "Including an Introduction in an E-Mail Message," on page 676). When you click the Blank E-Mail Message link in the New Document task pane, the e-mail pane includes a drop-down list that allows you to specify whether you want to format the message as HTML, rich text, or plain text.

After you display the e-mail pane in a document—regardless of whether it's a new document or an existing document—you are ready to configure the e-mail settings. Completing the e-mail pane is similar to addressing standard e-mail messages, as described here:

1. In the e-mail pane, enter recipient names in the To box and the Cc box, if necessary. (For more information about adding recipients, see the section "Specifying Sender and Recipient Identities," on page 676.)
2. Enter a subject in the Subject box, enter the document contents if necessary, and then click Send or Send A Copy (depending on how you created the e-mail message).

In addition to this basic procedure, you can use a number of other addressing and formatting features provided in Word. For example, you can include introductory text, specify a sender other than yourself, include an attachment, create a custom signature, and control a number of other e-mail related features, as described in the next few sections.

Including an Introduction in an E-Mail Message

If you click the E-Mail button on the Standard toolbar from an open document, Word includes an Introduction box in the e-mail pane. This box allows you to add text without inserting it into the existing document. You might want to do this if you're sending a document for review or sending a copy of a Web page. When you add an introduction, the recipient sees the introduction text separated from the main text by a horizontal rule, as shown in Figure 30-3.

Specifying Sender and Recipient Identities

When you send e-mail from within Word, you can specify the following participating parties:

- **Accounts.** If you have multiple e-mail accounts set up on your computer, you can specify from which account you'd like to send the current e-mail message. To do so, click the Accounts button in the e-mail pane, and select

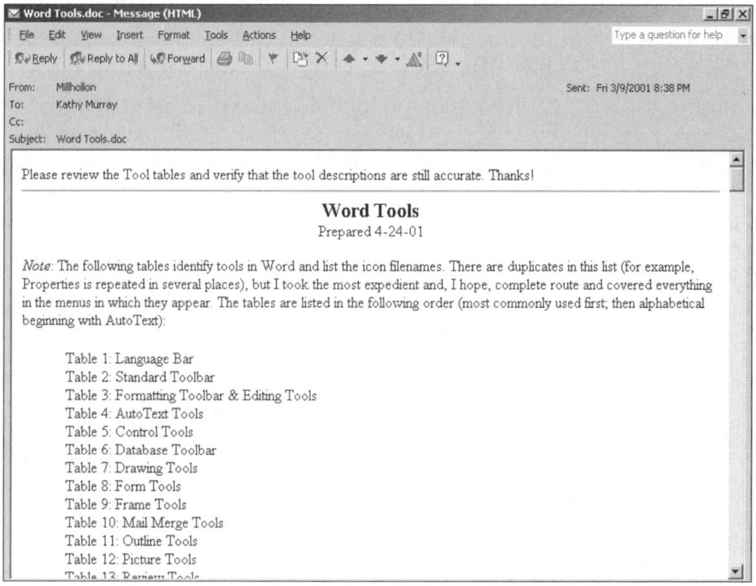

Figure 30-3. The Introduction box enables you to include ancillary text above your e-mail message's main contents.

the account you want to use to send the message. Figure 30-4 shows an Accounts drop-down list on a computer configured with three different e-mail accounts.

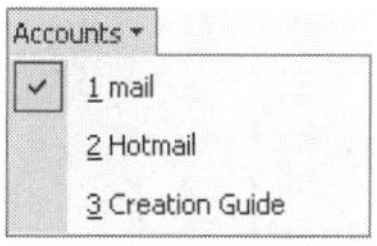

Figure 30-4. The Accounts drop-down list enables you to choose which account you want to use to send a message.

- **From.** You can choose to send an e-mail message on behalf of someone else by specifying a name in the From box. (If the From box isn't displayed in the e-mail pane, click the Options down arrow, and choose From on the drop-down menu.) When you send a message with a From name to a recipient using Outlook, the message header will show the From name in the Inbox, and the message itself will read **Your Name** *on behalf of* **Sender's Name** when the message is open. To specify a From name, type a name or an e-mail address in the From box, or click From in the e-mail pane to open the Sender dialog box. In the Sender dialog box, choose a name, and then click OK.

caution Be careful when using the From box because this option can produce misleading results. If the recipient is using Outlook, the *on behalf of* statement appears in the message header and the communication is clear. But if the recipient is using another e-mail application, such as Outlook Express, the message header will simply show the name you inserted in the From box—the recipient won't know that the message was created and sent by someone other than the listed name.

- To. Obviously, you need to specify a recipient (or recipients) for your message. You can do so by entering e-mail addresses in the To box. If you manually enter multiple recipients, separate each e-mail address with a semicolon followed by a space. You can also enter e-mail addresses by clicking To and choosing names in the Select Names dialog box, shown in Figure 30-5. To specify names in this dialog box, select each name, and click To. After you've added all the names you want to include, click OK.

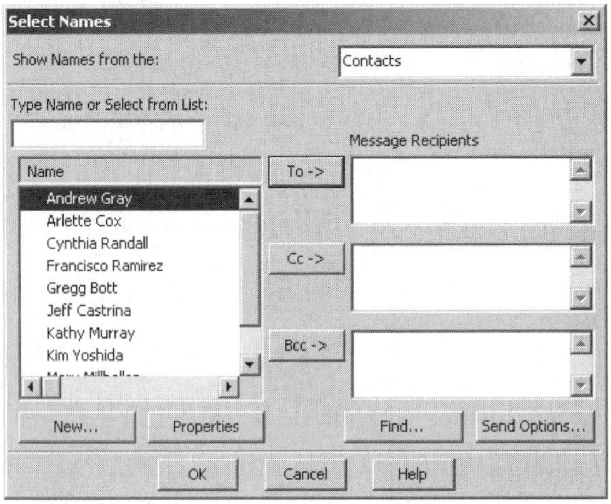

Figure 30-5. The Select Names dialog box enables you to specify e-mail addresses for the To, Cc, and Bcc boxes all at once.

- Cc. You can send copies of e-mail messages to other people by entering their e-mail addresses in the Cc (short for *carbon copy*) box, either by typing the addresses or by clicking Cc, selecting a name in the Select Names dialog box, clicking Cc, and then clicking OK. When you enter names in the Cc box, all recipients can see the names of all the people who've been sent a copy of the message.

- Bcc. You can use the Bcc (short for *blind carbon copy*) option to send a copy of an e-mail message to the person indicated in the Bcc box without revealing to the recipients specified in the To and Cc boxes that the additional copy was sent. To send blind copies of any e-mail messages, enter e-mail addresses in the Bcc box, either by typing the address or by clicking Bcc, selecting a name in the Select Names dialog box, clicking Bcc, and then clicking OK. If you don't see the Bcc box in the e-mail pane, click the Options down arrow, and choose Bcc in the drop-down list.

> **tip** **Verify the address resource**
>
> If you don't see the name you're looking for in the Choose Sender dialog box (which appears when you click From in the e-mail pane) or in the Select Names dialog box (which appears when you click To, Cc, or Bcc), verify that the proper address resource is displayed in the Show Names From The drop-down list. By default, Word presents the names stored in your Outlook Contacts folder, as shown in Figure 30-5.

Setting E-Mail Priority

At times, you might want to mark e-mail messages as urgent or not-at-all-urgent (also known as *low priority messages*). Marking your messages indicates instantly to recipients who are using Outlook or Outlook Express whether they should give special attention to a message. To set e-mail priority for a message, use the following techniques:

Importance: High

- **To send a high-priority message,** click the Importance: High button in the e-mail pane. A red exclamation point appears next to the message in the Importance column in the recipient's Inbox if the recipient is using Outlook or Outlook Express. (The treatment may vary in other e-mail applications.)

Importance: Low

- **To send a low-priority message,** click the Importance: Low button in the e-mail pane. In Outlook or Outlook Express, a blue down arrow appears next to the message in the Importance column in the recipient's Inbox.

By default, e-mail messages are classified as normal priority; normal priority messages aren't accompanied by any priority marker. You can also configure message priority levels by clicking the Options button in the e-mail pane to open the Message Options dialog box, clicking the Importance down arrow, and choosing Low, Normal, or High in the drop-down list.

Adding a Message Flag

You can add flags to e-mail messages to indicate that you or the recipient needs to perform some type of follow-up action in response to a message. The flag will appear only in Outlook (not Word), in the Sort By: Flag Status column. To flag a message, follow these steps:

Message Flag

1. In the e-mail pane, click the Message Flag button. The Flag For Follow Up dialog box appears.

2. Click the Flag To down arrow, choose a flag type, such as Call, Follow Up, Do Not Forward, and so forth.
3. Click the Due By down arrow, and choose a due date on the pop-up calendar. You can also click the down arrow for the adjacent drop-down list and specify a due by time.
4. Click OK to close the Flag For Follow Up dialog box.

When you send the message, it will be accompanied by a flag in your Sent box in Outlook and in the recipient's Inbox if the recipient is using Outlook or Outlook Express. You can also add flags to and remove flags from existing messages in your Inbox.

Sending an Attachment

One of the most frequent tasks associated with e-mail messages other than sending notes is transferring files and objects as attachments. You might want to send attachments if a recipient doesn't use an HTML e-mail application or if you're sending a large document, graphic, movie file, spreadsheet, or other file type. You attach files in Word in the same manner you attach files in other e-mail applications. To do so, use one of the following techniques:

Attachment

- Open the document you want to send as an attachment, and then choose File, Send To, Mail Recipient (As Attachment).
- In the e-mail pane, click the Insert File button to open the Insert File dialog box. Select the file you want to attach to the current e-mail message, and then click Insert. Notice that the file name appears in the Attach box in the e-mail pane, as shown in Figure 30-6.

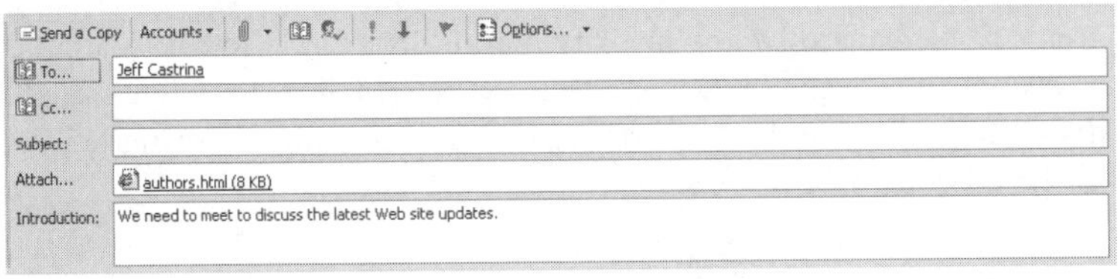

Figure 30-6. The e-mail pane displays the file names of any files attached to the current e-mail message.

- In Windows Explorer, right-click any document, and choose Send To, Mail Recipient.

When you send an attached file, recipients can save the file on their computers and view it locally.

Adding an E-Mail Signature

As you've probably seen during your e-mail travels, many people include a small blurb of information at the end of their e-mail messages. These blurbs are referred to as *signatures*. Signatures often supply extra contact information, links to Web pages, and sometimes witty or clever comments. Conveniently, you can edit or delete signatures just as you manipulate other text after it's inserted. To create a custom signature that you can use on an as-needed basis, follow these steps:

1. Choose Tools, Options, click the General tab, and then click the E-Mail Options button. If necessary, click the E-Mail Signature tab. The E-Mail Options dialog appears, as shown in Figure 30-7.

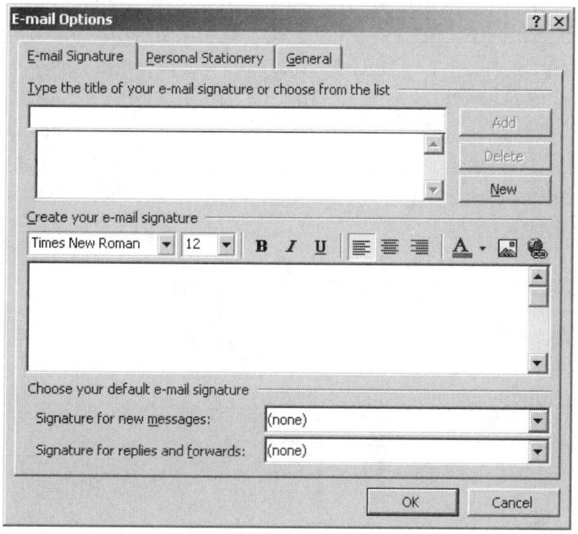

Figure 30-7. You can use the E-Mail Options dialog box to create a collection of signatures that you can choose from when you create e-mail messages in Word.

2. In the top box, enter a title for the signature you're creating.
3. Enter the signature's content (including text, graphics, and hyperlinks) in the box in the Create Your E-Mail Signature section, and click Add. By default, the newly created signature is assigned to be the default e-mail signature.

tip **Choose a default signature**

You can set any signature to be your default signature by configuring the E-Mail Signature tab in the E-Mail Options dialog box. To do so, select the signature's name in the Signature For New Messages and Signature For Replies And Forwards drop-down lists, and then click OK.

4 To add another signature, click New, name the signature, enter the signature information, and then click Add. You might see a message box asking whether you'd like to make the signature the default for all e-mail messages. If so, click Yes or No as appropriate, and then continue to add any additional signatures.

5 When you have finished creating signatures, click OK to close the E-Mail Options dialog box, and then click OK to close the Options dialog box.

After you create and set a default signature, Word inserts the default signature in future new, blank e-mail documents you create by clicking the Blank E-Mail Message link in the New Document task pane. In addition, your default signature will be added to messages that you create by replying to or forwarding messages sent to you. If you create a number of signatures in Word, you can easily change which signature is inserted into an e-mail message by right-clicking the existing signature and choosing another signature on the shortcut menu. When you do this, the existing signature is removed and the selected signature is inserted in your document. You can also use this shortcut menu to access the E-Mail Options dialog box (in which you can create a new signature, modify existing signatures, and change your default signature setting). Figure 30-8 shows a blank e-mail document containing a signature along with the shortcut menu showing other available signatures.

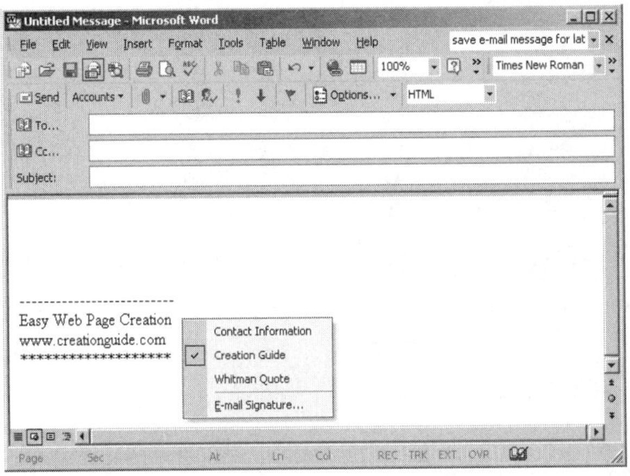

Figure 30-8. You can replace an existing signature by right-clicking it and then choosing another signature name on the shortcut menu.

Routing Documents via E-Mail

Most likely you're familiar with the *routing slips* used in office settings. In plain language, a routing slip is a list of names of people who need to review an item. When a person on the list reviews the item, she checks off her name, and passes the item to the next person on the list. Routed items can be anything from policy updates to "secret" birthday cards for a coworker. In Word, you can attach the online equivalent of a routing slip to a document, and you can route the document to each person on the list in sequence or all at once. You might want to use this feature if you want a number of people to review and return a particular document.

To create a routing slip, follow these steps:

1. Open the document you want to route, and then choose File, Send To, Routing Recipient. If a security warning appears, asking whether it's OK to check your Outlook Address Book, click Yes. The Routing Slip dialog box appears, as shown in Figure 30-9.

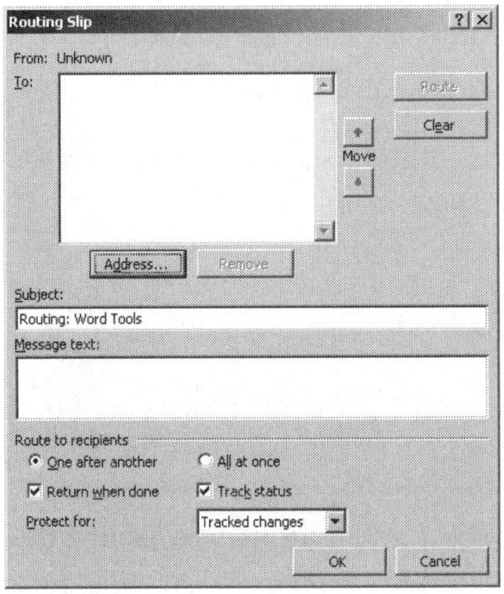

Figure 30-9. You can use the Routing Slip dialog box to create an online routing slip for a Word document.

2. In the Routing Slip dialog box, click the Address button. The Address Book dialog box appears.
3. In the name list, select the names you want to include on your routing slip (to select multiple names, press Ctrl as you select names), click To, and then click OK to close the Address Book dialog box. The selected names will appear in the To list in the Routing Slip dialog box, as shown in Figure 30-10, on the next page.
4. Adjust the order of recipients in the To list to suit your needs by selecting names and clicking the up or down arrow button to the right of the To list to move the selected name up or down in the list.
5. Enter text in the Message Text box, and in the Route To Recipients section, specify whether you want to route the document to each routing slip recipient in sequence or all at once.

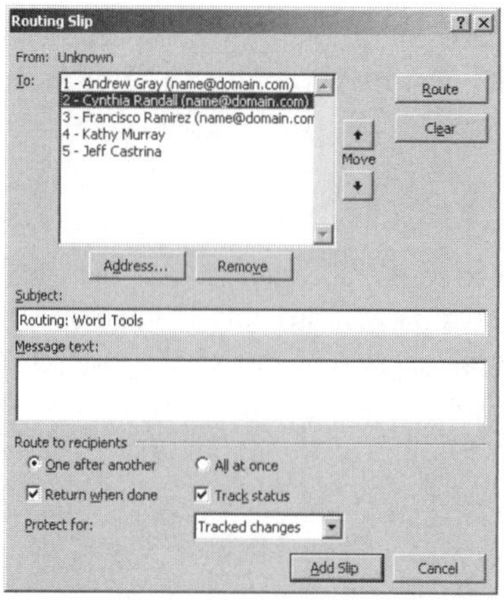

Figure 30-10. The To list in the Routing Slip dialog box specifies the users who will be included in the routing process.

6 Click the Route button to begin routing your document. If you receive a security warning, click Yes to continue.

Recipients of a document with a routing slip will receive an e-mail message stating that the attached document is being routed. After the recipient opens and reviews the document in Word, he should choose File, Send To, Next Routing Recipient to forward the document to the next person on the routing slip. If the recipient wants to route the document to another name on the list, he can choose File, Send To, Other Routing Recipient. As the document is routed, the originator of the routed document receives update e-mail messages indicating the latest action (such as *Bill routed the document* **name of document** *to Julie*).

Formatting Messages with Stationery and Themes

If you choose to send HTML-formatted e-mail messages, you can send highly customized messages. You can use the themes provided in Word to format your e-mail messages, as described in Chapter 23, "Using Word's Desktop Publishing Features." You can also add *stationery* to e-mail messages. Fundamentally, stationery is a scaled-down version of a theme, and the process of applying stationery is similar to applying themes, as shown here:

1 The E-Mail Options dialog box opens.

2 In the E-Mail Options dialog box, choose the Personal Stationery tab, shown in Figure 30-11.

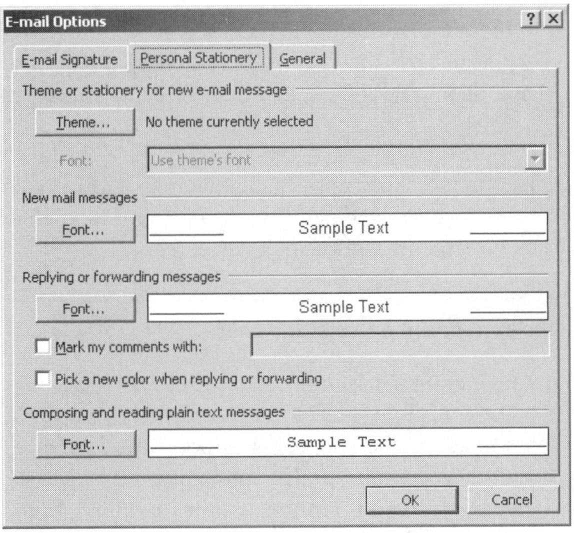

Figure 30-11. The Personal Stationery tab provides a number of format settings for e-mail messages, including the Theme button, which you can use to access the Theme Or Stationery dialog box.

3 Click the Theme button. The Theme Or Stationery dialog box appears, as shown in Figure 30-12.

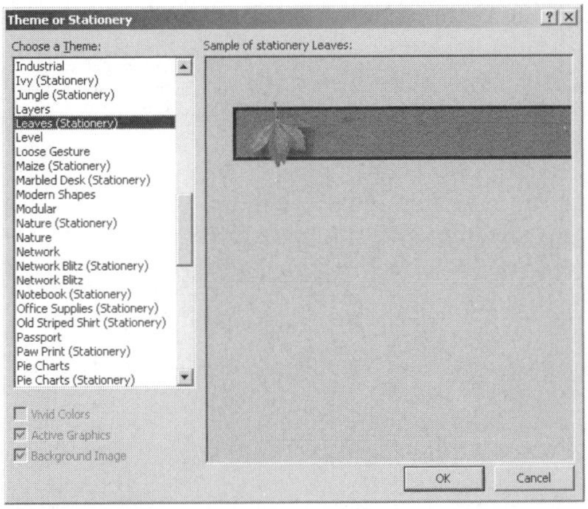

Figure 30-12. You can use the Theme Or Stationery dialog box to select and preview e-mail stationery and themes before applying them.

4 Choose a name in the Choose A Theme list. Notice that a number of themes include the word *Stationery* after the theme name; themes labeled as stationery are scaled-down themes that specify an e-mail message's background and standard text settings (such as color and font).

5 View themes in the preview box until you find one you want to use. Select the theme, click OK to close the Theme Or Stationery dialog box, click OK to close the E-Mail Options dialog box, and then click OK to close the Options dialog box.

When you set a default theme, Word applies the theme to all future e-mail messages you create until you reconfigure the default theme setting. The theme won't be applied to e-mail messages or documents you've already created.

tip **Apply a theme to the current e-mail message only**

You can apply a new theme to an existing e-mail message before you send it, regardless of whether the e-mail message has a theme already applied. To do so, choose Format, Theme to access the Theme dialog box. Select a theme, preview the theme, and then click OK. When you use this option, you won't see themes specially formatted as stationery, so you won't find themes listed with the *(Stationery)* identifier after the theme names.

Setting E-Mail Message Options

You can set a number of e-mail message options within Word by configuring settings in the Message Options dialog box, shown in Figure 30-13. To open the Message Options dialog box, click the Options button in the e-mail pane.

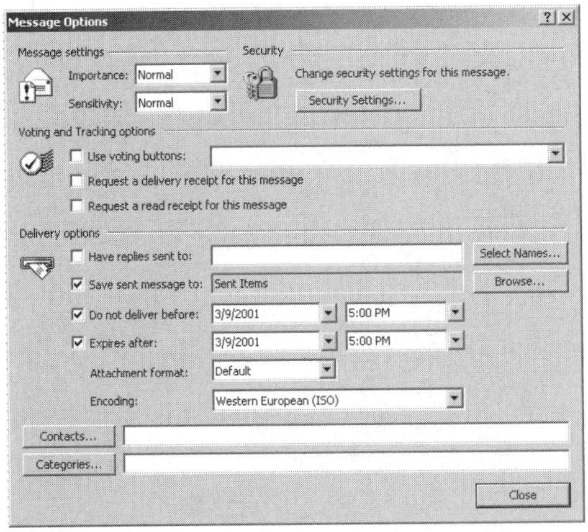

Figure 30-13. Click the Options button in the e-mail pane to access the Message Options dialog box.

The Message Options dialog box enables you to set the following options:

- **Importance** lets you mark a message as Low, Normal, or High importance. For more information about indicating an e-mail message's importance, see the section "Setting E-Mail Priority" on page 679.
- **Sensitivity** lets you specify whether the contents of a message are Normal, Personal, Private, or Confidential. This option serves as an indicator only; it doesn't protect your document in any way.
- **Security Settings** opens the Security Properties dialog box, which enables you to encrypt e-mail messages and add digital signatures. For more information about security, see Chapter 34, "Addressing Security Issues."
- **Use Voting Buttons** includes voting buttons in e-mail messages so that recipients can reply to a message by clicking buttons such as Approve or Reject.
- **Request A Delivery Receipt For This Message** sends a message to you when your e-mail message arrives at the recipient's address.
- **Request A Read Receipt For This Message** sends a message to you verifying the date and time your message was opened by the recipient. (Of course, this doesn't guarantee that the recipient actually read your message.)
- **Have Replies Sent To** sends replies to the current message to another e-mail address you specify, such as an assistant's address.
- **Save Sent Message To** saves the sent message in the specified folder. By default, sent messages are saved in the Sent Items folder in Outlook.
- **Do Not Deliver Before** stores the message in your Outbox until the specified date and time.
- **Expires After** allows you to specify a date after which the message becomes unavailable.
- **Attachment Format** specifies the format to use when sending an attachment. You can choose from Default, MIME, UUEncode, and BINHEX formats.
- **Encoding** lets you specify the character set used in the message.
- **Contacts** displays a list of contact names and addresses you can use to link the message to in Outlook.
- **Categories** assists you in assigning words you can use to find and group related items in Outlook.

After you configure the settings in the Message Options dialog box, click Close to accept the settings and continue creating your e-mail message.

Configuring HTML Options for E-Mail Messages

In addition to configuring settings in the Message Options dialog box, you can control a couple of HTML-specific options for e-mail messages you send that use HTML formatting. To access these HTML-specific options, follow these steps:

1. Choose Tools, Options, click the General tab, and then click the E-Mail Options button.
2. In the E-Mail Options dialog box, click the General tab, shown in Figure 30-14.

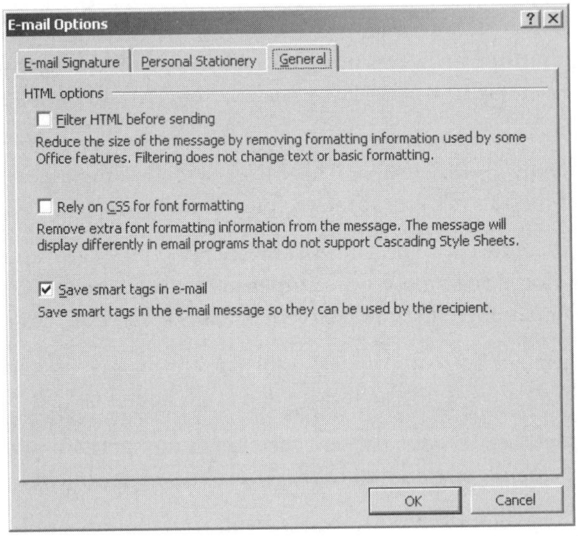

Figure 30-14. The General tab in the E-Mail Options dialog box presents three HTML-specific options you can control when you send HTML e-mail messages.

The General tab provides the following HTML-specific options:

- **Filter HTML Before Sending.** When you select this check box, Word reduces the file size of your HTML e-mail message without altering the message's appearance. The file size is reduced because Word strips out Word-specific formatting information from the message's HTML source code. If you plan to edit the document in Word later, you should keep this check box cleared.
- **Rely On CSS For Font Formatting.** When you select this check box, you instruct Word to create a cascading style sheet (CSS) and attach it to the e-mail message. The net result of this action usually reduces the size of the message. The drawback is that if the recipient uses an e-mail application that doesn't support CSS, your document will be displayed improperly.

- **Save Smart Tags In E-Mail.** If you know recipients will view your message in Outlook 2002, you can instruct Word to use smart tags in the e-mail message. Selecting this check box and sending a message to a recipient who uses an e-mail application other than Outlook 2002 will have no effect.

After you configure the settings in the E-Mail Options dialog box, click OK to save your settings, and then click OK again to close the Options dialog box.

Conducting Online Meetings with NetMeeting

Word, and other Office applications, work with Internet Explorer to provide online collaboration. This pairing of technologies enables you to conduct online interactive meetings by using NetMeeting. NetMeeting is a conferencing application that includes the following components:

- Application sharing
- Audio capabilities
- File distribution and sharing
- Text-based chat
- Video capabilities
- Virtual whiteboard

As you might imagine, using the audio and video capabilities requires that participants have speakers, microphones, and Web cameras installed on their systems. To use NetMeeting in Word, you must first configure NetMeeting in Internet Explorer, as described next.

Installing and Getting Familiar with NetMeeting

NetMeeting can be installed when you install Internet Explorer, so your system might already have NetMeeting installed. To find out whether NetMeeting is installed on your computer, open Internet Explorer and choose File, New, Internet Call. If NetMeeting is installed but you've never configured the application, the NetMeeting Wizard will appear. Simply complete the information in the NetMeeting Wizard welcome page, shown in Figure 30-15, on the next page, and then work through the wizard to set up your NetMeeting application.

Figure 30-15. The NetMeeting Wizard walks you through the NetMeeting setup process.

If NetMeeting isn't installed on your computer, you can download the latest version of NetMeeting from the Microsoft Web site, at *www.microsoft.com/netmeeting*. After you download NetMeeting, you'll need to work through the NetMeeting Wizard to configure your settings.

After you work through the NetMeeting Wizard, the NetMeeting window opens. You can check your video camera's operation and angle by clicking the Start Video button. Figure 30-16 shows the NetMeeting interface with video turned on.

Figure 30-16. The NetMeeting interface provides features you need to collaborate on line with others who have NetMeeting installed on their systems.

To get you up and running quickly, Table 30-1 describes the buttons available in the NetMeeting window.

Table 30-1. NetMeeting Tools

Button	Name	Description
	Place Call	Opens the Place A Call dialog box, from which you can place a call to another NetMeeting user.
	End Call	Disconnects your computer from the conference.
	Find Someone In A Directory	Opens the Find Someone dialog box and displays directory contents.
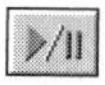	Start Video/ Stop Video	Starts and pauses video transmission.
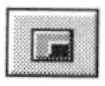	Picture-In-Picture	Displays your video as a small picture in the lower right corner of the video screen so that you can see your video as well as the video of the other conference participant. (Note that only two people at a time can use video during a meeting, even if more than two people have video cameras.)
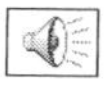 	Adjust Audio Volume/ View Participant List	Displays microphone and speaker audio controls. When speaker controls are displayed, the button changes to the View Participant List button; click this button to redisplay the list of meeting participants' user names.
	Share Program	Opens the Sharing dialog box, which enables you to share your computer's resources with other meeting participants.
	Chat	Opens the Chat window, which lets meeting participants communicate by entering text.
	Whiteboard	Opens the Whiteboard, which offers typical paint program capabilities.
	Transfer Files	Opens the File Transfer window, which enables you to transfer files to meeting participants.

For a full review of NetMeeting and its features, refer to *Running Microsoft Internet Explorer 5*, also from Microsoft Press.

Initiating and Joining NetMeeting Conferences

You can participate in NetMeeting conferences by initiating a call or accepting a call from another computer user. You can initiate a call in the following ways:

- In Word, choose Tools, Online Collaboration, Meet Now, and then click the name of the person you want to meet with in the Find Someone dialog box.
- In NetMeeting, click the Place Call button to open the Place A Call dialog box, complete the To box information, and click Call.

tip **Place a NetMeeting call directly**

The most direct way to initiate a call with another user is to open NetMeeting, click Place Call, and enter the other computer's IP address in the To box. You can easily find your computer's IP address in NetMeeting by choosing Help, About Windows NetMeeting. Your IP address is displayed at the bottom of the About Windows NetMeeting dialog box.

When you initiate a NetMeeting call while you're working in Word, Word displays the Online Meeting toolbar, shown in Figure 30-17, and displays your Word window to other meeting participants.

Figure 30-17. The Online Meeting toolbar is displayed automatically when you initiate a NetMeeting call from within Word.

Troubleshooting

I Can't Print or Save a File Shown During an Online Meeting

When you view a meeting participant's Word file during an online meeting, you can't print or save the file to your local resources. Instead, if you click Print while viewing a file, the document will be printed on the printer of the person hosting the online meeting. Similarly, if you click Save, the file will be saved on the meeting host's hard disk or server.

If you want a copy of the shared file that you can store or print, you should ask the meeting host to send you a copy of the file, or you can copy the document's contents to a file on your computer after the host grants you permission to make changes to the file.

Table 30-2 describes Word's Online Meeting toolbar buttons.

Table 30-2. Online Meeting Toolbar Buttons

Button	Name	Description
	Participant List	Displays a drop-down list containing the names of all meeting participants
	Call Participant	Opens the Find Someone dialog box
	Remove Participants	Disconnects the participant displayed in the Participant list
	Allow Others To Edit/ Stop Others From Editing	Allows others to edit the current Word document, or stops others from editing the Word document
	Display Chat Window	Opens the Chat window for real-time text communication
	Display Whiteboard	Opens the Whiteboard, which provides basic paint program capabilities
	End Meeting	Disconnects your computer from the conference

When another user initiates a NetMeeting conference with you, the NetMeeting – Incoming Call dialog box, shown in Figure 30-18, appears on your desktop along with the NetMeeting window. To join the conference, click Accept.

Figure 30-18. The NetMeeting – Incoming Call dialog box opens on your desktop automatically when someone attempts to start a NetMeeting conference with you.

Scheduling Meetings

You can schedule a meeting from within Word. To do so, choose Tools, Online Collaboration, Schedule Meeting. The Untitled – Meeting dialog box opens, as shown in Figure 30-19, on the next page. The Untitled – Meeting dialog box is the same as the Meeting dialog box found in Outlook 2002. To schedule a meeting, enter meeting participant names, configure the meeting's particulars in the appropriate boxes, and click Send.

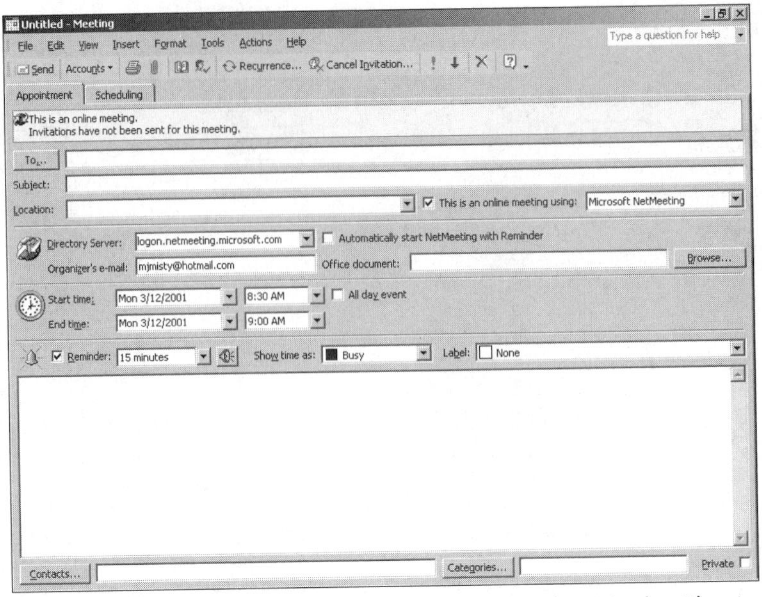

Figure 30-19. You can schedule a meeting from within Word, without opening Outlook.

> For more information about setting up meetings, refer to the Outlook Help files or consult an Outlook-specific resource.

Joining in Web Discussions

Another way to communicate on line is to take part in Web Discussions. The Web Discussions features in Office enable you to attach comments to and insert comments in a Web page or any file you can open in a Office application and view in a Web browser (including .htm, .xls, .doc, and .ppt files). The comments you attach to the document appear within the document when it is displayed on line but are stored on a discussion server, not in the document and not necessarily on the same server that stores the document. Figure 30-20 shows a document containing discussion comments that is stored on a SharePoint team Web site. Notice that some comments have been inserted directly in the document and others appear below the document. You can insert and view discussion comments in either location. Keep in mind that a server administrator must set up Web Discussions before you can use this feature.

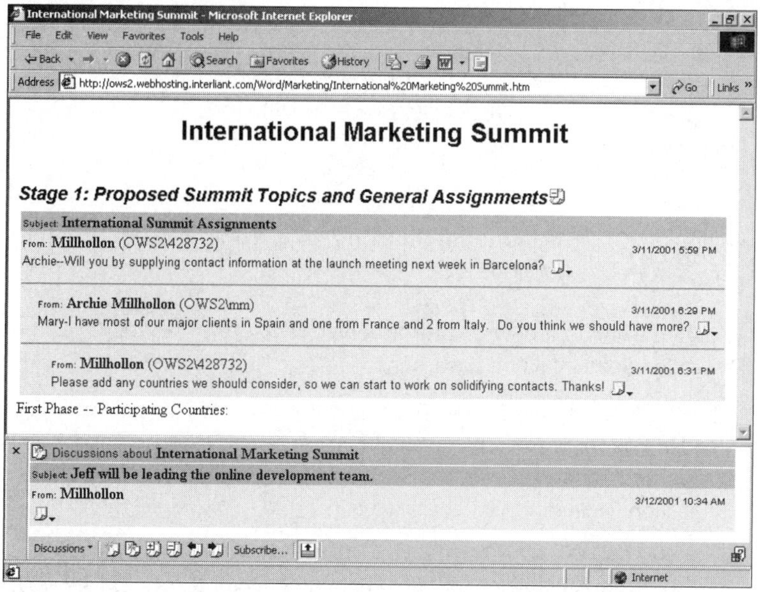

Figure 30-20. The Web Discussions feature in Office enables you to add comments to online documents for others to read and respond to.

For more information about team Web sites and SharePoint, see Chapter 32, "Sharing Information on Networks."

Connecting to a Discussion Server

After your server administrator sets up the Web Discussions feature, you can connect to the discussion server and participate in Web Discussions. To connect to a discussion server, follow these steps:

1. Choose Tools, Online Collaboration, Web Discussions. The Web Discussions toolbar appears, as shown in Figure 30-21.

Figure 30-21. The Web Discussions toolbar provides buttons you can use to connect to discussion servers and participate in Web Discussions.

2. On the Web Discussions toolbar, click the Discussions button to open the Discussions drop-down menu, shown in Figure 30-22, on the next page, and then choose Discussion Options. The Discussion Options dialog box appears.

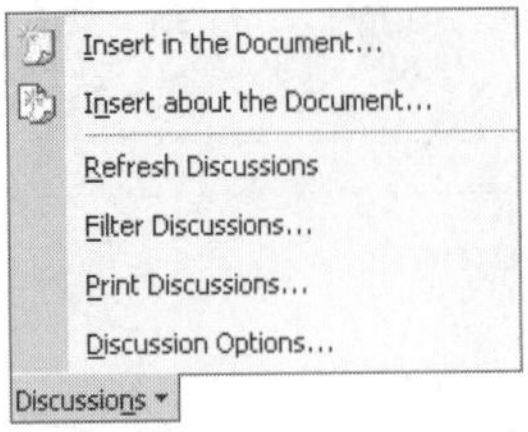

Figure 30-22. The Discussions button provides a drop-down menu of discussion-related options.

3. To create a link to a new discussion server, click Add. The Add Or Edit Discussion Servers dialog box opens.
4. In the Type The Name Of The Discussion Server Your Administrator Has Provided box, type the name of a discussion server. If security is set up on your discussion server using the Secure Sockets Layer (SSL), select the Secure Connection Required (SSL) check box.
5. In the You Can Type Any Name You Want To Use As A Friendly Name For The Discussion Server box, type the name you want to use for the server. Click OK to close the dialog box.
6. In the Discussion Options dialog box, click OK to connect to the discussion server listed in the Select A Discussion Server box.

After you connect to a discussion server, you can navigate to the online document you want to discuss and then add discussion comments, as described next.

Participating in a Discussion

After you've accessed an online document or a Web page, you can participate in Web Discussions by using the Web Discussions toolbar buttons. Table 30-3 describes the buttons contained on the Web Discussions toolbar.

Table 30-3. Web Discussions Toolbar Buttons

Button	Name	Description
	Discussions	Provides a selection of discussion-related actions you can perform, such as filtering, refreshing, and printing discussions
	Insert Discussion In The Document	Inserts a discussion comment at the insertion point location within a paragraph in the document
	Insert Discussion About The Document	Inserts a discussion comment in the Discussion pane, which is a separate pane that appears below the active document

Table 30-3. ***(continued)***

Button	Name	Description
	Previous	When discussions are showing in the Discussion pane, click this button to move to the preceding comment.
	Next	When discussions are showing in the Discussion pane, click this button to move to the next comment.
	Show General Discussion	Displays discussions below the document instead of as inline discussion comments
Subscribe...	Subscribe	Opens the Document Subscription window, which enables you to have the discussion server notify you when a file or folder changes by periodically sending you an e-mail message
	Stop Communication With Discussion Server	Disconnects your computer from the Web Discussions server
	Show/Hide Discussion Pane	Displays or hides the Discussion pane. You can drag the pane's border to adjust its viewing area
Close	Close Web Discussions	Closes the Web Discussions feature and toolbar

To add a discussion comment about an online document using the Web Discussion toolbar buttons, follow these steps:

1. To insert an inline discussion comment, position the insertion point in the paragraph you want to discuss, and click the Insert Discussion In The Document button. To insert a general discussion below the document, click the Insert Discussion About The Document button. The Enter Discussion Text dialog box opens.
2. In the Enter Discussion Text dialog box, click in the Discussion Subject box, and type a subject for your comment.
3. Click in the Discussion Text area, enter your comments, and then click OK. Your comment appears in the Discussion pane.

If you want to respond to an existing comment, you can click the Show A Menu Of Actions icon and choose an action on the shortcut menu, as shown in Figure 30-23, on the next page.

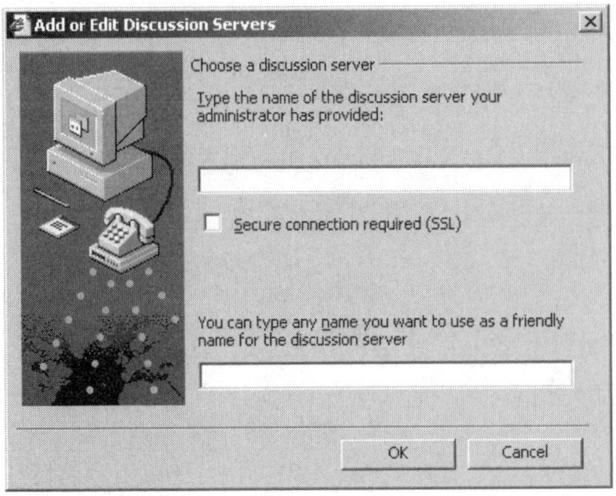

Figure 30-23. You can access a variety of actions by clicking the Show A Menu Of Actions icon that appears at the end of a discussion comment.

Most discussion features work with Office Server Extensions running on the network server. If you want to close and reactivate discussions or automatically store discussion comments on the same server as the document, the discussion server must be running Microsoft SharePoint Team Services. For more information about Microsoft SharePoint Team Services, see Chapter 32, "Sharing Information on Networks."

Using Word to Send Faxes

Faxing is another fast, convenient way to get information from your desktop to other desktops around the country or the world. Word provides a Fax Wizard that walks you through most of the process.

note Some of the items discussed in this section will be available on your computer only if you have fax capability on your system. If you do not have a fax modem, or if you have a stand-alone fax with fax software installed on your system, Windows will not recognize your fax and will not enable some of the menu options discussed here. You can, however, use Word's fax feature even if you don't have a fax modem or fax machine close by—by using the Fax Wizard to access an Internet faxing service and sending faxes via the Web to your intended recipients.

Sending a Document, Fax Style

If you have a fax modem installed on your computer, you can send a document as a fax directly to a recipient. For example, you might want to do this if you are finalizing the workshop assignments for a conference you are coordinating and you want to send the agenda to your committee leaders for review.

To send a document as a fax, follow these steps:

1. Save your finished document, and with the document still open, choose File, Send To to display a submenu of send options, as shown in Figure 30-24.

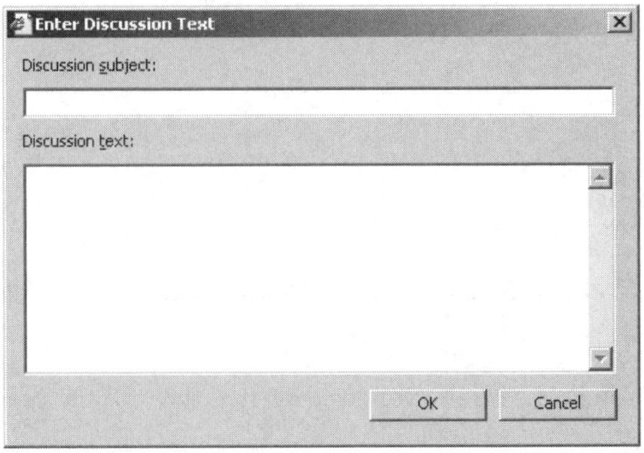

Figure 30-24. If you have fax capability on your system, you can fax an open document using the Send To submenu.

2. Choose Fax Recipient to start the Fax Wizard, which leads you through the steps necessary to send your fax.

Starting a Fax from Scratch

If you want to create fax without having created a document first—for those times when you simply want to send a file as an attachment or send only a cover page with a note—you start by creating a new document, as follows:

1. Choose File, New. The New Document task pane appears.
2. Click General Templates. The Templates dialog box appears.
3. On the Letters & Faxes tab, select Fax Wizard, and click OK. The Fax Wizard welcome page appears, as shown in Figure 30-25, on the next page, leading you through a series of questions that enable you to choose the document, select the fax program, and configure the specifications and recipients for your fax. (We'll work through these wizard steps in the remainder of this section.)

Figure 30-25. The Fax Wizard walks you step-by-step through the process of creating and sending your fax.

Troubleshooting

I Can't Find the Fax Wizard

If the Fax Wizard option is missing from the Letters & Faxes tab, you might need to install it. To do so, follow these steps:

1. Choose Start, Settings, Control Panel.
2. In Control Panel, double-click Add/Remove Programs, and in the Currently Installed Programs list, locate Microsoft Office.
3. Click Office, and click the Add/Remove button. The Microsoft Office XP Setup Wizard appears.
4. Click Add Or Remove Features, and click Next.
5. In the Features To Install list, expand Microsoft Word For Windows, Wizards And Templates, click Faxes, and choose Run From My Computer on the drop-down menu. Click the Update button to install the Fax Wizard.

If you are using Office on a network, be sure to check with your network administrator before installing any new features.

tip **Send a fax using the Internet**

You can also use Word to send and receive faxes over the Internet if you don't have a fax machine or fax capability on your system. To do so, connect to the Internet and then start the Fax Wizard as described. Click the Internet Faxing Options button on the first page of the Fax Wizard to access the Microsoft Office Update Web page, where you can find out more about online faxing or link to a Web faxing site.

Selecting the Document to Fax

On the Fax Wizard Start page, click Next to begin. The Document To Fax page allows you to specify which document you want to fax. By default, the current document is selected. If you have more than one document open and you want to choose a document other than the one shown, click the down arrow for the drop-down list and select the document you want to send. You can also make the following choices about cover sheets: to send a cover sheet along with the fax, click With A Cover Sheet; to send the document as is, without a cover sheet, leave Without A Cover Sheet selected; and to send the document as is, without a cover sheet, leave Without A Cover Sheet selected.

After you make your selections, click Next to proceed to the Fax Software page of the wizard.

note The options that are available on the Document To Fax page of the Fax Wizard depend on the fax software you are using to send the document. Some programs do not have the capacity to send a cover sheet with the fax. If you select different fax software (in the next step of the wizard), you can click Back to return to the Document To Fax page and select the cover page options you want.

Choosing a Fax Program

The Fax Software page of the Fax Wizard enables you to select the fax program you want to use. By default, Microsoft Fax might be selected on your system. If you want to choose a different fax program (and you already have one installed), click A Different Fax Program Which Is Installed On This System, and then click the down arrow to select the program name from the list of installed programs. If you don't see the program you want to use, click the Other button and navigate to the folder containing the fax program you need. Click Next to continue on to the Recipients page in the Fax Wizard.

tip If you will be walking down the hall and using the office fax machine to send a fax, you can click the I Want To Print My Document option to tell Word to print the selected document in fax format.

Specifying Recipients

The Recipients page of the Fax Wizard, shown in Figure 30-26, lets you specify who you want to receive your fax. Here you can select individuals from your Address Book or you can type names and fax numbers in the boxes provided.

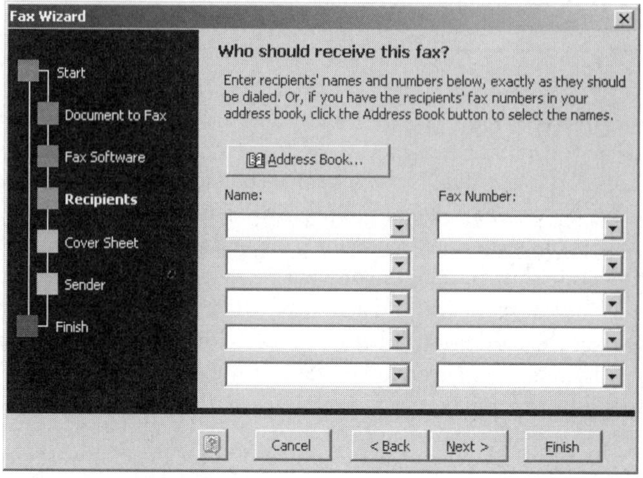

Figure 30-26. You can type the names and fax numbers of recipients or select them from your Address Book.

To choose recipients from your Address Book, follow these steps:

1. Click the Address Book button on the Recipients page of the Fax Wizard. If you have more than one e-mail profile configured on your computer, the Choose Profile dialog box appears; otherwise, the Select Name dialog box appears. If you have only one profile, skip to step 3.
2. If necessary, select the e-mail profile you want to use in the Choose Profile dialog box. (By default, the profile you use regularly will be displayed.) Click OK.
3. In the Select Name dialog box, click the Show Names From The down arrow, and choose the Address Book you want to use from the drop-down list.
4. Click the name you want in the list of recipients, and click OK. Word inserts the name in the first Name box on the Recipients page of the Fax Wizard.
5. Continue entering information, either by typing names and fax numbers or by selecting recipients from your Address Book. When you've finished identifying recipients, click Next.

> **tip** **Send merged faxes**
>
> You can send multiple faxes that you create by using the Mail Merge Wizard. Start by opening the document you want to fax, and then choose Tools, Letters And Mailings, Mail Merge Wizard. When you are asked to specify the document type you want to merge, select Faxes. For more information about creating and working with mail-merged documents, see Chapter 35, "Performing Mail Merges."

Selecting the Fax Style

Word provides three styles for the fax cover sheet you send: professional, contemporary, and elegant. Each is displayed on the Cover Sheet page of the Fax Wizard (which appears only if you selected a fax program that has cover sheet capability). Make your selection, and then click Next to move to the next page of the Fax Wizard.

Configuring Sender Info

The next page of the Fax Wizard, the Sender page, is about you—or your company. Fill in whatever information you want the recipient to know about you in the following boxes: Name, Company Information, Mailing Address, Phone, and Fax. Click Next to continue.

> **tip** **Save time by using the Address Book**
>
> If you have entered your company's info in the Address Book, you can have Word plug in the information automatically by clicking Address Book, choosing the address Book you want to use, and selecting your name from the list. Word inserts the information you've entered on the Sender page so that you don't have to retype it.

Completing and Sending the Fax

The last page of the Fax Wizard simply tells you to click Finish to send the fax. Word prepares the fax and displays the cover sheet (if you elected to send one) in your document window, as shown in Figure 30-27, on the next page. The Fax Wizard toolbar appears at the top of the document window. Make any last-minute changes, and click Send Fax Now on the Fax Wizard toolbar. Word launches your fax software, which dials the first number in your recipient list and begins to transmit the fax.

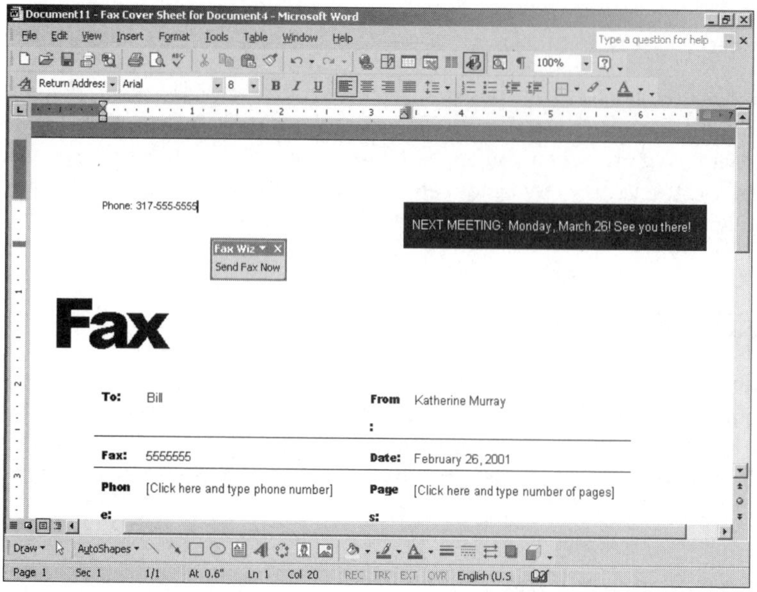

Figure 30-27. After you complete the Fax Wizard, Word displays the fax in the document window, where you can make final changes and send the fax.

> **tip** **Use Fax Service Management in Windows 2000**
>
> If you're using Windows 2000 Professional, another full-featured fax service is available to you. You can use the Fax Service Management utility to organize, manage, and send and receive faxes through your network. For more information about Fax Service Management, double-click Fax in Control Panel, and in the Fax Properties dialog box, click Advanced Options.

Chapter 31

Creating Professional Web Sites

Many people are finding their way onto the Web, and they're following a variety of paths to get there. One approach you can take to building an online presence is to create your Web pages and Web sites using Microsoft Word. As you'll see in this chapter, Word provides enough Web page creation features that you can create professional-looking Web pages and Web sites in the same manner you create Word documents. This functionality existed in Word 2000 as well, but a few key changes have made their way into Word 2002. For example, one notable change that experienced Web developers will appreciate is that you can now reduce the size of Web pages created in Word by filtering out Word commands added to your document's HTML source code. That might sound a little convoluted at this point, but it's a change well worth noting, and as you'll soon see this new filtering option is just one of the numerous features found in the Word arsenal of Web page building capabilities.

Understanding Web Page Creation Basics

In many ways, creating a Web page in Word is similar to creating any other document in Word. In fact, you can initiate Web page and Web site creation in Word by opening the New Document task pane (choose File, New) and then using any of the following methods:

- **Create a new, blank Web page.** Click the Blank Web Page link to get started.

- **Base a Web page on an existing document.** In the New From Existing Document section, click the Choose Document link. Then in the New From Existing Document dialog box, navigate to and select a copy of the file you want to use to create a Web page, and click Create New.

You can also save any open document as a Web page by choosing File, Save As Web Page or choosing File, Save As and specifying a file type of Web Page; Web Page, Filtered; or Web Archive. For more information about the various types of Web page file formats, see the section "Saving Your Web Pages," on page 718.

- **Use Web page templates.** Click the General Templates link to open the Templates dialog box. Then select the Web Page template on the General tab, or select another Web page template on the Web Pages tab and click OK.
- **Use the Web Page Wizard.** Click the General Templates link to open the Templates dialog box. Click the Web Pages tab, and double-click the Web Page Wizard.

Regardless of the method you use to create a Web page, you should know a bit about Web pages and how they differ from standard word processing documents before you start to create Web pages in Word. These two main differences stand out between standard Word documents and Web pages:

- **Most Web pages are created using multiple files.** A basic Web page generally consists of a text file that includes the HTML source code and a file for each graphic displayed on the Web page. The purpose of the source code in an HTML text file is to tell a browser how to display information. For example, the source code includes the page's text along with commands regarding how the text should be formatted. In addition, for each graphic on a Web page, the source code points to the location of the graphic file that should be displayed in a specified picture area within the Web page. When you view a Web page, you are actually viewing a number of files working together to create the appearance of a single page, as shown in Figure 31-1.
- **Most Web page layouts are fluid.** As you know, people around the world view Web pages using a variety of browsers, operating systems, computers, and display settings. Therefore, Web pages need to be flexible enough to be displayed under a wide array of circumstances. To gain flexibility, Web designers have had to give up complete control over their Web page layouts—instead of strategically placing each element on a page as in traditional print design, Web page designers merely suggest where information should appear and how the page should flow. Figure 31-2, on page 708, demonstrates how a Web page (in this case, the Web page example from Figure 31-1) can be displayed differently by viewing the same page at different resolutions.

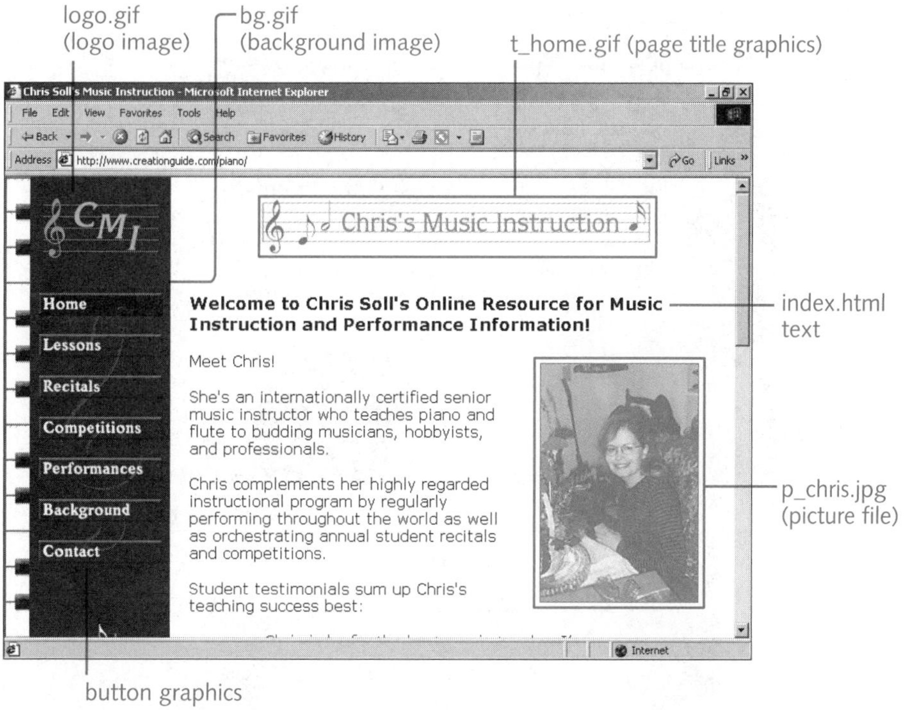

Figure 31-1. On this Web page, a number of graphics files—including GIF and JPEG files—are displayed in addition to the HTML text file's content to create a single Web page.

Of course, Web pages differ from printed documents in many other ways (for instance, hyperlinks are useless on printed pages), and Web design philosophies and opinions abound. If you're interested in Web page design theory, you can find lots of information in bookstores, at online reference sites, and in magazines. In this chapter, you'll learn how to use some of Word's features to help you gain the technical expertise you'll need to express your creative side in your Web site design endeavors.

Configuring Web-Related Options

Before you start creating Web pages in Word, you should review Word's Web page–related options. Setting options might sound a little tedious compared to the prospect of creating Web pages, but controlling your working environment up front can save you headaches later. By paying attention to the Web options, you'll also give yourself a chance to think about your Web pages before you get started, and you'll be alerted to the types of details you might have to take into consideration. The options discussed in this section can be found in the Web Options dialog box, which you can access by choosing Tools, Options, clicking the General tab, and then clicking the Web Options button. The first tab in the dialog box is the Browser tab, so we'll start there.

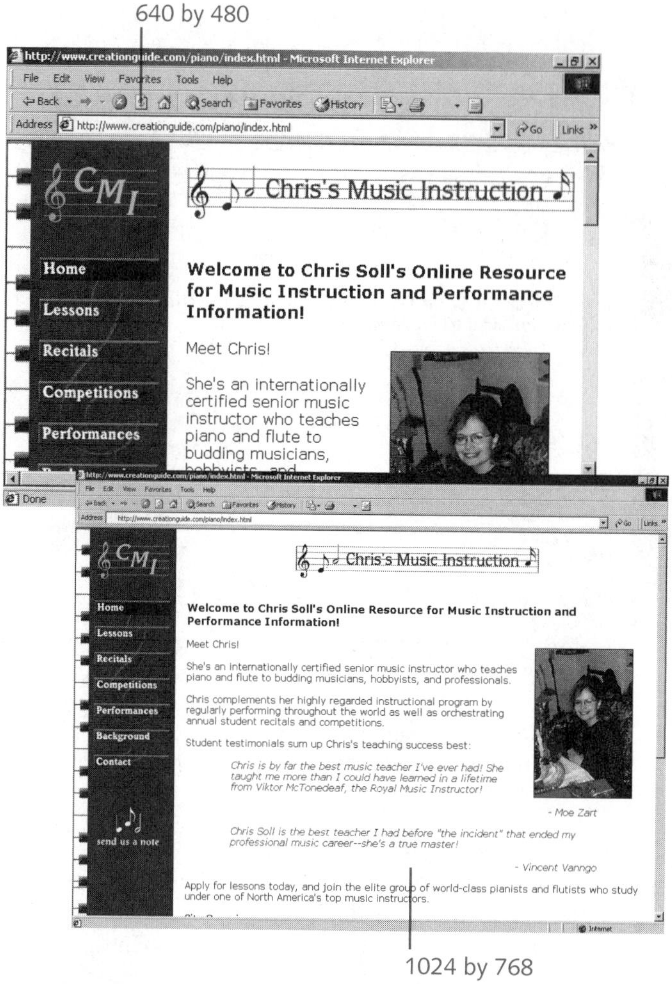

Figure 31-2. As a designer, you usually need to consider how your Web page will appear in a variety of circumstances. This figure shows the Web page example from Figure 31-1 with the monitor set to 640 by 480 and 1024 by 768 pixels instead of 800 by 600.

Specifying Target Browser Options

When you create Web pages, you have to consider how people will be viewing your pages. One detail you need to be aware of is which browsers users will be using. If you're publishing Web pages on an intranet for your company, chances are that most users will be using the same browser and similar computer configurations—in that case, design considerations are easy because you can design for the company standard. On the other hand, if you're planning to post your pages on the Internet for people around the world, you'll have to take a more liberal approach to design because you won't know how users will be viewing your pages. (Will they use Macs, PCs, Microsoft

Internet Explorer, Netscape Navigator, or something else?) In those cases, you need to define which browsers and versions of those browsers you're going to cater to as you design your Web pages.

Word helps you to design to a particular browser standard, which means that working within browser and version limitations is easier than it sounds. In Word, you can turn on or off features not supported by selected Web browsers. To configure this setting, follow these steps:

1. Choose Tools, Options, click the General tab, and then click the Web Options button. The Web Options dialog box appears, as shown in Figure 31-3.

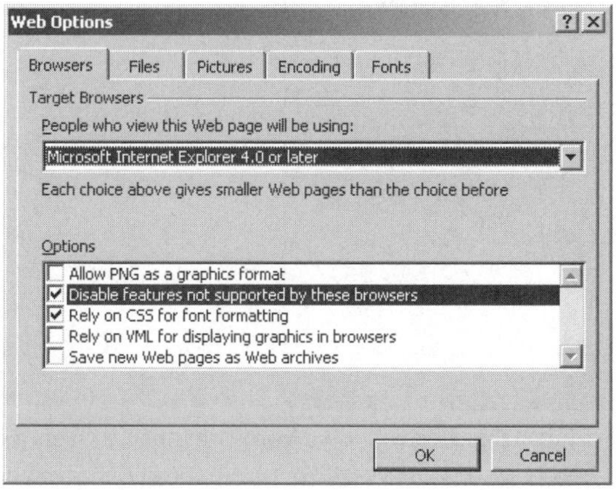

Figure 31-3. The Web Options dialog box provides options you can use to specify how Word handles some Web page creation tasks.

2. Click the Browsers tab, if necessary.
3. Ensure that the Disable Features Not Supported By These Browsers check box is selected.

caution If you clear the Disable Features Not Supported By These Browsers check box, you will be able to use every Web page feature built into Word regardless of whether any browser version can support it. In this case, "more" isn't better because you could very easily design a page that few people can view.

4. Click the People Who View This Web Page Will Be Using down arrow, and choose a browser type in the drop-down list. The check boxes in the Options list will be adjusted automatically based on the browser you select.

By default, Word is configured to use Internet Explorer 4 and Netscape Navigator 4 as target browsers. This setting is a fair standard, because those two browsers represent the most popular applications—and versions of the applications—in use today.

Reviewing File Options

After you specify a target browser for your intended Web audience, you should next consider how you want Word to handle your Web files. As mentioned, Web pages are made up of multiple files. When you create Web pages, you must keep your files organized—otherwise, you'll end up with pages containing broken links and missing components. Word offers a few ways you can organize your files, as well as a couple of default editor options, on the Files tab in the Web Options dialog box, shown in Figure 31-4.

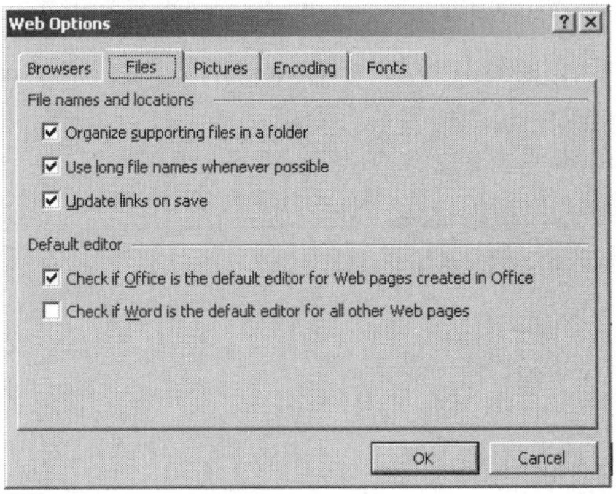

Figure 31-4. The Files tab helps control how Word organizes a Web page's files, and lets you specify whether you want Word to automatically check which program is registered as the default editor.

The Files tab enables you to specify the following preferences regarding files and folders:

- **Organize Supporting Files In A Folder.** By default, Word saves supporting Web page files (such as graphics) in a separate folder within the folder that contains the HTML document. Generally, this setup works best, because you'll be able to find your HTML document easily as well as group the supporting files together in a logical subfolder. You should clear this check box only if you're working on a Web page that already has an existing hierarchy of folders or if you prefer to have your HTML documents and supporting files stored in the same folder. Regardless of how you store your Web page's files, you should note the page's file organization. Later, when you upload your Web page to a server, you'll need to re-create the organizational structure on the Web server to ensure that your links work properly.
- **Use Long File Names Whenever Possible.** By default, this check box is selected. Nowadays, the only operating system that doesn't support long file names is Windows 3.x running on MS-DOS. If you know that some people who will be working with your files will be using Windows 3.x on MS-DOS, you'll want to clear this check box; otherwise, leave it selected.

- **Update Links On Save.** By default, this option is selected, which means that Word checks the Web page's links each time you save a Web page document. If Word finds a broken link, you'll receive an error message that provides an option for fixing the link before saving.

In addition to folder options, the Files tab provides two check boxes related to the default editing applications associated with Web pages. You can specify that you want Word to automatically check whether any Microsoft Office program or Word specifically is registered as the default Web page editor for a Web page. By default, the option to check whether Office is the default editor for Web pages created in Office is selected. This setting means that pages built in Word will be displayed in Word, whereas pages built in Microsoft Excel or Microsoft FrontPage will be opened in those programs. Keep in mind that you can open a Web page in any Web editor application, regardless of which application is set as the default editor. To do so, simply open the application you want to use as a Web page editor, and then open the document from within the application.

Targeting Monitor Specifications

The Pictures tab in the Web Options dialog box, shown in Figure 31-5, has been pared down in Word 2002. On this tab, you simply define a couple of target monitor settings for typical viewers. Basically, when you configure these settings you're instructing Word to optimize a Web page for the selected monitor. For most Web surfers, a typical monitor size is 800 by 600 pixels, with 96 pixels per inch. If you know that your audience uses other settings, you can optimize for those monitor settings. Regardless of your settings here, you should check all your Web pages using various screen settings before you post your pages live. As a Web designer, you want your Web pages to look their best for the largest possible number of people.

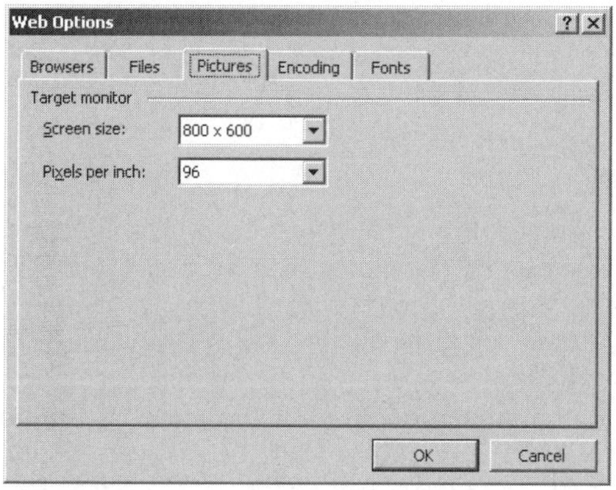

Figure 31-5. You can instruct Word to optimize a Web page for specific screen sizes and pixels-per-inch settings.

Selecting Encoding Options

The Encoding tab in the Web Options dialog box, shown in Figure 31-6, enables you to choose a language code from among those installed on your computer. *Encoding* refers to the byte or byte sequence that represents each character in your HTML or plain-text files. You can choose a language code for the current page if the page is not already displayed with the correct language encoding (by selecting a language code in the Reload The Current Document As drop-down list). You can also save the current document with a particular language code by clicking the Save This Document As down arrow, selecting a language code in the drop-down list, and then clicking OK. If you know that you always want to save Web pages using the encoding language selected in the Save This Document As list, you can select the Always Save Web Pages In The Default Encoding check box. This setting comes in handy if you reuse pages from other sources and want to store every page using one encoding language.

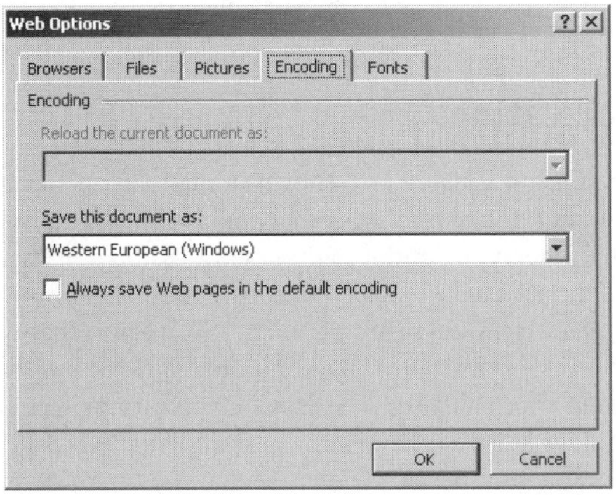

Figure 31-6. You can specify language encoding for documents that are currently displayed, for documents that are about to be saved, or for current and future Web pages you open in Word.

Choosing Default Fonts

The last tab in the Web Options dialog box is the Fonts tab, shown in Figure 31-7. On the Fonts tab, you can configure the following default settings:

- **Character Set** enables you to choose the character set that's used to encode the file. A character set is basically a mapping between the selected language's characters and a combination of numbers, letters, and symbols. For example, in ASCII (one of the most widely used character sets), the code 65 maps to the letter *A*. Most likely, the default setting is the character set you'll want to use for your Web pages.

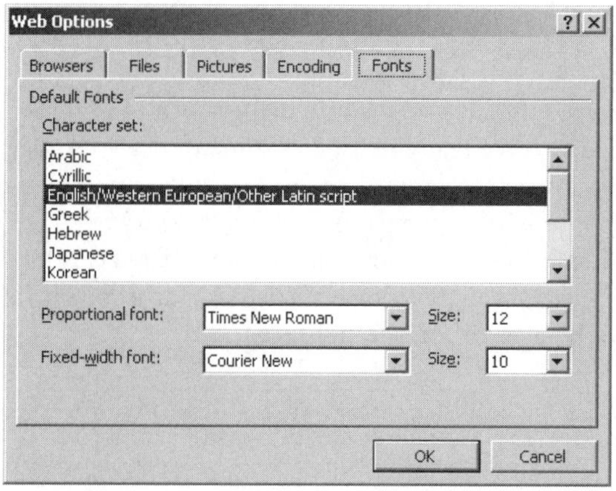

Figure 31-7. The Fonts tab enables you to set default font styles that will come into play when a Web page doesn't specifically assign a font style or size to text.

- **Proportional Font** specifies the font used for normal text if the Web page doesn't assign a font style. You can set a default font size in pixels in the Size box.
- **Fixed-Width Font** specifies the font used for fixed-width elements if a Web page doesn't assign a font style. You can set a default font size in pixels in the Size box.

Universal Web Page Fonts

When you use fonts in your Web pages, keep in mind that only the following select fonts are universally recognized as cross-platform fonts (which means they'll be displayed properly on both Macs and PCs):

- Arial
- Arial Narrow
- Comic Sans
- Courier New
- Georgia Times
- New Roman (or Times)
- Trebuchet
- Verdana

If your Web pages will be viewed by a large, diverse audience (as would be the case on the Internet), you should consider sticking with these fonts when you design Web pages.

Building Web Pages and Web Sites

Now that you've mastered the details of configuring Word to serve as a Web page editor according to your needs, you're ready to look at some of the Web page creation features in Word. As mentioned, you can choose from a variety of approaches when you're creating Web pages: You can save an existing document as a Web page, open a new blank Web page, base your Web page on templates, or create an entire site using the Web Page Wizard. In this section, we'll take a brief look at some of the techniques you can use to get your Web pages off on the right foot.

The process of saving existing documents as Web pages is discussed in the section "Saving Your Web Pages," on page 718.

Starting from Scratch

New Web Page

If you want to create a Web page without using a template, your best bet is to start by opening a blank Web page. To do so, open the New Document task pane (by choosing File, New), and click the Blank Web Page link. When you open a blank Web page, Word automatically disables features that aren't supported on the Web by the target browser(s) specified on the Browsers tab in the Web Options dialog box (as described in the section "Specifying Target Browser Options," on page 708). For example, underline colors aren't supported when you create Web pages. In addition, the New Blank Document icon on the Standard toolbar changes to a New Web Page icon, so when you're working on a Web page, you can quickly create a new, blank Web page by clicking the New Web Page button on the Standard toolbar.

To customize your Web pages, you can integrate of number of Word features, just as you do when you create other Word documents. The following features will come in especially handy when you're creating Web pages:

- **Frames.** You can display multiple Web pages at one time by using frames, as described in Chapter 23, "Using Word's Desktop Publishing Features." The most common way to use frames in Web pages is to present a menu bar in a side frame that contains hyperlinks to the Web site's Web pages. As users click the hyperlinks in the menu frame, the associated Web page's contents are displayed in the main frame.
- **Tables.** When you create Web pages, you can use tables to help control your page's layout. Using tables in Web pages is an extremely popular technique for page setup, and some of the Word Web page templates take advantage of tables, as you'll see in the next section, "Using Web Page Templates." For more information about working with tables, see Chapter 18, "Organizing Concepts in Tables," as well as the section "Using Tables to Align Web Page Elements," on page 724.

- **Themes.** You can quickly add a background, text formatting, bullets, and horizontal rules to Web pages by applying themes. For more information about themes, see Chapter 23, "Using Word's Desktop Publishing Features." If you work through the Web Page Wizard to create a Web site, you'll be able to apply a theme as you create your foundation Web site. For more information about the Web Page Wizard, see the section "Using the Web Page Wizard," on page 716.

Remember, creating a Web page from a blank Web page document is the same as creating a document from a new, blank document. If you'd like to jump-start your Web page creation project, you might want to try out the default Web page templates provided in Word, as described next.

Using Web Page Templates

If you need a little help getting started on your Web page, you can turn to the templates available in the Templates dialog box for ideas. You'll probably find that Word provides a template that will serve your needs nicely. By default, Word offers seven Web page templates (in addition to the Blank Web Page template): Column With Contents, Frequently Asked Questions, Left-Aligned Column, Personal Web Page, Right-Aligned Column, Simple Layout, and Table Of Contents.

To access the Web page templates, follow these simple steps:

1. Choose File, New to open the New Document task pane.
2. Click the General Templates link, and in the Templates dialog box, click the Web Pages tab, shown in Figure 31-8.

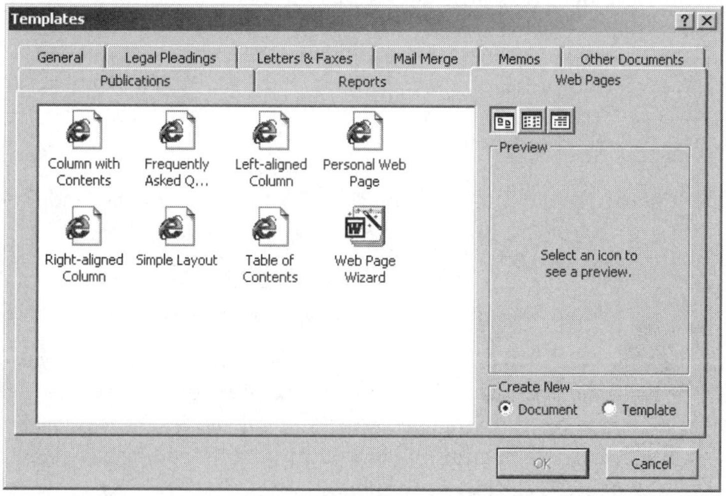

Figure 31-8. By default, Word includes seven Web page templates that contain preformatted page layouts and placeholder text.

3 Select the template you want to use, make sure that Document is selected in the Create New section, and then click OK.

4 When the template document opens, replace the placeholder text and graphics with your contents.

tip To best retain a Web page template's formatting and hyperlink settings, replace each placeholder element individually, instead of deleting the template's contents and attempting to rebuild the template's page layout.

The main advantage of using templates is that you can instantly start to focus on your Web page's contents instead of the page's layout and formatting.

Using the Web Page Wizard

To streamline Web page creation beyond using templates, you might want to put the Web Page Wizard to work. When you work though this wizard, you have the opportunity to add existing documents and Web pages to your Web site, apply a theme, insert a hyperlink bar (such as a navigation bar or a menu bar), and automatically use frames. By the time you complete the wizard, you'll have an almost complete Web page or Web site that you can fine-tune to suit your preferences.

tip **Prepare text before running the Web Page Wizard**

If possible, prepare a text file for each page you plan to include in your Web site using standard Word default styles, such as Heading 1, Normal, and so forth. If your existing Word documents use default Word headings, your Web pages' text will be automatically formatted according to the theme you select while working through the Web Page Wizard.

To use the Web Page Wizard, follow these steps:

1 Choose File, New to open the New Document task pane, and click the General Templates link to open the Templates dialog box.

2 Click the Web Pages tab, and double-click the Web Page Wizard. The Web Page Wizard Start page opens. Click Next to continue to the next page.

3 On the Title And Location page, enter a name for your Web site and the path where the main page of your Web site should be stored. Make sure that you enter short, descriptive text for the title text—this text will be displayed in viewers' title bars, so you'll want to be sure that it clearly identifies your Web page. Click Next to continue.

4. On the Navigation page, specify whether you want to use a vertical or horizontal frame for navigation by clicking Vertical Frame or Horizontal Frame, or click Separate Page to provide navigation via hyperlinks rather than a navigation or menu bar. Click Next to continue.
5. The Add Pages page allows you to specify which pages to include in your new Web site. You can add new pages, pages based on templates, or pages based on existing files. Click Next to move to the next page.
6. On the Organize Pages page, select a page in the list and click Move Up or Move Down to change the page's order in the navigation bar. You'll want your home page to be displayed at the top of your list. You can also select a page in the list and click Rename to open the Rename Hyperlink dialog box and change the name of the selected page. Click Next to continue.
7. On the Visual Theme page, specify whether to use a theme for your Web site. By default, the default theme will be selected for your Web site. If you want to select a different theme, click Browse Themes to open the Theme dialog box. Click Next to view the final page.
8. Click Finish on the End page to create your Web site.

You'll find that the Web Page Wizard will enable you to quickly pull together a functional Web page or Web site that you can customize to suit your needs. The wizard comes in especially handy when you're creating Web pages based on existing documents. For example, you might want to use the Web Page Wizard to create an online résumé based on an existing Word version of your résumé, or maybe you'd like to post your company's policies on line and you already have the policies in Word format. Using existing documents, the Web Page Wizard can help you to quickly create a Web site containing formatting and hyperlinks to related information.

tip **Modify your Web pages for your server**

Before you create a Web site using Word's Web Page Wizard, you should check with your Internet hosting service or network administrator regarding a few specifics. Namely, you should check your server's policies regarding .htm vs. .html extensions, default vs. index home-page naming schemes, and the use of spaces in file names. By default, the Web Page Wizard generates HTML files using .htm extensions and allows you to use file names that contain spaces. In addition, the wizard names your home page *default.htm* instead of *index.htm*. If your server doesn't support the wizard's defaults, you'll have to edit your Web page's HTML code to conform to your server's specifications.

Saving Your Web Pages

After you create a Web page document but before you get too far into Web page development, you need to save your Web pages. As with most document creation tasks, you should always (always, always, always) save your work frequently to avoid losing data due to unexpected system failures or power losses.

Saving Web pages involves a couple of key tasks that don't come into play when you save standard word processing documents. Specifically, you need to verify or add Web title bar text, and you need to determine whether you want to save your Web page so that you can continue to edit it in Word or save it in as streamlined a form as possible for publication on the Internet.

InsideOut

When you save a Web page, Word doesn't create a backup copy, even if you select the Always Create Backup Copy check box on the Save tab in the Options dialog box (choose Tools, Options, and click the Save tab). If you want to store a backup copy of a Web page, you'll need to use the Save As dialog box to manually save the document twice, using two different names or storing the files in two different locations.

Adding Title Bar Text

As you've probably noticed while surfing the Web, Web pages display text in your browser's title bar. The browser knows what text to display in the title bar by reading the HTML code in a Web page's header section. Using Word, you can add a title to a Web page without editing the document's source code. (If you've created a Web page using the Web Page Wizard, your page will already have title text assigned.) One of the most convenient ways to add title bar text to a Web page is to do so while saving the document, as described here:

1. With your Web page document open, choose File, Save As. The Save As dialog box opens.
2. In the Save As Type drop-down list, select Web Page or Web Page, Filtered. (The differences between these two file types are described in the next section, "Web Page vs. Web Page, Filtered.") As soon as you choose a Web page file type, the Save As dialog box changes to include the Change Title button, as shown in Figure 31-9.

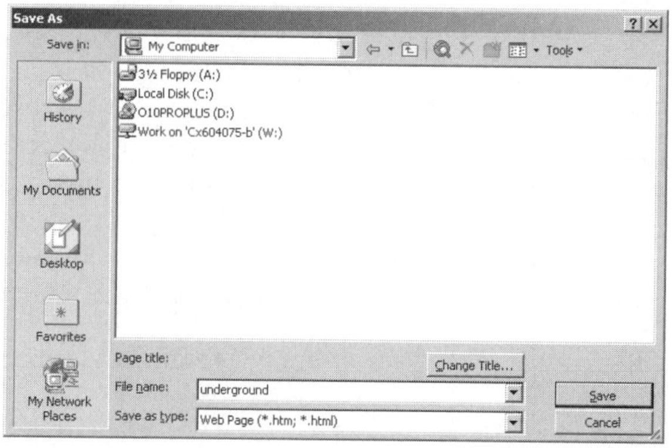

Figure 31-9. When you specify a Web page file type, the Save As dialog box changes to include the Change Title button.

3 Click the Change Title button. The Set Page Title dialog box opens, as shown in Figure 31-10.

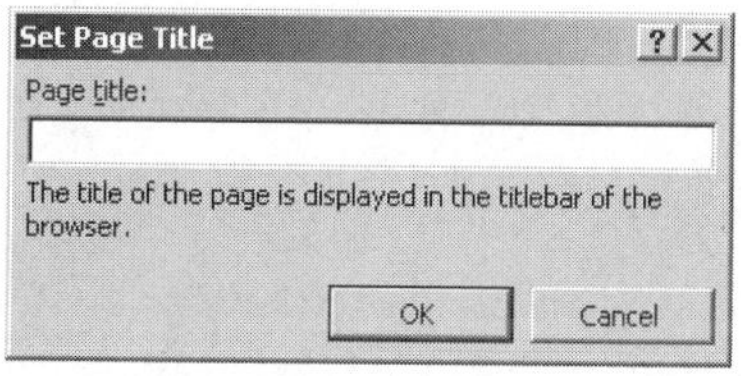

Figure 31-10. The Set Page Title dialog box enables you to add or modify a Web page's title bar text.

4 Type the title bar text for the Web page, and click OK.

5 Click Save to save your document.

When you display your Web page in a browser, the text you entered in the Set Page Title dialog box will be displayed in the browser's title bar. When you add title bar text, you should make the text as clear and descriptive as possible. The title text is also displayed on the Windows taskbar, so making the text concise and clear can help users find and return to your page if they're working with multiple windows open.

tip You can also change a document's title bar text by modifying the file's properties. To do so, open the file, choose File, Properties, click the Summary tab, and then type text in the Title box. Click OK to save your changes.

newfeature!

Web Page vs. Web Page, Filtered

As mentioned, you can save Web pages in two main formats: Web Page and Web Page, Filtered. Each file type serves a particular purpose. When you save a document using the Web Page file type, the document can be viewed on line. In addition, you can continue to edit the document in Word without a hitch. In contrast, when you save a document using the Web Page, Filtered format, tags specific to Microsoft Office are removed from the file's source code. This removal reduces the file size (and smaller file sizes mean faster download and display times when you're viewing files on the Web), but you lose some Office editing functionality. If you save a document using Web Page, Filtered and then reopen the file in an Office program, the text and general appearance of the page will be preserved, but some features might work differently or incorrectly.

You should follow these basic rules when saving Web pages in Word:

- If your Web page is a work in progress, save the document using the Web Page file type. That way, you'll retain full editing capabilities.
- If you've completed editing the Web page and you're ready to post it, save the document using the Web Page, Filtered file type to create the smallest possible document file with the cleanest HTML source code.

After you decide how you'd like to save your Web page document, you can do so as follows:

1. While your Web page document is open, choose File, Save As.
2. Type a name for the file in the File Name box, click the Save As Type down arrow, and choose Web Page (*.htm , *.html) or Web Page, Filtered (*.htm, *.html) in the drop-down list.
3. With the Save In drop-down list, navigate to the desired location, and then click Save.

When you save a Word document as a Web page that contains pictures, drawing objects, and other graphics not saved as JPEG (or JPG), GIF, or PNG files, Word saves copies of the graphics with the HMTL document using the JPG, GIF, or PNG format, as appropriate. (Pictures are saved as JPG graphics, and drawings are usually saved as GIF graphics.) When Word automatically converts images, it names and numbers the images image001.gif, image002.jpg, image003.png, and so forth.

tip **Maintain working versions of your Web pages**

If you think you'll need to edit a Web page in Word later but you need to post it on line now, consider maintaining two files—one in Web Page format and one in Web Page, Filtered format. You can edit the content in the Web Page document, save it as a Web Page document for future editing, and then save another copy of the file as Web Page, Filtered, which you can post on line.

newfeature!

Creating Web Archives (MHTML)

Web Archive

In addition to saving Web page documents, you can create *Web archives.* A Web archive contains all the elements of a Web page, including the text (HTML source code) and graphics files (pictures, background graphics, bullet images, and so forth), in a single file. An archive file can be likened to HTML-formatted messages and complete Web pages that can be sent in many e-mail applications. The Web archive encapsulation allows you to publish your entire Web site as a single MHTML (MIME [Multipurpose Internet Mail Extensions] encapsulation of aggregate HTML documents) file or send an entire Web site as an e-mail message or attachment. This format is supported by Internet Explorer 4 and later.

To save a Web page as a Web archive, you simply specify the Web Archive file type in the Save As dialog box, as follows:

1. Open the Web page, and choose File, Save As.
2. In the Save As dialog box, choose Web Archive in the Save As Type drop-down list.
3. Name the file, specify the location where you want to store the file, and click Save.

After you create a Web archive, you can move the file anywhere without losing the graphics. In addition, Web archives tend to be smaller overall than the original Web page and associated graphics stored as separate files. The major drawback to Web archives is that not all browsers support MHTML yet, so if you use this format to post Web pages, you risk losing viewers who use browsers that don't support the MHTML format.

Configuring Web View Options

After you create your core Web page documents and save your documents (including adding title bar text), you're well into Web page creation territory. As you start to design your Web pages, you're going to need to keep track of whether your content will be displayed according to your design plans when the page is displayed in Web browsers. To help you keep an eye on your pages, Word provides a number of Web-centric views you can use while you create and modify Web pages, as follows:

- **Web Layout view.** Web Layout view is the working view in Word when you're creating Web pages and documents that will be viewed on screen. When you're in this view, you can see backgrounds, text wrapping, and graphics in a manner similar to how the page will be displayed in a browser. To switch to Web Layout view, choose View, Web Layout, or click the Web Layout View button to the left of the horizontal scroll bar.

- **Web Page Preview.** You can view your Web page documents in your browser at any time. You should do this frequently to ensure that your page will be displayed as planned. To view an open Web page document in your browser, choose File, Web Page Preview. If your browser isn't open, it opens automatically, and the current Web page document is displayed in your browser. To return to Word, close or minimize your browser window, and redisplay the Word window.
- **HTML source code.** You can view and edit a Web page's HTML source code at any time. To do so, choose View, HTML Source. You might have to install the Microsoft Script Editor the first time you choose this option. If a message box appears, stating that you need to install the script editor, insert your installation CD, and then click OK in the installation message box. For more information about editing source code, see the section "Editing Source Code Using the Microsoft Script Editor," on page 750.

In addition to using these views, you should always check your Web pages in a variety of browsers (including past and present versions of Internet Explorer and Netscape Navigator) and on various platforms (at least on the Mac and PC) before you publish your Web pages on line. If you're designing for the Internet, you'll want your Web pages to look the best possible to the widest audience. Of course, if you're designing for a company network, you'll probably have to test your Web pages only on the browser types and versions used by employees.

tip **View your pages on various platforms**

Although checking your Web pages on various platforms is highly recommended, it's not always easily accomplished. If you don't have a test network set up for this purpose, you can use some creative ingenuity to check your Web pages. For example, consider posting your pages on line in a temporary directory. Then you can ask friends, relatives, and associates to view the temporary pages on their systems. You can also copy your files to a disk and take the disk to a nearby copy store to view your Web pages on their computers (for which you will probably be charged a fee). Or you can check out your Web pages on your local library's computers if it provides Internet access for members or allows you to bring your own disks. Finally, if you don't want to buy another computer or two for testing purposes, you can purchase software that enables you to install and run multiple operating systems on a single computer. Currently, VMWare is a popular software package that enables you to run multiple operating systems. You can find out about the software by visiting the company's Web site, at *www.vmware.com.*

Working with Web Page Text and Tables

When you create Web pages, you enter information in the same way you enter information in other Word documents. The main concerns you need to address when creating Web text are to keep formatting simple, ensure that text is concise, and provide guidance for aligning components.

Adding Text and Headings

When you add text and headings to your Web pages, you should try to use Word's default styles, available in the Normal template. That way, if you later apply a theme to your Web page, the formatting will be directly applied to your document, without extra formatting efforts on your part. Keep in mind that Web text is different from hard copy text. Generally, people read online text 25 percent more slowly than they read printed text. You can improve your Web pages' readability by keeping information concise and easily scannable. The following general rules of thumb might prove helpful when you create a Web page:

- Introduce a single idea per paragraph.
- Use simple sentence structure, and keep sentences short without dumbing down your content.
- Limit paragraphs to 75 words or fewer.
- Use bulleted lists whenever possible.
- Use numbered lists when you're presenting a series of steps.
- Insert headings and subheadings to break up text and highlight key points.
- Keep headings simple and direct. (When in doubt, choose meaningful headings over clever ones.)
- Make sure that your information is presented in a logical hierarchy.
- Separate paragraphs with empty space (commonly referred to as *white space*).
- Avoid adding too many hyperlinks to your page's body text.
- Carefully check your spelling and grammar.
- Avoid tiny print, busy backgrounds, hard-to-see colors, and the like.

You want to make your main ideas jump out at readers. If your main ideas strike a chord with a reader, the reader will then move on to read the more detailed information. In addition to these text rules, remember that although theoretically Web pages are infinitely wide and infinitely long, you don't have to create ultra-long and ultra-wide documents. In most cases, a long Web page is usually easier to digest if it's divided into a number of shorter pages that are linked by means of hyperlinks on a menu bar.

tip **Avoid underlining nonlinked text**

When you create Web text, avoid using underlining. Many people have become accustomed to associating underlined text in online documents with hyperlinks. If you underline nonhyperlinked text, viewers might become annoyed by clicking nonlinked text.

InsideOut

Using an Animated GIF to Create Animated Text for the Web

When you create Web text in Word, be aware that the Animate Text formatting feature found on the Text Effects tab in the Font dialog box doesn't work on line (even though it seems like a natural fit). If you want to include animated text, consider creating an animated GIF. A number of free animated GIF builders and prebuilt animated GIFs are available for download on the Internet.

Using Tables to Align Web Page Elements

Many browsers (old and new) support tables without a hitch. Therefore, hordes of Web designers have gravitated toward using tables to help align information on Web pages. A number of the Web page templates provided with Word use tables to align information. For example, Figure 31-11 shows the Left-Aligned Column template; notice the light gray lines used to denote the table cells. (The table borders are hidden when the page is displayed in a browser.)

For more information about creating and using tables, see Chapter 18, "Organizing Concepts in Tables."

When you design Web pages, you'll frequently find that using a table simplifies your task. Fortunately, creating tables in Web pages is the same as creating tables in standard Word documents. You can format cells, borders, backgrounds, and so forth in the same manner. The main "trick" to using tables effectively in Web pages is to ensure that at least one cell is formatted to be a relative size (meaning that after the other table cells are displayed in a user's browser according to the table size settings, the relative table cell resizes to fit the remainder of the user's browser window). When you use tables in this manner, your Web page will resize to fit a browser's window. The sidebar, on the facing page, illustrates this concept.

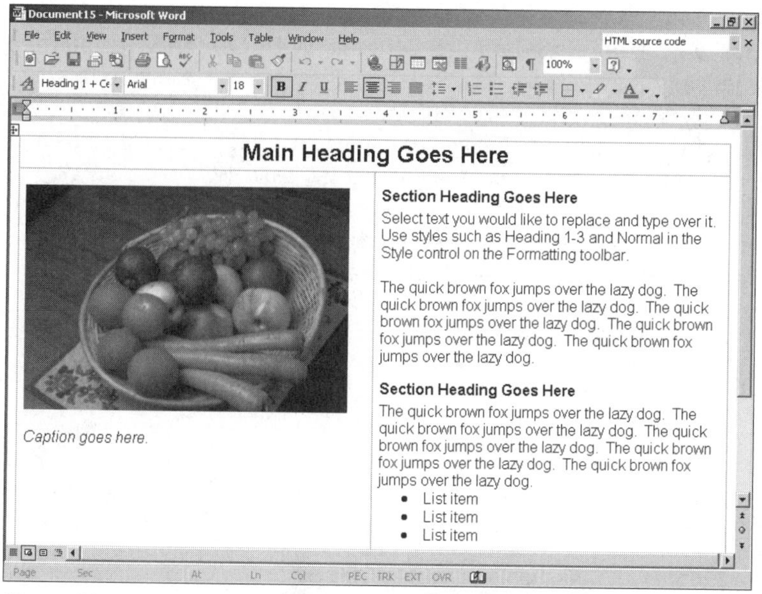

Figure 31-11. A number of Web page templates in Word use tables to align the Web page's content.

Troubleshooting

I Want a Web Page Based on the Columns With Contents Template to Resize Automatically

Word includes one default Web page template that's formatted as a table but isn't formatted to resize automatically—the Columns With Contents template. To fix this template's little oversight, you need to remove the width setting for the cell that contains the Web page's main content, as follows:

1. After you create a new document based on the Column With Contents template, click in the main content cell (the cell that contains the placeholder text *Section 1 Heading Goes Here*).
2. Choose Table, Table Properties.
3. Click the Cell tab, clear the Preferred Width check box so that the cell isn't formatted to be a specific width, and then click OK.

(continued)

I Want a Web Page Based on the Columns With Contents Template to Resize Automatically *(continued)* The page's content area will stretch to fill your window area regardless of how you resize your window, as shown in Figure 31-12. When you use tables to create other Web pages, determine which area should automatically resize to fill a user's browser, and then format the table cells accordingly. If you aren't sure at first which cell to format, experiment one at a time with a few cells, preview the Web page in a browser each time you make a change, and then resize the window to see whether the table specifications are effective.

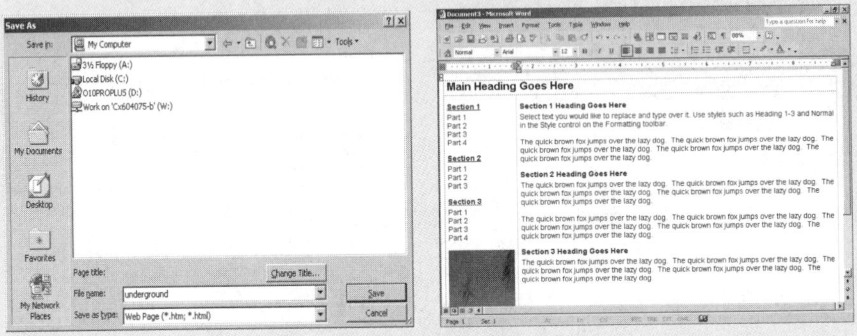

Figure 31-12. Here a document based on the Column With Contents template has been modified so that the page automatically fills the browser window.

Including Hyperlinks

If you create Web pages, you're going to want to include hyperlinks. After all, the ability to jump from document to document (or from file location to file location) using hyperlinks is a major drawing point of the Web. (Imagine entering a URL in the Address box every time you wanted to visit a Web page!) Because hyperlinks play such a large role in text navigation these days, Word provides convenient ways to create and modify hyperlinks in your documents.

As you probably know, hyperlinks are text or graphics that have been formatted to serve as links to other files or file locations when users click them. Every hyperlink consists of two main components: an *anchor* and a *target*. The part of the hyperlink you click is the anchor, and the information you see in response to clicking an anchor is the target. When you create hyperlinks, you must specify the anchor information and enter the address or location of the target information. In addition, you can add a third component to hyperlinks, called *ScreenTips*. A ScreenTip is the text that is displayed when you hover your mouse pointer over a hyperlink. Using Word, you can easily create text, graphic, and e-mail hyperlinks, as described in this section.

Controlling Automatic Hyperlinks

By default, Web and e-mail addresses are automatically formatted as hyperlinks when you type them in a Word document if Word can easily recognize the text as a Web address or an e-mail address. For example, if you type **www.creationguide.com**, Word will format the text as a Web address, but if you type **creationguide.com**, Word won't format the text as a hyperlink. To work around this, you could type **www.creationguide.com**, and then after Word formats the hyperlink, you could delete the *www.* portion of the Web address. Similarly, you could you could add *http://* in front of a Web address that doesn't start with *www.* to indicate that the text is a Web address, as in *http://creationguide.com*.

This automatic formatting feature is usually welcome, but at times you might prefer to turn off the feature. To change this setting, you must configure the AutoCorrect options, as follows:

1. Choose Tools, AutoCorrect Options, and click the AutoFormat As You Type tab.
2. Clear the Internet And Network Paths With Hyperlinks check box, and click OK.

After you turn off this AutoCorrect option, Word will no longer automatically format Web and e-mail addresses as hyperlinks in your documents. As you might expect, existing hyperlinks will not be affected.

tip **Change the Ctrl+click hyperlink setting in Word**

By default, you must press Ctrl+click to follow a hyperlink while you're working in Word. This setup is convenient because it enables you to click within a hyperlink to edit its text. At times, though, you might find the combination is unnecessary or cumbersome. If that's the case, you can turn off this setting (so that you can simply click hyperlinks to follow them when you're working in Word). To remove the Ctrl+click setting, choose Tools, Options, click the Edit tab, and then clear the Use Ctrl+Click To Follow Hyperlink check box.

Creating Text Hyperlinks

Any text, including characters, words, phrases, headings, paragraphs, and so forth can be formatted to serve as a hyperlink. To create a text hyperlink, follow these steps:

1. Select the text you want to format as a hyperlink, or position your insertion point where you want to insert a text hyperlink. Generally, it's easier to type and then select a hyperlink's text, but you can add the text as you build a hyperlink as well.

Hyperlink

2 Click the Hyperlink button on the Standard toolbar, or right-click the selected text or at the insertion point and choose Hyperlink on the shortcut menu. The Insert Hyperlink dialog box appears, as shown in Figure 31-13.

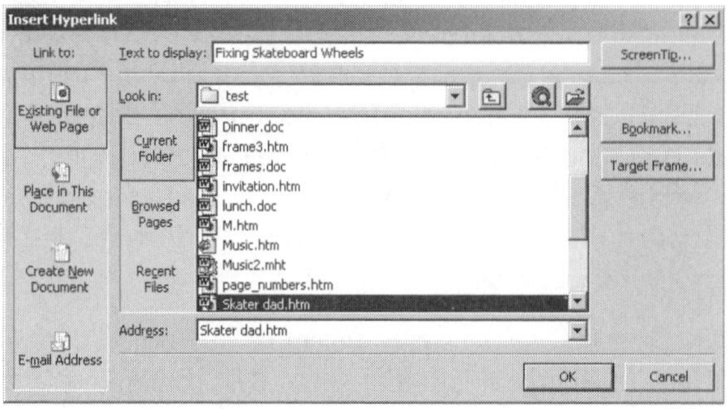

Figure 31-13. The Insert Hyperlink dialog box helps you specify the target for a hyperlink; you can choose any file, file location, or e-mail address to serve as a hyperlink target.

3 Verify that the Text To Display box shows the text you want to use to create the hyperlink. If not, you can modify the text to suit your needs. Keep in mind that the text you insert in this text box will be displayed on your page; it will be inserted at the insertion point or replace the text you selected in step 1.

4 Next you need to specify the hyperlink's target file, file location, or e-mail address. To do so, click a button in the Link To section to specify the type of hyperlink you'll be creating. You can select from among the following types of hyperlink targets:

- **Existing File Or Web Page.** You can use this option if your hyperlink will link to an existing file or Web page. If the page you're linking to contains headings or bookmarks, you can format the hyperlink to jump directly to a particular heading or bookmark location. To do so, specify the file you want to link to, click the Bookmark button, and then click the bookmark or heading you want users to see when they click the hyperlink.
- **Place In This Document.** You can create hyperlinks that jump to headings or bookmarks in the current document. When you click the Place In This Document button, the Insert Hyperlink dialog box changes to display a list of the headings and bookmarks in the current document. To create the hyperlink, verify the Text To Display text, click the Place In This Document button, click a listed heading or bookmark, and click OK. This type of hyperlink comes in handy

when you want to include a Return To Top link at the bottom of a page or if you have a long page with a list of links at the top of the page that enables viewers to jump to lower areas in the document.

> **tip** To create a bookmark in your document, position your insertion point where you want to insert a bookmark, and choose Insert, Bookmark. Then, in the Bookmark dialog box, type a bookmark name without spaces, and click Add.

- **Create New Document.** You can use this option to create a hyperlink to a page that hasn't been created yet. When you click the Create New Document button, the Insert Hyperlink dialog box changes to display a text box you can use to name a new document. You can then specify whether you want to edit the new document now or later. When you name a new document, make sure you include the .htm extension so that Word will create a Web page document instead of a Word document.
- **E-Mail Address.** You can use this option to create hyperlinks that users can click to open a preaddressed e-mail message window. For more information about creating e-mail hyperlinks, see the section "Inserting an E-Mail Hyperlink," on page 731.

5. After you choose one of the preceding options, select the file or file location you want the hyperlink to link to or type a Web address in the Address box. Figure 31-13 shows the Insert Hyperlink dialog box with information in the Address box, which links the hyperlink to another document stored in the current folder.
6. After you configure the hyperlink's target and text display information, click the ScreenTip button. The Set Hyperlink ScreenTip dialog box opens, as shown in Figure 31-14.

Figure 31-14. The Set Hyperlink ScreenTip dialog box enables you to specify the text that appears when users hover their mouse pointer over a hyperlink.

7. Type text in the ScreenTip Text box, and then click OK.
8. Click OK in the Insert Hyperlink dialog box to complete the hyperlink creation process.

Using Drag and Drop to Create Hyperlinks

If you want to create a hyperlink in one document to access information in another document, you can use the right-click and drag method, as follows:

1. Open both documents, and arrange them so that you can see both documents at once.
2. In the target file (the file containing the information you want to link to), select text you want to use as the hyperlink's display text. Then right-click the selected text, and drag it into the other document. When the insertion point is positioned where you want to insert the hyperlink, release the right mouse button.
3. On the shortcut menu that appears, choose Create Hyperlink Here.

Keep in mind that you can't drag drawing objects to create hyperlinks; for those types of objects, you have to use the standard hyperlink procedures, as described in the next section, "Linking Graphics." If you use the right-click and drag method to create hyperlinks and you plan to post the Web pages on line, you might find it easiest to store the files in the same folder. That way, you won't lose or confuse the hyperlink information when you upload the pages to the server.

tip **Set the hyperlink base**

You can set the base address for a document if you want all hyperlinks to automatically include the base address information in their paths. To specify a base address, choose File, Properties, click the Summary tab, enter the base address in the Hyperlink Base box, and then click OK.

Linking Graphics

You can create graphics hyperlinks in the same way you create text hyperlinks. When you design Web pages, you'll find that some graphics make particularly intuitive hyperlinks, including the following:

- Graphic buttons that link to subpages in a Web site
- Logos that consistently link to a company's home page
- Small (thumbnail) pictures that link to larger versions of the pictures
- E-mail graphics that link to preaddressed e-mail message windows
- Pictures that link to Web pages elaborating on the pictures, such as a picture of the company's president that's linked to a Letter From The President page.

To access the Insert Hyperlink dialog box when you're formatting a graphic as a hyperlink, click the image or drawing object and click the Hyperlink button, or right-click the picture or drawing object and choose Hyperlink on the shortcut menu. After you open the Insert Hyperlink dialog box, you configure the hyperlink information in the same way you configure text hyperlinks, as described in the section "Creating Text Hyperlinks," on page 727.

Creating Linked Banners and Navigation Buttons

You can combine Word features to create stylish linked banners and buttons. For example, you can create banners using WordArt (see Chapter 17, "Customizing Documents with WordArt"), and you can create buttons by using Word's drawing tools, AutoShapes, and text boxes (as described in Chapter 16, "Enlivening Documents with Drawings and AutoShapes"). After you create a banner or button in Word, you can format the object as a hyperlink by right-clicking the object and choosing Hyperlink on the shortcut menu or by clicking the object and then clicking the Hyperlink button on the Standard toolbar.

If you want to reuse a drawing object on several Web pages, you might want to save the object as a standard image file so that the button or banner appears consistently throughout your site. To turn a drawing object into an image, follow these steps. (You'll need a drawing program to complete this procedure, such as Microsoft Paint.)

1. Display the WordArt, button, or other drawing object on screen.
2. Press Print Scrn.
3. Open a drawing program, and paste the contents of your system Clipboard into the program. For example, in Paint, choose Edit, Paste, or press Ctrl+V.
4. Crop the WordArt or drawing object.
5. Resize the object to its approximate display size if necessary.
6. Save the image as a GIF file for use on your Web page.

After you create the GIF image, you can insert it in your Web page and format the image as a hyperlink, just as you insert and format other image files. For more information about inserting images in Web pages, see the section "Working with Web Graphics," on page 734.

Inserting an E-Mail Hyperlink

The last type of hyperlink we'll look at here is an e-mail hyperlink. E-mail hyperlinks are frequently used on Web pages to present an E-Mail The Webmaster link or other similar "contact us" types of link. When a user clicks an e-mail hyperlink, an e-mail message window opens, containing an e-mail address in the To box that you specified for the hyperlink. You can also automatically configure the Subject line's text.

To create an e-mail hyperlink, follow these steps:

1. Select the text or graphic you want to display as a hyperlink or position your insertion point where you want to insert the hyperlink, and then click the Hyperlink button on the Standard toolbar.
2. In the Link To section in the Insert Hyperlink dialog box, click the E-Mail Address button. The Insert Hyperlink dialog box changes to accommodate creating e-mail hyperlinks.
3. In the E-Mail Address box, enter the e-mail address you want to associate with the hyperlink, or, if available, click the e-mail address in the Recently Used E-Mail Addresses list, as shown in Figure 31-15. Notice that when you enter an e-mail address, Word automatically adds the *mailto:* prefix.

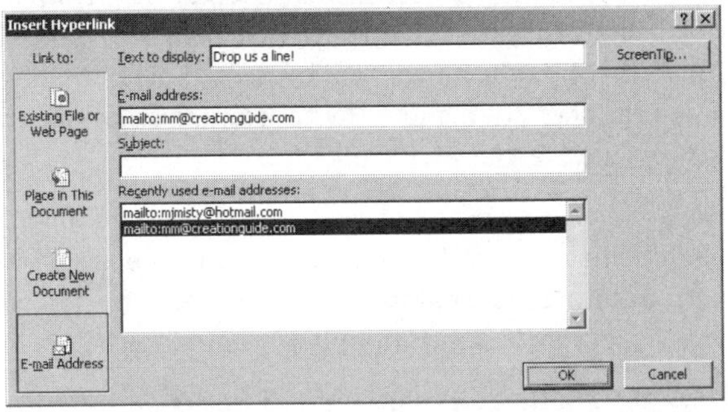

Figure 31-15. When you create an e-mail hyperlink, you can specify the To line e-mail address, ScreenTip information, and a Subject line for the e-mail message.

4. Verify or change the Text To Display text, and type text in the Subject box, if desired.
5. Click the ScreenTip button, enter ScreenTip information in the Set Hyperlink ScreenTip dialog box, and click OK.
6. Click OK in the Insert Hyperlink dialog box to complete the e-mail hyperlink.

tip **Use AutoCorrect to create e-mail hyperlinks**

As mentioned, you can also create e-mail hyperlinks automatically in your documents by simply typing an e-mail address directly in the body of your document. By default, AutoCorrect formats e-mail addresses typed in a document as e-mail hyperlinks.

Editing Hyperlinks

After you create text hyperlinks, you can customize their appearance just as you customize other text by using standard formatting techniques such as applying font colors and font styles.

> **tip** To easily select a hyperlink before applying formatting, right-click the hyperlink, and choose Select Hyperlink on the shortcut menu.

In addition, you can edit text, graphics, and e-mail hyperlinks by modifying the hyperlinks' properties. For example, you can make the following changes:

- **Change a hyperlink's target.** To change a hyperlink's target, right-click the hyperlink, and choose Edit Hyperlink on the shortcut menu. Then, in the Edit Hyperlink dialog box (which looks very much like the Insert Hyperlink dialog box), change the hyperlink's target information.
- **Change a text or an e-mail hyperlink's display text.** You can edit a hyperlink's text directly in the body of your document by typing over existing hyperlink text, or you can right-click a hyperlink, choose Edit Hyperlink on the shortcut menu, and change the Text To Display text in the Edit Hyperlink dialog box.
- **Remove hypertext formatting.** You can also remove hyperlink formatting from text, e-mail, and graphics hyperlinks. To do so, right-click the hyperlink, and choose Remove Hyperlink on the shortcut menu. When you remove hyperlink formatting, the hyperlink is converted to regular, nonlinked text or graphics. Keep in mind that formatted text retains its formatting (so if you manually applied boldface formatting or a font color to a hyperlink, the formatting remains intact even though the hyperlink is removed).

> **tip** To remove multiple instances of hyperlinks in a document, select the document's contents, and press Ctrl+Spacebar.

In addition to changing hyperlinks, you might want to occasionally delete hyperlinks. You delete hyperlinks in the same way you delete standard text and graphics. Select the information you want to delete, and press Delete or Backspace.

> **tip** **Modify hyperlink styles**
>
> If you want to change the style of all hyperlinks used in your Web page, your best bet is to alter the Hyperlink and FollowedHyperlink styles in the Styles And Formatting task pane. For more information about modifying styles, see Chapter 10, "Using Styles to Increase Your Formatting Power."

Working with Web Graphics

As you've seen up to now in the chapter, creating Web pages is much like creating standard Word documents, with a few twists here and there. So you won't be surprised to learn that adding graphics to your Web pages is similar to adding graphics in standard Word documents. The main difference is that Web page graphics have to be stored as one of the following graphic file types so that browsers can display them:

- **GIF.** GIFs (short for Graphics Interchange Format) are the most widely supported graphics type on the Web (which means that almost all browsers—old, new, and in-between—can display GIF images). GIF images can support up to 256 colors, and they are generally used for simple logos, line art, icons, cartoonlike illustrations, buttons, horizontal rules, bullets, backgrounds, and other graphics elements that require few colors. In addition, GIFs can include transparency and can be used to create simple animations, referred to as *animated GIFs*. (In a nutshell, an animated GIF can be likened a stack of GIF graphics that the browser flips through, like old movie flip cards, to create the appearance of movement.)

For more information about transparency, see Chapter 16, "Enlivening Documents with Drawings and AutoShapes."

- **JPEG (or JPG).** The JPEG image file format was created by and named after the Joint Photographic Experts Group. This image format supports millions of colors (24-bit color), and JPEGs are almost universally supported by browsers. Because JPEGs can contain millions of colors, this file format is usually used to display photographic images on line.
- **PNG.** PNG (pronounced "ping") stands for Portable Network Graphics. PNG images are similar to GIF images. They're small files that load quickly and are limited to 256 colors. PNG images transmit slightly faster than GIF files, but PNGs are supported only on newer browsers. At this point, if your Web pages are going to be viewed by a diverse audience using a variety of browsers, you should use GIF files instead of PNG files.

If you're creating a Web page in Word and you insert a graphic in your document that's stored as a file type other than these three file types, Word will create copies of the graphic and convert it to a JPG, GIF, or PNG file when you save the Web page document. Word will store copies of all graphics files in the HTML document's supporting files folder by default. This default action is desirable, because when you use graphics files in your Web pages, you must store your files in an orderly manner to ensure that your HTML code works properly. And when you upload your Web pages to a server, you must retain your Web page's HTML and graphics file organization so that the server can properly find all graphics files referred to in your HTML document.

Now that we have some of the Web graphics particulars taken care of, let's look at how you can use graphics in your Web pages. Generally, graphics are used in Web pages to create the following components:

- Photographs and illustrations
- Buttons and logos
- Icons, bullets, and horizontal rules
- Graphical text
- Backgrounds

As mentioned, inserting and adjusting graphics in Web pages is fundamentally the same as inserting and adjusting graphics in standard Word documents. But among Web graphics tasks, a few Web-specific topics stand out. In particular, when you create Web graphics, you'll want to specify alternative text for each graphic, and you'll probably want to know how to insert horizontal rules and graphics bullets. The next few sections briefly address these topics.

For more information about working with graphics, objects, and WordArt, see Part 2, "Adding Value with Graphics and Objects," and for more information about inserting backgrounds, see Chapter 23, "Using Word's Desktop Publishing Features."

Adding Alternative Text

When you use graphics on your Web pages, you should take a moment to think about the people who *won't* see your graphics, especially if your Web pages will be posted on the Internet. Because the Internet is worldwide, you can't accommodate all the types of Internet connections and browsers that people will be using to view your pages. It's highly likely that at least some of the people viewing your pages might be using text-only browsers or they might turn off the display of graphics in their browsers when they surf the Web so that they can display Web pages more quickly. As a Web page developer, you can specify alternative text (generally referred to as *ALT text* by Web designers) that will automatically be displayed while a graphic is loading or in a graphics area when a browser doesn't display graphics. Figure 31-16, on the next page, shows how ALT text appears in a Web page with the graphics display turned off.

ALT text is displayed in place of images under the following conditions:

- When a browser doesn't support graphics
- When a browser's settings are configured to not show graphics
- When a user experiences slow downloads
- When viewers have special needs due to visual impairment

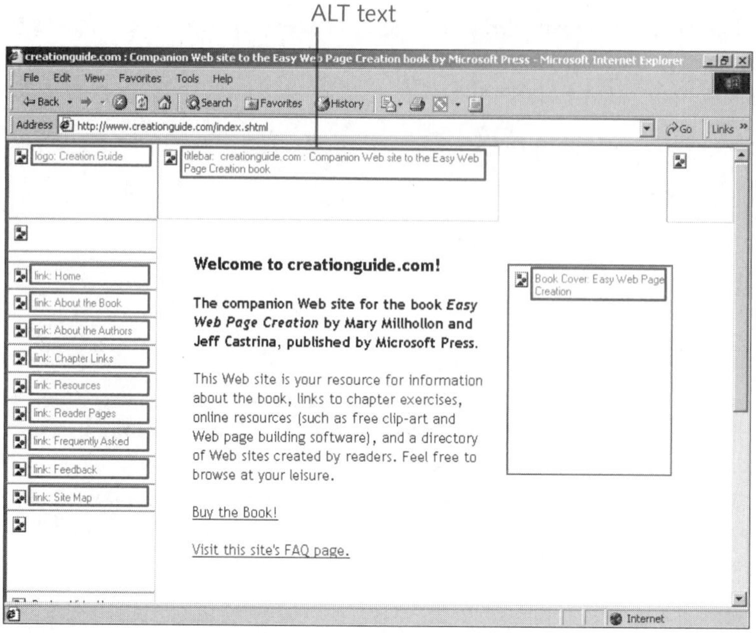

Figure 31-16. ALT text can be used to describe content areas to users who view your Web pages without graphics.

To specify ALT text for Web page graphics in Word, follow these steps:

1. With your Web page document open in Word, double-click the picture or drawing object in your Web page that you want to configure, and then click the Web tab in the Format Picture dialog box. Or click the picture or drawing object, choose Format, Picture (or Format, AutoShape), and click the Web tab.
2. In the Alternative Text box, type the text you want to display in place of the graphic, and click OK.

When you supply ALT text, you can insert as much text as you want, but keep in mind that some browsers might display only a limited number of characters. When you create ALT text, try to keep it concise and descriptive. Remember, ALT text's main purpose is to provide information to viewers who won't be viewing your graphics.

Adding Horizontal Rules

A typical type of graphic included on Web pages is a horizontal rule. Horizontal rules can be created in two main ways: by typing HTML code directly into a Web page's source code or by inserting a graphic divider. To enter HTML code for a horizontal rule (you use the <HR> tag), you need to open the Microsoft Script Editor and add the source code. The Microsoft Script Editor is introduced in the section "Editing Source

Code Using the Microsoft Script Editor," on page 750. This section looks at the other typical way to insert horizontal rules, by inserting a graphic divider.

Word makes inserting horizontal rules in Web pages easy. You can access Word's default horizontal line graphics in two main ways:

- Position the insertion point where you want to insert a divider, display the Insert Clip Art task pane, type **Web Dividers** in the Search For box, and press Enter.
- Position the insertion point where you want to insert a divider, choose Format, Borders And Shading, click the Borders tab, and click the Horizontal Line button.

As you can see in Figure 31-17, both approaches result in a similar display of available horizontal rules. To select a rule from either the Horizontal Line dialog box or the Insert Clip Art task pane, double-click the line you want to include in your Web page.

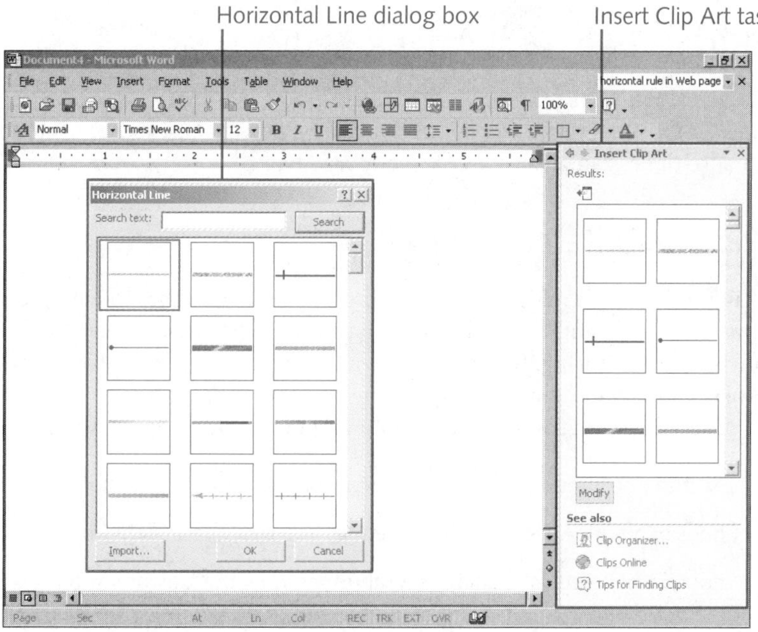

Figure 31-17. You can insert horizontal rules by displaying Word's default graphic lines and double-clicking the line you want to insert in your Web page.

After you insert a horizontal rule, you can modify its properties. If you inserted a rule using the Horizontal Line dialog box, you can right-click the line and choose Format Horizontal Line on the shortcut menu (or click the line, and choose Format, Horizontal Line) to display the Format Horizontal Line dialog box, shown in Figure 31-18, on the next page. If you inserted the rule using the Insert Clip Art task pane, you can right-click the line and choose Format Horizontal Line on the shortcut menu (or click the line, and choose Format, Picture) to display the Format Picture dialog box. (The Format Picture dialog box is discussed in Chapter 14, "Adding Visual Impact with Pictures.") Notice that you can control a line's width, height, color, and alignment using the Format Horizontal Line dialog box.

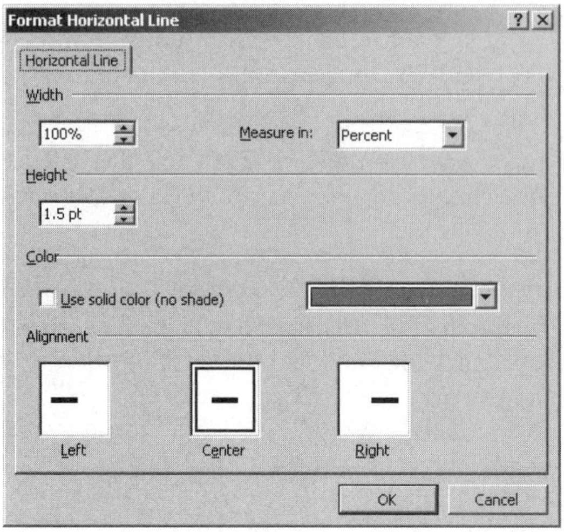

Figure 31-18. The Format Horizontal Line dialog box enables you to control the appearance of horizontal lines used in your Web pages.

Adding Picture Bullets

You can (and often should) use bulleted lists in your Web pages to help present information clearly and concisely. But being clear and concise doesn't have to be synonymous with boring. Instead of showing standard black dots every time you want to display a list, you might want to liven up your Web pages with graphics bullets. Word makes displaying a bulleted list with graphics a simple task, as described here:

1. Select the bulleted list you want to reformat with graphics bullets.
2. Choose Format, Bullets And Numbering, and click the Bulleted tab.
3. Choose a bulleted list display box, and then click the Customize button. The Customize Bulleted List dialog box appears, as shown in Figure 31-19.
4. In the Customize Bulleted List dialog box, click the Picture button to open the Picture Bullet dialog box.
5. Double-click the bullet you want to use. Notice that some bullet options have a star in the lower right corner. This star indicates that the bullet is displayed as an animated bullet when it is viewed in a browser.
6. Click OK in the Customize Bulleted List dialog box to reformat the bulleted list.

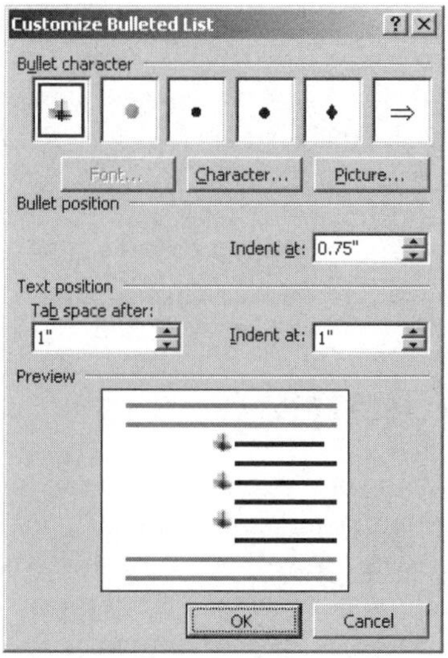

Figure 31-19. You can modify the layout of a bulleted list by configuring the Customize Bulleted List dialog box.

For more information about creating and modifying bulleted lists, see Chapter 8, "Enumerating with Lists, Lists, and More Lists."

Using Custom Graphics as Bullets

If you have a graphic that you want to use for a bulleted list, you can do so by importing a picture using the Bullets And Number dialog box (as described in Chapter 8 "Enumerating with Lists, Lists, and More Lists"), or you can follow these steps:

1. Create at least a couple of entries for your bulleted list using the Bullets button on the Formatting toolbar.
2. Right-click the bulleted list, and choose Bullets And Numbering on the shortcut menu.
3. On the Bulleted tab of the Bullets And Numbering dialog box, click the None box, and then click OK.
4. Click Insert, Picture, *file name* to insert the graphic in your document. Resize the graphic if necessary, and then select the graphic and press Ctrl+X to cut it.
5. Click at the beginning of the first bulleted list item, and press Ctrl+V to paste the graphic. Continue to paste the graphic in front of each list item.
6. If you need to add list items, click at the end of the last bulleted list item and press Enter. The graphic will be included in the next list entry automatically.

(continued)

Using Custom Graphics as Bullets *(continued)* When you add custom bullets, the Bullets And Numbering dialog box formats one of the bullet style boxes on the Bulleted tab with the bulleted list that uses your custom graphic. If you want to format other bulleted lists with the same custom graphic, you can select the bulleted list, choose Format, Bullets And Numbering, and then click the style box containing the custom graphic on the Bulleted tab in the Bullets And Numbering dialog box.

Inserting Web Page Components

In addition to adding text and graphics to your Web pages, you can present multimedia information, including movies, background sounds, and scrolling text. Word makes inserting these types of components easy by providing toolbar buttons on the Web Tools toolbar. To display the Web Tools toolbar, choose View, Toolbars, Web Tools, or right-click a toolbar, and choose Web Tools on the shortcut menu. In this section, you'll learn how to insert multimedia components. The Web Tools toolbar also provides buttons that help you create interactive Web forms. Creating interactive Web forms is discussed in the section "Creating Interactive Forms," on page 745.

InsideOut

Multimedia files are not automatically stored in the HTML folder when you save a Web page in Word. Therefore, the best way to approach inserting a movie or sound file into your document is to copy the multimedia elements into your HTML folder before you add the component to your page. That way, the links to the multimedia component will work properly after you upload your Web page files.

Inserting a Movie Component

When you create a Web page in Word, you can insert a movie directly in your Web page. Keep in mind that this option includes the movie directly on your page, similar to displaying a graphic. You can configure the movie to play when the Web page is opened, when the user moves the mouse cursor over the movie, or in both instances. To insert a movie in your Web page, follow these steps:

Movie

1 Position your insertion point where you want to insert a link to a movie, and then click the Movie button on the Web Tools toolbar.

   The Movie Clip dialog box opens, as shown in Figure 31-20, and a default Movie icon is displayed in your document.

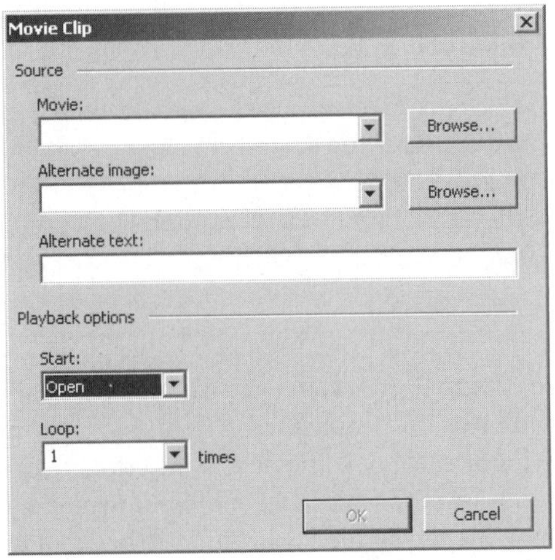

Figure 31-20. You use the Movie Clip dialog box to insert a movie in your Web page.

2 In the Movie box, type the path or Web address of the movie file you want to link to, or click Browse to locate the file.

> **tip** You can use AVI, MOV, ASF, and RM movie formats in Web pages.

3 In the Alternate Image box, type the path or Web address of the graphics file you want to designate as a substitute when the user's browser doesn't support movies or when the user turns off the display of movies.

4 In the Alternate Text box, type the text you want to appear in place of the movie or alternate image.

5 Click the Start down arrow, and select one of the following options in the drop-down list:

- **Open** plays the movie when the user downloads the Web page.
- **Mouse-Over** plays the movie when the user moves the mouse cursor over it.
- **Both** plays the movie when the user downloads the Web page or moves the mouse cursor over the movie image.

6 In the Loop box, enter the number of times you want the movie to repeat, or click the down arrow and select a specific number or Infinite, and then click OK.

> **tip** **Control the movie's display while you work**
>
> To review a movie while you're working on your Web page document in Word, you can right-click the image representing the movie and choose Play on the shortcut menu. To stop the movie, right-click the movie, and click Stop. To disable the movie altogether while you work, click the Design Mode button on the Web Tools toolbar to work in Design Mode. (To return to standard Web Layout view, click the Design Mode button again.)

Design Mode

Generally, inserting a movie directly into a Web page isn't the best approach to take to Web page design. For the same reasons people turn off graphics or can't view graphics, some users also disable movies or can't view movies. In addition, people with slow Internet connections might not want to wait while movies download. Better design practice dictates that you copy the movie file into your Web page folder and then create a hyperlink (text or graphic) that links to the movie file. That way, users can choose whether they want to view your movie instead of being forced to download it.

Movie placeholder

To delete a movie from your Web page, click the Design Mode button on the Web Tools toolbar to enter Design Mode. Then right-click the Movie placeholder icon, and choose Cut from the shortcut menu.

Including Background Sound

Another multimedia element you can add to Web pages is background sound. Background sound refers to a sound file that plays when users display your Web page. You should use background sound sparingly. Many people find background sound annoying and a waste of bandwidth. If you find an instance in which a background sound adds to your page (maybe you're displaying a page about cricket chirps), you should feel comfortable adding the feature. Otherwise, your best bet is to provide a link to a sound file so that users can choose whether they want to play the sound file, instead of being forced to run it. Here's how to add a background sound to a Web page in those instances in which a background sound adds significantly to your Web page:

Sound

1 On the Web Tools toolbar, click Sound. The Background Sound dialog box opens, as shown in Figure 31-21.

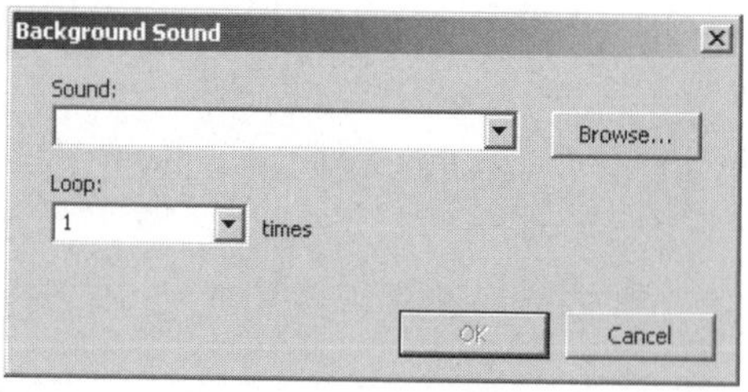

Figure 31-21. You can use the Background Sound dialog box to include background sound in your Web page.

2 In the Sound box, type the path or Web address of the sound file you want, or click Browse to locate the file.

> **tip** You can insert sound files in WAV, MID, AU, AIF, RMI, SND, and MP2 (MPEG audio) formats.

3 In the Loop box, type the number of times you want the background sound to repeat, or click the down arrow and select a specific number or Infinite.

To stop the background sound from playing while you work on the Web page, click the Design Mode button on the Web Tools toolbar. (This button stops both movies and background sounds from playing.) To hear your background sound, click the Design Mode button again to return to the standard Web Layout view.

Sound placeholder

To delete a sound from your Web page, click the Design Mode button, right-click the Sound placeholder icon, and choose Cut on the shortcut menu.

> **tip** To stop a background sound when you're viewing a Web page on line, press Esc.

Adding Scrolling Text

Scrolling Text

Another type of multimedia component you can easily include on Web pages you build in Word is *scrolling text,* which is more commonly called *marquee text* by Web designers. Scrolling text is displayed like stock-ticker text—it enters on one side of your document and slides across to the other.

> **caution** You should use scrolling text sparingly. Many browsers still don't support scrolling text and either will not display it at all or will display only part of it.

To insert scrolling text in your Web page document in Word, follow these steps:

1 On the Web Tools toolbar, click the Scrolling Text button. The Scrolling Text dialog box opens, as shown in Figure 31-22, on the next page.

2 In the Behavior drop-down list, select from the following options. (To preview an option, select it and watch the sample text in the Preview box.)

- **Scroll** scrolls text across the screen. This is the default setting.
- **Slide** scrolls text once, stops at the other edge of the page, and then continues to display the scrolling text as static text.
- **Alternate** bounces the text back and forth between the left and right margins of the page.

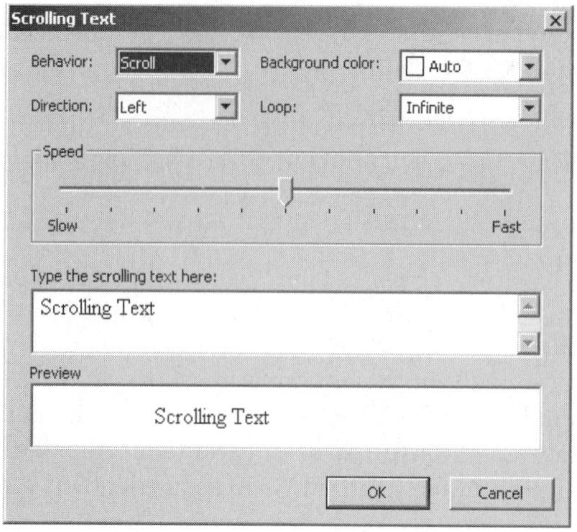

Figure 31-22. You use the Scrolling Text dialog box to include scrolling text in your Web page.

3. In the Direction drop-down list, specify whether you want the text to scroll in from the left or right edge of the page.
4. If desired, click the Background Color down arrow, and select a color from the drop-down list to be displayed behind the scrolling text. If you want to apply a background color, you must select one from the list; you can't apply custom colors to scrolling text items.
5. In the Loop box, type the number of times you want the text to scroll, or click the down arrow and select a value from the drop-down list. By default, scrolling text is configured to scroll infinitely (or as long as the page is displayed). If you select the Slide option in the Behavior drop-down list, the Loop option is unavailable, because a slide implies only one scrolling action.
6. Drag the Speed slider to modify how fast or slow your text scrolls (or bounces) across the page.
7. Type the text you want to display in the Type The Scrolling Text Here box.
8. Click OK when you're satisfied with your scrolling text settings.

After you insert scrolling text, you can further modify the component by working with it in Design Mode (click the Design Mode button on the Web Tools toolbar). In Design Mode, you can enhance your scrolling text in the following ways:

- **Resize the scrolling text area** by clicking the item and dragging the component box's selection handles.
- **Format the scrolling text** using Word's text formatting tools, such as the Font dialog box and the Formatting toolbar buttons. Select the scrolling text component (you can't select the text), and then apply the font

formatting settings. To view the settings, click the Design Mode button to run the scrolling text. To return to formatting mode, click the Design Mode button again.

- **Format the scrolling text component as a hyperlink** by right-clicking the scrolling text component in Design Mode and choosing Hyperlink on the shortcut menu. The Insert Hyperlink dialog box opens.

In general, you should use scrolling text to draw attention to a particular informational bit; you shouldn't include critical information in this component (unless the information also appears elsewhere on the page). If a user's browser doesn't support scrolling text, that user might not see the message, so you want to make sure the information is "expendable" to some extent.

Creating Interactive Forms

If you've ever ordered an item on line or used a Web search engine, you've used an interactive form. In Word, you can create online interactive forms in your Web page documents in the same way you create standard forms. The main difference between creating standard Word forms and online forms is that you need to configure the properties of your online form's controls to work with your Web server. Because online forms created in Word require additional support files and server support, you should work with your network or Web administrator when planning and creating interactive Web forms.

tip **Receive form responses as e-mail messages**

In addition to creating a *server-side online form* (a form that needs to work with a Web server that's configured to handle interactive forms), you can also create a Web form that sends an e-mail message to you each time the form is completed by a user. Whenever a user completes this type of form (often referred to as a *client-side form*) and clicks Submit, you receive an e-mail message containing the user's entries. To create this type of form, your best bet is to turn to a full-fledged HTML editor, such as FrontPage 2002.

When you create Web forms in Word, you can include 11 basic form controls, listed in Table 31-1, on the next page. Word organizes the Web form controls for you on the Web Tools toolbar (right-click a toolbar, and choose Web Tools on the shortcut menu). Using the Web Tools toolbar, you can create a form by using any combination of these controls.

For an in-depth look at creating forms in Word, see Chapter 36, "Working with Field Codes and Custom Forms."

Table 31-1. Interactive Web Form Components

Web Tools Button	Control Name	Description
	Checkbox Box	Provides an option that's not mutually exclusive in a group of options or that is displayed as an independent option.
	Option Button	Provides options that are mutually exclusive in a group of options. Users can select only one item in a group of items.
	Drop-Down Box	Creates a list of options that users can choose from in drop-down list format.
	List Box	Inserts a box containing a list of items users can choose from. If the list is longer than the box size, users can scroll through the list to access additional options.
	Textbox Box	Creates a control in which users can enter one line of text.
	Text Area	Creates a control in which users can enter multiple lines of text.
	Submit	Sends the data that a user enters in the Web form. Every online form needs to include a Submit button or a Submit With Image button.
	Submit With Image	Displays a graphic that users can click to submit information.
	Reset	Resets the form to its default settings and removes any information entered by the user.
	Hidden	Inserts a hidden control that's used to pass information to a Web server (such as information about a user's computer operating environment) when the user submits the form.
	Password	Creates a text box that displays an asterisk to mask each character the user types in the text box.

Properties

To set a Web form control's properties, select the form control, and click the Properties button on the Web Tools toolbar. To obtain information about the properties associated with each Web form control, consult the Word Help files. The Help topic titled "Form Controls You Can Use on a Web Page" provides property information for each of the 11 Web form controls.

Working with Cascading Style Sheets

Cascading style sheets (CSS) are used to format Web pages in much the same way traditional style sheets are used to format standard Word documents. The role of a cascading style sheet is to present a Web page's formatting information in a specific place—either at the beginning of an HTML document or in a separate document—in a format that browsers can easily interpret and apply to the associated Web page or Web pages. Using cascading style sheets provides a convenient way to format several Web pages or a whole Web site. When cascading style sheets are in use, you can change the format of Web pages by making changes to the style sheet information instead of editing individual Web pages.

Because Word automatically creates your source code, you don't actually see when Word creates cascading style sheets. By default, Word uses cascading style sheets if your target browser option is set to Internet Explorer 4 or Netscape Navigator 4. (For more information about configuring your target browser, see the section "Specifying Target Browser Options," on page 708.) When Word creates a cascading style sheet, Word embeds the style sheet at the top of each Web page.

In addition to generating cascading style sheet information, you can use Word to attach, remove, and manage cascading style sheets for Web pages. You can also use Word to attach more than one style sheet to a Web page if necessary. For example, you might have one style sheet that's part of a large Web site, such as a style sheet for an international corporation, and another style sheet that defines a smaller group of related pages, such as a style sheet for a regional office. You can then specify which style sheet takes precedence over the other, in case conflicting styles are defined for the same elements. When you attach a style sheet to your Web page in Word, the styles contained in the cascading style sheet will appear in the Styles And Formatting task pane.

> **For more information about the Styles And Formatting task pane, see Chapter 10, "Using Styles to Increase Your Formatting Power."**

Attaching Cascading Style Sheets

If you have a cascading style sheet file, you can attach it to a Web page. Cascading style sheets carry the .css extension. You attach a cascading style sheet to a document in the same way you attach a global template or an add-in. Specifically, you must complete the following steps:

1. Choose Tools, Templates And Add-Ins. The Templates And Add-Ins dialog box appears.
2. Click the Linked CSS button. The Linked CSS Style Sheets dialog box opens, as shown in Figure 31-23.

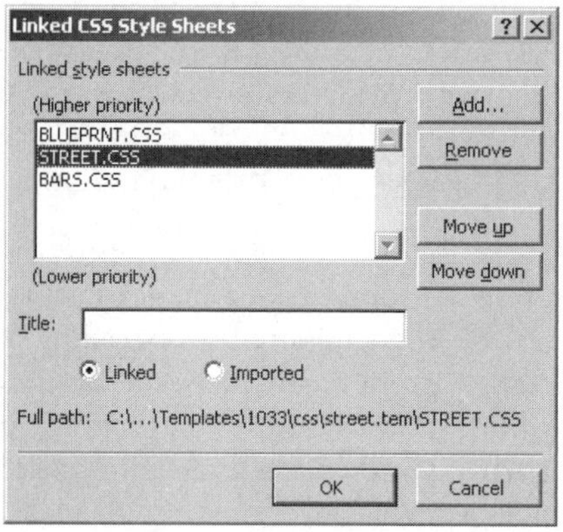

Figure 31-23. You can use the Linked CSS Style Sheets dialog box to attach, detach, and prioritize cascading style sheets.

3. Click the Add button. The Add CSS Link dialog box (which looks very similar to the Open dialog box) opens and displays any cascading style sheet files stored in your Templates folder.
4. Select the cascading style sheet you want to add, and then click OK.
5. To attach multiple style sheets to a document, repeat steps 3 and 4. After you've finished attaching cascading style sheets, click OK. A message box will appear, stating that the style sheet has changed and that you must save and reload the document. To have Word do this for you, click Yes.
6. Click OK to close the Templates And Add-Ins dialog box.

After you attach a cascading style sheet to a document, the styles from the cascading style sheet will appear in the Styles And Formatting task pane.

Changing the Order of Cascading Style Sheets

The order of cascading style sheets provides a precedence that determines which styles are applied if two or more style sheets have conflicting settings for the same element. When you move a style sheet up in the list, you assign a higher priority to the style sheet. Likewise, when you move a style sheet down in the list, you assign a lower priority to the style sheet. To configure precedence among style sheets, follow these steps:

1. Choose Tools, Templates And Add-Ins. The Templates And Add-Ins dialog box appears.
2. Click the Linked CSS button. The Linked CSS Style Sheets dialog box appears.
3. Select a style sheet in the list, and then click Move Up or Move Down to change the style sheet's precedence.
4. Click OK to close the Linked CSS Style Sheets dialog box, and click OK to close the Templates And Add-Ins dialog box.

Detaching Cascading Style Sheets

You can detach a cascading style sheet if you want to stop using the cascading style sheet to format a document. To do so, follow these steps:

1. Choose Tools, Templates And Add-Ins. The Templates And Add-Ins dialog box appears.
2. Clicked the Linked CSS button. The Linked CSS Style Sheets dialog box appears.
3. Select the style sheet you want to remove, and then click Remove.
4. Remove any other style sheets you want to detach, and then click OK when you've finished. A message box will appear, stating that the style sheet has changed and that you must save and reload the document. To have Word do this for you, click Yes.
5. Click OK to close the Templates And Add-Ins dialog box.

Keep in mind that when you remove a style sheet from the list, you don't delete the style sheet's file; you simply instruct the current document to stop referring to the style sheet.

Editing Source Code Using the Microsoft Script Editor

If you're comfortable working with HTML code, Web scripts, and cascading style sheet information, you might want to tweak your Web pages' source code directly from time to time. The Microsoft Script Editor allows you to view and edit your Web page documents' HTML source code. In addition, you can use the Microsoft Script Editor to add VBScript and JScript to your files.

To display a Web page's source code, open the document in Word, and then choose View, HTML Source. The first time you access the Microsoft Script Editor, you might see a message box stating that you have to install it. To do so, simply insert your installation CD, and click Install. After the installation is complete, your Web page's source code will be displayed in the Microsoft Script Editor window, as shown in Figure 31-24.

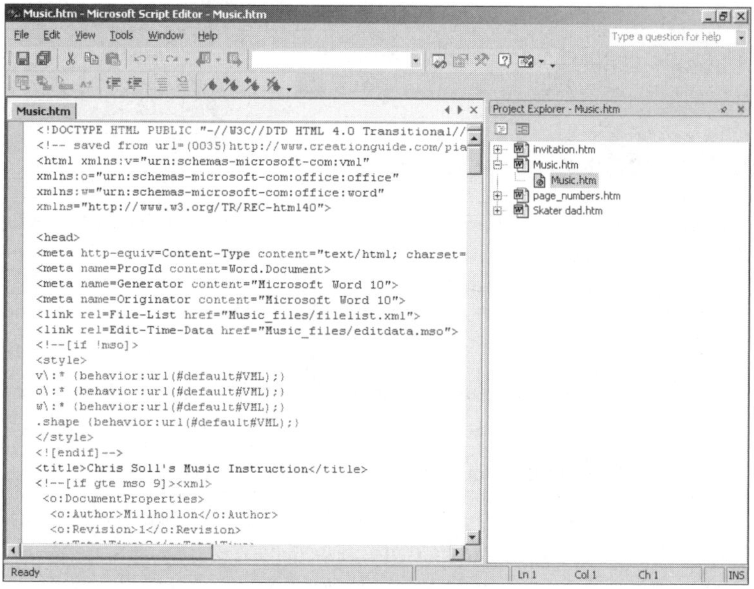

Figure 31-24. The Microsoft Script Editor provides a convenient way for Web page developers to edit Web page documents' source code.

You can edit and change the source code in the Microsoft Script Editor in the same way you edit source code in other applications. In addition to displaying the code for the current page, the Project Explorer pane displays all other open documents so that you can easily display the source code for those documents as well. Notice too that the Standard toolbar contains two save buttons: Save and Save All. Use the Save All button if you've been working on the source code in a number of open documents and you're ready to save all your changes to the documents. After you save changes you've made in a document's source code, the document is updated to incorporate the changes.

Publishing Your Web Pages

The last stage of Web page creation entails publishing your Web pages. After you create and save your Web page documents, you're ready to publish your pages for the world (or at least your fellow employees) to see. Publishing your Web pages simply means copying your Web page files and folders from your computer onto a Web server. Keep in mind that when you publish your Web pages, you must retain the hierarchical structure of your Web page files, including naming and organizational schemes. If your Web page stores all its graphics files in a subfolder, for example, you must publish the subfolder in addition to the contents of the folder without changing the name of the folder or files. (Remember, changing uppercase to lowercase constitutes changing a file's or folder's name.)

The most common way to publish Web pages is to copy the files and folders on your system to a server by using a File Transfer Protocol (FTP) application. When you create Web pages in Word, you have another option. You can save your Web page documents to a server by clicking the My Network Places button in the Save As dialog box and saving your Web page documents in a folder on your network location.

Whenever you publish Web pages, you should always view your live pages immediately after you upload them—that way, you'll be the first to see whether your pages are displayed properly. If your pages need to be fixed, change the local copy of your Web page document, and then save the updated file over the existing file on your Web server. After your Web pages are uploaded and live, you're ready for the next stage of Webmastering—maintaining and updating your Web site. (But that's a topic for another book!)

Chapter 32

Sharing Information on Networks

Many companies share information and resources on networks. In fact, many people work daily on intranets, extranets, and the Internet by transferring files, downloading information, storing information to networked backup systems, and printing using networked printers. Clearly, people benefit in a number of ways when they share information on networks.

As you've seen throughout this book, you can take advantage of several networking features in Microsoft Word (for example, using online collaboration tools is discussed in Chapter 30, "Collaborating On Line with E-Mail, NetMeeting, Discussions, and Faxes"). This chapter covers some network-specific topics about sharing information on line. In this chapter, you'll learn how to share folders and files, use workgroup templates, and work with team Web sites using Microsoft SharePoint Team Services.

Sharing Files and Folders

Part of the beauty of working on a network is that you can easily share files, folders, networked locations, and hardware resources (such as computers, Zip drives, printers, scanners, and so forth) with anyone linked to your network. In addition, you can frequently access networks from various locations. This capability can come in quite handy and can save you time because you won't have to continually copy information to a disk if you want to use the information on another computer and you won't be stranded in one location while your files sit in another. Because Word is a document creation program and sharing files and folders represents one of the most prominent reasons for networking, we'll look at sharing those resources in more depth here.

Sharing Word Information On Line

You can share information with other Word users in a number of ways. To share your information effectively, you should design your resource-sharing setup based on who will be accessing the information and how the information should appear. You can share files or folders using any of the following techniques:

- **Post the information to a public folder on Microsoft Exchange Server.** For example, you can open a file and choose File, Send To, Exchange Folder if your network has the Exchange Server extensions installed.
- **Save the information on a SharePoint team Web site.** SharePoint team Web sites are discussed in more detail in the section "Sharing Information on Team Web Sites," on page 763.
- **Save the information in a shared network or Internet folder.** To learn more about Internet folders and network locations, see Chapter 29, "Keeping an Eye on Word's Online Features."
- **Send a copy of a file to others using Word e-mail, fax, or NetMeeting features.** For more information about sending documents while working in Word, see Chapter 30, "Collaborating On Line with E-Mail, NetMeeting, Discussions, and Faxes."
- **Share a folder with others on your intranet using Windows 2000 sharing.** For more information about sharing resources in Windows 2000, see the sidebar "Using Windows 2000 to Share Folders on Your Intranet," on the facing page, as well as Appendix D, "Quick Guide to Peer-to-Peer Networks."
- **Store the information on a discussion server.** For more information about Web Discussions and discussion servers, see Chapter 30, "Collaborating On Line with E-Mail, NetMeeting, Discussions, and Faxes," as well as the section "Sharing Information on Team Web Sites," on page 763.)

Choosing how you want to share resources can be fairly straightforward. For example, if you're sharing a few computers on a peer-to-peer network made up of trusted resources, you'll probably feel comfortable simply specifying files and folders as shared resources in Windows 2000. On the other hand, if you know you have resources that people will need to access from many parts of the world, you'll be better served by sharing documents in an Internet folder. To take advantage of other sharing options, such as public folders and SharePoint team Web sites, you'll need to determine whether your server has Exchange Server extensions, Office Server extensions, or SharePoint Team Services installed.

For information about setting up a peer-to-peer network, see Appendix D, "Quick Guide to Peer-to-Peer Networks."

Using Microsoft Windows 2000 to Share Folders on Your Intranet

Windows 2000 makes it easy to share folders on intranets. The minor catch is that before you can share a folder with others on your intranet in Windows 2000, you must be logged on as a member of the Administrators group or as another type of user with sufficient privileges. After you've verified your logon status, follow these steps to share a resource:

1. In Windows Explorer, right-click the folder you want to share, and choose Sharing on the shortcut menu.
2. On the Sharing tab in the folder's Properties dialog box, click Share This Folder.
3. If desired, click the Permissions button on the Share tab to access the Permissions dialog box for the folder, and then specify permission settings, such as Full Control, Change, and Read for selected groups. Click OK to close the dialog box.
4. Click OK to close the Properties dialog box.

After you share a folder, the folder icon changes to a hand holding a folder. This lets you quickly determine which folders are shared on your computer. Others on your network can now navigate to your computer and view the contents of the folders you've shared.

Sharing Documents with People Using Other Versions of Word

As you know, the software world changes much more quickly than many offices and people tend to update their systems. In addition, people use a variety of hardware platforms and operating systems. Therefore, you'll find that you occasionally want to share Word documents with people who are using earlier versions of Word or using Macintosh versions of Word. Conveniently, Word includes several features that assist you when you want to share documents with people using other versions of Word (or people who aren't using Word at all).

note You can use Word 2002 to open documents created in Word 2000, Word 97, Word 95, Word 6.0, or Word 2.0. All data and formatting in documents using those versions of Word are fully supported in Word 2002.

Sharing Documents with Word 2000 and Word 97 Users

If you share documents with people who use Word 2000 or Word 97, you can save your documents in the standard Word document format. If desired, you can quickly create new documents or modify existing documents specifically for use in Word 97 by turning off features not supported in that version. To turn off features not supported in Word 97, follow these steps:

1. Ensure that the document you want to save is open in Word.
2. Choose Tools, Options, and click the Save tab. The Save tab in the Options dialog box is shown in Figure 32-1.

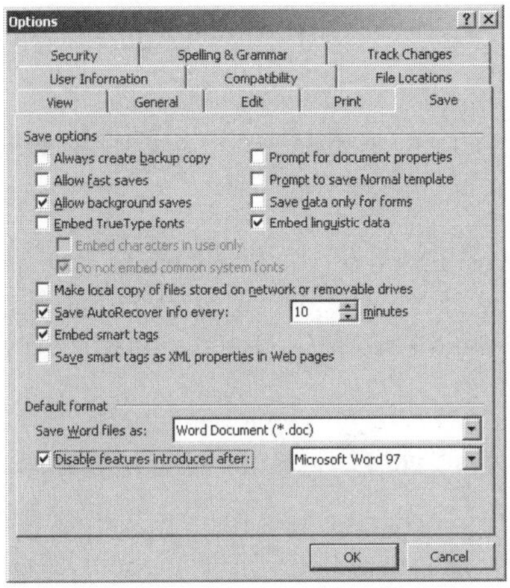

Figure 32-1. You can configure the settings on the Save tab to establish a default file format for new documents as well as disable features that aren't supported in earlier versions of Word.

3. Select the Disable Features Introduced After check box, select the version of Word you want in the drop-down list, and click OK. If appropriate, Word will display a summary of features in the document that aren't supported in the selected version of Word, as shown in Figure 32-2. Click the Tell Me More button to access additional information about features that aren't supported in the selected version of Word. After you finish reviewing the information, close the Help window, and then click Continue.

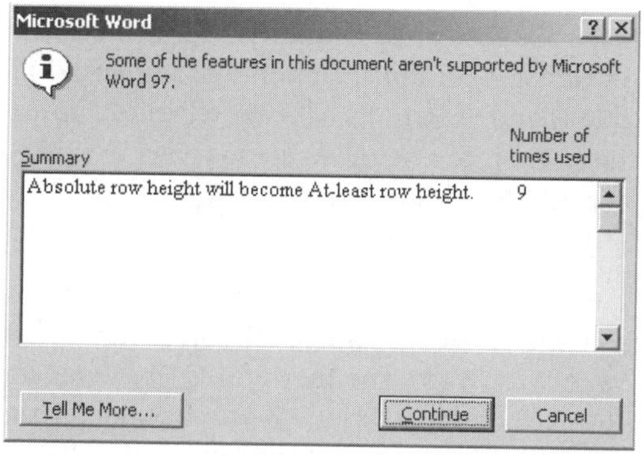

Figure 32-2. Word displays a summary of features found in the current document that aren't supported in the newly selected document format.

After you turn off features not supported by earlier versions of Word and save the document, the document can be used in the specified version of Word. If you work with the document in Word 2002, you'll notice that some of the features are unavailable on menus. If you choose an unavailable option (such as choosing Insert, Hyperlink when you're working on a document for Word 6.0), a dialog box will appear, stating that the feature is currently disabled. The dialog box includes a Tell Me More button that you can click to access further information about the disabled feature.

note You can't use the Disable Features Introduced After option when you're saving Web pages—Word 97 and earlier versions don't support HTML documents.

Sharing Documents with Word for Windows 95 Users

In addition to saving documents for people who use Word 2000 and Word 97, you can prepare your documents so that they're accessible in Word 6.0 or Word 95 for Microsoft Windows 95. You can achieve this compatibility using one of the following techniques:

- **Save existing documents in Word 6.0 or Word 95 format.** To save your document as a Word 6.0 or Word 95 file, choose File, Save As, and then select Word 6.0/95 in the Save As Type drop-down list. When you save a document in Word 6.0 or Word 95 format, Word replaces formatting in your document that isn't supported in Word 6.0 and Word 95 with formatting that is supported in those versions. Word then displays a dialog box showing the formatting changes that will be made in your document. In addition, when you work in a document that you saved in Word 6.0 or Word 95 format, Word automatically makes features unavailable that are not supported in Word 6.0 and Word 95. This makes it easy for you to create documents in Word 2002 that will not lose data or look different when viewed in Word 6.0 or Word 95.

- **Turn off unsupported features while you work.** To turn off unsupported features while you work, choose Tools, Options, click the Save tab, and configure the Disable Features Introduced After setting. (For more detailed information, see the section "Sharing Documents with Word 2000 and Word 97 Users," on page 756.) When you turn off unsupported features, you can create new documents or modify existing documents specifically for use in Word 6.0 or Word 95.
- **Send users a Word converter or viewer application.** Microsoft includes converters and viewers with Word, and they are also available for download from the Microsoft Office Update Web site Word downloads page. You can send a converter or a viewer application to users of Word 6.0, Word 95, or Microsoft Works, for Microsoft Windows, Microsoft Windows NT,

Receiving Notification When a Document Is Converted

If you want to know which converter (if any) is being used when you open a document, you can display the Convert File dialog box, shown here:

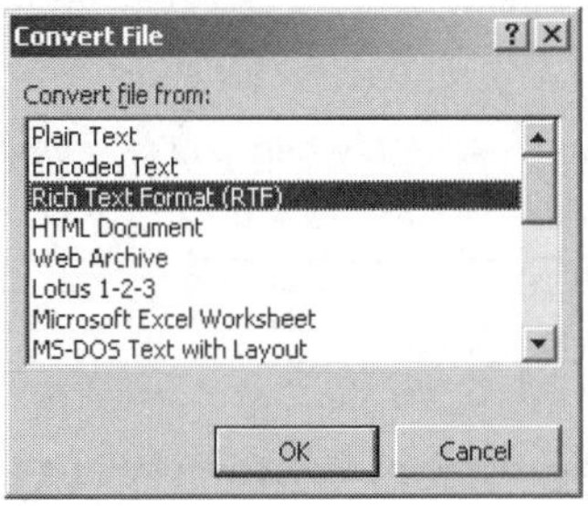

To configure Word to notify you when files are converted, follow these steps:

1. Choose Tools, Options, and click the General tab.
2. Select the Confirm Conversion At Open check box, and click OK.

After you set this option, the Convert File dialog box will be displayed when you open a file that must be converted. When you see the Convert File dialog box, simply click OK to open the document normally. (The file's default file format will be selected by default.) If you click Cancel, the process will be aborted, and the document won't be opened. If you select another file format in the Convert File dialog box, the document will be opened in the selected format. For example, if you select Plain Text in the Convert File dialog box when you're opening a Web page document, you'll see a text document that shows the HTML source code for the Web page instead of the standard WYSIWYG view Word normally displays when you open HTML documents.

or Apple Macintosh operating systems. Others can download a converter or viewer from the Microsoft Office Update Web site at *http://officeupdate.microsoft.com*. To download a converter or viewer from the Office Update Web site, display the Web page, click Word, click Download, choose Converters And Viewers on the downloads page, click Search Now, and then download the converter or viewer you need. After users install a converter or viewer, they can directly open Word 2002 documents.

Converting a Batch of Files to or from Word Format

In some cases, you might want to convert a number of Word files to another format. For example, you might want to convert a collection of files for a client who uses WordPerfect. You can easily convert a batch of files by using the Conversion Wizard included with Word. To do so, follow these steps:

1. Choose File, New to open the New Document task pane.
2. In the New Document task pane, click the General Templates link, and then choose the Other Documents tab.
3. Double-click the Batch Conversion Wizard icon. The Start page is shown in Figure 32-3.

Figure 32-3. The Conversion Wizard walks you through the process of converting a number of files at one time.

4. Click Next, and then specify whether you want to convert documents to Word format or convert Word documents to another format by selecting the appropriate option and choosing the file type in the drop-down list.

5 Click Next, and on the Folder Selection page, click the Source Folder Browse button. The Browse For Folder dialog box opens, as shown in Figure 32-4. Select the appropriate folder, and click OK.

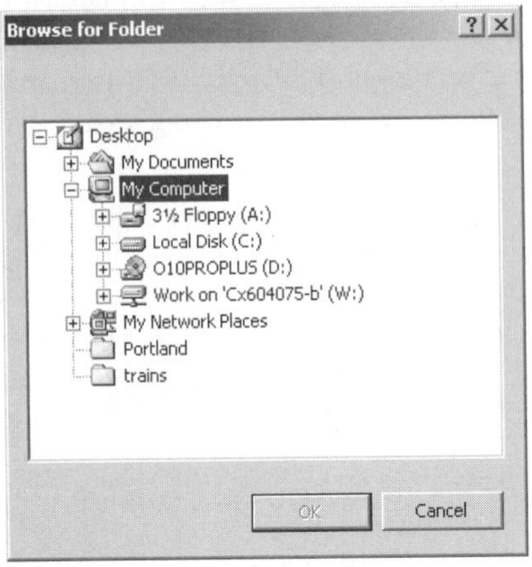

Figure 32-4. You can use the Browse For Folder dialog box to specify the folder that contains the files you want to convert and where you want to store the converted files.

6 Click the Destination Folder Browse button, select the folder in which you want to store the converted files, and click OK.

7 Click Next to display the File Selection page, shown in Figure 32-5, where you can specify the files you want to convert. To select a file, double-click the file name in the Available list; the file name will be displayed in the To Convert list. Continue to double-click file names in the Available list until all the files you want to convert appear in the To Convert list. If you want to convert all the files, click the Select All button. You can filter the Available list view by choosing a file type in the Type drop-down list.

8 After you've added files to the To Convert list, you can remove a single file by double-clicking it or click Remove All if you decide not to convert the specified files. When you've completed the File Selection page, click Next, and then click Finish to complete the conversion. You'll see the Batch Conversion Progress dialog box, and then a final message box will appear, asking whether you want to perform another conversion. Click Yes to perform another conversion, or click No to close the dialog box.

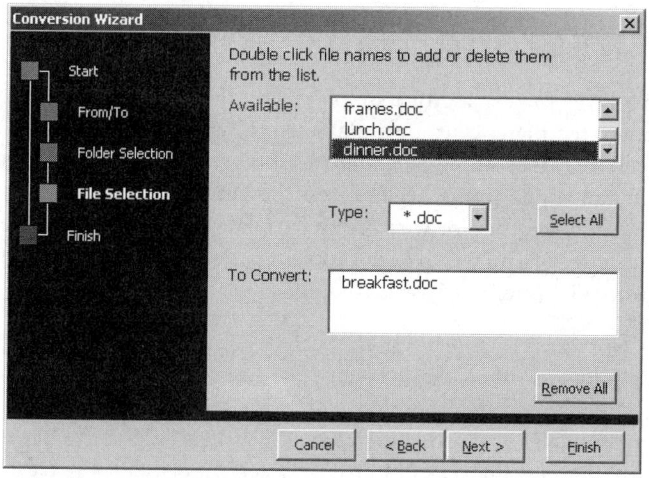

Figure 32-5. The File Selection page enables you to pick and choose the files you want to convert.

Keep in mind that when you perform a batch conversion, you don't delete or change the original files. Instead, you create copies of existing files that are stored in another file format.

Setting a Default File Format

If you frequently save documents in a particular format other than as standard Word 2002 documents (for example, perhaps you need to share most of the documents you create with a client who uses Word for Macintosh or WordPerfect), you can change the default file format Word uses to save new documents. To do so, follow these steps:

1. Choose Tools, Options, and click the Save tab.
2. In the Default Format section, click the Save Word Files As down arrow, and choose the file format you want to use as your default file format in the drop-down list.
3. Click OK.

Remember that when you configure the default file format, the setting affects only new documents you create. Word saves existing documents in the same format in which they were opened.

Using Workgroup Templates

A convenient way to keep a group supplied with the most up-to-date templates is to store common templates centrally on a network server. (These shared templates are generally referred to as *workgroup templates.*) By doing this, you can ensure that everyone working on similar projects can access the same version of these templates at any time. A central repository for workgroup templates also saves everyone the headache of distributing and obtaining individual copies of the latest templates and can greatly help to standardize documents across the board.

You create workgroup templates in the same way you create other templates. You then designate a folder as the workgroup template container and make sure that everyone's computers are configured to point to that particular file. Generally, you'll want to make workgroup templates read-only files so that no one accidentally changes the template information. If you want to ensure that only certain people can access the files, you might want to assign passwords to the templates or make the network share read-only.

For more information about creating templates, see Chapter 22, "Formatting Documents Using Templates, Wizards, and Add-Ins." For information about making documents read-only and password protected, see Chapter 34, "Addressing Security Issues."

To specify the location of workgroup templates on an individual's computer, follow these steps:

1. Choose Tools, Options, and click the File Locations tab.
2. In the File Types list, select Workgroup Templates, as shown in Figure 32-6.

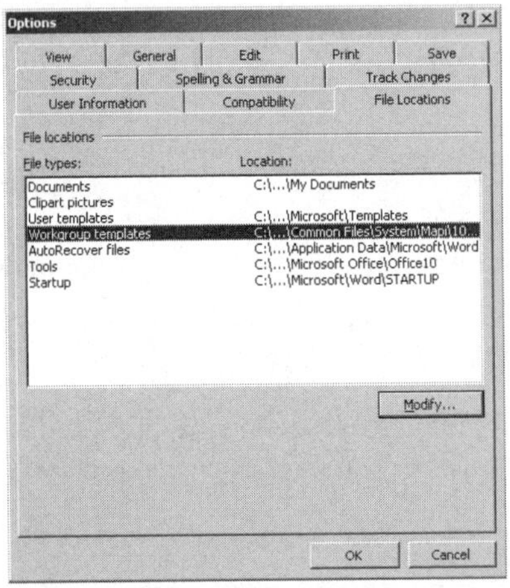

Figure 32-6. You can use the File Locations tab to specify locations for a number of file types, including workgroup templates.

3. Click Modify to open the Modify Location dialog box, which looks similar to the Open dialog box.

4. Navigate to and select the folder that contains the workgroup templates, click OK to close the Modify Location dialog box, and then click OK to close the Options dialog box.

To access templates stored in the workgroup templates folder, users can click the General Templates link in the New Document task pane and then click the General tab in the Templates dialog box. If workgroup templates are stored in a subfolder within the workgroup templates folder, the Templates dialog box will include a tab with the same name as the subfolder, and the templates stored within the subfolder will appear on that tab.

tip **Store workgroup templates in a Web folder**

You can't indicate an Internet location for your workgroup templates on the File Locations tab in the Options dialog box—the workgroup templates folder must be stored in a location on your computer or network. If you want to store templates in a Web folder, you should create a My Network Places link to the Web folder. You can then access the folder by clicking the Templates On My Web Sites link in the New Document task pane.

newfeature!

Sharing Information on Team Web Sites

Team Web sites provide a centralized area for groups that need to frequently share files, participate in discussions, distribute announcements, track tasks, create lists, store contact information, import spreadsheets, and communicate all sorts of information. Specifically, this Microsoft Office XP feature empowers groups to manage their projects and activities with a prebuilt Web site solution called SharePoint Team Services. SharePoint Team Services provides a way to create easy-to-use Web-based workspaces for teams. Figure 32-7, on the next page, shows a standard SharePoint team Web site interface. Keep in mind that SharePoint Team Services was designed to be highly customizable. For example, team Web site administrators can customize everything from the site layout to users' rights. Team Web site administrators can customize SharePoint Team Services using either a Windows-based Web browser (such as Internet Explorer 4 or later) or a SharePoint-compatible Web authoring tool, such as Microsoft FrontPage 2002.

For more information about using FrontPage 2002, see *Microsoft FrontPage Version 2002 Inside Out*, also from Microsoft Press. Further, to find out more about SharePoint, visit the SharePoint Portal Server Web site at *www.microsoft.com/sharepoint*.

Before you can create and use a team Web site, you must ask your system administrator or Internet service provider (ISP) for the URL for a Web server running SharePoint Team Services from Microsoft. After you obtain the URL, you can use the Add Network Place Wizard to link to a team Web site.

Understanding SharePoint Team Services

Once you access a server that's running SharePoint Team Services, you can create a working Web site in minutes, even if you don't know anything about HTML coding. SharePoint Team Services creates and maintains the site navigation links for you. For example, if you add an announcement to the site, the server displays it on the team Web site home page and provides a link to the complete announcement.

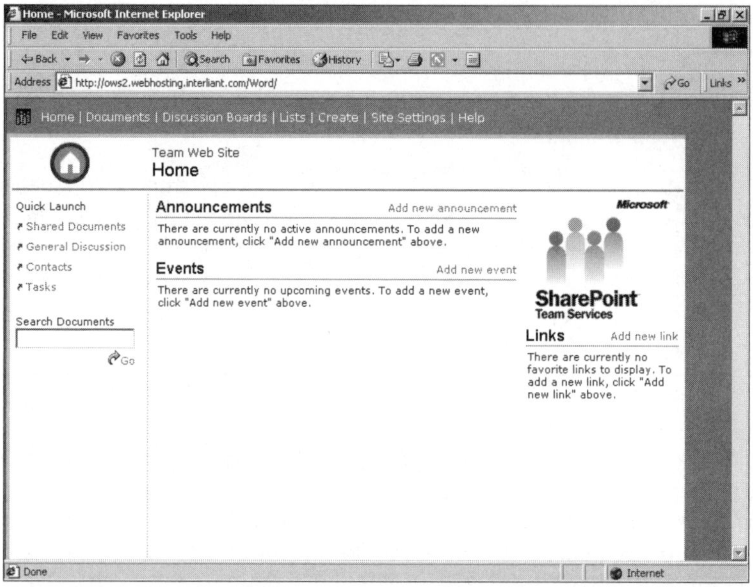

Figure 32-7. SharePoint team Web sites offer easy collaboration and can be customized to meet each group's particular needs.

Features available on team Web sites include the following:

- **Announcements** let you display the latest news on the home page. You can specify when and for how long announcements appear by providing an expiration date when you post the announcement.
- **Custom lists** can be created for any purpose. Click the Lists hyperlink on the team Web site to view the Lists page, shown in Figure 32-8, which shows existing lists and provides a hyperlink to create a new list.
- **Discussion boards** provide an efficient way to discuss issues relevant to the team. You can create topic-specific discussions to help organize the site's communication channels.
- **Document libraries** provide a way to share documents with others. When you add a document to a library, it is added to the document list on the team Web site. You can also include a template for any documents added to

the library, as described in the sidebar "Assigning a Template to a Document Library," on page 769.

- **Events** let you alert team members about upcoming events. Events are listed on the team Web site home page along with a link that enables users to add new events to the list.
- **Links** enable team members to share links to Web sites of interest. Links are displayed on the team Web site home page by default.
- **Surveys** provide a forum for team members to express their opinions about important issues. You can create a survey on a team Web site by providing information in a series of form fields; the survey serves as the equivalent of an online wizard.
- **Web document discussions** track and save document comments without modifying the document itself. The document appears within the user's Web browser, and a special toolbar provides options for adding comments.

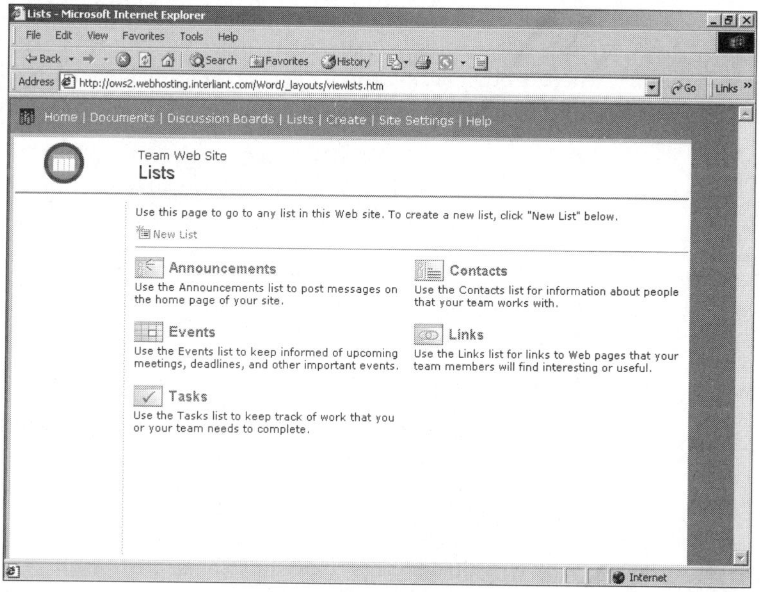

Figure 32-8. Creating a new resource, such as a list, on a team Web site is usually as straightforward as clicking a hyperlink and completing an online form. The team Web site takes care of posting the information, and it automatically creates hyperlinks in the appropriate locations.

Your team Web site can include any combination of the preceding elements, and you can customize each element by clicking the Site Settings hyperlink. The site settings available depend on your role as a site user, as described in the next section.

Setting Up a SharePoint Team Web Site

If you're in charge of setting up a SharePoint team Web site, you can create one directly from your Office XP program by clicking the Add Network Place link in the New Document task pane. Before you create a team Web site, you should gather the following information:

- **The URL of a Web server running SharePoint Team Services that will host the team Web site.** Your ISP or network administrator should be able to provide this information.
- **E-mail addresses of the members who will be using the team Web site.** Only members can browse or make changes to a team Web site. After you create the team Web site, you'll need to use the Site Settings page to send e-mail "invitations" to team members.
- **A list of access rights you want to assign to each user.** You can control the level of participation each user has regarding contributing, editing, and manipulating the Web site and the Web site's contents. For example, you might want to allow some users to edit and add documents to a document library, whereas others can only browse the Web site's contents. You assign access rights to members by assigning each member one of the following roles:
    - **Administrators** can view, add, and change all server content and can manage server settings and accounts.
    - **Advanced Authors** can create and edit content, contribute to Web document discussions, modify hyperlinks, and change documents, themes, and borders.
    - **Authors** can view, add, and change pages and documents.
    - **Contributors** can view the team Web site pages and documents and contribute to discussions.
    - **Browsers** can view pages and documents.
- **A list of team Web site features that you want to customize.** By default, team Web sites come configured to take advantage of a large collection of commonly used features. However, you might want to make some changes to suit your group's needs. You can make these changes up front during the Web site creation process or later as the need arises.

Ideally, you should gather this information before you create the team Web site, but rest assured that SharePoint team Web sites enable Web site administrators to customize the team Web site after it has been created. You can also manage users by adding and deleting users or changing existing users' roles after the site has been created. In other words, team Web sites can evolve over time in the same way most team projects evolve.

Working with Document Libraries

As a Word user using a team Web site, you'll most likely be working with documents stored in *document libraries.* Fundamentally, document libraries are collections of files that are shared on a team Web site. To view document libraries, click the Documents link on the team Web site's menu bar. As you can see in Figure 32-9, document libraries are similar to named folders; by default, they include brief descriptive text below the document library name.

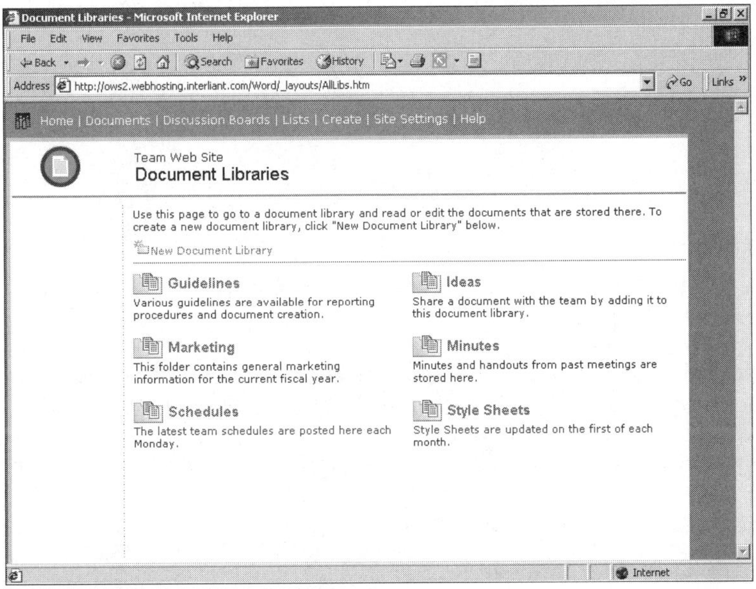

Figure 32-9. Document libraries can be used to organize the documents shared by team members in logical categories.

To view the documents stored in a document library, you simply click the document library's name. Figure 32-10, on the next page, shows the contents of a document library named Marketing. As you can see, one document is currently stored in the document library. Notice that you can use links to create a new document, upload an existing document, filter your view, and subscribe to the library (in which case, you'll receive an e-mail message containing a link to a changed document each time a change is made within the document library). In addition, you can edit the document if your role permits you to edit Web site content.

When you open a document in a document library by clicking the document's name, the document will be displayed in your browser. To edit a document in the document library, click the Edit icon to the right of the document's name. You'll be presented with a view similar to the one shown in Figure 32-11, on the next page, in which you can click the Edit In *Microsoft Office Program* hyperlink to open the document in the appropriate program (for example, if you're opening a text document, click the Edit in Microsoft Word hyperlink to open the document in Word 2002). You can then make

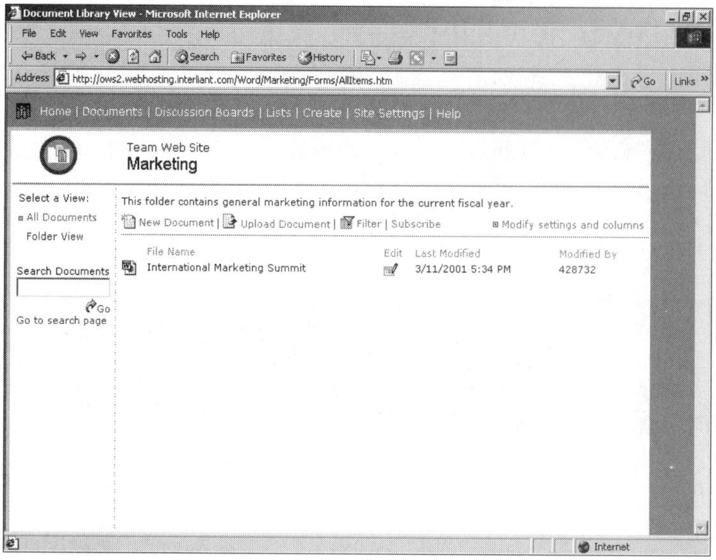

Figure 32-10. A document library containing a single file and links to create and edit the library's contents.

changes to the document by editing a local copy of the file. When you've finished, click Save to automatically upload and save the changed version of the document on the team Web site in place of the existing document. As you might expect, you'll need to supply your user name and ID before you can edit and save content on the team Web site.

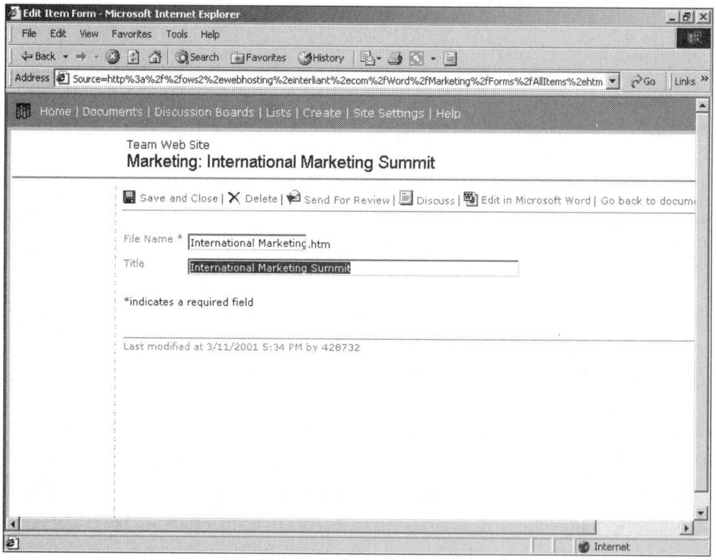

Figure 32-11. If your Web site role permits you to change Web site content, you can edit local versions of documents stored in document libraries using Office XP applications.

Assigning a Template to a Document Library

To ensure that all documents within a document library have a consistent look and feel, you can specify a template to be used when a new file is added to the library. You can modify this template by using Office XP programs just as you would any other template. You can associate only one template file per document library.

When you create a document library, you specify the type of files the library will contain by assigning a blank template. You can choose a blank Word, FrontPage, Microsoft Excel, or Microsoft PowerPoint template, and you can customize the blank template after you create a document library by following these steps:

1. Click the Documents link, and then display the contents of the document library in which you want to include a customized template.
2. Click the Modify Settings And Columns link.
3. In the General Settings section, click the Edit Template link in the Template section.
4. Enter your user name and ID to receive permission to edit the blank template.
5. Customize the file as desired, and then save the file.

The template will be applied to all new files created in the document library. Existing files will not be altered.

If you have an existing template that you'd like to apply to documents created in a document library, you can assign the existing template to the document library instead of modifying the default blank template. To associate an existing template with a document library, follow these steps:

1. Save the existing template on the current team Web site. (You can use the My Network Places link to the team Web site to save a document at the team Web site address.)
2. Display the contents of the document library in which you want to include a customized template.
3. Click Modify Settings And Columns.
4. In the General Settings section, click Change General Settings.
5. In the Document Template section, type the Web address of the template you want to use in the Template URL box, and then click OK.

The newly linked template applies only to new documents; existing documents remain unchanged.

Although the library files will be located on a Web server, the template file doesn't need to be in HTML (.htm) format. It's best to choose the format based on the type of files you'll be sharing in the library. For example, if you're sharing a library of Microsoft Word files, your template file should be in .dot format.

Part 8

Collaborating on Team Projects

Chapter 33

Revising Documents Using Markup Tools

As you probably know, many finished documents (this book is a prime example) reflect the efforts of a group of people who worked together to create a polished product. For example, you might be involved with a single document that was written by an author, modified by an editor, commented on by a technical reviewer, and inspected and approved by a project manager. This team collaboration can be simplified tremendously by using Microsoft Word.

In Word, numerous people can review the same document and incorporate their changes and comments with other people's changes and comments. After participants add their two cents worth in a document, others in the group can insert responses directly into the document. Throughout the process, Word can dutifully track and color-code everyone's comments and changes, as long as you configure Word's markup features properly. In this chapter, you'll learn to use Word's markup features and reviewing options so that you can maximize your collaboration efforts when you work with others on documents.

Familiarizing Yourself with Markup Tools

When you collaborate on a document, you can use Word to track and merge people's changes and comments, highlight information to draw attention to selected text and graphics, and store versions of documents throughout the development process. Specifically, Word provides the following reviewing and markup tools:

- **Comments** enable reviewers to annotate a document with suggestions and queries without changing the document. Comments are identified by comment markers in the text, which can be either insertion lines or parentheses, as described in the section "Adding and Managing Comments Effectively," on page 779.
- **The Highlight tool** enables you to draw attention to particular information (including a letter, word, phrase, sentence, paragraph, graphic, and so forth) by adding a color background behind the information, as described in the section "Using the Highlight Tool," on page 775.
- **The Track Changes feature** records editing changes, including deletions and added text, made to a document. Word can track changes from multiple reviewers, and the changes can later be evaluated and accepted or deleted on a case-by-case or global basis. For more information about the Track Changes feature, see the section "Tracking Changes," on page 797.
- **The Versions feature** maintains multiple versions of a document in a single file so that you can easily return to past versions of a changed document. The section "Working with Multiple Versions of a Document," on page 808, describes the Versions feature in more detail.

This chapter shows you how to make the most of these collaboration features. You'll find that many key collaboration features can be accessed from the Reviewing toolbar, shown in Figure 33-1. To open the Reviewing toolbar, right-click a toolbar and choose Reviewing on the shortcut menu, or choose View, Toolbars, Reviewing.

Figure 33-1. The Reviewing toolbar provides buttons you can use to add, modify, accept, and remove comments and tracked changes in documents.

As you can see in Figure 33-1, the Reviewing toolbar in Word 2002 is a modified version of the Reviewing toolbar found in Word 2000. The most notable additions to the Word 2002 Reviewing toolbar are the Display For Review drop-down list and the Show drop-down menu, which enable you to easily configure your reviewing options directly from the Reviewing toolbar. Table 33-1 describes the buttons found on the Reviewing toolbar.

Table 33-1. Reviewing Toolbar Buttons

Button	Name	Description
Display For Review	Display For Review	Controls how Word displays changes and comments in the current document.
Show	Show	Accesses a drop-down menu that enables you to configure the display and option settings for comments, reviewers, and tracked changes.
	Previous	Jumps to the previous tracked change or comment in the current document relative to the insertion point.
	Next	Jumps to the next tracked change or comment in the current document relative to the insertion point.
	Accept Change	Accepts a selected tracked change in the current document, or enables you to accept all changes at once.
	Reject Change/ Delete Comment	Rejects a selected change or deletes a selected comment and returns the text to its original state, or enables you to reject all changes or delete all comments at once.
	New Comment	Inserts a new comment. Clicking the down arrow enables you to edit and delete comments as well as record a voice comment.
	Track Changes	Controls whether the Track Changes feature is turned off or on.
	Reviewing Pane	Shows or hides the reviewing pane, which displays the complete text of tracked changes and comments.

Now that you've had a quick introduction to the main document collaboration features, let's look at the finer details. This chapter starts with the simplest feature associated with marking up documents—the Highlight tool.

Using the Highlight Tool

As in earlier versions of Word, the Highlight tool is available for use in Word 2002, and its functionality remains the same. Highlighting calls attention to important or questionable text in documents, as illustrated in Figure 33-2, on the next page. Highlighting parts of a document works best when the document is viewed on line, although you can use highlighting in printed documents if necessary. When you use the Highlight tool, the main tasks you'll perform are adding, removing, finding, and replacing highlighting. The next few sections briefly describe these procedures.

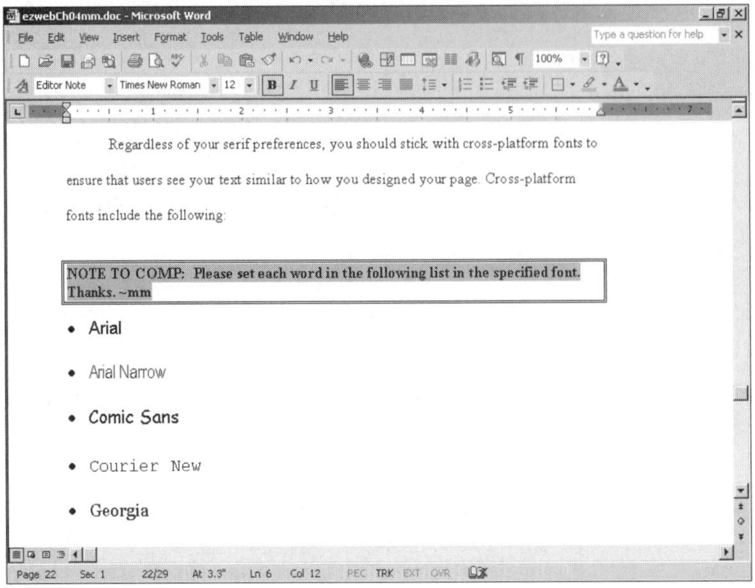

Figure 33-2. You can use the Highlight tool to draw attention to particular information in your Word document when you're collaborating with others.

> **note** In Word 2002, the Highlight tool is no longer included on the Reviewing toolbar. Instead, you have to access the Highlight tool directly from the Formatting toolbar.

Highlighting Information

Highlight

You can apply highlighting to a single block of selected text or graphics, or you can apply highlighting to a series of text areas or graphics. To apply a single instance of highlighting to information, select the information, and then click the Highlight button on the Formatting toolbar. To apply highlighting to multiple blocks of information, click the Highlight button, select the text or graphic you want to highlight, and then select the next item in the document you want to highlight. The Highlight tool continues to highlight information as you select it. To turn off highlighting, click the Highlight button again, or press Esc.

You can change the highlight color by clicking the Highlight button down arrow and choosing a color on the drop-down menu. The color you choose becomes the default highlight color until you select another color on the drop-down menu.

tip **Choose highlight colors wisely**

Be sure to choose a light highlight color if you're going to print your document with highlighted text, especially if the document will be printed in monochrome (including grayscale) or on a dot-matrix printer. If more than one person is going to be adding highlighting to a document, consider assigning highlight colors to each person or standardize highlight colors to indicate a particular issue (for example, reviewers could use turquoise highlighting to specify that a page reference needs to be completed, bright green highlighting to draw attention to repeated information, and so forth).

InsideOut

If you save highlighted text as part of a Web page, Word stores the highlighting information as part of the Web page's cascading style sheet (CSS). This information will be understood and displayed properly in Internet Explorer 3 and Netscape Navigator 4 browsers, but earlier versions of those browsers (and other less widely used browsers) might not display the highlighting properly. If you're not sure which browsers viewers will be using to display your Web page, you should consider using another method to draw attention to the text in place of highlighting. For example, you could color the text itself, create a graphic of the highlighted text, or build a table and color the text's table cell to simulate a highlighted paragraph.

Removing Highlighting from Documents

You can remove the highlighting in a document when you no longer need to draw attention to the text or graphic. To remove highlighting, follow these steps:

1. Select the information you want to remove highlighting from, or press Ctrl+A to select the entire document.
2. On the Formatting toolbar, click the Highlight button down arrow, and then choose None on the drop-down menu.

After you choose None, all instances of highlighting are removed from the selected text.

tip **Display and hide highlighting**

You can display or hide highlighting (but not the text itself) on screen and in the printed document without permanently removing the highlighting. To do so, choose Tools, Options, click the View tab, clear or select the Highlight check box in the Show section, and click OK.

Finding Highlighted Items

If you want to jump from highlighted item to highlighted item, you can do so by using the Find And Replace dialog box. To find instances of highlighted text, follow these steps:

1. Choose Edit, Find, or press Ctrl+F.
2. If necessary, click More to expand the Find tab.
3. Click Format, and choose Highlight.
4. Click Find Next to jump to the next occurrence of highlighted text, and click Close when you've finished reviewing all other instances of highlighted text.

You can also select all instances of highlighted text at one time by selecting the Highlight All Items Found In check box in the Find And Replace dialog box, verifying that Main Document is selected in the drop-down list below the check box, and clicking the Find All button.

For more information about the Find And Replace dialog box, see Chapter 12, "Honing Document Navigation Skills."

Reformatting Highlighted Items with Another Highlight Color

If your document contains a highlight color that you'd like to change, or if you'd like to change all instances of highlighting in a document to the same color, you can do so. To change a single instance of a highlight color, choose another highlight color on the Highlight button drop-down menu, and then select the highlighted text. The color changes to the newly selected color.

To change the color of multiple instances of highlighting, you can use the Find And Replace dialog box. Using this technique, you replace all highlighting (regardless of original highlight color) with a newly selected color, as follows:

1. Click the Highlight down arrow, and select the color you want to assign to all highlighting.
2. Choose Edit, Replace, or press Ctrl+H. The Find And Replace dialog box appears.
3. If necessary, click More to expand the Replace tab.
4. Make sure that no text appears in the Find What and Replace With boxes, position your insertion point in the Find What box, and then click Format and choose Highlight.

5. Click in the Replace With box, and choose Format, Highlight.
6. Click Replace All, and then click OK in the message box that tells you how many replacements were made.
7. Click Close to close the Find And Replace dialog box.

In addition to replacing all highlighted text with the newly selected color, you can also replace selected instances of highlighting with a new color. To do so, use the preceding procedure, but in step 6 click Find Next instead of Replace All. You can then specify which instances of highlighting are replaced with a new color on a case-by-case basis.

note You can also change all instances of highlighting to the same color by selecting all instances of highlighting using the Find tab, as described in the section "Finding Highlighted Items," on page 778, and then choosing a new color on the Highlight button drop-down menu.

newfeature!

Adding and Managing Comments Effectively

Comments allow people who collaborate on documents to ask questions, provide suggestions, insert notes, and generally annotate a document's contents without directly inserting any information into the body of the document. When you work with a document that contains comments, you can display the comments in the reviewing pane while viewing the document in any view or in a margin *balloon* if you're working in Web Layout or Print Layout view. When the reviewing pane is open, it is displayed below the document's editing window, along the bottom of the Word window. When you use balloons to display information, the balloons appear next to your document's contents in either the left or right margin. Figure 33-3, on the next page, shows a sample document in Print Layout view, with a comment balloon and the reviewing pane visible.

In addition to comment balloons, Word 2002 implements a number of visual cues when displaying comments. For example, notice in both the balloon and the reviewing pane (in the shaded comment bar) that the word *Comment* identifies the information as a comment. (You can also show insertions, deletions, and formatting changes in balloons and the reviewing pane, as described in the section "Tracking Changes," on page 797.) The balloons and comment bars in the reviewing pane can be color-coded to associate them with particular users, and each comment bar in the reviewing pane displays the user name of the person who inserted the comment. All these small modifications add up to create a new streamlined approach to using comments in Word.

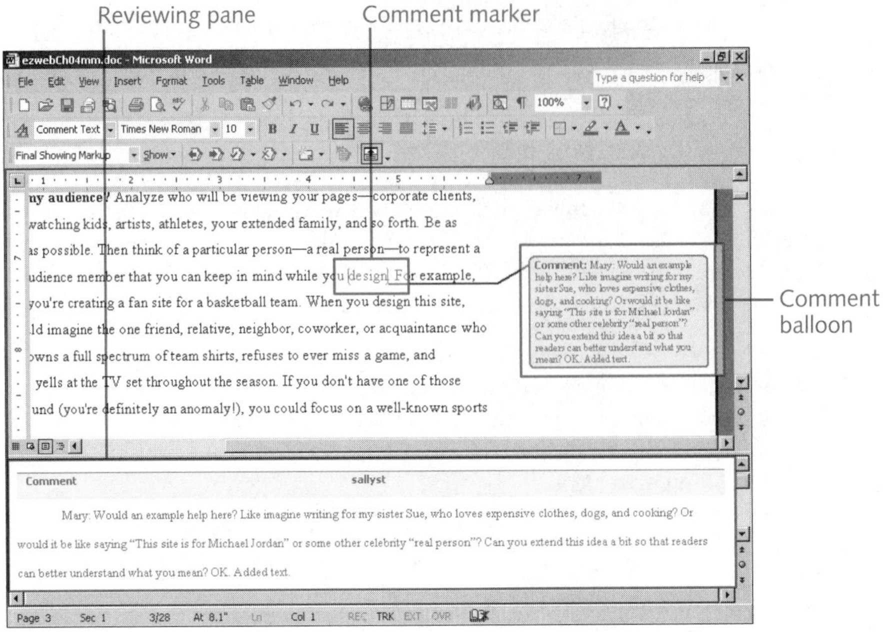

Figure 33-3. In Word 2002, you can display color-coded comments in comment balloons or in the reviewing pane.

Configuring Reviewers' User Names

Before you start inserting comments, you need to tell Word how to identify the comments you create. In other words, you need to configure your user name in Word. In fact, each person collaborating on the document must properly configure his or her user name to maximize Word's reviewing features. To set your user name information, you simply configure the settings on the User Information tab in the Options dialog box, as follows:

1. Choose, Tools, Options, and click the User Information tab.
2. In the Name box, type the name you want to use to identify your comments, and enter your initials in the Initials box, as shown in Figure 33-4.
3. Click OK to close the Options dialog box.

Keep in mind that the information you enter on the User Information tab is used by all Microsoft Office programs. Any changes you make to these settings will affect other Office programs in future documents as well. Fortunately, that's not as dire as it sounds. For example, if you're temporarily using someone else's machine to review a document, you can change the name on the User Information tab before you work without affecting existing documents. Then, when you've finished working with the document on that machine, reconfigure the User Information tab to contain the original information. That way, you can be sure that your comments will be marked with your name, even when you aren't working on your own computer.

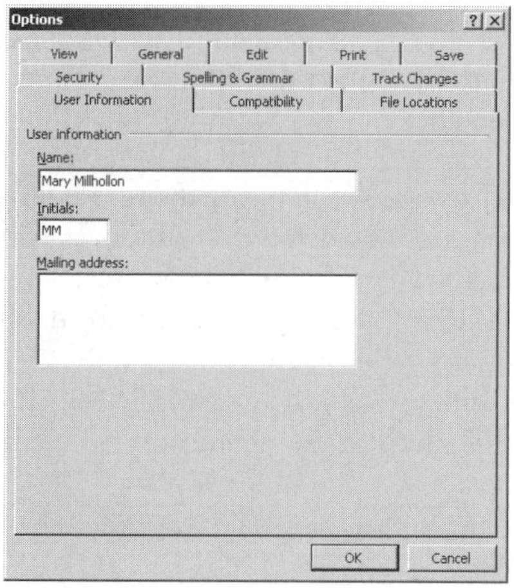

Figure 33-4. Word uses the User Information name to identify comments in documents.

Configuring Colors Associated with Reviewers

By default, Word automatically uses a different color for each reviewer's comments and tracked changes in a document. If you prefer all comments and tracked changes to be displayed in a single color, you can change the default setting by accessing the Track Changes options using one of the following techniques:

- On the Reviewing toolbar, click Show, and choose Options on the drop-down menu. The Track Changes dialog box opens, as shown in Figure 33-5.

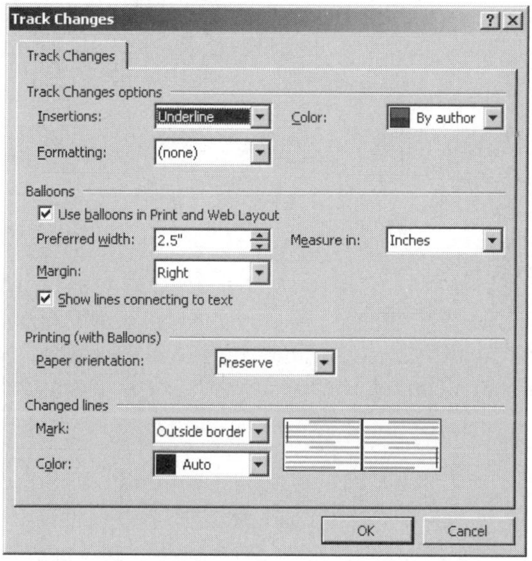

Figure 33-5. By default, comments and tracked changes are displayed in a different color for each reviewer.

- Choose Tools, Options, and click the Track Changes tab. The options on the Track Changes tab in the Options dialog box are the same options available in the Track Changes dialog box.

On the Track Changes tab, you can specify a color for all comments and tracked changes by selecting a color in the Color drop-down list. By default, By Author is selected in the Color box, which means that Word automatically assigns a different color to every person who inserts comments or tracked changes. Keep in mind that this setting doesn't always color-code each person's changes the same color every time. Instead, the By Author option simply guarantees that every person's marks will appear in a distinct color—each person's color will most likely change each time someone reopens the document.

For more information about configuring other Track Changes options, see "Adjusting the Appearance of Tracked Changes," on page 800.

If you're viewing a document that's color-coded for a number of reviewers, you can quickly see which colors are currently assigned to which reviewers. To do so, click Show on the Reviewing toolbar, and choose the Reviewers submenu. You'll see a list of reviewer names accompanied by color-coded check boxes, as shown in Figure 33-6. (Of course, you can't see the color-coding here, but you can get an idea of how the color-coding system works.) In addition to seeing the reviewer color assignments, you can use the Reviewers submenu to specify whose comments and tracked changes are displayed in the current document by selecting and clearing the check boxes next to reviewers' names. When you clear a check box while you're in Print Layout or Web Layout view, that reviewer's comment and tracked change balloons are hidden, and text inserted by the reviewer appears as regular body text. To redisplay a reviewer's comments and changes, reselect the reviewer's check box on the Reviewers submenu.

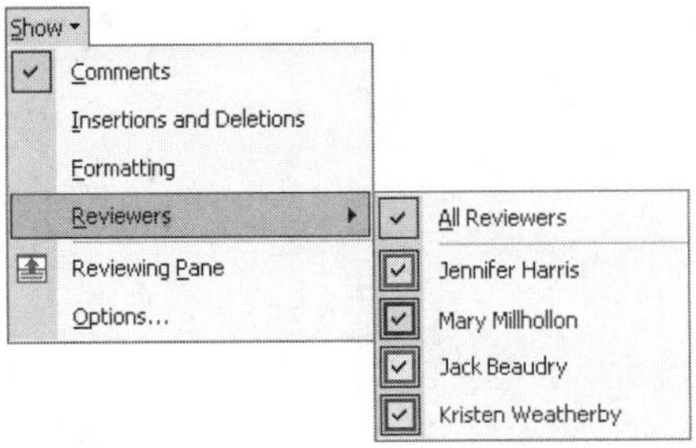

Figure 33-6. You can use the Reviewers submenu to quickly see the colors currently assigned to reviewers and to control whose comments and changes are displayed in the current document.

Marking Text You Insert in E-Mail Responses

If Microsoft Outlook is your e-mail client and Word is set to serve as your e-mail message editor, you can add comments to e-mail messages in the same way you add comments to standard documents. You can also configure Word to display your name or initials next to text you insert in e-mail responses, as follows:

1. Choose Tools, Options, and click the General tab.
2. Click E-Mail Options, and then click the Personal Stationery tab in the E-Mail Options dialog box.
3. Select the Mark My Comments With check box, and type the text (such as your name or initials) that you want to display in association with your comments, as shown here:

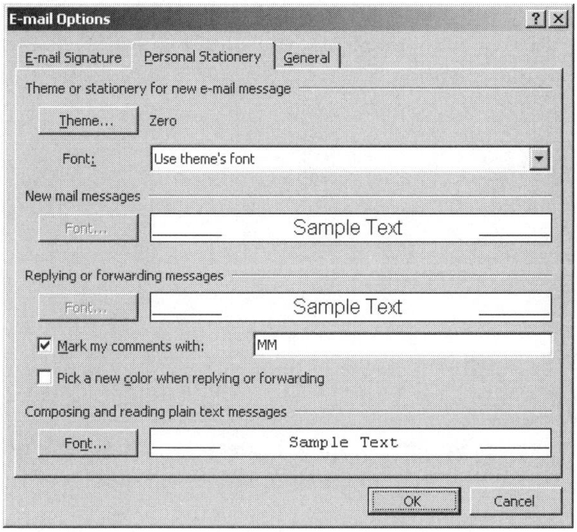

4. Click OK to close the E-Mail Options dialog box, and then click OK to close the Options dialog box.

When you select the Mark My Comments With check box, only text you type next to previously written text in a message will display your name or initials next to it. To turn off this formatting in e-mail messages, clear the Mark My Comments With check box.

InsideOut

If you're working in Normal view and you turn off the display of a reviewer's tracked changes, the text deleted by the reviewer appears restored and text inserted by the reviewer appears as regular text. As you can imagine, this can result in some strange mixtures of restored and added text. To avoid confusion, if you choose to hide a particular reviewer's comments and changes, be sure you're working in Print Layout or Web Layout view.

Allowing Reviewers to Use Only the Comments Feature

In addition to color-coding reviewers' comments, you can use Word to help control who may or may not add comments to a document during the review phases. To do this, you use the Protect Document dialog box, shown in Figure 33-7. Using this dialog box, you can ensure that the only modifications reviewers can make to your document is to add comments.

Figure 33-7. The Protect Document dialog box enables you to limit reviewers' actions and lets you assign a password that reviewers must enter before they can make changes to the document.

To arrange this setup, follow these steps:

1. Choose Tools, Protect Document.
2. In the Protect Document dialog box, click Comments.
3. If desired, type a password in the Password box, click OK, retype the password in the Confirm Password dialog box, and click OK again. If you specify a password, reviewers will have to enter the password before they can enter comments.

note Password protection created by using the Protect Document dialog box doesn't work with HTML (Web page) documents.

If you choose not to assign a password in step 3, reviewers will be restricted to inserting only comments by default. But if reviewers choose Tools, Unprotect Document, they'll be able to unlock the document and edit your document freely. In other words, this document protection plan is really more of a deterrent than a fail-safe protection, but many times a deterrent is all you really need.

For more information about protecting documents, see Chapter 34, "Addressing Security Issues."

Troubleshooting

I Forgot the Password for a Protected Document

If you forget the password for a protected document, you can recover the document by circumventing the password protection. To do so, select the entire document (by pressing Ctrl+A), copy the document (by pressing Ctrl+C), and paste the document (by pressing Ctrl+V) into a new, blank document. This process creates a new document based on the existing document.

newfeature!

Nicely enough, in Word 2002, when you copy and paste a document that contains tracked changes and comments, the newly created document retains all the reviewers' marks and color-coded settings. In earlier versions of Word, when you copy and paste text that contains tracked changes, the changes are accepted in the newly copied version of the text regardless of whether you're ready to accept the changes.

Inserting Standard Comments

After you configure your user name information, specify how to color comments, and set any reviewer limitations, you're ready to insert comments into documents. Inserting a comment is a straightforward process. You can insert your comment at the insertion point, or you can select text that you want to associate with your comment. If you insert a comment at the insertion point, Word indicates the existence of your comment in the text with a thin, color-coded insertion mark. (See Figure 33-3.) If you select text to be associated with a comment, Word marks the range of text by enclosing the text in thin, color-coded parentheses.

To insert a comment, follow these steps:

1. Position the insertion point where you want to insert a comment, or select the text or item you want to associate with your comment.
2. Perform any of the following three actions:
   - Choose Insert, Comment.
   - Click the New Comment button on the Reviewing toolbar.

- Press Ctrl+Alt+M.

  If you're working in Web Layout or Print Layout view, an empty balloon opens by default when you insert a comment. If you're working in Normal view, the reviewing pane opens.

> **note** By default, comment balloons are turned on in Print Layout and Web Layout views. If your balloons are hidden, you can type comments in the reviewing pane when you're working in Print Layout or Web Layout view.

3. Type the comment text in the comment balloon or the reviewing pane, and then click outside of the balloon or reviewing pane to complete the comment.

> **tip** If you're entering a comment in a balloon, you can press Esc when you've finished typing to return the insertion point to the body text.

If you want to change a comment after you create it, you can do so by clicking inside the comment balloon or reviewing pane and then editing the text just as you edit standard text. If a comment is long and its contents aren't entirely displayed in a balloon, you can modify the comment in the reviewing pane. If the reviewing pane isn't open, click the reviewing pane button on the Reviewing toolbar to open it. To close the reviewing pane, click the Reviewing Pane button on the Reviewing toolbar, or press Alt+Shift+C.

Inserting Voice Comments

Audio

In addition to inserting standard comments, you can include *voice comments* with documents. Basically, voice comments are recordings you make and attach to a document. To create voice comments, your computer must have a sound card and a microphone. Likewise, others who review the document and listen to your voice comments must be using computers equipped with a sound card and speakers. Unlike text comments (which appear in balloons and in the reviewing pane), voice comments appear as an audio icon in line with text. To create a voice comment, display the Reviewing toolbar, and then follow these steps:

1. Click the New Comment button down arrow.
2. Choose Voice Comment on the drop-down menu. Sound Recorder opens, as shown in Figure 33-8.

Record

3. Click the Record button, and then speak into your microphone to record your comment.

Stop

4. Click Stop when you've finished recording your comment, and close Sound Recorder or choose File, Exit & Return to complete the voice comment.

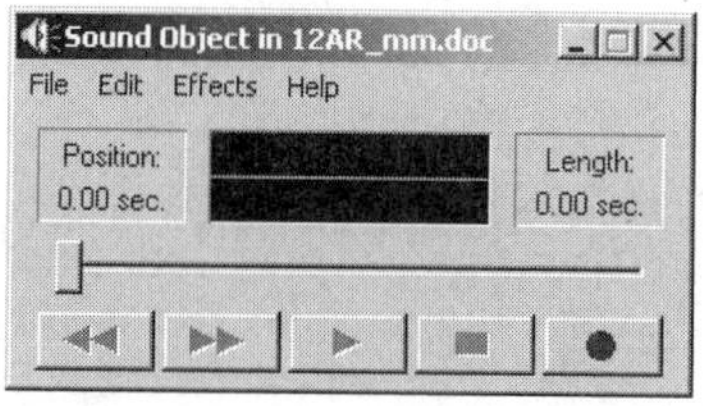

Figure 33-8. Sound Recorder is a simple application you can use to include voice comments in documents.

After you create a voice comment, you can manipulate it in the following ways:

- **Listen to the voice comment.** Double-click the audio icon in the document. The comment plays without opening Sound Recorder.
- **Open Sound Recorder before listening to the voice comment.** Right-click the audio icon, and choose Wave Sound Object, Edit on the shortcut menu.
- **Modify the voice comment.** Right-click the comment, and choose Wave Sound Object, Edit on the shortcut menu.
- **Delete the voice comment.** Select the audio icon and press Delete, or right-click the audio icon and choose Cut on the shortcut menu.

If you decide to use voice comments, you should keep your messages short. By default, voice comments are WAV audio files attached to the document, and as you know, audio files can grow in size fairly rapidly.

Configuring Comment Balloon and Reviewing Pane Options

When you work with comment balloons (and tracked change balloons, as discussed in the section "Tracking Changes," on page 797), you can control a variety of balloon options. Specifically, you can format balloon and reviewing pane label text (which is the text that is displayed on reviewing pane bars above each comment or tracked change), specify whether balloons will be displayed, and adjust balloon width and placement.

Changing the Style of Balloon and Reviewing Pane Labels

You can modify the style of balloon and reviewing pane labels (including the word *Comment* and user names) in the same manner you modify other styles in Word documents—by using the Styles And Formatting task pane. To modify the Balloon Text style, follow these steps:

1. Click the Styles And Formatting button on the Formatting toolbar to open the Styles And Formatting task pane.
2. In the Styles And Formatting task pane, click the Show down arrow, and choose Custom in the drop-down list to open the Format Settings dialog box.

InsideOut

If the Format Settings dialog box doesn't open when you choose Custom in the Show drop-down list in the Styles And Formatting task pane, your insertion point might be positioned in the reviewing pane. The Format Settings dialog box won't open when you're working in the reviewing pane. To work around this little peculiarity, simply click in the document's body text, and then choose Custom in the Show drop-down list again.

3. In the Styles To Be Visible list, select the Balloon Text check box, and then click OK.
4. In the list in the Pick A Formatting To Apply section, right-click the Balloon Text entry (this style also controls the reviewing pane label text), and choose Modify on the shortcut menu. The Modify Style dialog box appears.
5. Select any options you want, and click Format to access additional style attributes.
6. After you configure the options you want, select the Automatically Update check box if you want to update all instances of balloon and reviewing pane labels, and then click OK.

For more information about working with styles, see Chapter 10, "Using Styles to Increase Your Formatting Power."

Although most changes you make to balloon text affect only the balloon and the reviewing pane labels, changing the point size will affect the size of comment text. When you change the Balloon Text style point size, you'll also change the size of the comment text displayed in the balloons. To gain greater control over comment text within balloons and the reviewing pane, you should configure the Comment Text style, as discussed next.

Changing the Default Style for Text Inserted in Balloons and the Reviewing Pane

You can modify how comment text appears in balloons and in the reviewing pane by modifying the Comment Text style. When you modify this style, you change the appearance of text only in comment balloons (not text displayed in tracked change balloons, as discussed in the section "Tracking Changes," on page 797). To control how comment text appears, follow the steps in the preceding section, but in steps 3 and 4 choose Comment Text instead of Balloon Text.

Showing and Hiding Balloons

If you prefer to work with the reviewing pane and not balloons, you can turn off balloons. To control whether balloons are displayed in Web Layout and Print Layout views, you configure the Track Changes options, as follows:

1. On the Reviewing toolbar, click Show, and choose Options on the drop-down menu, or choose Tools, Options, and click the Track Changes tab.
2. In the Balloons section, select or clear the Use Balloons In Print And Web Layout check box, and click OK.

If you hide balloons, comments will be displayed as ScreenTips when you position your mouse pointer over the comment marker when the reviewing pane is closed, as shown in Figure 33-9. When the reviewing pane is open, comments will be displayed in the reviewing pane, and ScreenTips won't appear when you move your mouse pointer over a comment marker.

note When you hide balloons, insertions and deletions will be shown in the body of the document, and formatting changes will be visible when you view your document in Final or Final Showing Markup mode. Final and Final Showing Markup modes are discussed in the section "Tracking Changes," on page 797.

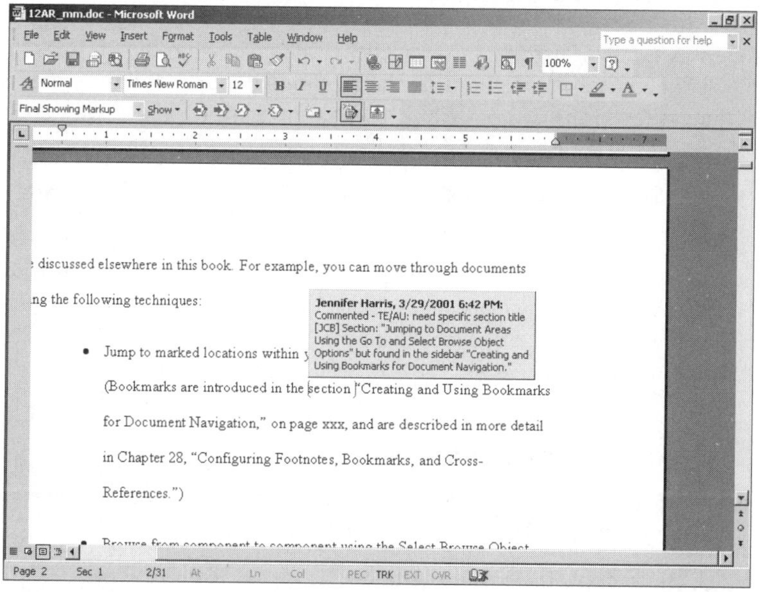

Figure 33-9. When balloons are hidden and the reviewing pane is closed, comments are displayed as ScreenTips.

tip **Hide or display lines connecting text and balloons**

You can also specify whether the lines used to connect balloons to text are displayed or hidden by selecting or clearing the Show Lines Connecting To Text check box on the Track Changes tab. When you clear the Show Lines Connect To Text check box, balloons are displayed with a thin dashed line when they aren't selected. Then, when you select a comment, the comment is displayed with a solid line that connects the balloon to the comment marker in the text.

Adjusting Balloon Size and Location for Online Viewing

Because balloons are a new feature in Word 2002, you might find that they take some getting used to, especially if you've frequently used comments and tracking tools in earlier versions of Word. To help you get more comfortable with this new feature, Microsoft provides a couple of options you can use to control the size and position of balloons when you choose to view them. In fact, you can control balloon width and location for online viewing as well as for printing purposes. In this section, we'll look at configuring the online presentation of balloons. For more information about configuring balloons for printing, see the section "Printing Comments," on page 794.

To set balloon width and specify whether balloons are displayed in the right or left margin, you must configure the Track Changes dialog box (or the Track Changes tab in the Options dialog box), as follows:

1. Open the Track Changes dialog box by clicking Show on the Reviewing toolbar and choosing Options on the drop-down menu, or display the Track Changes tab in the Options dialog box by choosing Tools, Options, and clicking the Track Changes tab.
2. Make sure that the Use Balloons In Print And Web Layout check box is selected.
3. Click the Measure In down arrow, and select an option in the drop-down list to specify whether you want the balloons to be measured in inches or percent. For more information about the Inches and Percent options, see the sidebar "Sizing Balloons—Inches vs. Percent," on the facing page.
4. In the Preferred Width box, enter a percentage or measurement (in inches) for the width of the balloons.
5. In the Margin box, choose the Left or Right option to specify on which side of the document text you want balloons to appear.
6. Click OK to apply the balloon settings.

Unfortunately, you can't preview how your balloon settings will be displayed from within the Track Changes tab. Your best bet when configuring balloons is to try a few settings and see which setting works best for you on your monitor.

Sizing Balloons—Inches vs. Percent

When you size balloons, Word configures them without compromising the document's content area. This is accomplished by expanding the view of your document (not by reducing the document's content area). To clarify, let's look at the two sizing options: Inches and Percent.

When you use the Inches setting, you provide a set size in which your balloons will appear in your document's margin. For example, if you specify 2 inches, your page's view will expand so that balloons will be displayed within a 2-inch-wide area, starting from the document's margin.

Similarly, if you size balloons using the Percent option, the balloons will be displayed as a percentage of the page's size without compromising the document's content area. For example, if you specify balloons to be 100 percent, the balloons will be sized equal to 100 percent of the page, and the width of your page's view will be expanded accordingly (doubled, in this case).

You can easily see how balloons will be displayed relative to the current document by saving a setting (using Inches or Percent) and then viewing your document in Print Preview mode by clicking the Print Preview button on the Standard toolbar.

Reviewing Comments

Let's say your document has made its rounds, and now it's up to you to review the comments reviewers have inserted into the document. You can review comments only, or you can review comments while you review tracked changes. In this section, we'll look at the process of reviewing comments only. (For more information about reviewing tracked changes, see the section "Tracking Changes," on page 797.) To review only comments, you must first hide tracked changes. To show comments without displaying tracked changes, display your document in Web Layout or Print Layout view, and then follow these steps:

1. If necessary, choose View, Markup to show tracked changes and comments in your document. The Markup command on the View menu is a toggle command that you can use to show and hide markup in documents.
2. On the Reviewing toolbar, make sure that either Final Showing Markup or Original Showing Markup is selected in the Display For Review box.
3. Click Show on the Reviewing toolbar, and make sure that only the Comments option is selected on the drop-down menu. To accomplish this, you'll probably have to choose Insertions And Deletions and Formatting to clear the check marks next to them.

After you complete these steps, comments and comment markers should be the only markup features visible in the current document. At this point, you can review the comments manually by scrolling through your document or the reviewing pane, or you can jump from comment to comment by clicking the Next and Previous buttons on the Reviewing toolbar. Depending on the current view, clicking the Next or Previous button displays the next or previous comment as follows:

- **In Normal view,** the comment is displayed in the reviewing pane. If the reviewing pane isn't open, Word opens it automatically.
- **In Print Layout or Web Layout view with balloons turned on,** the comment balloon is displayed on screen and appears as the active comment, indicated by a dark outline and solid connector line.
- **In Print Layout or Web Layout view with balloons turned off,** the comment is displayed in the reviewing pane. If the reviewing pane isn't open, Word opens it automatically.

note You can also browse from comment to comment by using the Select Browse Object feature (press Ctrl+Alt+Home) or the Go To tab in the Find And Replace dialog box. On the Go To tab, you can select Comment in the Go To What list and then choose to view all reviewers comments or a selected reviewer's comments by selecting Any Reviewer or a specific name in the Enter Reviewer's Name drop-down list. For more information about using the Browse Object feature and the Go To tab, see Chapter 12, "Honing Document Navigation Skills."

When you view comments in balloons, you might notice that some comments have an ellipsis in the lower-right corner, as shown in Figure 33-10. This symbol indicates that the entire comment text doesn't fit in the balloon. To view the remainder of the comment, click the ellipsis to open the reviewing pane, which will contain the entire contents of the comment.

Naturally, as you read through comments, you might want to respond to them while you work. You can do so in a couple of ways, including the following:

- Type directly in a comment, in which case your response won't be color-coded according to your user name. (This is a departure from earlier versions of Word, in which all text you add to a document is color-coded when the Track Changes feature is turned on.)
- Click in the comment you want to respond to, and then click New Comment on the Reviewing toolbar, press Ctrl+Alt+M, or choose Insert, Comment. A new balloon opens directly below the balloon you're responding to, or a blank entry opens in the reviewing pane. Then simply enter your response.

In addition to responding to comments, you might want to delete comments as you address them to help prepare the document for final publication, as described in the next section.

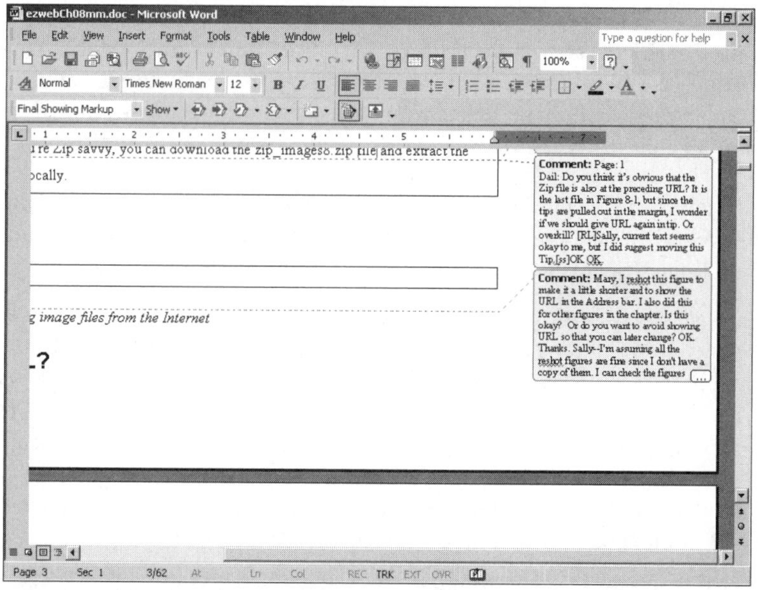

Figure 33-10. If a balloon contains more text than can be displayed in the balloon, you can click the ellipsis icon in the lower-right corner to open the reviewing pane, which will show the comment in its entirety.

> **tip** **See who created a comment and when**
>
> To quickly see when a comment was inserted and who created it, you can hover the mouse pointer over the comment balloon. When you do this, a ScreenTip appears that displays the comment's creation date and time as well as the user name of the person who created the comment. If you're working in the reviewing pane, each reviewing pane bar displays the user name and insertion date and time automatically.

> **note** If you notice that a name associated with tracked changes or comments changes to *Author* every time you save your document, you might have to reconfigure your Security tab settings in the Options dialog box. This automatic change from user names to *Author* occurs if you've selected the Remove Personal Information From This File On Save check box on the Security tab. When you select this option, names associated with tracked changes and comments are replaced with the word *Author*. For more information about configuring your security settings, see Chapter 34, "Addressing Security Issues."

Deleting Comments

Generally, comments serve a temporary purpose—reviewers insert comments, someone addresses the comments, and then the comments are removed before the document's final publication (either on line or in print). If you work with comments, you'll need to know how to delete them so that you won't unintentionally include them in your final publication. As you might expect, you can delete comments in several ways. Namely, you can delete a single comment, delete comments from a specific reviewer (or reviewers), or delete all comments, using the following techniques:

- **Delete a single comment.** Right-click a comment balloon and then click Delete Comment on the shortcut menu, or select a comment balloon and then click the Reject Change/Delete Comment button on the Reviewing toolbar.
- **Delete comments from a specific reviewer.** First clear the check boxes for all reviewers by clicking Show on the Reviewing toolbar and choosing Reviewers, All Reviewers. Next display only the comments you want to delete by clicking Show, choosing Reviewers, and then selecting the check box next to the reviewer's name whose comments you want to delete. (You can repeat this process to select additional reviewers as well.) To delete the displayed comments, click the Reject/Delete Comment down arrow, and choose Delete All Comments Shown on the drop-down menu.
- **Delete all comments in the document.** Make sure that all reviewers comments are displayed. (This is the default setting, but if all reviewers' comments aren't displayed, click Show on the Reviewing toolbar, and choose Reviewers, All Reviewers.) Click the Reject Change/Delete Comment down arrow, and then choose Delete All Comments In Document on the drop-down menu.

Keep in mind that when you delete all comments at once by choosing the Delete All Comments In Document option on the Reject Change/Delete Comment drop-down menu, you delete all comments in the document, regardless of whether they are displayed on screen.

tip **Delete a comment in the reviewing pane**

You can also delete comments one at a time from within the reviewing pane. To do so, click in the comment in the reviewing pane and click the Reject Change/Delete Comment button on the Reviewing toolbar, or right-click a comment in the reviewing pane and choose Delete Comment on the shortcut menu.

Printing Comments

As mentioned, you can control how comments are displayed on screen as well as in print. The section "Configuring Comment Balloons and Reviewing Pane Options," on page 787, addressed how to control the display of comments in balloons and in the reviewing pane. In this section, we'll look at the ways you can print comments. When you print a document containing comments (and tracked changes, for that matter), you can configure print settings in two areas: the Track Changes dialog box and the Print dialog box. Let's look first at the Track Changes dialog box.

In the Track Changes dialog box (accessed by clicking Show on the Reviewing toolbar and choosing Options), you can specify in the Printing (With Balloons) section how Word should adjust paper orientation to accommodate balloons. You can select any of the following settings in the Paper Orientation list:

- **Auto** specifies that Word can determine the best orientation layout for your document automatically, based on your margin settings and balloon width settings.
- **Preserve** prints the document with the orientation specified in the Page Setup dialog box.
- **Force Landscape** prints balloons and the document in landscape format to allow the most room for the display of balloons.

After you choose how you want Word to handle page orientation issues when you print documents with comment balloons, you're ready to configure the Print dialog box.

In the Print dialog box (choose File, Print), you can specify whether to print the document showing markup (the default setting when comments and tracked changes are displayed), or you can opt to print just a list of the markup changes made in a document. Most likely, if you want to print a document's changes, you'll want to print the document showing changes instead of printing a list of changes. When you print a list of changes, the list can become long and confusing.

The easiest way to print a document with its comments is to print the document with comment balloons in the margin and hide the other types of margin balloons (including balloons that show insertions, deletions, and formatting changes). To print comments in a document efficiently, follow these steps:

1. Display your document in Print Layout view.
2. On the Reviewing toolbar, click Show, and verify that only the Comments option is selected (and the Insertions And Deletions and Formatting options are cleared). By choosing just the Comments option, you'll be able to print the document and its comments, without cluttering up your view with balloons denoting inserted, deleted, and reformatted information.
3. Choose File, Print to open the Print dialog box.
4. In the Print dialog box, make sure that the Print What box shows Document Showing Markup, and click OK.

The document will be printed with comment balloons in the margin. Word will reduce the view of the page to accommodate printing balloons in the margins. This doesn't affect your document's layout parameters—it's just a temporary modification for printing purposes when you're printing balloons along with a document.

Saving a Document with Comments as a Web Page

You can save a document that contains comments and other marked up text as a Web page. When you do this, Word retains the comments and tracked changes in the text, although all reviewers' comments and changes are displayed in the same color. To save a reviewed document as a Web page, choose File, Save As, make sure in the Save As dialog box that the Save As Type box shows Web Page, and then click Save .

Keep in mind that the online display of comments and tracked changes in your document depends on your browser. In Microsoft Internet Explorer 4 and later, comments are shown as dynamic ScreenTips, as shown in Figure 33-11, and revised text appears in a color other than black with underlining and strikethrough formatting (but remember, color-coding based on reviewers' user names is lost), similar to how you see markup changes in Word when a single color is selected to show markup. In browsers earlier than Internet Explorer 4 and in Netscape Navigator 4 and later, comments appear as footnotes beneath the main Web page instead of as dynamic ScreenTips.

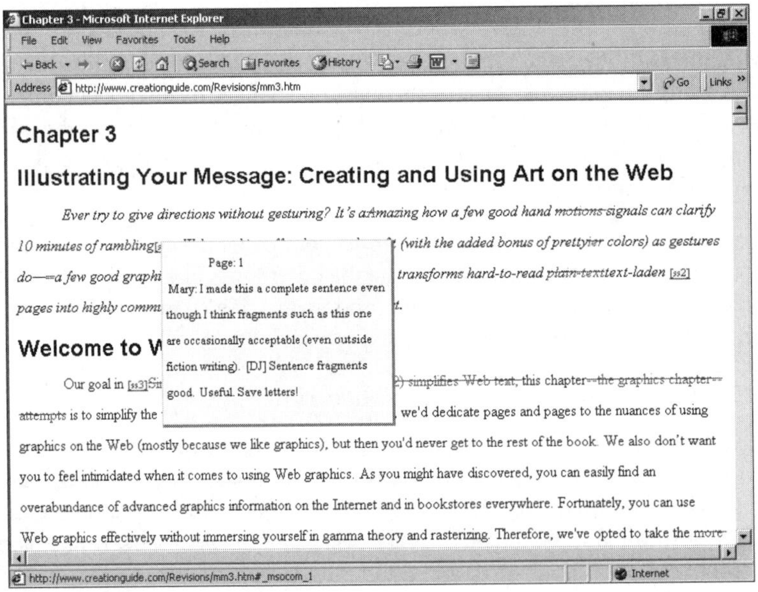

Figure 33-11. When you save a marked-up document as a Web page, users can view comments in the form of dynamic ScreenTips by positioning the mouse pointer over a comment link.

Tracking Changes

Adding comments to documents is invaluable when reviewers need to annotate and query text, but you need another set of features when you want reviewers to conduct line-by-line edits to help smooth a document's text and layout. When your document's ready for detailed editing, you'll want to turn to Word's Track Changes feature.

> **note** If you've been using Word for a few versions now, you might still think of the Track Changes feature as the Revision Marks feature, which was the name of this feature in Word 95 and earlier.

When you turn on the Track Changes feature, Word records the deletions, insertions, and formatting changes made by each reviewer who modifies the document. By default, Word displays each reviewer's changes in a different color so that you can easily identify the sources of changes within your document. When you work with a document that has been modified by reviewers, you can use the Display For Review drop-down list on the Reviewing toolbar to display the changed document in four views, as described here:

- **Final Showing Markup** shows deleted text in the balloons and displays inserted text and formatting changes in line.
- **Final** shows how the document would appear if you accepted all changes.
- **Original Showing Markup** shows the inserted text and formatting changes in balloons and shows deleted text in line with strikethrough lines.
- **Original** shows the original, unchanged document so that you can see how the document would look if you rejected all the changes.

Being able to display your document in these ways can help you as you add, accept, and reject tracked changes. In addition, many configuration settings you use to control how comments are displayed (as discussed earlier in this chapter) also apply to tracked changes. In the sections discussing tracked changes that follow, you'll find references to topics covered in the comments sections in this chapter if the topic applies to both comments and tracked changes.

Before we get to the details of working with tracked changes, you should note that Word doesn't track some changes when you modify a document, including changes you make involving the following:

- AutoCaptions
- Background colors
- Embedded fonts
- Resized figures and objects

- Routing information
- Some custom options, such as custom toolbar buttons
- Some types of mail merge information, such as whether a file is a main document or a data file

For the most part, you probably won't find that these limitations interfere with tasks involving tracked changes, but you should be aware of the exceptions, just in case.

note Although Word doesn't track changes when graphics and other objects are resized, it does track position changes to graphics and shapes. For example, when you move a graphic, Word shows the originally placed graphic as a deleted item and reinserts the graphic in the new location. Therefore, when you display a document with tracked changes showing, you might see a graphic in two locations (a deleted version of the graphic and a newly placed version of the graphic).

Tracking Changes While You Edit

When you track changes in a document, you can opt to display or hide the tracking marks while you work. Generally, it's easier to hide tracked changes if you're editing and writing text and better to view tracking marks when you're reviewing a document's changes. When Word tracks changes, it automatically records insertions or deletions in balloons (depending on your view, as described in the preceding section), which you can view in Web Layout and Print Layout view. Word marks tracked changes in a document as follows:

- **Added text** appears in the reviewer's color with underlining.
- **Deleted text** remains visible but is displayed in the reviewer's color with a strikethrough line indicating the deletion.
- **Text added and then deleted text by the reviewer** is displayed as if the text was never added. (In other words, no changed information appears in a document in places where a reviewer adds information and then deletes the added information.)

In addition to these actions, Word automatically inserts a vertical line, called a *changed line*, along the left margin to indicate that an editing change has been made. This line appears whenever text or formatting changes are made while the Track Changes feature is turned on.

Figure 33-12 shows a document in Final Showing Markup view, which displays inserted text in line, deleted text in balloons, and both deleted and inserted text in the reviewing pane. Notice the changed line in the left margin, which specifies that the text next to the line has been modified in some way. For more information about configuring changed lines, see the section "Customizing the Appearance of Changed Lines," on page 801.

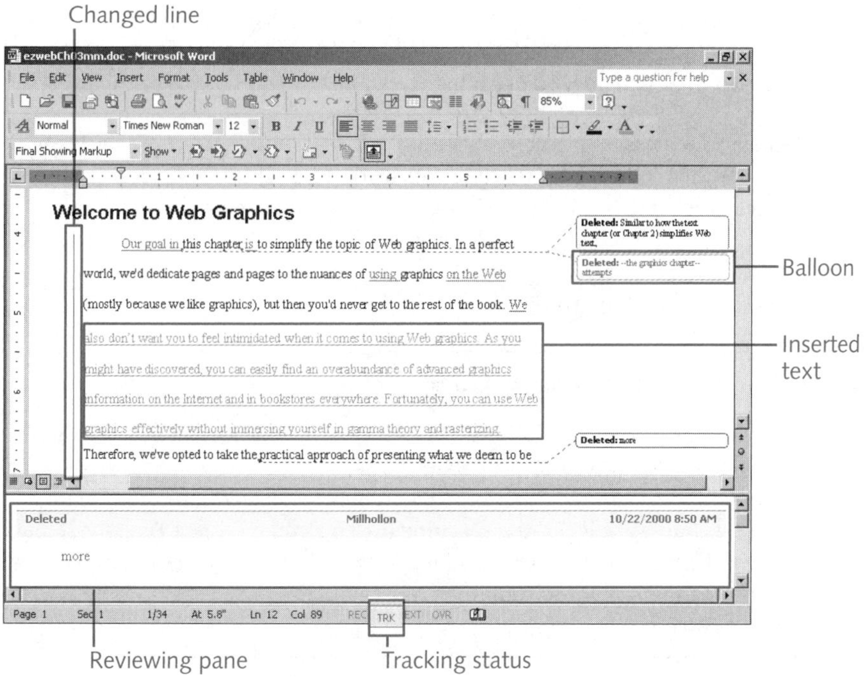

Figure 33-12. The Final Showing Markup view displays inserted text within the document and describes deletions in balloons in the margins. Of course, all changes are displayed in the reviewing pane regardless of the setting in the Display For Review box on the Reviewing toolbar.

Notice in Figure 33-12 that the TRK button on the status bar is turned on (not dimmed); this indicates that the Track Changes feature is currently turned on. You can control whether the Track Changes feature is turned on or off by double-clicking TRK on the status bar.

You can track changes in a document by following these steps:

1. Open the document you want to revise, and choose whether you want to edit the document in Normal, Web Layout, or Print Layout view.
2. Turn tracking on using one of the following techniques (all of which are toggle commands, which means that you can use the commands to turn Track Changes on or off):
   - Choose Tools, Track Changes.
   - Press Ctrl+Shift+E.
   - On the Reviewing toolbar, click the Track Changes button.
   - Double-click TRK on the status bar.

3. After Track Changes is turned on, make editorial changes, including inserting, deleting, moving, and reformatting. Word tracks your changes, regardless of whether your view reflects the tracked changes as marked-up text.

As mentioned, you can record changes while displaying tracked changes on screen or you can hide the tracking marks while you work. In addition, you can always tell whether changes are being tracked by looking at the TRK button on the status bar. If TRK appears black, you're tracking your changes, whether or not you can see the tracking marks on screen. If TRK appears dimmed, the Track Changes feature is turned off, and any changes you make will not be tracked.

> **tip** **Limit reviewers to making tracked changes only**
>
> You can control who can add tracked changes to your document by using the Protect Document dialog box, as described in the section "Allowing Reviewers to Use Only the Comments Feature," on page 784. To limit reviewers to making only tracked changes, choose Tools, Protect Document to open the Protect Document dialog box, click the Tracked Changes option, supply a password (if desired), and click OK. When tracked changes are protected, reviewers can't accept and reject changes made by other reviewers.

Adjusting the Appearance of Tracked Changes

Just as you can control the appearance of comments, you can control the appearance of tracked changes in your documents. A number of Track Changes options correspond to options available for comments, including the following:

- **Configuring user names.** See the section "Configuring Reviewers' User Names," on page 780.
- **Configuring colors associated with reviewers.** See the section "Configuring Colors Associated with Reviewers," on page 781.
- **Controlling balloon and reviewing pane options.** See the section "Configuring Comment Balloon and Reviewing Pane Options," on page 787.

In addition to these options, you can specify how inserted text and objects should be marked, how formatting changes should be identified, and how changed lines should appear in your document. These options are discussed in the next few sections.

> **note** The settings you configure for displaying tracked changes are global and will apply to all documents you open in Word that have Track Changes marks in them.

Specifying How Insertions and Formatting Changes Are Displayed

You can change how Word identifies inserted and reformatted information when the Track Changes feature is turned on. To configure these settings, you must access the Track Changes dialog box (or the Track Changes tab in the Options dialog box), as follows:

1. Click Show on the Reviewing toolbar and choose Options from the drop-down menu, or choose Tools, Options and click the Track Changes tab.
2. Click the Insertions down arrow, and select how you'd like inserted text to be identified. You can choose to show insertions without any special formatting (in which case inserted text looks like regular, non-color-coded text and is indistinguishable from the original text). Or you can display inserted text in the reviewer's color only or in the reviewer's color and formatted as boldface, italic, underlined, or double-underlined. By default, inserted text appears in the reviewer's color with an underline.
3. Click the Formatting down arrow, and select how you want Word to mark format changes. By default, formatting changes aren't marked in the body of the text (most likely because adding formatting to identify information that's been reformatted can sometimes create a confusing mix of formatting).
4. Click OK to save the settings.

Regardless of your selections for formatting inserted and reformatted information, you can still use changed lines to indicate in a general way where changes have occurred in a document. To learn how to configure changed lines, refer to the next section.

Customizing the Appearance of Changed Lines

As shown in Figure 33-12, Word automatically inserts a black vertical line, called a changed line, in the margin next to text that contains tracked changes. You can specify where changed lines are displayed on the page (along the right, left, or outside margins) and the color in which they are displayed. To configure how changed lines are displayed, follow these steps:

1. Click Show on the Reviewing toolbar and choose Options on the drop-down menu, or choose Tools, Options and click the Track Changes tab.
2. In the Changed Lines section, click the Mark down arrow, and specify whether you want changed lines to be displayed along the left, right, or outside border. You can select the (None) setting if you'd rather not display changed lines when you use the Track Changes feature. To see how a particular setting works, select the option and refer to the preview box in the Track Changes dialog box (or on the Track Changes tab in the Options dialog box). By default, changed lines are set to Outside Border.

3. To specify a color for changed lines, click the Color down arrow in the Changed Lines section, and then select a color in the Color drop-down list. (You can't create a custom color for changed lines.)
4. Click OK to save your settings.

After you configure the changed lines settings, all documents you open that contain tracked changes will use the newly configured settings. In addition, any currently opened documents that contain tracked changes will be reformatted automatically to reflect the new settings.

note In Normal view, all changed lines appear on the left, regardless of the setting you configure in the Mark drop-down list in the Track Changes dialog box (or on the Track Changes tab of the Options dialog box). The changed lines color settings applies in all views.

Accepting and Rejecting Proposed Edits

After a document has made the rounds and you receive a file containing a number of tracked changes, you can easily incorporate the edits by accepting or rejecting the changes. When you incorporate edits, you can address each edit on a case-by-case basis or you can accept multiple changes at once. In either case, you can reject and accept proposed changes by using the appropriate buttons on the Reviewing toolbar or by right-clicking changes and choosing options on the shortcut menu. Figure 33-13 shows the shortcut menu you see when you right-click deleted text. (If you right-click inserted text, the Accept Deletion and Reject Deletion options change to Accept Insertion and Reject Insertion.) In the next few sections, we'll look at the ways you can incorporate edits.

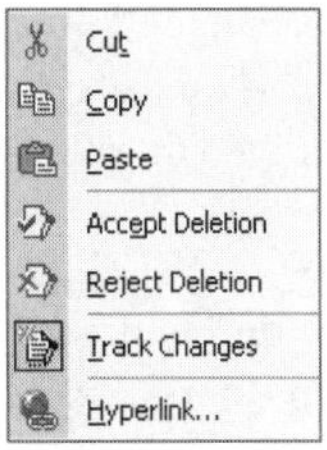

Figure 33-13. You can right-click tracked changes to access options that enable you to resolve the proposed changes.

tip **Save before incorporating edits**

Before you start accepting and rejecting tracked changes and comments, consider saving a version of the document with all the tracked changes and comments intact. That way, if you want to return to the originally marked-up version of the document, you'll have a copy on hand.

Addressing Tracked Changes One at a Time

The key to accessing the changes you want to review is to properly configure your view before you start navigating among changes and making editorial decisions. When you're ready to resolve tracked changes, you should configure the following settings:

- **Show document markup.** Show your document in either Final Showing Markup or Original Showing Markup view. You can do so by choosing either view name in the Display For Review drop-down list on the Reviewing toolbar or by choosing View, Markup.
- **Specify the type(s) of changes to display.** Use the Show drop-down menu on the Reviewing toolbar to specify which types of changes you want to review. Available options are Comments, Insertions And Deletions, and Formatting. You can review any combination of the three types of document changes.
- **Display selected user comments.** Click Show on the Reviewing toolbar, click Reviewers to open the list of reviewers, and then pick and choose which reviewer's markup changes you want to resolve. You can resolve all changes at one time (by selecting the All Reviewers option), or you can select any combination of listed reviewers.

After you display the changes you want to work with, you can move from tracked change to tracked change using the Next and Previous buttons on the Reviewing toolbar (in the same manner you jump from comment to comment), you can view and click edits in the reviewing pane, or you can scroll through the document and address edits in a less linear manner. Regardless of how you arrive at a tracked change, you can handle it in either of the following ways:

- Right-click a change (in the document body, in the reviewing pane, or in a balloon), and choose to accept or reject the addition or insertion.
- Click in a change, and click the Accept or Reject button on the Reviewing toolbar.

After you accept or reject a change, Word displays the revised text as standard text. If you change your mind about a change, you can undo it by clicking Undo on the Standard toolbar or pressing Ctrl+Z.

InsideOut

If you're working with a formatted list, Word allows you only to accept formatting changes made to the bullets or numbers; you cannot reject these changes. However, you can accept or reject changes made in the list's text. If you want to reject formatting changes made to your list, you'll need to accept the change and then reformat the list so that it is displayed in its original formatting.

Accepting and Rejecting All Tracked Changes at Once

At times, you might want to accept or reject all changes in a document. For example, maybe you've gone through the document with a fine-toothed comb, reading and changing the document in Final view. When you're satisfied with the document, you want to simply accept all changes instead of resolving each change one by one. You can do so by executing a single command.

To accept or reject all changes in a document, you use the Accept All Changes In Document or Reject All Changes In Document commands. To access these commands, click the Accept Change or Reject Change/Delete Comment down arrow on the Reviewing toolbar, and choose the appropriate command from the drop-down menu, as shown in Figure 33-14.

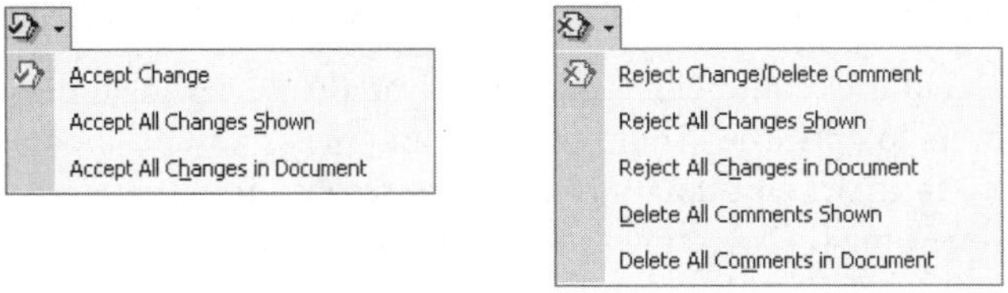

Figure 33-14. You can accept or reject all changes or displayed changes by using the Accept Change and Reject Change/Delete Comment drop-down menus, which are accessible from the Reviewing toolbar.

In addition to accepting and rejecting all changes in a document, you can show a subset of reviewers' changes and accept and reject just those changes. To control which changes are displayed in your document, click Show on the Reviewing toolbar, choose Reviewers, and then select which reviewers' changes you want to display and resolve. After you configure your display, click the Accept Change or Reject Change/Delete Comment down arrow, and choose the Accept All Changes Shown or Reject All Changes Shown option.

> **tip** **Accept or reject changes in selected text**
>
> Between resolving tracked changes one by one and accepting and rejecting all changes in one fell swoop lies the realm of accepting and rejecting edits contained in selected text. In other words, you can resolve editing issues on a piecemeal basis. To do so, select text—for example, you might want to select a paragraph or two that you've reviewed—and then click Accept Change or Reject Change/Delete Comment on the reviewing toolbar to accept or reject the tracked changes contained in the selected text.

Printing Documents That Contain Revisions

You can create printed versions of marked-up documents that include the revision marks and balloons. When you print a document with markup showing, by default Word chooses the zoom level and page orientation to best display your document's markup. In addition, you can print just a list of all markup in a document by selecting List Of Markup in the Print What box in the Print dialog box.

For more information about printing documents containing tracked changes, comments, and balloons, see the section "Printing Comments," on page 794.

To print a document showing markup, follow these steps:

1. Open your document, and switch to Print Layout view.
2. Display the tracked changes in the manner you want them to be printed by using the Display For Review drop-down list on the Reviewing toolbar. In addition, select which reviewers' comments you want to display and print by clicking Show on the Reviewing toolbar, clicking Reviewers, and specifying which reviewers' comments should be displayed (and subsequently printed).
3. Choose File, Print to open the Print dialog box, make sure that Document Showing Markup is selected in the Print What drop-down list, and then click OK to print the document.

tip **Creating a Web page that shows tracked changes**

You can save a document containing tracked changes as a Web page and post the page on line. For more information about saving a marked-up document as a Web page, see "Saving a Document with Comments as a Web Page," on page 796.

Comparing and Merging Documents

At times, you might want to expedite a reviewing process by sending reviewers separate copies of an original document. Then, when reviewers return the documents, you can merge their changes into the original version of the document. Using this approach to document revisions, you can merge any number of changed documents into a single document that will show each reviewer's changes.

note Although it's best if reviewers work with Track Changes enabled when you're planning to merge documents, Word can detect and show changes even if a reviewer didn't turn on the Track Changes feature.

To merge comments and changes from several reviewers into one document, follow these steps:

1. Open the document into which you want to merge changes. Most likely, this will be the original version of the document you sent to reviewers before they marked up their copy of the document.
2. Choose Tools, Compare And Merge Documents. The Compare And Merge Documents dialog box opens, as shown in Figure 33-15.

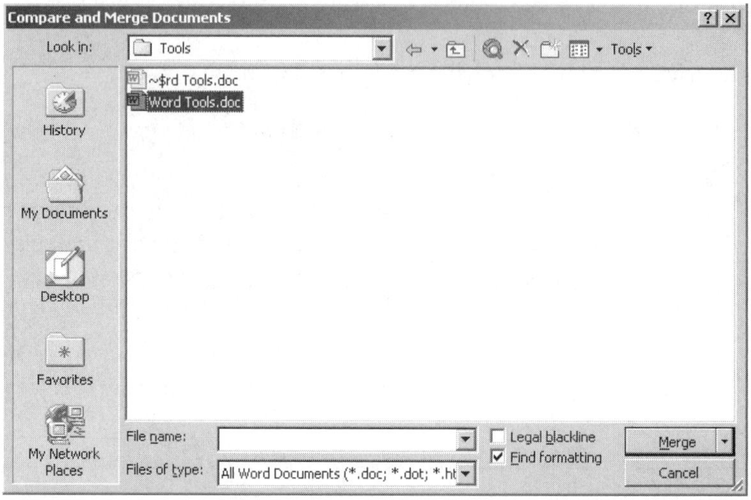

Figure 33-15. The Compare And Merge Documents dialog box looks similar to the Open dialog box, but it provides a couple of special merge-specific commands in the lower-right corner.

3. Navigate to and select the document that has changes to be merged.
4. Click the Merge button down arrow, and choose Merge Into Current Document on the drop-down menu, shown in Figure 33-16.

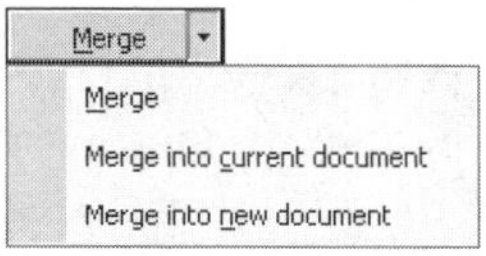

Figure 33-16. The Merge button enables you to control how Word merges the current and selected documents.

5. Repeat steps 2 through 4 to merge other reviewers' edits into the current document.

When you merge documents, you might see a message box stating that the documents being merged have one or more conflicting formatting changes, as shown in Figure 33-17. Word can store only one set of formatting changes at a time. When you merge multiple documents, you might have to choose whether you'd like to keep formatting from the current document or use the formatting in the document being merged. Select the document you want to use for formatting changes, and then click Continue With Merge. If you click Cancel, the merge procedure is aborted. If you don't want to incorporate formatting changes from the merged documents, you can clear the Find Formatting check box in the Compare And Merge Documents dialog box (shown in Figure 33-15) before you conduct a merge procedure.

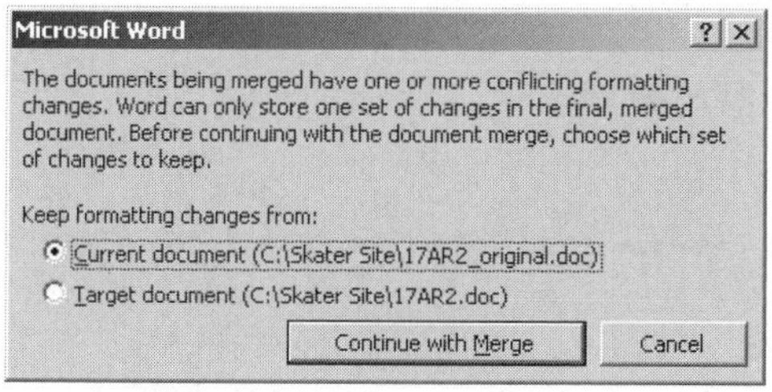

Figure 33-17. If you attempt to merge two documents with differing formatting, Word requires you to specify which document's formatting should take precedence.

tip For best results when merging changes from multiple reviewers, choose Tools, Options, click the Security tab, and verify that the Store Random Number To Improve Merge Accuracy check box is selected.

Displaying Changes Between Two Documents in a Separate File

You can use the Legal Blackline option in the Compare And Merge Documents dialog box to compare two documents and display the changes in a separate file. When you do this, both documents remain unaltered and a new third document is created automatically. You should use this option only when you're comparing two documents; if you need to compare more than two documents, you should use a different merge option.

To use the Legal Blackline option, follow these steps:

1. Open the edited copy of a document, and choose Tools, Compare And Merge Documents.
2. In the Compare And Merge Documents dialog box, select the original document, select the Legal Blackline check box, and then click Compare.
3. If either of the documents has tracked changes, you'll see a message box stating that Word will treat the tracked changes as if they've been accepted. Click Yes to continue the comparing procedure.

The new document displays the changed text in an unnamed document file. You'll need to save and name the file if you want to store the file for future use.

note If you've used the Versions command on the File menu to save versions of a document in one file and you want to compare the current version with an earlier saved version, you can do so. First you need to save the earlier version as a separate file using a different name. Then you can compare the current document with the newly created file. For more information about working with versions of documents, see the next section.

Working with Multiple Versions of a Document

Another way you can record changes made to a document is to store versions of the document. Using Word, you can save multiple versions of a document within the same document. This method saves you from having to manage multiple files (with potentially similar file names) and saves disk space because when you use the Versions feature, Word saves only the differences between versions, not an entire copy of the document for each version. After you've saved a version (or several versions) of a document, you can review, open, and delete earlier versions of a document.

You can create versions in two ways:

- **Manually.** You can save a "snapshot" of a document at any time. To do this, you manually instruct Word to save a version of the current document in its current state.
- **Automatically.** You can configure Word to automatically save a version of your document each time you close the document.

In the next few sections, you'll learn how to create and manage versions of documents manually as well as automatically.

InsideOut

Watch out when you're saving a document that contains versions as a Web page. Although Word maintains most aspects of your document when you save it as a Web page, it does not maintain versioning information. To preserve version information, save a copy of your file (as a Word document) before saving it as a Web page.

Saving a Version of a Document Manually

To manually take a snapshot of a document in its current state and save the snapshot as a version, follow these steps:

1. With the document open, choose File, Versions. The Versions dialog box appears, as shown in Figure 33-18. (The Versions dialog box in this example contains one saved version for illustrative purposes; when you create a version for the first time, the dialog box will be empty.)

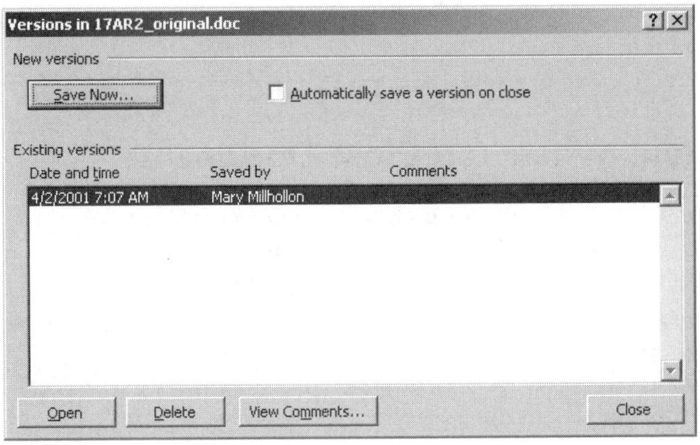

Figure 33-18. The Versions dialog box enables you to manually save a version of a document as well as access stored versions.

2. Click Save Now. The Save Version dialog box appears, as shown in Figure 33-19. You can use this dialog box to add comments regarding the version of the document you're saving.

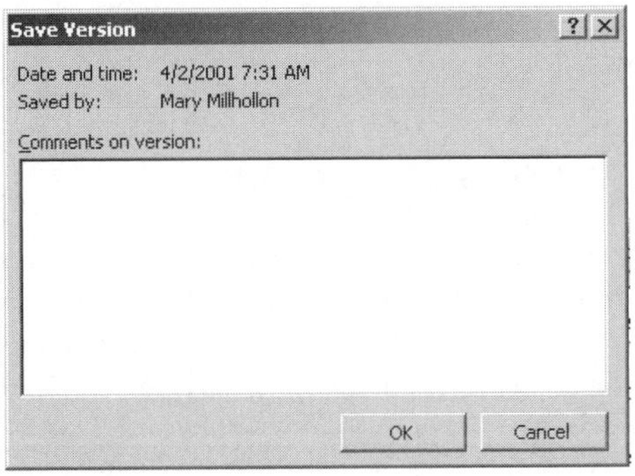

Figure 33-19. You can help differentiate between versions by entering comments about a version in the Save Version dialog box.

3. Enter descriptive information about the version you're saving, if desired, and then click OK.

The version of the document is saved, and an entry is inserted in the Versions dialog box. (You'll have to reopen the Versions dialog box to view the newly created entry.)

> **tip** **View comments associated with a version**
>
> By default, comments associated with versions are displayed only partially in the Versions dialog box. If you want to view the comments in their entirety, open the Versions dialog box (by choosing File, Versions), select a version, and then click the View Comments button. The View Comments dialog box opens, containing comments added when the version was created. Click Close to close the View Comments dialog box, and click Close to close the Versions dialog box.

Saving Versions When You Close Documents

In addition to creating versions manually, you can configure Word to save a version whenever you close the document. Setting this feature is helpful if you need to frequently record versions of a document but you don't want to manually execute extra steps to save multiple versions. To save a version of a document each time you close the document, follow these steps:

1. With the document open, choose File, Versions.
2. In the Versions dialog box, select the Automatically Save A Version On Close check box.
3. Click Close.

When you open the Versions dialog box later, you'll see a list of versions saved each time the document was closed. Each listed entry includes the date and time the version was created, the user name of the person who saved the document and version, and any comments associated with the version.

Opening an Earlier Version of a Document

The main point of saving versions is to be able to access earlier versions of the document from before changes were implemented. You can open any version of a document from within the Versions dialog box (and as you might guess, when you open a version, it contains all versions created prior to the opened version). To open a selected version of a document, follow these steps:

1. With the document open, choose File, Versions.
2. Select the version you want to open, and then click Open. The current document and the older version of the document appear tiled horizontally in your Word window.

Because you're accessing archived information about a document, you can't modify an earlier version of a document after you open it. Instead, after you open an earlier version, you must use the Save As command to save the version as a new separate file. After you create a new file based on the earlier version, you can modify the new file just as you modify any other Word document.

Deleting Version Information

The final action associated with using versions is deleting version information. You can delete version information from within the Versions dialog box. To do so, open the Versions dialog box (by choosing File, Versions), select the version you want to delete, and click the Delete button. Word will display a message box asking whether you're sure you want to delete the version. Click Yes to complete the task.

tip If you're planning to share a document with others (for review or other purposes), you might want to trim the document's size and avoid distributing unnecessary information by deleting past versions from the current document.

Chapter 34

Addressing Security Issues

With the proliferation of personal computing and the recent surge of networking at all levels, sharing Microsoft Word documents is more commonplace than ever. With this added increase in document swapping, you need to take an active role in making your information secure. Document security in Word comes in a number of forms. Most people know the importance of employing security measures at the network level, but you can also provide data integrity by securing your information at the document level. For example, you can perform the following document security tasks in Word:

- Control who can open and modify your documents.
- Specify the types of changes others can make to your document.
- Remove personal and hidden information.
- Identify yourself as the author of a document (by using digital signatures).
- Protect yourself and others from macro viruses.
- Control security settings when you send e-mail messages.

In this chapter, you'll learn about the various document protection schemes available in Word. Keep in mind that the security features offered by Word can work independently as well as in combination with each other. Not surprisingly, you'll often find that the best security setup for your situation involves taking advantage of a combination of Word's security features.

Adding Password Protection to Documents

You can restrict which users can open or modify a document by using *password protection*. When you use password protection, users must enter a password before they can open or change the password-protected document. Standard passwords in Word are case sensitive, they can be up to 15 characters long, and they can contain any combination of letters, numerals, spaces, and symbols.

> newfeature!
>
> **tip** **Create passwords longer than 15 characters**
>
> If you want to create passwords that are longer than 15 characters, you can do so (up to 255 characters) by choosing another encryption type for your document. To do this, choose Tools, Options, click the Security tab in the Options dialog box, click the Advanced button, and choose an RC4 encryption type in the Encryption Type dialog box.

To protect a document by assigning a password, open the document, choose Tools, Options, and click the Security tab in the Options dialog box, shown in Figure 34-1. Many of Word's security features are accessible from the Security tab.

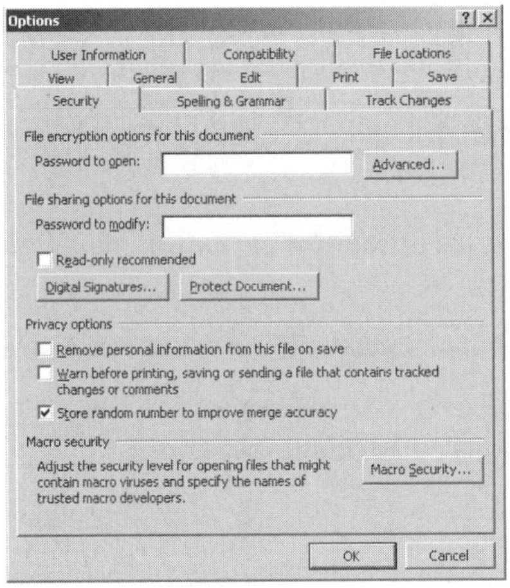

Figure 34-1. The Security tab in the Options dialog box provides a number of security-related settings.

After you display the Security tab, you can create a password that restricts who can open or modify the current document by performing one of the following actions:

- **Assign a password to open.** On the Security tab, enter a password in the Password To Open box, and click OK. The Confirm Password dialog box appears. In the Reenter Password To Open box, type your password again, and click OK. Save the document to complete the process.

- **Assign a password to modify.** On the Security tab, enter a password in the Password To Modify box, and click OK. The Confirm Password dialog box appears. In the Reenter Password To Open box, type your password again, and click OK. Save the document to complete the process.

After you assign a password to open a document, the Password dialog box will appear whenever someone attempts to open the document, as shown in Figure 34-2. To open the document, the user will have to enter the correct password and click OK. If a user doesn't know the password, he or she can click Cancel to abort the process.

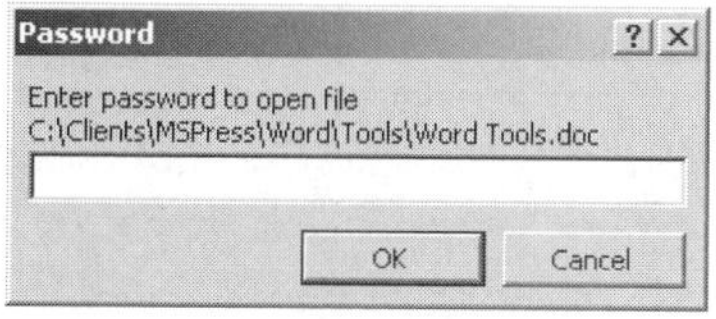

Figure 34-2. Before users can open a password-protected document, they must enter the correct password in the Password dialog box.

Similarly, after you assign a password to grant users modification privileges, they'll see a Password dialog box like the one shown in Figure 34-3 when they open the document.

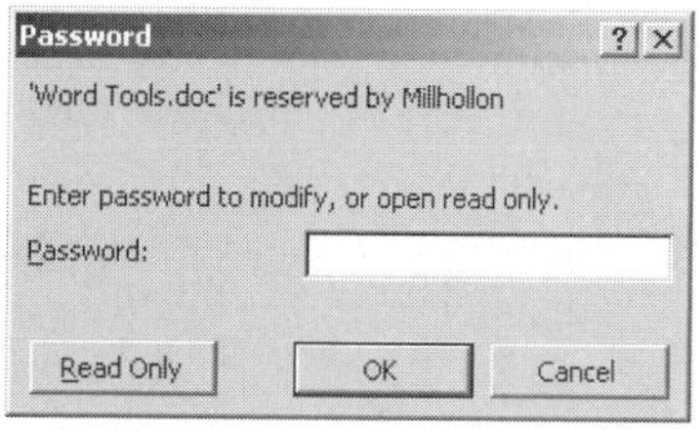

Figure 34-3. When a document is password protected for modification, users can open the document in read-only format, even if they don't know the password required to make changes.

In this Password dialog box, users can perform any of the following actions:

- **Enter a password in the Password box and click OK,** which enables users to open and modify the document.
- **Click Read Only,** which enables users to view the document without enabling them to modify the original version of the document.
- **Click Cancel,** which aborts the entire process.

If users open the document by clicking the Read Only button, they'll be able to make changes to the document, but they'll be able to save the modified document only as a new file—they won't be able to replace the existing version of the file with their modified version.

Chapter 34

> **tip** You can assign passwords to both the open and modify options on the Security tab, thereby providing two layers of protection and accessibility for your document.

To remove password protection, you must know the passwords to gain access to the document. After you open a password-protected document, you can delete the passwords (which appear as asterisks) on the Security tab; deleting password information on the Security tab removes the password protection. To do this, choose Tools, Options, click the Security tab, and delete the passwords in the Password To Open and Password To Modify boxes. Then click OK and save the document to complete the procedure.

> **caution** In most cases, you'll lose your password protection if you save your document in a format other than Word's document format. For example, if you save a Word document as a Web page, you'll lose your password protection. In addition, you cannot add password protection using Word's standard password protection options to Web page documents.

Suggesting That a File Be Opened as Read-Only

As mentioned, you can attach a password to a document and thereby allow only certain people (the people who know the password) to modify the document. When a password is required to modify the document, those who don't know the password can open the document only in read-only mode. In addition to configuring a password, you can also configure a document to display a dialog box suggesting that users open the document as read-only. When you configure this setting, users can choose whether they want to open the document in normal or read-only mode, without entering a password.

You might want to configure a document with the Read-Only Recommended option if the document is a template, for example, and you want to encourage users to use the template in read-only mode to ensure that they don't inadvertently change the template. On the other hand, some users might have to modify the template at times, so you don't want to make the template read-only in all cases.

To configure a document so that it suggests to viewers that they open the document in read-only mode, follow these steps:

1. Choose Tools, Options, and click the Security tab.
2. Select the Read-Only Recommended check box, click OK, and save your document.

When users open a file with the Read-Only Recommended option turned on, they'll see a dialog box similar to the one shown in Figure 34-4. The dialog box asks whether the user wants to open the document in read-only format, and the user can click Yes, No, or Cancel. If users open the document as read-only, they can make changes to the document, but they must save the changed version with a new name (thereby avoiding overwriting the original document).

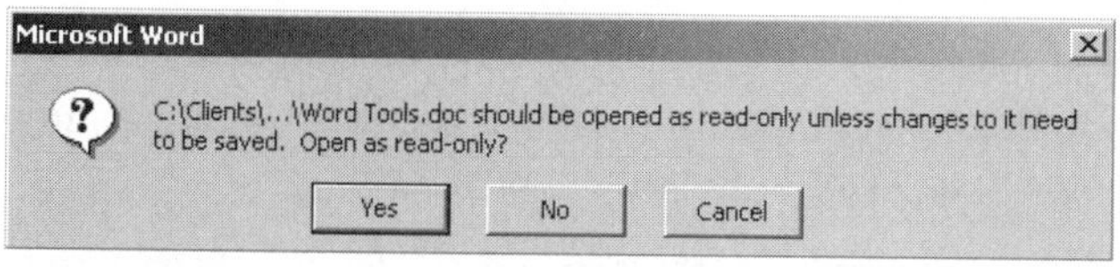

Figure 34-4. When the Read-Only Recommended check box is selected, users can click Yes to open a read-only version, click No to open the document normally, or click Cancel to bypass opening the document altogether.

Protecting Tracked Changes, Comments, and Forms

In addition to granting users access and modification rights to a document, you can control how users can manipulate information within a document. Specifically, you can choose any of the following options:

- **Force changes made to the document to be tracked.** This option lets users change a document but highlights all changes so that you can review any changes made to the document. When a document is protected for tracked changes, users can't turn off tracking, nor can they accept or reject changes.
- **Limit user changes to comments.** When this option is turned on, users can insert comments, but they can't make any other changes to the contents of the document.
- **Restrict data entry to forms.** This option protects a document from any changes other than entries in form fields or unprotected areas. You can also use this option to turn on or off protection for sections in a document, as described in the sidebar "Protecting Parts of a Document," on page 818.

To configure any of these editing limitations, follow these steps:

1. Open the document you want to protect, and then choose Tools, Protect Document (or choose Tools, Options, click the Security tab, and click the Protect Document button). The Protect Document dialog box opens, as shown in Figure 34-5, on the next page.

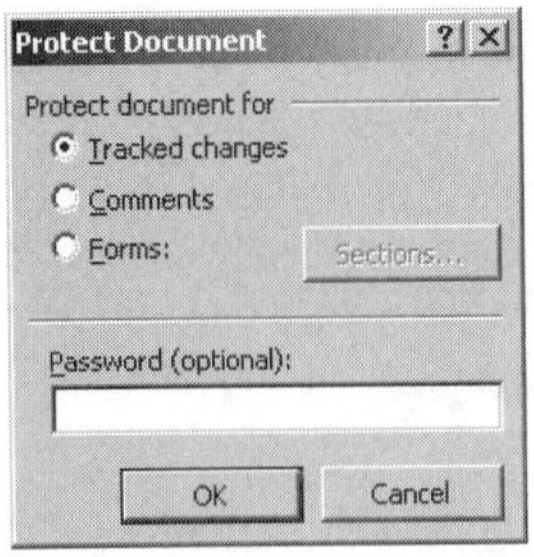

Figure 34-5. The Protect Document dialog box enables you to control the types of changes others can make to the current document.

2. Click the Tracked Changes, Comments, or Forms option, depending on how you want to protect the document.
3. To ensure that users can't easily unprotect the document, you can assign a password to protect the document. To do so, type a password in the Password box, click OK, type the password again in the Confirm Password dialog box, and click OK. If you don't include a password, users will be able to unprotect your document by choosing Tools, Unprotect Document. If you do assign a password, users will have to choose Tools, Unprotect Document and then enter the password before they can unprotect the document.

After you protect a document, users will be limited by the settings you've configured. You can turn off document protection by choosing Tools, Unprotect Document. If you assigned a password, you'll need to enter your password to unprotect the document. After you unprotect a document, it will remain unprotected until you reconfigure the settings in the Protect Document dialog box.

Protecting Parts of a Document

Protecting a document from changes doesn't have to be an all-or-nothing affair. With a little planning, you can protect certain sections of your document. You can use the Forms option in the Protect Document dialog box to pick and choose the sections of your document you want to protect. To do so, you must first divide your document by inserting section breaks and then specify which sections you want to protect. The steps to accomplish this are shown here:

1. Open the document you want to protect.
2. In your document, click where you want to insert a section break.
3. Choose Insert, Break to open the Break dialog box.
4. In the Section Break Types section, choose whether you want to create a Next Page, Continuous, Even Page, or Odd Page section break, and then click OK. This action divides your document into two sections (named Section 1 and Section 2).

(continued)

Protecting Parts of a Document *(continued)*

5. Continue to add section breaks as needed to offset all areas you want to protect.

> For more information about working with sections, see Chapter 9, "Formatting Columns and Sections for Advanced Text Control."

6. When you have finished creating section breaks, choose Tools, Protect Document, click Forms in the Protect Document dialog box, and then click the Sections button. The Section Protection dialog box appears, as shown here:

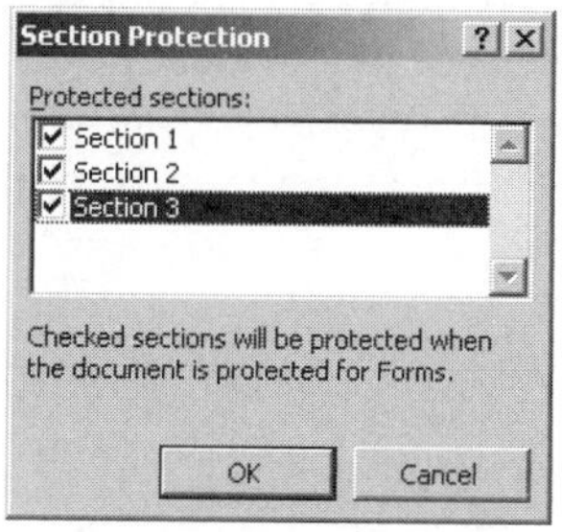

7. In the Protected Sections list, specify the sections you want to protect by selecting and clearing the check boxes. By default, all sections are selected for protection.
8. Click OK to close the Section Protection dialog box.
9. In the Protect Document dialog box, assign a password, if desired. Click OK, reenter the password in the Confirm Password dialog box (if necessary), click OK, and then save your document.

> **tip** To see section breaks in your document while you work, display hidden characters by clicking the Show/Hide button on the Standard toolbar.

After you complete these steps, only the sections of your document you selected will be protected from modifications. Users will be able to change the contents in the unprotected sections in the document, but they'll need to know the password to unprotect the document before they can alter any of the protected areas.

Removing Personal Information and Hidden Data

One easy security measure you can take when sharing documents with others is to remove information you don't intend others to see. For example, you can remove personal information so that people who view your document won't be able to see the names of reviewers, the author of the document, and so forth. If your document contains other hidden information, such as version information or changes recorded by Word's fast save option, you'll want to eliminate that information as well. If you don't delete hidden information, other people who view your document might see information you'd rather they didn't, especially if they save your Word document in another file format (because information hidden in a Word document doesn't remain hidden when a Word document is saved in another format and viewed in another application). In the next few sections, we'll take a more detailed look at ways in which you can clear unnecessary personal information from documents before you share the documents with others.

note In addition to removing personal information, removing version information, and removing fast save data, you should remove hidden text and accept or reject any tracked changes before you pass your document on to others. For more information about working with hidden text, see Chapter 5, "Adding Panache with Text Formatting and Special Characters," and for more information about accepting and rejecting tracked changes, see Chapter 33, "Revising Documents Using Markup Tools."

newfeature!

Removing Personal Information

Before you pass a document to others, you might want to remove hidden and personal information from the document. In Word, you can easily remove the following types of personal information:

- File properties, such as author name, manager name, company name, and last saved by information.
- Names associated with comments. (Word can change reviewers' names to *Author* automatically.)
- Routing slips.
- E-mail message header generated when you click the E-Mail button.
- Names associated with versions. (Word can change names associated with versions to *Author* automatically.)

To hide these informational tidbits, you must configure the Security tab in the Options dialog box as follows:

1. With your file open, choose Tools, Options, and click the Security tab.
2. Select the Remove Personal Information From This File On Save check box, and then click OK.
3. Save the document.

Keep in mind that when you use this option, the names associated with information are deleted, but the actual information remains. For example, setting this option changes all names associated with comments to *Author*, but the comments remain intact. The same holds true for versions—the name of the person who saved a version is changed to *Author*, but the version of the document remains available for display.

Sending Documents Without Version Information

If you use the Versions feature in Word when you work with documents, the versions are saved as hidden information in the document. This enables you to retrieve the information later. When you send a document that contains versions to others, they can open past versions just as you open versions. In addition, versions of a document do not remain hidden if you or someone else saves the document in another format. To avoid sending extraneous information to others, you might want to remove the version information in documents before you pass the document along. You can do so in two ways:

- **Distribute a separate document.** If you want to keep the previous versions of a document but you also need to pass the document on to others, you can save the current version as a separate document and then distribute the separate document instead of the document containing the versions. In this way, you create a "clean" document that doesn't include any version information. To do this, create a version to incorporate the latest changes (if necessary), and then choose File, Versions to open the Versions dialog box. Select the version of the document you want to save, and click Open. Then choose File, Save As to save this version as a new document.
- **Delete all version information.** If you don't need to retain information from prior versions, you can delete the version information stored in your document before you send the document to others. To do so, choose File, Versions to open the Versions dialog box, select the version(s) you want to remove (press Ctrl to select multiple versions), and click Delete.

After you remove versions from documents or create a clean copy of a document, you won't have to worry about others seeing version information if they open the document in an application other than Word. For more information about working with versions of documents, see Chapter 33, "Revising Documents Using Markup Tools."

Removing Fast Save Information

Another type of hidden information your Word documents might contain is information stored from fast saves. If you save a document with the Allow Fast Saves check box selected and then open the document as a text file, the document might contain information that you've deleted. This happens because fast saves save changes to a document instead of saving the entire document. To avoid this problem, before you share a document with someone else, you should fully save your document. To do so, follow these steps:

1. Open your document, choose Tools, Options, and click the Save tab in the Options dialog box.
2. Clear the Allow Fast Saves check box, and click OK.
3. Click the Save button on the Standard toolbar to save your document.

An added bonus of this procedure is that when you turn off the fast save option and perform a full save, you usually reduce your document's file size because you're no longer saving all the changes made to your document along with the document's contents.

Using Digital Certificates to Digitally Sign Files and Macros

Office XP applications use Microsoft Authenticode technology to enable you to digitally sign a file or macro by using a *digital certificate.* Digital certificates can be likened to online identification cards that are attached to macros and documents. These IDs help confirm to others that a macro or document originated from the signer and hasn't been altered along the way. Digital certificates contain information about the person who obtained the certificate as well as information about the certification authority that issued the certificate.

Obtaining Digital Certificates

To obtain a digital certificate, you can purchase one from a certification authority (such as VeriSign, at *www.verisign.com*, or E-Lock, at *www.elock.com*), you can obtain one from your organization's security administrator or IT professional, or you can create a digital signature for limited local use. Because a certification authority doesn't sign the digital certificates you create, your "homemade" certificates will be considered unauthenticated, which means they'll generate a security warning if you send the certificate to a user whose security level is set to Medium or be completely disabled if the user's security level is set to High. (For more information about security levels, see "Setting Word Security Levels," on page 828.)

Working with Certification Authorities and Security Administrators

When you obtain a digital certificate from a certification authority, you must submit an application to the authority and pay a fee (which is usually an annual rate based on the type of security you want to obtain). When you receive your digital certificate, the certification authority provides instructions for installation. Similarly, if you work with an in-house security administrator, you'll need to follow your organization's policies regarding how digital certificates are distributed and how digital signatures are added to your macros and files.

Creating Your Own Digital Certificates

If you want to create your own digital certificate to practice working with digital signatures or for your personal use, you can do so by using the Selfcert.exe application included with Office. Remember, this type of certification is unauthenticated, so it doesn't provide much security assurance to others.

Installing the Selfcert.exe Application By default, Selfcert.exe is not installed with Office, so your first step in creating a digital certificate is to install the application from the Office installation CD, as follows:

1. Run the Office setup application from your installation CD, click the Add Or Remove Features option on the Maintenance Mode Options page, and click Next.
2. In the Feature To Install tree, expand Office Shared Features, click Digital Signature For VBA Projects, and choose Run From My Computer.
3. Click Update.

After you click Update, the Selfcert.exe feature is installed on your system. Usually, the application is installed in the C:\Program Files\Microsoft Office\Office10 folder.

Creating a Certificate After you install the Selfcert.exe application, you're ready to create a digital certificate. To do so, follow these steps:

1. Double-click the Selfcert.exe application. If the file isn't stored in the C:\Program Files\Microsoft Office\Office10 folder, choose Start, Search, For Files Or Folders, and run a search for *selfcert.exe*. When the search is completed, double-click the Selfcert.exe application. You'll see the Create Digital Certificate dialog box, as shown in Figure 34-6, on the next page.

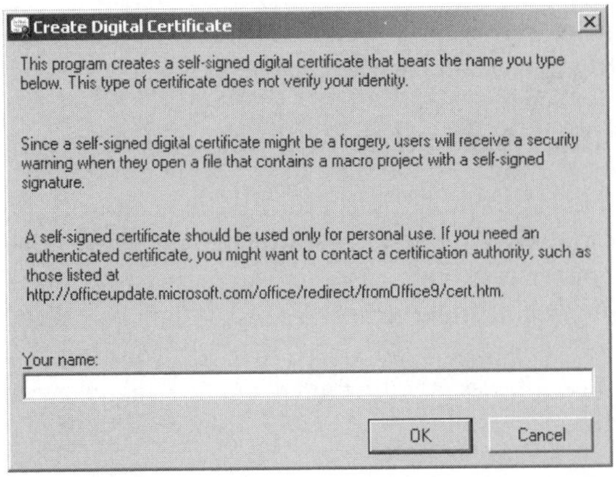

Figure 34-6. The Selfcert.exe application enables you to create an unauthenticated digital certificate that you can use for your own macros and files.

2 Type your name in the Your Name box, and click OK. A message box appears, stating that you've successfully created a certificate, as shown in Figure 34-7. Click OK.

Figure 34-7. A message box appears after your certificate has been created.

At this point, you've successfully created an unauthorized digital certificate that you can use to sign and run macros on your local machine. You can also use your unofficial certificate to practice working with digital certificates. You can view your newly created certificate and attach it to your files and macros, as described in the next section.

newfeature!

Attaching a Digital Certificate to a File

After you obtain a digital certificate, you can authenticate your files and macros by digitally signing them. Basically, digitally signing a file or macro means that you've attached your digital certificate to the document. In this section, you'll learn how to digitally sign a file. For information about digitally signing a macro, see Chapter 40, "Creating and Working with VBA Macros."

To attach a digital certificate to a file, follow these steps:

1 Open the document, and then choose Tools, Options and click the Security tab.

2 Click Digital Signatures. The Digital Signature dialog box appears, as shown in Figure 34-8.

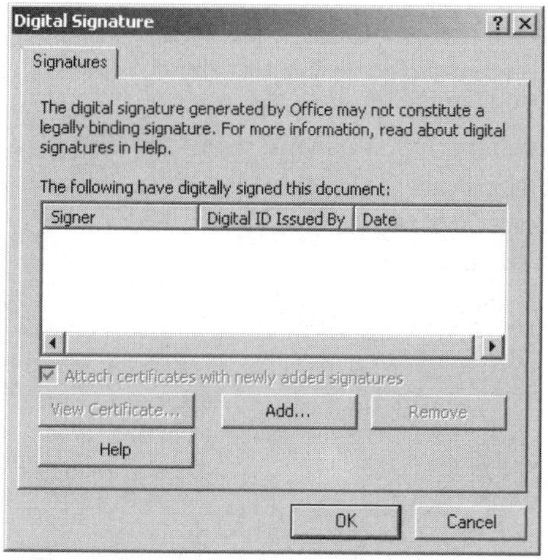

Figure 34-8. The Digital Signature dialog box lists the digital certificates attached to the current document and enables you to view, add, and remove certificates.

3 In the Digital Signature dialog box, click Add. The Select Certificate dialog box appears, as shown in Figure 34-9.

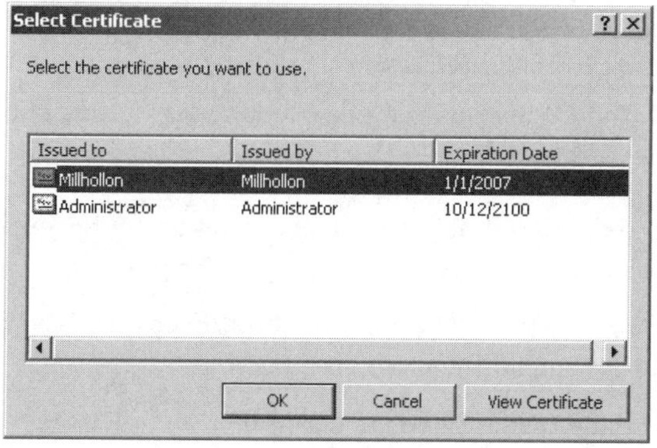

Figure 34-9. The Select Certificate dialog box lists the certificates you can use to digitally sign a file.

note If you're working in Normal view when you click Add in step 3, you might receive a message box that states that all text and pictures might not be visible in the current view. If you haven't saved the current document, you'll receive a message box stating that you must first save the document as a Word document before you can add a digital certificate. In either message box, click Yes to continue. If you need to save the current document, the Save As dialog box opens after you click Yes in the save message box.

4 Select the digital certificate you want to use. Click View Certificate to see more information about the selected certificate. The Certificate dialog box opens, displaying the General tab, as shown in Figure 34-10. Notice that the certificate icon has an X mark (in red on your screen) in the lower right corner, indicating that the certificate is unauthorized. This certificate was created using the Selfcert.exe application, which, as mentioned, creates unauthorized certificates for your personal use.

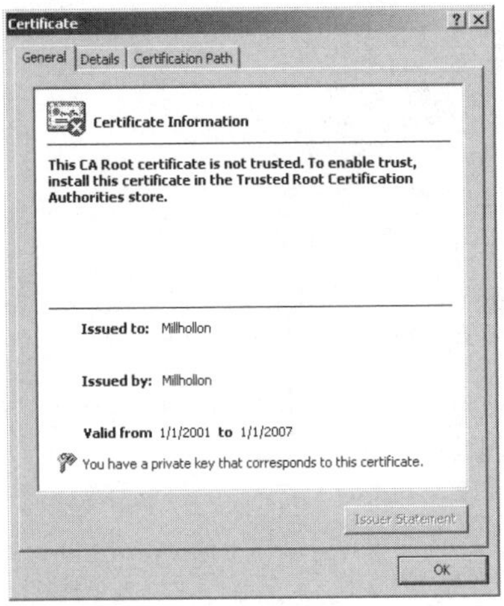

Figure 34-10. The Certificate dialog box shows you detailed information about a selected digital certificate.

5 Click OK to close the Certificate dialog box and return to the Select Certificate dialog box.

6 Click OK to add the certificate to the current document. The certificate will now be listed in the Digital Signature dialog box.

7 Click OK to close the Digital Signature dialog box, and click OK to close the Options dialog box.

After you add a certificate to a document, you can remove it at any time. To do so, choose Tools, Options, and click the Security tab. Click Digital Signatures, select the digital certificate you want to remove, click Remove, and then click OK twice. This action removes the certificate's association with the current document—it doesn't delete the certificate.

Checking for the Red X

As mentioned, a digital certificate you create using the Selfcert.exe application will be displayed with an X mark because the certificate is unauthenticated. A red X can also indicate the following security issues associated with a certificate:

- The signed file or macro has been tampered with.
- The certificate was not issued by a trusted certification authority.
- The certificate was issued without verification (such as a free certificate authority trial download).
- The certificate was invalid when it was used to sign the file or macros.

When you see a certificate with a red X, proceed with caution. This is a clear sign that something about the certificate is amiss.

Viewing Digital Certificates Attached to Files

If you're working with a file that's been digitally signed, you can easily view the digital certificates. The procedure for viewing digital signatures is similar to the digitally signing a file. To view a digital signature, follow these steps:

1. Choose Tools, Options, click the Security tab, and click the Digital Signatures button.
2. Select the digital signature you want to learn about, and click View Certificate. The Certificate dialog box opens, showing details about the certificate.
3. Click OK three times to close all open dialog boxes.

If you want to export a certificate to a file (for instance, you might want to copy your certificate to disk and then install it on another machine), you can do so by using the Certificate Export Wizard. To access this wizard, click the Details tab in the Certificate dialog box, and then click Copy To File. The wizard walks you through the process of exporting your digital certificate. Be careful when exporting your digital certificates. The security aspect of certificates relies entirely on the secrecy of the certificates' codes. If your codes become available to others, you've jeopardized your digital certificates' effectiveness.

Safeguarding Against Macro Viruses

Although the overriding purpose of macros is to streamline common tasks and procedures performed in Word and other applications, the unfortunate fact is that macros can also serve as a breeding ground for computer viruses. A macro virus is a type of computer virus that originates within a file, a template, or an add-in. As a Word user contemplating security issues, you need to be aware of macro viruses and how you can configure Word to assist you in recognizing when a macro might present a risk.

note Microsoft devotes a number of areas on its Web site to security issues. For example, if you want to find out more about security, visit *www.microsoft.com/technet/security* and *www.microsoft.com/security*. You can also visit the Office site, at *www.microsoft.com/office*, and search for *security* using the Search This Site box.

Preventing Viruses in Word Documents

One strategy you can use to combat macro viruses when working in Word is to attach digital signatures to macros to identify their origin. Then, if you trust the origin of the digital signature, you're safe to enable the macro. Keep in mind that digital signatures enable you to identify and run macros from trusted sources; they do not locate and eliminate viruses.

In addition to using digital certificates, which can provide assurance regarding the person from whom a file or macro originated (as discussed in the section "Using Digital Certificates to Digitally Sign Files and Macros," on page 822), you can specify how you want Word to react when it encounters documents that contain macros. To do this, you set Word security levels, as described next.

tip For the best protection against viruses, you should purchase and install third-party antivirus software to work in conjunction with Word's security settings.

Setting Word Security Levels

When Word encounters a document, it determines whether the document contains macros. If the document doesn't contain any macros, Word opens it without any warnings. If the document contains macros, Word opens it based on the current security settings. In Word, you can choose one of the following three levels of security:

- **High.** This setting allows only signed and trusted macros to run. When you use this setting, you can run only macros that have been digitally signed and are listed as from a trusted source. Unsigned macros are automatically disabled before the file is opened.
- **Medium.** When Word is set to medium-level security, you receive prompts asking whether you want to enable or disable macros on a file-by-file basis. Whenever a file containing macros is encountered that's signed by a source

that's not listed as a trusted source, Word allows you to choose whether you want to enable or disable the macros when you open the file.

- **Low.** This setting turns off all macro security warnings and trusts all macros. In other words, all files, including files that contain macros, will always open without a warning when you configure Word with the Low security level. You should consider using this setting only if you have installed the latest version of a virus scanner, if the most current virus signature files for your virus program are installed, and if you're absolutely sure that the documents you're opening can be trusted.

By default, Word's security is set to High, and this is the recommended setting. To display Word's security options, choose Tools, Options, click the Security tab, and then click Macro Security. In the Security dialog box, click the Security Level tab, shown in Figure 34-11. You can specify any security level, but you should consider retaining Word's High security-level setting unless a particular need arises that requires you to lower your security settings.

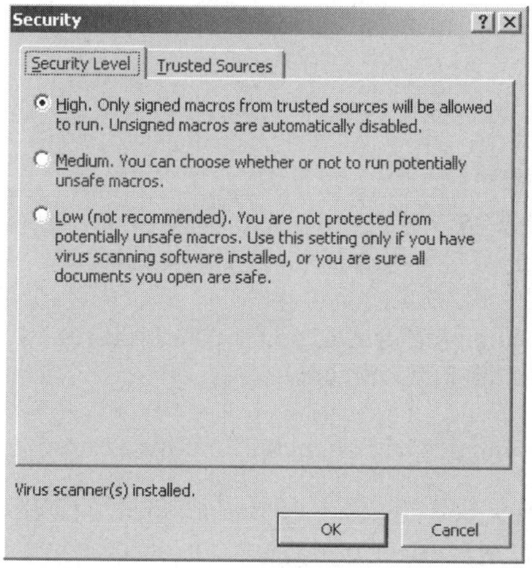

Figure 34-11. The Security Level tab in the Security dialog box enables you to specify how Word should react when you open a document that contains macros.

Viewing and Removing Trusted Sources

When you open a file that includes signed macros (and the signer isn't included on your trusted sources list, as described in this section), you'll be asked whether you want to trust all macros from the signer. If you click Yes, the signer will be added to your list of trusted sources. Before you add a signer, you should carefully review the source's certificate. You should especially review the certificate's Issued To, Issued By, and Valid

From fields. After you add a signer to your trusted sources list, Word will automatically enable macros signed by the source in the future.

If you later decide that you'd like to remove a signer from your trusted sources list, you can do so at any time, as follows:

1. Choose Tools, Options, and click the Security tab.
2. Click Macro Security to open the Security dialog box.
3. Click the Trusted Sources tab, shown in Figure 34-12.

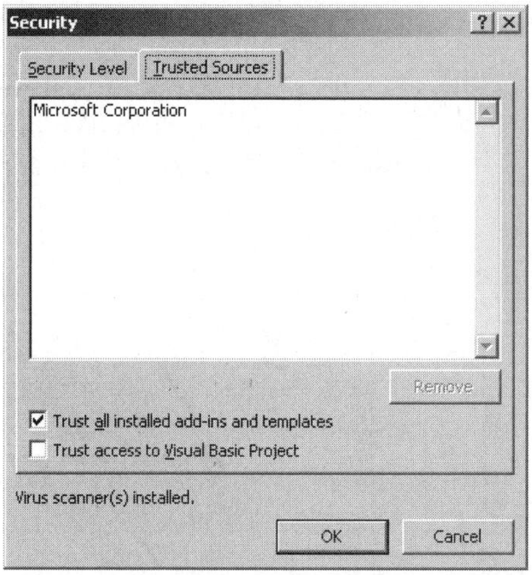

Figure 34-12. If you've added any sources to your trusted sources list, they'll appear on the Trusted Sources tab in the Security dialog box.

4. Select the source you want to remove, click Remove, and then click OK.

Microsoft digitally signs all templates, add-ins, and macros shipped with Office XP. After you add Microsoft to your list of trusted sources for one of these installed files, all subsequent interactions with these files will not generate messages.

tip **Add your Selfcert.exe certificate to trusted sources lists**

Office XP applications will allow you to add the owner of an unauthenticated certificate (such as a Selfcert.exe certificate) to the list of trusted sources only when the certificate is used on the same computer on which it was initially created. This means that you can create a certificate using Selfcert.exe and sign your own personal macros, and you can trust that certificate on your computer. But if you attempt to share your file with other users, they won't be able to run your macros if their security is set to High.

Accessing E-Mail Encryption Settings

One last type of security you might be concerned with when you're working in Word is e-mail security. If you're using Word to create e-mail messages, you should pay particular attention to the security settings associated with this feature. To access e-mail security settings, follow these steps:

1. If necessary, click the E-Mail button on the Standard toolbar to open the e-mail pane.

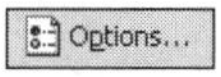

Options

2. In the e-mail pane, click the Options button. The Message Options dialog box opens.
3. In the Message Options dialog box, click Security Settings. The Security Properties dialog box opens, as shown in Figure 34-13. You can use this dialog box to encrypt your message and attach a digital signature to it.

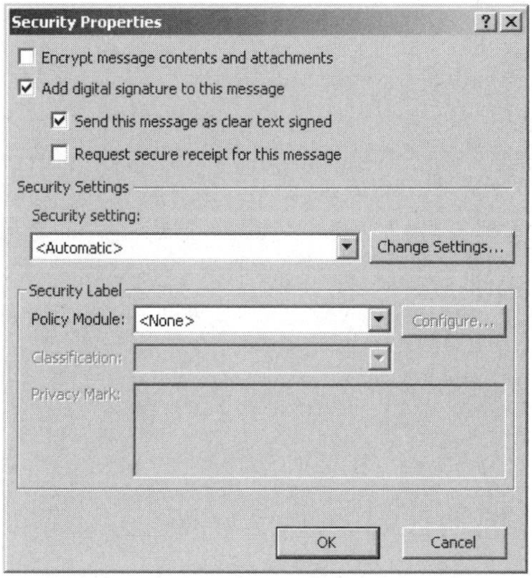

Figure 34-13. The Security Properties dialog box enables you to control security settings when you send e-mail messages from within Word.

4. After you configure your security settings, click OK, and then click Close to close the Message Options dialog box.

For additional information about providing security in e-mail messages, see the Microsoft Outlook Help files, visit the Outlook Web site (*www.microsoft.com/office/outlook*), and refer to an in-depth Outlook 2002 resource, such as "Microsoft Outlook Version 2002 Inside Out," from Microsoft Press.

Part 9

Mastering Advanced Data Functions

Chapter 35

Performing Mail Merges

If it's part of your job to create marketing mailings, surveys, broadcast e-mail messages, or distributed faxes, you'll be pleased to know that mail merge has been totally revamped in Microsoft Word 2002. Mail merge enables you to create a document once and use it many times, which cuts down on the time you spend creating and sending documents and enables you to use the data you've saved elsewhere, in a mailing list database, an address list, or your Microsoft Outlook Contacts list. You might use mail merge to create and send projects like these:

- A direct mail campaign sent to your top 1,000 customers announcing a new service
- An e-mail press release announcing a new product release
- Mailing labels to affix to catalogs you send to new customers
- A form letter announcing a new rate increase
- An address listing of all clients in your various databases

This chapter introduces you to the new mail merge features in Word and shows you how to master the techniques for individual merge projects. This means that you can capitalize on the work you've done by applying the "create-it-once, use-it-many-times" techniques mail merge offers.

newfeature!

Exploring New Mail Merge Features

The new mail merge features in Word 2002 make it easier than ever for you to create and modify merge documents. You can easily create the documents you want and attach the data sources you want to use. After that, printing or e-mailing is easy. The new features mail merge offers include these:

- The new Mail Merge makes all the mail merge tools available in a dockable toolbar you can place alongside your work area. This makes it easy for you to add, move to, highlight, and modify merge fields. You display the Mail Merge toolbar by choosing View, Toolbars, Mail Merge. Table 35-1 provides descriptions of each of the buttons on the Mail Merge toolbar.
- The Mail Merge Wizard appears in the task pane on the right side of the work area and leads you through all the steps in creating personalized letters, e-mail messages, envelopes, labels, and directories. You can begin by creating your own document, using an existing one, or starting with a Word template.
- Additionally, the Mail Merge Wizard gives you the ability to choose from a variety of data sources, including an existing data list, a prepared database, a Word data source you create yourself, or your Outlook Contacts list.
- In Word 2002, address lists, which were formerly called catalogs, are now known as *directories*. You can create a directory to make a list of all data items included in the data source file you select. This means, for example, that instead of paging one by one through all the form letters you intend to send, you can create a listing of all recipients to save along with your mailing.

Table 35-1. Mail Merge Tools

Button	Name	Description
	Main Document setup	Enables you to choose the type of merge document you want to create
	Open Data Source	Displays the Select Data Source dialog box so that you can choose your source file
	Mail Merge Recipients	Displays the Mail Merge Recipients dialog box, enabling you to select and deselect recipients in your list
	Insert Address Block	Displays the Insert Address Block dialog box so that you can choose the data and the format you want used for address data

(continued)

Table 35-1. *(continued)*

Button	Name	Description
	Insert Greeting Line	Displays the Greeting Line dialog box so that you can choose the greeting content and format
	Insert Merge Fields	Shows the Insert Merge Field dialog box so that you can choose and insert the merge fields you want to use
Insert Word Field	Insert Word Field	Displays a drop-down menu so that you can choose Word data fields for inclusion in the form document
	Show Fields/Values	After you run the merge, you can view the contents of the merge by clicking Show Values. To toggle the display to show fields, click Show Fields.
	Highlight Merge Fields	Highlights the merged fields in the selected document
	Match Fields	Enables you to match the fields in the mail merge operation to the fields in your database
	Propagate Labels	Changes the direction of the labels in the merge operation
	First Record	Displays the first merged record
	Previous Record	Displays the previous merge record
Record:	Go To Record	Allows you to move to a specific merged record
	Next Record	Moves to the next merged record
	Last Record	Displays the last merged record in the file
	Find Entry	Enables you to locate a specific entry

(continued)

Chapter 35

Table 35-1. *(continued)*

Button	Name	Description
	Error Check Merge	Lets you test the merge for errors before you run the merge operation
	Merge To Document	Merges the source and document file and places the results in the document
	Merge To Printer	Merges the source and document file and sends the results to the printer
	Merge To E-mail	Merges the source and document file and sends the results via e-mail
	Merge To Fax	Merges the source and document file and sends the results via fax

Getting an Overview of Mail Merge

Using Word's Mail Merge feature, you can create letters, faxes, e-mail messages, envelopes, labels, and directories that you can create once and use many times. Even though you can create a variety of document types, the merge process is basically the same. The Mail Merge Wizard will walk you through these basic steps, no matter which document type you're creating:

1. Select the document type you want to create. In this step, you tell Word whether you want to create a letter, e-mail message, envelope, labels, or directory.
2. Choose the document you want to start with. Here you select or create the file you want to use as the merge document.
3. Select the recipients. In this step, you choose your data list from an existing file, type data in the data source file, or select your Outlook Contacts list.
4. Write your letter (or e-mail message) and add the necessary merge fields.
5. Preview the merge operation and make any last-minute changes.
6. Merge the document and the data source and print or send the results.

The next several sections explain more about each of these steps.

Know Your Merge Terms

The following terms might be new to you if you are learning about mail merge for the first time:

- **Main document** is the letter, e-mail, envelope, or label into which the data will be merged.
- **Source file** or list is the file from which the merge data is taken.
- **Merge fields** are identifiers inserted in the text that indicate to Word the position and type of data you want to be inserted at that point in the document.
- **Address block** includes name and address information.
- **Greeting line** adds the opening salutation, along with the name of the recipient you select.

Starting the Mail Merge Wizard

To start the mail merge process, you can begin with the document you want to use open on your screen, or you can create or open a document while you are using the wizard. To launch the Mail Merge Wizard, choose Tools, Letters And Mailings, Mail Merge Wizard. The Mail Merge Wizard opens in the task pane on the right side of your Word window (shown in Figure 35-1).

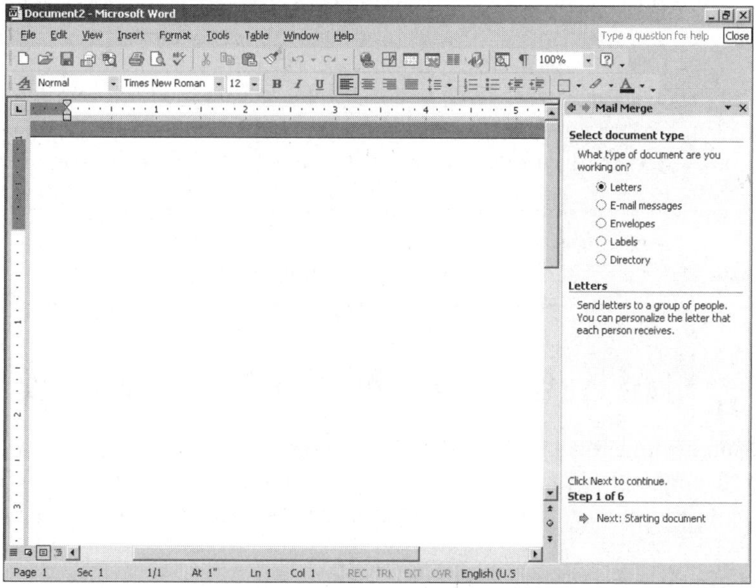

Figure 35-1. The Mail Merge Wizard leads you though a series of options to complete the merge operation.

tip **Choose commands quickly from the Mail Merge toolbar**

If you're comfortable working with merge commands on your own, you might want to close the wizard and work only with the Mail Merge toolbar. To close the wizard, click the Close box in the upper right corner of the Mail Merge task pane. To display the toolbar, choose Tools, Letters And Mailings, Show Mail Merge Toolbar.

Selecting the Document Type

Your first choice involves selecting the type of document you want to create. Will you be sending a direct mail letter, an e-mail message, or a fax? Perhaps you want to start with envelopes and labels, or create a directory to store listings of data such as customer names and addresses, product info, personnel contact data. This is where you'll make your choice. Follow these steps to make your selection:

1. Choose Tools, Letters And Mailings, Mail Merge Wizard. The Mail Merge task pane appears along the right side of the work area.
2. In the Select Document Type section, choose the document you want to create for the merge operation.

tip If the Mail Merge toolbar is displayed in your work area, you can click the Main Document Setup button to display the Main Document Type dialog box. You can then click the document type you want to use, and click OK.

3. Once you've selected the type of document you want to create, click the Next link in the task pane. The next step involves choosing the main document or form letter you want to use as the base document for the merge operation.

note If you select E-mail messages as the document type for your merge, Word automatically changes the display to Web Layout view.

Starting Out with the Main Document

The main document is the document that holds the text that doesn't change—in other words, the boilerplate text that will appear on all the sales letters you send out or all your past due notices (or, for a happier example, all the birth announcements you send via e-mail). Word gives you a number of choices for the way in which you select your main document. You can do any of the following:

- Use the current document
- Start from a template
- Start from an existing document

Using the Current Document

If you elect to use the current document as the main document for your merge operation, you can simply type the text for the document as you want it to appear. You can omit the address information and the greeting at this point, because Word provides the means to do that automatically later, when you add the merge fields to your document. Figure 35-2 shows an example of a form letter used in a merge print.

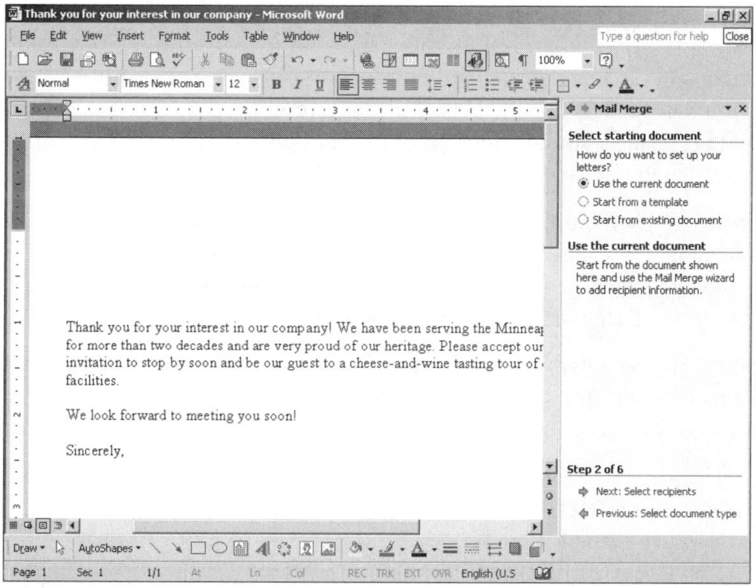

Figure 35-2. The main document stores the boilerplate text you'll use for the body of the message.

If you've used a letter in the past that was particularly effective, or if you want to save time by converting some of your marketing copy to an e-mail mailing, you can simply open that document and use it as the main document for your mailing. A main document can include text, images, borders, colors, shades, tables, and more—anything a traditional Word document can contain.

One consideration, however: If you're creating an e-mail message you want to broadcast in a merge operation, remember that many graphic images or special text formats can create larger files and might require more time for downloading. For the convenience of your readers, consider going light on the graphical enhancements if you're creating an e-mail message.

tip **Use existing form letters**

If you have a form letter that you used in a past mail merge operation, you can use it again, even if it was created in an earlier version of Word. Simply open the existing document before you start the Mail Merge Wizard and attach the data source as prompted. If you need to update any of the merge fields, you can delete, insert, or modify fields as needed as you go through the wizard steps.

Working with the Letter Wizard

Creating a letter is a straightforward process in Word, but there might be those times when you'd like to have a little help. For this purpose, Word 2002 includes a Letter Wizard that enables you to choose the page design and letter style you want, in addition to choosing sender information and other details.

To start the Letter Wizard, choose Tools, Letters And Mailings, Letter Wizard. The Letter Wizard dialog box appears, and you can make your choices about design, style, and information you want to add. When you click OK, the letter is created, with the format and style you selected, in the current document window.

If you're using the letter with a merge operation, you can now begin the Mail Merge Wizard by choosing Tools, Letters And Mailings, Mail Merge Wizard.

Starting from a Template

If you don't want to work with the current document, you can choose a template instead. Word includes 10 mail merge templates you can start with and then modify to fit the document you want to send.

note If you have a document open in the Word window, the program will prompt you that it will be replaced and any unsaved changes will be lost. If you want to leave that document open but also create a new merge document from a template, click New Document before starting the Mail Merge Wizard.

1. Start by clicking Start From A Template in step 2 of the Mail Merge Wizard.
2. Click the Select Template link in the Start From A Template section to display the Mail Merge tab of the Select Template dialog box (shown in Figure 35-3).

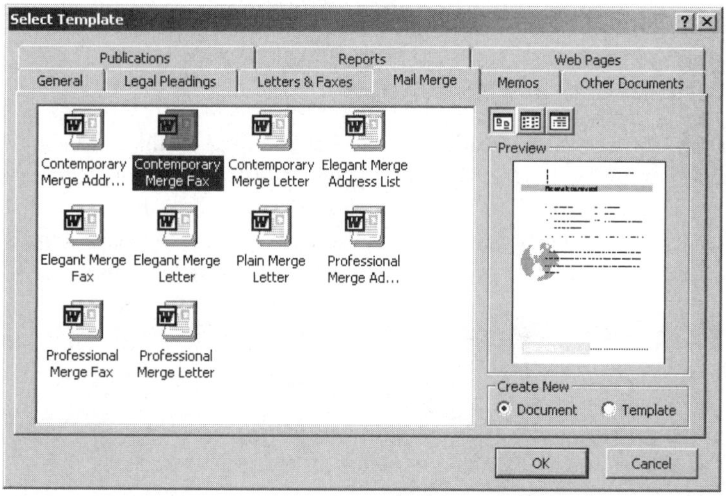

Figure 35-3. Word includes 10 different templates you can use for mail merge operations.

3. You'll find a variety of templates for each of three document types—address list, fax, and letter.
4. Click the template you want, and click Open. The template is displayed in the Word work area. You can then enter your text to personalize the letter, list, or fax for your purposes.

Starting from an Existing Document

When you click Start From Existing Document in the Select Starting Document section in step 2 of the Mail Merge Wizard, a list appears in the Start From Existing section so that you can choose the merge file you want to use. To choose an existing merge file, click the file you want and click Open. Word loads the file into the Word work area.

tip **Save time and substitute your text**

If you want to send a simple merge document and don't want to invest the time in creating one from scratch, you can open an existing merge document and simply modify it with your own text.

Choosing Your Recipients

When you get to the page in which you choose the recipients for your merge operations, it's time to select your data list, which was referred to as the data source in previous Word versions. You can use an existing list, choose Outlook Contacts, or type a new list.

Using an Existing Data Source

To select a list you've already created, click the Browse link in the Use An Existing List section of the Mail Merge Wizard. If you're using the Mail Merge toolbar, click the Open Data Source button. The Select Data Source dialog box appears so that you can choose a data list you've created. Navigate to the file you want; then click Open. The Mail Merge Recipients dialog box appears, as Figure 35-4 shows.

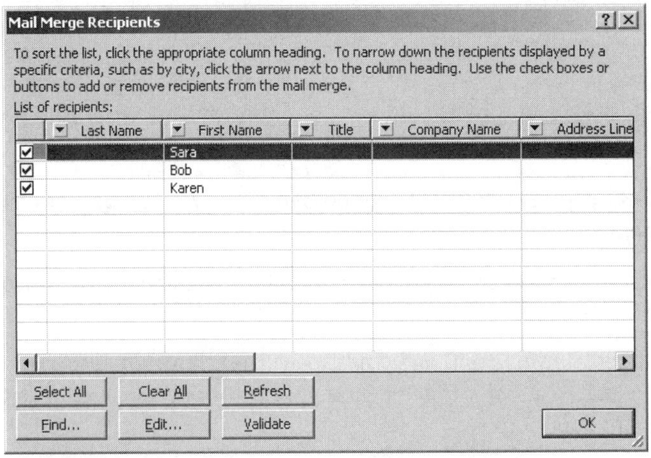

Figure 35-4. You can work with and modify the data in your data source in the Mail Merge Wizard.

If you don't want to change the recipient information in any way—in other words, you want to use the entire list just as it is—simply click OK to close the dialog box and continue using the Mail Merge Wizard.

tip **Check data again later**

If you decide to pass up your opportunity to change the data in your recipient list now, don't worry—before you complete the merge operation you'll have a chance to preview and modify the recipients you've selected.

Choosing, Sorting, and Editing Recipient Information

You'll use the Mail Merge Recipients dialog box to choose, sort, and edit the information in your data source file. If you plan to make changes, such as updating the address on a particular client, changing a company name, or deleting a customer you no longer work with, you can use the commands in this dialog box to carry out those tasks. (See Table 35-2.)

Table 35-2. Working with Merge Data

Action	Result
Clear the check mark in the first column to deselect the recipient row.	Removes a recipient from the merge operation
Select the check box in the first column to add a check mark.	Adds a recipient to the merge operation
Click the arrow in the heading of the column by which you want to sort (for example, Last Name or City).	Reorders recipient records based on a particular field (if the listing was A to Z, clicking the heading will arrange the list Z to A)
Click an existing entry and click Edit. When the address list dialog box appears, click New Entry and enter the new recipient data. Repeat as needed; then click Close to close the dialog box.	Adds a new recipient to the list
Click the Find button and type in the Find box the data you want to locate. Click Find Next to search for the recipient.	Finds a specific recipient (the first recipient record with the found data is highlighted in the Mail Merge Recipients dialog box)
Click the Select All button.	Selects all recipients (check marks appear in the left column in the dialog box)
Click the Clear All button.	Deselects all recipients (removes the checkmarks in the left column in the dialog box)
Click the Refresh button.	Updates the data displayed in the Mail Merge Recipient dialog box
Click the Validate button.	Checks the data validity for your address data if you have a validation program installed

Editing Your Data List

Once you've added the data list to the merge document, you can edit it at any time during the merge procedure by clicking the Edit Recipient List link in step 5 of the Mail Merge Wizard or by clicking the Mail Merge Recipients button on the Mail Merge toolbar. You might want to edit your list, for example, by selecting or deselecting fields to include, sorting data records, changing data entries, or modifying the order of fields.

When you click the Edit Recipient List link, the Mail Merge Recipients dialog box appears. Here you can make any needed changes and click OK to return to the wizard. Your changes are automatically saved.

Choosing Outlook Contacts

Perhaps the most seamless way of integrating up-to-date contact information with your main document for mailings and e-mail broadcasts is to use your contact manager, Microsoft Outlook. Because Outlook's Address Book is kept up to date as you work, with new features such as smart tags that enable you to insert and update Address Book information on the fly, your information is likely to be more current and complete. E-mail addresses are added automatically from messages you receive and send, which means data is gathered for you while you go through your daily routine. Of course, the most complete data records—client information, for example, that includes name, address, home and office phones, e-mail address, Web pages, and spouse names and birth dates—happen only because you enter them. This means that the degree to which Outlook can actually help you will depend on how consistently you've entered contact information.

tip **Get more data by importing address books**

Even if your Address Book in Outlook is incomplete, you can take heart: Because you can create and load new address books in Outlook, you can work from others' data and use that information in your merge operations. If you have address book files saved in Microsoft Exchange Server, Microsoft Outlook Express, Microsoft Internet Mail and News, Eudora Light and Pro, Netscape Mail and Messenger, or any other MAPI-compatible program, you can import them directly into Outlook and then use them in your Word merge operations.

Creating Your Own New Data Source

Word gives you the option of entering your own data as part of the Mail Merge Wizard if you're so inclined. When you're choosing the recipients for your document in the Mail Merge Wizard, click Type a New List in the Select Recipients section.

Click the Create link to display the New Address List dialog box (shown in Figure 35-5). You can now enter the information for the person or company you are adding.

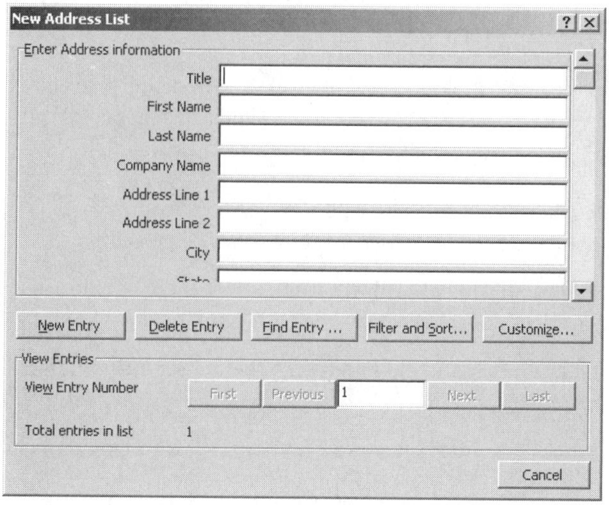

Figure 35-5. You can easily add your own data as you prepare your files for merging.

> **note** Any data you create in the Office Address List will be saved in its own .mdb (mailing database) file, which means that you can use it with other mailings as well.

To add recipient information to the data source file, simply click in the field you want and type the information. Press Tab to move to the next item or scroll down through the list as needed. When you've finished entering information for that entry, click New Entry to display another blank form or, if you're finished, click Close to close the dialog box.

When you click Close, the Save Address List dialog box appears, with My Data Sources selected as the current folder. (See Figure 35-6.) Enter a name for the file, and click Save. The information is displayed in the Mail Merge Recipients list, where you can sort, rearrange, and select or deselect recipients. Make any necessary selections, and click OK to close the dialog box and return to the wizard.

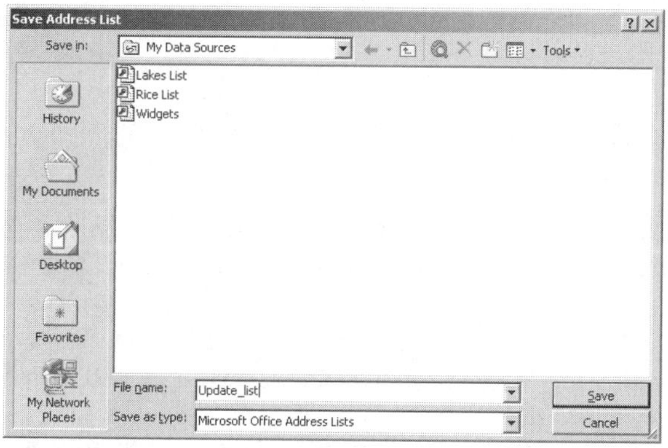

Figure 35-6. Microsoft Office Address List files are stored by default in the My Data Sources folder, where they can be accessed by all Office applications.

Customizing Address List Items

If you want to change the items listed in the New Address List dialog box, click Customize. The Customize Address List dialog box appears, as Figure 35-7 shows. You can make the following changes to the Field Names list:

- To add a field name, click Add. The Add Field dialog box appears. Type the name for the field you want to create, and click OK.
- To delete a field and all the field information, select the field, click Delete, and then click Yes in the confirmation message box.
- To rename a field, select it and click Rename; then enter a new name for the field, and click OK.
- To move a field, select it and click either Move Up or Move Down to change its position in the list.

When you're finished making modifications to the field list, click OK to return to the New Address List dialog box. Add or edit your data as needed; then click OK to return to the wizard.

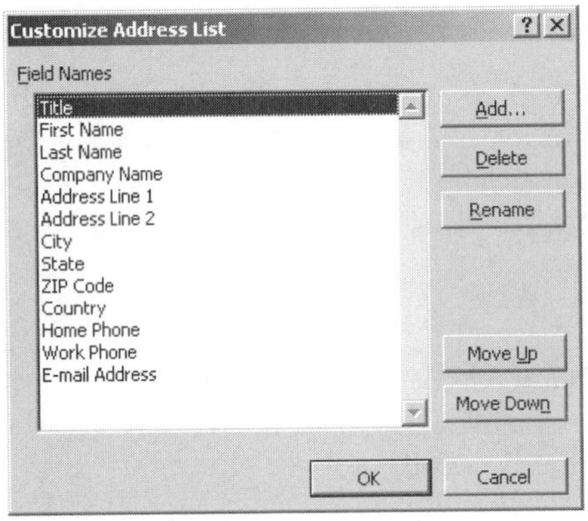

Figure 35-7. You can add, delete, or modify fields in your source file to fit the data items you need.

Adding Merge Fields

So now you've selected the document you want to use and you've identified the people to whom you want to send it. The next step involves adding the placeholders in the document where the data will be inserted for the individual recipients. When you click Next and the wizard displays the page on which you create the letter for your merge operation, you see the following merge fields you can insert in your document:

- **Address Block** displays the Insert Address Block dialog box so that you can add the name, address, and city, state, and ZIP code at the insertion point.

- **Greeting Line** displays the Greeting Line dialog box, allowing you to select the salutation you want to use as well as the format for the recipient name.
- **Electronic Postage** enables you to work with electronic postage if you've installed that feature.
- **Postal Bar Code** displays the Insert Postal Bar Code dialog box so that you can choose the field after which you'd like to display the postal bar code.
- **More Items** displays the Insert Merge Field dialog box, giving you the option of adding additional fields to your main document.

Inserting an Address Block

The Address Block includes the collection of data you're likely to use most often. The block includes the recipient name, address, city, state, and ZIP Code. You can also include the company name and the country and region in the address if you choose. To add the Address Block to your main document, follow these steps:

1. Place the insertion point where you want to insert the Address Block.
2. In step 4 of the Mail Merge Wizard, click the Address Block link, or click the Insert Address Block button on the Mail Merge toolbar. The Insert Address Block dialog box appears. (See Figure 35-8.)

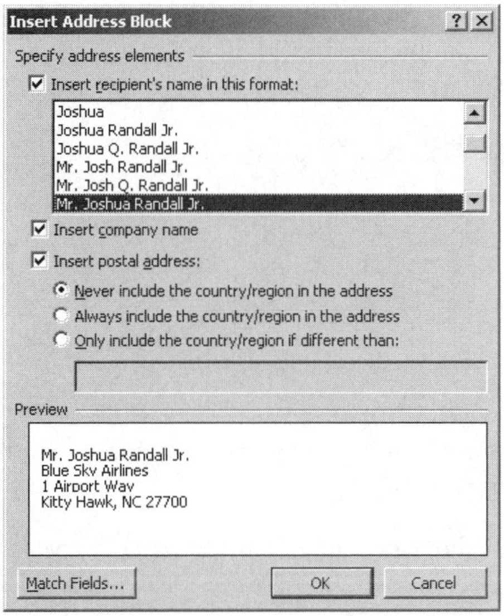

Figure 35-8. Specify the address format you want to use in the Insert Address Block dialog box.

3. Scroll through the Insert Recipient's Name In This Format list to choose the format you want to use for the recipient name; select the style you want to use.

4 If you want to omit the company name from the Address Block, clear the Insert Company Name check box.

5 To hide the postal information in the Address Block, clear the Insert Postal Address check box. The Preview section shows your current selections.

6 Click OK to close the dialog box. Word inserts the following code at the insertion point:

```
««AddressBlock»»
```

note You'll get a chance to preview your document with the data included before you do the actual merge. You can also use the Error Check Merge button on the Mail Merge toolbar to do a test run before you execute the merge operation.

Choosing a Greeting Line

The Greeting Line merge field enables you to say hello in the language and format you want. To add a Greeting Line, follow these steps:

1 Place the insertion point in the document where you want to add a Greeting Line.

2 Click the Greeting Line link in the Write Your Letter section of step 4 in the Mail Merge Wizard, or click the Insert Greeting Line button on the Mail Merge toolbar. The Greeting Line dialog box appears. (See Figure 35-9.)

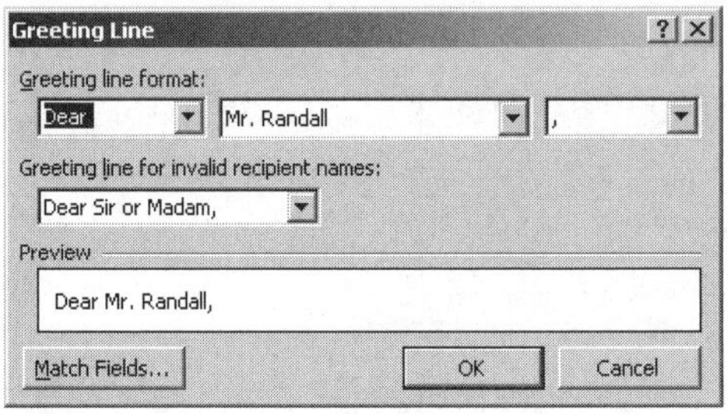

Figure 35-9. Choose the salutation and name format for your greeting in the Greeting Line dialog box.

3 For those recipients that show an empty or invalid name entry, you have the option of adding a generic phrase. Choose either Dear Sir Or Madam or To Whom It May Concern.

4 Click OK to close the dialog box and insert the Greeting Line. Word inserts the following code at the insertion point:

```
««GreetingLine»»
```

tip **Add a postal bar code**

If you're printing envelopes or labels on which you want a postal bar code to appear, click the Postal Bar Code link in step 4 of the Mail Merge Wizard. When the Insert Postal Bar Code dialog box appears, click the Merge Field With ZIP Code down arrow and choose the field to which the postal code should refer.

Next, click the Merge Field With Street Address down arrow to display the list of choices for the delivery address you want the postal code to reflect. Click your choice, and click OK.

Inserting Merge Fields

Word offers a number of preset merge fields you can insert by pointing and clicking. You can further personalize your main document by adding address or database fields. To display the additional merge fields you can use in your document, click the More Items link in step 4 of the Mail Merge Wizard. The Insert Merge Field dialog box appears, as Figure 35-10 shows.

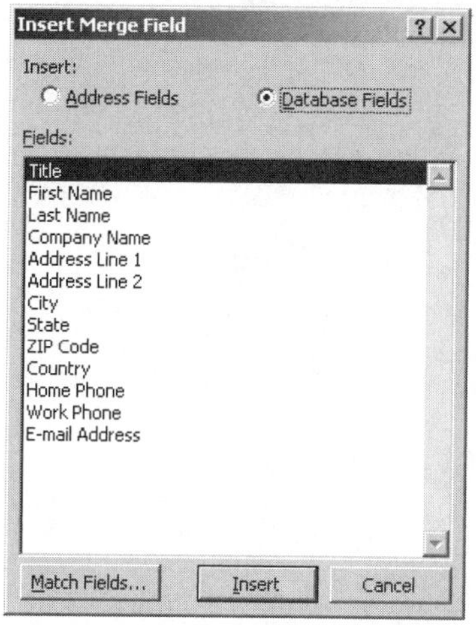

Figure 35-10. The Insert Merge Field dialog box enables you to choose either Address Fields or Database Fields.

If you want to use fields available in your Address Book, click the Address Fields option. You'll see quite a list of offerings, from basic contact info to spouse's name to nickname. When you click the Database Fields option, you see traditional database fields, including Title, First Name, Last Name, Company Name, Address Line 1, Address Line 2, City, State, ZIP Code, Country, Home Phone, Work Phone, and E-mail Address.

To insert one of Word's additional merge fields, follow these steps:

1. Place the insertion point where you want to add the field.
2. Click the More Items link in step 4 of the Mail Merge Wizard to display the Insert Merge Field dialog box, or click Insert Merge Fields on the Mail Merge toolbar.
3. Click Address Fields or Database Fields.
4. Click the field you want to add, and click Insert.
5. When you're finished, click Close to return to your main document.

Figure 35-11 shows a form letter after two database fields, <<First_Name>> and <<Email_Address>>, have been added. When you're ready to preview your document with the merge data intact, click Next to proceed to the next wizard step.

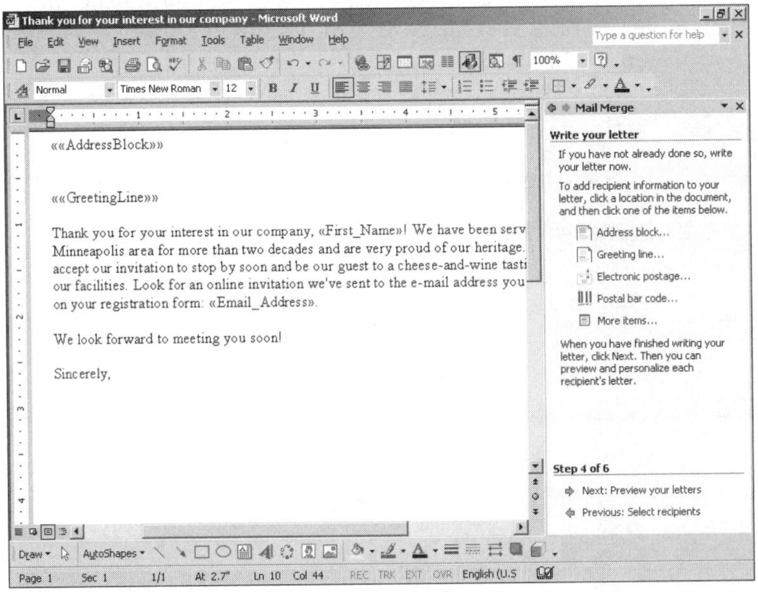

Figure 35-11. You can add database and address fields in the body of your document as needed.

> **tip** **Display paragraph marks for accurate spacing**
>
> When you're adding merge fields to your document, turn on paragraph marks by clicking Show All on the Standard toolbar. Displaying paragraphs shows all paragraph marks, spaces, and tab characters so that you can better control the placement of merge fields in your document.

Matching Fields with Your Database

Word enables you to use data you've entered and organized in other programs—such as Microsoft Access, Microsoft Excel, other database programs, or compatible e-mail utilities—to serve as the source for your mail merge. If the fields you've created in your database don't match the fields in the address list, don't worry—you can use Word's Match Fields tool to equate the fields so data flows into the right place automatically.

You can display the Match Fields dialog box in several different ways:

- Click the Match Fields button on the Mail Merge toolbar.
- Click the Match Fields button in the Insert Address Block dialog box.
- Click the Match Fields button in the Greeting Line dialog box.

Tell Word how to match fields by clicking the down arrow of the field you want to match. For example, if in your database file you have all addresses listed as Address Line 2, but in your Address List in the merge procedure you want it to be shown as Address Line 1, you can click the Address Line 1 down arrow (shown in Figure 35-12) and select Address Line 2. When you select Address Line 2, Word places in Address Line 1 any data it finds tagged for Address Line 2. After you make your matches, click OK to close the dialog box and return to the document.

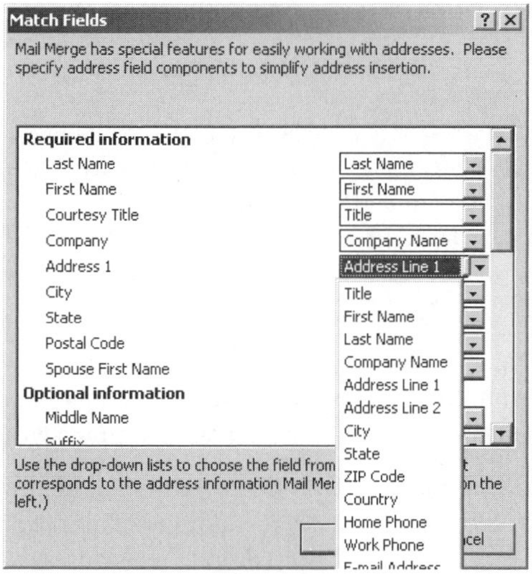

Figure 35-12. Use the Match Fields dialog box to tell Word how to correctly import the data you've created in other programs.

Adding Word Fields

Along with the merge fields you are given in the Mail Merge Wizard, you have another set of fields at your disposal. Word fields enable you to personalize your document, message, or form even further. You might want to add a Word field, for example, that skips a record based on the data in a particular field.

To add a Word field to your main document, follow these steps:

1. Place the insertion point in your document where you want to add the field.
2. Click the Insert Word Field button on the Mail Merge toolbar. A drop-down menu appears, listing the Word field choices. Click your choice, and Word prompts you to add additional information. Table 35-3 gives you an overview of the Word fields available in mail merge operations.

Table 35-3. Word Fields for Mail Merge

Field	Description	Options
Ask	Adds a customized dialog box that asks for more information during a merge	You can use a predefined bookmark or add a new one to mark the placement of the Ask field.
Fill-In	Prompts user for additional information	You can choose to have Word ask for information with each merged record or only once, at the beginning of the process.
If...Then...Else	Creates conditional text segments that insert one phrase in one situation and another phrase in another	You can control the fields you want to compare as well as the qualifier (Equal To, Not Equal To, Less Than, Greater Than, Less Than Or Equal, Greater Than Or Equal, Is Blank, Is Not Blank).
Merge Record #	Adds the number of the current record to the merged document	Place the insertion point where you want the number to appear; no dialog box is displayed.
Merge Sequence #	Inserts numbering for all documents in the merge	Place the insertion point where you want the number to appear; no dialog box is displayed.
Next Record	Includes data from the next record in the current record	You can include several records at once; however, to list many records, create a directory.
Next Record If	Includes data from the next record if a certain condition is met	You can include record data if a field contains a value you seek.

(continued)

Table 35-3. *(continued)*

Field	Description	Options
Set Bookmark	Adds a bookmark and attached text in every merged document	You can use existing bookmarks or add new ones to accommodate the merge.
Skip Record If	Omits records depending on a specific condition	You can choose the fields to compare and the qualifier (Equal To, Not Equal To, Less Than, Greater Than, Less Than Or Equal, Greater Than Or Equal, Is Blank, Is Not Blank).

Previewing the Merge

The next step in the merge process involves reviewing the data merged into your document. The first document is displayed by default with your first recipient's data in the Word window (shown in Figure 35-13). You can page through the recipients by clicking the previous (<<) or next (>>) button in the wizard task pane.

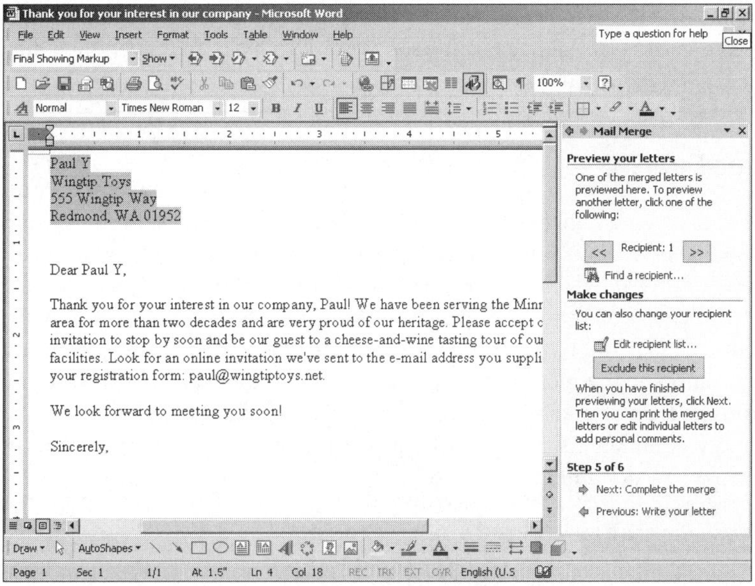

Figure 35-13. The merge data is shown automatically in your main document during Preview.

Finding a Specific Entry

If you want to locate a particular recipient in your list, click the Find A Recipient link in step 5 of the Mail Merge Wizard or click the Find Entry button on the Mail Merge toolbar. The Find Entry dialog box appears so that you can type in the Find box the data you'd like to locate. Specify the field you want to search, if necessary, and then click Find Next. Word locates the text you indicated in the merge document.

Excluding a Recipient

If you want to remove a recipient from the current merge operation, you can click Exclude This Recipient in the Make Changes section of the task pane. The entry is removed and the next recipient in the list is displayed.

If you change your mind and want to include the recipient after all, click the Edit Recipient List link to display the Mail Merge Recipients dialog box. Scroll to the recipient record you want to display, and select the check box in the left column. Click OK to close the dialog box. The recipient will be included in the merge.

> **tip** **Test before you print**
>
> Before you go too far in designing your letter, print a sample to make sure it fits on your company stationery. Particularly if you have a specialty logo or an unusual address line at the bottom of the page, test your printout to make sure everything fits before you start the merge operation.

Checking for Errors

If you're preparing a merge operation with hundred, or thousands, of records, it's an especially good idea to run a test before you do the actual merge. Word gives you an easy way to do a quick check for errors. Simply click the Error Check Merge button on the Mail Merge toolbar to display the Checking And Reporting Errors dialog box (shown in Figure 35-14). You have three choices for the way in which you test your merge: You can simulate the merge and save the errors in a new document; you can go ahead and run the merge operations, but have Word stop and alert you when an error is found; or you can complete the merge without pausing for errors and have Word report the errors in a new document.

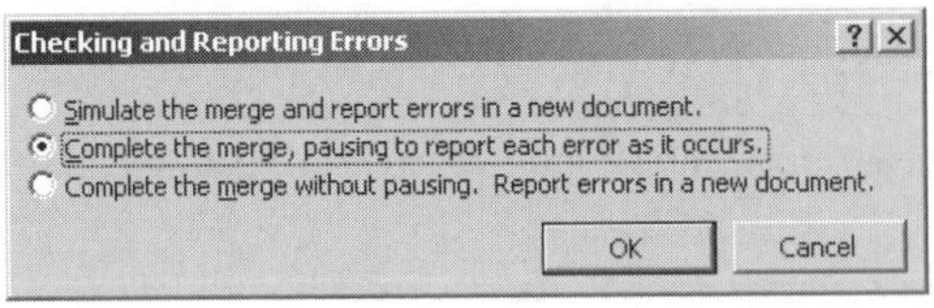

Figure 35-14. Select an error-checking method in the Checking And Reporting Errors dialog box.

The difference between these options is that one runs a "practice test" that reports on errors it finds but does not make changes in the document. The second option, the default, does the merge but alerts you immediately whenever an error is found. If this is the first time you've used Word's mail merge utility, it's a good idea to test it out using the simulation until you feel comfortable proceeding with the real thing.

Merging the Documents

The final step in the mail merge process involves printing, sending, or saving your document with the data intact. The actual merge is a bit anticlimactic. You simply click the Next button in the wizard or click the appropriate button on the Mail Merge toolbar—depending on whether you're merging to a new document, the printer, e-mail, or fax—to finalize the merge.

Choosing Merge Print Options

Merge To Printer

To prepare your merge documents for printing, click Print in step 6 of the Mail Merge Wizard or click the Merge To Printer button on the Mail Merge toolbar. The Merge To Printer dialog box appears, and you can choose from the following options:

- **All** prints all records in the current document.
- **Current Record** prints only the displayed record.
- **From / To** enables you to set a page range—from record 2 to 5, for example—so that you can select only those records you want to print.

Troubleshooting

Fields Are Printed in My Mail Merge Document Instead of Values

You went through all the steps in the Mail Merge Wizard, checked the merge for errors, and selected the merge process you wanted. Everything looked fine. But when you printed the merged documents, instead of the values, you see the merge field names in the document. What's going on?

It might be that the Field Codes check box has been selected in your Word options, which causes fields to be displayed by default rather than the values they store. To check this option and change it if necessary, choose Tools, Options. When the Options dialog box appears, click the Print tab. Clear the Field Codes check box in the Include With Document section, and then click OK to close the dialog box and return to the document.

Merge to a New Document

If you're working with a letter document type, Word gives you the option of merging to a new document after the Mail Merge Wizard finishes so that you can further personalize the documents you've created.

To merge the information to a document, click the Edit Individual Letters link in step 6 of the wizard or click the Merge To Document button on the Mail Merge toolbar. The Merge To New Document dialog box opens, and you can choose whether you want to merge all records, the current record only, or a range of records you specify. Make your choices, and click OK to complete the merge.

Merge to E-mail

If you select the E-mail Message document type when you began the Mail Merge Wizard, the merge process involves putting the source data together with the main document in e-mail messages. After you preview the records and click Next, step 6 of the Mail Merge Wizard appears. Your only choice is Electronic Mail. When you click the link, the Merge To E-mail dialog box appears. (See Figure 35-15.)

If you're creating your merge document by using the Mail Merge toolbar, you can click Merge To E-mail to begin the e-mail merge.

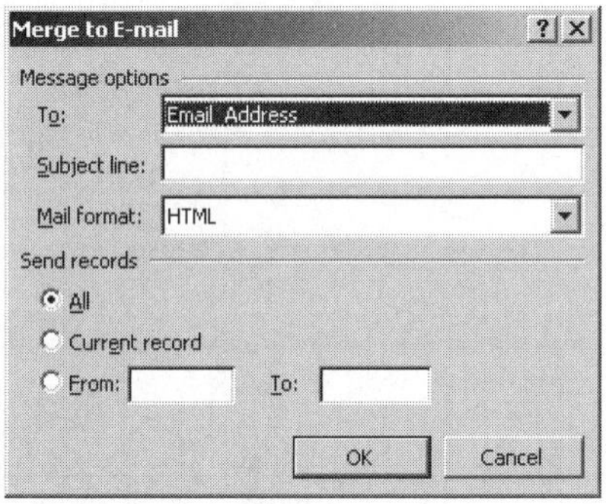

Figure 35-15. With Merge To E-mail, you combine source data with your main document and send the results to Outlook for delivery.

Your choices include the following:

- Click the To down arrow to display the list of choices for the field containing the e-mail addresses to which you want to send the messages.
- Enter a Subject in the Subject Line box to tell recipients something about the incoming message.

- In the Mail Format drop-down list, select Attachment, HTML, or Plain Text to control the method by which you want to send the e-mail messages.
- In the Send Records section, choose the records you want to send. Your choices are All, Current Record, or From and To, which enable you to choose the range of recipients for your message.

Merge to Fax

You have one final option for where and how to merge your documents. If you have fax support set up on your system, you can use the Merge To Fax button on the Mail Merge toolbar to send faxes to groups of people. The Merge To Fax dialog box appears so that you can select the records to send (your choices are All, Current, and From and To). Click OK to send the faxes.

Reviewing the Merge

After Word merges your document, take the time to page through and make sure the results are what you expected. Two tools will help you see where your inserted fields appear in the main document: Show Values and Highlight Merge Fields.

Click Show Values on the Mail Merge toolbar to toggle the display between the field and values display. When you click Show Values the first time, Word displays the names in place of the merged data. When you click Show Values the second time, Word displays the data values inserted in the document.

Using Highlight Merge Fields, also on the Mail Merge toolbar, enables you to see at a glance where all the inserted fields are in your main document. When you click Highlight Merge Fields, all fields in the document appear highlighted. To suppress the highlight, click the button again.

tip **Turn a merge document into a normal document**

If you want to change a form letter or merge document back into a standard Word document, simply display the document and then click Main Document Setup button on the Mail Merge toolbar. When the submenu appears, click Normal Word Document. The document is then displayed as a normal document without the marked fields in place.

Creating a Directory

All the merge operations in this chapter thus far have covered ways you can take multiple data items and plug them into documents you can replicate easily. There will be times, however, when you will want a complete listing of the records in your source file. You might, for example, want to keep a listing of all recipients to the catalog mailing you send in Fall 2002. To create a directory of records from your data source, you can use the Mail Merge Wizard. Here are the steps:

1 Start the wizard by choosing Tools, Letters And Mailings, Mail Merge Wizard. The wizard opens in the task pane.

2 In the Select Document Type section, click Directory. Click the Next link.

3 In the Select Starting Document section in step 2, choose whether you want to use the current document, select a template, or open an existing document for your directory; then click the Next link.

> **tip** **Save time formatting with templates**
>
> Word includes several address list templates you can use as the basis for your directories. Unless you have a certain format you need to stick to, you might as well benefit from the existing files already created.

4 In the Select Recipients section in step 3, choose your data source by opening an existing file, using your Outlook Contacts list, or typing new source data. Again, click the Next link.

5 In the Arrange Your Directory section of step 4, click the fields you want to insert (most likely you'll want only Address Block). If you want to add additional fields, click the More Items link to display the Insert Merge Field dialog box and make your choices. Click the Next link.

6 In step 5, preview your document. Don't worry that only one record is shown in the document window in preview; you'll see an entire list when the merge is completed. Click the Next link.

7 In step 6, click the To New Document link in the Merge section. Click All and then OK in the Merge To New Document dialog box. The merge is completed and the directory is displayed in your document window. You can now save the directory file and use it for future merge operations.

Printing Envelopes and Labels

In some cases, you might want to print only a single envelope or an individual sheet of labels. Here working with the data source and inserting fields in a document isn't necessary—no merge is needed. When you want to print a simple envelope or set of labels, choose Tools, Letters And Mailings, Envelopes And Labels. The Envelopes And Labels dialog box appears, as Figure 35-16 shows.

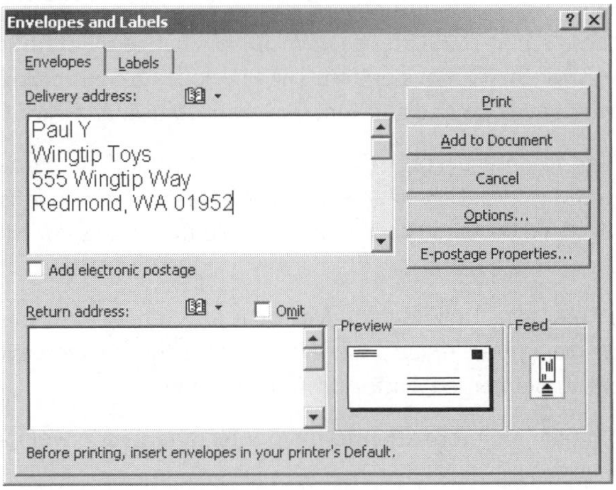

Figure 35-16. The Envelopes And Labels dialog box enables you to create and print individual envelopes and labels.

note If you're working with an open document that has an Address Block inserted (or a default address you've entered yourself), the address will be shown automatically in the Envelopes And Labels dialog box.

The Envelopes tab includes a number of quick options you can set before printing the envelope. Here's an overview:

- **Print** starts the print process—so make sure to set your other options and load the printer first!
- **Add To Document** adds the envelope to the current document so that the envelope and document can be printed together.
- **Cancel** closes the Envelopes And Labels dialog box without saving settings.
- **Options** displays the Envelope Options dialog box so that you can choose the envelope size and font specifications.
- **E-Postage Properties** enables you to work with an e-postage account if you've previously set one up on the Web.

To print an envelope, simply open the Envelopes And Labels dialog box and follow these steps:

1. If necessary, enter the recipient address in the Delivery Address box by typing it or by clicking the Insert Address button and selecting the recipient in the Select Name dialog box.
2. Enter the return address in the Return Address box by typing it or, again, you can click the Insert Address button and select the return address you want.
3. If you want to choose a non-standard size envelope or change the font used in the address blocks, click the Options button. The Envelope Options dialog box appears. Choose the envelope size and font you want to use, and click OK.
4. If you've subscribed to an e-postage service and want to add electronic postage to the envelope, click E-Postage Properties to set postage options and select the Add Electronic Postage check box to enable the feature for the current envelope.
5. Make sure your printer is ready and the envelope is inserted as shown in the Feed section of the dialog box. If you want Word to save the created envelope with the document to be merged, click Add To Document.
6. Click Print. Word sends the information to the printer, and your envelope is printed as your specified.

Creating Labels

Instead of printing directly on envelopes, you might want to print mailing labels. Word makes it easy for you to print labels in a wide range of shapes and sizes. If you want to print a single (or a few) labels and don't want to use mail merge to do it, you can use the Envelopes And Labels dialog box to print labels quickly. Here's how:

1. Choose Tools, Letters And Mailings, Envelopes And Labels. The Envelopes And Labels dialog box appears.
2. Click the Labels tab. The options here enable you to enter the label information, choose the way you want the label printed (a single label or a whole page of labels), and make selections about the label size and e-postage.
3. By default, Word prints a full page of labels. If you want to print only one, click the Single Label option in the Print section.
4. The selected label is shown in the Label section. If you want to select a different label, click Options to make a new choice.
5. When you're finished entering your choices, make sure your printer is loaded correctly and click Print. Word prints the labels as you selected.

tip **Print many labels fast**

If you have a number of labels that you want to print quickly, it's best to use the Mail Merge Wizard to lead you through the steps for printing labels.

Troubleshooting

I Can't Feed Envelopes from a Loaded Tray

If you've loaded envelopes in a paper tray and Word keeps prompting you to manually feed your envelopes to the printer, make sure that you've selected the correct paper feed choices. To check the settings, choose Tools, Letters And Mailings, Envelopes And Labels. Click the Envelopes tab, and then click the Options button. In the Envelope Options dialog box, click the Printing Options tab and click the Feed From down arrow. Choose the name of the tray in which you loaded the envelopes from the displayed list. Click OK to return to the Envelopes And Labels dialog box; click Print to print the envelope displayed.

Chapter 36

Working with Field Codes and Custom Forms

The flexibility of Microsoft Word 2002 gives you the means to create documents of all sorts—from simple letters to complex reports to documents that include indexes, footnotes and endnotes, diagrams, and more. But you aren't limited to creating documents you simply print and distribute or post on the Web; you can use Word's field capabilities to insert variable information on the fly or give users the choice of entering certain data items automatically. You also can create forms that prompt users for information they enter, either by making field selections or typing the requested data.

In this chapter, you'll learn to use Word's tools to work with fields and create forms. Along the way, you'll discover what makes a fast, effective form and find out how to make the most of Word's interactive data capabilities.

Why Use Fields and Forms in Word Documents?

A field is a kind of placeholder—a code inserted in your document that enables you to add variable data, launch another application, or ask for input from a user.

In its most basic sense, a field allows you to incorporate changeable data in your Word documents. For example, you might want to add information such as a product name, the number of pages in a document, or the current date. To do this, you insert field codes that tell Word to add text, graphics, page numbers, and other material to the document automatically. You can also use fields in your Word documents to do the following things:

- Calculate and display values in a document
- Add document information to headers and footers
- Prompt users to add more information during a mail merge operation
- Mark special items such as table of content entries, index entries, and more

A form is a Word document that helps you capture the data you need for your applications. The only difference between a traditional document and a form is the addition of data fields that allow you to gather information. Later in this chapter, you'll learn how to create and work with forms.

Understanding Fields

A field lets Word know that there's additional information you want to include, or an action you want to perform, in a document. You add a field by choosing Insert, Field. The Field dialog box opens so that you can make your choices about the particular field and options you want to use. (See Figure 36-1.)

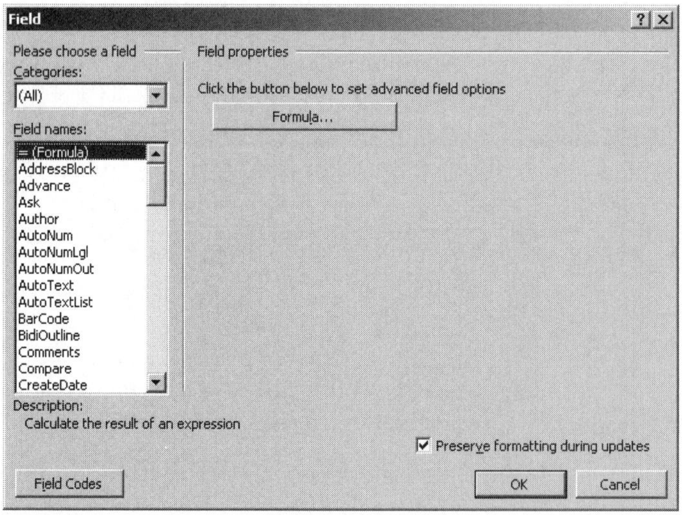

Figure 36-1. You insert a field by using the Field dialog box.

Field Anatomy

When you make the selections for the field, Word inserts a field code in the document at the insertion point. This is the code that tells Word what to insert or what action to call for when the user is working with the document. A field code like the following one includes four basic elements:

{ DATE \@ "dddd, MMMM dd, yyyy" * MERGEFORMAT }

- **Field identifiers.** The curly braces { } are inserted when you create the Field using the Field dialog box or press Ctrl+F9 to insert a field.
- **Field name.** The name of the field, in this case DATE, is the field you select or type between the braces.
- **Field instructions.** The instructions, here shown as "dddd, MMMM dd, yyyy," include any text you want to display as a prompt, a value or phrase, or a bookmark to be inserted.
- **Switches.** A switch, shown in this example as MERGEFORMAT, is an option you set to specify the way in which you want the field to be displayed or formatted.

Field Functions

Fields have three basic functions in Word. You might use a field to perform a certain kind of action, to mark a specific item, or to display the results of a calculation.

- **Action fields.** An action field asks for action from the user. Examples of fields include the ASK field and the FILL-IN field, which prompt the user to enter more information.
- **Marker fields.** A marker field is a field that marks an item for a specific purpose. For example, when you identify a word or phrase to be included in an index, Word inserts a field code to mark the index entry.
- **Result fields.** A result field, as you might expect, displays the results or a calculation or a file retrieval operation. One of the most common result fields you'll use is the Formula field; you'll also use Date and Time, as well as AutoText, to display results in the field.

Fields You're Already Using

For some procedures, Word adds fields behind the scenes. When you create a table of contents, for example, Word adds {TOC} codes in your document. When you create an index, Word adds the index entry {XE} codes as field codes. Other examples of field codes that might be in your document include these:

- A bookmark you've inserted is placed in your document as a {BOOKMARK} field code.
- If you've used Insert, Date And Time to add the current date, the {DATE} code is placed in your document.
- If you've added a page number, {PAGE} is already in your document.
- If you've added a hyperlink to a URL or another document, {HYPERLINK} is in your document.
- A footnote you've added shows up as {NOTEREF} in the document.

Inserting Fields

When you want to insert a field in the document, start by choosing your location. You can add a field to the body of your document or you can insert a field in a header or footer. The process for adding a field is as follows:

1. Place the insertion point in the document where you want to add the field.
2. Choose Insert, Field. The Field dialog box appears.
3. Click the Categories down arrow and choose the category of field you want to add. Table 36-1 lists the various categories and provides a description of each.
4. Select any options you want for the selected field, and click OK to add the field (see "Choosing Field Options" on page 871 for more information).

note When you first add a field, Word displays the result of the field, not the actual field code, in the document. If you want to view the code itself, press Alt+F9 to display it.

Table 36-1. Field Categories

Field Category	Description	Field Codes
Date and Time	Fields for entering, editing, printing, and saving the current date and time. These fields cannot be modified by an end user.	CreateDate Date EditTime PrintDate SaveDate Time IncludePicture
Document Automation	Fields for comparing documents, moving to another section, starting a macro, or printing.	Compare DocVariable GoToButton If MacroButton Print
Document Information	Fields for inserting information automatically, including author name, document properties, file name, keywords, template, and the number of characters, pages, or words.	Author Comments DocProperty FileName FileSize Info Keywords LastSavedBy NumChars NumPages NumWords Subject Template Title
Equations and Formulas	Fields for adding formulas or entering an offset amount, a scientific equation, or symbols.	=(Formula) Advance Eq Symbol
Index and Tables	Fields for entering index and table of contents entries. You can enter the codes from within the Field dialog box or allow Word to insert them automatically as you create the index or TOC.	Index RD TA TC TOA TOC XE

(continued)

Table 36-1. *(continued)*

Field Category	Description	Field Codes
Links and Reference	Fields for inserting text phrases and pictures and including links to various reference items, including footnote references, literal quotes, pictures, bookmark text, and paragraphs.	AutoText AutoTextList Hyperlink IncludePicture IncludeText Link NoteRef PageRef Quote Ref StyleRef
Mail Merge	Fields for inserting merge fields, including adding address book data, greeting lines, database records, and more. You can also use Ask and Fill-In fields to prompt users to enter information.	AddressBook Ask Compare Database Fill-In GreetingLine If MergeField MergeRec MergeSeq Next NextIf Set SkipIf
Numbering	Fields that insert automatic numbering of document pages, sections, as well as bar codes and list items.	AutoNum AutoNumLgl AutoNumOut BarCode ListNum Page RevNum Section SectionPages Seq
User Information	Fields that insert user information, including address, initials, and name.	UserAddress UserInitials UserName

Choosing Field Options

When you're working in the Field dialog box to enter field codes, you have a number of different options available to you, depending on what type of field you're adding. For example, when you insert an ASK field in your document, as shown in Figure 36-2, you need to provide the following additional information:

- The text prompt you want to use to prompt the user
- The bookmark name you want to use to mark the prompt

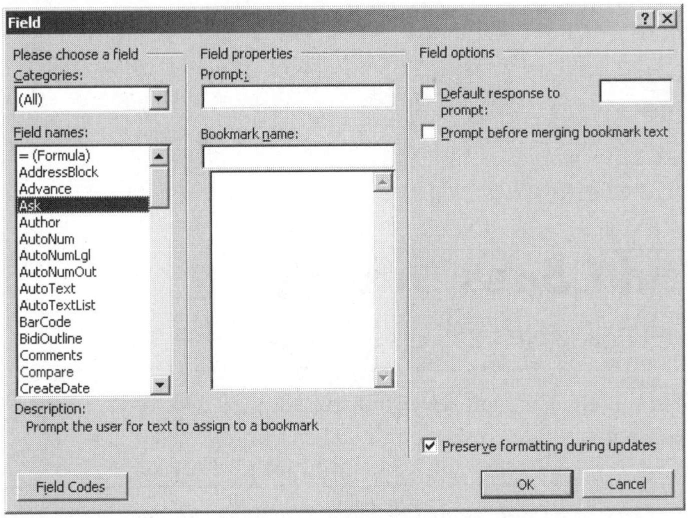

Figure 36-2. The Field dialog box provides field code options tailored to the field you select.

You can also add a default response to the prompt, if you want to provide one, and you can have Word provide a prompt before the information is merged in a mail merge operation. Finally, the last choice asks whether you want to preserve the formatting of the field code when you update the field.

If you select another type of field, such as the FILESIZE field, another set of options is displayed. (See Figure 36-3, on the next page.) With the FILESIZE field, you can choose

- The format of the number to be displayed
- The numeric format used
- Whether you want the file size to be displayed in kilobytes or megabytes

After you've made your field choices, click OK to close the Field dialog box. The field is placed in your document and the result will be displayed automatically.

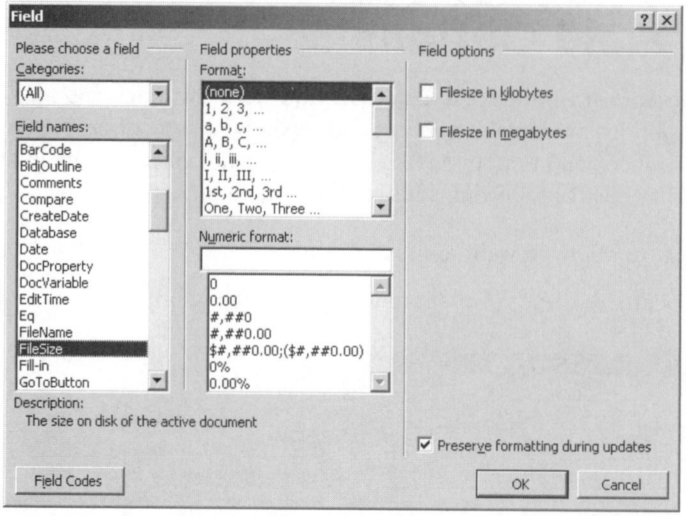

Figure 36-3. The Field dialog box gives different choices for a numeric field.

Typing Field Codes Directly

If you know the name of the field you want to insert, you can enter it directly in your document by placing the insertion point where you want to insert the field, pressing Ctrl+F9, and typing the field name. Word inserts the field code directly in the document at the insertion point.

note Although the curly braces surrounding the field code look like regular braces you type from the keyboard, they're actually special characters Word inserts when you press the keyboard shortcut for entering a field. Instead of typing the braces, press Ctrl+F9 to add the braces.

In order to insert the complete field, you need to be able to type the field code name, any arguments you want to include, and the necessary switches.

Using Arguments in Field Codes

An argument is an additional piece of information that the field needs in order to complete the operation and display a result. You enter arguments in quotation marks. For example, if you're entering a code specifying the author of a document, you might enter

{ AUTHOR "Patricia Doyle" }

The argument in this case is "Patricia Doyle," and the field code is AUTHOR. If you're entering a one-word argument, you can type it without quotation marks if you choose.

Entering Arguments in the Field Dialog Box

If you want to add arguments for the field code you're inserting by using the Field dialog box, follow these steps:

1. Place the insertion point where you want to insert the field.
2. Choose Insert, Field. The Field dialog box appears.
3. Choose the field you want to add.
4. Specify any necessary field options in the Field dialog box.
5. Click the Field Codes button in the lower left corner of the dialog box. The Advanced Field Properties section of the Field dialog box appears. (See Figure 36-4.)

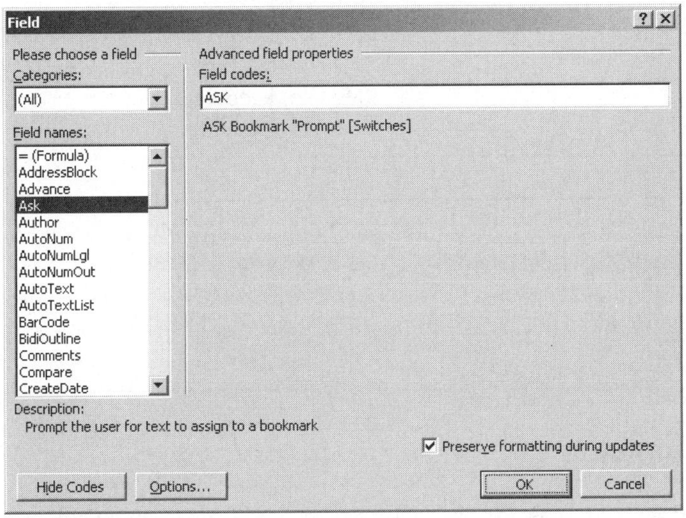

Figure 36-4. You can type field arguments in the Advanced Field Properties section of the Field dialog box.

Using Switches with Field Codes

Switches are special codes that change the way the field codes in your document act. There are two types of switches—general switches, which control the way the results of your field are formatted or displayed, and specific switches, which relate directly to the type of field you're using. Table 36-2, on the next page, gives you an overview of the general switches you'll use with Word's field codes.

Table 36-2. **Field Code Switches**

Category	Identifier	Description	Example
Format	*	Changes the way field results are displayed	{AUTHOR * Lower}
Numeric Picture	\#	Specifies format settings for displaying a numeric result	{NUMPAGES \# "0"}
Date-Time Picture	\@	Specifies the formatting for the display or a date or time	{PRINTDATE \@ "MMMM d, yyyy"}
Lock Result	\!	Locks a BOOKMARK, INCLUDETEXT, or REF field, keeping it from being updated	{BOOKMARK C:\\Text\Myreport.doc \!}

note The general switches shown in the preceding table will not work with the following fields: AUTONUM, AUTONUMGL, AUTONUMOUT, EMBED, FORMTEXT, TA, TC, XE, EQ, GOTOBUTTON, MACROBUTTON, RD, FORMCHECKBOX, FORMDROPDOWN, and LISTNUM. You'll be able to use field-specific switches with some of these fields, however.

Adding Switches

A field switch causes a specified action to be performed on a field result. For example, the * switch specifies a formatting action, and \@ indicates a switch that controls the display of a date, time, or picture entry.

If you're entering the switches by hand, you'll need to type the switches following the argument in the field code. If you're inserting the field using the Field dialog box, you can add the switches by following these steps:

1. Place the insertion point where you want to add the field.
2. Choose Insert, Field to display the Field dialog box.
3. Choose the field you want to add.
4. Make any necessary field choices in the Field dialog box.

5 Click the Field Codes button, and then click Options. The Field Options dialog box appears. (See Figure 36-5.)

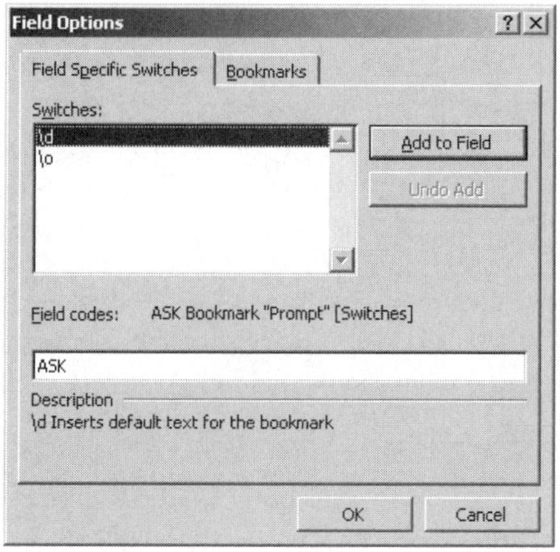

Figure 36-5. Add switches to your field in the Field Options dialog box.

6 Click the switch you want to use, and then click Add To Field.

7 Click OK to close the dialog box; click OK again to insert the field and return to the document.

tip **Display specific switch functions**

The switches shown in the Field Options dialog box are field-specific switches; that is, they perform a unique action on the selected field. If you want to find the function of individual switches, click each switch in the Field Options dialog box. The description of the switch's function appears in the Description section of the Field Options dialog box.

Viewing Codes and Fields

After you click OK in the Field dialog box to add the field, Word displays the field results in place of the field. This means that if you've inserted an AUTHOR field in your document, the name of the author will appear instead of the AUTHOR field code. If you've used the DATE field code to enter today's date, the date itself will appear instead of the code.

To switch between displaying field codes and field values, use one of these methods:

- To change a single field, click in the field and press Shift+F9.
- To change the display of all fields in the document, press Alt+F9.

tip **Change field code display**

If your field codes are displayed instead of the field values, choose Tools, Options to display the Options dialog box. If the Field Codes check box on the View tab is selected, the values will not be displayed. Clear the Field Codes check box to display values instead of codes, and click OK to close the dialog box.

Editing Fields

Once you've added a field to your document, you might want to make changes. To do this, simply right-click the field and click Edit Field on the shortcut menu. (See Figure 36-6.) The Field dialog box appears, and you can make field changes as needed.

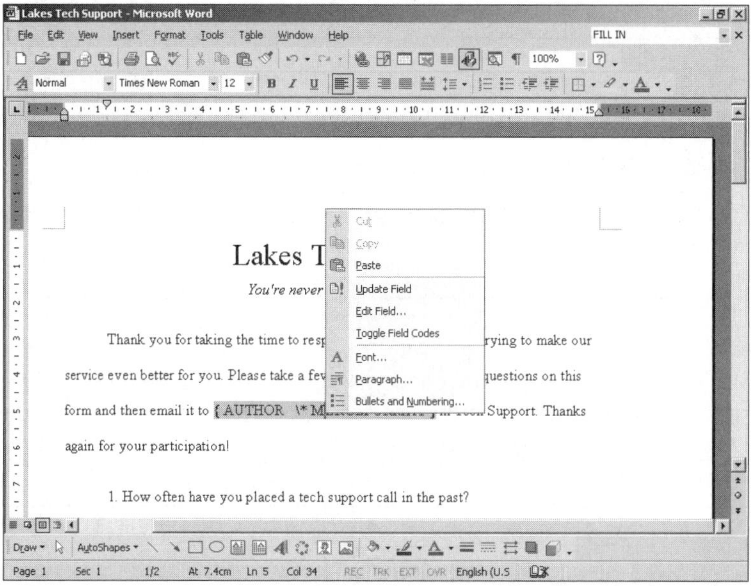

Figure 36-6. Right-click a field to display editing options.

note You can't make changes to a field in a form if the form is protected. If the form is protected, click the Protect Form button on the Forms toolbar to remove protection. For more information on creating and working with forms, see "Creating a Basic Form," on page 879, later in this chapter.

Adding Field Shading

Field shading can help you show users where to enter their response in a form you're creating. If you want to make field entries stand out, you can add a background shade that calls a reader's eye to the field on your form. To add a shade to a field, follow these steps:

1. Open the document in which you've created your form and unprotect it, if necessary, by clicking Protect Form on the Forms toolbar.
2. Click Tools, Options. The Options dialog box appears.
3. Click the View tab. Click the Field Shading down arrow to display your choices. (See Figure 36-7.) Choose Always, or When Selected.
4. Click OK to return to the document and have Word add the shading.

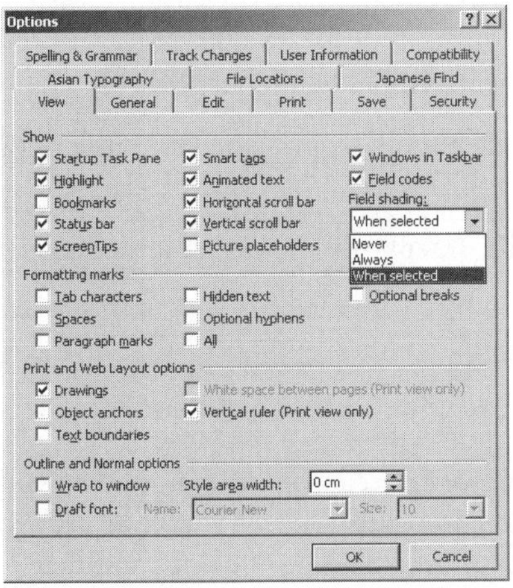

Figure 36-7. You can have Word add shading to field entries to highlight data-entry fields for users.

> **note** Field shading will appear only in those documents you use on line or in electronic form. When you print the form, the shading will not appear.

Nesting Fields

You can create a *nested* field, which is a field within a field, to provide multiple levels of variable information. You can create a nested field by following these steps:

1. Create the first field by choosing Insert, Field, and selecting the field options you want in the Field dialog box.
2. Click OK to close the Field dialog box and add the field to your document.

3. Press Alt+F9 to display the field codes if necessary; then place the insertion point inside the existing field, placing the insertion point in the field code at the point you want to insert the second field code.
4. Choose Insert, Field to display the Field dialog box; choose the field and enter your field choices.
5. Click OK to create the nested field.

Updating Fields

If you make changes to fields as you work, either by changing the arguments or by modifying the data on which the field is based, you need to have a way to update the field to reflect any changes. When you need to update the fields in your document, choose one of these methods:

- To update a single field, click in the field and press F9.
- To update multiple fields, select them by pressing Ctrl and clicking the fields; then press F9.
- To update all fields in the document, press Ctrl+A to select the entire document; then press F9.

Locking Fields

With all this work on the fields you've created, you don't want a coworker or user to be able to change the fields on the fly. To protect a field you've added, you can lock it. To do this, press Ctrl+F11. That keeps the field from being modified.

If you want to unlock the field, press Ctrl+Shift+F11. That returns the field to its normal, modifiable state.

> **If you want to protect an entire form, and not simply lock a field or two, you can use the Forms toolbar's Protect Form button to guard a form against further modification. For more information on protecting a form, see "Protecting Forms," later in this chapter.**

Printing Field Codes

Before you print a document that includes field codes, make sure that you've done an update to reflect all the latest changes. Here's how:

1. Choose Tools, Options and select the Print tab.
2. In the Printing Options section, select the Update Fields check box. When you choose Print to print the document later, field codes will be updated automatically before the document is printed.

note If you begin to print the document later and find that one of the borders isn't printing, try changing your page margins to move the boundary inward.

Creating a Basic Form

Forms enable you to create interactive documents that call for more information from readers. You can create a fill-in-the-blanks form, with text boxes, check boxes, and drop-down lists. You can create tables for your forms and use all standard Word elements, such as borders, shading, columns, background designs, graphics, and more.

Planning the Form

A good form requires some thought. What types of information do you want to capture? How long or short should the form be? What types of questions will you ask? Your answers to these and other questions will give you what you need to build a form that does what you intend it to do. Consider these issues as you plan:

- **The shorter the better.** Who likes to be held captive by a long form with seemingly endless questions? Forms that ask too many questions—or that won't let you proceed to the next application until you finish this one—can be a real turnoff for readers. Try to keep your form short, and limit the questions to those that ask the items you most need to know, in the order you need to know them.
- **Make it simple.** If you make your form easy for readers to understand and follow, with questions that are clear and to the point, you'll get a better response to your questions than if your form is complex and congested. Be concise and careful in your wording, and provide prompts and Help text where necessary, to explain to readers what you want them to do.
- **Order counts.** Readers will expect some kind of logical structure to your form. You might move from general questions to more specific questions, or you might follow a process. For example, if you're creating a customer response form that asks visitors to your Web site to evaluate their online shopping experience with your company, you might ask questions about their computer equipment and access, their ability to access your site, their experience using your site, how effective they feel your ordering system is, what they felt about your sales security, and how they would like to be notified when their order is shipped.
- **Invite suggestions.** Before you deploy your form for wide use, do a few tests to see how effective it is. Ask coworkers or a few customers to use the form and evaluate it. You can then make any necessary changes and incorporate suggestions to improve the form.

Starting a Form with an Existing Document

If you have a document you've used for other things—perhaps a questionnaire or interview sheet you've previously printed and handed out—you can easily turn the document into an interactive form. To use an existing document, follow these basic steps:

1. Open the document you'd like to use as a form.
2. Delete any unnecessary information, and add text if needed.
3. Apply the styles and formats you want to use, complete with borders and shading as needed.
4. In the spots where you want users to add information, add spaces or placeholder characters (such as * or &).
5. Choose File, Save As, and save the form as a template.

> **note** If you want to edit the form later, be sure to open the template and not the document. To make sure you're opening a template, choose File, Open, and in the Files Of Type field, select Document Templates.

Creating Your Own Form

You can create a form by starting with a new Word document and building your own. You might want to use a table to help provide the basic structure of the form; it'll make it easier for users to move from field to field by pressing Tab, and it helps provide an organized look for the document. (See Figure 36-8.)

When you're creating your own form, you can add, modify, and enhance text and graphics just as you would a regular text document. For example, you might want to do the following things:

- Include your company logo in the form heading
- Use styles to format headings and body text
- Select a Table AutoFormat to apply a predesigned look to your form
- Use the Draw Table button in the Tables And Borders toolbar to customize the way you draw lines for rows and columns
- Add shading to highlight certain sections of your form

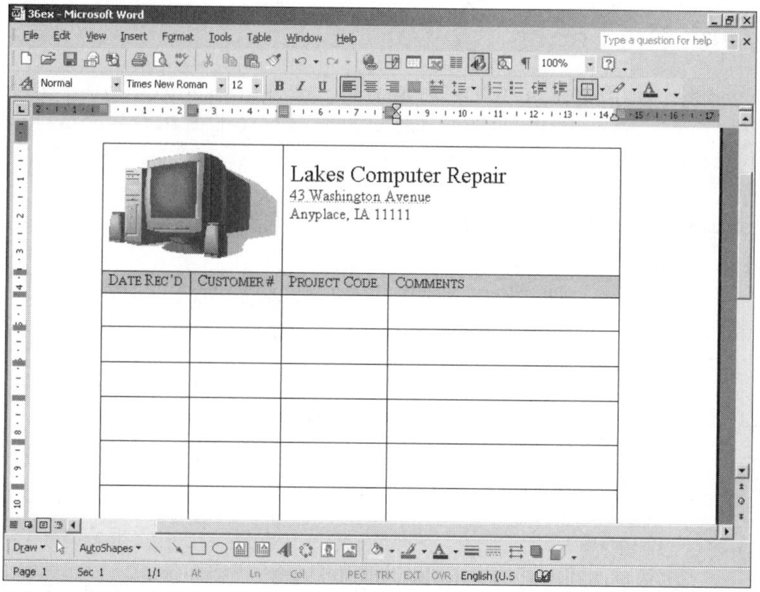

Figure 36-8. You can create a simple form quickly by using a Word table.

tip **Save your form as a template**

After you design your form the way you want it, remember to save it as a template so you can use it to build the interactive features that will capture the data for you. To save the file as a template, click File, Save As, and navigate to the folder in which you want to store the file. Click the Save As Type down arrow, and choose Document Template. Enter a name for the template in the File name box, and click Save.

Choosing a Form Template on the Web

Word also makes form templates available on the Web so that you can download existing forms and modify them to suit your needs. To find the form templates on line, follow these steps:

1. Establish your Internet connection.
2. Choose File, New. The New Document task pane appears.
3. Click the Templates On Microsoft.com link. Your Web browser opens and displays the Microsoft Office Template Gallery, where you can find and download the templates you want to use.
4. In the Browse By Category section, click the Business Forms hyperlink and browse the various forms available.
5. Close your Web browser after you've finished downloading new forms.

Working with the Forms Toolbar

You'll use the Forms toolbar to create and add form fields to your form. To display the toolbar, choose View, Toolbars, Forms. Table 36-3 describes the different functions of the Forms buttons.

Table 36-3. The Forms Toolbar

Button	Name	Description
	Edit Box	Adds a text field at the insertion point so users can enter information
	Check Box	Inserts a check box field in the document at the insertion point
	Combo Box	Enables users to display a drop-down list of choices
	Properties	Displays form field settings after a field has been added to the form
	Draw Table	Opens the Tables And Borders toolbar so that you can add tables and table elements to the form
	Insert Table	Lets you create a table with a selected number of rows and columns
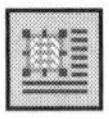	Frame	Adds a floating frame on the form
	Show Field Shading	Works as a toggle to display and hide shading for text, check boxes, and drop-down fields
	Reset Form Fields	Resets form fields to their default settings
	Protect Form	Works as a toggle to protect and unprotect parts of the form or the entire form

note Here's a quirk you might discover as you begin to create forms with Word. On the Forms toolbar, the name of the buttons may not seem to match the actual name of the tool you're using. For example, a combo box, which is the type of field that allows you to create a field that offers a combination of choices, is created with the Drop Down Form Field button.

Form Terminology

If you're creating a form for the first time, you might see some terms that are new to you. Here's a quick introduction to form terms and phrases:

- **Control** is an item you use on the form, such as a text box, check box, scroll bar, or command button. The item is called a control because it enables you to control the form by making selections or adding information.
- **Form fields** are the data receptacles into which you enter data. One form field, for example, might be Customer Name, which enables you to enter each customer's name on the form.
- **Property** is a characteristic of an object, such as the color, size, location, or display of an item.

Protecting Forms

The Protect Form button is an important form on the Forms toolbar. Before you can see the form in the way the user will see it, you must protect the form.

When you protect a form, you lock the fields in place so that no further changes can be made to field formats or specifications. You'll be able to use the drop-down lists as intended, select check boxes, and enter text in text fields. To protect the form, you click the Protect Form button; to unprotect the form, you click the Protect Form button again. When a form is protected, the fields appear as the user will see them. When the form is unprotected, you see the only field name or the sample data you've entered for the field.

Password Protecting the Form

You might want to assign a password to a form so that you can control when—and if—a form is unprotected. To protect a form in this way, follow these steps:

1. If necessary, unprotect the form by clicking the Protect Form button on the Forms toolbar.
2. Click Tools, Protect Document. The Protect Document dialog box appears, as shown in Figure 36-9, on the next page.
3. In the Password box, type a password of up to 15 characters.
4. Click OK. Word displays a Confirm Password dialog box so that you can re-enter the password you've chosen to verify that you've entered it correctly.
5. Type the password, and click OK. Word password protects the form.

Figure 36-9. You can use the Protect Document dialog box to assign a password to the form.

Unprotecting a Password Protected Form

If you want to modify a password protected form at a later time, you can use your password to enable editing. Open the form template and display the Forms toolbar. The Unprotect Document dialog box appears asking for your password. Type the password and click OK, and the form will be unprotected.

When you've finished making changes, click Protect Form a second time to return the protection. Save and close the file.

Entering Form Fields

Once you have all the basic text and design for your form in place, you can add the features that make it truly interactive: the form fields. Word enables you to enter three different types of fields to your forms:

- **Text fields** enable the user to type text, numbers, symbols, or perform calculations in text-entry boxes. Use this type of field when you're asking an open-ended question, when users are asked to provide comments or suggestions, or when you want to provide the flexibility for user-controlled input.
- **Check box** fields enable the user to click a box to add a check mark. Use this type of field when there can be only one selected response.
- **Drop-down fields** provide a list of options for the user to review. This type of field is also used when there can be only one selected response but the range of options needs to be shown.

The sections that follow go step by step through the process of adding each of these field types and choosing the options related to the type you selected.

note The options for adding macros to the various form fields and customizing help to assist users in filling out forms are available in each of the Form Field Options dialog boxes for the various field types. For more information on working with macros and customized help in Word forms, see "Adding Help to Forms," on page 891, and "Incorporating Form Macros," on page 892, later in this chapter.

Viewing Fields

In the next section, you'll learn how to add fields to your form. Before you'll be able to see a field the way your users will see it, however, you need to protect the field. Simply click the field and click the Protect Form button on the Forms toolbar. You'll then be able to see a field the way it'll appear to users. (See Figure 36-10.)

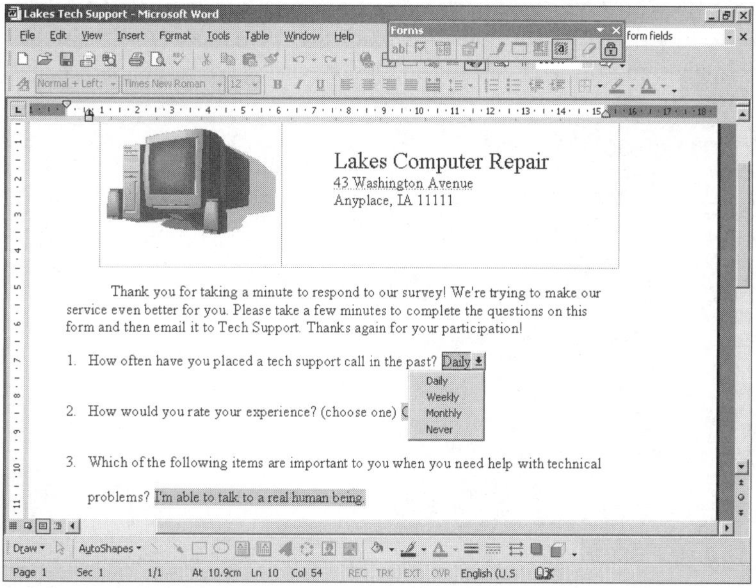

Figure 36-10. You can view a field you create by clicking the field and clicking the Protect Form button.

Inserting a Text Field

It's possible that the text field will be the type of field you use most often. A text field is a basic input tool—it records information you need that only the user can enter. For example, on a service request form, text fields would include the customer name, address, phone, and e-mail information. Another text field would record any comments on the service to be performed.

To add a text field to your form, follow these steps:

1. Place the insertion point where you want to add the text field.
2. Click the Text Form Field button on the Forms toolbar. Word inserts the field {FORMTEXT} in your document at the insertion point.

> **note** The field codes that Word inserts automatically can't be modified; to change the settings for the inserted field type, use the Form Field Options button on the Forms toolbar.

Selecting Text Field Options

Once the {FORMTEXT} field is placed in your form, you can select the Form Field Options you want to apply to the field. Click the Form Field Options button on the Forms toolbar, and the Text Form Field Options dialog box appears. (See Figure 36-11.)

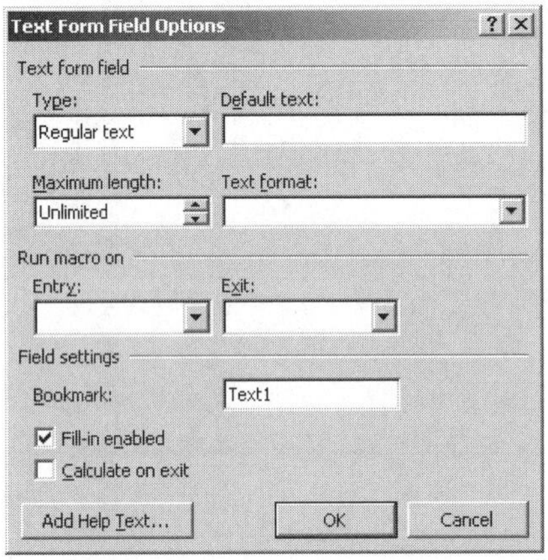

Figure 36-11. You make choices for the text field in the Text Form Field Options dialog box.

Choosing the Text Form Field Type

In the Text Form Field Options dialog box, you choose the type of text field you want to create, and Word changes the code accordingly. In the Type drop-down list, select one of the following field types:

- **Regular Text** form fields include text, numbers, symbols, and spaces.
- **Number** form fields accept numbers.

- **Date** form fields require dates.
- **Current Date** form fields display the current date and cannot be modified by users.
- **Current Time** form fields display the current time and cannot be modified by users.
- **Calculation** form fields calculate numbers and cannot be modified by users.

tip **Add default entries for users**

You can include a default entry in a text form fields so that your user doesn't have to enter it. Simply add the text you want in the field after creating the text form field. In the Text Form Field Options dialog box, type the text in the Default Text box and select the Fill-In Enabled check box The text you entered in the Default Text box will be displayed in the form until the user clicks in the field and types another entry.

Specifying Field Length

You can control the length of the text form field entry you will allow. If you've asked an open-ended question, perhaps requesting user comments about a new site feature you've added, you can leave a virtually unlimited space for user response. If, on the other hand, you want to limit the response to a few words, you can set the limit of the field length in the Text Form Field Options dialog box. Here are the steps:

1. Click the text form field code to select it.
2. Click the Form Field Options button on the Forms toolbar. The Text Form Field Options dialog box appears.

note In the Maximum Length box, click the up arrow to display the number of characters you want to allow. Or, as an alternative, you can click in the field and type the number. A character can be a text character, a number, or a symbol.

3. Click OK to close the dialog box and return to the form.

note If you want to link the text field to a bookmark you've previously created in your document, you can enter the name of the bookmark in the Bookmark box in the Text Form Field Options dialog box. Simply click in the box and type the bookmark name.

Controlling Text Display

If it matters to you, or to your data management personnel, how data is entered in the forms you create, you can control the capitalization of the text users enter in form fields. You can choose to display entries in all uppercase, lowercase, or in a variety of other displays. To choose the way text is shown, follow these steps:

1. Click the text form field code to select it.
2. Click the Form Field Options button on the Forms toolbar. The Text Form Field Options dialog box appears.
3. Click the Text Format down arrow. Choose from one of the following options:
   - **Uppercase** formats entries in uppercase letters.
   - **Lowercase** shows entries in lowercase letters.
   - **First capital** displays the entry with an initial first letter.
   - **Title case** treats the entry as though it is a title entry.
4. Click OK to close the dialog box and return to the form. Word adds the necessary field code so the information entered is displayed as you selected.

> **tip** **Calculate changes automatically**
>
> If you want Word to calculate the fields in your form each time you exit the form, select the Calculate On Exit check box in the Text Form Field Options dialog box and click OK. Each time you exit the form, Word updates the numeric fields and recalculates any equations in the form.

Adding a Check Box Field

If you want to include choices on your form in which users can select more than one option, you can create a list consisting of multiple check boxes. For example, suppose that your IT department is doing a survey to find out how happy the employees are with the technical support services. You might include a question such as the following:

1. Which of these services are important to you?

   A. Same-day response times

   B. Talking to a tech support person as opposed to an automated system

   C. Being able to get a loaner machine while yours is in the shop

You can turn the list items into check boxes so that users can select all that are important to them. To create a check box field, follow these steps:

1. Place the insertion point where you want to add the check box field.
2. Click the Check Box Form Field button on the Forms toolbar. Word inserts a check box symbol at the insertion point and places the code {FORMCHECKBOX} on the form.
3. Add the check box label by pressing the Spacebar and typing the label of your choice.
4. Repeat as needed to place additional check boxes.

> **tip** **Display the form field codes**
>
> If you want to see which code Word is inserting in your document when you add fields using the Forms toolbar, simply press Alt+F9. The display changes to show the field codes. When you're ready to change the display back, press Alt+F9 again.

Resizing the Check Box

By default, the check box field is created to match the size of surrounding text. If you want the box to stand out, you might want to modify the size of the check box character. To do this, you need to change the Check Box Size option in the Check Box Form Field Options dialog box. Here are the steps:

1. Double-click the check box, or select it and click the Form Field Options button on the Forms toolbar. The Check Box Form Field Options dialog box appears, as Figure 36-12 shows.

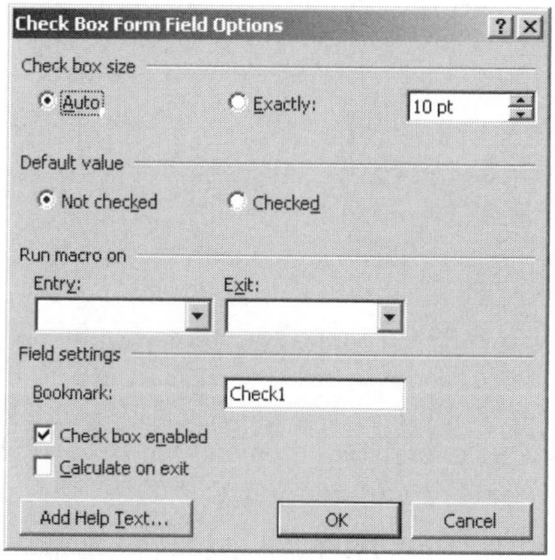

Figure 36-12. The Check Box Form Field Options dialog box enables you to make choices about the way your check box field will look and act.

2 In the Check Box Size section of the dialog box, click Exactly, and increase or decrease the size value in the text box to match the size you want.

3 Click OK to save your changes and return to the form.

> **note** If you want to lock a check box field so that users can't alter it, select the Check Box Enabled check box in the Check Box Form Field Options dialog box.

Creating a Drop-Down Field

You'll use a drop-down field when you want to provide a list of choices for the user. In the example, you might want to give users the choice of rating the kind of experience they most recently had with tech support. To create a drop-down field, follow these steps:

1 Place the insertion point where you want to add the field.

2 Select the Drop-Down Form Field button. Word adds a drop-down field to your form at the insertion point.

3 Double-click the form field or select it and click Form Field Options on the Forms toolbar to display the Drop-Down Form Field Options dialog box. (See Figure 36-13.)

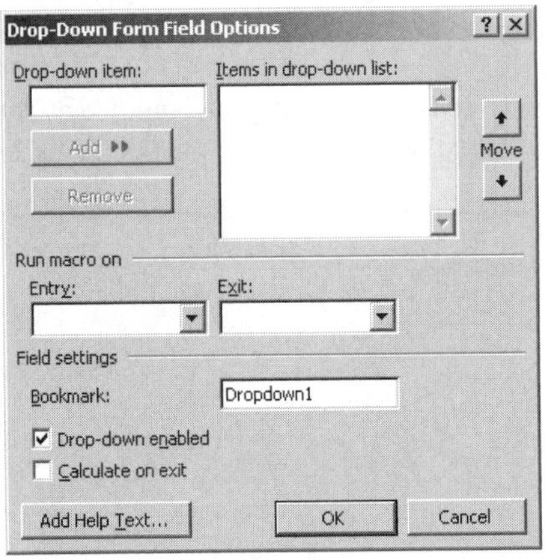

Figure 36-13. The Drop-Down Form Field Options dialog box is where you'll enter the items for the drop-down list.

4 Add entries to the drop-down list by typing items in the Drop-Down Item box and clicking Add. The item is added to the list.

5 Repeat adding items as needed. Click OK to close the dialog box.

Adding Help to Forms

If you think the users of your form need help knowing how to enter the information you seek, you can create customized help messages to help them along the way. To add help to your form, follow these steps:

1. Open the form template you want to use.
2. If necessary, click Protect Form on the Forms toolbar to unlock protection.
3. Double-click the form field you want to use. The Form Field Options dialog box for that field type appears (the text form, check box, and drop-down list fields all have different Form Field Options dialog boxes).
4. In the displayed dialog box, click the Add Help Text button. The Form Field Text Help dialog box appears, as Figure 36-14 shows.

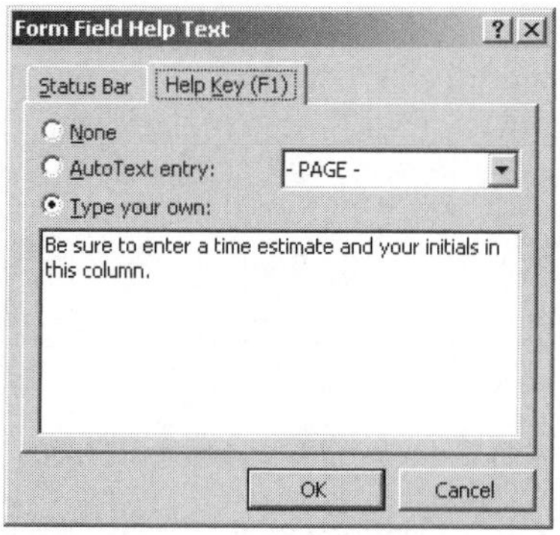

Figure 36-14. You can easily add your own help information to the form to help users know how to enter information.

5. Choose your option:
   - To display Help text in the status bar, click the Status Bar tab. Click in the text box, and type the text you want to appear in the status bar at the bottom of the Word window. Click OK to return to the form.
   - To show Help in a message box when the user presses F1, click the Help Key (F1) tab. Type the text you want to display in a help window when the user presses F1. Click OK to return to the form.
6. Click Protect Form on the Forms toolbar to enable form protection.

When you click in the form field, help will appear in the status bar if you selected status bar help. If you created help to be displayed in a Help window, click in the field and press F1 to display the help you entered in its own window. (See Figure 36-15, on the next page.)

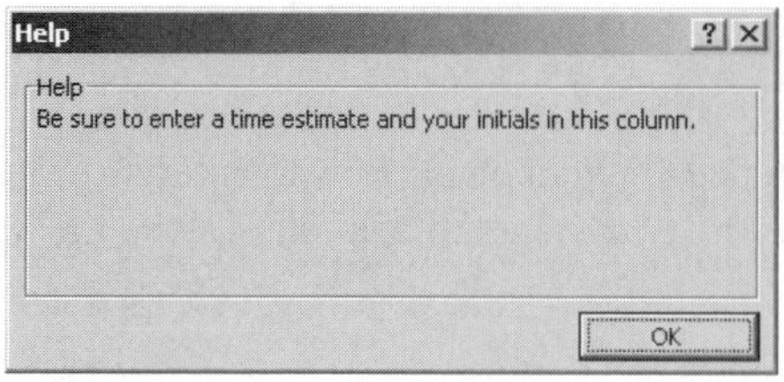

Figure 36-15. To display help you've created in a Help window, click in the protected field and press F1.

> **note** The message you enter for a Help window can contain up to 255 characters. If you create a message for the status bar, keep it to less than 138 characters.

Incorporating Form Macros

In some cases, you might want an action the user selects to execute a macro you've added to the form. You can add a macro to your form template just as you would add one to any other document. Here are the steps:

1. Open the template to which you want to add the macro.
2. Click the field you want to use, and click Protect Form on the Forms toolbar to unprotect the field.
3. Double-click the field to display its Form Field Options dialog box.
4. Select the macro you want to use by making a choice in the Run Macro On section of the dialog box:
   - If you want the macro to execute when the user enters, or selects, the field, click the Entry down arrow and choose the macro you want to use from the drop down list. (See Figure 36-16.) The macros displayed in the drop-down list as those that are available in the document you are currently using.
   - If you want the macro to execute after the user exits, or deselects, the field, click the Exit down arrow and choose the macro from the list.
5. Click OK to close the dialog box and save the settings.
6. Click Protect Form to protect the form once again. The macro is now enabled and will execute according to your selections when the user accesses the field.

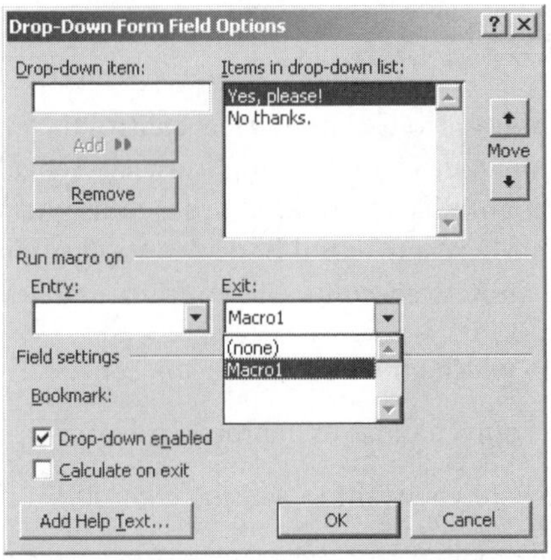

Figure 36-16. Choose whether you want Word to execute a macro when the user accesses or exits the field.

Troubleshooting

I Don't Have Any Macros in the Entry or Exit Drop-Down Lists

If you can't locate the macros you want to add, the trouble could be that you haven't added those macros to the current form. To add the macro to the current document, follow these steps:

1. Choose Tools, Templates And Add-Ins. The Templates And Add-Ins dialog box appears.
2. Click the Organizer button.
3. Click the Styles tab.
4. Click Close File on the left side of the dialog box; then click Open File and select the name of the file containing the macro you want to use.
5. Select the macro you want to use in the list on the left, and click Copy. The item is placed in the list on the right side of the dialog box.
6. Click Close to save the change and return to the document.

Adding ActiveX Controls

For special situations, you might want to use an ActiveX control to carry out actions when your user selects an item on your form. You might use an ActiveX control, for example, to run a macro that automates a task. In order to use ActiveX controls, you should be comfortable with Microsoft Visual Basic for Applications (VBA) or Microsoft Script Editor. To add an ActiveX control to your form, follow these steps:

1. Open the form template to which you want to add the control.
2. Click Protect Form on the Forms toolbar to unprotect the form.
3. Place the insertion point where you want to add the control.
4. Display the Control Toolbox toolbar by clicking View, Toolbars, Control Toolbox.
5. Click the ActiveX control button on the Control Toolbox toolbar that you want in the document. Word creates the control and displays the Exit Design Mode toolbar. (See Figure 36-17.)

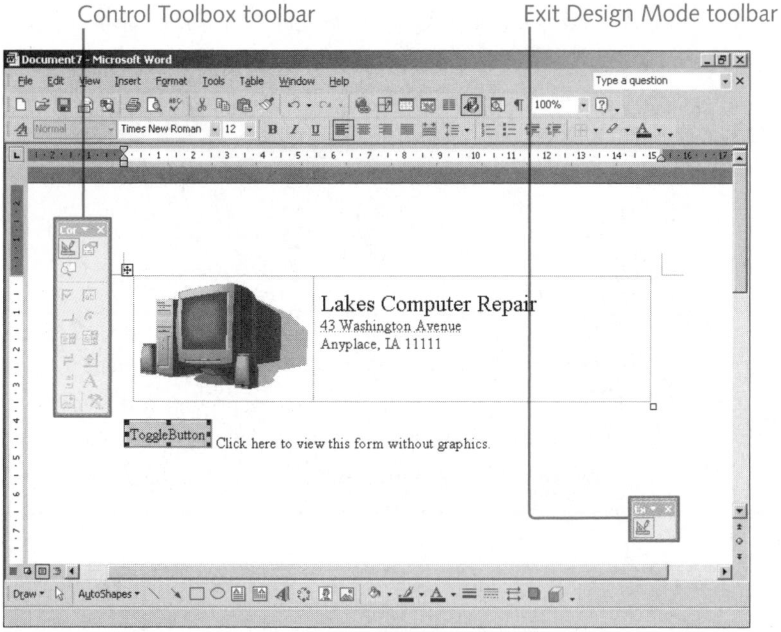

Figure 36-17. When you add an ActiveX control to your form, Word changes to Design Mode.

> **note** Use the controls you create with the Control Toolbox for forms you want to make available in Word, not for Web-based forms. Many browsers don't recognize the controls you create with the Control Toolbox toolbar.

Changing Control Properties

You can change the way the control appears by modifying the control's properties. Right-click the control to display the shortcut menu; then choose Properties. The Properties dialog box appears, as Figure 36-18 shows.

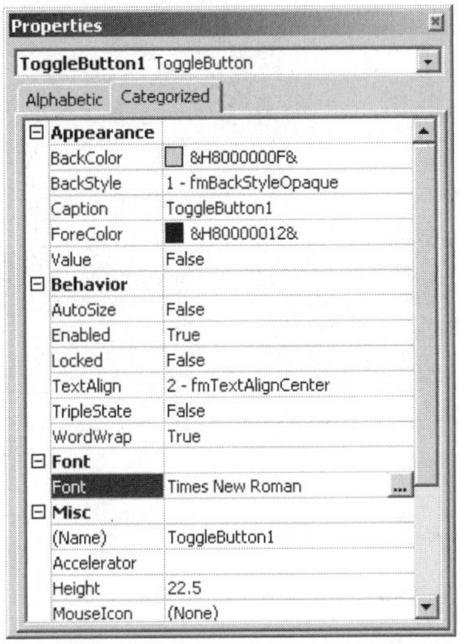

Figure 36-18. Change the way a control looks by making changes in the Properties dialog box.

Click the Categorized tab to see the various properties organized by category. If you want to make a change—for example, you might change the Font—double-click the setting in the right column. When you double-click the font selection, the Font dialog box appears so that you can make the necessary changes and click OK.

Programming a Control

Although an in-depth discussion of using VBA to program a control is beyond the scope of this chapter, you can easily access the code window for scripting from your form. To access the code window, follow these steps:

1. Click the control to select it. Unprotect the field if necessary by clicking Protect Form on the Forms toolbar.

2 Click the View Code button on the Control Toolbox toolbar. Word displays the Visual Basic Editor, as Figure 36-19 shows.

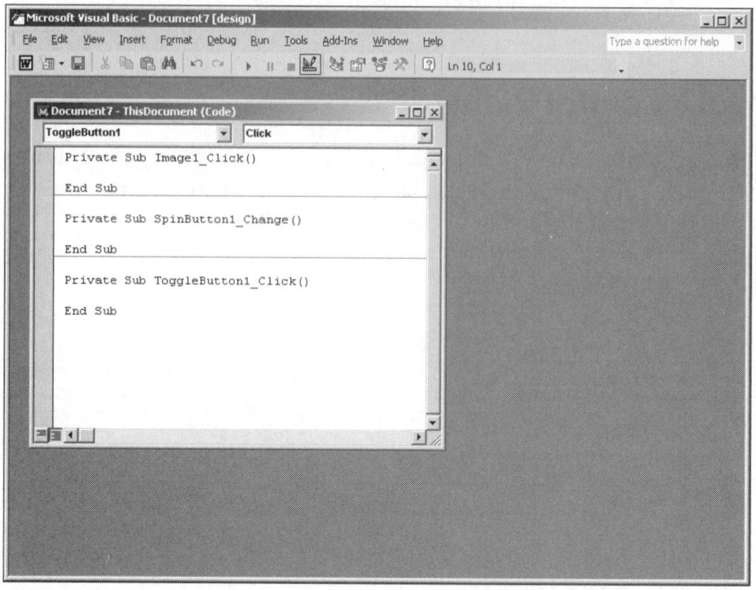

Figure 36-19. When you click View Code, the Visual Basic window opens so that you can enter the script for the control.

3 Enter the script for your Visual Basic program.

4 Click the Close box to exit the editor and return to your form.

Using a Form

Designing the form is the first part of the story; using the form is the second part. To use the form, follow these steps:

1 Click File, New. The New Document task pane opens.

2 Click General Templates. The Templates dialog box opens.

3 Click the General tab, and select the form template you created; click Open. The form is displayed in the Word window.

4 Enter your responses on the form as requested.

5 When you're finished, press Ctrl+S to save the form. The Save As dialog box appears.

6 Select the folder in which you want to save the form; click Save. This action saves the document as it is, complete with text, data, and any graphics you've included in the form.

Saving Form Data

You save a form as you would save any document, by pressing Ctrl+S and choosing the location and file name you want for the file. If you want to save only the data in the form instead of the entire form, you can do this using a selection in the Options dialog box. Here are the steps:

1. Create a new form using the form template you created.
2. Choose Tools, Options.
3. Click the Save tab, and select the Save Data Only For Forms check box.
4. Click OK to save the setting and return to the form.

The first time you elect to save form data as a text file, Word displays the File Conversion dialog box to enable you to select how you want to save the data. You can choose the way you want Word to handle individual data items; the Preview box shows you how the data will appear in the text file. (See Figure 36-20.) Make any necessary changes, and click OK to save the data.

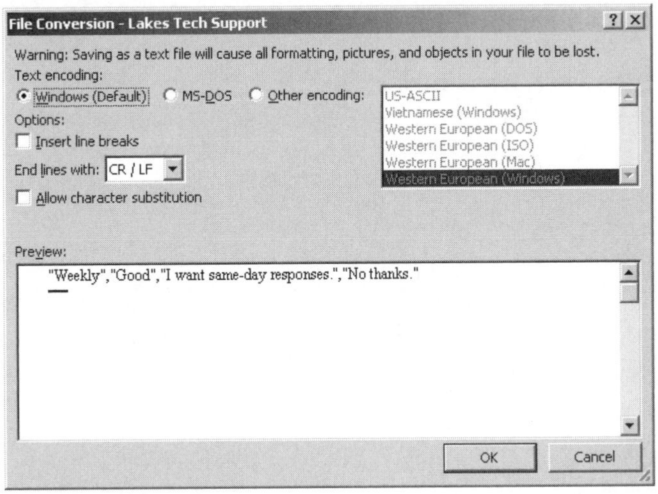

Figure 36-20. When you first save form data as a text file, Word displays your conversion options.

note Each time users open a copy of your form, they'll have to enable the Save Data Only for Forms option if you want only the data to be saved. You might want to add Help text or a form prompt to instruct users to select the option in the Options dialog box. You can also create a macro to handle the setting automatically for your users. For more about creating Word macros, see Chapter 40, "Creating and Working with VBA Macros."

Chapter 37

Implementing Multilanguage Features

If you work in a virtual office that spans the globe, or if you're often trading documents with clients or coworkers on other continents, you'll find that the multilanguage features in Microsoft Word 2002 are intuitive and easy to use. You might use multilanguage features, for example, when you want to do any of the following:

- Find out automatically in which language a document was written, and use the necessary styles, punctuation, and editing techniques to edit that document accurately
- Create documents that include text in other languages, using special characters and symbols
- Edit languages right to left
- Switch among documents in different languages to compare content and format
- Proofread documents created in other languages without having to use a third-party proofing program

This chapter introduces you to these multilanguage features and explains the enhancements now available with Word 2002. You'll find out how to enable multilanguage capability and work with the options related to multilanguage editing.

Understanding Multilanguage Support

The multilanguage support in Word comes to you courtesy of the Microsoft Office XP Multilingual User Interface Pack (MUI), which is available for Windows 98, NT 4.0, or Windows 2000. You'll find the Multilingual User Interface Pack on its own CD in your Microsoft Office package; the Pack has its own installation utility that you can use to setup the languages for use with Word. After you install the MUI Pack, you'll be able to use the following features:

- **Automatic language detection.** Word automatically detects up to 80 different languages and uses the correct dictionaries, punctuation rules, and sorting conventions for the language.
- **Font support.** All Office programs link to a second font for characters if the primary font is missing language-specific characters you need.

newfeature!

Multilanguage Enhancements in Word 2002

Working with multiple languages is easier than ever in Word 2002. The multilanguage support in Office XP has been streamlined and included in a way that makes installing and working with multiple languages a nearly seamless experience for the end user. Here are the major multilanguage changes in Word 2002:

- **Independent Setup for Languages.** You can set up each language independently by using the Office XP Multilingual User Interface Pack Setup. When you add a language by running setup and using the Windows Add/Remove Programs dialog box, you'll be able to see and load each language as a separate item.
- **Automated Installation.** The setup wizard walks you through the process of installing multilanguage support. If you're installing support on a network, you should contact your network administrator before proceeding, however.
- **Easy Office Integration.** Office XP automatically sets up the user interface, Help systems, and default language based on the selections you make during installation. Editing languages are enabled on each startup based on operating system support and keyboard/Input Method Editor (IME) support.
- **Changeable Language Options.** End users can now change application settings and the default language behavior of Office applications (such as default paper size, default labels, and default spellers).

In past versions of Word, you had to rely on Windows installation to provide multi-language features. Now Office XP not only includes the Multilingual User Interface, but it employs a setup wizard to help you install the languages you want to use.

- **Date, time, and number formats.** Word formats the date, time, and number formats in the manner applicable to the language selected.
- **Right-to-left editing.** If you're working in a language that requires right-to-left work, you can edit Word documents in that way.

note Word makes use of Unicode text for multilanguage documents. Unicode is a standard way of storing text characters that provides for more than one byte for each character, enabling you to use a single character set to represent all languages.

Installing the MultiLanguage Pack

To install the MultiLanguage features for Office XP, insert the Language Pack CD from your Office XP CD set. The setup utility launches automatically, and then the Microsoft software agreement is displayed. After you read the agreement, click the agreement permission and click Next. Then follow these steps:

1. The setup wizard asks you to choose the language you want to install. Select the check boxes next to the languages you wish to install, click your choice, and click Next.
2. Choose the way in which you want menus and Help to appear. The three choices offered are set by default to match the system settings and the language you've selected for your system. To make changes, click the option down arrows and click your choice. Click Next to continue.
3. Select the type of install you want: Click Install Now to use the same components selected during your Office installation; click Complete, Proofing Tools Only; or Custom (shown in Figure 37-1, on the next page) to install different configurations of the multilanguage features.
4. Click Install. Office installs the MultiLanguage Pack and prompts you to click OK when the installation is complete.

tip **Change multilanguage options with Add/Remove Programs**

After you install the MultiLanguage Pack, you can make further changes and enhancements to the feature. Choose Start, Settings, Control Panel, and then double-click Add/Remove Programs.

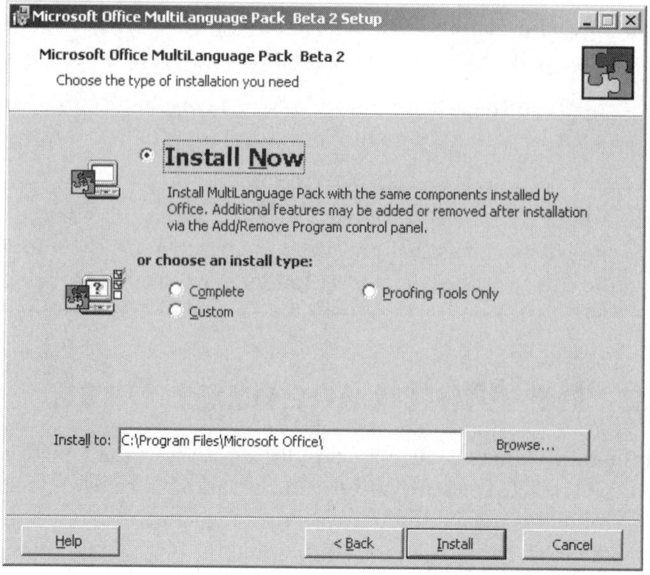

Figure 37-1. You use the MultiLanguage Setup utility to add multilanguage features.

Entering Windows Regional Options

You can set up Windows to automatically recognize dates, times, and numbers entered in different languages. After you've set up multilanguage support, you can configure Windows to address regional issues the way you want. To enter regional settings for multilanguage support, follow these steps:

1. Choose Start, Settings, Control Panel.
2. In the Control Panel window, double-click Regional Options. The Regional Options dialog box appears, as Figure 37-2 shows.
3. On the General tab, click the Your Locale down arrow and select the item that best describes your location.
4. In the Language Settings For The System section, scroll through the list to see which languages are configured on your system.
5. In the list, select the check box for a language for which you want to install regional settings for dates, times, and numbers.
6. Click Apply to change the settings for your system; then click OK to close the Regional Options dialog box.

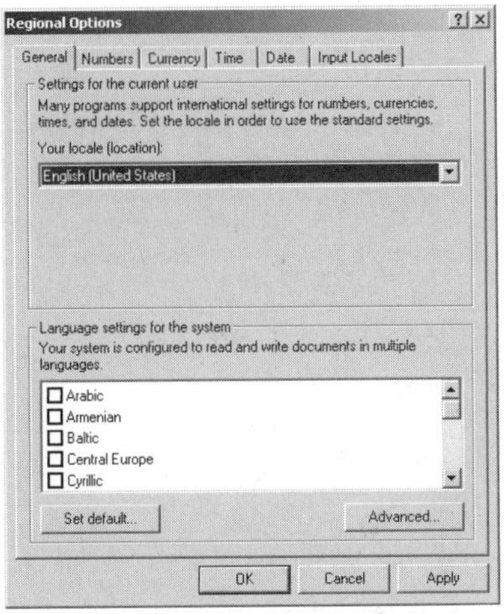

Figure 37-2. Enter regional options for dates, times, and number formats in the Regional Options dialog box.

Changing Menu and Dialog Box Display

If you want to have applications display menus and dialog boxes in another language, you can change the system locale setting. The system locale setting enables application programs to display all menu, dialog box, and Help information in the language you select. To change the language used in menus, follow these steps:

1. Choose Start, Settings, Control Panel.
2. In the Control Panel window, double-click Regional Options.
3. On the General tab, click Set Default. The Select System Locale dialog box appears.
4. Click the Select The Appropriate Locale down arrow, and choose the language you want to use.
5. Click OK to close the dialog box and return to the Regional Options dialog box. Click OK again to save your settings and return to Control Panel.

newfeature!

note You can choose code page conversion tables for the languages you want to use. To do this, open the Regional Options dialog box, and click Advanced On the General tab to display the Advanced Regional Options dialog box. To install additional code page conversion tables, select the check box next to a conversion table, and then click OK. Windows will prompt you to insert your Office CD so that the appropriate files can be installed.

Choosing Keyboard Layouts

Some languages rely on different character sets, and if you've selected one of those languages, you'll need to modify your keyboard so that you'll be able to enter the characters as needed. You can change your keyboard layout to reflect the language change. To do this, follow these steps:

1. Place your Office XP Language Pack CD in the drive.
2. Choose Start, Settings, Control Panel.
3. In the Control Panel window, double-click Text Services. The Text Services dialog box appears.
4. Click Add. The Add Input Language dialog box appears. (See Figure 37-3.)

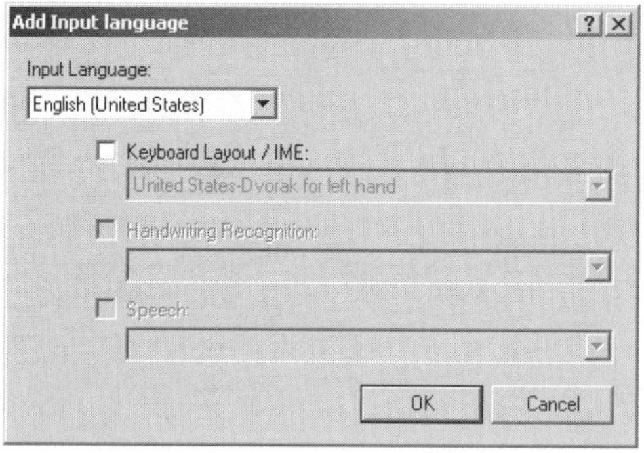

Figure 37-3. Add a keyboard layout using the Add Input Language dialog box.

5. Click the Input Language down arrow, and choose the language you want to use.
6. Select the Keyboard Layout/IME check box, click the Keyboard Layout/IME down arrow, and select the layout you want to use.
7. Click OK to close the Add Input Language dialog box and return to the Text Services dialog box.
8. Click Apply to change the settings currently used on your system, and click OK to close the Text Services dialog box.

Setting Keyboard Shortcuts for Switching Languages

If you want to create a keyboard shortcut so you can switch between keyboard layouts easily, open the Text Services dialog box by choosing Start, Settings, Control Panel, and then double-clicking Text Services. Follow these steps to select keyboard shortcuts for keyboard changes:

1. In the Text Services dialog box, click the Key Settings button. The Advanced Key Settings dialog box appears.
2. Select the action for which you want to assign a keyboard shortcut.
3. Click the Change Key Sequence button. The Change Key Sequence dialog box appears, as Figure 37-4 shows.

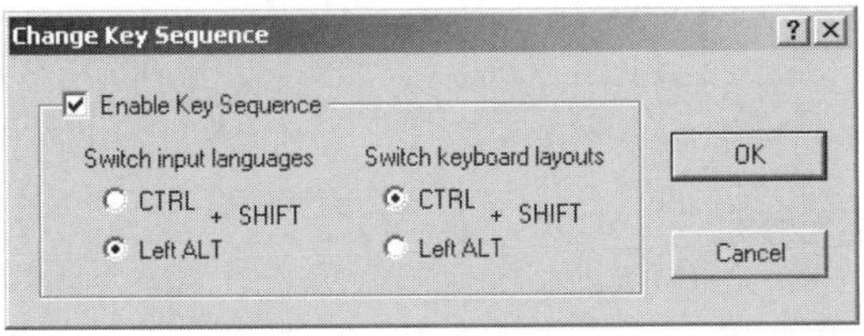

Figure 37-4. You can assign a keyboard shortcut to make a quick keyboard change.

4. Select the Enable Key Sequence check box. The defaults appear in the dialog box.
5. If you want to change the default selection (Left Alt+Shift) for the input languages, click the Ctrl option. The other option, Switch Keyboard Layouts, changes automatically.
6. Click OK to close the dialog box. The keyboard shortcut is recorded in the Advanced Key Settings dialog box.

> **note** If your keyboard doesn't work when you begin to enter text using the new language, make sure to use the keyboard shortcut sequence you selected to choose the new keyboard layout.

Enabling Languages

Before you can edit a document created in another language, you must make the language available in Word. When Word adds the new language, the program provides additional commands in the Format menu that allow you to work with punctuation and characters unique to that language. To enable a language, follow these steps:

1. Choose Start, Programs, Microsoft Office Tools, Microsoft Office XP Language Settings.
2. The Microsoft Office Language Settings dialog box appears, with the Enabled Languages tab selected. (See Figure 37-5.)

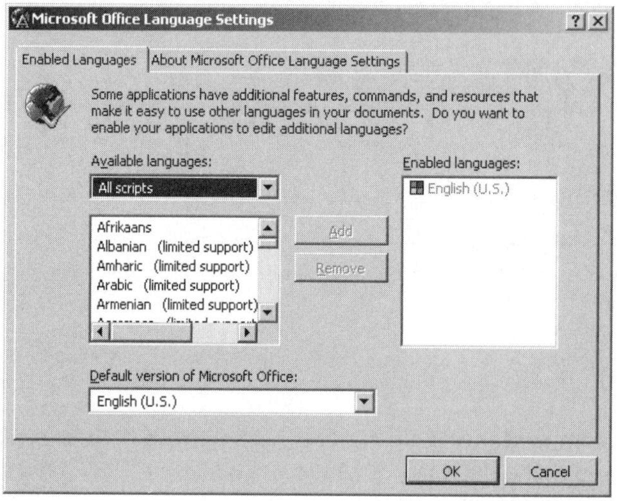

Figure 37-5. Choose the languages you want to work with using Microsoft Office Language Settings.

3. In the Available Languages list, click the language you want to use.
4. Click Add. Office adds the language to the Enabled Languages list. Repeat for any additional languages you want to add.
5. If you want to change the default language for Office, click the Default Version Of Microsoft Office down arrow and select the language you want to use.
6. Click OK. Office displays a message alerting you that you must restart your system before the new language becomes available.
7. Click Yes if you are ready to restart your system. Office updates your settings and makes the new language available for your use.

Working with Different Languages

While you're working in your document, you can switch between languages by using the Language bar. If the Language bar isn't currently displayed, click the EN symbol at the right side of the Windows taskbar to display it.

To change language selections, click the Language setting to display a shortcut menu with all installed languages listed. (See Figure 37-6.) Click the language you want to use and type your text.

Figure 37-6. You can select the language you want to use from the Language bar.

tip **Choose your keyboard layout**

Don't forget to use your keyboard shortcut to load the alternate keyboard with the character set unique to the language you've selected. The keyboard shortcut will be either Left Alt+Shift or Ctrl+Shift (depending on whether you changed the default setting). If you haven't yet set a keyboard shortcut for multilanguage keyboard use, see "Setting Keyboard Shortcuts for Switching Languages," on page 905.

When you use spelling and grammar checkers in your multilanguage document, Word uses the checker for the selected language. (See Figure 37-7.) Choose your options as needed, and continue the operation.

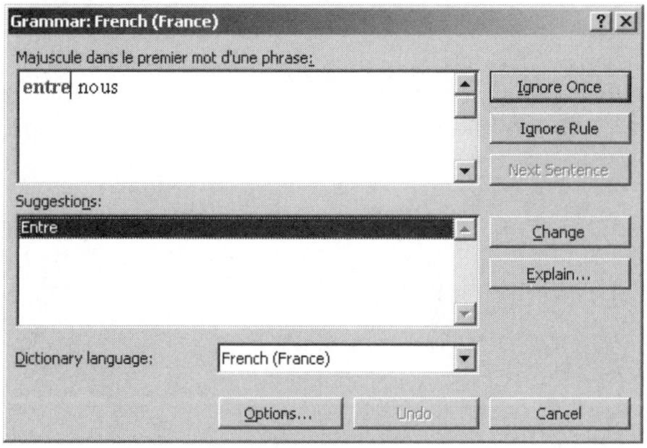

Figure 37-7. Word applies the language rules to the grammar and spelling checker.

Using Input Method Editors

Another utility that helps you work with different languages in your Word documents is an Input Method Editor (IME). An Input Method Editor allows you to enter Asian characters in your documents by using your traditional, 101-key keyboard. The IME functions as an add-on utility to the multilanguage features. When you type your information, Word converts the text to the appropriate characters in the language you've selected.

If the version of Office XP you use is in Simplified Chinese, Traditional Chinese, Japanese, or Korean, the necessary IMEs are already available with your software. If you use another version of Office and want to be able to use IMEs, you can go to the Microsoft Office Download Center (*office.microsoft.com/downloads*) and download the IMEs you need.

After you download and install the IMEs, they'll be available in your Language bar. To select the IME you want to use, simply click the keyboard selection on the Language bar to display the menu. Click your choice, and Office updates your keyboard settings.

Part 10

Optimizing Productivity

Chapter 38

Customizing Word and Maximizing Accessibility

As your experience with Microsoft Word grows, you'll look for ways to speed up routine tasks and streamline cumbersome procedures. You'll also discover things you like—and don't like—about the way Word operates and develop some preferences for what you'd like to see in menus, toolbars, and keyboard shortcuts.

This chapter shows you how to tailor Word to your liking and make the program more accessible for other users. Specific tasks include customizing toolbars, menus, keyboard shortcuts, and more. Additionally, you'll get ideas on how you can enhance accessibility to your document by making your documents easier to read and work with for a wide variety of users.

Saving Time by Starting Word Automatically

This first idea is a timesaving issue. If you launch Word every time you start Microsoft Windows, why not have Windows do it automatically? Follow these steps to add Word to your Startup window so that it launches automatically when you start your system:

1. Right-click the Windows taskbar, and choose Properties from the shortcut menu. The Taskbar And Start Menu Properties dialog box appears.
2. Click the Advanced tab, and then click Add. The Create Shortcut Wizard opens.

3 Navigate to the folder in which Winword.exe is stored, and click the file name. Word enters it in the text field.

4 Click Next. The Select Program Folder page appears.

5 Scroll down to Startup (shown in Figure 38-1), and double-click it.

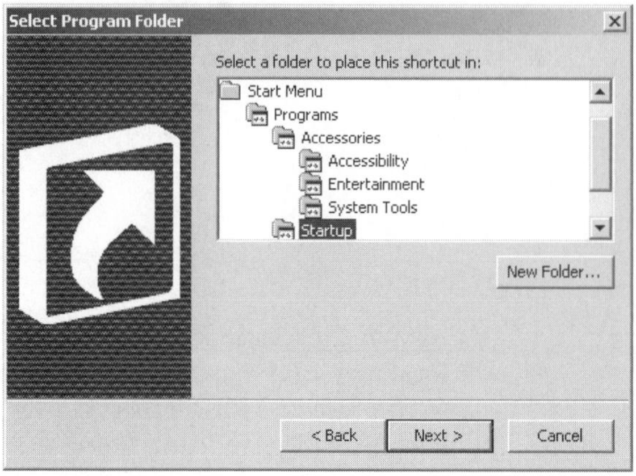

Figure 38-1. Starting Word automatically is a simple matter of adding it to your Startup folder.

6 Click Finish, and click OK. Word adds the shortcut icon to the Startup folder and the next time you launch Windows, Word will start automatically.

Specifying the Default Document's Location

If you often retrieve files from and save files to the same folder, you can automate that process to make the open and save procedures faster. You enter your settings for default file locations in the Options dialog box. To tell Word where you save your files by default, follow these steps:

1 Choose Tools, Options. The Options dialog box appears.

2 Click the File Locations tab, as shown in Figure 38-2. You see a listing of the various file location assignments that are currently active.

3 To change where Word stores the documents you create, click the Documents item and then click Modify.

4 Navigate to the folder you want Word to use as the default documents location. Click the folder, and then click OK. When you return to the dialog box, click OK again to return to the document. Word records the change and now, by default, both saves files to and retrieves files from the specified folder.

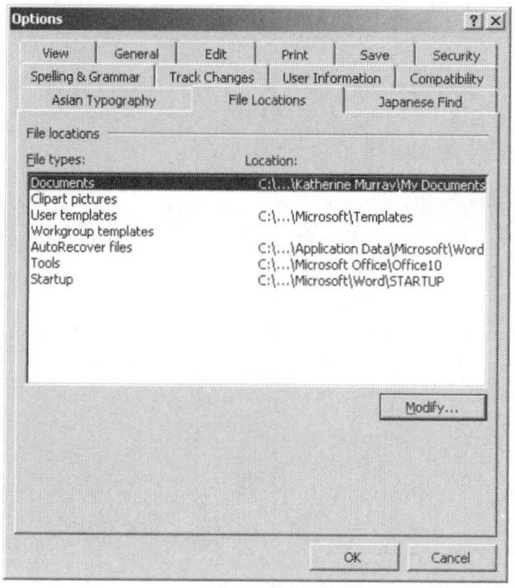

Figure 38-2. You can change the default folder in which Word stores and retrieves documents.

Customizing Word Toolbars

Word comes equipped with a great many toolbars—some old, some new. The toolbars customize themselves to suit you—the buttons you use most often are the ones that are displayed on the Standard and Formatting toolbars. You can also further customize the toolbars by electing to add or remove selected buttons or by creating new buttons and toolbars as you need them.

Showing ScreenTips and Shortcut Keys on Toolbars

By default, Word displays ScreenTips when you position the mouse pointer over buttons on your toolbars. You can disable ScreenTip display, if you choose, and you can decide to add shortcut keys to your ScreenTips. Here are the steps:

1. Choose Tools, Customize. The Customize dialog box appears.
2. Click the Options tab. (See Figure 38-3, on the next page.) Then select your options:
   - To disable ScreenTips, clear the Show ScreenTips On Toolbars check box.
   - To add shortcut keys to the ScreenTips, select both the Show ScreenTips On Toolbars and the Show Shortcut Keys On ScreenTips check boxes.
3. Click Close. If you've enabled both options, the ScreenTips now appear when you position the pointer over a button on a toolbar, and shortcut keys will be included in the ScreenTip, as follows:

   Font (Ctrl+Shift+F)

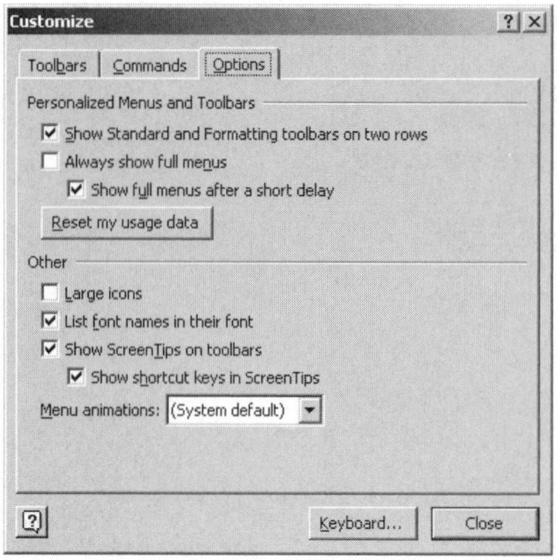

Figure 38-3. You can display or hide ScreenTips on the Options tab of the Customize dialog box.

Displaying Large Toolbar Buttons

If you want to increase the size of the buttons on your toolbars, you can magnify them using a Word customization setting. To increase the size of your toolbar buttons, follow these steps:

1. Choose Tools, Customize. The Customize dialog box appears.
2. Click the Options tab.
3. Select the Large Icons check box, but be forewarned: The icons on your workspace will be HUGE! If you want to reverse the effect, clear the Large Icons check box. Click OK to make the change.

Modifying Existing Toolbars

You can also change existing toolbars by adding or removing toolbar buttons, adding new buttons, moving buttons among menus, or reordering the buttons that are displayed on individual toolbars.

Adding a Button to an Existing Toolbar

Every toolbar you'll use in Word has its own Toolbar Options button. Position the mouse pointer over the small down arrow at the far right end of a toolbar, and the Toolbar Options ScreenTip will appear. Click the down arrow and a menu of toolbar choices appears.

To add a button to a toolbar, follow these steps:

1. Click the Toolbar Options button. A menu appears.
2. Choose Add Or Remove Buttons, and then choose toolbar name on the menu. (For example, for the Formatting toolbar you would choose Add Or Remove Buttons, Formatting.) A submenu appears, displaying all buttons available for the selected menu. (See Figure 38-4.) Buttons currently displayed on the toolbar are marked with a check mark; buttons not used show only the button image and name.

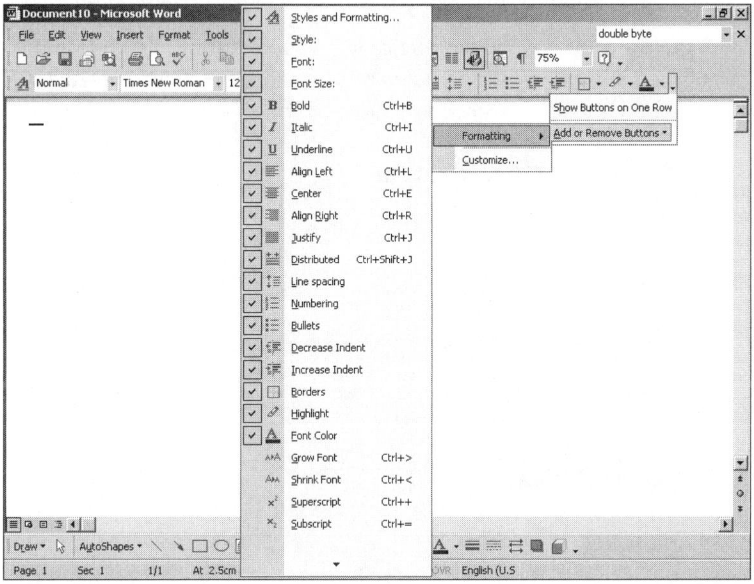

Figure 38-4. The Formatting submenu shows all the buttons available for the Formatting toolbar, with a check mark beside the ones currently shown on the toolbar.

3. Click the button or buttons you want to add. The button is added instantly to the toolbar you're working with.
4. Click outside the menu list to close it.

tip **Copy buttons between toolbars**

The process of creating a new toolbar requires that you copy buttons from one toolbar to another. The method? Just drag and drop. Whether you're creating a new toolbar or simply copying buttons from one toolbar to another, dragging works the same way: Select the button in the Commands list on the Commands tab of the Customize dialog box (choose Tools, Customize to open), and drag it to the new location on the toolbar you're modifying.

Creating Custom Toolbars

If you have special applications or a certain set of tools that you use most often, you can create your own custom toolbar to make those buttons available the way you want them. You can create a custom toolbar by using the Customize dialog box. Here are the steps:

1. Choose Tools, Customize. The Customize dialog box appears.
2. Click the Toolbars tab, and click the New button. The New Toolbar dialog box appears.
3. Type a name for the new toolbar in the Toolbar Name box.
4. Click the Make Toolbar Available To down arrow, and choose the name of the template in which you want to make the toolbar available. Click OK. A new toolbar is placed in your work area.

Adding Buttons to a New Toolbar

Next, you need to add tools to the toolbar you've just created. Follow these steps:

1. In the Customize dialog box, click the Commands tab. (See Figure 38-5.)

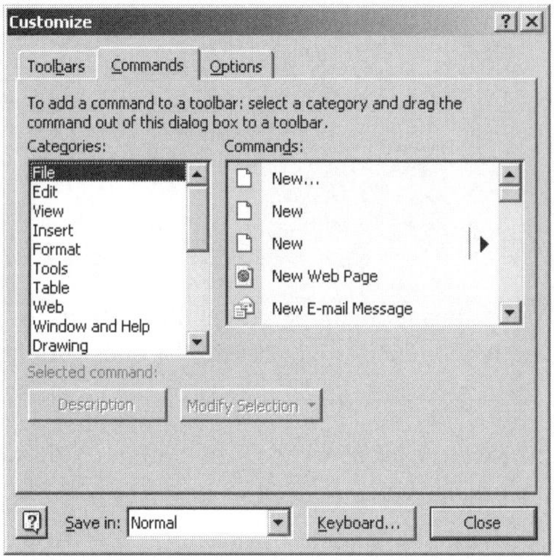

Figure 38-5. Create your own toolbar by copying and combining existing buttons.

2. In the Categories list, click the name of the menu that houses the command you want to add to your new toolbar.

3. In the Commands list, scroll to the command button you want to use. Drag the button to your new toolbar. A copy of the button is placed on the new toolbar.
4. Repeat steps 2 and 3, selecting first the menu and then the command, until you've added all desired buttons to your toolbar.
5. Click Close to close the Customize dialog box and begin working with your toolbar.

> **tip** **Reset toolbars**
>
> If you make changes to a toolbar and then decide to change what you've done, you can return the toolbar to the way it was before you made the modifications. To revert to your original toolbar, click Tools, Customize to display the Customize dialog box. Click the Toolbars tab. Click the name of the toolbar you want to reset, and then click the Reset button. The Reset Toolbar dialog box appears, asking you to indicate the name of the template storing the toolbar you want to restore the changes for. Click the down arrow and choose the template; then click OK to restore the original toolbar settings.

Changing the Look of Toolbar Buttons

When you're working with the buttons on your toolbars, you might want to change the look of a button you're adding or copying. To change a toolbar button, follow these steps:

1. Choose Tools, Customize to open the Customize dialog box.
2. Click the button on the toolbar you want to modify, and then click Modify Selection on the Commands tab of the Customize dialog box.
3. Choose Change Button Image. The following palette appears, giving you a number of images you can use in place of the current image on the selected button:

4. Click the image you want to use. The button image is updated on the toolbar. Click Close.

Chapter 38

Editing Button Images

If you really get into customizing your buttons, you might want to edit button images to create your own look. To edit a button image, follow these steps:

1. Display the Customize dialog box by clicking Tools, Customize.
2. Click the button on the toolbar you want to change.
3. Click Modify Selection on the Commands tab in the dialog box.
4. Click Edit Button Image from the menu. The Button Editor dialog box appears, as Figure 38-6 shows.

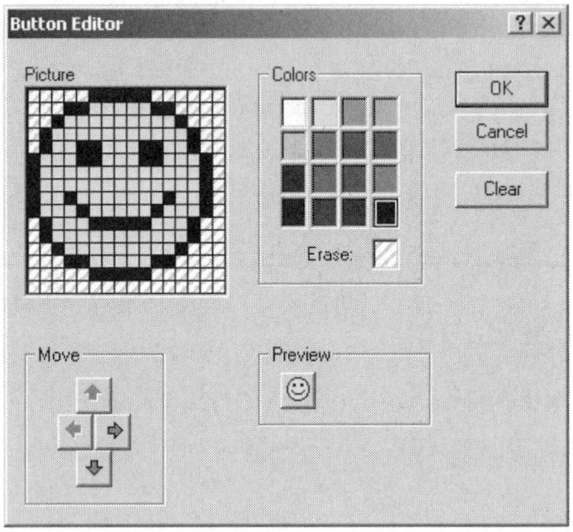

Figure 38-6. The Button Editor dialog box enables you to edit your button images.

To edit the button image, click the color you want to use and click the individual pixels to change the color of the image or turn the color on or off. Use the directional buttons in the lower right corner of the dialog box to move the image on the surface of the button. When you've made all the modifications you want, click OK to close the dialog box and record the changes.

Adding Divider Lines to Toolbars

Divider lines on toolbars help you visually group buttons with similar functions. If you've added a number of buttons to your custom toolbar, you might need to add divider lines to help you locate the tools you need more easily. To add a divider line, follow these steps:

1. Display the toolbar you want to change.
2. Choose Tools, Customize to display the Customize dialog box.
3. Click the Commands tab.

4 Click the button on the toolbar to the left of which you'd like to add the divider line.

5 Click Modify Selection, and then click Begin A Group on the menu that appears. (See Figure 38-7.) A divider line is added to the left of the button you selected.

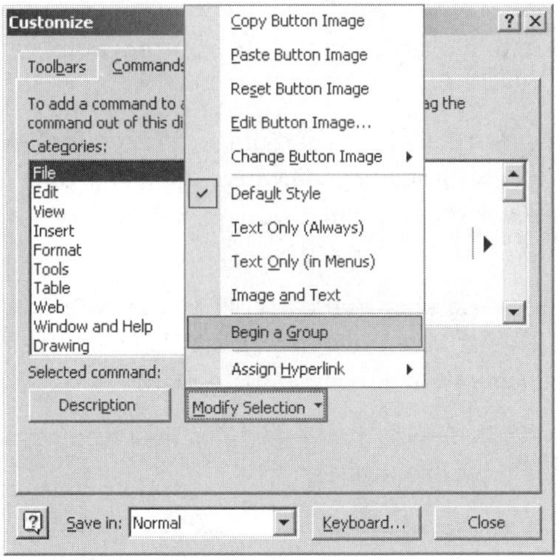

Figure 38-7. You can add a divider line to your custom toolbar to help organize your choices.

6 Click Close to close the dialog box.

tip **Rename a custom toolbar**

You can easily rename a toolbar you've created by choosing Tools, Customize and clicking the Toolbars tab. Next, select the toolbar you want to rename in the Toolbars list, and click the Rename button. When the Rename Toolbar dialog box appears, type the new name, and then click OK.

Customizing Menus for Added Functionality

In addition to all these toolbar changes, you can make modifications to the Word menus, as well. Not only can you change existing menus built into Word, but you can add new menus to the Word menu bar and add submenus to menus already in use.

Creating Your Own Menu

Creating custom menus in Word is a fun feature you can use to create a list of options you'll use most often and plug them into a menu you name and use yourself. To create a new menu for your Word menu bar, follow these steps:

1. Choose Tools, Customize. The Customize dialog box appears.
2. Click the Commands tab. In the Categories list, scroll down to New Menu and click it.
3. In the Commands list, click New Menu and drag it to the Word menu bar. The I-beam pointer appears, showing you where the menu name will be placed. When the menu is situated where you want it, release the mouse button.
4. With New Menu selected on the menu bar, click Modify Selection on the Commands tab of the Customize dialog box. Click Name on the menu that appears, and enter a name for the menu in the box.
5. Click Close to close the Customize dialog box. The new menu appears in the Word menu bar at the top of your screen.

> **tip** **Remove a menu**
>
> If you want to delete a menu, press and hold Alt while dragging the menu name down into the Word work area. The menu name is deleted from the menu bar.

Adding Menu Options to a New Menu

After you create a new menu, how do you add commands to it? The process is similar to adding a menu: You display the Commands tab of the Customize dialog box and drag the commands you want to the newly created menu. The I-beam pointer shows you where the command will be added; release the mouse button when you've positioned the command where you want it.

Rearranging Menu Commands

You can easily rearrange the commands in a menu by simply dragging them to the positions you want. Here's how:

1. Choose Tools Customize. The Customize dialog box appears.
2. On Word's menu bar, click the menu you wish to rearrange. The menu opens.
3. In the open menu, click the menu command you want to move and drag it to a new location.

4 Repeat as needed to move other commands in the menu.

5 Click Close to close the Customize dialog box and return to your document. The menu is updated so the new commands are displayed the next time you open the menu.

Removing Commands from Menus

If you want to remove a command from a menu, begin by displaying the Customize dialog box. On Word's menu bar, click the menu that contains the command. Drag the command off the menu and into the document window to remove it. Release the mouse button. The command is removed from the menu.

tip **Restore default menus**

If you decide that you've changed too much and don't like the way the new menu appears after all, you can return the menu to its configuration before the last change you made. To restore a menu to its previous setting, display the Customize dialog box, click the Commands tab, click the menu on the menu bar, click the Modify Selection button, and click Reset the menu that appears.

Creating Keyboard Shortcuts

If you like working quickly with the keyboard instead of opening menus and choosing commands using the mouse, you might be interested in working with and adding more keyboard shortcuts to your Word document. You can add shortcuts to existing buttons and include symbols and special characters while you're at it. This section gives you the steps for customizing your Word settings by adding keyboard shortcuts.

note All shortcut keys begin with ALT, CTRL, or a function key.

Assigning Keyboard Shortcuts to Existing Buttons and Commands

In the Customize dialog box, you'll find a Keyboard button that enables you to add keyboard shortcuts to commands you use often. When the Customize dialog box is displayed (choose Tools, Customize), click Keyboard to see the Customize Keyboard dialog box. (See Figure 38-8, on the next page.)

To add a keyboard shortcut, select the menu and the command you want to use. In the Press New Shortcut Key box, press the key combination you want to use. Click Assign to apply the change to the document, and then click Close to close the dialog box.

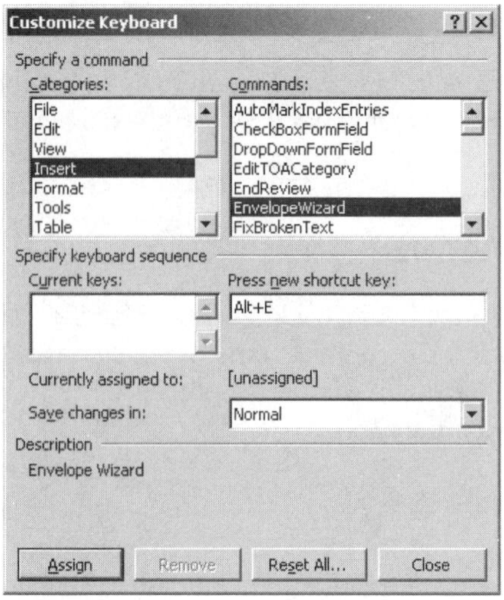

Figure 38-8. In the Customize Keyboard dialog box, you can choose a shortcut key for often-used commands.

note Any keyboard shortcuts you create will remain only with the current document. Be sure to save your changes to a template if you want to use the same settings with other files.

Using Symbols or Special Characters for Keyboard Shortcuts

You can assign a symbol or a special character to a keyboard shortcut if you want to create a quick key combination for a symbol or special character you use often. To use a symbol as a keyboard shortcut, follow these steps:

1. Choose Insert, Symbol. The Symbol dialog box appears. Click the Special Characters tab if you want to insert a special character; otherwise, leave the Symbols tab selected.
2. Click the Shortcut Key button. The Customize Keyboard dialog box appears. (See Figure 38-9.)
3. Click in the Press New Shortcut Key box, and press the new keyboard shortcut you want to assign to the symbol or special character.
4. Click Assign. Word applies the shortcut key to your selection.
5. Click Close twice to close both dialog boxes.

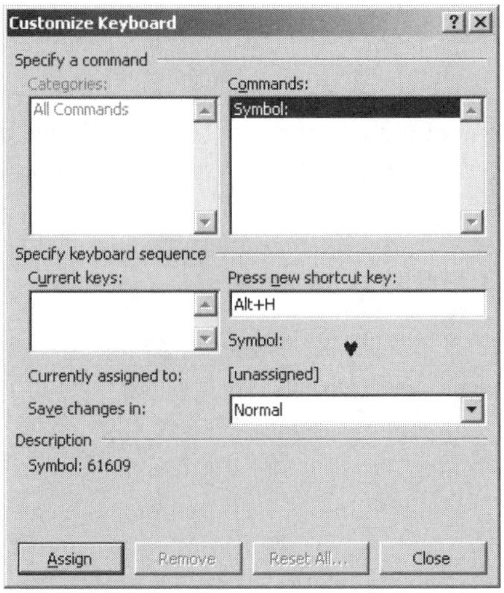

Figure 38-9. Assign a keyboard shortcut to a symbol or special character.

> **tip** **Reset keyboard shortcuts**
>
> You have the option of resetting all your keyboard shortcuts if you want to wipe the slate clean. To do this, display the Customize Keyboard dialog box by choosing Tools, Customize. Click the Keyboard button, and then click Reset All. Word alerts you that continuing with this operation will remove all macros you've previously assigned to the template you're currently using. Click Yes to continue; otherwise, click No to cancel the procedure. Click Close twice to close both dialog boxes.

Incorporating Additional Accessibility Ideas

The accessibility features in Word were created and developed over time to help make the program usable for a wide variety of users—including those with visual impairments, limited dexterity, and other physical challenges that make using a word processing program difficult. A number of the features in this chapter—such as the ability to enlarge command buttons, and the addition of keyboard shortcuts—can make the program easier to use. This section rounds out our customizing discussion by providing suggestions for ways in which you can make your documents more accessible to a wide variety of users.

Changing Text Color for Easier Reading

The color of your text and the color of the background on which it's displayed both play a large role in the readability of your document. You can change the color of your text easily by following these steps:

1. Select your text, and click the down arrow to the right of the Font Color button, on the Formatting toolbar.
2. Click a different color from the color palette.
3. Repeat as needed for other text sections.

tip **Choose a good contrast**

Experts tell us that the amount of contrast between background and text colors contributes as much to the readability of the text as the color of the text itself. Be sure, when you're creating your document, that there is a significant contrast between the text color and the color of the background of your document. If the two shades are too close, readers will find your document hard—or even impossible—to read.

Customizing Sound

Some people have difficulty hearing sounds that are easy for others to pick up; others are highly sensitive to certain kinds of sounds and might prefer that you not use sound at all in your document creations. You can tailor the sounds on your system to create the effect you want. You can customize the sound on your system with these simple procedures:

- To disable sound, choose Tools, Options, and click the General tab. Clear the Provide Feedback With Sound check box. Note, however, that selecting this option will affect all your Office XP applications, so disable the option only if you don't want to play sound with any of your applications.
- You can change the sounds that are used by making changes in Control Panel. Double-click Sounds And Multimedia in the Control Panel window. On the Sounds tab in the Sounds And Multimedia dialog box, click the event in the list in the Sound Events section to which you want to apply the sound. Click the Name down arrow, and choose the sound. Click Apply, and then click OK to close the dialog box. Windows makes the necessary changes in your sound settings, and you'll hear the new sounds you selected the next time the occasion presents itself.

tip **Add voice commands**

The sound events you hear while you're working on your document may be limited—you might hear a beep when you click a wrong command or a chime when a new e-mail message is delivered—but you can take sound a step further if need be. Word allows you to add audio clips and comments, adding real voice-over capability to your documents. This means you can add notes, suggestions, and instructions to documents, forms, or brochures, as well as use Word's dictation features to open menus, choose commands, and enter text with voice commands. For more about using voice commands in your Word documents, see Chapter 39, "Putting Speech and Handwriting Recognition Features to Work."

Chapter 39

Putting Speech and Handwriting Recognition Features to Work

People often have something to say to their computers–primarily in moments of frustration. In Microsoft Word 2002, the computer will actually listen and respond. With the addition of Speech Recognition, users can dictate text and control many Word functions by voice.

Speech isn't the only input method new to Word 2002: Handwriting Recognition and drawing capabilities also make an appearance. Although speech and handwriting recognition and drawing software have been on the market for some time, integrating these technologies into Word provides users many of the benefits of these separate applications in one place. Word 2002 users now have alternatives to traditional keyboard-and-mouse methods of document creation as well as faster ways to enter data. Computer data entry technology has advanced dramatically over the years, and Word has evolved with it.

This chapter introduces you to the new speech and handwriting recognition features in Word 2002 and shows you how to tailor them to suit your needs. Whether you're interested in dictating memos, sending audio notes, or making menu choices verbally instead of using your mouse, you'll find that the speech features save you time and give you additional flexibility in the way you work with documents. The handwriting features enable you to add signatures, logos, notes, and more to your document, whether you have a graphics tablet and stylus or a simple mouse or touchpad. The techniques in this chapter shows you how to install, set up, train, and work with speech and handwriting recognition and helps you customize the features so they will ultimately be able to follow your lead.

Introducing Speech and Handwriting Recognition Tools

The speech and handwriting input features might not be installed on your computer, depending on the setup method you use to install Word. When you run Setup, look for Alternative User Input (shown in Figure 39-1) under Office Shared Features in the Features To Install tree, and make sure that Run All From My Computer is selected. If you are planning only to use one or the other, you can select the Speech or Handwriting item and install only that feature.

Chapter 39

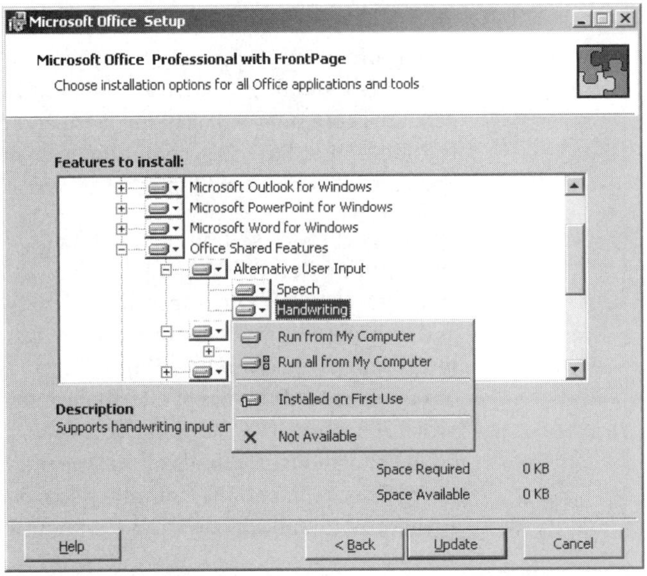

Figure 39-1. Choose to install speech and handwriting options during Word (or Office) installation.

If you didn't install speech or handwriting when you set up Word, you can add them by following these steps:

1. Click Start, and choose Settings, Control Panel. In Control Panel, double-click Add/Remove Programs.

2 In the list of currently installed programs, select either Microsoft Office XP or Microsoft Word, depending on which you installed, and click Change to launch Office Setup.

tip **Install the Language bar on first use**

If you're not sure whether you'll use the alternative input methods, use Setup's Installed On First Use option. This is especially handy if you're installing only one of the features. This way, the Language bar will be up and running as soon as you open Word, and when you use it to activate an uninstalled feature, Office Setup will prompt you to insert your CD so it can install the feature. If you installed from a networked source, Setup will go to the folder on the network and install the necessary software.

3 When the setup wizard appears, click the Add Or Remove Features option and click Next.

4 On the Features To Install page, click the plus sign (+) to the left of Office Shared Features to expand the item. Then click Alternative User Input, and choose Run All From My Computer to install both Speech Recognition and Handwriting Recognition.

note You can also install Speech Recognition alone by clicking the plus sign to the left of Alternative User Input, clicking Speech, and then choosing Run All From My Computer.

5 Click Update to install the additional components.

For more information on installing Office, see Appendix A, "Installing or Upgrading Word 2002."

Once either the Speech Recognition or Handwriting Recognition features are installed, the Language bar will be present by default, as shown in Figure 39-2, on the next page. Clicking the appropriate button on the Language bar will start the respective features. (See Table 39-1, on the next page.) The Language bar also enables you to set options and choose among several recognition feature modes. You can drag it with your mouse to move it to another location in your window, or you can minimize it.

Table 39-1. Language Bar Tools

Tool	Name	Description
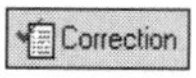	Correction	Allows you to automatically correct text you've entered with handwriting or speech features
	English (United States)	Displays a drop-down menu of keyboard layouts that are installed for your computer
	Microphone	Turns on the Speech Recognition feature and adds the Dictation and Voice Command buttons to the Language Bar
	Speech Tools	Displays a list of options you can use to fine-tune and edit text you entered using speech recognition
	Handwriting	Displays a menu of writing choices, enabling you to choose the method you will use to enter text
	Writing Pad	Opens the Writing Pad window.

If you minimize the Language bar, the System Tray will display a reference to the active language (such as EN for U.S. English). To restore the Language bar, click the System Tray icon and then click Show The Language bar on the shortcut menu that appears. You can also right-click the icon and click Show The Language bar on the longer shortcut menu that appears.

Figure 39-2. The new Language bar is the command center for Word's Speech and Handwriting Recognition features.

If you closed the Language bar, you can get it back by clicking Start and choosing Settings, Control Panel, and double clicking Text Services in Control Panel. In the Text Services dialog box, click the Language Bar Button, and in the Language Bar Settings dialog box, select the Show The Language Bar On The Desktop check box.

The Language Bar Settings dialog box, shown in Figure 39-3, also includes an option to show more icons (one for Speech and one for Handwriting Recognition) in the system tray, to include a text label or just icons on the Language bar, and to give the Language bar a cool, translucent effect when it's inactive. To set or change these Language bar options, select or clear the check boxes for the options you want to add or remove and click OK. Click OK again to close the Text Services dialog box and return to your document.

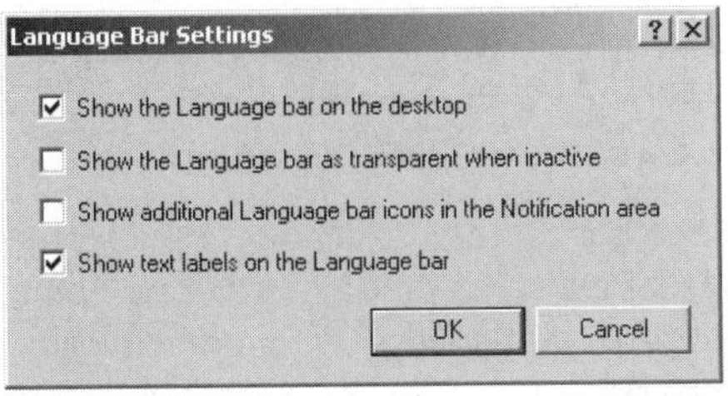

Figure 39-3. Set options for the Language bar in the Language Bar Settings dialog box.

Now that you've got a sense of the tools you'll be using to input text using speech and handwriting features, you are ready to put them to good use. The next section takes you quickly through the procedures for setting up, training, and working with speech recognition.

Using Speech Recognition to Reduce Typing Tasks

Aficionados of old movies are familiar with the archaic workplace scene consisting of an executive dictating a letter to a secretary. This doesn't occur often in the modern workplace, where we are expected to type our own letters.

Speech Recognition in Word brings dictation back into the mainstream of the working world. You dictate to your computer, and Word converts your speech into text on screen. You might even find yourself ordering: "Computer, take a letter …"

InsideOut

Speech recognition in Words is not a "hands-free" solution suitable for those who have physical disabilities that preclude use of the hands. (See the sidebar "Hands-Free Dictation.") This is because people who make regular use of speech recognition software have found that it's faster and more efficient to mix keyboard and mouse inputs rather than using voice commands alone. Word Speech Recognition takes this mixed input (voice and keyboard) approach.

Hands-Free Dictation

People who are not able to use their hands and arms need dictation software that is designed for hands-free use. The speech recognition capabilities of this class of products are not that different from those in Word. However, hands-free software adds more extensive navigation tools and voice macro support that allow users to write their own computer command instructions.

True hands-free solutions are installed by specialized consultants and resellers who configure hardware and software to meet the needs of individual users. Some consultants have developed their own software solutions. Your local disability agency or rehabilitation center might have recommendations of consultants and resellers in your area.

Preparing to Use Speech Recognition

The Speech Recognition feature in Word places heavy hardware demands on a computer. First the software loads into memory its vocabulary of words and its digital model of your speaking voice. Then the software performs complex computations to match your speech input to words in the vocabulary.

If you want to use speech recognition with Word, the *minimum* hardware recommendations are as follows:

- A microphone, ideally the headset-mounted type
- A 400 megahertz (MHz) or faster computer
- 128 MB or more of memory
- Microsoft Windows 98, Microsoft Windows NT 4.0, or later
- Microsoft Internet Explorer 5 or later

Memory is particularly critical because of the amount of system resources Speech Recognition requires. You should consider adding 64–128 MB of RAM to your system beyond your normal computing needs. In other words, if you need 128 MB to run your computer efficiently without Speech Recognition, you should have 192–256 MB to use this feature.

You'll also need a high quality sound card if you decide to use a conventional (analog) microphone. A better choice, however, would be to use one of the new USB digital microphone headsets. These contain their own digital signal processor (DSP) circuits to convert your voice's sound waves into digital code, and they plug into your computer's USB port. Typically there is a lot of electronic "noise" associated with a sound card because of its multifunction audio circuitry and because of its location inside the computer's case, where it's subject to noise emitted by the other computer components. DSP headsets are necessary if you're using a laptop, where system noise is too great for any accuracy in speech recognition. When you shop for a headset, be sure to look for one that has a noise-canceling microphone designed to filter out background noise in your workspace.

Shopping for a Microphone

Plantronics has been designated by Microsoft as its recommended supplier of headsets for Office XP. This company's monaural DSP-100 and stereo DSP units are well suited to Word, as is the analog LS-1. The USB models have nifty software that automatically switches your system from sound-card-and-speaker mode to the USB sound system when the headset is plugged in. Interesting products from VXI (a long-time supplier to the speech recognition market) include the Jamaica USB headset and the Bahama, which is an analog unit that connects to your telephone as well as your computer. And if you're a computer game addict, Microsoft's Game Voice controller has a Word-compatible headset that allows you to dictate letters and shoot aliens using the same piece of hardware.

tip **Position your microphone correctly**

Microphones work best for speech recognition if they are positioned in front and to the side of your mouth and if they remain in the same position throughout a dictation session. You can accomplish this with a desk-mounted microphone–provided you're willing to strap yourself rigidly in place at your workspace. Or you can use a headset microphone, which gives you the freedom to move around and still keep the microphone in place.

Activating Speech Recognition

The Speech Recognition function starts whenever you click the Microphone button on the Language bar. This works in any speech-enabled Office XP application, and, once started, Speech Recognition will continue to run until all Office applications are closed. You can also start Speech Recognition by choosing Tools, Speech in Word.

tip **Show the speech balloons**

By default, Show Speech Messages on the Language bar's Speech Tools drop-down menu is turned on. You should leave it on. The balloons provide helpful feedback, such as the last thing the system was able to recognize or warnings if you are talking too softly or too loudly. (For more on this feedback, see Table 39-1.)

When the Speech Recognition system is being activated, a speech balloon appears on the Language bar with the message Starting Speech. When the words disappear and the balloon turns blank, Speech Recognition has been loaded. (See Figure 39-4.) It is best to wait for the process to finish before running some other computer task; a lot of resources are being used and things will go more smoothly if you let the computer focus on that one task.

Figure 39-4. When the text Starting Speech appears in the balloon, the system is loading your Speech Recognition files. When the words disappear from the balloon, Speech Recognition is active.

Starting Speech Recognition for the First Time

The first time Speech Recognition runs, Word will present you with the Microphone Wizard to help you set up your microphone and sound system for use in recognition. The first wizard page guides you through microphone placement, and then you run a volume check and adjustment. To do this, simply pronounce the displayed text over and over–it usually takes three or four recitations–until the volume bar stays consistently in the green area. Word adjusts your Windows sound settings accordingly.

The last page in the Microphone Wizard requires you to say the phrase, **This papaya tastes perfect**, and then listen to a recording played back to you. (See Figure 39-5.) The object of this exercise is to ensure that the microphone is placed where there won't be too much "popping" from the breath you expel while talking.

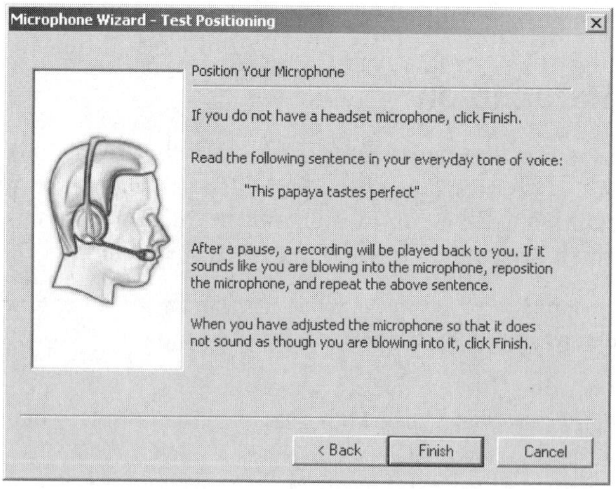

Figure 39-5. The last step of the training session helps you check that your microphone is positioned correctly.

Troubleshooting

My Computer Doesn't Hear Me

When you're troubleshooting Speech Recognition problems, don't forget the low-tech problems. Microphone cords can easily get tangled in things around your desk and yanked out of the computer, so check that first. Some microphones have volume controls in addition to or instead of mute switches, so if you're still experiencing problems be sure you have the microphone set to sufficient gain (volume) and that it isn't muted.

Also be sure that the Microphone is active in the Volume Control dialog box (sometimes referred to as the Windows Mixer) by following these steps:

1. If the Volume Control icon is present in your system tray, launch Volume Control by double-clicking the icon. In the Volume Control dialog box that appears, choose Options, Properties to open the Properties dialog box. In the Properties dialog box, click the Recording option. Make sure that the Microphone check box is selected in the Show The Following Volume Controls list. Then click OK, which will open up the Recording Control dialog box. Go to step 4.
2. If the Volume Control icon isn't in the System Tray, click the Start Menu and choose Settings, Control Panel, and double-click Multimedia in Control Panel (Windows 98 or Windows NT4) or double-click Sounds And Multimedia (Microsoft Windows 2000 and Microsoft Windows ME). Click the Audio tab, and click the Volume button in the Sound Recording Section to open the Recording Control dialog box.
3. If Microphone Balance isn't showing as one of the sound sources in the Recording Control dialog box, choose Options, Properties. Follow the procedures for setting the properties as described in step 1.
4. In the Recording Control dialog box, select the Select check box for the microphone. Note that the setting of the Microphone volume slider is not important, because Word will run a sound check and adjust those settings automatically. Click the close box to close the Recording Control dialog box and return to your document.

Training the Speech Recognition Feature

After you've finished the Microphone Wizard, Word opens the Voice Training Wizard so you can move on to a training process—for both you and Word. You dictate prepared text that gives you an introduction to Speech Recognition while Word builds a model of your voice. When Word "listens" to you, it's actually carrying out complex calculations in which the digital signals of what you dictated into the microphone are compared with Word's base phonetic models. Then, over time as you dictate and correct (see "Correcting Speech Recognition Errors" on page 944), Word modifies its phonetics to match your actual pronunciation patterns. To train Word to recognize your speech patterns, follow these steps:

1. When the Voice Training wizard opens, read the welcome page and then click Next.
2. In the next page, Word asks your age and gender. It's not being nosy; this is to establish a base voice model tied to the likely pitch of your voice. Select the appropriate options, and then click Next.

> **tip** Forget the gender stereotype. The real question is, do you have a high-pitched or low-pitched voice? For the former, answer female, and for the latter, answer male—regardless of your actual gender.

3. The next wizard page is informational. You are instructed to position your microphone properly and set aside some time and a quiet location for training. Quiet is very important in the early stages of Speech Recognition. You want the computer to hear only your voice, not background noise. After you've finished reading the page, click Next.
4. You then start working your way through a series of pages in which text is displayed for you to read. The wizard also instructs you in some basics of Speech Recognition. (See Figure 39-6.) As you read the words, the background behind them first turns light blue, and then dark blue to signify that Word has understood you. If the background turns white, go back and read those words again. If you are stuck on a word, click the Skip Word button.

> **note** You may use the Pause/Resume button as necessary to stop your training at any time. You do not need to do anything to advance the wizard; Word will do that automatically.

5. When you've completed the reading, a page showing a progress bar appears as the recorded data is converted into a computer model of your voice. When the process is done, click Finish.
6. A short tutorial video opens in an Internet Explorer window. You can let it play or close the window and go back to Word. This completes the initial voice training.

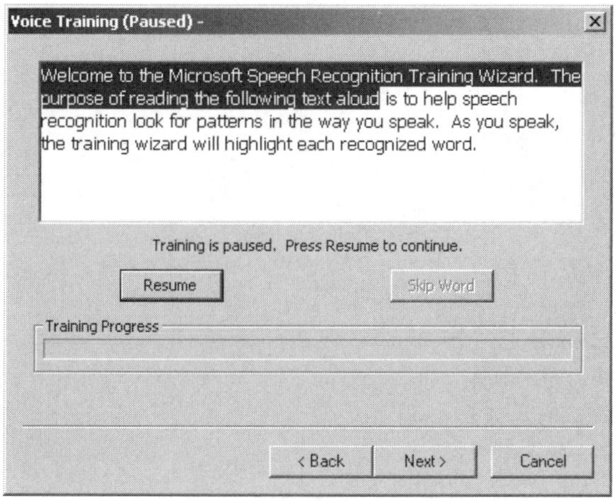

Figure 39-6. Reading the text helps Word "learn" your voice, and helps you learn about Speech Recognition.

note Patience is a virtue. Remember that Word has to learn how you speak. Don't expect great accuracy at first, since the software must develop its voice model over time. Realistically you will need several sessions before you can start using it efficiently. At first you ought to limit yourself to short sessions—a page or so of text. That way you won't get frustrated, and the frustration won't creep into your voice and make matters worse.

Using Speech Recognition Profiles

The central concept of a profile is that it is yours and yours alone. Your first profile was created when you went through the training process the first time you started Speech Recognition. If someone else is going to use the computer, he or she needs to create a separate voice profile. This is called *speaker dependent* recognition. You may also need to set up another profile for yourself to cover special situations—for example, one you can use on a day that you have a bad cold, so your "regular" voice model won't be corrupted by the way your voice sounds when you're sick.

You create a new profile by clicking Options on the Language bar's Speech Tools drop-down menu. You can also create a profile by clicking the Start and choosing Settings, Control Panel, and double-clicking Speech. Either method brings up the Speech Properties dialog box shown in Figure 39-7, on the next page. In the Recognition Profiles section, click New to create a new profile or click Delete to get rid of an old one. You can also run the Microphone Wizard again, which will be necessary if you change microphones, if noise levels change in your work environment, or if you want to refresh the settings. (For more details, see "Getting Situated before Starting" on page 940.)

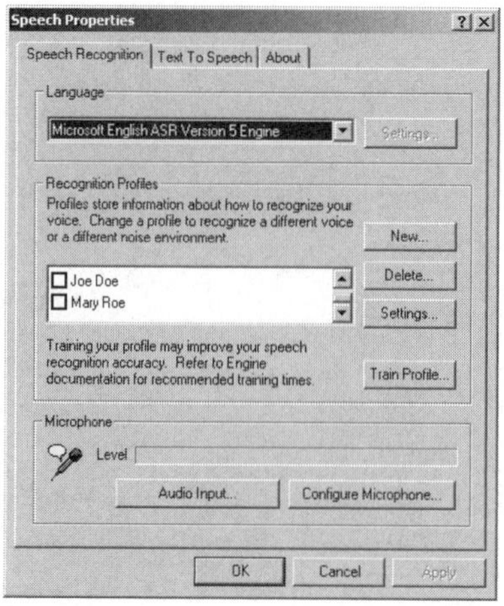

Figure 39-7. You can create additional profiles for Speech Recognition or eliminate obsolete ones.

Mastering the Art of Speaking to a Computer

Unless you are practiced at dictation, talking to your computer may seem strange at first. How, indeed, should you speak to a computer? Here are some pointers:

- **Don't mumble.** You don't need to have the diction of James Earl Jones, but you should make an effort to speak clearly.
- **Don't shout.** You don't need to yell, but you should try to keep a constant volume level.
- **Don't rush.** It isn't necessary to speak slowly—actually, that can hurt recognition. Just don't rush your words so that they slur together.

One of the principles of effective speech recognition is: speak in phrases. Word uses what is called continuous speech recognition, meaning that the program examines groups of words and tries to figure out what you said from context as well as from the sound of each word. It helps, therefore, to speak in phrases that convey the necessary context.

Consider, for example, the sentences, "I want to dictate something," and, "I want two dictation examples." Sound alone does not distinguish "to" from "two" (or "too"). But a *tu* sound followed immediately by a verb usually means "to," while the same sound followed by a noun is likely "two." In either case, if you pause after saying "I want *tu*," the computer would have no way to determine whether you wanted "to" or "two." (In that case, it just makes its choice on the basis of which version you use most frequently—a less accurate method.)

You switch between profiles by selecting the appropriate check box in the Recognition Profiles Section or by clicking the Speech Tools button on the Language bar and choosing Current User, and then the user from the drop-down menu, as shown in Figure 39-8.

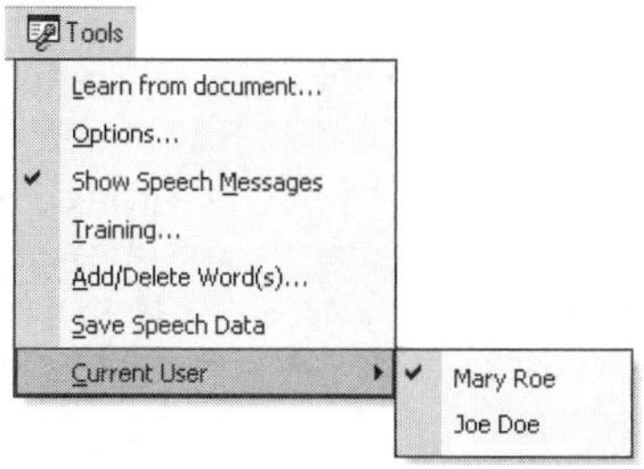

Figure 39-8. You can use the Speech Tools drop-down menu on the Language bar to specify the Speech Recognition user profile.

Providing Additional Training

Click Speech Tools on the Language bar and then choose Training to bring up other text passages to continue training Word. (See Figure 39-9.) It's a good idea to do at least two or three extra training sessions. The more data you give the computer, the better the voice profile it can create.

You probably ought to read the Bill Gates passage. Really. It's a businesslike description of the revisions he made in the second edition of his book, and it doesn't have many literary flourishes. This makes it the best approximation of routine business letters, reports, and memos.

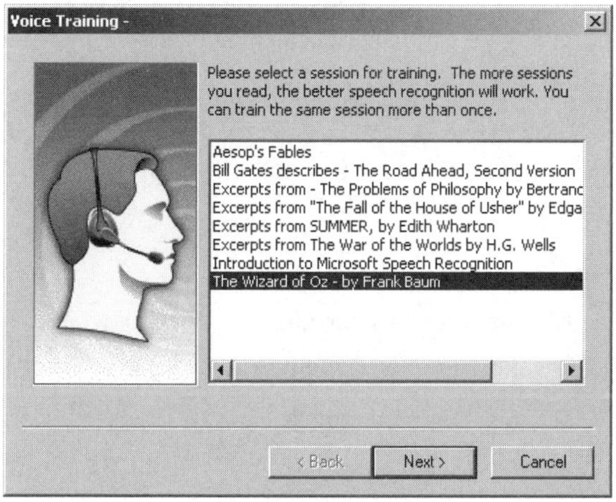

Figure 39-9. Selecting additional material to train Word helps improve your voice profile.

Getting Situated Before Starting

When you're ready to start dictating, you should begin by doing a microphone check. First make sure you have it positioned correctly, and then check the volume by clicking Tools, Options in the Language Bar. Click the Speech Recognition tab, if necessary, and speak into your microphone. The volume level is shown in the Level bar in the lower portion of the dialog box. If necessary, move your microphone to adjust the sound level or click the Configure Microphone button to launch the Microphone Wizard and readjust your volume levels. You rarely speak the same way at each sitting. You may be tired or bored and speak more softly than usual, or you may be exceptionally perky and loud on a given day. Your posture also affects your voice, so try to make sure you're seated comfortably and have a glass of water nearby in case your mouth gets dry as you speak.

Speech Recognition in Action

Now that your microphone is positioned, the sound levels are set, Word has developed a profile of your voice patterns, and all the other preliminaries are done, it's time to put Speech Recognition to work. Open a document, and start Speech Recognition using these simple steps:

1. Click the Microphone button on the Language bar. Two new icons appear on the bar: Dictation and Voice Command.
2. Click Dictation if you want to dictate text.
3. Click Voice Command if you want to use Speech Recognition to operate menu commands.

Once the Speech Recognition engine is started, you can swap modes by voice by saying **voice command** or **dictation.**

If you have selected Show Speech Messages in the Speech Tools menu, Word advises you on whether you're speaking correctly. If you're not, one of the messages in Table 39-1 appears.

Table 39-1. Dictation warning messages

Message	Means that you should
Too soft	Try speaking more loudly.
Too loud	Try speaking more quietly.
What was that?	Try repeating your words.
Too fast	Try speaking more slowly.

When you start to dictate text, the first thing you see is a blue bar—essentially a string of dots with blue shading—as shown in Figure 39-10. This signifies that Word has received data and is processing it.

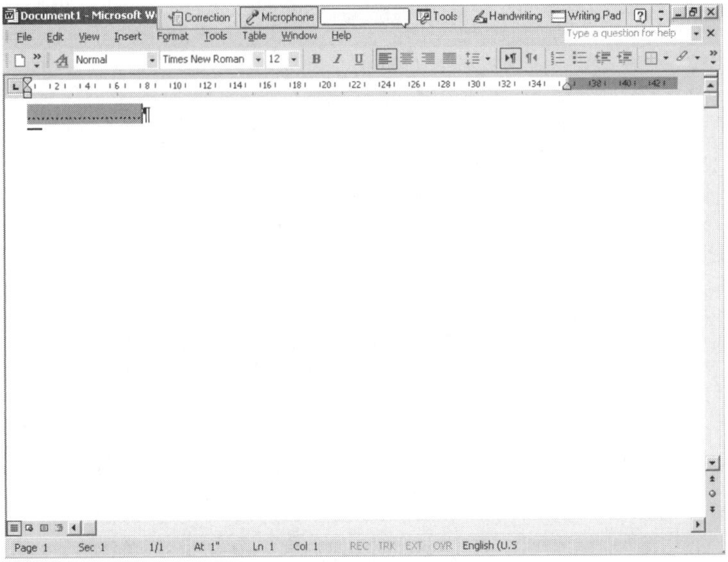

Figure 39-10. When you dictate, Word displays a blue bar on your screen that turns into recognized words.

When the processing is done, the bar turns into words. You do *not* need to wait for the blue bar to turn into words before dictating more words. Word displays the bar when it has finished its speech recognition and is ready for more words; meanwhile the previous dictation is working its way through the computers electronic pathways on its way to your screen.

Remember, when dictating you need to *say* the punctuation. Table 39-2 lists the punctuation terms that Word recognizes. The terms are straightforward, so your main task is to remember the more obscure marks; ~ is a tilde, for example.

InsideOut

Word's dictation allows only for standard plain text punctuation, such as, "--" (straight quotes and a double-hyphen) instead of "—" (curly quotes and an em dash). As a result, Word's "smart" formatting features for quotes, dashes, and so on aren't available directly by voice, which can make your documents look less professional.

Word's AutoCorrect fixes some of these formatting issues as you go. Be sure to check your AutoCorrect settings. (For more information about AutoCorrect, see Chapter 6, "Putting Text Tools to Work.") Use AutoFormat after you have finished dictating to resolve any remaining plain text formatting.

Table 39-2. Punctuation in Dictation mode

Say	To get
Period Dot	.
Comma	,
Colon	:
Semicolon	;
Question mark	?
Exclamation point	!
Ampersand	&
Asterisk	*
At sign At	@
Backslash	\
Slash	/
Vertical bar	|
Hyphen Dash	-
Double dash	--
Equals	=
Plus Plus sign	+
Pound sign	#
Percent Percent sign	%
Dollar sign	$
Underscore	_
Tilde	~
Ellipsis	...
Greater than	>
Less than	<
Caret	^

(continued)

Table 39-2. ***(continued)***

Say	To get
New line	Enter
New paragraph	Enter twice
Bracket Left bracket Open bracket	[
End bracket Right bracket Close bracket	]
Open brace Curly brace Left brace	{
Close brace End curly brace Right brace	}
Open parenthesis Left paren	(
Close parenthesis Right paren	)
Quote Open quote	"
Close quote	"
Single quote Open single quote	'
Close single quote	'
5 five	five (numbers less than 20 are spelled out when inserted)
21 twenty-one	21 (numbers greater than 20 are inserted as digits)
one half	1/2 (fractions)
five five five hyphen zero one eight seven	555-0187 (telephone numbers)

Correcting Speech Recognition Errors

You need to correct errors in dictation, otherwise Word will create an inaccurate voice profile and its recognition will become less accurate. You need to be particularly attentive during your first few Speech sessions, which is when Word makes the most changes to your voice model.

When you should make corrections while dictating is a matter of preference. You can correct as you go along, or you can input the text and then go back to make corrections. It's primarily a matter of how compulsive you are. In theory, going all the way through and then making corrections is more efficient. But if seeing those recognition errors on screen will make you crazy, fix them right away.

There are several different ways to make corrections:

- Right-click an error to open a shortcut menu containing list of alternative choices appear, as shown in Figure 39-11. Note that in this instance, "Microsoft Word" was recognized as "Microsoft word." The capitalized version is available on the shortcut menu. Click it, and it will replace the incorrect version. Word will then learn that you want capitalization when "word" follows "Microsoft."

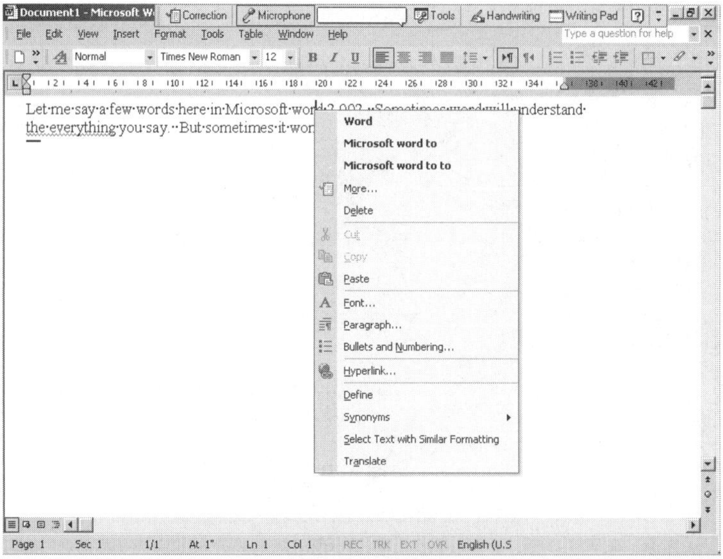

Figure 39-11. Right-clicking opens a shortcut menu with a list of possible corrections for dictation errors.

- Click the Correction button on the Language bar, or choose More on the shortcut menu when you right-click the error. Word will play back a recording of your dictation and then present you with an alternative choice. Click again to make the correction.

- Select the errant word with the mouse or keyboard and, in Dictation mode, say **spelling mode** and spell out your correction by voice. So if you wanted "sun" but got "son," say "**S-U-N**." You can also select a few words, including any error, and dictate over that. While you can select just a single word to correct by voice, dictating over a phrase will do more to improve accuracy.
- Select the word and type over the error.

tip **Select and correct by voice**

You can delete the last thing you said by saying, **scratch that.** You can also select text in Voice Command mode. For example, you can say, **select next word**, **select last word**, **select next line**, **select last line**, or **select paragraph**.

Controlling Word using Voice Commands

You can use Voice Command mode to navigate through a document and to make changes in it. Appendix B lists the available commands, giving both the actions you can execute and what you need to say. For example, say **right arrow** to move the insertion point to the right, or **new paragraph** to create a new paragraph. There are more than 50 voice functions, and many can be initiated by more than one voice command, so you might want to keep this book propped open on the table while learning these functions.

InsideOut

A limitation of Word Speech Recognition is you cannot directly add to the voice commands that are available. If you regularly use commands that are not shown in Appendix B or do not appear on a standard toolbar or menu, you cannot execute them by voice.

To work around this limitation, you must create a custom toolbar, or customize existing toolbars or menus (see the section "Creating Convenient Toolbar Displays," on page 27 for more information), and display them. You can then take advantage of Word's ability to read menus and toolbars to gain voice command over the functions on your custom menu or toolbar.

In addition to those commands, you can also operate Word's menus and toolbar buttons by saying their names (to operate buttons, say the names that appear in the buttons' ScreenTips). The toolbar must be visible for you to operate it by voice.

> **note** The actions that the commands in Appendix B carry out depend on the way in which Word "hears" what you want to do. This means that if you say "file save" as one phrase, Word will directly save the active file. If you say "file," pause, and then say "save," Word will open the File menu and select the Save command. Both methods do exactly the same thing, but using the command phrase saves a step.

Building Up Your Speech Vocabulary

While Word comes with a large speech recognition vocabulary, the built-in words will rarely meet all of your needs. There will be special terms you use, not to mention proper names. This process of building your Speech Recognition profile's vocabulary will continue as you create new documents by voice. But you can take some steps to give yourself a head start on tailoring Word's speech vocabulary to meet your needs.

Adding Words from a Document

One very effective way to increase Word's vocabulary is to have Word look for words it does not recognize in documents you've already created. This is a quick way to add words that you're likely to use in future documents to Word's speech dictionary. To do this, follow these steps:

1 Click Speech Tools on the Language bar, and then choose Learn From Document from the drop-down menu. Word scans the open document and then produces a list of words not in its vocabulary and displays them in the Learn From Document dialog box shown in Figure 39-12.

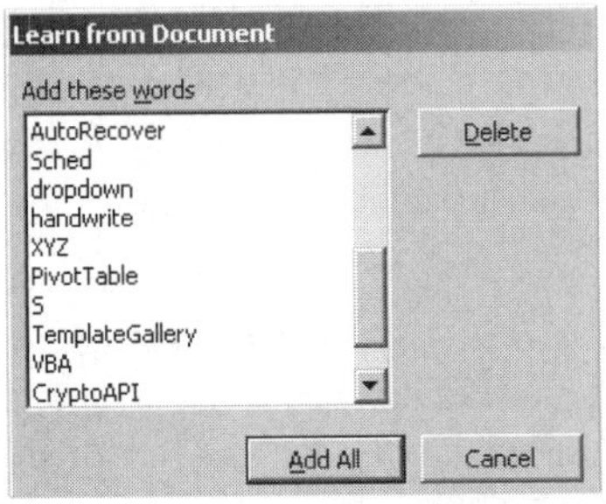

Figure 39-12. Use the Learn From Document dialog box to add words to your Speech Recognition vocabulary.

2 Review the list and delete each of the words that don't need to be added to your profile's vocabulary. For example, Word may have erroneously added parts of words (such as "to" and "gether" when you meant to say "together") that you can now delete. Select a word, and then click Delete to remove it from the Add These Words list.

3 When you're sure that the remaining list is what you want, click Add All to make the words a part of Word's vocabulary.

Adding Words by Dictating

You also can add words as you go. On the Language bar, click Speech Tools, and then choose Add/Delete Word(s) from the drop-down menu. A list of words appears, as shown in Figure 39-13. In the Word box, type the word you want to add. Click Record Pronunciation, and then pronounce the word. When the word is recognized, it will be added to the Dictionary list. You might need to say the word more than once before it is added to the list. Click Close to close the dialog box.

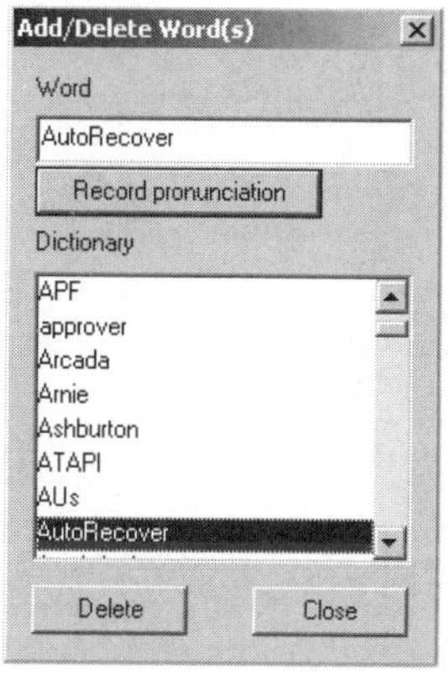

Figure 39-13. Word allows you to add or remove words from its speech vocabulary and to clarify pronunciation.

You can also use this process to add the correct pronunciation to words you added from a document. While the words were inserted into the dictionary, your pronunciation of them was not. This is especially necessary if the word is pronounced atypically; for example, the city of Quincy, MA is pronounced "quin-ZEE" and the city of Cairo, IL is pronounced "KAY-row."

Deleting Words from the Speech Dictionary

The Add/Delete Word(s) command can also prune unneeded words from the dictionary. Remember: the more words in your dictionary, the more data has to be loaded into your computer's memory. Select an unnecessary word, and then click Delete.

In addition, if words are being constantly misinterpreted, you will want to delete them, add them back in, and then record the pronunciation again.

Specifying whether to Save Speech Input

One other command available on the Language bar's Speech Tools drop-down menu is Save Speech Data. This refers to an audio recording of your actual spoken voice, which can be saved along with the words on the screen and linked to them. That is, if you said "**something**," Word would store a recording of that word and link the recording to the text "something" on screen. If the recording is saved with the document, you will have access to all of Word's speech correction features if you need to check and edit Word's Speech Recognition at a later point. Of course, that means a much larger file size since the document contains the text and the recording.

You should turn on Save Speech Data while you are working on a document. When you're done, turn the feature off and save the file in a more compact form.

> **tip** **Exit Office regularly so your voice files are saved**
>
> If you are doing a lot of dictating, particularly during your initial speech sessions, try closing all speech-enabled Office applications from time to time. Your voice files are not saved to your hard disk until Speech Recognition is shut down completely, and you could lose key changes if your system were to crash before a save.

Turning Off Speech Recognition

When you've finished dictating, you need to turn off Speech Recognition, otherwise the microphone will continue to record your every utterance. To turn off Speech Recognition, click the Microphone button on the Language bar, just as you did to start it. You can also simply say **Microphone** to disable the microphone. However, Speech Recognition is still running until you shut down Word and any other speech-enabled Office XP program that is running.

To uninstall Speech Recognition altogether, click the Start and choose Settings, Control Panel, and double-click Add/Remove Programs in Control Panel. Select Microsoft Word (or Microsoft Office XP) in the Add/Remove Programs dialog box, click Change and then Add Or Remove Features. Click Office Shared Features in the displayed list; then click Alternative User Input and Speech. Finally, select Not Available from the list of choices displayed when you click Speech. Click Update to Speech Recognition from your computer. For more information about installing Speech Recognition, see "Introducing Speech and Handwriting Recognition Tools" on page 928.

Speech Recognition Works, but Will It Work for You?

When determining whether speech recognition is right for your work style, the key question to ask yourself is: how well do you really type? If your typing speed is 80 words per minute with 95 percent accuracy, speech recognition will probably slow you down. If you're actually creating content as you type rather than just typing, your speed is going to be tied to how fast your brain can turn a phrase, not how fast your fingers can fly over the keyboard. In most cases, Word's Speech Recognition abilities won't slow down your writing process.

Real-world accuracy levels for speech recognition can consistently be 90-95%, going as high as 98% in optimal conditions. But you have to train Word patiently and build up its vocabulary to get to that kind of performance.

In the end, the choice between dictation and keyboarding is a matter of personal preference. But as you know, variety is the spice of life. And whether you use Word's Speech Recognition capabilities to dictate your next novel or simply to give your mouse-button-clicking finger a rest, it gives you yet another option that enables you to work with words in a way most comfortable for you.

Inputting Data using the Handwriting Recognition Feature

Handwriting recognition isn't yet deemed completely reliable because of the inaccuracies of very early implementations. Today, handwriting recognition is the main form of data entry on PDAs and handheld computers, and the same technology can be applied to desktop computers.

It might be best to think of this feature set in Word as handwriting recognition *and tablet* tools, as it has both graphical and text components. You can capture input from computer pens and pointing devices as text, graphics, or as a combination of both. Word attempts to read standard handwriting, rather than the stylized alphabets such as Character Recognizer on Pocket PCs.

Handwriting Recognition features impose no particular system requirements beyond the standard Word 2002 specifications; your computer typically deals with a handwriting device as if it were a mouse. To make the best use of Handwriting Recognition, you can use a tablet-PC, a pen-based input device (really a mouse shaped like a pen), or a graphics tablet used with 3-D drawing or Computer Aided Drafting (CAD) programs. Graphic tablets tend to be expensive, high-end solutions, but there are also low-priced units on the market that are perfectly suitable for Word. You can even use your mouse for handwriting recognition.

Handwriting recognition is installed through the same process as Speech, as described in the section "Introducing Speech and Handwriting Recognition Tools." During installation, make sure you choose Handwriting instead of Speech, as shown in Figure 39-1.

Familiarizing Yourself with Handwriting Recognition Capabilities

To get started with Handwriting Recognition, click the Language bar's Handwriting button to open the drop-down menu containing the five commands shown in Figure 39-14. When you choose one of the commands, Handwriting Recognition will be activated and the active tool's icon will be shaded. (If the Handwriting button doesn't appear automatically on your Language bar, click the Language Bar Options button to display a list of features and click Handwriting. The button will then be available on the Language bar.) The options on the Handwriting menu are described in the following sections.

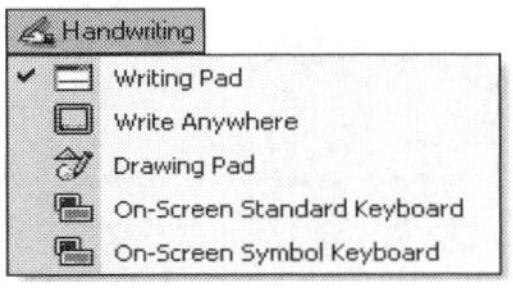

Figure 39-14. There are five choices for accessing Word's handwriting and tablet features

Writing Pad

The Writing Pad, shown in the following illustration, is the basic method for entering handwriting for recognition. It is a window that can be resized and moved to suit your needs, and there is a line (modeled after the rules on a paper pad) that serves as a guide to ascenders (the vertical line on an "h," for example) and descenders (for example, the loop in a "g" that falls below the line) in your electronic penmanship.

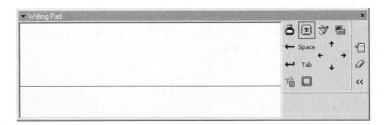

As with all the Handwriting tools, you close Writing Pad by clicking Close in the right-hand corner of the tool's title bar, or by clicking its button on the Language bar.

The buttons on the right-hand side of the Writing Pad window are for navigating and simple editing. You can click them to begin recognition, correct recognition errors, or erase what you wrote. You can also choose between inputting text or creating an Ink Object. This is a very new wrinkle in Word that we'll discuss later.

Write Anywhere

Write Anywhere mode is functionally identical to Writing Pad, except that you can write on the screen anywhere instead of in a special window. This mode is primarily intended to support tablet PCs and is activated by clicking Handwriting on the Language bar and choosing Write Anywhere on the drop-down menu. Be careful if you use it on a desktop computer or laptop: any movement you make with the mouse may be interpreted as text input. The Write Anywhere dialog box is shown in the following illustration.

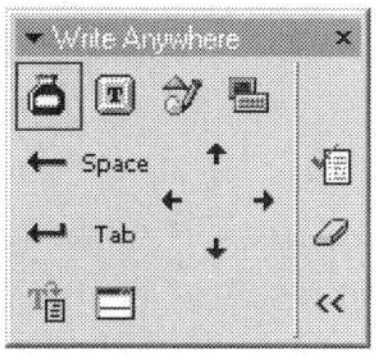

Drawing Pad

The Drawing Pad is intended purely for use of your pen device to input graphics into Word. It does not convert the drawings into text. It is, however, a good solution for making sketches or adding your signature to documents. It has a different set of icons from the Writing Pad or Write Anywhere mode: In addition to the standard Writing Pad and Clear icons, there is one to remove your last pen stroke, one to copy your drawing to the Windows Clipboard, and one to insert your drawing into your document, as shown in the following illustration.

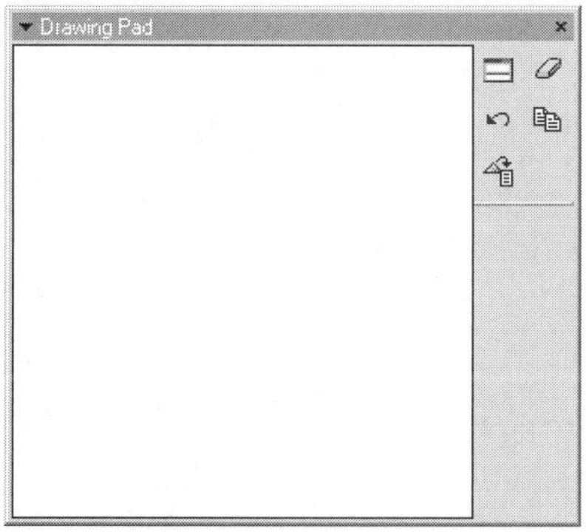

Keyboards

The On-Screen Standard Keyboard and the On-Screen Symbol Keyboard also are Tablet PC-oriented, providing a virtual keyboard for those who would rather avoid handwriting recognition or for those systems with touch-screen functionality. Word puts a picture of a keyboard on screen, and you tap the keys with your pen or pointing device.

note While seemingly redundant on a computer with a real keyboard, the Symbol Keyboard is a quick shortcut for inputting symbols in text. You might find it easier to use than choosing Symbol from the Insert menu in Word.

Configuring Handwriting Recognition Options

Word's Handwriting Recognition features can be configured to suit your tastes and needs. To change these settings, click Writing Pad or Write Anywhere on the Language bar. (If either command does not have a check next to it, choose them on the Language bar's Handwriting menu.) Click the down arrow in the left corner of the Writing Pad's title bar or the Write Anywhere toolbar, and then choose Options from the drop-down menu. The Handwriting Options dialog box appears, as shown in the following illustration, and contains two tabs: Common and Writing Pad. The Restore Default button appears on both tabs; clicking it will restore the default settings for all options.

Options on the Common tab (illustrated below) are as follows:

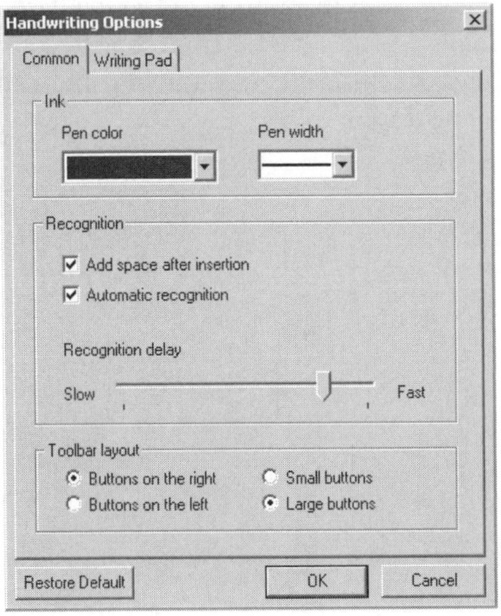

- **Pen Color and Pen Width.** These options are set using drop-down lists. This will determine how the input will look if you put it into your document as a graphic. (The default setting is blue and narrow width).
- **Add Space After Insertion.** When selected, Word will try to determine if you want a space between words when it performs recognition. (This option is turned on by default; turning it off will result in Word displaying a string of unbroken letters. This option is primarily intended for inputting data rather than text.)
- **Automatic Recognition.** When selected, Word automatically converts handwritten entries into text. (The option is turned on by default; turn it off if you are doing complicated writing that will require a lot of pen movement.)

tip You can turn off automatic recognition so you can write down phone numbers or other notes without having your writing interrupted by the text conversion process.

- **Recognition Delay.** This slider control sets the time lag before Word tries to convert your handwriting to text.

tip **Give yourself more time to write**

Until you are extremely proficient at electronic penmanship, keep the delay setting at the default setting, or better yet, slow it down by dragging the slider to the left. Slowing down the response time—and thus allowing yourself the time to write at a more leisurely pace—will substantially increase recognition accuracy.

- **Toolbar Layout.** With these options you can put the tools on the left or right, and use large or small buttons. The default is large buttons on the right.

note Drawing Pad has its own limited set of Options, also accessible from a down arrow in its dialog box. You can change the Pen Color, Pen Width, Toolbar Layout, and Restore Default options just as you would for the Writing Pad. Because the color and width you choose will affect the readability of the characters you write in Word, you might want to experiment with them.

The options on the Writing Pad tab (illustrated below) are as follows:

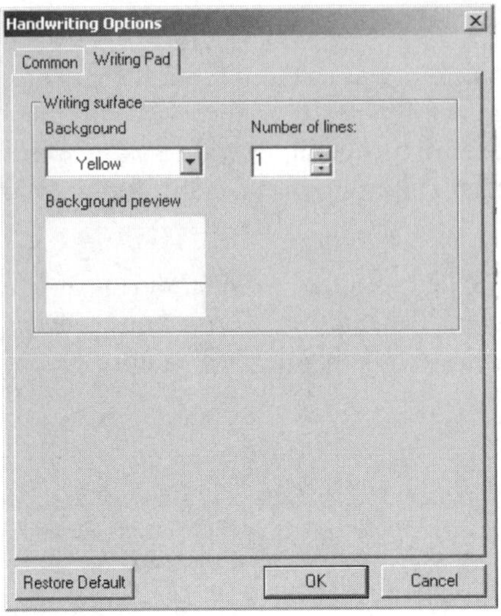

- **Background.** This drop-down list contains your choices for visual writing surfaces, including a rather stylish Parchment. The Background Preview box shows what the writing surface will look like.
- **Number Of Lines.** This box determines how many lines you can write on. You probably won't need more lines unless automatic recognition is turned off.

Converting Handwriting to Typed Text

If automatic recognition is enabled, just start writing. Word waits for you to pause, and then converts the handwriting to text. If automatic recognition is turned off, click the Recognize Now button on the Write Anywhere toolbar. Word then turns your handwriting into text and places it at the cursor position.

As you might imagine, neatness counts when you're entering text for recognition. Writing large characters also helps. Microsoft says cursive writing will work just as well as printing, but non-cursive block letters seem to be recognized most accurately.

Ink Objects

Ink Objects involve a hybrid format that allows you to insert graphics into documents and optionally convert them into text later. Figure 39-15 shows what writing **ABC 123** in the Writing Pad looks like as an Ink Object. To create an Ink Object, you simply click Handwriting, Writing Pad to display the Writing Pad, click Ink, and use your mouse or stylus to write the ink object in the Writing Pad window. The object is added to your document just the way it was written.

Word treats Ink Objects as words, even though they're displayed as graphics, so you can cut, paste, and insert between words (but not between the individual letters in each word). You can use Word's font settings (such as point size and bold, italic, and underline formatting) to modify the look of the Ink Object.

Once you add an Ink Object to your document, you need to tell Word to translate it into text. Right-click an Ink object and choose Ink Object from the shortcut menu to open a submenu of text recognition choices that you can use. Choose Recognize from the submenu to insert Word's Handwriting Recognition translation for the object; click Alternate List opens a list of possible translations you can choose from.

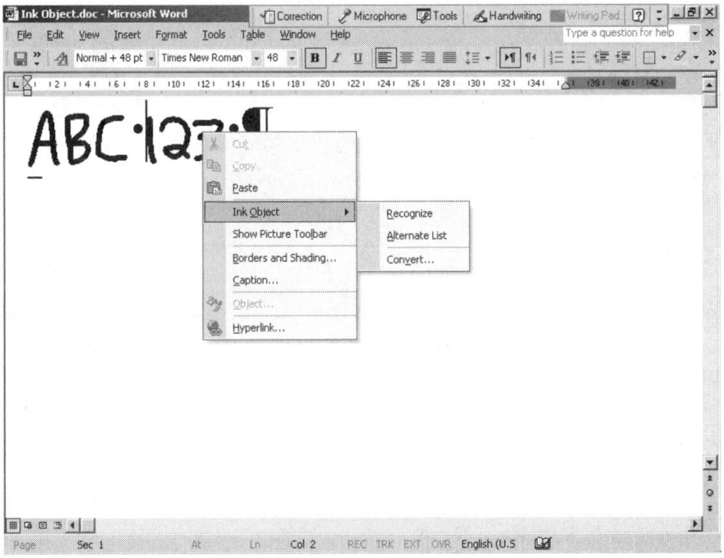

Figure 39-15. An Ink Object looks like it is a graphic, but it really is complex data that can be converted into text by Word's Handwriting Recognition.

Correct Handwritten Information

The procedures for correcting speech errors noted earlier in the section "Correcting Speech Recognition Errors" also apply to handwriting. To correct a word, click Correction on the Language bar or right-click the word, as shown in Figure 39-16. Either way, you get a list of alternative words from which to choose. You can also just type over an error. As with speech, Word learns from practice, so correcting the program's mistakes improves accuracy in the long term. And just as speech correction plays back a recording of what you dictated, a list of possible corrections for handwriting shows you a graphic of your original handwriting.

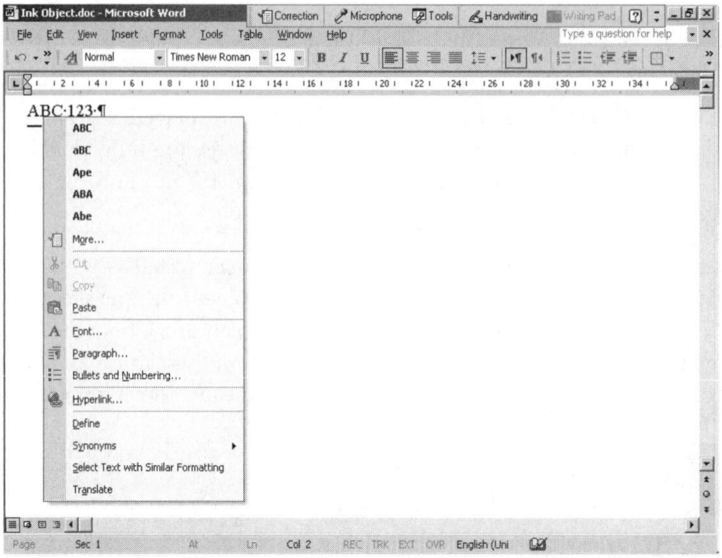

Figure 39-16. If there is error in recognition, you can correct it by choosing an alternate word.

Inserting a Quick Sketch

Operating Drawing Pad is straightforward: you simply use your pointing tool to draw a sketch in the pad, and when you click Insert Drawing, Word inserts the drawing in the document at the insertion point as a standard Word drawing object. To control your pointing tool's line color and thickness when you work with the Drawing Pad, perform the following steps:

1. Click Handwriting, Drawing Pad on the Language toolbar to open the Drawing Pad.
2. In the Drawing Pad, click the Down arrow in the title bar, and choose Options.
3. The Draw Options dialog box opens, as shown in Figure 39-17.
4. Choose a color in the Pen Color list box, and choose a line width in the Pen Width list box, and then click OK to apply the settings.

While the Drawing Pad is a convenient tool on the Language toolbar, if you want to create more complex drawings, you should use the Drawing Canvas instead of the Drawing Pad. To learn more about the Drawing Canvas, see Chapter 16, "Enlivening Documents with Drawings and AutoShapes."

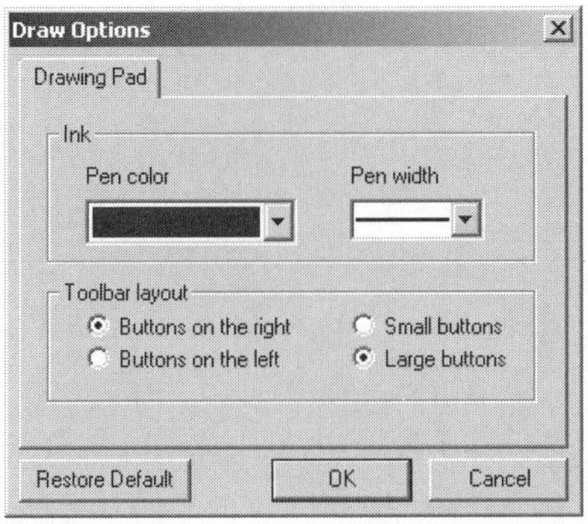

Figure 39-17. You can control how lines appear on your Drawing Pad by configuring the settings in the Draw Options dialog box.

tip **Insert your signature using Drawing Pad**

You can use Drawing Pad to "sign" your letters and other documents. Simply write your name with your pen or mouse, and your signature is placed in your document. Since it is an ordinary drawing object, it can be formatted and resized as needed. You can also turn it into an AutoText entry to reuse it later. Of course, keep in mind that electronic signatures aren't commonly accepted yet as reliable signatures for legal and identification purposes.

Saving and Turning Off Handwriting Recognition

As with Speech Recognition, you permanently remove Handwriting Recognition by using Windows Control Panel. Click Start and choose Settings, Control Panel, and double click Add/Remove Programs in Control Panel. Next, choose Microsoft Word (or Office), click Change, Add Or Remove Features. Navigate to the Handwriting feature by choosing Office Shared Features, Alternative User Input, and Handwriting. From the list of Handwriting options, click Not Available. Finally, click Update to save your changes and remove the Handwriting feature from your system. (For more information about installing Speech Recognition, see "Introducing Speech and Handwriting Recognition Tools" on page 928.)

note Closing Writing Pad, Drawing Pad, and the two on-screen keyboards will stop Handwriting Recognition in the current work session, but your input tool—be it pen, tablet, or whatever—will continue to be seen by Windows as a pointing device.

Chapter 40

Creating and Working with VBA Macros

If you find that you perform certain tasks repeatedly, you might be able to simplify your life by creating Visual Basic for Applications (VBA) macros. Properly used, VBA macros can perform some of your work for you. Many people find themselves cringing at the mere mention of the word macros, but there's really no reason to be intimidated. Simply put, a *macro* is a series of commands and instructions that are grouped together as a single command. For example, you can record a macro that creates a particularly formatted table and assign the macro to a toolbar button. Then, the next time you want to create a table with the same formatting, you simply click the toolbar button—nothing magical about it, but certainly a welcome convenience!

People typically create macros to perform the following tasks:

- Automate a complex series of steps
- Combine multiple commands (such as formatting and inserting tables with a single command)
- Make menu commands and submenu commands more quickly accessible
- Speed up editing and formatting procedures

As you start to use macros, you'll find that they come in handy in a number of situations and let you fully customize your working environment.

In Microsoft Word, you can create and run macros in a few main ways: You can view and run existing Word commands, record macros using the Macro Recorder, and hand-code macros using the Microsoft Visual Basic Editor (VBE). In this chapter, you'll be introduced to the built-in Word commands, and you'll also learn how to create a macro using the Macro Recorder. We'll also look briefly at the VBE (see the sidebar "Initiating a Macro in the VBE," on page 965), but learning all the ins and outs of using this tool is beyond the scope of this book.

Using Built-In Word Commands

Before you start to create your own macros, you should familiarize yourself with Word's built-in commands. As you might imagine, Word provides a number of built-in commands (over 900), and many of them are already associated with toolbar buttons, menu commands, and keyboard shortcuts. For example, the FileClose command is attached to the File menu's Close command. You can view, run, and associate Word commands with toolbar buttons, menus, and keyboard shortcuts in the same ways you perform these actions with macros you create.

Viewing Existing Word Commands

As mentioned, you can run Word's built-in commands in the same way you run macros. Some of these commands you use regularly without realizing it (such as when you click the Print button on the Standard toolbar), but others aren't assigned to toolbar buttons or menu commands by default.

To view a list of Word's built-in commands, follow these steps:

1. Choose Tools, Macro, Macros, or press Alt+F8. The Macros dialog box appears.
2. Click the Macros In down arrow, and select Word Commands in the drop-down list. The list of built-in Word commands appears, as shown in Figure 40-1.
3. Scroll through the list of Word commands. When you select a Word command's name, the Description box shows a brief description of the command's action. To perform the described action, click the Run button. If you'd rather not perform any actions at this point, click Cancel to close the Macros dialog box.

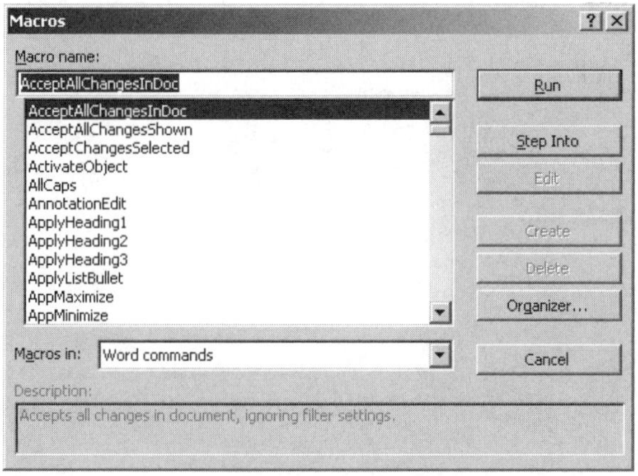

Figure 40-1. Using the Macros dialog box, you can display and run Word's built-in commands.

To see a list of built-in Word commands along with short descriptions, refer to Appendix C, "Word Macros." If you see any commands you think you might be able to use, you can create toolbar buttons, menu commands, or keyboard shortcuts based on the commands, as described in the next section.

Assigning Shortcuts to Word Commands

Once you're familiar with the built-in Word commands, you might find that you'd like quicker access to them. The process of displaying and running commands from the Macros dialog box isn't the most streamlined approach. To make selected Word commands more accessible, you can assign them to toolbar buttons, menu commands, or keyboard shortcuts, as follows:

1. Choose Tools, Customize. The Customize dialog box appears.
2. Click the Commands tab, and then select All Commands in the Categories list. The complete list of available Word commands that you can use for customization is displayed in the Commands list, as shown in Figure 40-2, on the next page. As you scroll through this list, notice that a number of the Word commands have a custom toolbar button already associated with them, which appears in the gray column to the left of the command names.

> **tip** If you want to remove a toolbar button or menu command—regardless of when it was added—you can drag the toolbar button or menu command off its toolbar or menu while the Customize dialog box is open.

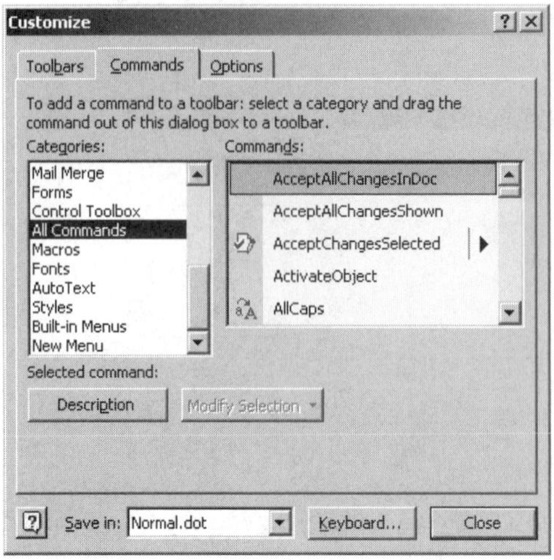

Figure 40-2. The Commands tab shows all the available commands when you click All Commands in the Categories list.

3 To see a description of a command, select the command in the Commands list, and click the Description button. The descriptions are displayed in a ScreenTip and are generally more in-depth than the descriptions provided in the Macros dialog box.

4 To add a command to a toolbar or menu, select the command in the Commands list, and drag the command to the toolbar or menu. To create a keyboard shortcut, click the Keyboard button, and configure the options in the Customize Keyboard dialog box. (For more information about creating toolbar buttons, menu commands, and keyboard shortcuts, see the section "Assigning a Macro to a Toolbar, a Menu, or a Keyboard Shortcut," on page 967.)

5 When you finish customizing your Word window, click Close in the Customize dialog box.

After you display a Word command as a menu command or toolbar button, you can right-click your newly created element to configure its display parameters, as described in the section "Assigning a Macro to a Toolbar or Menu," on page 967. Likewise, if you click the Keyboard button in the Customize dialog box to create a keyboard shortcut, you can configure your custom keyboard shortcut by completing the Customize Keyboard dialog box, as discussed in the section "Assigning a Macro to a Toolbar, a Menu, or a Keyboard Shortcut," on page 967.

Creating Macros Using the Macro Recorder

As mentioned, you can create macros by using the Macro Recorder, by entering VBA code in the VBE, or by using both tools in combination (for example, you could record the bulk of your macro's code using the Macro Recorder and then tweak the code in the VBE). In this section, we'll look at creating macros by using the Macro Recorder.

Planning a Macro

Regardless of how you create a macro, you need to gather your thoughts before you start. This is especially true when you're creating macros using the Macro Recorder. When you run the Macro Recorder, it tracks all your movements—including any corrections you make along the way. As you can imagine, because Word records every action, the more movements and commands you perform (including any commands you undo), the larger your macro becomes. Therefore, you'll want to make sure that you've outlined the most streamlined approach to creating your macro before you start to record the procedure. If necessary, you might even jot down some notes before you start the recorder. You should consider the following items before creating your macro:

- Carefully plan the steps and commands you want the macro to perform.
- Make sure that you know the keyboard shortcuts you need to use, especially for moving within the document text. (You can't use the mouse in the body of the document when you use the Macro Recorder.) Also keep in mind that using keyboard shortcuts to move around your document is generally more accurate than using the arrow keys. (For example, pressing Ctrl+End to move to the end of your document is more efficient than pressing the Down Arrow key 10 times.)

For more information about using keyboard shortcuts, see Chapter 2, "Creating Documents from Start to Finish."

- Take at least one practice run through the procedure, and take notes, if necessary.
- Anticipate any messages that Word might display that might halt your macro or seem confusing when the macro is run. (For example, if your macro includes using the Find or Replace command on the Edit menu, click More on the Find or Replace tab, and then click All in the Search box. Otherwise, if the macro searches only up or down in the document, it will stop when it reaches the beginning or end of the document and display a message box.)
- Make sure that your macro doesn't depend on the current document's content.

tip **Create a macro that formats text**

If you want to create a macro that formats text, select the text before you start the Macro Recorder, and then run the Macro Recorder and format the selected text as desired, preferably by using keyboard shortcuts or clicking toolbar buttons instead of opening the Font formatting dialog box.

After you've carefully planned the purpose and process of your macro, you're ready to run the recorder. Remember, running the recorder creates Visual Basic code, so you'll be able to view your macro and edit its code after you record it.

Initiating a Recording Procedure

To begin recording a macro, you must first open the Record Macro dialog box, shown in Figure 40-3, by choosing Tools, Macro, Record New Macro. The Record Macro dialog box enables you to set a number of macro parameters before you actually record your macro.

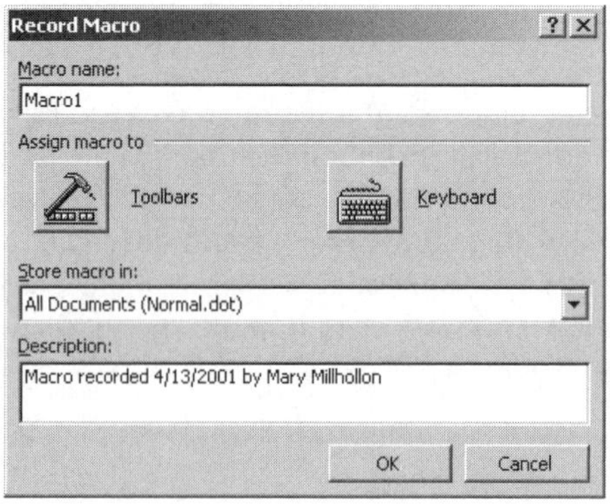

Figure 40-3. The Record Macro dialog box is a one-stop shop for configuring many macro settings.

Using the Record Macro dialog box, you can name your macro, specify how you'll access the macro after it's created, indicate where to store your macro, and add a description, if desired. Although you can configure and change these settings after you create the macro, your best bet is to address these issues up front, while the Record Macro dialog box is open and waiting for your input. If you postpone these tasks, you might overlook them later.

Initiating a Macro in the VBE

This chapter focuses on using the Macro Recorder to create macros, but you can hand-code your macros from the get-go if you want. To begin creating a macro in the VBE, follow these steps:

1. Choose Tools, Macro, Macros.
2. In the Macros dialog box, type a name for your macro in the Macro Name box. (For information about naming macros, see the section "Naming a Macro," below.)
3. If necessary, ensure that the Macros In drop-down list displays the template or document in which you want to create the macro.
4. Click Create.

The VBE opens (as shown later in this chapter, in Figure 40-9), in which you can enter VBA code to create your macro.

Naming a Macro

As you can see in Figure 40-3, the Record Macro dialog box contains a Macro Name box. By default, Word provides a name for your macro, such as Macro1, Macro2, and so forth. This default naming scheme is very vague. Most likely, you'll want to associate a more descriptive name with your macro (and this practice is highly recommended). Fortunately, you can supply any name for your macro as long as you abide by the following guidelines:

- The macro name must begin with a letter.
- The macro name can contain numbers.
- The macro name can contain up to 80 letters and numbers.
- The macro name can't contain spaces or symbols.

If you type a macro name that's invalid, an error message will appear after you click OK, as shown in Figure 40-4, on the next page. If you see this error message, click OK, and then choose Tools, Macro, Record New Macro to restart the macro creation process.

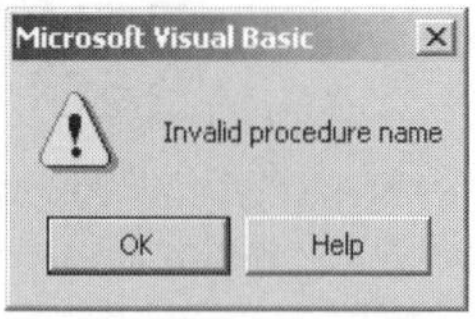

Figure 40-4. Word displays an error message if you type an invalid name in the Macro Name box in the Record Macro dialog box.

caution If you give a new macro the same name as an existing macro or Word command, the new macro's actions will replace the existing actions. You should be especially careful not to inadvertently replace existing Word commands. If you attempt to create a macro with the same name as an existing macro, Word will display a warning message box asking whether you would like to replace the existing macro. At that point, you can click Yes to replace the existing macro or click No to return to the Record Macro dialog box (in which case, you can enter a new name for your macro or click Cancel to halt the creation process).

Storing a Macro

In the Record Macro dialog box, you can also specify the location in which you'll store the macro. You can store macros in templates or in individual documents. Your macro is available only when the document or template in which it is stored is open. Most commonly, macros are stored in the Normal template, which means that the macros can be run at any time (because the Normal template is a global template, as described in Chapter 22, "Formatting Documents Using Templates, Wizards, and Add-Ins"). You can store macros in the following locations:

- **Active document.** If you plan to use a macro in a single document, you can store the macro directly in the document. When you choose this option, the macro will run only when the document is the active document.
- **All documents (Normal.dot).** You can store a macro in the Normal template, thereby making the macro available to all open files. By default, Word stores macros you create in the Normal template.
- **Template.** You can store a macro in a template other than the Normal template if a template is attached to the current document or open when you create the macro. When you do this, the macro is available only when the template is opened or attached to the active document.

To specify where you want to store a macro, open the Record Macro dialog box (by choosing Tools, Macro, Record New Macro), click the Store Macro In down arrow, and then select the location where you'd like to store the macro in the drop-down list.

Associating a Description with a Macro

The Record Macro dialog box also enables you to provide a brief description of macros you create. This description is helpful for future use, especially if you're planning to share the macro with others or if you modify or update an existing macro. By default, Word provides the date and author of a macro in the Description box. You can edit or delete this information and add custom information by typing in the Description box. Keep in mind that you can't edit text in the Description box for Word commands and other read-only macros.

Assigning a Macro to a Toolbar, a Menu, or a Keyboard Shortcut

When you create a macro, you can assign the macro to a keyboard shortcut, a toolbar button, or a menu command (or you can choose not to create an association). If you choose to create a toolbar, menu, or keyboard shortcut association, the recording process will begin directly after you make the assignment. If you opt not to associate the macro with a toolbar, menu, or keyboard shortcut, you're ready to begin recording, as described in the section "Recording a Macro," on page 970. In this section, you'll learn how to create associations for your macros.

note If you don't assign some sort of shortcut to your macro, you'll need to open the Macros dialog box, select the macro name, and then click Run each time you want to run your macro.

Assigning a Macro to a Toolbar or Menu

As mentioned, you can associate a macro with a toolbar button or menu command to make the macro easily accessible. As you'll see, customizing your toolbars or menus with macro commands is similar to customizing toolbars and menus in general. To create a toolbar button or menu command association for your macro, follow these steps:

1. In the Record Macro dialog box (choose Tools, Macro, Record New Macro), click the Toolbars button.
2. In the Customize dialog box, click the Commands tab, shown in Figure 40-5, on the next page.
3. In the Commands list, click the name of the macro you're recording, and drag the macro to the appropriate toolbar or menu.

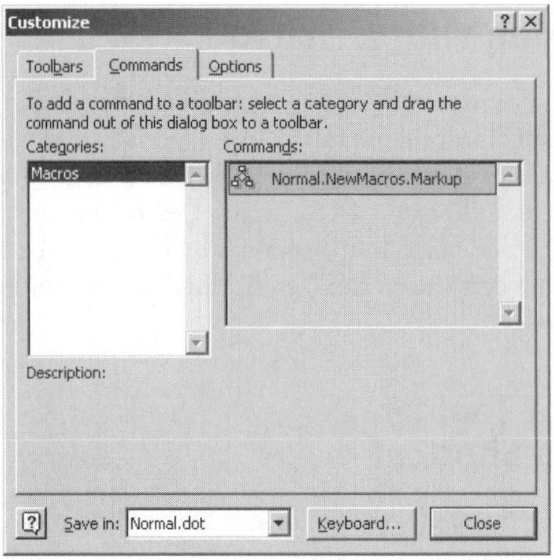

Figure 40-5. You can add a macro toolbar button or menu command by dragging the macro from the Customize dialog box onto a toolbar or menu.

4 After you add a macro to a toolbar or menu, you can customize the appearance of the macro by right-clicking it and choosing options on the shortcut menu. Figure 40-6 shows the shortcut menu you can use to customize a toolbar button. Notice that you can assign a button image to your newly created macro toolbar button.

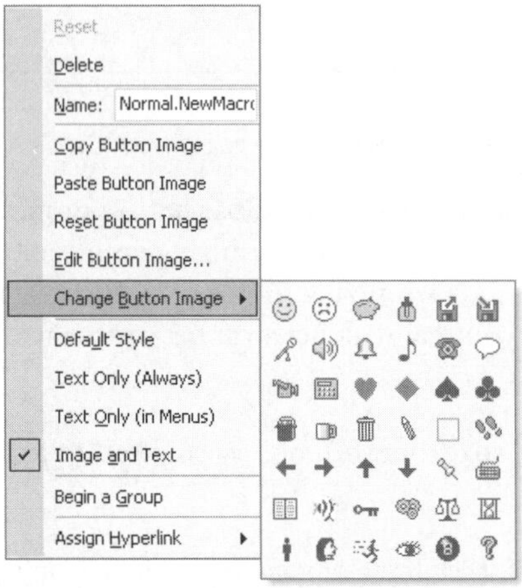

Figure 40-6. After you drag your macro to a toolbar or menu, you can customize its appearance by right-clicking it and choosing options on the shortcut menu.

The Customize dialog box also contains a Keyboard button (as shown in Figure 40-5). You can use this button to assign a keyboard shortcut to your macro in addition to creating a toolbar button or menu command, as described in the next section.

> For more information about customizing menus and adding toolbar buttons, see Chapter 38, "Customizing Word to Suit Working Environments and Maximize Accessibility."

Assigning a Macro to a Keyboard Shortcut

In addition to creating toolbar buttons and menu commands, you can associate your macros with keyboard shortcuts. You might want to do this if a menu command already exists but you prefer to use a keyboard command instead of continually opening the menu. Perhaps you'd like to create a macro that turns the markup feature on and off and assign a keyboard shortcut to the macro. That way, instead of choosing View, Markup each time you want to view the markup in the current document, you could simply press a keyboard shortcut that toggles the changes on and off.

To assign a macro to a keyboard shortcut, follow these steps:

1. In the Record Macro dialog box (choose Tools, Macro, Record New Macro) or in the Customize dialog box (discussed in the preceding section), click the Keyboard button. The Customize Keyboard dialog box opens.
2. By default, the insertion point is in the Press New Shortcut Key box. Press the key combination you want to assign to your macro, as shown in Figure 40-7, and then click Assign and click Close.

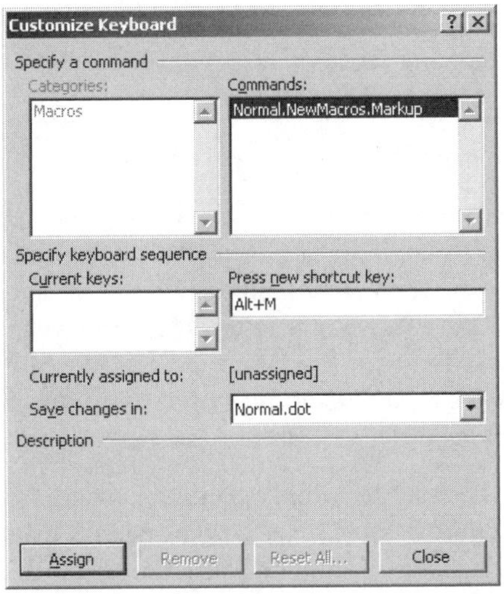

Figure 40-7. You can use the Customize Keyboard dialog box to assign keyboard shortcuts to your macros.

When you create keyboard shortcuts, make sure you don't overwrite an existing keyboard shortcut. In the example in Figure 40-7, the keyboard shortcut Alt+M is being assigned. The Currently Assigned To field indicates that the combination isn't assigned to another command in Word. If the command were already being used by another command, the dialog box would indicate that the combination is already in use and display the command that's using it. For example, if you attempt to assign Ctrl+P to a macro, Word would indicate that the FilePrint command already uses that keyboard shortcut. To assign another keyboard shortcut, delete the entry in the Press New Shortcut Key box, and try another combination.

> **tip** When you create keyboard shortcuts, consider using Alt+*letter* instead of Ctrl+*letter*. Many Ctrl+*letter* keyboard combinations already exist in Word, so you might find it a bit tricky to find an available combination.

Recording a Macro

After you configure the settings in the Record Macro dialog box, you're ready to record your macro. To begin recording, click OK in the Record Macro dialog box. (If you assigned your macro to a toolbar button, menu command, or keyboard shortcut, the Macro Recorder will begin automatically after you complete the assignment procedure.) When the Macro Recorder begins, the Record Macro dialog box closes, and the Stop Recording toolbar, shown in Figure 40-8, is displayed. You're officially in record mode. The actions you take from this point on will be recorded in your macro.

Figure 40-8. The Stop Recording toolbar is small, but it contains the buttons you need to stop and pause your recording session.

> **tip** **Avoid mixing macros and mice movements**
>
> As mentioned in the section "Planning a Macro," on page 963, when you use the Macro Recorder, you can use your mouse to click commands, toolbar buttons, and menu commands, but the recorder won't record mouse movements in your document window. You'll need to use keyboard commands to record those movements. For example, if you're adding column headings in a table, you'll need to press Tab to indicate a movement from one cell to another instead of clicking in each cell.

If you need to, you can pause the recorder while recording a macro. You might want to do this to avoid adding extra (unnecessary) steps to your macro's VBA code. To pause the recorder while recording a macro, you use the Pause button on the Stop Recording toolbar, as follows:

Pause Recording

1. On the Stop Recording toolbar, click the Pause Recording button.
2. Perform any actions you don't want to record.
3. To resume recording, click the Resume Recorder button on the Stop Recording toolbar.

tip You should avoid adding extra steps to your macros whenever possible because extra steps mean extra VBA coding, which in turn results in bigger macros and larger file sizes.

After you finish recording your macro, click the Stop button on the Stop Recording toolbar, or choose Tools, Macro, Stop Recording. Your macro is now ready to run.

Saving Macros

When you create macros, they aren't automatically saved. In fact, macros aren't saved until you save the documents in which the macros are stored. Therefore, after you create a macro, you should immediately save your documents. You can easily save all open documents and templates by using Word's Save All command. To do so, press Shift, and then choose File, Save All. After you save the documents containing your macros, you should run your macros to verify that they work as planned.

Editing and Viewing Macro VBA Code

If you encounter any undesirable traits or errors when you test a macro, you can edit the macro. To do so, you open the macro in the VBE, where you can make corrections, remove unnecessary steps, rename or copy the macro, or add instructions that you can't record in Word. To open a macro for editing in the VBE, follow these steps:

1. Choose Tools, Macro, Macros. The Macros dialog box opens.
2. In the Macro Name list, select the name of the macro you want to edit. If the macro you're looking for isn't displayed, click the Macros In down arrow, and select a different document or template in the drop-down list.
3. Click Edit. The VBE appears, as shown in Figure 40-9, on page 973.

note If you select a macro that's read-only, the Edit button will be disabled and appear dimmed.

Of course, if you prefer not to edit the VBA code to correct your macro, you can simply delete the macro and run the macro recorder again. Deleting macros is described in the section "Deleting Macros and Macro Projects," on page 978.

Keeping Your Macro Code Trim

When you record a macro and you add a command that displays a dialog box (such as choosing Format, Paragraph to open the Paragraph dialog box), Word records everything in the dialog box. In contrast, clicking toolbar buttons creates much more concise code. For example, let's say that part of your macro calls for right-aligning a paragraph. If you choose Format, Paragraph and set right-alignment by configuring the Paragraph dialog box settings while recording a macro, the following information will be inserted into your macro's code. (Notice that the alignment information is contained on a single line.)

```
With Selection.ParagraphFormat
        .LeftIndent = InchesToPoints(0)
        .RightIndent = InchesToPoints(0)
        .SpaceBefore = 0
        .SpaceBeforeAuto = False
        .SpaceAfter = 0
        .SpaceAfterAuto = False
        .LineSpacingRule = wdLineSpaceSingle
        .Alignment = wdAlignParagraphRight
        .WidowControl = True
        .KeepWithNext = False
        .KeepTogether = False
        .PageBreakBefore = False
        .NoLineNumber = False
        .Hyphenation = True
        .FirstLineIndent = InchesToPoints(0)
        .OutlineLevel = wdOutlineLevelBodyText
        .CharacterUnitLeftIndent = 0
        .CharacterUnitRightIndent = 0
        .CharacterUnitFirstLineIndent = 0
        .LineUnitBefore = 0
        .LineUnitAfter = 0
    End With
```

In contrast, if you click the Align Right button on the Formatting toolbar instead of opening the Paragraph dialog box, Word creates the following code for your macro:

```
Selection.ParagraphFormat.Alignment = wdAlignParagraphRight
```

In either case, your paragraph will be right-aligned, but the amount of VBA code used to create the effect differs dramatically. As you'd expect, using the single line of code

(continued)

Keeping Your Macro Code Trim *(continued)* approach is preferable because it's the more processor-efficient way of accomplishing a task.

You can compare how various procedures appear in VBA by creating your macro and noting the commands you use. Then view your macro's code in the VBE. You can rework your macro and view the VBA code each time until you find the combination that seems the most efficient.

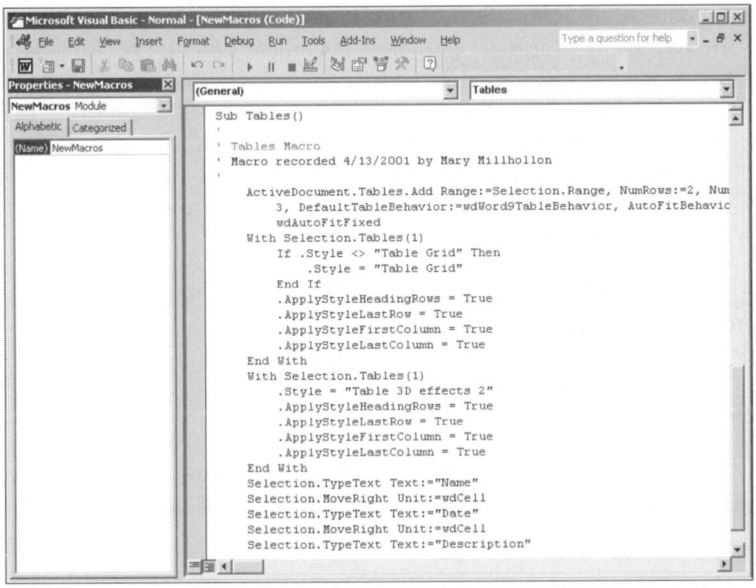

Figure 40-9. The VBE shows you the VBA code used to run your macros.

Running Macros

After you create a macro, you can run it using any of the following techniques:

- Click the macro's toolbar button or menu command.
- Press the macro's keyboard shortcut.
- Open the Macros dialog box (by pressing Alt+F8), select the macro in the Macro Name list, and click Run.

Users typically access macros by clicking toolbar buttons, choosing menu commands, or pressing keyboard shortcuts. But in some cases, you might want to store an infrequently used macro in your document or template, without making the macro instantly accessible—in other words, you might want a macro to be available when you need it, but you don't need to use it every time you work in Word. In those cases, you should simply create and store your macro in your document or template and then run the macro from within the Macros dialog box whenever you need to complete the desired procedure.

Copying Macros to Other Templates or Documents

When you create macros in a document or template, Word stores the macros as a single *macro project*. Simply stated, a macro project is a collection of macros grouped under one name and stored as a single entity in a document or template. Each document or template has one macro project that contains all the macros you've created for that document or template. By default, when you record macros, Word stores the VBA code in a macro project named NewMacros. You can manipulate a macro project in a number of ways by using the Organizer. For instance, you can copy a macro project from one document or template to another document or template, you can delete a macro project, or you can rename it.

In this section, we'll look at copying macro projects to other documents or templates by using the Organizer. To do so, follow these steps:

1. Choose Tools, Macro, Macros (or press Alt+F8) to open the Macros dialog box.

2. Click Organizer, and then click the Macro Project Items tab. Figure 40-10 shows the Organizer dialog box with the NewMacros macro project stored in the Normal template.

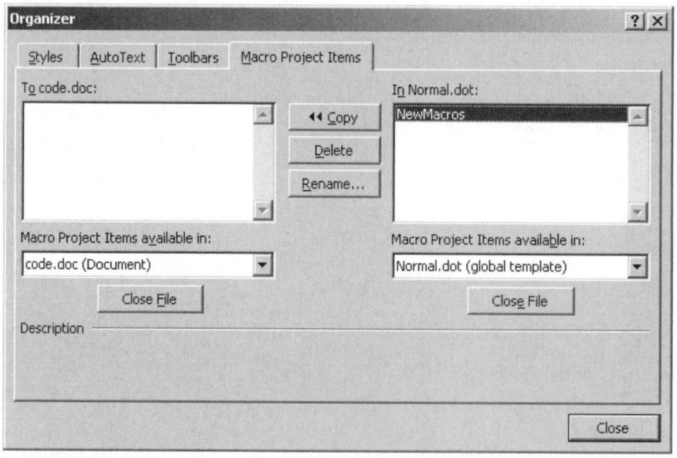

Figure 40-10. You can use the Organizer dialog box to copy, delete, and rename macro projects.

3. To copy the macro project from a template or document, display the desired documents or templates by clicking Close File and then clicking Open File to find and open the desired document or template.
4. Click the macro project you want to copy (in whichever list the item appears), and then click Copy to copy the macro project to the other currently displayed document or template (which should appear in the other list).
5. Click Close to close the Organizer dialog box.

tip If you have assigned macros to toolbars, you should also copy the toolbars by using the Toolbars tab in the Organizer dialog box.

When you copy a macro project to another document or template, you copy all the macros you've created to the other file. After you copy a macro project to another file, you can open the Macros dialog box in that file to edit, delete, or add individual macros.

Renaming Macro Projects

Renaming macro projects is similar to copying them. To rename a macro project, display the macro project in either list on the Macro Project Items tab in the Organizer dialog box (shown in Figure 40-10), select the macro project name, and then click the Rename button. The Rename dialog box appears, as shown in Figure 40-11. This dialog box is extremely straightforward—you simply type a new name for your macro project and then click OK.

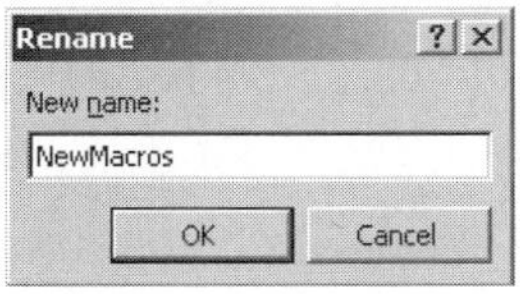

Figure 40-11. To rename a macro project, simply enter a new name in the Rename dialog box.

Signing a Macro with a Digital Signature

For added security, you can digitally sign your macros by attaching digital certificates to them. But before you can use this security measure, you must have a digital certificate installed on your computer. For more information about obtaining and using digital certificates, see Chapter 34, "Addressing Security Issues."

After you've installed a digital certificate, you can digitally sign a macro as follows:

1 Open the file that contains the macro project you want to sign.

2 Choose Tools, Macro, Visual Basic Editor, or press Alt+F11.

3 In the Project Explorer window of the VBE, select the macro project you want to sign in the Procedure drop-down list.

note You can also display a selected macro in the VBE by choosing Tools, Macro, Macros to open the Macros dialog box, selecting the macro you want to sign in the Macro Name list, and then clicking the Edit button. The VBE window opens and displays the code for the selected macro.

4 Choose Tools, Digital Signature. The Digital Signature dialog box opens, as shown in Figure 40-12.

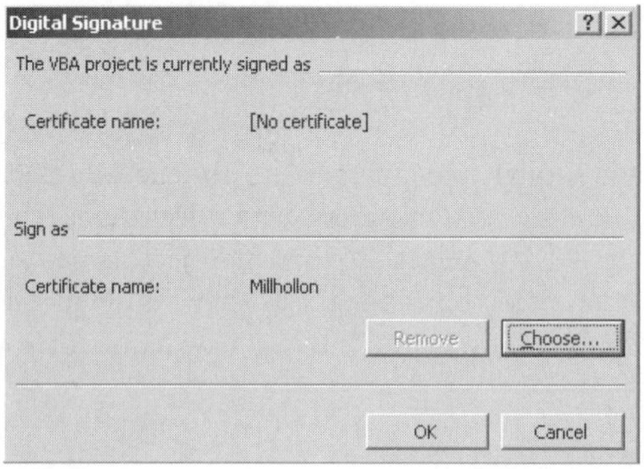

Figure 40-12. To help provide security, the Digital Signature dialog box enables you to sign your macros with a digital certificate.

5 In the Digital Signature dialog box, perform either of the following actions:

- If you haven't previously selected a digital certificate or want to assign a different certificate, click Choose. The Select Certificate dialog box appears, as shown in Figure 40-13. Select the certificate you want to use, and then click OK twice.
- To use the current certificate, if one is specified, click OK.

6 After you sign your macro, close the VBE and save your document.

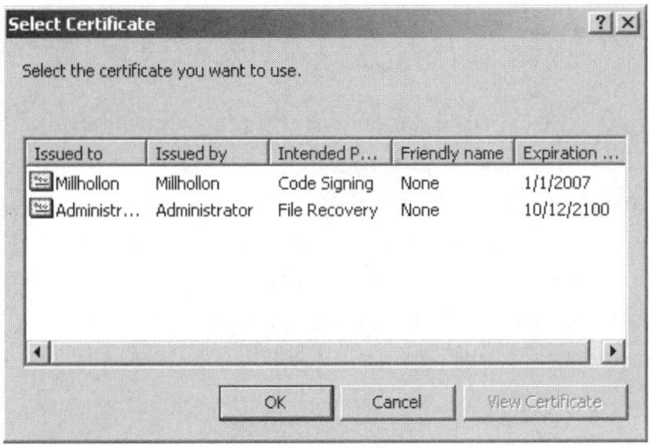

Figure 40-13. The Select Certificate dialog box displays a list of certificates that you can use to sign your macros.

As a rule, you should digitally sign a macro only after you've completed the creation process, including testing the macro. Whenever signed code is modified, the digital signature is removed. If you have the proper digital certificate on your computer, the macro will then be automatically resigned when it is saved. As you can see, editing a signed macro causes your computer to perform extra processing. In addition, if you're working on a computer that doesn't contain your digital certificate information, modifying your macro will remove the digital certificate, and the certificate won't be reattached when you save your changes.

Changing the Security Level for Macro Virus Protection

Another security-related macro issue involves setting the security level in Word. You can specify whether you want Word to treat documents that contain macros with a high, medium, or low security level. To configure your security level, follow these steps:

1. Choose Tools, Macro, Security.
2. In the Security dialog box, click the Security Level tab, and then specify whether you want High, Medium, or Low security.
3. Click OK to apply the security level.

For more information about Word's security levels and how Word handles each security level, see Chapter 34, "Addressing Security Issues."

Deleting Macros and Macro Projects

The last technique you should master when creating macros is how to delete them. You'll find that deleting macros sometimes comes into play during the creation process. For example, you might want to test-drive a few versions of a particular macro before you settle on a final version. Or you might want to delete a macro simply because you don't need it anymore or you're trying to reduce your document's file size. Regardless of your reason for deleting macros, you can do so in two ways: You can delete an individual macro, or you can delete an entire macro project (which contains all the macros in a selected document or template).

Deleting a Single Macro

You can easily delete any macro you create by opening the Macros dialog box and deleting the macro. To do so, follow these steps:

1. Choose Tools, Macro, Macros.
2. In the Macros dialog box, select the name of the macro you want to delete in the Macro Name list. If the macro isn't displayed, choose a different document, template, or list in the Macros In drop-down list.
3. Click Delete. Word displays a message box asking you to verify that you're sincere about deleting the macro.
4. Click Yes (unless you suddenly change your mind, in which case you should click No to end the process without deleting the macro).
5. Click Close to close the Macros dialog box.

Once you delete a macro, it's gone. If you decide that you'd like to use the macro after you've deleted it, you'll have to re-create the macro from scratch.

Deleting a Macro Project

In addition to deleting individual macros from within the Macros dialog box, you can delete an entire macro project by using the Organizer. When you delete a macro project, you delete all the macros you've created and added to a document or template.

caution After you delete a macro project and save the document or template, there's no way to recover the macro project.

To delete a macro project, follow these steps:

1. Choose Tools, Macro, Macros (or press Alt+F8) to open the Macros dialog box.
2. Click Organizer to open the Organizer dialog box.
3. Select the macro project you want to delete from the appropriate list, and click Delete.
4. Word displays a message box asking whether you're sure you want to delete the macro project. Click Yes to continue.
5. Click Close to close the Organizer dialog box.

By default, Word displays the macro projects contained in the current document in the left list and the macro projects stored in the Normal template in the right list. You can use either list to navigate to the document or template of your choice.

Part 11

Appendixes

Appendix A

Installing and Repairing Microsoft Word 2002

If you purchase Microsoft Word 2002 as part of the Microsoft Office XP package, as most people do, Word is installed by default when you install Office. Whether you're installing or upgrading your version of Word, you use the Microsoft Office XP Setup Wizard to lead you through the process. This appendix explains how to install and repair your version of Office XP.

note Office XP does not work with systems that are running Windows 3.x, Windows NT 3.5x, or Windows 95. For system hardware and software requirements, see the sidebar "Hardware and Software Requirements for Word 2002," on the next page.

Preparing to Install

The installation process is as simple as inserting the CD in the drive, launching the Setup utility, and following the prompts on the screen. As you prepare to install Office on your computer, however, here are a few things to keep in mind:

- If you're working on a corporate network, contact your system administrator before installing anything on your individual system.
- If you're working on a home network or a stand-alone system, make sure that you have the hardware and software required before beginning the installation (see the sidebar "Hardware and Software Requirements for Word 2002," for a listing of requirements).
- If you begin having trouble with your version of Word or want to add features you didn't install initially, you can run the Microsoft Office XP Setup Wizard at any time after the first installation.

note If you're installing, upgrading, or running Word 2002 on a network, check with your system administrator before making any changes to your existing system. If Word is already available on a network server, you can save time for your local installation by launching the Microsoft Office XP Setup Wizard directly from the server.

Hardware and Software Requirements for Word 2002

Basic System Requirements:

- Microsoft Windows 2000, Microsoft Windows 98, Microsoft Windows NT 4 with Service Pack 6a or later, or Microsoft Windows Millennium Edition
- An x86-compatible PC that is capable of running Windows 98 or Microsoft Windows NT 4
- A Pentium 90 MHz processor
- 32 MB RAM (minimum); 64 MB (recommended)
- 350 MB of available hard-disk space
- CD-ROM drive

Special Cconsiderations:

- For Windows NT systems, allow 4 MB space for Windows NT registry.
- If you're using multiple languages, allow 50 MB for each language user interface you'll be using. Microsoft recommends that you use the same language version for the operating system and the Office version you install.

Installing Office XP

Be sure that you've backed up all important files before you begin your install. Then follow these steps to install Office:

1. Insert the first Office XP CD in the drive and follow the instructions on your screen until the Choose The Type Of Installation page appears. (See Figure A-1.) (If setup doesn't start automatically when you insert the CD, display the contents of your CD and double-click Setup.exe to launch the setup utility.)
2. Select Install Now, Complete, or Custom for the installation. Selecting Install Now installs the typical Office configuration and settings. Complete installs all of the Office applications in your version of Office XP. Custom enables you to choose only the Office features you want to install.
3. Click Next, and follow the prompts on the screen to complete the installation.
4. When the Microsoft Office XP Setup Wizard is finished copying files, a message box appears, telling you that the setup completed successfully. Click OK to close the message box.

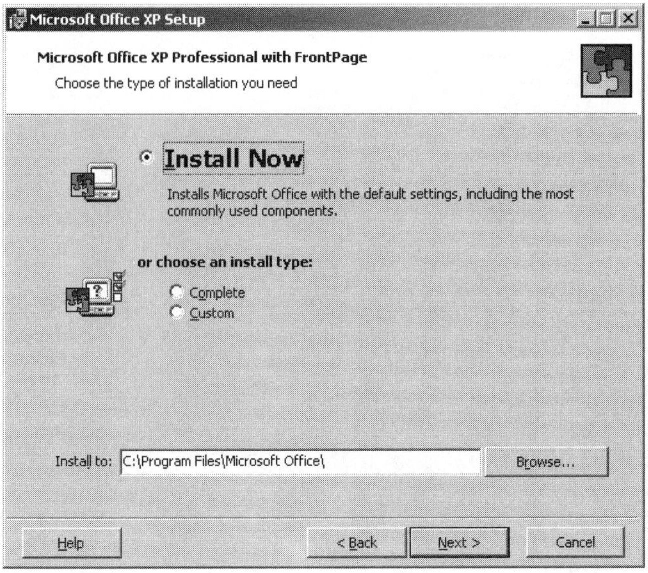

Figure A-1. The setup wizard presents you with the choices of a Complete or Custom installation.

> **tip** **Install the Multilanguage Pack**
>
> Office XP comes with a new and improved Multilanguage Pack, complete with its own installation wizard. To install the Multilanguage features, insert your Language Pack CD into the drive and follow the prompts on the screen. Select the languages you want to set up in Office, and click Next to continue. The wizard leads you through the process. For more information on working with Multilanguage features, see Chapter 37, "Implementing Multilanguage Features."

Adding and Removing Items

At any time during your use of Word, you can add or remove features or change the way the various items work. To make changes to the features installed in Word, use Add/Remove Programs in the Control Panel window. Here are the steps:

1. Choose Start, Settings, Control Panel.
2. Double-click Add/Remove Programs.
3. Scroll to the Microsoft Office XP icon, and click it.
4. Click the Change button. The wizard presents you with choices for modifying, repairing, or removing Office XP. (See Figure A-2, on the next page.)
5. Follow the prompts to make changes as needed.

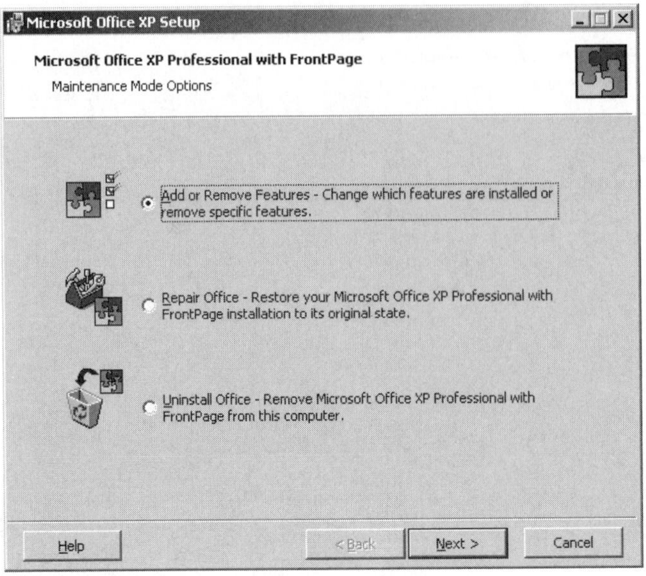

Figure A-2. The Microsoft Office XP Setup Wizard gives you choices for changing, repairing, or uninstalling Office.

Repairing Word

From time to time, you might notice problems with Word. It happens to the best of us—after a series of lock-ups or badly timed power outages, we have bits and pieces of files on our computer that can seem to hinder Word's performance or cause unexpected results.

Although Word 2002's Crash Recovery and AutoRecover features help to restore the data files you're using when a crash occurs, over time, repeated lock-ups can leave behind file fragments that slow down program performance. You can use Word's Detect And Repair command (available on the Help menu) to have Word look for and correct any of those barely noticed problems that might eventually get in your way.

Detect And Repair searches your Office installation for corrupted files and then reinstalls any damaged files it finds. To use Detect And Repair, follow these steps:

1. Insert the first Office XP CD in the drive.
2. Launch Word, and choose Help, Detect And Repair. The Detect And Repair dialog box appears. (See Figure A-3.)
3. If you want Word to automatically restore any damaged shortcuts found, select the Restore My Shortcuts While Repairing check box and then click Start. Word searches your installation and makes the necessary changes.

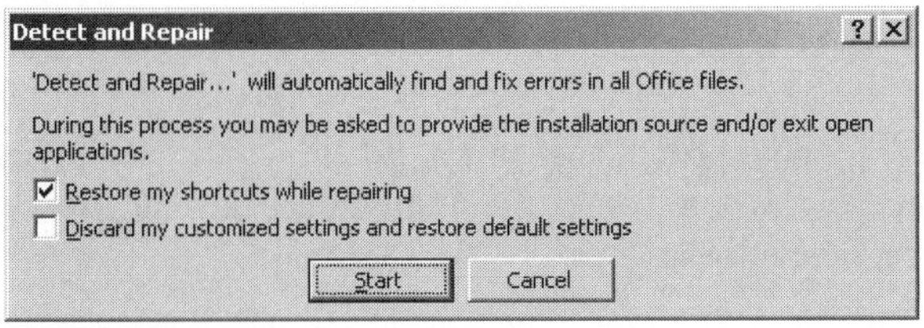

Figure A-3. Detect And Repair enables you to fix problems within Word.

Repairing Office XP

If you're concerned that something is wrong with your Office installation, you can use the Microsoft Office XP Setup Wizard to repair it. Here are the steps for repairing Office XP:

1. Place the first Office XP CD in the drive. If necessary, launch the setup utility by displaying the contents of the CD and double-clicking Setup.exe.
2. On the Maintenance Mode Options page of the wizard, select the Repair Office option and click Next.
3. On the Reinstall Or Repair Office Installation page, select Detect And Repair Errors In My Office Installation. If you want Office XP to restore your program shortcuts, select that check box before clicking Install. (See Figure A-4.)

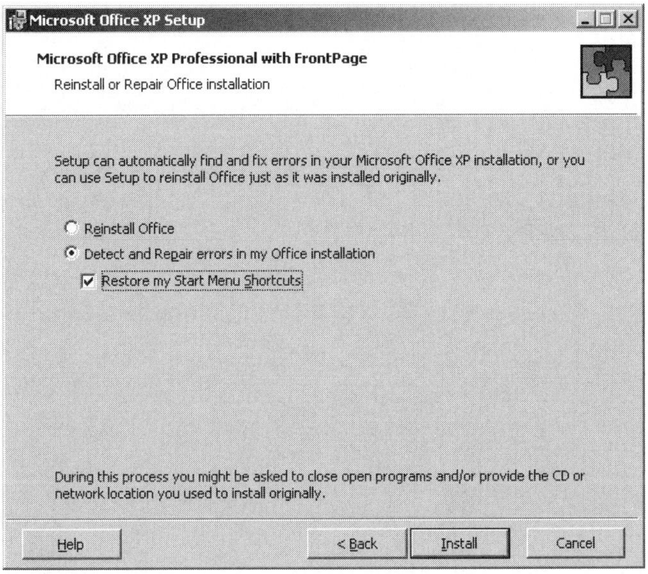

Figure A-4. You can repair Office from the Microsoft Office XP Setup Wizard.

Reinstalling Office

If you're continuing to have problems with Word even after you've tried to resolve them using Detect And Repair, you can reinstall Office and start over with a clean slate. To reinstall Office, follow these steps:

1. Insert the CD in the drive, and the Microsoft Office XP Setup Wizard launches. (If setup doesn't launch automatically, display the contents of the CD and double-click Setup.exe.)
2. On the Maintenance Mode Options page, click Uninstall Office and click Next.
3. A message box appears, asking you whether you want to remove the program. Click Yes to remove Office.

After Office is removed from your local system, start the setup wizard again and install Office as described in the section "Installing Office XP," on page 984.

Appendix B

Speech Recognition Commands in Word 2002

Say this	To do this
Expand More buttons	Display all the commands on a menu
Tab	In a dialog box, move to the next option or group of options
Shift tab	In a dialog box, move to the previous option or group of options
Escape Cancel	Close a dialog box without saving any changes and close menus
Return Enter New line Next line	Enter a new line
New paragraph	Enter a new paragraph
Go end	Go to the end of a line
Home Go home	Go to the beginning of a line
Backspace	Enter a backspace
Space Space bar	Enter a space
Left Left arrow Arrow left Go left	Move the insertion point one space to the left
Right Go right Right arrow Arrow right	Move the insertion point one space to the right

(continued)

Say this	To do this
Right one word Forward word Forward one word Go forward one word Next word Go right word Control right	Move the insertion point one word to the right
Left one word Back word Back one word Go back one word Last word Control left	Move the insertion point one word to the left
Up Go up Up arrow Arrow up	Go up one line
Down Go down Down arrow Arrow down	Go down one line
Page up Previous page	Scroll up
Page down Next page	Scroll down
Delete	Delete selected text
Right click Right click menu Show right click menu Context menu Show context menu	Display the right click menu
AutoCorrect options Options button	If the AutoCorrect Options button is visible, displays the AutoCorrect Options menu
Smart tag actions Smart tag options Options button	If the Smart Tag Actions button is visible, displays the Smart Tag Actions button menu

Say this	To do this
Paste options Options button	If the Paste Options button is visible, displays the Paste Options button menu
Shift control right Select next word	Select the next word
Shift control left Select last word	Select the last word
Shift control up Select last line	Select text going backward
Shift control down Select next line	Select text going forward
Open File open Open file	Open a file
New document New blank document	Open a new document
Close document File exit	Close a document
File open	Open a file
Task pane Show task pane View task pane	Show the task pane
Hide task pane	Hide the task pane
Select all	Select all
Cut	Cut selected text
Copy	Copy
Paste	Paste
Undo	Undo
Redo Repeat Same as before	Redo
Save	Save

(continued)

Say this	To do this
Office clipboard Show clipboard Show Office Clipboard Copy copy	Show the Office Clipboard
Hide clipboard Hide Office Clipboard	Hide the Office Clipboard
Turn on bold On bold Begin bolding	Add bold formatting
Turn off bold Remove bold Off bold Unbold Stop bolding	Remove bold formatting
Italicize Italic	Italicize and remove italics
Left justify Left justified Justify left	Left justify
Right justify Right justified Justify right	Right justify
Centered Center justify Center justified	Center justify
Ask a question Type a question for help	Move the insertion point to the Ask A Question box
Hide the assistant	Hide the Office Assistant
Print preview	Print preview

Appendix C
Word Macros

Word includes over 950 built-in commands that you can run as macros or add to your toolbars and menus. This appendix lists these commands and gives a brief description of each, as provided in the Macros dialog box.

To run a built-in Word command as a macro, choose Tools, Macro, Macros or press Ctrl+F8 to open the Macros dialog box, and select Word Commands in the Macros In drop-down list. Then select the desired command, and click Run.

To add a built-in Word command to a toolbar or menu, or to assign a keyboard shortcut to one of these commands, choose Tools, Customize, and click the Commands tab. In the Categories list, select All Commands. The Commands list displays the full list of Word commands, which you can select and customize. You can also select a command and then click the Description button to get a more detailed description of the command. Keep in mind that a number of Word commands are already assigned to toolbars and menus, and depending on your computer's setup, some of the Word commands listed in this appendix might not be available for selection on your computer.

Word Command	Description
AcceptAllChangesInDoc	Accepts all changes in document, ignoring filter settings
AcceptAllChangesShown	Accepts all changes that are highlighted in the current filter settings
AcceptChangesSelected	Accepts changes in current selection
ActivateObject	Activates an object
AllCaps	Makes the selection all capitals (toggle)
AnnotationEdit	Edits comment
ApplyHeading1	Applies Heading 1 style to the selected text
ApplyHeading2	Applies Heading 2 style to the selected text
ApplyHeading3	Applies Heading 3 style to the selected text
ApplyListBullet	Applies List Bullet style to the selected text
AppMaximize	Enlarges the application window to full size
AppMinimize	Minimizes the application window to an icon

(continued)

Word Command	Description
AppMove	Changes the position of the application window
AppRestore	Restores the application window to normal size
AppSize	Changes the size of the application window
AutoFitContent	AutoFits table to the contents
AutoFitFixed	Sets table size to a fixed width
AutoFitWindow	AutoFits table to the window
AutoMarkIndexEntries	Inserts index entries using an AutoMark file
AutomaticChange	Performs the suggested AutoFormat action
AutoScroll	Starts scrolling the active document
AutoSummarizeClose	Turns off AutoSummarize view
AutoSummarizePercentOfOriginal	Changes the size of the automatic summary
AutoSummarizeToggleView	Switches how Word displays a summary: highlighting summary text or hiding everything but the summary
AutoSummarizeUpdateFileProperties	Updates the file's properties information with the current summary
AutoText	Creates or inserts an AutoText entry, depending on the selection
Bold	Makes the selection boldface (toggle)
BoldRun	Makes the current run of letters (such as a word) in the selection boldface (toggle)
BorderAll	Changes all the borders of the selected table cells
BorderBottom	Changes the bottom border of the selected paragraphs, table cells, and pictures
BorderHoriz	Changes the horizontal borders of the selected table cells
BorderInside	Changes the inside borders of the selected paragraphs, table cells, and pictures

Word Command	Description
BorderLeft	Changes the left border of the selected paragraphs, table cells, and pictures
BorderLineColor	Changes border line color of the selected paragraphs, table cells, and pictures
BorderLineStyle	Changes border line styles of the selected paragraphs, table cells, and pictures
BorderLineWeight	Changes border line weights of the selected paragraphs, table cells, and pictures
BorderNone	Removes borders from the selected paragraphs, table cells, and pictures
BorderOutside	Changes the outside borders of the selected paragraphs, table cells, and pictures
BorderRight	Changes the right border of the selected paragraphs, table cells, and pictures
BorderTLtoBR	Changes the top left to bottom right diagonal of the selected table cells
BorderTop	Changes the top borders of the selected paragraphs, table cells, and pictures
BorderTRtoBL	Changes the top right to bottom left diagonal of the selected table cells
BorderVert	Changes the vertical borders of the selected table cells
BottomAlign	Aligns cell contents to the bottom of cell
BottomCenterAlign	Aligns cell contents to the bottom center of cell
BottomLeftAlign	Aligns cell contents to the bottom left of cell
BottomRightAlign	Aligns cell contents to the bottom right of cell
BrowseNext	Jumps to the next browse object
BrowsePrev	Jumps to the previous browse object
BrowseSel	Opens the Select Browse Object menu
Cancel	Terminates an action

(continued)

Word Command	Description
CellOptions	Changes the height and width of the rows and columns in a table
CenterAlign	Aligns cell contents to the center of cell
CenterPara	Centers paragraph between the indents
ChangeByte	Changes between wide and narrow versions of the letters in the selection
ChangeCase	Changes the case of the letters in the selection
ChangeKana	Changes the characters in the selection between Katakana and Hiragana
CharLeft	Moves the insertion point to the left one character
CharLeftExtend	Extends the selection to the left one character
CharRight	Moves the insertion point to the right one character
CharRightExtend	Extends the selection to the right one character
CharScale	Applies scaling to the selection
CheckBoxFormField	Inserts a check box form field
ClearFormatting	Clears formatting and styles from selected text
ClearFormField	Deletes the selected form field
ClosePane	Closes the active window pane
ClosePreview	Exits Print Preview mode
CloseUpPara	Removes extra space above the selected paragraph
CloseViewHeaderFooter	Returns to document text
ColumnSelect	Selects a columnar block of text
CommaAccent	Formats the selection with comma accents (toggle)
Connect	Connects to a network drive

Word Command	Description
ContextHelp	Turns on or off context-sensitive help accessed by pressing the F1 key
ContinueNumbering	Continues paragraph numbering
ControlRun	Displays Control Panel or the Clipboard
ConvertObject	Converts an object to another type or activates an object as another type
ConvertTextBoxToFrame	Converts a single selected text box to a frame
CopyFormat	Copies the formatting of the selection to a specified location
CopyText	Makes a copy of the selection at a specified location
CreateAutoText	Adds an AutoText entry to the active template
CreateSubdocument	Transforms the selected outline items into subdocuments
CreateTable	Inserts a table
CreateTask	Creates a Microsoft Outlook task from the current selection
CssLinks	Manages external cascading style sheet links
DecreaseIndent	Decreases indent or promotes the selection one level
DecreaseParagraphSpacing	Decreases paragraph spacing by 6 points
DefaultCharBorder	Applies the default character border
DefaultCharShading	Applies the default character shading
DeleteAllCommentsInDoc	Deletes all comments in document, ignoring filter settings
DeleteAllCommentsShown	Deletes all comments that are highlighted in the current filter settings
DeleteAnnotation	Deletes a comment
DeleteBackWord	Deletes the previous word without putting it on the Clipboard

(continued)

Word Command	Description
DeleteHyperlink	Removes a hyperlink
DeleteStyle	Deletes the current style
DeleteWord	Deletes the next word without putting it on the Clipboard
DemoteList	Demotes the selection one level
DemoteToBodyText	Applies Normal style and converts the selected headings to body text
DiacriticColor	Changes the color of the diacritics
DisplayDetails	Displays the details of the selected address
DisplayFinalDoc	Shows insertions in line and deletions in bubbles
DisplayForReview	Selects viewing mode for revisions and comments
DisplayOriginalDoc	Shows deletions in line and insertions in bubbles
DistributeColumn	Evenly distributes selected columns
DistributeGeneral	Evenly distributes selected rows and columns in a table
DistributePara	Distributes paragraph
DistributeRow	Evenly distributes selected rows
DocClose	Prompts to save the document and then closes the active window
DocMaximize	Enlarges the active window to full size
DocMinimize	Minimizes the active window to an icon
DocMove	Changes the position of the active window
DocRestore	Restores the window to normal size
DocSize	Changes the size of the active window
DocSplit	Splits the active window horizontally and then adjusts the split
DoFieldClick	Executes the action associated with the button fields

Word Command	Description
DotAccent	Formats the selection with dot accents (toggle)
DottedUnderline	Underlines the selection with dots (toggle)
DoubleStrikethrough	Formats the selection with a double strikethrough (toggle)
DoubleUnderline	Formats the selection with a double underline (toggle)
DrawAlign	Aligns the selected drawing objects with one another or the page
DrawCallout	Inserts a callout drawing object
DrawDisassemblePicture	Disassembles the selected metafile picture into drawing objects
DrawDuplicate	Duplicates the selected drawing objects
DrawInsertWordPicture	Opens a separate window for creating a picture object or inserts the selected drawing objects into a picture
DrawMenu3DColor	Applies the most recently used 3-D color to the selected AutoShape
DrawMenuShadowColor	Applies the most recently used shadow color to the selected AutoShape
DrawResetWordPicture	Sets document margins to enclose all drawing objects on the page
DrawReshape	Displays resizing handles on selected freeform drawing objects to enable resizing
DrawSelectNext	Selects the next drawn object
DrawSelectPrevious	Selects the previous drawn object
DrawSnapToGrid	Sets up a grid for aligning drawing objects
DrawTextBox	Inserts an empty text box or encloses the selected item in a tex box
DrawToggleLayer	Switches whether the drawing object appears in the front of or behind the text
DrawUnselect	Unselects a drawn object

(continued)

Word Command	Description
DrawVerticalTextBox	Inserts an empty vertical text box or encloses the selected item in a vertical text box
DropDownFormField	Inserts a drop-down form field
EditAutoText	Inserts or defines AutoText entries
EditBookmark	Assigns a name to the selection
EditClear	Performs a forward delete or removes the selection without putting it on the Clipboard
EditConvertAllEndnotes	Converts all endnotes to footnotes
EditConvertAllFootnotes	Converts all footnotes to endnotes
EditConvertNotes	Converts selected footnotes to endnotes or converts selected endnotes to footnotes
EditCopy	Copies the selection and puts it on the Clipboard
EditCopyAsPicture	Copies the selection and puts it on the Clipboard as a picture
EditCut	Cuts the selection and puts it on the Clipboard
EditFind	Finds the specified text or the specified formatting
EditGoTo	Jumps to a specified place in the active document
EditHyperlink	Edits a hyperlink
EditIMEReconversion	Reconverts using IME
EditLinks	Allows links to be viewed, updated, opened, or removed
EditObject	Opens the selected object for editing
EditOfficeClipboard	Displays the contents of the Office Clipboard
EditPaste	Inserts the Clipboard contents at the insertion point
EditPasteAppendTable	Inserts the Clipboard contents at the insertion point
EditPasteAsHyperlink	Inserts the Clipboard contents as a hyperlink object

Word Command	Description
EditPasteAsNestedTable	Inserts the Clipboard contents at the insertion point
EditPasteFromExcel	Inserts the Clipboard contents at the insertion point
EditPasteOption	Inserts the Clipboard contents at the insertion point using a specific recovery option
EditPasteSpecial	Inserts the Clipboard contents as a linked object, embedded object, or other format
EditPictureEdit	Converts the selected picture to a drawing canvas
EditRedo	Redoes the last action that was undone
EditRedoOrRepeat	Repeats the last action
EditReplace	Finds the specified text or the specified formatting and replaces it
EditSelectAll	Selects the entire document
EditSwapAllNotes	Changes all footnotes to endnotes and all endnotes to footnotes
EditTOACategory	Modifies the category names for the table of authorities
EditUndo	Reverses the last action
EditUpdateIMEDic	Updates IME dictionary
EditWrapBoundary	Edits the wrapping boundary for a picture or drawing object
EmailCheckNames	Verifies the recipient names in the e-mail pane
EmailEnvelope	Displays the e-mail pane
EmailFlag	Displays the e-mail pane's message flag dialog box
EmailFocusIntroduction	Switches focus to the e-mail pane's Introduction field
EmailFocusSubject	Switches focus to the e-mail pane's Subject field

(continued)

Word Command	Description
EmailMessageOptions	Displays the e-mail pane's Options dialog box
EmailOptions	Changes various categories of Word's e-mail options
EmailSaveAttachment	Saves the attachments of an e-mail pane message
EmailSelectBccNames	Displays the e-mail address book to add recipients to the Bcc field
EmailSelectCcNames	Displays the e-mail address book to add recipients to the Cc field
EmailSelectNames	Displays the e-mail address book
EmailSelectToNames	Displays the e-mail address book to add recipients to the To field
EmailSend	Executes the e-mail pane's Send command
EmailSignatureOptions	Creates or changes AutoSignature entries
EndOfColumn	Moves to the last cell in the current column
EndOfDocExtend	Extends the selection to the end of the last line of the document
EndOfDocument	Moves the insertion point to the end of the last line of the document
EndOfLine	Moves the insertion point to the end of the current line
EndOfLineExtend	Extends the selection to the end of the current line
EndOfRow	Moves the insertion point to the last cell in the current row
EndOfWindow	Moves the insertion point to the end of the last visible line on the screen
EndOfWindowExtend	Extends the selection to the end of the last visible line on the screen
EndReview	Ends the review for this document
EnvelopeSetup	Currently unavailable
EnvelopeWizard	Runs the Envelope Wizard

Word Command	Description
ExtendSelection	Turns on extend selection mode and then expands the selection with the direction keys
FileCheckin	Checks in a document
FileCheckout	Checks out a document
FileClose	Closes all the windows of the active document
FileCloseAll	Closes all the windows of all documents
FileCloseOrCloseAll	Performs FileClose or, if the Shift key is pressed, FileCloseAll
FileCloseOrExit	Currently unavailable
FileConfirmConversions	Toggles the display of a message box that asks the user to confirm the conversion when opening a file
FileExit	Quits Microsoft Word and prompts to save the documents
FileFind	Locates the documents in any directory, drive, or folder
FileNew	Creates a new document or template
FileNewContext	Creates a new document based on the Normal template
FileNewDefault	Creates a new document based on the Normal template
FileNewDialog	Creates a new document based on the Normal template
FileNewEmail	Creates a new e-mail message
FileNewPrint	Creates a new document based on the Normal template
FileNewWeb	Creates a new document based on the Normal template
FileOpen	Opens an existing document or template
FilePageSetup	Changes the page setup of the selected sections

(continued)

Word Command	Description
FilePost	Puts the active document into a Microsoft Exchange folder
FilePrint	Prints the active document
FilePrintDefault	Prints the active document using the current defaults
FilePrintPreview	Displays full pages as they will be printed
FilePrintPreviewFullScreen	Toggles full screen view on and off
FilePrintSetup	Changes the printer and printing options
FileProperties	Shows the properties of the active document
FileRoutingSlip	Adds or changes the e-mail routing slip of the active document
FileSave	Saves the active document or template
FileSaveAll	Saves all open files, macros, and AutoText entries, prompting for each one separately
FileSaveAs	Saves a copy of the document in a separate file
FileSaveAsWebPage	Saves a copy of the document in a separate file
FileSaveFrameAs	Saves a copy of the current frame document in a separate file
FileSaveHtml	Saves a copy of the file as an HTML document
FileSaveVersion	Saves a new version of a document
FileSearch	Opens the Search task pane
FileSendMail	Sends the active document through e-mail
FileSummaryInfo	Shows the summary information for the active document
FileTemplates	Changes the active template and the template options
FileVersions	Manages the versions of a document
FixBrokenText	Fixes broken text
FixMe	Verifies Microsoft Office

Word Command	Description
Font	Changes the font of the selection
FontColor	Changes the color of the selected text
FontSizeSelect	Changes the font size of the selection
FontSubstitution	Changes the document's font mapping
FormatAddrFonts	Formats the delivery address font for envelopes
FormatAutoFormat	Automatically formats a document
FormatAutoFormatBegin	Automatically formats a document
FormatBackgroundFillEffect	Provides fill effects for the background color
FormatBackgroundMoreColors	Provides more color choices for the background color
FormatBackgroundWatermark	Adds watermark background
FormatBulletDefault	Creates a bulleted list based on the current defaults
FormatBulletsAndNumbering	Creates a numbered or bulleted list
FormatCallout	Formats the selected callouts or sets callout defaults
FormatChangeCase	Changes the case of the letters in the selection
FormatChangeCaseFareast	Changes the case of the letters in the selection
FormatColumns	Changes the column format of the selected sections
FormatCombineCharacters	Combines characters
FormatConsistencyCheck	Checks for formatting consistency
FormatDrawingObject	Changes the properties of the selected drawing object
FormatDrawingObjectWrapBehind	Changes the selected drawing objects to no wrapping behind text
FormatDrawingObjectWrapFront	Changes the selected drawing objects to no wrapping in front of text
FormatDrawingObjectWrapInline	Changes the selected drawing objects to inline wrapping

(continued)

Word Command	Description
FormatDrawingObjectWrapNone	Changes the selected drawing objects to no wrapping
FormatDrawingObjectWrapSquare	Changes the selected drawing objects to square wrapping
FormatDrawingObjectWrapThrough	Changes the selected drawing objects to tight through wrapping
FormatDrawingObjectWrapTight	Changes the selected drawing objects to tight wrapping
FormatDrawingObjectWrapTopBottom	Changes the selected drawing objects to top or bottom wrapping
FormatDropCap	Formats the first character of current paragraph as a drop capital
FormatEncloseCharacters	Inserts an enclosed character
FormatField	Inserts a field in the active document
FormatFillColor	Applies the most recently used fill color to the selected AutoShape
FormatFitText	Applies the Fit Text property
FormatFont	Changes the appearance of the selected characters
FormatFrame	Changes the options for frame formatting
FormatFrameOrFramePicture	Changes the options for frame formatting
FormatHeaderFooterLink	Links this header or footer to the previous section
FormatHeadingNumbering	Changes numbering options for heading level styles
FormatHorizontalInVertical	Applies horizontal in the vertical property to format East Asian characters
FormatLineColor	Changes the line color
FormatMultilevelDefault	Creates a numbered list based on the current defaults
FormatNumberDefault	Creates a numbered list based on the current defaults
FormatPageNumber	Changes the appearance of page numbers

Word Command	Description
FormatParagraph	Changes the appearance and line numbering of the selected paragraphs
FormatPhoneticGuide	Inserts a Phonetic Guide field in the active document
FormatPicture	Changes the picture scaling, size, and cropping information
FormatRetAddrFonts	Formats the return address font for envelopes
FormatSectionLayout	Changes the page format of the selected sections
FormatSimpleNumberDefault	Creates a numbered list based on the current defaults
FormatStyle	Applies, creates, or modifies styles
FormatStyleByExample	Creates a style using the currently selected text
FormatStyleGallery	Applies styles from templates
FormatStyleModify	Modifies the selected style
FormatStyleVisibility	Changes the visibility state of the document's style
FormatTabs	Sets and clears tab stops for the selected paragraphs
FormatTextFlow	Changes the text flow direction and character orientation
FormatTheme	Applies a Web theme
FormattingPane	Applies, creates, or modifies styles and formatting
FormattingProperties	Shows or hides formatting properties
FormatTwoLinesInOne	Applies two lines in one property to format East Asian text
FormFieldOptions	Changes the options for a form field
FormShading	Changes shading options for the current form
FrameProperties	Changes the properties of the frame

(continued)

Word Command	Description
FrameRemoveSplit	Removes the current frame
FramesetTOC	Creates a frameset table of contents
FramesetWizard	Turns the current window into a frameset
FrameSplitAbove	Splits the active frame, adding the new frame above the current frame
FrameSplitBelow	Splits the active frame, adding the new frame below the current frame
FrameSplitLeft	Splits the active frame, adding the new frame to the left of the current frame
FrameSplitRight	Splits the active frame, adding the new frame to the right of the current frame
GoBack	Returns to the previous insertion point
GotoCommentScope	Highlights the text associated with a comment reference mark
GoToHeaderFooter	Jumps between header and footer
GoToNextComment	Jumps to the next comment in the active document
GoToNextEndnote	Jumps to the next endnote in the active document
GoToNextFootnote	Jumps to the next footnote in the active document
GotoNextLinkedTextBox	Selects the next linked text box
GoToNextPage	Jumps to the next page in the active document
GoToNextSection	Jumps to the next section in the active document
GoToPreviousComment	Jumps to the previous comment in the active document
GoToPreviousEndnote	Jumps to the previous endnote in the active document
GoToPreviousFootnote	Jumps to the previous footnote in the active document

Word Command	Description
GoToPreviousPage	Jumps to the previous page in the active document
GoToPreviousSection	Jumps to the previous section in the active document
GotoPrevLinkedTextBox	Selects the previous linked text box
GotoTableOfContents	Selects the first table of contents in the document
GreetingSentence	Runs the Japanese Greeting Wizard
GrowFont	Increases the font size of the selection
GrowFontOnePoint	Increases the font size of the selection by 1 point
HangingIndent	Increases the hanging indent
HanjaDictionary	Runs the Hanja dictionary
Help	Runs Help from the Office Assistant for the current task or command
HelpAbout	Displays the program information, Microsoft Word version number, and the copyright
HelpAW	Locates Help topics based on an entered question or request
HelpContentsArabic	Displays Arabic Help contents
HelpIchitaroHelp	Shows competitor (J Ichitaro, Korean WP) Help
HelpMSN	Currently unavailable
HelpPSSHelp	Displays information about the support available for Microsoft Word
HelpShowHide	Shows or hides the Office Assistant
HelpTipOfTheDay	Displays a Word Tip of the Day
HelpTool	Lets you get help with a command or screen region or examine text properties
HelpUsingHelp	Displays the instructions for how to use Help
HelpWordPerfectHelp	Shows the equivalent for a WordPerfect command

(continued)

Word Command	Description
HelpWordPerfectHelpOptions	Customizes WordPerfect Help
Hidden	Makes the selection hidden text (toggle)
Highlight	Applies color highlighting to the selection
HTMLSourceDoNotRefresh	Does not refresh HTML source code
HTMLSourceRefresh	Refreshes HTML source code
HyperlinkOpen	Opens a hyperlink
IgnoreAllConsistenceError	Ignores consistence error
IgnoreConsistenceError	Ignores consistence error
IMEControl	Disables IME
IncreaseIndent	Increases indent or demotes the selection one level
IncreaseParagraphSpacing	Increases paragraph spacing by 6 points
Indent	Moves the left indent to the next tab stop
IndentChar	Increases the indent by the width of a character
IndentFirstChar	Increases the hanging indent by the width of a character
IndentFirstLine	Increases the hanging indent by the width of two characters
IndentLine	Increases the indent by the width of two characters
InsertAddCaption	Adds a new caption type
InsertAddress	Inserts an address from your Personal Address Book
InsertAnnotation	Inserts a comment
InsertAutoCaption	Defines which objects are inserted with a caption
InsertAutoText	Replaces the name of the AutoText entry with its contents
InsertBreak	Ends a page, column, or section at the insertion point

Word Command	Description
InsertCaption	Inserts a caption above or below a selected object
InsertCaptionNumbering	Sets the number for a caption type
InsertChart	Inserts a Microsoft Graph object
InsertColumnBreak	Inserts a column break at the insertion point
InsertCrossReference	Inserts a cross-reference
InsertDatabase	Inserts information from an external data source into the active document
InsertDateField	Inserts a date field
InsertDateTime	Displays the Date And Time dialog box
InsertDrawing	Inserts a Microsoft Drawing object
InsertEmSpace	Inserts an em space
InsertEndnoteNow	Inserts an endnote reference at the insertion point
InsertEnSpace	Inserts an en space
InsertEquation	Inserts a Microsoft Equation object
InsertExcelTable	Inserts a Microsoft Excel worksheet object
InsertField	Inserts a field in the active document
InsertFieldChars	Inserts a field enclosed in field characters
InsertFile	Inserts the text of another file into the active document
InsertFootnote	Inserts a footnote or endnote reference at the insertion point
InsertFootnoteNow	Inserts a footnote reference at the insertion point
InsertFormField	Inserts a new form field
InsertFrame	Inserts an empty frame or encloses the selected item in a frame
InsertGraphicalHorizontalLine	Inserts a horizontal line graphic
InsertHorizontalLine	Inserts a horizontal line
InsertHTMLBGSound	Inserts a background sound

(continued)

Word Command	Description
InsertHTMLCheckBox	Inserts a check box
InsertHTMLDropdownBox	Inserts a drop-down list
InsertHTMLHidden	Inserts a hidden control
InsertHTMLImageSubmit	Inserts a Submit button with image
InsertHTMLListBox	Inserts a list box
InsertHTMLMarquee	Inserts a marquee control
InsertHTMLMovie	Inserts a movie control
InsertHTMLOptionButton	Inserts an Option button
InsertHTMLPassword	Inserts a password control
InsertHTMLReset	Inserts a Reset button
InsertHTMLSubmit	Inserts a Submit button
InsertHTMLTextArea	Inserts a text area
InsertHTMLTextBox	Inserts a text box
InsertHyperlink	Inserts a hyperlink
InsertIndex	Collects the index entries into an index
InsertIndexAndTables	Inserts an index or a table of contents, figures, or authorities into the document
InsertListNumField	Inserts a ListNum field
InsertMergeField	Inserts a mail merge field at the insertion point
InsertNewComment	Inserts a comment
InsertNumber	Inserts a number in the active document
InsertNumberOfPages	Inserts a number of pages field
InsertObject	Inserts an equation, chart, drawing, or some other object
InsertOCX	Inserts the selected OCX control or registers a new OCX control
InsertOCXButton	Inserts a button control
InsertOCXCheckbox	Inserts a check box control
InsertOCXDropdownCombo	Inserts a combo box control

Word Command	Description
InsertOCXFrame	Inserts a frame control
InsertOCXImage	Inserts an image control
InsertOCXLabel	Inserts a label control
InsertOCXListBox	Inserts a list box control
InsertOCXOptionButton	Inserts a radio button control
InsertOCXScrollbar	Inserts a scroll bar control
InsertOCXSpin	Inserts a spin control
InsertOCXTextBox	Inserts a text box control
InsertOCXToggleButton	Inserts a toggle button control
InsertOfficeDrawing	Inserts a Microsoft Draw 8 object
InsertPageBreak	Inserts a page break at the insertion point
InsertPageField	Inserts a page number field
InsertPageNumbers	Adds page numbers to the top or bottom of the pages
InsertPicture	Inserts a picture from a graphics file
InsertPictureBullet	Inserts a picture as a bullet
InsertSectionBreak	Ends a section at the insertion point
InsertSound	Inserts a sound object into the document
InsertSpike	Empties the Spike AutoText entry and inserts all of its contents into the document
InsertStyleSeparator	Joins two paragraphs together, creating leading emphasis
InsertSubdocument	Opens a file and inserts it as a subdocument in a master document
InsertSymbol	Inserts a special character
InsertTableOfAuthorities	Collects the table of authorities entries into a table of authorities
InsertTableOfContents	Collects the headings or the table of contents entries into a table of contents
InsertTableOfFigures	Collects captions into a table of figures

(continued)

Word Command	Description
InsertTimeField	Inserts a time field
InsertVerticalFrame	Inserts an empty vertical frame or encloses the selected item in a vertical frame
InsertWebComponent	Inserts a FrontPage Web component
Italic	Makes the selection italic
ItalicRun	Makes the current run in the selection italic (toggle)
JapaneseGreetingClosingSentence	Runs the Japanese Greeting Wizard closing sentence
JapaneseGreetingOpeningSentence	Runs the Japanese Greeting Wizard opening sentence
JapaneseGreetingPreviousGreeting	Runs the Japanese Greeting Wizard previous greeting
JustifyPara	Aligns the paragraph at both the left and the right indents
LabelOptions	Opens the Label Options dialog box
Language	Changes the language formatting of the selected characters
LearnWords	Learns words from the document for speech recognition
LeftPara	Aligns the paragraph at the left indent
LetterProperties	Formats a letter document
LettersWizardJToolbar	Displays or hides the Japanese Greeting Wizard toolbar
LetterWizard	Runs the Letter Wizard to create a letter document
LicenseVerification	Activates license verification
LineDown	Moves the insertion point down one line
LineDownExtend	Extends the selection down one line
LineSpacing	Applies line spacing to the selection
LineUp	Moves the insertion point up one line
LineUpExtend	Extends the selection up one line

Word Command	Description
ListCommands	Creates a table of Word commands, with key and menu assignments
ListIndent	Demotes the selection one level
ListOutdent	Promotes the selection one level
LockDocument	Toggles the file lock state of a document
LockFields	Locks the selected fields to prevent updating
LTRMacroDialogs	Makes macro dialog box display LTR (left to right)
LtrPara	Sets paragraph orientation to LTR
LtrRun	Makes the current run LTR
Magnifier	Toggles zoom-in and zoom-out mode
MailAsHTML	Converts the current message to HTML
MailAsPlainText	Converts the current message to plain text
MailAsRTF	Converts the current message to HTML
MailCheckNames	Checks the recipient names of an e-mail message
MailHideMessageHeader	Shows or hides the e-mail message header for Word when Word is used as an e-mail editor
MailMerge	Combines files to produce form letters, mailing labels, envelopes, and catalogs
MailMergeAddressBlock	Runs the mail merge address block
MailMergeAskToConvertChevrons	Toggles asking the user about converting Word for the Macintosh mail merge chevrons
MailMergeCheck	Checks for errors in a mail merge
MailMergeConvertChevrons	Toggles converting Word for the Macintosh mail merge chevrons
MailMergeCreateDataSource	Creates a new mail merge data source
MailMergeCreateHeaderSource	Creates a new mail merge header source
MailMergeCreateList	Creates an Office Address list
MailMergeDataForm	Edits a list or table in a form

(continued)

Word Command	Description
MailMergeEditAddressBlock	Edits the address block
MailMergeEditDataSource	Opens a mail merge data source
MailMergeEditGreetingLine	Edits the greeting lines
MailMergeEditHeaderSource	Opens a mail merge header source
MailMergeEditList	Edits an Office Address list
MailMergeEditMainDocument	Switches to a mail merge main document
MailMergeFieldMapping	Runs mail merge field mapping
MailMergeFindEntry	Finds a specified entry in a mail merge data source
MailMergeFindRecord	Finds a specified record in a mail merge data source
MailMergeFirstRecord	Displays the first record in the active mail merge data source
MailMergeGoToRecord	Displays the specified record in the active mail merge data source
MailMergeGreetingLine	Runs mail merge greeting line
MailMergeHelper	Prepares a main document for a mail merge
MailMergeInsertAsk	Inserts a Word ask field at the insertion point
MailMergeInsertFields	Inserts a Word insert field at the insertion point
MailMergeInsertFillIn	Inserts a Word fill-in field at the insertion point
MailMergeInsertIf	Inserts a Word if field at the insertion point
MailMergeInsertMergeRec	Inserts a Word record field at the insertion point
MailMergeInsertMergeSeq	Inserts a Word sequence field at the insertion point
MailMergeInsertNext	Inserts a Word next field at the insertion point
MailMergeInsertNextIf	Inserts a Word next if field at the insertion point

Word Command	Description
MailMergeInsertSet	Inserts a Word set field at the insertion point
MailMergeInsertSkipIf	Inserts a Word skip if field at the insertion point
MailMergeLastRecord	Displays the last record in the active mail merge data source
MailMergeNextRecord	Displays the next record in the active mail merge data source
MailMergeOpenDataSource	Opens a data source for a mail merge or inserts a database
MailMergeOpenHeaderSource	Opens a header source for mail merge
MailMergePrevRecord	Displays the previous record in the active mail merge data source
MailMergePropagateLabel	Propagates labels
MailMergeQueryOptions	Sets the query options for a mail merge
MailMergeRecipients	Sets mail merge recipients
MailMergeReset	Resets a mail merge main document to a normal document
MailMergeSetDocumentType	Sets or clears the mail merge document type
MailMergeShadeFields	Toggles shading of merge fields
MailMergeToDoc	Collects the results of the mail merge in a document
MailMergeToEMail	Sends the results of the mail merge to e-mail
MailMergeToFax	Sends the results of the mail merge to fax
MailMergeToolbar	Displays or hides the Mail Merge toolbar
MailMergeToPrinter	Sends the results of the mail merge to the printer
MailMergeUseAddressBook	Opens an address book as a data source for mail merge
MailMergeViewData	Toggles between viewing merge fields and actual data
MailMergeWizard	Runs the Mail Merge Wizard
MailMessageDelete	Deletes an e-mail message

(continued)

Word Command	Description
MailMessageForward	Forwards an e-mail message
MailMessageMove	Moves an e-mail message
MailMessageNext	Goes to the next e-mail message
MailMessagePrevious	Goes to the previous e-mail message
MailMessageProperties	Sets the properties of the e-mail message
MailMessageReply	Replies to an e-mail message
MailMessageReplyAll	Replies to all addresses in an e-mail message
MailSelectNames	Selects the recipients of an e-mail message
MarkCitation	Marks the text to include in the table of authorities
MarkIndexEntry	Marks the text to include in the index
MarkTableOfContentsEntry	Marks the text to include in the table of contents
MenuMode	Makes the menu bar active
MenuOrgChartInsert	Inserts an additional box in an organization chart
MenuShowChanges	Fine-tunes which bubbles are shown
MenuShowReviewers	Fine-tunes which bubbles are shown
MergeSplitGeneral	Merges or splits the selected table cells
MergeSubdocument	Merges two adjacent subdocuments into one subdocument
MicrosoftAccess	Starts or switches to Microsoft Access
MicrosoftExcel	Starts or switches to Microsoft Excel
MicrosoftFoxPro	Starts or switches to Microsoft FoxPro
MicrosoftMail	Starts or switches to Microsoft Mail
MicrosoftOnTheWeb*X*	Opens Microsoft Web site
MicrosoftPowerPoint	Starts or switches to Microsoft PowerPoint
MicrosoftProject	Starts or switches to Microsoft Project
MicrosoftPublisher	Starts or switches to Microsoft Publisher
MicrosoftSchedule	Starts or switches to Microsoft Schedule

Word Command	Description
MicrosoftScriptEditor	Starts or switches to Microsoft Script Editor
MicrosoftSystemInfo	Executes the Microsoft System Info application
MiddleCenterAlign	Aligns cell contents at the middle center of a cell
MiddleLeftAlign	Aligns cell contents at the middle left of a cell
MiddleRightAlign	Aligns cell contents at the middle right of a cell
MMEmailOptions	Runs the Mail Merge E-Mail Options dialog box
MMFaxOptions	Runs the Mail Merge Fax Options dialog box
MMNewDocOptions	Runs the Mail Merge New Document Merge Options dialog box
MMPrintOptions	Runs the Mail Merge Print Merge Options dialog box
MoveText	Moves the selection to a specified location
NewToolbar	Creates a new toolbar
NextCell	Moves to the next table cell
NextChangeOrComment	Goes to the next insertion, deletion, or comment
NextField	Moves to the next field
NextInsert	Returns to the next insertion point
NextMisspelling	Finds the next spelling error
NextObject	Moves to the next object on the page
NextPage	Moves to the next page
NextWindow	Switches to the next document window
NormalFontPosition	Removes the raised or lowered font attribute
NormalFontSpacing	Removes the expanded or condensed font attribute

(continued)

Word Command	Description
NormalizeText	Makes text consistent with the rest
NormalStyle	Applies the Normal style
NormalViewHeaderArea	Shows a list of headers and footers for editing
NoteOptions	Changes the options for footers or endnotes
OfficeOnTheWeb	Opens Microsoft Office on the Web
OK	Confirms a location for copying or moving a selection
OnlineMeeting	Starts or switches to an online meeting
OpenOrCloseUpPara	Sets or removes extra space above the selected paragraph
OpenSubdocument	Opens a subdocument in a new window
OpenUpPara	Sets extra space above the selected paragraph
Organizer	Opens the Organizer, which provides options to manage AutoText entries, styles, macros, and toolbars
OtherPane	Switches to another window pane
OutlineCollapse	Hides the lowest subtext of the selection
OutlineDemote	Demotes the selected paragraphs one heading level
OutlineExpand	Displays the next level of subtext of the selection
OutlineLevel	Sets the selected paragraphs to the heading level
OutlineMoveDown	Moves the selection to below the next item in the outline
OutlineMoveUp	Moves the selection to above the previous item in the outline
OutlinePromote	Promotes the selected paragraphs one heading level
OutlinePromoteHeading1	Promotes the selected text to Heading 1 style

Word Command	Description
OutlineShowFirstLine	Toggles between showing the first line of each paragraph only or showing all of the body text in the outline
OutlineShowFormat	Toggles the display of character formatting in Outline view
Overtype	Toggles the typing mode between replacing and inserting
PageDown	Moves the insertion point and document display to the next screen of text
PageDownExtend	Extends the selection and changes the document display to the next screen of text
PageUp	Moves the insertion point and document display to the previous screen of text
PageUpExtend	Extends the selection and changes the document display to the previous screen of text
ParaDown	Moves the insertion point to the beginning of the next paragraph
ParaDownExtend	Extends the selection to the beginning of the next paragraph
ParaKeepLinesTogether	Prevents a paragraph from splitting across page boundaries
ParaKeepWithNext	Keeps a paragraph and the following paragraph on the same page
ParaPageBreakBefore	Makes the current paragraph start on a new page
ParaUp	Moves the insertion point to the beginning of the previous paragraph
ParaUpExtend	Extends the selection to the beginning of the previous paragraph
ParaWidowOrphanControl	Prevents a page break from leaving a single line of a paragraph on one page
PasteFormat	Applies the previously copied formatting to the selection

(continued)

Word Command	Description
PauseRecorder	Pauses the macro recorder (toggle)
PostcardWizard	Runs the Postcard Wizard
PresentIt	Creates a Microsoft PowerPoint presentation from the current document
PrevCell	Moves to the previous table cell
PrevField	Moves to the previous field
PreviousChangeOrComment	Goes to the previous insertion, deletion, or comment
PrevObject	Moves to the previous object on the page
PrevPage	Moves to the previous page
PrevWindow	Switches to the previous document window
PromoteList	Promotes the selection one level
ProtectForm	Toggles protection for the active document
RedefineStyle	Redefines the current style based on the selected text
RejectAllChangesInDoc	Rejects all changes in the document, ignoring filter settings
RejectAllChangesShown	Rejects all changes that are highlighted in the current filter settings
RejectChangesSelected	Rejects changes and deletes comments in current selection
RemoveAllScripts	Removes all scripts
RemoveBulletsNumbers	Removes numbers and bullets from the selection
RemoveCellPartition	Removes cell partitions
RemoveFrames	Removes frame formatting from the selection
RemoveSubdocument	Merges contents of the selected subdocuments into the master document that contains them
RenameStyle	Renames the current style
RepeatFind	Repeats Go To or Find to find the next occurrence

Word Command	Description
ResetChar	Makes the selection the default character format of the applied style
ResetFormField	Resets the selected form field to its default value
ResetNoteSepOrNotice	Resets a separator, continuation separator, or continuation notice to the Word default
ResetPara	Makes the selection the default paragraph format of the applied style
RestartNumbering	Restarts paragraph numbering
ReturnReview	Sends the document under review
ReviewingPane	Opens a summary pane for viewing and editing document revisions (toggle)
RightPara	Aligns the paragraph at the right indent
RTLMacroDialogs	Makes macro dialog boxes display RTL (right to left)
RtlPara	Sets paragraph orientation to RTL
RtlRun	Makes the current run RTL
RunPrintManager	Displays the Print Manager
RunToggle	Toggles the insertion point between RTL and LTR runs
SaveTemplate	Saves the document template of the active document
ScheduleMeeting	Schedules an online meeting
ScreenRefresh	Refreshes the display
SelectCurAlignment	Selects all paragraphs with the same alignment
SelectCurColor	Selects all characters with the same color
SelectCurFont	Selects all characters with the same font name and point size
SelectCurIndent	Selects all paragraphs with the same indentation

(continued)

Word Command	Description
SelectCurSpacing	Selects all paragraphs with the same line spacing
SelectCurTabs	Selects all paragraphs with the same tabs
SelectDrawingObjects	Selects drawing objects (drag to create a rectangle enclosing the objects)
SelectNumber	Selects the paragraph number
SelectSimilarFormatting	Selects all similar formatting
SendForReview	Sends the document for review
SendToFax	Sends the document to fax
SendToOnlineMeetingParticipants	Sends the document to online meeting participants
SentLeft	Moves the insertion point to the beginning of the previous sentence
SentLeftExtend	Extends the selection to the beginning of the previous sentence
SentRight	Moves the insertion point to the beginning of the next sentence
SentRightExtend	Extends the selection to the beginning of the next sentence
SetDrawingDefaults	Changes the default drawing object properties
ShadingColor	Changes the shading color of the selected text
ShadingPattern	Changes the shading pattern of the selected paragraphs, table cells, and pictures
ShowAddInsXDialog	Displays the Office AddIn Manager dialog box
ShowAll	Shows or hides all nonprinting characters
ShowAllConsistency	Shows all relationships for consistency error
ShowAllHeadings	Displays all the heading levels and the body text
ShowChangesAndComments	Shows or hides markup balloons

Word Command	Description
ShowComments	Shows or hides comment balloons
ShowConsistency	Shows one relationship for consistency error
ShowFormatting	Shows or hides formatting markup balloons
ShowHeading1	Displays level 1 headings only
ShowHeading2	Displays level 1 and level 2 headings
ShowHeading3	Displays level 1 through level 3 headings
ShowHeading4	Displays level 1 through level 4 headings
ShowHeading5	Displays level 1 through level 5 headings
ShowHeading6	Displays level 1 through level 6 headings
ShowHeading7	Displays level 1 through level 7 headings
ShowHeading8	Displays level 1 through level 8 headings
ShowHeading9	Displays level 1 through level 9 headings
ShowInsertionsAndDeletions	Shows or hides markup balloons
ShowLevel	Displays the selected level headings only
ShowMe	Gives an in-depth explanation of the suggested tip
ShowNextHeaderFooter	Shows the next section's header and footer in Page Layout view
ShowPara	Shows or hides all nonprinting paragraph marks
ShowPrevHeaderFooter	Shows the previous section's header and footer in Page Layout view
ShowPropertyBrowser	Shows the Property Browser
ShowRepairs	Shows all repairs made to the document during Crash Recovery
ShowScriptAnchor	Shows all scripts
ShowSignatures	Shows digital signatures
ShrinkFont	Decreases the font size of the selection
ShrinkFontOnePoint	Decreases the font size of the selection by 1 point

(continued)

Word Command	Description
ShrinkSelection	Shrinks the selection to the next smaller unit
SignOutOfPassport	Signs out of Microsoft Passport
SkipNumbering	Makes the selected paragraphs skip numbering
SmallCaps	Makes the selection small capitals (toggle)
SpacePara1	Sets the line spacing to single space
SpacePara15	Sets the line spacing to one-and-one-half space
SpacePara2	Sets the line spacing to double space
Spike	Deletes the selection and adds it to the special AutoText entry
SplitSubdocument	Splits the selected part of a subdocument into another subdocument at the same level
StartOfColumn	Moves to the first cell in the current column
StartOfDocExtend	Extends the selection to the beginning of the first line of the document
StartOfDocument	Moves the insertion point to the beginning of the first line of the document
StartOfLine	Moves the insertion point to the beginning of the current line
StartOfLineExtend	Extends the selection to the beginning of the current line
StartOfRow	Moves the insertion point to the first cell in the current row
StartOfWindow	Moves the insertion point to the beginning of the first visible line on the screen
StartOfWindowExtend	Extends the selection to the beginning of the first visible line on the screen
Strikethrough	Formats the selection with a strikethrough (toggle)
Style	Applies an existing style or records a style by example
Subscript	Makes the selection subscript (toggle)

Word Command	Description
Superscript	Makes the selection superscript (toggle)
SymbolFont	Applies the Symbol font to the selection
TableAutoFormat	Applies the set of formatting to a table
TableAutoFormatStyle	Applies a table style to a table
TableAutoSum	Inserts an expression field that automatically sums a table row or column
TableColumnWidth	Changes the width of the columns in a table
TableDeleteColumn	Deletes the selected columns from the table
TableDeleteGeneral	Deletes the selected cells from the table
TableDeleteRow	Deletes the selected rows from the table
TableDeleteTable	Deletes the selected table
TableFormatCell	Changes the height and width of the rows and columns in a table
TableFormula	Inserts a formula field into a table cell
TableGridlines	Toggles table gridlines on and off
TableHeadings	Toggles the table headings attribute on and off
TableInsertColumn	Inserts one or more columns into the table
TableInsertColumnRight	Inserts one or more columns into the table to the right of the current column
TableInsertGeneral	Inserts a table
TableInsertRow	Inserts one or more rows into the table
TableInsertRowAbove	Inserts one or more rows into the table above the current row
TableInsertRowBelow	Inserts one or more rows into the table below the current row
TableMergeCells	Merges the selected table cells into a single cell
TableOptions	Opens the Table Options dialog box
TableProperties	Opens the Table Properties dialog box
TableRowHeight	Changes the height of the rows in a table

(continued)

Word Command	Description
TableSelectCell	Selects the current cell in a table
TableSelectColumn	Selects the current column in a table
TableSelectRow	Selects the current row in a table
TableSelectTable	Selects an entire table
TableSort	Rearranges the selection into a specified order
TableSortAToZ	Sorts records in ascending order (A to Z)
TableSortZToA	Sorts records in descending order (Z to A)
TableSplit	Inserts a paragraph mark above the current row in the table
TableSplitCells	Splits the selected table cells
TableToOrFromText	Converts a table to text
TableUpdateAutoFormat	Updates the table formatting to match the applied formatting set
TableWizard	Runs the Table Wizard
TableWrapping	Changes the wrapping in a table
TextBoxLinking	Creates a forward link to another text box
TextBoxUnlinking	Breaks the forward link to another text box
TextFormField	Inserts a text form field
ToggleCharacterCode	Toggles a character code and a character
ToggleFieldDisplay	Shows the field codes or the results for the selection (toggle)
ToggleFormsDesign	Enables form design
ToggleFull	Toggles full screen mode on and off
ToggleHeaderFooterLink	Links or unlinks the header and footer to or from the previous section
ToggleMainTextLayer	Toggles showing the main text layer in Page Layout view
ToggleMasterSubdocs	Switches between hyperlinks and subdocuments

Word Command	Description
TogglePortrait	Toggles between portrait and landscape mode
ToggleScribbleMode	Inserts a pen comment at the location of the insertion point
ToggleTextFlow	Changes the text flow direction and character orientation
ToggleWebDesign	Enables Web design
ToolsAddRecordDefault	Adds a record to a database
ToolsAutoCorrect	Adds or deletes AutoCorrect entries
ToolsAutoCorrectCapsLockOff	Selects or clears the AutoCorrect Caps Lock Off check box
ToolsAutoCorrectDays	Selects or clears the AutoCorrect Days check box
ToolsAutoCorrectExceptions	Adds or deletes AutoCorrect Capitalization exceptions
ToolsAutoCorrectHECorrect	Provides Hangul and alphabet correction
ToolsAutoCorrectInitialCaps	Selects or clears the AutoCorrect InitialCaps check box
ToolsAutoCorrectReplaceText	Selects or clears the AutoCorrect Replace Text check box
ToolsAutoCorrectSentenceCaps	Selects or clears the AutoCorrect SentenceCaps check box
ToolsAutoCorrectSmartQuotes	Selects or clears the AutoCorrect SmartQuotes check box
ToolsAutoManager	Changes various categories of Word Auto options
ToolsAutoSummarize	Automatically generates a summary of the active document
ToolsAutoSummarizeBegin	Automatically generates a summary of the active document
ToolsBookshelfDefineReference	Looks up a definition for the selected word in Microsoft Bookshelf

(continued)

Word Command	Description
ToolsBookshelfLookupReference	Looks up a reference for the selected word in Microsoft Bookshelf
ToolsBulletListDefault	Creates a bulleted list based on the current defaults
ToolsBulletsNumbers	Changes the numbered and bulleted paragraphs
ToolsBusu	Tools language Busu for Korea
ToolsCalculate	Calculates expressions in the selection
ToolsCompareVersions	Compares the active document with an earlier version
ToolsConsistency	Checks consistency in the active document
ToolsCreateDirectory	Creates a new directory
ToolsCreateEnvelope	Creates or prints an envelope
ToolsCreateLabels	Creates or prints a label or a sheet of labels
ToolsCustomize	Customizes the Word user interface (menus, keyboard, and toolbars)
ToolsCustomizeAddMenuShortcut	Provides a shortcut method for customizing menus
ToolsCustomizeKeyboard	Customizes the Word key assignments
ToolsCustomizeKeyboardShortcut	Provides a shortcut method for customizing keyboard settings
ToolsCustomizeMenus	Customizes the Word menu assignments
ToolsCustomizeRemoveMenuShortcut	Provides a shortcut method for customizing menus
ToolsCustomizeToolbar	Customizes the Word toolbars
ToolsDictionary	Translates the selected word
ToolsEnvelopesAndLabels	Creates or prints an envelope, a label, or a sheet of labels
ToolsEServices	Opens the eServices dialog box
ToolsFixSynonym	Accesses the Synonym feature
ToolsGrammar	Checks the grammar in the active document

Word Command	Description
ToolsGrammarHide	Hides background grammar errors
ToolsGramSettings	Customizes grammar settings
ToolsHHC	Finds a Hangul/Hanja word for the selected word
ToolsHyphenation	Changes the hyphenation settings for the active document
ToolsHyphenationManual	Hyphenates the selection or the entire document
ToolsInsertScript	Inserts a script
ToolsLanguage	Changes the language formatting of the selected characters
ToolsMacro	Runs, creates, deletes, or revises a macro
ToolsManageFields	Adds or deletes a field from a database
ToolsMergeRevisions	Merges changes from the active document to an earlier version of the document
ToolsNumberListDefault	Creates a numbered list based on the current defaults
ToolsOptions	Changes various categories of Word for Windows options
ToolsOptionsAutoFormat	Changes the AutoFormat options
ToolsOptionsAutoFormatAsYouType	Changes the AutoFormat As You Type options
ToolsOptionsBidi	Changes the bidirectional options
ToolsOptionsCompatibility	Changes the document compatibility options
ToolsOptionsEdit	Changes the editing options
ToolsOptionsEditCopyPaste	Opens the Settings dialog box
ToolsOptionsFileLocations	Changes the default locations Word uses to find files
ToolsOptionsFuzzy	Changes the fuzzy expressions options
ToolsOptionsGeneral	Changes the general options
ToolsOptionsGrammar	Changes the proofreader options

(continued)

Word Command	Description
ToolsOptionsHHC	Changes the HHC options
ToolsOptionsPrint	Changes the printing options
ToolsOptionsRevisions	Changes the track changes options
ToolsOptionsSave	Changes the save settings
ToolsOptionsSecurity	Changes the security options
ToolsOptionsSmartTag	Changes the smart tag options
ToolsOptionsSpelling	Changes the proofreader options
ToolsOptionsTypography	Changes the typography options
ToolsOptionsUserInfo	Changes the user information options
ToolsOptionsView	Sets specific view mode options
ToolsProofing	Checks the proofing in the active document
ToolsProtectUnprotectDocument	Sets protection for the active document
ToolsRecordMacroStart	Turns on the macro recorder
ToolsRecordMacroStop	Turns off the macro recorder
ToolsRecordMacroToggle	Turns macro recorder on or off
ToolsRemoveRecordDefault	Removes a record from a database
ToolsRepaginate	Recalculates page breaks
ToolsReviewRevisions	Reviews changes to the active document
ToolsRevisionMarksAccept	Accepts changes in the current selection
ToolsRevisionMarksNext	Finds the next change
ToolsRevisionMarksPrev	Finds the previous change
ToolsRevisionMarksReject	Rejects changes in the current selection
ToolsRevisionMarksToggle	Toggles track changes for the active document
ToolsRevisions	Sets track changes for the active document
ToolsSCTCTranslate	Translates a Chinese string
ToolsShrinkToFit	Attempts to make the document fit on one less page
ToolsSpeech	Turns on or off Speech Recognition

Word Command	Description
ToolsSpelling	Checks the spelling in the active document
ToolsSpellingHide	Hides background spelling errors
ToolsSpellingRecheckDocument	Resets spelling results for the current document
ToolsSpellSelection	Checks the spelling of the selected text
ToolsTCSCTranslate	Translates a Chinese string
ToolsTCSCTranslation	Translates a Chinese string
ToolsThesaurus	Finds a synonym for the selected word
ToolsTranslateChinese	Translates a Chinese string
ToolsWordCount	Calculates the word count statistics of the active document
ToolsWordCountList	Displays the word count statistics of the active document
ToolsWordCountRecount	Updates the word count statistics of the active document
TopAlign	Aligns cell contents at the top of the cell
TopCenterAlign	Aligns cell contents at the top center of the cell
TopLeftAlign	Aligns cell contents at the top left of the cell
TopRightAlign	Aligns cell contents at the top right of the cell
Translate	Displays the Translate task pane
TranslatePane	Translates text
TxbxAutosize	Changes the selected drawing object to AutoSize
Underline	Formats the selection with a continuous underline (toggle)
UnderlineColor	Changes the underline color of the selected text
UnderlineStyle	Formats the selection with a continuous underline
UnHang	Decreases the hanging indent

(continued)

Word Command	Description
UnIndent	Moves the left indent to the previous tab stop
UnIndentChar	Decreases the indent by the width of a character
UnIndentFirstChar	Decreases the hanging indent by the width of a character
UnIndentFirstLine	Decreases the hanging indent by the width of two characters
UnIndentLine	Decreases the indent by the width of two characters
UnlinkFields	Permanently replaces the field codes with the results
UnlockFields	Unlocks the selected fields for updating
UpdateFields	Updates and displays the results of the selected fields
UpdateSource	Copies the modified text of a linked file back to its source
UpdateTableOfContents	Updates the first table of contents in the document
UpdateToc	Selects the method of updating a table of contents or figures
UpdateTocFull	Rebuilds a table of contents or figures
ViewAnnotations	Shows or hides comment markup balloons
ViewBorderToolbar	Shows or hides the Tables And Borders toolbar
ViewChanges	Shows or hides markup balloons
ViewCode	Displays the Visual Basic Editor
ViewControlToolbox	Shows or hides the Control toolbox
ViewDocumentMap	Toggles the state of the Heading Explorer
ViewDraft	Displays the document without formatting and pictures for faster editing (toggle)
ViewDrawingToolbar	Shows or hides the Drawing toolbar

Word Command	Description
ViewEndnoteArea	Opens a pane for viewing and editing the endnotes (toggle)
ViewEndnoteContNotice	Opens a pane for viewing and editing the endnote continuation notice
ViewEndnotContSeparator	Opens a pane for viewing and editing the endnote continuation separator
ViewEndnoteSeparator	Opens a pane for viewing and editing the endnote separator
ViewFieldCodes	Shows the field codes or results for all fields (toggle)
ViewFooter	Displays the footer in Page Layout view
ViewFootnoteArea	Opens a pane for viewing and editing the footnotes (toggle)
ViewFootnoteContNotice	Opens a pane for viewing and editing the footnote continuation notice
ViewFootnoteContSeparator	Opens a pane for viewing and editing the footnote continuation separator
ViewFootnotes	Opens a pane for viewing and editing the notes (toggle)
ViewFootnoteSeparator	Opens a pane for viewing and editing the footnote separator
ViewFormatExToolbar	Shows or hides the Extended Formatting toolbar
ViewGridlines	Shows or hides the gridlines
ViewHeader	Displays the header in Page Layout view
ViewHTMLSource	Displays the HTML source code
ViewMasterDocument	Switches to Master Document view
ViewNormal	Changes the editing view to Normal view
ViewOnline	Displays the document optimized for reading on line
ViewOutline	Displays a document's outline
ViewOutlineMaster	Displays a document's outline

(continued)

Word Command	Description
ViewOutlineSplitToolbar	Shows or hides the Tables And Borders toolbar
ViewPage	Displays the page as it will be printed and allows editing
ViewRuler	Shows or hides the ruler
ViewSecurity	Displays the Security Level tab in the Security dialog box
ViewStatusBar	Shows or hides the status bar
ViewTaskPane	Shows or hides the task pane
ViewToggleMasterDocument	Switches between Outline and Master Document views
ViewTogglePageBoundaries	Switches between showing and hiding vertical margins in Print Layout view
ViewToolbars	Shows or hides the Word toolbars
ViewVBCode	Shows the Visual Basic editing environment
ViewWeb	Displays the document similar to how it would appear in a browser
ViewWebToolbox	Shows or hides the Web Toolbox
ViewZoom	Scales the editing view
ViewZoom100	Scales the editing view to 100 percent in Normal view
ViewZoom200	Scales the editing view to 200 percent in Normal view
ViewZoom75	Scales the editing view to 75 percent in Normal view
ViewZoomPageWidth	Scales the editing view to show the width of the page
ViewZoomWholePage	Scales the editing view to show the whole page in Page Layout view
WebAddHyperlnkToFavorites	Adds to Favorites list
WebAddress	Opens the Open Internet Address dialog box

Word Command	Description
WebAddToFavorites	Adds the active file to your Favorites list
WebCopyHyperlink	Copies a shortcut
WebGoBack	Opens the previous file or item
WebGoForward	Opens the next file or item in your history list
WebHideToolbars	Hides other toolbars
WebOpenFavorites	Opens the Favorites folder
WebOpenHyperlink	Jumps to a location
WebOpenInNewWindow	Opens a hyperlink's target in a new window
WebOpenSearchPage	Opens a search page
WebOpenStartPage	Opens the start page
WebOptions	Opens the Web Options dialog box
WebPagePreview	Displays full pages in a Web browser
WebRefresh	Refreshes the current page
WebSelectHyperlink	Edits text
WebStopLoading	Stops the current jump
WebToolbar	Toggles the Web toolbar
WindowArrangeAll	Arranges windows as nonoverlapping tiles
WindowList	Switches to the window containing the specified document
WindowNewWindow	Opens another window for the active document
WordLeft	Moves the insertion point to the left one word
WordLeftExtend	Extends the selection to the left one word
WordRight	Moves the insertion point to the right one word
WordRightExtend	Extends the selection to the right one word
WordUnderline	Underlines the words but not the spaces in the selection (toggle)

(continued)

Word Command	Description
WW7_DecreaseIndent	Decreases the indent or promotes the selection one level
WW7_DrawTextBox	Inserts a text box drawing object
WW7_DrawVerticalTextBox	Inserts a vertical text box drawing object
WW7_FormatDrawingObject	Changes the fill, line, size, and position attributes of the selected drawing objects
WW7_IncreaseIndent	Increases the indent or demotes the selection one level
WW7_ToolsOptions	Changes various categories of Word For Windows options

Appendix D

Quick Guide to Peer-to-Peer Networks

This appendix provides you with a basic understanding of computer networks, with an emphasis on peer-to-peer networks. The topics range from a discussion of standard network terms to setting up a computer for peer-to-peer network operation. This appendix starts by looking at some of the common network types in use today.

Reviewing Common Network Types

With the proliferation of computers came the need to connect them together in order to speed up the transfer of information. Large enterprises (such as universities, governments, and corporations) have been networked for several years. They were the only entities able to afford networks before the 1990s. Now, small business and home computer networks abound, because they can be achieved at reasonable cost and with minimal technical involvement. Of course, the types of networks vary between larger enterprise networks and small business and home networks. Many organizations use client/server networks and most small businesses and home users get along fine with peer-to-peer networks. Both client/server and peer-to-peer networks are referred to as local area networks (LANs).

Beyond the nucleus of LAN networks, you'll find wide area networks (WANs) and the Internet. A WAN typically connects LANs that are widely separated (such as LANs in New York, Los Angeles, Paris, and London). And the Internet is a publicly accessible global collection of WANs and LANs. Microsoft Word works very well within these networks, as does the entire Microsoft Office suite and many other recently developed applications. Using Word, you can open files on network computers, send files to network computers, create Web folders, store and send documents to Web folders, and work with document collaboration servers.

Client/Server Networks

Larger enterprises often use client/server networks, in which users' computers must send and receive information through a high-powered computer to communicate across a network. To understand how a client/server setup works, think of your favorite restaurant. When your computer requests a file from another computer, via a network, it's like you're ordering a sandwich for lunch at a restaurant. Both the computer and you are in client mode. When the computer sends a file to another computer, it's like the waiter bringing your sandwich. In this case, the computer and the waiter are in serving mode. Hence, the client/server relationship—the clients request a service, and the server finds and retrieves the requested item and serves it to the clients.

Generally, a small office with five computers or so would need only one server to handle the requests of all five computers. Figure D-1 shows a small client/server network.

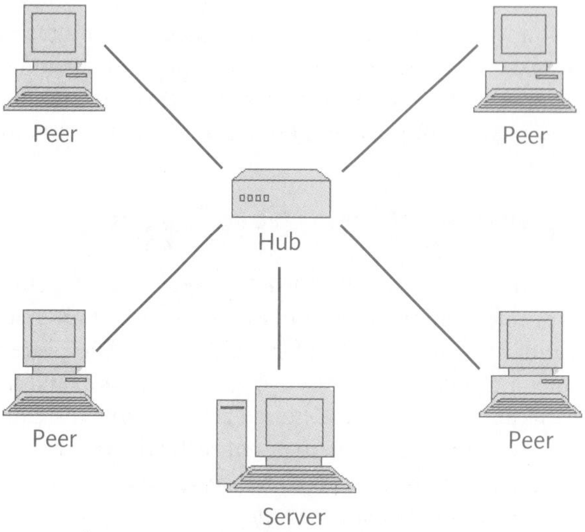

Figure D-1. A small client/server network is suitable for small offices.

Larger organizations, involving 50 or more computers on a network, generally require several server computers. Typically, in a large organization's network, each server is specialized to perform certain functions. For example, you'll often see networks with file servers, print servers, and applications servers. Generally, a *file server* is a central repository of files used by company employees (clients), and it transfers files to and from the employees as needed. A *print server* is commonly connected to one or more printers and handles the network printing for employees. An *application server* is usually dedicated to handling requests that require some processing beyond simple file transfers. A good example of an application server is a company billing and customer information setup, which typically involves searching a large database to assist employees in completing billing and customer-related tasks.

Two prime advantages enterprises gain by using client/server networks are uniformity and security:

- **Uniformity** means that a network user can sit down at any workstation and see screens of information identical to screens shown on any other workstation.
- **Security** is easy to maintain because all critical company information can be located on a few servers that require user IDs and passwords to access.

To help standardize network information and security, most client/server networks have a designated administrator. This administrator maintains the network and controls network security.

A main disadvantage of client/server networks is that they require dedicated computers to act as servers, which means the computers are not available for use as standard workstations. This can be an added expense—from both a hardware and a maintenance standpoint—because those extra computers must be purchased and maintained in addition to the users' workstations.

Peer-to-Peer Networks

Unlike client/server networks, peer-to-peer networks work without a dedicated server computer. In a peer-to-peer network, all computers are workstations, which are networked together. Figure D-2 shows an example of a small peer-to-peer network.

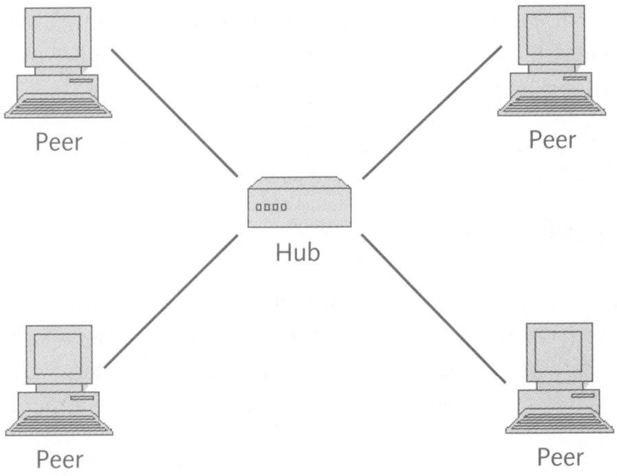

Figure D-2. In a small peer-to-peer network, each computer can act as a server.

In a peer-to-peer setup, each computer workstation on the network can act as either a client or a server. For example, let's say Julie needs information that's stored on Ronnie's computer. Julie uses her computer to send a request for the information (her computer acting as a client), and Ronnie's computer sends the information (his computer acting as a server). Likewise in reverse, Ronnie can use his computer to request information from Julie's computer (his computer acting as a client), and Julie's computer will send the information (her computer acting as a server).

Keep in mind that because information is distributed throughout many of the network computers (and not stored on a central server), the information might not be uniform in appearance. Likewise, security is not uniform across the network, because computer users establish and maintain security on their own computer workstations. For most users, security tends to be a secondary job function and often suffers (especially if their primary workload is high).

Overall, the main advantages of peer-to-peer networks are that they are easy to implement (most operating systems have built in peer-to-peer network functions) and there is no need for an extra computer to act as a server.

LANs, WANs, and the Internet

To help round out the discussion, let's quickly revisit LANs, WANs and the Internet. Basically, a LAN is a complex of computer and network equipment confined to a building or an area, such as a manufacturing plant or university. A WAN connects LANs. In other words, WANs connect LANs to make a geographically large network. A WAN can connect LANs located anywhere in the world. As you might imagine, the next step up from WANs is the Internet. The Internet, which is a global collection of interconnected WANs and LANs, is popular because it's far-reaching and publicly accessible.

Now that you're somewhat briefed on the various types of networks, let's move on to look more closely at peer-to-peer network setups. The remainder of this appendix presents information you can use to set up your own small peer-to-peer network on a Microsoft Windows-based machine.

Preparing to Set Up a Peer-to-Peer Network

At the simplest level, you can network two computers by using a couple of *network interface cards* (NICs) and a *crossover network cable*. Figure D-3 shows a simple two-computer peer-to-peer network. To network more than two computers, you'll need a connecting device called a *hub*. (These terms are defined later in this appendix.)

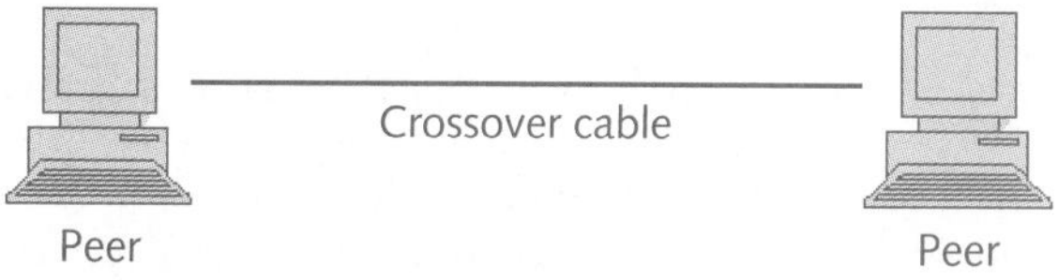

Figure D-3. You can create a two-computer network with a crossover network cable and two network interface cards (NICs).

After you have a peer-to-peer network set up, you can connect your network to another network via a device called a *gateway* or *router*. Figure D-4 shows a peer-to-peer network with a network printer, a broadband modem, and a router connection to another network. As this discussion moves along, you'll see how all these hardware pieces are used in a network.

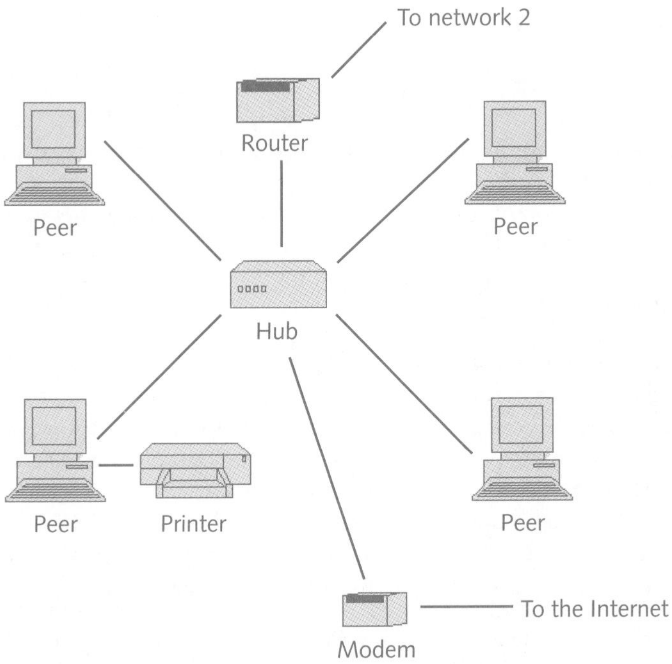

Figure D-4. This peer-to-peer network includes workstations, printer, broadband modem, and a router used to connect the network to another network.

In addition to the hardware, as you might suspect, you'll need to install and configure some Microsoft Windows networking software components. Specifically, you'll need Client For Microsoft Networks, a software driver for your NIC, some network protocol software (such as TCP/IP), and File And Printer Sharing For Microsoft Networks. All of these services come with the Windows operating system. The only exception could be the software driver for your NIC. In some cases, the NIC manufacturer might have a later version than the one it submitted to Microsoft for inclusion in Windows. Some of these terms might be new to you. If so, refer to the next few sections, which discuss the terms and components in more detail.

Network Hardware Components

NICs, cables, and hubs are the major hardware items needed to construct a network. In addition, while you might not need to use a router in your peer-to-peer setup, routers are discussed because they pertain to using a shared Internet connection on a small office and home office (SOHO) network. Let's take a closer look at these components.

Network Interface Card (NIC)

A NIC is a small circuit card that you plug into your computer's expansion bus. An *expansion bus* is a set of connectors inside your computer—it's called an *expansion bus* because it's used to expand the capability of your computer. Typical expansion cards include modems, sound cards, video cards, and network cards. In addition, several types of expansion bus sockets exist, including ISA (Industry Standards Architecture), EISA (Extended ISA), Micro Channel (IBM), VESA Local, and PCI (Peripheral Component Interconnect). ISA and PCI are the two most popular sockets in personal computers today.

Most current Ethernet NICs come with a PCI interface, and therefore, you'll need an available PCI slot on your expansion bus to install your NIC. The NIC provides the hardware interface between your computer and other Ethernet networked components. The most common network types used in home computers are Ethernet and Fast Ethernet. The Ethernet network speed is 10 Mbps (megabits per second) and the Fast Ethernet speed is 100 Mbps. Most currently available Ethernet NICs are 10/100 autoswitching, which means that they automatically sense the network speed (10 Mbps or 100 Mbps) and adjust their operation to that network speed.

While you'll probably create an Ethernet network, another common network type you might hear about is Token Ring. A Token Ring network connects all network computers in a ring configuration—each computer in turn receives the circulating token message. The computer that has the token can send any network messages it has in its queue. If the computer with the token has no message to send or has finished sending its message, it passes the token to the next computer.

Ethernet systems do not use tokens. Instead, an Ethernet computer listens to the network to see if any other computer is sending a message. If the network is quiet, the computer sends its message. Of course, this means that there's a chance that two computers might try to send a message at the same time and thus create a *collision*. When two messages collide, your network needs a way to resolve the situation or you'll end up with two hopelessly garbled messages. Therefore, Ethernet components have collision detection circuits that put a random delay time into message retransmit times. Usually, the random delay times separate two computers' retransmit attempts, so the collision is resolved. Adding a delay time for retransmission delays communication between your networked computers. A few collisions will not be noticeable, but as network traffic increases, more collisions are likely and you might notice the delay in network response.

Ethernet networks use a standard that specifies the information bit patterns and signal levels used on an Ethernet network. Most SOHO NICs are built to the Ethernet network standard, and they use RJ-45 network connectors.

note An RJ-45 jack is very similar to the standard wall telephone jack, which is an RJ-11 jack. The RJ-45 is bigger and uses eight conductors instead of the four conductors used in the RJ-11.

The job of the NIC is to receive Ethernet information from the network and convert it to bytes that the computer can understand. Conversely, the NIC must be able to receive bytes from the computer and convert them to Ethernet information for network transmission.

You're probably aware that printers and modems can be connected to networks. But they don't always connect to networks in the same way as they connect to a computer. In fact, printers and dial-up modems typically used in peer-to-peer networks do not contain NIC functions and connections. Instead, a printer usually connects to a computer's parallel port, and most dial-up modems are installed as internal cards on the computer's expansion bus. External dial-up modems connect to a computer's serial port.

note A parallel port is a 25-pin female connector found on the back of a computer's central processing unit (CPU). It is called a *parallel port* because it allows eight bits of information, or one whole byte, to cross the connector interface at the same time (eight bits in parallel). A serial port is a 9-pin male or 25-pin male connector on the back of a CPU. This type of connector is called *serial* because it sends only one bit at a time across the connector interface (and a byte is a serial stream of eight consecutive bits crossing the connector interface).

If you want to have a printer connect directly to the network, you need to buy a network-capable printer with a built-in NIC or buy an external *network adapter* for your parallel port printer. A network adapter is a small external unit with network and printer interface circuitry and connections for the printer parallel port cable, the network cable, and a power source. The network adapter converts the network serial data to parallel data needed by the printer.

Unlike most dial-up modems, broadband (high-speed) cable modems and DSL (digital subscriber line) modems are built with internal NIC functions and connections. Therefore, network printers, broadband modems, and DSL modems are good candidates for network connections, because they can efficiently support several users simultaneously

Crossover Cables

The easiest way to connect only two computers together is to use a crossover cable. It's called a *crossover cable* because it switches the function of the wire pairs (as described in the next paragraph) between NICs. You can avoid having to use a hub to connect the two computers by using a crossover cable.

You can identify the cables by looking at the cable's wire colors. For instance, on a normal network cable, if you hold the RJ-11 plugs on each end of the cable the same way, you can look at the plugs (which is easy if they are clear plastic plugs) and see that the color sequence of the wires from left to right is identical. On a crossover cable, the color sequence is altered because some of the wires are switched. This switching connects the transmit terminals from the first NIC to the receive terminals of the second NIC. Conversely, the receive terminals of the first NIC connect to the transmit terminals of the second NIC. These switches in the crossover cable ensure that each NIC transmitter is connected to a receiver at the other NIC. Without the wire switching, the NICs could not communicate, because their transmitters would be talking to each other and their receivers would be listening to each other—no one would be talking to the listeners and no one would be listening to the talkers!

Hubs and Interconnecting Cables

When you want to network more than two computers, you'll need to use a hub. A hub is basically a multi-connector repeater. It is multi-connector because it has 4, 8, 16, or more jacks to accommodate several network cables from computers, printers, modems, and other hardware you want to include on the network. A hub works by receiving a signal on the transmit pair of any of its jacks, and then repeating the signal on the receive pair of all the other jacks. The hub accomplishes the crossover function (as described in the section "Crossover Cables" on page 1045), thereby connecting all the NIC transmitters to the NIC receivers.

SOHO systems use UTP category 5 network cable. *UTP* stands for unshielded twisted pair, and category 5 means that the cable can work at speeds up to 100 mega*bits* per second (or 12 mega*bytes* per second). Unshielded twisted pair describes the wire pairs in the network cable. The network cable consists of eight wires arranged into four pairs. Each pair is twisted together about five or six turns per foot of wire. This twisting reduces the effect of interference signals from electrical appliances or equipment near the network cable. Interference signals can cause garbling of network messages thus leading to retransmissions and increased network traffic, with the worst case scenario being a complete overload of the network. For most SOHO environments, the unshielded twisted pair works very well. If the environment is electrically noisy, you can use shielded twisted pair (STP). In this case, each cable pair is wrapped with foil and then all four shielded pairs are again wrapped with foil before adding the outside plastic jacket. Category 5 cable is satisfactory for cable lengths of l00 meters (328 feet) or less. If you need greater speed or area, premium cables are available for network speeds above 100 megabits per second, and repeaters are available for extending cable runs beyond 100 meters in length.

If you're constructing a new building, you can easily have the builder include network cabling. Chances are, though, that you don't have that luxury. So, to install cables in your SOHO, you might have to drill holes in the walls and desks, and pull cables to the various computer stations, printer stations, and so forth.

> **tip** **Consider alternatives to standard network cables**
>
> Some alternatives to using standard networking cables exist. For example, some network systems can piggyback on AC (Alternating Current—110 volt) electrical wiring or telephone wiring. If you use those capabilities, you have to ensure that AC outlets and telephone jacks are near where you need network connections. In addition, you can choose a wireless networking system, which you'll be hearing more about in the next few years.

Routers

Another common network component is a router. The primary purpose of a router is to connect networks together. For example, a large organization might connect several smaller networks together by routers. Generally, a router connects two networks and has the function of passing, or *routing*, network messages between the two networks. A router checks the destination address of all the messages on both networks. If the sending computer and the receiving computer are on the same network, the router recognizes that it doesn't need to do any message routing. If the sending computer transmits a message for a computer on a different network, the router captures the message and retransmits it to the different network. Thus, you can connect your network to other networks by adding a router.

As you might expect, the Internet relies on the ability of thousands of routers to guide messages to their destinations. In a SOHO network, you might use a router if your network includes a cable modem or DSL modem with routing capabilities. In effect, if your networked computers share an Internet connection via a routing cable modem or DSL modem, your modem serves a routing function. When you browse the Internet, you're connecting a computer from your SOHO network to another network (the Internet) to reach the Web site you've selected. Thus, you're using your cable or DSL modem to connect networks together.

Not all cable and DSL modems have routing capabilities. If you have a cable or DSL modem that does not route messages, you can use the gateway feature of Windows 98, Windows Millennium Edition (Me), and Windows 2000, called Internet Connection Sharing (ICS). A *gateway* is a network computer connected to two networks that accomplishes the routing function between the two networks. ICS allows you to set up one of your network computers to connect to both your network and the Internet. Your Internet connection can be a dial-up, cable, or DSL connection. If you use a cable or DSL modem, you'll need two NICs—one for your network and one for the cable or DSL modem. ICS allows any of your network computers access to the Internet via the computer you set up as your Internet gateway, or host computer.

Network Software Components

After your network's hardware is in place, you're ready to break out the software and fire up the network. So, what do you need? For a peer-to-peer network you need the following:

- **Client/server software** to enable your computer to request information and supply information via the network
- **A software driver** for your NIC
- **A network protocol** so program applications know which rules to follow when sending and receiving information over a network
- **Sharing and security services** that you want to use on your network

The next few sections look at these software components in detail.

Client/Server Software

Client/server software allows your computer to ask for files and services from another computer. The Windows 95, Windows 98, Windows Me, and Windows 2000 operating systems all come with *Client For Microsoft Networks*. This software module can work as a client on a client/server network and can work as a client and a server on a peer-to-peer network. You can tell if you have Client For Microsoft Networks installed by looking at your network properties, as follows:

- **Windows 2000.** Right click My Network Places, and choose Properties from the shortcut menu. In the Network And Dial-Up Connections dialog box, right-click Local Area Connection, and choose Properties.
- **Windows 95/98/Me.** Right-click Network Neighborhood (for Windows Me right click on My Network Places) and choose Properties from the shortcut menu.

If Client For Microsoft Networks is installed, you'll see it listed. If you find that you don't have Client For Microsoft Networks installed on your system, don't worry; it's easy to install, as described in "Configuring a Network Client Setup" on page 1054.

NIC Driver Software

As you probably know, a *driver* is a small program that translates application program instructions into specific hardware (device) control instructions. For example, in Word, sending a document to a fax machine is almost like sending it to another computer on your network. In reality, the two functions differ only in which device driver Word requests. Word requests a Windows fax-modem driver to send information to a fax machine and a Windows NIC driver to send information to another network computer. If your computer came with a NIC, you probably already have a driver installed.

To see if your NIC driver is installed, check your network properties as described in the preceding section "Client/Server Software."

If your NIC driver is installed, you will see an adapter entry, such as "Netgear FA310TX Fast Ethernet PCI Adapter." You can also check for device drivers in Device Manager. In Windows 2000, choose Start, Settings, Control Panel, double-click System, click the Hardware tab, and then click the Device Manager button. If a Network Adapters entry is present, click the plus sign (+) that appears to the left of the entry. If your NIC driver is installed, you'll see it listed under the Network Adapters entry. In Windows 95, Windows 98, and Windows Me, you can access the Device Manager by choosing Start, Settings, Control Panel, double-clicking Systems, and clicking the Device Manager tab.

If you need to install a NIC and its driver, the section "Installing a Network Interface Card" on page 1051 tells you how to install a NIC, and the section "Configuring a Network Interface Card" on page 1053 explains how to install a NIC driver.

Network Protocol Software

In a nutshell, network protocols are simply standard sets of rules computers use to communicate across a network. The protocol used throughout the Internet is TCP/IP (Transmission Control Protocol/Internet Protocol). TCP/IP is a very sophisticated set of standards and software programs that handle the message formats, connection control, error control, routing, and other transmission tasks associated with network communication.

While TCP/IP is the protocol of choice for the Internet, you can also use it in your peer-to-peer network. With each new version of Windows, the installation of the TCP/IP protocol has become more automatic and easier. If you plan to connect to the Internet via a broadband modem or a dial-up modem, you'll have to install the TCP/IP protocol.

If you don't plan to have an Internet connection, you can use a non-routable fast protocol on your peer-to-peer network, like NetBEUI (Network BIOS Extended User Interface). A non-routable protocol is one that uses an addressing scheme that can't be decoded by a router. To see which network protocols you have installed on your computer, check your network properties as described in the section "Client/Server Software" on page 1048.

In Windows 2000 the protocol(s) should be listed and selected in the Components Checked Are Used By This Connection box. In Windows 95, 98 and Me the protocols will be listed but not checked in the Network (properties) window.

Network Services Software

Clearly, the benefit of constructing a network is to gain productivity from its use; network services software can help you realize this goal. When people work on a network, they usually look for flexibility and the ability to share resources. For example, when you create a network, you can increase productivity for network users by allowing them to perform any of the following actions from within Word:

- Send a document file to a coworker's computer for review or reference
- Transmit a document over a shared Internet connection to a customer
- Send a document to a network printer in your office or another office
- Set up a shared document folder that coworkers can access as they need

For more information about sharing information on a network while working in Word, see Chapter 30, "Collaborating On Line with E-Mail, NetMeeting, Discussions, and Faxes" and Chapter 32, "Sharing Information on Networks."

Network services provide all these capabilities. Windows 95, Windows 98, Windows Me, and Windows 2000 all have a network module called *File And Printer Sharing For Microsoft Networks*. This module allows you to set up your network computer for sharing folders and printers. To see if you have file and printer sharing installed, check your network properties as described in the section "Client/Server Software" on page 1048.

The File And Printer Sharing For Microsoft Networks service should be listed and selected in the Components Checked Are Used By This Connection box.

Installing Network Hardware

Up to this point in the appendix, you've been looking at the types of hardware and software you should expect to deal with when you're setting up a network. In this section, you'll find instructions for installing your network's hardware.

The fist step to building a network is to decide on the method you'll use for network communication. Your main choices are as follows:

- **Wireless network system.** A wireless system gives you total freedom in locating your network computers and it doesn't require you to modify your building with network jacks and cable installation. However, a wireless system is not as fast as a UTP cable Fast Ethernet system, and its NICs are the most expensive choice.
- **Phone network (PN) system.** With a phone network system, you can use existing home telephone wiring. The disadvantages are that it's not as fast as UTP cable and telephone jacks might not be in the best location for your computer.
- **UTP network cable system.** A UTP cable system is fast (100 Mbps) and the UTP cable NICs and hubs are the least expensive choice. However, it often requires drilling holes in walls and pulling in UTP cables.

After you decide on a network method, you are ready to install the network components, as described in the following sections.

Installing Network Cabling

The extent of cabling configuration you have to do depends on the type of network you're setting up. Obviously, if you choose a wireless system, you're done with wiring before you even start. Well, you have to plug the wireless network communicators into each network device (computer, printer, modem, and so forth) that you want to have on your network, but that's hardly considered a wiring project.

If you're setting up a phone network, your cable work consists of running phone network cables from each network device to a telephone jack. If you have multiple phone lines in your household or office, each network device (computer, printer, modem, and so forth) must connect to the same phone line.

Finally, if you choose to use a UTP cable system, you have to do some work. The first task is to select a location for the network hub. Remember, the maximum UTP cable length is 100 meters (328 feet). In some instances, this might have a bearing on where you locate the hub. If you suspect that you'll have a long cable running from a network device to the hub, consider placing the hub halfway between your most extreme network device locations. Once the hub is placed, it is just a matter of installing a UTP cable from each device to the hub. If you have devices in different rooms, you might need to drill holes in walls and pull UTP cables from each device to the hub.

Installing a Network Interface Card

The next hardware installation task you might face is installing NICs for one of the three main types of networks:

- **A wireless NIC** can be an external box that plugs into your computer's universal serial bus (USB) or it can be an internal circuit card that you plug into your computer's expansion bus.
- **A phone network NIC** can be an external box with two jacks. One jack connects to a phone cable going to a phone jack on the wall. The other jack plugs into your computer's USB. A phone network NIC can also be an internal circuit card.
- **A UTP cable system NIC** is almost always an internal circuit card.

To install an internal circuit card NIC, follow these steps:

1. Turn off your computer and remove the cover. Before handling your NIC or any internal computer parts make sure you wear a wrist strap or otherwise ground your body by touching the computer chassis to absorb any static electricity you develop by moving around.

> **tip** **Avoid damage from static electricity**
>
> The major hazard to computer equipment is damage due to static electricity. Computer circuit cards are very sensitive to static electricity. As little as 35 volts can damage a card; this voltage is so small you don't even feel the shock. The best preventative against static buildup on your body is to use a grounding wrist strap—available at most electronic supply stores for just a few dollars. The strap consists of a Velcro bracelet and an attached grounding lead. Strap on the bracelet and connect the grounding lead to your computer chassis to avoid static electricity problems.

2. Follow the manufacturer's directions for installing the internal NIC circuit card.

3. When finished with the physical installation of the internal NIC circuit card, remove your grounding lead from your computer and replace the cover on the processor box.

4. Before turning on your computer, connect your network cable to the newly installed NIC. Most of the internal NICs are plug-and-play, which means that after you finish the physical installation of a NIC and turn on your computer, Windows will detect and configure the new device.

After you install the NIC hardware, you'll have to ensure that the driver for it is installed properly. For more information about NIC software installation, see the section "Configuring a Network Interface Card" on page 1053.

Configuring Network Software in Windows

After you've completed the hardware side of your network, you'll need to set up your computer's software. Fortunately, all the networking software components you need to set up a peer-to-peer network, with the possible exception of the NIC driver module, come with Windows (Windows 95, Windows 98, Windows Me, and Windows 2000).

As mentioned in the section "Network Software Components" on page 1048, the software components you'll use to set up a peer-to-peer network are a NIC driver, a network client, a network protocol, and a network services module. Additionally, you'll need to assign a name for your network and assign names for each computer on your network. If you're using Windows 2000 on one of your computers, you'll also need to set up user IDs and passwords for all users (local and network) of that computer. You can easily set up all of these program modules using the network functions and user functions in your Control Panel. So, here we go—the next few sections lead you through the software side of your network installation and getting your network up and running.

Configuring a Network Interface Card

After completing the physical installation of your NIC, you can power up your computer and see if the plug-and-play system detects the newly installed NIC. In most cases, the system will detect your NIC, and you'll see the Found New Hardware dialog box, as shown in Figure D-5. All you have to do is follow the on-screen instructions. If Windows does not detect your NIC, you can use the Windows 2000 Add/Remove Hardware feature or the Windows 95, Windows 98, and Windows Me Add New Hardware feature in the Control Panel to install your NIC. Running the add new hardware wizard will start the hardware installation process, as shown in Figure D-5.

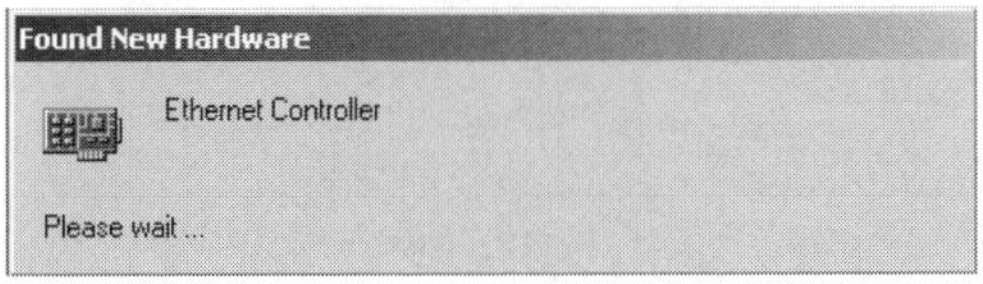

Figure D-5. The Found New Hardware dialog box opens if your system finds a newly installed NIC.

note The figures shown in this appendix are based on Windows 2000, but your network might include computers using other operating systems. Fortunately, the respective screens that you'll see in Windows 95, Windows 98, and Windows Me are very similar to the Windows 2000 screens shown in this appendix. You should be able to follow along while using Windows 95, Windows 98, or Windows Me.

Shortly after you see the Found New Hardware dialog box shown in Figure D-5, you'll see the Insert Disk dialog box shown in Figure D-6. A NIC comes with a floppy disk that contains several drivers, one for each operating system that can interface with the NIC. Insert your NIC driver floppy disk in your computer's floppy drive, and click OK.

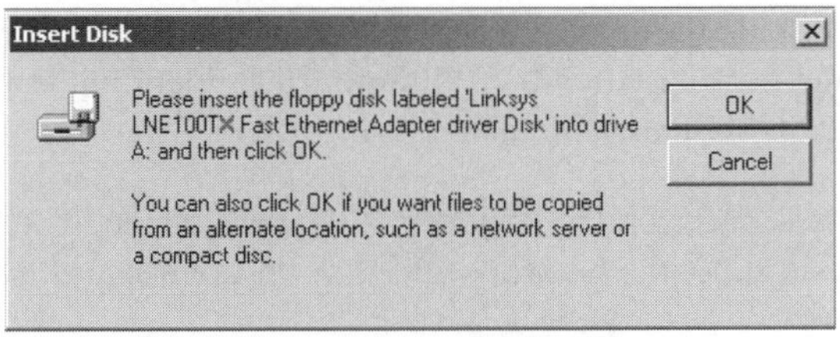

Figure D-6. The Insert Disk dialog box instructs you to insert your NIC's floppy disk so the NIC driver can be installed.

The Install Wizard should find the correct NIC driver for your operating system from the floppy disk. Sometimes, however, the system has trouble finding the correct directory for the driver it needs. In that case, you might receive a Files Needed dialog box similar to the one shown in Figure D-7. If this occurs, refer to the manufacturer's instructions that came with your NIC; they usually show separate procedures for software installation depending on the operating system. Locate the procedure appropriate for your operating system and the directory on your NIC disk you should use. After you find the correct directory, you can enter the path in the Copy Files From box in the lower part of the Files Needed dialog box. As an alternative, you can click the Browse button in the Files Needed dialog box to locate the directory that contains the NIC driver.

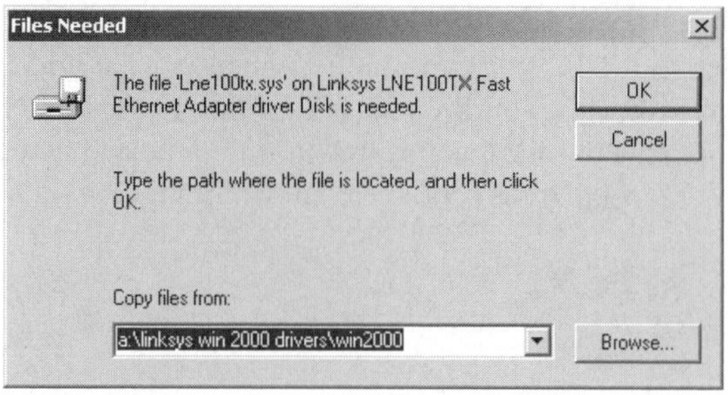

Figure D-7. The Files Needed dialog box opens if your system can't find the correct driver.

After the operating system finds the correct files, it will complete the NIC driver installation. In addition, Windows might need some files from your Windows CD-ROM; if so, you might need to insert your Windows CD in the CD-ROM drive.

When Windows completes the installation of all the files it needs, you'll see a dialog box stating that you need to restart your computer to complete the installation. Restart your computer and complete the installation of your NIC. Windows 2000 usually doesn't require the system CD-ROM or a restart to install your NIC, but don't be surprised if your setup requires these additional steps. At this point, you're ready to proceed to the installation of client, protocol, and service software, as described next.

Configuring a Network Client Setup

After the NIC drivers are installed, you need to set up your client software. To do so, follow these steps (these steps are based on the Windows 2000 operating system, but other operating system setups are fairly similar):

1. Right-click My Network Places on the Windows 2000 desktop, and choose Properties. In Windows 2000, the Network And Dial-Up Connections dialog box appears.
2. Right-click the Local Area Connection icon, and choose Properties. The Local Area Connection Properties dialog box opens, as shown in Figure D-8.

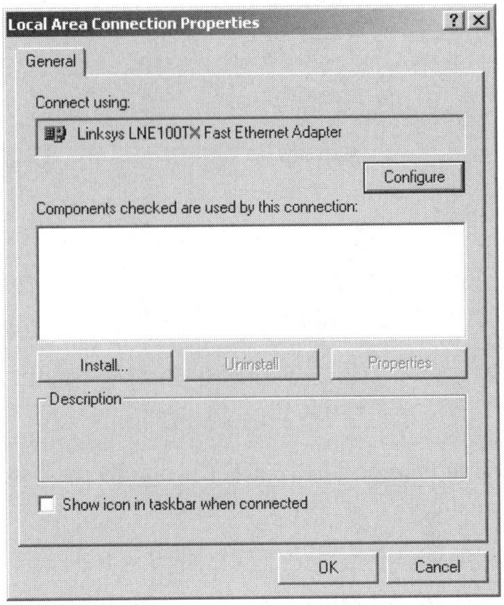

Figure D-8. This Local Area Connection Properties dialog box shows that no networking components are currently installed.

3 Click Install. The Select Network Component Type dialog box opens, as shown in Figure D-9. Notice that this dialog box has client, service, and protocol component types, which cover all the software elements you need to install in your computer to get a network up and running. Let's add the client first.

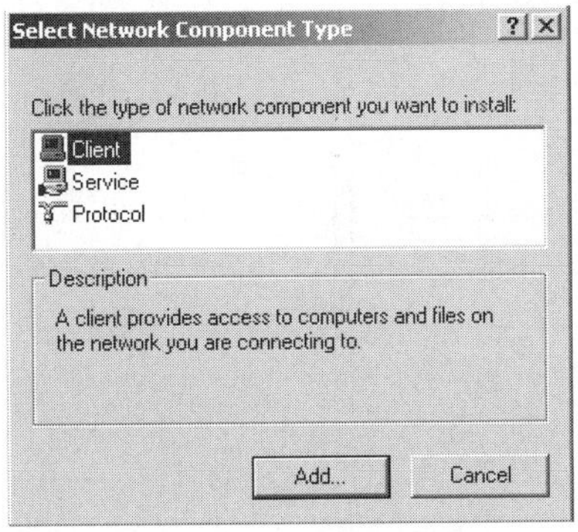

Figure D-9. Use the Select Network Component Type dialog box to select the type of network component you want to install.

4 Click Client, and click Add. The Select Network Client dialog box opens, as shown in Figure D-10, on the next page.

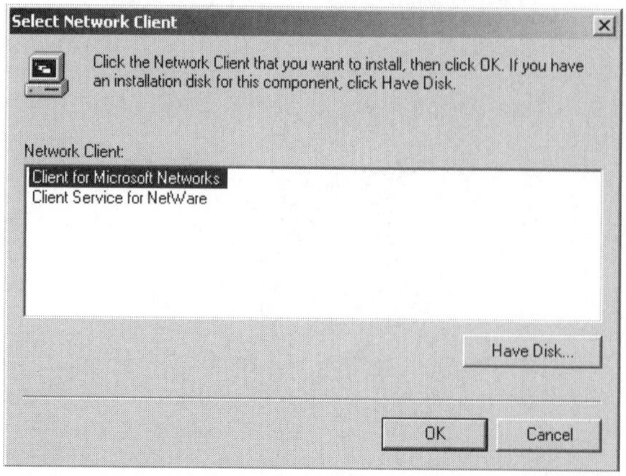

Figure D-10. Choose the type of network client you want to install in the Select Network Client dialog box.

5 Click Client For Microsoft Networks, and click OK. Now the Local Area Connection Properties dialog box lists the Client For Microsoft Networks, as shown in Figure D-11.

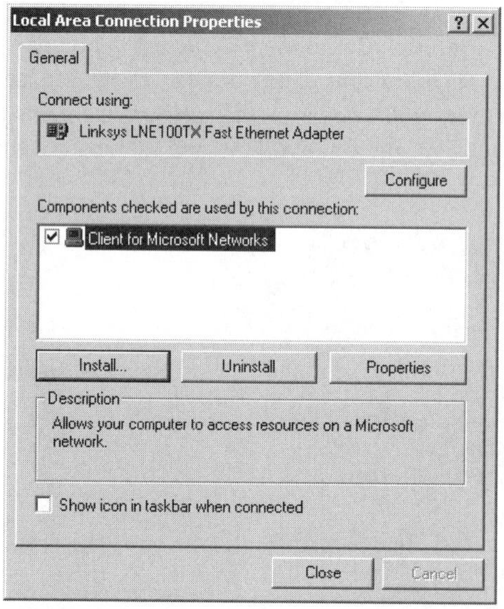

Figure D-11. The Local Area Connection Properties dialog box lists the clients currently installed on your network.

6 Click Close to complete the procedure.

Congratulations! You've just installed your first network component. Now for the next task—protocol setup.

Configuring a Protocol Setup

The steps you use to install a protocol are basically the same as you used to install the client. The steps to install a protocol are as follows:

1. Right-click My Network Places on the Windows 2000 desktop, and choose Properties. In Windows 2000, the Network And Dial-Up Connections dialog box appears.
2. Right-click Local Area Connection, and choose Properties. In the Local Area Connection Properties dialog box, click Install.
3. This time, select Protocol in the Select Network Component Type dialog box. The Select Network Protocol dialog box appears, as shown in Figure D-12.

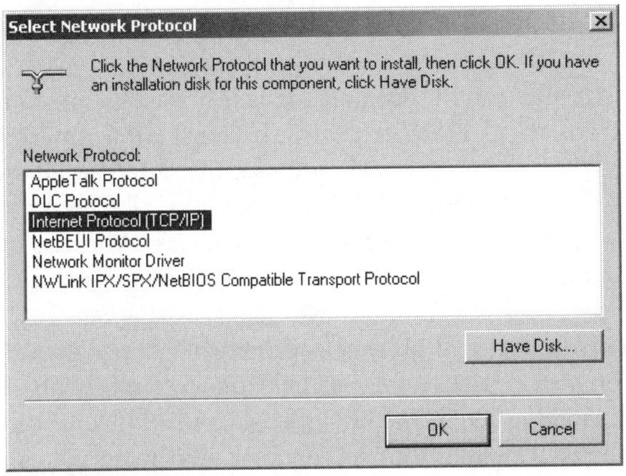

Figure D-12. Use the Select Network Protocol dialog box to choose the type of protocol you want to install for your network.

4. If you plan to share an Internet connection, select Internet Protocol (TCP/IP) and click OK. You'll see that the Local Area Connection Properties dialog box now lists Client For Microsoft Networks and Internet Protocol (TCP/IP). If you don't plan on sharing an Internet connection, you can select the NetBEUI protocol, which is a simple and quick protocol for a peer-to-peer network.
5. Click close to complete the procedure.

> **tip** Keep in mind that when you select protocols for your setup, you must have a common protocol on all computers in your network. The protocol must be the same in order for the computers to communicate with each other.

Check your TCP/IP Settings for Automatic IP Addressing

When you install the TCP/IP protocol, Windows usually sets the TCP/IP properties to obtain an IP address automatically. Automatic IP addressing means that a router, server, or gateway can assign an IP address to your computer to specifically identify your computer on the network. In the absence of any of those three devices, your computer will assign itself an IP address. Your computer will process all messages that contain your computer's IP address in the message destination field. If your network doesn't work after you finish setting it up, check the TCP/IP properties: Select Internet Protocol (TCP/IP) and then click the Properties button in the Local Area Connection Properties dialog box. Select the Obtain IP Address Automatically check box, and you'll be off and running with automatic IP addressing.

The easiest way to share an Internet connection is to use a DSL or cable modem with a National Address Translation (NAT) capability. If you share an Internet connection, every computer on your peer-to-peer network uses the same public Internet address assigned to the DSL or cable modem. NAT keeps track of all Internet request messages generated by any computer on your peer-to-peer network. When an Internet reply comes back to the modem, NAT correlates the reply to the original requesting computer on your peer-to-peer network. If your modem doesn't have NAT capability, you can also use a cable/DSL router in place of your network hub. Another option is to put two NICs in one computer and use the Internet Connection Sharing (ICS) features in Windows 2000 and Windows Me. One NIC would connect to your cable or DSL modem and the other NIC would connect to your peer-to-peer network hub. The ICS software does the work of the NAT software. Refer to the help files in Windows 2000 or Windows Me for more information about ICS.

Configuring a Service Setup

As with installing a protocol, installing a service (file and printer sharing) is basically the same procedure as you used to install the client. To install a service, follow these steps:

1. Right-click My Network Places on the Windows 2000 desktop, and choose Properties. In Windows 2000, the Network And Dial-Up Connections dialog box appears.
2. Right-click the Local Area Connection icon, and choose Properties.
3. In the Local Area Connection Properties dialog box, click Install.
4. Select Service in the Select Network Component Type dialog box, and click Add. The Select Network Service dialog box appears.

5. Select File And Printer Sharing For Microsoft Networks, and click OK. The Local Area Connection Properties dialog box appears, as shown in Figure D-13, which lists your network client, protocol, and service.

6. Click Close to complete the procedure.

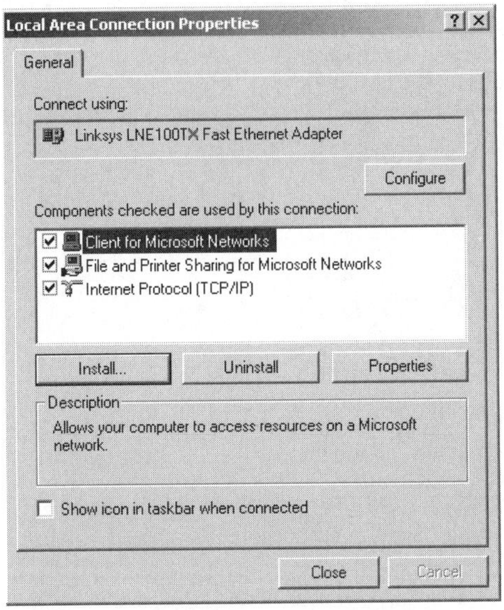

Figure D-13. This Local Area Connection Properties dialog box shows that a client, service, and protocol are installed.

Aha! You thought you were done? Not quite. You have three more tasks to complete before your network will be functional:

- You have to tag the files and printers you want to share.
- For each computer running Windows 2000, you need to set up a user ID and password for each user who will access a particular Windows 2000 computer.
- Ensure that each network computer has a unique computer name and a network-wide workgroup name.

The next three sections briefly describe how you can complete these tasks.

Share a File or Printer

Tagging a file or printer for sharing is simple. To do so, follow these steps:

1. Open Windows Explorer and right-click the drive, folder, or file you want to share.

2 Choose Properties from the shortcut menu, and click the Sharing tab, as shown in Figure D-14, on the next page.

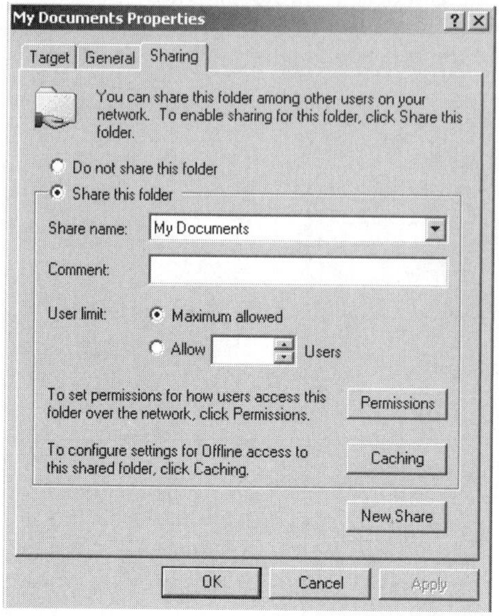

Figure D-14. The Sharing tab in the My Documents Properties dialog box enables you to share a drive, folder, or file stored on your computer.

3 Choose the Share This Folder option.

4 Click Permissions and select the permission you want to grant to each user as selected. Figure D-15 shows the Permissions for My Documents dialog box. The three permissions you can choose from are:

- **Read.** A user with Read permission can display folder names, filenames, file data, and attributes; run program files; and change folders within a shared folder. If you assign network users the Read permission, you'll be able to share your files yet still maintain file integrity, because you will be the only one able to change them.
- **Change.** A user with Change permission can do all the actions that Read permission allows plus create and delete folders, add and remove files, and change file data and attributes.
- **Full Control.** A user with Full Control permission can do all the actions that Change permission allows plus change file permissions and take ownership of files.

As a point of information, the preceding permissions are permissions available for a FAT (File Allocation Table) file format. The FAT format is the one used by Windows 95,

Windows 98, and Windows Me. Windows NT and Windows 2000 can also use the NTFS (New Technology File System) format. The NTFS format increases security over the FAT format. Within the NTFS format, you can choose from six levels of folder permissions. In addition to folder permissions, the NTFS format has five levels of file permissions. So, you can set permission at the file level in NTFS as contrasted to the folder level in FAT. You can find more information about NTFS in the Windows 2000 help files.

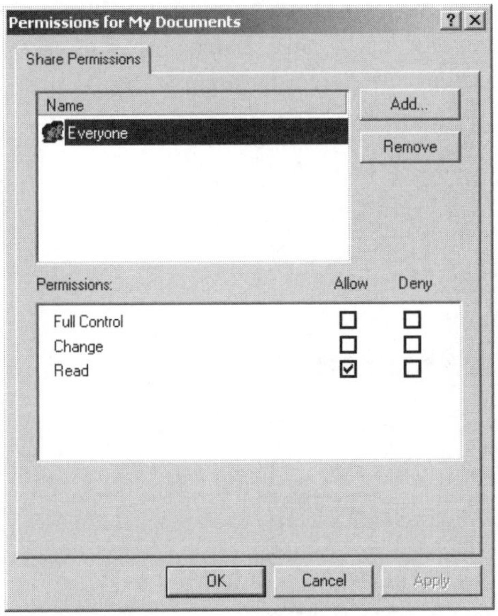

Figure D-15. Use the Permissions For My Documents dialog box to grant or deny Full Control, Change, and Read permissions.

Sharing a Printer

The procedure used to share a printer is very similar to the steps required to share a disk, folder, or file. To share a printer, complete these steps:

1. At the computer connected to the printer that you want to share, choose Start, Settings, Printers.
2. Right-click the printer you want to share, and choose Sharing.
3. In the printer Properties dialog box, click the Sharing tab, choose Shared As, and click OK to accept the suggested name for the shared printer. You can also enter a name of your own choosing in the Shared As Box.

Configuring a User Setup for Windows 2000 Computers

In Windows 2000, computer security is enforced through the use of user IDs and passwords that you set up. By contrast, in Windows 98 or Windows Me, you set up security by having a user sign in with a resource password before the user can access the resource. Setting up a user ID and password in Windows 2000 is easy:

1. Choose Start, Settings, Control Panel, and then double-click Users And Passwords. The Users And Passwords dialog box appears, as shown in Figure D-16. At this point, you can add, remove, check properties, or set the password for any user account.

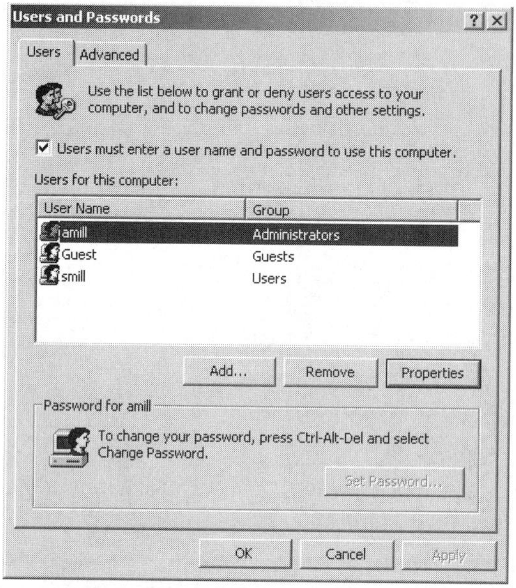

Figure D-16. The User And Passwords dialog box controls which users can access and configure your computer.

2. To add a user, click the Add button, and the Add New User box appears. Here, enter the user ID, name, and description. After you add your user information, click Next, and a dialog box opens that enables you to enter the user's password.

3. Enter the password, and click Next. A dialog box opens that asks you to specify your user's level of access. You can choose from Standard User, Restricted User, or Other. Select an access level, click Finish to complete the procedure, and then click OK to complete your user setup.

More About Access Levels and User Groups

In addition to choosing among Standard User or Restricted User, the Other option enables you to choose from additional access levels (including custom access levels you might have created) by selecting an access level from the drop-down list. For most network users, though, the Restricted User selection is adequate.

Also, if you're using Windows 2000, you'll see (Power Users Group) to the right of Standard User and (Users Group) to the right of Restricted User in the Add New User dialog box. In Windows 2000, you have the capability to assign users to groups and then share folders or assign permissions on a group basis. The advantage of using groups is that you can avoid repetitiously sharing folders and assigning permissions to individual users. Instead, you can place similar users in a group and share resources at the group level.

Windows 2000 includes six built-in local groups: Administrators, Power Users, Backup Operators, Replicator, Users, and Guests. Administrators have complete control over everything in the computer, while Guests usually have restricted read-only capability. The groups in between have specialized capabilities beyond those of the Guest group but not as liberal as the Administrators group. In a SOHO network, you would be the Administrator and most likely all other network users would be in the User group. You also have the option of creating your own group and assigning permission and sharing folders to meet your specific needs. For further information about groups, refer to the Windows 2000 help files.

Name Your Network and Your Computers

At this point, you're getting close to the finish line. One last task you need to take care of is to ensure that all your network computers have a computer name and a network name. You can verify whether your computers have the proper names in place in Windows 2000 as follows:

1. Right-click My Network Places and select Properties.
2. In the Network And Dial-up Connections window, click the Network Identification link. The Network Identification tab displays, as shown in Figure D-17, on the next page.

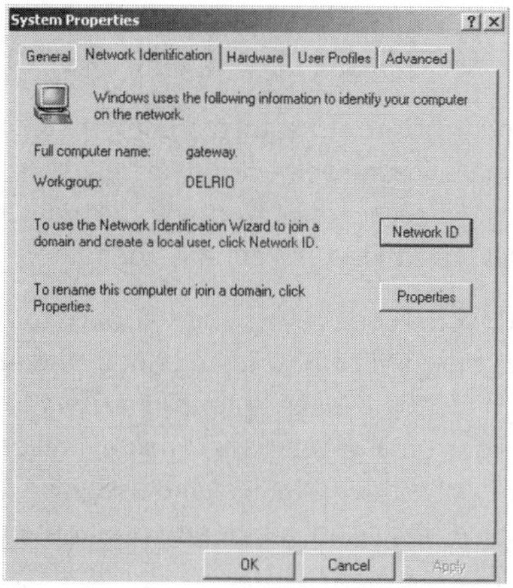

Figure D-17. Windows 2000 System Properties dialog box with the Network Identification tab open.

3. Ensure that you have a Full Computer Name and a Workgroup name for each computer on your network. At the time you installed your Windows operating system or the first time you turned on your computer when it was new, you probably entered your name. If you did not enter a computer name, the operating system will default to a computer name (such as your first name and the first few letters of your last name). Likewise, the operating system will supply a default network (workgroup) name, which usually is Workgroup.
4. Ensure that each network computer has a unique computer name, and ensure that each network computer has the same workgroup name. If you want or need to change either the computer name or the workgroup name, click the Properties button on the Network Identification tab, and the Identification Changes dialog box opens. Make any desired changes, and then click OK.
5. Click OK to close System Properties dialog box.

To access the equivalent of the Windows 2000 Network Identification tab in Windows 95, Windows 98, or Windows Me, right-click Network Neighborhood or My Network Places, and select Properties. The Network dialog box opens. Select the Identification tab. The computer and network identification information displays, as shown in Figure D-18. You can enter and edit your computer name and your network (workgroup) name as necessary. When you finish entering or changing the computer information, click OK, and Windows will store the new information. At this point, you might be asked to insert your Windows CD so the system can install some new files. If you receive this message, insert your CD. After the new files are installed, you'll probably have to restart your computer.

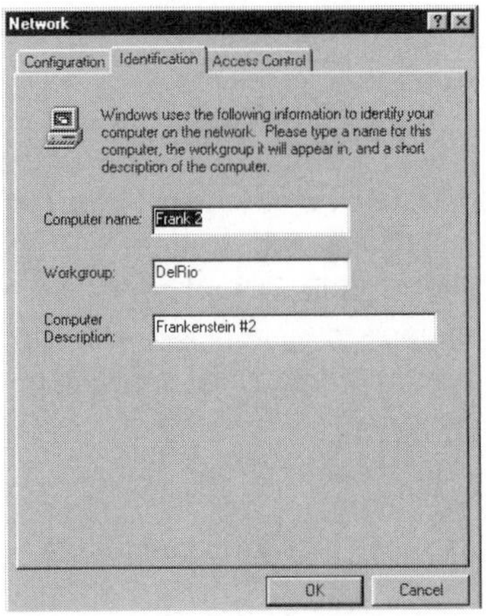

Figure D-18. Windows 95, Windows 98, and Windows Me Network Properties with the Network Identification tab open.

Ready to Roll

If you've made it this far, good job! You've completed the following tasks in setting up your network:

- You've successfully installed your networking hardware and software.
- Your network cables, hub, and NICs are installed, and your client, service, and protocol software configured.
- You've configured each computer with the shared files, folders, and printers you want to use as network resources.
- Your user accounts on all Windows 2000 computers are updated with user IDs and passwords.
- You network (workgroup) has a name and each network computer has a unique name.

After those tasks have been completed, check to make sure all your network devices are powered on and operating. Double-click My Network Places and double-click Computers Near Me; the Computers Near Me dialog box opens. This dialog box shows the computers and resources connected to your network. Congratulations! You've successfully set up a peer-to-peer network.

Troubleshooting

I Do Not See All My Network Computers when I Click on My Network Places.

If any computers are missing from your network, check that your network setup is correct and complete. Make sure all cables are fully plugged in and all NICs and hubs have power. Most NICs have a small green light that is lit when there's a link to the hub. Refer to the NIC manufacturer's documentation to identify indicator light functions. If everything seems OK, go to the computer that is not showing up on the network, and follow these steps:

1. Click Start, Help.
2. In the Help window, click the Contents tab, and click Troubleshooting And Maintenance.
3. Under the Troubleshooting And Maintenance entry, click Windows 2000 Troubleshooters. You'll find a troubleshooting routine for Networking (TCP/IP).
4. Click Networking (TCP/IP), and work through the troubleshooter's questions. The process requires you to answer questions and complete various checks to correct the problem.
5. Enjoy your networking!

Appendix E

Microsoft Office User Specialist (MOUS) Word 2002 Exam Objectives and Reference Guide

In today's competitive computer market, many people are earning certification status to help bolster their marketability and showcase their computer knowledge. One popular certification program targeted toward end users is the Microsoft Office User Specialist (MOUS) program. The MOUS program enables you to demonstrate your proficiency in Microsoft Office applications. As an experienced Word user, you can achieve two levels of MOUS certification to become a Microsoft Certified Professional (MCP) in Word by passing the Core Level and Expert Level exams. This appendix lists the objectives that you must master before you can become certified and points you to the sections in this book that describe the skills in detail. Once you're proficient in these skills, you'll be able to easily pass the MOUS exams and become an MCP.

> To find out more about the MOUS program and where you can take the exams, visit the Microsoft Training and Certification Web site at *www.microsoft.com/trainingandservices*. On the main page, click the Technical Certifications link on the navigation bar. Under the Desktop Certifications topic, you'll see a link to the MOUS informational pages.

MOUS Word 2002 Core Level Exam Objectives

The MOUS Word 2002 Core Level exam measures your ability to perform the following tasks:

- Create, modify, and print common business documents
- Collaboratively revise documents

This section presents the official list of specific skills you need to master before you can earn Core Level certification as a Word 2002 MCP.

Inserting and Modifying Text

Insert, Modify, and Move Text and Symbols

Inserting, cutting, copying, pasting, and using Paste Special

- See "Inputting Information," in Chapter 2.

- See "Cutting, Copying, and Pasting," in Chapter 2.
- See "Adding Linked Objects with Paste Special," in Chapter 15.

Finding and replacing text

- See "Finding Text and Elements Within the Current Document," in Chapter 12.
- See "Replacing Text," in Chapter 12.

Using AutoCorrect to insert frequently used text

- See "AutoCorrecting Your Typos Away," in Chapter 6.

Apply and Modify Text Formats

Applying and modifying character formats

- See "Formatting Text Efficiently," in Chapter 5.

Correct Spelling and Grammar Usage

Using spelling and grammar checks

- See "Building a Document's Credibility Using Spelling and Grammar Tools," in Chapter 13.

Using the Thesaurus

- See "Enlivening Your Vocabulary Using the Thesaurus," in Chapter 13.

Apply Font and Text Effects

Applying character effects (superscript, subscript, etc.) and text effects (animation)

- See "Adding Text Effects and Animation," in Chapter 5.

Applying highlights

- See "Using the Highlight Tool," in Chapter 33.

Enter and Format Date and Time

Inserting date/time fields and modifying field formats

- See "Inserting Date and Time Elements—The Quick Way," in Chapter 5.
- See "Inserting Fields," in Chapter 36.
- See "Editing Fields," in Chapter 36.

Apply Character Styles

Applying character styles

- See "Applying Existing Styles to Text," in Chapter 10.
- See "Selecting and Changing All Instances of a Style," in Chapter 10.

Creating and Modifying Paragraphs

Modify Paragraph Formats

Applying paragraph formats

- See "Formatting Paragraphs by Aligning and Indenting Text," in Chapter 7.
- See "Modifying Paragraph Attributes Using Reveal Formatting," in Chapter 7.

Applying borders and shading to paragraphs

- See "Perking Up Paragraphs with Borders and Shading," in Chapter 7.
- See "Adding Borders to Sections and Paragraphs," in Chapter 24.
- See "Shading Sections," in Chapter 24.

Indenting paragraphs

- See "Formatting Paragraphs by Aligning and Indenting Text," in Chapter 7.

Set and Modify Tabs

Setting and modifying tabs

- See "Controlling Alignment Using Tabs," in Chapter 7.

Apply Bullet, Outline, and Numbering Format to Paragraphs

Applying bullets and numbering

- See "Creating a Quick List," in Chapter 8.

Creating outlines

- See "Creating a New Outline," in Chapter 11.

Apply Paragraph Styles

Applying paragraph styles (e.g., Heading 1)

- See "Applying Existing Styles to Text," in Chapter 10.

Formatting Documents

Create and Modify a Header and Footer

Creating and modifying document headers and footers

- See "Controlling Header and Footer Placement," in Chapter 21.

Apply and Modify Column Settings

Applying columns and modifying text alignment

- See "Positioning Content Effectively," in Chapter 2.
- See "Formatting Paragraphs by Aligning and Indenting Text," in Chapter 7.
- See "Creating a Multi-Column Document," in Chapter 9.

Creating newsletter columns

- See "Creating a Multi-Column Document," in Chapter 9.

Revising column layout

- See "Creating a Multi-Column Document," in Chapter 9.

Modify Document Layout and Page Setup Options

Inserting page breaks

- See "Controlling Page Breaks," in Chapter 21.

Inserting page numbers

- See "AutoText in Headers and Footers," in Chapter 6.
- See "Controlling Header and Footer Placement," in Chapter 21.
- See "Inserting Page Numbers," in Chapter 21.

Modifying page margins, page orientation

- See "Changing Margins and Orientation," in Chapter 21.

Create and Modify Tables

Creating and modifying tables

- See "Creating a Simple Table," in Chapter 18.
- See "Editing Tables," in Chapter 18.

Applying AutoFormats to tables

- See "Enhancing Your Tables," in Chapter 18.

Modifying table borders and shading

- See "Adding Borders and Shading," in Chapter 18.

Revising tables (insert and delete rows and columns, modify cell formats)

- See "Editing Tables," in Chapter 18.
- See "Resizing Tables," in Chapter 18.

Preview and Print Documents, Envelopes, and Labels

Using Print Preview

- See "Previewing Before Printing," in Chapter 4.

Printing documents, envelopes, and labels

- See "Printing Quickly and Effectively," in Chapter 4.
- See "Printing Envelopes and Labels," in Chapter 35.

Managing Documents

Manage Files and Folders for Documents

Creating folders for document storage

- See "Saving Documents," in Chapter 2.

Create Documents Using Templates

Creating a document from a template

- See "Implementing Templates and Wizards," in Chapter 2.
- See "Choosing Predesigned Columns," in Chapter 9.
- See "Creating New Documents Based on Existing Templates," in Chapter 22.
- See "Using Web Page Templates," in Chapter 31.

Save Documents Using Different Names and File Formats

Using Save, Save As

- See "Saving Documents," in Chapter 2.
- See "Saving Your Web Pages," in Chapter 31.

Working with Graphics

Insert Images and Graphics

Adding images to documents

- See "Enhancing Your Documents with ClipArt," in Chapter 14.
- See "Inserting Pictures," in Chapter 14.

Create and Modify Diagrams and Charts

Creating and modifying charts and diagrams

- See "Creating a Basic Chart," in Chapter 19.
- See "Adding Organization Charts," in Chapter 20.
- See "Designing Conceptual Diagrams," in Chapter 20.

Workgroup Collaboration

Compare and Merge Documents

Comparing and merging documents

- See "Comparing and Merging Documents," in Chapter 33.

Insert, View, and Edit Comments

Inserting, viewing, and editing comments

- See "Adding and Managing Comments Effectively," in Chapter 33.

Convert Documents into Web Pages

Previewing documents as Web pages

- See "Previewing Before Printing," in Chapter 2.
- See "Configuring Web View Options," in Chapter 31.

Saving documents as Web pages

- See "Saving Documents," in Chapter 2.
- See "Understanding Web Page Creation Basics," in Chapter 31.
- See "Saving Your Web Pages," in Chapter 31.

MOUS Word 2002 Expert Level Exam Objectives

The MOUS Word 2002 Expert Level exam measures your ability to perform the following tasks:

- Create, edit, format, print, and collaboratively revise multiple-section business documents containing visual elements
- Perform mail merges using various data sources
- Create and apply document templates

This section presents the official list of specific skills you need to master before you can earn Expert Level certification as a Word 2002 MCP.

Customizing Paragraphs

Control Pagination

Managing orphans and widows

- See "Controlling Line and Page Breaks," in Chapter 7.

Setting line and page breaks

- See "Controlling Line and Page Breaks," in Chapter 7.
- See "Controlling Page Breaks," in Chapter 21.

Sort Paragraphs in Lists and Tables

Using the Sort feature

- See "Sorting Your Table Data," in Chapter 18.

Formatting Documents

Create and Format Document Sections

Using Page Setup options to format sections

- See "Working in Sections," in Chapter 21.

Verifying paragraph formats

- See "Modifying Paragraph Attributes Using Reveal Formatting," in Chapter 7.
- See "Understanding Styles," in Chapter 10.

Clearing formats

- See "Clearing Formatting in Selected Text," in Chapter 10.

Create and Apply Character and Paragraph Styles

Creating and applying character and paragraph styles

- See "Making Styles Work for You," in Chapter 10.
- See "Creating New Styles," in Chapter 10.

Create and Update Document Indexes and Tables of Contents, Figures, and Authorities

Inserting an index

- See "Indexing with Word," in Chapter 27.

Inserting a table of contents, table of figures, or table of authorities

- See "Creating a Table of Contents," in Chapter 26.
- See "Building a Table of Figures," in Chapter 26.
- See "Generating a Table of Figures," in Chapter 26.
- See "Building a Table of Authorities," in Chapter 26.
- See "Generating a Table of Authorities," in Chapter 26.

Create Cross-References

Inserting cross-references

- See "Using Cross-References," in Chapter 28.

Add and Revise Endnotes and Footnotes

Create, format, and edit footnotes and endnotes

- See "Adding Footnotes and Endnotes," in Chapter 28.

Create and Manage Master Documents and Subdocuments

Creating master documents with three or more subdocuments

- See "Creating a Master Document," in Chapter 25.
- See "Creating Subdocuments," in Chapter 25.
- See "Navigating to and from the Master Document," in Chapter 25.

Move Within Documents

Using automation features for document navigation (bookmarks and Document Map)

- See "Accessing Document Areas Using the Document Map," in Chapter 12.
- See "Jumping to Document Areas Using the Go To and Select Browse Objects Options," in Chapter 12.

Create and Modify Forms Using Various Form Controls

Creating custom forms using two or more form controls

- See "Creating a Basic Form," in Chapter 36.

Create Forms and Prepare Forms for Distribution

Protecting forms

- See "Protecting Tracked Changes, Comments, and Forms," in Chapter 34
- See "Protecting Forms," in Chapter 36.

Distributing forms

- See "Creating Interactive Forms," in Chapter 31.
- See "Routing Documents via E-Mail," in Chapter 36.

Customizing Tables

Use Excel Data in Tables

Using object linking to display Excel worksheet data as a Word table or worksheet object

- See "Linking Objects," in Chapter 15.
- See "Importing Data from Other Programs," in Chapter 19.

Perform Calculations in Word Tables

Using formulas in tables

- See "Working with Functions in Tables," in Chapter 18.

Modifying table formats by merging or splitting table cells

- See "Merging Cells," in Chapter 18.
- See "Splitting Cells," in Chapter 18.

Creating and Modifying Graphics

Create, Modify, and Position Graphics

Creating and inserting graphics in documents

- See "Inserting Pictures," in Chapter 14.
- See "Controlling Objects in Drawings," in Chapter 16.
- See "Integrating the Drawing Canvas with Document Text," in Chapter 16.

Modifying graphics

- See "Working with Pictures," in Chapter 14.
- See "Controlling Objects in Drawings," in Chapter 16.

Create and Modify Charts Using Data from Other Applications

Creating and revising charts using Excel or Access data

- See "Importing Data from Other Programs," in Chapter 19.

Align Text and Graphics

Using advanced text wrapping and layout options with graphics

- See "Working with Pictures," in Chapter 14.

Customizing Word

Create, Edit, and Run Macros

Creating macros

- See "Creating Macros," in Chapter 40.

Editing a macro using the Visual Basic Editor

- See "Editing and Viewing Macro VBA Code," in Chapter 40.

Running macros

- See "Running Macros," in Chapter 40.

Customize Menus and Toolbars

Creating a custom menu

- See "Customizing Menus for Added Functionality," in Chapter 38.

- See "Assigning Shortcuts to Word Commands," in Chapter 40.
- See "Assigning a Macro to a Toolbar, Menu, or Keyboard Shortcut," in Chapter 40.

Adding and removing buttons from a toolbar

- See "Customizing Word Toolbars," in Chapter 38.
- See "Adding Shortcuts to Word Commands," in Chapter 40.
- See "Assigning a Macro to a Toolbar, Menu, or Keyboard Shortcut," in Chapter 40.

Workgroup Collaboration

Track, Accept, and Reject Changes to Documents

Tracking changes

- See "Tracking Changes," in Chapter 33.

Reviewing changes by type and reviewer

- See "Adjusting the Appearance of Tracked Changes," in Chapter 33.

Responding to proposed changes

- See "Resolving Proposed Edits," in Chapter 33.

Merge Input from Several Reviewers

Distributing documents for revision via e-mail

- See "Routing Documents via E-Mail," in Chapter 30.

Merging three or more revisions of the same document

- See "Comparing and Merging Documents," in Chapter 33.

Insert and Modify Hyperlinks to Other Documents and Web Pages

Inserting and modifying hyperlinks

- See "Including Hyperlinks," in Chapter 31.

Create and Edit Web Documents in Word

Opening Web pages in Word

- See "Looking at Your Documents from the Web's Perspective," in Chapter 29.

- See "Configuring Web View Options," in Chapter 31.

Saving Word documents to the Web

- See "Saving a File as a Web Page," in Chapter 2.
- See "Saving a File on a Network," in Chapter 2.
- See "Working with My Network Places," in Chapter 29.
- See "Saving Your Web Pages," in Chapter 31.
- See "Publishing Your Web Pages," in Chapter 31.

Create Document Versions

Creating versions of documents

- See "Working with Multiple Versions of a Document," in Chapter 33.

Protect Documents

Setting document protection

- See "Allowing Reviewers to Use Only the Comments Feature," in Chapter 33.
- See "Protecting Tracked Changes, Comments, and Forms," in Chapter 34.
- See "Protecting Forms," in Chapter 36.

Define and Modify Default File Locations for Workgroup Templates

Modifying and re-posting HTML documents

- See "Using Workgroup Templates," in Chapter 32.

Attach Digital Signatures to Documents

Using digital signatures to authenticate documents

- See "Using Digital Certificates to Digitally Sign Files and Macros," in Chapter 34.
- See "Signing a Macro with a Digital Signature," in Chapter 40.

Using Mail Merge

Merge Letters with a Word, Excel, or Access Data Source

Completing an entire mail merge process for form letters

- See "Starting the Mail Merge Wizard," in Chapter 35.
- See "Merging the Documents," in Chapter 35.

Merge Labels with a Word, Excel, or Access Data Source

Completing an entire mail merge process for mailing labels

- See "Starting the Mail Merge Wizard," in Chapter 35.
- See "Merging the Documents," in Chapter 35.

Use Outlook Data as a Mail Merge Data Source

Completing a mail merge using Outlook information as the data source

- See "Choosing Outlook Contacts," in Chapter 35.

Index to Troubleshooting Topics

Index

B

C

E

J

K

L

O

P

U

X

Y

Z

About the Authors

Mary Millhollon is a certified Expert-level Microsoft Office User Specialist in Word, a recognized Internet expert, and the owner of Bughouse Productions. She has more than enough years of publishing, design, and computer experience to count, including hands-on experience in the book, magazine, newspaper, courseware, and Web publishing industries. Mary is a freelance writer, Web designer, editor, sometimes instructor, and Internet expert, working daily (and nightly) with desktop applications and online technologies. Mary's educational background is a blend of art, English, journalism, and computer science, which lends itself well to today's constantly morphing computer technology. Her most recent publications include *Easy Web Page Creation* (Microsoft Press) and a collection of other computer-related books about Microsoft Office applications, Internet browsers, HTML (beginner and advanced), online communities, Web graphics, online auctions, and other desktop, Internet, network, application, and design topics. You can contact Mary via email at mm@creationguide.com or visit www.bughouseproductions.com.

Katherine Murray has been using technology to write about technology since the early 80s. With more than 40 computer books (and a number of parenting books) to her credit, Katherine enjoys working on projects that teach new skills, uncover hidden talents, or develop mastery and efficiency in a chosen area. From books on general computer use to more specialized books on presentation graphics, Internet use, and Web animation, Katherine gets most excited about the programs that help people communicate, through print, sound, electronic, or visual expression—on or off the Web. For the last 14 years, Katherine has owned and operated reVisions Plus, Inc., a writing and publishing services company that relies on Word as the program of choice. You can contact Katherine via email at kmurray@revisionsplus.com or visit her company on the web at www.revisionsplus.com.

The manuscript for this book was prepared and galleyed using Microsoft Word 2000. Pages were composed by Studioserv (www.studioserv.com) using Adobe PageMaker 6.52 for Windows, with text in Minion and display type in Syntax. Composed pages were delivered to the printer as electronic prepress files.

coverdesigner
GIRVIN/Strategic Branding & Design

interiorgraphicdesigner
James D. Kramer

coverillustration
Daman Studio

manuscripteditors
Jennifer Harris and Gail Taylor

technicaleditor
Jack Beaudry

principalcompositors
Sharon Bell, Presentation Desktop Publications, and Steve Sagman, Studioserv

principalproofreader
Tom Speeches

indexer
Caroline Parks, Indexcellence

Proof of Purchase

Use this page as proof of purchase if participating in a promotion or rebate offer on this title. Proof of purchase must be used in conjunction with other proof(s) of payment such as your dated sales receipt—see offer details.

Microsoft® Word Version 2002 Inside Out

0-7356-1278-1

CUSTOMER NAME

Microsoft Press, PO Box 97017, Redmond, WA 98073-9830